S0-BZZ-272

LUTHERAN WORSHIP

Hymnal Companion

LUTHERAN WORSHIP

Hymnal Companion

Fred L. Precht

Prepared under the auspices of
The Commission on Worship
of
The Lutheran Church—Missouri Synod

Publishing House
St. Louis

3558 S. Jefferson Avenue, St. Louis, MO 63118-3968
Manufactured in the United States of America

The LaserGREEK™ font used in this publication is available from Linguist's Software, Inc., P.O. Box 580, Edmonds, WA 98020-0580, (206) 775-1130.

Library of Congress Cataloging-in-Publication Data

Precht, Fred L., 1916–
Lutheran worship hymnal companion / Fred L. Precht.
p. cm.
Includes index.
ISBN 0-570-01345-3
1. Lutheran Church—Hymns. 2. Hymns, English. 3. Lutheran Church—Hymns—History and criticism. 4. Hymns, English—History and criticism. I. Title.
BV410.P74 1992
264'.04132202—dc20

1 2 3 4 5 6 7 8 9 10 RMc 02 01 00 99 98 97 96 95 94 93 92

To my sainted mother and father,
Anna and Fred, who early taught
me to love and appreciate
the Christian hymn

CONTENTS

PREFACE

"I will sing with my spirit, but I will also sing with my mind" (1 Cor. 14:15b). With these words St. Paul emphasizes in unmistakable terms that corporate worship must be with understanding—with the "mind." Speaking in tongues without interpretation of what has been said negates the first great principle of public worship, namely, "the strengthening of the Church" (1 Cor. 14:26), or its edification. Interestingly, in this chapter 14 the word *mind*, that great gift from God, occurs three times in the seven verses from 13–19, attesting the intense intellectual activity which the Holy Spirit produces. While pleasurable hymn singing entails no more than a sound voice and the ability to read the texts with understanding, a knowledge of their history and background can lead the worshiper to a fuller and deeper meaning and to the capture of their power and import. Hymns are an important part of Christianity's history. They can rarely be fully appreciated without some knowledge of their authors and composers. Such knowledge adds not only to our appreciation; it can add to our spiritual profit. And it is especially the function of pastors and teachers to convey, from time to time, this knowledge to their congregations and classes.

Although not readily evident in the contents, basically the body of this book is comprised of two large sections: notes on texts and tunes; and biographical information on the authors, translators, composers, and arrangers. In the first section every effort has been made briefly to present facts that are historically accurate and to shed some light on the Christian faith as adorned in the hymn under discussion—all with the hope that this might possibly enhance one's appreciation of that hymn. Sometimes, however, my research has come up against a wall of silence, as can readily be gathered by the reader in certain instances. At other times I have encountered a maze of conflicting statements demanding a decision as to which might happily be the more correct course of events. Thus I entertain no illusions that this book is error-free. For any errors and inadequacies that may be discovered, I alone am responsible.

It may come as a surprise to some that oftentimes little is reliably known about the circumstances surrounding the authorship of a well-known hymn. Moreover, much still remains obscure and uncertain, especially regarding some medieval hymns and tunes. Then too, a goodly amount of mythology has grown up around some well-known hymns; there are tales which have no foundation in fact. These had either to be omitted or recognized as such. Unfortunately, space did not permit an in-depth treatment of the hymn text itself. Actually, that constitutes another, separate assignment.

Since hymns are meant to be sung, tunes deserve due attention, for in a good hymn, text and tune are mutually supportive. As Louis Benson says, "A great tune . . . adds something to the printed words by way of suggesting things of the spirit unprinted between the lines" *(The Hymnody of the Christian Church)*. Admittedly, vital congregational singing is in direct proportion to the quality of the tunes people are asked to sing. Moreover, the popularity of many a hymn text is readily attributed to the tune to which it is coupled. With this in mind, we have attempted, when possible, to say a little bit more than simply to note where the tune first appeared. Frequently also, the evolution of the tune, especially if a chorale, is demonstrated by giving an example of its early appearance(s) from Johannes Zahn's monumental work, *Die Melodien Der deutschen evangelischen Kirchenlieder*. The consistent use of full capitals in the tune names makes them readily recognized as such whenever mention is made of them.

Incidentally, in announcing portions of hymns or printing them in the worship folder, it is well to distinguish between *stanza* and *verse*. According to Webster, *verse* is "a line of metrical writing"; *stanza* is a "division of a poem consisting of a series of lines . . . in a usually recurring pattern of meter and rhyme." The use of *verse* for *stanza* is thus contrary to good usage.

In the biographical information section regarding authors, composers, arrangers, and even a few printers, the length of an individual sketch is not necessarily a measure of the importance or significance of the individual under discussion. In some instances, living individuals wrote their own biographies or at least were given opportunity to revise, update, and enlarge what had previously appeared in some other publications; in other instances only scant information was available. When seeking information on a given hymn or spiritual song, the person is encouraged to read also the pertinent biographies, thus to gain a fuller understanding and possibly a broader perspective of the matter.

References to the select bibliography are made both to give credit and to afford the reader opportunity further to pursue the specific subject. Frequently the reference is only to authors. In the case of multiple titles by the same author, both author and title are mentioned.

The debt that I owe to others who have plowed this vast field—editors, authors, librarians, historians, as well as representatives of numerous other professions—is truly immense, individual mention of which would go on *ad infinitum*. I would be remiss, however, if I did not express special thanks to the Commission on Worship of The Lutheran Church—Missouri Synod, the knowledgeable, scholarly, and committed group responsible for producing *Lutheran Worship* (1982) while I was its executive director, for the privilege it accorded me in authorizing that I prepare this *Companion*; to Kay Cogswell, my secretary at the time, for her initial logistical planning and other contributions to the project prior to my retirement, July 1, 1987; to my successor James Brauer for providing an office, equipment, and secretarial help in Sandra Kohlmeier; to Dorothy Richterkessing, music department of Concordia Publishing House, for tracking down various historical bits of information; to Shari Siemsen, librarian at the International Center of the Synod, for making available to me the extended loan of certain reference books and providing other research material from various libraries; and finally to my wife Louise for her patience in my frequent absence from home and for her unflagging encouragement.

It is hoped that this volume will be of interest and usefulness to pastors, teachers, students of hymnology and liturgy, organists, choir directors, and worship planners, and that through them it will bring enrichment and greater understanding of our great hymnological heritage whenever and wherever "the faith that was once for all entrusted to the saints" (Jude 3b) is expressed in song by the worshiping congregation.

Fred L. Precht

St. Philip and St. James, Apostles, 1990

NOTES ON TEXTS AND TUNES OF CANTICLES, HYMNS, AND SPIRITUAL SONGS

OH, COME, OH, COME, EMMANUEL 1

Oh, come, oh, come, Emmanuel,
And ransom captive Israel,
That mourns in lonely exile here
Until the Son of God appear.

Refrain
Rejoice! Rejoice! Emmanuel
Shall come to you, O Israel.

Veni veni Emmanuel;
captivum solve Israel,
qui gemit in exilio,
privatus Dei Filio.

Gaude, gaude, Emmanuel
nascetur pro te, Israel.

Prescribed during Advent as an alternate canticle to the Gloria in Excelsis in Divine Service I (see *LW*, p. 137), stanza 1 of *LW* 31 has been placed here for such use.

For comments on the text and tune see hymn 31.

Paul G. Bunjes, music editor of *Lutheran Worship* (1982), prepared the setting contained in *Lutheran Worship: Accompaniment for the Liturgy* (1982).

THE ROYAL BANNERS FORWARD GO 2

The royal banners forward go:
The cross shows forth redemption's flow
Where he, by whom our flesh was made,
Our ransom in his flesh has paid.

Vexilla regis prodeunt,
Fulget crucis mysterium,
Quo carne carnis conditor
Suspensus est patibulo:

Prescribed during Lent as an alternate canticle to the Gloria in Excelsis in Divine Service I (see *LW*, p. 137), stanza 1 of *LW* 104 has been placed here for such use.

For comments on the text see hymn 103; on the tune see hymn 104.

Paul G. Bunjes, music editor of *Lutheran Worship* (1982), prepared the setting contained in *Lutheran Worship: Accompaniment for the Liturgy* (1982).

GLORY BE TO THE FATHER 3

Known as the Gloria Patri, or the Lesser Doxology, it is traditionally sung or said to conclude a canticle or psalm or portion thereof. Dating as far back as the seventh century, it is not only a beautiful ascription of praise but a confession of the Holy Trinity. Its scriptural basis is evident in Romans 16:27; Ephesians 3:21; Philippians 4:20; and Revelation 1:6.

The chant formula, source of which is unknown, was that used for the Gloria Patri in Matins and Vespers in *The Lutheran Hymnal* (1941).

Paul G. Bunjes prepared the setting contained in *Lutheran Worship: Accompaniment for the Liturgy* (1982).

4 I BELIEVE IN ONE GOD

This is the traditional prose form of the Nicene Creed (the Niceno-Constantinopolitan) dating from the year 381. Named after the first word of the Latin "Credo in unum Deo" (I believe), the creed is a formal summary and authoritative statement of Christian doctrine, belief of which is held to be necessary to salvation. Nowhere in the liturgy is the unity between the *fides quae creditur* (the faith, or doctrine, which is believed [objective faith]) and the *fides qua creditur* (the faith by which one believes [subjective faith]) given such special emphasis as in the creed (in this case the Nicene). Moreover, to say or sing the creed is not to say or sing something that everybody in the Christian congregation already knows. No, it is an act of faith!

The Nicene is one of three so-called ecumenical creeds, that is, creeds professed by Christianity as a whole, the other two being the Apostles' and the Athanasian. This English text is originally from *The Book of Common Prayer* (1549).

The plainsong, or Gregorian, chant setting represents Credo III, dating from the 17th century.

Paul G. Bunjes prepared the setting contained in *Lutheran Worship: Accompaniment for the Liturgy* (1982).

5 CREATE IN ME

This is the familiar offertory (Ps. 51:10–12) from the Order of Morning Service without Communion in *The Lutheran Hymnal* (1941), here given, with updated text, as an alternate to the other familiar one now in Divine Service I.

The chant tune was composed by J. G. Winer (1583–1651) for the corresponding German text beginning "Schaffe in mir Gott ein reines Herze," which resulted in an offertory sentence that enjoyed wide usage in German Lutheranism following the Reformation.

The setting contained in *Lutheran Worship: Accompaniment for the Liturgy* (1982) was prepared by Paul G. Bunjes.

HOLY, HOLY, HOLY 6

More musically than textually, this constitutes a new Sanctus, provided as an alternate to the familiar Sanctus in Divine Service I or, for that matter, for use in place of either of the two Sanctus settings in Divine Service II. This so-called ordinary (unchangeable part) in the liturgy represents the work of Paul G. Bunjes, music editor of *Lutheran Worship* (1982), who adapted and harmonized a Sanctus melody by Lucas Lossius (1508–82), Lutheran clergyman, theologian, teacher, and music theorist, student and friend of Melanchthon (*LW* 189) while at the University of Wittenberg. Lossius was wont to apply Gregorian chant melodies to the evolving Lutheran liturgy, thus greatly influencing Lutheran music in northern Germany. Congregations with the patience to learn this setting will, it is believed, find it rewarding. Its accompaniment, prepared by Paul G. Bunjes, is contained in *Lutheran Worship: Accompaniment for the Liturgy* (1982).

O CHRIST, THE LAMB OF GOD 7

This is the familiar Agnus Dei from the Communion service in *The Lutheran Hymnal* (1941) that originally appeared in the Brunswick Church Order of 1528 with the text, "Christe, du Lamm Gottes, der du trägst die Sünd der Welt, erbarm dich unser." Derived from the words of John the Baptist (John 1:29), it was brought into the Latin Mass of the Western Church by Pope Sergius I (fl. 687–701) in the words: "Agnus Dei, qui tollis peccata mundi, miserere nobis." It is said that wars and disorders in the 11th century prompted the change to "Dona nobis pacem" (Grant us peace) in the third and last repetition.

"Lamb of God, pure and sinless" (*LW* 208) is a metrical paraphrase of this text.

Paul G. Bunjes prepared the setting contained in *Lutheran Worship: Accompaniment for the Liturgy* (1982).

WE PRAISE YOU, O GOD 8

This is the familiar text and setting contained in Matins in *The Lutheran Hymnal* (1941), here slightly revised in the pointing of text to chant. The two so-called Anglican chant formulas used here are an adaptation by R. Cooke, 18th-century organist and choir director at Westminster Abbey, of the work of Henry Lawes, English composer and singer, leading song writer of the mid-17th century. This canticle has been placed in the Canticles and Chants section to serve as an alternate to the newly composed setting by Paul G. Bunjes located in Matins itself.

The Te Deum, named after the first words of the Latin, consists of three sections—two prose hymns and a litany. Of unknown authorship, without doubt it is the great and ancient canticle of adoration and praise, as such, the festive canticle of Matins. Martin Luther (*LW* 13, et al.) considered it second only to the Apostles' and Athanasian Creeds as a symbol of faith.

Paul G. Bunjes prepared the harmonization contained in *Lutheran Worship: Accompaniment for the Liturgy* (1982).

9 ALL YOU WORKS OF THE LORD

This canticle of high praise (Latin: Benedicite Omnia Opera, named so after the opening words) was included in *The Lutheran Hymnal* (1941), page 120, but, lacking a chant setting (it could have been chanted to an Anglican chant contained in the hymnal or to a psalm tone), it was seldom, if ever, sung. Often called Song of the Three Children (here, Song of the Three Young Men), its text appeared in the Apocrypha, following Daniel 3:23, where it is the song sung by them in the fiery furnace. It ends with an added ascription of praise to the Holy Trinity (verse 21), which, of course, is a Christian addition.

Addressing inanimate objects or persons (usually deceased) as here done is a poetic device called apostrophic, a usage that occurs, for instance, in Psalm 148. This is another canticle for Matins, most appropriately sung for festivals and especially during the Easter season with its week of weeks—the Sundays of Easter.

The use of two psalm tones—the composition of and arrangement by Paul G. Bunjes—lends a pleasing variety to the whole. (See *Lutheran Worship: Accompaniment for the Liturgy*, pp. 142–43.)

10 CHRISTIANS TO THE PASCHAL VICTIM

This represents a revised and updated form of the Victimae Paschali (Easter) Celebration contained in the *Worship Supplement* (1969) to *The Lutheran Hymnal* (1941). The dialog between choir (singing the more difficult plainsong) and the congregation (singing the familiar chorale "Christ Is Arisen," *LW* 124) can serve as an effective and edifying vehicle of praise between the Epistle and Gospel or at some other appropriate place in the Divine Service. For information about this sequence hymn and the chorale, see *LW* 124. For the accompaniment, provided by Paul G. Bunjes, see *Lutheran Worship: Accompaniment for the Liturgy* (1982), pages 143–45.

LORD, NOW LET YOUR SERVANT DEPART IN PEACE

11

This is the familiar post-Communion canticle, the Song of Simeon, or Nunc Dimittis (Luke 2:29–32), contained in the Communion service in *The Lutheran Hymnal* (1941), slightly revised and updated, textually and musically. Based as it is on the Gregorian, or plainsong, psalm tone V, it is provided here as an alternate to the Nunc Dimittis composed by Paul G. Bunjes included in Divine Service I.

The setting of this canticle, prepared by Paul G. Bunjes, is contained in *Lutheran Worship: Accompaniment for the Liturgy* (1982).

12 THE ADVENT OF OUR GOD

The advent of our God Shall be our theme for prayer; Come, let us meet him on the road And place for him prepare.	Instantis adventum Dei Poscamus ardenti prece, Festisque munum inclytum Praeoccupemus canticis.
The everlasting Son Incarnate stoops to be, Himself the servant's form puts on To set his people free.	Aeterna proles feminae Non horret includi sinu; Ipse servus, ut jugo Non servitutis eximat.
Come, Zion's daughter, rise To meet your lowly king, Nor let your faithless heart despise The peace he comes to bring.	Mansuetus et clemens venit; Occurre, festina, Sion: Ultro tibi quam porrigit, Ne dura pacem respuas.
As judge, on clouds of light, He soon will come again And all his scattered saints unite With him on high to reign.	Mox nube clara fulgurans Mundi redibit arbiter, Suique membra corporis Caelo triumphator vehet.
Before the dawning day Let sin be put to flight; No longer let the law hold sway, But walk in freedom's light.	Fetus tenebrarum, die Cedant propinquo crimina; Adam reformetur vetus, Imago succedat novi.
All glory to the Son, Who comes to set us free, With Father, Spirit, ever one Through all eternity.	Qui liberator advenis, Fili, tibi laus maxima Cum Patre et almo Spiritu In sempiterna saecula.

Charles Coffin wrote this original Latin hymn, which was included in the *Paris Breviary* (1736). Nearly a century later John Chandler began translating the hymns from that publication into English; he titled his volume of translations *The Hymns of the Primitive Church* (1837) as he was unaware of the *Breviary's* origin. *Lutheran Worship,* like most other modern hymnals, has altered Chandler's translations considerably. Says Percy Dearmer in *Songs of Praise Discussed,* "As we are not bound to re-echo the theology of Paris in the reign of Louis XIV, [we have] modernized it rather freely, and we thus have here a paraphrase rather than a translation of Coffin."

ST. THOMAS, a notably bright, sturdy short meter tune, is an extraction from a tune found in Aaron Williams' *New Universal Psalmodist* (1763), there called HOLBORN, which was probably composed by Williams himself. HOLBORN was a long tune set to four stanzas of Charles Wesley's "Soldiers of Christ, Arise." In the fifth edition of his book, *New Universal Psalmodist* (1770), Williams took lines 5 through 8 (Wesley's second stanza) of HOLBORN and set them to Psalm 48 under the title ST. THOMAS'S. The tune is also called WILLIAMS.

The setting, originally taken from *Lutheran Book of Worship* (1978), was altered in the fifth printing of *Lutheran Worship* in 1984 to correct the parallel octaves in the second measure.

SAVIOR OF THE NATIONS, COME 13

Savior of the nations, come,
Show yourself the virgin's son.
Marvel, heaven, wonder, earth,
That our God chose such a birth.

No man's pow'r of mind or blood
But the Spirit of our God
Made the Word of God be flesh,
Woman's offspring, pure and fresh.

Here a maid was found with child,
Virgin pure and undefiled.
In her virtues it was known
God had made her heart his throne.

Then stepped forth the Lord of all
From his pure and kingly hall;
God of God, becoming man,
His heroic course began.

God the Father was his source,
Back to God he ran his course.
Into hell his road went down,
Back then to his throne and crown.

Father's equal, you will win
Vict'ries for us over sin.
Might eternal, make us whole;
Heal our ills of flesh and soul.

From the manger newborn light
Sends a glory through the night.
Night cannot this light subdue,
Faith keeps springing ever new.

Glory to the Father sing,
Glory to the Son, our king,
Glory to the Spirit be
Now and through eternity.

Nun komm, der Heiden Heiland,
Der Jungfrauen Kind erkannt!
Dass sich wundre alle Welt,
Gott solch' Geburt ihm bestellt.

Nicht von Mann's Blut noch von Fleisch,
Allein von dem Heil'gen Geist
Ist Gott's Wort worden ein Mensch
Und blüht ein' Frucht Weibesfleisch.

Der Jungfrau Leib schwanger ward,
Doch blieb Keuschheit rein bewahrt,
Leucht't hervor manch' Tugend schön,
Gott da war in seinem Thron.

Er ging aus der Kammer sein,
Dem kön'glichen Saal so rein,
Gott von Art und Mensch ein Held,
Sein'n Weg er zu laufen eilt.

Sein Lauf kam vom Vater her
Und kehrt' wider zum Vater,
Fuhr hinunter zu der Höll'
Und wieder zu Gottes Stuhl.

Der du bist dem Vater gleich,
Führ' hinaus den Sieg im Fleisch,
Dass dein' ew'ge Gott'sgewalt
In uns das krank' Fleisch erhalt'.

Dein' Krippe glänzt hell und klar,
Die Nacht gibt ein neu Licht dar,
Dunkel muss nicht kommen drein,
Der Glaub' bleibt immer im Schein.

Lob sei Gott dem Vater g'tan,
Lob sei Gott sein'm ein'gen Sohn,
Lob sei Gott dem Heil'gen Geist
Immer und in Ewigkeit!

This hymn is derived from the Latin text of St. Ambrose, bishop of Milan, with whom the real history of hymns in the West begins.

1 Veni, Redemptor gentium;
Ostende partum virginis;
Miretur omne saeculum.
Talis decet partus Deo.

2 Non ex virili semine,
Sed mystico spiramine
Verbum Dei Factum est caro,
Fructusque ventris floruit.

3 Alvus tumescit virginis
Claustrum pudoris permanet;
Vexilla virtutum micant,
Versatur in templo Deus.

4 Procedit e thalamo suo,
Pudoris aulo regia,
Geminae gigans substantiae,
Alacris ut currat viam.

5 Egressus eius a Patre,
Regressus eius ad Patrem;
Excursus usque ad inferos,
Recursus ad sedem Dei.

6 Aequalis aeterno Patri,
Carnis tropaeo accingere,
Infirma nostri corporis
Virtute firmans perpeti.

7 Praesepe iam fulget tuum
Lumenque nox spirat novum,
Quod nulla nox interpolet
Fideque iugi luceat.

8 Gloria tibi, Domine,
Qui natus es de virgine,
Cum Patre et sancto Spiritu
In sempiterna saecula.

Luther's German version is a rather literal translation of the Latin except that he substitutes a doxology for the final stanza by Ambrose. This version appeared with its tune in both editions of *Eyn Enchiridion* (Erfurt, 1524), as well as in Johann Walter's *Geystliche Gesangk Büchleyn* (Wittenberg, 1524).

The translation of Luther's version is by F. Samuel Janzow.

NUN KOMM, DER HEIDEN HEILAND. This tune is also known as VENI, REDEMPTOR GENTIUM, the first words of the Latin text sung originally to Gregorian chant, or plainsong. Luther simplified the melodic line, thus making it easier for congregations to sing. In the history of hymnody this hymn is the Advent hymn *par excellence.*

The harmonization, or setting, is by Paul G. Bunjes.

14 ON JORDAN'S BANK THE BAPTIST'S CRY

On Jordan's bank the Baptist's cry
Announces that the Lord is nigh;
Awake and hearken, for he brings
Glad tidings of the King of kings!

Then cleansed be ev'ry life from sin;
Make straight the way for God within,
And let us all our hearts prepare
For Christ to come and enter there.

We hail you as our Savior, Lord,
Our refuge and our great reward;
Without your grace we waste away
Like flow'rs that wither and decay.

Jordanis oras praevia
Vox ecce Baptistae quatit:
Praeconis ad grandes sonos
Ignavus abscedat sopor.

Mundemus et nos pectora
Deo propinquanti viam
Sternamus, et dignam domun
Tanto paremus hospiti.

Tu nostra, tu, Jesu, salus;
Tu robur et solacium:
Arens ut herba, te sine
Mortale tabescit genus.

Stretch forth your hand, our health restore,
And make us rise to fall no more;
Oh, let your face upon us shine
And fill the world with love divine.

All praise to you, eternal Son,
Whose advent has our freedom won,
Whom with the Father we adore,
And Holy Spirit, evermore.

Aegris salutarem manum
Extende; prostratos leva;
Ostende vultum; jam suus
Mundo reflorescet decor.

Qui liberator advenis,
Fili, tibi laus maxima
Cum Patre et almo Spiritu
In sempiterna saecula.

Charles Coffin published his Latin text in *Hymni Sacri* (1736). Mistaking it for an ancient text, John Chandler translated it for inclusion in his *Hymns of the Primitive Church* (1837); his translation has been altered for various hymnals, including *Lutheran Worship*. The final doxological stanza is from the original edition of *Hymns Ancient and Modern* (1861).

PUER NOBIS NASCITUR. Set to a German translation of an old Latin carol, "Geborn ist Gottes Söhnelein," the melody appeared in Michael Praetorius's *Musae Sioniae* VI (1609). Apparently it is based on the 15th–century tune used with the carol. It is also known sometimes as SPLENDOR. George R. Woodward's setting appeared in the *Service Book and Hymnal* (1958).

LO, HE COMES WITH CLOUDS DESCENDING 15

This four-stanza text by Charles Wesley, a great hymn of Christ's Second Advent, was first published in a 1758 tract entitled *Hymns of Intercession for All Mankind*. Although it may have been suggested by an earlier and similar six-stanza hymn by John Cennick that appeared in the 1752 edition of his *Collection of Sacred Hymns*, beginning with "Lo! he cometh, countless trumpets Blow before his bloody sign," it should not be confused with that inferior text. Unfortunately, what has added to the confusion is that Martin Madan (1726–90) made a cento of Wesley's and Cennick's texts which he included in his *Collection of Psalm and Hymn Tunes* (1769).

Taken from *Lutheran Book of Worship* (1978) with but slight alterations—"Once, for favored sinners slain" in stanza 1 was, for the sake of clarification, changed to "Once for ev'ry sinner slain"—the text is by Charles Wesley.

PICARDY. Instead of using HELMSLEY as *LBW* did, the Commission on Worship decided to stay with the usage in *Worship Supplement* (1969) and used PICARDY, the tune for "Let All Mortal Flesh Keep Silence" (*LW* 241), a lovely folk song from northern France, where it was traditionally sung to a legend about Jesus, who, dressed as a beggar, wanders from door to door asking for food and lodging. For additional comments see hymn 241.

The harmonization is by Paul G. Bunjes.

16 HOSANNA NOW THROUGH ADVENT

This children's hymn by Claudia F. Hernaman appeared in George R. Woodward's *Songs of Syon* (1910). Later it appeared in *The Children's Hymnal* (Concordia Publishing House, 1955) and, with language updated, passed into *Lutheran Worship*. Hernaman's stanza 3 has been omitted:

For we who sing Hosanna
Must like our Savior be,
In gentleness and meekness,
In love and purity.

MARIA IST GEBOREN first appeared in *Geistliche Kirchengesäng* (Köln, 1623). It was coupled to this text in *The Children's Hymnal* (1955).

Paul G. Bunjes prepared the harmonization for *Lutheran Worship* (1982).

17 O LORD OF LIGHT, WHO MADE THE STARS

O Lord of light, who made the stars, O Dawn, by whom we see the way, O Christ, redeemer of the world: Come now and listen as we pray!	Conditor alme siderum, Aeterna lux credentium Christe, redemptor omnium, Exaudi preces supplicum:
In lowliness you came on earth To rescue us from Satan's snares; O wondrous love that healed our wounds By taking on our mortal cares!	Qui, condolens interitu Mortis perire saeculum, Salvasti mundum languidum, Donans reis remedium:
To pay the debt we owed for sin, Your painful cross was made the price; From blessed Mary's womb you came, A victim pure for sacrifice.	Vergente mundi vespere, Uti sponsus de thalamo, Egressus honestissima Virginis matris clausula.
But now you reign, the King of kings, Adored in highest majesty; Your very name is held in awe From pole to pole and sea to sea!	Cuius forti potentiae Genu curantur omnia; Caelestia, terrestria Fatentur nutu subdita.
Great judge of all, on earth's last day Have pity on your children's plight; Rise up to shield us with your grace, Deliver us from Satan's might.	Te deprecamur, hagie, Venture iudex saeculi, Conserva nos in tempore Hostis a telo perfidi.
To God the Father and the Son And Holy Spirit, Three in One, Praise, honor, might, and glory be From age to age eternally. Amen	Laus, honor, virtus, gloria Deo Patri cum Fili Sancto simul Paraclito In sempiterna saecula.

The vesper office hymn for Advent in the monastic cycle, this beautiful Latin hymn appears in a ninth-century manuscript at Bern, and again in the Canterbury Hymnal of the 10th century. It was revised, beginning "Creator alme siderum," for the new Breviary sponsored by Pope Urban VIII about 1632. Clemens Blume in the *Catholic Encyclopedia* (1907–22) describes this mutilated Breviary: "Hymnody then received its death blow as . . . the medieval rhythmical hymns were forced into more classical forms by means of so-called corrections." Modern translators have attempted to undo the damage by restoring the original Latin meanings and rhythms.

This is a new translation by Melvin Farrell, replacing that of John Mason Neale which began, "Creator of the stars of night." Farrell's text appeared in the second edition of *The People's Hymnal* (Cincinnati, 1961).

CONDITOR ALME SIDERUM is the traditional plainsong melody for this text. Carl Schalk's setting first appeared in *Lutheran Book of Worship* (1978)

HARK! A THRILLING VOICE IS SOUNDING 18

Hark! A thrilling voice is sounding!
"Christ is near," we hear it say.
"Cast away the works of darkness,
All you children of the day!"

Startled at the solemn warning,
Let the earthbound soul arise;
Christ, its sun, all sloth dispelling,
Shines upon the morning skies.

See, the Lamb, so long expected,
Comes with pardon down from heav'n.
Let us haste, with tears of sorrow,
One and all, to be forgiv'n;

So, when next he comes in glory
And the world is wrapped in fear,
He will shield us with his mercy
And with words of love draw near.

Honor, glory, might, dominion
To the Father and the Son
With the everliving Spirit
While eternal ages run!

Vox clara ecce intonat,
Obscura quaeque increpat;
Pellantur eminus somnia,
Ab aethere Christus promicat.

Mens iam resurgat torpida,
Quae sorde exstat saucia:
Sidus refulget iam novum,
Ut tollat omne noxium.

E sursum Agnus mittitur
Laxare gratis debitum;
Omnes pro indulgentia
Vocem demus cum lacrimis:

Secundo ut cum fulserit
Mundumque horror cinxerit,
Non pro reatu puniat,
Sed pius nos tunc protegat.

Laus, honor, virtus, gloria
Deo Patri cum Filio
Sancto simul Paraclito
In sempiterna saecula.

Assigned to Lauds during Advent, this Latin hymn dates back at least to the 10th century, perhaps earlier. Some credit St. Ambrose with the hymn, but no proof has been offered in support of this suggestion. Edward Caswall's translation originally began, "Hark, an awful voice is sounding"; other slight changes have been made to the text since its first publication in *Lyra Catholica* (1849).

FREUEN WIR UNS ALL IN EIN. This interesting tune appeared in Michael Weisse's *Ein Neugesängbuchleyn* (1531), the first hymnal for the German Bohemian Brethren, where it was set to a text beginning with the same words.

The setting was done by Richard Hillert for *Worship Supplement* (1969).

19 O LORD, HOW SHALL I MEET YOU

O Lord, how shall I meet you,
How welcome you aright?
Your people long to greet you,
My hope, my heart's delight!
Oh, kindle, Lord most holy,
Your lamp within my breast
To do in spirit lowly
All that may please you best.

Your Zion strews before you
Green boughs and fairest palms;
And I too will adore you
With joyous songs and psalms.
My heart shall bloom forever
For you with praises new
And from your name shall never
Withhold the honor due.

I lay in fetters, groaning;
You came to set me free.
I stood, my shame bemoaning;
You came to honor me.
A glorious crown you give me,
A treasure safe on high
That will not fail or leave me
As earthly riches fly.

Love caused your incarnation;
Love brought you down to me.
Your thirst for my salvation
Procured my liberty.
Oh, love beyond all telling,
That led you to embrace
In love, all love excelling,
Our lost and fallen race.

Rejoice, then, you sad–hearted,
Who sit in deepest gloom,
Who mourn your joys departed
And tremble at your doom.
Despair not; he is near you,
There, standing at the door,
Who best can help and cheer you
And bids you weep no more.

He comes to judge the nations,
A terror to his foes,

Wie soll ich dich empfangen,
Und wie begegn' ich dir,
O aller Welt Verlangen,
O meiner Seele Zier?
O Jesu, Jesu, setze
Mir selbst die Fackel bei,
Damit, was dich ergötze
Mir kund und wissend sei.

Dein Zion streut dir Palmen
Und grüne Zweige hin,
Und ich will dir in Psalmen
Ermuntern meinen Sinn.
Mein Herze soll dir grünen
In stetem Lob und Preis
Und deinem Namen dienen,
So gut es kann und weiss.

Ich lag in schweren Banden,
Du kommst und machst mich los;
Ich stund in Spott und Schanden,
Du kommst und machst mich gross
Und hebst mich hoch zu Ehren
Und schenkst mir grosses Gut,
Das sich nicht lässt verzehren,
Wie irdisch Reichtum tut.

Nichts, nichts hat dich getrieben
Zu mir vom Himmelszelt
Als das geliebte Lieben,
Damit du alle Welt
In ihren tausend Plagen
Und grossen Jammerlast,
Die kein Mund aus kann sagen,
So fest umfangen hast.

Das schreib dir in dein Herze,
Du hochbetrübtes Heer,
Bei denen Gram und Schmerze
Sich häuft je mehr und mehr.
Seid unverzagt! Ihr habet
Die Hilfe vor der Tür;
Der eure Herzen labet
Und tröstet, steht allhier.

Er kommt zum Weltgerichte,
Zum Fluch dem, der ihm flucht;

A light of consolations
And blessed hope to those
Who love the Lord's appearing.
O glorious Sun, now come,
Send forth your beams so cheering
And guide us safely home.

Mit Gnad' und suessem Lichte
Dem, der ihn liebt und sucht.
Ach komm, ach komm, o Sonne,
Und hol uns allzumal
Zum ew'gen Licht und Wonne
In deinen Freudensaal!

If "Savior of the Nations, Come" (*LW* 13) is the Advent hymn *par excellence*, then this great hymn for the same season by Paul Gerhardt can certainly be considered as next in rank. While other hymns of his made their way into various hymnals rather slowly, this one was soon included during his lifetime.

With Paul Gerhardt the more individualistic and introspective hymn comes to the fore, compared to earlier developments in German hymnody. Yet his hymns express the most beautiful and fervent faith; they are the finest in all German sacred poetry and are probably next in importance to those of Martin Luther.

"O Lord, how shall I meet you" first appeared in Christoph Runge's hymnal for the Reformed churches in Berlin entitled *Dr. Martin Luther's und anderer vornehmen und geistreichen und gelehrten Männer geistliche Lieder und Psalmen* (Berlin, 1653), for which Johann Crüger was the music editor. The English translation, based on Catherine Winkworth's in her *Chorale Book for England* (1863), except for the omission of three stanzas and the text having been updated, is that which appeared in *The Lutheran Hymnal* (1941). It is based on Matthew 21:1–9, the Gospel for the First Sunday in Advent in the Old Standard Series.

WIE SOLL ICH DICH EMPFANGEN, a chorale tune of great merit, was composed by Johann Crüger, the most significant tune-maker after Luther, specifically for Gerhardt's Advent text, and this union first appeared in the above-mentioned Runge hymnal. It is the second tune for the Gerhardt text in *The Lutheran Hymnal* (1941) and thus possibly the less familiar of the two tunes offered therein, the other being VALLET WILL ICH DIR GEBEN by Melchior Teschner, also an excellent chorale tune. The Commission on Worship chose to use the latter tune for "O Jesus, King of glory" (*LW* 79) and for the great Palm Sunday hymn "All Glory, Laud and Honor" (*LW* 102).

The harmonization of WIE SOLL ICH DICH EMPFANGEN was prepared for *Lutheran Worship* (1982) by Wilhelm Quampen, a *nom de plume*, or pen name, of Paul G. Bunjes.

O BRIDE OF CHRIST, REJOICE 20

O bride of Christ, rejoice;
Exultant raise your voice.
Now comes the King, who glorious
Reigns over all victorious.

Hosanna! Now adore him,
Our king; we bow before him!

Fryd dig, du Kristi Brud,
Imod din Herre Gud!
For Haanden er hans Naade,
Som dig Profeten spaade.

Hosianna, Hder og Äre
Skal denne vor Konning väre!

Let shouts of gladness rise
Triumphant to the skies.
The King who comes in meekness
Is strong to heal our weakness.

Your heart now open wide;
Bid Christ with you abide.
He graciously will hear you
And be forever near you.

Gak ud af dit Paulun,
Og se et glädligt Syn:
Her rider Ärens Konning,
Gläd dig, du Zions Dronning!

Lad op dine Porte vid',
Kristus ind til dig rid!
Han agter dig at gjeste,
Din Salighed til Bedste.

Of unknown authorship, this Swedish hymn may date back to the 17th century. It was translated by Victor O. Petersen in 1899 and appeared in *The Lutheran Hymnary* (1913).

WO SOLL ICH FLIEHEN HIN. This tune appeared in Kasper Stieler's *Der Bussfertige Sünder oder Geistliches Handbüchlein* (Nürnberg, 1679), where it was set to Johann Herman's confident hymn of repentance beginning with the same words. It is uncertain whether this tune was composed or simply used by Stieler.

The setting is by Wilhelm Quampen, a *nom de plume* of Paul G. Bunjes.

21 "COMFORT, COMFORT," SAYS THE VOICE

"Comfort, comfort," says the voice,
"My people that they may rejoice."
The weight of sin, the judgment rod,
Removed by Christ, the Son of God.

Gladness, gladness let them hear,
With God's own peace the weary cheer:
"The prison's open, slaves are free,
Forgiven their iniquity."

Even, even out God's path,
Set straight what might invite his wrath.
The voice calls out, "Repent today,
The King of kings is on his way."

Witness, witness to the world
The glory of the Lord unfurled.
The hour now strikes, the dawnlight breaks,
God keeps the promises he makes.

Withered, withered human might,
Its bloom cut off by frost and blight.
All flesh, like grass, wilts to the core,
But God's Word lives forevermore.

Lift your voice, speak words of pow'r
That none may fear the awesome hour.
Now comes the Lord, your God is here,
His grace and might rule far and near.

"Tröstet, tröstet," spricht der Herr,
"Mein Volk, dass es nicht zage mehr."
Der Sünde Last, des Todes fron
Nimmt von euch Christus, Gottes Sohn.

Freundlich, freundlich rede du
Und sprich dem müden Volke zu:
"Die Qual ist um, der Knecht ist frei,
All Missetat vergeben sei."

Ebnet, ebnet Gott die Bahn,
Bei Tal und Hügel fanget an.
Die Stimme ruft: "Tut Busse gleich,
Denn nah ist euch das Himmelreich."

Sehet, sehet, alle Welt
Die Herrlichkeit des Herrn erhellt.
Die Zeit ist heir, es schlägt die Stund,
Geredet hat es Gottes Mund.

Alles, alles Fleisch ist Gras,
Die Blüte sein wird bleich und blass.
Das Gras verdorrt, das Fleisch verblich,
Doch Gottes Wort bleibt ewiglich.

Hebe deine Stimme, sprich
Mit Macht, dass niemand fürchte sich.
Es kommt der Herr, eur Gott ist da
Und herrscht gewaltig fern und nah.

This well-crafted text by Waldemar Rode, Lutheran pastor in Hamburg-Uhlenhorst, is based on the Old Testament reading of the Old Standard pericopes, viz., Isaiah 40:1–8, designated for the Third Sunday in Advent. Pastor Rode wrote it in connection with a sermon he preached on the above text in Advent 1937. It is in the original German text that one especially notices the almost literal presentation of the biblical text. The translation is by F. Samuel Janzow.

TRÖSTET, TRÖSTET, SPRICHT DER HERR. This tune was composed by Hans Friedrich Micheelsen, who, at the time the text was written, was music director at Rode's church. When Pastor Rode showed his text to Micheelsen, the latter happily decided to write the tune. Micheelsen had composed music for numerous contemporary poets, especially the works of Rudolph Alexander Schroeder. Regarding the tune under consideration Micheelsen said:

> I often listen to pre-Reformation hymns in order to learn from them, but I never attempted to imitate them. The tunes to the strong texts of Schroeder came to my mind all at once. I didn't have to fuss or take great pains with them. Naturally one must know the rules of a good melody, and one must work at it. Knowledge of structure must blend with the idea, or concept. One thing I must emphasize: They [the melodies] do not grow out of 'inner voices.' With Schroeder I pursued the masterly formed texts; with Rode, the smooth, folklike verse. (Büchner, *Die Lieder Unserer Kirche*)

The harmonization is by Paul G. Bunjes.

COME, O LONG-EXPECTED JESUS 22

This hymn by Charles Wesley first appeared in an 18-hymn collection titled *Hymns for the Nativity of Our Lord* (1744). Alterations to the text are slight, mostly for updating of the personal pronouns. John Wesley did not include this text in his *Collection of Hymns for the Use of the People Called Methodists* (1780), so it remained unfamiliar to Methodists until 1875, although not to Anglicans: Martin Madan included it in his *Psalms and Hymns* (1760), and Augustus Toplady in his *Psalms and Hymns* (1776).

JEFFERSON. This tune appeared in William Walker's *Southern Harmony* (1835) as the setting for "Glorious things of you are spoken" (*LW* 294).

The setting is by Donald A. Busarow from *Lutheran Book of Worship* (1978).

23 LIFT UP YOUR HEADS, YOU MIGHTY GATES

Lift up your heads, you mighty gates!
Behold, the King of glory waits.
The King of kings is drawing near,
The Savior of the world is here.
He brings salvation down to earth.
Greet him with shouts of holy mirth.
Our highest praise we bring,
Our God, Creator, King.

Macht hoch die Tür, die Tor' macht weit,
Es kommt der Herr der Herrlichkeit,
Ein König aller Königreich',
Ein Heiland aller Welt zugleich,
Der Heil und Leben mit sich bringt;
Derhalben jauchzt, mit Freuden singt:
Gelobet sei mein Gott,
Mein Schöpfer, reich von Rat!

The righteous King is bringing peace;
He comes the pris'ners to release.
His royal crown, self–sacrifice,
Its jewel, mercy without price.
He brings our sorrows to an end.
Shout out your joy to God, our friend.
Our highest praise we bring,
Our God, Redeemer, King.

Er ist gerecht, ein Helfer wert,
Sanftmütigkeit is sein Gefährt,
Sein Königskron' ist Heiligkeit,
Sein Zepter ist Barmherzigkeit,
All unsre Not zum End' er bringt,
Derhalben jauchzt, mit Freuden singt:
Gelobet sei mein Gott,
Mein Heiland, gross von Tat!

O happy town, O blessed land
That keeps our gracious King's command,
And blest the heart when he comes in
His holy reign there to begin.
His entrance is the dawn of bliss;
He fills our lives and makes them his.
Our highest praise we bring,
God, Comforter and King.

O wohl dem Land, o wohl der Stadt,
So diesen König bei sich hat!
Wohl allen Herzen insgemein,
Da dieser König ziehet ein!
Er ist die rechte Freudensonn',
Bringt mit sich lauter Freud' und Wonn:
Gelobet sei mein Gott,
Mein Tröster, früh und spat!

Unbar the gate, fling wide the door,
Your heart to God's design restore.
Adorn its walls with all things right,
With peace and love and joy and light.
Your King will then be glad to come
And live within you as his home.
Our highest praise we bring
To God, our Lord and King.

Macht hoch die Tür, die Tor' macht weit,
Eu'r Herz zum Tempel zubereit't,
Die Zweiglein der Gottseligkeit
Steckt auf mit Andacht, lust und Freud'!
So kommt der König auch zu euch,
Ja Heil und Leben mit zugleich.
Gelobet sei mein Gott,
Voll Rat, voll Tat, voll Gnad'!

Christ Jesus, Lord and Savior, come,
I open wide my heart, your home.
Oh, enter with your radiant grace,
On my life's pattern shine your face,
And let your Holy Spirit guide
To gracious vistas rich and wide.
Our God, we praise your name,
Forevermore the same.

Komm, o mein Heiland Jesu Christ,
Mein's herzens Tür dir offen ist!
Ach zeuch mit deiner Gnade ein,
Dein' Freundlichkeit auch uns erschein',
Dein Heil'ger Geist uns führ' und leit'
Den Weg zur ew'gen Seligkeit!
Dem Namen dein, o Herr,
Sei ewig Preis und Ehr'!

This is perhaps the most folklike and widely sung of all the German Advent hymns in the hymnal, undoubtedly the result of the two buoyant swinging tunes to which it has been sung. In German hymnals this hymn frequently began the Advent section, thus heeding the original intent of Georg Weissel, its author. Based on Psalm 24:7–10, it appeared in Part I of the *Preussische Festlieder* (Elbing, 1642), issued by Johann Eccard

(*LW* 103), at that time director of the royal orchestra in Königsberg. The translation is by F. Samuel Janzow.

MACHT HOCH DIE TÜR. The hymn beginning with these words failed to become popular until the text appeared in Johann Freylinghausen's *Geistreiches Gesangbuch* (Halle, 1704) set to this tune, evidently composed by him. When the text was first published in the *Preussische Festlieder* (see above), it was coupled to a tune by Johann Stobäus (*LW* 358) and intended for choir use, not congregation. By any standards, this is a catchy, ingratiating tune in triple meter that congregations love to sing.

The harmonization is essentially the work of Freylinghausen as it appeared in *The Lutheran Hymnal* (1941), except for occasional changes in the voice leading.

LIFT UP YOUR HEADS, YOU MIGHTY GATES 24

For discussion of the text see hymn 23.

MILWAUKEE. The popularity of this tune, the third of three tunes set to Georg Weissel's text and included in *The Lutheran Hymnal* (1941), prompted the Commission on Worship to include it in *Lutheran Worship* (1982). Composed for this text by August Lemke, it was sung in Trinity Lutheran Church, Milwaukee, where Lemke was teacher, organist, and choir director.

The harmonization is from *The Lutheran Hymnal* (1941).

O PEOPLE, RISE AND LABOR 25

O people, rise and labor,
To renovate the heart
That mankind's mighty Savior,
Whom God's love set apart
To free you all from sin,
May do the promised wonder
And with his life and splendor,
Victorious, enter in.

Mit Ernst, ihr Menschenkinder,
Das Herz in euch bestellt,
Damit das Heil der Sünder,
Der grosse Wunderheld,
Den Gott aus Gnad' allein
Der Welt zum Licht und Leben
Versprochen hat zu geben,
Bei allen kehre ein.

Prepare with earnest rigor
The way for your great guest.
Make straight his path with vigor,
Rebuild your lives with zest.
The sunken valleys fill,
Restore eroded places,
Where sin-bursts leave their traces,
Cut down the prideful hill.

Bereitet doch fein tüchtig
Den Weg dem grossen Gast,
Macht seine Steige richtig,
Lasst alles, was er hasst;
Macht alle Bahnen recht,
Das Tal lasst sein erhöhet;
Macht niedrig, was hoch stehet,
Was krumm ist, gleich und schlecht.

A heart that humbly serves him
Stands highest in his sight.
The haughty heart, the proud whim
Go down in anguished night.
But those who love God's Word
And go where he is pointing
Are fit by his anointing
To host their gracious Lord.

Dear Lord, in high compassion
Bend down with Advent grace.
My heart, I pray, refashion
With mercy from your face.
Come from the thankless inn
To make my heart your manger
That I, no more a stranger,
Eternal praise begin.

Ein Herz, das Demut übet,
Bei Gott am höchsten steht;
Ein Herz, das Hochmut liebet,
Mit Angst zugrunde geht;
Ein Herz, das richtig ist
Und folget Gottes Leiten,
Das kann sich recht bereiten,
Zu dem kommt Jesus Christ.

Ach, mache du mich Armen
In dieser Gnadenzeit,
Aus Güte und Erbarmen,
Herr Jesu, selbt bereit!
Zieh in mein Herz hinein
Vom Stall und von der Krippen,
So werden Herz und Lippen
Dir ewig dankbar sein.

This sincere, imploring Advent hymn by Valentin Thilo (the Younger) first appeared in Part I (Advent to Easter) of *Preussische Festlieder* (Elbing, 1642) issued by Johann Stobäus. Its emphasis on repentance reminds one that in earlier times Advent had a more penitential character than it has today. One can picture John the Baptist crying out, "Repent, for the kingdom of heaven is near. . . . Prepare the way of the Lord" (Matt. 3:2–3). Regrettably the specific mention of John the Baptist in the original stanza 4 was deleted, and other lines, as here given in German and in translation, were substituted in the Hannover *Gesangbuch* of 1657.

The translation is by F. Samuel Janzow.

AUS MEINES HERZENS GRUNDE was not the tune originally set to the above text in the *Preussische Festlieder* (Elbing, 1642). Similar to the procedure with respect to "Macht hoch die Tür," Stobäus set the text to more of an art song for the choir, rather than for the congregation. Cognizant of congregations' familiarity with and love for the union of text and tune as contained in *The Lutheran Hymnal* (1941), the Commission on Worship chose to retain AUS MEINES HERZENS GRUNDE, a beautiful, now somewhat modified version of the tune published in *New Katechismus Gesangbüchlein* (Hamburg, 1598), edited by David Walder, who used it, however, with the text of Johann Walter's hymn "Herzlich tut mich erfreuen" (*LW* 176).

Another splendid tune that can well serve as an alternate is VON GOTT WILL ICH NICHT LASSEN (*LW* 409), a tune having its origin in folksong, and almost inseparably wedded to Valentin Thilo's Advent hymn in the current hymnals of the Lutheran territorial churches in Germany.

The harmonization of AUS MEINES HERZENS GRUNDE was prepared for *Lutheran Worship* (1982) by Paul G. Bunjes.

THE KING SHALL COME 26

John Brownlie's seven-stanza hymn is evidently a translation from the Greek, although its antecedent is unknown. He included it in his *Hymns from the East, being Centos and Suggestions from the Service Books of the Holy Eastern Church* (1907). Stanzas 5 and 6 have been omitted:

The King shall come when morning dawns
And earth's dark night is past;
O haste the rising of that morn,
The day that aye shall last;

And let the endless bliss begin,
By weary saints foretold,
When right shall triumph over wrong,
And truth shall be extolled.

It is possible that Brownlie, a scholar well-acquainted with the Eastern Church, wrote an original text in the spirit of eastern worship and included it in his collection as an example rather than as a translation.

CONSOLATION, also called MORNING SONG, is from Wyeth's *Repository of Sacred Music,* Part II (Harrisburg, 1813). Several southern "shaped-note" hymnals used this collection as a resource for their tunes; CONSOLATION appeared in *Kentucky Harmony* (1816) and several other collections, under this name, in the Aeolian mode (see essay: The Church Modes, p. 832). There the composer is listed as a Mr. Dean, which has been interpreted as a misprint for Elkanah Kelsay Dare, a Methodist minister and musician, for a time dean of boys at Wilmington College, Wilmington, Delaware. Although Dare was given credit in Wyeth's index for a number of tunes, this one was not among them.

The arrangement, from *Worship Supplement* (1969), is by Theodore Beck.

PREPARE THE ROYAL HIGHWAY 27

Prepare the royal highway;
The King of kings is near!
Let ev'ry hill and valley
A level road appear!
Then greet the king of glory
Foretold in sacred story:

Refrain
Oh, blest is he that came
In God the Father's name!

Bereden väg för Herran!
Berg, sjunken, djup, stan' opp!
Han kommer, han som fjärran
Var sedd av fädrens hopp,
Rättfärdighetens Förste,
Av Davids hus den störste.

Välsignad vare han
Som kom i Herrens namm.

God's people, see him coming:
Your own eternal king!
Palm branches strew before him!
Spread garments! Shout and sing!
God's promise will not fail you!
No more shall doubt assail you!

Guds folk, für dig han träder
En evig konung opp.
Strö palmer, bred ut kläder,
Sjung ditt uppfyllda hopp.
Guds löften äro sanna,
Nu ropa: Hosianna!

Then fling the gates wide open
To greet your promised king!
Your king, yet ev'ry nation
Its tribute too should bring.
All lands, bow down before him!
All voices, join in singing:

Gör dina portar vida
För Herens härlighet.
Se, folken kring dig bida
Att na din salighet.
Kring jordens länder alla
Skall denna lovsang skalla:

His is no earthly kingdom;
It comes from heav'n above.
His rule is peace and freedom
And justice, truth, and love.
So let your praise be sounding
For kindness so abounding:

Ej kommer han med härar
Och ej med stat och prakt;
Dock ondskan han forfarar
I all dess stolta makt.
Med Andens svärd han strider
Och segrar, när han lider.

By Frans Mikael Franzen, this hymn, rich in scriptural allusions, was originally published in Franzen and Johan Olof Wallin's *Prof-Psalmer* (1812). After the text was given a poor review, Franzen revised it before including it in the *Psalm-Boken* (1819). Augustus Nelson, pastor of a rural parish in Minnesota, translated it for inclusion in the first English hymnal of the Augustana Lutheran Church (1901), beginning, "Prepare the way, O Zion." Except for the last two lines of stanza 3, *Lutheran Worship* (1982) uses instead the new translation prepared by the Inter-Lutheran Commission on Worship for *Lutheran Book of Worship* (1978). Considering the original two lines in that hymnal—"All lands will bow before him; Their voices join your singing"—readily construed as millennialistic, the Synod's commission altered these lines to read: "All lands, bow down before him! All voices, join in singing."

BEREDEN VÄG FÖR HERRAN. The form of the tune used in *Lutheran Book of Worship* appeared in the 1697 tune edition of the "Svedberg Hymnal," a revision of Jesper Svedberg's (*LW* 434) offering to the Swedish Church of a year earlier. According to the *Koralbok för Svenska Kyrkan* (1939), the form of the tune used there is from an 18th–century manuscript of the Ovikens Church in Jämtland. The repetitive nature of the rhythmic pattern of that tune (♩ | 𝅗𝅥 ♩ 𝅗𝅥 ♩ | 𝅗𝅥. 𝅗𝅥) prompted the commission to alter it as contained in *Lutheran Worship.*

The setting in *Lutheran Worship* was prepared by Richard W. Gieseke.

28 COMFORT, COMFORT THESE MY PEOPLE

"Comfort, comfort these my people,
Speak of peace!" so says our God.
Comfort these who sit in darkness

Tröstet, tröstet meine Lieben,
Tröstet mein Volk, spricht mein Gott;
Tröstet, die sich jetzt betrüben

Groaning under sin's dread rod.
"To my people I proclaim
Pardon now in Jesus' name.
Tell them that their sins I cover,
That their warfare now is over!"

Über Feindes Hohn und Spott.
Weil Jerusalem wohl dran,
Redet sie gar freundlich an;
Denn ihr Leiden hat ein Ende,
Ihre Ritterschaft ich wende.

Yes, our sins the Lord will pardon,
Blotting out each dark misdeed.
All that well deserved his anger
He no more will see nor heed.
We who languished many a day
Under guilt now washed away
We exchange our pining sadness
For his comfort, peace, and gladness!

Ich vergeb' all ihre Sünden,
Ich tilg' ihre Missetat,
Ich will nicht mehr sehn noch finden,
Was die Straf' erwecket hat;
Sie hat ja zweifältig Leid
Schon empfangen; ihre Freud'
Soll sich täglich neu vermehren
Und ihr Leid in Freud' verkehren.

Now the herald's voice is crying
In the desert far and near,
Calling us to true repentance,
For the kingdom now is here!
Oh, that warning cry obey,
Oh, prepare for God a way,
Let the valleys rise to meet him,
Let the hills bow down to greet him!

Eine Stimme lässt sich hören
In der Wüste weit und breit,
Alle Menschen zu bekehren:
Macht dem Herrn den Weg bereit,
Machet Gott ein' ebne Bahn;
Alle Welt soll heben an,
Alle Tale zu erhöhen,
Dass die Berge niedrig stehen.

Straight must be what long was crooked;
Make the roughest places plain!
Let your hearts be true and humble,
Ready for his holy reign!
Here the glory of the Lord
Stands so graciously revealed
That all people see the token
That God's word is never broken!

Ungleich soll nun eben werden
Und, was höckricht, gleich und schlecht;
Alle Menschen hier auf Erden
Sollen leben schlecht und recht;
Denn des Herren Herrlichkeit,
Offenbar zu dieser Zeit,
Macht, dass alles Fleisch kann sehen,
Wie, was Gott spricht, muss geschehen.

Catherine Winkworth translated this German hymn for her *Chorale Book for England* (1865). The original, intended for the festival of St. John the Baptist (June 24), was written by Johann Olearius and included in his *Geistliche Singe-Kunst* (Leipzig, 1671), one of the most renowned German hymnbooks of the 17th century, containing more than 1,200 hymns, over 300 by Olearius himself. As with many of Winkworth's translations, this one has been considerably altered, retaining the essence of her wording and rhyming.

FREU DICH SEHR (PSALM 42). Originally set to an early 16th-century folksong, "Ne l'oseray je dire," this sturdy, rhythmically interesting tune was adapted by Louis Bourgeois (*LW* 216, et al.) for the Genevan Psalter, *Trente quatre Pseaumes de David* (1551). There it accompanied Theodore de Beze's version of Psalm 42, "Ainsi que la biche ree" ("As Pants the Hart for Cooling Streams," *LBW* 452). In 1613 it appeared in Rhamba's *Harmoniae sacrae* with the funeral hymn "Freu dich sehr, O meine Seele," by which name the tune is known in Germany.

The tune was first linked with Olearius' text in the *Chorale Book for England* (1863), where its irregular rhythm (see essay: Polyrhythmic and Isometric Chorales, p. 822) was forced into straight 4/4 time.

The harmonization was prepared by Richard W. Gieseke for *Lutheran Worship.*

29 HARK THE GLAD SOUND

This hymn by Philip Doddridge, originally in seven stanzas, was written to accompany his Christmas sermon delivered on December 28, 1735. It was first published in England in the posthumous edition of Doddridge's *Hymns, Founded on Various Texts in the Holy Scriptures* (1755). Since then it has appeared in many hymnals of Scotland and England, often with extensive alterations. Sir Roundel Palmer, later Lord Selbourne, literary figure who compiled the famous *The Book of Praise from the Best English Hymn Writers* (Macmillan, 1862), said of this hymn: "A more sweet, vigorous, and perfect composition is not to be found in the whole body of ancient hymns." *Lutheran Worship* (1982) contains Doddridge's original text with only the personal pronouns updated.

CHESTERFIELD. Since it originally appeared in Thomas Haweis' *Carmina Christo* (1792), this tune is usually attributed to him. Originally extended by a repetition of the last line of Haweis' text, "O thou from whom all goodness flows," as such it exemplified a rather typical 18th-century hymn tune with its somewhat florid character in triple meter and repetitions of parts of the text. The present form of the tune as shortened and revised by Samuel Webbe, Jr.—a notable improvement over the original—is variously called HAWEIS, RICHMOND (for a friend of the composer, Leigh Richmond), ALDWINKLE (after Haweis' parish in Northamptonshire), MT. CALVARY, or SPA FIELDS CHAPEL (chapel of Selina Shirley, Countess of Huntingdon). The name CHESTERFIELD derives from Lord Chesterfield, a frequent visitor at Lady Huntingdon's chapel, where Haweis was chaplain.

The harmonization is by Paul G. Bunjes.

30 ONCE HE CAME IN BLESSING

Once he came in blessing,
All our sins redressing;
Came in likeness lowly,
Son of God most holy;
Bore the cross to save us;
Hope and freedom gave us.

Still he comes within us;
Still his voice would win us
From the sins that hurt us;
Would to truth convert us

Gottes Sohn ist kommen
Uns allen zu Frommen
Hier auf diese Erden
In armen Gebärden,
Dass er uns von Sünde
Freiet' und entbünde.

Er kommt auch noch heute
Und lehret die Leute,
Wie sie sich von Sünden
Zur Buss' sollen wenden,

From our foolish error
Ere he comes in terror.

Thus, if we have known him,
Not ashamed to own him,
Nor have spurned him coldly
But will trust him boldly,
He will then receive us,
Heal us, and forgive us.

Those who then are loyal
Find a welcome royal.
Come, then, O Lord Jesus,
From our sins release us;
Let us here confess you
Till in heav'n we bless you.

Von Irrtum und Torheit
Treten zu der Wahrheit.

Die sich sein nicht schämen
Und sein'n Dienst annehmen
Durch ein'n rechten Glauben
Mit ganzem Vertauen,
Denen wird er eben
Ihre Sünd' vergeben.

Ei nun, Herre Jesu,
Schicke unser Herz zu,
Dass wir alle Stunden
Rechtgläubig erfunden,
Darinnen verscheiden
Zur ewigen Freuden.

This lovely Advent hymn by Johann Horn, originally in seven stanzas, was first published in *Ein Gesangbuch der Brüder inn Behemen und Merherren* (Nürnberg, 1544). Relating the confession of sin to Advent themes makes it a good opening hymn for corporate worship in that season.

Except for stanzas 3 and 4, which have been altered and updated, the translation is that of Catherine Winkworth in her *Chorale Book for England* (1863).

GOTTES SOHN IST KOMMEN takes its name from the first line of the above German text. Its origin, however, is from the 14th-century Marian song, "Ave ierarchia celestis et pia," sung at times by the Bohemian congregations in corporate worship after the Kyrie or sequence. Michael Weisse (*LW* 18), in his *New Gesangbuchlen* (1531), turned this Marian song into a German Advent hymn of 15 stanzas beginning with "Menschenkind merk eben" (Zahn 3294).

The harmonization was prepared by Paul G. Bunjes.

OH, COME, OH, COME, EMMANUEL 31

Oh, come, oh, come, Emmanuel,
And ransom captive Israel,
That mourns in lonely exile here
Until the Son of God appear.

Refrain
Rejoice! Rejoice! Emmanuel
Shall come to you, O Israel.

Oh, come, our Wisdom from on high,
Who ordered all things mightily;
To us the path of knowledge sow,
And teach us in her ways to go.

Veni, veni, Emmanuel,
Captivum solve Israel
Qui gemit in exilio,
Privatus Dei Filio.

Gaude! Gaude! Emmanuel
Nascetur pro te, Israel.

Veni, O Sapientia,
Quae hic disponis omnia;
Veni, viam prudentiae
Ut doceas et gloria.

Oh, come, oh, come, our Lord of might, Who to your tribes on Sinai's height In ancient times gave holy law, In cloud and majesty and awe.	Veni, veni, Adonai, Qui populo in Sanai Legem dedisti vertice In majestate gloriae.
Oh, come, O Rod of Jesse's stem, From ev'ry foe deliver them That trust your mighty pow'r to save; Bring them in vict'ry through the grave.	Veni, O Jesse Virgula, Ex hostis tuos ungula; De secu tuos tartari Educ et antro barathri.
Oh, come, O Key of David, come, And open wide our heav'nly home; Make safe the way that leads on high, And close the path to misery.	Veni, Clavis Davidica, Regna reclude caelica, Fac iter tutum superum, Et claude vias inferum.
Oh, come, our Dayspring from on high, And cheer us by your drawing nigh; Disperse the gloomy clouds of night, And death's dark shadows put to flight.	Veni, veni, O Oriens Solari nos adveniens, Noctis depelle nebulas, Dirasque mortis tenebras.
Oh, come, Desire of nations, bind In one the hearts of all mankind; Oh, bid our sad divisions cease, And be yourself our King of Peace.	Veni, veni, Rex gentium Veni, Redemptor omnium, Ut salvas tuos famulos Peccati sibi conscios.

Sometime prior to the ninth century the custom arose of chanting an antiphon before and after the Magnificat at Vespers from December 17 to 23 (see *Lutheran Worship*, p. 288–89). Thus there arose seven such antiphons, not necessarily of Roman origin, each beginning with "O" and saluting the coming of the Messiah by one of the many titles ascribed to him in Holy Scripture, and closing with a petition based on the salutation. In the Middle Ages it was customary, at least in some places, for each of the chief officers of the monastery to be assigned a given "O" to be sung on a particular day and then to provide a pittance or feast for the monks.

Some unknown author, probably in the 12th or 13th century, cast these antiphons into verse form and added the refrain. This version first appeared in the Appendix to *Psalteriolum Cantionum Catholicarum* (Cologne, 1710), and was translated into English by John Mason Neale (*LW* 36, et al.) in his *Mediaeval Hymns and Sequences* (1851), with the opening line, "Draw nigh, draw nigh, Emmanuel." In the original edition of *Hymns Ancient and Modern* (1861) Neale's translation was included in considerably altered form. The version here used is basically his in altered and updated form. The parallel Latin text here given is the early prose form, except that the seventh becomes stanza 1 of the hymn, the first becomes stanza 2 and so on.

VENI EMMANUEL. Until quite recently the exact origin of this tune was a mystery. In Neale's music edition of the *Hymnal Noted* (1854) it is stated that the tune is from a French Missal in the National Library at Lisbon, Portugal. Since the source could not be located there, it was assumed that Thomas Helmore, a priest and musician who worked with Neale in producing the 1854 edition of the *Hymnal Noted*, constructed the tune from fragments of various Kyrie melodies. Thus it was indeed welcome news when Mother Thomas More (now better known as Doctor Mary Berry), in the September

1966, issue of *The Musical Times*, stated that the tune had been found in a small 15th-century *Processional* belonging to a community of French Franciscan nuns, where it served as the tune to some verses of the funeral responsory, "Libera me," beginning with "Bone Iesu dulcis cunctis."

Here is truly a noble plainsong tune, skillfully and economically constructed from a single phrase and its inversion. Notice also that the refrain is almost identical to the opening phrases except for the change in rhythm. Reflecting its character, the tune should be sung lightly, flexibly, and not too slowly, the rhythm largely controlled by the movement of the words and phrases.

The harmonization was prepared by Paul G. Bunjes.

O SAVIOR, REND THE HEAVENS WIDE 32

O Savior, rend the heavens wide;
Come down, come down with mighty stride;
Unlock the gates, the doors break down;
Unbar the way to heaven's crown.

O Father, light from heaven lend;
As morning dew, O Son, descend.
Drop down, you clouds, the life of spring:
To Jacob's line rain down the King.

O earth, in flow'ring bud be seen;
Clothe hill and dale in garb of green.
Bring forth, O earth, a blossom rare,
Our Savior, sprung from meadow fair.

O Morning Star, O radiant Dawn,
When will we sing your morning song?
Come, Son of God! Without your light
We grope in dread and gloom of night.

Sin's dreadful doom upon us lies;
Grim death looms fierce before our eyes.
Oh, come, lead us with mighty hand
From exile to our promised land.

There shall we all our praises bring
And sing to you, our Savior King;
There shall we laud you and adore
Forever and forevermore.

O Heiland, reiss die Himmel auf,
Herab, herab vom Himmel lauf;
Reiss ab vom Himmel Tor und Tür,
Reiss ab, wo Schloss und Riegel für.

Gott, ein' Tau vom Himmel giess,
Im Tau herab, o Heiland, fliess.
Ihr Wolken, brecht und regnet aus
Den König über Jakobs Haus.

O Erd, schlag aus, schlag aus, o Erd,
Dass Berg und Tal grün alles werd.
O Erd, herfür dies Blümlein bring,
O Heiland, aus der Erden spring.

O klare Sonn, du schöner Stern,
Dich wollten wir anschauen gern;
O Sonn, geh auf, ohn deinen Schein
In Finsternis wir alle sein.

Hier leiden wir die grösste Not,
Vor Augen steht der ewig Tod.
Ach komm, führ uns mit starker Hand
Vom Elend zu dem Vaterland.

Da wollen wir all danken dir,
Unserm Erlöser, für und für;
Da wollen wir all loben dich
Zu aller Zeit und ewiglich.

The German text of this notable hymn first appeared in *Ausserlesene Catholische Geistliche Kirchengesäng* (Cologne, 1623), printed by Peter Brachel (Bäumker I, p. 248). More recent Roman Catholic hymnals ascribe its authorship to Friedrich von Spee.

A somewhat unique characteristic of this Advent hymn is its direct reference to numerous bold images, or metaphors, from Holy Scripture. Its theme reflects the ancient Introit for the Fourth Sunday in Advent with its dramatic call: "You heavens above, reign down righteousness; let the clouds shower it down. Let the earth open wide, let salvation spring up" (Is. 45:8). Closely associated with this are "Oh, that you would rend the heavens and come down" (Is. 64:1) and "A shoot will come up from the stump of Jesse; from his roots a Branch will bear fruit" (Is. 11:1). Not to be overlooked are the references to Christ as the sun (more direct in the German)—"His face was like the sun shining in all its brilliance" (Rev. 1:16b)—and as the "bright Morning Star" (Rev. 22:16b), all pointing directly to him as the Redeemer, whose coming is entreated with deep fervor.

The translation is an altered form of that prepared by Martin L. Seltz for inclusion in *Worship Supplement* (1969).

O HEILAND, REISS DIE HIMMEL AUF. The German text first appeared with "Conditor alme siderum," an old vesper tune (*LW* 17) dating perhaps from the sixth century. The present strong, solid tune first appeared in a German Roman Catholic hymnal for Rhein-Pfalz, printed in Augsburg in 1666. Choir directors may remember the beautiful set of variations on this tune composed by Johannes Brahms (1833–97).

In American Lutheranism this hymn and tune first appeared in *Worship Supplement* (1969).

The harmonization is by Paul G. Bunjes.

33 LET THE EARTH NOW PRAISE THE LORD

Let the earth now praise the Lord, Who has truly kept his word And at last to us did send Christ, the sinner's help and friend.	Gott sei Dank durch alle Welt, Der sein Wort beständig hält Und der Sünder Trost und Rat Zu uns hergesendet hat.
What the fathers most desired, What the prophets' heart inspired, What they longed for many a year, Stands fulfilled in glory here.	Was der alten Väter Schar Höchster Wunsch und Sehnen war, Und was sie geprophezeit, Ist erfüllt nach Herrlichkeit.
Abram's promised great reward, Zion's helper, Jacob's Lord— Him of twofold race behold— Truly came, as long foretold.	Zions Hilf' und Abrams Lohn, Jakobs Heil, der Jungfrau'n Sohn, Der wohl zweigestammte Held, Hat sich treulich eingestellt.
Welcome, O my Savior, now! Joyful, Lord, to you I bow. Come into my heart, I pray; Oh, prepare yourself a way!	Sei willkommen, o mein Heil! Hosianna, o mein Teil! Richte du auch eine Bahn Dir in meinem Herzen an.
As your coming was in peace, Quiet, full of gentleness,	Und gleichwie dein' Ankunft war Voller Sanftmut, ohn' Gefahr,

Let the same mind dwell in me
Which is yours eternally.

Bruise for me the Serpent's head
That, set free from doubt and dread,
I may cling to you in faith,
Safely kept through life and death.

Then when you will come again
As the glorious king to reign,
I with joy will see your face,
Freely ransomed by your grace.

Also sei auch jederzeit
Deine Sanftmut mir bereit.

Tritt der Schlange Kopf entzwei,
Dass ich, aller Ängste frei,
Dir im Glauben um und an
Selig bleibe zugetan.

Das, wenn du, o Lebensfürst,
Prächtig wiederkommen wirst,
Ich dir mög' entgegengehn
Und vor Gott gerecht bestehn.

This hymn first appeared in a publication by Heinrich Held's Altenburg friend, Johann Niedling, *Neuerfundener Geistlicher Wasserquelle* (Frankfort-am-Oder, 1658). Suggested by St. Ambrose's "Veni redemptor gentium," as was also Luther's "Nun komm, der Heiden Heiland" (*LW* 13), it differs greatly from the latter both in form and content. Here the rules of Martin Opitz regarding German poetry are discreetly employed and clearly in evidence. And while Luther took pains to give a somewhat literal translation of this well-known and much-loved Latin hymn, Held is not interested in such literalness. Instead, with Ambrose's hymn as a model, he is more concerned with what might be looked upon as the theme that he enunciates in the first stanza, "The Lord has kept his Word." Indeed, promise and fulfillment answer each other; they represent the deepest yearning of mankind. The hymn concludes with a look to the final coming of the Lord and the perfect fulfillment of all promises. Truly this ranks among the best of Advent hymns.

The translation, altered and updated, is by Catherine Winkworth in the *Chorale Book for England* (1863).

NUN KOMM, DER HEIDEN HEILAND. See hymn 13 for a discussion of this tune.
The harmonization is by Paul G. Bunjes.

COME, O PRECIOUS RANSOM 34

Come, O precious Ransom, come,
Only hope for sinful mortals!
Come, O Savior of the world;
Open are to you all portals.
Come, your beauty let us view;
Anxiously we wait for you.

Enter now my waiting heart,
Glorious King and Lord most holy.
Dwell in me and never leave,
Though I am but poor and lowly.
What vast riches will be mine
When you are my guest divine!

Komm, du wertes Lösegeld,
Dessen alle Heiden hoffen;
Komm, o Heiland aller Welt,
Tor' und Türen stehen offen;
Komm in ungewohnter Zier,
Komm, wir warten mit Begier!

Zeuch auch in mein Herz hinein,
O du grosser Ehrenkönig,
Lass mich deine Wohnung sein!
Bin ich armer Mensch zu wenig,
Ei, so soll mein Reichtum sein,
Dass du bei mir ziehest ein.

My hosannas and my palms
Graciously receive, I pray you;
Evermore, as best I can,
Homage I will gladly pay you,
And in faith I will embrace
Life eternal by your grace.

Hail! Hosanna! David's Son!
Jesus, hear our supplication!
Let your kingdom, scepter, crown
Bring us blessing and salvation
That forever we may sing:
Hail! Hosanna to our king!

Nimm mein Hosianna an
Mit den Siegespalmenzweigen!
Soviel ich nur immer kann,
Will ich Ehre dir erzeigen
Und im Glauben dein Verdienst
Mir zueignen zum Gewinst.

Hosianna, Davids Sohn!
Ach Herr, hilf, lass wol gelingen!
Lass dein Zepter, Reich und Kron'
Uns viel Heil und Segen bringen,
Dass in Ewigkeit besteh':
Hosianna in der Höh'!

This popular and frequently sung Advent hymn, based on Matthew 21:1–9, the Gospel for the First Sunday in Advent in the Old Standard Series, was written and first published by Johann Gottfried Olearius in his *Primitiae poeticae oder Erstlinge an deutschen Liedern und Madrigalien* (Halle, 1664).

The translation is by August Crull, somewhat altered and updated.

MEINEN JESUM LASS ICH NICHT appeared in the *Neu verfertiges Darmstädisches Gesangbuch* (Darmstadt, 1699) set to a text by Christian Keimann (1607–62) beginning with these words. It is one of several tunes used with the Keimann text. The composer of this neatly crafted and popular tune is not known.

The harmonization is from *The Lutheran Hymnal* (1941), slightly altered.

WE PRAISE, O CHRIST, YOUR HOLY NAME

35

We praise, O Christ, your holy name.
Truly human child you came,
From virgin born; this word is true.
Your angels are rejoicing too.
Alleluia!

Now in the manger one may see
God's Son from eternity,
The gift from God's eternal throne
Here clothed in our poor flesh and bone.
Alleluia!

The virgin mother lulls to sleep
Him who rules the cosmic deep;
This infant is the Lord of day,
Whom all the turning worlds obey.
Alleluia!

The Light Eternal, breaking through,
Made the world to gleam anew;
His beams have pierced the core of night,
He makes us children of the light.
Alleluia!

The Prince, God's very Son, came here,
Guest among the sons of fear.
His banner leads us out of woe,
And to his royal hall we go.
Alleluia!

Such grace toward us now fills with light
Length and breadth and depth and height!
O endless ages, raise your voice;
O Christendom, rejoice, rejoice!
Alleluia!

Gelobet seist du, Jesu Christ,
Dass du Mensch geboren bist
Von einer Jungfrau, das ist wahr;
Des freuet sich der Engel Schar.
Kyrieleis!

Des ew'gen Vaters einig Kind
Jetzt man in der Krippen findt;
In unser armes Fleisch und Blut
Verkleidet sich das ewig Gut.
Kyrieleis!

Den aller Welt Kreis nie beschloss,
Der liegt in Marien Schoss;
Er ist ein Kindlein worden klein,
Der alle Ding' erhält allein.
Kyrieleis!

Das ewig Licht geht da herein,
Gibt der Welt ein'n neuen Schein;
Es leucht't wohl mitten in der Nacht
Und uns des Lichtes Kinder macht.
Kyrieleis!

Der Sohn des Vaters, Gott von Art,
Ein Gast in der Welt hier ward
Und führt uns aus dem Jammertal,
Er macht uns Erben in sein'm Saal.
Kyrieleis!

Das hat er alles uns getan,
Sein' gross' Lieb' zu zeigen an.
Des freu' sich alle Christenheit
Und dank' ihm des in Ewigkeit.
Kyrieleis!

Stanza 1 represents a pre-Reformation German *Leisen* hymn, a hymn frequently sung by the congregation on Christmas Day in response to the sequence "Grates nunc omnes." Essentially, *Leisen* hymns such as this, dating from about the ninth century, exhibit the German congregational hymn in its earliest stage. One very evident characteristic of such hymns is the concluding *Kyrie eleison* ("Lord, have mercy") or *Kyrieleis* or simply *Eleison* to each stanza.

To the original single stanza Luther added six, and the hymn first appeared in broadsheet form in Augsburg around Christmas 1523. Both text and tune appeared in the two Erfurt *Enchiridia* (1524). The translation was prepared by F. Samuel Janzow.

GELOBET SEIST DU. It is difficult to ascertain the exact origin of this tune. Most likely Luther retained the tune originally associated with the text. Notice the absence of the so-called *Freudensprung* (upbeat or pick-up note, so characteristic of many of the tunes of this period) at the beginning of the second lines of the stanzas, effecting an interesting alternation of iambic and trochaic rhythms.

The harmonization is by Paul G. Bunjes under the *nom de plume* of George Leonard.

36 OF THE FATHER'S LOVE BEGOTTEN

Of the Father's love begotten
Ere the worlds began to be,
He is Alpha and Omega,
He the source, the ending he,
Of the things that are, that have been,
And that future years shall see
Evermore and evermore.

Oh, that birth forever blessed,
When the virgin, full of grace,
By the Holy Ghost conceiving,
Bore the Savior of our race,
And the babe, the world's redeemer,
First revealed his sacred face
Evermore and evermore.

This is he whom seers in old time
Chanted of with one accord,
Whom the voices of the prophets
Promised in their faithful word;
Now he shines, the long-expected;
Let creation praise its Lord
Evermore and evermore.

Let the heights of heav'n adore him;
Angel hosts, his praises sing;
Pow'rs, dominions, bow before him
And extol our God and King;
Let no tongue on earth be silent,
Ev'ry voice in concert ring
Evermore and evermore.

Christ, to you, with God the Father
And the Spirit, there shall be
Hymn and chant and high thanksgiving
And the shout of jubilee:
Honor, glory, and dominion
And eternal victory
Evermore and evermore!

Corde natus ex Parentis
Ante mundi exodium,
Alpha et omega cognominatus,
Ipse fons et clausula
Omnium quae sunt, fuerunt,
Quaeque post futura sunt,
Saeculorum saeculis.

O beatus ortus ille,
Virgo cum puerpera
Edidit nostram salutem,
Feta sancto Spiritu
Et puer, redemptor orbis,
Os sacratum protulit,
Saeculorum saeculis.

Ecce, quem vates vetustis
Concinebant saeculis,
Quem prophetarum fideles
Paginae spoponderant,
Emicat promissus olim;
Cuncta conlaudent eum,
Saeculorum saeculis.

Psallat altitudo caeli,
Psallant omnes angeli;
Quidquid est virtutis usquam
Psallat in laudem Dei:
Nulla linguarum silescat,
Vox et omnis consonet,
Saeculorum saeculis.

Tibi, Christe, sit cum Patre
Hagioque Pneumate
Hymnus, decus, laus perennis
Gratiarum actio,
Honor, virtus, victoria,
Regnum aeternaliter,
Saeculorum saeculis.

This hymn, a cento by Prudentius, the illustrious Spanish poet of the early Christian church, is taken from the *Hymna omnis horae* in his *Cathemerinon*, a book containing 12 extended poems, one for each hour of the day. It is based on the ninth poem beginning "Da puer plectrum, choreis est canam fidelibus." Parts of this poem were used at Compline in the York and Hereford rites or at the lesser hours during Christmastide. Elsewhere parts were sometimes used on Marian festivals.

The first translation in the meter of the original was done by John Mason Neale and appeared in *The Hymnal Noted* (1852) beginning with "Of the Father, sole-begotten." Henry W. Baker revised this translation for inclusion in *Hymns Ancient and Modern* (1861), wherein he included also a translation of the final doxological stanza, which, like the refrain "saeculorum saeculis," had been added later to the poem of Prudentius.

DIVINUM MYSTERIUM. This beautiful plainsong melody in the Ionian mode, also called CORDE NATUS, is not that associated with the text in the aforementioned sources but is a Sanctus trope appearing in the 12th to 15th century manuscripts in Italy and Germany with the text "Divinum mysterium." In 1582 a young Finnish student at the University of Rostock, Didrik Pedersen (Theodorici Petri), published a collection of Protestant hymns and carols from Nyland, Finland, with the title *Piae Cantiones Ecclesiasticae et Scholasticae*. Included in the collection was DIVINUM MYSTERIUM. In 1853, almost three hundred years later, a rare copy of this book came into the hands of Thomas Helmore, priest-teacher, master of the Children of the Chapel Royal in England. As music editor of *The Hymnal Noted* (London, 1851), he set this tune to Neale's translation.

The arrangement in *Lutheran Worship*, prepared by Paul G. Bunjes, follows the original plainsong as closely as possible, although the former uses notes (or neums) which have no precise time value.

FROM HEAVEN ABOVE TO EARTH I COME — 37

WELCOME TO EARTH, O NOBLE GUEST — 38

From heav'n above to earth I come
To bring good news to ev'ryone!
Glad tidings of great joy I bring
To all the world and gladly sing:

To you this night is born a child
Of Mary, chosen virgin mild;
This newborn child of lowly birth
Shall be the joy of all the earth.

This is the Christ, God's Son most high,
Who hears your sad and bitter cry;
He will himself your Savior be
And from all sin will set you free.

The blessing which the Father planned
The Son holds in his infant hand
That in his kingdom, bright and fair,
You may with us his glory share.

Vom Himmel hoch, da komm' ich her,
Ich bring' euch gute neue Mär,
Der guten Mär bring' ich so viel,
Davon ich sing'n und sagen will.

Euch ist ein Kindlein heut' gebor'n
Von einer Jungfrau auserkor'n,
Ein Kindelein, so zart und fein,
Das soll eur' Freud' und Wonne sein.

Es ist der Herr Christ, unser Gott,
Der will euch führ'n aus aller Not,
Er will eu'r Heiland selber sein,
Von allen Sünden machen rein.

Er bringt euch alle Seligkeit,
Die Gott der Vater hat bereit,
Dass ihr mit uns im Himmelreich
Sollt leben nun und ewiglich

These are the signs which you will see
To let you know that it is he:
In manger bed, in swaddling clothes
The child who all the earth upholds.

So merket nun das Zeichen recht,
Die Krippe, Windelein so schlecht,
Da findet ihr das Kind gelegt,
Das alle Welt erhält und trägt.

How glad we'll be to find it so!
Then with the shepherds let us go
To see what God for us has done
In sending us his own dear Son.

Des lasst uns alle fröhlich sein
Und mit den Hirten gehn hinein,
Zu sehn, was Gott uns hat beschert,
Mit seinem lieben Sohn verehrt.

Look, look, dear friends, look over there!
What lies within that manger bare?
Who is that lovely little one?
The baby Jesus, God's dear son.

Merk auf, mein Herz, und sieh dorthin!
Was liegt dort in dem Krippelein?
Wer ist das schöne Kindelein?
Es ist das liebe Jesulein.

Welcome to earth, O noble Guest,
Through whom this sinful world is blest!
You turned not from our needs away!
How can our thanks such love repay?

Bis willekomm, du edler Gast!
Den Sünder nicht verschmähet hast
Und kommst ins Elend her zu mir,
Wie soll ich immer danken dir?

O Lord, you have created all!
How did you come to be so small
To sweetly sleep in manger bed
Where lowing cattle lately fed?

Ach Herr, du Schöpfer aller Ding',
Wie bist du worden so gering,
Dass du da liegst auf dürrem Gras,
Davon ein Rind und Esel asz!

Were earth a thousand times as fair
And set with gold and jewels rare,
Still such a cradle would not do
To rock a prince so great as you.

Und wär die Welt vielmal so weit,
Von Edelstein und Gold bereit't,
So wär sie doch dir viel zu klein,
Zu sein ein enges Wiegelein.

For velvets soft and silken stuff
You have but hay and straw so rough
On which as king so rich and great
To be enthroned in humble state.

Der Sammet und die Seide dein,
Das ist grob Heu und Windelein,
Darauf du König gross und reich
Herprangst, als wär's dein Himmelreich.

O dearest Jesus, holy child
Prepare a bed, soft, undefiled,
A holy shrine, within my heart,
That you and I need never part.

Ach mein herzliebes Jesulein,
Mach dir ein rein, sanft Bettelein,
Zu ruhen in mein's Herzens Schrein,
Dass ich nimmer vergesse dein!

My heart for very joy now leaps;
My voice no longer silence keeps;
I too must join the angel throng
To sing with joy his cradlesong:

Davon ich allzeit fröhlich sei,
Zu springen, singen immer frei
Das rechte Susaninne schon,
Mit Herzenslust den süssen Ton.

"Glory to God in highest heav'n,
Who unto us his Son has giv'n."
With angels sing in pious mirth:
A glad new year to all the earth!

Lob, Ehr' sei Gott im höchsten Thron,
Der uns schenkt seinen ein'gen Sohn!
Des Freuen sich der Engel Schar
Und singen uns solch neues Jahr.

The happiness in Luther's household is reflected in this delightful, folklike hymn which Luther wrote for his children's Christmas Eve celebration, perhaps in 1534 or 1535. Whereas his earlier Christmas hymns were derived largely from early Latin hymns, this German text is original with him. He called it *Ein Kinderlied auf die Weinacht vom Kindlein Jesu*. Stanzas 1–5 were sung by someone dressed as an angel, stanzas 7–14 by the individual children as a response to the angel, and stanzas 6 and 15 were done by the entire family group. *Lutheran Worship* has simplified this arrangement by designating the first seven stanzas as part 1—The Angel's Message, and the remaining stanzas as part 2—Our Response.

Stanza 1 is actually a paraphrase of a pre-Reformation folk song popular with the young people of Luther's day as a singing game. A young man would sing:

Good news from far abroad I bring,
Glad tidings for you all I sing.
I bring so much you'd like to know,
Much more than I shall tell you, though.

Thereafter he would propose a riddle to one of the girls. Failure to solve the riddle required that she forfeit to him the wreath she wore as headdress.

Catherine Winkworth's translation, contained in her *Lyra Germanica* (first series, 1855), served as the basis for this text when it was prepared by the Inter-Lutheran Commission on Worship for *Lutheran Book of Worship*. Missing from the original by Luther is stanza 12, which Winkworth translates:

Thus hath it pleased thee to make plain The truth to us poor fools and vain, That this world's honor, wealth, and might Are naught and worthless in thy sight.	Das hat also gefallen dir, Die Wahrheit anzuzeigen mir: Wie aller Welt Macht, Ehr' und Gut Vor dir nichts gilt, nichts hilft noch tut.

VOM HIMMEL HOCH. Originally Luther set this text to the tune of the riddle song, "Aus fremden Landen komm ich her." The Klug hymnal of 1535 as well as various subsequent hymnals contained it thus. The popularity of this text and its gradual use in the churches seems to have prompted him to prepare a new tune, a tune that first appeared in Schumann's *Geistliche Lieder* (1539) and that ultimately became the proper tune. By fashioning this tune, among several others, in the Ionian mode—the equivalent of the major diatonic scale pattern—rather than in the more traditional church modes (see essay: The Church Modes, p. 832), Luther exhibited himself as a rather daring innovator.

Paul G. Bunjes prepared a separate harmonization for each use of the tune.

38

Text is treated with hymn 37.

ONCE AGAIN MY HEART REJOICES — 39

Once again my heart rejoices As I hear Far and near Sweetest angel voices. "Christ is born!" their choirs are singing	Fröhlich soll mein Herze springen Dieser Zeit, Da vor Freud' Alle Engel singen. Hört, hört, wie mit vollen Chören

Till the air
Ev'rywhere
Now with joy is ringing!

Should we still fear God's displeasure,
Who, to save,
Freely gave
His most precious treasure?
To redeem us, he has given
His own Son,
Cherished one,
From his throne in heaven.

Hark! his voice, our hearts delighting,
Softly greets,
It entreats,
All the world inviting:
"Children, from the sins that grieve you
You are freed;
All you need
I will surely give you!"

Come, then, banish all your sadness,
One and all,
Great and small,
Come with songs of gladness!
Let your thankful hearts now hold him
Savior dear,
Ever near,
Lovingly enfold him!

Alle Luft
Laute ruft:
Christus ist geboren!

Sollt' uns Gott nun können hassen,
Der uns gibt,
Was er liebt
Über alle Massen?
Gott gibt, unserm Leid zu wehren,
Seinen Sohn
Aus dem Thron
Seiner Macht und Ehren.

Nun, er liegt in seiner Krippen,
Ruft zu sich
Mich und dich,
Spricht mit süssen Lippen:
Lasset fahr'n, o liebe Brüder,
Was euch quält,
Was euch fehlt,
Ich bring' alles wieder.

Ei, so kommt und lasst uns laufen!
Stellt euch ein,
Gross und klein,
Eilt mit grossem Haufen!
Liebt den, der vor Liebe brennet;
Schaut den Stern,
Der uns gern
Licht und Labsal gönnet.

This hymn by Paul Gerhardt, in its original of 15 stanzas, is perhaps the most fervent and profound of his Christmas hymns. Gerhardt is and always remains a teacher and pastor. Here he lovingly invites the sorrowful, the heavy laden with sin, the poor and the distressed to the manger, there to thank and adore the Christ child.

This hymn first appeared in Johann Crüger's monumental *Praxis pietatis melica* (1653), for a long time the classic source for Lutheran praise.

The translation is an altered and updated form of that by Catherine Winkworth in her *Lyra Germanica* (second series, 1858).

FRÖHLICH SOLL MEIN HERZE SPRINGEN, a fitting and moving tune, was composed by Johann Crüger specifically for this Gerhardt text and published together with it.

The harmonization was prepared by Wilhelm Quampen, a *nom de plume*, or pen name, of Paul G. Bunjes.

OH, REJOICE, ALL CHRISTIANS, LOUDLY 40

Oh, rejoice, all Christians, loudly,
For our joys have now begun:
Christ is born as Mary's son.
Tell abroad his goodness proudly,
Who our race has honored so,
That he lives with us below.

Refrain
Joy, O joy, all hearts embracing,
God in Christ himself abasing,
Our adoring love enshrining,
Here the sun of grace lies shining!

See, my soul, your Savior choosing
Poverty and weakness too,
In such love he comes to you.
Neither crib nor cross refusing,
All he suffers for your good,
To redeem you by his blood.

Lord, how shall I thank you rightly?
I am saved eternally
By your life and death for me.
Let me not regard you lightly
But on you in faith depend,
Praising you, my heav'nly friend.

Jesus, guard and guide your members,
Make us children of your grace,
Hear our prayers in ev'ry place.
Quicken now faith's glowing embers,
Give all Christians, far and near,
Holy peace, a glad new year.

Freuet euch, ihr Christen, alle!
Freue sich, wer immer kann,
Gott hat viel an uns getan.
Freuet euch mit grossem Schalle,
Dass er uns so hoch geacht't,
Sich mit uns befreund't gemacht.

Freude, Freude über Freude!
Christus wehret allem Leide.
Wonne, Wonne über Wonne!
Er ist die Genadensonne.

Siehe, siehe, meine Seele,
Wie dein Heiland kommt zu dir,
Brennt in Liebe für und für.
Dass er in der Krippe Höhle
Harte lieget dir zugut,
Dich zu lösen durch sein Blut.

Jesu, wie soll ich dir danken?
Ich bekenne, dass von dir
Meine Seligkeit herrühr.
O lass mich von dir nicht wanken,
Nimm mich dir zu eigen hin,
So empfindet Herz und Sinn.

Jesu, nimm dich deiner Glieder
Ferner in Genaden an!
Schenke, was man bitten kann,
Zu erquicken deine Brüder;
Gib der ganzen Christenschar
Frieden und ein sel'ges Jahr.

This hymn by Christian Keimann, so popular with Lutheran congregations, was written for a Christmas play to be enacted by his students. The Zittau *Gymnasium*, where he was rector, was an institution that cultivated and promoted such customary plays, and in 1646 this play appeared in Görlitz with the title "Der neugeborne Jesus" ("The Newborn Jesus"). In writing the text Keimann was undoubtedly influenced by the words of St. Paul to the Philippians: "Rejoice in the Lord always. I will say it again: Rejoice! Let your gentleness be evident to all. The Lord is near" (Phil. 4:4–5), as well as those of Martin Luther in his "Dear Christians, one and all, rejoice" (*LW* 353).

The translation is an altered and updated version of that by Catherine Winkworth in her *Chorale Book for England* (1863).

FREUET EUCH, IHR CHRISTEN is the tune that Andreas Hammerschmidt set to Keimann's text beginning with the same words and which he published in his *Musikalische Andachten* (Freiberg, Saxony, 1646). Introduced and concluded by a twelvefold alleluia, the overall tone of the tune unquestionably reflects the practice of the 17th century.

The harmonization was prepared by Wilhelm Quampen, a *nom de plume* of Paul G. Bunjes

41 OH, COME, ALL YE FAITHFUL

Oh, come, all ye faithful, Joyful and triumphant! Oh, come ye, oh, come ye to Bethlehem; Come and behold him Born the king of angels:	Adeste, fidelis, laeti triumphantes; venite, venite in Bethlehem; natum videte regem angelorum.
Refrain Oh, come, let us adore him, Oh, come, let us adore him, Oh, come, let us adore him, Christ the Lord!	Venite, adoremus Dominum.
Highest, most holy, Light of light eternal, Born of a virgin, a mortal he comes; Son of the Father Now in flesh appearing!	Deum de Deo, lumen de lumine, gestant puellae viscera, Deum verum, genitum, non factum.
Sing, choirs of angels, Sing in exultation, Sing, all ye citizens of heaven above! Glory to God In the highest:	Cantet nunc "Io" chorus angelorum; cantet nunc aula caelestium, Gloria in excelsis Deo.
Yea, Lord, we greet thee, Born this happy morning; Jesus, to thee be glory giv'n! Word of the Father, Now in flesh appearing!	Ergo, qui natu die hodierna Iesu, tibi sit gloria: Patris aeterni verbum caro factum!

All of the five existing manuscript copies of this Latin text were signed and dated by John Francis Wade, with the exception of the earliest about 1743, whose title page is missing; however, it has been established by graphology that this copy was also executed by Wade. Described as "a man who made his living by copying and selling plain chant and other music," Wade was also a teacher of Latin and church music. Thus it is conceivable that he composed some original texts and music as well.

In *Adeste Fideles: A study on its origin and development* (Buckfast Abbey, 1947) John Stephen presents a convincing argument for the authorship of both text and tune by John E. Wade.

The early manuscripts consist of only four stanzas, each beginning with:

1 Adeste, fidelis
2 Deum de Deo

3 Cantet nunc io
4 Ergo, qui natus

Having heard "Adeste fidelis" sung in England while exiled there during the French Revolution, Jean Francois Borderies, a French abbé, introduced it to his catechism classes in Paris after the fall and execution of Robespierre (July 28, 1794). He used the first stanza as written, adding three new stanzas of his own:

2 En grege relicto,
Humiles ad cunas,
Vocate pastores approperant,
Et nos ovanti
Gradu festinemus.

2 See how the shepherds.
Summoned to his cradle
Leaving their flocks, draw nigh to gaze;
We too will thither
Bend our joyful footsteps:

3 Aeterni Parentis
Splendorem aeternum,
Velaturm sub carne videbimus,
Deum infantem,
Pannis involutum.

3 No translation available

4 Pro nobis egenum
et foeno cubantem
piis foveamus amplexibus;
sic nos amantem
quis non redamaret?

4 Child, for us sinners
Poor in the manger,
Fain we embrace thee with love and awe;
Who would not love thee,
Loving us so dearly?

Borderies' four stanzas make up the hymn as it is sung in France today. Yet another stanza was added by an unknown source:

Stella duce, Magi
Christum adorantes,
Aurum, tuus, et myrrham dant munera.
Jesu Infanti
Corda praebeamus:

Lo, star led chieftans,
Magi, Christ adoring,
Offer him incense, gold, and myrrh;
We to the Christ-child
Bring our hearts's oblations:

Together these eight stanzas—four attributed to Wade, three by Borderies, and one anonymous stanza—appeared in *Thesaurus Animae Christianae* (Mechlin, c. 1850) in the following order:

1 Adeste, fidelis
2 Deum de Deo
3 En grege relicto
4 Stella duce, Magi
5 Aeterna Parentis
6 Pro nobis egenum
7 Cantet nunc io (altered to Cantet nunc hymnos)
8 Ergo, qui natus

From this "full text" various centos have been used, and more than 40 English translations are listed in Julian's *A Dictionary of Hymnology.* In America, the most popular of these is by Canon Frederick Oakeley, prepared in 1841 for his Margaret

Street Chapel, London. Beginning "Ye faithful, approach ye, joyfully triumphant," it was not published by Oakeley, but it soon became popular through use in the chapel and was included in the *People's Hymnal* (1867). A revised version, "O come all ye faithful, joyfully triumphant" soon came into use, first appearing in F. H. Murray's *A Hymnal for Use in the English Church* (1852). Various alterations have been made to the text, which still remains a favorite in all hymnals.

ADESTE FIDELES. In all the previously mentioned manuscripts, the music was in triple rhythm. It was only in part II of the *Essay or Instruction for Learning the Church Plain Chant* (London, 1782) by Samuel Webbe, Senior, that it appeared in duple time. It was apparently first published in the United States in 1795 in broadsheet form, of which there is a copy in the Newberry Library, Chicago; thereafter it appeared in Benjamen Carr's *Musical Journal*, II, No. 29 (December 1800). In Vincent Novello's *The Psalmist*, the tune is called PORTUGUESE HYMN, so named, according to Novello, by the Duke of Leeds who heard it in 1785 in the Chapel of the Portuguese Embassy.

The harmonization of this great tune is from *The Hymnal 1940*.

42 LET US ALL WITH GLADSOME VOICE

Let us all with gladsome voice Praise the God of heaven, Who, to make our hearts rejoice, His own Son has given.	Lasst uns alle fröhlich sein, Preisen Gott den Herren, Der sein liebes Söhnelein Uns selbst tut verehren!
To this place of fears he came, Servant, healer, mender; Through his death we heaven claim, There to reign in splendor.	Er kommt in das Jammertal, Wird ein Knecht auf Erden, Damit wir in Himmelssaal Grosse Herren werden.
We are rich, for he was poor; Is not this a wonder? Therefore praise God evermore Here on earth and yonder.	Er wird arm, wir werden reich, Ist das nicht ein Wunder? Drum lobt Gott im Himmelreich Allzeit wie jetzunder!
Christ, our Lord and Savior dear, Oh, be ever near us. Be our joy throughout each year. Amen, Jesus, hear us.	O Herr Christ, nimm unser wahr Durch dein'n heil'gen Namen! Gib uns ein gut neues Jahr! Wer's begehrt, sprech': Amen.

The authorship of this charming little Christmas hymn is uncertain. Zahn mentions that it is ascribed to Urban Langhans, a 16th-century choirmaster and deacon. James Mearns, assistant editor of Julian's *A Dictionary of Hymnology*, says that the first stanza was included in a Christmas sermon by Martin Hammer, published in Leipzig in 1620. The earliest appearance of both text and tune is in the *Dresdenisch Gesang-Buch, Ander Teil* (Dresden, 1632).

The translation is an altered and updated form of that by Catherine Winkworth in her *Chorale Book for England* (1863).

LASST UNS ALLE first appeared with the text beginning with the same words in the *Dresdenisch Gesang-Buch, Ander Teil* (Dresden, 1632). The unaffected simplicity of this tune undoubtedly contributed to the popularity of the hymn text. Both found their way into numerous German hymnals of the 18th and 19th centuries.

The harmonization is from *The Lutheran Hymnal* (1941), slightly altered.

FROM EAST TO WEST 43

From east to west, from shore to shore
Let ev'ry heart awake and sing
The holy child whom Mary bore,
The Christ, the everlasting king.

Behold, the world's creator wears
The form and fashion of a slave;
Our very flesh our maker shares,
His fallen creatures all to save.

For this how wondrously he wrought!
A maiden, in her lowly place,
Became, in ways beyond all thought,
The chosen vessel of his grace.

And while the angels in the sky
Sang praise above the silent field,
To shepherds poor the Lord most high,
The one great shepherd, was revealed.

All glory for this blessed morn
To God the Father ever be;
All praise to you, O Virgin-born,
And Holy Ghost eternally.

A solis ortus cardine
ad usque terra limitem,
Christum canamus principem
natum Maria virgine.

Beatus auctor saeculi
servile corpus induit,
ut carne carnem liberans
ne perderet quod condidit.

Clausa puellae viscera
caelestis intrat gratia;
venter puellae bajulat
secreta quae non noverat.

Gaudet chorus caelestium,
et angeli canunt Deum,
palamque fit pastoribus
pastor creator omnium.

Gloria tibi, Domine,
qui natus es de virgine,
cum Patre et sancto Spiritu,
in sempiterna saecula.

Coelius Sedulius' poem, in iambic dimeter, dates to the early fifth century. It was in 23 stanzas, each beginning with a successive letter of the alphabet, describing the life of Christ, and was accordingly titled *Paean alphabeticus de Christo*. Liturgically it has been divided into two hymns: the first, "A solis ortus cardine" (stanzas *a* through *g*), was designated for Lauds on Christmas Day and on the Epiphany; the second, "Hostis Herodes impie" (stanzas *h, i, l, n,* and *s*), for first and second Vespers on the Epiphany and throughout the octave. (See *LW* 81, "When Christ's appearing was made known.") The doxology was added at a later date.

John Ellerton first prepared a translation in common meter, published in *Church Hymns* (1871), on which he based this later long meter translation. This appeared in the *Supplement* (1889) to the 1875 edition of *Hymns Ancient and Modern*. Alterations to Ellerton's text are limited to the second stanza, which originally ended "His fallen *creature, man*, to save," and the doxology, where personal pronouns were updated. It was thus included in *Lutheran Book of Worship* (1978).

CHRISTUM WIR SOLLEN LOBEN SCHON. Martin Luther translated the above cento of Sedulius into German, beginning "Christum wir sollen loben schon." It appeared in *Eyn Enchiridion* (Erfurt, 1524), set to this strong tune. Luther's translation of "Hostis Herodes impie," not completed until 1541, was published in 1544 in Klug's *Geistliche Lieder* as "Was fürcht'st du Feind Herodes sehr."

Richard W. Hillert's setting appeared in *Worship Supplement* (1969).

44 LET ALL TOGETHER PRAISE OUR GOD

Let all together praise our God
Before his glorious throne;
Today he opens heav'n again
To give us his own Son.

The Father sends him from his throne
To be an infant small
And lie here poorly mangered now
In this cold, dismal stall.

Within an earth-born form he hides
His all-creating light;
To serve us all he humbly cloaks
The splendor of his might.

He undertakes a great exchange,
Puts on our human frame,
And in return gives us his realm,
His glory, and his name.

He is a servant, I a lord:
How great a mystery!
How strong the tender Christ child's love!
No truer friend than he.

He is the key and he the door
To blessed paradise;
The angel bars the way no more.
To God our praises rise.

Your grace in lowliness revealed
Lord Jesus, we adore
And praise to God the Father yield
And Spirit evermore;
We praise you evermore.

Lobt Gott, ihr Christen alle gleich,
In seinem höchsten Thron,
Derr heut' aufschleusst sein
Himmelreich Und schenkt uns seinen Sohn!

Er kommt aus seines Vaters Schoss
Und wird ein Kindlein klein,
Er liegt dort elend, nackt und bloss
In einem Krippelein.

Er äussert sich all seiner G'walt,
Wird niedrig und gering
Und nimmt an sich ein's Knechts Gestalt,
Der Schöpfer aller Ding'.

Er wechselt mit uns wunderlich:
Fleisch und Blut nimmt er an
Und gibt uns in sein's Vaters Reich
Die klare Gottheit dran.

Er wird ein Knecht und ich ein Herr,
Das mag ein Wechel sein!
Wie könnt' es doch sein freundlicher
Das herz'ge Jesulein?

Heut' schleusst er wieder auf die Tür
Zum schönen Paradeis;
Der Cherub steht nicht mehr dafür.
Gott sei Lob, Ehr' und Preis!

This popular hymn and tune by Nikolaus Herman first appeared in his *Die Sanntags Evangelia Über das ganze Jahr* (Wittenberg, 1560), a collection of 101 hymns on the

Gospel readings of the church year. This hymn was the first of the three for Christmas, under the heading "Three Spiritual Christmas Songs of the Newborn Child Jesus, for the Children in Joachimsthal," the town where he served as teacher of the Latin school and cantor in the Lutheran Church. The subtitle of the book in which this hymn appeared—*In Geseng Verfasset für die Kinder und christliche Haus-Väter* (The Sunday Gospels . . . composed in song for the children and Christian fathers)—seems to indicate that it did not occur to Herman that the contents of his collection could, and would, eventually be sung in corporate worship.

The translation by F. Samuel Janzow first appeared in *Worship Supplement*. The final doxological stanza, for which there is no German equivalent, is also his creation.

LOBT GOTT, IHR CHRISTEN. This tune is also by Herman. It first appeared in his *Ein Christlicher Abendreihen* (1554), set to his text, "Kommt her, ihr liebsten Schwesterlein" (cf. Zahn 198), a children's song on the life and work of John the Baptizer. Later Herman included the tune in *Die Sonntags-Evangelia über das ganze Jahr* (Wittenberg, 1560), set to the above hymn text.

This tune, constructed by Herman from the old Mixolydian Gregorian melody of the Introit for the third Christmas Mass, is a good example of tone painting. To appreciate this technique one must go back to the original German text, the first two lines of which read: "Lobt Gott, ihr Christen alle gleich, In seinem höchsten Thron." Notice the leap of a fifth on the opening "Lobt Gott" and the emphasis given the word "alle" on the sixth tone (the submediant); also the return to this sixth tone on the word *höchsten*, the tone that serves as the pitch-height accent to the entire melody. This is a degree of text treatment that is not often found in this period of chorale development (but see Luther, p. 684). Moreover, Herman casts this tune, with its lyrical, childlike rhythm, in the Ionian mode, a harbinger of the trend away from the old church modes to major tonality.

The harmonization is from the *Württembergisches Choralbuch* (1953).

O SAVIOR OF OUR FALLEN RACE 45

O Savior of our fallen race,
O Brightness of the Father's face,
O Son who shared the Father's might
Before the world knew day or night,

O Jesus, very Light of light,
Our constant star in sin's deep night:
Now hear the prayers your people pray
Throughout the world this holy day.

Remember, Lord of life and grace,
How once, to save our fallen race,
You put our human vesture on
And came to us as Mary's son.

Jesu Redemptor omnium,
Quem lucis ante originem,
Parem paternae gloriae,
Pater supremus edidit.

Tu lumen et splendor Patris,
Tu spes perennis omnium:
Intende quas fundunt preces
Tui per orbem servuli.

Memento, rerum Conditor,
Nostri quod olim corporis,
Sacrata ab alvo Virginis
Nascendo, formam sumpseris.

Today, as year by year its light
Bathes all the world in radiance bright,
One precious truth outshines the sun:
Salvation comes from you alone.

For from the Father's throne you came,
His banished children to reclaim;
And earth and sea and sky revere
The love of him who sent you here.

And we are jubilant today,
For you have washed our guilt away.
Oh, hear the glad new song we sing
On this, the birthday of our king!

O Christ, redeemer virgin-born,
Let songs of praise your name adorn,
Whom with the Father we adore
And Holy Spirit evermore.
Amen

Testatur hoc praesens dies,
Currens per anni circulum,
Quod solus e sinu Patris
Mundi salus adveneris.

Hunc astra, tellus, aequora,
Hunc omne quod caelo subest,
Salutis auctorem novae
Novo salutat cantico.

Et nos, beata quos sacri
Rigavit unda sanguinis,
Natalis ob diem tui,
Hymni tributum solvimus.

Jesu, tibi sit gloria,
Qui natus es de Virgine,
Cum Patre et almo Spiritu,
In sempiterna saecula.
Amen

The lovely Christmas vesper hymn, dating perhaps as far back as the sixth century, made its way into various breviaries (liturgical books containing complete texts of the canonical hours: matins, lauds, prime, terce, sext, nones, vespers, compline) such as the Sarum, York, Aberdeen, and Roman. The text was considerably revised in the Roman Breviary of 1632 and in the two collections of Charles Coffin (*LW* 12, 14): *Hymni Sacri* (1736) and the *Paris Breviary* (1736). Various translations of the Latin have appeared. This translation was prepared by Gilbert E. Doan for *Lutheran Book of Worship* (1978).

CHRISTE REDEMPTOR is the plainsong, or Gregorian, tune associated with the Latin text. Of its various versions, this one is from the Sarum rite, namely, that used in Salisbury, England.

The harmonization was prepared for *Lutheran Worship* (1982) by Wilhelm Quampen, a *nom de plume* of Paul G. Bunjes.

While choirs can readily be taught such plainsong tunes, considerable time and effort may be required to teach them to a congregation to a point where it will appreciate and enjoy them. Lest this beautiful text be dismissed as a congregation hymn because of its tune, it is suggested that a familiar long meter (LM) tune be substituted, one that matches the mood and spirit of the text. In doing so, however, care should be exercised that the accentuation scheme of the text matches that of the tune.

46 LOVE CAME DOWN AT CHRISTMAS

Christina Rossetti's great talent for expressing the Gospel in words children can understand shows itself in this hymn where, as Percy Dearmer notes, "so much is said in so little space." It first appeared in *Time Flies: A Reading Diary* (1885); later, Rossetti changed the last line from "Love for universal sign" to its present form.

GARTAN. This traditional Irish melody was included in Stanford's *A Complete Collection of Irish Music as Noted by George Petrie* (1902). It is named after Lough Gartan, a small lake in Donegal, Ireland.

The harmonization is by Wilhelm Quampen, a *nom de plume* of Paul G. Bunjes.

NOW SING WE, NOW REJOICE 47

Now sing we, now rejoice
With heart and soul and voice.
Life's most precious treasure
Here poor in manger lies;
He brings purer pleasure
Than sunlight from the skies.
Christ is born today!
Christ is born today!

God's Son, come from above,
Your grace and saving love
To my spirit bringing,
O pure and holy Child,
Fill my heart with singing
For grace so great and mild.
Draw me, Lord, to you!
Draw me, Lord, to you!

We see God's love divine
For us in Jesus shine.
Guilt of sin had taught us
But death and misery;
Then our Ransom bought us
God's bright eternity.
Oh, that we were there!
Oh, that we were there!

Where is that place so fair?
Oh, nowhere else but there
Where the angel voices
With God's redeemed unite,
Awed that he rejoices
To share his joy and light.
Oh, that we were there!
Oh, that we were there!

In dulci iubilo,
Nu singet und seyt fro!
Unsers herzens Wonne
Leyt in praesepio
Und leuchtet als die Sonne
Matris in gremio
Alpha es et O!
Alpha es et O!

O Iesu, parvule,
Nach dir ist mir so we;
Tröst mir myn Gemüte,
O puer optime,
Durch aller juncfrawen Güte,
O princeps gloriae.
Trahe me post te!
Trahe me post te!

O Patris caritas!
O Nati lenitas!
Wir weren all verloren
Per nostra crimina;
So hat er uns erworben
Coelorum gaudia.
Eya, wär wir da!
Eya, wär wir da!

Ubi sunt gaudia?
Nirgend mer denn da,
Da die Engel singen
Nova cantica,
Und die schellen klingen
In Regis curia.
Eya, wär wir da!
Eya, wär wir da!

According to Hoffman von Fallersleben, mixed, or "macaronic" (part Latin, part vernacular), nonliturgical songs were popular as far back as the 14th century. Their simple folk song character beautifully served the desire of pre-Reformation people to express themselves in the vernacular and thus to participate actively in religious services, especially on the high festivals. Examples of such are "Dies est laetitiae"

("Hail the Day So Rich in Cheer," *TLH* 78), "Resonet in laudibus" ("Joseph Dearest, Joseph, Mine"), "Quem pastores" (*LW* 54), a popular component of German Christmas Eve services, and "In dulci jubilo" ("In Sweet Jubilation"), the one that, with its waltz-like tune and interesting combination of Latin and German, became a special favorite, and that lent itself so beautifully to singing in alternation (*alternatim praxis*).

Tradition has it that "In dulci jubilo" was first sung by angels to the Dominican monk and mystic Heinrich Suso (d. 1366), who became so enthralled, he joined the celestial hosts in a "circle dance" ("carolle"). The earliest version of this hymn, in a Leipzig University manuscript of about 1400, first appeared in Martin Luther's *Geistliche Lieder auffs new gebessert* (Wittenberg, 1539), the so-called *Klug Gesängbuch*. From there it made its way into numerous Evangelical and Roman Catholic collections. In England it appeared in an anonymous collection of Latin and German hymns entitled *Lyra Davidica* (1708). Current German as well as American hymnals omit the Latin and sing only the all-vernacular versions. Choirs have ready access to both Latin-English and Latin-German versions in *The Oxford Book of Carols*.

By far the most widely sung English translation is that by John Mason Neale (*LW* 31, et al.), beginning "Good Christian men, rejoice." The translation here given was prepared by F. Samuel Janzow for *Lutheran Worship* (1982).

IN DULCI JUBILO. Both text and tune have been inseparably united. The tune included here is identical to that which appeared with the text in the so-called *Klug Gesängbuch* (1529).

The harmonization is by Richard W. Hillert, as prepared for *Lutheran Book of Worship* (1978).

48 COME, YOUR HEARTS AND VOICES RAISING

Come, your hearts and voices raising,
Christ the Lord with gladness praising;
Loudly sing his love amazing,
Worthy folk of Christendom.

Christ, from heav'n to us descending
And in love our race befriending;
In our need his help extending,
Saved us from the wily foe.

Jacob's star in all its splendor
Beams with comfort sweet and tender,
Forcing Satan to surrender,
Breaking all the pow'rs of hell.

From the bondage that oppressed us,
From sin's fetters that possessed us,
From the grief that sore distressed us,
We, the captives, now are free.

Kommt und lasst uns Christum ehren,
Herz und Sinnen zu ihm kehren!
Singet fröhlich, lasst euch hören,
Wertes Volk der Christenheit!

Seine Seel' ist uns gewogen,
Lieb' und Gunst hat ihn gezogen,
Uns, die Satanas betrogen,
Zu besuchten aus der Höh'.

Jakobs Stern ist aufgegangen,
Stillt das sehnliche Verlangen,
Bricht den Kopf der alten Schlange
Und zerstört der Hölle Reich.

Unser Kerker, da wir sassen
Und mit Sorgen ohne Massen
Uns das Herze selbst abfrassen,
Ist entzwei, und wir sind frei.

Oh, the joy beyond expressing When by faith we grasp this blessing And to you we come confessing Your great love has set us free.	O du hochgesegn'te Stunde, Da wir das von Herzensgrunde Glauben und mit unserm Mund Danken dir, o Jesulein!
Gracious Child, we pray, oh, hear us, From your lowly manger cheer us, Gently lead us and be near us Till we join your choir above.	Schönstes Kindlein in dem Stalle, Sei uns freundlich, bring uns alle Dahin, wo mit süssem Schalle Dich der Engel Heer erhöht!

This hymn by Paul Gerhardt, originally in eight stanzas—as such the shortest of all his hymns—was first published by Johann G. Ebeling (*LW* 370, et al.) in his *P. Gerhardi Geistliche Andachten* (Berlin, 1666). Based on the words of the shepherds in Luke 2:15, "Let us go to Bethlehem and see this thing that has happened, which the Lord has told us about," and reflecting the words of the psalmist, "Come, let us bow down in worship" (Ps. 95:6a), Gerhardt evidently wrote the text as sort of a sequel to the old Latin "Quem pastores laudaveri" (*LW* 54), even to the point of following the rhyme scheme of the Latin—notice the rhyming of the first three lines of each stanza, with the fourth line independent.

The translation, in updated form, is from *The Lutheran Hymnal* (1941).

QUEM PASTORES is the delightful and popular tune of a German carol from a 14th-century manuscript. Its first appearance in print seems to be in Valentin Triller's *Ein Schlesich Singebüchlein aus Göttlicher Schrifft* (Breslau, 1555) with both a Latin text beginning with the same words and a German text beginning with "Preis sei Gott im höchsten Throne."

The harmonization was prepared for *Lutheran Worship* (1982) by George Leonard, a *nom de plume* of Paul G. Bunjes.

HARK! THE HERALD ANGELS SING 49

Hark! The herald angels sing, Glory to the newborn king; Peace on earth and mercy mild, God and sinners reconciled. Joyful, all you nations, rise; Join the triumph of the skies; With angelic hosts proclaim, Christ is born in Bethlehem!	Hark, how all the welkin rings Glory to the King of Kings, Peace on earth and mercy mild, God and sinners reconciled. Joyful, all ye nations, rise Join the triumph of the skies; Universal nature say Christ the Lord is born today.
Refrain Hark! The herald angels sing, Glory to the newborn king!	
Christ, by highest heav'n adored, Christ, the everlasting Lord, Late in time behold him come, Offspring of a virgin's womb.	Christ, by highest heaven adored, Christ the everlasting Lord, Late in time behold him come Offspring of a virgin's womb.

Veiled in flesh the Godhead see! Hail, incarnate deity! Pleased as man with us to dwell, Jesus, our Emmanuel!	Veil'd in flesh, the Godhead see, Hail the incarnate deity! Pleased as man with men to appear Jesus! our Immanuel here!
Hail the heav'n-born Prince of Peace! Hail the sun of righteousness! Light and life to all he brings, Ris'n with healing in his wings. Mild he lays his glory by, Born that we no more may die, Born to raise each child of earth, Born to give us second birth.	Hail the heavenly Prince of Peace! Hail the sun of righteousness, Light and life to all he brings Risen with healing in his wings. Mild he lays his glory by, Born—that man no more may die. Born—to raise the sons of earth, Born—to give them second birth.

The history of this celebrated hymn text by Charles Wesley disproves two common assertions: 1) that hymns be sung exactly as originally written; 2) that composite efforts of revision invariably result in a mere patchwork.

This hymn, originally in 10 four-line stanzas, first appeared in Charles Wesley's *Hymns and Sacred Poems* (1739) and thereafter in a form revised by him and included in the new edition of the foregoing published in 1733. This revised text is given above in parallel column to the text in *Lutheran Worship*. The final four stanzas by Wesley, omitted in *Lutheran Worship*, read as follows laid out in two stanzas:

Come, Desire of nations, come, Fix in us thy humble home; Rise, the woman's conquering Seed Bruise in us the serpent's head. Now display thy saving power, Ruin'd nature now restore Now in mystic union join Thine to ours, and ours to Thine.	Adam's likeness, Lord, efface; Stamp thy image in its place; Second Adam from above, Reinstate us in thy Love. Let us thee, though lost, regain, Thee the life, the inner man O! to all thyself impart, Form'd in each believing heart.

Space precludes giving the details of subsequent revisions. Suffice it to say that the eloquent preacher George Whitefield (1714–70), founder of Calvinistic Methodism, gave the hymn its more common form of today in his *Hymns for social worship, collected from various authors* of 1753. Martin Madan (1726–90) made revisions in his *Psalms and Hymns* (1760), as did others. The popular refrain was not added until it appeared in *The Supplement* to the Tate and Brady Psalter (1782). The present tune, so integral to the text, had not yet seen the light of day. The Wesleys must not have regarded the text too highly, for it did not appear in any Methodist collection until the *Supplement to Wesley's Hymns* (1831). The inclusion of both text and the Mendelssohn tune in the 1861 edition of *Hymns Ancient and Modern* gave it wide currency. It is interesting to note the outcry that resulted when the 1904 edition of *Hymns Ancient and Modern* altered the first line back to the original "Hark, how all the welkin rings!" The dispute finally died down when *The English Hymnal* (1906) included both the current common revised version and the 1743 "welkin" version exactly as Charles Wesley had written it, except for the omission of stanzas 9 and 10, set to an English traditional melody.

The slightly-revised common text here given was prepared by the Inter-Lutheran Commission on Worship for inclusion in the *Lutheran Book of Worship* (1978).

MENDELSSOHN (BERLIN, BETHLEHEM, HERALD ANGELS, JESU REDEMPTOR, NATIVITY, PRAISE, ST. VINCENT) is an adaptation of the second chorus from Mendelssohn's *Festgesang an die Künstler*, Op. 68, for male voices and brass instruments, written for and first performed at the Gutenberg Festival in Leipzig, June 1840, to commemorate the fourth centenary of the invention of printing. Sometime later it occurred to William H. Cummings, organist at Waltham Abbey, that this tune would serve as a suitable setting for "Hark! The herald angels sing." When he noticed that the combination was favorably received by his choir, he published the same in 1856, and it soon found its way into numerous hymnals, the first of which was Richard R. Chope's *Congregational Hymn and Tune Book* (1857). Thus was created perhaps the most popular English hymn in the world, noted not only for its scriptural and literary merit, but also its jubilant spirit, due in no small part to its somewhat unique trochaic meter.

The harmonization is by William H. Cummings.

ANGELS FROM THE REALMS OF GLORY — 50

James Montgomery wrote this hymn in five stanzas, of which *Lutheran Worship* has retained the first three. The doxological stanza 4, here given in updated form, comes from the *Salisbury Hymn Book* (1857).

This hymn, titled "Nativity," was first printed on Christmas Eve of 1816 in the newspaper, the Sheffield *Iris,* of which Montgomery was editor. It was reprinted in the eighth edition of Thomas Cotterill's (1779–1823) *A Selection of Psalms and Hymns for Public and Private Use* (1819). This hymnal, largely due to Montgomery's influence, was such a creative departure from the first seven editions that, the Church of England considering a return to psalm singing, it was withdrawn from publication. The hymn appeared again in Cotterill's ninth edition, which was accepted because of its dedication to and approval by the Archbishop of York. From the very first, this text became popular on both sides of the Atlantic.

Montgomery himself made a few small revisions to the text before the hymn was published in his *Christian Psalmist* (1825), and, as the revisions were retained in his *Original Hymns* (1853), they are accepted as constituting the authorized text.

REGENT SQUARE is perhaps Henry Smart's best and most celebrated tune. Composed for the English Presbyterian Church's *Psalms and Hymns for Divine Worship* (1867), it was first set in that volume to Horatius Bonar's "Glory be to God the Father" (*LW* 173). James Hamilton, editor of the hymnal and pastor of London's Regent Square Church, gave the tune its name.

George Leonard, a *nom de plume* of Paul G. Bunjes, provided the harmonization for *Lutheran Worship* (1982).

51 A GREAT AND MIGHTY WONDER

The Greek original by St. Germanus (c. 634–734) is designated in the *Menaea* (Greek Orthodox calendar) to be sung on Christmas Day. John M. Neale's translation appeared in his *Hymns of the Eastern Church* (1862), where he erroneously attributed the Greek to St. Anatolius, perhaps because of the proximity of several Anatolius hymns in the *Menaea*.

The *English Hymnal* (1906) adapted Neale's version to the tune ES IST EIN ROS by forming a refrain from his third stanza (omitting the first line):

And we with them triumphant
Repeat the hymn again:
"To God on high be glory,
And peace on earth to men!"

This combination of text and tune has proved very popular and has thus been copied by various hymnals.

ES IST EIN ROS. For comments on this tune see hymn 67.

The harmonization is from the *Musae Sioniae* (1605) by Michael Praetorius.

52 FROM HEAVEN CAME THE ANGELS BRIGHT

From heaven came the angels bright
To shepherds watching in the night.
A newborn royal child, they said,
Lies yonder in a manger bed.

To Bethlehem, King David's town,
As Micah saw, comes great renown;
Your Lord Christ is incarnate there
To save you all from sin and care.

Rejoice therefore that through his Son
Your God with you is now at one.
He took on human flesh and bone,
And you, his brothers, are God's own.

God came to share himself with you;
Your sin and death he overthrew.

Vom Himmel kam der Engel Schar,
Erschien den Hirten offenbar,
Sie sagten ihn:Ein Kindlein zart,
Das liegt dort in der Krippen hart.

Zu Bethlehem in Davids Stadt,
Wie Micha das verkündet hat.
Es ist der Herre Jesus Christ,
Der euer aller Heiland ist.

Des sollt ihr billig fröhlich sein,
Dass Gott mit euch ist worden ein.
Er ist gebor'n eu'r Fleisch und Blut,
Eu'r Bruder ist das ew'ge Gut.

Was kann euch tun die Sünd' und Tod?
Ihr habt mit euch den wahren Gott.

The foe may send his fiery dart, Your friend, God's Son, will shield your heart.	Lasst zürnen Teufel und die Höll', Gott's Sohn ist worden eu'r Gesell.
He never will abandon you. Trust King Immanuel the True. Yield not to any evil might. Walk in the Christ child's saving light.	Er will und kann euch lassen nicht, Setzt ihr auf ihn eur' Zuversicht. Es mögen euch viel fechten an: Dem sei Trotz, der's nicht lassen kann!
Then in the end you will prevail; God's friends and brothers cannot fail. In praise to God then raise your voice, Prepare forever to rejoice.	Zuletzt müsst ihr doch haben recht, Ihr seid nun worden Gott's Geschelcht. Des danket Gott in Ewigkeit, Geduldig, fröhlich allezeit!

Luther perhaps wrote this hymn for Christmas 1542, and its first appearance was in Joseph Klug's *Geistliche Lieder* (Wittenberg, 1543). It is one of the two hymn texts, the other being "Our Father, Who from Heaven Above" (*LW* 431), that is known to exist in Luther's own handwriting.

In comparing the exquisite, childlike "From Heaven Above to Earth I Come" (*LW* 37) to "From Heaven Came the Angels Bright," one notices the latter to be more serious and instructive, and designed more for the mature Christian. Moreover, in force of expression and simple beauty of form the latter certainly ranks high among Luther's hymns.

The translation is by F. Samuel Janzow.

PUER NOBIS. This lovely tune is from Michael Praetorius' *Musae Sioniae* VI (1609), where it is set to a German translation of an old Latin carol "Geborn ist Gottes Söhnelein." Because of its association with the text "O Splendor of the Father's light" (LW 481), the tune has sometimes been called SPLENDOR.

Strangely, "From Heaven Came The Angels Bright" never was given a proper tune. The hymnals during Luther's lifetime used VOM HIMMEL HOCH (*LW* 37, 38), and while Berlin hymnals used the early folksong tune *Aus fremden Landen komm ich her* (see Zahn 344a), today's hymnals of the Lutheran territorial churches in Germany again use the former.

The harmonization is by Paul G. Bunjes under the *nom de plume* of Wilhelm Quampen.

JOY TO THE WORLD — 53

This popular hymn by Issac Watts, a free paraphrase based on Psalm 98:2–9, first appeared in his *The Psalms of David, imitated in the language of the New Testament* (1719) with the heading "The Messiah's Coming and Kingdom."

ANTIOCH (COMFORT, HOLY TRIUMPH, MESSIAH) appeared in Lowell Mason's *Occasional Psalms and Hymn Tunes* (Boston, 1838) as "arranged from Handel." If one accepts Mason's statement, one can see the correspondence between the opening four notes of this tune with those for the sopranos in the first measure of the chorus "Lift Up Your Heads, O Ye Gates" in the *Messiah;* also the music for the two short phrases "and heaven and nature sing" from the introduction to the recitative "Comfort Ye My People" in the same oratorio.

Why Mason called the tune ANTIOCH can only be conjectured. He often chose biblical names, apparently at random. It was in Antioch, the ancient city in Syria, that the disciples were first called Christians. In England this tune is known as COMFORT; HOLY TRIUMPH may reflect the sentiment of the hymn; MESSIAH aludes to the tune's possible source, namely, Handel's *Messiah.*

In America, text and tune have been so inseparably wedded and so associated with Christmas that one cannot imagine the hymn as being a paraphrase of Psalm 98. Some of England's standard hymnals do not include this hymn text nor the tune. *The Hymnal 1940* of the Protestant Episcopal Church includes the text set to RICHMOND, otherwise known as CHESTERFIELD (*LW* 29). Interestingly, the successor to this hymnal, *The Hymnal 1982*, uses Lowell Mason's ANTIOCH.

The harmonization of ANTIOCH is by Lowell Mason.

54 HE WHOM SHEPHERDS ONCE CAME PRAISING

Quem pastores

He whom shepherds once came praising, Awed by heav'nly light ablazing, Cheered by angel news amazing: "King of glory, Christ is born!"	Quem pastores laudavere, Quibus angeli dixere Absit vobis iam timere, Natus est Rex gloriae.
He whom sages, westward faring, Myrrh and gold and incense bearing, Humbly worshiped, off'rings sharing, Judah's lion reigns this morn!	Ad quem reges ambulabant, Auram, thus, myrrham portabant Immolabant haec sincere Leoni victoriae.
Sing with Mary, virgin mother; Praise her Son, our newborn brother; Angel ranks, lead one another, Hailing him in holy joy!	Exsultemus cum Maria, In caelesti hierarchia, Natum promat voce pia, Laus honor et gloria.
To our king, God ever reigning, Yet of Mary manhood gaining, Heav'nly gifts for us obtaining, Raise your hymns of homage high!	Christo Regi, Deo nato, Per Mariam nobis dato, Merito resonet vere Laus, honor et gloria.

Nunc angelorum

The glorious angels came today, Aglow with light into the night of darkness deep,	Nunc angelorum gloria hominibus Resplenduit in mundo,

To shepherds who by moon's bright ray
Did in the field o'er sheep their silent vigil keep.
"Joy, great joy and tidings glad we bring
from heav'n resounding,

For you, for you and all the world
abounding."

"God's majesty has come to earth
And sent his only Son to you in humankind;
A chosen virgin gave him birth.
In David's town the holy infant you will find,
Lying helpless in a manger, poor and bare and lowly,
To set you free from all your sorrow wholly."

Then sang the angels this refrain:
"To God on high alone give praise and glory,
And peace on earth again shall reign.
Let all on earth with gladness heed this story
And rejoice in his goodwill."
The Savior came in meekness
For you, for you, to bear your flesh in weakness.

The wond'ring shepherds said: "Behold!
Let us now go with all good speed to Bethlehem
To see this thing the Lord has told;
The sheep are safe; he will indeed take care of them."
There they found the wonder child,
in lowly swaddling clothes lying,
Yet all the world with his free grace supplying.

Quam celebris victoria recolitur
In corde laetabundo;

Novi partus gaudia
Virgo mater produxit,
Et sol verus in tenebris illuxit.

Pastores, palam dicite in Bethlehem
Quem genuit Maria,
Deum verum et hominem,
Errantium qui est salus et vita.
Lux de caelo claruit
Pace iam reparata,
Et genetrix permansit illibata.

Magnum nomen domini Emanuel,
Quod est nobiscum deus.
Culpae datur hodie remissio;
Laetetur homo reus.
Redemptori domino
Redempti iubilemus;
Hic est dies at annus iubilaeus.

"Rex regum natus hodie de virgine
Conserva nos constantes,
Ut post hanc vitam fragilem
Sempiternam simus participantes."
Laus, honor et gloria
Sit Deo in excelsis,
Hominibus pax bonae voluntatis.

Resonet in laudibus

God's own Son is born a child, is born a child;
God the Father is reconciled, is reconciled!

Magnum nomen Domini Emanuel,
quod annuntiatum est per Gabriel.

The so-called Quempas Celebration recaptures a worshipful and beautiful Christmas Eve custom dating back to the Middle Ages, the procedure of which approximated the directions given at the bottom of the first page of the hymn . The term *Quempas* is derived from the first two syllables of the Latin text "Quem pastores laudavere" the first of the three Latin carol texts that make up the whole. The Quempas evidently arose in southern Bohemia, for it is in a Hohenfurth Abbey manuscript (now in the Prague Museum) dating from about 1410, that the text and tunes of the "Quem pastores" and the "Nunc angelorum" are contained. The third carol is from the 14th-century "Resonet in laudibus," to which the text "Joseph lieber, Joseph mein" and other German texts were sung. Actually it is only a portion of the entire tune RESONET IN LAUDIBUS that is here used with the text "God's own Son is born a child, . . ." This portion was the setting for "Magnum nomen Domini Emmanuel, quod annuntiatum est per Gabriel," often attached to "Resonet in laudibus."

Valentin Triller's *Ein Schlesisch Singbüchlein aus göttlicher Schrift* (Breslau, 1555) not only is the oldest printed German source for part 1 of this hymn (Zahn 1380), but Triller also added, in due time, the German text of parts 2 and 3. Triller, a pastor in Panthenau, Bohemia, was a follower of Kasper von Schwenkfeld (c. 1489–1561), a mystic lay person who helped introduce the Reformation in Silesia but who soon deserted its cause for theological reasons. His theological aberrations, incidently, were rejected by the *Formula of Concord* (1577). Loyalty to Schwenkfeld perhaps accounts for the fact that Triller avoided including any hymns and tunes of Luther and his colleagues in the above hymnals, concentrating instead on folk songs, approximately 145 in all. Some songs in this collection constitute the earliest source available to hymnologists and musicologists. With due regard to this source, Michael Praetorius (*LW* 14, et al.) supplied notable settings for eight of them.

In 1543 "Resonet in laudibus" and "Nunc angelorum" appeared in Joseph Klug's *Geistlche Lieder* (Zahn 8573) and from then on they appeared in various Lutheran hymnals, sometimes side by side.

Johann Leisentritt's Roman Catholic hymnal, *Geistliche Lieder und Psalmen* (Bautzen, 1567), is the first to note something about the performance of the Quempas by stating, "A beautiful song for the boys to sing in four choirs." Performance instructions were further spelled out in a choir office book printed by Matthaeus Luedtke in Wittenberg in 1589, and these, generally speaking, became the norm.

The English translation of "Quem pastores laudavere," based on that by C. Winfred Douglas in *The Hymnal 1940* of the Episcopal Church, was prepared by Martin Seltz for inclusion in *Worship Supplement* (1969). The four stanzas beginning "The glorious angels came today" represent a free paraphrase by Herbert Bouman of the Latin stanzas beginning with "Nunc angelorum gloria hominibus," which Bouman did for the same book.

QUEM PASTORES, NUNC ANGELORUM, RESONET IN LAUDIBUS are treated in the above.

The harmonizations are by Richard W. Hillert.

55 ANGELS WE HAVE HEARD ON HIGH

Angels we have heard on high,
Sweetly singing o'er the plains,
And the mountains in reply,
Echoing their joyous strains.

Les anges dans nos campagnes
Ont etonne l'hymne des cieux,
Et l'echo de nos montagnes
Redit ce chant melodieux:

Refrain
Gloria in excelsis Deo;
Gloria in excelsis Deo.

Shepherds, why this jubilee?
Why your joyous strains prolong?
What the gladsome tidings be
Which inspire your heav'nly song?

Bergers pour qui cette fete?
Quel est l'objet de tous ces chants?
Quel vainqueur, quelle conquete
Merite ces cris triomphants?

Come to Bethlehem and see
Him whose birth the angels sing;
Come, adore on bended knee
Christ the Lord, the newborn king.

Cherchons tous l'heureux village
Qui l'a vu naitre sous ses toits;
Offrons-lui le tendre hommage
Et de nos coeurs et de nos voix.

In his *Les Noels et al tradition popularie* (1932), Jan R. H. de Smidt opines that this French carol text and tune date from the 18th century and were first published in 1855 in the *Nouveau recueil de cantiques*. The translation here used is from a Roman Catholic collection entitled *Crown of Jesus Music*, Part II (London, 1862), by Henri Frederick Hemy. Whether he himself actually made the English translation is uncertain. Slight variations of this text are common today, the original French authorship of which is completely unknown.

GLORIA, also known as IRIS, is the traditional French tune associated with this text. The harmonization is from a setting by Edward Shippen Barnes in *The New Church Hymnal* (New York, 1937).

I AM SO GLAD WHEN CHRISTMAS COMES 56

I am so glad when Christmas comes,
The night of Jesus' birth,
When Bethl'em's star shone as the sun
And angels sang with mirth.

The little child of Bethlehem,
The King of heav'nly grace,
Came down from his exalted throne
To save our fallen race.

He's now returned to heav'n above,
God's Son he is alway;
He ne'er forgets his little ones
But hears them when they pray.

I too would sing my Savior's praise,
My joy, my crown, my Lord;
For he has made me his own child
By Water and the Word.

I love this precious Christmas eve
And my dear Savior mild,
And I shall not forget the truth:
He loves me as his child.

I am so glad when Christmas comes:
Let anthems fill the air!
He opens wide for every child
His paradise so fair.

Jeg er sa glad hver julekveld,
For da blev Jesus født;
Da lyste stjernen som en sol,
Og engler sang sa søtt.

Det lille barn i Bethlehem,
Han var en konge stor
Som kom fra himlens høie slott
Ned til vår arme jord.

Nu bor han høit i himmerik,
Han er Guds egen Sønn,
Men husker alltid pa de små
Og hører deres bønn.

Å gid jeg kunde synge så
Da blev visst Jesus glad;
Ti jeg ja ogsa blev Guds barn
Engang i dåpens bad.

Jeg holder av vår julekveld
Og av den Herre Krist
Og at han elsker mig igjen,
Det vet jeg ganske visst

Jeg er så glad hver julekveld,
Da synger vi hans pris;
Da åpner han for alle små
Sitt søte paradis.

This is a translation of Marie Wexelsen's Norwegian carol, "Jeg er saa glad hver Julekveld," which appeared in *Nynorsk Salmebog* (1926). The original hymn had nine stanzas; two of them were omitted in an earlier translation by Peter Sveegen, "How Glad I Am Each Christmas Eve," which appeared in the *Concordia Hymnbook* (Norwegian Edition, 1918). The present translation was prepared by Norman Madson at the request of Alfred Fremder (*LW* 375, 423) for use by the choir of Bethany College, Mankato, Minnesota, of which he was conductor at the time.

JEG ER SAA GLAD, also known as CHRISTMAS EVE, was once thought to be a Norwegian folk tune. The melody is now known, however, to have been composed by Peder Knudsen while he was organist in Alesund, Norway. The setting is from the *Service Book and Hymnal* (1958).

57 GENTLE MARY LAID HER CHILD

Joseph S. Cook wrote this text for a carol competition sponsored by the *Christian Guardian* in 1919. In five stanzas of four lines each, it took first prize and appeared in the Christmas issue of the magazine. For the *Hymnary* (1930) of the United Church of Canada, another quatrain was added to accommodate the tune, creating the three eight-line stanzas now in use.

TEMPUS ADEST FLORIDUM is from the famous collection *Piae Cantiones,* compiled in 1582 by Theodoricus Petrus of Nyland, Finland. It became associated with Christmas through John Mason Neale's legend of "Good King Wenceslas," written for this delightful tune; in the *Hymnary* (1930) the tune was set to the above text.

The harmonization by Theodore Beck is from *Worship Supplement* (1969).

58 ONCE IN ROYAL DAVID'S CITY

To make the church's catechism more interesting and meaningful, Cecil F. Alexander decided to present various subjects in a series of catechism hymns. This hymn was one of those based on the Second Article of the Apostles' Creed, specifically "I believe . . . in Jesus Christ . . . , who was conceived by the Holy Spirit, born of the virgin Mary." Readers may recall another rather popular versification of hers, namely, "There is a green hill far away," based on the words of the same article, particularly the words "was crucified, died, and was buried." The various hymn texts in this catechism series were first published in her *Hymns for Little Children* (1848).

IRBY. This beautiful and celebrated tune first appeared set to the above text in a little pamphlet entitled *Christmas Carols, Four Numbers* published by Henry J. Gauntlett in 1849. There it was a unison melody with simple piano accompaniment. In 1858 he included it in a four-part setting in his music edition of Alexander's book, *Hymns for Little Children with Piano Accompaniment*. Why Gauntlett called the tune IRBY—the name of two townships in Lincolnshire—is uncertain.

Pastors and choir directors who have used the Service of Nine Lessons and Carols from King's College, Cambridge, will recall that "Once in Royal David's City" serves as the stately and thrilling opening processional. Indeed, young and old alike enjoy the noble simplicity and honesty of this lovely tune, always associated with Alexander's text.

The harmonization was prepared by George Leonard, a *nom de plume* of Paul G. Bunjes.

O LITTLE TOWN OF BETHLEHEM 59

Written by Phillips Brooks for a Sunday School Christmas festival service in 1868, this carol was at first slow to gain popularity, but has since become a favorite in the United States and England. The lyrics were probably inspired by Brooks' visit to the Holy Land in December of 1865 when, on Christmas Eve, he traveled by horseback from Jerusalem to Bethlehem.

Six teachers and 36 Sunday school students sang "O Little Town of Bethlehem" at its first performance at Holy Trinity Church, Philadelphia. A local bookseller then printed it in leaflets for sale, and it first appeared in a hymn collection in William R. Huntington's *The Church Porch* (1874), a hymn and tune book for children. The Episcopal Church published it for use as a church hymn in its *Hymnal* (1892).

Brooks originally penned five stanzas for this hymn. Stanza 4, here omitted, originally read:

Where children pure and happy
Pray to the blessed Child,
Where misery cries out to Thee,
Son of the undefiled,
Where Charity stands watching
And Faith holds wide the door,
The dark night wakes, the glory breaks
And Christmas comes once more.

Of this stanza, Louis F. Benson in *Studies of Familiar Hymns*, First Series, quotes Brooks' organist, Lewis Redner, as writing:

> The fourth line led to some amusing criticism lest it should smack of the doctrine of the Immaculate Conception. Brooks then changed that line to 'Son

> of the Mother mild,' [and so it appears in the Christmas program of 1868], but he afterwards decided to omit the fourth verse altogether from the carol.

FOREST GREEN is an adaptation by Ralph Vaughan Williams of the lovely English folk tune, "The Ploughboy's Dream," heard by Williams at Forest Green, Surrey, in 1903. Its first use as a hymn tune was in the *English Hymnal* (1906), of which Williams was the music editor. It is his harmonization in that hymnal that is here used.

60 O LITTLE TOWN OF BETHLEHEM

The text of hymn 60 is treated with hymn 59.

ST. LOUIS, by Lewis H. Redner, is the tune which accompanied "O Little Town of Bethlehem" at its first performance in 1868. Redner, organist and Sunday school superintendent at Holy Trinity Church, where the hymn's author Phillips Brooks was rector, related the following story:

> As Christmas of 1868 approached, Mr. Brooks told me that he had written a simple little carol for the Christmas Sunday-school service, and he asked me to write the tune to it. The simple music was written in great haste and under great pressure. We were to practice it on the following Sunday. Mr. Brooks came to me on Friday, and said, "Redner, have you ground out that music yet to 'O Little Town of Bethlehem'? I replied, 'No,' but that he should have it by Sunday.
>
> On the Saturday night previous my brain was all confused about the tune. I thought more about my Sunday-school lesson than I did about the music. But I was roused from sleep late in the night hearing an angel-strain whispering in my ear, and seizing a piece of music paper I jotted down the treble of the tune as we now have it, and on Sunday morning before going to church I filled in the harmony. Neither Mr. Brooks nor I ever thought the carol or the music to it would live beyond that Christmas of 1868.
>
> My recollection is that Richard McCauley, who then had a bookstore on Chestnut Street west of 13th Street, printed it on leaflets for sale. Rev. Dr. Huntington, rector of All Saints' Church, Worcester, Mass., asked permission to print it in his Sunday-school hymn and tune book, called *The Church Porch*, and it was he who christened the music "Saint Louis" (Benson, *Studies of Familiar Hymns*, First Series).

Further illumination on the tune name comes from *Stories of Christmas Carols* by Ernest K. Emurian. The story here is that Brooks, having requested Redner to compose a melody, remarked that it might be called ST. LEWIS after the composer's Christian name. Redner in all modesty answered that a more suitable name might be ST. PHILLIPS. Emurian then comments:

> Brooks paid his organist a worthy tribute without embarrassing him by naming the new tune "St. Louis," changing the spelling of the superintendent's first name from "Lewis" to "Louis," an alteration which gave rise to many conjectures about a possible but nonexistent connection between the midwestern city of that name and the name of the tune (Reynolds, *Hymns of Our Faith*).

The harmonization is from the *Service Book and Hymnal* (1958), slightly altered.

WHAT CHILD IS THIS 61

One of William C. Dix's many Christmas poems, this three-stanza carol is drawn from *The Manger Throne* (c. 1865), which Dix is said to have written on the Epiphany, taking his cue from that day's Gospel, Matthew 2:1–12.

GREENSLEEVES was no doubt a very popular ballad in 1580, as it was licensed to several individuals for printing in that year. Its first license in the record of the Stationers' Company, September 1580, was to Richard Jones for "A new Northern Dittye of the *Lady Greene Sleeves*." The ballad's traditional text begins:

> Alas, my love, you do me wrong
> To cast me off discourteously,
> For I have loved you oh, so long,
> Delighting in your company.
> Greensleeves was all my joy,
> Greensleeves was my delight,
> Greensleeves was my heart of gold,
> And who but my Lady Greensleeves?

The popularity of GREENSLEEVES is evidenced by a perusal of Shakespeare's *The Merry Wives of Windsor*, wherein two references are made to the ballad.

Twelve days after the first printing license was granted, the melody was adapted for religious use, as the Stationers' Company records reflect: "*Green Sleves* [sic] moralized to the Scripture, declaring the manifold benefits and blessings of God bestowed on sinful man." In 1642 it appeared in *New Christmas Carols* to "The old year now away is fled."

This English ballad tune has been sung to a great variety of texts.

The harmonization is from the *Service Book and Hymnal* (1958), slightly altered.

62 IT CAME UPON THE MIDNIGHT CLEAR

Edmund H. Sears composed this Christmas poem in 1849 and sent it to the editor of the *Christian Register*, where it appeared December 29, 1850. One of its claims to fame is its unique situation, being a nativity hymn written by a Unitarian; another is its social implication of the Christmas message, seen particularly in Sears' omitted third stanza:

Yet with the woes of sin and strife
The world hath suffered long;
Beneath the angel-strain have rolled
Two thousand years of wrong;
And man, at war with man, hears not
The love song which they bring;
O hush the noise, ye men of strife,
And hear the angels sing.

Stanza 4 has been considerably altered to obviate the false chiliastic hope of universal peace with the entire converted world joining in the hymn of praise.

CAROL comes from Study No. 23 in Richard S. Willis' *Church Chorals and Choir Studies* (New York, 1850), where it was set to "See Israel's Gentle Shepherd Stand." In a letter written in 1887, Willis said that while he was a vestryman in the Church of the Transfiguration, New York City, he adapted the tune to its present form as a Christmas carol for "While Shepherds Watched Their Flocks by Night." The arrangement was accomplished by adding a new third phrase and repeating the second as a closing phrase.

The harmonization is from the *Service Book and Hymnal* (1958).

63 WHO ARE THESE THAT EARNEST KNOCK

This hymn by Henry L. Lettermann appeared already in the *Worship Supplement* (1969), there also coupled to this delightful tune. Its 10 uneven phrases—76 76 77 57 76—with a rhyme scheme of ABABCCDEFG, together with its fresh flavor by the use of "earnest," "docile," and "silent" as adjectives rather than as adverbs, combine to give the whole a sense of naivete.

DIES EST LAETITIAE. The foregoing textual impression is amplified by this tune, named after the incipit of a Latin Christmas song contained in a number of 15th-century manuscripts. Zahn (7869) gives this tune with the German text, "Als Jesus geboren war zu Herodis Zeiten." Both the Latin and German texts were well known and found their way into various early hymnals of the Reformation.

The harmonization is by Paul G. Bunjes.

AWAY IN A MANGER 64

Referring to this text as "Luther's Cradle Hymn" is an error that by now should have run its course. Admittedly this text, however, may have had some connection with German Lutherans in Pennsylvania, for its earliest-known source is in the *Little Children's Book for Schools and Families*, published in 1885 in Philadelphia under the Evangelical Lutheran Church in North America. There it had two anonymous stanzas set to a tune by J. E. Clark called ST. KILDA. When, two years later, the text appeared with the tune AWAY IN A MANGER, prefixed with the initials J. R. M., in J. R. Murray's *Dainty Songs for Little Lads and Lasses* (Cincinnati, 1887), it was described as "Luther's Cradle Hymn. Composed by Martin Luther for his children, and still sung by German mothers to their little ones." But, as one scholar's research of this rather charming children's hymn reveals, there is no evidence in Luther's (*LW* 13, et al.) works of his having written this hymn for his children; moreover, the hymn appears in no German book nor was it translated into German until 1934 (see R. S. Hill "Not so far away in a manger: Forty-one settings of an American Carol," *Music Library Association Notes*, December 1945). Thus the Luther myth regarding text and tune has been exposed for what it is. Stanza 3, incidentally, is a later addition that appeared in *Gabriel's Vineyard Songs* (1892), collected by C. H. Gabriel, Louisville, Kentucky, a popular composer of gospel songs during the Billy Sunday-Homer Rodeheaver evangelistic crusades in the early 1900s. Whether he himself wrote the stanza is uncertain.

CRADLE SONG. Of the more than forty tunes associated with this text, three are perhaps most preferred and well-known. The Commission on Worship chose CRADLE SONG for *Lutheran Worship*, a tune composed by William J. Kirkpatrick that first appeared in *Around the World with Christmas*, published in Cincinnati, Chicago, and St. Louis in 1895. As an American tune that has been popularly coupled to this text in Great Britain, Canada, and Australia, the commission considered it most superior of the three here mentioned. AWAY IN A MANGER, also called MUELLER, the tune that appeared in the above-mentioned *Dainty Songs for Little Lads and Lasses*, undoubtedly composed by J. R. Murray, has perhaps wider use in American Lutheranism. Finally, many people in the United States still prefer to sing this carol to the tune of "Flow gently, sweet Afton," written in 1838 by J. S. Spilman.

The simple, lilting harmonization of CRADLE SONG in *Lutheran Worship* is by Ralph Vaughan Williams.

65 ON CHRISTMAS NIGHT ALL CHRISTIANS SING

Little is known about this text and tune, taken from the *Oxford Book of Carols* (1928), except that it is there said to be "from Mrs. Verrall, Monks Gate, Sussex." Arranged by Ralph Vaughan Williams, it has long been a favorite of choral groups in this country. The unison melody with the choir singing in parts should result in a joyous and pleasing effect. Only stanzas 1, 3, and 4 of the four stanzas in the *Oxford Book of Carols* are here utilized.

The harmonization by Ralph Vaughan Williams is from the *Hymnal for Colleges and Schools* (1956).

66 EVERY YEAR THE CHRIST CHILD

Ev'ry year the Christ child Comes to us on earth To proclaim redemption Through his holy birth.	Alle Jahre wieder, Kommt das Christus Kind. Auf die Erde nieder Wo wir Menschen sind.
He would with his blessing In each home abide And on ev'ry pathway Travel by our side.	Kehrt mit seinem Segen Ein in jedes Haus, Geht auf allen Wegen Mit uns ein und aus.
All unseen, the Savior At my side does stand, Evermore to guide me With his loving hand.	Ist auch mir zur Seite Still und unerkannt, Dass er treu mich leite An der lieben Hand.

Johann Wilhelm Hey's text appeared in the appendix to the second series of his *Fabeln für Kinder* (Hamburg, 1837). A translation by Mrs. H. R. Spaeth, beginning "As each happy Christmas," was published in the *Little Children's Book* (Philadelphia, 1885) and repeated in the *Common Service Book* (1918) and the *Hymnal and Order of Service* (Augustana Lutheran, 1927).

The translation of stanza 1 was provided by Erich Allwardt. W. Gustave Polack (*LW* 209, et al.) prepared the translation of stanzas 2 and 3.

ALLE JAHRE WIEDER. Attributed to Friedrich Silcher, a collector and arranger of folk songs, the tune is frequently identified as having been sung to a German folk song beginning with "Aus dem Himmel ferne."

The harmonization is by Paul G. Bunjes.

LO, HOW A ROSE IS GROWING 67

Lo, how a rose is growing,
A bloom of finest grace;
The prophets had foretold it:
A branch of Jesse's race
Would bear one perfect flow'r
Here in the cold of winter
And darkest midnight hour.

The rose of which I'm singing,
Isaiah had foretold.
He came to us through Mary,
Who sheltered him from cold.
Through God's eternal will
This child to us was given
At midnight calm and still.

The shepherds heard the story
The angels sang that night;
How Christ was born of Mary;
He was the Son of light.
To Bethlehem they ran
To find him in the manger
As angel heralds sang.

This flow'r, so small and tender,
With fragrance fills the air;
His brightness ends the darkness
That kept the earth in fear.
True God and yet true man,
He came to save his people
From earth's dark night of sin.

O Savior, child of Mary,
Who felt all human woe;
O Savior, king of glory,
Who triumphed o'er our foe:
Bring us at length, we pray,
To the bright courts of heaven
And into endless day.

Es ist ein Reis (Ros') entsprungen
Aus einer Wurzel zart,
Als uns die Alten sungen,
Von Jesse kam die Art,
Und hat ein Blümlein bracht
Mitten im kalten Winter
Wohl zu der halben Nacht.

Das Reislein, das ich meine,
Davon Jesaias sagt,
Hat uns gebracht alleine
Marie, die reine Magd.
Aus Gottes ew'gem Rat
Hat sie ein Kind geboren
Wohl zu der halben Nacht.

Den Hirten auf dem Felde
Verkünd't das englisch' Heer,
Wie zur selbigen Stunde
Christus geboren wär'
Zu Bethle'm in der Stadt,
Da sie das Kindlein finden,
Wie ihn'n der Engel g'sagt.

Das Blümelein so kleine,
Das duftet uns so süss,
Mit seinem hellen Scheine
Vertreibt's die Finster nis,
Wahr'r Mensch and wahrer Gott,
Hilft uns aus allen Leiden,
Rettet von Sünd' und Tod.

Wir bitten dich von Herzen,
O Heiland, edles Kind,
Durch alle deine Schmerzen,
Wann wir fahren dahin
Aus diesem Jammertal,
Du wollest uns geleiten
Bis in der Engel Saal.

This popular Christmas carol, of unknown authorship and uncertain origin, was to all appearances current in the 15th century, although its earliest appearance is not until 1599, when it was included in the *Alte Catholische Geistliche Kirchengeseng*, published in Cologne. Taking its cue from Isaiah 11:1, and relating the events in Luke 1–2 and Matthew 2, the hymn originally contained 23 stanzas. Two stanzas in the original clearly indicate that this was a hymn addressed to the virgin Mary. Stanza 2 identified her as the *shoot*, or *rose*, prophesied in Isaiah 11:1: "A shoot will come up from the stump of Jesse; from his roots a branch will bear fruit." She thus bears the *branch* who is Christ. Stanza 2 as here given is an altered form of the original that shifts the identification from the virgin Mary to the Christchild; he is the "rose" of which is sung. Stanza 22 originally prayed that Mary, queen of heaven, accompany the believers out of this valley of sorrows to the heavenly, angelic realm. Notice how that stanza, here given as stanza 5, has artfully shifted the emphasis and action to Christ the Savior, child of Mary.

Referring to the virgin Mary as the "rose" was not uncommon in the Middle Ages. In the 14th century the poet Heinrich Frauenlob, for instance, refers to her as the blooming rose of Jesse without a thorn ("Die blühend Rose von Jesse ohne Dorn"); similarly do Herman von Sachsenheim and Heinrich von Laufenberg. The Italian poet Dante (1265–1321) refers to Mary as the rose in whom the Word became incarnate.

From its very beginning this carol was included in various German hymnals, usually with the appropriate alterations and in various cento arrangements.

The original German of stanza 4, as here given, is uncertain. It is not in the earliest appearance of this long hymn. The assertion that it comes from the second supplement to *Geistliche Liederschatz* (Berlin, 1853) or possibly from the *Kleine Missionsharfe* (Berlin, 1836), has up to now not been proven. Should perchance any of these sources be confirmed, then Gustav Knak (1806–78), gifted poet, pastor of Bethlehem Lutheran Church in Berlin, staunch advocate of foreign mission work, might well be the author, for he, together with Samuel Elsner and E. Langbecker, edited the aforementioned.

The translation of this cento was prepared by Gracia Grindall for inclusion in *Lutheran Book of Worship* (1978).

EST IS EIN ROS. This lovely carol tune, dating perhaps from the fourteenth or fifteenth century, first appeared with the above text in the *Alte Catholische Geistliche Kirchengeseng* (Cologne, 1599), where it differs from that here given only in its relative note values (Bäumker I, 156, and No. 78).

This popular setting is from the *Musae Sioniae* VI (1609) of Michael Praetorius.

68 SILENT NIGHT, HOLY NIGHT

Silent night, holy night!
All is calm, all is bright
Round yon virgin mother and child.
Holy Infant, so tender and mild,
Sleep in heavenly peace,
Sleep in heavenly peace.

Stille Nacht, heilige Nacht!
Alles schläft, einsam wacht,
Nür das heilige Elternpaar,
Das im Stalle zu Bethlehem war
Bei dem himmlischen Kind,
Bei dem himmlischen Kind.

Silent night, holy night!
Shepherds quake at the sight;
Glories stream from heaven afar,
Heav'nly hosts sing, Alleluia!
Christ, the Savior, is born!
Christ, the Savior, is born!

Stille Nacht, heilige Nacht!
Hirten erst kundgemacht;
Durch der Engel Halleluja
Tönt es laut von fern und nah:
Christ, der Retter, ist da!
Christ, der Retter, ist da!

Silent night, holy night!
Son of God, love's pure light
Radiant beams from your holy face
With the dawn of redeeming grace,

Stille Nacht, heilige Nacht!
Gottes Sohn, o wie lacht
Lieb' aus deinem göttlichen Mund,
Da uns schläget die rettende Stund',

Jesus, Lord, at your birth,	Christ, in deiner Geburt!
Jesus, Lord, at your birth.	Christ, in deiner Geburt!

Breakdown of the organ in St. Nikolaus Church in Ober ndorf, Austria, created the need for music other than originally planned for the Christmas Eve Midnight Mass. Thus on December 24, 1818, Joseph Mohr, the church's young assistant priest, brought the six-stanza carol text he had written to Franz Gruber, parish organist and teacher in the village school, with the request that he set it to music. That night the work—for two solo voices (soprano and alto; or tenor or bass) and choir (in four-part harmony in the last four bars)—was sung with Mohr singing the tenor, Gruber singing the bass while accompanying with his guitar, and with a small choir of girls from the village repeating the final two lines of each stanza in harmony. 20 years elapsed before the tune and text were published in Leipzig in the *Katholisches Gesang-und Gebetbuch für den öffentlichen und häuslichen Gottesdienst Zunächst zum Gebrauche der katholischen Gemeinden im Königreiche Sachsen* (known as *Leipziger Gesangbuch*, 1838). In the meantime, however, the carol was disseminated to other Tyrolean towns by Karl Mauracher of Zillerthal, the man who repaired the organ in St. Nickolaus, and from there it gradually traveled around the world, being sung, as someone has said, "as reverently in the Himalayas of India as in the Alps of Austria." Its simple language and design readily lent itself to being translated into almost any language. It was introduced to the United States by the Renner family, a folk-singing group that toured America in 1827, and was further popularized by Ernestine Schumann-Heink (1861–1936), renowned Austrian operatic contralto, later naturalized American.

In 1913 St. Nikolaus Church was razed because of danger of collapse from a flood. A small memorial chapel, consecrated in 1937, now stands on this site, to which hundreds of people come yearly to attend the outdoor Christmas Eve memorial service, with "Silent Night" played and sung as originally done.

Among the dozen or so English versions, the most popular and familiar is that here given, the source of which, for almost one hundred years, was uncertain. Thanks to the research of Byron E. Underwood, rector of St. Ann's Episcopal Church, Revere, Massachusetts (see his article in *The Hymn* 8, 4 [October 1957]: 123–130), it is now known to be the work of John F. Young, a translation of stanzas 1, 6, and 2 of the original Mohr text that first appeared in the *Sunday-School Service and Tune Book: Selected and arranged by John Clark Hollister* (New York and Boston, 1863) and later included in Young's posthumous collection, *Great Hymns of the Church* (1887). The general acceptance and apparent exclusive use of these three particular stanzas is undoubtedly the result of Young's selection. The remaining original stanzas 3, 4, and 5 are here given for anyone who might wish simply to see them or actually to use them on some occasion.

3. Stille Nacht! Heilige Nacht	3. Silent night! Holy night!
Die der Welt Heil gebracht,	Brings to earth saving light;
Aus des Himmels goldenen Höhn	Grace fulfilled to us is giv'n,
Uns der Gnader Fülle läßt sehn:	From the golden heights of heaven,

Jesum in Menchengestalt,
Jesum in Menchengestalt.

4. Stille Nacht! Heilige Nacht!
Wo sich heut alle Macht
Väterlicher Liebe ergoß
Und als Bruder huldvoll umschloß
Jesus die Völker der Welt.
Jesus die Völker der Welt.

5. Stille Nacht! Heilige Nacht!
Lange schon und bedacht,
Als der Herr vom Grimme befreit
In der Väter urgrauer Zeit
Aller Welt Schonung verhieß,
Aller Welt Schonung verhieß.

Comes in lowly birth,
Comes in lowly birth.

4. Silent night! Holy night!
Shows to each his great might.
Love descends from heaven above;
Dwells with us in brotherly love,
Hailed by nations afar,
Hailed by nations afar.

5. Silent night! Holy night!
Grants us grace, from sin's plight;
Stills God's wrath as was foretold
By his prophets in days of old.
Peace, goodwill to all,
Peace, goodwill to all.

STILLE NACHT. As indicated above, this tune is unquestionably the composition of organist and teacher Franz X. Gruber. Although for a time generally considered to have been a Tyrolean folk-song, and even sometimes attributed to others, including Mozart and Michael or Franz Joseph Haydn (*LW* 294), an inquiry in 1854, commissioned by the Emperor William Frederick in Berlin, resulted in a letter by Gruber himself in which he gave a detailed account of the origin of both text and music.

The extreme simplicity of both tune and text, reminiscent of folk song, though perhaps a little sentimental, caused it to become an essential part of Christmas celebrations in many lands. Oddly enough, it does not appear in the hymnals of Lutheran territorial churches in Germany nor in the *Oxford Book of Carols* (1928). Though Gruber's original manuscript is not extant, he made a number of arrangements of the tune with varying accompaniments for different instruments that survive (see J. Gassner, *Franz Xaver Gruber's Autographen von Stille Nacht, heilige Nacht*, Orberndorf und Salzach, 1958), one of which is reproduced in C. Cudworth's article, "The True 'Stille Nacht,' " *The Musical Times* CV/1642 (December 1964): 892–94.

The setting is from the *Service Book and Hymnal* (1958).

69 LET OUR GLADNESS HAVE NO END

Let our gladness have no end, Alleluia!
For to earth did Christ descend. Alleluia!

Refrain
On this day God gave us
Christ, his Son, to save us;
Christ, his Son, to save us.

See, the loveliest blooming rose,
Alleluia!
From the branch of Jesse grows.
Alleluia!

Narodil se Kristus Pán, Veselme se;
Z ruze kvet vykvetl nàm, Radujme se!

Z zivota cisteho,
Z rodu královského
Jiz nám narodil se.

Ktery prorokován jest, Veselme se;

Ten na svet k nám poslán jest, Radujme se!

Into flesh is made the Word, Alleluia!
He, our refuge and our Lord. Alleluia!

Aj, clovecenstvi nase, Veselme se,
Rácil jest vziti na se, Radujme se!

This jubilant Bohemian text, of unknown authorship and originally in six stanzas, appeared in Jiri Tranovsky's *Tranocius* (1636). According to Jaroslav Vajda (*LW* 132, et al.), the first four stanzas were discovered in 1872 in a manuscript, dated 1420, in Jestebnice, Bohemia, one of the oldest Hussite hymnals. Later the hymn appeared in the handwritten Latin and Czech gradual with music notation by Jan Franus in 1505, and again in the posthumously published hymnal by Vaclav Mirinsky (d. 1492). Thus this hymn enjoyed a two-century circulation and popularity prior to its inclusion in Tranovsky's Lutheran hymnal.

This three-stanza version, based loosely on the first three stanzas of the original text, is that prepared by the Inter-Lutheran Commission on Worship for inclusion in *Lutheran Book of Worship* (1978). Actually, the Vincent Pisek translation in *The Lutheran Hymnal* (1941), beginning "Christ the Lord to us is born," is much closer to the original first three stanzas.

NARODIL SE KRISTUS PÁN, named SALVATOR NATUS in *The Lutheran Hymnal*, is the anonymous tune originally associated with this carol.

The harmonization by Richard W. Hillert is that which he prepared for inclusion in *Lutheran Book of Worship* (1978).

WHILE SHEPHERDS WATCHED 70

This famous paraphrase, or metrical version, of Luke 2:8–14 by the poet laureate Nahum Tate first appeared in six stanzas of four lines in the *Supplement* (1700) to *A New Version of the Psalms of David, Fitted to the Tunes used in Churches* (1696), generally known as the New Version or as "Tate and Brady" (see essay: Metrical Psalms, p. 825). This *Supplement*, in addition to versions of the customary canticles, Ten Commandments, and the "Veni Creator," contained six hymns—hymns, so to speak, of human composure—one for Christmas, two for Easter, and three for Holy Communion. The one for Christmas, the hymn here being considered, is the only one to survive in common use, having been translated into many languages and included in practically every large hymnal. Moreover, "While Shepherds Watched" enjoys the distinction of being one of the few hymns allowed to be sung in English churches alongside the metrical psalms.

WHILE SHEPHERDS WATCHED. The above text has been and continues to be sung to numerous tunes—WINCHESTER OLD (*LW* 196), UNIVERSITY (*EH* 93), CROWLE (*EH* 463), CORNWALL (*EH* Appendix 8), CHRISTMAS (*PH* 362)—to mention but a few. *The Lutheran Hymnal* (1941) used BETHLEHEM, a tune that Sir Arthur Sullivan used and called OLD CAROL. Considering that tune and its harmonization to be of inferior quality, the Commission on Worship chose a rather charming old English carol, as in the *Oxford Book of Carols* (1928), and named it WHILE SHEPHERDS WATCHED.

That this tune not be sung too slowly, but lightly and with rhythmic vitality, it is suggested that it be interpreted in 2/2.

The harmonization was prepared by George Leonard, a *nom de plum* of Paul G. Bunjes.

71 FROM SHEPHERDING OF STARS

This hymn by F. Samuel Janzow first appeared in the November 1963 issue of *Lutheran Education*. Its inclusion in the *Worship Supplement* (1969) marked its first appearance in a full-fledged hymnal.

SHEPHERDING was composed by Richard W. Hillert for the above text at the request of the editors of *Lutheran Education*. Later it appeared with Janzow's text in *A New Song* (St. Louis, 1967), a collection of 13 hymns, new, so to speak, to congregations of the Synod, authorized by its Commission on Worship as a preview to the proposed contents of *Worship Supplement* (1969), where it was given its present title.

This simple, charming pentatonic tune (five-tone scale with, for instance, the intervallic pattern of the black keys of the piano beginning on F♯) and its harmonization reflect the pastoral nature of the text in a pleasing and effective manner.

THE ONLY SON FROM HEAVEN 72

The only Son from heaven,
Foretold by ancient seers,
By God the Father given,
In human form appears.
No sphere his light confining,
No star so brightly shining
As he, our Morning Star.

O time of God appointed,
O bright and holy morn!
He comes, the king anointed,
The Christ, the virgin-born,
Grim death to vanquish for us,
To open heav'n before us
And bring us life again.

Awaken, Lord, our spirit
To know and love you more,
In faith to stand unshaken,
In spirit to adore,
That we, through this world moving,
Each glimpse of heaven proving,
May reap its fullness there.

O Father, here before you
With God the Holy Ghost
And Jesus, we adore you,
O pride of angel host:
Before you mortals lowly
Cry, "Holy, holy, holy,
O blessed Trinity!"

Herr Christ, der einig Gotts Sohn
Vaters in Ewigkeit,
Aus sein Herzen entsprossen,
Gleichwie geschrieben steht,
Er ist der Morgensterne,
Sein Glänzen streckt er ferne
Vor andern Sternen klar;

Für uns ein Mensch geboren
Im letzten Teil der Zeit,
Dass wir nicht wärn verloren
Vor Gott in Ewigkeit,
Den Tod für uns zerbrochen,
Den Himmel aufgeschlossen,
Das Leben wiederbracht:

Lass uns in deiner Liebe
Und Kenntnis nehmen zu,
Dass wir am Glauben bleiben,
Dir dienen im Geist so,
Dass wir hie mögen schmecken
Dein Süssigkeit im Herzen
Und dürsten stets nach dir.

Among the various individuals who contributed to early evangelical hymnody was also a woman, namely, Elizabeth Cruciger, the author of this touching Epiphany hymn, "The Only Son from Heaven." It appeared in the two hymnals containing Luther's first hymns known as the Erfurt *Enchiridia* (1524). This hymn enjoys the distinction of being the first "Jesus Hymn" of the Evangelical Church. Its poetically tender lines, with perhaps a touch of late medieval mystical piety, stand in contrast to the more contesting and combative verses of the early male hymn writers. The picture in stanza 1 of Christ's going forth from the heart of God the Father has its roots in the Prudentius hymn, "Corde natus ex parentis" ("Of the Father's Love Begotten," *LW* 36).

Originally consisting of five stanzas, it is the first three stanzas of Cruciger, translated by Arthur T. Russel, that are here used. They appeared in his *Psalms and Hymns, partly Original, partly Selected, for the Use of the church of England* (1851). The fourth concluding doxological stanza was prepared by the Hymn Text Committee of the Inter-Lutheran Commission on Worship for *Lutheran Book of Worship* (1978).

HERR CHRIST DER EINIG GOTTS SOHN is a folk tune coupled to a secular love song, "Mein Freud möcht sich wohl mehren," no. 7 in the *Lochheimer Liederbuch* (1455–60), a collection of music manuscripts by various persons, a notable source of early German folksong in the vicinity of Nürnberg. Elizabeth Cruciger herself evidently chose this tune to go with her text, as both were published in the previously mentioned Erfurt *Enchiridia* (1524).

The setting was prepared by Jan O. Bender for *Lutheran Book of Worship* (1978).

73 O MORNING STAR, HOW FAIR AND BRIGHT

O Morning Star, how fair and bright!
You shine with God's own truth and light,
Aglow with grace and mercy!
Of Jacob's race, King David's son,
Our Lord and master, you have won
Our hearts to serve you only!
Lowly, holy!
Great and glorious,
All victorious,
Rich in blessing!
Rule and might o'er all possessing!

Come, heav'nly bridegroom, light divine,
And deep within our hearts now shine;
There light a flame undying!
In your one body let us be
As living branches of a tree,
Your life our lives supplying.
Now, though daily
Earth's deep sadness
May perplex us
And distress us,
Yet with heav'nly joy you bless us.

Lord, when you look on us in love,
At once there falls from God above
A ray of purest pleasure.
Your Word and Spirit, flesh and blood,
Refresh our souls with heav'nly food.
You are our dearest treasure!
Let your mercy
Warm and cheer us!
Oh, draw near us!
For you teach us
God's own love through you has reached us.

Almighty Father, in your Son
You loved us when not yet begun
Was this old earth's foundation!
Your Son has ransomed us in love
To live in him here and above:
This is your great salvation.
Alleluia!
Christ the living,

Wie schön leuchtet der Morgenstern
Voll Gnad und Wahrheit von dem Herrn,
Die süsse Wurzel Jesse.
Du Sohn Davids aus Jakobs Stamm,
Mein König und mein Bräutigam,
Hast mir mein Herz besessen;
Lieblich, freundlich,
Schön und herrlich,
Gross und ehrlich,
Reich an Gaben,
Hoch und sehr prächtig erhaben.

Geuss sehr tief in das Herz hinein,
Du leuchtend Kleinod, edler Stein,
Mir deiner Liebe Flamme,
Dass ich, o Herr, ein Gliedmass bleib
An deinem auserwählten Leib,
Ein Zweig an deinem Stamme.
Nach dir wallt mir
Mein Gemüte
Ewge Güte
Bis es findet
Dich, des Liebe mich entzündet.

Von Gott kommt mir ein Frendenschein,
Wenn du mich mit den Augen dein
Gar freundlich tust anblicken.
O Herr Jesu, mein trautes Gut,
Dein Wort, dein Geist, dein Leib und Blut
Mich innerlich erquicken.
Nimm mich freundlich
In dein Arme,
Herr, erbarme
Dich in Gnaden;
Auf dein Wort komm ich geladen.

Herr Gott Vater, mein starker Held,
Du hast mich ewig vor der Welt
In deinem Sohn geliebet.
Dein Sohn hat mich ihm selbst vertraut,
Er ist mein Schatz, ich seine Braut,
Drum mich auch nichts betrübet.
Eia, eia,
Himmlisch Leben

To us giving
Life forever,
Keeps us yours and fails us never!

Wird ergeben
Mir dort oben;
Ewig soll mein Herz ihn loben.

What joy to know, when life is past,
The Lord we love is first and last,
The end and the beginning!
He will one day, oh, glorious grace,
Transport us to that happy place
Beyond all tears and sinning!
Amen! Amen!
Come, Lord Jesus!
Crown of gladness!
We are yearning
For the day of your returning.

Wie bin ich doch so herzlich froh,
Dass mein Schatz ist das A und O,
Der Anfang und das Ende.
Er wird mich doch zu seinem Preis
Aufnehmen in das Paradeis;
Des klopf ich in die Hände.
Amen, Amen,
Komm, du schöne
Freudenkrone,
Bleib nicht lange;
Deiner wart ich mit Verlangen.

Oh, let the harps break forth in sound!
Our joy be all with music crowned,
Our voices gaily blending!
For Christ goes with us all the way—
Today, tomorrow, ev'ry day!
His love is never ending!
Sing out! Ring out!
Jubilation!
Exultation!
Tell the story!
Great is he, the King of glory!

Zwingt die Saiten in Cythara
Und lasst die süsse Musika
Ganz freudenreich erschallen,
Dass ich möge mit Jesulein,
Dem wunderschönen Bräutgam mein,
In steter Liebe wallen.
Singet, springet,
Jubilieret,
Triumphieret,
Dankt dem Herren;
Gross ist der König der Ehren.

Both hymns of Philipp Nicolai contained in *Lutheran Worship* (1982)—this one, called the "queen of chorales," and "Wake, awake, for night is flying" (*LW* 177), called the "king of chorales"—must be numbered among the gems of the hymnal. Their style of diction, poetic structure, and grand tunes are nothing short of the unique and sublime. Both exhibit traces of the author's background in their acrostic structure, that is, the initial letters of each stanza of the original German form a word or phrase. In the case of this hymn, originally in seven stanzas (the second is here omitted), the W, E, G, U, H, Z, W refer to *Wilhelm Ernst, Graf und Herr zu Waldeck*, a friend and student of Nicolai as well as referring to his birthplace. Finally, both hymns, of which Nicolai is both author and composer, were published by him in the Appendix to his *Frewden Spiegel des ewigen Lebens* (Frankfurt-am-Main, 1599).

As indicated by Nicolai himself, the hymn is based on Psalm 45. Reference to "Morning Star" in stanza 1, however, is reflective of Revelation 22:16, and "The end and the beginning" in stanza 5 (originally the final stanza) is reflective of Revelation 22:13. Upon close examination one cannot but agree with the churchman who stated that nearly every word of the text is taken from Holy Scripture. The hymn became a great favorite and enjoyed wide usage at festival occasions, not only of the church year, but especially at weddings.

The translation was prepared by the Inter-Lutheran Commission on Worship for inclusion in *Lutheran Book of Worship* (1978).

WIE SCHÖN LEUCHTET (also known as MORGENSTERN, FRANKFURT). This celebrated tune first appeared with Nocolai's text in the above-mentioned *Frewden*

Spiegel (Zahn V, 8359). Although generally attributed to him, it was undoubtedly based on the melody of "Jauchst dem Herren, alle Land," a setting for Psalm 100 in the Strasbourg Psalter of 1538, for whole sections of this melody are identical with phrases of Nicolai's chorale tune.

The popularity of this tune, in this and later forms, is evidenced by its frequent use on the part of composers (J. S. Bach, Dietrich Buxtehude, Felix Mendelssohn-Bartholdy, to mention but a few) as well as by its inclusion in numerous denominational hymnals other than Lutheran.

In her *Christian Singers of Germany* (1869) Catherine Winkworth says of this hymn:

> So popular did it soon become, that its tune was often chimed by city chimes, lines and verses from it were printed by way of ornament on the common earthenware of the country, and it was invariably used at weddings and certain festivals.

The harmonization is from the *Choralbuch* (1955).

74 FROM GOD THE FATHER, VIRGIN-BORN

From God the Father, virgin-born To us the only Son came down; By death the font to consecrate, The faithful to regenerate.	A patre unigenitus, Ad nos venit per virginem Baptisma cruce consecrans Cunctos fideles generans.
Beginning from his home on high, In human flesh he came to die; Creation by his death restored, And shed new joys of life abroad.	De caelo celsus prodiit, Excepit forman hominis, Facturam morte redimens, Gaudia vite largiens.
Glide on, O glorious Sun, and bring The gift of healing on your wing; To ev'ry dull and clouded sense The clearness of your light dispense.	Hoc te, redemptor, quaesumus: Illabere propitius Klarumque nostris sensibus Lumen praebe fidelibus.
Abide with us, O Lord, we pray; The gloom of darkness chase away; Your work of healing, Lord, begin, And take away the stain of sin.	Mane nobiscum, domine, Noctem obscuram remove, Omne delictus ablue, Piam medelam tribue,
Lord, once you came to earth's domain And, we believe, shall come again; Be with us on the battlefield, From ev'ry harm your people shield.	Quem iam venisse novimus, Redire item credimus, Sceptrumque tuum inclitum Tuum defende populum.
To you, O Lord, all glory be For this your blest epiphany; To God, whom all his hosts adore, And Holy Spirit evermore.	Gloria tibi domine, Qui apparuisti hodie, Cum patre et sancto spiritu In sempiterna saecula.

Monasticism produced a great cycle of office hymns designed to be sung in the canonical hours. Although most of them may be of antiquarian interest, many, in their devotional quality, scriptural substance, and objective directness have been successfully adapted for modern use. "From God the Father, Virgin-born" ("A patre unigenitus"), a Latin text from at least the 11th century, if not earlier, is such a hymn, the authorship of which is unknown.

The translation, based on that by John Mason Neale (*LW* 31, et al.) but with considerable number of alterations, was prepared by the Inter-Lutheran Commission on Worship for inclusion in *Lutheran Book of Worship* (1978).

DEUS TUORUM MILITUM is a French church melody from the *Grenoble Antiphoner* of 1753 and 1868, where it served as the setting for the office hymn for martyrs, "Deus tuorum militum." It is a type of tune that came into use in French Roman Catholic dioceses toward the end of the 17th and early 18th centuries to replace the old Gregorian, or plainsong, tunes. Some were adapted from plainsong; others from secular tunes; but all, in their regular rhythms and non-modal tonality (see essay: The Church Modes, p. 000), represent a departure from plainsong in their shape and purpose. Their meters are largely long meter (LM) in triple time as here, or sapphic. (Cf. HERZLIEBSTER JESU, 11 11 11 5, *LW* 119.)

The Hymnal Noted (1851), prepared by John Mason Neale and Thomas Helmore (1811–90), English clergy-teacher and choir trainer, introduced a number of such French tunes into England, taken from *La Feillee's Methode de Plain-Chant* (1750, 1782, and 1808). As for the tune under discussion, although J. B. Croft included it in his *Melodies of the Evening Office* (1902), it was most effectively introduced to English-speaking congregations in *The English Hymnal* (1906). It appeared in *Songs of Syon* (1910) and in the United States in *The De LaSalle Hymnal* (New York, 1913).

The harmonization was prepared by Basil Harwood for *The Hymn Book* (1971) of the United Church of Canada and the Anglican Church of Canada. This notable, powerful tune should be sung rhythmically and with vigor.

AS WITH GLADNESS MEN OF OLD 75

Sick in bed on the Epiphany of Our Lord, about 1858, while convalescing from a serious illness, William C. Dix read the Gospel for the day and by evening had composed this poem based on that Gospel. Although first published in *Hymns of Joy and Love* (1861), a small collection for private circulation, in 1859 it was already slated for inclusion in the original edition of *Hymns Ancient and Modern* (1861).

Since the Wise Men came to a house (Matt. 2:11) and not to a stable, the revised edition of *Hymns Ancient and Modern* (1875) made several changes—"manger-bed" to "lowly-bed"; "manger, rude and bare," to "cradle, rude and bare"—revisions that were approved by Dix. They were incorporated both in *The Lutheran Hymnal* (1941) and in *Lutheran Book of Worship* (1978) as well as here in *Lutheran Worship* (1982).

DIX, also known as TREUER HEILAND, originally appeared in Conrad Kocher's *Stimmen aus dem Reiche Gottes* (1738) set to "Treuer Heiland, wir sind hier," a text of seven lines (Zahn 4809). The tune gained popularity after it was shortened to six lines by William H. Monk (*LW* 405, 490) for inclusion in *Hymns Ancient and Modern* (1861) to fit the text "As with Gladness Men of Old." Dix disliked the tune, which nevertheless carries his name because of its association with his text. Admittedly the flow of the tune is somewhat restricted by the similar cadences. The union, however, has proven to be effective and popular.

The setting is from the *Service Book and Hymnal* (1958).

76 O CHIEF OF CITIES, BETHLEHEM

O chief of cities, Bethlehem,
Of David's crown the fairest gem,
But more to us than David's name,
In you, as man, the Savior came.

Beyond the sun in splendor bright,
Above you stands a wondrous light
Proclaiming from the conscious skies
That here in flesh the Godhead lies.

The Wise Men, seeing him so fair,
Bow low before him and with prayer
Their treasured eastern gifts unfold
Of incense, myrrh, and royal gold.

The golden tribute owns him king,
But frankincense to God they bring,
And last, prophetic sign, with myrrh
They shadow forth his sepulcher.

O Jesus, whom the Gentiles see,
With Father, Spirit, One in Three:
To you, O God, be glory giv'n
By saints on earth and saints in heav'n.

O sola magnarum urbium
Maior Bethlem, cui contigit
Ducem salutis caelitus
Incorporatum gignere:

Quem stella, quae solis rotam
Vincit decore ac lumine,
Venisse terris nuntiat
Cum carne terrestri Deum.

Videre postquam illum magi,
Eoa prumunt munera,
Stratique votis offerunt
Tus, myrram, et aurum regium.

Regem Deumque adnuntiant
Thesaurus et fragrans odor
Turis Sabaei, ac myrreus
Pulvis sepulcrum praedocet.

Gloria tibi, Domine,
Qui apparuisti hodie,
Cum Patre et sancto Spiritu
In sempiterna saecula.

This cento from Marcus Aurelius Clemens Prudentius' *Cathemerinon*, a collection of hymns for the hours of daily prayer and the festivals of the church year, is from the section called Hymnus *Epiphaniae*, beginning with line 77, "Quicumque Christum quaeritis." After the Council of Trent (1545–63) the hymn was designated in the Roman Breviary for use at Lauds (sunrise) on the Epiphany of our Lord.

The translation is a composite. Nathaniel B. Smithers' *Translations of Latin Hymns of the Middle Ages* (1879) is the source for stanzas 1–2, and 4, while stanza 3 is from Charles Winfred Douglas' *The Monastic Diurnal* (1932). The doxology first appeared in John Patrick Crichton-Stuart's four-volume translation of *The Roman Breviary* (1879).

TRUTH FROM ABOVE. Ralph Vaughan Williams included this delightful tune in his *Eight Traditional English Carols* (1919), noting that it was sung by Mr. W. Jenkins of Kyng's Pyon, Herefordshire, to the carol "This Is the Truth Sent from Above." The harmonization is by Williams. Note that the meter shifts between 5/4 and 6/4.

THE PEOPLE THAT IN DARKNESS SAT 77

John Morison's paraphrase of Isaiah 9:2–8, originally in seven stanzas, was first published in the Church of Scotland's *Translations and Paraphrases in Verse* (1781), beginning with "The race that long in darkness pined." Disquieted over various expressions in the original, hymnal editors have made various changes in the course of time. A thoroughgoing revision was made by the compilers of the first edition of *Hymns Ancient and Modern* (1861), with the result that the opening line read: "The people that in darkness sat." The text in *Lutheran Worship* is essentially that in the latter but with updated pronouns.

LOBT GOTT, IHR CHRISTEN. For comments on this tune see hymn 44.
The harmonization is by Paul G. Bunjes.

JESUS HAS COME AND BRINGS PLEASURE 78

Jesus has come and brings pleasure eternal, Alpha, Omega, Beginning and End; Godhead, humanity, union supernal, O great Redeemer, you come as our friend! Heaven and earth, now proclaim this great wonder: Jesus has come and brings pleasure eternal!	Jesus ist kommen, Grund ewiger Freude; A und O, Anfang und Ende steht da. Gottheit und Menschheit vereinen sich beide; Schöpfer, wie kommst du uns Menschen so nah! Himmel und Erde, erzählets den Heiden: Jesus ist kommen, Grund ewiger Freuden.
Jesus has come! Now see bonds rent asunder! Fetters of death now dissolve, disappear. See him burst through with a voice as of thunder! He sets us free from our guilt and our fear, Lifts us from shame to the place of his honor. Jesus has come! Hear the roll of God's thunder!	Jesus ist kommen, nun springen die Bande, Stricke des Todes die reissen entzwei. Unser Durchbrecher ist nunmehr vorhanden; Er, der Sohn Gottes, der machet recht frei, Bringet zu Ehren aus Sünde und Schande; Jesus ist kommen, nun springen die Bande.
Jesus has come as the mighty Redeemer. See now the threatening strong one disarmed! Jesus breaks down all the walls of death's fortress, Brings forth the pris'ners triumphant, unharmed. Satan, you wicked one, own now your master! Jesus has come! He, the mighty Redeemer!	Jesus ist kommen, der starke Erlöser, Bricht dem gewappneten Starken ins Haus, Sprenget des Feindes befestigte Schlösser, Führt die Gefangenen siegend heraus. Fühlst du den Stärkeren, Satan, du Böser? Jesus ist kommen, der starke Erlöser.
Jesus has come as the King of all glory! Heaven and earth, oh, declare his great pow'r, Capturing hearts with the heavenly story.	Jesus ist kommen, der König der Ehren; Himmel und Erde, rühmt seine Gewalt! Dieser Beherrscher kann Herzen bekehren;

Welcome him now in this fast-fleeting hour!
Ponder his love! Take the crown he has for you!
Jesus has come! He, the King of all glory!

Öffnet ihm Tore und Türen fein bald!
Denkt doch, er will euch die Krone gewähren.
Jesus ist kommen, der König der Ehren.

The hymns of the Cöthen circle of poets, of which Allendorf was chief, were at first not widely disseminated but were circulated among the Pietists in small group situations. In 1736 the first notable collection appeared with the title *Einige ganz neue Lieder zum Lobe des Dreyeinigen Gottes und zur gewünschten reichen Erbauung vieler Menschen* (Some Brand-New Hymns for the Praise of the Triune God and toward the Wished-For Rich Edification of Many People). Included in this collection, in 23 stanzas, was "Jesus Has Come and Brings Pleasure."

This hymn clearly exhibits both the distinct craftsmanship of the author and the common style of later Pietistic poets. The verse structure, so typical of the Pietistic school, is purely dactylic (´˘˘). To strict orthodoxists such meter might prove unbearable. But the movement and joy of such hymns invariably capture the imagination of young and old alike.

The present translation was done by Oliver Rupprecht for *Lutheran Worship* (1982).

JESUS IST KOMMEN, GRUND EWIGER FREUDE. This tune first appeared, about 1733, in a single printing (*Einzeldruck*) of five hymns coupled to Allendorf's text "Einer ist König." Johann Georg Hille, cantor in Glaucha near Halle, who later issued, or published, Cöthen hymns with melodies and figured bass, may have been the composer. This is a strong, moving tune in the style of what might be called solo-aria, and it represents a classic example of dactylic, triple-meter form, so frequently evident in the Freylinghausen tradition of the chorale.

The setting is by Paul G. Bunjes.

79 O JESUS, KING OF GLORY

O Jesus, King of glory,
Both David's Lord and son!
Your realm endures forever,
In heaven is your throne.
Help that in earth's dominions,
From pole to farthest pole,
Your reign may spread salvation
To each benighted soul.

O König aller Ehren,
Herr Jesu, Davids Sohn,
Dein Reich soll ewig währen,
Im Himmel ist dein Thron.
Hilf, dass allhier auf Erden
Den Menschen weit und breit
Dein Reich bekannt mög' werden
Zur ew'gen Seligkeit!

The eastern sages, kneeling,
Their richest tributes bring,
Where witnessing your glory,
They worship you, their King.
To you the star is pointing,
The sure prophetic Word;
So joyously we hail you:
Our Savior and our Lord!

Von deinem Reich auch zeugen
Die Leut' aus Morgenland;
Die Knie sie vor dir beugen,
Weil ihnen bist bekannt;
Der neu' Stern auf dich weiset,
Dazu das göttlich' Wort,
Drum man dich billig preiset,
Dass du bist unser Hort.

You are a mighty monarch, As by your Word is told, Yet you care very little For earthly goods or gold; You come not proudly riding, You seek no great renown, You dwell in no high castle, You wear no jeweled crown.	Du bist ein grosser König, Wie uns die Schrift vermeld't; Doch achtest du gar wenig Vergänglich Gut und Geld, Prangst nicht auf einem Rosse, Trägst keine güldne Kron', Sitzt nicht im festen Schlosse, Hier hast du Spott und Hohn.
Yet you are decked with beauty, With rays of glorious light; Your works proclaim your goodness, And all your ways are right. O Lord, protect your people With your almighty arm That they may dwell in safety From those who mean them harm.	Doch bist du schön gezieret, Dein Glanz erstreckt sich weit, Dein' Güt' allzeit florieret Und dein' Gerechtigkeit. Du woll'st die Frommen schützen Durch dein' Macht und Gewalt, Dass sie im Frieden sitzen, Die Bösen stürzen bald.
Oh, look on me with pity Though I am weak and poor; Admit me to your kingdom To dwell there, blest and sure. I pray, Lord, guide and keep me Safe from my bitter foes, From sin and death and Satan; Free me from all my woes.	Du woll'st dich mein erbarmen, In dein Reich nimm mich auf, Dein Güte schenk mir Armen Und segne meinen Lauf. Mein'n Feinden woll'st du wehren, Dem Teufel, Sünd' und Tod, Dass sie mich nicht versehren; Rett mich aus aller Not!
Then let your Word within me Shine as the fairest star, Your reign of love revealing How wonderful you are. Help me confess you truly And with your Christendom Here own you King and Savior With all the world to come.	Du woll'st in mir entzünden Dein Wort, den schönsten Stern, Dass falsche Lehr' und Sünden Sei'n von mein'm Herzen fern; Hilf, dass ich dich erkenne Und mit der Christenheit Dich meinen König nenne Jetzt und in Ewigkeit!

This hymn is the result of Pastor Martin Behm's custom of writing a hymn reflecting the thoughts in the Sunday or festival Gospel and using this as a prayer before his sermon, based on that day's Gospel. This laudable Epiphany hymn, based on Matthew 2:1–12, originally in six stanzas, was first published in his *Centuria precationum rhythmicarum* (Wittenberg, 1606). The "bright Morning Star" (Rev. 22:16b), customarily referring to Christ, here includes the prophetic, or godly (*göttlich*) Word (cf. stanzas 2 and 6).

The translation is an altered form of that by Catherine Winkworth (*LW* 28, et al.) in her *Choralebook for England* (London, 1865).

VALET WILL ICH DIR GEBEN. For comments on the tune see hymn 102.

The harmonization is by Paul G. Bunjes.

80 WITHIN THE FATHER'S HOUSE

This notable hymn on the Gospel (Luke 2:41–52) for the First Sunday after the Epiphany in the Old Standard Series of pericopes, now for the First Sunday after Christmas in the Three Year Lectionary, Series C, was written by James R. Redford and first published in *The Parish Hymn Book* (1863), of which he was one of the editors. Stanza 6 of the original has been omitted and the language of the remaining stanzas updated.

FRANCONIA was constructed by W. H. Havergal (*LW* 392, 404) for a beautiful tune in Johann B. König's (*LW* 80, et al.) *Harmonischer Lieder-Schatz, oder allgemeines evangelisches Choral-Buch* (Frankfurt, 1738), where it was set to "Was ist, das mich betrübt?" The adaptation is virtually a new tune, consisting of König's first, second, fourth, and last phrases, somewhat altered, that appeared in Havergal's *Old Church Psalmody* (London, 1847). The tune's name is apparently derived from the fact that König lived most his life in Frankfurt-am-Main in Old Franconia.

The harmonization is from *The Hymnal 1940*, slightly altered.

81 WHEN CHRIST'S APPEARING WAS MADE KNOWN

When Christ's appearing was made known,
King Herod trembled for his throne;
But he who offers heav'nly birth
Seeks not the kingdoms of this earth.

Hostis Herodes impie,
Christum venire quid times?
Non eripit mortalia,
Qui regna dat caelestia.

The eastern sages saw from far
And followed on his guiding star;
By light their way to light they trod,
And by their gifts confessed their God.

Ibant magi, quam viderant,
Stellam sequentes praeviam:
Lumen requirunt lumine,
Deum fatentur munere.

Within the Jordan's sacred flood
The heav'nly Lamb in meekness stood
That he, of whom no sin was known,
Might cleanse his people from their own.

Lavacra puri gurgitis
Caelestis Agnus attigit;
Peccata, quae non detulit,
Nos abluendo sustulit.

And oh, what miracle divine,
When water reddened into wine!
He spoke the word, and forth it flowed
In streams that nature ne'er bestowed.

Novum genus potentiae,
Aquae ruescunt hydriae,
Vinumque iussa fundere
Mutavit unda originem.

For this his glad epiphany
All glory unto Jesus be,
Whom with the Father we adore,
And Holy Ghost forevermore.

Gloria tibi, Domine,
Qui apparuisti hodie,
Cum Patre et Sancto Spiritu
In sempiterna saecula.

This is a continuation of *LW* 43, the Coelius Sedulius poem describing the life of Christ entitled *Paean Alphabeticus De Christo*. This section was historically designated for first and second Vespers on the Epiphany of Our Lord and throughout its octave in the Roman, Sarum (Salisbury), and Mozarabic rites. In *The Lutheran Hymnal* (1941) this began with "The star proclaims the King is here" (*TLH* 131) as translated by John Mason Neale (*LW* 31, et al.) in his *The Hymnal Noted* (1852). The first stanza here in *Lutheran Worship* is from *The Hymn Book* (1971) of the United Church and the Anglican Church of Canada; stanzas 2–5, altered and updated, are from *The Hymnal Noted.*

PUER NOBIS. For comments on this tune see hymn 14.

The harmonization by George R. Woodward is from *The Cowley Carol Book* (1901).

HAIL TO THE LORD'S ANOINTED 82

This hymn by James Montgomery, based on messianic Psalm 72, originally in eight stanzas, was written for a Christmas service in a Moravian settlement in Yorkshire, England, in 1821. When, on April 4, 1822, Montgomery addressed a Wesleyan missionary conference in Pitt Street Wesleyan Chapel, the lights went out during his speech. A wooden chair was broken by the crowd with a resounding crash, and confusion reigned until Montgomery, inspired by the chairman's assurance, "There is still light within," ended his address with "Hail to the Lord's anointed" as the lighting was restored. Dr. Adam Clarke, preacher and chairman of the meeting, was so impressed that he asked Montgomery for a copy of the hymn. Clarke published it in connection with Psalm 72 in his *Commentary on the Bible* (1822), concluding:

> I need not tell the intelligent reader that he [Montgomery] has seized the spirit and exhibited some of the principal beauties of the Hebrew bard; though (to use his own words in a letter to me) his "hand trembled to touch the harp of Zion." I take the liberty here to register a wish, which I have strongly expressed to himself, that he would favor the Church of God with a metrical version of the whole book.

In May 1822 part of the hymn entitled "Imitation of the 72nd Psalm" appeared in the *Evangelical Magazine*. Its next appearance, in complete form, was in Montgomery's own *Songs of Zion: being Imitations of the Psalms* (London, 1822). It was also included in his *Poetical Works* (1828) and in his *Original Hymns* (1853). The text in *Lutheran Worship* includes Montgomery's stanzas 1, 2, 4, with stanza 6 combining the first quatrains of his stanzas 6 and 7.

A comparison of even these four stanzas with "Jesus Shall Reign Where'er the Sun," another metrical version of the same psalm by Issac Watts, will readily demonstrate the emphasis placed on literary form in Montgomery's time as opposed to Watts' more strict adherence to Scripture. Apropos is the statement of Bailey: "Montgomery absorbed from the Psalm the essential intent of the psalmist as he saw it, then proceeded to create his own imagery" (*The Gospel in Hymns*, p. 157). An excellent hymn, the finest of Montgomery's imitations of the psalms, it is appropriate not only for Epiphany, but also for Advent, for missions, and for general use.

FREUT EUCH, IHR LIEBEN is by Leonard Schröter and was published in his Newe Weyhnachtliedlein (1587), set to the Christmas hymn "Freut euch, ihr lieben Christen, Freut euch von Herzen sehr" (Zahn 5374, 5375a) by an unknown author of the early 16th century.

The harmonization is by Paul G. Bunjes.

83 O GOD OF GOD, O LIGHT OF LIGHT

John Julian penned this hymn for the tune PETERBOROUGH by John Goss (1800–90), leader of English church music in the early 19th century. Written for the Sheffield Church Choir's Union Festival on April 16, 1883, the text was first published in the festival book. Its first appearance in a public worship book was in W. Garrett Horder's *Congregational Hymns* (1884).

The text was adapted by the Inter-Lutheran Commission on Worship for Lutheran Book of *Worship* (1978), as above, and omitting Julian's fourth stanza:

Nations afar, in ignorance deep,
Isles of the sea, where darkness lay,
These hear His voice, they wake from sleep,
And throng with joy the upward way.
They cry with us, "Send forth Thy light,
O Lamb, once slain for sinful men;
Burst Satan's bonds, O God of might;
Set all men free!" Amen, Amen.

The text in *Lutheran Worship* (1982) is taken from *Lutheran Book of Worship* with slight alterations in punctuation.

O GROSSER GOTT is by an unknown composer. A fine tune, it appeared in the *Schlag-Gesang- und Notenbuch* (Stuttgart, 1744). A problem of long meter tunes (88 88) in duple time, whether single or double, is that the measures are often so filled with quarter notes, organists tend to insert fermatas at the ends of phrases, thus to give the singers occasion for breath. The better alternative is to retain the steady pulse (*Takt*) of the tune by playing eighth notes at such points followed by an eighth rest, thus to afford singers a catch-breath.

Paul Bouman's harmonization was originally prepared for *Lutheran Book of Worship* (1978).

HAIL, O SOURCE OF EVERY BLESSING 84

The most popular of Basil Woodd's hymns, this text, here slightly altered and updated, first appeared in his *The Psalms of David and other portions of the Sacred Scriptures, etc.* (c. 1810–20). It was erroneously attributed to Robert Robinson (1735–90), author of "Come, Thou Fount of Every Blessing" (*LBW* 499) in *Christian Psalmody* (1833), and this error has persisted in several subsequent collections.

O DURCHBRECHER. The melody, also called CONQUEROR, appeared in Johann Freylinghausen's *Neues geistreiches Gesangbuch* (Halle, 1704), set to the hymn "O Durchbrecher aller Bande" by Gottfried Arnold (1666–1714). Paul G. Bunjes provided the setting for *Lutheran Worship* (1982).

ARISE AND SHINE IN SPLENDOR 85

Arise and shine in splendor,
Let night to day surrender;
Your light is drawing near.
Above, the day is beaming,
In matchless beauty gleaming;
The glory of the Lord is here.

See earth in darkness lying,
The heathen nations dying
In hopeless gloom and night.
To you the Lord of heaven,
Your light, your hope, has given
Great glory, honor, and delight.

The world's remotest races,
Upon whose weary faces
The sun looks from the sky,
Shall run with zeal untiring,
With joy your light desiring
That breaks upon them from on high.

Lift up your eyes in wonder;
See, nations gather yonder,
They all come to be free.
The world has heard your story,
Your sons come to your glory,
And daughters haste your light to see.

Brich auf und werde lichte,
Lass gehn die Nacht zunichte,
Dein Licht kommt her zu dir;
Die Herrlichkeit des Herren
Glänzt prächtig weit und ferren
Und zeigt sich um und über dir.

Zwar finster ist die Erde,
Der armen Heiden Herde
Liegt dunkel weit und breit;
Dich hat der Herr, dein Leben,
Dein Heil und Trust, umgeben
Mit grosser Ehr' und Herrlichkeit.

Die Völker auf der Erden,
So je beschienen werden
Durchs klare Sonnenlicht,
Die sollen dein Licht kennen,
Zum Glanze fröhlich rennen,
Der aus der Höh' des Himmels bricht.

Heb auf, heb dein Gesichte:
Das Volk folgt deinem Lichte,
Die Welt kommt ganz zu dir;
Sie hat von dir vernommen,
Die Söhn' und Töchter kommen
Und suchen deinen Ruhm und Zier.

Your heart will leap rejoicing When multitudes come voicing Desire to share your peace. Your eyes will fill with wonder When people without number Come thronging to you for God's grace.	Dein Herze wird dir wallen, Wenn dir kommt zu Gefallen Die Anzahl um das Meer; Du wirst die Augen weiden Am Volke vieler Heiden, So dringt mit Haufen zu dir her.

Martin Opitz, poet and metrical reformer, headed this hymn "On the Holy Three Kings' Day, Isaiah 60" on its first publication in his *Die Episteln der Sontage und fürnemsten Feste des gantzen Jahrs* (Breslau, 1628). The translation by Gerhard Gieschen appeared in a publication called *Faith-Life* and was revised by Gieschen himself for *The Lutheran Hymnal* (1941). *Lutheran Worship* has revised the language in several instances and updated the pronouns. The omitted stanza 6 read as follows, translated by Emmanuel Cronenwett (*LW* 189, 340) for the Ohio *Lutheran Hymnal* (1880):

There are glad delegations From Ephah and far nations And clouds from Midian; With gold shall Sheba cheer thee And incense; all that near thee Shall sing thy praise, O chosen one!	Es kommen alle Seelen Aus Epha mit Kamelen, Mit Läufern Midian. Gold wird dir Saba bringen Und Weihrauch, es wird singen Dein Lob und Preis ein jedermann.

WELT, ICH MUSS DICH LASSEN is usually attributed to Heinrich Isaac (c. 1450–1517), although some scholars have opined that Isaak prepared only the harmonization, the melody being a traditional German folk tune. This magnificant melody, also called INNSBRUCK, was the top voice of a four-part polyphonic setting of the folk song, "Innsbruck, ich muss dich lassen," in Georg Forster's *Ein auszug guter alter und neuer Teutschen liedlein* (1539), a collection of songs in four part books. From this form it was adapted to Johann Hesse's hymn for the dying, "O Welt, ich muss dich lassen," in the *Eisleben Gesangbuch* of 1598. The tune appears in various forms in German hymnals from that point on, usually as the setting for Paul Gerhardt's "Nun ruhen alle Wälder" (*LW* 485).

The harmonization was prepared for *Lutheran Worship* by Herbert Gotsch.

86 BRIGHTEST AND BEST OF THE STARS OF THE MORNING

Reginald Heber's Epiphany hymn first appeared in the November 11, 1811, edition of the *Christian Observer*, to be sung to the Scottish tune WANDERING WILLIE, and was later included in his posthumous *Hymns, written and adapted to the Weekly Church Service of the Year* (1827). Julian writes:

> Few hymns of merit have troubled compilers more than this. Some have held that its use involved the worshipping of a star, whilst others have been offended with its meter as being too suggestive of a solemn dance.

Although excluded from the early editions of *Hymns Ancient and Modern* (1861ff.), it fully merits its general popularity today.

The text in *Lutheran Worship* is verbatim from *Lutheran Book of Worship* (1978), in which alterations from the original are minimal. Since Heber's "sons of the morning" in the opening line appeared, to some at least, to refer to Isaiah 14:12, where, in the Authorized Version, Lucifer is so described, or where, according to Job 38:7, "morning stars" and "sons of God" are perhaps angels joining in the praise of God for his wonderful act of creation, the Inter-Lutheran Commission on Worship deemed it advisable to avoid such possible misinterpretations by changing "sons of the morning" to "stars of the morning," thus referring perhaps less mistakably to the "star of the east," the star which the Magi saw, as indicated in Matthew 2:1–2. Other changes include the updating of the personal pronouns, the change of Heber's "Odors of Edom" to "Fragrance of Edom" in stanza 3, line 2, and of "and" to "or" in line 4 of the same stanza.

MORNING STAR derives its name from association with the above text. The melody is part of an anthem written by James P. Harding for use at Gifford Hall Mission, London, in 1892. Its first publication in an American hymnal was in the Presbyterian *The New Psalms and Hymns* (Richmond, Virginia, 1901).

The harmonization is taken from the *Service Book and Hymnal* (1958).

OH, WONDROUS TYPE! OH, VISION FAIR 87

Oh, wondrous type! Oh, vision fair
Of glory that the Church may share,
Which Christ upon the mountain shows,
Where brighter than the sun he glows!

With Moses and Elijah nigh
The incarnate Lord holds converse high;
And from the cloud the Holy One
Bears record to the only Son.

With shining face and bright array
Christ deigns to manifest today
What glory shall be theirs above
Who joy in God with perfect love.

And faithful hearts are raised on high
By this great vision's mystery,
For which in joyful strains we raise
The voice of prayer, the hymn of praise.

O Father, with th'eternal Son
And Holy Spirit ever one,
We pray you, bring us by your grace
To see your glory face to face.

Caelestis formam gloriae,
Quam spes quaerit ecclesiae,
In monte Christus indicat
Quo supra solem emicat.

Res memoranda saeculis,
Hic cum tribus discipulis
Cum Moyse et Helia
Grata promit eloquia.

Glorificata facie
Christus declarat hodie,
Quia sit honor credentium
Deo pie fruentium.

Visionis mysterium
Corda levat fidelium,
Unde sollemni gaudio
Clamat nostra devotio.

Pater cum Unigenito
Et Spiritu Paraclito
Unus nobis hanc gloriam
Largire per praesentiam.

Although the Benedictines on the Continent, for instance, had observed the Transfiguration of Our Lord centuries earlier, it was evidently not until the 15th century that such observance became common in England, for it is in the *Sarum Breviary* (1495) that this anonymous hymn, one of several written for that occasion, first appears.

The translation by John Mason Neale (*LW* 31, et al.) in his *The Hymnal Noted* (1852), beginning "A type of those bright rays on high," was considerably altered for the original edition of *Hymns Ancient and Modern* (1861). A somewhat altered version was included in *The Hymnal 1940*, which version appeared in *Worship Supplement* (1969). From there, with updated personal pronouns, it was included in *Lutheran Book of Worship* (1978) and subsequently in *Lutheran Worship* (1982).

DEO GRATIAS (also known as AGINCOURT). After his victory over the French at the Battle of Agincourt, 1415, London was prepared to celebrate the return of King Henry V amid great pageantry. According to Raphael Holinshed's *Chronicle* (1577), however, the king ordered this pageantry to cease and commanded that "no ditties should be made or sung by minstrels or others . . . for that he would whollie have the praise and thankes altogether given to God." This song evidently survived the censorship. The following version comes from an 15th-century manuscript at Trinity College, Cambridge:

ci- as an - gli - a, red - de pro vic- to - ri - a.

The melody is undoubtedly a well-known folk tune, considerably older than the manuscript copy. The long cantilena at the beginning and end to the words "Deo gracias Anglia redde pro victoria" were embellishments added perhaps in response to the king's express wish. It was *The English Hymnal* (1906) that first adapted the tune for congregational use. The unexpected accent on the second beat of various phrases is strikingly interesting and effective. Archibald Jacob, in *Songs of Praise Discussed* (1933), describes the tune as "a magnificently direct and stirring tune, with a vehement dignity, and a remarkable expression of triumphant pride."

Paul G. Bunjes prepared the harmonization for *Lutheran Worship*.

SONGS OF THANKFULNESS AND PRAISE 88

This hymn by Christopher Wordsworth appeared in his *Holy Year: or Hymns for Sundays, Holidays, and Other Occasions throughout the year* (1862) with the caption "Sixth Sunday after the Epiphany. A recapitulation of the Subjects presented in the Services of former weeks throughout the season of Epiphany; and Anticipation of the future great and glorious Epiphany, at which Christ will appear again to judge the world." The rhyming of the archaic personal pronouns in stanza four prevented the Commission on Worship from updating the text, for to do so would have involved considerable restructuring.

ST. GEORGE'S, WINDSOR (or ST. GEORGE) was composed by George J. Elvey for James Montgomery's "Hark, the song of jubilee" and first appeared in E. H. Thorne's *A Selection of Psalm and Hymn Tunes* (1858). Named after St. George's Chapel, Windsor, where George Elvey, one of the better composers of the Victorian period, was organist for 47 years, it was confusing to call it simply ST. GEORGE, for there exist other tunes with that name. Coupled to Henry Alford's "Come, Ye Thankful People, Come" (*LW* 495) in the original edition of *Hymns Ancient and Modern* (1861), this tune was not only popularized but virtually wedded to that text. Thus the decision of the Intersynodical Committee on Hymnology to use this tune with "Songs of Thankfulness and Praise" in *The Lutheran Hymnal* (1941) constituted a somewhat bold move. Its predecessor, *The Evangelical Lutheran Hymn-Book* (1912), had used the overly disjunct and not a little sticky ST. EDWARD, a tune that evidently was infrequently used, and deservedly so. In contrast, the combination in *The Lutheran Hymnal* and *Lutheran Worship* is decidedly more felicitous.

The harmonization is from *The Lutheran Hymnal.*

89 HOW GOOD, LORD, TO BE HERE

Another notable hymn for the Lord's Transfiguration (cf. *LW* 87), occurring on the Last Sunday after the Epiphany, this text, here in updated form, was written by Joseph A. Robinson in 1888 and first published in the 1904 edition of *Hymns Ancient and Modern.*

POTSDAM. This simple, stepwise, attractive tune is an adaptation from the theme of the E-Major Fugue in Book II of J. S. Bach's *Well-Tempered Clavichord.* Thus it was not originally a so-called chorale tune. Its name is probably derived from Bach's famous visit to the castle at Potsdam, where King Frederick the Great, an accomplished flute player, invited him, first of all, to try the newly invented piano, of which he had just acquired several examples by Silbermann. The skill of Bach's improvisations whetted the king's appetite for more. The next evening, desirous of hearing a fugue in six parts, the king suggested a theme and asked Bach to improvise such a fugue, which Bach did. Following his brilliant performance, the king is said to have exclaimed, "There is only one Bach!" After his return to Leipzig, Bach worked out the theme more fully, added other movements, and sent the whole to the king with the title *Musikalisches Opfer* (Musical Offering). And what an interesting, inventive, and ingenious offering it was!

POTSDAM was adapted for use as a hymn tune in William Mercer's *The Church Psalter and Hymn Book* (1854).

The setting is from *The Lutheran Hymnal* (1941).

JESUS, REFUGE OF THE WEARY 90

This is a translation by Jane F. Wilde of Girolamo Savonarola's Italian hymn, "Gesu, sommo conforto," ending in a fervent prayer in which Jesus is implored to help Christians gain a deeper measure of love for him. Wilde submitted her translation to R. R. Madden for his *Life and Martyrdom of Savonarola* (1853), a reprint of which was later included in her *Poems by Speranza* (1864), "Speranza" ("Hope") being her *nom de plume*. The first use of her translation as a hymn appeared in F. H. Murray's *A Hymnal for Use in the English Church* (1852).

O DU LIEBE MEINER LIEBE. This chorale melody was probably a folk tune originally. First published in Johann Thommen's *Erbaulicher Musikalischer Christenschatz oder 500 Geistliche Lieder* (Basel, 1745), where it was set to an anonymous hymn of the same name, it was already in use at the Moravian settlement at Herrnhut before that time. Also called CASSEL and LUCERNE, it is supposed to have been sung to a popular song, "Sollen nun die grünen Jahre," dating from the early 18th century.

The harmonization is from the *Service Book and Hymnal* (1958).

MY SONG IS LOVE UNKNOWN 91

Samuel Crossman preceded Issac Watts in writing English hymns in a free use of Scripture as opposed to the metrical paraphrases of the psalms or other portions of Scripture. His small pamphlet entitled *The Young Man's Meditation, or some few Sacred Poems upon Select Subjects and Scriptures* (London, 1664) contains nine poems, including this one. This beautiful Lenten text, with its strong, naive directness and charm, is free from the sometimes unwholesome coarse treatment of the Passion by, for instance, Count Zinzendorf's Moravians.

Crossman probably expected his verses to be read, not sung, for they carried the motto, "A verse may find him whom a sermon flies."

The text is unaltered and unabridged.

LOVE UNKNOWN. This tune, written in 15 minutes on a scrap of paper immediately after a request from Geoffrey Shaw for a setting of these words, was contributed by John Ireland to *The Public School Hymn Book* (1919), where it was set to "My Song Is Love Unknown." Text, tune, and setting next appeared in *Songs of Praise* (1925). LOVE UNKNOWN is both an unusual and an especially attractive tune with its art song-like character and its irregular rhythm. Once learned, congregations will thoroughly enjoy its moving, buoyant qualities.

92 O LORD, THROUGHOUT THESE FORTY DAYS

This hymn is a paraphrase of Claudia F. Hernaman's hymn, "Lord, who throughout these forty days," included in her *The Child's Book of Praise* (London, 1873). It was prepared by Gilbert E. Doan, chairman of the Hymn Text Committee of the Inter-Lutheran Commission on Worship, for *Lutheran Book of Worship* (1978).

CAITHNESS is one of 31 "common tunes" included in the 1635 Scottish Psalter, *The Psalmes of David in Prose and Meeter*, where it was called "Cathnes Tune." The common tunes were provided to be sung to any of the psalms in common meter. *The Hymnal 1940 Companion* notes a similarity between the first phrase of this tune and that of DUNDEE (*LW* 283), which appeared in the predecessor to the 1635 psalter, *The CL Psalmes of David* (1615).

Supposed to be a Scottish tune, CAITHNESS is so called after a county in northeast Scotland. The harmonization is from *The Hymnal 1940*, slightly altered.

93 SAVIOR, WHEN IN DUST TO YOU

This "Litany" by Robert Grant, originally in five stanzas, was first published in *The Christian Observer*, November 1815. Later it appeared in *Sacred Poems by the late R. Hon. Sir R. Grant* (1839), edited by a certain Lord Glenelg.

This text is the altered and updated form that was included in *Lutheran Book of Worship* (1978).

ABERYSTWYTH. Named for the Welsh port city at the mouth of the river Ystwyth (*aber*, "river mouth"; *ystwyth*, "flexible"), this strong, rondo-like Welsh tune was composed by Joseph Parry while he was professor of music at the University College there. It was set to the hymn "Beth sydd i mi yn y byd" in the new 1879 edition of E. Stephen and J. D. Jones's *Ail Lyfr Tonau ac Emynau* (Second Book of Hymns and Tunes). Later Parry used it in his cantata *Ceridwen* with "Jesus, Lover of My Soul" (*LW* 508), for which it has become the rather standard setting.

The few hymnals of this century that include "Savior, When in Dust to You" set it either to ABERYSTWYTH or to SPANISH CHANT (*TLH* 166). The Inter-Lutheran Commission on Worship, considering the merits of each, chose to use the former for *Lutheran Book of Worship*. The compilers of *Lutheran Worship* followed suit.

The harmonization is from the *Hymnal for Colleges and Schools* (1956).

CHRIST, THE LIFE OF ALL THE LIVING 94

Christ, the life of all the living,
Christ, the death of death, our foe,
Christ, yourself for me once giving
To the darkest depths of woe:
Through your suff'ring, death, and merit
Life eternal I inherit.
Thousand, thousand thanks are due,
Dearest Jesus, unto you.

You have suffered great affliction
And have borne it patiently,
Even death by crucifixion,
Fully to atone for me;
For you chose to be tormented
That my doom should be prevented.
Thousand, thousand thanks are due,
Dearest Jesus, unto you.

Then, for all that bought my pardon,
For the sorrows deep and sore,
For the anguish in the garden,
I will thank you evermore,
Thank you for the groaning, sighing,
For the bleeding and the dying,
For that last triumphant cry,
Praise you evermore on high.

Jesu, meines Lebens Leben,
Jesu, meines Todes Tod,
Der du dich für mich gegeben
In die tiefste Seelennot,
In das äusserste Verderben,
Nur dass ich nicht möchte sterben:
Tausend-, tausendmal sei dir,
Liebster Jesu, Dank dafür!

Du hast dich in Not gestecket,
Hast gelitten mit Geduld,
Gar den herben Tod geschmecket,
Um zu büssen meine Schuld;
Dass ich würde losgezählet,
Hast du wollen sein gequälet.
Tausend-, tausendmal sei dir,
Liebster Jesu, Dank dafür!

Nun, ich danke dir von Herzen,
Jesu, für gesamte Not:
Für die Wunden, für die Schmerzen,
Für den herben, bittern Tod,
Für dein Zittern, für dein Zagen,
Für dein tausendfaches Plagen,
Für dein Angst und tiefe Pein
Will ich ewig dankbar sein.

This touching Lenten text with its striking refrain originally appeared in the first part of *E. C. Homburg's Geistliche Lieder,* published in two parts at Jena and Naumberg in 1659. Homburg headed it: "Hymn of thanksgiving to his Redeemer and Savior for his bitter sufferings." The first line immediately calls to mind verse 4 from the prolog of John's Gospel: "In him was life, and that life was the light of men." This is truly a hymn of soul-stirring fervor, the product of a gifted poet who, so he stated, turned from writing secular things to Christian hymns "by the anxious and sore afflictions by which God . . . has for some time laid me aside."

The translation of this cento, from an original of eight stanzas, is an altered form of that by Catherine Winkworth in her *Chorale Book for England* (1861).

JESU, MEINES LEBENS LEBEN was originally the tune set to "Alle Menschen müssen sterben" (*TLH* 601) by J. G. Albinus that appeared in the *Kirchengesanbuch* (Darmstadt, 1687). It became especially associated with this text in the *Anhang, An das Gothaische Cantional* (1726). For numerous variants of this fine tune see Zahn 6779a.

The harmonization is from *The Lutheran Hymnal* (1941), slightly altered.

95 GRANT, LORD JESUS, THAT MY HEALING

Grant, Lord Jesus, that my healing
In your holy wounds I find.
Cleanse my spirit, will, and feeling;
Heal my body, soul, and mind.
When some evil thought within
Tempts my wayward heart to sin,
Work in me for its eviction,
Weighted by your crucifixion.

If some lust in current fashion
Rises like a fi'ry flood,
Draw me to your cross and Passion,
Quench the fire, Lord, by your blood.
Lest I to the tempter yield,
Let me front him with the shield,
Thorn-crowned, blood-marked tree displaying,
Sign the devils find dismaying.

Beckoned by the world's old question,
"Going my broad, easy road?"
Let me turn from its suggestion
To the agonizing load
Which for me you did endure.
Let me thus flee thoughts impure
Lest I toy with soiled emotions,
Losing joy in blest devotions.

Where the wound is and the hurting,
Pour in oil and cleansing wine.
Let your cross, its pow'r asserting,
Touch my life with grace divine.
Ev'ry bitter cup make sweet,
Bread of comfort let me eat.
For you won my soul's salvation
By your death for ev'ry nation.

Jesus, rock of strength, my tower,
In your death I put my trust.
When you died, death lost its power,
When you rose, it turned to dust.
Let your bitter agony,
Suffered for us, comfort me.
Dying, Lord, in its protection,
I have life and resurrection.

Jesu, deine tiefen Wunden,
Deine Qual und bittern Tod
Lass mir geben alle Stunden
Trost in Leib's- und Seelennot!
Wenn mir fällt was Arges ein,
Lass mich denken deiner Pein,
Dass ich deine Angst und Schmerzen
Wohl erwäg' in meinem Herzen!

Will sich gern in Wollust weiden
Mein verderbtes Fleisch und Blut,
Lass mich denken, dass dein Leiden
Löschen muss der Hölle Glut!
Dringt der Satan ein zu mir,
Hilf, dass ich ihm halte für
Deiner Wunden Mal' und Zeichen,
Dass er von mir müsse weichen!

Wenn die Welt mich will verführen
Auf die breite Sündenbahn,
Woll'st du mich also regieren,
Dass ich alsdann schaue an
Deiner Marter Zentnerlast,
Die du ausgestanden hast,
Dass ich kann in Andacht bleiben,
Alle böse Lust vertreiben!

Gib für alles, was mich kränket,
Mir aus deinen Wunden Saft;
Wenn mein Herz hinein sich senket,
So gib neue Lebenskraft,
Dass mich stärk' in allem Leid
Deines Trostes Süssigkeit,
Weil du mir das Heil erworben,
Da du bist für mich gestorben.

Lass auf deinen Tod mich trauen,
O Mein Gott und Zuversicht!
Lass mich feste darauf bauen,
Dass den Tod ich schmecke nicht!
Deine Todesangst lass mich
Stets erquicken mächtiglich;
Herr, lass deinen Tod mir geben
Auferstehung, Heil und Leben!

This notable hymn by Johann Heermann, originally in six stanzas, appeared in the fourth edition of his *Devoti Musica Cordis. Haus- und hertz-Musica* (Leipzig and Breslau, 1644). There it is entitled "Consolation from the wounds of Jesus in all manner of temptation. From the *Manual* of St. Augustine, Chapter XXII." This manual is a medieval compilation from various church fathers, and chapter XXII, upon which this hymn is based, is by Bernard of Clairvaux (*LW* 113, 274). Heermann's version became a favorite in the Lutheran Church. Nicolaus Ludwig von Zinzendorf (*LW* 362,

386) alludes to it as "The Crown of all our old hymns . . . in which our entire teaching and practice is contained."

DER AM KREUZ, by Johann B. König, first appeared in the *Harmonischer Liederschatz* (Frankfurt, 1738) as a setting for "Der am Kreutz ist meine Liebe," a Lenten hymn commonly attributed to Johann Mentzer (*LW* 293, 448).

The harmonization is by Paul G. Bunjes.

COME TO CALVARY'S HOLY MOUNTAIN 96

This hymn by James Montgomery is based on Zechariah 13:1: "On that day a fountain will be opened to the house of David and the inhabitants of Jerusalem, to cleanse them from sin and impurity." First published in 1819 as "The Open Fountain" in Thomas Cotterill's (1779–1823) famous eighth edition of *A Selection of Psalms and Hymns for Public and Private Use*, it appeared later in Montgomery's *The Christian Psalmist* (1825). In his *Original Hymns for Public, Private and Social Devotion* (1853) it was entitled "A Fountain Opened for Sin and Uncleanness."

It seems somewhat strange that most American hymnals, while containing numerous hymns by the gifted Montgomery, failed to include this notable Lenten hymn. Its inclusion appears almost confined to Lutheran hymnals.

The hymn as here given has been considerably altered and updated. In the former process "He that drinks shall live forever" in stanza 4 was changed to "Take the life that lasts forever."

NAAR MIT ÖIE. This tune by Ludvig M. Lindeman is called NAAR MIT ÖIE for having been set in Lindeman's *Koralbog for den Norska Kirke* (1871) to Hans Brorson's hymn of the same name. The *Service Book and Hymnal* (1958) calls the tune HOLY MOUNTAIN because of its association with Montgomery's text.

The harmonization is from *The Lutheran Hymnal* (1941), slightly altered.

ALAS! AND DID MY SAVIOR BLEED 97

Isaac Watts headed this hymn "Godly sorrow arising from the Sufferings of Christ" in Book II of his *Hymns and Spiritual Songs* (1707). The second stanza was marked with an option to be omitted, and usually is:

Thy Body slain, sweet Jesus, thine,
And bath'd in its own Blood,
While all expos'd to Wrath divine
The glorious Sufferer stood?

Further alterations in this hymn, taken from *Lutheran Book of Worship*, include line 4 of the first stanza, from "For such a worm as I"—what Percy Dearmer calls "vermicular theology"; "sins" for "crimes" in stanza 2, line 1; and the last line of stanza 3, which originally read "For man the creature's sin."

MARTYRDOM. Hugh Wilson penned this tune in common time shortly before the turn of the 19th century. In melody and bass lines only, it was intended for use by singing classes. On its first publication in *Sacred Music Sung in St. George's Church* (Edinburgh, 1825) the tune was altered to triple time and described as an "Old Scottish Melody." Litigation after Wilson's death served to establish him as the composer of MARTYRDOM, also called FENWICK or DRUMCLOG.

The harmonization is from the *Service Book and Hymnal* (1958), slightly altered.

98 GLORY BE TO JESUS

Glory be to Jesus,
Who in bitter pains
Poured for me the lifeblood
From his sacred veins.

Grace and life eternal
In that blood I find;
Blest be his compassion,
Infinitely kind.

Blest through endless ages
Be the precious stream
Which from endless torment
Did the world redeem.

Abel's blood for vengeance
Pleaded to the skies;
But the blood of Jesus
For our pardon cries.

Oft as earth exulting
Wafts its praise on high,
Angel hosts rejoicing
Make their glad reply.

Lift we then our voices,
Swell the mighty flood;
Louder still and louder
Praise the precious blood.

Viva! Viva! Gesu! che per mio bene
tutto il sangue verso dalle sue vene.

Il sangue di Gesu fu la mia vita;
Benedetta la Sua bonta infinita.

Questo sangue in eterno sia lodato,
Che dall' inferno il mondo ha riscattato.

D'Abele il sangue gridava venedetta,
Quel di Gesu per noi perdono aspetta.

Se di Gesu si esalta il divin sangue,
Tripudia il ciel, Trema l'abisso e langue.

Diciamo dunque insiem con energia
Al sangue di Gesu gloria si dia. Amen

The author of this Italian hymn, thought to be from the 18th century, is unknown. According to an 1880 translation of the collection, it represents one of the *Aspirazioni Devote* in *Raccolta di Orazioni de Pie Opere colle Indulgenze* compiled by Telesforo Galli, a Roman priest who died in 1845. F. W. Faber (1814–63), Anglican priest turned Roman, in a note to his translation of the hymn, says, "To all the faithful who say or sing the above hymn, Pius VII grants an indulgence of 100 days; applicable to the souls in purgatory."

The commonly used translation, as here, is that by Edward Caswall as published in his *Hymns for the Use of the Birmingham Oratory* (1857). Originally in nine stanzas, stanza 4, 5, and 7 are here omitted.

WEM IN LEIDENSTAGEN (also known as CASWALL, FILITZ) was published in Filitz's *Vierstimmiges Choralbuch* (Berlin, 1847), where it was set to Heinrich Siegmund Oswald's hymn beginning with "Wem in Leidenstagen." (Zahn 1127)

The harmonization is from *The Lutheran Hymnal* (1941).

NOT ALL THE BLOOD OF BEASTS 99

The eminent hymnologist Louis F. Benson considers this hymn by Isaac Watts as being sermonic—as are most of his hymns. This came naturally to Watts for, among the dissenters for whom he wrote, the homiletical aspect of corporate worship was considered the ideal. The hymn, sung after the sermon and reflecting its content, confirmed and helped drive home the point in the sermon. The sermonic hymn had a great day, but, sad to state, to some extent it still survives among pastors who would throw out the historic liturgy with its sacramental and sacrificial poles and supplant it with a homocentrically centered program. Granted the importance of the homilitical aspect, corporate worship in Word and Sacrament is more than listening to a sermon.

Watts published "Not All the Blood of Beasts" in the enlarged editions of his *Hymns and Spiritual Songs* (1709). The language has here been updated and slightly altered. Originally line four in stanza 4 read, "and *hopes* her guilt was there."

SOUTHWELL is one of two tunes by that name. This one, in Short Meter (SM—66 86)—the other by Herbert S. Irons is in Common Meter (CM—86 86)—is one of the earliest such tunes in English hymnody. It first appeared as the setting for Psalm 45 in William Daman's *The Psalmes of David in English meter, with Notes of foure parts set unto them by Guilielmo Daman* (1579) printed by John Day (*LW* 342, 502). It was Ravenscroft who, in his psalter of 1621, called the tune SOUTHWELL, after the cathedral city in Nottinghamshire. There it was set to Psalms 50, 70, and 134. As in Daman's Psalter, it was in the Dorian mode, the pattern of which can be noted by sharping the Cs in the soprano line. Daman's setting is given at hymn 122 in the *Historical Companion to Hymns Ancient and Modern* (1962).

Benjamin Britten (1913–76) makes effective use of this hymn tune in his "Noyes Fludde" ("Noah's Flood").

The setting is from *The English Hymnal* (1906), slightly altered.

100 ON MY HEART IMPRINT YOUR IMAGE

On my heart imprint your image, Blessed Jesus, king of grace, That life's riches, cares, and pleasures Never may your work erase; Let the clear inscription be: Jesus, crucified for me, Is my life, my hope's foundation, And my glory and salvation!	Skriv dig, Jesu, paa mit Hjerte, O min Konge og min Gud, At el Vellyst eller Smerte Dig formaar at slette ud. Denne Opskrift paa mig set: Jesus udaf Nazaret, Den korsgästede, min Äre Og mion salighed skal väre!

Thomas Kingo included in his *Vinterparten* (1689) a Passion hymn of 29 stanzas beginning "Bryder frem, I hule Sukke." The above translation, composed in 1898 by Peer Olsen Strömme, represents stanza 15. It was first published in the *Lutheran Hymnary* (1913). The text as here given has been updated.

Another translation of this stanza, "Print thine image pure and holy," was prepared by Jens Christian Aaberg (1877–1970) and included in the *Service Book and Hymnal* (1958).

DER AM KREUZ. For comments on this tune see hymn 95.

The harmonization is by Paul G. Bunjes.

101 IN THE CROSS OF CHRIST I GLORY

This text by John Bowring entitled "The Cross of Christ" appeared first in the author's *Hymns* (1825). The original had a fifth stanza which repeated the first. Similar to Watts's "When I Survey the Wondrous Cross," the hymn is based on Galatians 6:14.

It is said that Bowring was inspired to write the hymn by the sight of an old Portuguese cathedral at Macao, in China, built 300 years earlier, and which time and the elements had turned into a crumbling ruin—all but the spire, at the top of which an old bronze cross reflected the rays of the setting sun. The story is interesting, but whether true is doubtful. Bowring did not visit China until 1849, the year of his appointment as British consul at Canton. That was 24 years after the hymn had been published in his *Hymns*. He may have learned about this cathedral from another source.

RATHBUN was composed in 1849 by Ithamar Conkey while he was serving as organist at Central Baptist Church, Norwich, Connecticut. Discouraged by the lack of choir attendance at the service one rainy Sunday, Conkey left church early and went home to practice the piano. Going through his mind were the words of "In the cross of Christ I glory," the hymn proposed by his minister for use with a series of sermons on Christ's words from the cross. Although his mood at the time was far from glorying, he composed the tune which he later named "RATHBUN" after one of his choir members, the lead soprano, a Mrs. Rathbun.

The harmonization is from the *Service Book and Hymnal* (1958), slightly altered.

102 ALL GLORY, LAUD, AND HONOR

Refrain All glory, laud, and honor To you, Redeemer, King, To whom the lips of children Made sweet hosannas ring.	Gloria, laus et honor tibi sit, rex, Christe, redemptor, cui puerile decus prompsit hosanna pium.
You are the king of Israel And David's royal Son, Now in the Lord's name coming, Our King and Blessed One. *Refrain*	Israel tu rex, Davidis et inclyta proles, nomine qui in Domini, rex benedicte, venis.
The company of angels Are praising you on high; Creation and all mortals In chorus make reply. *Refrain*	Coetus in excelsis te laudat caelicus omnis et mortalis homo, cuncta creata simul.
The multitude of pilgrims With palms before you went, Our praise and prayer and anthems Before you we present. *Refrain*	Plebs Hebraea tibi cum palmis obvia venit; cum prece, voto, hymnis adsumus ecce tibi.
To you, before your Passion, They sang their hymns of praise. To you, now high exalted, Our melody we raise. *Refrain*	Hi tibi passuro solvebant munia laudis; nos tibi regnanti pangimus ecce melos.
Their praises you accepted; Accept the prayers we bring, Great author of all goodness, O good and gracious King. *Refrain*	Hi placuere tibi; placeat devotio nostra, rex pie, rex clemens, cui bona cuncta placent.

History seems to have disproved the legend surrounding this hymn, related by Clichtoveus in *Elucidatorium* (1516), which states that Theodulf, bishop of Orleans, imprisoned for allegedly conspiring against Louis I, chanted his newly composed poem at the window of his cloister prison cell on Palm Sunday, 821, as the emperor, popularly known as Louis the Pious, passed by in procession. According to the story, the ruler was so impressed by the song that he ordered Theodulf's immediate release and restoration to his bishopric; and he further declared that the song should be sung every Palm Sunday thereafter. It appears likely that the hymn was indeed written by Theodulf during his confinement in the cloister at Angers, but since this confinement began in 818 and ended with his death in 821, and since there is no record of Louis having visited Angers after 818, the legend was almost certainly manufactured.

In any case, the hymn began its long association with Palm Sunday processionals very soon after its composition, and it appears in the ancient Sarum, York, Hereford, Roman, and other missals. Medieval rites called for a choir of seven boys to sing the first four stanzas from a high point near the south end of the church, possibly to recall Theodulf's imprisonment. The 39 couplets comprising the Latin original were not too many for congregations to sing, as the processions often moved through the town.

John M. Neale made two translations of parts of the hymn. The first, "Glory and honor and laud," was published in his *Medieval Hymns and Sequences* (1851) in the same meter as the original. Neale then retranslated the hymn for *The Hymnal Noted* (1854) in the more popular 76 76 D meter. This second translation was altered with Neale's approval for the 1859 trial edition of *Hymns Ancient and Modern*, where the first line read, "All glory, laud, and honor." Also in that edition stanza 5 was retranslated to its now familiar form from Neale's irregular stanza:

Thou wast hast'ning to thy Passion
When they raised their hymns of praise:
Thou art reigning in thy glory,
When our melody we raise.

This retranslated and revised stanza appears as number 4 in *Lutheran Worship*, for the refrain which begins the hymn was designated as number 1 in Neale's collection. Neale included another stanza, here omitted:

Receive instead of palm-boughs,
Our victory o'er the foe,
That in the conqueror's triumph
This strain may overflow.

Neale writes that another stanza was "usually sung, until the 17th century, at the pious quaintness of which we can scarcely avoid a smile:

Be thou, O Lord, the rider,
And we the little ass,
That to God's holy city
Together we may pass."

As well as updating the second-person pronouns, *Lutheran Worship* has made a few small revisions to the text. Stanza 2 originally ended, "And mortal men and all things Created make reply." Stanza 3, line 1, was changed from "The people of the Hebrews"; and stanza 5 was written, "Thou didst accept their praises, Accept the prayers we bring, Who in all good delightest, Thou good and gracious King."

Scriptural references, among others, reflected in the hymn are Psalms 24:7–10; 118:25–27; Matthew 21:1–17; and Luke 19:37–38.

VALET WILL ICH DIR GEBEN (ST. THEODOLPH). This celebrated and popular tune by Melchior Teschner was first published in a small six-page pamphlet entitled *Ein andächtigtes Gebet* (Leipzig, 1615), where it was set in five voices to a text of the same name from the pen of Valerius Herberger (1562–1627), pastor of *Kripplein Christi* (Manger of Christ) Lutheran Church in Fraustadt, Germany, where Teschner was cantor for five years. As indicated by its opening line, the hymn, written during the years of the great plague—no less than 2,135 people died in Fraustadt and its environs—was intended for the dying as a farewell to the world. Teschner wrote two tunes for it, and it is the second, the one here discussed, that has been adopted by most hymnals for "All

Glory, Laud, and Honor," having been thus introduced by the 1861 edition of *Hymns Ancient and Modern*.

As in the case of other chorales, this tune has seen its share of variations. Originally the tune went thus, here lowered a whole step—into the key of B♭, for ease of unison singing:

In the 1861 *Hymns Ancient and Modern* editor William H. Monk (*LW* 405, 490) changed the three notes beginning at (1) to C A A. J. S. Bach (*LW* 89), using this tune in his *St. John Passion,* changed the G at (2) to B♭, thus imitating the alteration (possibly a misprint!) in the *Gothaer Cantional* of 1648, a procedure not perpetuated by Lutheran congregations. That same cantional altered the sequence of five notes beginning at (3) with F, D, E, F, G thus following the practice in the previously mentioned cantional, a sequence included in *The Lutheran Hymnal* (1941). Congregation members singing this hymn from *Lutheran Worship* (1982) undoubtedly have noticed a change at this point—perhaps at first somewhat annoying—the result of the commission's decision to go back to Teschner's original sequence as indicated beginning at (3), a procedure exhibited also in *Lutheran Book of Worship* (*LW* 108). Thus the tune as now given in both hymnals corresponds to the usage in European Lutheranism, especially in the Lutheran territorial and Free churches in Germany, except for one note: instead of the D at (4), as in the original Teschner version, F is used to introduce the concluding line of text. Here both *Lutheran Book of Worship* and *Lutheran Worship* followed the lead of Peter Sohren (*LW* 246), cantor and organist in Elbing, Germany, who made this change in one of his editions of Johann Crüger's (*LW* 19, 39, et al.) *Praxis pietatis melica*, a change, considered by the Commission on Worship, to be preferred.

In the *Companion to Congregational Praise* (1953), Erik Routley (1917–82) deplores the practice of repeating the first half of the tune as a refrain, thereby ending it in the middle; but he concedes that this usage has acquired the authority of commonality.

A slight similarity between VALET WILL ICH DIR GEBEN and "Sellinger's Round," a 16th-century round dance, has been noted, and the tune therefore ascribed to

William Byrd (c. 1540-1623), English organist and composer of the madrigalian era, in the *Oxford Hymn Book*. The evidence for such ascription is, however, extremely weak.

The *Lutheran Worship* setting is by Paul G. Bunjes, from *New Organ Accompaniments for Hymns* (1976).

THE ROYAL BANNERS FORWARD GO 103

The royal banners forward go; The cross shows forth redemption's flow Where he, by whom our flesh was made, Our ransom in his flesh has paid:	Vexilla regis prodeunt, Fulget crucis mysterium, Quo car ne carnis conditor Suspensus et patibulo.
Where deep for us the spear was dyed, Life's torrent rushing from his side, To wash us in the precious flood Where flowed the water and the blood.	Quo vulneratus insuper Mucrone dirae lanceae, Ut nos lavaret crimine, Magnavit unda, sanguine.
Fulfilled is all that David told In sure prophetic song of old, That God the nation's king should be And reign in triumph from the tree,	Impleta sunt, quae concinit David fidelis carmine, Dicens: in nationibus Regnavit a ligno Deus.
On whose hard arms, so widely flung, The weight of this world's ransom hung, The price of humankind to pay And spoil the spoiler of his prey.	Beata, cuius brachiis Saecli pependit praemium, Statera facta corporis, Praedam quae tulit tartari.
To you, eternal Three in One, Let homage meet by all be done, By all you ransomed and restore; Oh, guide and gladden evermore.	Te, summa Deus trinitas, Collaudet ominis spiritus, Quos per crucis mysterium Salvas, rege per saecula.

The text of this great processional hymn by Venantius Honorius Fortunatus is supposed to have been written and first sung during a procession headed by Fortunatus to meet the bearers of fragments of the supposed true cross. Queen Rhadegunde had petitioned Emperor Justin II to send these relics to her convent, Ste. Croix, which had been so named because of Rhadegunde's reverence for the cross. The emperor complied with her request, but routed the relics to Euphronius, Bishop of Tours, with instructions to deliver them with due honor to Ste. Croix. At the reception of the pieces of the true cross, on November 19, 569, the "Vexilla regis" was chanted.

In the eighth century two additional stanzas were added by an unknown author. Used first as a processional, the hymn became a part of Vespers in Passion Week and appeared in the Roman Missal designated to be sung following the adoration of Christ on the cross. (See Good Friday I, rubric 14 in *Lutheran Worship: Agenda*, p. 56.)

The word *vexilla* in the opening line refers to the standards borne by the Roman cavalry, whose eagle ornament of earlier times was replaced with a cross by Emperor Constantine (c. 280–337).

Over 40 translations of the Latin and variants of them in English have been made, as well as various alterations of John Mason Neale's (*LW* 31, et al.) eight-stanza translation in his *Medieval Hymns and Sequences* (1851) and, with one stanza omitted, in his *Hymnal Noted* (1852). The translation of the stanzas used in *Lutheran Worship* are largely based on Neale's work.

HERR JESU CHRIST, WAHR MENSCH UND GOTT was published in Johann Eccard's chorale collection, *Der Erste Theil Geistliche Lieder* (1597), where it accompanied the text, "Herr Jesu Christ, wahr Mensch und Gott," by Paul Eber (*LW* 189, 428). Shortly after that appearance the melody, in various forms, was included in several other collections. This fact led some to believe it was a "discovered" rather than an original tune by Eccard.

The harmonization by Paul G. Bunjes is from *Worship Supplement* (1969).

104 THE ROYAL BANNERS FORWARD GO

See hymn 103 regarding the text of this hymn.

VEXILLA REGIS. This beautiful plainsong melody in Mode 1 (see essay: The Church Modes, p. 832) is the traditional tune for "The Royal Banners Forward Go," and may be as old as the text. It is the proper melody for the text in the Sarum use (Salisbury, England), to be sung at Evensong on Passion Sunday and daily until Wednesday in Holy Week. The setting is by Paul G. Bunjes for *Lutheran Worship*.

Following the commission's suggestion that the choir sing this plainsong tune (the more difficult of the two tunes to learn) in alternation with the congregation singing the chorale tune (*LW* 103), should prove to be devotionally effective.

105 RIDE ON, RIDE ON IN MAJESTY

Henry H. Milman wrote this hymn at the age of 30, just before he became professor of poetry at Oxford. First published in Reginald Heber's (*LW* 86, et al.) posthumous *Hymns Written and Adapted to the Weekly Church Services of the Year* (1827), the manuscript prompted Heber to write Milman, "You have indeed sent me a most powerful reinforcement to my projected hymnbook. A few more such and I shall neither need nor wait for the aid of Scott and Southey." Milman later included "Ride On, Ride On in Majesty" in his *Selection of Psalms and Hymns* (1837).

Stanza 1, line 3, which originally read, "Thine humble beast pursues his road," was altered to "O Savior meek, pursue thy road" by F. H. Murray in *A Hymnal for Use in the English Church,* 1852 edition. This change and one other, the substitution of "expects" for "awaits" in stanza 4, have been adopted by most modern hymnals. *Lutheran Worship* (1982) returned to the author's original "winged squadrons" in stanza 3 from "angel armies" in *The Lutheran Hymnal* (1941), and updated the personal pronouns.

THE KING'S MAJESTY was composed by Graham George for this text, to replace its former setting, WINCHESTER NEW (*TLH* 162), also known as FRANKFORT or CRASSELIUS. Describing his inspiration, George wrote:

> It originated as a result of a choir practice before Palm Sunday in, I suppose, 1939, during which I had been thinking 'Winchester New' is a fine tune, but it has nothing whatever to do with the 'tragic trumpets,' as one might theatrically call them, of Palm Sunday. At breakfast the following morning I was enjoying my toast and marmalade when the first two lines of this tune sang themselves unbidden into my mind. This seemed too good to miss, so I went to my study, allowed the half-tune to complete itself—which it did with very little trouble—and there it was (Ronander and Porter, *Guide to the Pilgrim Hymnal*).

The tune was first published with "Ride On, Ride On in Majesty" in *The Hymnal 1940*.

The harmonization is by Graham George.

HOSANNA, LOUD HOSANNA 106

This text was published by Jennette Threlfall in a collection of her poetry called *Sunshine and Shadow* (1873). Threlfall claimed that almost all her verses were written in idle moments; she then sent them anonymously to various periodicals. This is the only hymn of hers that has survived.

Stanza 2 is a composite made up of the first four lines of Threlfall's second stanza and the last four lines of her third. The original stanza 2 ended:

> Bright angels joined the chorus,
> Beyond the cloudless sky—
> "Hosanna in the highest!
> Glory to God on high!"

and stanza 3 began:

> Fair leaves of silvery olive
> They strowed upon the ground,
> While Salem's circling mountains
> Echoed the joyful sound.

ELLACOMBE. This fine tune is vaguely foreshadowed in the *Gesangbuch . . . der Herzogl. Württembergischen katholischen Hofkapelle* (1784), set to an early *Marienlied* "Ave Maria, klarer und lichter Morgenstern" in a book used in the private chapel of the Duke of Württemberg. In Xavier Ludwig Hartig's *Vollständige Sammlung der gewöhnlichen Melodien zum mainzer Gesangbuche* (c. 1833) the tune appears in more recognizable form, set to the hymn "Der du im heil'gsten Sakrament." (Cf. Bäumker IV, 533–36, for a number of variants.)

The tune appears to have been brought to England by being included in the 1868 Appendix to *Hymns Ancient and Modern*, set to J. J. Daniell's hymn for children, "Come, Sing with Holy Gladness." Thus it was accorded wide use and soon became popular. The name ELLACOMBE may have been given the tune by an English editor, perhaps designating a locality, for instance, a village in Devonshire.

The harmonization was prepared for *Lutheran Worship* by Paul G. Bunjes.

107 THE DEATH OF JESUS CHRIST, OUR LORD

The death of Jesus Christ, our Lord,
We celebrate with one accord;
It is our comfort in distress,
Our heart's sweet joy and happiness.

He blotted out with his own blood
The judgment that against us stood;
He full atonement for us made,
And all our debt he fully paid.

That this is now and ever true
He gives an earnest ever new:
In this his holy Supper here
We taste his love so sweet, so near.

His Word proclaims and we believe
That in this Supper we receive
His very body, as he said,
His very blood for sinners shed.

A precious food is this indeed—
It never fails us in our need—
A heav'nly manna for our soul
Until we safely reach our goal.

Oh, blest is each believing guest
Who in this promise finds his rest;
For Jesus will in love abide
With those who do in him confide.

The guest that comes with true intent
To turn to God and to repent,
To live for Christ, to die to sin,
Will thus a holy life begin.

War Herres Jesu Kristi dod
Hugswalar oss i all war nöd,
Och när wi tänke deruppa,
En hjertans glädje wi da fa.

Afplanat har han med sitt blod
Den handskrift, some emot oss stod;
Ty han war oss sa god och huld,
Att han betalte all war skuld.

Att detta trofast ärh och sant,
Han gifwer oss en säker pant
Uti sin helga nattward, der
Wi smake huru ljuf han är.

Hans heliga lekamen sann,
Hans dyra blod, som för oss rann,
Wi undfa wid hans helga bord,
Som han har lofwat i sitt ord.

En harlig spis är detta wisst,
Pa hwilken aldrig blifwer brist,
Ett himmelskt manna, som war själ
Till ewigt lif bewarar wäl.

Säll är da hwarje wärdig gäst,
Som lit till Jesu ord har fäst;
Ty Jesus will med kärlek bo
Hos den, som har en stadig tro;

Och som will helgad bli i Gud,
Ej wika fran hans ord och bud,
Men Kristo lefwer, synden dör
Och sa Guds helga wilja gör.

They who his Word do not believe
This food unworthily receive,
Salvation here will never find—
May we this warning keep in mind!

Men den owärdig gar härtill,
Ej tror, ej sig omwanda will,
Han äter döden uti sig
Och blir fördömd ewinnerlig.

Help us sincerely to believe
That we may worthily receive
Your Supper and in you find rest.
Amen, he who believes is blest.

Gif oss att tro af hjertans grund,
Att wi fa frälsning och miskund
Utaf din nades fullhet stor.
Åmen, wälsignad den det tror!

Haquin Spegel's notable Communion hymn, originally in 10 stanzas, was written in 1686 and included in the *Psalm-Book* (1696) prepared by Jesper Svedberg in collaboration with Spegel. The translation by Olof Olsson appeared in the *Evangelical Lutheran Hymn-Book* (1912), predecessor to *The Lutheran Hymnal* (1941), as well as in the latter.

The omitted ninth stanza read:

O Jesus Christ, our Brother dear,
Unto Thy cross we now draw near;
Thy sacred wounds indeed make whole
A wounded and afflicted soul.

GOTTLOB, ES GEHT NUNMEHR ZU ENDE derives its name from poet and playwright Christian Weise's (1726–1804) burial hymn beginning with that line. It is an old German melody of unknown origin, found in various forms in German collections. Its first appearance was in *Sammlung alter und neuer . . . Melodien*, by Johann G. Wagner (1742). The present form of the tune is from J. S. Bach's *Vierstimmige Choralgesänge* (1769).

Paul G. Bunjes prepared the setting of this fine chorale tune for *Lutheran Worship* (1982).

FROM CALVARY'S CROSS I HEARD CHRIST SAY — 108

From Calv'ry's cross I heard Christ say:
"Father, forgive these men, for they
In truth know not what they do."
Forgive us too, for often we
In ignorance offend you.

Zum ersten: Vater, strafe nicht
An ihnen, was mir jetzt geschicht,
Weil sie es nicht verstehen.
Vergib uns, Gott, wenn wir auch noch
Aus Irrtum was begehen!

Now to the contrite thief he cries:
"You, truly, will in paradise
Meet me before tomorrow."
Lord, take us soon to heav'n with you,
Who linger here in sorrow.

Zum andern er des Schächers dacht':
Fürwahr, du wirst noch vor der Nacht
In meinem Reich heut' leben.
O Herr, nimm uns aus bald zu dir,
Die wir im Elend schweben.

To weeping Mary standing by,
"Behold your son," we hear him cry;

Zum dritten: Deinen Sohn sieh, Weib!
Johannes, ihr zu Dienste bleib

To John, "Behold your mother." So when we die, let those we leave In love befriend each other.	Und sie als Mutter liebe! Versorg, Herr, die wir lassen hier, Dass niemand sie betrübe!
The Savior's fourth word was "I thirst!" O mighty prince of life, your thirst Yearns for my full salvation. Your love, your mercy's sacrifice Compel my adoration.	Zum vierten sagte er: Mich dürst't! O Jesu, grosser Lebensfürst, Du hast Durst und Verlangen Nach unsrer Seligkeit; drum hilf, Dass wir sie auch empfangen.
The fifth, "My God, my God, oh, why Do you not hear my earnest cry?" Lord, you were here forsaken That we may never be so lost; Let lively faith awaken.	Zum fünften: O mein Gott, mein Gott, Wie lässt du mich so in der Not? Hier wirst du, Herr, verlassen, Dass uns Gott wieder dort aufnehm'. Den Trost lass uns wohl fassen.
With "It is finished!" you have done, The course your Father set is run, The victory achieving. So let us do your work on earth, Your promises believing.	Zum sechsten: Hiermit ist vollbracht Und alles nunmehr gutgemacht. Gib, dass wir auch durchdringen, Und was du Herr, uns auferlegt, Hilf seliglich vollbringen.
And last, as life and suff'rings end: "O God my Father, I commend Into your hands my spirit." Be this, dear Lord, my dying prayer; O gracious Father, hear it.	Zum siebenten: Ich meine Seel' O Gott, mein Vater, dir befehl' Zu deinen treuen Händen. Dies Wort sei unser letzter Wunsch, Wenn wir das Leben enden.
Our Lord thus spoke these seven times When on his cross, for all our crimes, He died that we not perish. Let us his last and dying words In our remembrance cherish.	Da Jesus an des Kreuzes Stamm Der ganzen Welt Sünd' auf sich nahm, Sprach er in seinen Schmerzen Noch sieben Wort', die lasset uns Erwägen wohl im Herzen.

James Mearns in Julian's *A Dictionary of Hymnology* concludes that this hymn, as first published in the *Hanover Gesang-Buch* (1646), was written to supersede an earlier hymn accredited to Johann Böschenstain, beginning "Da Jesus an dem Kreuze stund." The latter has been traced to an undated leaflet, c. 1515, where it appeared in nine stanzas. However, the above text may be simply an expansion of Böschenstain's original, since its author has not been determined.

The new translation, in eight stanzas, was prepared by Henry Lettermann for *Lutheran* Worship. Congregations may be familiar with the earlier translation, beginning "Our blessed Savior sev'n times spoke," that appeared in *The Lutheran Hymnal* (1941).

DA JESUS AN DES KREUZES is a reworking of an old German folksong. It first appeared in the Babst *Gesangbuch* (1545) set to the hymn, "In dich hab' ich gehoffet, Herr" (*LW* 406) by Adam Reusner.

The harmonization is by Paul G. Bunjes.

JESUS, I WILL PONDER NOW 109

Jesus, I will ponder now
On your holy Passion;
With your Spirit me endow
For such meditation.
Grant that I in love and faith
May the image cherish
Of your suff'ring, pain, and death
That I may not perish.

Make me see your great distress,
Anguish, and affliction,
Bonds and stripes and wretchedness
And your crucifixion;
Make me see how scourge and rod,
Spear and nails did wound you,
How you died for those, O God,
Who with thorns had crowned you.

Yet, O Lord, not thus alone
Make me see your Passion;
But its cause to me make known
And its termination.
For I also and my sin
Brought your deep affliction;
This the shameful cause has been
Of your crucifixion.

Grant that I your Passion view
With repentant grieving,
Let me not bring shame to you
By unholy living.
How could I refuse to shun
Ev'ry sinful pleasure
Since for me God's only Son
Suffered without measure?

If my sins give me alarm
And my conscience grieve me,
Let your cross my fear disarm,
Peace and pardon give me.
Grant that I may trust in you
And your holy Passion;
If his Son forgives anew,
God must have compassion.

Jesus, Lord, my heart renew,
Let me bear my crosses,
Learning humbleness from you,
Peace despite my losses.
May I give you love for love!
Hear me, O my Savior,
That I may in heav'n above
Sing your praise forever.

Jesu, deine Passion
Will ich jetzt bedenken;
Wollest mir vom Himmelsthron
Geist und Andacht schenken.
In dem Bild jetzund erschein,
Jesu, meinem Herzen,
Wie du, unser Heil zu sein,
Littest alle Schmerzen!

Meine Seele sehen mach
Deine Angst und Bande,
Deine Speichel, Schläg' und Schmach,
Deine Kreuzesschande,
Deine Geissel, Dornenkron',
Speer- und Nägel Wunden,
Deinen Tod, o Gottessohn,
Und den Leib voll Schrunden!

Doch so lass mich nicht allein
Deine Marter sehen,
Lass mich auch die Ursach' fein
Und die Frucht verstehen!
Ach, die Ursach' war auch ich,
Ich und meine Sünde;
Diese hat gemartert dich,
Nicht das Heideng'sinde.

Jesu, lehr bedenken mich
Dies mit Buss' und Reue;
Hilf, dass ich mit Sünden dich
Martre nicht aufs neue!
Sollt' ich dazu haben Lust
Und nicht wollen meiden,
Was Gott selber büssen musst'
Mit so grossem Leiden?

Wenn mir meine Sünde will
Machen heiss die Hölle,
Jesu, mein Gewissen still,
Dich ins Mittel stelle!
Dich und deine Passion
Lass mich gläubig fassen;
Liebet mich sein lieber Sohn,
Wie kann Gott mich hassen?

Gib auch, Jesu, dass ich gern
Dir das Kreuz nachtrage,
Dass ich Demut von dir lern'
Und Geduld in Plage,
Dass ich dir geb' Lieb' um Lieb'!
Indes lass dies Lallen
(Bessern Dank ich dorten geb'),
Jesu, dir gefallen!

This favorite Lenten hymn in the Lutheran Church was written by Sigismund von Birken. Its first appearance was in *Passions-Andachten zu Johann Michael Dilherrn heiliger Charwochen* (Nürnberg, 1653).

The translation is an altered form of that by August Crull, first included in the *Evangelical Lutheran Hymn-Book* (Baltimore, 1889).

JESU KREUZ, LEIDEN UND PEIN represents the tune coupled to Peter Herbert's hymn beginning with these words, a tune included in Melchior Vulpius' *Ein schön geistlich Gesangbuch* (Jena, 1609).

The harmonization is that contained in *Lutheran Book of Worship* (1978), slightly altered.

110 GO TO DARK GETHSEMANE

Go to dark Gethsemane,
All who feel the tempter's pow'r;
Your Redeemer's conflict see.
Watch with him one bitter hour;
Turn not from his griefs away;
Learn from Jesus Christ to pray.

Follow to the judgment hall,
View the Lord of life arraigned;
Oh, the wormwood and the gall!
Oh, the pangs his soul sustained!
Shun not suff'ring, shame, or loss;
Learn from him to bear the cross.

Calv'ry's mournful mountain climb;
There, adoring at his feet,
Mark that miracle of time,
God's own sacrifice complete.
"It is finished!" hear him cry;
Learn from Jesus Christ to die.

Early hasten to the tomb
Where they laid his breathless clay;
All is solitude and gloom.
Who has taken him away?
Christ is ris'n! He meets our eyes.
Savior, teach us so to rise.

Go to dark Gethsemane,
Ye that feel the tempter's power;
Your Redeemer's conflict see;
Watch with Him one bitter hour;
Turn not from his griefs away;
Learn from Him to watch and pray.

See Him at the judgment-hall,
Beaten, bound, reviled, arraign'd:
See Him meekly bearing all!
Love to man His soul sustain'd!
Shun not suffering, shame or loss;
Learn of Christ to bear the cross.

Calvary's mournful mountain view;
There the Lord of Glory see,
Made a sacrifice for you,
Dying on the accursed tree:
"It is finish'd," hear Him cry:
Trust in Christ, and learn to die.

Early to the tomb repair,
Where they laid his breathless clay;
Angels kept their vigil there:
Who hath taken Him away?
"Christ is risen!" He seeks the skies;
Saviour! teach us so to rise.

James Montgomery's original version of this hymn (above in the right column) was written in 1820 and first printed in the ninth edition of Thomas Cotterill's (1779–1823) *A Selection of Psalms and Hymns for Public and Private Use* (London, 1820). Montgomery himself revised the hymn to the form which, with minor changes, appears in *Lutheran Worship*. This revised version was first published in the *Selection of Hymns for the Use of the Protestant Dissenting Congregations of the Independent Order in Leeds* (1822). Montgomery used this second version in the *Christian Psalmist* (1825), and both it and the original from Cotterill's *Selection* have been in common usage.

Many hymnals omit the fourth stanza. Referring to such shortened versions, Bailey (*The Gospel in Hymns*) lists "the lessons one may learn from three of the final incidents in the life of Jesus: Gethsemane—learn the spirit of prayer; the Praetorium—learn how to bear the Cross; Calvary—learn how to die." One wonders at the omission of the greatest and final lesson: the Resurrection—learn how to live anew!

GETHSEMANE. Richard Redhead's tunes were unnamed by the composer and therefore designated numerically; this one, set to Toplady's "Rock of Ages" (*LW* 361), for which it was written, appeared as No. 76 in Redhead's *Church Hymn Tunes, Ancient and Modern* (1853) and hence is often called REDHEAD NO. 76. In England it is still frequently used with "Rock of Ages," from which it derives its popular name PETRA (Greek for "rock"); Americans more commonly refer to it as GETHSEMANE because of its association with Montgomery's "Go to Dark Gethsemane."

Although Erik Routley considers Richard Redhead to be a "trivial" composer and the tune REDHEAD NO. 76 to be one of the "holy terrors" that Redhead wrote (*Music of Christian Hymnody*), this tune still appears in a goodly number of present-day hymnals as the vehicle either for "Rock of Ages" or "Go to Dark Gethsemane."

The setting is that contained in *The Lutheran Hymnal* (1941), slightly altered.

A LAMB ALONE BEARS WILLINGLY 111

A lamb alone bears willingly
Sin's crushing weight for sinners;
He carries guilt's enormity,
Dies shorn of all his honors.
He goes to slaughter, weak and faint,
Is led away with no complaint
His spotless life to offer.
He bears the stripes, the wrath, the lies,
The mockery, and yet replies,
"Willing all this I suffer."

This lamb is Christ, our soul's great friend,
The Lamb of God, our Savior,
Whom God the Father chose to send
Our rebel guilt to cover.
"Go down, my Son," the Father said,
"To free my children from their dread
Of death and condemnation.
The wrath and stripes are hard to bear,
But in your death they all can share
The joy of your salvation!"

"Yes, Father, yes, most willingly
I bear what you command me;

Ein Lämmlein geht und trägt die Schuld
Der Welt und ihrer Kinder;
Es geht und träget in Geduld
Die Sünden aller Sünder;
Es geht dahin, wird matt und krank,
Ergibt sich auf die Würgebank,
Verzeiht sich aller Freuden;
Es nimmet an Schmach, Hohn und Spott,
Angst, Wunden, Striemen, Kreuz und Tod
Und spricht: Ich will's gern leiden.

Das Lämmlein ist der grosse Freund
Und Heiland meiner Seelen;
Den, den hat Gott zum Sündenfeind
Und Sühner wollen wählen.
Geh hin, mein Kind, und nimm dich an
Der Kinder, die ich ausgetan
Zur Straf' und Zornesruen.
Die Straf' ist schwer, der Zorn ist gross,
Du kannst und sollst sie machen los
Durch Sterben und durch Bluten.

Ja, Vater, ja, von Heerzensgrund,
Leg' auf, ich will dir's tragen;

My will conforms to your decree,
I risk what you have asked me."
O wondrous love, what have you done?
The Father offers up his Son,
The Son, content, agreeing!
O Love, how strong you are to save,
To put God's Son into his grave,
All people thereby freeing!

Mein Wollen hängt an deinem Mund,
Mein Wirken ist dein Sagen.
O Wunderlieb', o Liebesmacht,
Du kannst, was nie kein Mensch gedacht,
Gott seinen Sohn abzwingen!
O Liebe, Liebe, du bist stark,
Du streckest den ins Grab und Sarg,
Vor dem die Felsen springen!

Then, when we come before God's throne,
This little lamb shall lead us;
His righteousness shall be our crown,
His innocence precede us.
His grace our dress of royalty;
His all-forgiving loyalty
Unites us with our Father,
Where we shall stand at Jesus' side,
His Church, redeemed and glorified,
Where all his faithful gather!

Wenn endlich ich soll treten ein
In deines Reiches Freuden,
So soll dies Blut mein Purpur sein,
Ich wil mich darein kleiden.
Es soll sein meines Hauptes Kron',
In welcher ich will vor dem Thron
Des höchsten Vaters gehen
Und dir, dem er mich anvertraut,
Als eine wohlgeschmückte Braut
An deiner Seite stehen.

Dear to Paul Gerhardt's heart was the doctrine of justification by faith; and so he graces the church year—to him the Christ-year—with hymns that are clear and objective expressions of the Christian faith. He sings of the love of God in Christ for the world's redemption with inexhaustible freshness and spiritual depth. Of the 13 hymns that he authored on the Lord's Passion, this hymn, based on John 1:29 and Isaiah 53:4–7, is as Koch says, "the masterpiece of all Passion hymns." From the first to the last stanza—originally 10 stanzas—it is a praise of God's love unmatched in any other Passion hymn, a hymn that first appeared in the third edition of Johann Crüger's *Praxis pietatis melica* (Berlin, 1648).

The translation was prepared for *Lutheran Worship* (1982) by Henry L. Lettermann.

AN WASSERFLÜSSEN BABYLON. While Luther and his colleagues in Wittenberg were concerned about providing hymn texts reflecting and based on Scripture as a whole, in Germany, particularly in Strassburg, for instance, there were individuals who busied themselves exclusively with psalmody, considering this the true, God-pleasing vehicle of praise and devotion. Such an one was Wolfgang Dachstein, to whom this tune, touted as a "lovely melody" ("melodia suavissima"), is credited. Set to his metrical paraphrase of Psalm 137, beginning "An Wasserflüssen Babylon," it first appeared in the third part of *Teutsch Kirchenamt, wie es die Gemeind zu Strassburg singt* (Strassburg, 1525). Incidentally, Luther took over both this text and tune for inclusion in Valentin Babst's *Geystliche Lieder* (Leipzig, 1545), the last hymnal publication Luther had occasion to supervise.

The harmonization was prepared by Walter Gresens for *Lutheran Worship* (1982).

JESUS, IN YOUR DYING WOES 112

This seven-part hymn, three stanzas to each part, represents a versified litany on the seven words of Jesus on the cross from the pen of Thomas B. Pollock as contained in his *Metrical Litanies for Special Services and General Use* (Oxford, 1870). Litany is an ancient form of prayer consisting of petitions or biddings with certain fixed congregational responses, so called from the Greek word meaning "supplication."

Except for the updating of the personal pronouns the text is essentially as originally conceived.

Scriptural references to these seven words are:

I. Luke 23:34
II. Luke 23:43
III. John 19:26–27
IV. Matthew 27:46
V. John 19:28
VI. John 19:30
VII. Luke 23:46

Julian states that the metrical litanies came into vogue about 1854. Prose litanies, however, are more common today in corporate worship.

SEPTEM VERBA, the Latin for seven words, is the tune that Bernard Schumacher composed for the Pollock text for inclusion in *The Lutheran Hymnal* (1941), the hymnal produced by the Intersynodical Committee on Hymnology and Liturgics for the Evangelical Lutheran Synodical Conference, of which he was a member. The almost exclusive conjunct, or stepwise, movement of the notes, although appropriate to the solemnity of the text, is somewhat enervating. Only one tune in *Lutheran Worship* surpasses its stepwise character, namely, HAMBURG (*LW* 115), which is completely stepwise, or conjunct.

O SACRED HEAD, NOW WOUNDED 113

O sacred head, now wounded, With grief and shamed weighed down, Now scornfully surrounded With thorns, your only crown. O sacred head, what glory And bliss did once combine; Though now despised and gory, I joy to call you mine!	O Haupt voll Blut und Wunden, Voll Schmerz und voller Hohn, O Haupt, zum Spott gebunden Mit einer Dornenkron' O Haupt, sonst schön gezieret Mit höchster Ehr' und Zier Jetzt aber höchst schimpfieret: Gegrüsset sei'st du mir!

How pale you are with anguish,
With sore abuse and scorn!
Your face, your eyes now languish,
Which once were bright as morn.
Now from your cheeks has vanished
Their color once so fair;
From loving lips is banished
The splendor that was there.

Die Farbe deiner Wangen,
Der roten Lippen Pracht
Ist hin und ganz vergangen;
Des blassen Todes Macht
Hat alles hingenommen,
Hat alles hingerafft,
Und daher bist du kommen
Von deines Leibes Kraft.

All this for my transgression,
My wayward soul to win;
This torment of your Passion,
To set me free from sin.
I cast myself before you,
Your wrath my rightful lot;
Have mercy, I implore you,
O Lord, condemn me not!

Nun, was du, Herr, erduldet,
Ist alles meine Last;
Ich hab' es selbst verschuldet,
Was du getragen hast.
Schau her, hier steh' ich Armer,
Der Zorn verdienet hat;
Gib mir, o mein Erbar mer,
Den Anblick deiner Gnad'!

Here will I stand beside you,
Your death for me my plea;
Let all the world deride you,
I clasp you close to me.
My awe cannot be spoken,
To see you crucified;
But in your body broken,
Redeemed, I safely hide!

Ich will hier bei dir stehen,
Verachte mich doch nicht!
Von dir will ich nicht gehen,
Wenn dir dein Herze bricht;
Wenn dein Haupt wird erblassen
Im letzten Todesstoss,
Alsdann will ich dich fassen
In meinen Arm und Schoss.

What language can I borrow
To thank you, dearest friend,
For this your dying sorrow,
Your mercy without end?
Bid me to you forever,
Give courage from above;
Let not my weakness sever
Your bond of lasting love.

Ich danke dir von Herzen,
O Jesu, liebster Freund,
Für deines Todes Schmerzen,
Da du's so gut gemeint.
Ach gib, dass ich mich halte
Zu dir und deiner Treu'
Und, wenn ich nun erkalte,
In dir mein Ende sei!

Lord, be my consolation,
My constant source of cheer;
Remind me of your Passion,
My shield when death is near.
I look in faith, believing
That you have died for me;
Your cross and crown receiving,
I live eternally.

Erscheine mir zum Schilde,
Zum Trost in meinem Tod,
Und lass mich sehn dein Bilde
In deiner Kreuzesnot!
Da will ich nach dir blicken,
Da will ich gaubensvoll
Dich fest an mein Herz drücken.
Wer so stirbt, der stirbt wohl.

This classic hymn by Paul Gerhardt, originally in 10 German stanzas, is based on a Latin poem generally attributed to the illustrious and influential Bernard of Clairvaux; more probably it was authored by a writer of the 14th century. The Latin original, *Rhythmica Oratio*, is a rhythmical prayer beginning "Salve, mundi salutare," a seven-part adoration of Christ on the Cross, a part for each of the seven days of Holy Week. Each five-stanza part addresses a different member of Christ's body: *Ad Pedes* (to the feet), *Ad Genua* (to the knees), *Ad Manus* (to the hands), *Ad Latus* (to the side), *Ad Pectus* (to the breast), *Ad Cor* (to the heart), and *Ad Faciem* (to the face, or the head). This last part, from which Gerhardt drew his hymn, begins:

Salve, caput cruentatum,
Totum spinis corontatum,
Conquassatum, vulneratum,
Arundine sic verberatum
Facie sputis illita
Salve, cuius dulcis vultus,
Immutatus et incultus
Immutavit suum florem
Totus versus in pallorem
Quem coeli tremit curia.

The enormous popularity of Gerhardt's German version, included in Johann Crüger's (*LW* 19, 39, et al.) *Praxis pietatis melica* (Frankfurt, 1656), has been maintained in numerous English translations by various hymnal committees. Moreover, the concern to present this great hymn as beautifully and effectively as possible has led to many composite versions and centos.

Such is the case also with the version in *Lutheran Worship*. Desirous of presenting more than the four stanzas contained in *Lutheran Book of Worship* (see *LBW* 116 with rhythmic setting; 117 with isometric setting), the Hymn Text and Music Committee, with the approval of the Commission on Worship, instructed Henry Lettermann, a member of the former, to update the *LBW* version (a translation essentially by James Waddell Alexander that appeared in Joshua Leavitt's *The Christian Lyre* [New York, 1830]) and to add thoughts and/or stanzas from *The Lutheran Hymnal* (1941). The result was a skillfully prepared, composite version of six stanzas, including a beautiful final stanza, popularly used as a prayer for the dying—partly from the *LBW* version and partly from the *TLH* version in updated, altered, and sometimes rearranged form. Thus is perpetuated, in abbreviated form, a hymnic jewel of which historian Philipp Schaff has said:

> This classical hymn has shown an imperishable vitality in passing from the Latin into the German, and from the German into the English, and proclaiming in three tongues, and in the name of three Confessions—the Catholic, Lutheran, and Reformed—with equal effect, the dying love of our Savior and our boundless indebtedness to him (Schaff, *Christ in Song*, 1869).

HERZLICH TUT MICH VERLANGEN (PASSION CHORALE, O HAUPT VOLL BLUT UND WUNDEN) was first published in Hans Leo Hassler's *Lustgarten neuer teutscher Gesäng* (Nürnberg, 1601) coupled with the secular text "Mein Gmüt ist mir verwirret, das macht ein Jungfrau zart" (Zahn 5385a). As a hymn setting it was first used in *Harmoniae Sacrae* (Görlitz, 1613), set to Christoph Knoll's funeral hymn, "Herzlich thut mich verlangen," which gave the tune the name by which it is best known. It was early adopted for Roman Catholic use in D. G. Corner's *Gross Catholisch Gesangbuch* (1631) and in his *Geistliche Nachtigal* (1649). As previously stated, it first appeared with Gerhardt's "O Haupt voll Blut und Wunden" in Johann Crüger's *Praxis pietatis melica* (Frankfurt, 1656).

This undeniably magnificent chorale tune was evidently a great favorite of J. S. Bach (*LW* 89), for he included it five times in his *St. Matthew Passion,* where it is central to and casts a spell over the entire work; twice in the *Christmas Oratio*; as well as in five cantatas (24, 135, 153, 159, and 161); and in a number of organ compositions.

The harmonization in *Lutheran Worship* (1982) was prepared by Wilhelm Quampen, a *nom de plume* of Paul G. Bunjes.

114 WHEN I SURVEY THE WONDROUS CROSS

Often called Watts's greatest hymn, this text first appeared in Book III of his *Hymns and Spiritual Songs* (1707). In the first edition Watts's second line read, "Where the young Prince of Glory dy'd," but he altered it in the second edition of 1709, probably because of criticism he solicited from friends, to the now-familiar line. Dearmer in *Songs of Praise Discussed* blames the change on "someone who had no feeling for poetry," noting that a return to the original would be desirable but well-nigh impossible due to familiarity and sentimental associations.

Watts also included an optional fourth stanza, which has been customarily omitted:

His dying Crimson, like a Robe,
Spreads o'er his Body on the Tree;
Then am I dead to all the Globe,
And all the Globe is dead to me.

The only other change in the *Lutheran Worship* text, as also in its predecessor hymnals, is the substitution of "tribute" for "present" in line 2 of the final stanza. Several anecdotes have cropped up concerning the practical application of this stanza. Haeussler describes the reaction of Father Ignatius at St. Edmund's Church, London: "Well, I'm surprised to hear you sing that. Do you know that altogether you put only fifteen shillings in the collection bag this morning?" The spirit of total consecration found in this hymn has given it top ranking in all denominations, sharing the position with "Rock of Ages" (*LW* 361), "Jesus, Lover of My Soul" (*LW* 508), and "All Hail the Power of Jesus' Name" (*LW* 272). And well it should be held in high esteem, for the cross, the symbol of Christ's atoning death, is also the most significant and eloquent symbol of the Christian faith!

ROCKINGHAM OLD. Edward Miller apparently adapted this tune from an anonymous one that appeared in Aaron Williams' (*LW* 12) *A Second Supplement to Psalmody in Miniature* (c. 1780), where it was set to Charles Wesley's (*LW* 15, et al.) "All Ye That Pass By" and appeared thus:

In a copy of that volume possessed by Miller, he had noted that this anonymous tune would make a good long meter (LM) tune. When, 10 years later, Miller published his *The Psalms of David for Use of Parish Churches* (1790), he included his adaptation—a long meter version—of that anonymous tune and called it ROCKINGHAM to honor his friend and patron, twice prime minister of Great Britain, the Marquis of Rockingham. In this volume his tune was set to several different texts and annotated "Part of the melody taken from a hymn tune."

According to Marilyn Stulken the above anonymous tune was unidentified until an article in the *Musical Times* (May 1909) identified it as TUNBRIDGE.

Robert Bridges (*LW* 460, 486) in his notes on the *Yattendon Hymnal* claims ROCKINGHAM to be derived from the tune BROMLEY, by Jeremiah Clarke, and adds this comment:

> It is easy to see how Dr. Miller came to write a popular tune, if he vulgarised the work of a man of genius; also why ROCKINGHAM has won the favour of musicians; because the force of Clarke's melodious invention supports the coarse fabric of Dr. M.'s garment. He certainly concocted a tune which any congregation can sing, and one which, alas! the average congregation is never tired of singing. His maudlin composition is still chosen by our church musicians to be sung to the most sacred words.

Erik Routley in the *Companion to Congregational Praise* notes:

> Those are the words of the late Poet Laureate, and although they exemplify admirably that astringently critical attitude which was one of the chief forces in the great musical revival which took place in our hymnody at the beginning of this century, we can now, having reaped the good fruit of the revival, judge their eminent author pedantic and extreme at this point. Nor may we regard his derivation of ROCKINGHAM from BROMLEY as more trustworthy than his opinion of it.

Known as COMMUNION in Scotland because of its association with Paraphrase 35 (Matt. 26:26–29), which is used as a Communion hymn, the tune is also called MAYHEW in Lowell Mason's collections. In *Lutheran Worship*, as well as in other hymnals, it is called ROCKINGHAM OLD to distinguish it from a later tune by Mason.

The tune was coupled to "When I Survey the Wondrous Cross" in William Mercer's (*LW* 492) *The Church Psalter and Hymnbook* (1854), if not earlier. Its inclusion in *Hymns Ancient and Modern* (1861) both stamped and gained widespread approval of this combination. Christians acquainted with *The Lutheran Hymnal* (1941) will have noticed that ROCHINGHAM OLD is the second tune for the text under discussion, the first being HAMBURG. The latter tune, however, is also provided with this text in *LW* 115.

The harmonization is from *The Worshipbook: Services and Hymns* (Westminster, 1972).

115 WHEN I SURVEY THE WONDROUS CROSS

For comments on the text see hymn 114.

HAMBURG. This tune was first used in 1824 at the Presbyterian Church in Savannah, Georgia, where the composer, Lowell Mason, worked as a bank clerk. It was included in the *Boston Handel and Haydn Society Collection of Church Music* (Boston, 1825), labeled as being derived from Gregorian chant. Mason later elaborated, "Arranged from Gregorian Tone I by L. Mason." The tune as it appeared in the *Boston Handel and Haydn Society Collection* (1828) is given below, with the text to which it was then set:

Sing to the Lord with joy - ful voice; Let ev - 'ry land his name a - dore;
Let earth, with one u - nit - ed voice, Re-sound his praise from shore to shore.

Mason's reference to "Gregorian Tone I" refers to the ancient, or Gregorian, psalm tones, flexible melodic formulas used for chanting the psalms, of which there are eight in number, one for each of the church modes (see essay: The Church Modes, p. 832). Resemblance of the above tune to Gregorian Tone I can be readily seen:

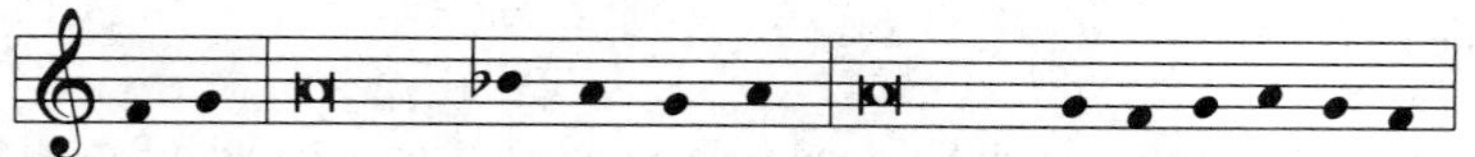

The harmonization of HAMBURG is from *The Lutheran Hymnal* (1941), slightly altered.

STRICKEN, SMITTEN, AND AFFLICTED 116

Both the content and popularity (it was in both the 1912 and 1941 Lutheran hymnals) of this Passion hymn by the fervent Irish evangelical Thomas Kelly prompted its inclusion in *Lutheran Worship*. It first appeared in his *Hymns on various passages of Scripture* (Dublin, 1804) and is here given in updated language.

O MEIN JESU, ICH MUSS STERBEN is the tune set to the text beginning with the same words, first appearing in *Geistliche Volkslieder* (Paderborn, 1850). Its inclusion in the third section of Friedrich Layriz's *Kern des deutschen Kirchengesangs* (Nördlingen, 1853) evidently gave it wide currency in the Missouri Synod (Zahn 6762).

The harmonization was provided by George Leonard, a *nom de plume* of Paul G. Bunjes.

SING, MY TONGUE, THE GLORIOUS BATTLE 117

Sing, my tongue, the glorious battle; Sing the ending of the fray. Now above the cross, the trophy, Sound the loud triumphant lay; Tell how Christ, the world's redeemer, As a victim won the day.	Pange, lingua, gloriosi praelium certaminis, et super crucis tropaeum dic triumphum nobilem, qualiter redemptor orbis immolatus vicerit.
Tell how, when at length the fullness Of the appointed time was come, He, the Word, was born of woman, Left for us his Father's home, Blazed the path of true obedience, Shone as light amidst the gloom.	quando venit ergo sacri plenitudo temporis, missus est ab arce Patris Natus, orbis conditor, atque ventre virginali carne factus prodiit.
Thus, with thirty years accomplished, He went forth from Nazareth, Destined, dedicated, willing, Did his work, and met his death; Like a lamb he humbly yielded On the cross his dying breath.	lustra sex qui jam peracta, tempus inplens corporis, se volente, natus ad hoc, passioni deditus, Agnus in crucis levatur immolandus stipite.
Faithful cross, true sign of triumph, Be for all the noblest tree; None in foliage, none in blossom, None in fruit your equal be; Symbol of the world's redemption, For your burden makes us free.	crux fidelis, inter omnes arbor una nobilis, nulla talem silva profert flore, fronde, germine, dulce lignum dulce clavo dulce pondus sustinens!
Unto God be praise and glory; To the Father and the Son,	gloria et honor Deo usquequo altissimo,

To the eternal Spirit honor Now and evermore be done; Praise and glory in the highest While the timeless ages run.	una Patri, Filioque, inclito Paraclito, cujus honor et potestas in aeterna saecula.

One of the finest of Latin hymns and perhaps one of the greatest hymns on the cross—although originally containing legendary material and a crude doctrine of atonement—this hymn by Fortunatus has traditionally been associated with "The Royal Banners Forward Go" (*LW* 103) and with the reception given the relics of the true cross, which Queen Rhadegunda had procured from the East, when these were brought to her new monastery at Poitiers in November 569. Originally consisting of 10 stanzas of unrhymed trochaic tetrameter verse, to which an 11th doxological stanza was added, in its liturgical use as an office hymn it was divided into two parts of five stanzas, each part concluded with the doxology. Part 1 was sung at Matins (after midnight) and part 2 at Lauds (sunrise), daily from Passion Sunday to Maundy Thursday. In some areas of Christendom it was sung after the Reproaches (*Improperia*) on Good Friday (see Good Friday I, rubric 14 in *Lutheran Worship: Agenda* [1984]).

The translation here used is by John Mason Neale in *Medieval Hymns and Sequences* (1851), slightly altered.

FORTUNATUS NEW, a strong rugged tune by Carl F. Schalk, well mated to the text, first appeared in *Spirit* (March 1967), a Lutheran youth magazine, then in *Worship Supplement* (1969).

118 WE SING THE PRAISE OF HIM WHO DIED

This hymn was first published in *Hymns by Thomas Kelly, not before Published* (Dublin, 1815), where the last two lines read:

'Tis all that sinners want below;
'Tis all that angels want above.

These lines were changed to the present form in the sixth edition (1826) of Kelly's *Hymns on Various Passages of Scripture* (Dublin, 1826).

Although, in the estimation of Benson (*The English Hymn*), most of Kelly's 765 hymns are rather commonplace, this is one of three hymns by him on the crucified and exalted Christ—the other two being "Look, Ye Saints the Sight Is Glorious" (*TLH* 222) and "The Head That Once Was Crowned with Thorns" (*TLH* 219)—that is a classic, a hymn that continues to be well known and sung with a joyous heart.

WINDHAM. First published in *The American Singing Book* (New Haven, 1785), the tune is attributed to Daniel Read and appeared in various collections with "Broad Is the Road That Leads to Death" by Isaac Watts (*LW* 53, et al.). In its earlier form it was printed in duple rhythm.

In *The Lutheran Hymnal* (1941) Kelly's text is set to O JESU CHRIST, WAHRES LICHT (*TLH* 178; *LW* 314), incorrectly labeled O JESU CHRIST, MEINS. WINDHAM, on the other hand, is therein coupled to "That Day of Wrath, That Dreadful Day" (*TLH* 612). Since the latter text and tune were seldom sung, WINDHAM may here be new to many people. Congregations should feel free to use either of these two laudable tunes with Kelly's text.

O DEAREST JESUS, WHAT LAW HAVE YOU BROKEN 119

O dearest Jesus, what law
    have you broken
That such sharp sentence
    should on you be spoken?
Of what great crime have you
    to make confession,
What dark transgression?
	Herzliebster Jesu, was hast du
	    verbrochen,
	Dass man ein solch scharf
	    Urteil hat gesprochen?
	Was ist die Schuld?
	    In was für Missetaten
	Bist du geraten?

They crown your head with thorns,
    they smite, they scourge you;
With cruel mockings to the cross
    they urge you;
They give you gall to drink,
    they still decry you;
They crucify you.
	Du wirst verspeit, geschlagen
	und verhöhnet,
	Gegeisselt und mit Dornen
	    scharf gekrönet,
	Mit Essig, als man dich
	    ans Kreuz gehenket,
	Wirst du getränket.

What is the source of all your
    mortal anguish?
It is my sins for which you, Lord,
    must languish;
Yes, all the wrath, the woe
    that you inherit,
This I do merit.
	Was ist die Ursach' aller
	    solcher Plagen?
	Ach, meine Sünden
	    haben dich geschlagen!
	Ich, ach Herr Jesu,
	    habe dies verschuldet,
	Was du erduldet.

How strange is this great paradox
    to ponder:
The shepherd dies for sheep who
    love to wander;
The master pays the debt
    his servants owe him,
Who would not know him.
	Wie wunderbarlich ist doch
	    diese Strafe!
	Der gute Hirte leidet
	    für die Schafe,
	Die Schuld bezahlt der Herre,
	    der Gerechte,
	Für seine Knechte.

The sinless Son of God must die
    in sadness;
The sinful child of man
    may live in gladness;
We forfeited our lives
	Der Fromme stirbt, so recht
	    und richtig wandelt;
	Der Böse lebt, so wider Gott
	    misshandelt;
	Der Mensch verwirkt den Tod

yet are acquitted;
God is committed!
O wondrous love, whose depth
no heart has sounded,
That brought you here, by foes
and thieves surrounded,
Conquer my heart, make love
its sole endeavor
Henceforth forever!

und ist entgangen,
Gott wird gefangen.
O grosse Lieb', o Lieb'
ohn' alle Masse,
Die dich gebracht auf diese
Marterstrasse!
Ich lebte mit der Welt
in Lust und Freuden,
Und du musst leiden

When, dearest Jesus, at your throne
in heaven
To me the crown of joy
at last is given,
Where sweetest hymns your saints
forever raise you,
I too shall praise you!

Wenn dort, Herr Jesu, wird vor
deinem Throne
Auf meinem Haupte stehn die
Ehrenkrone,
Da will ich dir, wenn alles wird
wohl klingen,
Lob und Dank singen.

This great hymn by Johann Heermann, originally in 15 stanzas, first appeared in his *Devoti Musica Cordis, Hauss-und Hertz-Musica*, published in Breslau in 1630 with the caption, "The cause of the bitter sufferings of Jesus Christ and consolation from his love and grace. From Augustine's *Meditations*, Chapter VII." Taking his cue from Martin Moller (1547–1606) of Görlitz, who published the *Meditationes sanctorum patrum* in two volumes (1584, 1591) and attributed the work to St. Augustine of Hippo (354–430), the great Latin church father, Heermann thought he was putting the words of the latter into rhyme. Actually, the *Meditationes* was a medieval compilation from various church fathers, including Augustine, Gregory the Great, and Anselm of Canterbury. It is more likely that Chapter VII, to which Heermann refers and on which he based this hymn text, was written by Anselm (1033–1109), archbishop of Canterbury.

The translation is an altered as well as updated form of that by Catherine Winkworth in her *Chorale Book for England* (1863).

HERZLIEBSTER JESU was composed by Johann Crüger for Heermann's text and first published in his *Newes vollkömliches Gesangbuch Augsburgische Confession* (Berlin, 1640), a hymnal that contains some of his earliest tunes, of which this simple, syllabic, rhythmically decisive tune, so typical of his work, is perhaps the most famous. It may not be completely original, for part of it is a direct quotation from the tune to Psalm 23 in the final edition of the Genevan Psalter of 1562 (Zahn 3199):

er mich wei=det, zum ſchö=nen fri=ſchen Waſ=ſer er mich lei = tet,
er=quickt mein Seel von ſei = nes Na=mens we = gen, ge = rad er
mich führt auf den rech = ten Ste = gen. (Lobwaſſer.)

The harmonization is by Paul G. Bunjes.

UPON THE CROSS EXTENDED 120

1 Upon the cross extended
See, world, your Lord suspended.
Your Savior yields his breath.
The Prince of Life from heaven
Himself has freely given
To shame and blows and bitter death.

O Welt, sieh hier dein Leben
Am Stamm des Kreuzes schweben,
Dein Heil sinkt in den Tod!
Der grosse Fürst der Ehren
Lässt willig sich beschweren
Mit Schlägen, Hohn und grossem Spott.

3 Who is it, Lord, that bruised you?
Who has so sore abused you
And caused you all your woe?
We all must make confession
Of sin and dire transgression
While you no ways of evil know.

Wer hat dich so geschlagen,
Mein Heil, und dich mit Plagen
So übel zugericht't?
Du bist ja nicht ein Sünder
Wie wir und unsre Kinder,
Von Übeltaten weisst du nicht.

5 Your soul in griefs unbounded,
Your head with thorns surrounded,
You died to ransom me.
The cross for me enduring,
The crown for me securing,
You healed my wounds and set me free.

Du setzest dich zum Bürgen,
Ja lässest dich gar würgen
Für mich und meine Schuld.
Mir lässest du dich krönen
Mit Dornen, die dich höhnen,
Und leidest alles mit Geduld.

7 Your cross I place before me;
Its saving pow'r restore me,
Sustain me in the test.
It will, when life is ending,
Be guiding and attending
My way to your eternal rest.

Ich will's vor Augen setzen,
Mich stets daran ergötzen,
Ich sei auch, wo ich sei.
Es soll mir sein ein Spiegel
Der Unschuld und ein Siegel
Der Lieb' und unverfälschten Treu'.

121 UPON THE CROSS EXTENDED

1 Upon the cross extended See, world, your Lord suspended. Your Savior yields his breath. The Prince of Life from heaven Himself has freely given To shame and blows and bitter death.	O Welt, sieh hier dein Leben Am Stamm des Kreuzes schweben, Dein Heil sinkt in den Tod! Der grosse Fürst der Ehren Lässt willig sich beschweren Mit Schlägen, Hohn und grossem Spott.
2 Come, see these things and ponder, Your soul will fill with wonder As blood streams from each pore. Through grief beyond all knowing From his great heart came flowing Sighs welling from its deepest core.	Tritt her und schau mit Fleisse: Sein Leib ist ganz mit Schweisse Des Blütes überfüllt; Aus seinem edlen Herzen Vor unerschöpften Schmerzen Ein Seufzer nach dem andern quillt.
4 I caused your grief and sighing By evils multiplying As countless as the sands. I caused the woes unnumbered With which your soul is cumbered, Your sorrows raised by wicked hands.	Ich, ich und meine Sünden, Die sich wie Körnlein finden Des Sandes an dem Meer, Die haben dir erreget Das Elend, das dich schläget, Und das betrübte Marterheer.
6 Your cords of love, my Savior, Bind me to you forever, I am no longer mine. To you I gladly tender All that my life can render And all I have to you resign.	Ich bin, mein Heil, verbunden All' Augenblick' und Stunden Dir überhoch und sehr. Was Leib und Seel' vermögen, Das soll ich billig legen Allzeit an deinen Dienst und Ehr'.

This "profound meditation on the Lord's Passion," as Polack calls it, originally in 16 stanzas, a cento of which is given here, first appeared in the third edition of Johann Crüger's *Praxis pietatis melica* (Berlin, 1648). It is to be noted that the hymn was undoubtedly written while Paul Gerhardt was studying at Wittenberg University, toward the end of the Thirty Years' War (1618–48), a time when the destructive and miserable consequences were much on his mind. Hence he calls the suffering world, of which he is a part, to the cross and to Christ's sufferings for the world's salvation. His preaching of repentance is not over against the world, but it is such in which he accuses also himself as having caused the Savior's sorrows and woes. Having begun his hymn as a song of dying, he concludes it on a joyous note of eternal rest in stanza 16, here omitted and reading as follows:

Your groaning and your sighing,
Your bitter tears and dying,
With which you were oppressed.
They shall, when life is ending,
Be guiding and attending
My way to your eternal rest.

The reader may recall J. S. Bach's use of two stanzas of this great hymn in his *St. Matthew Passion* and *St. John Passion*, namely, stanza three above and the original stanza five, here omitted and reading as follows:

'Tis I who should be smitten
My due should here be written,
Bound hand and foot in hell.
The fetters and the scourging,
The floods around you surging,
'Tis I who have deserved it well.

The translation in *Lutheran Worship* (1982) is an altered and updated form of that by John Kelly in his *Paul Gerhardt's Spiritual Songs* (London, 1867).

O WELT, SIEH HIER, the tune for *LW* 120, is ascribed to Heinrich Friese, 1703 (Zahn 2278), of whom little is known.

O WELT, ICH MUSS DICH LASSEN is a traditional German tune, dating perhaps as early as the 15th century, and first structured and harmonized by Heinrich Isaac in the Nürnberg physician and composer Georg Forster's *Ein Ausszug guter alter und newer teutscher Liedlein* (Nürnberg, 1539; see Zahn 2293a). There it was set to a song of praise and farewell to Innsbruck, Austria, "Innsbruck, ich muss dich lassen"; hence the tune is also called INNSBRUCK. In later hymnals as, for instance, the Eisleben *Gesangbuch* (1598), the tune was adapted and set to the hymn text, "O Welt, ich muss dich lassen," considered originally to have been a secular folk song, later turned into a Christian hymn, the authorship of which is uncertain. More as a prayer to be spoken for a Christian about to die than as a congregational hymn, it is today still included in the hymnals of the Lutheran territorial churches in Germany (see *EKG* 312).

Finally, the tune under discussion is most commonly associated with Paul Gerhardt's notable and popular evening, "Now Rest Beneath Night's Shadow" (*LW* 485).

Before leaving this lovely tune one cannot escape mentioning that J. S. Bach evidently was fond of it, for he used it frequently, exhausting its harmonic possibilities: four times in the *Choralgesänge*; in Cantatas 11, 12, and 97; and in both the *St. Matthew* and *St. John* Passions.

The settings of both O WELT, SIEH HIER and O WELT, ICH MUSS DICH LASSEN were prepared by Richard W. Gieseke for *Lutheran Worship* (1982).

122 O DARKEST WOE

O darkest woe!
Tears overflow!
What heavy grief we carry!
God the Father's only Son
In a grave lies buried.

Deep, deep the pain!
God's Son is slain,
The Lord, who came from heaven,
Who for us upon the cross
His dear life has given.

Our load of sin,
Our guilt within
Brought low him who is lying
In a stone-cold garden tomb,
Silent mid our sighing.

The Bridegroom dead!
The Lamb stained red,
His lifeblood freely flowing,
Wine poured out to cleanse our wound,
Health on us bestowing.

O Ground of faith,
Brought low in death!
Fair lips, your silence keeping.
Must not all throughout the world
Join in bitter weeping?

But how blest he
Eternally
Who here will rightly ponder
Why the Prince of Life has died,
Why God made this wonder!

O Jesus blest,
My help and rest,
My tears flow to entreat you:
Make me love you to the last
Till in heav'n I greet you.

O Traurigkeit,
O Herzeleid!
Ist das nicht zu beklagen?
Gott des Vaters einig Kind
Wird ins Grab getragen.

O grosse Not!
Gott selbst ist tot,
Am Kreuz ist er getstorben,
Hat dadurch das Himmelreich
Uns aus Lieb' erworben.

O Menschenkind,
Nur deine Sünd'
Hat dieses angerichtet,
Da du durch die Missetat
Warest ganz vernichtet.

Dein Bräutigam,
Das Gotteslamm,
Liegt hier mit Blut beflossen,
Welches er ganz mildiglich
Hat für dich vergossen.

O süsser Mund,
O Glaubensgrund,
Wie bist du doch zerschlagen!
Alles, was auf Erden lebt,
Muss dich ja beklagen.

O selig ist
Zu aller Frist,
Der dieses recht bedenket,
Wie der Herr der Herrlichkeit
Wird ins Grab versenket!

O Jesu, du
Mein' Hilf' und Ruh',
Ich bitte dich mit Tränen:
Hilf, dass ich mich bis ins Grab
Nach dir möge sehnen!

Among the many medieval customs connected with Christ's burial is one where a canopy is erected in a side chapel, surrounded with anywhere from six to 12 candles, thus typifying Christ's holy grave. On Good Friday evening a covered monstrans, containing the transubstantiated host, or a white veiled crucifix, is carried in festive procession into the grave to the singing of "O Traurigkeit, O Herzeleid," a hymn of seven stanzas contained in the Mainz and Würzburg hymnals of 1628, as also the setting contained in David Corner's large Roman Catholic hymnal of 1631. Although the Reformation did away with this ceremony, Lutherans observed Christ's Passion and burial liturgically in various ways. For one such observance Johann Rist, retaining the first stanza (here ascribed to the Jesuit Friedrich von Spee from Kaiserswerth, but more likely anonymous) from the Mainz and Würzburg hymnals, added seven more, which he published in *Erstes Zehen: Fest-und Passionsgesänge* of his *Himlische Lieder* (Lüneberg, 1641). In an accompanying note Rist stated: "The first stanza of this burial hymn, together with its devotional tune, came accidently into my hands. While I could not share the thoughts of the other stanzas, I composed seven more." Stanza 6, here omitted, reads:

O lieblich Bild,
Schön zart und mild,
Du Söhnlein der Jungfrauen,
Niemand kann dein heisses Blut
Sonder Reu' anschauen.

The translation of stanzas 1–6 was done for *Lutheran Worship* by F. Samuel Janzow. Stanza 7 is an updated form of that which appeared in *The Lutheran Hymnal* (1941), originally the work of Catherine Winkworth in her *Chorale Book for England* (1863).

O TRAURIGKEIT is the expressive tune to which the hymn originally appeared in the Mainz and Würzburg hymnals (Zahn 1915).

The harmonization is by Paul G. Bunjes.

123 CHRIST JESUS LAY IN DEATH'S STRONG BANDS

Christ Jesus lay in death's strong bands
For our offenses given;
But now at God's right hand he stands
And brings us life from heaven.
Therefore let us joyful be
And sing to God right thankfully
Loud songs of alleluia!
Alleluia!

It was a strange and dreadful strife
When life and death contended;
The victory remained with life,
The reign of death was ended.
Holy Scripture plainly says
That death is swallowed up by death,
Its sting is lost forever.
Alleluia!

Here the true Paschal Lamb we see,
Whom God so freely gave us;
He died on the accursed tree—
So strong his love—to save us.
See, his blood now marks our door;
Faith points to it; death passes o'er,
And Satan cannot harm us.
Alleluia!

So let us keep the festival
To which the Lord invites us;
Christ is himself the joy of all,
Sun that warms and lights us.
Now his grace to us imparts
Eternal sunshine to our hearts;
The night of sin is ended.
Alleluia!

Then let us feast this Easter Day
On Christ, the bread of heaven;
The Word of grace has purged away
The old and evil leaven
Christ alone our souls will feed;
He is our meat and drink indeed;
Alleluia!

Christ lag in Todesbanden,
Für unsre Sünd' gegeben,
Der ist wieder erstanden
Und hat uns bracht das Leben.
Des wir sollen fröhlich sein,
Gott loben und dankbar sein
Und singen: Halleluja!
Halleluja!

Es war ein wunderlicher Krieg,
Da Tod und Leben rungen;
Das Leben, das behielt den Sieg,
Es hat den Tod verschlungen.
Die Schrift hat verkündet das,
Wie ein Tod den andern frass,
Ein Spott der Tod ist worden.
Halleluja!

Hier ist das rechte Osterlamm,
Davon Gott hat geboten,
Das ist dort an des Kreuzes Stamm
In heisser Lieb' gebraten;
Des Blut zeichnet unsre Tür,
Das hält der Glaub' dem Tod für,
Der Würger kann nicht würgen.
Halleluja!

So feiern wir dies hohe Fest
Mit Herzensfreud' und Wonne,
Das uns der Herre scheinen lässt;
Er ist selber die Sonne,
Der durch seiner Gnaden Glanz
Erleucht't unsre Herzen ganz,
Der Sünd' Nacht ist vergangen.
Halleluja!

Wir essen nun und leben wohl
In rechten Osterfladen;
Der alte Sauerteig nicht soll
Sein bei dem Wort der Gnaden.
Christus will die Koste sein
Und speisen die Seel' allein;
Halleluja!

Luther's superscription, or title, "The Hymn of Praise 'Christ Is Arisen' Improved," points to the existence of a very old popular German Easter folk song of perhaps the 12th century, namely, the *leise*, "Christ ist erstanden" (see *LW* 124). The term *improved* has reference to the tune, not to the text. However, it should be stated that the text, too, is quite independent of its precursor. Notice the reflection of the Old Standard Epistle for Easter Day (1 Cor. 5:6–8) in stanza 5.

This folk song, in turn, has its roots in the mighty sequence "Victimae paschali laudes" by Wipo of Burgundy (d. 1048), the Easter sequence in the Roman rite. In early usage the choir sang the sequence in Latin, the congregation sang the folk song immediately thereafter.

Luther's strong love for this hymn with its comforting theology is evidenced by his frequent reference to it. On one occasion he said, "In time one becomes tired of other hymns, but 'Christ ist erstanden' one can sing year after year." The translation is that of Richard Massey, slightly altered, as contained in his *Martin Luther's Spiritual Songs* (1854).

CHRIST LAG IN TODESBANDEN. Originally two versions of this tune, a reconstruction of the Dorian CHRIST IST ERSTANDEN (*LW* 124), appeared, one in the Erfurt *Enchiridia*, the other as the *cantus firmus* in Johann Walter's *Geistliche gesangk Buchleyn*, both in 1524. The tune here used is almost identical to Walter's; it is the one preferred by the later Wittenberg and Strassburg hymnals.

The harmonization is by Richard W. Gieseke.

CHRIST IS ARISEN 124

Christ is arisen From the grave's dark prison. So let our song exulting rise: Christ with comfort lights our eyes. Alleluia!	Christ ist erstanden Von der Marter alle; Des soll'n wir alle froh sein, Christ will unser Trost sein. Kyrieleis!
All our hopes were ended Had Jesus not ascended From the grave triumphantly Our never-ending life to be. Alleluia!	Wär' er nicht erstanden, So wär' die Welt vergangen; Seit dass er erstanden ist, So lob'n wir den Herrn Jesum Christ. Kyrieleis!
Alleluia, alleluia, alleluia! So let our song exulting rise: Christ, our comfort, fills the skies. Alleluia!	Halleluja! Halleluja! Halleluja! Des soll'n wir alle froh sein, Christ will unser Trost sein. Kyrieleis!

Partly for utilitarian reasons, but more reasonably due to the natural desire for creativity, there arose in the Roman liturgy of the ninth to 13th centuries textual additions to the authorized liturgical texts in what are called tropes, and as an activity called troping. Tropes ranged from a few amplifying words interpolated between "Kyrie eleison" (e.g.,"Kyrie—*fons bonitatis*—Eleison," called farced Kyrie) to more lengthy explanatory sentences and even entire poems. This practice represented an important development in the history of the chorale, for the Kyrie Eleison, Christe Eleison, originally derived from the Eastern Church, were sung or shouted by German Christians on all possible occasions—processions, pilgrimages, burials, and in some minor liturgical services. The inserted texts, underlaid to the single notes of a Gregorian melisma (a florid grouping of notes) gradually developed into hymn-like stanzas. At times the Kyrie Eleison might serve as a refrain to the text; at other times the text might be prefaced with Kyrie and concluded with Eleison (cf. *LW* 209). These words were often abbreviated into *Kyrieleis*, *Kyrieles*, *Kyrieeleis*, and even *Kerleis*. These vernacular songs, which became so popular in German, came to be called *leisen* (singular: *leise*), or *kirleisen*, and they exhibit the German congregational hymn in its earliest form, hence they are referred to as pre-Reformation chorales.

The anonymous Easter hymn "Christ is arisen" ("Christ ist erstanden")—Wackernagel gives four versions extant in the 12th century from which numerous variations ensued—is one of the most famous of such hymns (see *LW* 137), a hymn, based on the sequence "Victimae paschali laudes," dear to the heart of Luther. Notice that the *Kyrieleis* in the original German text has been supplanted with alleluia, an acclamation of Easter joy.

The translation is by F. Samuel Janzow.

CHRIST IST ERSTANDEN is based on the Gregorian, or plainsong, tune for the Latin Easter sequence, "Victimae paschali laudes," ascribed to Wipo of Burgandy (d. 1048).

The sequence is the oldest and the more important type of the trope briefly discussed above. As early as perhaps the ninth century it became customary to sing the Alleluia of the Gradual of the Roman Mass to a florid, or ornate, chant, with the final vowel extended into a very elaborate flourish of notes (*jubilus*). According to his own report, Notker Balbulus (d. 912), a German monk at the famous monastery in St. Gall, first conceived the idea of providing appropriate and suitable texts to these long vocalizations (recent research to the contrary), thus constructing a brief form of rhythmic prose hymn. Others followed Notker's example, and before long these creations—texts set to music in a rather strict syllabic style—called sequences (from the Latin *sequi*, to follow; the sequence immediately follows the Alleluia of the Gradual, replacing its verse), were, with papal authority, given honored place in the ritual at festival and solemn occasions. Later French poets proceeded to write sequences in rhymed verse. What now distinguishes the sequence from other Latin hymns (office hymns) is that the sequence is admitted as a liturgical piece in the Mass on certain festival days. Gradually the number of sequences and their use increased to the point (see the extensive listing in Julian, *A Dictionary of Hymnology*) that in the reforms of the liturgy pursuant to the directions of the Council of Trent (1545–63), only five were retained and admitted in the Mass:

Victimae paschali laudes	Easter Sunday
Veni Sancte Spiritus	Pentecost
Lauda Sion	Corpus Christi
Dies Irae	Mass for the Dead
Stabat Mater Dolorosa (added in 1727)	Good Friday

To return to the tune CHRIST IST ERSTANDEN, the form used here is from Joseph Klug's *Geistliche Lieder* (1533). The harmonization was prepared by Paul G. Bunjes.

HAIL THEE, FESTIVAL DAY 125

Perhaps shortly before the death of Bishop Felix of Nantes, France, about 582, Venantius Honorius Fortunatus wrote a long 110–line poem about the spring season, the Resurrection, the Baptism in elegiac couplets beginning "Tempora florigero rutilant distincta sereno," which he dedicated to Bishop Felix, copy of which is extant as early as the *Echtenach Gradual* (c. 1000). During the Middle Ages numerous versions of it were made for various festivals, some containing no more of Fortunatus than the first line of the 20th couplet: "Salve, festa dies, toto venerabilis aevo." The more authentic and lasting versions were those for Easter, Ascension (*LW* 148), and Pentecost (*LW* 159). This version of the Easter hymn, based largely on that in *Songs of Praise* (1931), was prepared by the Inter-Lutheran Commission on Worship for inclusion in *Lutheran Book of Worship* (1978).

Whereas some hymnals combine various festivals into a single processional hymn with appropriate lines for the specific observance of the day (*Songs of Praise* 389; *LBW* 142), the Commission on Worship, when preparing *Lutheran Worship* (1982), to avoid confusion on the part of the singing congregation as well as to encourage the more frequent selection of this hymn on the part of pastors, chose to separate the observances into three hymn categories: Easter (*LW* 125); Ascension (*LW* 148); and Pentecost (*LW* 159).

It might not be taken amiss to remind planners of corporate worship that processional hymns such as these, or parts of them, can be used as ordinary hymns, just as some ordinary hymns can be used effectively as processionals.

SALVE FESTA DIES is a broad, expansive, festive tune by Ralph Vaughan Williams from *The English Hymnal* (1916) that, once learned by congregations, will be a joy to sing. The harmonization is also the work of Ralph Vaughan Williams.

AT THE LAMB'S HIGH FEAST WE SING 126

At the Lamb's high feast we sing
Praise to our victorious king,
Who has washed us in the tide
Flowing from his pierced side.
Alleluia!

Ad regias Agni dapes
Stolis amicti candidis
Post transitum maris rubri
Christo canamus principi;

Praise we him, whose love divine
Gives his sacred blood for wine,
Gives his body for the feast—
Christ the victim, Christ the priest.
Alleluia!

Divina cuius caritas
Sacrum propinat sanguinem,
Almique membra corporis
Amor sacerdos immolat.

Where the paschal blood is poured,
Death's dread angel sheathes the sword;
Israel's hosts triumphant go
Through the wave that drowns the foe.
Alleluia!

Sparsum cruorem postibus
Vastator horret angelus,
Fugitque divisum mare,
Merguntur hostes fluctibus.

Praise we Christ, whose blood was shed,
Paschal victim, paschal bread;
With sincerity and love
Eat we manna from above.
Alleluia!

Iam pascha nostrum Christus est,
Paschalis idem victima,
Et pura puris mentibus
Sinceritatis azyma.

Mighty Victim from the sky,
Hell's fierce pow'rs beneath you lie;
You have conquered in the fight,
You have brought us life and light.
Alleluia!

O vera caeli victima,
Subjecta cui sunt tartara,
Soluta mortis vincula,
Recepta vitae praemia.

Now no more can death appall,
Now no more the grave enthrall;
You have opened paradise,
And your saints in you shall rise.
Alleluia!

Victor subactis inferis
Tropaea Christus explicat,
Caeloque aperto subditum
Regem tenebrarum trahit.

Easter triumph, Easter joy!
This alone can sin destroy;
From sin's pow'r, Lord, set us free,
Newborn souls in you to be.
Alleluia!

Ut sis perenne mentibus
Paschale, Iesu, gaudium,
A morte dira criminum
Vitae renatos libera.

Father, who the crown shall give,
Savior, by whose death we live,
Spirit, guide through all our days:
Three in One, your name we praise.
Alleluia!

Gloria tibi, Domine,
qui surrexisti a mortuis,
cum Patre et sancto Spiritu
in sempiterna saecula.

The original Latin text beginning with "Ad coenam Agni providi" is of uncertain origin, dating anywhere from the sixth to the ninth centuries. It was used in the Ambrosian and Mozarabic rites as well as in the Latin cycle in addition to appearing in the Roman and several English breviaries. Maurice Frost notes: "The hymn abounds in references to the Paschal services, especially those of Easter Even, when the catechumens, clothed in white, were first baptized and then confirmed, and so went to their first communion on Easter morning." Another feature of these services was the commemoration of the Israelites' deliverance from the Egyptian bondage with its passage through the Red Sea and journey to the Promised Land. A vestige of this is noticeable in stanza 3.

The influence of humanism in the 16th and 17th centuries prompted the revision of many of the early Latin hymns. Thus, at the instigation of Pope Urban VIII, this hymn fell victim to this procedure for its inclusion in his *Breviary* (1632). "At the Lamb's High Feast We Sing" is more specifically based on this revised Latin version given above, beginning with "Ad regias Agni dapes." The English translation by Robert Campbell, here in updated form, was originally published in his *Hymns and Anthems for use in the Holy Services of the Church within the United Diocese of St. Andrew's,*

Dunkeld, and Dunblane (1850). In the process of updating Campbell's translation, the final doxological stanza has undergone considerable alteration.

The statement in stanza 2, "Gives his sacred blood for wine, gives his body for the feast," has evoked some concern with respect to the Lutheran view of the real presence of Christ in the Lord's Supper. In considering this matter it is first of all important to realize that this is essentially an Easter hymn, a feast-like or festival celebrating of Christ's triumphant resurrection after defeating sin, death, and hell for us by his sacrificing himself as the Paschal Lamb. The first four stanzas set the tone of joy and celebration over the great victory of Christ by establishing an analogy between the "high feast" (faith's celebration of Easter) and the annual joyous passover feast of the Israelites with its wine, song, and its eating of the passover lamb in celebration of the first Passover and Israel's deliverance. The high feast of Easter is the New Testament counterpart to Israel's annual Passover feast.

In response to several inquiries, F. Samuel Janzow, one of the text editors of the *Lutheran Worship*, a member of the then Commission on Worship, has rightly stated:

> The Easter joy of faith's feeding upon Christ and his sin-and-death-and-hell-conquering crucifixion and resurrection is poetically pictured [in this hymn] as a feast at which the blood of the Lamb is the wine which faith drinks, and the Lamb's flesh, or body, is the food upon which it feeds during this victory banquet.

Admittedly the phrases "sacred blood for wine" and "body for the feast" are most unusual but highly appropriate within their poetical context. They cannot possibly refer to the Lord's Supper; in terms of the doctrine of the Sacrament, they make no sense. But they beautifully fit the celebratory and feasting imagery introduced by the hymn's references to Israel's Passover.

A Good Friday and Easter faith that rejoices in the sacrificial death and the triumphant resurrection of Christ and their meaning for our eternal salvation, feasting upon Christ and his Gospel as it sings this wonderful hymn, is eating the flesh and drinking the blood of the Son of Man, who was the Lamb of God; and this faith is doing so in the sense of John 6. The Christian's heart is gladdened as with wine; his soul is sustained as with bread. Christ crucified and risen for him is his food and drink; for him, Christ is the bread and the water, the feast and the wine of life.

SONNE DER GERECHTIGKEIT. This buoyant tune, originally a 15th-century folk song to the text "Der reich Mann war geritten aus," was included in the *Kirchengeseng* (Prague, 1566) of the Bohemian Brethren, edited by Michael Tham, Johannes Geletzky, and Petrus Herbert. In reality this hymn book constituted the third edition of Johann Horn's hymnal of 1544, printed in Nürnberg.

"At the Lamb's High Feast We Sing" has been sung to various tunes. This happy union of text and tune was suggested by Edward W. Klammer for inclusion in *Worship Supplement* (1969). At that time Klammer was manager of the Music Department of

Concordia Publishing House and a member of the Hymn Committee of the Commission on Worship of The Lutheran Church—Missouri Synod.

The harmonization was originally prepared by Jan O. Bender for *Worship Supplement* (1969).

127 JESUS CHRIST IS RISEN TODAY

Jesus Christ is ris'n today, Alleluia!
Our triumphant holy day, Alleluia!
Who did once upon the cross, Alleluia!
Suffer to redeem our loss. Alleluia!

Hymns of praise then let us sing, Alleluia!
Unto Christ, our heav'nly king, Alleluia!
Who endured the cross and grave, Alleluia!
Sinners to redeem and save. Alleluia!

But the pains which he endured, Alleluia!
Our salvation have procured; Alleluia!
Now above the sky he's king, Alleluia!
Where the angels ever sing, Alleluia!

Sing we to our God above, Alleluia!
Praise eternal as his love; Alleluia!
Praise him, all you heav'nly host, Alleluia!
Father, Son and Holy Ghost. Alleluia!

Surrexit Christus hodie
Humano pro solamine.
Mortem qui passus pridie
Miserrimo pro homine.

Mullieres ad tumulum
Dona ferunt aromatum,
Album cernentes angelum
Anuntiantes gaudium.

Mulieres, o tremulae,
In Galilaeam pergite,
Discipulis hoc dicite,
Quod surrexit rex gloriae.

Ubique praecedet suos,
Quos dilexit, discipulos.
Sit benedictus hodie,
Qui nos redemit sanguine.

Ergo cum dulci melodo
Benedicamus Domino.
Laudetur sancta trinitas,
Deo dicamus gratias.

This triumphant Easter hymn is based on an anonymous Latin text, "Surrexit Christus hodie," the older, according to Bäumker (I, pp. 516–17), of several German manuscripts of the 14th century, "Erstanden ist der Heilig Christ." The latter appears to have been the chief basis of the English translation that appeared in *Lyra Davidica, or a Collection of Divine Songs and Hymns, partly new composed, partly translated from German and Latin Hymns: and set to easy and pleasant tunes* (London, 1708), published by John Walsh, a well-known music printer. Containing 25 tunes and 31 hymns, the compiler or editor of which is unknown, this little volume is a rare book, the copy in the British Museum being the only one known to exist. In the preface of this book the compiler says that the object of the book has been to introduce "a little freer air than the grave movement of the Psalm-tunes, as being both reasonable and acceptable." The tune and text appear therein as follows:

Jesus Christ is risen today, Halle-hale-lujah.
Our triumphant Holyday
Who so lately on the Cross
Suffer'd to redeem our loss.

Haste ye females from your fright
Take to Galilee your flight
To his sad disciples say
Jesus Christ is risen today.

In our Paschal joy and feast
Let the Lord of life be blest
Let the Holy Trine be prais'd
And thankful hearts to heaven be rais'd.

One can immediately see the affinity between the first stanza above and stanza 1 of the hymn under discussion. Interestingly, the reference to females in stanza 2 above may have represented common, dignified use in the 18th century England. Today, however, it is unquestionably out of place, militating at least against one qualification of a good hymn, namely, liturgical propriety. Fortunately when the now current form of the hymn first appeared in the second edition of John Arnold's *The Compleat Psalmodist* (London, 1749), the reference was given a more felicitous recast. It is from this book that the present stanzas 1 to 3 are derived. The thrilling doxological stanza 4, especially so when trumpets and other instruments are added, is the work of Charles Wesley as contained in his *Hymns and Sacred Poems* (1740), a stanza first attached to this hymn text and popularized in the supplement to Tate and Brady's New Version (c. 1816; see essay: Metrical Psalms p. 825).

EASTER HYMN (ANGLIA, EASTER MORN, THE RESURRECTION, WORGAN) represents the tune that appeared with this text in the *Lyra Davidica* published by John Walsh (see above) and again later in John Wesley's *Collection of Tunes . . . sung at the Foundry* (1742). Admittedly the tune has seen some revisions since its first appearance, but its basic shape is still that which appeared in Arnold's *The Compleat Psalmodist.* A delightfully joyous tune, written with an eye to the early jubilation on the final "a" of the Alleluia of the Gradual of the Roman Mass, it is no small wonder that congregations and choirs love to sing it.

The harmonization is from *The Worshipbook: Services and Hymns* (Westminster, 1972).

128 AWAKE, MY HEART, WITH GLADNESS

Awake, my heart, with gladness, See what today is done; Now, after gloom and sadness, Comes forth the glorious sun. My Savior there was laid Where our bed must be made When to the realms of light Our spirit wings its flight.	Auf, auf, mein Herz, mit Freuden, Nimm wahr, was heut' geschieht! Wie kommt nach grossem Leiden Nun ein so grosses Licht! Mein Heiland war gelegt Da, wo man uns hinträgt, Wenn von uns unser Geist Gen Himmel ist gereist.
The foe in triumph shouted When Christ lay in the tomb; But lo, he now is routed, His boast is turned to gloom. For Christ again is free; In glorious victory He who is strong to save Has triumphed o'er the grave.	Er war in Grab gesenket, Der Feind trieb gross Geschrei. Eh' er's vermeint und denket Ist Christus wieder frei Und ruft: Victoria! Schwingt fröhlich hier und da Sein Fähnlein als ein Held, Der Feld und Mut behält.
This is a sight that gladdens— What peace it does impart! Now nothing ever saddens The joy within my heart. No gloom shall ever shake, No foe shall ever take The hope which God's own Son In love for me has won.	Das ist mir anzuschauen Ein rechtes Freudenspiel; Nun soll mir nicht mehr grauen Vor allem, was mir will Entnehmen meinen Mut Zusamt dem edlen Gut, So mir durch Jesum Christ Aus Lieb' erworben ist.
Now hell, its prince, the devil, Of all their pow'r are shorn; Now I am safe from evil, And sin I laugh to scorn. Grim death with all its might Cannot my soul affright; It is a pow'rless form, Howe'er it rave and storm.	Die Höll' und ihre Rotten, Die krümmen mir kein Haar; Der Sünden kann ich spotten, Bleib' allzeit ohn' Gefahr; Der Tod mit seiner Macht Wird schlecht bei mir geacht't; Er bleibt ein totes Bild, Und wär er noch so wild.
Now I will cling forever To Christ, my Savior true; My Lord will leave me never, Whate'er he passes through. He rends death's iron chain; He breaks through sin and pain; He shatters hell's grim thrall; I follow him through all.	Ich hang' und bleib' auch hangen An Christo als ein Glied; Wo mein Haupt durch ist gangen, Da nimmt er mich auch mit. Er reisset durch den Tod, Durch Welt, durch Sünd' und Not, Er reisset durch die Höll', Ich bin stets sein Gesell.

He brings me to the portal That leads to bliss untold, Whereon this rhyme immortal Is found in script of gold: "Who there my cross has shared Finds here a crown prepared; Who there with me has died Shall here be glorified."	Er bringt mich an die Pforten, Die in den Himmel führt, Daran mit güldnen Worten Der Reim gelesen wird: Wer dort wird mit verhöhnt, Wird hier auch mit gekrönt; Wer dort mit sterben geht, Wird hier auch mit erhöht.

One looks in vain for hymns of the 16th century that address the individual heart or that begin with a rousing or cheering "Auf, mein Herz" ("Awake, my heart"). Admittedly some hymns of the Reformation begin with the more full, or broad, "Wach auf" or "Wachet auf," as for example, Philipp Nicolai's "Wake, Awake, for Night Is Flying" (*LW* 177). Credit must be given Martin Opitz (1597–1639), poet and metrical reformer, for introducing such expressions into the language of hymnody. As a result, a goodly number of hymns of the 17th century begin with "Auf, auf, mein Herz," "Auf, auf, mein Geist" ("Awake, my spirit"), or "Auf, auf, mein Seel" ("Awake, my soul").

Despite the personal aspect of this great Easter hymn by Paul Gerhardt, the hymn cannot help but move and arouse the congregation to express its joy in the resurrection of Jesus Christ, the keynote of which is unquestionably victory—the victory of which Micah foretold: "Your hand will be lifted up in triumph over your enemies, and all your foes will be destroyed" (Micah 5:9); the victory of which the psalmist speaks: "Shouts of joy and victory resound in the tents of the righteous" (Ps. 118:15); the victory that St. Paul boldly and joyfully proclaims: "Death has been swallowed up in victory" (1 Cor. 15:54b) and for which he joyously asserts: "But thanks be to God! He gives us the victory through our Lord Jesus Christ" (1 Cor. 15:57).

This hymn, originally in nine stanzas, first appeared in Johann Crüger's *Praxis pietatis melica* (1648). The translation by John Kelly appeared in his *Paul Gerhardt's Spiritual Songs* (1867) and was included, in altered form, in *The Lutheran Hymnal* (1941). From there, in updated form, it made its way into *Lutheran Book of Worship* (1978) and in turn was taken over by *Lutheran Worship* (1982).

AUF, AUF, MEIN HERZ. This buoyant tune was composed by Johann Crüger for Gerhardt's text, and the union appeared in the third edition of *Praxis pietatis melica* (1648). It is a tune made famous, without alteration, by J. S. Bach (*LW* 89).

The setting is from *The Lutheran Hymnal* (1941), slightly altered.

GOOD CHRISTIAN FRIENDS, REJOICE AND SING 129

This joyous text was written by Cyrill A. Alington, headmaster of Eton, specifically for the tune here used and for inclusion in *Songs of Praise* (London, 1931), for which Percy Dearmer (*LW* 175, et. al.) served as text editor and Ralph Vaughan Williams and Martin

Shaw as music editors. The combination soon became popular in England, and deservedly so. It became known in American Lutheranism by its inclusion in the *Worship Supplement* (1969) and in the *Service Book and Hymnal* (1958).

The text has been slightly altered in the process of updating, as well as revised with the change of the opening appellation "Good Christian men" to "Good Christian friends."

GELOBT SEI GOTT, also known as VULPIUS, is the excellent tune that was included in Melchior Vulpius' celebrated *Ein schön geistlich Gesangbuch* (Jena, 1609), where it was set to "Gelobt sei Gott im höchsten Thron" (Zahn 283), a hymn of 20 stanzas by Michael Weisse (*LW* 18). Vulpius composed a triple Alleluia as substitute for the single Alleluia of the Weisse text. This shout of joy, which in the threefold Alleluia amounts to sort of a holy laughter, is hardly outdone by any other Easter tune.

The harmonization, from *Worship Supplement* (1969), is by Richard W. Hillert.

130 O SONS AND DAUGHTERS OF THE KING

Alleluia, alleluia, alleluia!

O sons and daughters of the King, Whom heav'nly hosts in glory sing, Today the grave has lost its sting! Alleluia!	O filii et filiae, Rex caelestis, Rex gloriae, Morte revixit hodie. Alleluia!
That Easter morn, at break of day, The faithful women went their way To seek the tomb where Jesus lay. Alleluia!	Et Maria Magdalene Et Iacobi et Salome Venerunt corpus ungere. Alleluia!
An angel clad in white they see, Who sits and speaks unto the three, Your Lord will go to Galilee." Alleluia!	In albis sedens angelus Praedixit mulieribus, "In Galilaea est Dominus." Alleluia!
That night the apostles met in fear; Among them came their master dear And said, "My peace be with you here." Alleluia!	Discipulis adstantibus In medio stetit Christus, Dicens, "Pax vobis omnibus." Alleluia!
When Thomas first the tidings heard That they had seen the risen Lord, He doubted the disciples' word. Alleluia!	Postquam audivit Didymus Quia surrexerat Iesus, Remansit fide dubius. Alleluia!
My pierced side, O Thomas, see, And look upon my hands, my feet; Not faithless but believing be." Alleluia!	"Vide, Thomas, vide latus, Vide pedes, vide manus; Noli esse incredulus." Alleluia!

No longer Thomas then denied;
He saw the feet, the hands, the side;
You are my Lord and God!" he cried.
Alleluia!

Quando Thomas vidit Christum,
Pedes, latus suum, manus,
Dixit, "Tu es Deus meus."
Alleluia!

How blest are they who have not seen
And yet whose faith has constant been,
For they eternal life shall win.
Alleluia!

Beati, qui non viderunt
Et firmiter crediderunt;
Vitam aeternam habebunt.
Alleluia!

On this most holy day of days
Be laud and jubilee and praise:
To God your hearts and voices raise.
Alleluia!

In hoc festo sanctissimo
Sit laus et iubilatio:
Benedicamus Domino.
Alleluia!

The authorship of the original joyous, nine-stanza Latin poem is attributed to the Franciscan friar Jean Tisserand (d. 1494). Called "L'aleluya du jour des Pasques," it is contained both in an untitled booklet, printed between 1518 and 1536, now in the *Bibliotheque Nationale*, Paris, and in *L'Office de la Semaine Sainte* (Paris, 1674), with the caption "Joyous chant for the time of Easter." This folklike carol was popularly sung in many French dioceses on the evening of Easter Day. Bäumker gives a German translation of 1671 together with the tune that appears in the Jesuit book, Nordstein's *Führer zur Seligkeit*, mentioning the text to be from the Latin "O filii et filiae" (I, No. 292, p. 569).

Although there exists a number of translations, the translation by John Mason Neale in his *Medieval Hymns and Sequences* (1851) and with changes in the *The Hymnal Noted* (1854) is the most frequently used today. It is here given in altered and updated form as prepared by the Inter-Lutheran Commission on Worship for inclusion in *Lutheran Book of Worship* (1978).

O FILII ET FILIAE is undoubtedly an adaptation of the traditional tune for these words. Probably of French origin, its earliest known printed form with Latin text is in a Paris collection entitled *Airs sur les hymnes sacrez, odes et noels* (1623). Varied forms of the tune as well as harmonizations are contained in present-day hymnals. In America the first printing of "this happy dance of the Spirit" was in Philadelphia in John Aiken's *A Compilation of the Litanies and Vespers, Hymns and Anthems as they are sung in the Catholic church* (1787). The Solesmes version with 12 stanzas appears in the *Liber Usualis*, pages 1875–76. The form of the tune in *Lutheran Worship* appears in Samuel Webbe's *Collection of Motets or Antiphons* (c. 1840, Vincent Novello edition).

The harmonization is that prepared by Richard W. Hillert for *Worship Supplement* (1969).

131 NOW ALL THE VAULT OF HEAVEN RESOUNDS

Paul Zeller Strodach penned these words for the tune LASST UNS ERFREUEN, and submitted them to the hymnal committee for the *Service Book and Hymnal* (1958), of which he was a member. The language was updated somewhat for *Lutheran Book of Worship* (1978).

LASST UNS ERFREUEN first appeared in *Ausserlesene, Catholische, Geistliche Kirchengesäng* (Cologne, 1623), coupled to the Easter hymn "Lasst uns erfreuen herzlich sehr." Thus the tune is sometimes called COLOGNE or EASTER SONG, also EASTER ALLELUIA (cf. Bäumker I, No. 280). The melody is perhaps based on an earlier folk song tune; it bears some resemblance, especially the first phrase, to the tune for Psalm 36 in *Aulcuns Pseaumes et Cantiques mys en Chant* (Strassburg, 1539). Placement of the alleluias resulted in two forms of the tune. Although both text and tune were popular with German-speaking Roman Catholics in Europe in the 17th century, the hymn was not in use among Protestants. Its inclusion in *The English Hymnal* (1906) as the tune for "Ye Watchers and Ye Holy Ones" (*LW* 308), by Athelstan Riley, gradually brought it into prominence and quickly increased its popularity. There the eminent composer Ralph Vaughan Williams barred the tune in triple meter throughout and, together with his harmonization, created a form of the music that is nothing short of classic. It is, as Percy Dearmer states:

> This now-famous tune is built altogether on a single musical unit of four notes, by imitations and inversions. It is a remarkable example not only of economy of structure but of the accumulating force of repetition—when the repeated phrase, as here, is strong enough to bear it. (*Songs of Praise Discussed*)

This tune, so expressive of "natural" effects, lends itself well to variety, especially antiphonal treatment, for example, the choir singing the alleluias, the stanzas distributed among men's and women's voices. The tune should be sung with festal and rhythmic verve. Notice that the second-to-last note is held for three beats (in contrast to two in *The Lutheran Hymnal*), following the practice of Ralph Vaughan Williams.

The harmonization by Ralph Vaughan Williams is from *The English Hymnal* (1906).

MAKE SONGS OF JOY 132

Make songs of joy to Christ, our head; Alleluia!
He lives again who once was dead! Alleluia!

Our life was purchased by his loss; Alleluia!
He died our death upon the cross. Alleluia!

O death, where is your deadly sting? Alleluia!
Assumed by our triumphant King! Alleluia!

And where your victory, O grave, Alleluia!
When one like Christ has come to save? Alleluia!

Behold, the tyrants, one and all, Alleluia!
Before our mighty Savior fall! Alleluia!

For this be praised the Son who rose, Alleluia!
The Father, and the Holy Ghost! Alleluia!

Zpivejmez vsickni vesele: Hallelujah,
Ke cti Krista Spasitele: Hallelujah.

Kteryz nás k sobe vykoupil: Hallelujah,
Kdyz na krizi smrt podstoupil: Hallelujah.

Smrti, kams osten podela? Hallelujah,
Smrt Kristova jej odjala: Hallelujah.

Kdez jest vitezstvi tve, paklo? Hallelujah,
Co muzes. bys se i vzteklo? Hallelujah.

Ty vsecky, hle, ukrutniky: Hallelujah,
Premohl Pán nás veliky: Hallelujah.

Sláva Otci nebeskému: Hallelujah,
Synu i Duchu Svatému: Hallelujah.

The hymn by Jire Tranovsky, originally in 12 stanzas, appeared in his *Cithara Sanctorum*, popularly known as the "Tranoscius." This translation/paraphrase was prepared by Jaroslav J. Vajda for inclusion in *Lutheran Book of Worship* (1978). It was done, he says, "in an effort to salvage the tune and some of the thoughts of the original text, especially the reference to 'tyrants.' "

ZPIVEJMEZ VSICKNI VESELE was originally the tune for the Ascension hymn, "Ustoupil jest Kristus na nebe: Hallelujah."

The harmonization is from the Chorvat, *Velka Partitura* (1936).

THE DAY OF RESURRECTION 133

The day of resurrection!
Earth, tell it out abroad,
The passover of gladness,
The passover of God.
From death to life eternal,
From sin's dominion free,
Our Christ has brought us over
With hymns of victory.

Let hearts be purged of evil
That we may see aright
The Lord in rays eternal
Of resurrection light
And, list'ning to his accents,
May hear, so calm and plain,
His own "All hail!" and, hearing,
May raise the victor strain.

᾿Αναστάσεως ἡμέρα,
λαμπρυνθῶμεν λαοί.
Πάσχα Κυρίου, πάσχα.
᾿Εκ γὰρ θανάτου πρὸς ζωήν,
καὶ ἐκ γῆς πρὸς οὐρανόν,
Χριστὸς ὁ θεὸς
ἡμᾶς διεβίβασεν,
ἐπινίκιον ᾄδοντας.

Καθαρθῶμεν τὰς αἰσθήσεις,
καὶ ὀψόμεθα
τῷ ἀπροσίτῳ φωτὶ
τῆς ἀναστάσεως Χριστὸν
ἐξαστράπτοντα, καὶ
»Χαίρετε« φάσκοντος
τρανῶς ἀκουσόμεθα,
ἐπινίκιον ᾄδοντες.

Now let the heav'ns be joyful,
Let earth its song begin,
Let all the world keep triumph
And all that is therein.
Let all things, seen and unseen,
Their notes of gladness blend;
For Christ the Lord has risen,
Our joy that has no end!

Then praise we God the Father,
And praise we Christ his Son,
With them the Holy Spirit,
Eternal Three in One,
Till all the ransomed number
Fall down before the throne
And honor, pow'r, and glory
Ascribe to God alone!

Οὐρανοὶ μὲν ἐπαξίως
εὐφραινέσθωσαν,
γῆ δὲ ἀγαλλιάσθω·
ἑορταζέτω δὲ κόσμος
ὁρατός τε ἅπας
καὶ ἀόρατος,
Χριστὸς γὰρ ἐγήγερται,
εὐφροσύνη αἰώνιος.

Πάτερ παντοκράτωρ
καὶ λόγε καὶ πνεῦμα,
τρισὶν ἑνιζομένη
ἐν ὑποστάσεσι φύσις,
ὑπερούσιε
καὶ ὑπέρθεε, εἰς σὲ βεβαπτίσμεθα
καὶ σὲ εὐλογοῦμεν
εἰς πάντας τοὺς αἰῶνας.

This hymn by the great Greek theologian and talented poet John of Damascus is from what is called the "Golden Canon for Easter," written about the middle of the eighth century. The canon is a form of hymn introduced into the Greek Church toward the close of the seventh century, usually comprised of nine odes, each containing any number of stanzas, on the nine canticles of Holy Scripture. The translation here used is an altered form of the rather free translation by John Mason Neale in his *Hymns of the Easter Church* (1862). First published as a congregational hymn in the *Parish Hymn Book* (1863), it is rarely omitted today in any hymnal.

According to Neale's account of a midnight service on Easter Eve in Athens, worshipers carry unlighted tapers which, upon a given signal, are lighted, filling the church with a brilliant glow. At this point the Golden Canon is sung, accompanied by drums and trumpets and with the joyous greeting "Christos anesti" ("Christ Is Risen").

HERZLICH TUT MICH ERFREUEN. While the tunes ELLACOMBE (*LW* 106, 203) and LANCACHIRE (*TLH* 205) generally share the honor in various denominational hymnals of being set to this great Easter hymn, the Commission on Worship, when producing the *Worship Supplement* (1969) decided to use HERZLICH TUT MICH ERFREUEN, a tune that it considered superior to LANCACHIRE as well as being a rhythmic chorale tune that should be retrieved and used as another contribution from the Lutheran heritage. Thus this union of text and tune is contained in both *Lutheran Book of Worship* (1978) and *Lutheran Worship* (1982).

Originally a folk tune associated with the secular text, "Herzlich tut mich erfreuen die fröhlich Sommerzeit" (Zahn 5361), it was first printed in Georg Rhau's (*LW* 382) *Bicinia Gallica, latina et germanica* (Wittenberg, 1544). Seven years later it appeared in Nürnberg with the secular text, "Papiers Natur ist Rauschen." It was Johann Walter (*LW* 265) who recast the "Herzlich tut mich erfreuen" text into a sacred one and published the combined text and tune in his *Ein Schöner Geistlicher und Christlicher newer Berckreyen* (1552). It is this form of the tune that is used here at hymn 133.

The harmonization used here is the one that Theodore A. Beck prepared for inclusion in the *Worship Supplement* (1969).

WITH HIGH DELIGHT 134

With high delight
Let us unite
In songs of sweet jubilation.
You pure in heart,
Each take your part,
Sing Jesus Christ, our salvation.
To set us free
Forever, he
Is ris'n and sends
To all earth's ends
Good news to save ev'ry nation.

True God, he first
From death has burst
Forth into life, all subduing.
His enemy
Shall vanquished lie;
His death has been death's undoing.
And yours shall be
Like victory
O'er death and grave,"
Said he, who gave
His life for us, life renewing.

Let praises ring;
Give thanks, and bring
To Christ our Lord adoration.
His honor speed
By word and deed
To ev'ry land, ev'ry nation.
So shall his love
Give us above,
From misery
And death set free,
All joy and full consolation.

Mit Freuden zart
Zu dieser Fahrt
Lasst uns zugleich fröhlich singen,
Beid, gross und klein,
Von Herzen rein
Mit hellem Ton frei erklingen.
Das ewig Heil
Wird uns zuteil,
Denn Jesus Christ
Erstanden ist,
Welchs er lässt reichlich verkünden.

Er ist der Erst,
Der starck und fest
All unsre Feind hat bezwungen
Und durch den Tod
Als wahrer Gott
Zum neuen Leben gedrungen,
Auch seiner Schar
Verheissen klar
Durch sein rein Wort
Zur Himmelspfort
Desgleichen Sieg zu erlangen.

Singt Lob und Dank
Mit freiem klang
Unserm Herrn zu allen Zeiten
Und tut sein Ehr
Je mehr und mehr
Mit Wort und Tat weit ausbreiten:
So wird er uns
Aus Lieb und Gunst
Nach unserm Tod,
Frei aller Not,
Zur ewigen Freud geleiten.

This spirited Easter hymn by Georg Vetter, a priest of the Unity of Brethern (Unitas Fratrum), originally comprised of 13 stanzas, first appeared in 1566 in a hymnal of the Bohemian Brethern entitled *Kirchengeseng darinnen die Heubtartickel das Christlichen Glaubens gefasset und ausgelegt sind* (Zahn 8186). Here given are the first two stanzas plus the final stanza of that hymn.

Although not clearly evident because of the omission of 10 stanzas, the hymn praises Christ in exuberant terms, who, through his resurrection and ascension, became mediator between heaven and earth. In its strong eschatological ring it reflects 1 Corinthians 15:22–23 and Colossians 1:18.

The hymn is also notable from a poetic and artistic standpoint. Each stanza has 11 lines; lines one and two, four and five, seven and eight, nine and 10 rhyme with each other, while lines three, six, and 11 are tied together in rhyme.

The translation by Martin Franzmann was included in *Worship Supplement* (1969).

MIT FREUDEN ZART. This grand, exciting tune appeared with Georg Vetter's text in the above mentioned *Kirchengeseng* (1566). The tune is undoubtedly older than 1566, for it is quite similar to that set to Psalm 138 in the Geneva Psalter of 1562 (see *Songs of Praise* 661) as well as to a French pastoral song, "Une pastourelle gentille," published by Pierre Attaignant (1529–30), French music printer and publisher. Blume thinks it originated in the late Middle Ages (p. 598).

The harmonization was prepared by Carl F. Schalk for inclusion in *Worship Supplement* (1969).

135 WELCOME, HAPPY MORNING

For a discussion of this hymn text see hymn 125. The translation is an adaptation of that by John Ellerton.

PRINCE RUPERT. Named after the famous cavalry leader, this tune is an adaptation of the old English march, "Prince Rupert's March." Contained in the *Bellerophon* (*Gesang der Zeeden*, Amsterdam, 1648), Playford's *The Dancing Master* (1650), and other collections, it was arranged by Gustav Holst to provide a stirring substitute tune for "Onward, Christian Soldiers" (*LW* 518) in *Songs of Praise* (1925). Since the original march contained only the tune form the verse, Holst adapted the refrain from another traditional tune.

The harmonization, from *Songs of Praise*, is also by Holst.

136 TODAY IN TRIUMPH CHRIST AROSE

Today in triumph Christ arose
And conquered all his hellish foes.
Alleluia, alleluia!
Great splendor marks his victory.
Sing praise to God eternally!
Alleluia, alleluia!

Now hell has lost its pow'r and might;
Our Lord puts all its hosts to flight.
Alleluia, alleluia!
He brings the end of all our woe;
He routs our foes and lays them low.
Alleluia, alleluia!

Though Satan rage, his pow'r is gone;
His thund'ring roar can harm us none.

Heut triumphieret Gottes Sohn,
Der von dem Tod erstanden schon,
Alleluia, alleluia!
Mit grosser Pracht und Herrlichkeit,
Das dankn wir ihm in Ewigkeit.
Alleluia, alleluia!

Dem Teufel hat er sein Gewalt
Zerstört, verheert in alle Gestalt,
Alleluia, alleluia!
Wie pflegt zu tun ein grosser Held,
Der seinen Feind gewaltig fällt.
Alleluia, alleluia!

Nun kann uns kein Feind schaden mehr,
Ob er gleich murrt, ists ohn Gefähr.

Alleluia, alleluia!
Our strong Defender hurls him down
But wins for us a heav'nly crown.
Alleluia, alleluia!

O Christ, our Savior, Helper, Friend,
Be with us till our journey's end.
Alleluia, alleluia!
In mercy guide us by your grace
Till we behold your glorious face.
Alleluia, alleluia!

To God the Lord, on highest throne,
To Christ, the Father's own dear Son,
Alleluia, alleluia!
To God the Holy Spirit be
All praise and thanks eternally
Alleluia, alleluia!

Alleluia, alleluia!
Er liegt im Staub, der arge Feind,
Wir aber Gottes Kinder seind.
Alleluia, alleluia!

O süsser Herre Jesu Christ,
Der du der Sünder Heiland bist,
Alleluia, alleluia!
Führ uns durch dein Barmherzigkeit
Mit Freunden in dein Herrlichkeit.
Alleluia, alleluia!

Gott Vater in dem höchsten Thron
Samt Christo, seinem lieben Sohn,
Alleluia, alleluia!
Dem Heilgen Geist in gleicher Weis'
In Ewigkeit sei Lob und Preis!
Alleluia, alleluia!

This moving hymn first appeared in 1591 in the *Kinderspiegel oder Hauszucht-und Tischbüchlein* (Eisleben), issued by Kaspar Stolshagen, and headed: "A good hymn about the triumph and resurrection of Christ." Strangely, it was only as recent as 1883 that Stolshagen was assumed to be the author of this hymn, an assumption difficult to prove since his name was not attached to it in the *Kinderspiegel* nor can it be imagined that Stolshagen would be responsible for such garbled German as exhibited in the original. It is likely that the hymn experienced various alterations and is of much older vintage (cf. *Die Lieder unserer Kirche*, p. 143). At any rate, this is a notable hymn, a newcomer in the Synod's English hymnals but included in the German hymnals of the early Synod as well as presently in the hymnals of the Lutheran territorial churches in Germany. The translation is by Oliver C. Rupprecht.

In reflecting on St. Paul's assertion: "Having disarmed the powers and authorities, he [Christ] made a public spectacle of them, triumphing over them by the cross" (Col. 2:15), one is struck by the close correspondence between Stolshagen's hymn and that of Fortunatus, beginning "Pange, lingua gloriosi proelium certamimis," translated by John Mason Neale:

Sing, my tongue, the glorious battle;
Sing the ending of the fray.
Now above the cross, the trophy,
Sound the loud triumphant lay;
Tell how Christ, the world's redeemer,
As a victim won the day. (see *LW* 117, st. 1)

HEUT TRIUMPHIERET GOTTES SOHN. This laudable tune appeared with this text in *Geistlichen deutschen Liedern* (1601), issued by Bartholomäus Gesius (Zahn 2585). Since the text originally consisted of three-line stanzas, it is probable that prior to this the hymn may have been sung to the tune of "Resurrexit Dominus, qui pro nobis omnibus passus est serotinus." It appears that Gesius (*LW* 379, 421) joined two stanzas, resulting in six-line stanzas, setting a tune to the whole that he may have constructed from the Christmas hymn, "Puer natus in Bethlehem."

The harmonization was prepared by George Leonard, a *nom de plume* of Paul G. Bunjes.

137 CHRIST THE LORD IS RISEN TODAY; ALLELUIA

Christ the Lord is ris'n today; Alleluia!
Christians, hasten on your way; Alleluia!
Offer praise with love replete, Alleluia!
At the paschal victim's feet. Alleluia!

For the sheep the Lamb has bled, Alleluia!
Sinless in the sinner's stead. Alleluia!
Christ the Lord is ris'n on high; Alleluia!
Now he lives, no more to die. Alleluia!

Hail, the victim undefiled, Alleluia!
God and sinners reconciled, Alleluia!
When contending death and life, Alleluia!
Met in strange and awesome strife. Alleluia!

Christians, on this holy day, Alleluia!
All your grateful homage pay; Alleluia!
Christ the Lord is ris'n on high; Alleluia!
Now he lives, no more to die. Alleluia!

Victimae paschali laudes
Immolent christiani.

Agnus redemit oves;
Christus innocens Patri
Reconcilavit peccatores.

Mors et vita duello
Conflixere mirando;
Dux vitae mortuus regnat vivus.

Dic nobis, Maria,
Quid vidisti in via?
Sepulchrum Christi viventis,
Et gloriam vidi resurgentis;

Angelicos testes,
Suarium et vestes.
Surrexit Christus, spes mea,
Praecedet suos in Galilea.

Credendum est magis soli Mariae veraci,
Quam Iudaeorum turbae fallaci.

Scimus Christum surrexisse
Ex mortuis vere.
Tu nobis, victor rex, miserere.

This stirring hymn is based on the Latin sequence (see discussion at hymn 124) of the 11th century, the authorship of which is credited to Wipo (d.c. 1050) of Burgundy, noted successor of Notker at the monastery in St. Gall, chaplain to German Emperors Konrad II and his son Heinrich III. (Cf. Bäumker I, pp. 536–42.)

The translation by Jane E. Leeson, slightly altered, is that which first appeared in Henry Formby's *Catholic Hymns* (1851).

LLANFAIR. This simple but pleasing Welsh tune is indictative of early Welsh tunes in its economy of form—AABA, without development and embellishment—when compared, for instance, to ABERYSTWYTH with its rondolike repetitions. The name LLANFAIR (Llan, "church"; fair, "Mary") is the initial part of the long name of a little village in Wales. In his manuscript book, composer Robert Williams named the tune BETHEL. It appeared in J. Parry's collection, *Peroriaeth Hyfreyd* (1837), where, as also here, it was harmonized by John Roberts.

HE'S RISEN, HE'S RISEN 138

He's risen, he's risen, Christ Jesus, the Lord;
Death's prison he opened, incarnate, true Word.
Break forth, hosts of heaven, in jubilant song
While earth, sea, and mountain the praises prolong.

Erstanden, erstanden ist Jesus Christ,
Es freue sich, was auf Erden ist,
Es jauchze der Himmel mit seinem Heer;
O hüpfet, ihr Berge, und brause, du Meer!
Kyrieleis.

The foe was triumphant when on Calvary
The Lord of creation was nailed to the tree.
In Satan's domain his hosts shouted and jeered,
For Jesus was slain, whom the evil ones feared.

Der Feind triumphierte auf Golgatha,
Die Hölle durchtönte Viktoria,
Denn endlich hatte der Finster nis Macht
Den Fürsten der Lebens ans Kreuz gebracht.
Kyrieleis.

But short was their triumph, the Savior arose,
And death, hell, and Satan he vanquished, his foes;
The conquering Lord lifts his banner on high.
He lives, yes, he lives, and will nevermore die.

Doch Trotz dir, du Hölle, und Trotz dir, o Welt,
Der Herzog des Heiles behält das Feld.
Kaum waren vergangen der Tage drei,
So war dein Gefangener los und frei.
Kyrieleis.

Oh, where is your sting, death? We fear you no more;
Christ rose, and now open is fair Eden's door.
For all our transgressions his blood does atone;
Redeemed and forgiven, we now are his own.

Wo ist nun dein Stachel, O Todesgestalt?
Wo ist nun dein cieg, O Höllengewalt?
Wo ist nun, o Sünde, deine Kraft?
Wo sind nun, Gesetz, deine Flüche und Haft?
Kyrieleis.

Then sing your hosannas and raise your glad voice;
Proclaim the blest tidings that all may rejoice.
Laud, honor, and praise to the Lamb that was slain;
In glory he reigns, yes, and ever shall reign.

Der Herr ist erstanden, das Grab ist leer,
Entschlafen ist nun unsrer Sünden Heer;
Nun jauchze alles, was Sünder heisst,
Und preise den Vater, Sohn und Geist.
Kyrieleis.

This hymn and tune appear in Martin Günther's *C. F. W. Walther* (1890), a biography of the first president of The Lutheran Church—Missouri Synod, the leading force in the publication of its first official hymnal titled the *Kirchengesangbuch für evangelisch-Lutherische Gemeinden der ungeändenter-Augsburgischer Confession* (1847). Originally in 11 stanzas (stanzas 5–9 are here omitted), it there appears with the heading "On the First Easter Day, April 8, 1860 on the Ocean." Thus both text and tune were evidently done by him that year while on a trip to Germany for health reasons.

The somewhat free translation is the work of Anna M. Meyer, first published in the Synod's periodical *Lutheran Witness* (1937). Thereafter, both text and tune, now named WALTHER, appeared in *The Lutheran Hymnal* (1941).

The harmonization, based on that in *The Lutheran Hymnal*, was revised by Paul G. Bunjes, member of the Commission on Worship and music editor of *Lutheran Worship* (1982).

139 JESUS LIVES! THE VICTORY'S WON

Jesus lives! The vict'ry's won!
Death no longer can appall me;
Jesus lives! Death's reign is done!
From the grave will Christ recall me.
Brighter scenes will then commence;
This shall be my confidence.

Jesus lebt, mit ihm auch ich;
Tod, wo sind nun deine Schrecken?
Jesus lebt und wird auch mich
Von den Toten auferwecken.
Er verklärt mich in sein Licht:
Dies ist meine Zuversicht.

Jesus lives! To him the throne
There above all things is given.
I shall go where he is gone,
Live and reign with him in heaven.
God is faithful; doubtings, hence!
This shall be my confidence.

Jesus lebt. Ihm ist das Reich
Über alle Welt gegeben.
Mit ihm werd' ich auch zugleich
Ewig herrschen, ewig Leben.
Gott erfüllt, was er verspricht:
Dies ist meine Zuversicht.

Jesus lives! For me he died,
Hence will I, to Jesus living,
Pure in heart and act abide,
Praise to him and glory giving.
All I need God will dispense;
This shall be my confidence.

Jesus lebt. Sein Heil ist mein:
Sein sei auch mein ganzes Leben;
Reines Herzens will ich sein
Und den Lüsten widerstreben.
Er verlässt den Schwachen nicht:
Dies ist meine Zuversicht.

Jesus lives! And I am sure
Neither life nor death shall sever
Me from him. I shall endure
In his love, through death, forever.
God will be my sure defense;
This shall be my confidence.

Jesus lebt. Ich bin gewiss;
Nichts soll mich von Jesu scheiden,
Keine Macht der Finsternis,
Keine Herrlichkeit, kein Leiden.
Er gibt Kraft zu jeder Pflicht:
Dies ist meine Zuversicht.

Jesus lives! And now is death
But the gate of life immortal;
This shall calm my trembling breath
When I pass its gloomy portal.
Faith shall cry, as fails each sense:
Jesus is my confidence!

Jesus lebt. Nun ist der Tod
Mir der Eingang in das Leben.
Welchen Trost in Todesnot
Wird er meiner Seele geben,
Wenn sie gläubig zu ihm spricht:
Herr, Herr, meine Zuversicht!

This hymn text by Christian Fürchtegott Gellert first appeared in his *Geistliche Oden und Lieder* (Leipzig, 1757). The confidence that "Jesus lives" fills the heart with unspeakable joy regarding the Christian's own resurrection to life eternal.

Soon included in most major German hymnals, this Easter hymn became known in English-speaking countries by the translation of Frances E. Cox. Her misleading original first line, "Jesus lives! no longer now," was altered with her approval to "Jesus lives! thy terrors now." First included in Cox's *Sacred Hymns from the German* (1841), the translation underwent revisions by her own hand in subsequent publications, and further alterations by hymnal editors.

JESUS, MEINE ZUVERSICHT, also called RATISBON, appeared anonymously in its present form with the text beginning with the same words in Johann Crüger's *Praxis pietatis melica* of 1653 (Zahn 3432b). The tune is not definitely attributed to Crüger, however, until the 1668 edition of that work. It may be based on an older tune that

Crüger recast or it may be an original composition of his. At any rate, among chorale tunes it is a jewel.

The harmonization is from the *Württembergisches Choralbuch* (1953).

THIS JOYFUL EASTERTIDE 140

This modern carol first appeared in George Woodward's *Carols for Easter and Ascension* (1894) and reprinted in the 1901 and 1902 editions of *The Cowley Carol Book for Christmas, Easter, and Ascension Tide*, of which he was the gifted music editor. With the words written for the tune, this hymn certainly ranks with the best in *Lutheran Worship* (1982), and as an Easter hymn will undoubtedly become a celebrated and indispensable one. It was introduced to the members of the Synod by its inclusion in *Worship Supplement* (1969).

VRUECHTEN (EASTERTIDE) is the tune of a popular Dutch song of the 17th century, "De Liefde voortgebracht," that was turned to sacred use in Joachim Oudaen's *David's Psalmen* (Amsterdam, 1685). There it was set to "Hoe groot de Vruechten Zign," from which the tune got its name.

A vigorous, swinging tune with an attractive meter, care should be taken that it not be sung too slowly. Organists would do well to "lean" on the tempo, especially in the refrain, giving the whole a sense of urgency—an urgency reflected also in the splendid harmonization by Paul G. Bunjes—to get to the pitch-height accent E♭ in the second-to-last measure.

COME, YOU FAITHFUL, RAISE THE STRAIN 141

Come, you faithful, raise the strain Of triumphant gladness! God has brought his Israel Into joy from sadness, Loosed from Pharaoh's bitter yoke Jacob's sons and daughters, Led them with unmoistened foot Through the Red Sea waters.	Αἴσωμεν, πάντες λαοί. τῷ ἐκ πικρᾶς δουλείας· Φαραὼ τὸν Ἰσραὴλ ἀπαλλάξαντι καὶ ἐν βυθῷ θαλάσσης ποδὶ ἀβρόχως ὁδηγήσαντι ᾠδὴν ἐπινίκιον, ὅτι δεδόξασται.
This the spring of souls today: Christ has burst his prison And from three days' sleep in death	Σήμερον ἔαρ ψυχῶν, ὅτι Χριστὸς ἐκ τάφου, ὥσπερ ἥλιος, ἐκλάμψας τριήμερος

As a sun has risen;
All the winter of our sins,
Long and dark, is flying
From his light, to whom is giv'n
Laud and praise undying.

τὸν ζοφερὸν χειμῶνα
ἀπήλασε τῆς ἁμαρτίας ἡμῶν,
αὐτὸν ἀνυμνήσωμεν,
ὅτι δεδόξασται.

Now the queen of seasons, bright
With the day of splendor,
With the royal feast of feasts
Comes its joy to render;
Comes to gladden faithful hearts
Which with true affection
Welcome in unwearied strain
Jesus' resurrection!

῾Η βασιλὶς τῶν ὡρῶν
τῇ λαμπροφόρῳ ἡμέρα
ἡμερῶν τε βασιλίδι φανότατα
δωροφοροῦσα, τέρπει
τὸν ἔγκριτον τῆς ἐκκλησίας λαόν,
ἀπαύστως ἀνυμνοῦσα
τὸν ἀναστάντα Χριστόν.

For today among his own
Christ appeared, bestowing
His deep peace, which evermore
Passes human knowing.
Neither could the gates of death
Nor the tomb's dark portal
Nor the watchers nor the seal
Hold him as a mortal.

Πύλαι θανάτου, Χριστέ,
οὐδὲ τοῦ τάφου σφραγῖδες,
οὐδὲ κλεῖθρα τῶν θυρῶν Σοι ἀντέστησαν,
ἀλλ᾽ ἀναστὰς ἐπέστης
τοῖς φίλοις σου εἰρήνην, Δέσποτα,
δωρούμενος τὴν πάντα
νοῦν ὑπερέχουσαν.

Alleluia! Now we cry
To our King immortal,
Who, triumphant, burst the bars
Of the tomb's dark portal.
Come, you faithful, raise the strain
Of triumphant gladness!
God has brought his Israel
Into joy from sadness!

This hymn by one of the fathers of the Greek Church of the eighth century, the greatest of her hymn writers, John of Damascus, is based on the first ode of the canon for St. Thomas Sunday (Sunday after Easter), an ode based on the song of Moses in Exodus 15 (cf. *LW* 133). A look at stanza 1 points to and relates the deliverance effected by Moses with that effected by Christ and his resurrection.

The translation, prepared by the Inter-Lutheran Commission on Worship for inclusion in *Lutheran Book of Worship* (1978), is an altered and updated version of that by John Mason Neale that first appeared in four stanzas in an article by him in the *Christian Remembrancer* (April 1859). From there it made its way into the first edition of *Hymns Ancient and Modern* (1861) and then into Neale's own *Hymns of the Eastern Church* (1862).

GAUDEAMUS PARITER. Perhaps a traditional German tune, this joyous rhythmic chorale first appeared in *Ein Gesangbuch der Brüder im Behemen* [Bohemia] *und Merherrn* [Moravia] (Nürnberg, 1544) set to Johann Horn's Advent hymn, "Nun Lasst uns zu dieser Frist." There it was captioned "Gaudeamus pariter omnes," apparently an appropriate Latin motto (Zahn 6285).

The harmonization was prepared by Theodore A. Beck for inclusion in *Worship Supplement* (1969).

CHRIST THE LORD IS RISEN TODAY 142

This is a cento, consisting of stanzas 1–5 and 10, of Charles Wesley's popular Easter hymn, originally consisting of 11 stanzas, which first appeared in his *Hymns and Sacred Poems* (1739).

ORIENTIS PARTIBUS. This tune is from a "sacred folk song" for the Festival of the Donkey, a medieval mystery play venerating the donkey that carried Mary to Bethlehem and then to Egypt with the baby Jesus. The "Prose de l'Asne," or "Donkey's Sequence," is ascribed to Pierre de Corbeille, archbishop of Sens from 1200–22. Appearing in a number of medieval manuscripts, it began:

Orientis partibus
Adventavis Asinus,
Pulcher et fortissimus,
Sarcinis aptissimus.
Hez, sire Asne, hez.

Out from lands of Orient
Was the ass divinely sent,
Strong and very fair was he,
Bearing burdens gallantly.
Heigh, sir Ass, oh heigh.

Thomas J. Williams in *The Hymn* 6:4 describes the Festival of the Donkey:

> On January first, the Feast of the Circumcision, at the Hour of Terce (9 a.m.), immediately before the singing of High Mass, the donkey, wearing a cope and other episcopal vestments (including a mitre tied under his jaws by its *infulae* [bands]), was met at the west portal of the church by the canons and other clergy and conducted in solemn procession up the nave and into the chancel where he was duly censed and enthroned in the archbishop's *cathedra* in the choir. The sung parts of the Mass were chanted 'in a harsh braying tone.' After the Epistle, Gradual and Alleluia before the Gospel, the Sequence, or Prose, of the Ass was sung, set to the melody composed by the Archbishop. At the close of the Sequence, instead of the usual Alleluia, everyone present sang "Hez-va, hez-va, hez-va, hez!"—the Old French equivalent of "Hee-haw, hee-haw, hee-haw, hee!"

The Festival of the Donkey was celebrated at Rouen in the 10th century, and as late as 1634 at Sens.

In *Church Hymn Tunes* (1853), Richard Redhead (*LW* 110, 285) arranged the tune, originally in the mixolydian mode (reading the *E*s as E♭ will reproduce that effect), for devotional use, without the refrain. It appeared in *Hymns Ancient and Modern* (1868), and then passed into common usage. The present harmonization was prepared for *Lutheran Book of Worship* by Donald A. Busarow.

143 THE STRIFE IS O'ER

Alleluia, alleluia, alleluia!

The strife is o'er, the battle done;
Now is the victor's triumph won;
Now be the song of praise begun.
Alleluia!

The pow'rs of death have done their worst,
But Christ their legions has dispersed.
Let shouts of holy joy outburst.
Alleluia!

The three sad days have quickly sped,
He rises glorious from the dead.
All glory to our risen head!
Alleluia!

He broke the age-bound chains of hell;
The bars from heav'n's high portals fell.
Let hymns of praise his triumph tell.
Alleluia!

Lord, by the stripes which wounded you
From death's sting free your servants too
That we may live and sing to you.
Alleluia!

Alleluia, Alleluia, Alleluia.

Finita iam sunt proelia,
Est parta iam victoria;
Gaudeamus et canamus:
Alleluia!

Post fata mortis barbara
Devicit Iesus tartara;
Applaudamus et psallamus:
Alleluia!

Surrexit die tertia
Caelesti clarus gratia
Insonemus et cantemus:
Alleluia!

Sunt clausa stygis ostia,
Et caeli patent atria;
Gaudeamus et canamus:
Alleluia!

Per tua, Iesu, vulnera
Nos mala morte libera.
Ut vivamus et canamus:
Alleluia!

Although some scholars—even John Mason Neale (*LW* 31, et al.)—considered this hymn of unknown authorship to go back as far as the 12th century, the oldest source appears to be the Jesuit hymnal, *Symphonia Sirenum Selectarum* (Cologne, 1695). Among those in 19th-century England desirous of recovering for use early Greek and Latin hymns was Francis Pott. It was he who translated this hymn, beginning "Finita iam sunt proelia," including it in his *Hymns Fitted to the Order of Common Prayer* (1861). It is here given in somewhat altered and updated form.

VICTORY (PALESTRINA) is an adaptation from the Gloria Patri of the *Magnificat Tertii Toni*, contained in a collection published by Giovanni Pierluigi Palestrina in 1591:

It appears that William H. Monk (*LW* 405, 490), impressed by this work, decided to make out of it a melody for the use of the Church of England, an adaptation that appeared in the *Parish Choir* (c. 1850), set to John Cosin's "Come, Holy Ghost" (*LW* 157, 158). This went as follows:

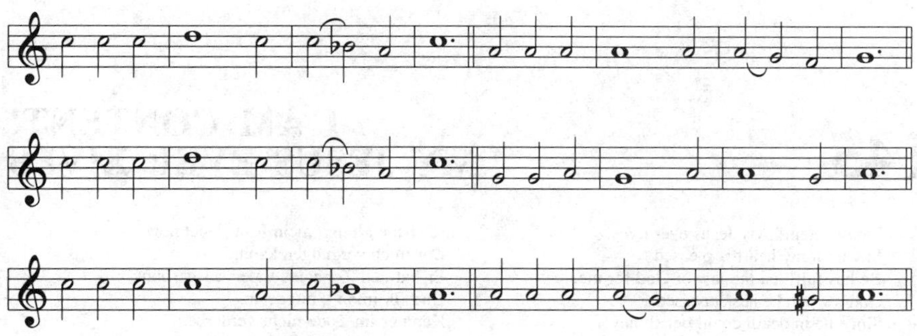

Harmonized in simple, vertical, chordal style, it was not a little dull. His second effort is the tune under discussion, which he made for *Hymns Ancient and Modern* (1861).

Here he uses only the first two phrases of the original and rounds off the whole with alleluias of his own making, setting the tune firmly in the major key.

Interestingly, some editors, following the example of *The English Hymnal* (1906), omit the introductory and concluding alleluias, so prone to getting the hymn off to a bad start.

Granted, Monk's VICTORY is a tune of considerable solemnity that has gained popular favor. It should be taken broadly and rhythmically for best effect.

144 TRIUMPHANT FROM THE GRAVE

As editor of *The Northwestern Lutheran* from 1956–1968, Werner H. Franzmann, desirous of including a hymn in a given festival issue, occasionally tried his hand at hymn writing. This is one such hymn, one of 17 that became appreciated and was occasionally sung here and there in corporate worship. Congregations acquainted with the *Worship Supplement* (1969), prepared by the Commission on Worship of The Lutheran Church—Missouri Synod, may remember Franzmann's notable hymn for Christ's Transfiguration, "Down from the Mount of Glory" (*WS* 724), contained therein.

TRIUMPH represents the sturdy tune that Bruce Backer, professor of music at Dr. Martin Luther College, New Ulm, Minnesota, composed for Franzmann's text. The harmonization here used was prepared by James Engel.

145 I AM CONTENT! MY JESUS EVER LIVES

I am content! My Jesus ever lives,
In whom my heart is pleased.
He has fulfilled the law of God for me,
God's wrath he has appeased.
Since he in death could perish never,
I also shall not die forever.
I am content! I am content!

Ich habe g'nug: mein Jesus lebet noch,
Der mich vergnügen kann;
Er hat den Zorn des Vaters ausgesöhnt
Und für mich g'nuggetan.
Kann er im Tode nicht verderben,
So werd' ich auch nicht ewig sterben.
Ich habe g'nug. Ich habe g'nug.

I am content! My Jesus is my head;
His member I shall be.
He bowed his head when on the cross he died
With cries of agony.

Ich habe g'nug: mein Jesus ist mein Haupt,
Ich bin sein teures Glied.
Das neigte sich mit grossem Angstgeschrei,
Als er am Kreuz verschied;

Now death is brought into subjection
For me too by his resurrection.
I am content! I am content!

I am content! My Jesus is my light,
My radiant sun of grace.
His cheering rays beam blessings forth for all,
Sweet comfort, hope, and peace.
This Easter sun has brought salvation
And everlasting exultation.
I am content! I am content!

I am content! At length I shall be free,
Awakened from the dead,
Arising glorious evermore to be
With you, my living head.
My Lord, earth's binding fetters sever,
Then shall my soul rejoice forever.
I am content! I am content!

Nun hat er's wieder aufgerichtet
Und meinen Tod zugleich vernichtet.
Ich habe g'nug. Ich habe g'nug.

Ich habe g'nug: mein Jesus ist mein Glanz
Und heller Gnadenschein.
Dies Freudenlicht lässt keinen ohne Trost
Und unvergnüget sein;
Denn von derselben Ostersonne
Kommt Leben, Seligkeit und Wonne.
Ich habe g'nug. Ich habe g'nug.

Ich habe g'nug, nur zeuch mich, Herr, nach dir,
Damit ich aufersteh',
Wenn du aufstehst, und endlich wohlvergnügt
Zu deiner Freud' eingeh'.
Zeuch mich aus dieses Leibes Höhle,
So rufet die erfreute Seele:
Ich habe g'nug. Ich habe g'nug.

This hymn, reflecting Elijah's state of mind when Jezebel vowed to kill him (1 Kings 19:4), has stilled the anxieties of many hopeless souls. In the *Kirchengesangbuch für Evangelisch-Lutherische Gemeinden* (St. Louis, n.d.) it is attributed to Johann Joachim Möller (1660–1733), about whom little information has been available.

The translation is an altered and updated form of that by August Crull in the *Evangelical Lutheran Hymn-Book* (1912), the predecessor to *The Lutheran Hymnal* (1941).

ES IST GENUG is the fine chorale tune in Johann R. Ahle's *Drittes Zehn neuer geistlicher Lieder* (Mühlhausen, 1662), where it was set to the hymn "Es ist genug, so nimm, Herr, meinen Geist zu Zion's Geistern hin" by Franz J. Burmeister (Zahn 7173). The use of the tritone between the first and fourth notes (E to C♯) gives this tune the joyously unrestrained expressive quality of an aria; and the folklike rhythmic changes remind one of earlier times.

The harmonization was prepared for *Lutheran Worship* (1982) by Paul G. Bunjes.

LO, JUDAH'S LION WINS THE STRIFE 146

Lo, Judah's Lion wins the strife
And conquers death to give us life.
Alleluia!
Come, join in joyful praises!

As David, so our David too
The jeering huge Goliath slew.

Aj, ten silny lev udatny
Kristus vstal z mrtvych, Pán mily:
Hallelujah,
Vesele sezpívejme!

Kteréhozto ruku silnou
David znamenal udatnou.

Alleluia!
Oh, sing with festive voices!

Our strongest, fiercest foe he foils
And waves aloft the victor's spoils.
Alleluia!
Now let us sing his praises!

Our Samson storms death's citadel
And carries off the gates of hell.
Alleluia!
Oh, praise him for his conquest!

The pow'r of death he broke in two
When he arose to life anew.
Alleluia!
To him all praise be given!

He frees the prisoned and oppressed
And pardons all whom sin possessed.
Alleluia!
Oh, praise him for his mercy!

In festal spirit, song, and word,
To Jesus, our victorious Lord,
Alleluia!
All praise and thanks be rendered.

Praise God, all-holy and triune,
For this all-gracious, glorious boon;
Alleluia!
Now gladly sing we Amen.

Hallelujah,
Rcemez vsickni vesele!

On obra toho silného
Premoh', vzav loupeze jeho:
Hallelujah,
Bud Jemu z toho chvála!

Tot jest Samson preudatny,
Jenz pobral pekelné brány:
Hallelujah,
Vsickni spolu spévejme!

Jakzto Samgar sám hrdinsky
Pobil zástup nepratelsky:
Hallelujah!
Rcemez vsickni vesele!

Sprostil nás jeho trápeni,
Odnal od nás pohanení:
Hallelujah,
Smiloval se nad námi.

V téchto hodech preveselych,
Slavného Vítezitele:
Hallelujah,
Písne Jemu zpívejme!

Pochvalmez Svatou Trojici,
Boha nerozdilné moci:
Hallelujah,
Rcemez: Amen! vesele.

This hymn of unknown authorship first appeared in Zavorka's Bohemian Neo-Utraquist *Kancional* in 1602. From there it entered the second Trencin (Slovakia) edition, 1659, of the *Cithara Sanctorum*, popularly known as the "Tranoscius," printed by Nikodem Czizaka. The revised and updated translation, prepared by Jaroslav J. Vajda, is based on that done by John Bajus for *The Lutheran Hymnal* (1941), predecessor to *Lutheran Worship* (1982).

It is to be noted that the English of the Bohemian stanza 5 simply paraphrases the thought of the original with its strange reference to "Samgar" (Jer. 39:37), who single handedly slew a horde of enemies. This possibly reflects Samson's killing a thousand Philistines with a donkey's jawbone (Judges 15:15). The biblical strength of the text, with its unique three-line structure, prompted the Commission on Worship to include this hymn in *Lutheran Worship*, albeit coupled to a new tune.

BRONXVILLE. This tune was composed by Ralph Schultz specifically for this Bohemian hymn text. In a meeting of the Commission on Worship, of which Schultz was a member, the opinion was expressed that this great Easter text suffered disuse because of the tune to which it was coupled in *The Lutheran Hymnal*. Schultz was asked to provide a new tune, a task he accomplished on his return flight to New York. This robust tune was meant by him to capture the aspects of celebrating Christ's hard-fought victory as described in the text. The name Bronxville was chosen by Schultz as representing the city and the state of New York, where Concordia College, of which he is president, is located. The harmonization is likewise by Schultz.

THAT EASTER DAY WITH JOY WAS BRIGHT 147

That Easter day with joy was bright;
The sun shone out with fairer light,
When, to their longing eyes restored,
The apostles saw their risen Lord!
Alleluia!

O Jesus, king of gentleness,
With constant love our hearts possess;
To you our lips will ever raise
The tribute of our grateful praise.
Alleluia!

O Christ, you are the Lord of all
In this our Easter festival,
For you will be our strength and shield
From ev'ry weapon death can wield.
Alleluia!

All praise, O risen Lord, we give
To you, once dead but now alive!
To God the Father equal praise,
And God the Holy Ghost, we raise!
Alleluia!

Claro paschali gaudio
sol mundo nitet radio
cum Christum jam apostoli
visu cernunt corporeo.

Rex Christi clementissime,
tu corda nostra posside,
ut tibi laudes debitas
reddamus omni tempore.

Quaesumus, auctor omnium,
in hoc paschali gaudio
ab omni mortis impetu
tuum defende populum.

Gloria tibi, Domine
qui surrexisti a mortuis,
cum patre et sancto spiritu
in sempiterna saecula.

Sometimes ascribed to Ambrose (*LW* 481), this Latin hymn from the fourth or fifth century is a cento from the third part of the poem beginning "Aurora lucis rutilat." This hymn, together with the Easter hymn "Ad coenam Agni" (*LW* 126), were the first hymns adopted for a particular season of the church year, and thus they constitute the germ of *de tempore* (of the time) hymns.

The translation by John Mason Neale in his *The Hymnal Noted* (1852) is here, as well as in other hymnals, including the original editions of *Hymns Ancient and Modern* (1861), given in considerably altered form. Stanza 1, for instance, appeared thus:

In this our bright and pascal day
The sun shines out in purer ray;
When Christ, to earthly sight made plain,
The glad apostles see again.

ERSCHIENEN IST DER HERRLICH TAG. This tune by Nikolaus Herman is used with three Easter hymns in his *Die Sonntags Evangelia über das ganze Jahr* (Wittenberg, 1560), best known of which is "Erschienen ist der herrlich Tag." The tune, in the Dorian mode, has as its basis the Easter antiphon "Ad monumentum venimus gementes." Recent research indicates that it has close resemblance to the tenor line of an anonymous motet from the early 16th century beginning with the words "Sing euch hie on als gefer." It is a splendid tune, with a rather striking leap of a fifth in the fourth line.

The harmonization is by George Leonard, a *nom de plume* of Paul G. Bunjes.

HAIL THEE, FESTIVAL DAY 148

For comments on the text and tune see hymn 125.

A HYMN OF GLORY LET US SING 149

The original Latin of this hymn, beginning with "Hymnum canamus gloriae," is ascribed to the Venerable Bede and is first found in an 11th-century manuscript in the British Museum. Three other 11th-century manuscripts begin with "Hymnum canamus domino."

The English text of this great Ascension hymn was done for *Lutheran Book of Worship* (1978) and represents a synthesis of two earlier translations—"A Hymn of Glory Let Us Sing" by Elizabeth Rundle Charles, contained in her *Voice of Christian Life in Song* (1858), and "Sing We Triumphant Hymns of Praise," contributed to *The Hymnal Noted* (1854) by Benjamin Webb (*LW* 275), with certain revisions.

LASST UNS ERFREUEN. For comments on the tune and harmonization see hymn 131.

ON CHRIST'S ASCENSION I NOW BUILD 150

On Christ's ascension I now build
The hope of my ascension;
This hope alone has always stilled
All doubt and apprehension;
For where the head is, there as well
I know his members are to dwell
When Christ will come and call them.

Since Christ returned to claim his throne,
Great gifts for me obtaining,
My heart will rest in him alone,
No other rest remaining;
For where my treasure went before,
There all my thoughts will ever soar
To still their deepest yearning.

Oh, grant, dear Lord, this grace to me,
Recalling your ascension,
That I may serve you faithfully,
Adorning your redemption;
And then, when all my days will cease,
Let me depart in joy and peace
In answer to my pleading.

Auf Christi Himmelfahrt allein
Ich meine Nachfahrt gründe
Und allen Zweifel, Angst und Pein
Hier mit stets überwinde;
Denn weil das Haupt im Himmel ist,
Wird seine Glieder Jesus Christ
Zur rechten Zeit nachholen.

Weil er gezogen himmelan
Und grosse Gab' empfangen,
Mein Herz auch nur im Himmel kann,
Sonst nirgend Ruh' erlangen;
Denn wo mein Schatz ist kommen hin,
Da ist auch stets mein Herz und Sinn,
Nach ihm mich sehr verlanget.

Ach Herr, lass diese Gnade mich
Von deiner Auffahrt spüren,
Dass mit dem wahren Glauben ich
Mög' meine Nachfahrt zieren
Und dann einmal, wenn dir's gafällt,
Mit Freuden scheiden aus der Welt.
Herr, höre doch mein Flehen!

This beautiful Ascension hymn—but it is more than that, encompassing as it does St. Paul's words to the Colossians for holy living (3:1–4)—is the result of misfortune suffered by its author Josua Wegelin when, due to the Thirty Years' War (1618–48), he had to leave his pastorate in Augsburg and assume a new one in Pressburg. In this situation he wrote a devotional booklet for his former congregation in Augsburg entitled *Andächtige Versöhung mit Gott, welche hilfet aus aller Not* (Pious Reconciliation with God, which helps in All Troubles), and it is in this little work in 1635 that the hymn under discussion appeared. (Later this booklet came to be referred to as *Ausburger Betbüchlein.*)

The German text here given as well as that included in the present hymnals of the Lutheran territorial churches in Germany is not Wegelin's but the one recast for the Lüneberg hymnal of 1661 by Ernst Sonnenmann, senior assistant of the Latin school in Celle. Wegelin's text began: "Allein auf Christi Himmelfahrt mein Nachfahrt ich tu gründen."

The translation is an altered and updated form of that prepared by William M. Czamanske for inclusion in *The Lutheran Hymnal* (1941).

NUN FREUT EUCH. For comments on the tune see hymn 353.

The harmonization is by Wilhelm Quampen, a *nom de plume* of Paul G. Bunjes.

151 O CHRIST, OUR HOPE

O Christ, our hope, our hearts' desire,
Creation's mighty Lord,
Redeemer of the fallen world,
By holy love outpoured:

How vast your mercy to accept
The burden of our sin
And bow your head in cruel death
To make us clean within.

But now the bonds of death are burst,
The ransom has been paid;
You now ascend the Father's throne
In robes of light arrayed.

Oh, let your mighty love prevail
To purge us of our pride
That we may stand before your throne
By mercy purified.

Christ Jesus, be our present joy,
Our future great reward;
Our only glory, may it be
To glory in the Lord!

Jesu, nostra redemptio,
Amor et desiderium,
Deus creator omnium,
Homo in fine temporum:

Quae te vicit clementia,
Ut ferres nostra crimina,
Crudelem mortem patiens
Ut nos a morte tolleres:

Inferni claustra penetrans,
Tuos captivos redimens,
Victor triumpho nobili
Ad dextram Patris residens.

Ipsa te cogat pietas,
Ut mala nostra superes
Parcendo, et voti compotes
Nos tuo vultu saties.

Tu esto nostrum gaudium
Qui es futurus praemium;
Sit nostra in te gloria
Per cuncta semper saecula.

All praise to you, ascended Lord;
All glory ever be
To Father, Son, and Holy Ghost
Through all eternity!

Gloria tibi, Domine,
Qui scandis super sidera,
Cum Patre et sancto Spiritu
In sempiterna saecula.

This seventh- or eighth-century Latin hymn of unknown authorship was evidently quite popular in the canonical, or prayer, hours from Ascension to Pentecost, for it was included in no less than four 11th-century hymn collections. In York it was used at Lauds (sunrise), in Roman use at Vespers (sunset), in Sarum (Salisbury) used at Compline (nightfall).

The translation is an adaptation of that by John Chandler which appeared in his *Hymns of the Primitive Church* (1837).

ICH SINGE DIR. This short but delightful anonymous tune appeared in Belthasar König's *Harmonischer Liederschatz* (Frankfurt, 1738), where it was set to Paul Gerhardt's notable hymn of praise "ich singe dir mit Herz und Mund."

The harmonization is by Richard W. Gieseke.

UP THROUGH ENDLESS RANKS OF ANGELS 152

At the request of Augsburg Publishing House Jaroslav Vajda wrote this stirring Ascension hymn in 1973 to the 19th-century tune, OUR LADY, TRONDHEIM, by Ludvig Lindeman (*LW* 96, 291), a factor that determined the metric scheme. After studying again the implications of the Ascension for Christians, Vajda says:

> Taking the scriptural phenomenological viewpoint, I originally began the text with the word 'Up.' The publishers, however, preferred to avoid the three-tiered universe imagery and so substituted the word 'There,' in which version they published a setting by Carl Schalk. When the Inter-Lutheran Commission on Worship chose the text as the Hymn of the Day for Ascension, the original opening preposition was restored and a last-minute substitution for both OUR LADY TRONDHEIM [sic] and the Carl Schalk tune was made (Vajda, *Now the Joyful Celebration*).

ASCENDED TRIUMPH was composed for Vajda's text by Henry V. Gerike while attending summer sessions at Concordia Seminary, St. Louis, in 1973. The ascending leap of a fifth to the octave in the opening phrase, plus the same leaps leading to the pitch-height accents to introduce the final cadence, beautifully reflect the spirit of the Lord's Ascension. The contour of the tune reflects especially the first stanza.

This text and its tune were included in *Lutheran Book of Worship* (1978) and from there were taken over into *Lutheran Worship* (1982). The harmonization is also by Henry V. Gerike.

153 DRAW US TO YOU

Draw us to you,
And we will do
What you have taught forever
And hasten on
Where you have gone
To be with you, dear Savior.

Draw us to you
Each day anew.
Let us depart with gladness
That we may be
Forever free
From sorrow, grief, and sadness.

Draw us to you
That we stay true
And walk the road to heaven.
Direct our way
Lest we should stray
And from your paths be driven.

Draw us to you;
Our hope renew;
Into your kingdom take us.
Let us all there
Your glory share;
Your saints and joint heirs make us.

Zeuch uns nach dir,
So laufen wir
Mit herzlichen Verlangen
Hin, da du bist,
O Jesu Christ,
Aus dieser Welt gegangen.

Zeuch uns nach dir
In Liebsbegier,
Ach reiss uns doch von hinnen,
So dürfen wir
Nicht länger hier
Den Kummerfaden spinnen.

Zeuch uns nach dir,
Herr Christ, ach führ
Uns deine Himmelsstege!
Wir irr'n sonst leicht
Und sind verscheucht
Vom rechten Lebenswege.

Zeuch uns nach dir
Nur für und für
Und gib, dass wir nachfahren
Dir in dein Reich,
Und mach uns gleich
Den auserwählten Scharen!

This excellent Ascension hymn, originally in five stanzas, was written by Friedrich Funcke, cantor in Lüneberg and later Lutheran pastor in Römstedt, and first published in the *Lüneberg Stadt Gesang Buch* (1686), a hymnal of almost 2,000 hymns that he and Caspar Hermann Sandhagen (1639–97), Lutheran superintendent at Lüneberg, compiled. Having identified his hymn with only the initials F. F. created some doubt as to its authorship. Some, following the lead of Edward Emil Koch, have attributed the hymn to Friedrich Fabricius (1642–1703); others to Countess Ludämilie Elisabeth von Schwarzburg-Rudolstadt.

While the opening lines reflect Song of Songs 1:4: "Take me away with you—let us hurry," the hymn in general is reminiscent of John 12:32: "But I, when I am lifted up from the earth, will draw all men to myself."

Stanzas 1–3, and 5 of the original five appear here in the translation of August Crull, altered and updated.

ACH GOTT UND HERR. For comments on this tune see hymn 232.

The harmonization is by Paul G. Bunjes.

COME, HOLY GHOST, GOD AND LORD

154

Come, Holy Ghost, God and Lord,
With all your graces now outpoured
On each believer's mind and heart;
Your fervent love to them impart.
Lord, by the brightness of your light
In holy faith your Church unite;
From ev'ry land and ev'ry tongue
This to your praise, O Lord our God be sung:
Alleluia, alleluia!

Come, holy Light, guide divine,
Now cause the Word of life to shine.
Teach us to know our God aright
And call him Father with delight.
From ev'ry error keep us free;
Let none but Christ our master be
That we in living faith abide,
In him, our Lord, with all our might confide.
Alleluia, alleluia!

Come, holy Fire, comfort true,
Grant us the will your work to do
And in your service to abide;
Let trials turn us not aside.
Lord, by your pow'r prepare each heart,
And to our weakness strength impart
That bravely here we may contend,
Through life and death to you, our Lord, ascend.
Alleluia, alleluia!

Komm, Heiliger Geist, Herre Gott,
Erfüll mit deiner Gnaden Gut
Deiner Gläubigen Herz, Mut und Sinn,
Dein brünstig Lieb' entzünd' in ihn'n!
O Herr, durch deines Lichtes Glast
Zu dem Glauben versammelt hast
Das Volk aus aller Welt Zungen;
Das sei dir, Herr, zu Lob gesungen!
Halleluja! Halleluja!

Du heiliges Licht, edler Hort,
Lass uns leuchten des Lebens Wort
Und lehr uns Gott recht erkennen,
Von Herzen Vater ihn nennen!
O Herr, behüt vor fremder Lehr',
Dass wir nicht Meister suchen mehr
Denn Jesum mit rechtem Glauben
Und ihm aus ganzer Macht vertrauen!
Halleluja! Halleluja!

Du heilige Brunst, süsser Trost,
Nun hilf uns fröhlich und getrost
In dein'm Dienst beständig bleiben,
Die Trübsal uns nicht abtreiben!
O Herr, durch dein' Kraft uns bereit
Und stärk des Fleisches Blödigkeit,
Dass wir hier ritterlich ringen,
Durch Tod und Leben zu dir dringen!
Halleluja! Halleluja!

This hymn, undoubtedly one of the greatest and most powerful hymns of the Lutheran Church, is based on a well-known pre-Reformation German antiphon, which in turn was based on an earlier Latin antiphon for the Vigil of Pentecost, namely, "Veni, Sancte Spiritus, reple tuorum corde fidelium." In his *Table Talk* Luther expressed his fondness for the German version by stating: "The hymn 'Come, Holy Ghost, God and Lord,' was composed by the Holy Ghost himself, both words and music."

Luther not only polished and improved the original German version, he also amplified it with the addition of two stanzas so neatly crafted and joined to the original that one cannot distinguish the old from the new.

KOMM, HEILIGER GEIST, HERRE GOTT. The tune as here used is the one that gained prevalence. As such it represents a simplified form of the more melismatic tune used with the German antiphon, the form that appeared in the Erfurt *Enchiridion* and in Johann Walter's *Geystliche gesangk Buchleyn*, both in 1524. The Latin antiphon had its own tune, a tune that enjoyed no currency in the German versification.

The harmonization is by Paul G. Bunjes.

155 TO GOD THE HOLY SPIRIT LET US PRAY

To God the Holy Spirit let us pray
Most of all for faith upon our way
That he may defend us when life is ending
And from exile home we are wending.
Lord, have mercy!

O sweetest Love, your grace on us bestow;
Set our hearts with sacred fire aglow
That with hearts united we love each other,
Ev'ry stranger, sister, and brother.
Lord, have mercy!

Transcendent Comfort in our ev'ry need,
Help us neither scorn nor death to heed
That we may not falter nor courage fail us
When the foe shall taunt and assail us.
Lord, have mercy!

Shine in our hearts, O Spirit, precious light;
Teach us Jesus Christ to know aright
That we may abide in the Lord who bought us,
Till to our true home he has brought us.
Lord, have mercy!

Nun bitten wir den Heiligen Geist
Um den rechten Glauben allermeist,
Dass er uns behüte an unserm Ende,
Wenn wir heimfahrn aus deisem Elende.
Kyrieleis.

Du süsse Lieb, schenk uns deine Gunst,
Lass uns empfinden der Liebe Brunst,
Dass wir uns von Herzen einander lieben
Und im Frieden auf einem Sinn bleiben.
Kyrieleis.

Du höchste Tröster in aller Not,
Hilf, dass wir nicht fürchten Schand noch Tod,
Dass in uns die Sinne nicht verzagen,
Wenn der Feind wird das Leben verklagen.
Kyrieleis.

Du wertes Licht, gib uns deinen Schein,
Lehr uns Jesum Christ kennen allein,
Dass wir an ihm bleiben, dem treuen Heiland,
Der uns bracht hat zum rechten Vaterland.
Kyrieleis.

The first stanza of this hymn is what is called a *Leise* hymn, a form of hymn that exhibits the German congregational hymn in its first estate. Down to the 10th century the only practice among the Germans that could come close to popular church song was the shouting of the words "Kyrie eleison, Christe eleison" from the ancient Mass. In processions, on pilgrimage, at burials these words were repeated over and over. When formally sung, the Gregorian tones proper to these words were used. Gradually texts were inserted between the Kyrie eleison and the Christe eleison, resulting in what became known as tropes, or "farced Kyries." These in turn developed into a more regular type of hymn with the Kyrie eleison serving as conclusion to each stanza.

"To God the Holy Spirit Let Us Pray" is one of the earliest of popular *Leisen* hymns. The people were frequently permitted to sing it in the Mass on Pentecost, immediately following the choir's rendition of the Latin sequence "Veni, Sancte Spiritus." It was a favorite of both Martin Luther and Johann Walter. In his *Formula Missae* (1523) Luther recommended that it be sung after the distribution of the body and blood of Christ; in the *Deutsche Messe* (1526) he suggested that it be sung between the reading of the Epistle and Gospel. It is interesting to note that in 1542 he included it in the book of funeral hymns. Shortly after the appearance of the *Deutsche Messe* Luther added three stanzas, thus converting a medieval *Leise* into, what later would be called, a Lutheran chorale. Its first appearance was as a choral work in Walter's *Geystliche gesangk Buchleyn* (1524). Before long, however, every Lutheran hymnal included it.

The text in *Lutheran Worship* is an adaptation of an earlier version prepared by the Commission on Worship for inclusion in *Worship Supplement* (1969).

NUN BITTEN WIR. This tune, built on a five-tone scale—d, f, g, a, c, d—is strongly suggestive of an old folk melody. In Walter's *Geistliche gesangk Buchleyn* it is joined to Luther's text.

The setting is from the *Württembergisches Choralbuch* (1953).

CREATOR SPIRIT, HEAVENLY DOVE 156

Creator Spirit, heav'nly dove, Descend upon us from above; With graces manifold restore Your creatures as they were before.	Veni, creator Spiritus, Mentes tuorum visita, Imple superna gratia Quae tu creasti pectora.
To you, the Comforter, we cry, To you, the gift of God most high, True fount of life, the fire of love, The soul's anointing from above.	Qui Paracletus diceris, Donum Dei altissimi, Fons vivus, Ignis, Caritas, Et spiritalis Unctio.
In you, with graces sevenfold, We God's almighty hand behold While you with tongues of fire proclaim To all the world his holy name.	Tu septiformis munere, Dextrae Dei tu digitus, Tu rite promisso Patris, Sermone ditas guttura.
Your light to every sense impart, And shed your love in ev'ry heart; Your own unfailing might supply To strengthen our infirmity.	Accende lumen sensibus, Infunde amorem cordibus, Infirma nostri corporis Virtute firmans perpeti.
Keep far from us our cruel foe, And peace from your own hand bestow; If you be our protecting guide, No evil can our steps betide.	Hostem repellas longius, Pacemque dones protinus, Ductore sic te praevio Vitemus omne noxium.
Oh, make to us the Father known; Teach us the eternal Son to own; And you, whose name we ever bless, Of both the Spirit, to confess.	Per te sciamus, da, Patrem, Noscamus atque Filium, Te utriusque Spiritum Credamus omni tempore.
Praise we the Father and the Son And Holy Spirit, with them one; And may the Son on us bestow The gifts that from the Spirit flow.	Sit laus Patri cum Filio, Sancto simul Paracleto, Nobisque mittat Filius Charisma Sancti Spiritus.

For a discussion of the Latin basis of this hymn see hymn 158. Martin Luther (*LW* 13, et al.) prepared a seven-stanza German translation of this, beginning "Komm, Gott Schöpfer, Heiliger Geist," which appeared in the Erfurt *Enchiridia* of 1524.

The translation here given is a composite: stanzas 1 and 3 are from Richard Massie's (*LW* 123, et al.) *Martin Luther's Spiritual Songs* (1854); stanzas 2, 4, 6–7 are from Edward Caswall's (*LW* 18, et al.) *Lyrica Catholica* (1849); and stanza 5 is from Robert Campbell's (*LW* 126) *Hymns and Anthems* (1850).

KOMM, GOTT SCHÖPFER is the simple syllabic version, based on the plainsong melody proper to the Latin "Veni, creatur Spiritus," that appeared in Joseph Klug's (*LW* 124, et al.) *Geistliche Lieder* (1533), example of which is here given:

Zünd vns ein liecht an jm verstand/ gib vns jns hertz der liebe brunst/ Das schwach fleisch jnn vns dir bekand / erhalt fest dein krafft vnd gunst.

Du bist mit gaben siebenfalt/der finger an Gotts rechter hand/Des Vaters wort gibstu gar bald / mit zungen jnn alle land.

Des feindes list treib von vns fern/ den fried schaff bey vns deine gnad/ Das wir deim leiten folgen gern / vnd meiden der selen schad.

Ler vns den Vater kennen wol / das zu Jhesum Christ seinen son / Das wir des glaubens werden vol / Dich beyder geist zuuerstehon.

Gott Vater sey lob vnd dem son/ der von den todten aufferstund / Dem Tröster sey dasselb gethon / jnn ewigkeit alle stund. Amen.

The melody in the Erfurt *Enchiridia* (1524), according to Zahn 294, appeared thus:

The harmonization is from *The Lutheran Hymnal* (1941).

This hymn has enjoyed a long tradition of use for ordination in the Western Church as well as in the Lutheran and Episcopal communions.

COME, HOLY GHOST, OUR SOULS INSPIRE 157

This text is the same as hymn 158.

KOMM, GOTT SCHÖPFER. For comments on this tune see hymn 156.

The harmonization was prepared by George Leonard, a *nom de plume* of Paul G. Bunjes.

COME, HOLY GHOST, OUR SOULS INSPIRE 158

Come, Holy Ghost, our souls inspire, Ignite them with celestial fire; Spirit of God, you have the art Your gifts, the sev'nfold, to impart.	Veni, creator Spiritus, Mentes tuorum visita, Imple superna gratia Quae tu creasti pectora.
Your blest outpouring from above Is comfort, life, and fire of love. Illumine with perpetual light The dullness of our blinded sight.	Tu septiformis munere, Dextrae Dei tu digitus, Tu rite promisso Patris, Sermone ditas guttura.
Anoint and cheer our much-soiled face With the abundance of your grace. Keep far our foes; give peace at home; Where you guide us, no ill can come.	Hostem repellas longius, Pacemque dones protinus, Ductore sic te praevio Vitemus omne noxium.
Teach us to know the Father, Son, And you, of both, to be but one That, as the ceaseless ages throng, Your praise may be our endless song!	Per te sciamus, da, Patrem, Noscamus atque Filium, Te utriusque Spiritum Credamus omni tempore.

A cursory examination of various denominational hymnals reveals that hymns addressed to or focusing on the Holy Spirit are relatively few in comparison with those that dwell either on God the Father or on his Son Jesus Christ. Two hymns that enjoy wide usage today in various denominations are "Breathe on Me, Breath of God" (*LBW* 488) by Edwin Hatch (1835–89), Oxford scholar whom the Anglo-Catholic movement repelled, and "Spirit of God, Descend upon My Heart" (*LBW* 486) by George Croly (1780–1860), successful literary figure. Both men were clergy of the Anglican Church. The deeply individualistic character of these two hymns, and the apparent espousal of a sort of mysticism apart from God's Word and the Sacraments in the second, militated against their inclusion in *Lutheran Worship*.

The oldest extant hymn on the Holy Spirit is the "Veni, creator Spiritus" from the ninth century, generally attributed to that great Frankish scholar and theologian Rhabanus Maurus. Since its first use in the latter part of the ninth century it has had a long and distinguished history, having been included in numerous breviaries as the office hymn for Terce to commemorate the outpouring of the Holy Spirit on the third hour of the day, namely, 9:00 a.m. (Acts 2:15). In the Middle Ages it was one of the oldest, best loved, and most frequently and widely used invocations of the Holy Spirit, the singing of which in medieval rites was accompanied by the use of incense, lights, bells, and the richest of vestments. Its use for the ordination service is first mentioned in the 11th century, a custom that has been perpetuated to the present. It is the first of the two hymns prescribed at ordination in *Lutheran Worship: Agenda* (1984), the other being "Creator Spirit, Heav'nly Dove" (*LW* 156), based on a translation by Luther of the same Latin text. Its use at the coronation of Edward II in 1307 has been continued for the coronation of English monarchs ever since.

Translations of this text have been numerous. According to Julian, 35 had been made by 1907. The translation by John Cosin, here in slightly revised and updated form, was first published in his *Collection of Private Devotions in the Practice of the Ancient Church, called the Hours of Prayer* (1627). Cosin's translation was inserted in the 1662 edition of the *Book of Common Prayer* as an alternative to the 16-stanza translation in the Anglican ordinals. Initially included in the Prayer Book for responsive reading, it was the 1861 edition of *Hymns Ancient and Modern* that first introduced Cosin's text for singing.

VENI CREATOR SPIRITUS as here given is a somewhat simplified form of the tune considered proper to this text as it appears in the *Vesperale Romanum cum cantu emendato* (Mechlin [Malines], Belgium, 1848), a collection of Gregorian, or plainsong, tunes intended to restore this idiom to French Catholic churches at a time when plainsong had fallen into desuetude. The tune in its original form may be older than the "Veni, creator" text, having been first associated with the Ambrosian Easter hymn, "Hic est dies verus dei." It is a beautiful tune in the mixolydian mode (see essay: The Church Modes, p. 832), one that has withstood the test of time, having served both Catholics and Protestants. The Solesmes version can be seen in the *Liber Usualis*, page 885. Congregations and/or choirs, once having learned it, will enjoy it if sung fairly quickly with a free rhythm dictated by the text.

The harmonization was prepared for *Lutheran Worship* (1982) by Paul G. Bunjes.

159 HAIL THEE, FESTIVAL DAY

For comments on the text and tune see hymn 125.

O HOLY SPIRIT, ENTER IN

160

O Holy Spirit, enter in,
And in our hearts your work begin,
And make our hearts your dwelling.
Sun of the soul, O Light divine,
Around and in us brightly shine,
Your strength in us upwelling.
In your radiance
Life from heaven
Now is given
Overflowing,
Gift of gifts beyond all knowing.

O Heil'ger Geist, kehr bei uns ein
Und lass uns deine Wohnung sein,
O komm, du Herzenssonne!
Du Himmelslicht, lass deinen Schein
Bei uns und in uns kräftig sein
Zu steter Freud' und Wonne,
Dass wir in dir
Recht zu leben
Uns ergeben
Und mit Beten
Oft deshalben vor dich treten.

Left to ourselves, we surely stray;
Oh, lead us on the narrow way,
With wisest counsel guide us;
And give us steadfastness that we
May follow you forever free,
No matter who derides us.
Gently heal those
Hearts now broken;
Give some token
You are near us,
Whom we trust to light and cheer us.

Steh uns stets bei mit deinem Rat
Und führ uns selbst den rechten Pfad,
Die wir den Weg nicht wissen!
Gib uns Beständigkeit, dass wir
Getreu dir bleiben für und für,
Wenn wir nun leiden müssen!
Schaue, baue,
Was zerrissen
Und geflissen,
Dir zu trauen
Und auf dich allein zu bauen!

O mighty Rock, O Source of life,
Let your good Word in doubt and strife
Be in us strongly burning
That we be faithful unto death
And live in love and holy faith,
From you true wisdom learning.
Lord, your mercy
On us shower;
By your power
Christ confessing,
We will cherish all your blessing.

Du starker Fels und Lebenshort,
Lass uns dein himmelsüsses Wort
In unsern Herzen brennen,
Dass wir uns mögen nimmermehr
Von deiner weisheitreichen Lehr'
Und reinen Liebe trennen!
Fliesse, giesse
Deine Güte
Ins Gemüte,
Dass wir können
Christum unsern Heiland nennen!

First published in 1640 in Crüger's *Newes Vollkommliches Gesangbuch Augspurgischer Confession* (Berlin), this Pentecost hymn by Michael Schirmer was originally comprised of seven stanzas. It was greatly altered for inclusion in the Hanoverian *Gesangbuch* (Lüneberg, 1659), wherein Schirmer's fifth stanza was reworked and placed second. Later hymnbooks retained this revision, also restoring Schirmer's original fifth stanza, thus creating a hymn of eight stanzas, of which *Lutheran Worship* has retained three. Here omitted are stanzas 2–3,5,7–8.

Schirmer's third stanza—stanza 2 in *Lutheran Worship*—is a recast of stanza 7 of Johann Heermann's "Wir wissen nicht, Herr Zabaoth." The translation is from Catherine Winkworth's *Chorale Book for England* (1863), slightly altered.

WIE SCHÖN LEUCHTET. For comments on the tune see hymn 73.

161 COME, GRACIOUS SPIRIT, HEAVENLY DOVE

Simon Browne patterned this hymn on that of Isaac Watts. Few hymns in the English language have been subjected to so many alterations and changes as this one. The hymn goes back to Browne's *Hymns and Spiritual Songs*, Book 1 (London, 1720), headed "The Soul giving itself up to the Conduct and Influence of the Holy Spirit." There were seven stanzas of which none escaped alterations, which began as early as 1769 in Ash and Evans, *A collection of Hymns adapted to Public Worship*. The present form crystallized in Mercer's (*LW* 206, 492) *Church Psalter and Hymn Book* (1864): omitting and substituting certain lines, and changing the personal pronoun from singular to plural, thus making the text a corporate rather than individual appeal.

WAREHAM is from William Knapp's *Sett of New Psalm Tunes and Anthems in Four Parts*, where, with the melody in the tenor part, it was set to Psalm 36:5–10 and headed, "For the Holy Sacrament." Named for the birthplace of the composer, the tune appears to have proved popular (as indeed other of Knapp's compositions), for it appeared in at least ten different collections between 1747 and 1786. Notice its remarkable smoothness, moving stepwise (conjunct) except between the fifth and sixth notes.

In his later book, *New Church Melody* (1754), Knapp changed the tune to duple time, set to Psalm 139, calling it "Blandford." This version, however, never won favor. When the first, the triple-meter tune, set to the same psalm text, appeared in *Psalms, Hymns, and Anthems* (1774), a publication of the London Foundling Hospital, it had essentially the form as exhibited in *Lutheran Worship* (1982).

The harmonization is from the *Service Book and Hymnal* (1958) slightly altered.

162 COME DOWN, O LOVE DIVINE

Come down, O Love divine;
Seek out this soul of mine,
And visit it with your own ardor glowing;
O Comforter, draw near;
Within my heart appear,
And kindle it, your holy flame bestowing.

Oh, let it freely burn
Till worldly passions turn
To dust and ashes in its heat consuming;
And let your glorious light
Shine ever on my sight
And clothe me round, the while my path illuming.

Discendi, amor santo
Visita la mie mente
Del tuo amore ardente,
Si che di te m'infiammi tutto quanto.

Vienne, consolatore,
Nel mio cuor veramente:
Del tuo ardent amore
Ardel veracemente:
Del tuo amor cocente
Si forte sie ferito:
Vada come smarrito
Dentro e di fuore ardendo tutto quanto.

Let holy charity
My outward vesture be
And lowliness become my inner clothing—
True lowliness of heart,
Which takes the humbler part
And over its shortcomings weeps with loathing.

And so the yearning strong,
With which the soul will long,
Shall far outpass the pow'r of human telling;
No soul can guess his grace
Till it become the place
Wherein the Holy Spirit makes his dwelling.

Arda si fortemente
Che tutto mi consumi,
Si che veracemente
Lassi mondan costumi:
Li splendienti lumi
Lucenti, illuminanti
Mi stien sempre davanti,
Per il quali mi vesta il vero manto.

El manto ch'i'mi vesta
Sie la carita santa:
Sott'una bigia vesta
Umilita si canta,
La qual mai non si vanta
Per se nullo ben fare,
Non si sa inalzare,
Ma nel profondo scende con gran pianto.

Si grande e quel disio
Ch'allor l'anima sente,
Che dir nol sapre' io,
A cio non son potente:
Nulla umana mente
Entender nol potria,
Se nol gustasse pria
Per la vertu dello Spirito Santo.
Deo gratias.

This is a cento from the original eight stanzas that appeared in Bianco da Siena's *Laudi Spirituali* (1851), published by Telesforo Bini at Lucca, Italy. The translation, here altered largely in the process of updating, was done by Richard Littledale for inclusion in the *Peoples Hymnal* (1867).

Laudi Spirituali represent hymns of praise and devotion in the Italian language, set to simple melodies, that flourished in the 13th–14th centuries. They were especially popularized by the Flagellants of northern Italy, an enthusiastic sect of penitents that marched about seeking atonement for the sins of the time by scourging themselves. Later, groups of Christians called "Laudisti" cultivated and perpetuated devotional singing among the Italian people, thus outside the official auspices of the Roman Catholic, or Western, Church.

DOWN AMPNEY was composed for this hymn by Ralph Vaughan Williams, first published in *The English Hymnal* (1906) and named for his birthplace in Glaucestershire. It is a strong, dignified, moving tune, made especially interesting by its unusual metrical scheme. Parry and Routley assert that "it is perhaps the most beautiful hymn-tune composed since the *Old Hundredth*" (*LW* 216).

The harmonization, also by Vaughan Williams, is the one that appeared in the above hymnal.

163 O DAY FULL OF GRACE

O day full of grace that now we see
Appearing on earth's horizon,
Bring light from our God that we may be
Replete in his joy this season.
God, shine for us now in this dark place;
Your name on our hearts emblazon.

O day full of grace, O blessed time,
Our Lord on the earth arriving;
Then came to the world that light sublime,
Great joy for us all retrieving;
For Jesus all mortals did embrace,
All darkness and shame removing.

For Christ bore our sins, and not his own,
When he on the cross was hanging;
And then he arose and moved the stone
That we, unto him belonging,
Might join with angelic hosts to raise
Our voices in endless singing.

God came to us then at Pentecost,
His Spirit new life revealing,
That we might no more from him be lost,
All darkness for us dispelling.
His flame will the mark of sin efface
And bring to us all his healing.

When we on that final journey go
That Christ is for us preparing,
We'll gather in song, our hearts aglow,
All joy of the heavens sharing,
And walk in the light of God's own place,
With angels his name adoring.

Den signede Dag, som vi nu ser
Med Blide til os opkomme,
Den lyse af Himlen meer og meer
Os alle til Lyft og Fromme!
Det kjendes pá os, som Lysets Born,
At Natten den er nu omme!

Den signede Stund, den Midnats Tid,
Vor Herre han lod sig fode,
Da klarned det op i Oster-Lid
Til deiligste Morgenrode,
Da Lyset oprandt, som Jordens Kreds
Skal lysne udi og glode.

Thi takke vi Gud, vor Fader god,
Som Fuglen i Morgenrode,
For Dagen han os oprinde lod,
For Livet, hav gav af Dode!
For alt, pa vor Mark i tusind Ar,
Der grode til Sjaele-Fode!

Nu sagtelig skrid, du Pintsedag
Med Straler i Krans om Tinde!
Hver Time til Herrens Velbehag
Som Bekke i Eng henrinde,
Til frydelig sig tilsidst de sno
Op under de gronne Linde!

Sa reise vi til vort Faedreland,
Der ligger ei Dag i Dvale,
Der stander en Borg sa prud og grand
Med Sammen i gyldne Sale,
Sa Frydelig der til evig Tid
Med Venner i Lys vi tale!

This hymn is based on a pre-Reformation vernacular folk hymn popular in Scandinavia, a Swedish version of which, dating from about 1450, is in the library of Uppsala University. It was in Hans Thomissön's *Den Danske Psalmebog* (1569) that the hymn first appeared in the Danish language, revised for use in the cause of the Protestant Reformation. To commemorate the thousandth anniversary of the introduction of Christianity in Denmark, Bishop Nikolai Grundtvig (*LW* 291, 333) recast the hymn, an English translation of which appeared in the *Concordia Hymnal* (1932). The translation in *Lutheran Worship* (1982) is that from the older text prepared by Gerald Thorson for *Lutheran Book of Worship* (1978).

DEN SIGNEDE DAG is a splendid Scandinavian tune, composed in 1826 for the Grundtvig text by Christoph E. F. Weyse, organist at the Church of Our Lady, Copenhagen, from 1805–42. Users of *The Lutheran Hymnal* (1941) will recognize the tune as having been coupled to Magnus Landstad's (*LW* 234, 464, 466) "I Know of a Sleep in Jesus' Name (*TLH* 592). The harmonization is by Paul G. Bunjes.

HOLY SPIRIT, EVER DWELLING 164

This laudable Pentecost text by Timothy Rees first appeared in his *The Mirfield Mission Hymn Book* (c. 1922) and again in *Sermons and Hymns by Timothy Rees, Bishop of Landaff* (London and Oxford, 1946). Except for a few alterations ("Sons of earth" to "Those of earth;" "In a fellowship unending" to "In communion never ending") and the updating of personal pronouns (see essay: The Matter of Alterations, p. 817), the text is that which appeared in the latter publication. The hymn's inclusion in present-day hymnals—*Hymns for the church and school* (1964), *Hymns and Songs* (1969), and *The Hymnal* (1982)—attests to its ever gaining popularity.

IN BABILONE is an ingratiating Dutch tune (notice the similarity of three of its phrases, thus AABA) found in *Oude en Nieuwe Hollantse Boerenlities en Contradanseu* (c. 1710), a collection of old and new Dutch peasant songs and country dances, some of which were edited in modern arrangements by Julius Röntgen (1855–1932), distinguished Dutch conductor, composer, pianist, professor at and director of the Amsterdam Conservatory (1914–24), friend of Liszt, Brahms, and Grieg. In the course of preparing *The English Hymnal* (1906), this collection came to the attention of Ralph Vaughan Williams who then, recognizing the merit of this tune, included it in that hymnal, set to "See the Conqueror mounts in triumph" by Christopher Wordsworth (1807–85), Bishop of Lincoln.

The harmonization was prepared by Carl Schalk for the hymn's inclusion in *Worship Supplement* (1969).

COME, OH COME, O QUICKENING SPIRIT 165

Come, oh come, O quick'ning Spirit, God before the dawn of time! Fire our hearts with holy ardor, Blessed Comforter sublime! Let your radiance fill our night, Turning darkness into light.	Komm, o komm, du Geist des Lebens, Wahrer Gott von Ewigkeit! Deine Kraft sei nicht vergebens, Sie erfüll' uns jederzeit; So wird Geist und Licht und Schein In dem dunkeln Herzen sein.
Only that which you desire Be our object; with your hand Lead our ev'ry thought and action, Let them be at your command. All our sinfulness erase With the increase of your grace.	Gib ins unser Herz und Sinnen Weisheit, Rat, Verstand und Zucht, Dass wir andres nichts beginnen, Denn was nur dein Wille sucht! Dein'Erkenntnis werde gross Und mach uns von Irrtum los!

Blessed Spirit, still renewing
All who dwell upon the earth,
When the evil one assails us
Help us prove our heav'nly birth;
Arm us with your mighty sword
In the legions of the Lord.

Help us keep the faith forever;
Let not Satan, death, or shame
Draw us from you or deprive us
Of the honor of your name.
When the foe would lure us hence,
Be, O God, our sure defense.

O du Geist der Kraft und Stärke,
Du gewisser, neuer Geist,
Fördre in uns deine Werke,
Wenn der Satan Macht beweist;
Schenk uns Waffen in dem Krieg
Und erhalt in uns den Sieg!

Herr, bewahr auch unern Glauben,
Dass kein Teufel, Tod noch Spott
Uns denselben möge rauben!
Du bist unser Schutz und Gott.
Sagt das Fleish gleich immer nein,
Lass dein Wort gewisser sein.

This splendid hymn of invocation of the Holy Spirit first appeared in a publication by Heinrich Held's Altenburg friend, Johann Niedling, *Neuerfundener Geistlicher Wasserquelle* (Frankfort-am-Oder, 1658) with the caption: "On Holy Pentecost, to the French psalm tune 146." The translation by Edward Traill Horn III was originally done for the *Service Book and Hymnal* (1958).

KOMM, O KOMM, DU GEIST DES LEBENS. This tune first appeared in the *Neu-vermehrtes und zu übung Christliche Gottseligkeit eingerichtetes meinigisches Gesangbuch* (1693), where it was coupled to J. C. Werner's text, "Ich begehr nicht mehr zu leben." There it appeared thus (Zahn 3651):

The tune is undoubtedly older than 1693, for it is contained in a notebook of variations by Johann Christoph Bach (1642–1702), the uncle of Johann Sebastian Bach (1685–1750). Whether it is actually a creation of his is uncertain. The union of this tune to Held's Pentecost text first occurred in the *Geistreiches Gesangbuch* (Darmstadt, 1698).

Barry L. Bobb's setting is original to *Lutheran Worship.*

166 HOLY SPIRIT, LIGHT DIVINE

Desirous of including in *Lutheran Worship* "Holy Ghost, with Light Divine" from *The Lutheran Hymnal* (hymn 234) and recognizing the merit of "Holy Spirit, Truth Divine in *Lutheran Book of Worship* (hymn 257), the Commission on Worship accepted a composite text constructed by F. Samuel Janzow and Henry Lettermann of its Hymn Text and Music Committee. Thus this text includes some lines by the Congregational minister Andrew Reed, from his *Supplement* (1817) to Watts' hymns, and a considerable number by the Unitarian minister Samuel Longfellow, from *Hymns of the Spirit*, a collection he edited in collaboration with Samuel Johnson, a fellow student at Harvard.

SONG 13, also called GIBBONS, CANTERBURY, LIGHT DIVINE, NORWICH, ST. IRENAEUS, AND SIMPLICITY, was "put into its hat and boots," so Henry Alford (*LW* 495) describes the melody and bass lines, by Orlando Gibbons for George Wither's *Hymnes and Songs of the Church* (1623) where it was the setting for Song XIII, a metrical paraphrase of a part of the Song of Solomon (NIV, *Song of Songs*), beginning "O my love, how comely now." When one compares the original version below with that in the hymnal, one readily notices the rhythmic simplification and the harmonic changes that have occurred.

The harmonization was prepared by Richard W. Gieseke for *Lutheran Worship* (1982).

167 CREATOR SPIRIT, BY WHOSE AID

This is another translation of the "Veni Creator Spiritus, Mentes" (see *LW* 156) attributed to Rhabanus Maurus, here translated by John Dryden and included in a work published by Jacob Tonson entitled *Examen Poeticum: being the Third Part of Miscellany Poems, Containing a Variety of New Translations of the Ancient Poets, Together with many Original Copies, by the Most Eminent Hands* (1693). Originally in seven stanzas, those used here have been altered and updated.

ALL EHR UND LOB. For comments on this tune see hymn 210.
The setting is from *The Lutheran Hymnal* (1941), slightly altered.

HOLY, HOLY, HOLY 168

Reginald Heber wrote this hymn for the Sunday of the Holy Trinity, but its use has been almost universal. It appeared in *A Selection of Psalms and Hymns of the Parish Church of Banbury* (third edition, 1826) and later in Heber's posthumous collection of *Hymns, Written and Adapted to the Weekly Church Service of the Year* (1827). In a meter unusual for its time, this was one of Tennyson's favorite hymns. Percy Dearmer in *Songs of Praise Discussed* (1933) notes:

> It was the more valuable because in the Victorian books there were so few hymns about God; and this, free from all subjectivity, filled a large gap, expressing the pure spirit of worship in stately language based upon Rev. 4:8–11. Heber perhaps inaugurated the more flowing measures of our later hymnody, with its increasing width of metrical range.

One line has been changed from Heber's original: the second line of stanza 3 read, "Though the eye *of sinful man* thy glory may not see."

NICAEA was composed by John Dykes for Heber's text, although it is not the only or first tune to which the text has been sung. Inclusion of this combination in the first edition of *Hymns Ancient and Modern* (1861) has, however, solidly established the relationship. Routley opines that NICAEA "is perhaps the only really great and timeless tune that he [Dykes] wrote" (*The Music of Christian Hymnody*), because its style is reminiscent of the German chorale. Dykes appropriately named the tune NICAEA, for it was there (about 48 miles south of Constantinople) that some 300 bishops convened in 325 A.D. to settle the controversy about the Holy Trinity, with the resultant formulation of the Nicene Creed.

The harmonization is from *The Worship Book: Services and Hymns* (Westminster, 1972).

COME, O ALMIGHTY KING 169

This anonymous hymn entitled "An Hymn to the Trinity" first appeared in a four-page tract of unknown date containing also Charles Wesley's hymn on "The Backslider," beginning "Jesus, let thy pitying eye." This tract is bound up with the copies of George Whitefield's *Collection of Hymns for Social Worship* (1757, 1759, and 1760 editions) located in the British Museum. Later editions of Whitefield's *Collection* incorporated both above-mentioned hymns in the body of the work. Although this hymn is sometimes attributed to Charles Wesley, evidence for this is slight. The hymn appears in *Lutheran Worship* in updated form.

ITALIAN HYMN, a title referring to the composer's country of birth, also called MOSCOW, referring to his place of death, is the tune composed by Felice de Giardini that since 1769 has been sung to the text above for which it was written. It first appeared in Martin Madan's *A Collection of Psalm and Hymn Tunes Never Published Before* (1769), published for the benefit of Lock Hospital at Hyde Park in London.

The harmonization by Robert Carwithen is from *The Worshipbook: Services and Hymns* (Westminster, 1972).

170 TRIUNE GOD, OH, BE OUR STAY

Triune God, oh, be our stay; Oh, let us perish never! Cleanse us from our sins, we pray, And grant us life forever. Keep us from the evil one; Uphold our faith most holy, And let us trust you solely With humble hearts and lowly. Let us put God's armor on, With all true Christians running Our heav'nly race and shunning The devil's wiles and cunning. Amen, amen! This be done; So sing we "Alleluia!"	Gott der Vater wohn' uns bei Und lass' uns nicht verderben, Mach' uns aller Sünden frei Und helf' uns selig sterben! Vor dem Teufel uns bewahr', Halt uns bei festem Glauben Und auf dich lass uns bauen, Aus Herzensgrund vertrauen, Dir uns lassen ganz und gar, Mit allen rechten Christen Entfliehen Teufels Listen, Mit Waffen Gott's uns fristen! Amen, Amen, Das sei wahr, So singen wir: Halleluja!
Jesus Christ, oh, be our stay;	Jesus Christus wohn' uns bei
Holy Spirit, be our stay;	Heilig Geist, der wohn' uns bei

This hymn has its roots in the numerous medieval German folklike litanies invoking the aid of St. Mary, St. Peter, St. Nicholas, and others in versified form. This text is very similar to a litany to the virgin Mary preserved in a Crailshaim manuscript of 1480. Instead of addressing a saint, Luther invokes each person of the Trinity.

In its first appearance, namely, in Johann Walter's *Geistliche gesangk Buchleyn* (Wittenberg, 1524), this hymn stands between the Pentecost hymns and the Creed, "We All Believe in One True God, Maker" (*LW* 213), a position that identifies it with the Trinity. A number of church orders also give it this identification. Because of the close association of this text with the Gospel account of the temptation of our Lord, this hymn is given an alternate ending for use during Lent.

The English translation here given is by Richard Massey from *Martin Luther's Spiritual Songs* (London, 1854), slightly altered.

GOTT DER VATER WOHN' UNS BEI. The tune as it originally appeared in Walter's book shows that Luther took over the pre-Reformation tune without change.

The setting is by Paul G. Bunjes.

HOLY GOD, WE PRAISE YOUR NAME 171

Holy God, we praise your name;
Lord of all, we bow before you.
All on earth your scepter claim,
All in heav'n above adore you.
Infinite your vast domain,
Everlasting is your reign.

Hark! The glad celestial hymn
Angel choirs above are raising;
Cherubim and seraphim,
In unceasing chorus praising,
Fill the heav'ns with sweet accord:
Holy, holy, holy Lord!"

Lo, the apostolic train
Join your sacred name to hallow;
Prophets swell the glad refrain,
And the white-robed martyrs follow;
And from morn to set of sun
Through the Church the song goes on.

You are King of Glory, Christ;
Son of God, yet born of Mary.
For us sinners sacrificed,
As to death a Tributary,
First to break the bars of death,
You have opened heav'n to faith.

Holy Father, holy Son,
Holy Spirit, three we name you,
Though in essence only one;
Undivided God we claim you
And, adoring, bend the knee
While we own the mystery.

Grosser Gott, wir loben dich,
Herr, wir preisen deine Stärke,
Vor dir beugt die Erde sich
Und bewundert deine Werke.
Wie du warst vor aller Zeit,
So bleibst du in Ewigkeit.

Alles, was dich preisen kann,
Cherubim und Seraphinen,
Stimmen dir ein Loblied an.
Alle Engel, die dir dienen,
Rufen dir in sel'ger Ruh':
Heilig, heilig, heilig! zu.

Der Apostel heil'ger Chor,
Der Propheten grosse Menge
Schickt zu deinem Thron empor
Neue Lob- und Dankgesänge.
Der Blutzeugen grosse Schar
Lobt und preist dich immerdar.

Du, des ewgen Vaters Sohn,
Hast die Menschheit angenommen,
Du bist auch von deinem Thron,
Zu uns auf die Welt gekommen.
Gnade hast du uns gebracht,
Von der Sünde frei gemacht.

Sie verehrt dein Heil'gen Geist,
Welcher uns mit seinen Lehren
Und mit Troste kräftig speist;
Der, o König aller Ehren,
Der mit dir, Herr Jesu Christ,
Und dem Vater ewig ist.

This is a portion of the very popular versified German *Te Deum*, "Grosser Gott, wir loben dich," that appeared, together with the tune, in eight stanzas in the *Katholisches Gesangbuch*, published in Vienna in 1774 at the request of the Austrian Empress Maria Theresa, a devout Roman Catholic and an important political figure in 18th-century Europe. Although both author and composer are unknown, the hymn became immediately popular and was included in, among others, *Catholic Hymns* (Albany, 1860), *The Catholic Psalmist* (Dublin, 1858), and Alfred Young's *Complete Sodalist's Manual and Hymn Book* (1863). It became used in Protestant denominations in the United States through its appearance in Hall and Lasar's *Evangelical Hymnal* (New York, 1880), in the translation by Clarence A. Walworth, which bore the date of 1853. It is his translation, altered and updated, that appears in *Lutheran Worship* (1982). It is said that Walworth's lines were inspired by the singing of "Grosser Gott, wir loben dich" that he heard on pilgrimages during his seminary days in Belgium.

GROSSER GOTT (TE DEUM) is the anonymous tune that appeared with "Gosser Gott, wir loben dich" in the *Katholiches Gesangbuch* mentioned above. There, according to Bäumker (III, 219, p. 285), it went thus:

This tune has seen its share of variants (Bäumker III, pp. 286–87). Its present form is from Johann G. Schicht's *Allgemeienes Choral-Buch für Kirchen, Schulen, Gesangvereine, Orgel-und Piano forte-Spieler*, published in Leipzig in 1819 (Zahn 3495).

The harmonization in *Lutheran Worship* is from *The Worshipbook: Services and Hymns* (Westminster, 1972).

This metrical setting of the Te Deum can occasionally well serve as a substitute for the prose setting (*LW*, canticle 8). This applies also to a lesser known version, namely, "We Worship You, O God of Might" (*LW* 199).

It is interesting to note that "Holy God, We Praise Your Name," is a well-loved hymn in Roman Catholic churches. It warmed one's heart to hear it played as the late President Kennedy's casket was carried out of St. Matthew's Cathedral, Washington, D.C., November 25, 1963; it was sung by a large crowd in Yankee Stadium, New York City, following the historic celebration of the Mass by Pope Paul VI, October 4, 1965.

172 I BIND UNTO MYSELF TODAY

Known as the "Lorica of St. Patrick," or "St. Patrick's Breastplate," this text is found in two 11th-century manuscripts, one in the library of Trinity College, Dublin, reproduced in John H. Bernard and Robert Atkinson's *The Irish Liber Hymnorum* (1898). Tradition ascribes the text to St. Patrick, whose refusal to honor the heathen festival headed by King Loegaire caused the latter to plot his assassination. According to the legend, Patrick and his men invoked this *lorica* as they fled from the king's wrath, at which point they appeared as wild deer and escaped unharmed.

The Irish know the hymn as *Faeth Fiada*, sometimes translated as "Deer's Cry." However, "cry" or "scream" would actually be *faed*, while the manuscripts unquestionably call it *faeth*. Bernard and Atkinson believe that *feth fiadha* was a "*spell*, peculiar to druids and poets, who by pronouncing certain verses made themselves invisible. And thus this Lorica may have gained its title not from any tradition about St. Patrick and the deer at Tara, but from its use as a charm or incantation to ensure invisibility." This type of superstitious incantation has long been a part of the religion of Ireland, incorporated into the early Christianity of the region.

While Bernard and Atkinson have found in the Irish text "uncouthness of grammatical forms" that could easily point to St. Patrick, others claim it to be no earlier than eighth century in origin.

Cecil F. Alexander, the greatest of women hymn writers in English, prepared the spirited metrical paraphrase for St. Patrick's Day, 1889. It was comprised of two parts with doxology, of which *Lutheran Worship* omits the second section:

> Christ be with me, Christ within me,
> Christ behind me, Christ before me,
> Christ beside me, Christ to win me,
> Christ to comfort and restore me,
> Christ beneath me, Christ above me,
> Christ in quiet, Christ in danger,
> Christ in hearts of all that love me,
> Christ in mouth of friend and stranger.

Because of the layout of the Irish text, with its separate parts and unusual indentations, it is thought possible that it was intended to fill a particular shape, perhaps that of a physical breastplate. The opening line, "Atomriug indiu," has been translated several different ways; it is generally agreed that the literal meaning is closer to "I arise today" than "I bind unto myself today," but that the following lines include the sense of invocation.

ST. PATRICK'S BREASTPLATE is from George Petrie's *Complete Collection of Irish Music*, edited by C. V. Stanford, 1902, where it bears the caption "The hymn by St. Bernard, 'Jesu dulcis memoria' from Mr. Southwall." The present form of the tune is from *The English Hymnal* (1906).

The harmonization was prepared by Carl Schalk for *Worship Supplement* (1969).

This hymn and tune early on became especially associated with the Baptism of new converts at the Easter Vigil. The records in Westminster Abbey indicate that it was used at weddings. As a processional it is best sung in a slow and dignified manner.

GLORY BE TO GOD THE FATHER 173

Although first published in Bonar's *Hymns of Faith and Hope* (third series, 1866), this hymn was written specifically for *Psalms and Hymns for Divine Worship*, a compilation for the English Presbyterian Church which came off the press a year later. It calls to mind the joyful praise: "To him who loves us and has freed us from our sins by his blood, and has made us to be a kingdom of priests to serve his God and Father—to him be the glory and power for ever and ever! Amen" (Rev. 1:5b–6). In some churches the first stanza is sung at times in place of the long meter doxology.

WORCESTER was composed by Walter Grenville Whinfield. Diligent research has been unsuccessful in discovering the original or first appearance of this fine tune. Repeating the opening phrase and using the third phrase as the climax, gives the congregation's singing a powerful boost. Originally this text was set to REGENT SQUARE (*LW* 50).

The harmonization was prepared by George Leonard, a *nom de plume* of Paul G. Bunjes.

174 THE LORD, MY GOD, BE PRAISED

The Lord, my God, be praised, My light, my life from heaven; My maker, who to me Has soul and body given; My Father, who will shield And keep me day by day And make each moment yield New blessings on my way.	Gelobet sei der Herr, Mein Gott, mein Licht, mein Leben, Mein Schöpfer, der mir hat Mein Leib und Seel' gegeben, Mein Vater, der mich schützt Von Mutterleibe an, Der alle Augenblick' Viel Gut's an mir getan!
The Lord, my God, be praised, My trust, my life from heaven, The Father's own dear Son, Whose life for me was given, Who for my sin atoned With his most precious blood And gives to me by faith The highest heav'nly good.	Gelobet sei der Herr, Mein Gott, mein Heil, mein Leben, Des Vaters liebster Sohn, Der sich für mich gegeben, Der mich erlöset hat Mit seinem teuren Blut, Der mir im Glauben schenkt Das allerhöchste Gut!
The Lord, my God, be praised, My hope, my light from heaven, The Spirit, whom the Son In love to me has given. His grace revives my heart And gives my spirit pow'r, Help, comfort, and support In sorrow's gloomy hour.	Gelobet sei der Herr, Mein Gott, mein Trost, mein Leben, Des Vaters werter Geist, Den mir der Sohn gegeben, Der mir mein Herz erquickt, Der mir gibt neue Kraft, Der mir in aller Not Rat, Trost und Hilfe schafft!
The Lord, my God, be praised, My God, the ever-living, To whom the heav'nly host Their laud and praise are giving. The Lord, my God, be praised, In whose great name I boast, God Father, God the Son, And God the Holy Ghost.	Gelobet sei der Herr, Mein Gott, der ewig lebet, Den alles lobet, was In allen Lüften schwebet! Gelobet sei der Herr, Des Name heilig heisst: Gott Vater, Gott der Sohn Und Gott der werte Geist.

Of the hymns for Trinity Sunday in *Lutheran Worship*, this hymn by Johannes Olearius, member of the illustrious family of German Lutheran theologians, noted poet, hymn scholar and collector, ranks certainly among the best. First published in his monumental *Geistliche Singe-Kunst* (Leipzig, 1671), it appeared therein with the caption: "Encouragement from the festival Gospel, John 3, to thankful meditation on the great mystery of the Trinity." Originally in seven stanzas, the doxological and conclusive character of stanza 4 prompted the Commission on Worship to drop stanza 5.

The translation by August Crull has been updated.

NUN DANKET ALLE GOTT was evidently the tune Olearius had in mind when he wrote the text. For comments on the tune see hymn 443.

The harmonization was prepared by Richard W. Gieseke.

FATHER MOST HOLY, MERCIFUL, AND TENDER 175

Father most holy, merciful, and tender;
Jesus, our Savior, with the Father reigning;
Spirit of comfort, advocate, defender,
Light never waning.

Trinity blessed, unity unshaken;
Goodness unbounded, very God of heaven,
Light of the angels, joy of those forsaken,
Hope of all living.

Maker of all things, all thy creatures praise thee;
All for thy worship were and are created;
Now, as we also worship thee devoutly,
Hear thou our voices.

Lord God Almighty, unto thee be glory,
One in three persons, over all exalted!
Glory we offer, praise thee and adore thee,
Now and forever.

O Pater sancte, mitis atque pie,
O Iesu Christe, Fili venerande,
Paracliteque Spiritus o alme,
Deus aeterne,

Trinitas sancta unitasque firma,
Deitas vera, bonitas immensa,
Lux angelorum, salus orphanorum,
Spesque cunctorum,

Serviunt tibi cuncta, quae creasti;
Te tuae cunctae laudant creaturae;
Nos quoque tibi psallimus devoti;
Tu nos exaudi.

Gloria tibi, omnipotens Deus,
Trinus et unus, magnus et excelsus;
Te decet hymnus, honor, laus, et decus
Nunc et in aevum. Amen

This anonymous Latin hymn is found in several 10th-century French manuscripts and it appears in the breviaries of Sarum, York, Aberdine, Old Roman, and others, assigned to the office for Trinity Sunday.

The translation, based on that done by Percy Dearmer for *The English Hymnal* (1906), was prepared by the Inter-Lutheran Commission on Worship for inclusion in *Lutheran Book of Worship* (1978). It retains the interesting sapphic meter (11 11 11 5), a favorite of Latin hymn writers. This is a rather notable hymn in that it contains a concentrated summary of trinitarian doctrine.

CHRISTE SANCTORUM is an anonymous French church tune first found in the *Paris Antiphoner* (1681), set to a hymn for the visitation of the Blessed Virgin beginning "Ceteri numquam nisi vagiendo," and also in the *Cluny Antiphoner* (1686), set to "Mille quem stipant" for the festival of St. Michael, as well as in La Feillee *Methode du plain-chant* (1750), a manual of instruction for choirmasters written by a priest and singer connected with the choir of Chartres Cathedral. Although printed as plainsong, or Gregorian chant, these French church tunes were somewhat on the order of measured music and they were predominantly in the major and minor tonality as against the old church modes (see essay: The Church Modes, p. 832). Their source was the French breviaries of the 17th and 18th centuries, the result of the breviary revision and modernization begun by Pope Urban VIII (1568–1644). La Feillee's *Methode* concerned itself not only with singing the traditional plainsong but in singing the new church tunes as well. It was a book that continued to be printed and augmented by other editors well into the 19th century; it constituted a source of seven fine tunes in *The Hymnal Noted* (1852, 1854), prepared by John Mason Neale (*LW* 31, et al.) and Thomas Helmore, and of a number in *The English Hymnal* (1906) and in subsequent English hymnals. For an excellent account of these French tunes see Pocknee, *The French Diocesan Hymns and Their Melodies* (1954).

The name of the splendid tune under discussion is due to its association with the medieval office hymn "Christe sanctorum, decus angelorum." The harmonization was prepared by Carl F. Schalk for inclusion in *Worship Supplement* (1969).

THE BRIDEGROOM SOON WILL CALL US

176

The Bridegroom soon will call us,
"Come to the wedding feast."
May slumber not befall us
Nor watchfulness decrease.
But may our lamps be burning
With oil enough and more
That, with our Lord returning,
We find an open door.

Then, oh, what jubilation
To see our Savior's face,
His glorious exaltation
Since winning us God's grace.
Then kings will come to meet us
And psalmists rich in song,
Apostles, prophets greet us,
A great and splendid throng.

Then Christ, his glory sharing,
Will give us crowns of gold
He won for us by wearing
Thorned agonies untold.
The Father with embraces
Will welcome us, each one,
Robed in the Spirit's graces
As princely as God's Son.

Like skies in joyous motion
Or music after tears,
New song will fill the ocean
Of heaven's ageless years
While angel hosts are raising
With saints from great to least
The anthem tides for praising
The Giver of this feast.

Der Bräut'gam wird bald rufen:
Kommt all', ihr Hochzeitsgäst'!
Hilf, Gott, dass wir nicht schlafen,
In Sünden schlummern fest,
Bald hab'n in unsern Händen
Die Lampen, Ol und Licht
Und dürfen uns nicht wenden
Von deinem Angesicht.

Da werden wir mit Freuden
Den Heiland schauen an,
Der durch sein Blut und Leiden
Den Himmel aufgetan,
Die lieben Patriarchen,
Propheten allzumal,
Die Märt'rer und Apostel
Bei ihm, ein' grosse Zahl.

Gott wird sich zu uns kehren,
Ein'm jeden setzen auf
Die güldne Kron' der Ehren
Und herzen freundlich drauf,
Wird uns an sein' Brust drücken
Aus Lieb' ganz väterlich,
An Leib und Seel' uns schmücken
Mit Gaben mildiglich.

Da wird man hören klingen
Die rechten Saitenspiel';
Die Musikkunst wird bringen
In Gott der Freuden viel.
Die Engel werden singen,
All' Heil'gen Gottes gleich,
Mit himmelischen Zungen
Ewig in Gottes Reich.

In the 16th century, or earlier, there existed a popular folk song in seven stanzas, the first stanza of which read:

Herzlich tut mich erfreuen
Die frölich Sommerzeit
All mein Geblüt verneuen,
Der Mai viel Wullust geit.
Die Lerch tut sich erschwingen
Mit ihrem süssem Schall,
Lieblich die Vöglein singen,
Voraus die Nachtigall.

Using this folk song as a basis, Johann Walter, cantor in Torgau, Luther's musician and friend, constructed a 34-stanza hymn, first published in Wittenberg in 1552, entitled "A

Beautiful Spiritual Christian and New Miner's Song [Alpine Song] of the Last Day and Eternal Life."

Melchior Franck's (*LW* 306) fondness for Walter's version prompted him to create, using Walter's stanzas 31, 8, 9, 16, 18, 17, 13, a shorter hymn beginning "Der Bräutgam wird bald rufen" ("The bridegroom soon will call us"), which he included in his *Rosetulum Musicum* (Coburg, 1627), and again in his *Gotha Cantional* of 1647. From there it made its way into numerous 18th-century hymnals. Granted, with its emphasis now on the parable of the ten virgins (Matt. 25:1–13), the folk character of Walter's spiritual song is lost. The gain, however, is that many German hymns on the glories of life everlasting find their roots in this original version of Johann Walter.

The translation by F. Samuel Janzow is an altered and updated cento based on the translation by Matthias Loy (*LW* 235, et al.) that appeared in the Ohio Synod's *Hymnal* (1880).

ACH GOTT VOM HIMMELREICHE. This laudable tune is from Michael Praetorius' *Musae Sioniae* VII of 1609 (Zahn 5368). Friedrich Layriz' inclusion of this tune in his chorale book *Geistliche Melodien* (1848) evidently brought into common use and popularized it in German worshiping congregations to the point of causing it to appear in the *Evangelical Lutheran Hymn-Book* (1912), *The Lutheran Hymnal* (1941), and now in *Lutheran Worship* (1982), wherein it is used twice (see *LW* 244).

The harmonization is by Paul G. Bunjes.

177 WAKE, AWAKE, FOR NIGHT IS FLYING

"Wake, awake, for night is flying,"
The watchmen on the heights are crying;
"Awake, Jerusalem, arise!"
Midnight hears the welcome voices
And at the thrilling cry rejoices:
"Where are the virgins, pure and wise?
The bridegroom comes, awake!
Your lamps with gladness take!
Alleluia!
With bridal care
And faith's bold prayer,
To meet the bridegroom, come, prepare!"

Zion hears the watchmen singing,
And in her heart new joy is springing.
She wakes, she rises from her gloom.
For her Lord comes down all-glorious,
The strong in grace, in truth victorious.
Her star's arising light has come!
"Now come, O blessed one,
Lord Jesus, God's own Son.
Hail! Hosanna!
We answer all

Wachet auf! ruft uns die Stimme
Der Wächter sehr hoch auf der Zinne,
Wach auf, du Stadt Jerusalem!
Mitternacht heisst diese Stunde,
Sie rufen uns mit hellem Munde:
Wo seid ihr klugen Jungfrauen?
Wohlauf, der Bräut'gam kömmt,
Steht auf, die Lampen nehmt!
Halleluja!
Macht euch bereit
Zu der Hochzeit,
Ihr müsset ihm entgegengehn!

Zion hört die Wächter singen,
Das herz tut ihr vor Freuden springen,
Sie wacht und stehet eilend auf.
Ihr Freund kommt vom Himmel prächtig,
Von Gnaden stark, von Wahrheit mächtig,
Ihr Licht wird hell, ihr Stern geht auf.
Nun komm, du werte Kron',
Herr Jesu, Gottes Sohn!
Hosianna!
Wir folgen all'

In joy your call, We follow to the wedding hall."	Zum Freudensaal Und halten mit das Abendmahl.
Now let all the heav'ns adore you, Let saints and angels sing before you With harp and cymbals' clearest tone. Of one pearl each shining portal, Where, joining with the choir immortal, We gather round your radiant throne. No eye has seen that light, No ear the echoed might Of your glory; Yet there shall we In your vict'ry Sing shouts of praise eternally!	Gloria sei dir gesungen Mit menschen- und mit Engelzungen, Mit Harfen und mit Zimbeln schön. Von zwölf Perlen sind die Pforten An deiner Stadt, wir sind Konsorten Der Engel hoch um deinen Thron. Kein Aug, hat je gespürt Kein Ohr hat mehr gehört Solche Freude. Das sind wir froh, I-o, i-o, Ewig in dulci iubilo.

Philipp Nicolai composed both text and music for this hymn while a pastor at Unna in Westphalia. During this time the bubonic plague was ravaging the country; no less than 1400 people died in the course of the first seven months in 1597. Pondering the many deaths in his parish and the eternal life to follow, Nicolai wrote:

> Day by day I wrote out my meditations, found myself, thank God, wonderfully well, comforted in heart, joyful in spirit, and truly content; gave to my manuscript name and title of a *Mirror of Joy*, and took this, thus composed, to leave behind (if God should call me from the world) as the token of my peaceful, joyful, Christian departure, or (if God should spare me in health) to comfort other sufferers whom he should also visit with the pestilence.

This description of the state of mind which allowed Nicolai to produce "the king of chorales" amid the fear and horror of the time appeared in the appendix to his *Frewden-Spiegel des ewigen Lebens* (Frankfurt-am-Main, 1599), wherein the hymn first appeared.

The text is based on Matthew 25:1–13, the Parable of the Ten Virgins; Revelation 19:6–9; 21:21; 1 Corinthians 2:9; Ezekiel 3:17; and Isaiah 3:8. Described by Nicolai as "a spiritual bridal hymn of the believing soul concerning Jesus Christ, her heavenly bridegroom," it became a favorite marriage hymn in Germany. In the original German the text forms a reversed acrostic—W, Z, G— the initial letter of each of its three stanzas referring to Count Wilhelm Ernst, the *Graf zu Waldeck*, a friend and former student of Nicolai.

With its unique trochaic-iambic meter, this hymn is patterned after the "watchmen's songs" of the Middle Ages but, where the latter warned workers of darkness to escape discovery, Nicolai's hymn calls Christians to the light.

The original translation, here considerably altered, is by Catherine Winkworth. It appeared in her *Lyra Germanica* (second series, 1858).

WACHET AUF. This tune, also by Nicolai, was first published with the text in 1599. It bears some resemblance to the "Silberweisse" by Hans Sachs (1494–1576), the cobbler-poet of Nürnberg. Winterfeld says it is the greatest and most solemn melody of evangelical Christendom.

The setting is by Paul G. Bunjes.

178 AT THE NAME OF JESUS

Caroline M. Noel's long illness produced some of her finest work in *The Name of Jesus, and Other Verses for the Sick and Lonely* (1861), later enlarged and changed to *The Name of Jesus and Other Poems* (1870). This hymn, originally beginning "In the name of Jesus," appeared in the latter. It is based on Philippians 2:9-11, which passage may itself have been a paraphrase of an early Christian hymn. Noel intended the hymn for use as a processional on Ascension Day.

The doxology was added to Noel's text by *Songs of Praise* (1925). The only other alterations are in the sixth stanza, "*Brothers*, this Lord Jesus," and "*With* his Father's glory."

The hymn's concern, based as it is on Philippians 2:9–11, is that in consequence of his humiliation and self-sacrafice Christ is given "the name that is above every name"; it is not specifically a title that is meant, but the highest honor and authority over all creation, a status befitting his divine majesty and glory.

KING'S WESTON was both composed and harmonized for this Ascension Day processional by Ralph Vaughan Williams for inclusion in *Songs of Praise* (1925), of which he was music editor with Martin Shaw. A solid tune, in triple time with strongly stressed rhythm, it seems to march forward toward the pitch-height accent note D in measure 13 and then recede with a contrasting rhythmic pattern: 𝅗𝅥 𝅗𝅥 ♩ ♩ against the earlier ♩ ♩ 𝅗𝅥 𝅗𝅥. Also, the B♮ in measure 11 gives the impression of the strong Dorian mode. (See essay: The Church Modes, p. 832.)

According to McCutchan, KING'S WESTON is "a country house on the River Avon near Bristol, England, noted for its beautiful park" (*Hymn Tune Names*).

179 REJOICE, THE LORD IS KING

Charles Wesley's Pentecost hymn in six stanzas appeared in John Wesley's *Moral and Sacred Poems* (1744), and again in *Hymns for our Lord's Resurrection* (1746). The final two stanzas are omitted:

He all his foes shall quell,
And all our sins destroy;
Let every bosom swell
With pure seraphic joy;

Rejoice in glorious hope;
Jesus the Judge shall come,
And take his servants up
To their eternal home;

and the final refrain ran:

> We soon shall hear the angel's voice;
> The trump of God shall sound—Rejoice!

Otherwise, alterations are confined to stanza 1, line 3: "*Mortals*, give thanks and sing" and stanza 2, line 1: "*Jesus, the Savior*, reigns."

Although composed for Whitsuntide, or Pentecost, the hymn has a general significance and is appropriate for various occasions. In the meter of 66 66 88, the first stanza is a masterpiece in its use of the short sixes for imperative exhortations followed by the longer eights in the refrain.

DARWALL'S 148th (DARWELL, ZION, OLNEY) was the tune composed by John Darwall for Aaron Williams' *New Universal Psalmodist* (London, 1770) for the New Version (see essay: Metrical Psalms, p. 825) of Psalm 148, beginning "Ye boundless realms of joy." Although Darwall set the entire Psalter to two-part tunes, this is the only tune of his that remains in use. An excellent tune, undoubtedly one of the best in what is sometimes referred to as the Hallelujah Meter—66 66 88, it represents one of the many ways of combining sixes and eights in addition to that in the basic Short, Common, and Long meters, and thus creating a refreshing and delightful "unsquare" form. Moreover, the usual rhyme scheme of ABABCC—admittedly there are variations—adds to the pleasure of singing this type of tune. Its upward general movement makes it, in this instance, very suitable to the text.

This setting is from *The Lutheran Hymnal* (1941).

180 OUR GOD, OUR HELP IN AGES PAST

This hymn, undoubtedly the greatest hymn in the English language, was first published by Isaac Watts in his *Psalms of David, Imitated* (1719). Originally in nine stanzas, based on Psalm 90:1–5, it was headed "Man Frail and God Eternal." Watts probably wrote this hymn about 1714, in a time of great national anxiety just before the death of Queen Anne in August of that year. Her death halted the enactment of the Schism Act that would have suppressed Dissenters (of whom Watts was one) and would undoubtedly have brought persecution upon them.

George Sampson, in his Warton Lecture to the British Academy in 1943, asks and answers:

> What is the greatest of all English hymns? The hymn that suits all sorts and condition of men, at church or at chapel, on ship or at church parade anywhere; the hymn we can sing in triumph or in adversity, the hymn of consolation, comfort and resignation? It is the first part of Psalm 90, written in common meter by Isaac Watts, and bearing the title 'Man Frail and God Eternal' (*The Century of Divine Songs).*

How true! But this hymn, based as it is on the profoundest psalm on the mystery of time, rises above occasions and situations. Reflecting on the inexorable passing of time, expressed in the Greek word *chronos*, it looks with hope to the *kairos*, the proper, the right time for something, to the God of our eternal salvation. In the final analysis it is the *kairos*-time that gives meaning and purpose to the *chronos*.

In his *Collection of Psalms and Hymns* (1737), John Wesley printed the hymn with the opening, "O God, our help," a form that many subsequent hymnals have followed. Perhaps this was prompted by his dislike for overfamiliarity with God; perhaps he thought the fourfold repetition of "our" stylistically clumsy. The editors of *Lutheran Worship*, however, chose to retain the original, the more personal style of the Lord's Prayer. Also, stanza 5, line 2 was changed from the author's "Bears all its sons away" to the inclusive "Soon bears us all away;" and "They fly forgotten" in line 3 was changed to "We fly forgotten." In keeping with the updated language, line 3 of stanza 6 reads "Still be our guard" instead of "Be thou our guard."

ST. ANNE was probably composed by William Croft. It appeared anonymously in the sixth edition of *A supplement to the New Version of Psalms* (1708) by Tate and Brady, set to a paraphrase of Psalm 42, "As pants the heart for cooling streams," but it was attributed to Croft in two later collections—in Philip Hart's (d.c. 1749) *Melodies Proper to be sung to any of ye versions of ye Psalms of David* (1720), and in John Church's (1679–1741) *Introduction to Psalmody* (1723). Both these editors were contemporaries of Croft, and Church was master of the choristers at Westminster Abbey while Croft was organist there.

In the 1708 volume the tune is called ST. ANNE, the name of the Soho church where Croft served at the time. It appears as LEEDS in Abraham Barber's *Book of Psalm Tunes*, and credited to a "Mr. Denby." This collection was licensed in 1687, before the 6th *Supplement*, but the edition which contains the tune is the seventh, dated 1715; so unless an edition is found that includes the tune dated earlier than 1708, it must be assumed that the ascription to Croft is correct, and that Denby merely prepared a new arrangement.

The opening phrase of the tune is a common one of the early 18th century, and indeed is said to be traceable to a French chanson of the 16th century. Henry Lawes used this phrase in three tunes, including FARLEY CASTLE (*LW* 243). Handel used it in his sixth Chandos anthem, "O Praise the Lord" (1734), and Bach made it the theme of his *Fugue in E Flat major*, which in England is often called "St. Anne's Fugue," although there is really no evidence to suggest that Bach was familiar with the English tune.

The melody as it appears in the 1708 *Supplement* mentioned above begins and ends each line with a note of double length. A passing tone between the first and second notes of the penultimate bar is the only other difference between the tune's original and present forms; both changes were incorporated in the 1861 edition of *Hymns Ancient and Modern*, which first associated the tune with this text. This now almost legendary and traditional association illustrates the influence that *Hymns Ancient and Modern* exerted on the hymn singing of the whole Church in England.

The harmonization is from *The Lutheran Hymnal* (1941).

ACROSS THE SKY THE SHADES OF NIGHT 181

This New Year's Eve hymn by James Hamilton, originally in six stanzas, appeared in Godfrey Thring's (*LW* 218, et al.) *Collection* (1882). Hamilton designed the hymn, here in altered and updated form, to be sung to the chorale tune, ALLEIN GOTT IN DER HÖH.

ALLEIN GOTT IN DER HÖH. For comments on this tune see hymn 215.

The harmonization is by Wilhelm Quampen, *a nom de plume* of Paul G. Bunjes.

JESUS! NAME OF WONDROUS LOVE 182

This hymn by William Walsham How first appeared in the original edition of *Psalms and Hymns* (1854), which he prepared with Thomas Baker Morrell. Based essentially on the angel's words to Joseph, "You are to give him the name Jesus, because he will save his people from their sins," it is especially appropriate for corporate worship on

New Year's Eve. Included in the Synod's English hymnals as far back as the *Evangelical Lutheran Hymn-Book* (1912), this text has also enjoyed popularity in the Episcopal Church since the *Hymnal* of 1874, including *The Hymnal 1982*. Except for slight alterations and updating of the final two lines in stanza 6, the hymn appears as in *The Lutheran Hymnal* (1941).

GOTT SEI DANK (LÜBECK, BERLIN) is an altered form of the tune in minister-musician Johann A. Freylinghausen's celebrated *Geistreiches Gesangbuch* (Halle, 1704), where it was set to "Gott sei Dank in aller Welt" and went thus (from Zahn 1230):

Gottfried Heinrich Stölzel's 1744 hymnal was the first to print the present melodic form. It is a fine, song-like tune that the compilers of numerous present-day hymnals have not overlooked. In contrast to the more austere form of it in *The Lutheran Hymnal* (1941), the Commission on Worship added two passing tones (eighth notes F and A), more reflective of the original, thus giving the tune more lilt.

The harmonization is by Wilhelm Quampen, a *nom de plume* of Paul G. Bunjes.

183 GREET NOW THE SWIFTLY CHANGING YEAR

Greet now the swiftly changing year
With joy and penitence sincere.
Rejoice! Rejoice! With thanks embrace
Another year of grace.

Remember now the Son of God
And how he shed his infant blood.
Rejoice! Rejoice! With thanks embrace
Another year of grace.

This Jesus came to end sin's war;
This name of names for us he bore.
Rejoice! Rejoice! With thanks embrace
Another year of grace.

His love abundant far exceeds
The volume of a whole year's needs.
Rejoice! Rejoice! With thanks embrace
Another year of grace.
With him as Lord to lead our way

Rok novy zase k nám prisel,
v nemz má byti kazdy vesel:
Radujme se, veselme se
v tomto novém rose!

Zacal krev svou vylévati
a nád ní vykupovati:
Radujme se . . .

Jezis, pusobce spasení,
nazván jest nám k potesení:
Radujme se . . .

Vic ucinil dobrodini,
nez jest v roce okamzení:
Radujme se . . .

Ten verny Spasitel sveta

In want and in prosperity, What need we fear in earth or space In this new year of grace!	chránil nás jiz mnohá léta: Radujme se . . .
"All glory be to God on high, And peace to earth!" the angels cry. Rejoice! Rejoice! With thanks embrace Another year of grace.	Sláva bud Bohu na nebi, a pokoj lidem na zemi: Radujme se . . .
God, Father, Son, and Spirit, hear! To all our pleas incline your ear; Upon our lives rich blessing trace In this new year of grace.	Otce, Synu, Duchu Svaty, slys pokorné nase prosby: Otevri své stedré ruce v tomto novém roce.

This old and popular text, originally in 12 stanzas, appeared with the tune below in the *Kancional* (Prague, 1602), a hymnal of the Bohemian Brethren compiled by Tobias Závorka. In his concern for providing doctrinally sound hymns for Slovak Lutheran congregations, Jiri Tranovsky (*LW* 132) included text and tune in his *Pisne duchovni stare i move . . . cili Cithara Sanctorum* (1636) popularly identified by Slovak Lutherans as the "Tranoscius."

The translation was originally prepared by Jaroslav Vajda for inclusion in the *Worship Supplement* (1969). The slightly revised and updated text here given was prepared by Vajda for inclusion in *Lutheran Book of Worship* (1978).

Interestingly, both text and tune (and its harmonization) are included in the *Psalter Hymnal* (1987) of the Christian Reformed Church. *The Hymnal 1982* of the Episcopal Church has also included the text, beginning "Now greet the swiftly changing year," but with a new tune by Alfred V. Fedak (b. 1953).

ROK NOVY. This lovely tune of Slovak flavor is undoubtedly older than the date of 1602 when it appeared with the above text in Tobias Zavorka's *Kancional.* The harmonization was prepared by Theodore Beck for inclusion in the *Worship Supplement* (1969).

NOW LET US COME BEFORE HIM 184

Now let us come before him, With song and prayer adore him Who for our life has given The strength we need from heaven.	Nun lasst uns gehn und treten Mit Singen und mit Beten Zum Herrn, der unserm Leben Bis hierher Kraft gegeben.
The storms in battle clashing, The hooves of thunder crashing, True mothers guard the slumber Of children without number.	Denn Wie von treuen Müttern In schweren Ungewittern Die Kindlein hier auf Erden Mit Fleiss bewahret werden:
So when events are fright'ning And slash like lurid lightning, God hides us in embraces To shield his children's faces.	Also auch und nicht minder Lässt Gott sich seine Kinder, Wenn Not und Trübsal blitzen, In seinem Schosse sitzen.

God helps all those forsaken
When to their plight they waken,
Our counselor, our treasure,
Our friend in pain or pleasure.

Lord, show your tender feeling;
For sickness give your healing;
To minds, when dark thoughts frighten,
Come with your joy, bring light in.

Above all else, Lord, send us
Your Spirit to attend us,
His peace in us abiding,
Our footsteps heav'nward guiding.

Lass ferner dich erbitten,
O Vater, und bleib mitten
In unserm Kreuz und Leiden
Ein Brunnen unsrer Freuden.

Hilf gnädig allen Kranken,
Gib fröhliche Gedanken
Den hochbetrübten Seelen,
Die sich mit Schwermut quälen!

Und endich, was das meiste,
Füll uns mit deinem Geiste,
Der uns hier herrlich ziere
Und dort zum Himmel führe!

This is one of the few "we" hymns of Paul Gerhardt (in contrast to his more personal "I" hymns) that first appeared in the so-called Runge *Gesangbuch* (Berlin, 1653) produced for the Reformed churches in Berlin under the music editorship of Johann Crüger. Originally in 15 stanzas, it is the Thirty Years' War (1618–48) with its suffering and woe (more noticeable in the stanzas here omitted) that looms as the backdrop for this fine hymn. Recognizing its appropriateness for other than times of war, it soon began to be sung in worship on New Year's Eve or New Year's Day.

The translation is by F. Samuel Janzow.

NUN LASST UNS GOTT DEM HERREN. This tune by Nikolaus Selnecker first appeared in *Christliche Psalmen, Lieder und Kirchengesenge* (Leipzig, 1587), where it was set to a text by Ludwig Helmbold (*LW* 409, et al.) beginning with the same words. In the aforementioned Runge *Gesangbuch*, Johann Crüger revised and enhanced the tune, and it is this version that is here used. Departures from the version used in *The Lutheran Hymnal* (1941) will thus be readily noticed.

The harmonization was prepared by Paul G. Bunjes for *Lutheran Worship* (1982).

185 IN PEACE AND JOY I NOW DEPART

In peace and joy I now depart
Since God so wills it.
Serene and confident my heart;
Stillness fills it.
For God promised death would be
No more than quiet slumber.

This is what you have done for me,
My faithful Savior.
In you, Lord, I was made to see
All God's favor.
I now know you as my life,
My help when I am dying.

Mit Fried' und Freud' ich fahr' dahin
In Gottes Willen;
Getrost ist mir mein Herz und Sinn,
Sanft und stille,
Wie Gott mir verheissen hat:
Der Tod ist mein Schlaf worden.

Das macht Christus, wahr'r Gottessohn,
Der treue Heiland,
Den du mich, Herr, hast sehen lan
Und g'macht bekannt,
Dass er sei das Leben mein
Und Heil in Not und Sterben.

It was God's love that sent you forth
As man's salvation,
Inviting to yourself the earth,
Ev'ry nation,
By your wholesome healing Word
Resounding round our planet.

You are the health and saving light
Of lands in darkness;
You feed and lighten those in night
With your kindness.
All God's people find in you
Their treasure, joy and glory.

Den has du allen vorgestellt
Mit grossen Gnaden,
Zu seinem Reich die ganze Welt
Heissen laden
Durch dein teuer, heilsam Wort,
An allem Ort erschollen.

Er ist das Heil und selig Licht
Für all die Heiden,
Zu 'rleuchten, die dich kennen nicht,
Und zu weiden.
Er ist dein's Volks Israel
Der Preis, Ehr', Freud' und Wonne.

Luther's fondness for the Gospel appointed for the Presentation of Our Lord (Luke 2:22–32, Song of Simeon), February 2, evidently led him to turn his thoughts into a hymn that could be sung by the congregation. Thus in 1524 this hymn appeared in Johann Walter's *Geistliche gesangk Buchleyn* (Wittenberg). When one compares other 16th-century versifications of this Scripture text, one cannot but be impressed with the beauty of Luther's version. His overview of the Gospel message therein gives it the stamp of originality far exceeding a mere versification of Simeon's words in the Gospel text. Although primarily conceived for the Presentation of Our Lord, it was also sung as a funeral hymn and included in Klug's *Burial Hymns* (Wittenberg, 1542).

The translation is by F. Samuel Janzow.

MIT FRIED UND FREUD. This tune, in the Dorian mode, is the one that originally appeared in Walter's hymnbook. Its rhythmic pattern is reflective of the 16th-century polyphonic *cantus firmi*. Opinions differ as to whether it is by Luther or Walter.

The harmonization is by Paul G. Bunjes.

IN HIS TEMPLE NOW BEHOLD HIM 186

Henry J. Pye, in his collection of *Hymns* (1851), included this hymn for the Purification of the Blessed Virgin Mary. While few hymnals have found a place for it, the text is eminently suited to the Presentation of Our Lord, February 2.

The text also appeared in the Cooke and Denton *Hymnal* (1853), with an additional stanza by William Cooke.

WESTMINSTER ABBEY. From Henry Purcell's anthem, "O God, Thou Art My God," Ernest Hawkins made an arrangement of the terminal Alleluias for use as a hymn tune. The result was published in Vincent Novello's *The Psalmist: A Collection of Psalm and Hymn Tunes* (fourth series, 1843), named BELLEVILLE. *Hymns Ancient and Modern* (1861) used the tune, with harmonization essentially intact, calling it WESTMINSTER ABBEY. There is a certain grandeur and strength in a trochaic 87 87 87 such as this, a tune with room to carry weighty theological ideas.

Richard W. Gieseke prepared the setting for *Lutheran Worship* (1982).

187 WHEN ALL THE WORLD WAS CURSED

When all the world was cursed
By Moses' condemnation,
Saint John the Baptist came
With words of consolation.
With true forerunner's zeal
The greater one he named,
And him, as yet unknown,
As Savior he proclaimed.

Before he yet was born,
He leaped in joyful meeting,
Confessing him as Lord
Whose mother he was greeting.
By Jordan's rolling stream,
A new Elijah bold,
He testified of him
Of whom the prophets told:

Behold the Lamb of God
That bears the world's transgression,
Whose sacrifice removes
The enemy's oppression.
Behold the Lamb of God,
The bearer of our sin,
Who for our peace and joy
Will full atonement win.

Thrice blest is ev'ryone
Who heeds the proclamation
Which John the Baptist brought,
Accepting Christ's salvation.
He who believes this truth
And comes with love unfeigned
Has righteousness and peace
In fullest measure gained.

Our Lord of love, oh, grant
That we receive, rejoicing,
The word proclaimed by John,
Our true repentance voicing,
That gladly we may walk
Upon our Savior's way
Until we live with him
In his eternal day.

Es war die ganze Welt
Von Mosis Fluch erschrecket,
Bis Sankt Johannes hat
Den Finger ausgestrecket
Auf Jesum, welchen er
Zum Heiland aller Welt
Als sein Vorläufer hat
Gezeigt und vorgestellt,

Vor dem er ungebor'n
Mit Freuden aufgesprungen,
Zu dem er sich bekannt
Mit unberedter Zungen
In seiner Mutter Leib
Und mit Elias' Geist
Bei Gross' und Kleinen ihn
Gepredigt und geweist:

Sieh, das ist Gottes Lamm,
Das unsre Sünde träget,
Das sich der ganzen Welt
Zum Opfer niederleget;
Sieh, das ist Gottes Lamm,
Bei dem man aller Sünd'
Vergebung, Friede, Ruh'
Und alle Gnade find't!

Wohl dem, der dieses Lamm,
Das uns Johannes weiset,
Im Glauben fest ergreift
Und in dem Leben preiset!
Wer dieser Tauf' gedenkt
Und wahre Busse übt,
Der wird von ihm auch sein
Begnadet und geliebt.

So gib, du grosser Gott,
Dass wir Johannis Lehre
Von Herzen nehmen an,
Dass sich in uns bekehre,
Was bös und sündlich ist,
Bis wir nach dieser Zeit
Mit Freuden gehen ein
Zu deiner Herrlichkeit!

According to Julian, this hymn by Johann G. Olearius first appeared in his *Primitiae poeticae oder Erstlinge an deutschen Liedern und Madrigalien* (Halle, 1664). Olearius designated it for the festival of St. John the Baptist, observed on June 24.

The translation, prepared by Paul E. Kretzmann for *The Lutheran Hymnal* (1941), is slightly altered.

WAS FRAG ICH NACH DER WELT. For comments on this tune see hymn 418.

The harmonization was prepared for *Lutheran Worship* (1982) by Ralph Schultz. Other settings of this tune are at *LW* 371, 372, and 418.

SWEET FLOWERETS OF THE MARTYR BAND 188

Sweet flow'rets of the martyr band,
Plucked by the tyrant's ruthless hand
Upon the threshold of the morn,
Like rosebuds by a tempest torn;

First victims for th'incarnate Lord,
A tender flock to feel the sword;
Beside the altar's ruddy ray,
With palm and crown, you seemed to play.

Ah, what availed King Herod's wrath?
He could not stop the Savior's path.
Alone, while others murdered lay,
In safety Christ is borne away.

O Lord, the virgin-born, we sing
Eternal praise to you, our King,
Whom with the Father we adore
And Holy Spirit evermore.

Salvete, flores martyrum,
quos lucis ipso in limine
Christi insecutor sustulit,
ceu turbo nascentes rosas.

Quid crimen Herodem juvat?
vos, prima Christi victima,
grex immolatorum tener,
palma et coronis luditis.

Quid proficit tantum nefas?
inter coaevi sanguinis
fluenta solus integer
impune Christus tollitur.

Gloria tibi, Domine,
qui natus es de virgine,
cum Patre et sancto Spiritu
in sempiterna saecula.

This hymn, a cento by Prudentius, the notable Spanish poet of the early Christian Church, is taken from the 12th poem of his *Cathemerinon*, entitled "Hymnus Epiphaniae," which begins with "Quicumque Christum quaeritis." The present poem consists of lines 125–136 and a doxology. Especially heartwarming are the stanzas that picture the holy innocents, the first martyrs for Christ, gathered up to heaven and there, by the side of God's altar, playing childlike with the palms and crowns, the tokens of their reward.

The translation is by Henry W. Baker and first appeared in the revised edition of *Hymns Ancient and Modern* (1875), slightly altered.

DAS WALT GOTT VATER. This tune appeared as no. 37 in part 2 of Daniel Vetter's *Musicalische Kirchen- und Haus-Ergötzlichkeit* (Leipzig, 1713), for use with Martin Behm's text "Das walt Gott Vater und Gott Sohn."

The setting is from *The Lutheran Hymnal* (1941), altered. The tune itself reflects the more strict quarter-note notation by J. S. Bach. The original tune with its frequent passing tones was considerably more lyrical. It appeared as here given (Zahn 673):

Das walt Gott Vater u. Gott Sohn, Gott heilger Geist ins Himmels Thron;
man dankt dir, eh die Sonn aufgeht, wenns Licht anbricht, man vor dir steht.

189 LORD GOD, TO YOU WE ALL GIVE PRAISE

Lord God, to you we all give praise,
To you with joy our thanks we raise
For angel multitudes that shine
In your great throne room crystalline.

From them flow light and heav'nly grace
Reflecting splendors of your face.
They heed your voice, they know it well,
In godly wisdom they excel.

They never rest nor sleep as we;
Their whole delight is but to be
With you, Lord Jesus, and to keep
Your little flock, your lambs and sheep.

Increase, we plead, our song of praise
For angel hosts that guard our days;
Teach us to ceaselessly adore,
To serve as they do evermore.

Herr Gott, dich loben alle wir
Und sollen billig danken dir
Für dein Geschöpf der Engel schön,
Die um dich schweb'n vor deinem Thron.

Sie glänzen hell und leuchten klar
Und sehen dich ganz offenbar,
Dein' Stimm' sie hören allezeit
Und sind voll göttlicher Weisheit.

Sie feiern auch und schlafen nicht,
Ihr Fleiss ist gar dahin gericht't
Dass sie, Herr Christe, um dich sei'n
Und um dein armes Häufelein.

Darum wir billig loben dich
Und danken dir, Gott, ewiglich,
Wie auch der lieben Engel Schar
Dich preiset heut' und immerdar.

This hymn by Philip Melanchthon for the festival of St. Michael and All Angels (September 29) first appeared in Latin in a pamphlet that he published in Wittenberg in 1543 entitled *De angelis duo hymni Philippi Melanchthonis et Ionnis Stigelii*. (John Stigel [1515–62] lectured on early Latin literature at the University of Wittenberg.) This sapphic meter hymn (11 11 11 5, a combination of dactylic [´ ˘ ˘] and trochaic [´ ˘]), considered a consummate masterpiece, is here given in the four stanzas used in *Lutheran Worship*:

Dicimus grates tibi, summe rerum
Conditor, gnato tua quod ministros
flammeos finxit manus angelorum
agmina pura.

Qui tuae lucis radiis vibrantes
te vident laetis oculis, tuasque
hauriunt voces, sapientiaeque
fonte fruuntur.

Nos non ignavum finis esse vulgus,
nec per ingentes volitare frustra
aetheris tractus, temere nec inter
ludere ventos.

Hos tum munus celebramus una,
et tibi noster chorus angelique
gratias dicunt simul accinentes,
Conditor alme.

Paul Eber, a friend and colleague of Melanchthon, made a somewhat free German translation of the Latin text in the more simple, eight-syllable, four-line Ambrosian verse form. His version, in 13 stanzas, appeared in a separate print entitled *Ein schön neu geistlich Lobgesang* (Nürnberg, 1554).

The English translation by Emanuel Cronenwett first appeared in the Ohio *Lutheran Hymnal* (1880).

KOMM, GOTT SCHÖPFER. For comments on this tune see hymn 156.

The harmonization was prepared by George Leonard, a *nom de plume* of Paul G. Bunjes.

STARS OF THE MORNING, SO GLORIOUSLY BRIGHT 190

Stars of the morning, so gloriously bright,
Filled with celestial resplendence and light,
These, where no darkness the glory can dim,
Praise the Thrice Holy One, serving but him.

These are your ministers, these are your own,
Lord God of Sabaoth, nearest your throne,
These are your messengers, these whom you send,
Helping your helpless ones, Helper and Friend.

Then, when the earth was first poised in midspace,
Then, when the planets first sped on their race,
Then, when were ended the six days' employ,
Then all the sons of God shouted for joy.

Still let them be with us, still let them fight,
Lord of the angelic hosts, battling for right,
Till, where their anthems they ceaselessly pour,
We with the angels may bow and adore.

Φωστῆρες τῆς ἀΰλου οὐσίας,
τῶν νοερῶν δυνάμεων
προστατεύοντες
καὶ τῆς Τρισηλίου Δόξης
ταῖς μαρμαρυγαῖς
φωτοδοτοῦντες τὴν οἰκουμένην,
ἀρχιστράτηγοι,

ἀλήκτῳ φωνῇ,
τὸν τρισάγιον ὕμνον ἐξᾴδετε·
διὸ πρεσβεύσατε
σωθῆναι τὰς ψυχὰς ἡμῶν.

In his *Hymns of the Eastern Church* (1862) John Mason Neale refers to this hymn as "a cento from the Canon of the 'bodiless ones', Tuesday in the Week of the First Tone." He attributes it to St. Joseph the Hymnographer, whereas H. J. W. Tillyard credits it to St. John of Damascus (*Hymns of the Sticherarium for November. Monumenta Musicae Transcripta* II, [1938]). As opined by both Julian and Tillyard, Neale's lines are more inspired by the entire Greek Canon for this festival than as a rendering of this specific hymn.

The text in *Lutheran Worship* (1982) is an altered and updated form of that by Neale that appeared in *The Lutheran Hymnal* (1941).

O QUANTA QUALIA takes its name from having been set to a hymn text beginning with the same words in John Mason Neale's *The Hymnal Noted* (1852), a hymn written by the great scholar and theologian Peter Abelard (1079–1142) for the Abbey of the Paraclete at Nogent-sur-Seine, over which Heloise presided. The tune is an adaptation from the *Accompanying Harmonies to The Hymnal Noted* (1858) of a tune from a copy of Aynes' 1808 edition of La Feillees *Methode du Plain-chant*, where it was the setting for J. B. Santeuil's "Regnator orbis," thus the alternate name REGNATOR ORBIS. It is not an ancient plainsong tune but one of the French church melodies that came into use in the latter half of the 17th century. More correctly, it is from the *Paris Antiphoner* of 1681, where it was set to "Fumant sabaeis," a hymn for the Purification of the Virgin Mary.

The harmonization is by John B. Dykes in the Appendix (1868) to *Hymns Ancient and Modern* (1861).

191 FOR ALL THE SAINTS

When first published in Earl Nelson's *Hymns for Saints' Day, and Other Hymns* (1864), this magnificent hymn by William Walsham How contained 11 stanzas. The customarily omitted stanzas 3, 4, and 5 read thus:

For the apostles' glorious company
Who, bearing forth the cross o'er land and sea,
Shook all the mighty world, we sing to thee.
Alleluia! Alleluia!

For the evangelists, by whose pure word
Like fourfold stream, the garden of the Lord
Is fair and fruitful, be thy name adored.
Alleluia! Alleluia!

For martyrs who with rapture-kindled eye
Saw the bright crown descending from the sky
And, dying, grasp it, thee we glorify.
Alleluia! Alleluia!

Originally the first line began with "For all *thy* saints." The change to "For all *the* saints" was later made by the author himself. Slight alterations in the text have occurred in the process of updating the personal pronouns. Notice the rhyming of all last words, a customary procedure with three-line stanzas.

While other hymns on the saints may equal or surpass the merits of this hymn, what makes this hymn text stand out is that already in the second line it points to the essential trait of sainthood, that is, faith—"all who by faith before the world confessed." That is undoubtedly the most important line in the hymn. The saints boldly confessed Jesus, the Savior of the world. One is reminded of the 11th chapter of Hebrews, where the author gives that famous catalog of heroes of Old Testament history, each introduced with "By faith."

SINE NOMINE was composed by Ralph Vaughan Williams specifically for How's text and included in *The English Hymnal* (1906). It is a strong, buoyant tune, described by Percy Dearmer (*Songs of Praise Discussed*) as "one of the finest hymn tunes written during the present century." Once learned, it is sung with vigor and pleasure by congregations.

The harmonization is by Ralph Vaughan Williams.

BEHOLD A HOST ARRAYED IN WHITE 192

Behold a host arrayed in white
Like thousand snow-clad mountains bright.
They stand with palms
And sing their psalms
Before the throne of light.
These are the saints who kept God's Word;
They are the honored of the Lord.
He is their prince
Who drowned their sins,
So they were cleansed, restored.
They now serve God both day and night;
They sing their songs in endless light.
Their anthems ring
When they all sing
With angels shining bright.

On earth their work was not thought wise,
But see them now in heaven's eyes;
Before God's throne
Of precious stone
They shout their vict'ry cries.
On earth they wept through bitter years;
Now God has wiped away their tears;
Transformed their strife
To heav'nly life,
And freed them from their fears.
For now they have the best at last;
They keep their sweet eternal feast.
At God's right hand
Our Lord commands;
He is both host and guest.

Den store hvide Flok vi se
Som tusind Berge fuld' af Sne,
Med Skov omkring
Af Palmesving,
For Thronen. Hvo er de?
Det er den Helteskare, som
Af hin den store Trängsel kom,
Og har sig toed
I Lammets Blod,
Til Himlens Helligdom.
Der holde de nu Kirkegang
Med uophörlig Jubelklang
I höie Kor,
Hvor Gud han bor
Blandt alle Englers Sang.

Her gik de under stor Foragt,
Men se dem nu i deres Pragt
For Thronen staa
Med Kroner paa
I Himlens Prästedragt!
Sandt er deit, i saa mangen Nöd
Tidt Taareström paa Kinden flöd,
Men Gud har dem,
Straks de kom hjem,
Aftörret paa sit Sköd.
Nu holde de, og har tilbedst'
Hos ham en evig Lövsals-Fest,
Og Lammet selv
Ved Livets Elv
Er baade Vert og Gjest.

O blessed saints, now take your rest;	Til Lykke, Kjämpe-Samling! ja,
A thousand times shall you be blest	O tusindfold til Lykke da,
For keeping faith	At du var her
Firm unto death	Saa tro isör,
And scor ning worldly trust.	Og slap saa vel herfra!
For now you live at home with God;	Du har foragtet Verdens Tröst,
You harvest seeds once cast abroad	Saa lev nu evig vel, og höst,
In tears and sighs.	Hvad du har sand
See with new eyes	Med Suk og Graad,
The patter n in the seed.	I tusind Engle-Lyst!
The myriad angels raise their song.	Ophöi den Röst, slaa Palme-Takt,
O saints, sing with that happy throng;	Og syng af Himmel-Kraft og Magt:
Lift up one voice;	Pris väre dig
Let heav'n rejoice	Evindelig,
In our Redeemer's song!	Vor Gud og Lammet, sagt!

This is one of 70 hymns, originally in nine stanzas, included in Hans A. Brorson's *Svanga-Sang* (Swan Song) published in 1765, a year after his death. After appearing in the *Psalmbog for Kirke Og Huus-Andagt* (Copenhagen, 1855) and Landstad's *Salemebog* (Kristinia, 1869) and other Scandanavian hymnals, it soon made its way into various hymnals in American Lutheranism, including the *Service Book and Hymnal* (1958), *The Lutheran Hymnal* (1941), and *Lutheran Book of Worship* (1978).

A goodly number of individuals have set their hands to translating this triumph song of the saints of God, most of them coming up with composite versions. *Lutheran Worship* (1982) uses a slightly altered translation of that prepared by Gracia Grindal, with the assistance of her father, Harold K. Grindal, for *Lutheran Book of Worship* (1978).

DEN STORE HVIDE FLOK (BEHOLD A HOST, GREAT WHITE HOST) is the well-known and loved Norwegian folk tune of the 17th century, the tune used in all American hymnals as well as in the *Norsk Koralbok* (1936), popularized by the St. Olaf College Choir, Northfield, Minnesota.

The interesting harmonization is by Edvard Grieg from his opus 3, no. 10, for four-part male choir with baritone solo.

193 BY ALL YOUR SAINTS IN WARFARE

Horatio, third Earl of Nelson, included this text in his *Hymns for the Saints' Days, and other Hymns, By a Layman* (1864). The format of the hymn, allowing individual stanzas to be inserted for particular commemorations, was suggested to Nelson by John S. B. Monsell's (*LW* 260, et al.) "Ye saints! in blest communion," in his *Hymns of Love and Praise* (1863). Should a congregation desire a specific stanza for St. Barnabas (observed June 11) and one for St. Peter and St. Paul (observed June 29), Henry Simon, pastor of Signal Hill Lutheran Church, Bellville, Illinois, has written the following:

All praise, Lord, for the Levite
Who gave your church his best,
Encouraging your people
That they, too, might be blest.
Like Bar nabas, let us be,
And serve in any way,
So we with him may join you
In heav'n's eternal day.

Praise, Lord, for your apostles
Who spread the joyous Word,
To Jew and Gentile telling
The Gospel they had heard.
May we be bold and willing
To give your lives to you
And show your love outreaching
In all we say and do.

KING'S LYNN is named for the Norfolk seaport where Ralph Vaughan Williams first heard this delightful traditional English melody. Vaughan Williams arranged the tune for use with G. K. Chesterton's hymn, "O God of Earth and Altar" (*WS* 784), in *The English Hymnal* (1906). *LW* 193 is as harmonized by Williams; Paul G. Bunjes prepared the setting for *LW* 194, which first appeared in *Worship Supplement* (1969).

BY ALL YOUR SAINTS IN WARFARE 194

Hymn 194 is treated with hymn 193.

FOR ALL YOUR SAINTS, O LORD 195

This hymn by Richard Mant, originally in six stanzas, first appeared in his *Ancient Hymns from the Roman Breviary, for Domestick Use . . . to which are added Original Hymns* (1837), and represents one of such original hymns. It comes to *Lutheran Worship* from *Lutheran Book of Worship* (1978), slightly altered.

FESTAL SONG, a fine short meter tune (SM) composed by William H. Walter, first appeared in John Ireland Tucker's *The Hymnal with Tunes Old and New* (1872) of the Episcopal Church, where it was coupled to "Awake and sing the song" by William Hammond.

The harmonization was prepared by Paul O. Manz.

196 WHEN ALL YOUR MERCIES, O MY GOD

Written by Joseph Addison, the hymn in its present form was included on the list prepared by the Consultation on Ecumenical Hymnody for the *Lutheran Book of Worship* (1978) and is based on stanzas 1, 10, 11, and 13 of the original, here slightly altered and updated. This 13-stanza hymn was appended to an essay on "Gratitude" which appeared in Addison's newspaper *The Spectator* on August 9, 1712. There he had written:

> There is not a more pleasing exercise of the mind than gratitude. It is accompanied with such an inward satisfaction that the duty is sufficiently rewarded by the performance. If gratitude is due from man to man, how much more from man to his Maker! Every blessing we enjoy, by what means soever it may be derived upon us, is the gift of Him who is the great Author of good and Father of mercies.

WINCHESTER OLD, perhaps the most famous of the old common meter psalm tunes (see essay: Metrical Psalms, p. 825), first appeared in Thomas Este's *Whole Booke of Psalmes with their wonted Tunes, composed into foure parts* (1592), where it was set to Psalm 84. Este gave the tune no name. Next the tune appeared in Thomas Ravenscroft's *Whole Booke of Psalms* (1621), where it was set to the same psalm and, for the first time, named WINCHESTER. The word OLD was appended later, after the appearance of WINCHESTER NEW in 1690.

The tune is evidently derived from the second half of Christopher Tye's (c. 1497–1572) music to chapter eight of his *Actes of the Apostles* (1553):

The adaptation has been credited to George Kirbye because the name "G. Kirbye" is attached to this lovely tune in Este's book, presumably as being the arranger.

The association of this tune with "While Shepherds Watched Their Flocks by Night" (*LW* 70) was made in *Hymns Ancient and Modern* (1861).

The setting here used is a somewhat altered form of that in *The Lutheran Hymnal* (1941).

LORD, OPEN NOW MY HEART TO HEAR 197

Lord, open now my heart to hear,
And through your Word to me draw near,
Preserve that Word in purity
That I your child and heir may be.

Your Word it is that heals my heart,
That makes me whole in ev'ry part;
Your Word of joy within me sings,
True peace and blessedness it brings.

To God the Father, God the Son,
To God the Spirit, three in one,
Honor and praise forever be
Now and through all eternity!

Herr, öffne mir die Herzenstür,
Zeuch mein Herz durch dein Wort zu dir,
Lass mich dein Wort bewahren rein,
Lass mich dein Kind und Erbe sein!

Dein Wort bewegt des Herzens Grund;
Dein Wort macht Leib und Seel' gesund;
Dein Wort ist, das mein Herz erfreut;
Dein Wort gibt Trost und Seligkeit.

Ehr' sei dem Vater und dem Sohn,
Dem Heil'gen Geist in einem Thron;
Der Heiligen Dreieinigkeit
Sei Lob und Preis in Ewigkeit!

This hymn by Johannes Olearius appeared in his *Geistliche Singe-Kunst* (Leipzig, 1671) entitled "Special meditation of the hearer at the close of the sermon." The sense of the first lines, however, appear to make the hymn more appropriate before the sermon or at the beginning of the worship rather than after the sermon.

The translation was prepared by Henry L. Lettermann for *Lutheran Worship* (1982).

ERHALT UNS HERR. For comments on this tune see hymn 334.

The harmonization is by Wilhelm Quampen, a *nom de plume* of Paul G. Bunjes.

OPEN NOW THY GATES OF BEAUTY 198

Open now thy gates of beauty,
Zion, let me enter there,
Where my soul in joyful duty
Waits for God, who answers prayer.
Oh, how blessed is this place,
Filled with solace, light, and grace!

Gracious God, I come before thee;
Come thou also unto me;
Where we find thee and adore thee,
There a heav'n on earth must be.
To my heart, oh, enter thou,
Let it be thy temple now!

Here thy praise is gladly chanted,
Here thy seed is duly sown;
Let my soul, where it is planted,
Bring forth precious sheaves alone,

Tut mir auf die schöne Pforte,
Führt in Gottes Haus mich ein!
Auch, wie wird an diesem Orte
Meine Seele Fröhlich sein!
Hier ist Gottes Angesicht,
Hier ist lauter Trost und Licht.

Herr, ich bin zu dir gekommen;
Komme du nun auch zu mir!
Wo du Wohnung hast genommen,
Ist der Himmel hell vor mir.
Zeuch in meinem Herzen ein,
Lass es deinen Himmel sein!

Mache mich zum guten Lande,
Wenn dein Saatkorn auf mich fällt;
Gib mir Licht in dem Verstande,
Und was mir wird vorgestellt,

So that all I hear may be Fruitful unto life in me.	Präge du dem Herzen ein; Lass es mir zur Frucht gedeihn
Thou my faith increase and quicken, Let me keep thy gift divine; Howsoe'er temptations thicken, May thy Word still o'er me shine As my guiding star through life, As my comfort in all strife.	Stärk in mir den schwachen Glauben, Lass dein teures Kleinod mir Nimmer aus dem Herzen rauben, Halte mir dein Wort stets für; Ja, das sei mein Morgenstern, Der mich führet zu dem Herrn!
Speak, O God, and I will hear thee, Let thy will be done indeed; May I undisturbed draw near thee While thou dost thy people feed. Here of life the fountain flows; Here is balm for all our woes.	Rede, Herr, so will ich hören, Und dein Wille werd' erfüllt! Lass nichts meine Andacht stören, Wenn der Brunn' des Lebens quillt. Speise mich mit Himmelsbrot Tröste mich in aller Not!

This Sunday, or Lord's Day, hymn by Benjamin Schmolck, originally in seven stanzas, first appeared in his *Kirchen-Gefährte* (1732). He later included this text in his *Klage und Reigen* (1734), where it was titled "The First Step into the Church" (Third Commandment).

In translating the hymn, Catherine Winkworth (1827–78) omitted stanzas 3 and 7, possibly because of difficult idioms therein. Her five-stanza translation was first published in her *Chorale Book for England* (1863). The frequent rhyming of the traditional English pronouns in her translation, necessitating an extensive recast for their removal, prompted the Commission on Worship to abandon the updating of this text.

UNSER HERRSCHER, by Joachim Neander, was published in his *Glaub- und Liebes-übung* (Bremen, 1679), where it was set to his text, "Unser Herrscher, Unser König." It is sometimes known by the names NEANDER, MAGDEBURG, and EPHESUS.

The setting is by Paul G. Bunjes, from his *New Organ Accompaniment for Hymns* (1976).

199 WE WORSHIP YOU, O GOD OF MIGHT

This hymn by the eminent Johan Olof Wallin, archbishop of Uppsala, is a Swedish metrical version of the Latin *Te Deum laudamus* (cf. Canticles and Chants, *LW* 8; also *LW* 171 for a German metrical version). Based on an earlier metrical version, "Dig vare lov och pris, o Krist," which appeared in *Senska Psalm-Boken* (1695), both Wallin's version and the earlier one were included in the *Psalmer* (1811).

The translation here used is an altered form of that by Joel W. Lundeen.

The *Service Book and Hymnal* (1958) included this hymn in a translation by Charles Wharton Stork, beginning "We Worship Thee, Almighty Lord" (no. 174), as did also the Presbyterian *Pilgrim Hymnal* of 1931 (no. 28). The *Worship Supplement* (1969) contained the hymn in a composite translation, beginning "Jehovah, You We Glorify" (no. 771).

VI LOVA DIG, O STORE GUD, also WALLIN, after Bishop Wallin, and TER SANCTUS (Thrice Holy), is from *Een ny Handbog, med Psalmer oc anndelige Lofsange* (Rostock, 1529), which represents its first use as a hymn tune. This was an enlarged edition of the earliest Danish-Norwegian Lutheran hymnal, issued by Klaus Mortensen Tönderbinder at Malmö in 1528, a book that with changes and editions in 1569 became Hans Thomissön's *Den danske Psalmebog* (see *LW* 222).

The interesting harmonization of this stately tune was prepared by Richard W. Hillert for *Worship Supplement* (1969).

THIS IS THE DAY THE LORD HAS MADE 200

The last of four poems loosely based on Psalm 118, this appeared in Isaac Watts' *Psalms of David* (1719). He called it "Hosanna: The Lord's Day; or, Christ's Resurrection and our Salvation." While little else in the hymn other than stanza 1 bears close resemblance to Psalm 118, it must be remembered that Watts was trying to make the Church of England accept hymns of human composition in worship over against strict metrical psalmody.

NUN DANKET ALL was composed by Johann Crüger to serve as the setting for Paul Gerhardt's (*LW* 19, et al.) text "Nun danket all' und bringet Ehr'," a union that first appeared in the second edition of Crüger's *Praxis pietatis melica* (Berlin, 1647).

This triadic type of melody, so typical of many of Crüger's tunes, injects a "fresh, outspoken, sometimes earthy vigor into the world of Lutheran hymnody" (Riedel).

The harmonization is by Paul G. Bunjes.

LORD JESUS CHRIST, BE PRESENT NOW 201

Lord Jesus Christ, be present now; Our hearts in true devotion bow. Your Spirit send with light divine, And let your truth within us shine.	Herr Jesu Christ, dich zu uns wend, Dein'n Heil'gen Geist du zu uns send! Mit Lieb' und Gnad', Herr, uns regier Und uns den Weg zur Wahrheit führ.
Unseal our lips to sing your praise In endless hymns through all our days; Increase our faith and light our minds; And set us free from doubt that blinds.	Tu auf den Mund zum Lobe dein, Bereit das Herz zur Andacht fein, Den Glauben mehr, stärk den Verstand, Dass uns dein Nam' werd' wohl bekannt,

Then shall we join the hosts that cry, "O holy, holy Lord Most High!" And in the light of that blest place We then shall see you face to face.	Bis wir singen mit Gottes Heer: Heilig, heilig ist Gott der Herr! Und schauen dich von Angesicht In ew'ger Freud' und sel'gem Licht.
All glory to the Father, Son, And Holy Spirit, Three in One! To you, O blessed Trinity, Be praise throughout eternity!	Ehr' sei dem Vater und dem Sohn, Dem Heil'gen Geist in einem Thron; Der Heiligen Dreieinigkeit Sei Lob und Preis in Ewigkeit!

Of unknown authorship, this hymn appeared in the second edition, 1648, of Johann Niedling's *Lutherisch Handbüchlein* in four 4-line stanzas. Koch claims it was also included in the first edition of 1638, but this may be purely conjecture. In 1651 the text was published in *Cantionale Sacrum*, set to the tune below. While the hymn is often attributed to Wilhelm August II (1598–1662), Duke of Saxe-Weimar, his name is not linked with the text earlier than 1676.

In 1678 a command was issued that this hymn be sung in all the churches of Saxony on Sundays and festivals. The English translation by Catherine Winkworth first appeared in her *Chorale Book for England* (1863).

HERR JESU CHRIST, DICH ZU UNS WEND. This tune by an unknown composer first appeared in the *Cantionale Germanicum* (Gochsheim, 1628), coupled to another text. It was in the *Gotha Cantionale* (1651) that it appeared with this text ("Lord Jesus Christ, Be Present Now").

In its rigidly formed measures the tune reflects the style of the first half of the 17th century. Moreover, as herein, the tunes of this period evidence a distinct dancelike rhythm, a trait or characteristic that had made inroads into the Italian social, or drawing room, songs and early Baroque suites.

The setting is from the *Service Book and Hymnal* (1958).

202 DEAREST JESUS, AT YOUR WORD

Dearest Jesus, at your word We have come again to hear you; Let our thoughts and hearts be stirred And in glowing faith be near you As the promises here given Draw us wholly up to heaven.	Liebster Jesu, wir sind hier, Dich und dein Wort anzuhören; Lenke Sinnen und Begier Auf die süssen Himmelslehren, Dass die Herzen von der Erden Ganz zu dir gezogen werden.
All our knowledge, sense, and sight Lie in deepest darkness shrouded Till your Spirit breaks the night, Filling us with light unclouded. As good thoughts and all good living Come but by your gracious giving.	Unser Wissen und Verstand Ist mit Finsternis umhüllet, Wo nicht deines Geistes Hand Uns mit hellem Licht erfüllet. Gutes denken, Gutes dichten Musst du selbst in uns verrichten.
Radiance of God's glory bright, Light of light from God proceeding,	O du Glanz der Herrlichkeit, Licht vom Licht aus Gott geboren,

Jesus, send your blessed light;
Help our hearing, speaking, heeding,
That our prayers and songs may please you
As with grateful hearts we praise you.

Father, Son, and Holy Ghost,
Praise to you and adoration!
Grant us what we need the most:
Your blest Gospel's consolation
While we here on earth await you
Till in heav'n with praise we greet you.

Mach uns allesamt bereit,
Öffne Herzen, Mund und Ohren!
Unser Bitten, Flehn und Singen
Lass, Herr Jesu, wohl gelingen!

Vater, Sohn, Heiliger Geist,
Dir sei ewig Preis und Ehre!
Tröst die Herzen allermeist
Mit dem Wort der reinen Lehre
Hier in diesen Sterblichkeiten,
Bis wir dort dein Lob ausbreiten.

First published anonymously in the *Altdorffisches Gesang-Büchlein*, either in 1663 or in 1667, the German hymn in three stanzas was intended for Sunday worship, to be sung before the sermon. Tobias Clausnitzer's name appeared with the text in the *Nürnberg Gesangbuch* (1676); the doxology was added by an unknown hand for the *Berliner Gesangbuch* (1707).

Catherine Winkworth's three-stanza translation, beginning "Blessed Jesus, at thy Word" in her *Lyra Germanica* (second series, 1858), has been adapted for *Lutheran Worship*.

LIEBSTER JESU, WIR SIND HIER. This tune by Johann R. Ahle, also known as DESSAU, first appeared in *Neue Geistliche auf die Sonntage durch's gantze Jahr gerichtete Andachten* (Mühlhausen, 1664), set to Franz Joachim Burmeister's Advent hymn, "Ja, er ist's, das Heil der Welt." There it appeared as follows (Zahn 3498a):

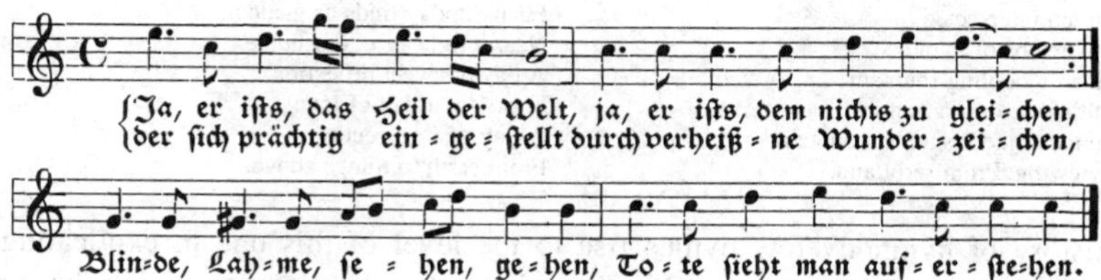

The influence of Italian opera is clearly in evidence. In fact, Ahle himself referred to such church melodies as "solo arias."

When coupled to Clausnitzer's text in *Das Grosse Cantionale: oder Kirchen-Gesangbuch* (Darmstadt, 1687), this fine tune, as exhibited below, appears greatly simplified (Zahn 3498b):

It is to be noted, however, that it still retains subtle passing tones, reflecting one of the *gallant* niceties of the Freylinghausen tradition. This is in stark contrast to the stripped-down version given in *The Lutheran Hymnal* (1941).

The harmonization was prepared for *Lutheran Worship* (1982) by Wilhelm Quampen, a *nom de plume* of Paul G. Bunjes.

203 O DAY OF REST AND GLADNESS

Christopher Wordsworth included this hymn in six stanzas in *The Holy Year* (1862). Eight years later he changed the ending of the first stanza from

> Before th' eternal throne
> Sing, "Holy, holy, holy,"
> To the great Three in One

to its present form for the book's sixth edition.

While most major denominations in the United States use some form of this hymn, the number of stanzas differs widely. *Lutheran Worship* (1982) omits the author's stanzas 3 and 4:

> Thou art a port protected
> From storms that round us rise;
> A garden intersected
> With streams of Paradise.
> Thou art a cooling fountain
> In life's dry, dreary sand;
> From thee, like Pisgah's mountain
> We view the Promised Land.

> Thou art a holy ladder,
> Where angels go and come;
> Each Sunday finds us gladder,
> Nearer to heav'n, our home.
> A day of sweet reflection
> Thou art, a day of love,
> A day of resurrection
> From earth to things above.

In the history of hymnody few hymns rise to the level of this one in explicating the meaning and purpose of the Lord's Day. In a time when Sunday has largely become a weekly holiday for so many people, this hymn deserves some serious study and reflection.

ELLACOMBE. For comments on the tune see hymn 106.

The setting is an altered form of that in *The Covenant Hymnal* (no. 183).

COME, LET US JOIN OUR CHEERFUL SONGS 204

This hymn by Issac Watts, among the most widely esteemed of his hymns, first appeared in his *Hymns and Spiritual Songs* (1707) with the heading "Christ Jesus, the Lamb of God, worshipped by all the Creation; Revelation 5: 11, 12, 13." Hymnals invariably omit stanza 4 of Watts' original. It reads:

Let all that dwell above the sky
And air and earth and seas
Conspire to lift thy glories high
And speak thine endless praise.

NUN DANKET ALL. For comments on this tune see hymn 200.
The harmonization is from the *Choralbuch* (1955).

OH, SING JUBILEE TO THE LORD 205

Oh, sing jubilee to the Lord, ev'ry land: Glory be to God! Oh, serve him with gladness as in halls we stand; Sing praises to God out of Zion!	Al verden nu raabe for Herren med fryd, Lovet väre Gud! Träd frem for hans ansigt med sang his og jubellyd, Guds menighed love nu Herren!
He made us his own and has given us breath; Glory be to God! The sheep of his pasture, we need not fear our death; Sing praises to God out of Zion!	Kom, kjend Gud, din herre, du intet selv formaar, Lovet väre Gud! Han, han har dig gjort til sit folk og födes faar, Guds menighed love nu Herren!
Oh, come to his feast with thanksgiving and praise; Glory be to God! Give glory to him, and your brightest banners raise; Sing praises to God out of Zion!	Gaar ind ad hans porte med lov og takkesang, Lovet väre Gud! Velsigner, höilover evindelig hans navn, Guds menighed love nu Herren!
His mercy is ours; he is Lord over all; Glory be to God! May all generations find power in his call; Sing praises to God out of Zion!	Guds godhed og miskundhed er ny i evighed, Lovet väre Gud! Fra slegt og til slegt skal hans sandhed vare ved, Guds menighed love nu Herren!

This Norwegian hymn by Ulrik V. Koren, intended as a metrical version of Psalm 100, first appeared in a Norwegian hymn book and thereafter in *The Lutheran Hymnary* of the Evangelical Lutheran Church (Augsburg, 1913, 1935), in a translation by Harriet Reynolds Spaeth. From there it made its way into *The Lutheran Hymnal* (1941).

The translation here used was prepared by the Inter-Lutheran Commission on Worship for inclusion in *Lutheran Book of Worship* (1978).

GUDS MENIGHED, SYNG (HOFF), a spirited tune in an unusual meter, is considered to have been composed by Erik C. Hoff and was included in his *Melodibog til samtlige authorisered Salmeboger*, set to a text beginning with the same words.

The setting is contained in the *Service Book and Hymnal* (1958), slightly altered.

206 GOD HIMSELF IS PRESENT

God himself is present;
Let us now adore him
And with awe appear before him.
God is in his temple;
All within keep silence,
Prostrate lie with deepest rev'rence.
Him alone
God we own,
Him, our God and Savior;
Praise his name forever!

Gott ist gegenwärtig!
Lasset uns anbeten,
Und in Ehrfurcht vor ihn treten.
Gott ist in der Mitten;
Alles in uns schweige,
Und sich innigst vor ihm beuge.
Wer ihn kennt,
Wer ihn nennt,
Schlagt die Augen nieder;
Kommt, ergebt euch wieder!

God himself is present;
Hear the harps resounding;
See the hosts the throne surrounding!
"Holy, holy, holy!"
Hear the hymn ascending,
Songs of saints and angels blending.
Bow your ear
To us here:
Hear, O Christ, the praises
That your Church now raises.

Gott ist gegenwärtig,
Dem die Cherubinen
Tag und Nacht mit Ehrfurcht dienen;
Heilig, heilig singen
Alle Engelchören,
Wenn sie Gott mit Jauchzen ehren.
Herr, vernimm
Unsre Stimm',
Da auch wir Geringen
Unsre Opfer bringen.

Light of light eternal,
All things penetrating,
For your rays our soul is waiting,
As the tender flowers,
Willingly unfolding,
To the sun their faces holding:
Even so
Would we do,
Light from you obtaining,
Strength to serve you gaining.

Du durchdringest alles,
Lass dein schönstes Lichte,
Herr, berühren mein Gesichte.
Wie die zarten Blumen
Willig sich entfalten
Und der Sonne stille halten,
Lass mich so
Still und froh
Deine Strahlen fassen
Und dich wirken lassen.

Come, celestial Being,
Make our hearts your dwelling,
Ev'ry carnal thought dispelling.
By your Holy Spirit
Sanctify us truly,
Teaching us to love you only.
Where we go
Here below,
Let us bow before you
And in truth adore you.

Herr, komm in mir wohnen,
Lass mein Geist auf Erden
Dir ein Heiligtum noch werden!
Komm, du treuer Heiland,
Dich in mir verkläre,
Dass ich dich stets lieb' und ehre.
Wo ich geh',
Sitz' und steh',
Lass mich dich erblicken
Und vor dir mich bücken.

This excellent hymn by Gerhard Tersteegen first appeared in his *Geistliches Blumengärtlein* (1729) with the heading "Remembrance of the Glorious and Delightful Presence of God." The translation is a composite: stanzas 1 and 2 were done by

Frederick William Foster, bishop in the Moravian Church, and John Miller for the *Moravian Hymn Book* (1789), a translation that was somewhat altered in William Mercer's (*LW* 492) *The Church Psalter and Hymn Book* (1855); stanzas 3 and 4, also here altered, were done by Herman Brueckner for inclusion in the *American Lutheran Hymnal* (1930).

WUNDERBARER KÖNIG, also called ARNSBERG and GOTT IST GEGENWÄRTIG, was attributed to Joachim Neander (*LW* 198) in his *Alpha and Omega, Joachimi Neandri Glaub- und Liebes-Übung* (Bremen, 1679), where it was set to his hymn, "Wunderbarer König."

The concentration given the simple musical figure in this tune (♩♩♩♩𝅗𝅥𝅗𝅥), with its sequential treatment of all phrases, although perhaps helpful in focusing on the single theme of adoration, can readily tend to create a sense of boredom.

The harmonization is from the *Service Book and Hymnal* (1958), slightly altered.

The category, Beginning of Service, in which this hymn occurs, evokes a comment. If, as advocated by Carl F. Schalk, hymns in corporate worship should serve a specific purpose: to underscore, complement, introduce, conclude a certain action in the liturgy, and not simply as a filler—then designations such as Opening Hymn, Sermon Hymn, Closing Hymn are best avoided. The Entrance Hymn of the Liturgy fulfills the first; the Hymn of the Day, the second; and the Closing Hymn, although not called for in the liturgy, if one is desired or custom demands, can well follow the blessing without a label.

TO YOUR TEMPLE, LORD, I COME 207

This hymn by James Montgomery was titled "A Sabbath Hymn" in William Collyer's (1782–1854) *Hymns, partly collected and partly original* (1812). Originally "To thy temple I repair," it has been altered in various hymnals to "To thy presence I repair" or "In thy presence we appear." The *Lutheran Worship* version has been updated in language; otherwise it follows Montgomery's original seven stanzas.

GOTT SEI DANK. For comments on the tune and harmonization see hymn 182.

208 LAMB OF GOD, PURE AND SINLESS

Lamb of God, pure and sinless,
Once on the cross an off'ring,
Patient, meek, though guiltless,
Forsaken in your suff'ring!
You died our guilt to banish
That none in sin need perish!
Grant us your mercy, O Jesus!

Lamb of God, pure and sinless,
Once on the cross an off'ring,
Patient, meek, though guiltless,
Forsaken in your suff'ring!
You died our guilt to banish
That none in sin need perish!
Grant us your mercy, O Jesus!

Lamb of God, pure and sinless,
Once on the cross an off'ring,
Patient, meek, though guiltless,
Forsaken in your suff'ring!
You died our guilt to banish
That none in sin need perish!
Your peace be with us, O Jesus!
Amen

O Lamm Gottes, unschuldig
Am Stamm des Kreuzes geschlachtet,
Allzeit funden geduldig,
Wiewohl du warest verachtet:
All' Sünd' hast du getragen,
Sonst müssten wir verzagen.
Erbarm dich unser, O Jesu!

O Lamm Gottes, unschuldig
Am Stamm des Kreuzes geschlachtet,
Allzeit funden geduldig,
Wiewohl du warest verachtet:
All' Sünd' hast du getragen,
Sonst müssten wir verzagen.
Erbarm dich unser, O Jesu!

O Lamm Gottes, unschuldig
Am Stamm des Kreuzes geschlachtet,
Allzeit funden geduldig,
Wiewohl du warest verachtet:
All' Sünd' hast du getragen,
Sonst müssten wir verzagen.
Gib uns dein'n Frieden, O Jesu!

This is an English translation by Joel W. Lundeen of a German metrical version of the Agnus Dei by Nicolaus Decius which first appeared in Low German (*Plattdeutsch*) in *Geystliche leder* (Rostock, 1531), and thereafter in High German (*Hochdeutsch*) in Valentin Schumann's *Gesang Buch* (Leipzig, 1539). The Latin/plainsong Agnus Dei, dating from the 13th century, if not earlier, from which Decius made his adaptation of both text and tune, is in Mass X (Cum jubilo) for the Feast of the Blessed Virgin (*Liber Usualis*, p. 41). The form of the tune here used appeared in *Christliche Kirchen Ordnung* (Erfurt, 1542) published by Anton Corvinus. The hymn became a favorite in Lutheranism, frequently sung in the midweek Lenten services as well as on Good Friday.

It is interesting to note that both text and tune found their way into David Gregor Corner's *Gross Catolisch Gesangbuch* of 1631 (Bäumker I, p. 456).

O LAMM GOTTES, UNSCHULDIG. The harmonization is from the *Württembergisches Choralbuch* (1953).

209 KYRIE, GOD FATHER

Kyrie, God Father in heav'n above,
You abound in gracious love,
Of all things the maker and preserver.

Kyrie, Gott Vater in Ewigkeit,
Gross ist dein' Barmherzigkeit.
Aller Ding' ein Schöpfer und Regierer.

Eleison, eleison!
Kyrie, O Christ, our king,
Salvation for all you came to bring.
O Lord Jesus, God's own Son,
Our mediator at the heav'nly throne,
Hear our cry and grant our supplication.
Eleison, eleison!
Kyrie, O God the Holy Ghost,
Guard our faith, the gift we need the most,
And bless our life's last hour
That we leave this sinful world with gladness.
Eleison, eleison!

Eleison, eleison!
Christe, aller Welt Trost
Uns Sünder allein du hast erlöst.
O Jesu, Gottes Sohn,
Unser Mittler bist in dem höchsten Thron;
Zu dir schreien wir aus Herzensbegier:
Eleison, eleison!
Kyrie, Gott Heiliger Geist,
Tröst, stärk uns im Glauben aller meist,
Dass wir am letzten End'
Fröhlich abscheiden aus diesem Elend.
Eleison, eleison!

This has as its basis the troped "Kyrie, fons bonitatis" (Font of Kindness), dating from the 12fth century, if not earlier; it constitutes another example of Lutheran indebtedness to the Roman Mass. It was in the 16th century that a German translation of unknown authorship appeared, beginning "Kyrie, Gott Vater in Ewigkeit," apparently in Wittenberg in 1541 (Wackernagel III, 250). As such it soon either supplanted Luther's brief Kyrie or served as its alternate in those Lutheran areas in Europe using Luther's *German Mass* (1526); in some places both the German and the Latin Kyries were sung on festivals from Trinity to Christmas. This Kyrie constituted also the prescribed Kyrie in the Chief Service (*Hauptgottesdienst*) in the *Kirchen-Agende*, the first official agenda issued by the Missouri Synod in 1856.

The translation is an altered form of that prepared by W. Gustav Polack (*LW* 66, et al.) for inclusion in *The Lutheran Hymnal* (1941).

KYRIE, GOTT VATER is based on the original plainsong tune of the "Kyrie, fons bonitatis." Zahn (8600a) gives this setting as in the *Teutsch Kirchenant* (Erfurt, 1525), stating that the tune at that time used only the abbreviated text:

Herr, erbarm dich unser. (Lord, have mercy on us.)
Christ, erbarm dich unser.
Herr, erbarm dich unser.

The harmonization was prepared for *Lutheran Worship* (1982) by Paul G. Bunjes.

ALL GLORY BE TO GOD ALONE 210

All glory be to God alone,
Forevermore the Highest One.
He is our sinful race's friend;
His grace and peace to us extend.
May humankind see his goodwill,
May hearts with deep thanksgiving fill.

We praise you, God; your name we bless
And worship you in humbleness;
From day to day we glorify

All' Ehr' und Lob soll Gottes sein,
Er ist und heisst der Höchst' allein.
Sein Zorn auf Erden hab' ein End',
Sein' Fried' und Gnad' sich zu uns wend'.
Den Menschen das gefalle wohl,
Dafür man herzlich danken soll.

Ach lieber Gott, dich loben wir
Und preisen dich mit ganzer B'gier,
Auch kniend wir anbeten dich,

Our everlasting God on high.
Your splendor's glorious light we sing,
And to your throne our thanks we bring.

Lord God, our King on heaven's throne,
Our Father, the Almighty One.
O Lord, the Sole-begotten One,
Lord Jesus Christ, the Father's Son,
True God from all eter nity,
O Lamb of God, to you we flee.

You take the whole world's sin away;
Have mercy on us, Lord, we pray.
You take the whole world's sin away;
Oh, listen to the prayer we say.
From God's right hand, oh, send today
Your mercy on us, Lord, we pray.

You are the only Holy One,
The Lord of all things, you alone.
O Jesus Christ, we glorify
You and the Spirit, Lord Most High;
With him you ever more will be
One in the Father's majesty.

This truth divine, this mystery
The angels sing adoringly.
By all creation, far and wide,
You, Lord, are ever glorified;
For all your people sing your praise
Now and through everlasting days.

Dein' Ehr' wir rühmen stetiglich;
Wir danken dir zu aller Zeit
Um deine grosse Herrlichkeit.

Herr Gott, im Himmel König du bist,
Ein Vater, der allmächtig ist.
Du Gottes Sohn vom Vater bist
Einig gebor'n, Herr Jesu Christ.
Herr Gott, du zartes Gotteslamm,
Ein Sohn aus Gott des Vaters Stamm,

Der du der Welt Sünd' trägst allein,
Woll'st uns gnädig, barmherzig sein!
Der du der Welt Sünd' trägst allein,
Lass dir unsre Bitt' g'fällig sein!
Der du gleich sitzt dem Vater dein,
Woll'st uns gnädig, barmherzig sein!

Du bist und bleibst heilig allein,
Über alles der Herr allein.
Der Allerhöchst' allein du bist,
Du lieber Heiland, Jesu Christ,
Samt dem Vater und Heil'gen Geist
In göttlicher Majestät gleich.

Amen, das ist gewisslich wahr,
Das bekennt aller Engel Scharr
Und alle Welt, so weit und breit,
Dich lobt und ehret allezeit.
Dich rühmt die ganze Christenheit
Von Anfang bis in Ewigkeit.

This is a so-called metrical paraphrase of the *hymnus angelicus*, the "Gloria in excelsis Deo," in the Mass of the Western Church, the authorship of which is uncertain. On the basis of such authorities, among others, as Friedrich Spitta (1822–1924) and Konrad Ameln, *Lutheran Worship* attributes it to Martin Luther. In any case, this hymn first appeared in an order of worship for a church in Naumburg, 1537, formulated by Nikolaus–Medler. Thereafter it appeared in the Klug *Gesangbuch* (Wittenberg, 1543).

When one compares this text to the metrical paraphrase of the same Latin text by Nikolaus Decius, namely, "All Glory Be to God on High (*LW* 215), one cannot but note that Luther's text follows the Latin much more closely than the latter. The translation is that prepared by W. Gustave Polack for *The Lutheran Hymnal* (1941), slightly altered.

ALL EHR UND LOB, by an unknown composer, it first appeared in the *Kirchengesangbuch* (Strassburg, 1541). A through-composed tune—without repeated phrases—it moves along in a dignified, light, restrained manner, never detracting from the text. In six eights—88 88 88, a variant of the Long Meter (LM—88 88)—it is the interesting pattern that John Wesley found so convenient for translating Paul Gerhardt's "Jesus, Your Boundless Love So True" (*LW* 280), and that his brother Charles found so to his liking, he wrote over 1,100 poems in this form.

The setting is from *The Lutheran Hymnal* (1941), slightly altered.

MY SOUL NOW MAGNIFIES THE LORD 211

As a metrical paraphrase of the Magnificat (Luke 1:46–55), this hymn by Stephanie Kristian Frey was written in the summer of 1974 at the suggestion of Gracia Grindal (*LW* 67, et al.). Regarding the inspiration for the task, the author has stated:

> Mary's song has always been a special one to me because it is such a moving declaration of praise and thanksgiving spoken with deep humility on the part of a woman whose life was to be radically changed by the work of the Creator.

In Long Meter form (LM—88 88), the meter in which St. Ambrose (*LW* 13, et al.) gave the church its first "modern" hymns, the author avoided the singsonginess of rhymed couplets (AABB), choosing the more felicitous pattern of cross rhyming (ABAB). Moreover, it is a meter that lends itself well to majestic subjects.

SONG 34 (ANGELS' SONG, ANGELS'). Considering the tune by Heinrich Schütz used to this text in *Lutheran Book of Worship* (1978) a bit too ponderous, and the two descending leaps of a fourth too difficult for the average singer, the Commission on Worship chose to use SONG 34. This stately tune, yet with an attractive innocence, appeared in George Wither's *The Hymns and Songs of the Church* (1623) set to the 34th Song, Wither's four-line paraphrase of Luke 2:13, beginning "Thus angel's sung, and thus sing we," hence the alternate tune names ANGELS' SONG or ANGELS'. This book contained a number of fine tunes in two parts, treble and bass, by Orlando Gibbons, this being one of them.

The harmonization was prepared by Carl F. Schalk.

WE ALL BELIEVE IN ONE TRUE GOD, FATHER 212

We all believe in one true God, Father, Son, and Holy Ghost, Ever-present help in need, Praised by all the heav'nly host; All he made his love enfolds, All creation he upholds.	Wir glauben all' an einen Gott, Vater, Sohn und Heil'gen Geist, Der uns hilft in aller Not, Den die Schar der Engel preist, Der durch seine grosse Kraft Alles wirket, tut und schafft.
We all believe in Jesus Christ, Son of God and Mary's son, Who descended from his throne And for us salvation won; By whose cross and death are we Rescued from all misery. We all confess the Holy Ghost, Who from both in truth proceeds,	Wir glauben auch an Jesum Christ, Gottes und Marien Sohn, Der vom Himmel kommen ist Und uns führt in's Himmels Thron Und uns durch sein Blut und Tod Hat erlöst aus aller Not. Wir glauben auch an Heil'gen Geist, Der von beiden gebet aus,

Who sustains and comforts us
In all trials, fears, and needs.
Blest and holy Trinity,
Praise forever yours shall be.

Der uns Trost und Beistand leist't
Wider alle Furcht und Graus.
Heilige Dreifaltigkeit,
Sei gepreist zu aller Zeit!

This metrical paraphrase of the Apostles' Creed by Tobias Clausnitzer first appeared in the *Kulmbach-Bayreuth Gesangbuch* (1668).

The translation, an altered form of that prepared by Catherine Winkworth in her *Chorale Book for England* (1863), comes to *Lutheran Worship* by way of *The Lutheran Hymnal* (1941), except that the altered form has been slightly updated.

WIR GLAUBEN ALL AN EINEN GOTT, an anonymous tune, was originally set to Clausnitzer's text in the Darmstadt *Kirchengesangbuch* (1699). Its present form, from Hiller's *Choralbuch* (1793), appeared with Catherine Winkworth's translation in the *Chorale Book for England* (1863).

Although the rubric in the Chief Service (*Hauptgottesdienst*) in the *Kirche-Agende* (1856), the first official Agenda of the Synod, directed the singing of Luther's metrical setting of the Nicene Creed (*LW* 213), this more simple text and tune became a popular alternate.

The harmonization is by Wilhelm Quampen, a *nom de plume* of Paul G. Bunjes.

213 WE ALL BELIEVE IN ONE TRUE GOD, MAKER

We all believe in one true God,
Maker of the earth and heaven.
"Our Father," he would have us say;
Children's place to us has given.
He has pledged a*lw*ays to feed us,
Body, soul, to keep, to nourish.
Through all evil he will lead us,
Guards us well that we may flourish.
He cares for us by day and night
And governs all things by his might.

We all believe in Christ, his Son,
Whom as Lord we are addressing,
Of equal Godhead, throne, and might,
Source of ev'ry grace and blessing.
Born of Mary, virgin mother,
By the power of the Spirit,
Made true man, our human brother
Through whom sonship we inherit;
He, crucified for sinful men,
Through God's pow'r rose to life again.

We all confess the Holy Ghost,
Who grants comfort, grace, and power.

Wir glauben all' an einen Gott,
Schöpfer Himmels und der Erden,
Der sich zum Vater geben hat,
Dass wir seine Kinder werden.
Er will uns allzeit ernähren,
Leib und Seel' auch wohl bewahren,
Allem Unfall will er wehren,
Kein Leid soll uns widerfahren;
Er sorget für uns, hüt't und wacht,
Es steht alles in seiner Macht.

Wir glauben auch an Jesum Christ,
Seinen Sohn und unsern Herren,
Der ewig bei dem Vater ist,
Gleicher Gott von Macht und Ehren;
Von Maria, der Jungfrauen,
Ist ein wahrer Mensch geboren
Durch den Heil'gen Geist im Glauben,
Für uns, die wir war'n verloren,
Am Kreuz gestorben und vom Tod
Wieder auferstanden durch Gott.

Wir glauben an den Heil'gen Geist,
Gott mit Vater und dem Sohne,

He, with the Father and the Son,
Robes us for the triumph hour,
Keeps the Church, his own creation,
In true unity of spirit;
Here forgiveness and salvation
Come to us through Jesus' merit.
The body ris'n, we then shall be
In life with God eternally.
Amen

Der aller Blöden Tröster heisst
Und mit Gaben zieret schöne,
Die ganz' Christenheit auf Erden
Hält in einem Sinn gar eben;
Hier all' Sünd' vergeben werden,
Das Fleisch soll auch wieder leben.
Nach diesem Elend ist bereit
Uns ein Leben in Ewigkeit.
Amen

A one-stanza versification of the Nicene Creed, beginning with "We all believe in one true God," was in existence prior to Luther's time. It is possible that Luther's friend, Stephen Roth, of Zwickau, informed Luther concerning the existence of this hymn, for in the Zwickau library there is a handwritten antiphon by Roth as well as a one-stanza German creed. A Breslau manuscript preserves this versification of the creed together with the notes to both Latin and German texts.

Luther turned the medieval one-stanza summary of the Creed into three, devoting a stanza to each of its three articles. The hymn first appeared in Johann Walter's *Geystliche gesangk Buchleyn* (1524), where it followed the Easter and the Pentecost hymns, next to "Gott der Vater, wohn uns bei" (*LW* 170). This seems to indicate that Luther thought of it first as a Trinity hymn. In 1525 the Erfurt *Enchiridion* put it under the heading, "The *Patrem*, or the Creed," and in his *German Mass* (1526) Luther prescribed that it be sung in the service as the creed. It was occasionally also sung outside the Divine Service, for instance, at the funeral of Kurfurst Friedrich in 1525. Later it was included in the collection of burial hymns published by Joseph Klug in Wittenberg in 1542.

The translation is by F. Samuel Janzow.

WIR GLAUBEN ALL. This plainsong tune is that of the single-stanza medieval hymn. The version used in *Lutheran Worship* is from Klug's *Geistliche Lieder* (1533), a more felicitous form than what appeared in Walter's *Geystliche gesangk Buchleyn* (1524).

The harmonization is by Paul G. Bunjes.

ISAIAH, MIGHTY SEER, IN SPIRIT SOARED 214

Isaiah, mighty seer, in spirit soared
And saw enthroned in majesty the Lord,
Around whose throne shone glory from his face,
Whose robe of light filled all the holy place.
Beside the throne two six-winged seraphim,
Who with their wings showed reverence to him.
With two each hid his face in holy awe,
With two his feet, these angels without flaw,
And with the third wing pair ascended high
To span the heavens with this mighty cry:
"Holy is God, the Lord of Sabaoth!

Jesaia, dem Propheten, das geschah,
Dass er im Geist den Herren sitzen sah
Auf einem hohen Thron in hellem Glanz,
Seines Kleides Saum den Chor füllet' ganz.
Es stunden zween Seraph bei ihm daran,
Sechs Flügel sah er einen jeden han:
Mit zween verbargen sie ihr Antlitz klar,
Mit zween bedeckten sie die Füsse gar,
Und mit den andern zween sie flogen frei,
Genander riefen sie mit grossem G'schrei:
Heilig ist Gott, der Herre Zebaoth!

Holy is God, the Lord of Sabaoth!
Holy is God, the Lord of Sabaoth!
His grace and might and glory fill the earth!"
Then shook the roof beam and the lintel stone,
And smoke of incense swirled around the throne.

Heilig ist Gott, der Herre Zebaoth!
Heilig ist Gott, der Herre Zebaoth!
Sein' Ehr' die ganze Welt erfüllet hat.
Von dem G'schrei zittert' Schwell' und Balken gar,
Das Haus auch ganz voll Rauchs und Nebels war.

This is Luther's German Sanctus, a metrical paraphrase of the Latin, based on Isaiah 6:1–4. It first appeared in his *Deutsche Messe* (1526). In the rubrics Luther suggests that this Sanctus, or his "Gott sei gelobet und gebenedeiet" (*LW* 238), or John Hus' "Jesus Christus nostra salus" (*LW* 236) be sung after the consecration, or blessing, of the bread, i.e., during the distribution of the body of our Lord, before the blessing of the cup. Thereafter the cup was to be consecrated and administered while the remainder of the aforementioned hymns or the German Agnus Dei are sung. Before long this hymn appeared in various hymnals, and it was sung largely at Communion celebrations.

The translation is by F. Samuel Janzow.

JESAIA, DEM PROPHETEN. This tune, in the Lydian mode, represents a rather free adaptation of a plainsong Sanctus appointed for the Sundays during Advent and Lent (see *Liber Usualis*, XVII of Ordinary Chants of the Mass, p. 61, for the original plainsong). Johann Walter praises the mastery of Luther in adapting the notes to this hymn text. Tone painting was not foreign to Luther. Notice the melody rise on "Around whose throne shone," also the melodic height on "Holy is God." It is interesting to note that later 16th-century services frequently dictated that the "Holy is God" sections be sung with pronounced dignity and gravity.

The form of the melody here used was included in Valentin Babst's *Geistliche Lieder* (1545). The harmonization in *Lutheran Worship* (1982) is by Paul G. Bunjes.

215 ALL GLORY BE TO GOD ON HIGH

All glory be to God on high
And thanks to him forever!
Whatever Satan's host may try,
God foils their dark endeavor.
He bends his ear to ev'ry call
And offers peace, goodwill to all,
And calms the troubled spirit.

O Father, for your lordship true
We give you praise and honor;
We worship you, we trust in you,
We give you thanks forever.
Your will is perfect, and your might
Relentlessly confirms the right;
Your lordship is our blessing.

Allein Gott in der Höh' sei Ehr'
Und Dank für seine Gnade,
Darum dass nun und nimmermehr
Uns rühren kann kein Schade.
Ein Wohlgefall'n Gott an uns hat,
Nun ist gross' Fried' ohn' Unterlass,
All' Fehd' hat nun ein Ende.

Wir loben, preis'n anbeten dich
Für deine ehr'; wir danken,
Dass du, Gott Vater, ewiglich
Regierst ohn' alles Wanken.
Ganz ungemess'n ist deine Macht,
Fort g'schieht, was dein Will' hat bedacht;
Wohl uns des feinen Herren!

Lord Jesus Christ, the only Son Of God, creation's author, Redeemer of your wand'ring ones, And source of all true pleasure: O Lamb of God, O Lord divine, Conform our lives to your design, And on us all have mercy.	O Jesu Christ, Sohn eingebor'n Deines himmlischen Vaters, Versöhner der'r, die war'n verlor'n, Du Stiller unsers Haders, Lamm Gottes, heil'ger Herr und Gott, Nimm an die Bitt' von unsrer Not, Erbarm' dich unser aller!
O Holy Spirit, perfect gift, Who brings us consolation: To men and women saved by Christ Assure your inspiration. Through sickness, need, and bitter death, Grant us your warm, life-giving breath; Our lives are in your keeping.	O Heil'ger Geist, du höchstes Gut, Du allerheilsamst' Tröster, Vor's Teufels G'walt fortan behüt', Die Jesus Christ erlöset Durch grosse Mart'r und bittern Tod, Abwend all unsern Jamm'r und Not! Darauf wir uns verlassen.

This metrical version by Nikolaus Decius of the prose "Gloria in excelsis" in the liturgy first appeared in the *Gesang Buch* (Rostock, 1525) in Low German (*Plattdeutsch*), the oldest known hymnal in that German, beginning "Allene Godt in der höge sey eer." In High German, together with the tune in the Ionian mode (see essay: The Church Modes, p. 832), it first appeared in Valentin Schumann's *Geistliche Lieder auffs new gebessert und gemehrt*, published in Wittenberg in 1539. Thereafter its popularity caused it to be included in numerous hymnals.

The new and fresh translation was prepared by Gilbert E. Doan for inclusion in *Lutheran Book of Worship* (1978).

ALLEIN GOTT IN DER HÖH. This tune appeared in Valentin Schumann's *Geistliche Lieder* (Leipzig, 1539), coupled to Nikolaus Decius' hymn text beginning with the same words. Both text and tune are generally ascribed to Decius. The tune appears to be an adaptation of the 10th-century plainsong tune to a "Gloria in excelsis," beginning with the "et in terra pax" (see *Liber Usualis*, p. 16). Its triple meter has sometimes caused it be referred to as "the Lutheran waltz."

Carl F. Schalk prepared the setting for *Lutheran Worship* (1982).

216 ALMIGHTY FATHER, BLESS THE WORD

This translation of a Scandinavian hymn of unknown origin appeared in *The Lutheran Hymnary* (1913), set to the tune WENN WIR IN HÖCHSTEN NÖTEN SEIN. The personal pronouns referring to God have been updated.

OLD HUNDREDTH, composed or adapted by Louis Bourgeois, first appeared in the *Trente-quatre Psalmes de David* (Genevan Psalter) in 1551, for which Bourgeois was the music editor. There it was set to Theodore de Beze's version of Psalm 134, "Or sus, serviteurs du Seigneur." Ever since William Kethe's metrical paraphrase of Psalm 100 (*LW* 435) appeared in the Anglo-Genevan Psalter (1561), and again in the English Psalter of the same year, set to this tune (hence the title OLD HUNDREDTH), the text and tune have been inseparably united. (See essay: Metrical Psalms, p. 825.)

The harmonization is from *The Lutheran Hymnal* (1941).

217 ON WHAT HAS NOW BEEN SOWN

This cento is an interesting example of how some hymns have evolved into their final popular form. Stanza 1, for instance, is the final stanza of John Newton's (*LW* 217, et al.) interesting hymn entitled "Travailing in Birth for Souls" (cf. Gal. 4:19), first appearing in the *Olney Hymns* (1779), Book 2. (For the complete text see Polack, p. 40.) Stanzas 2 and 3 represent a separate hymn, a "Short Hymn for Close of Divine Service," also from the *Olney Hymns* (1779), Book 3. This cento made its first appearance in the *Irish Hymnal* (1873).

The text here given is that which was altered and updated by the Inter-Lutheran Commission on Worship for inclusion in *Lutheran Book of Worship* (1978).

DARWALL'S 148TH. For comments on the tune see hymn 179.

The harmonization is from *The Lutheran Hymnal* (1941).

218 LORD, DISMISS US WITH YOUR BLESSING

First appearing anonymously in *A Supplement to The Shawbury Hymn Book* (Shrewsbury, 1773), in John Harris's *Collection of Psalms and Hymns* (York, 1780) it is credited to John Fawcett, Yorkshire Nonconformist minister. (See the long discussion about authorship in Julian.) Originally the last line in stanza 1 read, "In this dry and barren place." Godfrey Thring rewrote the third stanza, and it is his version that appears here with updated personal pronouns.

REGENT SQUARE. See hymn 50 for comments on this tune.

GRANT PEACE, WE PRAY, IN MERCY, LORD 219

Grant peace, we pray, in mercy, Lord;
Peace in our time, oh, send us!
For there is none on earth but you,
None other to defend us.
You only, Lord, can fight for us.
Amen

Verleih uns Frieden gnädiglich,
Herr Gott, zu unsern Zeiten.
Es ist doch ja kein andrer nicht,
Der für uns könnte streiten,
Denn du unser Gott alleine.

This hymn is a free paraphrase of an old Latin antiphon, "Da pacem, Domine, in diebus nostris," based on 2 Kings 20:19; 2 Chronicles 20:12; and Psalm 122:7, dating from the sixth century. It is likely that Luther wrote it shortly before its presumed appearance in Joseph Klug's *Geistliche Lieder* (1529), for in that year the evangelicals had ample reason to pray for peace: there was the uncertainty of the forthcoming second Diet of Spires plus the threat of the Turks approaching Vienna. In his "Vermahnung zum Gebet wider den Türken" (Exhortation to Prayer against the Turks) Luther expressly recommended that this hymn be sung.

In many publications of this hymn there is appended the ancient Collect for Peace:

> O God, from whom come all holy desires, all good counsels, and all just works, give to us, your servants, that peace which the world cannot give, that our hearts may be set to obey your commandments; and also that we, being defended from the fear of our enemies, may live in peace and quietness; through the merits of Jesus Christ, our Savior, who lives and reigns with you and the Holy Spirit, God forever (*LW* p. 260).

Moreover, this hymn was often appended to "Lord, Keep Us Steadfast in Your Word" (*LW* 334) and sung after the sermon.

The English translation is from *Laudamus*, first edition (Hanover, 1952), hymnal of the Lutheran World Federation.

VERLEIH UNS FRIEDEN. It is only the first line that bears some resemblance to the early plainsong tune to "Da pacem, Domine." The rest of the tune bears reminders of "Erhalt uns Herr" and "Nun komm der Heiden Heiland."

The harmonization is by Carl F. Schalk.

220 GUIDE ME EVER, GREAT REDEEMER

Guide me ever, great Redeemer,
Pilgrim through this barren land.
I am weak, but you are mighty;
Hold me with your pow'rful hand.
Bread of heaven, bread of heaven,
Feed me now and evermore;
Feed me now and evermore.

Open now the crystal fountain
Where the healing waters flow;
Let the fire and cloudy pillar
Lead me all my journey through.
Strong deliv'rer, strong deliv'rer,
Shield me with your mighty arm;
Shield me with your mighty arm.

When I tread the verge of Jordan,
Bid my anxious fears subside;
Death of death and hell's destruction,
Land me safe on Canaan's side.
Songs and praises, songs and praises
I will raise forevermore;
I will raise forevermore.

Arglwydd, arwain trwy'r anialwch
Fi bererin gwael ei wedd,
Nad oes ynof nerth na bywyd,
Fel yn gorwedd yn y bedd;
Hollaluog
Ydyw'r un a'm cwyd i'r lan.

Colofn dân rho'r nos i'm harwain
A rho'r golofn niwl y dydd;
Dal fi pan bwy'n teithio'r manau
Geirwon yn fy ffordd y sydd;
Rho imi fanna,
Fel na bwyf yn llwfrhau.

Agor y ffynnonau melus
Sydd yn tarddu o'r Graig i maes;
'Rhyd yr anial mawr canlyned
Afon iachawdwriaeth gras
Rho imi hyny;
Dim i mi ond dy fwynhau.

Pan bwy'n myned trwyr Iorddonen—
Angeu creulon yn ei rym,
Ti est trwyddi gynt dy hunan,
P'am yr ofnaf bellach ddim?
Buddugoliaeth!
Gwna imi waeddi yn y llif!

Ymddiriedaf yn dy allu,
Mawr yw'r gwaith a wnest erioed;
Ti gest angau, ti gest uffern,
Ti gest Satan dan dy droed,
Pen Calfaria,
Nac aed hwnw byth o'm cof.

Written in Welsh by William Williams, this hymn in five stanzas was first published in his hymnbook titled *Alleluia* (Bristol, 1745). Peter Williams (not related), a friend and co-worker of the author, translated stanzas 1, 3, and 5 into English for his *Hymns on Various Subjects* (1771); the first of these translated stanzas was joined with three others (stanzas 3 and 4 of the original plus a new stanza), translated by either the author himself or his son, John, and published in a leaflet the following year. Headed "A Favourite Hymn sung by Lady Huntingdon's young Collegians; Printed by the desire of many Christian Friends," the leaflet was printed for Trevecca College, of which John Williams was later principal. The fourth English stanza, as follows, is never used today:

Musing on my habitation,
Musing on my heav'nly Home
Fills my soul with holy longing,

Come, my Jesus, quickly come:
Vanity is all I see,
Lord, I long to be with Thee!

With its abundant analogies between the Israelites in the wilderness and the Christian traveling through earthly life, the hymn is embraced by English-speaking people everywhere and has been translated into at least 75 other languages. The text appearing here was prepared by the Inter-Lutheran Commission on Worship for inclusion in the *Lutheran Book of Worship* (1978).

CWM RHONDDA, a strong, moving tune, was composed by John Hughes for the annual Baptist Cymanfâu Ganu (singing festival) at Capel Rhondda, Pontypridd, Wales, in 1905 or 1907, and first printed in the festival program. From that time it is said to have been sung at thousands of such festivals. It appeared in the United States in 1918 as the setting for "Angels from the realms of glory" (*LW* 50) in *Cân a Mawl: Song and Praise*, a bilingual hymnal of the Calvinistic Methodist Church of the USA. In 1927 it was copyrighted in the United States when it appeared in *The Voice of Thanksgiving No. 4*. Its appearance in the revised *Fellowship Hymnbook* (1933) seems to mark its entrance into Great Britain. The composer's widow states that the tune was written on a Sunday morning during the worship service at a country church called Salem Chapel.

Hughes first called the tune RHONDDA, but was forced to retitle it to avoid confusion with another melody of the same name. CWM RHONDDA (pronounced "koom rawn'tha") means "valley of the Rhondda." The Rhondda is a river running through Wales; its valley is the heart of the Welsh coal-mining industry.

The harmonization is the work of Paul G. Bunjes.

SAVIOR, AGAIN TO YOUR DEAR NAME WE RAISE 221

John Ellerton wrote this hymn, the most popular of his hymns, for the 1866 festival of the Malpas, Middlewich, and Nantwich Choral Association, which organization Ellerton had founded. The original, in six stanzas, was written on the back of a note from the previous Sunday's sermon, and began:

Father, once more before we part, we raise
With one accord our parting hymn of praise.

Ellerton himself made several revisions; he shortened the hymn to four stanzas, with more revisions, for the Appendix to the 1868 edition of *Hymns Ancient and Modern*.

Louis F. Benson in his *Studies of Familiar Hymns* (second series, 1923) says of this hymn, "It could have been written only by one to whom the reverent conduct of public worship meant a great deal. Its very atmosphere is churchly. . . . And the thought of the hymn is that lips and heart so engaged in reverent offices should carry with them to the life outside the peace of that benediction and the purity of that worship." Small wonder that it is included in the latest hymnals, for instance, *The United Methodist Hymnal* (1989), *The Hymn Book* of the Anglican and United Churches of Canada (1971), the *Psalter Hymnal* (1987) of the Christian Reformed Church, and *The Hymnal 1982* of the Episcopal Church.

ELLERS. Edward S. Hopkins wrote this tune, first called BENEDICTION, for this text. It was first published in E. Brown-Borthwick's *Supplemental Hymn and Tune Book* (1869), for unison voices with a different accompaniment for each stanza. Hopkins later prepared a four-part arrangement for the *Appendix to the Bradford Tune Book* (1872). Ellerton approved of the tune, and used it in the Society for the Promotion of Christian Knowledge's *Church Hymns* (1871), for which he served as co-editor with William W. How (*LW* 182, et al.).

The setting is from *The Lutheran Hymnal* (1941).

222 HOW BLEST ARE THEY WHO HEAR GOD'S WORD

How blest are they who hear God's Word,
Who keep in faith what they have heard,
Who daily grow in wisdom.
From light to light they shall increase
And journey on life's way in peace;
They have the oil of gladness
To soothe their pain and sadness.

Through sorrow's night my sun shall be
God's Word, a treasure dear to me,
My shield and buckler ever.
My title as his child and heir
The Father's hand has written there,
His promise failing never:
"You will be mine forever."

Today his voice with joy I heard
And fed upon his holy Word,
That bread so freely given.
May grace a stronger faith maintain
So that its fruit shall all remain
When my account is given
Before God's throne in heaven.

O salig den, Guds Ord har hört,
Bevaret og til Nyte fört!
Han daglig Visdom lärte;
Fra Lys til Lys han vandre kan,
Og har i Livets Prövestand
En Salve for sit Hjerte
Mod al sin Nöd og Smerte.

Guds Ord det er min rige Skat,
Min Sol i Sorgens mörke Nat,
Mit Sverd i Troens Krige.
Guds Finger selv i Ordet skrev
Min Barne-Ret, mit Arve-Brev;
Den Skrift skal aldrig svige:
Kom, arv et evigt Rige!

Jeg gik smo til et däkket Bord
Idag og hörte Herrens Ord
Og Själen sanked Föde.
Gid Troen derved vokse saa,
At Troens Frugt ei savnes maa,
Naar jeg for ham skal möde,
Som for os alle döde!

This hymn appeared in *Evangeliske Sange* (1786), a collection of hymns written and published by the Norwegian defender of orthodox Lutheranism, Bishop Johan Nordahl Brun. This book was intended to supplement Ove Guldberg's *Psalmebog* (1778) then in use. Regarding his hymns the pious bishop stated: "Our divine worship is that garden from which I have gathered many flowers." The hymn is based on the last portion of the

Gospel for the Third Sunday in Lent (Old Standard series): "Blessed . . . are those who hear the word of God and obey it" (Luke 11:28).

The translation is from the *Service Book and Hymnal* (1958).

OM HIMMERIGES RIGE, also known as ISLAND, is an anonymous tune that first appeared in Hans Thomissön's *Den danske Psalmebog* (1569) coupled to the text beginning with the same words. This *Psalmebog* was the first hymnal prepared especially for Lutherans in Denmark, a book that was also quite generally used in Sweden.

The harmonization is from the *Service Book and Hymnal* (1958).

223 TO JORDAN CAME THE CHRIST, OUR LORD

To Jordan came the Christ, our Lord,
To do his Father's pleasure;
Baptized by John, the Father's Word
Was given us to treasure.
This heav'nly washing now shall be
A cleansing from transgression
And by his blood and agony
Release from death's oppression.
A new life now awaits us.

Oh, hear and mark the message well,
For God himself has spoken.
Let faith, not doubt, among us dwell
And so receive this token.
Our Lord here with his Word endows
Pure water, freely flowing.
God's Holy Spirit here avows
Our kinship while bestowing
The baptism of his blessing.

These truths on Jordan's banks were shown
By mighty word and wonder.
The Father's voice from heav'n came down,
Which we do well to ponder:
"This man is my beloved Son,
In whom my heart has pleasure.
Him you must hear, and him alone,
And trust in fullest measure
The word that he has spoken."

There stood the Son of God in love,
His grace to us extending;
The Holy Spirit like a dove
Upon the scene descending;
The triune God assuring us,
With promises compelling,
That in our baptism he will thus
Among us find a dwelling
To comfort and sustain us.

To his disciples spoke the Lord,
"Go out to ev'ry nation,
And bring to them the living Word
And this my invitation:
Let ev'ryone abandon sin
And come in true contrition
To be baptized and thereby win
Full pardon and remission
And heav'nly bliss inherit."

But woe to those who cast aside
This grace so freely given;
They shall in sin and shame abide
And to despair be driven.
For born in sin, their works must fail,

Christ unser Herr zum Jordan kam
Nach seines Vaters Willen,
Von Sankt Johann die Taufe nahm,
Sein Werk und Amt zu 'rfüllen.
Da wollt er stiften uns ein Bad,
Zu waschen uns von Sünden,
Ersäufen auch den bittern Tod
Durch sein selbst Blut und Wunden;
Es galt ein neues Leben.

So hört und merket alle wohl,
Was Gott heisst selbst die Taufe
Und was ein Christe lauben soll,
Zu meiden Ketzerhaufen.
Gott spricht und will, dass Wasser sei,
Doch nicht allein schlicht Wasser,
Sein heiligs Wort ist auch dabei
Mit reichem Geist ohn Massen:
Der ist allhie der Täufer.

Solchs hat er uns beweiset klar
Mit Bildern und mit Worten.
Des Vaters Stimm man offenbar
Daselbst am Jordan hörte;
Er sprach: "Das ist mein lieber Sohn,
An dem ich hab Gefallen;
Den will ich euch befohlen han,
Dass ihr ihn höret alle
Und folget seinem Lehren."

Auch Gotts Sohn hie selber steht
In seiner zarten Menschheit,
Der Heilig Geist herniederfährt
In' Taubenbild verkleidet,
Dass wir nicht sollen zweifeln dran:
Wenn wir getaufet werden,
All drei Person' getaufet han,
Damit bei uns auf Erden
Zu wohnen sich begeben.

Sein Jünger heisst der Herre Christ:
"Geht hin, all Welt zu lehren,
Dass sie verlorn in Sünden ist,
Sich soll zur Busse kehren;
Wer glaubet und sich taufen läst,
Soll dadurch selig werden;
Ein neugeborner Mensch er heisst,
Der nicht mehr könne sterben,
Das Himmelreich soll erben."

Wer nicht glaubt dieser grossen Gnad,
Der bleibt in seinen Sünden
Und ist verdammt zum ewgen Tod
Tief in der Höllen Grunde.
Nichts hilft sein eigen Heiligkeit,

Their striving saves them never; Their piteous acts do not avail, And they are lost forever, Eternal death their portion.	All sein Tun ist verloren, Die Erbsünd machts zur Nichtigkeit, Darin er ist geboren, Vermag sich selbst nicht helfen.
All that the mortal eye beholds Is water as we pour it. Before the eye of faith unfolds The pow'r of Jesus' merit. For here it sees the crimson flood To all our ills bring healing; The wonders of his precious blood The love of God revealing, Assuring his own pardon.	Das Aug allein das Wasser sieht, Wie Menschen Wasser giessen; Der Glaub im Geist die Kraft versteht Des Blutes Jesu Christi, Und ist vor ihm ein rote Flut, Von Christi Blut gefärbet, Die allen Schaden heilen tut, Von Adam her geerbet, Auch von uns selbst begangen.

With the appearance of his hymn on the Lord's Prayer in 1539, Luther had completed all his so-called Catechism Chorales except one, namely, the one on Baptism. If, as the evidence indicates, "To Jordan Came the Christ, Our Lord" appeared in 1541, then the gap in the catechism chorales is filled.

A Lübeck hymnal of 1556 indicates that this hymn may first have appeared in broadsheet form in 1541. In 1543 it appeared in Christian Rödinger's Ein schön geistlich Sangbuch (Magdeburg); in Johann Walter's *Geistliche Leyder und Psalmen*; in Klug's *Geistliche Lieder zu Wittenberg*; and in the appendix to Valentin Schumann's *Geistliche Lieder auffs new gebessert und gemehrt.*

The theological content of this hymn bears strong resemblance to the thoughts expressed by Luther in his two sermons on Baptism in 1540 as well as in his Small and Large Catechisms. This leads to the assumption that Luther here created a new text.

The translation is that done by Elizabeth Quitmeyer, originally solicited by Carl Schalk. Then director of music for "The Lutheran Hour" radio program, Schalk asked Quitmeyer to supply a new English translation of Luther's hymn for a future program. When, in 1965, the Inter-Lutheran Commission on Worship was formed, of which the Missouri Synod became a part, Schalk transmitted her translation to that commission.

CHRIST, UNSER HERR. The aforementioned hymnals used the tune coupled to Luther's "Es wolle Gott uns gnädig sein," first published in Johann Walter's *Geystliche gesangk Buchleyn* (Wittenberg, 1524). It was not associated with the text "To Jordan came the Christ, our Lord" until 1543, and may well be an original tune by Luther. The harmonization is by Richard W. Hillert.

BAPTIZED INTO YOUR NAME MOST HOLY 224

Baptized into your name most holy, O Father, Son, and Holy Ghost, I claim a place, though weak and lowly,	Ich bin getauft auf deinen Namen, Gott Vater, Sohn und Heil'ger Geist, Ich bin gezählt zu deinem Samen,

Among your seed, your chosen host.
Buried with Christ and dead to sin,
I have your Spirit now within.

My loving Father, here you take me
Henceforth to be your child and heir;
My faithful Savior, here you make me
The fruit of all your sorrows share;
O Holy Ghost, you comfort me
Though threat'ning clouds around I see.

O faithful God, you never fail me;
Your cov'nant surely will abide.
Let not eternal death assail me
Should I transgress it on my side!
Have mercy when I come defiled;
Forgive, lift up, restore your child.

All that I am and love most dearly,
Receive it all, O Lord, from me.
Oh, let me make my vows sincerely,
And help me your own child to be!
Let nothing that I am or own
Serve any will but yours alone.

Zum Volk, das dir geheiligt heisst,
Ich bin in Chritum eingesenkt,
Ich bin mit seinem Geist beschenkt.

Du hast zu deinem Kind und Erben,
Mein lieber Vater, mich erklärt,
Du hast die Frucht von deinem Sterben,
Mein treuer Heiland, mir gewährt.
Du willst in aller Not und Pein,
O guter Geist, mein Tröster sein.

Mein treuer Gott, auf deiner Seite
Bleibt dieser Bund wohl feste stehn;
Wenn aber ich ihn überschreite,
So lass mich nicht verlorengehn!
Nimm mich, dein Kind, zu Gnaden an,
Wenn ich hab' einen Fall getan!

Ich gebe dir, mein Gott, aufs neue
Leib, Seel' und Herz zum Opfer hin.
Erwecke mich zu neuer Treue
Und nimm Besitz von meinem Sinn!
Es sei in mir kein Tropfen Blut,
Der nicht, Herr, deinen Willen tut.

This popular Baptism hymn by Johann J. Rambach first appeared in his *Erbauliches Handbüchlein für Kinder* (Giessen, 1734). Originally the hymn had seven stanzas. Catherine Winkworth translated six for her *Chorale Book for England* (1863), from which the present form was drawn by the Inter-Lutheran Commission on Worship for inclusion in *Lutheran Book of Worship* (1978).

O DASS ICH TAUSEND ZUNGEN HÄTTE (Dretzel). Not to be confused with Johann König's tune of the same name (see *LW* 360), this melody by Kornelius Heinrich Dretzel first appeared in *Des evangelischen Zions Musicalische Harmonie* (Nürnberg, 1731) as the setting for "Weil nichts gemeiner ist als sterben" (Zahn 2858). The tune name is derived from its association with Johann Mentzer's hymn beginning with "O dass ich tausend Zungen hätte" (*LW* 448).

225 ALL WHO BELIEVE AND ARE BAPTIZED

All who believe and are baptized
Shall see the Lord's salvation;
Baptized into the death of Christ,
They are a new creation;
Through Christ's redemption they will stand
Among the glorious heav'nly band
Of ev'ry tribe and nation.

Enhver som tror og bliver döbt,
Han skal vist slaig blive,
Thi han ved Jesu Blod er kjöbt,
Som vil sig ham indlive,
Og blandt Guds Börns det hellig' Tal
Til Himmeriges Äres Val
Med Korsets Blod indskrive.

With one accord, O God, we pray,
Grant us your Holy Spirit;
Help us in our infirmity
Through Jesus' blood and merit;
Grant us to grow in grace each day
By holy Baptism that we may
Eternal life inherit.

Vi sukke alle hjertelig,
Og udi Troen sige
Med Hjertens Bön, enhver for sig:
O Jesu, lad os stige
Ved Daabens Kraft i Dyder frem,
Og for os saa ved Troen hjem
Til Ärens evig' Rige!

The Danish original of this hymn by Thomas Kingo, so popular in Denmark and Norway, first appeared in his proposed hymnal of 1689, and again in the official Danish *Psalmbog* (1699). Headed as a hymn for use after Holy Baptism, it was deemed worthy of inclusion in Guldberg's *Psalmebog* (1778).

George T. Rygh's translation was prepared in 1909 for *The Lutheran Hymnary* (1913). The first stanza was written in the third person singular (masculine gender); other than changing this stanza to plural and updating the pronouns, alterations to Rygh's text are slight.

ES IST DAS HEIL. For comments on the tune see hymn 355.

The setting is that contained in *The Lutheran Hymnal* (1941), slightly altered.

DEAREST JESUS, WE ARE HERE 226

Dearest Jesus, we are here,
Gladly your command obeying.
With this child we now draw near
In response to your own saying
That to you it shall be given
As a child and heir of heaven.

Your command is clear and plain,
And we would obey it duly:
"You must all be born again,
Heart and life renewing truly,
Born of water and the Spirit,
And my kingdom thus inherit."

This is why we come to you,
In our arms this infant bearing;
Lord, to us your glory show;
Let this child, your mercy sharing,
In your arms be shielded ever,
Yours on earth and yours forever.

Gracious head, your member own;
Shepherd, take your lamb and feed it;
Prince of Peace, make here your throne;
Way of life, to heaven lead it;
Precious vine, let nothing sever
From your side this branch forever.

Liebster Jesu, wir sind hier,
Deinem Worte nachzuleben.
Dieses Kindlein kommt zu dir,
Weil du den Befehl gegeben,
Dass man sie zu Christo führe,
Denn das Himmelreich ist ihre.

Ja, es schallet allermeist
Dieses Wort in unsern Ohren:
Wer durch Wasser und durch Geist
Nich zuvor ist neugeboren,
Wird von dir nicht aufgenommen
Und in Gottes Reich nicht kommen.

Darum eilen wir zu dir.
Nimm das Pfand von unsern Armen,
Tritt mit deinem Glanz herfür
Und erzeige dein Erbarmen,
Dass es dein Kind hier auf Erden
Und im Himmel möge werden!

Hirte, nimm dein Schäflein an;
Haupt, mach es zu deinem Gliede;
Himmelsweg, zeig ihm die Bahn;
Friedefürst, schenk ihm den Frieden;
Weinstock, hilf, dass diese Rebe
Auch im Glauben dich umgebe!

Now into your heart we pour	Nun, wir legen an dein Herz,
Prayers that from our hearts proceeded.	Was vom Herzen ist gegangen;
Our petitions heav'nward soar;	Führ die Seufzer himmelwärts
May our fond desires be heeded!	Und erfülle das Verlangen;
Write the name we now have given;	Ja, den Namen, den wir geben,
Write it in the book of heaven!	Schreib ins Lebensbuch zum Leben!

Benjamin Schmolck published this hymn in seven stanzas in his *Heilige Flammen der himmlischgesinnten Seele* (Striegau, 1704), titled "Good Thoughts of the Sponsors Who Journey with a Child to Baptism." Catherine Winkworth's six-stanza translation, beginning "Blessed Jesus, here we stand," contained in her *Lyra Germanica* (second series, 1858) as well as in her *Chorale Book for England* (1863), served as the basis for the altered and updated form included in *Lutheran Book of Worship* (1978) and *Lutheran Worship* (1982).

LIEBSTER JESU, WIR SIND HIER. See hymn 202 for comments on the tune.

The harmonization, which differs somewhat from *LW* 202, is also by Wilhelm Quampen, a *nom de plume* of Paul G. Bunjes.

227 THIS CHILD WE NOW PRESENT TO YOU

The popularity of this hymn, the result of its inclusion and use in the *Evangelical Lutheran Hymn-Book* (1912) and in *The Lutheran Hymnal* (1941), prompted the Commission on Worship to include it in *Lutheran Worship* (1982).

Although this hymn text by Samuel Gilman, dated 1823, is said to be a translation from the German (so Alfred P. Putnam, *Singers and Songs of the Liberal Faith* [Boston, 1875]), no mention is made of the German original, nor has this writer been able to find anything resembling these four stanzas. Stanza 2 of a hymn by Christoph F. Neander (1724–1802), beginning "Dir Herr, sei dieses Kind befohlen," contained in the *Württembergisches Gesangbuch* (1791), constitutes perhaps a hint, but no more than that.

Comparing this text with that in *The Lutheran Hymnal* (1941), one notices that not only have the personal pronouns been updated, but a textual change has been made: "And would renew its solemn vow" (st. 3 , line three) has been altered to "Its covenant we here renew." Since the context of the stanza appears to refer to the members of the congregation having been baptized in infancy, when no such "solemn vow" was made by the individual, the change was considered by the Commission on Worship to be theologically appropriate.

UXBRIDGE, not to be confused with a tune with the same name in Common Meter (CM—86 86), also called BURFORD, this tune UXBRIDGE is the work of Lowell

Mason that appeared set to A. M. Toplady's (*LW* 361) "At anchor laid, remote from home" in the Boston Handel and Haydn Society Collection (ninth edition, 1830).

The harmonization is from *The Lutheran Hymnal* (1941), slightly altered.

OUR CHILDREN JESUS CALLS 228

The text in five stanzas was first published in Job Orton's posthumous edition of Doddridge's *Hymns Founded on Various Texts in the Holy Scriptures* (London, 1755). Its title was "Christ's Condescending Regard to Little Children. Mark 10:14." In *A Collection of Hymns and a Liturgy for the Use of Evangelical Lutheran Churches* (New York, 1834), Doddridge's text occurs in six stanzas as follows:

See Israel's gentle Shepherd stand
With all-engaging charms.
Hark how He calls the tender lambs
And takes them in His arms!

"Permit them to approach," He cries,
"Nor scorn their humble name;
It was to save such souls as these
With power and love I came."

We bring them, Lord, with grateful hearts
And yield them up to Thee;
Rejoiced that we ourselves are Thine;
Thine let our offspring be.

Thus Lydia's house was sanctified
When she received the Word;
Thus the believing jailer gave
His family to the Lord.

Ye little flock, with pleasure hear;
Ye children, seek his face
And fly with transport to receive
The Gospel of his grace.

If orphans they are left behind,
Thy care, O God, we trust;
And let Thy promise cheer our hearts
If weeping o'er their dust.

Stanza 4 of this version is probably an insertion by an unknown hand.
To this hymn Duffield remarks:

> Perhaps we forget the little phrases of the evangelists as to this incident. Matthew says that Christ was expected "to put His hands on them and pray"; Luke, that He should "touch" them; and Mark adds that He "took them up in His arms, put His hands upon them, and blessed them." And if it was a precious

memory for such a child later in life to know that he had once been in the Savior's arms, how precious it must also be to one who knows—even in our days— that he has been committed to the Lord's love in his earliest moments!

Henry Ustic Onderdonk adapted the first three stanzas of Doddridge's hymn in his *Prayer Book Collection* (1826), the first line reading: "The gentle Savior calls." This appears to be a recasting of the hymn, "See Israel's Gentle Shepherd Stand." One is Common Meter, and the other is Short Meter.

FRANCONIA is from *Harmonischer Lieder-Schatz*, oder *Allgemeines Evangelisches Choral-Buch . . . gestellet von Johann Balthasar König*, where it is set to the hymn "Was ist, das mich betrübt?" The original melody, which may be by König himself, runs as follows (Zahn 2207):

The tune was abbreviated by dropping the third and fifth phrases in William Henry Havergal's *Old Church Psalmody* (1847).

The harmonization is from *The Lutheran Hymnal* (1941), slightly altered.

JESUS SINNERS WILL RECEIVE 229

Jesus sinners will receive;
May they all this saying ponder
Who in sin's delusions live
And from God and heaven wander!
Here is hope for all who grieve:
Jesus sinners will receive.

We deserve but grief and shame,
Yet his words, rich grace revealing,
Pardon, peace, and life proclaim.
Here our ills have perfect healing;
We with humble hearts believe
Jesus sinners will receive.

When their sheep have lost their way,
Faithful shepherds go to seek them;
Jesus watches all who stray,
Faithfully to find and take them
In his arms that they may live—
Jesus sinners will receive.

Come, O sinners, one and all,
Come, accept his invitation;
Come, obey his gracious call,
Come and take his free salvation!
Firmly in these words believe:
Jesus sinners will receive.

Jesus sinners will receive.
Even me he has forgiven;
And when I this earth must leave,
I shall find an open heaven.
Dying, still to him I cleave—
Jesus sinners will receive.

Jesus nimmt die Sünder an;
Saget doch dies Trostwort allen,
Welche von der rechten Bahn
Auf verkehrten Weg verfallen!
Hier ist, was sie retten kann:
Jesus nimmt die Sünder an.

Keiner Gnade sind wir wert,
Doch hat er in seinem Worte
Eidlich sich dazu erklärt.
Sehet nur, die Gnadenpforte
Ist hier völlig aufgetan:
Jesus nimmt die Sünder an.

Wenn ein Schaf verloren ist,
Suchet es ein treuer Hirte;
Jesus, der uns nie vergisst,
Suchet treulich das Verirrte,
Dass es nicht verderben kann:
Jesus nimmt die Sünder an.

Kommet alle, kommet her,
Kommet, ihr betrübten Sünder!
Jesus rufet euch, und er
Macht aus Sündern Gottes Kinder.
Glaubet's doch und denket dran:
Jesus nimmt die Sünder an.

Jesus nimmt die Sünder an,
Mich hat er auch angenommen
Und den Himmel aufgetan,
Dass ich selig zu ihm kommen
Und auf den Trost sterben kann:
Jesus nimmt die Sünder an.

This hymn, originally in eight stanzas, is the result of Erdmann Neumeister's custom of often closing his sermon with an appropriate hymn of his making. It is the hymn that followed his sermon on the Gospel, Luke 15:1–10, for the Third Sunday after Trinity Sunday in the year 1718, the year in which he dwelt on the Gospels of the church year. Later that year they were published and disseminated in his *Evangelischer Nachklang*, in the preface of which—not written by Neumeister—it was stated that these hymns constitute the "sweet kernel of the powerful Gospel of Mark . . . in contrast to the new hymns of the fanatical Enthusiasts (*Schwärmer*, i.e., Pietists) in which they subtly hide the poison of their new teaching."

The translation is an altered and updated form of that contained in *The Lutheran Hymnal* (1941), a version prepared by the Inter-Lutheran Commission on Worship for inclusion in *Lutheran Book of Worship* (1978).

MEINEN JESUM LASS ICH NICHT is here a simplified form of the tune by Johann Ulich that appeared in *Siebenfache Welt- und Himmels-kapell* (1674), set to Christian Keimann's (*LW* 40) hymn beginning with the same words. This was a volume issued by Michael Schernack, skilled Wittenberg musician. Originally the tune appeared thus (Zahn 3451a):

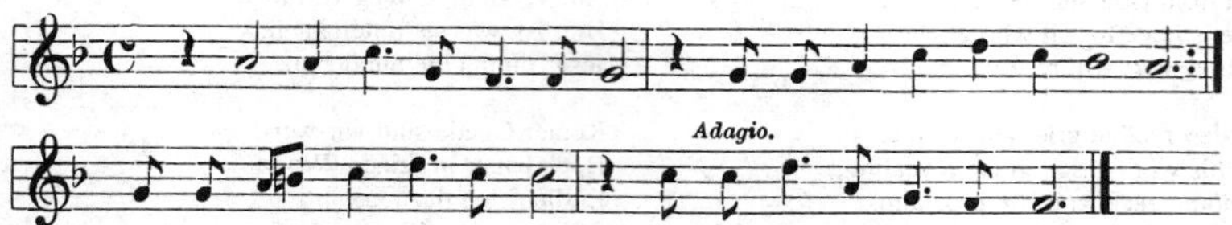

The harmonization is from the *Württembergisches Choralbuch* (1953).

230 FROM DEPTHS OF WOE I CRY TO YOU

From depths of woe I cry to you.
O Lord, my voice is trying
To reach your heart and, Lord, break through
With these my cries and sighing.
If you keep record of our sin
And hold against us what we've been,
Who then can stand before you?

Your grace and love alone avail
To blot out sin with pardon.
In your gaze our best efforts pale,
Develop pride, and harden.
Before your throne no one can boast
That he escaped sin's deadly coast.
Our haven is your mercy.

In God I anchor all my trust,
Discarding my own merit.
His love holds firm; I therefore must
His fullest grace inherit.
He tells me, and my heart has heard,
The steadfast promise of his Word,
That he's my help and haven.

Though help delays until the night
Or waits till morning waken,
My heart shall never doubt his might
Nor think itself forsaken.
All you who are God's own indeed,
Born of the Spirit's Gospel seed,
Await his promised rescue.

Though sins arise like dunes of sand,
God's mercy-tides submerge them.

Aus tiefer Not schrei ich zu dir,
Herr Gott, erhör mein Rufen.
Dein gnädig Ohren kehr zu mir
Und meiner Bitt sie öffen;
Denn so du willst das sehen an,
Was Sünd und Unrecht ist getan,
Wer kann, Herr, vor dir bleiben?

Bei dir gilt nichts denn Gnad und Gunst,
Die Sünde zu vergeben;
Es ist doch unser Tun umsonst
Auch in dem besten Leben.
Vor dir niemand sich rühmen kann,
Des muss dich fürchten jedermann
Und deiner Gnade leben.

Darum auf Gott will hoffen ich,
Auf mein Verdienst nicht bauen;
Auf ihn mein Herz soll lassen sich
Und seiner Güte trauen,
Die mir zusagt sein wertes Wort
Das ist mein Trost und treuer Hort,
Des will ich allzeit harren.

Und ob es währt bis in die Nacht
Und wieder an den Morgen,
Doch soll mein Herz an Gottes Macht
Verzweifeln nicht noch sorgen.
So tu Israel rechter Art,
Der aus dem Geist erzeuget ward,
Und seines Gotts erharre.

Ob bei uns ist der Sünden viel,
Bei Gott ist viel mehr Gnade;

Like oceans pouring from his hand, Strong flows the grace to purge them. Our shepherd will his Israel lead To uplands out of every need And ransom us from sinning.	Sein Hand zu helfen hat kein Ziel, Wie gross auch sei der Schade. Er ist allein der gute Hirt, Der Israel erlösen wird Aus seinen Sünden allen.

Already as early as 1523 in his *Formula Missae* Luther bemoaned the fact that there were not more German hymns that the congregations might sing during the Mass and he encouraged poets to compose them. Toward the end of that year he wrote to his friend George Spalatin, court chaplain of Frederick the Wise, inviting him to turn some psalms into German hymns. In the course of the letter he mentions that he has already completed Psalm 130 (*De profundis*) and that he is enclosing it as an example.

There is no evidence that Spalatin honored the request. The sample Luther mentions is undoubtedly the metrical paraphrase of Psalm 130, "From depths of woe I cry to you," contained in *Lutheran Worship* (1982) and its predecessors. This psalm, with its portrayal of deepest repentance and highest assurance of forgiveness, constituted for Luther an expression of his own experience. Hence he was concerned that the forgiveness of sins, the very heart of biblical and Reformation doctrine, be impressed on people's hearts.

Two versions of this hymn began to circulate, a longer and shorter. The longer, now more common five-stanza version, appeared in Johann Walter's *Geistliche gesangk Buchleyn* (1524) and in Luther's *Christliche Gesengts und Begrebnes* (Wittenberg, 1542). The shorter version, with its conflation of the second and fourth stanzas, first appeared in the *Achtliederbuch* (1523), thereafter in the two Erfurt *Enchiridia* (1524), and in some southwest German, especially Strassburg, hymnals.

It should be mentioned that, so far as is known, Luther had nothing to do with the publishing of the *Achtliederbuch*. It was strictly an undertaking of Jobst Gutknecht's printing establishment in Nürnberg. It is opined that Gutknecht received a recreated or corrupted version of the hymn from a Nürnberg student who had heard it while attending Wittenberg University.

Since it is the belief in the forgiveness of sins through Jesus Christ that alone can be of comfort to the Christian in the hour of death, it is quite natural that this hymn would become popular at funerals. It was sung in the Wittenberg Castle Church at the burial of Frederick the Wise as well as at the burial of John the Steadfast. It was sung by the congregation in the Church of Our Dear Lady in Halle as Luther's body lay in state there, February 20, 1546, on its way from Eisleben to Wittenberg.

The translation is by F. Samuel Janzow.

AUS TIEFER NOT I. The text has been coupled to a number of tunes. The *Achtliederbuch* (*Etlich christlich lider*) prescribed ES IST DAS HEIL (*LW* 225, 355); one of the Erfurt *Enchiridia* uses ACH GOTT VOM HIMMEL (*TLH* 260); and the Strassburg hymnals from 1525 on used what is known as AUS TIEFER NOT II (*LW* 248), a tune by Wolfgang Dachstein (*LW* 111). The other Erfurt *Enchiridion* and Johann Walter's *Geistliche gesangk Buchleyn* (1524) used the tune here called AUS TIEFER NOT I. This beautiful Phrygian tune, undoubtedly the work of Luther, fits the text beautifully. Notice the tone painting: the low note on "depths"; the pitch height on "woe"; the descending Phrygian leading tone on "trying"; and the questioning ring of the final Phrygian cadence. Truly a masterpiece!

The harmonization is by Paul G. Bunjes.

231 LORD JESUS, THINK ON ME

Lord Jesus, think on me
And purge away my sin;
From selfish passions set me free
And make me pure within.

Lord Jesus, think on me,
By anxious thoughts oppressed;
Let me your loving servant be
And taste your promised rest.

Lord Jesus, think on me,
Nor let me go astray;
Through darkness and perplexity
Point out your chosen way.

Lord Jesus, think on me
That, when the flood is past,
I may th'eternal brightness see
And share your joy at last.

Μνώεο, Χριστέ,
υἱὲ Θεοῖο
ὑψιμέδοντος,
οἰκέτεω Σοῦ,
Κῆρ' ἀλιτροῖο
Τάδε γράψαντος·
Καί μοι ὄπασσον
λύσιν παθέων
κηριτρεφέων
τά μοι ἐμφυῆ
ψυχᾷ ῥυπαρᾷ·
δὸς δὲ ἰδέσθαι,
Σῶτερ 'Ιησοῦ,
ζαθέαν αἴγλαν
Σάν, ἔνθα φανεὶς
μέλψω ἀοιδὰν
παίονι ψυχᾶν,
παίονι γυίων,
Πατρὶ σὺν μεγάλῳ
Πνεύματί Θ' 'Αγνῷ.

This is Allen W. Chatfield's "paraphrase or simplification," as he says, of this last of 10 Greek odes by Synesius, Bishop of Cyrene. Originally in five stanzas, published in his *Songs and Hymns of the earliest Greek Christian poets, Bishops, and others, translated into English Verse* (1876), Chatfield later added four more stanzas. Admittedly his version is more somber than the original Greek lines. Given here are stanzas 2, 3, 5, and 7 of that larger work.

SOUTHWELL. For comments on the tune see hymn 99.

The setting is that which appeared in *The Lutheran Hymnal* (1941), slightly altered.

ALAS, MY GOD, MY SINS ARE GREAT

232

Alas, my God, my sins are great,
My conscience must upbraid me;
And now I find that in my strait
No human pow'r can aid me.

Were I to flee in my despair
In some lone spot to hide me,
My grief would still be with me there
And peace still be denied me.

I must, O Lord, by you be sought;
Oh, pity and restore me.
Just God, make not your wrath my lot;
Your Son has suffered for me.

If pain and woe must follow sin,
Then be my path still rougher.
Here spare me not; if heav'n I win,
On earth I gladly suffer.

But curb my heart, forgive me still,
Oh, make my patience firmer;
For they ignore your kindly will
Who at your chast'nings murmur.

All that you do is for my best;
Your grace will help me bear it
If but at last I see your rest
And with my Savior share it.

Ach Gott und Herr, wie gross und schwer
Sind mein' begangne Sünden!
Da ist niemand der helfen kann,
In dieser Welt zu finden.

Lief' ich gleich weit zu dieser Zeit
Bis an der Welt ihr' Enden
Und wollt' los sein des Kreuzes mein,
Würd' ich doch solch's nicht wenden.

Zu dir flieh' ich, verstoss mich nicht,
Wie ich's wohl hab' verdienet!
Ach Gott, zürn nicht, geh nicht ins G'richt,
Dein Sohn hat mich versöhnet.

Soll's ja so sein, dass Straf' und Pein
Auf Sünden folgen müssen,
So fahr hier fort und schone dort
Und lass mich hier wohl büssen!

Gib, Herr, Geduld, vergiss der Schuld,
Verleih ein g'horsam Herze;
Lass mich nur nicht, wie's oft geschicht,
Mein Heil murrend verscherze!

Handle mit mir, wie's dünket dir,
Auf dein' Gnad' will ich's leiden;
Lass mich nur nicht dort ewiglich
Von dir sein abgeschieden!

On July 2, 1613, Johann Major preached a sermon at Jena about a natural disaster that took place May 29 of that year, all but destroying the surrounding community. The sermon was printed at Jena the same year, and a second edition, published at Eisleben later in 1613, was followed by the six stanzas of this hymn that was to become a popular and widely used confessional hymn.

Major's authorship of the hymn itself has been disputed in favor of two others, Johann Göldel and Martin Rutilius. While early appearances of the text were either anonymous or labeled "J. G.," taken to mean Johann Gross (or Major), the second edition of J. Clauder's *Psalmodia Nova* (Altenburg, 1630) credited "J. Gö." with the first part, having added four new stanzas. This attribution stood, as referring to Göldel, for nearly 100 years.

By this time the hymn appeared in any combination of the six stanzas of 1613, the four added in Clauder, and/or two additional stanzas first found in Melchior Franck's *Geistlichen Musikalischen Lustgartens* (Nürnberg, 1616). Rutilius' claim to its origin was made in 1726 by Caspar Binder, a pastor at Mattstedt. Binder based his theory on the discovery of Rutilius' inscription in an autograph album, in which appeared the six stanzas of 1613. Although Binder gives the date of the inscription as May 29, 1604, Mearns in Julian's *Dictionary of Hymnology* presumes this to be a misreading or misprint; assuming the correct date to be May 29, 1614, he concludes that Rutilius, who was not of a particularly poetic bent, chose to commemorate the anniversary of the 1613 disaster by repeating Major's lines.

Thus Major remains the most likely candidate for author of the original text. The translation by Catherine Winkworth, using the six stanzas printed with Major's sermon, appeared in her *Chorale Book for England* (1863). It is her text that appears here slightly altered and updated form.

ACH GOTT UND HERR first appeared in a major key in Christoph Peter's *Andachts-Zymbeln* (Freyberg, 1655), but it had been through a number of appearances and revisions prior to that. In *As hymnodus sacer* (Leipzig, 1625) it accompanied the above text in the following form:

Johann Crüger presented the melody in his *Newes vollkömmliches Gesangbuch* (1640) with changes in the second line; from Peter's 1655 form it fell into the hands of J. S. Bach, who regularized the rhythm for his *Vierstimmige Choralgesänge* (1769).

The composer of the original tune is unknown. Paul G. Bunjes prepared the present harmonization for *Lutheran Worship* (1982).

233 LORD, TO YOU I MAKE CONFESSION

Lord, to you I make confession: I have sinned and gone astray, I have multiplied transgression, Chosen for myself my way. Led by you to see my errors, Lord, I tremble at your terrors.	Herr, ich habe missgehandelt, Ja mich drückt der Sünden Last; Ich bin nicht den Weg gewandelt, Den du mir gezeiget hast, Und jetzt wollt' ich gern aus Schrecken Mich vor deinem Zorn verstecken.
Though my conscience' voice appall me, Father, I will seek your face; Though your child I dare not call me, Yet receive me in your grace. Do not for my sins forsake me; Let your wrath not overtake me.	Drum ich muss es nur bekennen: Herr, ich habe missgetan, Darf mich nicht dein Kind mehr nennen. Ach, nimm mich zu Gnaden an; Lass die Menge meiner Sünden Deinen Zorn nicht gar entzünden!
Your Son came to suffer for me, Gave himself to rescue me, Died to heal me and restore me,	Aber, Christe, deine Wunden, Ja ein einzigs Tröpflein Blut, Das kann meine Wunden heilen,

Reconciled and set me free.
Jesus' cross alone can vanquish
These dark fears and soothe this anguish.

Lord, on you I cast my burden.
Sink it to the depths below.
Let me know your gracious pardon,
Wash me, make me white as snow.
Let your Spirit leave me never;
Make me only yours forever.

Löschen meiner Sünden Glut;
Drum will ich, mein' Angst zu stillen,
Mich in deine Wunden hüllen.

Dir will ich die Last aufbinden,
Wirf sie in die tiefe See;
Wasche mich von meinen Sünden,
Mache mich so weiss wie Schnee;
Lass dein'n guten Geist mich treiben,
Einzig stets bei dir zu bleiben!

This heartfelt hymn of confession by Johann Frank first appeared in Johann Crüger's *Geistliche Kirchenmelodien* (Leipzig, 1649) coupled to a tune composed by Crüger himself. Originally consisting of eight stanzas, it is stanzas 1, 3, 7, and 8 that are here given.

The translation is a revised and updated form of that by Catherine Winkworth in her *Chorale Book for England* (1863).

HERR, ICH HABE MISSGEHANDELT is a splendid tune by Johann Crüger that fits hand-in-glove with the text for which it was originally composed.

The harmonization is by Paul G. Bunjes.

TO YOU, OMNISCIENT LORD OF ALL 234

To you, omniscient Lord of all,
With grief and shame I humbly call;
I see my sins against you, Lord,
The sins of thought, of deed and word.
They press me sore; to you I flee:
O God, be merciful to me!

My Lord and God, to you I pray,
Oh, cast me not in wrath away;
Let your good Spirit ne'er depart,
But let him draw to you my heart
That truly penitent I be:
O God, be merciful to me!

O Jesus, let your precious blood
Be to my soul a cleansing flood.
Turn not, O Lord, your guest away,
But grant that justified I may
Go to my house, at peace to be:
O God, be merciful to me!

Jeg staar for Gud, som alting veed,
Og slaar mit Öie skamfuld ned,
Jeg ser min Synd, at den er stor
I Tanker, Gjerninger og Ord,
Det mig igjennem Hjertet skjär;
O Gud, mig Synder naadig vär!

O Herre Gud, hvad jeg har gjort,
Kast mig ei fra dir Aasyn bort,
Tag ei din Helligaand fra mig,
Men lad ham drage mig til dig,
Den rette Angers Vei mig lär;
O Gud, mig Synder naadig vär!

O Jesu, lad dit Blod, din Död
Mig redde ud af Syndens Nöd,
Forstod mig ei, hjölp, at jeg maa
Retfärdiggjort ved dig faa gaa
Ned til mit Hus, og glädes der;
O God, mig Synder naadig vär!

This hymn by Magnus B. Landstad first appeared in his *Udkast til Kirkesalmebog* (1861), which revised would become the *Kirkesalmebog* (1869), an officially authorized Norwegian hymnbook. The scriptural basis of each stanza is as follows: stanza 1, Ezra 9:6, 15; stanza 2, Psalm 51:11; stanza 3, Luke 18:14.

The translation, originally beginning "Before thee God, who knowest all," was prepared by Carl Döving for inclusion in *The Lutheran Hymnary* (Minneapolis, 1913).

VATER UNSER. For comments on the tune see hymn 431.
The harmonization is by Paul G. Bunjes.

235 AS SURELY AS I LIVE, GOD SAID

As surely as I live, God said,
I would not see the sinner dead.
I want him turned from error's ways,
Repentant, living endless days.

To us therefore Christ gave command:
"Go forth and preach in ev'ry land;
Bestow on all my pard'ning grace
Who will repent and mend their ways.

"All those whose sins you thus remit
I truly pardon and acquit,
And those whose sins you will retain
Condemned and guilty shall remain.

What you will bind, that bound shall be;
What you will loose, that shall be free;
To my dear Church the keys are giv'n
To open, close the gates of heav'n."

The words which absolution give
Are his who died that we might live;
The minister whom Christ has sent
Is but his humble instrument.

When ministers lay on their hands,
Absolved by Christ the sinner stands;
He who by grace the Word believes
The purchase of his blood receives.

All praise to you, O Christ, shall be
For absolution full and free,
In which you show your richest grace;
From false indulgence guard our race.

Praise God the Father and the Son
And Holy Spirit, Three in One,
As was, is now, and so shall be
World without end, eternally!

So wahr ich leb', spricht Gott der Herr,
Des Sünders Tod ich nicht begehr',
Sondern dass er bekehre sich,
Tu' Buss' und lebe ewiglich.

Drum Christ, der Herr, sein' Jünger sandt':
Geht hin, predigt in allem Land
Vergebung der Sünd' jedermann,
Dem's leid ist, glaubt und will alban.

Wem ihr die Sünd' vergeben werd't,
Soll ihr'r los sein auf dieser Erd'.
Wem ihr sie b'halt't im Namen mein,
Dem sollen sie behalten sein.

Was ihr bind't, soll gebunden sein;
Was ihr auflöst, das soll los sein.
Die Schlüssel zu dem Himmelreich
Hiermit ich euch geb' allen gleich.

Wenn uns der Beicht'ger absolviert,
Sein Amt der Herr Christ durch ihn führt
Und spricht uns selbst von Sünden rein;
Sein Werkzeug ist der Dein'r allein.

Wem der Beicht'ger auflegt sein' Hand,
Dem löst Christ auf der Sünden Band
Und absolviert ihn durch sein Blut;
Wer's glaubt, aus Gnad' hat solches Gut.

Wen nun sein G'wissen beisst und nagt,
Die Sünd' quäilt, dass er schier verzagt,
Der halt'sich zu dem Gnadenthron,
Zum Wort der Absolution.

Lob sei dir, wahrer Gottessohn,
Für die heil'g' Absolution,
Darin du zeigst dein' Gnad' und Güt';
Vor falschem Ablass uns behüt!

Nikolaus Herman first published this hymn, originally in 11 stanzas, in his *Die Sonntags Evangelia über das ganze Jahr* (Wittenberg, 1560) with the title "A hymn on the power of the Keys and the virtue of holy absolution; for the children in Joachimsthal." The reference to the laying on of hands in stanza 6 implies private, or individual, confession to the pastor. It is this type that the Lutheran Symbols praise so highly in pastoral care, a type that, somewhat unfortunately, has given way to a general confession of sins in the Preparation (*Confiteor*) in the Divine Service or in a service of corporate confession.

ST. LUKE. This fine tune by Jeremiah Clarke, so complementary to the text, first appeared in Henry Playford's *The Divine Companion* (1701).

The harmonization was prepared by George I. Leonard, a *nom de plume* of Paul G. Bunjes, for *Lutheran Worship* (1982). Notice the interesting harmonic progression of line 3 of each stanza leading into line 4, a device frequently employed by J. S. Bach (*LW* 89).

236–237 JESUS CHRIST, OUR BLESSED SAVIOR

Jesus Christ, our blessed Savior,
Turned away God's wrath forever;
By his bitter grief and woe
He saved us from the evil foe.

He, to pledge his love undying,
Spreads this table, grace supplying,
Gives his body with the bread,
And with the wine the blood he shed.

Banquet gifts God here is sharing;
Take them—after well preparing;
For if one does not believe,
Then death for life he shall receive.

Praise the Father, who from heaven
To his own this food has given,
Who, to mend what we have done,
Gave into death his only Son.

Firmly hold with faith unshaken
That this food is to be taken
By the sick who are distressed,
By hearts that long for peace and rest.

Agony and bitter labor
Were the cost of God's high favor;
Do not come if you suppose
You need not him who died and rose.

Christ says: "Come, all you that labor,
And receive my grace and favor:
They that feel no want nor ill
Need no physician's help nor skill."

If your heart this truth professes
And your mouth your sin confesses,
You will be your Savior's guest,
Be at his banquet truly blest.

Let this food your faith so nourish
That by love its fruit may flourish
And your neighbor learn from you
How much God's wondrous love can do.

Jesus Christus, unser Heiland,
Der von uns den Gotteszorn wandt',
Durch das bitter Leiden sein
Half er uns aus der Hölle Pein.

Dass wir nimmer des vergessen,
Gab er uns sein'n Leib zu essen,
Verborgen im Brot so klein,
Und zu trinken sein Blut im Wein.

Wer sich will zu dem Tisch machen,
Der hab' wohl acht auf sein' Sachen;
Wer unwürdig hinzugeht,
Für das Leben den Tod empfäht.

Du sollst Gott den Vater preisen,
Dass er dich so wohl wollt' speisen
Und für deine Missetat
In den Tod sein'n Sohn geben hat.

Du sollst glauben und nicht wanken,
Dass es Speise sei den Kranken,
Den'n ihr Herz von Sünden schwer
Und vor Angst ist betrübet sehr.

Solch' gross' Gnad' und Barmherzigkeit
Sucht ein Herz in grosser Arbeit.
Ist dir wohl, so bleib davon,
Dass du nicht kriegest bösen Lohn!

Er spricht selber: Kommt, ihr Armen,
Lass mich über euch erbarmen!
Kein arzt ist dem Starken not,
Sein' Kunst wird an ihm gar ein Spott.

Glaubst du das von Herzensgrunde
Und bekennest mit dem Munde,
So bist du recht wohl geschickt,
Und die Speise dein' Seel' erquickt.

Die Frucht soll auch nicht ausbleiben,
Deinen Nächsten sollst du lieben,
Dass er dein geniessen kann,
Wie dein Gott an dir hat getan.

The authorship of this notable hymn on the Lord's Supper and its worthy and salutary reception, although generally ascribed to John Hus, Bohemian forerunner of the Reformation, still remains in doubt. The fact that it is still sung today in Lutheran churches is due to Luther's having made a 10-stanza translation of the early 15th-century Latin text, improving it theologically, a translation that first appeared in *Eyn Enchiridion* (Erfurt, 1524). The thoughts about this blessed Sacrament contained in Luther's translation are reminiscent of words and phrases that he used in his sermons on

Palm Sunday and Maundy Thursday in 1524. Later on, the Latin text appeared in the second part of the *Historia et Monumenta Joh. Hus atque Hieronymi Pragensis* (Nürnberg, 1558).

The translation given here is that prepared by F. Samuel Janzow.

JESUS CHRISTUS, UNSER HEILAND. The form of the tune designated at *LW* 236 is the familiar tune that appeared in *The Lutheran Hymnal* (1941), the tune set to Luther's German text in J. Klug's *Geistliche Lieder* (1533). The harmonization by Paul G. Bunjes first appeared in his *New Organ Accompaniments for Hymns* (St. Louis, 1976).

The tune designated at *LW* 237 is from a Wittenburg choir book of 1524; it is the tune used in present-day hymnals of the Lutheran territorial churches in Germany. The harmonization was also prepared by Paul G. Bunjes, music editor of *Lutheran Worship* (1982), a member of the Commission on Worship.

Notice the distribution of the nine stanzas to the two settings and the note that they "may be sung in numerical order to either tune, or they may be sung in alternation as the stanza numbers indicate." A suggestion: Using this hymn during the distribution of the Lord's body and blood, with the congregation singing odd-numbered stanzas to the familiar tune at *LW* 236 and the choir singing (in unison) the even-numbered stanzas to the unfamiliar tune (after thorough rehearsing!) at *LW* 237 should, prove to be effective and uplifting.

O LORD, WE PRAISE YOU 238

O Lord, we praise you, bless you, and adore you, In thanksgiving bow before you. Here with your body and your blood you nourish Our weak souls that they may flourish. O Lord, have mercy! May your body, Lord, born of Mary, That our sins and sorrows did carry, And your blood for us plead In all trial, fear and need: O Lord, have mercy!	Gott sei gelobet und gebenedeiet, Der uns selber hat gespeiset Mit seinem Fleische und mit seinem Blute, Das gib uns, Herr Gott, zugute! Kyrieleison! Herr, durch deinen heiligen Leichnam, Der von deiner Mutter Maria kam, Und das heilige Blut Hilf uns, Herr, aus aller Not! Kyrieleison!
Your holy body into death was given, Life to win for us in heaven. No greater love than this to you could bind us; May this feast of that remind us! O Lord, have mercy! Lord, your kindness so much did move you That your blood now moves us to love you. All our debt you have paid; Peace with God once more is made. O Lord, have mercy!	Der heil'ge Leichnam ist für uns gegeben Zum Tod, dass wir dadurch leben; Nicht grössre Güte konnt' er uns geschenken, Dabei wir sein soll'n gedenken. Kyrieleison! Herr, dein Lieb' so gross dich zwungen hat, Dass dein Blut an uns gross' Wunder tat Und bezahlt' unsre Schuld, Dass uns Gott ist worden hold. Kyrieleison!
May God bestow on us his grace and favor To please him with our behavior And live together here in love and union	Gott geb' uns allen seiner Gnade Segen, Dass wir gehn au seinen Wegen In rechter Lieb' und brüderlicher Treue,

Nor repent this blest communion.	Dass uns die Speis' nicht gereue.
O Lord, have mercy!	Kyrieleison!
Let not your good Spirit forsake us,	Herr, dein Heil'ger Geist uns nimmer lass,
But that heav'nly-minded he make us;	Der uns geb' zu halten rechte Mass,
Give your Church, Lord, to see	Dass dein' arm' Christenheit
Days of peace and unity.	Leb' in Fried' und Einigkeit!
O Lord, have mercy!	Kyrieleison!

Luther first mentions this hymn in his *Formula Missae* (1523). Bemoaning the lack of vernacular evangelical hymns that might be sung by the congregation during the Mass, he suggests that, until more such hymns are forthcoming, the hymn, "O Lord, We Praise You," be sung following the Communion. He stipulates, however, that the line "and holy Sacrament, at our last end, from the consecrated priest's hand" be omitted. This line, he says, was appended by someone of the cult of St. Barbara, who, having neglected the Sacrament all his life, hoped that at the point of death he might gain eternal life by his good work rather than through faith in Christ.

The hymn to which Luther refers was a popular German pre-Reformation *Leise* sung by the congregation on Corpus Christi festival (observed on the Thursday after Trinity Sunday by the Roman Catholic church) after the choir's singing of the sequence, "Laude Sion Salvatorem" ("Zion, lift your voice and sing"), by Thomas Aquinas (c. 1225–1274). By taking over this *Leise*, with the exception of the aforementioned lines, and adding two stanzas of his own, Luther provided the Lutheran church one of its finest hymns on Holy Communion. This was perhaps done shortly before the hymn, without the tune, appeared in the Erfurt *Enchiridia* (1524).

It is in the *Formula Missae* that Luther advocated, among other things, that the distribution of both bread and wine to the people be restored, in agreement with Christ's institution of the Sacrament. In his *Of Secret Masses and Priestly Consecration* (1533), Luther refers to this pre-Reformation *Leise* as proof of the custom of Communion in both kinds in the medieval church.

GOTT SEI GELOBET UND GEBENEDEIET. This tune was coupled to the one-stanza pre-Reformation text as early as the 15th century (Bäumker, I, pp. 719f.). It appeared with Luther's text in Johann Walter's *Geystliche gesangk Büchleyn* (1524). The harmonization is by Carl F. Schalk.

In the German worship of bygone years, this hymn, a rubrical option in the Chief Service (*Hauptgottesdienst*) of the Synod, was invariably sung in spirited fashion after the Benediction to conclude the Communion service.

239 SOUL, ADORN YOURSELF WITH GLADNESS

Soul, adorn yourself with gladness,	Schmücke dich, o liebe Seele,
Leave the gloomy haunts of sadness,	Lass die dunkle Sündenhöhle,
Come into the daylight's splendor,	Komm ans helle Licht gegangen,

There with joy your praises render.
Bless the one whose grace unbounded
This amazing banquet founded:
He, though heav'nly, high, and holy,
Deigns to dwell with you most lowly.

Hasten as a bride to meet him,
Eagerly and gladly greet him.
There he stands already knocking;
Quickly, now, your gate unlocking,
Open wide the fast-closed portal,
Saying to the Lord immortal:
"Come, and leave your loved one never;
Dwell within my heart forever."

Now in faith I humbly ponder
Over this surpassing wonder
That the bread of life is boundless
Though the souls it feeds are countless:
With the choicest wine of heaven
Christ's own blood to us is given.
Oh, most glorious consolation,
Pledge and seal of my salvation.

Jesus, source of lasting pleasure,
Truest friend, and dearest treasure,
Peace beyond all understanding,
Joy into all life expanding:
Humbly now, I bow before you;
Love incarnate, I adore you;
Worthily let me receive you
And, so favored, never leave you.

Jesus, sun of life, my splendor,
Jesus, friend of friends, most tender,
Jesus, joy of my desiring,
Fount of life, my soul inspiring:
At your feet I cry, my maker,
Let me be a fit partaker
Of this blessed food from heaven,
For our good, your glory, given.

Jesus, Bread of Life, I pray you,
Let me gladly here obey you.
By your love I am invited,
Be your love with love requited;
By this Supper let me measure,
Lord, how vast and deep love's treasure.
Through the gift of grace you give me
As your guest in heaven receive me.

Fange herrlich an zu prangen!
Denn der Herr, voll Heil und Gnaden,
Will dich jetzt zu Gaste laden;
Der den Himmel kann verwalten,
Will jetzt Herberg' in dir halten.

Eile, wie Verlobte pflegen,
Deinem Bräutigam entgegen,
Der da mit dem Gnadenhammer
Klopft an deine Herzenskammer!
Öffn' ihm bald des Geistes Pforten,
Red ihn an mit schönen Worten:
Komm, mein Liebster, lass dich küssen,
Lass mich deiner nicht mehr missen!

Nein, Vernunft, die muss hier weichen,
Kann dies Wunder nicht erreichen,
Dass dies Brot nie wird verzehret,
Ob es gleich viel Tausend' nähret,
Und dass mit dem Saft der Reben
Uns wird Christi Blut gegeben.
O der grossen Heimlichkeiten,
Die nur Gottes Geist kann deuten!

Jesu, meines Lebens Sonne,
Jesu, Meine Freud' und Wonne,
Jesu, du mein ganz Beginnen,
Lebensquell und Licht der Sinnen,
Hier fall' ich zu deinen Füssen;
Lass mich würdiglich geniessen
Dieser deiner Himmelsspeise
Mir zum Heil und dir zum Preise!

Jesu, meines Lebens Sonne,
Jesu, meine Freud' und Wonne,
Jesu, du mein ganz Beginnen,
Lebensquell und Licht der Sinnen,
Hier fall' ich zu deinen Füssen;
Lass mich würdiglich geniessen
Dieser deiner Himmelsspeise
Mir zum Heil und dir zum Preise!

Jesu, wahres Brot des Lebens,
Hilf, dass ich doch nicht vergebens
Oder mir vielleicht zum Schaden
Sei zu deinem Tisch geladen!
Lass mich durch dies Seelenessen
Deine Liebe recht ermessen,
Dass ich auch, wie jetzt auf Erden,
Mög dein Gast im Himmel werden!

The first stanza of this hymn by Johann Franck appeared in Johann Crüger's *Geistliche Kirchenmelodien* (Leipzig, 1649) set to the tune that Crüger composed for it. Exactly when the entire hymn of nine stanzas was written is uncertain. It appeared thus in the so-called Runge *Gesangbuch* (Berlin, 1653) of which Johann Crüger was music editor, and also in Crüger's *Praxis pietatis melica*. Franck published it in section 1 of his

Geistliches Zion (Guben, 1672) with the heading "Preparation for the Holy Communion."

This is, without doubt, a great hymn. Small wonder that Julian states:

> This hymn is perhaps the finest of all German Hymns for the Holy Communion. It is an exhortation to the soul to arise and draw near to partake of the Heavenly Food and to meditate on the wonders of Heavenly Love, ending with a prayer for final reception of the eternal feast.

Albert F. W. Fischer characterizes it as "a hymn of purest metal in consummate form" (*Kirchenlieder-Lexicon*, Band 1, 1878). Indeed, its unique form exibits the craftsmanship of Franck. Notice that in the original German the final syllable of each line contains the vowel *e*; moreover, all rhymes are feminine, that is, two-syllable. Yet the poetry is not monotonous!

The composite translation is based on the translation of Catherine Winkworth published in her *Lyra Germanica* (second series, 1858) and revised in her *Chorale Book for England* (1863). The first four stanzas were prepared by the Inter-Lutheran Commission on Worship for inclusion in *Lutheran Book of Worship* (1978). Although stanza 4 in that hymnal, intended as the final stanza, includes some thoughts from Franck's subsequent German stanzas, the Commission on Worship decided to add stanzas 7 and 9 from *The Lutheran Hymnal* (1941). Hence it requested Jaroslav Vadja to revise and update them. This accounts for the repetition of the German stanza 4 as parallel to the English stanzas 4 and 5.

It is to be noted that later printings of *Lutheran Worship* corrected the error of *By* in line 4, stanza 6, changing it to "*Be* your love. . . ."

SCHMÜCKE DICH is the tune that Johann Crüger composed for Johann Franck's text when it first appeared in Crüger's *Geistliche Kirchenmelodien* (Leipzig, 1649). An old judgment, or opinion, about this tune says that it is so well crafted, the angels in heaven could do no better.

The harmonization is by Paul G. Bunjes.

240 DRAW NEAR AND TAKE THE BODY OF THE LORD

Draw near and take the body of the Lord, And drink the holy blood for you outpoured; Offered was he for greatest and for least, Himself the victim and himself the priest.	Sancti, venite, Christi corpus sumite, Sanctum bibentes, quo redempti sanguine. Pro universis immolatus Dominus, Ipse sacerdos exstitit et hostia.
He who his saints in this world rules and shields, To all believers life eternal yields; With heav'nly bread he makes the hungry whole, Gives living waters to the thirsting soul.	Sanctorum custos, rector quoque, Dominus, Vitae perennis, largitur credentibus. Caelestem panem dat esurientibus, De fonte vivo praebet sitientibus.

Come forward then with faithful hearts sincere, And take the pledges of salvation here. O Lord, our hearts with grateful thanks endow As in this feast of love you bless us now.	Accedant omnes pura, mente creduli, Sumant aeternam salutis custodiam. Alpha et Omega, ipse Christus Dominus, Venit venturus iudicare homines.

Legend has it that this Latin hymn was sung by the angels when, after a heated theological argument, St. Patrick and his nephew Sechnall were reconciled in their church's graveyard. More factual is the assertion that this Communion hymn was written toward the end of the seventh century by an unknown author at the Monastery of Bangor County Down, Ireland, and that it is contained in the Bangor *Antiphoner*, an Irish manuscript dating from the aforementioned century. From Ireland the manuscript was carried to Bobbio, a famous Italian monastery, and then to the Ambrosian Library in Milan. There it was discovered and first published by Ludovico Antonio Muratori (1672–1750), Roman Catholic priest, historian, theologian, and librarian, better known for having discovered in 1740, what came to be called, the Muratorian Fragment, an 85-line fragment of an early Latin treatise on the Bible canon.

Although this may be one of the earliest metrical Communion hymns of Western Christianity, one is reminded of the contributions in this category of Thomas Aquinas (c. 1227–74), the distinguished "Angelic Doctor," among which are: "Of the Glorious Body Telling" (*LBW* 120) and "Thee We Adore, O Hidden Savior" (*LBW* 199).

The translation of "Sancte, venite, corpus Christi sumite" is an altered and updated form of that by John M. Neale in his *Medieval Hymns* (1851), of which two of its five stanzas have here been omitted.

OLD 124TH, abbr. is the magnificent tune first appearing in the Genevan Psalter (1551) set to Psalm 124, "Or peut bien dire Israel maintenant." It made its way into the Anglo-Genevan Psalter (1558), also with Psalm 124, and thus came to be called OLD 124TH. The desire to use this exemplary tune for other hymns was frustrated by the lack of texts in this meter, namely, 10 10 10 10 10. Thus it came about that a form of tune was produced by omitting the third phrase of the original psalm tune and by squaring up the remaining four phrases into 16 symmetrical measures having a meter of 10 10 10 10. This came to be called TOULON, or as here, OLD 124TH, abbr.

This became a popular meter for 19th-century hymn writers. Granted that the lines are long; the thought processes involved. Thus couplet rhyming (AABB) is best, thereby facilitating the mind's recall. While Charles Wesley wrote numerous poems in such decasyllabic lines, he avoided this form in his hymns. On the other hand, notice the quantity and quality of the hymns in this meter in *Lutheran Worship* (p. 998): the familiar "Abide with Me, Fast Falls the Eventide" (*LW* 490); the beautiful "Here, O My Lord, I See You Face to Face" (*LW* 243; notice the ABAB rhyming) to the lovely tune FARLEY CASTLE; and "Stars of the Morning, So Gloriously Bright" (*LW* 190) to O QUANTA QUALIA—to mention but a few.

The harmonization is from *The Lutheran Hymnal* (1941), slightly altered.

241 LET ALL MORTAL FLESH KEEP SILENCE

Let all mortal flesh keep silence
And with fear and trembling stand;
Ponder nothing earthly-minded,
For with blessing in his hand
Christ our God to earth descending
Comes our homage to demand.

King of kings yet born of Mary,
As of old on earth he stood,
Lord of lords in human vesture,
In the body and the blood,
He will give to all the faithful
His own self for heav'nly food.

Rank on rank the host of heaven
Spreads its vanguard on the way
As the Light of Light, descending
From the realm of endless day,
Comes the pow'rs of hell to vanquish
As the darkness clears away.

At his feet the six-winged seraph,
Cherubim with sleepless eye,
Veil their faces to the presence
As with ceaseless voice they cry:
"Alleluia, alleluia!
Alleluia, Lord Most High!"

Σιγησάτω πᾶσα σὰρξ βροτεία
καὶ στήτω μετὰ φόβου καὶ τρόμου,
καὶ μηδὲν γήϊνον ἐν ἑαυτῇ λογιζέσθω·
ὁ γὰρ βασιλεὺς τῶν βασιλευόντων καὶ
Κύριος τῶν κυριευόντων, Χριστὸς ὁ
Θεὸς ἡμων προέρχεται σφαγιασθῆναι
καὶ δοθῆναι είς βρῶσιν τοῖς πιστοῖς·

προηγοῦνται δὲ τούτου οἱ χοροὶ
τῶν ἀγγέλων μετὰ πάσης ἀρχῆς
καὶ ἐξουσίας, τὰ πολυόμματα
Χερουβίμ, καὶ τὰ ἑξαπτέρυγα
σεραφὶμ τὰς ὄψεις καλύπτοντα,
καὶ βοῶντα τὸν ὕμνον,
ἀλληλούϊα, ἀλληλούϊα, ἀλληλούϊα.

Hardly a single present-day hymnal excludes this beautiful hymn found in the Liturgy of St. James—James the Less, first bishop of Jerusalem—and sung in the Eastern Orthodox churches probably as early as the fifth century at the Great Entrance, when the Communion elements were brought into the sanctuary at the beginning of the Liturgy of the Faithful (*Missa Fidelium*). Translated by J. M. Neale (*LW* 31, et al.) and R. F. Littledale (*LW* 162) as the "Prayer of the Cherubic Hymn" in their *Translations of the Primitive Liturgies* (1868–69), Gerard Moultrie, Anglican clergyman, was acquainted with its translation before its publication, for he paraphrased it into a metric pattern of four stanzas, beginning "Let all mortal flesh keep silence," in his *Lyra Eucharistica* (1864).

Notice the trochaic (´ ˘) 87 87 87 meter, so expressive of grandeur and strength and its ability of conveying weighty thoughts in its 15 syllables per double line.

PICARDY is a glorious French carol tune, probably of the 17th century, printed in *Chansons populaires des provinces de France* IV (Paris, 1840) edited by Jean Fleury-Weckerlin, where it is headed "The Ballad of Jesus Christ" as sung by Mme. Pierre Dupont, a folk song she remembered from her childhood in Picardy, northern France. The tune is also in Julien Tiersot's *Melodies* (Paris, 1887) with the mention that among French folk songs it is one of a few of a religious nature (apart from carols). It is in *The English Hymnal* (1906) that it appeared in its present form.

Apropos are the words of Archibald Jacob:

> This tune is not of the type to which the previous French carol tunes in this book [i.e., in *Songs of Praise*, 1931] have conformed; there is no childlike mirth or gaiety here whether the tune be sung fast or slow. In the present instance it must be sung very slowly, when its character appears very somber, but at the same time dignified and ceremonious; if, however, it is sung fast the somberness changes to fierceness, and though it may suggest a dance, it is a dance of no amenable kind. All tunes change their character, to a certain degree, with a considerable change of speed, but the cleavage here is of a remarkable nature, and denotes an unusual tune (*Songs of Praise Discussed*).

The harmonization is by Paul G. Bunjes.

I COME, O SAVIOR, TO YOUR TABLE 242

I come, O Savior, to your table, For weak and weary is my soul; You, Bread of Life, alone are able To satisfy and make me whole.	Ich komm' zu deinem Abendmahle, Weil meine Seele hungrig ist, Der du wohnst in dem Freudensaale Und meiner Seele Speise bist;
Refrain Lord, may your body and your blood Be for my soul the highest good!	Mein Jesu, lass dein Fleisch und Blut Sein meiner Seele höchstes Gut!
Restless am I and heavy laden, With sin my soul is sore oppressed; Receive me graciously, and gladden My heart that here is now your guest.	Mühselig bin ich und beladen Mit einer schweren Sündenlast; Doch nimm mich Sünder zu umfangen, Und speise mich als deinen Gast!
Your heart is filled with fervent yearning That I, a sinner, come to you; I, Lord, to your sure mercy turning, My ancient bond of faith renew.	Dein Herz ist stets voll von Verlangen Und brennt von sehnlicher Begier, Die armen Sünder zu umfangen, Drum komm' ich Sünder auch zu dir.
In hope I come to your high table, Your testament of deepest love; For by its grace I now am able To know the heart of God above.	Ich kann dein Abendmahl wohl nennen Nur deiner Liebe Testament; Denn, ach, hier kann ich recht' erkennen, Wie sehr dein Herz vor Liebe brennt!
What greater gift can I inherit? It is faith's bonded solid base; It is the strength of heart and spirit, The covenant of hope and grace.	Es ist das Hauptgut aller Güter Und unsers Glaubens Band und Grund, Die grösste Stärke der Gemüter, Die Hoffnung und der Gnadenbund.
Your body crucified, O Savior, Your blood which once for me was shed,	Der Leib, den du für mich gegeben, Das Blut, das du vergossen hast,

These are my life and strength forever, By them my hungry soul is fed.	Gibt meiner Seele Kraft und Leben Und meinem Herzen Ruh' und Rast.

The importance of the Lord's Supper in the corporate worship of Lutherans as well as in the life of its members is readily attested by the numerous Lutheran hymn writers dwelling on this subject and the inclusion of many such hymns in their hymnals. This hymn by Friedrich C. Heyder was a favorite in the *Kirchengesangbuch für Evangelisch-Lutherische Gemeinden ungeänderter Augsburgischer Confession* (St. Louis, 1847), the first official hymnal of the Synod, as well as in its successive printings. Therein it contained 21 stanzas and was commonly sung during the distribution. According to A. F. W. Fischer (*Kirchenlieder-Lexicon*), the hymn's first appearance—in 28 stanzas!—was in Brumberg's *Gesangbuch* (Zwickau, 1710).

The translation is an updated cento of the 15-stanza version that appeared in *The Lutheran Hymnal* (1941).

ICH STERBE TÄGLICH. Originally set to Benjamin Schmolk's (*LW* 198, 226) burial hymn, "Ich sterbe täglich und mein Leben eilt immerfort zum Grabe hin," it was included in the *Emskirchner Choral-Buch* (1756), a manuscript collection in Leipzig Municipal Library containing 295 tunes in four-part settings, familiar tunes not only from the 16th and 17th centuries, but also from Freylinghausen's (*LW* 23, et al.) *Geistreiches Gesangbuch* and from the *Melodienbüchlein* (Bayreuth, 1733).

The harmonization is by Paul G. Bunjes.

243 HERE, O MY LORD, I SEE YOU FACE TO FACE

At the close of the celebration of the Lord's Supper at St. Andrew's Free Church, Greenock, Scotland, a printed leaflet with notices of forthcoming services and a suitable hymn was customarily given to each departing communicant at the church door. For the observance on the first Sunday of October, 1855, the pastor, John James Bonar, requested his younger brother, Horatius Bonar, to provide a Communion poem for this leaflet. This hymn was promptly written and made its first appearance on that Sunday; two years later this laudable and popular hymn with its eschatological close was included in Horatius Bonar's *Hymns of Faith and Hope*, first series. Some hymnals use the following remaining stanza, here updated, as are also the other stanzas:

I have no wisdom, save in him who is
My Wisdom and my Teacher, both in one;
No wisdom can I lack while you are wise,
No teaching do I crave save yours alone.

FARLEY CASTLE appears in *A Paraphrase upon the Divine Poems* by George Sandys (1638), set to Psalm 72. This, the second edition of Sandys's metrical version of the

Psalms, contains a number of tunes in two parts, treble and bass, which are therein anonymous, but, in later editions, ascribed to Henry Lawes (*LW* 243).

The interesting arrangement of this charming tune is by Carl F. Schalk, as prepared for *Worship Supplement* (1969).

O LIVING BREAD FROM HEAVEN 244

O living Bread from heaven, How well you feed your guest! The gifts that you have given Have filled my heart with rest. Oh, wondrous food of blessing, Oh, cup that heals our woes! My heart, this gift possessing, With praises overflows.	Wie wohl hast du gelabet, O liebster Jesu, deinen Gast, Ja mich so reich begabet, Da ich jetzt fühle Freud' und Rast! O wundersame Speise, O süsser Lebenstrank! O Lieb'smahl, das ich preise Mit einem Lobgesang, Indem es hat erquicket Mein Leben, Herz und Mut! Mein Geist, der hat erblicket Das allerhöchste Gut.
My Lord, you here have led me Within your holiest place And here yourself have fed me With treasures of your grace; For you have freely given What earth could never buy, The bread of life from heaven, That now I shall not die.	Du hast mich jetzt geführet, O Herr, in deinen Gnadensaal, Daselbst hab' ich berühret Dein' edle Güter allzumal; Da hast du mir gegeben, Geschenket mildiglich Das werte Brot zum Leben, Das sehr ergötzet mich; Du hast mir zugelassen, Dass ich den Seelenwein Im Glauben möchte fassen, Und dir vermählet sein.
You gave me all I wanted; This food can death destroy. And you have freely granted The cup of endless joy. My Lord, I do not merit The favor you have shown, And all my soul and spirit Bow down before your throne.	Ein Herz, durch Reu' zerschlagen, Ein Herz, das ganz zerknirschet ist, Das, weiss ich, wird behagen, Mein Heiland, dir zu jeder Frist; Du wirst es nicht verachten, Demnach ich emsig bin, Nach deiner Gunst zu trachten. Nimm doch in Gnaden hin Das Opfer meiner Zungen; Denn billig wird jetzund Dein teurer Ruhm besungen, Herr Gott, durch meinen Mund.
Lord, grant me then, thus strengthened With heav'nly food, while here My course on earth is lengthened, To serve with holy fear. And when you call my spirit To leave this world below, I enter, through your merit, Where joys unmingled flow.	Hilf ja, dass dies Geniessen Des edlen Schatzes schaff' in mir Ein heil'ges Tränenfliessen, Dass ich mich wende stets zu dir. Lass mich hinfüro spüren Kein' andre Lieblichkeit, Als welche pflegt zu rühren Von dir zu dieser Zeit.

Lass mich ja nichts begehren
Als deine Lieb' und Gunst;
Denn niemand kann entbehren
Hier deiner Lieb' und Brunst.

Wohl mir, ich bin versehen
Mit Himmelsspeis' und Engeltrank;
Nun will ich rüstig stehen,
Zu singen dir Lob, Ehr' und Dank.
Ade, du Weltgetümmel,
Du bist ein eitler Tand!
Ich seufze nach dem Himmel,
Dem rechten Vaterland.
Ade, dort werd' ich leben
Ohn' Unglück und Verdruss;
Mein Gott, du wirst mir geben
Der Wollust Überfluss.

This notable Communion hymn by Johann Rist, originally in nine stanzas, first appeared in his *Neuer Himlischer Lieder Sonderbares Buch* (Lüneberg, 1651). While in her *Lyra Germanica* (second series, 1858) Catherine Winkworth translated eight 12-line stanzas of this hymn, in her *Chorale Book for England* (1865) she kept but five of those stanzas representing stanzas 1-2 and 7–9 of the German original, which stanzas, somewhat altered, were included in *The Lutheran Hymnal* (1941). The four-stanza altered form, both textually and metrically, that appeared in the *Service Book and Hymnal* (1958) was from the *Church Book* (Philadelphia, 1868). It is this version, altered and updated by the Inter-Lutheran Commission on Worship for inclusion in *Lutheran Book of Worship* (1978), that is here given. The German text is presented here with no pretense of matching parallel stanzas.

ACH GOTT VOM HIMMEL REICHE. For comments on the tune and setting see hymn 176.

245 O JESUS, BLESSED LORD, MY PRAISE

O Jesus, blessed Lord, my praise,
My heartfelt thanks to you I raise;
You have so lovingly bestowed
On me your body and your blood.

Break forth, my soul, in joy and say:
What wealth has come to me today,
What health of body, mind, and soul!
Christ dwells within me, makes me whole.

O Jesus, sode Jesus, dig
Ske Hjertens Tak evindelig,
Som med dit eget Kod og Blod
Saa kjärlig mig bespise lod!

Bryd ud, min Själ, med Tak og sig:
O, hvor er jeg nu bleven rig!
Min Jesus i mit Hjerte bor,
Tak, tak, hvad er min Glade stor!

Thomas Kingo's Swedish text appeared in *En Ny Kirke-Psalme-Bog* (the so-called *Vinterparten*) as a "Thanksgiving after the Lord's Supper." The translation by Arthur

James Mason has been slightly altered to update the text; it was prepared for the 1889 Supplement to *Hymns Ancient and Modern*.

OLD HUNDREDTH. For comments on the tune see hymn 216.
The harmonization is by Paul G. Bunjes.

LORD JESUS CHRIST, YOU HAVE PREPARED 246

Lord Jesus Christ, you have prepared
This feast for my salvation,
Your very body and your blood;
Thus, at your invitation,
With weary heart, by sin oppressed,
I come to you for needed rest;
I need your peace, your pardon.

Though into heaven you have gone,
Ascending far above me,
Yet here in earthly food I see
How much indeed you love me.
You are not bound to any place;
No contrite heart escapes your grace;
Your love unsought surrounds me.

I eat this bread, I drink this cup,
Your promise firm believing;
In truth your body and your blood
My lips are here receiving.
Your word remains forever true;
All things are possible for you;
Your searching love has found me.

Unaided reason cannot see
What eager faith embraces,
But this consoling supper, Lord,
Each restless doubt displaces.
Your wondrous ways are not confined
Within the limits of my mind;
Your promise wholly triumphs.

I should have died eternally,
But here, repentant kneeling,
Newborn I rise to live the love
Found in your strength, your healing.
Lord, in this sacrament impart
Your joy and courage to my heart;
Dead yet alive I praise you!

Herr Jesu Christ, du hast bereit't
Für unsre matten Seelen
Dein Leib und Blut zu ein'r Mahlzeit,
Tust uns zu Gästen wählen.
Wir tragen unsre Sündenlast,
Drum kommen wir zu dir zu Gast
Und suchen Rat und Hilfe.

Ob du schon aufgefahren bist
Von dieser Erde sichtig
Und bleibst nunmehr zu dieser Frist
Von uns allhier unsichtig,
Bis dein Gericht dort wird angehn
Und wir vor dir all' werden stehn
Und dich fröhlich anschauen:

Du sprichst: Nehmt hin, das ist mein Leib,
Den sollt ihr mündlich essen;
Trinkt all' mein Blut, bei euch ich bleib',
Mein sollt ihr nicht vergessen.
Du hast's gered't, drum ist es wahr;
Du bist allmächtig, drum ist gar
Kein Ding bei dir unmöglich.

Und ob mein Herz hier nicht versteht,
Wie dein Leib an viel Orten
Zugleich sein kann, und wie's zugeht,
So trau' ich doch dein'n Worten;
Wie das sein kann, befehl' ich dir,
An deinem Worte g'nüget mir,
Dem stehet nur zu glauben.

Für solch dein tröstlich Abendmahl,
Herr Christ, sei hochgelobet!
Erhalt uns das, weil überall
Die Welt dawider tobet!
Hilf, dass dein Leib und Blut allein
Mein Trost und Labsal möge sein
Im letzten Stündlein! Amen

This notable hymn by Samuel Kinner, originally in eight stanzas, first appeared in Jeremiah Weber's *Gesang Buch* (Leipzig, 1638), entitled "A Beautiful Hymn on the Supper of Our Lord."

The popularity of this Communion hymn in the bygone years of German worship in the Synod evidently prompted its inclusion in *The Lutheran Hymnal* (1941), in *Lutheran Book of Worship* (1978), and now in *Lutheran Worship* (1982). Although it was not included in the *Evangelical Lutheran Hymn-Book* (1912), the first official English hymnal of the Synod, it had appeared in a translation by Emmanuel Cronenwett in the 1880 Lutheran Hymnal of the Ohio Synod.

The translation was prepared by the Inter-Lutheran Commission on Worship for inclusion in *Lutheran Book of Worship* (1978).

DU LEBENSBROT, HERR JESU CHRIST (also known as HERR JESU CHRIST, DU HAST BEREITT) first appeared in 1668 in Peter Sohren's edition of Johann Crüger's *Praxis pietatis melica* (Frankfurt-am-Main, 1668) set to Johann Rist's (*LW* 122, et al.) "Du lebensbrot, Herr Jesu Christ."

Notice the interesting iambic 87 87 887 meter—unsquare and asymmetrical, in contrast to the usual English type of hymn—a form so typical of numerous chorales (see listing of such tunes in *LW*, p. 998). Notice also the effectiveness of the rhyme scheme ABABCCD.

The harmonization was prepared by Paul A. Bouman for inclusion in *Lutheran Book of Worship* (1978).

247 SENT FORTH BY GOD'S BLESSING

Christians recognize that the reception of Christ's body and blood involves dedication. The divine self-giving prompts the grateful response of offering their lives for the cause of Christ and the welfare of God's children. Thus is the life of God enacted in their ordinary, everyday occupations.

Illustrative of such understanding is this splendid text that appeared in *The People's Mass Book* (1964) under the pseudonym "J. Clifford Evers." Written by Omer J. Westendorf, it was altered somewhat for inclusion in *Contemporary Worship 4* (1972), issued by the Inter-Lutheran Commission on Worship. Further alterations were made for *Lutheran Book of Worship* (1978) and *Lutheran Worship* (1982).

THE ASH GROVE. A Welsh folk melody, this tune was picked up by Katherine K. Davis from a pamphlet entitled *Book of National Songs* (Novello) for a choral piece she penned in the 1920s, "Let All Things Now Living," published by E. C. Schirmer (1939). The popularity of this piece, coupled to THE ASH GROVE, is attested by its inclusion in various recent hymnals: *Worship* (1986): A Hymnal and Service Book for Catholics; the *Psalter Hymnal* (1987); and *Lead Me, Guide Me* (1987)—to mention but a few. The *United Methodist Hymnal* (1987) uses the Westendorf text.

The harmonization of this tune was prepared by Leland Sateren for inclusion in *Contemporary Worship 4*, a tune that he describes as "charming, cool-water-fresh."

LORD JESUS CHRIST, LIFE-GIVING BREAD

248

Lord Jesus Christ, life-giving bread,
May I in grace possess you.
Let me with holy food be fed,
In hunger I address you.
Prepare me well for you, O Lord,
And, humbly by my prayer implored,
Give me your grace and mercy.

To pastures green, Lord, safely guide,
To restful waters lead me;
Your table well for me provide,
Your wounded hand now feed me.
Though weary, sinful, sick, and weak,
Refuge in you alone I seek,
To share your cup of healing.

O bread of heav'n, my soul's delight,
For full and free remission
I come with prayer before your sight
In sorrow and contrition.
Your righteousness, Lord, cover me
That I receive you worthily,
Assured of your full pardon.

I do not merit favor, Lord,
My weight of sin would break me;
In all my guilty heart's discord,
O Lord, do not forsake me.
In my distress this comforts me
That you receive me graciously,
O Christ, my Lord of mercy!

Du Lebensbrot, Herr Jesu Christ,
Mag dich ein Sünder haben,
Der nach dem Himmel hungrig ist
Und sich mit dir will laben,
So bitt' ich dich demütiglich,
Du wollest so bereiten mich,
Dass ich recht würdig werde.

Auf grüner Aue wollest du
Mich diesen Tag, Herr, leiten,
Den frischen Wassern führen zu,
Den Tisch für mich bereiten.
Ach, ich bin sündlich, matt und krank,
Lass, Herr, mich deinen Gnadentrank
Aus deinem Becher schmecken!

Du angenehmes Himmelsbrot,
Du wollest mir verzeihen,
Dass ich in meiner Seelennot
Zu dir muss kläglich schreien;
Dein Glaubensrock bedecke mich,
Auf dass ich möge würdiglich
An deiner Tafel sitzen!

Zwar ich bin deiner Gunst nicht wert,
Als der ich jetzt erscheine
Mit Sünden allzuviel beschwert,
Die schmerzlich ich beweine.
In solcher Trübsal tröstet mich,
Herr Jesu, dass du gnädiglich
Der Sünder dich erbarmest.

This hymn by Johann Rist, originally in eight stanzas and based on Psalm 23, first appeared in his *Frommer und gottseliger Christen Alltägliche Hausmusik* (Lüneberg, 1654), where it was headed "A devotional hymn which may be sung when the people are about to take their place at the Holy Communion of our Lord." The cento includes stanzas 1, 2, 3, and 5.

The translation is an altered and updated form of that by Arthur T. Russel in his *Psalms and Hymns, partly original, partly selected* (Cambridge, 1851), a work in which German hymns played a large part and in which its arrangements of hymns reflected old Lutheran hymnbooks.

AUS TIEFER NOT II is a fine chorale tune that is named after Luther's text "Aus tiefer not schrei ich zu dir" ("From Depths of Woe I Cry to You," *LW* 230) to which it was set in the *Teutsch Kirchenamt* (Strassburg, 1525). The Roman numeral II has been added to distinguish it from Luther's tune at *LW* 230, where it has been designated as AUS TIEFER NOT I. The AUS TIEFER NOT II is also known as HERR WIE DU WILLST from the first words of the text by Kaspar Bienemann (1540–1610) to which it was often set in some earlier hymnals.

The harmonization is by George Leonard, a *nom de plume* of Paul G. Bunjes.

249 YOUR TABLE I APPROACH

Your table I approach;
Dear Savior, hear my prayer.
Oh, let no unrepented sin
Prove hurtful to me there.

Lord, I confess my sins
And mourn their wretched bands;
A contrite heart is sure to find
Forgiveness at your hands.

Your body and your blood,
Once slain and shed for me,
Are taken at your table, Lord,
In blest reality.

Search not how this takes place,
This wondrous mystery;
God can accomplish vastly more
Than what we think could be.

Oh, grant, most blessed Lord,
That earth and hell combined
May not about this sacrament
Raise doubt within my mind.

Oh, may I never fail
To thank you day and night
For your true body and true blood,
O God, my peace and light.

Ich trete frisch
Zu Gottes Tisch,
Hilf, Vater, hilf mit Gnaden,
Dass mir keine Missetat
Hierbei möge schaden!

Ich leugne nicht,
Was mir gebricht,
Ich beichte meine Schulden;
Reu' für Sünden pflegst du ja,
Frommer Gott, zu dulden.

Dein Leib und Blut,
Das mir zugut
Gebrochen und vergossen,
Wird, o tiefe Wundertat!
Hier am Tisch genossen.

O grüble nicht,
Wie dies geschicht,
Noch ob es mag geschehn!
Gott kann überschwenglich tun,
Was wir nicht verstehen.

Verleih, o Gott,
Durch Christi Tod,
Dass weder Welt noch Teufel
Mir an diesem Glaubenspunkt
Rege ein'gen Zweifel!

So will ich nie,
Nicht spät noch früh
Ermüden, sonder Wanken
Für dein teu'rvergossnes Blut
Dir, mein Gott, zu danken.

A cento from the 11-stanza hymn by Gerhard W. Molanus, this represents the author's stanzas 1, 2, 5, 7, 10, and 11. The text first appeared in the *Rinteln Gesang Buch* (1673). The translation is altered and updated from a version by Matthias Loy, published in the Ohio *Lutheran Hymnal* (1880).

ST. MICHAEL (OLD 134TH, GENEVA 101) first appeared in the Genevan Psalter (1551), composed or arranged by Louis Bourgeois (*LW* 216, et al.) for Clement Marot's metrical version of Psalm 101 (see essay: Metrical Psalms, p. 825). The rhythm was chastened and squared off to make it work with the short meter version of Psalm 104 in the Anglo-Genevan Psalter (1561), hence the name OLD 134TH, thus becoming one of the few four-line tunes in early psalters. Subsequent variants occurred in various Scottish and English psalters. After 1595 the tune fell into disuse until William Crotch (1775–1847), prominent composer, teacher, and lecturer, revised it in its abbreviated short meter form in his *Psalm Tunes* (London, 1836), where, omitting the gathering notes and casting the last phrase into its present melodic form, he called it ST. MICHAEL. The result is a somewhat drab, albeit useful tune, that Erik Routley has characterized as "a pathetic, twisted torso, no more."

The harmonization was prepared by Wilhelm Quampen, a *nom de plume* of Paul G. Bunjes.

LORD JESUS CHRIST, WE HUMBLY PRAY 250

In compiling the hymns for the *Common Service Book* (Philadelphia, 1917), Luther D. Reed (1873–1972) remarked that a Lutheran hymnal should give fuller expression to the sacraments, since the church stressed them so strongly. By way of reply, Henry E. Jacobs submitted this hymn, which was then published with the collection.

Notice the eschatological outlook in stanza 5, the joyous aspect of Holy Communion mentioned by the evangelists (Matt. 26:29; Mark 14:25; Luke 22:16) but so often overlooked in thoughts on this Sacrament. (See also *LW* 243, st. 7.)

Included also in *The Lutheran Hymnal* (1941), the *Service Book and Hymnal* (1958), and the *Lutheran Book of Worship* (1978), the text appears here, however, in altered and updated form.

HERR JESU CHRIST, DICH ZU UNS WEND. For comments on the tune see hymn 201.

The harmonization was prepared by George Leonard, a *nom de plume* of Paul G. Bunjes.

251 O FATHER, ALL CREATING

John Ellerton was requested by the Duke of Westminster to write a hymn for the marriage of his daughter to the Marquis of Ormonde in 1876. Within a few days Ellerton had composed "O Father, all creating" and sent the manuscript to his Grace, who was pleased with it. The hymn was not published until 1880, when it appeared in Godfrey Thring's *A Church of England Hymn-book*; in that collection the second line was altered to read, "Whose wisdom *and whose* power." *Lutheran Worship* has restored to it the word "love" from Ellerton's original.

AURELIA was composed by Samuel S. Wesley and introduced into English hymnody as the setting for "Jerusalem the Golden" (*LW* 309) in *A Selection of Psalms and Hymns* (1864) edited by Samuel Wesley and Charles Kemble. In 1872 the tune was set to the same text in the composer's *European Psalmist*.

The name AURELIA, taken from the Latin for "gold," was suggested by the composer's wife. Used by *Hymns Ancient and Modern* (1868) as the setting for "The Church's One Foundation" (*LW* 289), it has become so closely linked to that text as to become almost a proper.

Henry J. Gauntlett (*LW* 58) criticized the tune as "decidedly inferior" in an article which appeared in *The Choir* (1872). Haeussler remarks that Gauntlett's article "really amounted to an intemperate denunciation. . . . That his judgment has not been accepted by posterity is borne out by the continued popularity of the tune."

The harmonization is by Samuel S. Wesley.

252 LORD, WHEN YOU CAME AS WELCOME GUEST

This prayerful marriage hymn is the work of F. Samuel Janzow, a member of the Commission on Worship that produced *Lutheran Worship* (1982).

RESIGNATION is a lovely early American tune of uncertain origin that appeared in William Walker's *Southern Harmony* (1835), a collection of hymn tunes in four-note notation with symbols for mi, fa, sol, la. The tune was popularized in a choral setting by Virgil Thomson (1896–1989), American composer and music critic.

Paul G. Bunjes prepared the laudable harmonization for inclusion in *Lutheran Worship*.

O PERFECT LOVE 253

Dorothy Frances Gurney, *née* Blomfield, wrote this hymn for the marriage of her sister to Hugh Redmayne at Ambleside, England, in 1883. The bride wished the John B. Dykes tune STRENGTH AND STAY to be performed at the ceremony, but the standard text to which it was sung seemed unsuitable. So, according to Mrs. Gurney, her sister suddenly asked, "What is the use of a sister who composes poetry if she cannot write me new words for this tune?" The poet agreed to try her hand at it, and within 15 minutes had composed the present text. Mrs. Gurney adds: "The writing of it was no effort whatever after the initial idea had come to me of the two-fold aspect of perfect union, love and life, and I have always felt that God had helped me to write it."

After a few years of popularity at private weddings, the text was published in the 1889 Supplement to *Hymns Ancient and Modern*, where it achieved still greater popularity. Coupled to the tune below, it was included in *The Hymnal* (1892) of the Protestant Episcopal Church. From there it made its way into numerous hymnals.

O PERFECT LOVE, also called SANDRINGHAM after a British royal residence, is the first section minus a brief introduction, from an anthem, or choir, setting for Gurney's text which Joseph Barnby composed in 1889 for the marriage of the Duke of Fife to Princess Louise of Wales.

The harmonization is from the *Service Book and Hymnal* (1958).

Despite the fact that this text with this tune undoubtedly constitutes the most famous of wedding hymns, this author feels constrained to make a few comments.

The metric scheme of 11 10 11 10, in which the text of "O Perfect Love" is cast, unfortunately shares some of the shortcomings of its relative, the pattern of 10 10 10 10. Appearing to be the dominant meter of the 19th century, the latter comprises few excellent hymns, for most sound like poems, with the tune as an afterthought. The lines are long, the thought process involved; thus the AABB rhyme scheme—the closer rhyme scheme—is best; it guards the mind from losing the rhyme pattern. Interestingly, although Charles Wesley wrote numerous poems in 10 10 10 10, he never used this pattern for hymns. The 11 10 11 10 scheme compounds the situation, or problem, in that lines one and three end in what is considered to be the tedious feminine rhyme—the rhyming of the two final syllables. Notice this occurring in the two other hymns in *Lutheran Worship* that are in this metric pattern: *LW* 377 and 86. While the rhyme scheme of AABB is preferred in these long-line stanzas, in the instance of 11 10 11 10 the rhyme scheme of ABAB appears to be more felicitous in that it spaces the feminine rhymes farther apart, thus reducing their tediousness.

The tune O PERFECT LOVE exhibits, in Routley's words, "the less endearing aspects of Victorianism," a tune that he says is "regrettable." Admittedly the harmony is a bit soggy. Sung too slowly, the combined tune and harmony can readily become lugubrious. Lest it thus detract from the nuptial cheerfulness, it is suggested that it be sung at M. M. 112.

While hymnal committees have sought to use other tunes for Gurney's text (*TLH* used CARITAS PERFECTA by English organist Frederick Atkinson—not a great improvement), with but few exceptions (*The Hymnal 1982* has dropped both text and tune) Barnby's tune hangs on stubbornly in present-day hymnals.

A tune called HIGHWOOD that Richard R. Terry (1865–1938), noted organist, composer, director of music at Westminster Cathedral, London, wrote for Dorothy F. Gurney's text is worthy of consideration. An excellent tune that suits the text very well, although perhaps somewhat difficult for the congregation, its use as a wedding solo would, in this writer's estimation, prove very effective and rewarding. For the person who dares give it a try, the tune and setting is contained in *The Methodist Hymn Book* (London, 1933), no. 254. This tune enjoys precedence of place over Barnby's tune in a more recent hymnal, namely, *The Australian Hymn Book* (Sydney, 1977), no. 526.

MAY GOD THE FATHER OF OUR LORD

254

Dorothy Hoyer Scharlemann wrote this text at the request of a friend who anticipated including it in a collection of old German tunes he considered publishing. Inspired by the expressions of the confirmation rite used by her sainted father Theodore Hoyer, pastor and professor at Concordia Seminary, St. Louis, the text failed to appear in the intended publication. Rather, it appeared with the title "Confirmation Blessing" in the *Concordia Journal* (May 1980). Thereafter the author submitted it to the Commission on Worship for possible inclusion in *Lutheran Worship* (1982).

TALLIS' CANON. For comments on the tune see hymn 484.

The setting is from *Ravenscroft's Psalter* (1621).

MY MAKER, NOW BE NIGH

255

My Maker, now be nigh
The light of life to give,
And guide me with your eye
While here on earth I live.
To you my heart I tender
And all my pow'rs surrender;
Make it my one endeavor
To love and serve you ever.
Upon your promise I rely;
My Maker, now be nigh.

My Savior, wash me clean
With your most precious blood,
That takes away all sin
And seals my peace with God.
My soul in peace abiding,
Within your deep wounds hiding,
I there find full salvation
And freedom from damnation.
Without you lost, defiled by sin,
My Savior, wash me clean.

My Comforter, give pow'r
That I may stand secure
When in temptation's hour
The world and sin allure.
The Son to me revealing,
Inspire my thought and feeling,
His Word of grace to ponder,
Nor let me from him wander.
On me your gifts and graces show'r:
My Comforter, give pow'r!

Mein Schöpfer, steh mir bei,
Sei meines Lebens Licht!
Dein Auge leite mich,
Bis mir mein Auge bricht!
Hier leg' ich Herz und Glieder
Vor dir zum Opfer nieder;
Bestimme meine Kräfte
Für dich und dein Geschäfte!
Du willst, dass ich der Deine sei:
Mein Schöpfer, steh mir bei!

Mein Heiland, wasche mich
Durch dein so teures Blut,
Das alle Flecken tilgt
Und lauter Wunder tut!
Schliess die verirrte Seele
In deine Wundenhöhle,
Dass sie von Zorn und Sünde
Hier wahre Freiheit finde!
Ich bin verloren ohne dich:
Mein Heiland, wasche mich!

Mein Tröster, gib mir Kraft,
Wenn sich Versuchung zeigt!
Regiere meinen Geist,
Wenn er zur Welt sich neigt!
Lehr mich den Sohn erkennen,
Ihn meinen Herrn auch nennen,
Sein Gnadenwort verstehen,
Auf seinen Wegen gehen!
Du bist, der alles Gute schafft:
Mein Tröster, gib mir Kraft!

O Holy Trinity,
To whom I all things owe,
Your image graciously
Within my heart bestow.
Choose me, though weak and lowly,
To be your temple holy
Where praise shall rise unending
For grace so condescending.
Oh, heav'nly bliss, your own to be,
O Holy Trinity!

Gott Vater, Sohn und Geist,
Dir bin ich, was ich bin.
Ach, drücke selbst dein Bild
Recht tief in meinen Sinn!
Erwähle mein Gemüte
Zum Tempel deiner Güte,
Verkläre an mir Armen
Dein gnadenreich Erbarmen!
Wohl mir, wenn du der Meine heisst:
Gott Vater, Sohn und Geist!

This is one of two hymns of merit by Johann J. Rambach, one of the leaders of Pietism, that became almost indispensable at confirmation in Lutheranism.The other is "Baptized into Your Name Most Holy" (*LW* 224). First published posthumously in *Gesammelte Geistliche Gedichte* (Jena, 1740) entitled "Offering to the Triune God," it made its way into the Hanover *Kirchen Gesangbuch* (1740), set to the tune mentioned below, to which it has since been wedded. Notice the sequential vocatives at the beginning of each stanza: "My Maker," "My Savior," "My Comforter," and "O Holy Trinity."

The translation by R. E. Taylor, except for having been updated and slightly altered, is that which appeared in *The Lutheran Hymnal* (1941).

MEIN SCHÖPFER, STEH MIR BEI, to which the text beginning with the same words was originally set, was composed by Franz H. Meyer.

The harmonization is from *The Lutheran Hymnal* (1941), slightly altered.

256 YOURS FOREVER, GOD OF LOVE

This confirmation hymn by Mary F. Maude, originally in seven stanzas, was written for her class at St. Thomas. She explains:

> In 1847 my husband was minister of the Parish Church of St. Thomas, Newport, Isle of Wight. We had very large Sunday-schools, in which I taught the first class of elder girls, then preparing for their confirmation by the Bishop of Winchester. Health obliged me to go for some weeks to the seaside, and while there I wrote 12 letters to my class, which were afterward printed by the Church of England Sunday-School Institute. In one of the letters I wrote off, almost impromptu, "Thine forever." (Benson, *Studies of Familiar Hymns*, first series)

First published in 1848 in the above-mentioned *Twelve Letters on Confirmation*, the hymn was picked up by the Society for the Promotion of Christian Knowledge and included in its *Church Hymns* (1871), edited by William W. How (*LW* 182, et al.). Queen Victoria chose it to be sung at the confirmation of a royal princess.

Lutheran Worship, in addition to altering and updating the language of the original, has followed *The Lutheran Hymnal* (1941) in reversing Maude's stanzas 2 and 3, thus to provide greater continuity of context.

SONG 13. For comments on the tune see hymn 166.
The setting is from the *Hymnal for Colleges and Schools* (1956), slightly altered.

LET ME BE YOURS FOREVER 257

Let me be yours forever,
My gracious God and Lord;
May I forsake you never
Nor wander from your Word.
Preserve me from the mazes
Of error and distrust,
And I shall sing your praises
Forever with the just.

Lord Jesus, bounteous giver
Of light and life divine,
You did my soul deliver;
To you I all resign.
You have in mercy bought me
With blood and bitter pain;
Let me, since you have sought me,
Eternal life obtain.

O Holy Spirit, pouring
Sweet peace into my heart
And all my soul restoring,
Let me in grace depart.
And while his name confessing
Whom I by faith have known,
Grant me your constant blessing
And take me as your own.

Lass mich dein sein und bleiben,
Du treuer Gott und Herr;
Von dir lass mich nichts treiben,
Halt mich bei reiner Lehr';
Herr, lass mich nur nicht wanken,
Gib mir Beständigkeit!
Dafür will ich dir danken
In alle Ewigkeit.

Herr Jesu Christ, mein Leben,
Mein Heil und ein'ger Trost,
Dir tu' ich mich ergeben,
Du hast mich teu'r erlöst
Mit deinem Blutvergiessen,
Mit grossem Weh und Leid;
Lass mich des auch geniessen
Zu meiner Seligkeit!

O Heil'ger Geist, mein Tröster,
Mein Licht und teures Pfand,
Lass mich Christ, mein'n Erlöser,
Den ich im Glaub'n erkannt,
Bis an mein End' bekennen,
Stärk mich in letzter Not,
Von dir lass mich nichts trennen,
Gib einen sel'gen Tod!

This simple, touching hymn for faithfulness and steadfastness, so popular for confirmation—at least in the Missouri Synod—first appeared as a single stanza in Nikolaus Selnecker's *Passio. Das Leiden und Sterben unsers Herrn Jesu Christi aus den Vier Evangelisten* (Wolfenbüttel, 1572), where it was titled "Prayer," a prayer that he daily prayed. Originally the fourth line read: "Ich bleib bei deiner Lehr" instead of "Halt mich bei reiner Lehr." In continental usage the hymn was frequently sung as a close to corporate worship. Interestingly, even today the hymnals of the Lutheran territorial churches in Germany place the single stanza in the category of Close of Worship.

Stanzas 2 and 3, of unknown authorship, were not added until 1688 with the issuance of the *Rudolstädter Gesangbuch*.

The translation by Matthias Loy (*LW* 235, et al.), included in the Ohio *Lutheran Hymnal* (1880), here in altered and updated form, was prepared by the Inter-Lutheran Commission on Worship for inclusion in *Lutheran Book of Worship* (1978).

LOB GOTT GETROST MIT SINGEN was originally a popular 15th-century secular folk song, "Erlaubt ist uns der Walde gen disem Winter kalt." The oldest printed source is in *Musica Teutsch, auf die Instrument der Grossen und Kleinen Geygen auch Lautten* (Nürnberg, 1532), issued by Hans Gerle (d. 1570), German instrumentalist, lute maker, compiler of several volumes of instrumental music. In 1544 Johann Horn (*LW* 141) adopted the tune to "Lob Gott getrost mit singen" in his *Ein Gesangbuch der Brüder inn Behemen und Merherrn* (Nürnberg). In 1545 it appeared in Valentin Babst's *Geystliche Lieder* (Leipzig) set to Johann Kolross's "Ich dank dir, lieber Herre," by which title it is also known.

The setting is from *The Lutheran Hymnal* (1941), slightly altered.

GOD OF THE PROPHETS, BLESS THE PROPHETS' SONS 258

Denis Wortman submitted this hymn, originally in seven stanzas, to New Brunswick Theological Seminary (Reformed), New Jersey, on the occasion of its centennial in October 1884. It was first published in the volume entitled *Centennial of the Theological Seminary of the Reformed Church in America* (1885); eight years later it appeared in the *Church Hymnal* (1892) of the Episcopal Church, with one stanza omitted.

An 1860 graduate of the seminary, Wortman accompanied the hymn, entitled "Prayer for Young Ministers," with the message:

> May I take the liberty of sending you the enclosed verses; a very humble attempt to express the prayer that our Class of 1860, and indeed all loyal sons of New Brunswick Seminary, lift to God at this unusual anniversary, for His blessing upon her and all who go forth from her instructions.

This hymn, popularly sung at the ordination or installation of pastors, appears here in altered and updated form.

OLD 124TH, abbr. For comments on the tune and setting see hymn 240.

PREACH YOU THE WORD AND PLANT IT HOME 259

In spite of the fact that this hymn uses images from the Parable of the Sower (Luke 8:4–15), in reality it is actually based on "Preach the Word" (2 Tim. 4:2), the motto of Concordia Theological Seminary, Springfield, Illinois (now at Fort Wayne, Indiana). Martin Franzmann wrote this hymn commemorating the seminary's 125th anniversary while he was visiting professor during the winter and spring terms of the 1972–73 academic year. Though he wrote the text with the tune WAREHAM (*LW* 161) in mind, the present tune seems to be the better match.

O HEILAND, REISS DIE HIMMEL AUF. For comments on the tune and setting see hymn 32.

260 LORD OF THE LIVING HARVEST

Headed "For Ember Days and Ordinations," this hymn by John S. B. Monsell was first published in four stanzas in the second edition of his *Hymns of Love and Praise for the Church's Year* (1866). The omitted stanza 3, here updated, read:

> Come down, O Holy Spirit,
> And fill their souls with light.
> Clothe them in spotless raiment,
> In linen clean and white.
> Beside your sacred altar.
> Be with them where they stand
> To sanctify your people
> Through all this happy land.

The entire text has been altered and updated.

Eminently suitable for ordinations, the three-stanza hymn is used in some churches with first-person pronouns, to be sung by the newly ordained themselves. The *Companion to the Hymnal of the Service Book and Hymnal* (1976) explains the heading given the hymn by Monsell:

> Ember Days were certain days in each season of the year set aside for prayer and fasting, to thank God for the gift of nature and to ordain candidates to the holy priesthood. The Ember Days are Wednesday, Friday, and Saturday after the First Sunday in Lent, the week after Pentecost, the week after September 14 (Exaltation of the Holy Cross), and after December 13 (St. Lucy's Day). Three of these Ember Day seasons correspond to the ancient pagan Roman celebrations connected with the grain harvest (Pentecost), vintage harvest (September), sowing of the seed (December).

AURELIA. For comments on the tune and setting see hymn 251.

261 LORD OF THE CHURCH, WE HUMBLY PRAY

This laudable prayer-hymn for pastors by the Cornish medical doctor Edward Osler first appeared in W. J. Hall's *Psalms and Hymns adapted to the services of the Church of England* (1836). Sometimes called the *Mitre Hymn Book* because of the mitre embossed on its cover, this mitre, plus the book's arrangement of hymns according to the Sundays and festivals of the church year, caused the volume to be considered as high church, despite the fact that it was unacceptable to the leaders of the Oxford Movement. The following year it appeared in his *Church and King*. Based on Charles Wesley's

"Thou Jesus, thou my breast inspire," it was first published in the *Wesleyan Hymn Book* (1780), which in turn is a cento from the much longer Charles Wesley's "O thou who at thy creature's bar," that was published in *Hymns and Sacred Poems* (1749). It is here given in updated form.

KOMMT HER ZU MIR is from a 15th-century German folk tune, a *Lindenschmidton*, to which were sung both secular and spiritual texts. As a setting for Georg Grüenwald's "Kommt her zu mir spricht Gottes Sohn" it appeared in 1530 described as "Ein schöns newes Christlichs lyed" and looked thus (Zahn 2496a):

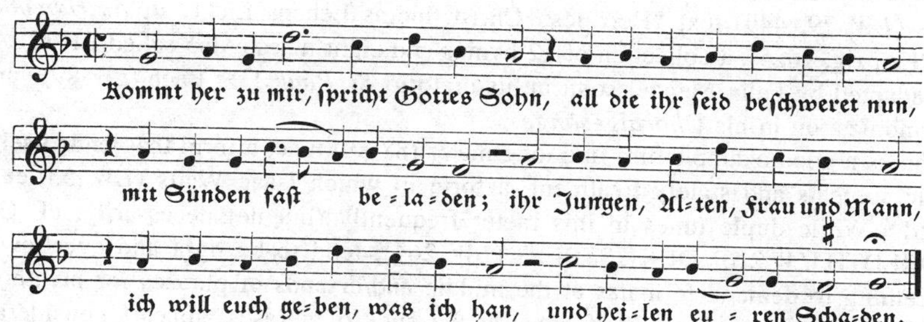

Thereafter certain modifications of the tune occurred in various hymnals, one of which closely resembling that given in *Lutheran Worship* (1982).

The harmonization is by Paul G. Bunjes.

WE BID YOU WELCOME IN THE NAME 262

Considering such a hymn as this appropriate for the installation of a pastor—a hymn that was included in *The Lutheran Hymnal* (1941) and in the *Evangelical Lutheran Hymn-Book* (1912), the first official English hymnal of the Synod, but rare in present new hymnals—the Commission on Worship thought it well to include it in *Lutheran Worship* (1982).

First published in the author's *Christian Psalmist* (1825), this hymn by James Montgomery was headed "On the Appointment of a Minister." Stanzas 3 and 4 of the six-stanza original have customarily been omitted:

Come as a watchman; take thy stand
Upon the tower amidst the sky,
And when the sword comes on the land,
Call us to fight or warn to fly.

Come as an angel—hence to guide
A band of pilgrims on their way,
That softly walking at thy side,
We fail not, faint not, turn nor stray.

In addition to updating the second-person pronouns, *Lutheran Worship* has altered stanza 3, line 3, from "Lift o'er our ranks the prophet's rod" to "Our ranks encourage, laggards prod;" and "behold" to "enjoy" in stanza 4, line 3.

HERR JESU CHRIST, MEINS. This tune, derived from a folk song ("Ich fahr dahin") which appeared in the *Locheimer Liederbuch* (c. 1455–60), was published with Martin Behm's (*LW* 79, 449) text "Herr Jesu Christ, meins Lebens Licht" in *As Hymnodus Sacer* (Leipzig, 1625), a collection of 12 hymns and eight tunes. Also called BRESLAU, it was adapted by Felix Mendelssohn in his oratorio *St. Paul*; J. S. Bach (*LW* 89) varied the harmonization in his *Choralgesänge*.

This is a good example of a fine long meter (88 88) tune, a form that lends itself to majestic subjects and stately treatment, a form in which Isaac Watts (*LW* 53, et al.) excelled. While duple tunes in this meter frequently (but not necessarily, cf. OLD HUNDREDTH [*LW* 216], DUKE STREET [*LW* 264]) tend to be tight and overflowing, thus seeming to demand fermatas at the middle and/or ends of phrases for breath, the triple pattern, with its dotted half notes at the ends of phrases, appears considerably more user-friendly, affording the singer easy opportunity for breath.

Paul G. Bunjes provided the setting for *Lutheran Worship* (1982).

263 SEND, O LORD, YOUR HOLY SPIRIT

Send, O Lord, your Holy Spirit
On your servant now, we pray,
Let him prove a faithful shepherd
That no lamb is led astray.
Your pure teaching to proclaim,
To extol your holy name,
And to feed your lambs, dear Savior,
Make his aim and sole endeavor.

You, O Lord, yourself have called him
For your precious lambs to care;
But to prosper in his calling,
He the Spirit's gifts must share.
Give him wisdom from above,
Fill his heart with holy love;
In his weakness, Lord, be near him,
In his prayers, Good Shepherd, hear him.

Help, Lord Jesus, help him nourish
All our children with your Word
That in fervent love they serve you
Till in heav'n their song is heard.

Segne, Herr, mit deinem Geiste
Deinen Diener immerdar,
Dass den rechten Dienst er leiste
Dir an deiner Lämmerschar.
Deines Wortes reine Lehr',
Deines heil'gen Namens Ehr',
Deinen Lämmlein Seligkeit
Sei sein Ziel zu aller Zeit.

Du, o Herr, hast ihn erwählet
Zu dem Amt, so schön, doch schwer;
Ohne deinen Geist ihm fehlet
Alle Hilfe, Kraft und Wehr.
Schenk ihm Weisheit und Verstand,
Stärk ihm Herz und Mund und Hand.
Hör uns, o Herr Jesu Christ,
Der du Hirt und Helfer bist!

Hilf, Herr Christ, ihm treulich weiden
Unsre Kindlein auf den Au'n
Deines Worts, hilf ihm sie leiten,
Dass sie selig einst dich schaun.

Boundless blessings, Lord, bestow
On his faithful toil below
Till by grace to him be given
His reward, the crown of heaven.

Hilf ihm tragen all' Beschwer,
Die sein Amt bringt mit sich her;
Krön ihn auch mit Herrlichkeit
Einst in sel'ger Ewigkeit.

Extensive research for the author of this hymn, most likely stemming from the 19th century, has produced no results. Inclusion of the German texts in the supplement to *Lieder-Perlen* (St. Louis, 1894), a collection of both sacred and secular songs (some in English) for Lutheran day schools, wherein it was headed "For the Installation of a Teacher," evidently caused it to become known and used. Recognizing its laudable contents and appropriateness for the ordination and/or installation of pastors and the commissioning and/or installation of teachers prompted the Intersynodical Committee on Hymnology and Liturgics to include it, in the translation by Frederick W. Herzberger, in *The Lutheran Hymnal* (1941). Its general acceptance and use, as well as the scarcity of such hymns, resulted in its inclusion in *Lutheran Worship* (1982), slightly altered.

WERDE MUNTER is a notable tune by Johann Schop that appeared in *Das Dritte Zehn* (Lüneberg, 1642) of Johann Rist's (*LW* 122, et al.) *Himmlische Lieder* (issued in five sets of ten), where it was the setting for Rist's evening hymn "Werde Munter mein Gemüte" (Zahn 6551a).

The tune evidently appealed to J. S. Bach (*LW* 89), for he used it not only twice in the *St. Matthew Passion*, but also in Cantatas 46, 55, and 144. It is in Cantata 147, for the Feast of the Visitation, that he uses Schop's tune in the popular and familiar "Jesu, Joy of Man's Desiring."

Richard W. Gieseke prepared the harmonization in *Lutheran Worship* (1982).

264 I KNOW THAT MY REDEEMER LIVES

This great Easter and Death and Burial hymn by Samuel Medley, originally in nine stanzas, first appeared in George Whitefield's *Psalms and Hymns* (21st edition, 1775). Surprisingly, it fails to appear in many present-day hymnals, except, but possibly also among others not examined, in *The Australian Hymn Book* (1977); *Rejoice in the Lord* (1985); the *Baptist Hymnal* (1975); *Worship: A Hymnal and Service Book for Roman Catholics* (1986); and *Lead Me, Guide Me: The African American Catholic Hymnal* (1977).

DUKE STREET first appeared anonymously as a tune in Henry Boyd's posthumous *A Select Collection of Psalm and Hymn Tunes* (Glasgow, 1793), intended for use with Joseph Addison's (*LW* 196) version of Psalm 19 ("The spacious firmament on high"). It is named DUKE STREET and credited to John Hatton in William Dixon's *Euphonia, containing Sixty-Two Psalm and Hymn Tunes . . . Harmonized, Arranged and Composed by W. Dixon* (Liverpool, 1805). The tune exhibits the type of tune popularized by Wesley and his followers and is an example of the later development of the type.

The setting is from the *Service Book and Hymnal* (1958).

265 IN THE VERY MIDST OF LIFE

In the very midst of life
Death has us surrounded.
When shall we a helper find
Hear his coming sounded?
For you, our Lord, we're waiting.
We sorrow that we left your path,
Doing what deserves your wrath.
Holy, most righteous God!
Holy, most mighty God!
Holy and most merciful Savior!
Forever our Lord!
Keep us from despairing
In the bitter pain of death.
Have mercy, O Lord!

In the midst of bitter death,
Sharp the hell-drawn harrow.
Who will break its teeth and save
Faith's most inner marrow?
Lord, you alone, our Savior.
Though you were grieved by our misdeed,
Pity drew you to our need.
Holy, most righteous God!
Holy, most mighty God!
Holy and most merciful Savior!

Mitten wir in Leben sind
Mit dem Tod umfangen.
Wen suchen wir, der Hilfe tu,
Dass wir Gnad erlangen?
Das bist du, Herr, alleine.
Uns reuet unser Missetat,
Die dich, Herr, erzürnet hat.
Heiliger Herre Gott,
Heiliger starker Gott,
Heiliger barmherziger Heiland,
Du ewiger Gott,
Lass uns nicht versinken
In des bittern Todes Not.
Kyrieleison.

Mitten in dem Tod ansicht
Uns der Höllen Rachen.
Wer will uns aus solcher Not
Frei und ledig machen?
Das tust du, Herr, alleine.
Es jammert dein Barmherzigkeit
Unser Klag und grosses Leid.
Heiliger Herre Gott,
Heiliger starker Gott,
Heiliger barmherziger Heiland,

Forever our Lord!
Let despair not bind us
With its threats of deepest hell.
Have mercy, O Lord!

Du ewiger Gott,
Lass uns nicht verzagen
Vor der tiefen Höllen Glut.
Kyrieleison.

Through the midst of hells of fear
Our transgressions drive us.
Who will help us to escape,
Shield us, and revive us?
Lord, you alone, our Savior.
Your shed blood our salvation won;
Sin, death, hell are now undone.
Holy, most righteous God!
Holy, most mighty God!
Holy and most merciful Savior!
Forever our Lord!
Give us grace abounding;
Keep us, keep us in the faith.
Have mercy, O Lord!

Mitten in der Höllen Angst
Unser Sünd uns treiben.
Wo solln wir denn fliehen hin,
Da wir mögen bleiben?
Zu dir, Herr Christ, alleine.
Vergossen ist dein teures Blut,
Das gnug für die Sünde tut.
Heiliger Herre Gott,
Heiliger starker Gott,
Heiliger barmherziger Heiland,
Du ewiger Gott,
Lass uns nicht entfallen
Von des rechten glaubens Trost.
Kyrieleison.

In the medieval Church there existed the following popular hymn about death that was sung on days of supplication and prayer as well as used as a battle song:

Media vita in morte sumus,
quem quaerimus adjutorem
nisi te, domine?
Qui pro peccatis nostris
juste irasceris.
Sancte deus,
sancte fortis,
sancte et misericors salvator,
amarae morti ne tradas nos.

The appearance of this text in 14th-century codices from the Benedictine monastery at St. Gaul, Switzerland, has caused some scholars to ascribe this hymn to the musician and scholar, Notker Balbulus (d. 912), the famed originator of the Latin sequence hymn. However, its appearance in English manuscripts more accurately marks it as an 11th-century work. It is to be noted that the second part, beginning with "Sancte deus," bears strong resemblance to the *Trisagion* in the Greek liturgy, dating from the fifth century.

German translations of the "Media vita" appeared prior to Luther, both in prose and in rhyme. A Basil Plenarium, or Gospel Book, 1480, has it thus:

In mittel unsers lebens zeyt
im tod seind wir umbfangen:
Wen suchen wir, der uns hilffe geyt,
von dem wir huld erlangen.
denn dich, Herr, alleine?
Der du umb unser missetat
rechtlichen zür nen thust.
Heiliger herre gott,
Heiliger starker gott,
Heiliger und bamherziger Heiler, ewiger got,
lass uns nit gewalt thun des bitteren tods not.

When one compares this version to the first stanza of Luther's hymn, one notices immediately that the emphasis is more on the Christian sorrow over sin and its eternal consequences than on the nearness of death and deliverance from bodily corruption. Especially in the two stanzas that Luther adds there is evidence of the confidence of faith in the grace of God through the blood of Christ, coupled with a plea for forgiveness.

Luther's German text appeared, without tune, in the Erfurt *Enchiridia* (1524). Its inclusion in Joseph Klug's small collection of burial hymns in 1542, for which Luther wrote the preface, made it become a popular hymn for the dying.

The English translation is by F. Samuel Janzow.

MITTEN WIR IM LEBEN SIND. The tune is that adapted by Johann Walter from the tune associated with the medieval Latin text. It first appeared in his *Geystliche gesang Buchleyn*, (Wittenberg, 1524). The harmonization is from the *Württembergisches Choralbuch* (1953).

266 JESUS CHRIST, MY SURE DEFENSE

Jesus Christ, my sure defense
And my Savior, now is living!
Knowing this, my confidence
Rests upon the hope here given
Though the night of death be caught
Still in many an anxious thought.

Jesus, my redeemer, lives;
Likewise I to life shall waken.
He will bring me where he is;
Shall my courage then be shaken?
Shall I fear, or could the head
Rise and leave his members dead?

No, I am too closely bound
By my hope to Christ forever;
Faith's strong hand the rock has found,
Grasped it, and will leave it never;
Even death now cannot part
From its Lord the trusting heart.

I am flesh and must return
To the dust, whence I am taken;
But by faith I now discern
That from death I will awaken
With my Savior to abide
In his glory, at his side.

Then these eyes my Lord will know,
My redeemer and my brother;
In his love my soul will glow—
I myself and not another!

Jesus, meine Zuversicht
Und mein Heiland, ist im Leben;
Dieses weiss ich, sollt' ich nicht
Darum mich zufrieden geben,
Was die lange Todesnacht
Mir auch für Gedanken macht?

Jesus, er, mein Heiland, lebt;
Ich werd' auch das Leben schauen,
Sein, wo mein Erlöser schwebt;
Warum sollte mir denn grauen?
Lässet auch ein Haupt sein Glied,
Welches es nicht nach sich zieht?

Ich bin durch der Hoffnung Band
Zu genau mit ihm verbunden;
Meine starke Glaubenshand
Wird in ihn gelegt befunden,
Dass mich auch kein Todesbann
Ewig von ihm trennen kann.

Ich bin Fleisch und muss daher
Auch einmal zu Asche werden;
Das gesteh' ich, doch wird er
Mich erwecken aus der Erden,
Dass ich in der Herrlichkeit
Um ihn sein mög' allezeit.

Dieser meiner Augen Licht
Wird ihn, meinen Heiland, kennen;
Ich, ich seibst, kein Fremder nicht,
Werd' in seiner Liebe brennen;

Then the weakness I feel here
Will forever disappear.

Nur die Schwachheit um und an
Wird von mir sein abgetan.

Then take comfort and rejoice,
For his members Christ will cherish.
Fear not, they will hear his voice;
Dying, they will never perish;
For the very grave is stirred
When the trumpet's blast is heard.

Seid getrost und hocherfreut,
Jesus trägt euch, meine Glieder!
Gebt nicht Raum der Traurigkeit!
Sterbt ihr, Christus ruft euch wider,
Wenn die letzt' Drommet' erklingt,
Die auch durch die Gräber dringt.

Oh, then, draw away your hearts
From all pleasures base and hollow.
Strive to share what he imparts
While you here his footsteps follow.
As you now still wait to rise,
Fix your hearts beyond the skies.

Nur dass ihr den Geist erhebt
Von den Lüsten dieser Erden
Und euch dem schon jetzt ergebt,
Dem ihr beigefügt wollt werden
Schick das Herze da hinein,
Wo ihr ewig wünscht zu sein!

This hymn, originally in nine stanzas, appeared in 1653 in two Berlin hymnals—in *D. M. Luthers und anderer vornehmen geistreichen und gelehrten Männer geistliche Lieder und Psalmen*, edited by Christoph Runge, with Johann Crüger as music editor, and in Johann Crüger's own *Praxis pietatis melica*. The first, the so-called Runge *Gesangbuch*, was produced at the behest of Luise Henriette von Brandenburg (1627–66) for the purpose of uniting the Lutheran and Reformed communions. The statement of Runge in its introduction, acknowledging Luise Henriette's contribution of four hymns, including "Jesus, meine Zuversicht," has resulted in frequently attributing the authorship to her. Proof of this, however, is difficult. All four appeared anonymously in the Runge collection. They may simply have been favorites of hers that she wanted included. Moreover, of Dutch extraction, it is doubtful she had the command of High German to write such fine poetry. And if she wrote in Dutch, the hymns would certainly have required a recast in German.

Despite its anonymity, this is truly a great hymn on the blessed resurrection of the Christian to life everlasting. It is, as someone has said, "an acknowledged masterpiece of first rank." Although essentially an Easter hymn and not a funeral hymn, its frequent and appropriate use at the graveside in the committal service prompted the Commission on Worship to include it in the category of Death and Burial.

The translation, based largely on Catherine Winkworth's in her *Chorale Book for England* (1863), is a slightly revised and updated version of that which appeared in *The Lutheran Hymnal* (1941). It was prepared by the Inter-Lutheran Commission on Worship for inclusion in the *Lutheran Book of Worship* (1978).

JESUS, MEINE ZUVERSICHT. This excellent tune that appeared with the above text in Johann Crüger's *Praxis pietatis melica* (Berlin, 1653) digresses a bit from the anonymous tune attached to the same text in Christoph Runge's *D. M. Luthers und anderer vornehmen geistreichen und gelehrten Männer geistliche Lieder und Psalmen* (Berlin, 1653). All editions of the *Praxis pietatis melica* published this tune anonymously until the Peter Sohren edition of 1668 affixed to it the initials "J C" (Zahn 3432b). It is possible that Johann Crüger personally avoided taking credit for it, since he simply reworked and refined the tune that originally appeared in the Runge hymnal.

The harmonization was prepared for *Lutheran Worship* (1982) by Wilhelm Quampen, a *non de plume* of Paul G. Bunjes.

267 FOR ME TO LIVE IS JESUS

For me to live is Jesus,
To die is gain for me;
So, when my Savior pleases,
I meet death willingly.

For Christ, my Lord, my brother,
I leave this world so dim
And gladly seek another,
Where I shall be with him.

My woes are nearly over,
Though long and dark the road;
His merits my sin cover,
And I have peace with God.

Lord, when my pow'rs are failing,
My breath comes heavily,
And words are unavailing,
Let my sighs plead for me.

In my last hour, oh, grant me
A slumber soft and still,
No doubts to vex or haunt me,
Safe anchored in your will;

This anchor of your making
Forever holding me,
I will, in heav'n awaking,
Sing heaven's melody.

Christus, der ist mein Leben,
Sterben ist mein Gewinn,
Dem tu' ich mich ergeben,
Mit Fried fahr' ich dahin.

Mit Freud fahr ich von dannen
Zu Christ, dem Bruder mein,
Dass ich mög" zu ihm kommen
Und ewig bei ihm sein.

Nun hab' ich überwunden
Kreuz, Leiden, Angst und Not,
Durch sein' heilig' fünf Wunden
Bin ich versöhnt mit Gott.

Wenn meine Kräfte brechen,
Mein Atem schwer geht aus
Und kann kein Wort mehr sprechen:
Herr, nimm mein Seufzen auf!

Alsdann fein sanft und stille,
Herr, lass mich schlafen ein
Nach deinem Rat und Willen,
Wenn kommt mein Stündelein,

Und lass mich an dir kleben
Wie eine Klett' am Kleid
Und ewig bei dir leben
In Himmelswonn' und -freud'!

This hymn, of unknown authorship and originally in seven stanzas, first appeared in *Ein schön geistlich Gesangbuch* (Jena, 1609), coupled to the tune here used, published by Melchior Vulpius. Thereafter it appeared, in slightly altered form and with an eighth stanza, in *Christliches Gesangbüchlein* (Hamburg, 1612).

Based as it is on St. Paul's statement "to live is Christ and to die is gain" (Phil. 1:21), in addition to reflecting the Nunc Dimittis of Luke 2 and the overcoming of life's struggles as exemplified in the Revelation of St. John, small wonder that the hymn enjoyed immediate popular acceptance, and that its dissemination, often by word of mouth, resulted in numerous textual variations.

The translation is an altered form of that which Catherine Winkworth made for inclusion in her *Chorale Book for England* (1863).

CHRISTUS, DER IST MEIN LEBEN is the tune, composed by Melchior Vulpius, to which the text was coupled when it appeared in his *Ein schön geistlich Gesangbuch* (Jena, 1609). It is a splendid chorale tune, and the union of this tune and text unquestionably belongs to that group of excellent and much-loved hymns that has brought rich blessings to many Christians.

The harmonization is by George Leonard, a *nom de plume* of Paul G. Bunjes.

OH, HOW BLEST ARE YOU 268

Oh, how blest are you whose toils are ended,
Who through death have to our God ascended!
You have arisen
From the cares which keep us still in prison.

We are still as in a dungeon living,
Still oppressed with sorrow and misgiving;
Our undertakings
Are but toils and trouble and heartbreakings.

You meanwhile are in your chambers sleeping,
Quiet and set free from all our weeping;
No cross or sadness
There can hinder your untroubled gladness.

Christ has wiped away your tears forever;
You have that for which we still endeavor;
To you are chanted
Songs that to no mortal ear are granted.

Ah, who would, then, not depart with gladness
To inherit heav'n for earthly sadness?
Who here would languish
Longer in bewailing and in anguish?

Come, O Christ, and loose the chains that bind us;
Lead us forth and cast this world behind us.
With you, th'Anointed,
Finds the soul its joy and rest appointed.

O wie selig seid ihr doch, ihr Frommen,
Die ihr durch den Tod zu Gott gekommen!
Ihr seid entgangen
Aller Not, die uns noch hält gefangen.

Muss man hier doch wie im Kerker leben
Und in Sorgen, Furcht und Schrecken schweben.
Was wir hier kennen,
Ist nur Müh' und Herzeleid zu nennen.

Ihr hingegen ruht in eurer Kammer
Sicher und befreit von allem Jammer;
Kein Kreuz und Leiden
Ist euch hinderlich in euren Freuden.

Christus wischet ab all eure Tränen,
Habt das schon, wonach wir uns erst sehnen;
Euch wird gesungen,
Was in keines Ohr allhier gedrungen.

Ach wer wollte denn nicht gerne sterben
Und den Himmel für die Welt ererben?
Wer wollt' hier bleiben,
Sich den Jammer länger lassen treiben?

Komm, o Christe, komm, uns auszuspannen;
Lös uns auf und führ uns bald von dannen!
Bei dir, o Sonne,
Ist der frommen Seelen Freud' und Wonne.

This hymn by the gifted poet Simon Dach was written as a memorial to Job Lepner, mayor of Königsberg Altstadt, unforgettable lover and promoter of music, who died May 6, 1635. With the setting provided by Johann Stobäus, cantor at the cathedral church, the hymn first appeared in broadsheet form. Before long, however, it began to be included in various hymnals. With the horrors and deprivation of the Thirty Years' War (1618–48) as the backdrop—although East Prussia, wherein Königsberg was situated, was of all Germany less affected by that catastrophe—it was the Königsberg poets, of which Dach was the leader, that devoted themselves to the subject of death and that have bequeathed to the church some of the most valuable and precious hymns in that category. Few hymns on that subject match the intensity of those by Simon Dach.

Witness for instance the cry in stanza 6: "Come, O Christ, and loose the chains that bind us; Lead us forth and cast this world behind us." Dach's artistic skill is also exhibited in the rare metrical form 10 10 5 10, in which iambic and trochaic lines alternate. Moreover, the five-syllable line in each stanza highlights both the content and poetic tone.

The translation is a slightly altered and updated form of that by Henry Wadsworth Longfellow in his *Poets and Poetry of Europe, with introductions and biographical notices* (New York, 1845).

O WIE SELIG was evidently composed for Dach's text by J. Georg Stoezel, a court cantor of whom little is known, for inclusion in the third edition of J. G. Christian Störtz's *Choralbuch*, which Stoezel produced for publication at Stuttgart in 1744. A fine chorale tune, it was used to this text in *The Evangelical Lutheran Hymn-Book* (1912), the first official English hymnal in the Synod, as well as in *The Lutheran Hymnal* (1941), predecessor to *Lutheran Worship* (1982). It is one of numerous tunes sung to this text that Zahn lists (nos. 1583–92), another of which, by Johann Crüger, appeared in the first edition of *Praxis pietatis melica* (Berlin, 1644). The latter well-crafted tune is presently used by the various Lutheran territorial churches in Germany.

The harmonization is from *The Lutheran Hymnal*, slightly altered.

269 JESUS, SHEPHERD, IN YOUR ARMS

Jesus, Shepherd, in your arms
You have held this child once weeping.
Willed it should be free from harm
And the moaning end in sleeping,
Carried it then through the door
To where crying is no more.

There your peace ends ev'ry care;
No more wail of wind through stubble.
There bloom only meadows fair,
Never chilled by any trouble.
Your lamb, robed in radiant white,
Lives there, Lord, now crowned with light.

Shepherd us to that bright place,
Into fields where joy is ringing,
Where this lamb, in your embrace,
Has its sighs all tuned to singing.
Bring us, like this child we love,
To that life in heav'n above.

Guter Hirt, du hast gestillt
Deines Lämmchens langen Jammer;
Ach, wie ruhig, blass und mild
Liegt's in seiner kleinen Kammer,
Und kein Seufzer bang und schwer
Quälet seinen Busen mehr.

In der Welt voll Angst und Grau'n
Willst du es nicht länger leiden;
Auf den Paradiesesau'n
Soll dein liebes Lamm nun weiden
Und mit unbeflecktem Kleid
Schweben in der Herrlichkeit.

O Herr Jesu, möchten wir,
Wo es schwebt, auch einmal schweben,
Und dein sel'ges Lustrevier
Uns auch Himmelsnahrung geben!
Dann sind Not und Tod Gewinn,
Nimmst du auch das Liebste hin.

No category on Death and Burial would be complete without at least one hymn referring to the death of a child.

This touching hymn-prayer by Johann W. Meinhold was written to be sung for the burial of his 15-month-old son Joannes Ladislaus on July 5, 1833. It first appeared in print in the author's *Gedichte* (Leipzig, 1835), and was later included in the *Newverfertiges Gesangbuch* (Darmstadt, 1699). The quality and the appropriateness of this hymn was recognized by its having been included in the first edition of *Hymns Ancient and Modern* (1861) in the translation of Catherine Winkworth as contained in the second series of her *Lyra Germanica* (1858). Regrettably editors of present-day hymnals have overlooked this hymn.

The English version in *Lutheran Worship*, by F. Samuel Janzow, is more of a paraphrase of the original German than a translation.

MEINEN JESUM LASS ICH NICHT. For comments on this tune see hymn 34.

The harmonization is by Wilhelm Quampen, a *nom de plume* of Paul G. Bunjes.

270 JESUS, PRICELESS TREASURE

Jesus, priceless treasure,
Source of purest pleasure,
Truest friend to me,
Long my heart was burning,
And my soul was yearning,
Lord, with you to be!
Yours I am, O spotless Lamb;
Nothing I'll allow to hide you,
Nothing ask beside you.

In your arms I rest me;
Foes who would molest me
Cannot reach me here.
Though the earth be shaking,
Ev'ry heart be quaking,
Jesus calms my fear.
Sin and hell in conflict fell
With their bitter storms assail me;
Jesus will not fail me.

Satan, I defy you;
Death, I now decry you;
Fear, I bid you cease.
World, you cannot harm me
Nor your threats alarm me
While I sing of peace.
God's great pow'r guards ev'ry hour;
Earth and all its depths adore him,
Silent bow before him.

Hence, all earthly treasure!
Jesus is my pleasure,
Jesus is my choice.
Hence, all empty glory!
What to me your story
Told with tempting voice?
Pain or loss or shame or cross
Shall not from my Savior move me
Since he chose to love me.

Hence, all fears and sadness,
For the Lord of gladness,
Jesus, enters in.
Those who love the Father,
Though the storms may gather,
Still have peace within.
For, whatever I must bear,
Still in you lies purest pleasure,
Jesus, priceless treasure!

Jesu, meine Freude,
Meines Herzens Weide,
Jesu, meine Zier,
Ach, wie lang, ach lange
Ist dem Herzen bange
Und verlangt nach dir!
Gotteslamm, mein Bräutigam,
Ausser dir soll mir auf Erden
Nichts sonst Liebers werden!

Unter deinem Schirmen
Bin ich vor den Stürmen
Aller Feinde frei.
Lass den Satan wittern,
lass die Welt erschütern,
Mir steht Jesus bei.
Ob es jetzt gleich kracht und blitzt,
Obgleich Sünd' und Hölle schrecken,
Jesus will mich decken.

Trotz dem alten Drachen,
Trotz dem Todesrachen,
Trotz der Furcht dazu!
Tobe, Welt, und springe,
Ich steh' hier und singe
In gar sichrer Ruh';
Gottes Macht hält mich in acht;
Erd' und Abgrund muss verstummen,
Ob sie noch so brummen.

Weg mit allen Schätzen,
Du bist mein Ergötzen,
Jesu, meine Lust!
Weg, ihr eitlen Ehren,
Ich mag euch nicht hören,
Bleibt mir unbewusst!
Elend, Not, Kreuz, Schmach und Tod
Soll mich, ob ich viel muss leiden,
Nicht von Jesu scheiden.

Weicht, ihr Trauergeister,
Denn mein Freudenmeister,
Jesus, tritt herein!
Denen, die Gott lieben,
Muss auch ihr Betrüben
Lauter Zucker sein.
Duld' ich schon hier Spott und Hohn,
Dennoch bleibst du auch im Leide,
Jesu, meine Freude.

This moving hymn by Johann Franck first appeared in the fifth edition of Johann Crüger's *Praxis pietatis melica* (Berlin, 1653). Franck himself did not publish it until his *Johann Frankens Teutsche Gedichte, bestehend im Geistlichen Sion* (Guben, 1674), nearly 20 years after its appearance in Christoph Peter's *Andachts-Zymbeln* (Freiberg, Saxony 1656). Peter was Franck's cantor in Guben.

Franck modeled this hymn in 1641 after a love song by Heinrich Albert that began with "Flora, meine Freude, meiner Seelen Weide," using the same stanzaic structure. In this hymn, one of the three Nelle considers the crown of Franck's poetry, faith boldly walks into the abyss; it trusts Jesus in spite of all sadness and trouble. Small wonder that shortly after its appearance it made its way into most hymnals. Even Peter the Great, Czar of Russia, not known for his piety, had it translated into Russian in 1724. True, some older Lutherans considered it too subjective and emotional for corporate worship.

JESU MEINE FREUDE. Much of this hymn's popularity can be attributed to the tune, first printed along with the text in Johann Crüger's *Praxis pietatis melica* (Berlin, 1653), a tune to which he alluded as being a "traditional melody." Superbly dignified and intense, without doubt it ranks among the finest of German chorales.

J. S. Bach made frequent use of this chorale in his cantatas (12, 64, 81, 87), in organ literature and, not to forget, in "Jesu, meine Freude," the most beautiful and intimate of his motets.

The harmonization was prepared by Paul G. Bunjes for *Lutheran Worship* (1982).

CHRIST IS THE WORLD'S REDEEMER 271

Christ is the world's Redeemer,
The lover of the pure,
The font of heav'nly wisdom,
Our trust and hope secure,
The armor of his soldiers
The Lord of earth and sky,
Our health while we are living,
Our life when we shall die.

Christ has our host surrounded
With clouds of martyrs bright,
Who wave their palms in triumph
And fire us for the fight.
Then Christ the cross ascended
To save a world undone
And, suff'ring for the sinful,
Our full redemption won.

Down in the realm of darkness
He lay, a captive bound,
But at the hour appointed
He rose, a victor crowned.
And now, to heav'n ascended,
He sits upon the throne
Whence he had ne'er departed,
His Father's and his own.

Christus redemptor gentium
Christus amator virginum
Christus fons sapientium
Christus fides credentium
Christus lorica militum
Christus creator omnium
Christus calus viuentium
et vita morientium

Coronauit exercitum costrum
cum turba martirum
Christus crucem ascenderat
Christus mundum salvauerat
Christus et nos redemeret
Christus pro nobis passus est
Christus infernum penetrat

Christus caelum ascenderat
Christus cum deo sederat
ubi nunquam defuerat

Gloria haec est altissimo
deo patri ingenito
honor ac summo
filio unico unigenito

Glory to God the Father,
The unbegotten One,
All honor be to Jesus,
His sole-begotten Son;
And to the Holy Spirit,
The perfect Trinity,
Let all the worlds give answer,
Amen—so let it be.

Spirituique obtimo
sancto perfecto sedulo
amen fiat perpetua
in sempiterna saecula
In te Christe credentium

This hymn is a translation of "Christus redemptor gentium," the second part of a longer Latin hymn beginning "In te Christi credentium miserearis omnium," plausibly ascribed to St. Columba. This hymn is contained in *The Book of Hymns of the Ancient Church of Ireland*, Part II (1869), edited by J. H. Todd for the Irish Archeological and Celtic Society, as well as in the Irish *Liber Hymnorum*, edited by J. H. Bernard and R. Atkinson (1898).

The most celebrated hymn ascribed to Columba is, of course, the "Altus prosator." It tells the story of the creation, the fall of the angels and of man, and concludes with a terrible "Dies irae," reminiscent of Zephaniah's "That day will be a day of wrath, a day of distress and anguish . . . a day of trumpet and battle cry" (Zeph. 1:15–16).

Tradition has it that when the objection was raised that the "Altus prosator" nobly praised God for his work of creation but gave too feeble expression of the work of redemption, Columba, admitting the criticism to be just, composed another hymn to make up the deficiency, namely, the previously mentioned "In te Christi." It consists of two parts, the first describing what Christ is to believers, the second what Christ has done for the redemption of mankind.

The translation of "Christus redemptor gentium" is by Duncan Macgregor, apparently made for the evening service, at which he preached, during a commemoration of St. Columba in Iona in 1897. It appeared in his *St. Columba: A Record and a Tribute* (1897), among "Offices for the Commemoration of St. Columba, June 9, 1897."

MOVILLE. This charming tune is an adaptation of a traditional Irish melody for "Scorching is this love" in *A Complete Collection of Irish Music as Noted by George Petrie* (1902), edited by C. V. Stanford (1852–1924), British composer, teacher and conductor.

The harmonization is by Charles Herbert Kitson as contained in *The Church Hymnal with Tunes* (1919).

ALL HAIL THE POWER OF JESUS' NAME

272

The first stanza of this great hymn by Edward Perronet was printed anonymously in the *Gospel Magazine* for November 1779 with the tune SHRUBSOLE or MILES LANE (*LBW* 329). The complete seven-stanza poem first appeared in the April 1870 issue of the same magazine entitled "On the Resurrection, the Lord is King" and again in the author's *Occasional Verses, Moral and Sacred, Published for the Instruction and Amusement of the candidly Serious and Religious* (1785).

Here is another example where credit must be given to later editors and revisors for the high place which this hymn enjoys in Christendom. Perronet's stanza 2, for instance, went thus:

Let highborn seraphs tune the lyre,
And, as they tune it, fall
Before his face who tunes their choir,
And crown him Lord of all.

In the bygone days when the parish clerk "lined out" hymns for the congregation, it must have sounded somewhat ludicrous to hear him read out, "Let highborn seraphs tune the lyre," and the congregation thereafter sing the line, and next having the clerk follow this by reading out, "and, as they tune it, fall."

The version now most frequently used comes from John Rippon's *A Selection of Hymns from the Best Authors intended to be an Appendix to Dr. Watts's Psalms and Hymns* (1787), wherein some stanzas of Perronet were either altered or completely replaced. In *Lutheran Worship* the first five stanzas are from Perronet, the last two from Rippon, all slightly altered and with updated personal pronouns.

CORONATION was composed for Perronet's text by Oliver Holden, a Massachusetts carpenter and self-taught musician. The phrase "crown him Lord of all" evidently prompted him to name the tune CORONATION when it first appeared in the two-volume *Union Harmony, or Universal Collection of Sacred Music* (Boston, 1793), a work to which he contributed 35 tunes.

While CORONATION has become the most popular setting for this hymn in the United States, British congregations still use the tune that first accompanied this text in the *Gospel Magazine*, namely, SHRUBSOLE or MILES LANE (*LBW* 329).

The harmonization is from the *Service Book and Hymnal* (1958), slightly altered.

273 AMID THE WORLD'S BLEAK WILDERNESS

This hymn was written by Jaroslav Vajda at the suggestion of the sainted E. Theodore DeLaney, former executive director of the Missouri Synod's Commission on Worship, that the former supply a hymn on the Vine and Branches (John 15:1-8) for inclusion in the proposed *Lutheran Book of Worship*, a hymn that might serve as a Hymn of the Day for the Fifth Sunday of Easter. To depict the interwoven nature of a vine, Vajda used the classic form of *terza rima*, so effectively used by Alighiere Dante (1265–1321) in his *Divine Comedy* (*Divina Commedia*), a verse form in which the second of three lines rhymes with lines 1 and 3 of the succeeding stanza (ABA, BCB, CDC, etc.).

GRANTON, by Richard W. Hillert, was named for the composer's birthplace in Wisconsin, and written at the suggestion of the Hymn Music Committee of the Inter-Lutheran Commission on Worship to go with Jaroslav Vajda's "Amid the world's bleak wilderness."

Regarding the tune Hillert comments:

> The distinctive structure of the text, terza rima, is reflected in the form of the tune. There are three phrases constructed so that in the fifth stanza, the second phrase will form a satisfactory conclusion to the whole. The third phrase, with its lowered seventh degree, employs a mixolydian characteristic.

The setting is also the work of Hillert.

274 O JESUS, KING MOST WONDERFUL

O Jesus, King most wonderful! O Conqueror renowned! O Source of peace ineffable, In whom all joys are found:	Iesu, rex admirabilis Et triumphator nobilis, Dulcedo ineffabilis, Totus desiderabilis,
When once you visit darkened hearts, Then truth begins to shine, Then earthly vanity departs, Then kindles love divine.	Quando cor nostrum visitas, Tunc lucet ei veritas, Mundi vilescit vanitas, Et intus fervet caritas.
O Jesus, light of all below, The fount of life and fire, Surpassing all the joys we know, All that we can desire:	Iesu, dulcedo cordium, Fons vitae, lumen mentium, Excedis omne gaudium Et omne desiderium.
May ev'ry heart confess your name, Forever you adore,	Iesum omnes agnoscite, Amorem eius poscite,

And, seeking you, itself inflame
To seek you more and more!

Oh, may our tongues forever bless,
May we love you alone
And ever in our lives express
The image of your own!

Iesum ardenter quaerite,
Quaerendo inardescite.

Te nostra, Iesu, vox sonet,
Nostri te mores exprimant,
Te corda nostra diligant
Et nunc et in perpetuum.

For years the Latin poem "Iesu dulcis memoria," has been attributed to Bernard of Clairvaux. Though this rhapsody on the person of Christ is in keeping with Bernard's spirit and medieval piety, proof of his authorship is lacking. F. J. E. Raby's study of this matter appears to supply the most plausible answer. In his article in *The Bulletin* of the Hymn Society of Great Britain and Ireland (October 1945) he doubts Bernard's authorship. After analyzing and assessing the research of Dom Andre Wilmart, OSB, published in Rome in 1944, he considers the poem to be the work of an Englishman, written about the end of the 12th century. From there it moved to the continent.

David Livingstone (1813–73), noted Scottish missionary and explorer, greatly moved by the poem, said of it in his diary: "That hymn of St. Bernard, on the name of Christ, although in what might be termed dog-Latin, pleases me so; it rings in my ears as I wander across the wide, wide wilderness."

Originally in 42 stanzas, the poem was expanded in the 15th century to 51 stanzas of which the present cento begins with stanza 9. Edward Caswall's 15-stanza translation, appearing in his *Lyra Catholica* (1849) and in his *Hymns and Poems* (1873), has been considerably altered over the years by hymnal editors. The cento appears here in altered and updated form.

HIDING PLACE, a rather sprightly hexatonic anonymous tune, appeared in Joshua Leavitt's *Christian Lyre* (1830) set to a hymn text by Jehoiada Brewer beginning "Hail, sovereign love that first began." Related to CONSOLATION (*LW* 26), George Pollen Jackson, in his *Down-East Spirituals* (1939), notes its secular relatives to be "The Bailaiffs Daughter of Islington" (musicians will remember the delightful illustration pointing up the mechanical novelties of Anglican chant in the Cathedral Psalter set to the line "And he loved the bailaiff's daughter dear That lived at Islington," in Douglas, *Church Music in History and Practice*, p. 133), "Heart's ease," and "Gernutus the Jew of Venus."

Paul G. Bunjes prepared the harmonization for *Lutheran Worship* (1982).

OH, LOVE, HOW DEEP — 275

Oh, love, how deep, how broad, how high,
Beyond all thought and fantasy,
That God, the Son of God, should take
Our mortal for m for mortal's sake!

O amor quam exstaticus,
Quam effluens, quam nimius,
Qui Deum Dei filium
Unum fecit mortalium!

He sent no angel to our race,
Of higher or of lower place,
But wore the robe of human frame
And to this world himself he came.

Non invisit nos angelo
Seu supremo seu infimo;
Carnis assumens pallium
Venit ad nos per se ipsum.

For us baptized, for us he bore
His holy fast and hungered sore;
For us temptation sharp he knew;
For us the tempter overthrew.

Nobis baptisma suscipit,
Nobis jejunans esurit,
Nobis et Satan hunc temptat,
Nobis temptantem superat.

For us he prayed; for us he taught;
For us his daily works he wrought,
By words and signs and actions thus
Still seeking not himself but us.

Nobis orat et praedicat,
Pro nobis cuncta factitat,
Verbis signis et actibus
Nos quaerens non se penitus.

For us by wickedness betrayed,
For us, in crown of thorns arrayed,
He bore the shameful cross and death;
For us he gave his dying breath.

Pro nobis comprehenditur
Flagellatur, conspuitur,
Crucis perfert patibulum,
Pro nobis tradit spiritum.

For us he rose from death again;
For us he went on high to reign;
For us he sent his Spirit here
To guide, to strengthen, and to cheer.

Nobis surgit a mortuis,
Nobis se transfert superis,
Nobis suum dat Spiritum
In robur, in solacium.

All glory to our Lord and God
For love so deep, so high, so broad;
The Trinity whom we adore
Forever and forevermore.

Deo Patri sit gloria
Per infinita saecula,
Cujus amore nimio
Salvi sumus in Filio.

This beautiful hymn on the incarnation of Christ, which G. M. Dreves attributes to Thomas à Kempis and whom others have followed in such attribution, is undoubtedly an anonymous work of the 15th century. Originally consisting of 23 stanzas and beginning with “Apparuit benignitas,” it was translated by Benjamin Webb for inclusion in John Mason Neale’s *The Hymnal Noted* (1854), where it is the hymn for the Sundays after the Epiphany.

The translation here used consists of stanzas 2, 4, 9, 10, 11, 12, and 23 of the original, in altered form, prepared by the Inter-Lutheran Commission on Worship for inclusion in *Lutheran Book of Worship* (1978). The final doxological stanza, differing considerably from that of Webb, is from *The Pilgrim Hymnal* (1962).

Didactic in character, the hymn begins with the incarnation of Jesus Christ and proceeds through his Baptism, his temptation, his works and signs, his trial and death, culminating in his resurrection.

DEO GRACIAS. For comments on the tune see hymn 87.

The harmonization is that which Carl F. Schalk prepared for inclusion in the *Worship Supplement* (1969).

OH, FOR A THOUSAND TONGUES TO SING 276

On the first anniversary of his spiritual rebirth that had taken place on Sunday, May 21, 1738, Charles Wesley wrote this hymn to commemorate the event. Originally in 18 stanzas and beginning with "Glory to God, and praise and love," it was first published in the Wesley brothers' *Hymns and Sacred Songs* (1740). The present arrangement and use of Wesley's stanzas, varying, of course, somewhat in different hymnals, is the result of R. Conyers' *Psalms and Hymns* (1767) in which he reduced the overall length by omitting stanzas and by placing the first stanza last and the seventh stanza first, thus making the hymn begin with "Oh, for a thousand tongues to sing." This opening line is credited to a remark made to Charles Wesley by Peter Böhler, the Moravian missionary who was instrumental in Wesley's spiritual change: "Had I a thousand voices, I would praise him with them all," a statement that may have reflected Thomas Mentzer's earlier hymn of 1704, beginning "Oh, that I Had a Thousand Voices" (*LW* 448).

Beginning with *A Collection of Hymns for the use of the People called Methodists* (1780), this hymn of praise invariably constitutes the first hymn in Methodist hymnals, under the category of Praise and Thanksgiving. In this, *The United Methodist Hymnal* (1989), the latest such hymnal, is no exception. In second place this hymnal reproduces the entire hymn in 18 stanzas as originally conceived by Wesley. Of late both *Lutheran Book of Worship* (1978) and *Lutheran Worship* (1982), following the lead of the Lutheran territorial churches in Germany, begin their hymn sections with the church year, thus emphasizing Christ and his coming in Advent, reserving hymns of praise and adoration as the Christian's response in the category of The Christian Life.

Wesley's stanzas are here given with updated second-person pronouns.

BEATITUDO was composed by John B. Dykes for inclusion in *Hymns Ancient and Modern* (revised edition, 1875) set to "How bright these glorious spirits shine," a text begun by Isaac Watts as probably altered by W. Cameron (1751–1811). The success of Dykes, the typical Victorian composer, is in no small way due to the success of *Hymns Ancient and Modern* (1861), for in this edition he is represented with seven tunes, with 24 in the 1868 edition, and with 56 in the 1875 edition. This tune of Dykes, whom Routley calls the "typical Victorian composer," ranks certainly among his better tunes in its congregational character, a far cry from the excesses so evident in some of his later imitators.

The harmonization is from *The Lutheran Hymnal* (1941).

Coming out of and so deeply rooted in the Methodist tradition, it appears strange that "Oh, for a thousand tongues," is sung to so many different tunes, even to chorale tunes. *The Hymn Book* of the Anglican and the United Church of Canada (1971), for instance, uses Nikolaus Herman's LOBT GOTT, IHR CHRISTEN (*LW* 44). AZMON appears to be the favorite in some more recent hymnals: in *The United Methodist Hymnal* (1989); *The Psalter Hymnal* (1987) of the Christian Reformed Church; and *The*

Hymnal 1982 of the Episcopal Church. Previously the hymnal of the latter church—*The Hymnal 1940*—had used STRACATHRO and ARLINGTON (no. 325).

277 ONE THING'S NEEDFUL

One thing's needful; Lord, this treasure
Teach me highly to regard;
All else, though it first give pleasure,
Is a yoke that presses hard.
Beneath it the heart is still fretting and striving,
No true, lasting happiness ever deriving.
The gain of this one thing all loss can requite,
Can teach me in all things to find true delight.

If you seek this one thing needful,
Turn from all created things;
Turn to Jesus and be heedful
Of the peace and joy he brings.
For where God and man both in one are united,
With love and forgiveness the heart is delighted;
There, there is the worthiest lot and the best,
Where Jesus alone is your joy and your rest.

How were Mary's thoughts devoted
Her eternal joy to find
As intent each word she noted
At her Savior's feet reclined!
How kindled her heart, how devout was its feeling
While hearing the wisdom that Christ was revealing!
For Jesus all earthly concerns she forgot
In love and devotion to what Jesus taught.

So my longings, upward tending,
Jesus, rest alone on you.
All my life on you depending,
Teach me what to will and do.
Although all the world should forsake and forget you,
In love I would follow, I'll never desert you.
The words of your teaching, O Lord, are my life,
My joy and my peace in this vain world of strife.

Wisdom's highest, noblest treasure,
Jesus, is revealed in you.
Let me find in you my pleasure,
Make my will and actions true,
Humility there and simplicity reigning,
In paths of true wisdom my steps ever training.
If I learn from Jesus this knowledge divine,
The blessing of heavenly wisdom is mine.

Therefore you alone, my Savior,
Shall be all in all to me;
Search my heart and my behavior,
Root out all hypocrisy.

Eins ist not, ach Herr, dies Eine
Lehre mich erkennen doch!
Alles andre, wie's auch scheine,
Ist ja nur ein schweres Joch,
Darunter das Herze sich naget und plaget
Und dennoch kein wahres Vergnügen erjaget.
Erlang' ich dies eine, das alles ersetzt,
So werd' ich mit einem in allem ergötzt.

Seele, willst du dieses finden,
Such's bei keiner Kreatur;
Lass, was irdisch ist, dahinten,
Schwing dich über die Natur.
Wo Gott und die Menschheit in einem vereinet,
Wo alle vollkommene Fülle erscheinet:
Da, da ist das beste, notwendigste Teil,
Mein ein und mein alles, mein seligstes Heil.

Wie Maria war beflissen
Auf des einigen Geniess,
Da sie sich zu Jesu Füssen
Voller Andacht niederliess—
Ihr Herze entbrannte, dies einzig zu hören,
Was Jesus, ihr Heiland, sie wollte belehren;
Ihr alles war gänzlich in Jesum versenkt,
Und wurde ihr alles in einem geschenkt—,

Also ist auch mein Verlangen,
Liebster Jesu, nur nach dir;
Lass mich treulich an dir hangen,
Schenke dich zu eigen mir!
Ob viel' auch umkehrten zum grössesten Haufen,
So will ich dir dennoch in Liebe nachlaufen,
Denn dein Wort, o Jesu, ist Leben und Geist;
Was ist wohl, das man nicht in Jesu geneusst?

Aller Weisheit höchste Fülle
In dir ja verborgen liegt.
Gib nur, dass sich auch mein Wille
Fein in solche Schranken fügt.
Worinnen die Demut und Einfalt regieret
Und mich zu der Weisheit, die himmlisch ist, führet.
Ach, wenn ich nur Jesum recht kenne und weiss,
So hab' ich der Weisheit vollkommenen Preis.

Drum auch, Jesu, du alleine,
Sollst mein ein und alles sein.
Prüf, erfahre, wie ich's eine,
Tilge allen Heuchelschein!

Through all my life's pilgrimage, guard and uphold me,
In loving forgiveness, O Jesus, enfold me.
This one thing is needful, all others are vain;
I count all but loss that I Christ may obtain!

Sieh, ob ich auf bösem, betrüglichem Stege,
Und leite mich, Höchster, auf ewigem Wege!
Gib, dass ich hier alles nur achte für Kot
Und Jesum gewinne! Dies eine ist not.

This hymn by Johann H. Schröder first appeared in the *Geistreiches Gesangbuch* (Halle, 1697) with the title "Concerning the denial of self and the world, Luke 10:42." Originally in 10 stanzas, the first four dwell on the words of Jesus to Mary; the next four inject the thoughts of St. Paul from 1 Corinthians 1:30; the last two close with thanks and entreaty. This cento omits stanzas 6–9 of the original German.

The translation by Frances E. Cox appeared in her *Sacred Hymns from the German* (1841). The stanzas here used have been altered and updated.

A unique feature of this hymn is its metric structure. To Schröder the old hymns appeared too smooth and meek. The dactylic meter must be added to the mild iambic and trochaic to give the text more interest and verve. This results in the aria, or solo-like, chorale style so characteristic of the late 17th and early 18th centuries.

Theologically and poetically Wilhelm Nelle is inclined to call this the most blessed hymn of the entire circle of Halle Pietists. Its popularity prompted its immediate inclusion in the Darmstadt hymnal of 1698 and the Freylinghausen hymnal of 1704.

EINS IST NOT. This tune is a newcomer to *Lutheran Worship* (1982). Whereas *The Lutheran Hymnal* (1941) used a tune with the same name composed by Friedrich Layriz (1808–59), this tune is the product of Adam Krieger, often referred to as "the Schubert of the 17th century." Once learned, the metric grid as well as melodic progression will prove interesting.

Paul G. Bunjes prepared the harmonization for *Lutheran Worship.*

CROWN HIM WITH MANY CROWNS 278

Matthew Bridges wrote this hymn, originally titled "In capite ejus diademata multa" (On His Head Were Many Crowns), in 1851. It was published in the same year in Bridges' *Hymns of the Heart*.

Seldom printed the same way twice, this was originally a six-stanza poem, each stanza beginning "Crown him." Godfrey Thring (*LW* 218, et al.) in 1874 wrote six new stanzas with different crowns. Most current hymnals use a combination of Bridges' and Thring's hymns; Thring himself took Bridges' stanza 1 plus four of his own for *A Church of England Hymn Book* (1880; revised in 1882 as *The Church of England Hymn Book*).

The textual version in *Lutheran Worship* is comprised of the following: stanzas 1–3 are by Bridges; stanzas 4 is by Thring; stanza 5 is comprised of lines 1–4 of Bridges' stanza 5 and lines 5–8 of his original stanza 6; and stanza 6 is by Thring.

DIADEMATA. George J. Elvey wrote this fine tune for the hymn. Named after the Greek word for "crowns," it first appeared in the 1868 *Appendix* to the first edition of *Hymns Ancient and Modern* (1861).

The harmonization is from the *Service Book and Hymnal* (1958), slightly altered.

279 HOW SWEET THE NAME OF JESUS SOUNDS

This popular hymn by John Newton, invariably included in most present-day hymnals, first appeared in the memorable volume, *Olney Hymns* (1779), produced by Newton and William Cowper. Newton's past as an infidel, libertine, and slave trader, as he called himself, is undoubtedly reflected in this personal meditation of his. Toward the end of his life he remarked: "My memory is nearly gone, but I remember two things, that I am a great sinner and that Jesus is a great Savior."

In stanza 5, line 1 Newton originally had "Jesus, my Shepherd, *Husband*, Friend," apparently following St. Bernard in interpreting the Bride in the Song of Solomon (NIV: Song of Songs) as the individual Christian and not as the Church.

The text is here in the altered and updated form.

ST. PETER was originally the tune set to a version of Psalm 118 beginning "Far better 'tis to trust in God" in Alexander R. Reinagle's *Psalm Tunes for the Voice and Pianoforte* (Oxford, c. 1830), thus as a solo with piano accompaniment. In 1840 it appeared in Reinagle's *A Collection of Psalm and Hymn Tunes, Chants, and other music, as such in the Parish Church of St. Peter's in the East, Oxford. Arranged for the Organ or Pianoforte* (Oxford), where it was called ST. PETER. The composer reharmonized the tune for the present text in the original edition of *Hymns Ancient and Modern* (1861). Routley considers it to be a tune of excellent quality from the early 19th century.

The harmonization was prepared for *Lutheran Worship* (1982) by Paul G. Bunjes.

280 JESUS, YOUR BOUNDLESS LOVE SO TRUE

Jesus, your boundless love so true
No thought can reach, no tongue declare;
Unite my thankful heart to you,
And reign without a rival there.
Yours wholly, yours alone I am;
Be you alone my sacred flame.

O Jesu Christ, mein schönstes Licht,
Der du in deiner Seelen
So hoch mich liebst, dass ich es nicht
Aussprechen kann noch zählen:
Gib, dass mein Herz dich wiederum
Mit Lieben und Verlangen

Mög umfangen
Und als dein Eigentum
Nur einzig an dir hangen!

Oh, grant that nothing in my soul
May dwell but your pure love alone;
Oh, may your love possess me whole,
My joy, my treasure, and my crown!
All coldness from my heart remove;
My ev'ry act, word, thought be love.

Gib, dass sonst nichts in meiner Seel'
Als deine Liebe wohne;
Gib, dass ich deine Lieb' erwähl'
Als meinen Schatz und Krone!
Stoss alles aus, nimm alles hin,
Was dich und mich will trennen
Und nicht gönnen,
Dass all mein Mut und Sinn
In deiner Liebe brennen!

This love unwearied I pursue
And dauntlessly to you aspire.
Oh, may your love my hope renew,
Glow in my soul like heav'nly fire!
And day and night be all my care
To guard this sacred treasure here.

O dass ich wie ein kleines Kind
Mit Weinen dir nachginge
So lange, bis dein Herz, entzünd't,
Mit ar men mich umfinge
Und deine Seel' in mein Gemüt
In voller, süsser Liebe
Sich erhübe
Und also deiner Güt'
Ich stets vereinigt bliebe!

In suff'ring be your love my peace,
In weakness be your love my pow'r;
And when the storms of life shall cease,
O Jesus, in that final hour
Be then my rod and staff and guide
And draw me safely to your side.

Lass sie sein meine Freud' in Leid,
In Schwachheit mein Vermögen,
Und wenn ich nach vollbrachter Zeit
Mich soll zur Ruhe legen,
Alsdann lass deine Liebestreu',
Herr Jesu, bei mir stehen,
Luft zuwehen,
Dass ich getrost und frei
Mög' in dein Reich eingehen!

Based on a prayer in the *Paradiesgärtlein* (Magdeburg, 1612), a devotional book by Johann Arndt (1555–1621), the most influential author of such works in the Lutheran Church, Johann Gerhardt's notable hymn of love to Christ, originally in 16 stanzas, first appeared in Johann Crüger's *Praxis pietatis melica* (Berlin, 1653).

Becoming acquainted with Gerhardt's hymn as contained in the *Herrnhut Gesangbuch* (1635) when he was in Savannah, Georgia, and recognizing its singular character, John Wesley translated the entire hymn in another meter and published the same in his *Hymns and Sacred Poems* (1739).

This cento includes stanzas 1, 2, 8, and 16, in altered and updated form.

VATER UNSER. For comments on this tune see hymn 431.

The harmonization is from the *Württembergisches Choralbuch* (1953).

281 LORD, ENTHRONED IN HEAVENLY SPLENDOR

This hymn by George H. Bourne, originally in 10 stanzas, was included in his *Seven Post-Communion Hymns* (1874), a private publication for use at St. Edmond's College, Salisbury, England. Its first appearance in a more general hymnal was in the *Supplement* (1889) to *Hymns Ancient and Modern* (1861). Not only is it an appropriate hymn in the category of Redeemer, but it serves well as a post-communion hymn. Moreover, it is useful for processions at Ascension and at other festive occasions.

BRYN CALFARIA, meaning "Mount Calvary," was written by William Owen to go with the rather revivalistic and evangelistic Welsh hymn, "Gwaed y groes sy'n cody fynny," words touching deep about Jesus and the cross. It seems first to have appeared in his *Y Perl Cerddorol* (The Pearl of Music) in 1886. However well another text might go to this tune, the Welsh person cannot separate the two. It is said that when tragedy strikes in Wales, as in the case of a mine disaster when families gather at the pit to see if their kin are safe, the singing of this Welsh hymn brings special strength and comfort. The inclusion of this tune in *The English Hymnal* (1906), not to the original but to the above text, introduced it to English congregations.

Once learned, the tune is recognized as one of solemn grandeur, possessing a strong individuality all its own. Its trochaic metrical scheme gives it a determined, somewhat vehement character. Small wonder that Erik Routley has described it as "a piece of real Celtic rock."

The harmonization is by Theodore A. Beck.

282 O SAVIOR, PRECIOUS SAVIOR

Frances R. Havergal wrote this hymn at Leamington, England, November 1870, and it first appeared in her *Under the Surface* (1874), entitled "Christ Worshiped by the Church." Her text appears here in the updated and slightly altered form.

ANGEL'S STORY (WATERMOUTH, SUPPLICATION) was contributed by Arthur H. Mann to the *Methodist Sunday-school Tune-Book* (London, c. 1881) where it was set to Emily Miller's "I love to hear the story which angel voices tell."

Paul G. Bunjes prepared the harmonization for *Lutheran Worship* (1982).

YOU ARE THE WAY; TO YOU ALONE 283

First published in George W. Doane's *Songs by the Way* (1824), this was the only hymn by an American author included in the original edition of *Hymns Ancient and Modern* (1860), retaining its place in all the revisions of that hymnal. The text originally began "Thou art the way;" updating the language for *Lutheran Worship* necessitated a change in the last line of stanza 1, from "Must seek him, Lord, by thee."

DUNDEE. The tune first appeared in Andro Hart's Scottish *The CL* (150) *Psalms of David* (1615), where it was called FRENCH TUNE. Thomas Ravenscroft in his *The Whole Book of Psalms, etc.* (1621), renamed the tune DUNDY, after the town in Scotland now known as Dundee. The tune called DUNDIE in the Scottish Psalter is known as WINDSOR today; to avoid confusion, some hymnals which include both tunes call the present one DUNDEE (FRENCH) and refer to the other as DUNDEE (WINDSOR).

The harmonization is from *The English Hymnal* (1906).

HAIL, O ONCE REJECTED JESUS 284

Although this hymn is often attributed to John Bakewell, one of John Wesley's (*LW* 280, 362) lay preachers, there seems to be no basis for this assumption. Two stanzas appeared in 1757 in a small pamphlet titled *Hymns Addressed to the Holy, Holy, Holy, Triune God* (London):

Hail, thou once-despised Jesus,
Hail, thou Galilean King!
Who didst suffer to release us,
Who didst free salvation bring!
Hail, thou universal Saviour,
Who hast borne our sin and shame;
By whose merits we find favour,
Life is given thro' thy name!

Jesus, hail, enthron'd in glory,
There for ever to abide;
All the heav'nly host adore thee,
Seated at thy Father's side:
Worship, honour, pow'r, and blessing,
Thou art worthy to receive—
Loudest praises without ceasing
Meet it is for us to give!

Martin Madan included an expanded version, similar to the present text, in his *Collection of Psalms and Hymns* (1760); it is not known whether Madan or the original author made the revisions. Next Augustus Toplady (*LW* 361) published the hymn in

Psalms and Hymns (1776), omitting the stanza beginning "Paschal Lamb by God appointed" as un-Calvinistic. And so alterations have continued to the present. The hymn's inclusion in two previous hymnals of the Synod—the *Evangelical Lutheran Hymn-Book* (1912) the first English hymnal, and *The Lutheran Hymnal* (1941)—and its resultant popularity, prompted the Commission on Worship to include it in *Lutheran Worship* (1982), where it is given in updated form.

O DURCHBRECHER. Set to Gottfried Arnold's hymn "O Durchbrecher aller Bande," the tune appeared in Johann Freylinghausen's *Neues geistreiches Gesangbuch* (Halle, 1704). Sometimes called CONQUEROR, it is a notable tune in the solo-aria style—one of the two styles of the chorale prevalent in the second half of the 17th century and in Pietism, the other being the isometric form.

The harmonization is by Fred L. Precht.

285 CHIEF OF SINNERS THOUGH I BE

William McComb, Irish bookseller, published this hymn in his *The Poetical Works of William McComb* (1864), where it was titled "Christ All in All." With the opening line based on St. Paul's assertion: "Christ Jesus came into the world to save sinners of whom I am chief" (AV, 1 Tim. 1:15; NIV translates: "the worst") and the body of the hymn text reflecting Romans 5:8–11, it constitutes a rather notable hymn on the Redeemer. Few hymnals, however, include it. Its popular use in previous hymnals of the Synod—*The Evangelical Lutheran Hymn-Book* (1912) and *The Lutheran Hymnal* (1941)—prompted its inclusion in *Lutheran Book of Worship* (1978) and subsequently here. Admittedly, while the trochaic metric pattern of six sevens (77 77 77) can be effectively used, in this instance the AABBCC rhyming pattern can prove somewhat enervating.

GETHSEMANE. For comments on the tune see hymn 110.

The setting is from the *Service Book and Hymnal* (1958), slightly altered.

286 LOVE DIVINE, ALL LOVE EXCELLING

This much-loved hymn by Charles Wesley first appeared in *Hymns for those that Seek, and those that have, Redemption in the Blood of Christ* (1747), the first line beginning "Love divine, all loves excelling." With but several alterations—Wesley had "Take away our power of sinning" in stanza 2, line 5 and "Pure and sinless let us be" in stanza

4, line 2—alterations common in many hymnals, the hymn appears here basically as Wesley wrote it.

While some may construe certain expressions in stanza 4 as reflecting the Wesleyan doctrine of Christian perfectionism, these should be interpreted as in the paradoxical *simul iustus et peccator,* namely, at one and the same time we, as Christians, through the blood and righteousness of Christ, are saints and sinners.

Cast in the trochaic 87 87D meter, a meter of strength and ability to carry weighty ideas in its 15 syllables per double line, the pattern used for some of Christendom's great and most popular hymns, small wonder that this hymn was included in collections by Martin Madan (see his biography, p. 800), Augustus M. Toplady (*LW* 361), and in innumerable hymnals since.

HYFRYDOL. Considering both the tune O DU LIEBE and its harmonization used with this text in *The Lutheran Hymnal* (1941) not a good match, the Commission on Worship, following the lead of *Lutheran Book of Worship* (1978), chose to use HYFRYDOL, meaning "pleasant" or "good cheer." Written by Rowland H. Prichard when he was but twenty years old, it is a strong, simple tune within the compass of a fifth except for one note in the last phrase. Printed in his *Cyfaill y Cantorion* (1844) with some 40 other of his tunes, it also appeared in *Halelwiah Drachefn* (1855), edited by Griffith Roberts. Its first appearance in English hymnody seems to have been in *The English Hymnal* (1906), set to "Alleluia, sing to Jesus" (no. 301), and as an alternate tune to "Once to every man and nation" (no. 563). It has enjoyed a long association with Wesley's "Love divine, all love excelling."

The setting is from the *Service Book and Hymnal* (1958), slightly altered.

287 ABIDE WITH US, OUR SAVIOR

Abide with us, our Savior,
Nor let your mercy cease;
From Satan's might defend us,
And give our hearts your peace.

Abide with us, our Helper,
Sustain us by your Word;
Let us and all your people
To living faith be stirred.

Abide with us, Redeemer,
O Light, eternal Light;
Your truth direct and guide us
To flee from error's night.

Abide in princely bounty
With us, large-hearted Lord,
Our lives with grace and wisdom
Enriching through your Word.

Abide as our protector
Among us, Lord, our strength;
Let world and wily Satan
Be overcome at length.

Abide among us always,
O Lord, our faithful friend,
And take us to your mansions
When time and world shall end.

Ach bleib mit deiner Gnade
Bei uns, Herr Jesu Christ,
Dass uns hinfort nicht schade
Des bösen Feindes List!

Ach bleib mit deinem Worte
Bei uns, Erlöser wert,
Dass uns beid' hier und dorte
Sei Güt' und Heil beschert!

Ach bleib mit deinem Glanze
Bei uns, du wertes Licht;
Dein' Wahrheit uns umschanze,
Damit wir irren nicht!

Ach bleib mit deinem Segen
Bei uns, du reicher Herr!
Dein' Gnad' und all's Vermögen
In uns reichlich vermehr!

Ach bleib mit deinem Schutze
Bei uns, du starker Held,
Dass uns der Feind nicht trutze,
Noch fäll' die böse Welt!

Ach bleib mit deiner Treue
Bei uns, mein Herr und Gott!
Beständigkeit verleihe,
Hilf uns aus aller Not!

A popular hymn in Lutheranism, both in the United States and in Europe, this immortal hymn by Josua Stegmann first appeared in his *Christliches Gebetbüchlein* (Rinteln, 1627) under the rubric "Prayer in behalf of the Maintenance of God's Teaching and Church." It was later editors who linked it with the two disciples on the road to Emmaus (Luke 24:13–35). More specifically, it was the hardships of the Thirty Years' War (1618–48) to which the territory of Schaumburg was subjected, wherein Stegmann worked as superintendent and professor of theology, that served as the background for this hymn. Noting that the hymn has been sung as a prayer for all sorts of occasions other than originally intended (though not inappropriately so), the Commission on Worship restored it to its rightful place, namely, under the category of The Church, where its original character and purpose are not lost.

Regarding the translation, indicated as being composite, stanza 1 is from *The Church Book* (Philadelphia, 1868); the remaining stanzas represent a rather free translation of the German, prepared by the Hymn Text and Music Committee of the Commission on Worship.

CHRISTUS, DER IST MEIN LEBEN. For comments on the tune see hymn 267.

The setting is from *The Lutheran Hymnal* (1941), slightly altered.

MAY GOD EMBRACE US WITH HIS GRACE 288

May God embrace us with his grace,
Pour blessings from his fountains,
And by the brightness of his face
Guide toward celestial mountains,
So that his saving acts we see
Wherein his love takes pleasure.
Let Jesus' healing power be
Revealed in richest measure,
Converting ev'ry nation.

Es woll' uns Gott genädig sein
Und seinen Segen geben;
Sein Antlitz uns mit hellem Schein
Erleucht' zum ew'gen Leben,
Dass wir erkennen seine Werk',
Und was ihm liebt auf Erden,
Und Jesus Christus Heil und Stärk'
Bekannt den Heiden werden
Und sie zu Gott bekehren.

All people living on his globe,
Praise God with exultation!
The world puts on a festive robe
And sings its jubilation
That your rule, Lord, is strong and true
And curbs sin's evil hour.
Your Word stands guard and will renew
Your people's health and power
To live, Lord, in your presence.

So danken, Gott, und loben dich
Die Heiden überalle,
Und alle Welt, die freue sich
Und sing' mit grossem Schalle,
Dass du auf Erden Richter bist
Und lässt die Sünd' nicht walten;
Dein Wort die Hut und Weide ist,
Die alles Volk erhalten,
In rechter Bahn zu wallen.

Our praises grow from living roots
When we thank God by action,
Improve the field, grow righteous fruits
Drawn by the Word's attraction.
Oh, bless us, Father and the Son
And Spirit, ever holy.
May people ev'rywhere be won
To love and praise you truly.
To this our heartfelt amen.

Es danke, Gott, und lobe dich
Das Volk in guten Taten;
Das Land bringt Frucht und bessert sich,
Dein Wort ist wohl geraten.
Uns segne Vater und der Sohn,
Uns segne Gott der Heil'ge Geist,
Dem alle Welt die Ehre tu',
Vor ihm sich fürchte allermeist.
Nun sprecht von Herzen: Amen!

Luther's *Formula Missae* (1523) had hardly been published when Paul Speratus, castle preacher and hymnist at Königsberg, the man who helped Luther prepare the *Achtliederbuch*, made a German translation of it, a work that appeared in Wittenberg in 1524. In the *Formula Missae* Luther stated that the customary benediction contained in the Roman Mass be given ("May almighty God bless you, the Father, and the Son, and the Holy Spirit") or also the benediction from Numbers 6:24–27, which the Lord himself appointed. To this Luther added one more option, namely, Psalm 67:6b–7: "God, our God, will bless us. God will bless us, and all the ends of the earth will fear him." It is at this point that Speratus appends Luther's hymn, "May God bestow on us his grace," a paraphrase of Psalm 67, written by Luther about this time, perhaps to serve this very purpose of supplanting the spoken psalm verses.

It is worthy of note that this is the first Protestant hymn with a mission thrust.

The translation is by F. Samuel Janzow.

ES WOLLE GOTT UNS GNÄDIG SEIN. This beautiful Phrygian tune (see essay: The Church Modes, p. 832) comes from an old German hymn to the virgin Mary, "Maria, du bist genaden voll." The first-published form of this hymn, both text and tune, appeared in a broadsheet printed by Hans Knappe the Younger in Magdeburg (1524). Thereafter it appeared in the Erfurt *Enchiridia* (1524) and in Johann Walter's *Geistliches gesangk Buchleyn* (1524).

The setting is by Paul G. Bunjes.

289 THE CHURCH'S ONE FOUNDATION

A shot in the battle of doctrine raging at the time, this hymn was one of 12 published by Samuel J. Stone in 1866 as *Lyra Fidelium*, each hymn addressing an article in the Apostles' Creed. "The Church's One Foundation" was no. 9, based on "I believe in . . . the holy Christian [ancient text: catholic] Church." Stone's hymns were written in support of Bishop Gray of Capetown, who deposed Bishop John W. Colenso for calling into question the historicity of certain Old Testament texts.

Originally in seven stanzas, these were reorganized into five stanzas in the Appendix (1868) to *Hymns Ancient and Modern* (1861), using Stone's stanzas 1, 2, 4, 5, and the final four lines of each of stanzas 6 and 7. The version now commonly used is from 1868, dropping one stanza for a total of four.

It was the conviction and belief of the Commission on Worship that the above creedal statement refers to the worldwide, universal, or invisible Church, the Una Sancta, the one holy Christian Church to which belong only those true believers who, by the working of the Holy Spirit, have been brought to faith in Jesus Christ and his vicarious atonement. Hence, omitted here are stanzas by Stone that speak of "False sons within her pale" and "By schisms rent asunder, By heresies distressed," expressions that refer to the so-called visible church, the body of professing Christians among whom there are divisions, false believers, and even hypocrites.

An expanded, 10-stanza version was made in 1885 for use as a processional at Salisbury cathedral. Set to AURELIA in the aforementioned Appendix to *Hymns Ancient and Modern*, the hymn became immensely popular and was frequently sung at church conferences.

AURELIA. For comments on this tune see hymn 251.

The harmonization is that of Samuel S. Wesley.

290 CHRIST IS OUR CORNERSTONE

Christ is our cornerstone,
On him alone we build;
With his true saints alone
The courts of heav'n are filled.
On his great love
Our hopes we place

Angularis fundamentum
lapis Christus missus est
Qui conpage parietis
in utroque necitur,
Quem Sion sancta suscepit,
in quo credens permanet.

Of present grace
And joys above.

Oh, then, with hymns of praise
These hallowed courts shall ring;
Our voices we will raise
The Three in One to sing
And thus proclaim
In joyful song,
Both loud and long,
That glorious name.

Omnis illa Deo sacra
et dilecta civitas,
Plena modulis in laude
et canore jubilo,
Trinum Deum unicumque
cum favore praedicat.

Here, gracious God, do now
And evermore draw near;
Accept each faithful vow,
And ev'ry suppliant hear.
In copious show'r
On all who pray
Each holy day
Your blessing pour.

Hoc in templo, summe Deus,
exoratus adveni,
Et clementi bonitate
precum vota suscipe;
Largam benedictionem
hic infunde iugiter.

Here may we gain from heav'n
The grace which we implore,
And may that grace, once giv'n,
Be with us evermore
Until that day
When all the blest
To endless rest
Are called away.

Hic promereantur omnes
petita adquirere,
Et adepta possidere
cum sanctis perenniter,
Paradisum introire,
translati in requiem.

This is an updated version of John Chandler's (*LW* 12) translation of four stanzas of a Latin hymn as it appeared in his *Hymns of the Primitive Church* (1837). The original anonymous Latin hymn of nine stanzas, dating perhaps from the seventh century, was a favorite for dedication festivals. Originally divided into two parts, the first four stanzas, beginning with "Urbs beata Ierusalem" ("Blessed city, heavenly Salem"), emphasized the vision of heavenly Jerusalem descending to earth; the last five stanzas, beginning "Angularis fundamentum lapis Christus missus est" ("Christ is made the sure foundation," here, "Christ is our cornerstone"), emphasize and invoke the Lord's continued blessings on his Church. John Mason Neale (*LW* 31) made a translation of the complete hymn and included it in his *Medieval Hymns and Sequences* (1851). Here Chandler has translated and utilized only the first four stanzas of the second part of the original hymn.

DARWALL'S 148TH. For comments on this tune see hymn 179.

The harmonization is from *The Lutheran Hymnal* (1941), slightly altered.

291 BUILT ON THE ROCK

Built on the Rock the Church shall stand,
Even when steeples are falling;
Crumbled have spires in ev'ry land,
Bells still are chiming and calling,
Calling the young and old to rest,
Calling the souls of those distressed,
Longing for life everlasting.

Not in our temples made with hands
God, the Almighty, is dwelling;
High in the heav'ns his temple stands,
All earthly temples excelling.
Yet he who dwells in heav'n above
Deigns to abide with us in love,
Making our bodies his temple.

We are God's house of living stones,
Built for his own habitation;
He fills our hearts, his humble thrones,
Granting us life and salvation.
Were two or three to seek his face,
He in their midst would show his grace,
Blessings upon them bestowing.

Yet in this house, an earthly frame,
Jesus the children is blessing;
Hither we come to praise his name,
Faith in our Savior confessing.
Jesus to us his Spirit sent,
Making with us his covenant,
Granting his children the Kingdom.

Through all the passing years, O Lord,
Grant that, when church bells are ringing,
Many may come to hear God's Word
Where he this promise is bringing:
I know my own, my own know me;
You, not the world, my face shall see;
My peace I leave with you. Amen.

Kirken den er et gammelt Hus,
Staar, om end Tarrmene falde;
Taarne fuld mange sank i Grus,
Klokker end kime og kalde,
Kalde paa Gamel og paa Ung,
Meest dog paa Själen trät og tung,
Syg for den evige Hvile.

Herren vor Gud vist ei bebor
Huse, som Händer mon bygge,
Arke-Paulunet var paa Jord
Kun af hans Tempel en Skygge,
Selv dog en Bolig underfuld
Bygde han sig i os af Muld,
Reiste af Gruset i Naade.

Vi er Guds Hus og Kirke nu,
Bygget af levende Stene,
Sm under Kors med ärlig Hu
Troen og Daaben forene;
Var vi paa Jord ei meer end To,
Bygge dog vilde han og bo
Hos os med hele sin Naade.

Husene dog med Kirke-Navn,
Bygde til Frelserens Äre,
Hvor han de Smaa tog tidt i Favn,
Er os, som Hjemmet, saa kjäre,
Deilige Ting i dem er sagt,
Sluttet har der med os sin Pagt
Han, som os Himmerig skjänker.

Give da Gud, at hvor vi bo,
Altid, naar Klokkerne ringe,
Folket forsamles i Jesu Tro
Der, hvor det pleied at klinge:
Verden vei ei, men I mig ser,
Alt hvad jeg siger, se, det sker!
Fred väre med eder alle!

In the attempt to stem the tide of Rationalism and skepticism so prevalent in 19th-century Denmark, two men stand out, namely, Nikolai F. S. Grundtvig and Sören A. Kierkegaard (1813–55). While the latter is more generally known today for his popularization of the radical existentialism as related to the character of the Christian faith, the former, with his emphasis on Word and Sacrament, on congregational life and hymnody, undoubtedly made the greater impact during their lifetimes.

This classic, widely known Scandinavian hymn—a stirring affirmation of faith—appeared, originally in seven stanzas, in the first of Grundtvig's published collections, *Sang-värk til den Danske Kirke* (1837). Later it appeared, revised and abbreviated, in his *Festsalmer* (sixth edition, 1854). In 1855 the text appeared in *Psalmebog for Kirke-og Huus-Andagt* in seven stanzas.

First translated by Carl Döving, a Norwegian-American Lutheran pastor, for *The Lutheran Hymnary* (Minneapolis, 1913), this translation was revived by Fred C. Hansen, a member of the Commission on Liturgy and Hymnal from the Danish Lutheran Church, for inclusion in the *Service Book and Hymnal* (1958). It is the latter's version that appears in *Lutheran Book of Worship* (1978) and in *Lutheran Worship* (1982).

KIRKEN DEN ER ET GAMMELT HUS (Church it is an old house) was composed by Ludwig M. Lindemann expressly for Grundtvig's hymn, after which it is named. A sturdy chorale tune, it was first published in W. A. Wexel's *Christelige Psalmer* (1840) and is the first of many tunes that he provided for the Lutheran Church in Norway.

Paul G. Bunjes prepared the setting for inclusion in *Lutheran Worship* (1982).

IN ADAM WE HAVE ALL BEEN ONE 292

This is another of the six hymns by Martin Franzmann included in *Lutheran Worship* (1982), hymns that largely made their way into this hymnal via the *Worship Supplement* (1969). Written by Franzmann in 1961, this hymn was included in *A New Song* (1963). The text appears here in updated and altered form (compare with *WS* 759 for original).

THE SAINTS' DELIGHT is an abbreviated form of an anonymous tune that appeared in William Walker's (*LW* 22) collection of anthems, fuguing and hymn tunes, in manuscript form, titled *Miss Elizabeth Adams' Music Book* and published in 1832 (see article by Milburn Price, "Miss Elizabeth Adams' Music Book: A Manuscript Predecessor of William Walker's Southern Harmony" in *The Hymn* 29, 2 [April 1978]: 70–75). In 1835 the tune was included in *Southern Harmony* as the setting for Isaac Watts' (*LW* 53, et al.) "When I can read my title clear To mansions in the skies."

Paul G. Bunjes prepared the harmonization for inclusion in *Lutheran Worship* (1982).

LORD JESUS CHRIST, THE CHURCH'S HEAD 293

Lord Jesus Christ, the Church's head,
You are her one foundation;
In you she trusts, before you bows,
And waits for your salvation.
Built on this rock secure,
Your Church shall endure

O Jesu, einig wahres Haupt
Der heiligen Gemeine,
Die an dich, ihren Heiland, glaubt,
Und nur auf dir alleine
Als ihrem Felsen steht,
Der nie untergeht,

Though all the world decay
And all things pass away.
Oh, hear, oh, hear us, Jesus!

O Lord, let this your little flock,
Your name alone confessing,
Continue in your loving care,
True unity possessing.
Your sacraments, O Lord,
And your saving Word
To us, Lord, pure retain.
Grant that they may remain
Our only strength and comfort.

Help us to serve you evermore
With hearts both pure and lowly;
And may your Word, that light divine,
Shine on in splendor holy
That we repentance show,
In faith ever grow;
The pow'r of sin destroy
And evils that annoy.
Oh, make us faithful Christians.

And for your Gospel let us dare
To sacrifice all treasure;
Teach us to bear your blessed cross,
To find in you all pleasure.
Oh, grant us steadfastness
In joy and distress,
Lest we, Lord, you forsake.
Let us by grace partake
Of endless joy and gladness.

Wenngleich die ganze Welt
Zertrümmert und zerfällt:
Erhör, erhör uns, Jesu!

Lass uns, dein kleines Häufelein,
Das sich zu dir bekennet,
Dir ferner anbefohlen sein;
Erhalt uns ungetrennet.
Wort, Tauf' und Abendmahl
Lass in seiner Zahl
Und ersten Reinigkeit
Bis an den Schluss der Zeit
Zu unserm Troste bleiben.

Hilf, dass wir dir zu aller Zeit
Mit reinem Herzen dienen.
Lass uns das Licht der Seligkeit,
Das uns bisher geschienen,
Zur Buss' kräftig sein
Und zum hellen Schein,
Der unsern Glauben mehrt,
Der Sünden Macht zerstört
Und fromme Christen machet.

Lass uns beim Evangelio
Gut, Blut, und Leben wagen;
Mach uns dadurch getrost und froh,
Das schwerste Kreuz zu tragen.
Gib Beständigkeit,
Dass uns Lust und Leid
Von dir nicht scheiden mag,
Bis wir den Jubeltag
Bei dir im Himmel halten.

Although not included in the Synod's early *Kirchengesangbuch* (St. Louis, 1847) nor in the *Evangelical Lutheran Hymn-Book* (1912), the Intersynodical Committee on Hymnology and Liturgics did well to include this noteworthy hymn on the church in *The Lutheran Hymnal* (1941), and it now appears here in *Lutheran Worship* (1982).

Written by the gifted poet Johann Mentzer, it first appeared in *Reibersdorfer Gesang Buch* (1726) in seven stanzas, of which this cento includes stanzas 1–4. Notice the effective uneven number of phrases, for a total of nine—87 87 65 66 7—with the rhyme scheme ABCBDDEEF.

The translation by William J. Schaefer, appearing here in updated and slightly altered form, was prepared by him in 1938 for inclusion in *The Lutheran Hymnal* (1941).

REUTER. This fine tune, although a product of the 20th century, is reflective of a 17th century chorale, the result of its uneven metric pattern to fit the text. The pulse (*Takt*) should be rigidly kept throughout by the organist, even though this means that the quarter note which ends certain phrases should be played as an eighth note, thus to afford the congregation a catch-breath on the remaining eighth-value rest.

The harmonization is from *The Lutheran Hymnal* (1941), slightly altered.

GLORIOUS THINGS OF YOU ARE SPOKEN 294

This great, joyful hymn by John Newton, practically a part of every Christian's vocabulary, first appeared in *Olney Hymns* (1779), which he edited jointly with William Cowper (*LW* 426, 506). Originally in five stanzas, stanzas 1, 2, 3 and 5, the choice in most hymnals, are here given in updated form. While Cowper's contributions in the *Olney Hymns* (these number 281) excel more in personal devotion, Newton's hymns focus more on the church. And this hymn is undoubtedly his finest in that area.

While the scriptural text written over the hymn in the original is Isaiah 33:20–21, beginning "Look upon Zion, the city of our festival; your eyes will see Jerusalem, a peaceful abode, a tent that will not be moved," the entire hymn is a mosaic of scriptural thought (Ps. 87:3; Matt. 16:18; Matt. 7:24; Ps. 46; Ezek. 47; Rev. 22; Ex. 17:6), to cite but a few examples, all reflecting a sense of pride and joy in being, by God's grace, a member of the church, a place of "solid joys and lasting pleasures."

AUSTRIA. With but few exceptions, most hymnals have used and continue to use this tune by Franz Joseph Haydn with John Newton's "Glorious Things of You Are Spoken." While on a visit to England, Haydn was moved by the spiritual singing of "God save the King" and he expressed to individuals in high government circles regrets that his own people had no such national anthem. As a result the imperial chancellor Count von Saurau commissioned poet Leopold Haschka to write such a text. Early in 1797 Haydn set this text, which began with "Gott, erhalte Franz den Kaiser," to the tune now named AUSTRIA. The tune soon became the most popular of all Haydn's songs as well as his own favorite tune, and it greatly increased his popularity. William H. Hadow (1859–1937), English writer on music, composer, editor, and educator, in his *A Croatian Composer: Notes towards the Study of Joseph Haydn* (London, 1897) considers the Croatian folk song, "Vjatvo rano se ja vstanem," to be the basis for Haydn's tune. Incidently, the slow movement of Haydn's Emperor Quartet, op. 76, no. 3, consists of four variations of this tune.

The first use of AUSTRIA as a hymn tune in an English hymnal was in Edward Miller's *Sacred Music* (1802). In 1804 the tune appeared in German in a Roman Catholic hymnal printed in Breslau coupled to "Christen! singt mit frohen Herzen."

The *Evangelical Lutheran Hymn-Book* (1912), the first official English hymnal of the Synod, gave SILCHER first place (*ELH* 464), with AUTUMN (*ELH* 335) and HARWELL (*ELH* 451) as alternates, not one of which is a tune of quality. The *Service Book and Hymnal* (1958), produced by a commission representing the American Lutheran Church, Lutheran Church in America, Evangelical Lutheran Church, and others, offered two tunes to this text (*SBH* 152), HARWELL and AUSTRIA. In the production of *Lutheran Book of Worship* (1978), the Inter-Lutheran Commission on Worship decided to include the more popular of the two, namely, AUSTRIA. A few years later, the Commission on Worship, in producing *Lutheran Worship*, followed suit, even though

The Lutheran Hymnal (1941) used the less felicitous tune by Joseph Barnby (*LW* 253, et al.) titled GALILEAN (*TLH* 469; *LW* 318).

Two other tunes, both of merit, have been and continue to be used with Newton's text. The first is RUSTINGTON, composed by Charles Hubert Hastings Parry (1848–1918), English professor of composition, lecturer, and author. This tune first appeared in the *Westminster Abbey Hymn Book* (1897), and later in *Hymns Ancient and Modern* (1904). It presently appears, among others, in *The Hymn Book* (1971) of the Anglican Church of Canada and the United Church of Canada, also in the *Psalter Hymnal* (1987) of the Christian Reformed Church. The other tune is ABBOT'S LEIGH, composed by Cyril Vincent Taylor in 1937 for use of the religious broadcasting department of the British Broadcasting Company during World War II, and first printed with "Glorious Things" in a leaflet by Oxford University Press in 1941. This tune presently appears, among others, in *Rejoice in the Lord* (1985), hymnal of the Reformed Church in America, and in *The Australian Hymn Book* with Catholic Supplement (1971), an ecumenical hymn book representing Anglicans, Congregationalists, Methodists, and Presbyterians.

Admittedly, for German immigrants and people of countries occupied by the Nazis in World War II the tune AUSTRIA brings painful and horrible memories of those frightful days, when also, for instance, they were forced to sing "Deutschland, Deutschland, über alles" to it. The fact that, according to Erik Routley, the tune "stands as one of the very few examples of a first-class hymn tune written by a symphonic composer of the front rank" is of no comfort to such Christians. In such circumstances, pastors and/or organists will be sufficiently sensitive to the feelings of these Christians, thus to sing, lest the precious Gospel be hindered, Newton's splendid hymn text to another tune, perhaps to one of those previously mentioned.

The setting in *Lutheran Worship* is that contained in the *Service Book and Hymnal* (1958).

295 BLEST BE THE TIE THAT BINDS

This hymn by John Fawcett commemorates his decision to remain in tiny, destitute Wainsgate, Yorkshire, after accepting a call to London in 1772. Fawcett had preached his farewell sermon, and the family's belongings had been loaded onto carts, when the time came for the final goodbyes to the congregation. So much emotion was felt and exhibited that Fawcett's wife finally exclaimed, "Oh, John, John, I cannot bear this! I know not how to go!" Her husband replied, "Nor I either—nor will we go. Unload the wagons!" A letter was immediately dispatched to London, and the family stayed among their beloved friends. The resultant hymn, "Blest Be the Tie That Binds," was published 10 years later in Fawcett's *Hymns Adapted to the Circumstances of Public Worship*, where it contained six stanzas. The omitted stanzas 4 and 5 read:

When we asunder part
It gives us inward pain,
But we shall still be joined in heart,
And hope to meet again.

This glorious hope revives
Our courage by the way;
While each in expectation lives,
And longs to see the day.

BOYLSTON, a tune by Lowell Mason, first appeared in his *The Choir, or Union Collection of Church Music* (1832) as the setting for "Our days are as grass." It may have been named for a town in Massachusetts which has been incorporated into Boston. Popularity of and familiarity with both text and tune in *The Lutheran Hymnal* (1941) as well as in its predecessor, the *Evangelical Lutheran Hymn-Book* (1912), prompted the inclusion in *Lutheran Worship* (1982). DENNIS (*LBW* 370), first published by Lowell Mason in his *Psaltery* (1845), where it was set to "How gentle God's commands," is another popular alternative tune in present-day hymnals. It is a tune that Mason arranged from Johann (Hans) Georg Nägeli (1708–1836), Swiss publisher and pioneer in music education.

The harmonization is also by Lowell Mason.

I LOVE YOUR KINGDOM, LORD 296

While president of Yale College, Timothy Dwight, at the request of the General Association of the Presbyterian Churches of Connecticut, made a revision of Isaac Watts' (*LW* 53, et al.) *The Psalms of David Imitated* (1719), thus to make them more palatable to Americans following the American Revolution. It is in the resultant *Psalms of David by Isaac Watts . . . by Timothy Dwight* (Hartford, 1800) that "I Love Thy Kingdom, Lord," appeared, constituting the last part of Psalm 137 and entitled "Love to the Church." Originally in eight stanzas, the cento here given in updated form was prepared by the Inter-Lutheran Commission on Worship for inclusion in *Lutheran Book of Worship* (1978).

Incidentally, Dwight's addition to Watts of 33 of his own hymns and paraphrases contributed so greatly to the success of, what was called, Dwight's Watts, that it was used extensively in Congregational and Presbyterian churches in Connecticut.

ST. THOMAS (WILLIAMS) is an abbreviated version of HOLBURN, set to Charles Wesley's "Soldiers of Christ, Arise" (*SBH* 564) in the 1763 edition of Aaron Williams' *The Universal Psalmodist*. Containing the note "never before printed" has caused the tune to be thought of as a composition of Williams. The shortened form, called ST. THOMAS, appeared in Williams' *New Universal Psalmodist* (1770) set to "Great Is the Lord Our God," a version of Psalm 48, and again in Isaac Smith's *Collection of Psalm-Tunes in Three Parts* (c. 1780).

This bright, sturdy, moving tune has been sung by Christians on both sides of the Atlantic for two centuries and still appears fresh at every turn. Unquestionably it ranks among the best of the short meter tunes—a stanza-form made up of two couplets, the first containing 12 syllables and the second 14, resulting in brevity that rules out wordiness!

The harmonization is from *Lutheran Book of Worship* (1978).

A MIGHTY FORTRESS IS OUR GOD 297

A mighty fortress is our God,
A sword and shield victorious;
He breaks the cruel oppressor's rod
And wins salvation glorious.
The old satanic foe
Has sworn to work us woe.
With craft and dreadful might
He arms himself to fight.
On earth he has no equal.

Ein feste Burg ist unser Gott,
Ein gute Wehr und Waffen;
Er hilft uns frei aus aller Not,
Die uns jetzt hat betroffen.
Der alt' böse Feind,
Mit Ernst er's jetzt meint,
Gross' Macht und viel List
Sein' grausam' Rüstung ist,
Auf Erd' ist nicht seinsgleichen.

No strength of ours can match his might.
We would be lost, rejected.
But now a champion comes to fight,
Whom God himself elected.
You ask who this may be?
The Lord of hosts is he,
Christ Jesus, mighty Lord,
God's only Son, adored.
He holds the field victorious.

Mit unsrer Macht ist nichts getan,
Wir sind gar bald verloren;
Es streit't für uns der rechte Mann,
Den Gott hat selbst erkoren.
Fragst du, wer der ist?
Er heisst Jesus Christ,
Der Herr Zebaoth,
Und ist kein andrer Gott,
Das Feld muss er behalten.

Though hordes of devils fill the land
All threat'ning to devour us,
We tremble not, unmoved we stand;
They cannot overpow'r us.
Let this world's tyrant rage;
In battle we'll engage.
His might is doomed to fail;
God's judgment must prevail!
One little word subdues him.

Und wenn die Welt voll Teufel wär'
Und wollt' uns gar verschlingen,
So fürchten wir uns nicht so sehr,
Es soll uns doch gelingen.
Der Fürst dieser Welt,
Wie sau'r er sich stellt,
Tut er uns doch nicht,
Das macht, er ist gericht't,
Ein' Wörtlein kann ihn fällen.

God's Word forever shall abide,
No thanks to foes, who fear it;
For God himself fights by our side
With weapons of the Spirit.
Were they to take our house,
Goods, honor, child, or spouse,
Though life be wrenched away,
They cannot win the day.
The Kingdom's ours forever!

Das Wort sie sollen lassen stahn
Und kein'n Dank dazu haben;
Er ist bei uns wohl auf dem Plan
Mit seinem Geist und Gaben.
Nehmen sie dein Leib,
Gut, Ehr', Kind und Weib:
Lass fahren dahin,
Sie haben's kein'n Gewinn,
Das Reich muss uns doch bleiben.

The English version of Martin Luther's German text given here was prepared by the Inter-Lutheran Commission on Worship for inclusion in *Lutheran Book of Worship*. (Cf. *LW* 298.)

EIN FESTE BURG. The tune is based on the form that appeared in Johann König's *Harmonischer Lieder-Schatz* of 1738 (Zahn 7377d). The harmonization is from the *Service Book and Hymnal* (1958).

This tune differs from that in *LW* 298 in its rhythmic makeup. It is in the isorhythmic form, in contrast to the polyrhythmic, or rhythmic, form in which Luther cast *LW* 298. Characteristic of the latter is the liberal mixture of different metric patterns, a quality manifested in some of the early Reformation chorales that gives them a distinctive, fast-flowing motion. Added to this is the frequent appearance of a shortened note value at the beginning of a phrase—the so-called *Freudensprung*. Once learned, congregations have little difficulty singing these delightfully varied polyrhythmic chorales. Their beat differs little from that of the Negro spiritual or jazz idiom. (See essay: Polyrhythmic and Isometric Chorales, p. 822.)

In contrast, the isorhythmic form (*LW* 297) is a smoothed-out version; both tune and harmony move in the same rhythmic values, exemplifying a more vertical, chordlike progression on a strict metric grid. The chorales of this sort are generally of later vintage than the 16th century. Incidentally, J. S. Bach (*LW* 89) is not the first to come out with the isorhythmic form of Luther's rhythmic tune. Already in 1616 a somewhat smoothed-out version appeared in a Strassburg hymnal (Zahn 7377b); in 1715 it even appeared in triple meter (Zahn 7377c).

298 A MIGHTY FORTRESS IS OUR GOD

A mighty fortress is our God,
A trusty shield and weapon.
He helps us free from ev'ry need
That hath us now o'ertaken.
The old evil foe
Now means deadly woe;
Deep guile and great might
Are his dread arms in fight;
On earth is not his equal.

With might of ours can naught be done,
Soon were our loss effected;
But for us fights the valiant One,
Whom God himself elected.
Ask ye, Who is this?
Jesus Christ it is,
Of sabaoth Lord,
And there's none other God;
He holds the field forever.

Though devils all the world should fill,
All eager to devour us,
We tremble not, we fear no ill,
They shall not overpow'r us.
This world's prince may still
Scowl fierce as he will,
He can harm us none,
He's judged; the deed is done;
One little word can fell him.

The Word they still shall let remain
Nor any thanks have for it;
He's by our side upon the plain
With his good gifts and Spirit.
And take they our life,
Goods, fame, child, and wife,

Ein feste Burg ist unser Gott,
Ein gute Wehr und Waffen;
Er hilft uns frei aus aller Not,
Die uns jetzt hat betroffen.
Der alt' böse Feind,
Mit Ernst er's jetzt meint,
Gross' Macht und viel List
Sein' grausam' Rüstung ist,
Auf Erd' ist nicht seinsgleichen.

Mit unsrer Macht ist nichts getan,
Wir sind gar bald verloren;
Es streit't für uns der rechte Mann,
Den Gott hat selbst erkoren.
Fragst du, wer der ist?
Er heisst Jesus Christ,
Der Herr Zebaoth,
Und ist kein andrer Gott,
Das Feld muss er behalten.

Und wenn die Welt voll Teufel wär'
Und wollt' uns gar verschlingen,
So fürchten wir uns nicht so sehr,
Es soll uns doch gelingen.
Der Fürst dieser Welt,
Wie sau'r er sich stellt,
Tut er uns doch nicht,
Das macht, er ist gericht't,
Ein' Wörtlein kann ihn fällen.

Das Wort sie sollen lassen stahn
Und kein'n Dank dazu haben;
Er ist bei uns wohl auf dem Plan
Mit seinem Geist und Gaben.
Nehmen sie dein Leib,
Gut, Ehr', Kind und Weib:

Though these all be gone, Our vict'ry has been won; The Kingdom ours remaineth.	Lass fahren dahin, Sie haben's kein'n Gewinn, Das Reich muss uns doch bleiben.

Numerous views have been advanced as to the time and place of the origin of this hymn that Heinrich Heine (1799–1856), German poet and critic, called the Marseillaise of the Reformation. All of them are simply conjecture. Friedrich Lucke, editor of volume 35 of Luther's Works, Weimar edition, considers it likely that this hymn appeared in Hans Weiss's Wittenberg hymnal of 1528 as well as in Joseph Klug's hymnal, 1529, both not extant. Leupold states that Andrew Rauscher's Erfurt hymnal, 1531, is the earliest extant hymnal in which it appeared. Based on Psalm 46, "Deus noster refugium et virtus," this hymn is more of an original production on the theme of David's psalm than a metrical paraphrase of it (Polack). F. Samuel Janzow says of it:

> This hymn is no outpouring of subjective religious lyric feeling but application of promises of God's inspired Scriptures to the needs and struggles of the Church. Its integrity and strength flow from the genuine faith with which Luther grasps the ancient promises of God and from the power with which this fusion of faith to the divine Word of grace arms the singer with Christ's victory.

Small wonder that among Luther's hymns (some 37 in all), this hymn takes first place. It was sung at the Diet of Augsburg (1555) and in all the churches of Saxony; sung on the streets and, thus heard, comforted Philip Melanchthon, Justus Jonas, and Kaspar Kreutziger as they entered Weimar, banished from Wittenberg in 1547. Etched in the history of Reformation times, it also became the national hymn of Protestant Germany. It was the battle hymn of the army of Gustavus Adolphus against the forces of Wallenstein at the battle of Lützen, 1632, in the Thirty Years' War, in which the king was slain but the battle was won for Protestantism.

This hymn has been translated into more languages than any other hymn in Christendom; its English translations number more than 100. While an exile in Germany, Miles Coverdale (c. 1488–c. 1568) became acquainted with Luther's hymns and made translations of a number of them, which he printed in *Goostly Psalmes and Spiritualle Songes* (c. 1537). His version of "A mighty fortress," although using Luther's meter and tune, reproduces only the first four lines of stanza 1. The first complete English translation appeared anonymously in *Lyra Davidica, or a Collection of Divine Songs and Hymns, Partly New Composed, Partly Translated from German and Latin Hymns: and set to easy and pleasant tunes*, published in 1708 by John Walsh, a well-known music printer. Of the numerous English translations, two versions merit special note. The first is by the Scottish historian, essayist, moral teacher, and rector Thomas Carlyle (1795–1881), beginning with "A safe stronghold our God is still." It first appeared in *Frasers Magazine* (1831). Carlyle's knowledge of Luther and his poetic gift resulted in what, in many respects, is the best English version. The second is by the Unitarian clergyman, professor of church history and German at Harvard, Fredrick Henry

Hedge (1805–90), beginning with "A mighty fortress is our God." It first appeared in the second edition of Dr. Furness's *Gems of German Verse* (1852). Except for the change of one word—the use of "Though" instead of "Let" in the seventh line of stanza 4—the translation in *Lutheran Worship* is that which appeared in *The Lutheran Hymnal* (1941). It is the composite translation taken from the Pennsylvania Lutheran *Church Book* (1868), prepared by the editorial committee of that book, based on Carlyle's version and on a version by W. M. Reynolds based on Carlyle's, which was included in the General Synod's *Collection* of 1850 (Polack). It is one of the many translations that captures the ruggedness of Luther's German as well as being a familiar one.

EIN FESTE BURG. This tune is also the work of Luther. Presumably it appeared in Joseph Klug's *Geistliche Lieder* (Wittenberg, 1529), copy of which is not extant. The earliest version extant today is in *Kirchegesang, mit vil schönen Psalmen vnd Melodey, gantz geendert un gemert* (Nürnberg, 1531). The harmonization is by Paul G. Bunjes. (For a discussion of this rhythmic type of chorale tune see hymn 297 as well as the essay: Polyrhythmic and Isometric Chorales, p. 822.)

Rightly does W. G. Polack say of this hymn:

> The good this hymn has done, the faith it has inspired, the hearts it has comforted, the influence it has exerted, cannot be measured and will first be revealed to us in eternity, where the saints of God will praise their Lord and redeemer for many blessings, not the least of which will be the privilege of having known and sung this hymn here on earth.

299 FIGHT THE GOOD FIGHT WITH ALL YOUR MIGHT

John S. B. Monsell, vicar of Guildford, wrote this hymn on February 14, 1834, for the Nineteenth Sunday after Trinity Sunday. It was published in his *Hymns of Love and Praise for the Church's Year* (1863) after first appearing in Ferguson's *Selection of Hymns for British Seamen* (1838). Based on 1 Timothy 6:12, it also recalls other texts of Scripture, namely, 2 Timothy 4:7–8; 1 Corinthians 9:24,26; and Ephesians 3:13.

The text in *Lutheran Worship* was taken over verbatim from *Lutheran Book of Worship* (1978). In it the second-person pronouns are updated, and stanzas 3 and 4 altered somewhat. The present form of stanza 3 is based on that in *The Hymnal 1940* of the Protestant Episcopal Church.

GRACE CHURCH, GANANOQUE. Composer Graham George named this tune for the church on the St. Lawrence Seaway where he served as organist from 1962–66. The tune was written for this text around 1950 and revised in 1962 for publication in *The Methodist Hymnal* (1964). From 1874, when Arthur Sullivan's (*LW* 515, 518) *Church Hymns* was published, William Boyd's (1847–1928) tune PENTECOST (*SBH* 557) was the standard setting for "Fight the Good Fight." Boyd himself at first objected to the coupling of text and tune, but it was 90 years before a more suitable tune supplanted it. George writes:

> There are two things wrong with the way this fine hymn is usually sung. One is that people don't recognize the fight is that of the Happy Warrior, though the words say it quite clearly; and the other is PENTECOST, which sings well, partly because the singer has only to establish and hold tight. I don't in fact deny the validity of very simple tunes which have this roof-raising capacity. I was brought up a Baptist, and anyone who has ever heard a churchfull of Baptists roaring their battle-song "Blest Be the Tie That Binds," must be incurably obstinate if he denies that something is going on. But "Fight the Good Fight," as to a lesser degree "Blest Be the Tie That Binds," has more in it than to serve merely as a sort of religious "Sieg Heil," and my purpose in GRACE CHURCH, GANANOQUE was to design a tune sufficiently obvious to have some chance of competing with the obviousness of PENTECOST, which would yet catch something of that "more-than-that" (Osborne, *If Such Holy Song*).

Admittedly, George's tune will undoubtedly present a serious challenge to many congregations.

The setting is from *The Methodist Hymnal* (1964).

DO NOT DESPAIR, O LITTLE FLOCK 300

Do not despair, O little flock,
Although the foes' fierce battle shock
Loud on all sides assail you!
Though at your fall they laugh, secure,
Their triumph cannot long endure;
Let not your courage fail you!

The cause is God's; obey his call
And to his hand commit your all
And fear no ill impending!
Though not yet seen by human eyes,
His Gideon shall for you arise,
God's Word and you defending.

As sure as God's own Word is true,
Not Satan, hell, nor all their crew
Can stand against this power.
Scorn and contempt their cup will fill,
For God is with his people still,
Their help and their strong tower.

Verzage nicht, du Häuflein klein,
Obschon die Feinde willens sein,
Dich gänzlich zu verstören,
Und suchen deinen Untergang,
Davon dir wird recht angst und bang;
Es wird nicht lange währen.

Dich tröste nur, dass deine Sach'
Ist Gottes, dem befiehl die Rach'
Und lass allein ihn walten!
Er wird durch seinen Gideon,
Den er wohl weiss, dir helfen schon,
Dich und sein Wort erhalten.

So wahr Gott ist und sein Wort,
Muss Teufel, Welt und Höllenpfort',
Und was dem will anhangen,
Endlich werden zu Hohn und Spott;
Gott ist mit uns und wir mit Gott,
Den Sieg woll'n wir erlangen!

Then help us, Lord! Now hear our prayer. Defend your people ev'rywhere For your own name's sake. Amen. Then with a mighty hymn of praise Your Church in earth and heav'n will raise Their songs of triumph. Amen	Amen, das hilf, Herr Jesu Christ, Dieweil du unser Schutzherr bist, Hilf uns durch deinen Namen: So wollen wir, deine Gemein', Dich loben und dir dankbar sein Und fröhlich singen Amen.

This hymn has been variously attributed to King Gustavus Adolphus of Sweden, to Johann Michael Altenburg, and to Jacob Fabricius.

Shortly after the death of Gustavus Adolphus in the battle of Lützen, November 9, 1632, there appeared a pamphlet with a long title beginning "Epicedeon Lamentabile... Lament and Praise Hymn over the departure in death of King Gustavus Adolphus . . ." in which this text, in three stanzas, appears, a text that is called the King's Swansong, a song that his majesty sang fervently to God before his fall at Lützen. That the king actually sang it is unquestioned. He can hardly, however, be considered the author. In a Leipzig hymn book of 1638 provided by Jeremiah Weber, this hymn appeared with the heading "A heart-rejoicing hymn of Consolation upon the watchword God with us used by the Evangelical army in the Battle of Leipzig, 17 September 1631 composed by M. Johann Altenburg, pastor at Gross Sommern in Düringen." This has resulted in generally attributing the hymn's authorship to Altenburg, despite the fact that it is evidently the musical setting that is here referred to. Today, based on a brief reference in a 17th century German manuscript indicating that Gustavus Adolphus wrote the prose version of the hymn prior to the Battle of Lützen and that at his request Chaplain Jacob Fabricius versified the same, the text is credited to Fabricius. The foregoing represents the case for his authorship in *Die Lieder unserer Kirche* by Johannes Kulp.

As to the origin of stanza 4 (the present hymnals of the Lutheran territorial churches in Germany give only stanzas 1, 2, 3), this was perhaps added by an unknown hand. In times past, the hymn's popularity (it was often sung in battles against Napoleon) is attested by the numerous stanzas that were gradually added—three, then five, later 10, and in 1673 there were 25.

The translation appearing in *Lutheran Worship* (1982) was prepared by the Inter-Lutheran Commission on Worship, based on that of Catherine Winkworth in her *Lyra Germanica* (1855), for inclusion in *Lutheran Book of Worship* (1978).

KOMMT HER ZU MIR. For comments on this tune see hymn 261.

The harmonization was prepared by Paul G. Bunjes for inclusion in *Lutheran Worship* (1982).

301 LORD OF OUR LIFE

Lord of our life and God of our salvation, Star of our night and hope of ev'ry nation: Hear and receive your Church's supplication, Lord God Almighty.	Christe, du Beistand deiner Kreuzgemeine, Eile, mit Hilf' und Rettung uns erscheine; Steure den Feinden, ihre Blut-gerichte Mache zunichte!

See round your ark the hungry billows curling, See how your foes their banners are unfurling. Lord, while their poisoned arrows they are hurling, You can preserve us.	Streite doch selber für uns arme Kinder, Wehre dem Teufel, seine Macht verhinder'; Alles was kämpfet wider deine Glieder, Stürze danieder!
Lord, you can help when earthly armor fails us; Lord, you can save when deadly sin assails us; And in the day when hell itself appalls us, Grant us your peace, Lord:	Frieden bei Kirch' und Schulen uns beschere, Frieden zugleich der Obrigkeit gewähre, Frieden dem Herzen, Frieden dem Gewissen Gib zu geniessen!
Peace in our hearts, where sinful thoughts are raging, Peace in your Church, our troubled souls assuaging, Peace when the world its endless war is waging, Peace in your heaven.	Also wird zeitlich deine Güt' erhoben, Also wird ewig und ohn' Ende loben Dich, o du Wächter deiner armen Herde, Himmel und Erde.

It is in the sorrow and afflictions of the Thirty Years' War (1618–48) that the strong, objective faith of former times in hymnody is brought into closer relationship to actual life situations, a fact clearly evidenced in the so-called Cross-and-Comfort hymns (see hymns 420–29). But from that war is also noted a certain heroism of faith, as, for instance, reflected in this, what might be called, battle-hymn by Matthäus Apelles Löwenstern, a hymn that appeared in the Breslau *Geistliche Kirchen-und Haus-Music* (1644). Entitled "Sapphic ode. For spiritual and temporal peace," it is a hymn in which he vividly describes the perils faced by the church and bravely affirms the supremacy of God. Personally suffering his share during the ravaging Thirty Years' War, he fervently prays for the church's deliverance and peace.

The English translation is the result of that passionate and protracted controversy in the English Church aroused by the Oxford Movement. Now, two centuries after Löwenstern's time, Philip Pusey appropriates the former's thoughts in his paraphrase, "Lord of Our Life and God of Our Salvation," an English version published in Alexander Reinagle's *Psalms and Hymn Tunes* (Oxford, 1840). Of this hymn Pusey said, "It refers to the state of the Church . . . the Church of England, 1834—assailed from without, enfeebled and distracted within, but on the eve of a great awakening." Pusey may have over painted the picture, but the hymn has become one of the great battle-hymns of the Church Militant.

ISTE CONFESSOR is one of those French church melodies briefly discussed at hymn 175. Perhaps the finest of such tunes, it served as the setting for the eighth-century Latin hymn, "Iste confessor domini sacratus," in the Poitiers *Antiphoner* (1746). Because of its appearance also in the *Rouen Processionale* (1763), it is sometimes called ROUEN.

The harmonization is by Paul G. Bunjes.

302 RISE, MY SOUL, TO WATCH AND PRAY

Rise, my soul, to watch and pray;
From your sleep awaken;
Be not by the evil day
Unawares o'ertaken.
Satan's prey
Oft are they
Who secure are sleeping
And no watch are keeping.

Watch against the world that frowns
Darkly to dismay you;
Watch when it your wishes crowns,
Smiling to betray you.
Watch and see,
You are free
From false friends who charm you
While they seek to harm you.

Watch against yourself, my soul,
Lest with grace you trifle;
Let not self your thoughts control
Nor God's mercy stifle.
Pride and sin
Lurk within,
All your hopes to shatter
Heed not when they flatter.

But while watching, also pray
To the Lord unceasing.
God alone can make you free,
Strength and faith increasing,
So that still
Mind and will
Heartfelt praises tender
And true service render.

Mache dich, mein Geist, bereit,
Wache, fleh und bete,
Dass dich nicht die böse Zeit
Unverhofft betrete;
Denn es ist
Satans List
Über viele Frommen
Zuer Versuchung kommen.

Wach, dass dich nicht die Welt
Durch Gewalt bezwinge
Oder, wenn sie sich verstellt,
Wieder an sich bringe.
Wach und sieh,
Damit nie
Viel von falschen Brüdern
Unter deinen Gliedern!

Wache dazu auch für dich,
Für dein Fleisch und Herze,
Damit es nicht liederlich
Gottes Gnad' verscherze;
Denn es ist
Voller List
Und kann sich bald heucheln
Und in Hoffart schmeicheln.

Bete aber auch dabei
Mitten in dem Wachen;
Denn der Herre muss dich frei
Von dem allem machen,
Was dich drückt
Und bestrickt,
Dass du schläfrig bleibest
Und sein Werk nicht treibest.

Johann B. Freystein's laudable German text, originally in 10 stanzas and based on the Lord's words in Matthew 26:41, first appeared, according to Koch, in the *Geistreiches Gesangbuch* (Darmstadt, 1698). The English form given here is an adaptation of that by Catherine Winkworth in her *Chorale Book for England* (1863) as prepared by the Inter-Lutheran Commission on Worship for inclusion in *Lutheran Book of Worship* (1978).

STRAF MICH NICHT. One concern of Winkworth's *Chorale Book for England* (1863) was that her hymn translations be accompanied by their "proper" tunes. This tune was set to "Rise, my soul" in that volume. It comes from the *Hundert ahnmüthig- und sonder-bahr geistlichen Arien* (1694), published as an appendix to the Dresden *Geist- und Lehr-reiches Kirchen- und Hauss-Buch* of the same year. Zahn states that the tune, set to Johann G. Albinus' "Straf mich nicht in deinem Zorn" in the *Hundert Arien*, appeared in an earlier (prior to 1681) manuscript collection of dance music, but it is unknown whether it was originally a dance tune or a hymn tune. A fine, notable tune in isometric form, it represents one of the two quite dissimilar chorale styles in the latter half of the 17th century and in Pietism, the other being the solo-aria style (cf., for instance, *LW* 77, 277, and 445, to mention but a few).

The setting was prepared by Wilhelm Quampen, a *nom de plume* of Paul G. Bunjes.

RISE! TO ARMS! WITH PRAYER EMPLOY YOU 303

Rise! To arms! With prayer employ you,
O Christians, lest the foe destroy you;
For Satan has designed your fall.
Wield God's Word, the weapon glorious;
Against all foes be thus victorious.
God will set you above them all.
Fear not the hordes of hell,
Here is Emmanuel.
Hail the Savior!
The strong foes yield
To Christ, our shield,
And we, the victors, hold the field.

Cast afar the world's vain pleasure
And boldly strive for heav'nly treasure.
Be steadfast in the Savior's might.
Trust the Lord, who stands beside you,
For Jesus from all harm will hide you.
By faith you conquer in the fight.
Take courage, weary soul!
Look forward to the goal!
Joy awaits you,
The race well run,
Your long war won,
Your crown shines splendid as the sun.

Wisely fight, for time is fleeting;
The hours of grace are fast retreating;
Short, short is this our earthly way.
When the Lord the dead will waken
And sinners all by fear are shaken,
The saints with joy will greet that day.
Praise God, our triumph's sure.
We need not long endure
Scorn and trial.
Our Savior King
His own will bring
To that great glory which we sing.

Rüstet euch, ihr Christenleute!
Die Feinde suchen euch zur Beute,
Ja Satan selbst hat eu'r begehrt.
Wappnet euch mit Gottes Worte
Und kämpfet frisch an jedem Orte,
Damit ihr bleibet unversehrt!
Ist euch der Feind zu schnell,
Hier ist Immanuel!
Hosianna!
Der Starke fällt
Durch diesen Held,
Und wir behalten mit das Feld.

Reinigt euch von euren Lüsten,
Besieget sie, die ihr seid Christen
Und stehet in des Herren Kraft!
Stärket euch in Jesu Namen,
Dass ihr nicht strauchelt wie die Lahmen!
Wo ist des Glaubens Eigenschaft?
Wer hier ermüden will,
Der schaue auf das Ziel,
Da ist Freude.
Wohlan, so seid
Zum Kampf bereit,
So krönet euch die Ewigkeit!

Streitet recht die wenig Jahre,
Eh' ihr kommt auf die Totenbahre!
Kurz, kurz ist unser Lebenslauf.
Wenn Gott wird die Toten wecken
Und Christus wird die Welt erschrecken,
So stehen wir mit Freuden auf.
Gott Lob, wir sind versöhnt!
Dass uns die Welt noch höhnt,
Währt nicht lange,
Und Gottes Sohn
Hat längstens schon
Uns beigelegt die Ehrenkron'.

This is one of three hymns credited to Wilhelm E. Arends that Freylinghausen included in his *Geistreiches Gesangbuch* (1714). Koch describes it as "a call to arms for spiritual conflict and victory," a hymn that soon received wider circulation.

The translation is by John M. Sloan in Wilson's *Service of Praise* (1865), slightly altered.

WACHET AUF. For comments on the tune see hymn 177.

Richard W. Gieseke prepared the harmonization for inclusion in *Lutheran Worship* (1982).

304 THE SON OF GOD GOES FORTH TO WAR

Reginald Heber's posthumous *Hymns written and adapted to the Weekly Church Services of the Year* (1827) included this text for the day of St. Stephen, First Martyr, referred to in the second stanza.

Refuting those who would change the war imagery of this hymn, pacifist William P. Merrill stated in a sermon to the Hymn Society of America:

> It would be a distinct loss, and a great one, to the kingdom of God, if we should cease to sing "The Son of God Goes Forth to War," or to change it as has been definitely suggested, to the statement, "The Son of God Goes Forth for Peace." The "blood-red banner" is stained with His own blood, not with that of His foes; and the whole hymn is full of the martyr spirit at its noblest. To let that die out would mean the death of Christianity. (Jan. 20, 1935, at The Brick Presbyterian Church, New York City)

Lutheran Worship's version follows Heber's original except in two words, "those who" for "them that" in stanza 2.

ALL SAINTS NEW, also known as CUTLER, was written by Henry S. Cutler for the above text and first appeared in John Ireland Tucker's *Hymnal with Tunes Old and New* (1872). Thereafter it entered the *Hymnal* of the Protestant Episcopal Church in 1874.

The setting of this strong, moving tune is from the *Service Book and Hymnal* (1958).

305 STAND UP, STAND UP FOR JESUS

George Duffield based this hymn, originally in six stanzas, on the dying words of a personal friend and fellow clergyman, Dudley Atkins Tyng, minister of Epiphany Episcopal Church in Philadelphia. Tyng had preached to a crowd of 5,000 members of the Philadelphia Young Men's Christian Association one Sunday morning in 1858; the following Wednesday, taking a study break, he visited the barn where a mule was operating a threshing machine. As he patted the mule's neck, Tyng's sleeve was caught in the machinery, wrenching his arm from the socket. His death occurred a short time later. Because Tyng had been criticized for championing the oppressed, some feel the words "Stand up for Jesus" had special significance for him; at any rate, they had formed his final message to the YMCA.

Duffield used his hymn, incorporating some specific references to Tyng and his accidental death, the following Sunday, after preaching from Ephesians 6:14. The text was printed on a flyleaf for the Sunday school; from there it "found its way into a Baptist newspaper" and then was included in the *Church Psalmist* (1859). Samuel W. Duffield, son of George Duffield, in notes on the hymn in his *English Hymns* (1886), modestly states:

> This hymn has had such a history and has been so extensively honored of the Lord in the work of the Church that it absolves the present writer from any feeling of delicacy which he might otherwise have experienced in its annotation. It will remain to him as one of his own happiest memories that the same hand which pens these lines made the first copy of this fine lyric for the press.

The altered and updated text here given is that prepared by the Inter-Lutheran Commission on Worship for inclusion in *Lutheran Book of Worship* (1978).

WEBB (MORNING LIGHT, GOODWIN), a tune that is known the world over, was composed by George J. Webb, while on a voyage from England to America, as a vehicle for the secular song, "'Tis dawn, the lark is singing." It was first published in *The Odeon: a Collection of Secular Melodies, designed for adult singing schools and for social music parties* (Boston, 1837), edited by Webb and Lowell Mason (*LW* 115, et al.). The Odeon was a vacant theatre in Boston which Mason and Webb initially used for some of the classes of their Boston Academy of Music. Webb's tune was first used with a hymn text in *The Wesleyan Psalmist* (Boston, 1842), a small pocket-size book for use at "Camp meetings . . . prayer meetings and other occasions of social devotion." Therein it was set by its Methodist editor, M. L. Scudder, to Samuel F. Smith's "The morning light is breaking" (*TLH* 497) and named MILLENIAL DAWN. Text and tune soon became popular and appeared in various other collections with a variety of names: GOODWIN in Mason and Webb publications; WEBB in *The Shawm* (1853) by Bradbury and Root; MORNING LIGHT by editors of English hymnals. The association of the tune with Duffield's text in Sankey's songbooks and in the 1875 edition of *Hymns Ancient and Modern* confirmed the tune as the proper one for this text.

Despite the fact that the tune exhibits no distinguishing marks of craftsmanship, it is invariably sung with gusto provided it is not sung too frequently.

The harmonization is from the *Service Book and Hymnal* (1958).

306 JERUSALEM, O CITY FAIR AND HIGH

Jerusalem, O city fair and high,
Your tow'rs I yearn to see;
My longing heart to you would gladly fly.
It will not stay with me.
Elijah's chariot take me
Above the lower skies,
To heaven's bliss awake me,
Released from earthly ties.

O happy day, O yet far happier hour,
When will you come at last,
When by my gracious Father's love and pow'r
I see that portal vast?
From heaven's shining regions
To greet me gladly come
Your blessed angel legions
To bid me welcome home.

The patriarchs' and prophets' noble train,
With all Christ's foll'wers true,
Who washed their robes and cleansed sin's guilty stain,
Sing praises ever new!
I see them shine forever,
Resplendent as the sun,
In light diminished never,
Their glorious freedom won.

Unnumbered choirs before the shining throne
Their joyful anthems raise
Till heaven's arches echo with the tone
Of that great hymn of praise.
And all its host rejoices,
And all its blessed throng
Unite their myriad voices
In one eternal song.

Jerusalem, du hochgebaute Stadt,
Wollt' Gott, ich wär in dir!
Mein sehnlich Herz so gross Verlangen hat
Und ist nicht mehr bei mir.
Weit über Berg und Tale,
Weit über blaches Feld
Schwingt es sich überalle
Und eilt aus dieser Welt.

O schöner Tag und noch viel schönre Stund',
Wann wirst du kommen schier,
Da ich mit Lust, mit freiem Freudenmund
Die Seele geb' von mir
In Gottes treue Hände
Zum auserwählten Pfand,
Dass sie mit Heil anlände
In jenem Vaterland!

Propheten gross und Patriarchen hoch,
Auch Christen insgemein,
Die weiland dort trugen des Kreuzes Joch
Und der Tyrannen Pein,
Schau' ich in Ehren schweben,
In Freiheit überall,
Mit Klarheit hell umgeben,
Mit sonnenlichtem Strahl.

Mit Jubelklang, mit Insrumenten schön,
In Chören ohne Zahl,
Dass von dem Klang und von dem süssen Ton
Erbebt der Freudensaal;
Mit hundertausend Zungen,
Mit Stimmen noch viel mehr,
Wie von Anfang gesungen
Das himmelische Heer.

Johann Meyfart's *Tuba Novissima* (Coburg, 1626) contained four sermons on death, judgment, eternal life, and eternal punishment. This hymn, originally in eight stanzas, concluded the third sermon, based on Matthew 17:1–9, and was headed "On the joy and glory which all the elect are to expect in the life everlasting."

Richard Lauxmann, editor/reviser of the eighth edition of Koch, writes:

> The hymn is a precious gem in our Treasury of Song, in which one clearly sees that from it the whole heart of the poet shines out on us. Meyfart had his face turned wholly to the future, to the Last Things; and with a richly fanciful mysticism full of deep and strong faith he united a flaming zeal for the House of the Lord and against the abuses of his times.

Winkworth published her translation in *Lyra Germanica* (second series, 1858) and again in the *Chorale Book for England* (1863), where it was set to this tune. It appears here in altered and updated form.

JERUSALEM, DU HOCHGEBAUTE STADT. Although ascribed to Melchior Franck, the origin of this tune cannot be established with certainty. It first appeared with the above hymn text in 1663 in an Erfurt hymnal entitled *Christlich neu-vermehrt und gebessertes Gesangbuch*, 40 years after the appearance of the text and almost 25 years after the death of the alleged composer.

The popularity of Meyfart's hymn is unquestionably enhanced by this notable tune that, in the words of Koch, "is a pearl among evangelical hymns." Winterfeld says of it: "While Philipp Nicolai begins his beautiful hymn, 'Wake, awake,' about the heavenly Jerusalem with a strong soaring flight, this tune, on the other hand, sinks to the depths of an unfathomable mystery, however, not in gloomy dreaming but in joyful, blessed surrender, sounding forth with genuine ecstasy."

The setting was prepared by George Leonard, a *nom de plume* of Paul G. Bunjes, for inclusion in *Lutheran Worship* (1982).

JERUSALEM, MY HAPPY HOME 307

A manuscript in the British Museum, dating from perhaps the late 16th or early 17th centuries, may possibly be the earliest source of this hymn text. This manuscript contains a poem of 26 stanzas entitled "A Song Mad(e) by F. B. P. to the tune of Diana." Attempts to ascertain the identity of F. B. P. have proven less than satisfactory. A suggestion that continues to be given precedence is that the initials may mean Francis Baker, Presbyter, a priest who is said to have been imprisoned in the Tower of London. John Julian concludes that both this hymn and a similar one by W. P. Prid, "O Master Dear, Jerusalem" are based on passages in an earlier 16th-century translation of the volume, often falsely attributed to St. Augustine of Hippo (354–430), known as *Liber Meditationum*, published in Venice in 1553. About this work Julian says, "At the time of the Reformation, Roman Catholic and Protestant alike vied in translations of it, in whole or in part." In all such versions there is an intense longing to be released from earthly bonds and received into the joys of the heavenly Jerusalem. Leonard Ellinwood has said, "Here is sacred folk-literature at its very finest, coming at a time when the singing of English congregations was limited to the metrical paraphrases of the Psalms." (*The Hymnal 1940 Companion*)

LAND OF REST is a traditional tune edited and harmonized by Annabel Morris Buchanan in her *Folk Hymns of America* (New York, 1938). She states that as a child she first heard it from her grandmother, Sarah Ann (Love) Foster, who sang it to the lines:

O land of rest, for thee I sigh,
When will the moment come
When I shall lay my armor by
And dwell in place at home?

Of possibly Scottish or north English origin, she found it widely sung in the Appalachian region. Similarities between LAND OF REST and the tune of "Swing Low, Sweet Chariot" have been observed. The Negro spiritual is a pentatonic tune; LAND OF REST is hexatonic but with a strong pentatonic flavor, since the fourth degree of the scale (B♭) appears only twice.

The original instruction "to the tune of Diana" refers to the English folk song ("Diana and her darlings deare"), also known as ROGERO in William Chappell's *Popular Music of the Olden Time*. The text of "Diana and her darlings deare" may be seen in Hyder E. Rollins' edition of *A Handful of Pleasant Delights* (1566, reprint 1924).

308 YE WATCHERS AND YE HOLY ONES

This popular hymn by J. Athelstan Riley bids Christians to lift up their voices with the whole creation in the praise of God. Originally in four stanzas, it was written for inclusion in the English Hymnal (1906), a book in which Riley was a leading figure. Clearly in evidence is his knowledge of early Eastern churches and their liturgies.

In stanza 1, he calls upon the nine orders of angels codified by Dionysius the Areopagite (c. 500) in *Celestial Hierarchy*. The original stanza 2, inadvertently omitted in *Lutheran Worship* (1982), is a direct paraphrase of the *Theotokion*, a stanza (*troparion*) of liturgical hymnography addressed to the virgin Mary and calling on her (*theotokos*, literally God-bearer) in praise of the Lord. It was this term that Cyril (376–444), patriarch of Alexandria, defended against Nestorius (d. c. 451), patriarch of Constantinople, a term upheld by the Third Ecumenical Council at Ephesus in 431. The *Theotokion* was sung in the early Eastern churches as the conclusion to the choir office. Riley's omitted stanza reads:

O higher than the cherubim
More glorious than the seraphim,
Lead their praises, Alleluia!
Thou Bearer of th' eternal Word,
Most gracious, magnify the Lord, Alleluia! (*TLH* 475, st. 2)

Stanza 2 in *Lutheran Worship*—Riley's original stanza 3—is reflective of early litanic prayers in its calling on the souls, patricarchs, and prophets to praise the Lord, forms of prayer that appeared and were developed in the East from the end of the third century and in the West from the late fifth century.

Calling on God's creatures—animate and inanimate, as well as persons—to praise God is a poetic device called *apostrophic*, a device that occurs frequently in psalmody (see, for instance, Psalm 148).

LASST UNS ERFREUEN. Riley's text was originally coupled to this tune. It matches the tune's unusual meter so well that it is sometimes thought, mistakenly, to be a translation of a German hymn. For comments on the tune and its harmonization see hymn 131.

JERUSALEM THE GOLDEN 309

Jerusalem the golden,
With milk and honey blest,
Beneath your contemplation
Sink heart and voice oppressed.
I know not, oh, I know not
What joys await us there,
What radiancy of glory,
What bliss beyond compare.

They stand, those halls of Zion,
Conjubilant with song
And bright with many an angel
And all the martyr throng.
The prince is ever in them;
The daylight is serene;
The pastures of the blessed
Are decked in glorious sheen.

There is the throne of David,
And there, from care released,
The shout of those who triumph,
The song of those who feast.
And they, who with their leader
Have conquered in the fight,
Forever and forever
Are clad in robes of white.

Oh, sweet and blessed country,
The home of God's elect!
Oh, sweet and blessed country
That eager hearts expect!
In mercy, Jesus, bring us
To that dear land of rest!
You are, with God the Father
And Spirit, ever blest.

Urbs Sion aurea,
patria lactea,
cive decora,
omne cor obruis,
omnibus obstuis
et cor et ora.

Nescio, nescio, quae iubilatio,
lux tibi qualis,
quam socialia gaudia,
gloria
quam specialis.

Sunt Sion atria
coniubilantia,
martyre plena, cive micantia,
principe stantia,
luce serena.

Sunt ibi pascua
mentibus afflua
praestita sanctis;
regis ibi thronus,
agminis et sonus est epulantis.

Gens duce splendida,
contio candida
vestibus albis,
sunt sine fletibus
in Sion aedibus,
aedibus almus. Amen

This hymn and also "The Clouds of Judgment Gather" (*LW* 463) are portions of the great hymn of nearly 3,000 lines entitled *De contemptu mundi*, written in the difficult dactylic hexameter meter by Bernard of Cluny, a work in which he attacks the evils of his time in contrast to the joys of heaven. Small wonder that, upon completion of the work, Bernard remarked, "Unless the Spirit of wisdom and understanding had flowed in upon me, I could have not put together so long a work in so difficult a meter."

Regarding the translation of this section of Bernard's long hymn, with but one alteration it is the altered and updated form prepared by the Inter-Lutheran Commission on Worship for inclusion in *Lutheran Book of Worship* (1978) based on John Mason Neale's translation from his *Medieval Hymns and Sequences* (1851) that is here used. The alteration: "What social joys are there" in stanza 1 was changed to "What joys await us there," the wording in *The Lutheran Hymnal* (1941).

EWING, also called ARGYLE, ST. BEDE'S, and BERNARD, was composed by Alexander Ewing and originally set to "For thee, O dear, dear country," Part IV of Bernard of Cluny's hymn, and published in Grey's *Manual of Psalm and Hymn Tunes* (1857). It appeared with the present text in the first edition of *Hymns Ancient and Modern* (1861) and has been associated with it ever since. William H. Monk changed the original 3/2 meter of the tune to 4/2 for inclusion in *Hymns Ancient and Modern*, and that without the consent of the composer, who was out of the country at the time. In 1861 John M. Neale, whose translation was set to EWING, wrote:

> I have so often been asked as to what tune the words of Bernard may be sung, that I may mention that of Mr. Ewing, the earliest written, the best known, and with children the most popular; no small proof in my estimation of the goodness of church music.

Concerning the rhythmic change, Alexander Ewing stated: "In my opinion the alteration of the rhythm has very much vulgarized my little tune. It now seems to me a good deal like a polka. I hate to hear it." Actually, the change added dignity to the tune, ridding it of its jerky rhythm! The wide range of the tune (a 10th) necessitates a careful choice of key, lest the tune be either too high or too low. The upward movement of phrases five and six, arriving at the pitch-height accent in the latter, contributes greatly to the tune's impressiveness.

Paul G. Bunjes prepared the harmonization for inclusion in *Lutheran Worship* (1982).

310 LOOK TOWARD THE MOUNTAINS

For some unknown reason this hymn was placed in the category of The Church Triumphant when, according to its author F. Samuel Janzow, it was specifically intended as a processional or entrance hymn with banners and led by the cross on its way to the chancel. In the words of the author, "The hymn invites worshipers to look both toward Sinai's Law and Mount Calvary's Gospel and for the distinctive, contrasting, vital message of each." The author explains:

The appropriate response to 'love's ten standards' unfurled on Mt. Sinai (that show how tattered lie lives' 'best banners') is penitent awe and dread amid the flarings of the moral Law's holy lightnings. This experience prepares one to see with great joy the surpassing glory from the heights where the Gospel trumpets sound forth the messages of that saving grace that takes the Christian worshipers up into God's forgiving and loving embrace. Since Christ is the way to the Father (st. 5), therefore follow his cross (st. 6), the cross that stands both for sin's penalty and the divine rescue from it, follow it into the Law and Gospel's heights to adore the Triune God who is both perfect in holiness and infinite in grace.

Such are the powerful and yet comforting thoughts that inspired the author to write this hymn text while engaged at the time in newly translating C. F. W. Walther's (*LW* 138) classic *Die rechte Unterscheidung von Gesetz und Evangelium* (The Proper Distinction between Law and Gospel [St. Louis, 1929]), a task never completed, impressed as he also was with Walther's method of proclaiming repentance and the remission of sins.

ERSCHIENEN IST DER HERRLICH TAG. For comments on this tune and its harmonization see hymn 147.

311 LIFT HIGH THE CROSS

The original version was written by George W. Kitchin, Anglican clergyman, for a festival of the Society for the Propagation of the Gospel held in his cathedral at Winchester, June 1887. Very likely it owes something to Emperor Constantine's vision in 312 of the Cross of Christ in the sky and the words, "In hoc signo vinces" (In this sign you shall conquer) as related by the historian Eusebius (c. 260–c. 339). The text generally sung today is the revision by Michael R. Newbolt, canon of Chester Cathedral, that he prepared, in 12 stanzas, the refrain counted as the first, for inclusion in the 1916 Supplement to *Hymns Ancient and Modern* (1861).

The omitted stanzas, in updated form, are as follows:

This is the sign which Satan's legions fear
And angels veil their faces to revere.

Saved by this cross whereon their Lord was slain,
The sons of Adam their lost home regain.

From north and south, from east and west they raise
In growing unison their songs of praise.

Let every race and every language tell
Of him who saves our souls from death and hell.

From farthest regions let them homage bring,
And on his cross adore their Savior King.

Set up your throne, that earth's despair may cease
Beneath the shadow of its healing peace.

For your blest cross which does for all atone
Creation's praises rise before your throne.

Intended for use as a processional, the 1916 text calls for the following versicle to be said at the entrance into the chancel:

V God forbid that I should glory,
R save in the cross of our Lord Jesus Christ.

Alterations of the *Lutheran Book of Worship* text for inclusion in *Lutheran Worship* are slight. Stanza 3 was originally singular in number: "Each newborn soldier . . . Bears on his brow." Updating the second-person pronouns demanded that the fourth stanza, which originally read, "As thou hast promised, draw men unto thee," be reworded but still reflect John 12:32. As in *LBW*, so also here, stanza 5 was added to replace the final stanza of Kitchin/Newbolt.

CRUCIFER. Sydney H. Nicholson composed the tune for the above text and also prepared the harmonization for their inclusion in the 1916 Supplement to *Hymns Ancient and Modern.*

Stanley L. Osborne is undoubtedly correct when he avers that *The Hymn Book* (1971) of the Anglican Church of Canada and the United Church of Canada "is the first North American hymnal that has published the [namely this] hymn." Other recent hymnals of mainline denominations, among undoubtedly others, that have followed suit are: *The Australian Hymn Book* (1977), representing Anglicans, Congregationalists, Methodists, Presbyterians, and, with Catholic Supplement, also Roman Catholics; *Rejoice* (1985) of the Reformed Church in America; *Worship: A Hymnal and Service Book for Roman Catholics* (1986); the *Psalter Hymnal* (1987) of the Christian Reformed Church; and *The United Methodist Hymnal* (1989).

JESUS SHALL REIGN 312

This popular mission hymn by Isaac Watts, perhaps the most successful writer in long meter (88 88), a meter suited to lofty themes, has been translated into more languages than practically any other English hymn. It was included in his *The Psalms of David Imitated* (1719) as a metrical version of Psalm 72. Explaining the inclusion of Jesus' name in a supposed psalm, Watts wrote in the preface to that volume:

> Where the original runs in the form of prophecy concerning Christ and his salvation, I have given an historical turn to the sense; there is no necessity that we should always sing in the obscure and doubtful style of prediction when the things foretold are brought into open light by a full accomplishment.

Watts wrote eight stanzas; those omitted from *Lutheran Worship* follow.

2 Behold the islands with their kings,
And Europe her best tribute brings;
From north to south the princes meet
To pay their homage at his feet.

3 There Persia, glorious to behold,
There India shines in Eastern gold,
And barbarous nations at his word
Submit and bow and own their Lord.

7 Where he displays his healing power,
Death and the curse are known no more;
In him the tribes of Adam boast
More blessings than their father lost.

How the geographic and religious landscape has changed since Watts' days!

DUKE STREET. The composer, John Hatton, died in 1793, the year this tune was apparently first published anonymously in *A Select collection of Psalm and Hymn Tunes . . . by the Late Henry Boyd*, where it was called "Addison's 19th Psalm." Hatton's name was first associated with the tune in a collection of tunes called *Euphonia* (1805).

Hatton lived in a home on Duke Street, St. Helen's, Windle, Lancaster, England, from which various names for the tune have been derived, such as WINDLE, NEWRY, and ST. HELEN'S.

The harmonization is from *The Worshipbook: Services and Hymns* (Westminster, 1972), no. 443.

313 RISE, CROWNED WITH LIGHT

Alexander Pope's poem, *The Messiah*, in 107 lines, appeared in the *Spectator* of May 14, 1712. Beginning "Ye nymphs of Solyma! begin the song," it was headed, "Messiah. A sacred eclogue, composed of several passages of Isaiah the Prophet. Written in imitation of Virgil's *Pollio*." Joseph Addision (*LW* 196), editor of the *Spectator*, introduced the poem by writing:

> I will make no apology for entertaining the reader with the following poem, which is written by a great genius, a friend of mine, in the country, who is not ashamed to employ his wit in the praise of his Maker.

This hymn is a cento from the last portion of the poem, which reads:

Rise, crowned with light, imperial Salem, rise!
Exalt thy towery head and lift thy eyes!
See a long race thy spacious courts adorn;
See future sons and daughters, yet unborn,
In crowding ranks on every side arise,
Demanding life, impatient for the skies!
See barbarous nations at thy gates attend,
Walk in thy light, and in thy temple bend;
See thy bright altars thronged with prostrate kings
And heaped with products of Sabean springs!
For thee Idume's spicy forests blow,
And seeds of gold in Ophir's mountains glow.
See heaven its sparkling portals wide display
And break upon thee in a flood of day.
No more the rising sun shall gild the morn
Nor evening Cynthia fill her silver horn;
But lost, dissolved in thy superior rays,
One tide of glory, one unclouded blaze
O'erflow thy courts: the light himself shall shine
Revealed, and God's eternal day be thine!
The seas shall waste, the skies in smoke decay,
Rocks fall to dust, and mountains melt away;

But fixed His Word, His saving power remains;
Thy realm forever lasts, thy own Messiah reigns!

A perusal of some of the most recently published hymnals reveals that *Lutheran Worship* stands alone in having included this hymn. From 1826 on it was included in successive hymnals of the Protestant Episcopal Church, including *The Hymnal 1940*, but in its latest, *The Hymnal 1982*, this hymn has been dropped. Conversely, its inclusion in the *Evangelical Lutheran Hymn Book* (1912), the first official English hymnal of the Synod, as well as in *The Lutheran Hymnal* (1941), plus its sustained usage and popularity in the cause of missions, prompted the Commission on Worship to include it in *Lutheran Worship* (1982).

OLD 124TH, abbr. The success of this hymn is due, in part at least, to this splendid tune. For comments on it see hymn 240.

The harmonization is from *The Lutheran Hymnal* (1941), slightly altered.

O CHRIST, OUR LIGHT, O RADIANCE TRUE 314

O Christ, our light, O Radiance true, Shine forth on those estranged from you, And bring them to your home again, Where their delight shall never end.	O Jesu Christe, wahres Licht, Erleuchte, die dich kennen nicht, Und bringe sie zu deiner Her', Dass ihre Seel' auch selig werd'!
Fill with the radiance of your grace The wand'rers lost in error's maze. Enlighten those whose secret minds Some deep delusion haunts and blinds.	Erfüll mit deinem Gnadenschein, Die in Irrtum verführet sein, Auch die, so heimlich fichtet an In ihrem Sinn ein falscher Wahn!
Lord, open all reluctant ears, And take away the childish fears Of those who tremble to express The faith their secret hearts confess.	Den Tauben öffne das Gehör, Die Stummen richtig reden lehr', Die nicht bekennen wollen frei, Was ihres Herzens Glaube sei!
Lord, let your mercy's gentle ray Shine down on others strayed away. To those in conscience wounded sore Show heaven's waiting, open door.	Erleuchte, die da sind verblend't, Bring her, die sich von uns getrennt, Versammle, die zerstreuet gehn, Mach feste, die im Zweifel stehn!
Make theirs with ours a single voice Uplifted, ever to rejoice With wond'ring gratitude and praise To you, O Lord, for boundless grace.	So werden sie mit uns zugleich Auf Erden und im Himmelreich, Hier zeitlich und dort ewiglich Für solche Gnade preisen dich.

The most widely used of Johann Heermann's hymns in English translation, this was one of the "Songs of Tears" in his *Devoti musica cordis* (Breslau, 1630). Heermann's hymns, written during the Thirty Years' War (1618–48), are described by Wackerngel, translated by Polack:

When we consider the many kinds of trials, sufferings of body and soul, under which many would have lost courage and given up in despair, then Heermann's hymns will loom up before us as among the most exalted of spiritual poems.

The background of this hymn text is not a little extraordinary, for the thoughts expressed therein are not exactly original with Johann Heermann, but are based on the prayer headed, "Toward averting the destructive Schism of the Christian Religion," that appeared in a booklet issued by Philipp Kegel in Hamburg, 1592, entitled *A New Christian and very necessary Prayer Book*. Little did Heermann know that the prayer on which he based his hymn was actually a prayer by the Jesuit Peter Brillmacher for the return of the faithless and mislead Protestants who had forsaken the Roman Catholic faith. Today's congregations naturally construe and sing it as a fitting and beautiful prayer on behalf of home and foreign missions.

O JESU CHRISTE, WAHRES LICHT. Heermann originally specified for use with his hymn text a little-known tune today that he called "Nimm von uns Herr, du treuer Gott." The more popular tune for this text, as named above, is an anonymous one, in duple time, that appeared in the *Andächtige Haus-Kirche . . . Gesängen* (Nürnberg, 1676) looking thus (Zahn 535):

Usage has altered the tune rhythmically.

The harmonization is from the *Württembergisches Choralbuch* (1953).

315 AWAKE, THOU SPIRIT OF THE WATCHMEN

Awake, thou Spirit of the watchmen Who never held their peace by day or night, Contending from the walls of Zion Against the foe, confiding in thy might. Throughout the world their cry is ringing still And bringing peoples to thy holy will.	Wach auf, du Geist der ersten Zeugen, Die auf der Mauer als treue Wächter stehn, Die Tag und Nächte nimmer schweigen, Und die getrost dem Feind entgegen gehn; Ja, deren Schall die ganze Welt durchdringt, Und aller Völcker Schaaren zu dir bringt!

O Lord, now let thy fire enkindle
Our hearts that ev'rywhere its flame may go
And spread the glory of redemption
Till all the world thy saving grace shall know.
O harvest Lord, look down on us and view
How white the fields, the laborers, how few!

O dass dein Feur doch bald entbrennte!
O möcht' es doch in alle Lande gehn.
Ach Herr! gib doch in deine Ernte
Viel Knechte, die in treuer Arbeit stehn.
O Herr der Ernt'! ach siehe doch darein!
Die Ernt' ist gross, die zahl der Knechte klein.

The prayer thy Son himself hath taught us
We offer now to thee at his command;
Behold and hearken, Lord; thy children
Implore thee for the souls of ev'ry land:
With yearning hearts they make their ardent plea;
Oh, hear us, Lord, and say, "Thus shall it be."

Dein Sohn hat ja mit klaren Worten
Uns diese Bitte in den Mund gelegt.
O siehe, wie an allen Orten
Sich deiner Kinder Herz und Sinn bewegt,
Dich herzinbrünstig hierum anzuflehn;
Drum hör, o Herr, und sprich: Es soll geschehn!

This cento is from Karl H. von Bogatzky's famous missionary hymn of 14 stanzas that appeared in his *Die Übung der Gottseligkeit in allerley-geistlichen Liedern*, published in Halle in 1750 and entitled "For faithful laborers in the harvest of the Lord, for the blessed spread of the Word to all the world." The cento is constructed of stanzas 1, 2, and 3 of the original.

The translation was prepared by C. Winfred Douglas and Arthur W. Farlander for inclusion in *The Hymnal 1940*, in the production of which they were members of the Committee on Translations.

DIR, DIR, JEHOVAH, a moving tune, sometimes erroneously ascribed to Bartholomäus Crasselius, first appeared anonymously in Georg Wittwe's *Musicalische Hand-Buch der Geistlichen Melodien* (Hamburg, 1690), where it was coupled to Georg Neumark's "Wer nur den lieben Gott lässt walten" (*LW* 420). In 1704 Johann Freylinghausen included the tune in his *Geistreiches Gesangbuch*, set to Bartholomäus Crasselius' hymn "Dir, dir, Jehovah will ich singen" (*LW* 446).

The tune's popularity prompted its use in England where, altered to fit the long meter, it became known as WINCHESTER NEW.

The harmonization was prepared by George Leonard, a *nom de plume* of Paul G. Bunjes.

SEND NOW, O LORD, TO EVERY PLACE 316

This hymn by Mary C. Gates, written in 1888, was introduced at a convention of the Christian Endeavor Society in 1890 and thereafter published in *Sursum Corda* (1898). Its inclusion in the *Evangelical Lutheran Hymn-book* (1912), the first official English hymnal of the Synod, and in *The Lutheran Hymnal* (1941), and its resultant popularity, prompted its inclusion in *Lutheran Worship* (1982), appearing here in updated form.

ISLEWORTH was composed by Samuel Howard for a metrical version of Psalm 6 in *Melodies of the Psalms of David, according to the Version of Christopher Smart* (1765). This is one of those tunes in 4/4 where, in quarter notes, the measures are filled to overflowing, leaving little room for a breath. Rather than placing a fermata at the end of the second line of each stanza, it is suggested that the pulse (*Takt*) be kept strict by singing an eighth note at that point, permitting an eighth rest for a catch-breath.

The harmonization is from *The Lutheran Hymnal* (1941), slightly altered.

317 GOD, WHOSE ALMIGHTY WORD

John Marriott never published any of his hymns. This fine hymn, according to his son, was written about 1813. Six weeks after the author's death the hymn was quoted by Thomas Mortimer in a speech, and it was first printed with excerpts from the speech in the *Evangelical Magazine* III (1825): 262. In 1867 the hymn appeared in *Lyra Britannica*, with other hymnals soon following suit. The altered and updated text was prepared by the Inter-Lutheran Commission on Worship for inclusion in *Lutheran Book of Worship* (1978). Although rarely represented in present-day hymnals, this text and tune made it into *Worship: A Hymnal and Service Book for Roman Catholics* (1986).

ITALIAN HYMN. For comments on the tune see hymn 169.

Richard W. Gieseke prepared the harmonization for inclusion in *Lutheran Worship* (1982).

318 HARK, THE VOICE OF JESUS CALLING

Daniel March, a Congregational pastor in Philadelphia, was asked to speak at the Philadelphia Christian Association meeting on October 18, 1868. Finding no suitable hymns for his sermon text, Isaiah 6:8, he composed this original hymn shortly before the service, where it was sung from manuscript. It was first included in Robert Lowry's *Bright Jewels for the Sunday School* (New York, 1869).

March's first line originally read, "Hark, the voice of Jesus *crying*." In addition, his second stanza has been omitted:

> If you cannot cross the ocean,
> And the heathen lands explore,
> You can find the heathen nearer,
> You can help them at your door;
> If you cannot give your thousands,
> You can give the widow's mite,
> And the least you give for Jesus
> Will be precious in his sight.

This stanza has been called into question because its last four lines are ambiguous; it is possible to interpret them wrongly. The editors of *The Lutheran Hymnal* (1941) omitted the stanza for this reason, substituting stanza 3 by an unknown author. The entire text in that hymnal was altered and updated by the Inter-Lutheran Commission on Worship for inclusion in *Lutheran Book of Worship* (1978); it has also been included here.

GALILEAN. This tune is by Joseph Barnby, who seldom gave names to his hymn tunes; it was probably so christened by a later hymnal editor.

The setting is from *The Lutheran Hymnal.*

O GOD, O LORD OF HEAVEN AND EARTH 319

Martin H. Franzmann wrote this stirring text to commemorate the 450th anniversary of the Reformation in 1967. First appearing in the *Worship Supplement* (1969), it was included in *Lutheran Book of Worship* (1978) in updated form. The original text is given here:

O God, O Lord of heaven and earth,
Thy living finger never wrote
That life should be an aimless mote,
A death-ward drift from futile birth.
Thy word meant life triumphant hurled
Through every cranny of thy world.
Since light awoke and life began,
Thou hast desired thy life for man.

Our fatal will to equal thee.
Our rebel will wrought death and night.
We seized and used in thy despite
Thy wondrous gift of liberty.
We housed us in this house of doom,
Where death had royal scope and room,
Until thy Servant, Prince of peace,
Breached all its walls for our release.

Thou camest to our hall of death,
O Christ, to breathe our poisoned air,
To drink for us the dark despair
That strangled man's reluctant breath.
How beautiful the feet that trod
The road that leads us back to God.
How beautiful the feet that ran
To bring the great good news to man.

O Spirit, who didst once restore
Thy Church that it may be again
The bringer of good news to men,
Breathe on thy cloven Church once more,

That in these gray and latter days
There may be men whose life is praise,
Each life a high doxology
To Father, Son, and unto thee.

WITTENBERG NEW was composed by Jan O. Bender for Franzmann's text for inclusion in the *Worship Supplement* (1969). The tune is named after Wittenberg University, Springfield, Ohio, where Bender was at the time professor of music. The harmonization is also by Bender.

Interesting and effective long meter double (LM D—88 88 88 88) tunes that are congregational in character are difficult to write and few and far between. With patience, this one can be learned and sung with pleasure.

320 ON GALILEE'S HIGH MOUNTAIN

Commissioned by Christ to witness to the reconciling, life-transforming love of God revealed in Christ and his atoning work, the church joyfully and enthusiastically bends every effort, by Word and Sacrament, to arouse in human beings at home and abroad, faith in Christ and commitment to him, thus to lead them into righteous, loving relationships with God and other persons of all nations and races. In the final analysis, it is only in this Gospel that people will find purpose and meaning in this life and eternal salvation in the next. Such is the spirit of this hymn written by Henry L. Lettermann.

MISSIONARY HYMN was composed by Lowell Mason, distinguished musical figure in early American hymnody, and first printed in the *Boston Handel and Haydn Society's Collection of 1829*. While perhaps lacking in musical content by today's standards, the austere and restrained character of Mason's tunes was deliberate, namely, to counteract the extravagance and sentimentality of American church music of his time.

The setting is from *The Lutheran Hymnal* (1941).

321 SPREAD THE REIGN OF GOD THE LORD

Spread the reign of God the Lord,
Spoken, written, mighty Word;
Ev'rywhere his creatures call
To his heav'nly banquet hall.

Tell how God the Father's will
Made the world, upholds it still,

Walte, walte nah und fern,
Allgewaltig Wort des Herrn,
Wo nur seiner All-macht Ruf
Menschen für den Himmel schuf!

Wort vom Vater, der die Welt
Schuf und in den Armen hält

How his own dear Son he gave
Us from sin and death to save.

Tell of our Redeemer's grace,
Who, to save our human race
And to pay rebellion's price,
Gave himself as sacrifice.

Tell of God the Spirit giv'n
Now to guide us on to heav'n,
Strong and holy, just and true,
Working both to will and do.

Enter, mighty Word, the field;
Ripe the promise of its yield.
But the reapers, oh, how few
For the work there is to do!

Lord of harvest, great and kind,
Rouse to action heart and mind;
Let the gath'ring nations all
See your light and heed your call.

Und aus seinem Schoss herab
Seinem Sohn zum Heil ihr gab;

Wort von des Erlösers Huld,
Der der Erde schwere Schuld
Durch des heil'gen Todes Tat
Ewig weggenommen hat;

Kräftig Wort von Gottes Geist,
Der den Weg zum Himmel weist
Und durch seine heil'ge Kraft
Wollen und Vollbringen schafft;

Auf zur Ernt' in alle Welt!
Weithin wogt das weisse Feld,
Klein ist noch der Schnitter Zahl,
Viel der Garben überall.

Herr der Ernte, gross und gut,
Wirk zum Werke Lust und Mut,
Lass die Völker allzumal
Schauen deines Lichtes Strahl.

Jonathan F. Bahnmaier first printed this German hymn privately in 1827, in seven stanzas, with the first line, "Walte, fürden, nah und fern." In 1828 it appeared in the same form in the *Kern des deutschen Liederschatzes*. The first line of stanza 1 was changed to "Walte, walte, nah und fern" in Christian Carl Bunsen's *Versuch eines allgemeinen evangelischen Gesang- und Gebetbuchs* (1833).

Lutheran Worship's translation was prepared by a subcommittee of the Hymn Texts and Music Committee in 1979, utilizing earlier translations by Catherine Winkworth (*LW* 28, et al.) and others. Julian considers this hymn to be "one of the best and most useful of hymns for foreign missions."

GOTT SEI DANK. For comments on the tune see hymn 207.

The harmonization is by George Leonard, a *nom de plume* of Paul G. Bunjes.

FROM GREENLAND'S ICY MOUNTAINS 322

The original hymn with this title, in four stanzas, was written by Reginald Heber on Pentecost Eve at Wrexham, 1819, where he was staying with his father-in-law Dr. Shipley, dean of St. Asaph and vicar of Wrexham. The next day it was sung in the latter church, when the royal letter authorized collections throughout England on behalf of the Society for the Propagation of the Gospel. It was first published in the *Evangelical Magazine* XXIX (July 1821) and thereafter in Heber's *Hymns* (1827) with the heading "Before a collection made for the Society for the Propagation of the Gospel."

While W. G. Polack could label this as "one of the most famous missionary hymns ever written," a hymn included in numerous hymnals as late as the early half of this century, it is given little place in present-day hymnals. Among the reasons for this, S. Paul Schilling states:

> Readers of Christian missionary endeavors have become painfully aware of the linkages between missionary enterprise and Western colonialism and imperialism, political and economic. Widespread revolutionary movements and the demands of the Third World countries for independence have often made missionary activity precarious or impossible. The stark realities of poverty, racism, and oppression have compelled reexamination of the nature and goals of the Christian mission and reassessment of what accomplishments may be expected.

Cognizant of the above and mindful of the implied imperial and cultural sense of superiority toward peoples of non-western lands "where only man is vile," the commission, desirous of including the hymn, sought to obviate the problems of Heber's text. To that end it requested F. Samuel Janzow, one of its members, to make, what he considered to be, the necessary revisions. *LW* 322 constitutes the result, especially stanza 2.

MISSIONARY HYMN. For comments on the tune and harmonization see hymn 320.

ONLY-BEGOTTEN, WORD OF GOD ETERNAL 323

Only-begotten, Word of God eternal,
Lord of creation, merciful and mighty:
Hear us, your servants, as our tuneful voices
Rise in your presence.

Holy this temple where our Lord is dwelling:
This is none other than the gate of heaven.
Ever your children, year by year rejoicing,
Chant in your temple.

Hear us, O Father, as we throng your temple.
By your past blessings, by your present bounty,
Smile on your children, and in grace and mercy
Hear our petition.

God in three Persons, Father everlasting,
Son coeternal, ever blessed Spirit:
To you be praises, thanks, and adoration,
Glory forever.

Christe, cunctorum dominator alme,
Patris aeterni genitus ab ore,
Suplicum vota pariterque hymnum
Cerne benignus.

Hic locus nempe vocitatur aula
Regis immensi niveaque caeli
Porta, quae vitae patriam petentes
Accipit omnes;

Quaesumus ergo, Deus, ut sereno
Adnuas vultu famulos gubernans,
Qui tui summo celebrant amore
Gaudia templi.

Gloria summum resonet parentem,
Gloria natum pariterque sanctum
Spiritum, dulci moduletur hymno
Omne per aevum.

A ninth-century manuscript in Bern, Switzerland, exhibits the earliest occurrence of this anonymous office hymn in 12 stanzas beginning "Christe, cunctorum dominator alme," and designated for use in the consecration of a church. Sometimes beginning "Christe, *sanctorum* dominator alme," this hymn was generally used in Matins in all the important western liturgies.

The altered and updated translation here used is based on that by Maxwell J. Blacker which he made from the Roman Breviary of 1632 for use at St. Barnabas Church, Pimlico, England, where he was curate for a time. It represents four stanzas of the six that were prepared by the Inter-Lutheran Commission on Worship for inclusion in *Lutheran Book of Worship* (1978).

ISTE CONFESSOR. For comments on the tune see hymn 301.

The harmonization is by Paul G. Bunjes.

AS MOSES, LOST IN SINAI'S WILDERNESS 324

This text by Henry Lettermann was written to commemorate the centennial of Concordia Teachers College, River Forest, Illinois, in 1964. Written in the somewhat unusual meter of 10 10 10 10 and refrain, possibly to give it room for exposition and depth, with the unique and sparse rhyme scheme of stanza-ending with refrain-ending, the text still comes off well, ably supported by the music setting.

RIVER FOREST was composed and harmonized by Richard W. Hillert for Lettermann's text. Text and tune result in a compatible combination. The tune's name identifies the place of the college, the centennial of which was being celebrated.

325 FOR MANY YEARS, O GOD OF GRACE

William M. Czamanske, pastor of St. Mark's Lutheran Church, Sheboygan, Wisconsin, wrote this text for the congregation's 25th anniversary celebration in 1934. It was included in *The Lutheran Hymnal* (1941), and has often been used for congregational anniversaries. It is given here in an updated form.

WIE SCHÖN LEUCHTET. For comments on the tune see hymn 73.

The harmonization was prepared by Ralph Schultz for inclusion in *Lutheran Worship* (1982).

326 OUR FATHERS' GOD IN YEARS LONG GONE

This notable hymn, originally in five stanzas, by W. Harry Krieger, onetime president of the Michigan District of the Missouri Synod, was written to commemorate the 125th anniversary of The Lutheran Church—Missouri Synod and introduced in a special service on June 27, 1972, at Holy Trinity Chapel, Concordia College, Ann Arbor, Michigan, during the 85th convention of the Michigan District.

Written in long meter (88 88), the meter that lends itself to majestic subjects and stately treatment, the meter that Ambrose used to give the church its first "modern" hymns (*LW* 481, 487), it originally began "Oh Lord, our God, in years long gone."

O GROSSER GOTT. For comments on the tune see hymn 83.

The harmonization was prepared by Richard W. Gieseke for inclusion in *Lutheran Worship* (1982).

327 HOW BLESSED IS THIS PLACE, O LORD

Ernest E. Ryden, coeditor of the *The Hymnal* (1925) of the then-Augustana Lutheran Church, now part of the Evangelical Lutheran Church in America, wrote this fine text for that volume as a hymn for the dedication of an altar. It is based on Genesis 28:17 and 35:1–7.

STEHT AUF, IHR LIEBEN KINDERLEIN. This tune, also known as O HEILIGE DREIFALTIGKEIT, exhibits a strong resemblance to the tune, *Lobt sei dem almächtigen Gott*, from a Bohemian Brethren hymnal of 1544. Although difficult to establish, it is likely that both have their source in a common folk tune, or folk song.

Nikolaus Herman wrote this tune for his text, "Der hie für Gott will sein gerecht," in his *Die Sonntags Evangelia über das gantze Jar* (Wittenberg, 1560). Several years later Herman used the tune with "Freut euch, ihr Christen alle gleich." Thereafter the tune was used with various texts. The *Evangelisches Kirchengesangbuch* (1959) uses it with "Steht auf, ihr lieben Kinderlein," a text by Erasmus Alber (c. 1500–53), Lutheran pastor and skillful poet. In Johann Stötzel's *Harfen- und Psalterspiel*, published in Stuttgart, 1744, the tune appears with "O Heilige Dreifaltigkeit." Its folklike character, rhythmic interest, and overall fine craftsmanship is better evidenced in its original form as here given (Zahn 376):

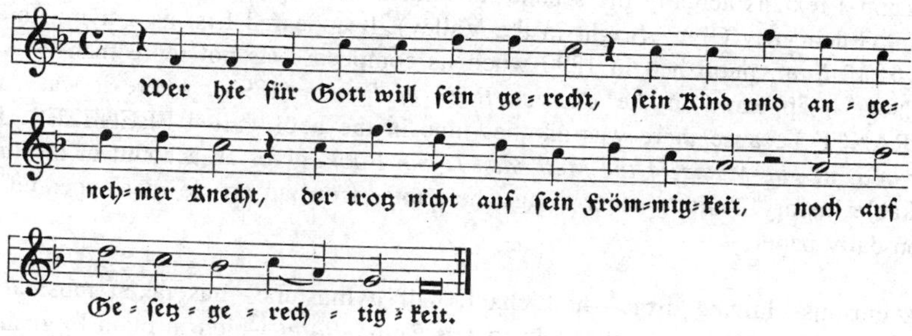

The harmonization was prepared by Wilhelm Quampen, a *nom de plume* of Paul G. Bunjes.

328 THY STRONG WORD

Martin H. Franzmann wrote this text in 1954 for Concordia Seminary, St. Louis, Missouri. Based on the seminary's motto, "Ανωθεν τὸ φῶς ("The Light Comes from Above"), it was first used there in chapel services. Presently it is sung as the processional in every baccalaureate and commencement service of that seminary. Included in *Worship Supplement* (1969), it made its way into *Lutheran Book of Worship* (1978) and now in *Lutheran Worship* (1982).

The strong trochaic 87 87 D meter is one that can carry weighty ideas while reflecting a spirit of grandeur. Small wonder that it has contributed to some of Christendom's most popular hymns: "Love Divine, All Love Excelling," (*LW* 286), "Come, O Long Expected Jesus" (*LW* 22), "Glorious Things of You Are Spoken" (*LW* 294), to mention but a few.

EBENEZER (TON-Y-BOTEL), a vigorous and majestic tune so compatible with Franzmann's text, is actually the second movement of Thomas J. William's memorial anthem "Golen yn y Glyn" (Light in the Valley). It appeared first as a hymn tune in *Llawlyfr Moliant*, published in 1890 when its composer was not more than 21 years old. Next it appeared in the *Baptist Book of Praise* (1893), where it was called ASSURANCE because there was another tune in the book called EBENEZER. J. T. Lightwood, in *The Music of the Methodist Hymn Book*, gives an account of the tune's remarkable history. Among other things, he quotes from an article that appeared in a London daily paper:

> A curious slurring dirge—half chant, half hymn-tune—has taken musical Wales by storm. It is popularly known as *Ton-y-Botel* which in plain English means "The Tune in the Bottle," for it is generally believed to have been picked up on the Welsh coast sealed up in a bottle, cast ashore by the waves.

Lightwood adds that the legend about the bottle arose when a young man, who had sung at a private engagement and was asked about the tune's history, laughingly told his friends that it had been picked up by a yokel on the coast of Lleyn, in a sealed bottle that had washed ashore. At any rate, the tune spread like wild fire from one Welsh village to another. And rightly so. For it has, as Routley says, "an effect of accumulating grandeur that is almost hypnotic when sung by a large gathering." *The English Hymnal* (1906) is said to have introduced the tune into English hymnody.

The harmonization was prepared by Richard W. Hillert for inclusion in *Worship Supplement* (1969).

THE LAW OF GOD IS GOOD AND WISE 329

THE GOSPEL SHOWS THE FATHER'S GRACE 330

These two companion hymns were contributed by Matthias Loy to the Ohio Synod's *Collection of Hymns* (fourth edition, 1863); subsequently they appeared in the Ohio *Evangelical Lutheran Hymnal* (1880). These hymns illustrate, to a degree at least, the importance that Lutheranism attaches to the distinction between the Law and the Gospel, for the Word of God, both Old and New Testaments, meets the hearts of people with two diametrically opposite teachings, namely, either Law or Gospel. The Law in its narrow sense reveals the righteousness and the immutable will of God. It shows how human beings are to act in order to be acceptable to God and it threatens transgressors of the Law with temporal and eternal punishment. It leads to a knowledge of sin and it condemns sin.

The Gospel in its narrow sense teaches the person condemned by the Law because of sin that Christ through his suffering, death, and resurrection has fulfilled God's Law, has satisfied its demands, and has won for humanity the forgiveness of sins, life, and salvation. It calls on the sinner to accept this gift of salvation in faith; it even supplies that faith through the Holy Spirit who is at work in the Gospel.

Luther rightly held that the proclamation of the Law is the indispensable and necessary presupposition for preaching the Gospel. For without the Law the person will not recognize his or her sinfulness, but remain secure and proud in his or her moral capacity.

On the other hand, the Scriptures also use the terms Law and Gospel in the broad sense, with each including both teachings (for instance, Law: Is. 2:3; Gospel: Mark 1:1). When doing so they do not contradict each other; they are the same Word of God, in both the Old Testament and New Testament, applicable to all people and at all times, Christians and non-Christians.

Properly to distinguish between Law and Gospel is intrinsic to a full and proper understanding of God's Word. Failure to do so leads to wrong conclusions such as: Since God is loving and caring, there can be no threat connected with his Word. Such reasoning, however, leads to love without cost, and grace without response, something that Dietrich Bonhoeffer (1906–45) calls "cheap grace," and against which he protested.

To master making the proper distinction between Law and Gospel is not an easy matter. Luther, who often addressed this subject, confesses in his *Table Talk*:

> There's no man living on earth who knows how to distinguish between the Law and the Gospel. We may think we understand it when we are listening to a sermon, we're far from it. Only the Holy Spirit knows this. . . . Because I've been writing so much and so long about it, you'd think I'd know the

distinction, but when a crisis comes I recognize very well that I am far, far from understanding. So God alone should be our holy master. (*Luther's Works* 54: 127)

To bring to the fore this distinction between Law and Gospel, these two hymns have been conveniently placed on facing pages so that they can readily and fittingly be sung in alternation, stanza by stanza.

ERHALT UNS, HERR. For comments on the tune see hymn 334.
The harmonization is by Paul G. Bunjes.

HERR JESU CHRIST, DICH ZU UNS WEND. For comments on the tune see hymn 201.
The setting is from *The Lutheran Hymnal* (1941).

331 HERE IS THE TENFOLD SURE COMMAND

Here is the tenfold sure command
God gave to men of ev'ry land
Through faithful Moses standing high
On holy Mount Sinai.
Have mercy, Lord!

I, I alone, am God, your Lord;
All idols are to be abhorred.
Trust me, step boldly to my throne,
Sincerely love me alone.
Have mercy, Lord!

Do not my holy name disgrace,
Do not my Word of truth debase.
Praise only that as good and true
Which I myself say and do.
Have mercy, Lord!

And celebrate the worship day
That peace may fill your home, and pray,
And put aside the work you do,
So that God may work in you.
Have mercy, Lord!

You are to honor and obey
Your parents, masters, ev'ry day,
Serve them each way that comes to hand;
You'll then live long in the land.
Have mercy, Lord!
Curb anger, do not harm or kill,
Hate not, repay not ill with ill.

Dies sind die heil'gen Zehn Gebot',
Die uns gab unser Herre Gott
Durch Moses, seinen Diener treu,
Hoch auf dem Berg Sinai.
Kyrieleis!

Ich bin allein dein Gott, der Herr,
Kein' Götter sollst du haben mehr;
Du sollst mir ganz vertrauen dich,
Von Herzensgrund lieben mich.
Kyrieleis!

Du sollst nicht führen zu Unehr'n
Den Namen Gottes, deines Herrn;
Du sollst nicht preisen recht noch gut,
Ohn' was Gott selbst red't und tut.
Kyrieleis!

Du sollst heil'gen den Feiertag,
Dass du und dein Haus ruhen mag;
Du sollst von dein'm Tun lassen ab,
Dass God sein Werk in dir hab'.
Kyrieleis!

Du sollst ehr'n und gehorsam sein
Dem Vater und der Mutter dein,
Und wo dein' Hand ihn'n dienen kann,
So wirst du lang's Leben hab'n.
Kyrieleis!
Du sollst nicht töten zorniglich,
Nicht hassen noch selbst rächen dich,

Be patient and of gentle mind, Convince your foe you are kind. Have mercy, Lord!	Geduld haben und sanften Mut Und auch dem Feind tun das Gut'. Kyrieleis!
Be faithful, keep the marriage vow; The straying thought do not allow. Keep all your conduct free from sin By self-controlled discipline. Have mercy, Lord!	Dein Eh' sollst du bewahren rein, Dass auch dein Herz kein' andre mein', Und halten keusch das Leben dein Mit Zucht und Mässigkeit fein. Kyrieleis!
You shall not steal or cheat away What others worked for night and day, But open up a gen'rous hand To feed the poor in the land. Have mercy, Lord!	Du sollst nicht stehlen Geld noch Gut, Nicht wuchern jemands Schweiss und Blut; Du sollt auftun dein' milde Hand Den Armen in deinem Land. Kyrieleis!
A lying witness never be, Nor foul your tongue with calumny. The cause of innocence embrace, The fallen shield from disgrace. Have mercy, Lord!	Du sollst kein falscher Zeuge sein, Nicht lügen auf den Nächsten dein; Sein Unschuld sollst auch retten du Und seine Schand' decken zu. Kyrieleis!
The portion in your neighbor's lot, His goods, home, wife, desire not. Pray God he would your neighbor bless As you yourself wish success. Have mercy, Lord!	Du sollst dein's Nächsten Weib und Haus Begehren nicht noch etwas draus; Du sollst ihm wünschen alles Gut', Wie dir dein Herz selber tut. Kyrieleis!
You have this law to see therein That you have not been free from sin But also that you clearly see How pure toward God life should be. Have mercy, Lord!	Die Gebot all' uns geben sind, Dass du dein' Sünd', o Menschenkind, Erkennen sollst und lernen wohl, Wie man vor Gott leben soll. Kyrieleis!
Lord Jesus, help us in our need; Christ, you our go-between indeed. Our works, how sinful, marred, unjust! Christ, you our one hope and trust. Have mercy, Lord!	Das helf' uns der Herr Jesu Christ, Der unser Mittler worden ist; Es ist mit unserm Tun verlor'n, Verdienen doch eitel Zorn. Kyrieleis!

Luther's concern for instructing and firmly grounding the people in God's Word and the way of salvation prompted him to versify the Ten Commandments in both a long and short version, one with 12 stanzas and another with five. Only the long version is included in *Lutheran Worship*. As early as 1525 these two hymns were sung in the weekday Lenten services when the sermons were based on the Catechism. The Wittenberg church order of 1533 prescribed that the choirboys sing this hymn before the Catechism sermons and the shorter one afterward. It is to be noted that Luther was not alone in his concern for such hymns. The Genevan Psalter (see essay: Metrical Psalms, p. 825) and early English psalters also contained versifications of this nature.

The translation contained in *Lutheran Worship* (1982) is by F. Samuel Janzow, professor emeritus at Concordia College, River Forest, Illinois.

It is of interest to note Luther's enumeration of the commandments. Stanza 1 serves as the prologue. Thereafter follow the commandments, the first through the eighth (stanzas 2–9), in the order that Luther employs in his Small and Large

Catechisms. (He, however, includes the "graven image," or "idol," matter [Ex. 20:4] with the first [in st. 2].) Stanza 10 appears to combine the ninth and 10th commandments, which in the catechisms, following the tradition of the Western Church, Luther divides into two commandments. This hymn then represents only nine commandments from the simple standpoint of enumeration.

It should be mentioned that while the Anglican, Reformed, and Eastern Orthodox combine the Lutheran-Roman Catholic ninth and 10th commandments, they arrive at ten by subsuming the "no other gods" statement (Ex. 20:3) into the prologue and making the "graven image," or "idol," matter stand for the second commandment. Such enumeration might appear to be intimated in the layout of some contemporary versions of the Bible, including the New International Version (see Ex. 20:2–17; Deut. 5;6–21), although these texts themselves do not explicitly give ordinals or numerals. It is in Exodus 34:28 and Deuteronomy 4:13, 10:4 that the numeral 10 occurs: contextually "10 words" (Decalog), or, as most translations have it, "10 commandments." Moreover, the fact that in the Exodus 20:2–7 and Deuteronomy 5:6–21 accounts the negative Hebrew *lo'* (not *'al*) in each instance is followed by an indicative verb, not imperative, brings Horace Hummel to the conclusion that the Decalog consists of:

> statements of what the believer who has experienced God's grace *will* voluntarily do, not commands of what he *must* do to deserve or earn God's love. They represent the perimeters or boundaries of God's kingship, beyond which the believer will not stray, but *within* which he is essentially free to respond joyfully and voluntarily, as illustrated by the rest of the 'laws' or 'codes' of the Old Testament.

IN GOTTES NAMEN FAHREN WIR. Luther guaranteed the ready acceptance of his hymn text by setting it to a popular pre-Reformation pilgrimage *Leise*, "In God's name we go." Gottfried von Strassburg (fl. c. 1210) mentions this song in his *Tristan and Isolde*. In Bavaria it was early sung in this form:

> In Gotes Namen fara wir,
> Der Wein ist pesser dann das Pier
> So helfe uns das grosser Vas,
> Do der pesser Wein in was
> So trinck wir alle dester Pas,
> Kirie eleison.

In the 14th century this was sung as the army of Albrecht von Hapsburg entered the battle of Göllheim.

The setting is by Paul G. Bunjes.

HOW PRECIOUS IS THE BOOK DIVINE 332

First published in the author's *Hymns Adapted to the Circumstances of Public Worship and Private Devotion* (1782), this hymn by John Fawcett, based on Psalm 119:105, is used almost exclusively in America. A few words have been changed from the original: "doctrines" to "teachings" in stanza 1; "a Savior" to "our Savior," stanza 2; masculine language made inclusive in stanza 3; and in stanza 4, "sweetly" to "gladly" and "light" to "peace."

Duffield in *English Hymns* uses an old Hebrew parable to explain the imagery of the hymn:

> A traveller, it is said, was passing through a gloomy forest in the night. He feared the robbers, and he could not see his way. Finally he discovered a torch, by whose light he went on without fear of pitfalls and wild beasts. But still he was in mortal dread of the robbers. At length he emerged into the highway, and then felt at ease. The darkness, so the interpreters add, is the lack of religious knowledge; the torch is God's precepts; the forest is the world; beyond the forest shines out the unclouded sun of divine love.

WALDER. The tune takes its name from the composer, Johann J. Walder, and is dated 1788. Its stepwise, diatonic character goes well with the gentleness of the text.

The setting is from *The Lutheran Hymnal* (1941).

GOD'S WORD IS OUR GREAT HERITAGE 333

God's Word is our great heritage
And shall be ours forever;
To spread its light from age to age
Shall be our chief endeavor.
Through life it guides our way,
In death it is our stay.
Lord, grant, while worlds endure,
We keep its teachings pure
Throughout all generations.

Guds Ord det er vort Arvegods,
Det skal vort Afkoms väre;
Gud giv os i vor Grav den Ros,
Vi holdt det hölt in Äre!
Det er vor Hälp i Nöd,
Vor Tröst i Liv og Död;
O Gud, ihvor det gaar,
Lad dog, mens Verden staar,
Det i vor Ät nedarves!

First published in *Salmer ved Jubelfesten* (1817), this is the fifth stanza of Nicolai F. S. Grundtvig's Danish version of Martin Luther's "A Mighty Fortress." Later this single stanza appeared in Danish and Norwegian hymnals as a separate hymn, frequently used on festival occasions and as a closing hymn in corporate worship.

The translation is by Ole G. Belsheim (1909) as it appeared in *The Lutheran Hymnary* (1913).

REUTER. For comments on the tune see hymn 293.

The harmonization is from *The Lutheran Hymnal* (1941), slightly altered.

334 LORD, KEEP US STEADFAST IN YOUR WORD

Lord, keep us steadfast in your Word;
Curb those who by deceit or sword
Would wrest the kingdom from your Son
And bring to naught all he has done.

Lord Jesus Christ, your pow'r make known,
For you are Lord of lords alone;
Defend your holy Church that we
May sing your praise triumphantly.

O Comforter of priceless worth,
Send peace and unity on earth;
Support us in our final strife
And lead us out of death to life.

Erhalt uns, Herr, bei deinem Wort
Und steur des Papsts und Türken Mord,
Die Jesum Christum, deinen Sohn,
Wollen stürzen von deinem Thron!

Beweis dein' Macht, Herr Jesu Christ,
Der du Herr aller Herren bist;
Beschirm' dein' arme Christenheit,
Dass sie dich lob' in Ewigkeit!

Gott Heil'ger Geist, du Tröster wert,
Gib dein'm Volk ein'rlei Sinn auf Erd',
Steh bei uns in der letzten Not,
G'leit uns ins Leben aus dem Tod!

The occasion for this hymn is undoubtedly attributable to the difficult times for the Empire. In August of 1541 King Ferdinand suffered a severe defeat by the Mohammedan Turks at Budapest, a fact that Luther mentions in correspondence the following September and October. In October a hurricane destroyed the fleet of Emperor Charles V near Algiers, an event to which Luther responded with his *Vermahnung zum Gebet wider den Türken* (Admonition to Pray against the Turk). In July of 1542 Francis I of France made an alliance with Sultan Suleiman over against the emperor. Reports had it that the Pope had sided with this pact. Thus, of all things—Pope and Turk in alliance against Christendom!

In a letter to the pastors in the confines of Wittenberg, Luther urged devout prayers after the sermon and he frequently stressed the importance of prayers by the children. Such were the conditions that prompted this hymn, the hymn of Luther that, of all his hymns, has perhaps enjoyed widest use.

The hymn may first have appeared in broadsheet form in Wittenberg in 1542. That same year a Low German version of it was included in the *Magdeburg Gesangbuch*. The following year a High German version appeared in Joseph Klug's *Geistliche Lieder*, entitled "A Children's Hymn, to be sung against the two Archenemies of Christ and his Holy Church, the Pope and the Turk." This title has led some to believe that Luther wrote this hymn in 1541 for a special Wittenberg service of prayer against the Turkish threat. The reference to children in the title may indicate that it was to be sung in the service by the boys' choir (Polack).

Originally the second line of stanza 1, translated into English, read: "Restrain the murderous Pope and Turk." Opposition to this line together with the waning of the actual threat gradually caused it to be changed to a general petition for protection from the opponents of God's Word.

The translation is that of Catherine Winkworth in her *Chorale Book for England* (1863), slightly altered.

ERHALT UNS, HERR, named after the first words of Luther's text to which it was coupled in Joseph Klug's *Geistliche Leider* (Wittenberg, 1543), is a tune believed by some scholars to be the work of Luther. This, however, is little more than conjecture, for in its plainsong notation in Klug's hymnal it bears a strong resemblance to the 15th-century form of the "Veni, Redemptor gentium" (*LW* 13) and also to the antiphon "Da pacem, Domine." Appearing in a goodly number of hymnals, the tune is also called SPIRES, WITTENBERG, and PRESERVE US, LORD.

Originally in the Dorian mode, the tune in *Lutheran Worship* (1982) retains this flavor by not sharping the seventh scale step in the final cadence.

The harmonization is from the *Württembergisches Choralbuch* (1953).

O WORD OF GOD INCARNATE 335

William W. How included this hymn in the Supplement to *Psalms and Hymns* (1867), which he coedited with Thomas Morrell. Originally in four stanzas (here stanza 2 is comprised of the first four lines of the original stanza 2 plus the last four lines of the original stanza 3), the hymn was headed "Proverbs 6:23: The commandment is a lamp, and the law is a light." Appearing here in slightly altered and updated form, this hymn, addressed to Christ the incarnate Word, in notable terms of poetic beauty, it praises him for the divine gift of the Holy Scriptures, shining like a lantern throughout the centuries, and which the church uses to guide men and women through the shadowy mists to the truth. The final stanza is a prayer that the church be a worthy bearer of the light to the world till the Savior's final coming when we shall no longer "see but a poor reflection; . . . we shall see face to face" (1 Cor. 13:12a).

MUNICH (MEININGEN, KÖNIGSBERG, ELIJAH). This tune as here used is an adaptation of the quartet, "Cast thy burden upon the Lord," from Mendelssohn's *Elijah* (1846). It is essentially a recast of a chorale melody that appeared in the *Neu-Vermehrtes und zu Übung Christliche Gottseligkeit* (Meiningen, 1693), where it was set to Johann Heermann's great hymn, "O Gott, du frommer Gott" (*LW* 371), and appeared thus (Zahn 5148):

This combination of tune and text appeared also in Catherine Winkworth's *Chorale Book for England* (1865).

Zahn traces various parts of this splendid tune to the psalter of Wolf Helmhard von Hohenberg entitled *Lust und Artzneigarten des königlichen Propheten Davids* (Regensburg, 1675), in which most of the tunes were composed by organist Hieronymous Gradenthaller (1637–1700). Zahn comments on the many variations of the tune that evolved in Germany during the 18th and 19th centuries. J. S. Bach (*LW* 89) used the tune with some modifications in cantatas 24 and 71.

Both text and setting contained in *Lutheran Worship* (1982) were originally prepared for inclusion in *Lutheran Book of Worship* (1978).

The harmonization is from *The Lutheran Hymnal* (1941), slightly altered.

The abiding popularity of this hymn with its tune is attested by its inclusion in such recent hymnals as *The Hymnal 1982* of the Episcopal Church; the *Psalter Hymnal* (1987) of the Christian Reformed Church; and the *United Methodist Hymnal* (1989).

336 GRANT, HOLY GHOST, THAT WE BEHOLD

Grant, Holy Ghost, that we behold
The grace of Christ our Savior,
Whose wounds and agony untold
Made good for our behavior.
The last hour cannot bring us loss
When we are sheltered by the cross
That canceled our transgressions.

Your living Word shine in our heart
And to a new life win us.
With seed of light implant the start
Of Christlike deeds within us.
Help us uproot what is impure,
And while faith's fruits in us mature,
Prepare us for your harvest.

Then when our earthly course is run,
Death's bitter hour impending,
May your good work in us begun
Bring peace to our life's ending,
The joy of surely being brought,

Gott Heil'ger Geist, hilf uns mit Grund
Auf Jesum Christum schauen,
Damit wir in der letzten Stund'
Auf seine Wunden bauen,
Die er für uns nach Gottes Rat
Am heil'gen Kreuz empfangen hat
Zu Tilgung unsrer Sünden.

Durchs Wort in unsre Herzen schein
Und tu uns neu gebären,
Dass wir als Gottes Kinder rein
Vom bösen Wandel kehren
Und in dir bringen Früchte gut,
So viel, als unser blöder Mut
In diesem Fleisch kann tragen.

In Sterbensnöten bei uns steh
Und hilf uns Wohl verscheiden,
Dass wir fein sanft aus allem Weh
Hinfahren zu den Freuden,
Die uns der fromme Vater wert

By Christ, who our salvation bought,
Into our Father's mansion.

Aus lauter Gnade hat beschert
In Christo, seinem Sohne.

This fine hymn was written by Bartholomäus Ringwaldt while serving as Lutheran pastor at Langenfeld, Brandenburg, Germany. Based on the Gospel reading for Pentecost Sunday, it appeared in his *Evangelia, auff alle Sontag und Fest* (Frankfurt-an-der-Oder, 1581).

The translation is by F. Samuel Janzow, a member of the Commission on Worship that prepared *Lutheran Worship* (1982).

ES IST GEWISSLICH. For comments on the tune see hymn 462.

The harmonization is by Wilhelm Quampen, a *nom de plume* of Paul G. Bunjes.

PRESERVE YOUR WORD, O SAVIOR 337

Preserve your Word, O Savior,
To us this latter day,
And let your kingdom flourish;
Enlarge your Church, we pray.
Oh, keep our faith from failing;
Keep hope's bright star aglow.
Let nothing from truth turn us
While living here below.

Preserve, O Lord, your honor,
The bold blasphemer smite;
Convince, convert, enlighten
The souls in error's night.
Reveal your will, dear Savior,
To all who dwell below,
Great light of all the living,
That all your name may know.

Preserve, O Lord, your Zion,
Bought dearly with your blood;
Protect what you have chosen
Against the hellish flood.
Be always our defender
When dangers gather round;
When all of earth is crumbling,
Safe may your Church be found.

Preserve your Word and preaching,
The truth that makes us whole,
The mirror of your glory,
The pow'r that saves the soul.
Oh, may this living water,
This dew of heav'nly grace,
Sustain us while here living
Until we see your face.

Erhalt uns deine Lehre,
Herr zu der letzten Zeit,
Erhalt dein Reich, vermehre
Dein' edle Christenheit;
Erhalt standhaften Glauben,
Der Hoffnung Leitsternstrahl;
Lass uns dein Wort nicht rauben
In diesem Jammertal!

Erhalt dein' Ehr' und wehre
Dem, der dir widerspricht;
Erleucht, Herr, und bekehre,
Allwissend ewig Licht,
Was dich bisher nicht kennet;
Entdecke doch der Welt
(Der du dich Licht genennet),
Was einzig dir gefuallt!

Erhalt, was du gebauet
Und durch dein Blut erkauft,
Was du dir hast vertrauet,
Die Kirch', auf welch' anlauft
Der grimme Sturm des Drachen;
Sei du ihr Schutz und Wall,
Dass, ob die Welt will krachen,
Sie nimmermehr verfall'!

Erhalt und lass uns hören
Dein Wort, das selig macht,
Den Spiegel deiner Ehren,
Das Licht in dieser Nacht,
Dass dieser Brunn uns tränke,
Der Himmelstau uns netz',
Dass diese Richtschnur lenke,
Der Honigseim ergötz'!

Preserve in wave and tempest Your storm-tossed little flock; Assailed by wind and weather, May it endure each shock. Stand at the helm, our pilot, And set the course aright; Then we will reach the harbor In your eternal night.	Erhalt in Sturm und Wellen Dein Häuflein, lass dochnicht, Uns Wind und Wetter Fällen, Steur selbst dein Schiff und richt Den Lauf, dass wir erreichen Die Anfurt nach der Zeit Und hilf uns Segel streichen In sel'ger Ewigkeit!

This is Andreas Gryphius' recast of an earlier hymn by Josua Stegmann (*LW* 287) that originally appeared in the latter's *Herzen-Seufzer* (Lüneberg, 1630). The recast first appeared in the Saubert *Gesangbuch* (Nürnberg, 1676) entitled "About God's Word and Christian Doctrine." Gryphius is a dramatic poet, one who holds a certain disdain for the world, whose faith is true and deep.

The translation is an altered and updated form of that by William J. Schaefer which appeared in *The Lutheran Hymnal* (1941).

Although this hymn enjoys little use today in the Lutheran territorial churches in Germany, its inclusion and popularity in the Synod's early German hymnals and in *The Lutheran Hymnal* prompted its inclusion in *Lutheran Worship* (1982).

IST GOTT FÜR MICH. This Dorian tune (see essay: The Church Modes, p. 832), new to American Lutheranism, has a rather interesting history. It was first sung January 14, 1590, in London, to celebrate the victory of England's armed forces under the leadership of Lord Willoughby of Cresby (1555–1601) against the Spaniards. Thereafter a ballad and tune arose, extolling Willoughby as a folk hero, beginning "The fifteenth day of July with glistening sword and shield," to which a musician no less than William Byrd (1546–1623) made a setting for the virginal. Capturing the fancy of the people, this admirable setting spread like wildfire. The story is told that already in 1596 some English comedians entertained an audience in Frankfurt-am-Main, singing a song about "Roland and Margaret" to this tune—a hilarious jig about a less than faithful maiden. It was through this musical comedy that the tune became famously known throughout Europe under the name "Rolandtune" (not to be confused with the medieval Rolandlied). Before long poets of spiritual texts began to utilize this fine tune, first of whom was David Spaiser (d.c. 1627), whose "O Gott, ich tu dirs klagen" was included in his *Vierundzwanzig geistliche Lieder* that appeared in Augsburg in 1609. Others soon followed. Thereafter the tune was forgotten until 1890 when Johannes Zahn produced his monumental *Die Melodien der deutschen evangelischen Kirchenlieder* in which he included this tune (see 5492, 5493). From there it entered the present *Evangelisches Kirchengesangbuch* of the Lutheran territorial churches in Germany, where it is the setting for Paul Gerhardt's (*LW* 19, et al.) "Ist Gott für mich, so trete gleich alles wider mich." Acquaintance with this tune therein led the Commission on Worship to choose it for Gryphius' "Preserve Your Word, O Savior" rather than use the overworked HERZLICH TUT MICH as done in *The Lutheran Hymnal* (1941).

The harmonization is from the *Württembergisches Choralbuch* (1953).

WHEN SEED FALLS ON GOOD SOIL 338

This fine text, reflecting the Parable of the Sower (Matt. 13:8, 23; Mark 4:8, 20; Luke 8:8, 15), is the same as that included in *Lutheran Book of Worship* (1978) except for one alteration: instead of "For it must find in humankind The fertile soil in heart and mind" in stanza 2, lines 3 and 4, *Lutheran Worship* has "And it would work in humankind, The fertile soil in heart and mind."

WALHOF was composed by Frederick F. Jackisch while waiting at the Minneapolis airport for a flight to Springfield, Ohio, following a meeting of the Inter-Lutheran Commission on Worship. While there are numerous ways to combine sixes and eights other than in the basic short (66 86), common (86 86), and long (88 88) meters, not all come off as well as this one in 66 88 66, with its simple diatonic movement, its well-placed pitch-height accent, and its moving harmonization (also by Jackisch)—all contributing to a refreshing unsquare feeling.

The name WALHOF was chosen by the composer, as he has stated, "to honor Karen Walhof who served as secretary, scorekeeper, policewoman, paper-pusher, mail-sender, encourager, critic, all of the above and then some, for the music committees of the Inter-Lutheran Commission on Worship. Without her attention to detail we all would have been hopelessly lost in a morass of hymnological materials."

SPEAK, O LORD, YOUR SERVANT LISTENS 339

Speak, O Lord, your servant listens,
Let your Word to me come near:
Newborn life and spirit give me,
Let each promise still my fear.
Death's dread pow'r, its inward strife,
Wars against your Word of life;
Fill me, Lord, with love's strong fervor
That I cling to you forever!

Oh, what blessing to be near you
And to listen to your voice;
Let me ever love and hear you,
Let your Word be now my choice!
Many hardened sinners, Lord,
Flee in terror at your Word,
But to me, who know my burden,
Show me now your Word of pardon!

Lord, your words are waters living,
When my thirsting spirit pleads;
Lord, your words are bread life-giving,
On your words my spirit feeds.

Rede, liebster Jesu, rede,
Denn dein Kind gibt acht darauf;
Stärke mich, denn ich bin blöde,
Dass ich meinen Lebenslauf
Dir zur Ehre setze fort,
Ach, lass stets dein heilig Wort
In mein Herz sein eingeschlossen,
Dir zu folgen unverdrossen!

Ach, wer wollte dich nicht hören,
Dich, du liebster Menschenfreund?
Sind doch deine Wort' und Lehren
Alle herzlich wohl gemeint.
Sie vertreiben alles Leid,
Selbst des Todes Bitterkeit
Muss vor deinen Worten weichen,
Nichts ist ihnen zu vergleichen.

Jesu, dein Wort soll mich laben;
Deine trosterfüllte Lehr'
Will ich in mein Herz eingraben.
Ach, nimm sie doch nimmermer

Lord, your words will be my light Through death's vale, its dreary night; Yes, they are my sword prevailing, And my cup of joy unfailing!	Von mir weg in dieser Zeit, Bis ich in der Ewigkeit Werde kommen zu den Ehren, Dich, o Jesu, selbst zu hören.
Precious Jesus, I entreat you, Let your words in me take root; Let this gift of heav'n enrich me So that I bring gen'rous fruit: Never take them from my heart Till I see you as you are, When in heav'nly bliss and glory I will meet you and adore you!	Unterdes vernimm mein Flehen; Liebster Jesu, höre mich! Lass bei dir mich feste stehen; So will ich dich ewiglich Preisen mit Herz, Sinn und Mund Ich will dir zu jeder Stund' Ehr' und Dank in Demut bringen Und dein hohes Lob besingen.

Some indication of the importance that Lutherans attach to the Word of God is exhibited by the 16 hymns contained in *Lutheran Worship* (1982) in that category. Such Word of God is not essentially a Word about God, but a Word from God, and hence a Word through which God discloses himself to mankind. Since it enacts history, God's Word is not separable from his actions. Jesus Christ is God's final Word both in the sense of his ultimate disclosure and in bringing his history with mankind to completion through Christ's redemptive Word and work. This finality of Jesus as God's disclosive or verbal history is plainly indicated in the statement: "In the past God spoke to our forefathers through the prophets at many times and in various ways, but in these last days he has spoken to us by his Son. . . . The Son is the radiance of God's glory and the exact representation of his being" (Heb. 1:1–3). It is only through this avenue of history that mankind can hear God. Hence Luther asserts: "We must not, as the sectarians do, imagine that God comforts us immediately, without his Word . . . which the Holy Spirit effectively calls to mind and enkindles in our hearts, even though it has not been heard for ten years" (*Luther's Works* 14:62). Therefore he insisted on preaching, hearing, and reading the Word of God, and that the means of grace, Word and Sacrament, are vital for God's communication of himself to mankind—this Word, often described as Law and Gospel. (See *LW* 329, 330.)

The preciousness of that Word in the life of a Christian is beautifully exhibited in this hymn by the pious and educated Anna Sophia, countess of Hesse Darmstadt, a hymn that first appeared in her devotional book, *Der Treue Seelenfreund Christus Jesus* (Jena, 1658).

The translation is an altered and updated form of that originally done by George T. Rygh for inclusion in *The Lutheran Hymnary* (1913), later included in *The Lutheran Hymnal* (1941).

WERDE MUNTER. For comments on the tune see hymn 263.

The harmonization is by Paul G. Bunjes.

WE HAVE A SURE PROPHETIC WORD 340

This hymn by Emmanuel Cronenwett was first published in the Ohio *Lutheran Hymnal* (1880) under the category of Holy Scripture.

WO GOTT ZUM HAUS. This fine anonymous tune first appeared in J. Klug's *Geistliche Lieder auffs new gebessert* (Wittenberg, 1533) where it was set to "Wo Gott zum Haus nicht gibt sein' Gunst," a text based on Psalm 127 and ascribed to Johann Kolrosz, teacher in Basel, Switzerland.

The harmonization was prepared for *Lutheran Worship* (1982) by Paul G. Bunjes.

O GOD, OUR LORD, YOUR HOLY WORD 341

O God, our Lord,
Your holy Word
Was long a hidden treasure
Till to its place
It was by grace
Restored in fullest measure.
For this today
Our thanks we say
And gladly glorify you.
Your mercy show
And grace bestow
On all who still deny you.

Salvation true
By faith in you,
That is your Gospel's preaching,
The heart and core
Of Bible lore
In all its sacred teaching.
In Christ we must
Put all our trust,
Not in our deeds or labor;
With conscience pure
And heart secure
Love you, Lord, and our neighbor.

Lord, you alone
This work have done
By your free grace and favor.
All who believe
Will grace receive
Through Jesus Christ, our Savior.
And though the foe
Would overthrow
Your Word with grim endeavor,

O Herre Gott,
Dein göttlich Wort
Ist lang verdunkelt blieben,
Bis durch dein' Gnad'
Uns ist gesagt,
Was Paulus hat geschrieben
Und andere
Apostel mehr
Aus dein'm göttlichen Munde;
Des danke wir
Mit Fleiss, was wir
Erlebet hab'n die Stunde.

Willst du nun fein
Gut Christe sein,
So musst du erstlich glauben:
Setz dein Vertraun—
Darauf fest bau
Hoffnung und Lieb' im Glauben!—
Allein auf Christ
Zu aller Frist,
Dein'n Nächsten lieb daneben;
Das G'wissen frei,
Rein Herz dabei
Kein' Kreatur kann geben.

Allein, Herr, du
Musst solches tun
Doch ganz aus lauter Gnaden;
Wer sich des tröst't,
Der ist erlöst,
Und kann ihm niemand schaden.
Ob wollten gleich
Papst, Kaiser, Reich
Sie und dein Wort vertreiben,

What plan he tries,
It always dies;
Your Word will stand forever.

You are my Lord,
And by your Word
Death holds no dreadful terrors;
Your precious blood,
My highest good,
Has blotted out my errors.
My thanks to you!
Your Word is true,
You keep your promise ever.
While here I live,
Your grace you give
And heaven's bliss forever.

Ist doch ihr' Macht
Geg'n dich nichts g'acht't,
Sie werden's lassen bleiben.

Gott ist mein Herr,
So bin ich der
Dem Sterben kommt zugute,
Weil du uns hast
Aus aller Last
Erlöst mit deinem Blute.
Das dank' ich dir,
Drum wirst du mir
Nach dein'r Verheissung geben,
Was ich dich bitt';
Versag mir's nicht
Im Tod und auch im Leben!

As to the authorship of this powerful and popular Reformation hymn, originally in eight stanzas, the reference to it with the initials A. H. Z. W. in a work by the eminent hymnologist Georg Serpilius (Latin for Quendal, 1668–1723) that appeared in Regensburg in 1710 elicited numerous conjectures, most of which have little to commend them. Later research reports a 1526 pamphlet, or fly sheet, discovered in the Tübingen Library in 1888 that attaches the initials A. H. W. S. V. R. to this hymn, a series that considerably limits the possibilities of authorship and that points undoubtedly to *A*rnag, *H*err *zu* *W*ildenfels, *S*chönkirchen *u*nd *R*onneburg. In fact, his name is actually mentioned with this hymn in a Ratzeburger *Gesangbuch* (1735).

Of noble birth (c. 1490–1539), his name first appears when invested with a fief by his godfather Fredrick the Wise (1463–1525), befriender of Martin Luther (*LW* 13, et al.). Arnag helped introduce the Lutheran Reformation in Wildenfels as well as in other German territories, even to the point of supplying evangelical preachers in the monasteries of Saxony. His last position appears to have been as counsel to Johann Friedrich, who in 1532 came to rule Saxony. (Büchner, *Die Lieder unserer Kirche*)

Well known and sung everywhere in Germany up to the time of the Enlightenment in the 18th century, Nelle says of this hymn:

> Like Luther's "Erhalt uns Herr bei deinem Wort" [*LW* 334], this hymn was forbidden by the authorities, pastors were deposed from office for having it sung, in short, it has a history of battle and victory similar to Luther's best hymns. It deeply made its impression on the hearts of the congregation as a solid and forceful hymn.

The translation is an altered and updated form of that prepared by W. Gustav Polack for inclusion in *The Lutheran Hymnal* (1941).

O HERRE GOTT. This splendid tune appeared anonymously with the above text in the Wittenberg *Enchiridion* of 1526, a tune to which this text has since been inseparably wedded. Its basis lies in the secular folksong, "Weiss mir ein Blümlein blaue" (Show me a blue flower) that arose about the beginning of the 16th century.

The setting was prepared by Paul G. Bunjes for inclusion in *Lutheran Worship* (1982).

ALMIGHTY GOD, YOUR WORD IS CAST 342

Written about 1815 by John Cawood and based on the Parable of the Sower in Matthew 13 and Mark 4, this hymn was first published in Thomas Cotterill's *Selection of Psalms and Hymns* (eighth edition, 1819) in 5 stanzas and 4 lines, and stipulated for use "after the sermon." Its inclusion in James Montgomery's (*LW* 50, et al.) *The Christian Psalmist* (1825) increased its use as a congregational hymn in English-speaking countries, in some cases with the omission of one or more stanzas, in others, with the addition of a doxology. Strangely, present-day hymnals of mainline denominations give it no place except for *The Hymnal 1982* of the Protestant Episcopal Church.

Text and tune in *Lutheran Worship* (1982) are those prepared by the Inter-Lutheran Commission on Worship for inclusion in *Lutheran Book of Worship* (1978).

ST. FLAVIAN (OLD 132ND, REDHEAD, PRESCOT) is the tune set to Psalm 132 in John Day's monumental *The Whole Book of Psalmes* (1562), often called Day's Psalter or the English Psalter (see essay: Metrical Psalms, p. 825). There the tune appeared thus:

Readily noted is the fact that the present form of the tune resembles only the first half as included in Day. The first appearance of the present form was in Richard Redhead's (*LW* 110, 285) *Church Hymn Tunes* (1853). In the original edition of *Hymns Ancient and Modern* (1861) the tune was called REDHEAD, a name changed to ST. FLAVIAN (an early bishop of Constantinople) in the revised edition of 1875.

The harmonization is from the *Service Book and Hymnal* (1958).

343 GOD HAS SPOKEN BY HIS PROPHETS

This text by George W. Briggs was included in *Ten New Hymns on the Bible*, printed by the Hymn Society in America in 1952 in celebration of the publication of the Revised Standard Version of the Bible by Thomas Nelson publishers, New York.

REX GLORIAE, by Henry T. Smart, appeared in the Appendix (1868) to *Hymns Ancient and Modern* (1861). Although confident, vigorous, and rather soundly constructed, the tune lacks a certain originality in both phrase and rhythm.

The harmonization was done for *Lutheran Worship* (1982) by Richard W. Gieseke.

344 LORD JESUS CHRIST, WILL YOU NOT STAY

Lord Jesus Christ, will you not stay?
It is now toward the end of day.
Oh, let your Word, that saving light,
Shine forth undimmed into the night.

Rekindle for the end-time stress
Faith's ancient strength and steadfastness
That we keep pure till life is spent
Your holy Word and Sacrament.

To hope grown dim, to hearts turned cold
Speak tongues of fire and make us bold
To shine your Word of saving grace
Into each dark and loveless place.

May glorious truths that we have heard,
The bright lance of your mighty Word,
Spurn Satan that your Church be strong,
Bold, unified in act and song.

Restrain, O Lord, the human pride
That seeks to thrust your truth aside
Or with some man-made thoughts or things
Would dim the words your Spirit sings.

The cause is yours, the glory too.
Then hear us, Lord, and keep us true,
Your Word alone our heart's defense,
The Church's glorious confidence.

Ach bleib bei uns, Herr Jesu Christ,
Weil es nun Abend worden ist;
Dein göttlich Wort, das helle Licht,
Lass ja bei uns auslöschen nicht!

In dieser, letzt'n, betrübten Zeit
Verleih uns, Herr, Beständigkeit,
Dass wir dein Wort und Sakrament
Rein b'halten bis an unser End'!

Herr Jesu, hilf, dein' Kirch' erhalt,
Wir sind gar sicher, faul und kalt!
Gib Glück und Heil zu deinem Wort,
Damit es schall' an allem Ort!

Ehalt uns nur bei deinem Wort
Und wehr des Teufels Trug und Mord!
Gib deiner Kirche Gnad' und Huld,
Fried', Einigkeit, Mut und Geduld!

Den stolzen Geistern wehre doch,
Die sich mit G'walt erheben hoch
Und bringen stets was Neues her,
Zu fälschen deine rechte Lehr'.

Dein Wort ist unsers Herzens Trutz
Und deiner Kirche wahrer Schutz;
Dabei erhalt uns, lieber Herr,
Dass wir nichts anders suchen mehr!

This splendid hymn on the Word of God and the preservation of the Church is a cento of the nine-stanza hymn that first appeared in *Geistliche Psalmen, Hymnen, Liedern und Gebeten* in two simultaneous Nürnberg printings in 1611, one by Georg L. Fuhrmann and the other by Abraham Wagenmann. Stanza 1 represents a German translation that appeared in 1579 of a Latin stanza written by Philipp Melanchthon (*LW* 189) in 1551: "Vespera iam venit. Nobiscum, Christe maneto, exstingui lucem nec patiare tuam." One can readily recognize this as based on Jesus' appearance to the two disciples on the road to Emmaus on Easter morning and their statement to Jesus: "Stay with us, for it is nearly evening; the day is almost over" (Luke 24:29). Stanza 2 represents an addition to the first that appeared in the book *Christliche Gebet und Psalmen, Welche die Kinder in der Jungfrauschulen zu Freiberg zu Beten und zu singen Phlegen* (1602), a stanza that exhibits a definite affinity to the rhymed prayer with which Nikolaus Selnecker concludes Psalm 29 in his *Der Psalter mit Kurzen Summarien und Gebetlein für die Hausväter und ihre Kinder* (Leipzig, 1572). Stanzas 3–6 are by Selnecker as contained in this *Psalter*; they stand therein with Psalm 122 and with the heading "Gebetlein" (Little Prayer).

The translation of this cento in *Lutheran Worship* (1982) is by F. Samuel Janzow.

ACH BLEIB BEI UNS. This laudable chorale tune is from *Geistliche Lieder D. Martini Lutheri und anderer frommen Christen* (Leipzig, 1589).

The harmonization is by George Leonard, a *nom de plume* of Paul G. Bunjes.

345 COME UNTO ME, YE WEARY

This hymn by William Chatterton Dix first appeared in *The People's Hymnal* (1867). Dix wrote to F. A. Jones, author of *Famous Hymns and Their Authors*:

> I was ill and depressed at the time, and it was almost to idle away the hours that I wrote the hymn. I had been ill for many weeks, and felt weary and faint, and the hymn really expresses the languidness of body from which I was suffering at the time. Soon after its completion I recovered, and I always look back to that hymn as the turning point in my illness.

A few minor alterations have been made to the text.

ANTHES. For comments on the tune see hymn 347.

The harmonization is by George Leonard, a *nom de plume* of Paul G. Bunjes.

346 O KINGLY LOVE, THAT FAITHFULLY

This hymn by Martin H. Franzmann, then professor at Concordia Seminary, St. Louis, is the result of Concordia Publishing House's music committee commissioning him to write an appropriate hymn for the 450th Reformation anniversary observance in 1967. Apparently the committee reacted unfavorably to the completed text, for in a letter dated October 1966 Franzmann wrote:

> Regarding the topic we discussed at luncheon on Thursday last: I think we're in an impossible situation. Asking me to write a hymn such as your committee expects, apparently is like asking Healey Willan to write in Duke Ellington's idiom; I don't address God as "you" even in my private devotions. I cannot see how any amount of doctoring up on the present hymn would bring it much closer to the committee's expectations, and I do not have any time for another attempt. So I suggest we just forget about the whole thing.

Evidently Edward Klammer, then head of Concordia's music department and member of the aforementioned music committee, did not completely share the committee's sentiments, for in a letter in which he sent payment to Franzmann for his efforts he wrote:

We are still planning to ask Prof. Hillert of Concordia Teacher's College in River Forest to provide music for it and we are hopeful that congregations will use it. If not, we are certain that choirs will use it.

KINGLY LOVE was composed, harmonized, and so named by Richard W. Hillert at the request of Concordia Publishing House's music committee, but the text and setting was neither used nor promoted by Concordia in its Reformation anniversary materials. It remained for the Synod's Commission on Worship, shortly thereafter engaged in the task of producing the *Worship Supplement* (1969), to include it in that volume, largely at the encouragement of Edward Klammer, who brought the text and tune to the attention of the commission, of which he was a member.

Granted that the text and tune have probably not enjoyed great popularity—its lofty but well-crafted language; its irregular meter, lumped in the category of peculiar meter (PM, *LW* p. 999); its sound with the setting's pan-modal (see essay: The Church Modes, p. 832) features (Aeolian and Mixolydian characteristics)—these may evoke a negative reaction at first attempts. With patience and endurance, however, its use can result in an edifying and rewarding experience. At least such proved to be the case at Lutheran Church of the Resurrection, Sappington, Missouri, where Edward Klammer, then director of music, patiently taught the hymn to both choir and congregation, and where it was frequently sung and appreciated during the distribution of Holy Communion.

TODAY YOUR MERCY CALLS US 347

The comfort of salvation through Christ Jesus by the grace of God, not by works, is beautifully expressed in this hymn by Oswald Allen, an invalid bank manager. It first appeared in *Hymns of the Christian Life* (London, 1861), a collection of his hymns that he produced during England's severe winter of 1859–60. The original had first-person singular pronouns throughout.

The text appears here in updated form.

ANTHES is named after its composer Johann A. Anthes. It first appeared in a *Choralbuch* (1847) to the Nassau, Germany, hymnal of 1842 set to a German translation of a Latin text beginning "Ergrünt, ihr Siegespalmen ihr Himmel werdet klar" and it soon became a popular and much-loved tune (Zahn 8786). It appeared with Oswald Allen's text, "Today Your Mercy Calls Us," in both *The Lutheran Hymnal* (1941) and it's predecessor *The Evangelical Lutheran Hymn-Book* (1912).

The harmonization is from *The Lutheran Hymnal* (1941).

348 I HEARD THE VOICE OF JESUS SAY

This popular hymn, written by Horatius Bonar while he was a minister at Kelso in Scotland, first appeared in his *Hymns Original and Selected* (1846) and later in his *Hymns of Faith and Hope* (1862) under the title "The Voice from Galilee—John 1:16." The scriptural reference, which reads, "From the fullness of his grace we have all received one blessing after another," appears to be somewhat marginal when, upon examining the hymn text, there come to mind such obvious references as Matthew 11:28, John 4:14, and John 1:9. But give Bonar credit. His was the day when hymn singing was still restricted to metrical psalmody (see essay: Metrical Psalms, p. 825). Bonar's early attempt at hymn writing while assistant to the minister at Leath was the result of the total lack of interest in such psalmody on the part of the children in Sunday school.

THIRD MODE MELODY is the third of Thomas Tallis' nine tunes included in Archbishop Parker's Psalter (c. 1567), where the melody was originally in the tenor. The beautiful and haunting Phrygian mode melody has served as the setting for various texts in English hymnals; the combination with Bonar's text is in *The Hymnal 1940* of the Episcopal Church and also in its successor *The Hymnal 1982*. Ralph Vaughan Williams' (*LW* 59, et al.) *Fantasy for Strings*, based on this melody, well exhibits its beauty.

The setting is from the *Service Book and Hymnal* (1958).

349 DELAY NOT, DELAY NOT, O SINNER DRAW NEAR

This call to repentance by Thomas Hastings was first published in his *Spiritual Songs for Social Worship* (1832). Duffield gives the hymn little credit when he says:

> It is upon the same page with Knox's "Acquaint thyself quickly, O Sinner, with God," is of the same meter, and perhaps was suggested by it, and written in order that the vacant space upon the page might be filled by a hymn of similar purport.

Strangely, too, of the numerous hymnals examined, both old and new, only the *Lutheran Hymnal* (1973) of the Lutheran Church of Australia, *The Lutheran Hymnal* (1941), and *Lutheran Worship* (1982) include this hymn.

MALDWYN is a Welsh melody dating from the 17th century from the collection of tunes entitled *Moliant, Cenedl Dinbych* (1920) by David E. Evans (1843–1913), Welsh music critic, teacher, and composer. Cast in the dactylic (´ ˘ ˘) four elevens (11 11 11 11), although technically anapestic since each line ends with an accented syllable, the triple movement, so characteristic of such meters, lends a sense of urgency to the thoughts of the text.

The setting is from *The Lutheran Hymnal* (1941).

THE SAVIOR CALLS; LET EVERY EAR 350

This hymn by Anne Steele, perhaps the most popular and best follower of Isaac Watts (*LW* 53, et al.), was first published in her *Poems on Subjects Chiefly Doctrinal* (1760), where it was entitled "The Invitation." Few present-day hymnals include this hymn, a hymn that became popular in the Missouri Synod by its inclusion both in the *Evangelical Lutheran Hymn-Book* (1912) and *The Lutheran Hymnal* (1941).

AZMON (GASTON, DENFIELD) was composed by Carl G. Gläser, a native of Wessenfels, Germany, a tune brought into American hymnody by Lowell Mason (*LW* 115, et al.) in his *Modern Psalmodist* (1839). There it appeared in duple time set to "Come, Let Us Lift Our Joyful Eyes." In his *Carmina Sacra* (1841) it appeared with the same text but in triple time.

Notice that this hymn is in common meter (86 86), the workhorse of hymnody, a meter that uses simple, direct, mostly single-syllable words in language that is brief and to the point. Moreover, the strong accent with which each of the four lines ends lends strength to the tune. The musical imbalance of eights and sixes is solved in several ways. In 4/4 (duple) the dotted half note at the ends of lines two and four provides the two extra pulses to balance things out (cf. ST. ANNE, *LW* 180). In 3/2 or 3/4 (triple), as in Azmon, the balance is gained by providing six basic pulses in each phrase.

Mason's name for the tune, AZMON, is the Hebrew word for "Fortress," an identified place mentioned in Numbers 34:4. Present-day hymnals most frequently use AZMON as the tune for Charles Wesley's "Oh, for a Thousand Tongues to Sing" (*LW* 276).

The setting in Lutheran Worship (1982) is from the *Service Book and Hymnal* (1958).

351 BY GRACE I'M SAVED

By grace I'm saved, grace free and boundless;
My soul, believe and doubt it not.
Why stagger at this word of promise?
Has Scripture ever falsehood taught?
No; then this word must true remain:
By grace you too will life obtain.

By grace God's Son, our only Savior,
Came down to earth to bear our sin.
Was it because of your own merit
That Jesus died your soul to win?
No, it was grace, and grace alone,
That brought him from his heav'nly throne.

By grace! This ground of faith is certain;
As long as God is true, it stands.
What saints have penned by inspiration,
What in his Word our God commands,
Our faith in what our God has done
Depends on grace—grace through his Son.

By grace to timid hearts that tremble,
In tribulation's furnace tried,
By grace, in spite of fear and trouble,
The Father's heart is open wide.
Where could I help and strength secure
If grace were not my anchor sure?

By grace! On this I'll rest when dying;
In Jesus' promise I rejoice;
For though I know my heart's condition,
I also know my Savior's voice.
My heart is glad, all grief has flown
Since I am saved by grace alone.

Aus Gnaden soll ich selig werden!
Herz, glaubst du's, oder glaubst du's nicht?
Was willst du dich so blöd' gebärden?
Ist's Wahrheit, was die Schrift verspricht,
So muss auch dieses Wahrheit sein:
Aus Gnaden ist der Himmel dein.

Aus Gnaden kam sein Sohn auf Erden
Und übernahm die Sündenlast.
Was nötigt' ihn, dein Freund zu werden?
Sag's, wo du was zu rühmen hast!
War's nicht, dass er dein Bestes wollt'
Und dir aus Gnaden helfen sollt'?

Aus Gnaden!—Dieser Grund wird bleiben
Solange Gott wahrhaftig heisst.
Was alle Knechte Jesu schreiben,
Was Gott in seinem Wort anpreist,
Worauf all unser Glaube ruht,
Ist Gnade durch des Lammes Blut.

Aus Gnaden bleibt dem blöden Herzen
Das Herz des Vaters aufgetan,
Wenn's unter grösster Angst und Schmerzen
Nichts sieht und nichts mehr hoffen kann.
Wo nähm' ich oftmals Stärkung her,
Wenn Gnade nicht mein Anker wär'!

Aus Gnaden!—Hierauf will ich sterben.
Ich fühle nichts, doch mir ist wohl;
Ich kenn' mein sündliches Verderben,
Doch auch den, der mich heilen soll.
Mein Geist ist froh, die Seele lacht,
Weil mich die Gnade selig macht.

When one looks seriously at the God-disclosed history of the Judeo-Christian tradition, one is struck with the continuum of one word among all other words, namely, the beautiful word *grace* and its continuum in the midst of judgment; grace—mercy and compassion for one who by every act has forfeited his or her claim on love. Such is the grace of God to the sinner! Moreover, any admixture of merit, as constituting a claim on mercy, destroys the very essence of grace. Thus, merit and grace are mutually exclusive.

Few hymns surpass this one on the subject of grace, a hymn that was included in and popularly sung from the *Evangelical Lutheran Hymn-Book* (1912). Written by Christian L. Scheidt and based on Ephesians 2:8–9 and Romans 4:4, it first appeared, originally in 10 stanzas, in the Ebersdorfer *Gesangbuch* (1742).

The translation is a slightly altered and updated version of the composite form that appeared in *The Lutheran Hymnal* (1941).

O DAS ICH TAUSEND ZUNGEN HÄTTE. For comments on this tune see hymn 224.

The harmonization is from *The Lutheran Hymnal* (1941), slightly altered.

GOD LOVED THE WORLD SO THAT HE GAVE 352

God loved the world so that he gave
His only Son the lost to save
That all who would in him believe
Should everlasting life receive.

Christ Jesus is the ground of faith,
Who was made flesh and suffered death;
All who confide in Christ alone
Are built on this chief cornerstone.

If you are sick, if death is near,
This truth your troubled heart can cheer:
Christ Jesus saves your soul from death;
That is the firmest ground of faith.

Be of good cheer, for God's own Son
Forgives all sins which you have done;
You're justified by Jesus' blood;
Baptized, you have the highest good.

Glory to God the Father, Son,
And Holy Spirit, Three in One!
To you, O blessed Trinity,
Be praise now and eternally!

Also hat Gott die Welt geliebt,
Dass er uns seinen Sohn hergibt,
Dass, wer ihm traut und glaubt allein,
Kann und soll ewig selig sein.

Der Glaubensgrund ist Jesus Christ,
Der für uns selbst Mensch worden ist.
Wer seinem Mittler fest vertraut,
Der bleibt auf deisen Grund gebaut.

Bist du krank, kommst du gar in Tod,
So merk dies wohl in aller Not;
Mein Jesus macht die Seel' gesund,
Das ist der rechte Glaubensgrund.

Drum sei getrost, weil Gottes Sohn
Die Sünd' vergibt, der Gnadenthron;
Du bist gerecht durch Christi Blut,
Die Tauf' schenkt dir das höchste Gut.

Ehr' sei dem Vater und dem Sohn
Samt Heil'gem Geist in einem Thron,
Welch's ihm auch also sei bereit't
Von nun an bis in Ewigkeit.

In the *Kirchengesanbuch für Evangelisch-Lutherische Gemeinden ungeändertes Augsburgischer Konfession* (1847), the first official hymn book of the Missouri Synod, Bollhagen's *Gesangbuch* (1791) is given as the source of this hymn, one of the numerous hymns based on John 3:16. This occurs as well in its three subsequent editions, the 1848, 1857, and the 1917. More recent research, however, on the part of August Suelflow, head of Concordia Historical Institute, St. Louis, has discovered that the hymn appeared in an earlier, undated edition of this Pomeranian hymnal, published in Stettin with a prayer book dated 1778 and entitled *Heiliges Lippen-und Herzens-Opfer einer gläubigen Seele oder Vollständiges Gesang-Buch*. This book with the two supplements and an additional section of new hymns had a total of 1,313 hymns.

August Crull's translation, beginning "God loved the world so that he gave," which was used in the *Evangelical Lutheran Hymn-Book* (1912) and in *The Lutheran Hymnal* (1941), appears here in altered and updated form. To the first four stanzas prepared by the Inter-Lutheran Commission on Worship for inclusion in *Lutheran Book of Worship* (1978) the Commission on Worship added the doxological stanza 5.

DIE HELLE SONN LEUCHT. While the *Kirchengesangbuch* mentioned above called for the tune HERR JESU CHRIST, MEINS (*LW* 262) for this hymn, *Lutheran Worship* (1982), following the lead of *Lutheran Book of Worship* (1978), uses DIE HELLE SONN LEUCHT. Composed by Melchior Vulpius, it was included in his *Geistliches Gesangbuch* (Jena, 1609) as the setting for Nikolaus Herman's (*LW* 44, 235) "Die helle Sonn' leucht jetzt herfür" (see "The Radiant Sun Shines in the Skies," *TLH* 547).

Paul G. Bunjes prepared the harmonization for *Lutheran Worship* (1982).

353 DEAR CHRISTIANS, ONE AND ALL

Dear Christians, one and all, rejoice,
With exultation springing,
And with united heart and voice
And holy rapture singing,
Proclaim the wonders God has done,
How his right arm the vict'ry won.
What price our ransom cost him!

Fast bound in Satan's chains I lay,
Death brooded darkly o'er me,
Sin was my torment night and day;
In sin my mother bore me.
But daily deeper still I fell;
My life became a living hell,
So firmly sin possessed me.

My own good works all came to naught,
No grace or merit gaining;
Free will against God's judgment fought,
Dead to all good remaining.
My fears increased till sheer despair
Left only death to be my share;
The pangs of hell I suffered.

But God had seen my wretched state
Before the world's foundation,
And mindful of his mercies great,
He planned for my salvation.
He turned to me a father's heart;
He did not choose the easy part
But gave his dearest treasure.

God said to his beloved Son:
"It's time to have compassion.
Then go, bright jewel of my crown,
And bring to all salvation;
From sin and sorrow set them free;
Slay bitter death for them that they
May live with you forever."

The Son obeyed his Father's will,
Was born of virgin mother;
And God's good pleasure to fulfill,

Nun freut euch, liebe Christen g'mein,
Und lasst uns fröhlich springen,
Dass wir getrost und all' in ein
Mit Lust und Liebe singen,
Wass Gott an uns gewendet hat,
Und seine süsse Wundertat;
Gar teu'r hat er's erworben.

Dem Teufel ich gefangen lag,
Im Tod war ich verloren,
Mein' Sünd' mich quälte Nacht und Tag,
Darin ich war geboren.
Ich fiel auch immer tiefer drein,
Es war kein Gut's am Leben mein,
Die Sünd' hatt' mich besessen.

Mein' gute Werk', die galten nicht,
Es war mit ihn'n verdorben;
Der frei' Will' hasste Gott's Gericht,
Er war zum Gut'n erstorben.
Die Angst mich zu verzweifeln trieb,
Dass nichts denn Sterben bei mir blieb,
Zur Hölle musst' ich sinken.

Da jammert' Gott in Ewigkeit
Mein Elend übermassen,
Er dacht' an sein' Barmherzigkeit,
Er wollt' mir helfen lassen;
Er wandt' zu mir das Vaterherz,
Es war bei ihm fürwahr kein Scherz,
Er liess's sein Bestes kosten.

Er sprach zu seinem lieben Sohn:
Die Zeit ist hier zu 'rbarmen;
Fahr hin, mein's Herzens werte Kron',
Und sei das Heil dem Armen
Und hilf ihm aus der Sündennot,
Erwürg' für ihn den bittern Tod
Und lass ihn mit dir leben!

Der Sohn dem Vater g'horsam ward,
Er kam zu mir auf Erden
Von einer Jungfrau rein und zart,

He came to be my brother.
His royal pow'r disguised he bore,
A servant's form, like mine, he wore
To lead the devil captive.

Er sollt' mein Bruder werden.
Gar heimlich führt' er sein' Gewalt,
Er ging in meiner armen G'stalt,
Den Teufel wollt' er fangen.

To me he said: "Stay close to me,
I am your rock and castle.
Your ransom I myself will be;
For you I strive and wrestle;
For I am yours, and you are mine,
And where I am you may remain;
The foe shall not divide us.

Er sprach zu mir: Halt dich an mich,
Es soll dir jetzt gelingen;
Ich geb' mich selber ganz für dich,
Da will ich für dich ringen;
Denn ich bin dein, und du bist mein,
Und wo ich bleib', da sollst du sein,
Uns soll der Feind nicht scheiden.

"Though he will shed my precious blood,
Of life me thus bereaving,
All this I suffer for your good;
Be steadfast and believing.
Life will from death the vict'ry win;
My innocence shall bear your sin;
And you are blest forever.

Vergiessen wird er mir mein Blut,
Dazu mein Leben rauben;
Das leid' ich alles dir zugut.
Das halt mit festem Glauben!
Den Tod verschlingt das Leben mein,
Mein' Unschuld trägt die Sünde dein:
Da bist du selig worden.

"Now to my Father I depart,
From earth to heav'n ascending,
And, heav'nly wisdom to impart,
The Holy spirit sending;
In trouble he will comfort you
And teach you always to be true
And into truth shall guide you.

Gen Himmel zu dem Vater mein
Fahr' ich von diesem Leben,
Da will ich sein der Meister dein,
Den Geist will ich dir geben,
Der dich in Trübnis trösten soll
Und lehren mich erkennen wohl
Und in der Wahrheit leiten.

"What I on earth have done and taught
Guide all your life and teaching;
So shall the kingdom's work be wrought
And honored in your preaching.
But watch lest foes with base alloy
The heav'nly treasure should destroy;
This final word I leave you."

Was ich getan hab' und gelehrt,
Das sollst du tun und lehren,
Damit das Reich Gott's werd' gemehrt
Zu Lob und seinen Ehren,
Und hüt' dich vor der Menschen G'satz,
Davon verdirbt der edle Schatz!
Dass lass' ich dir zur Letze.

According to Zahn this hymn first appeared in broadsheet form in 1523 and thereafter in *Etlich Christlich lieder* (1524), entitled, "A Christian hymn of Dr. Martin Luther, setting forth the unspeakable grace of God and the true faith." It is debatable whether this is Luther's first hymn or whether that honor should be accorded "Flung to the Heedless Winds" (*TLH* 259), the balladlike hymn written to commemorate the martyrdom of two young Augustinian monks, Heinrich Voes and Johann Esch, who were burned at the stake in Brussels, June 30, 1523. As a personal confession, or testimony, "Dear Christians, One and All, Rejoice" portrays in a moving and forthright manner the course of Luther's early adult life, from his entry into the Augustinian monastery to his attainment of complete peace in the doctrine of justification by faith in Jesus Christ, not by works. As such it beautifully mirrors his inner spiritual development.

This hymn can unquestionably be considered the greatest confessional hymn of the Lutheran Church. It may be readily outlined thus:

1. God's compassion (sts. 1–4)
2. God's method of redemption—the life of the Savior according to the church year (sts. 5–9)
3. Exhortation (st. 10)
   a. Spread the Gospel (lines 1–4)
   b. Preserve the *Sola Scriptura* (lines 5–7)

The translation, by Richard Massey in his *Martin Luther's Spiritual Songs* (1854), was included in *The Lutheran Hymnal* (1941) in altered form and is further altered and updated here in *Lutheran Worship.*

NUN FREUT EUCH. Of the three tunes associated with the above text, this tune with its leap of fourths in the first, third, fifth, and seventh lines is the one that captures the exuberance of the text. Based on a pre-Reformation folksong, "Nun freut euch, Frauen, unde Mann," it still exhibits Luther's creative hand. Notice the *Freudensprung* at the beginning of each line. This tune appeared with the above text in *Etlich Christlich lieder* (1524). The two other tunes early associated with this text are "Es ist das Heil uns kommen her" (*LW* 355) and "Es ist gewisslich an der Zeit" (*LW* 462).

The harmonization is by Carl F. Schalk.

354 I KNOW MY FAITH IS FOUNDED

I know my faith is founded
On Jesus Christ, my God and Lord;
And this my faith confessing,
Unmoved I stand on his sure Word.
Man's reason cannot fathom
The truth of God profound;
Who trusts its subtle wisdom
Relies on shifting ground.
God's Word is all-sufficient,
It makes divinely sure,
And trusting in its wisdom,
My faith shall rest secure.

Increase my faith, dear Savior,
For Satan seeks by night and day
To rob me of this treasure
And take my hope of bliss away.
But, Lord, with you beside me,
I shall be undismayed;
And led by your good Spirit,
I shall be unafraid.
Abide with me, O Savior,
A firmer faith bestow;
Then I shall bid defiance
To ev'ry evil foe.

Ich weiss, an wen ich gläube:
Mein Jesus ist des Glaubens Grund;
Bei dessen Wort ich bleibe,
Und das bekennet Herz und Mund.
Vernunft darf hier nichts sagen,
Sie sei auch noch so klug;
Wer Fleisch und Blut will fragen,
Der fällt in Selbstbetrug.
Ich folg' in Glaubenslehren
Der Heil'gen Schrift allein;
Was diese mich lässt hören,
Muss unbeweglich sein.

Herr, stärke mir den Glauben;
Denn Satan trachtet Nacht und Tag,
Wie er dies Kleinod rauben
Und um mein Heil mich bringen mag.
Wenn deine Hand mich führet,
So werd' ich sicher gehn;
Wenn mich dein Geist regieret,
Wird's selig um mich stehn.
Ach segne mein Vertrauen
Und bleib mit mir vereint!
So lass' ich mir nicht grauen
Und fürchte keinen Feind.

In faith, Lord, let me serve you;
When persecution, grief, and pain
From you, Lord, seek to swerve me,
Let me a steadfast trust retain;
And then at my departure,
Lord, take me home to you
Your riches to inherit
As all you said holds true.
In life and death, Lord, keep me
Until your heav'n I gain,
Where I by your great mercy
The end of faith attain.

Lass mich im Glauben leben;
Soll auch Verfolgung, Angst und Pein
Mich auf der Welt umgeben,
So lass mich treu im Glauben sein!
Im Glauben lass mich sterben,
Wenn sich mein Lauf beschliest,
Und mich das Leben erben,
Das mir verheissen ist!
Nimm mich in deine Hände
Bei Leb- und Sterbenszeit,
So ist des Glaubens Ende
Der Seelen Seligkeit.

Erdmann Neumeister, Hamburg pastor and poet, strong defender of orthodoxy against Pietism, first published this notable hymn in his *Evangelischer Nachklang* (first part, Hamburg, 1718), where it was designated for *Quasimodogeniti* (As Newborn Babes)—historically the First Sunday after Easter, in *Lutheran Worship* the Second Sunday of Easter—to be sung after the sermon.

The translation is an altered and updated form of that which appeared in *The Lutheran Hymnal* (1941).

NUN LOB, MEIN SEEL. For comments on this tune see hymn 453.

The harmonization was prepared for *Lutheran Worship* (1982) by Wilhelm Quampen, a *nom de plume* of Paul G. Bunjes.

SALVATION UNTO US HAS COME 355

Salvation unto us has come
By God's free grace and favor;
Good works cannot avert our doom,
They help and save us never.
Faith looks to Jesus Christ alone,
Who did for all the world atone;
He is our one redeemer.

What God did in his Law demand
And none to him could render
Caused wrath and woe on ev'ry hand
For man, the vile offender.
Our flesh has not those pure desires
The spirit of the Law requires,
And lost is our condition.

It was a false, misleading dream
That God his Law had given
That sinners could themselves redeem
And by their works gain heaven.
The Law is but a mirror bright
To bring the inbred sin to light
That lurks within our nature.

Es ist das Heil uns kommen her
Von Gnad' und lauter Güte,
Die Werke helfen nimmer mehr,
Sie mögen nicht behuten,
Der Glaub' sieht Jesum Christum an
Der hat g'nug für uns all' getan,
Er ist der Mittler worden.

Was Gott im G'setz geboten hat,
Da man es nicht konnt' halten,
Erhub sich Zorn und grosse Not
Vor Gott so mannigfalten;
Vom Fleisch wollt' nicht heraus der Geist,
Vom G'setz erfordert allermeist,
Es war mit uns verloren.

Es war ein falscher Wahn dabei,
Gott hätt' sein G'setz drum geben,
Als ob wir möchten selber frei
Nach seinem Willen leben;
So ist es nur ein Spiegel zart,
Der uns zeigt an die sünd'ge Art,
In unserm Fleisch verborgen.

Since Christ has full atonement made And brought to us salvation, Each Christian therefore may be glad And build on this foundation. Your grace alone, dear Lord, I plead, Your death is now my life indeed, For you have paid my ransom.	Und wenn es nun erfüllet ist Durch den, der es konnt' halten, So lerne jetzt ein frommer Christ Des Glaubens recht' Gestalte. Nicht mehr, denn: Lieber herre mein, Dein Tod wird mir das Leben sein, Du hast für mich bezahlet!
Faith clings to Jesus' cross alone And rests in him unceasing; And by its fruits true faith is known, With love and hope increasing. For faith alone can justify; Works serve our neighbor and supply The proof that faith is living.	Die Werk', die kommen g'wisslich her Aus einem rechten Glauben; Denn das nicht rechter Glaube wär', Wollt'st ihn der Werk' berauben. Doch macht allein der Glaub' gerecht, Die Werke sind des Nächsten Knecht'. Dabei wir'n Glauben merken.
All blessing, honor, thanks, and praise To Father, Son, and Spirit, The God who saved us by his grace; All glory to his merit. O triune God in heav'n above, You have revealed your saving love; Your blessed name we hallow.	Sei Lob und Ehr' mit hohem Preis Um dieser Gutheit willen Gott Vater, Sohn, Heiligem Geist! Der woll' mit Gnad' erfüllen, Was er in uns ang'fangen hat Zu Ehren seiner Majestät, Dass heilig werd' sein Name.

This great hymn, a bold, instructive statement of the Reformation's faith, was written by Paul Speratus, at the time a priest in the Western Church, while imprisoned for espousing Luther's cause and openly and freely preaching Luther's biblical and evangelical doctrine. In this circumstance, apparently Luther's "Dear Christians, One and All, Rejoice" (*LW* 353) came into his hands. In connection with it, he wrote this hymn, sending it as a comfort to his beloved congregation in Olmütz. Interestingly, he used the same metric pattern—87 87 887—as Luther had, a pattern that became typical of so many German chorales. Shortly thereafter Speratus' hymn appeared in *Etlich Christlich lider Lobgesang* (Wittenberg, 1524) with the heading "A Hymn of Law and Faith, Powerfully furnished with God's Word." This little book, commonly known as the *Achtliederbuch*, in the preparation of which he assisted Luther, enjoys the distinction of being, what might be called, the first Lutheran hymnal.

Since this hymn helped spread the Reformation teachings on wings of song, it was esteemed similar to Luther's hymns and happily included in all Lutheran hymnals. Up to the time of Pietism it was considered among the *Kernlieder*—the splendid normative core of Reformation hymnody. As a teaching and confessional hymn—a mark of orthodoxy—Pietism sought every excuse to put it aside. The Enlightenment would have nothing to do with it. And even in the confessional revival of the early 19th century, some considered it simply as a rhymed paraphrase of the doctrine of justification by faith; others, seeing it as a venerable relic, were reluctant to include it in a Lutheran hymnal since the hymnal should not be a shrine for relics. And of all things, Claus Harms (1778–1855), one of the leaders of the confessional revival, affirming the hymn's importance in the Reformation as a teaching device in rhyme, but denying it to be really a hymn, considered the hymn unnecessary, since the Catechism and the evangelical sermons were sufficiently acquainting congregations with the doctrine of justification by faith.

On the other hand, there were those who considered it one of the finest of *Kernlieder*, a hymn that dare not be cast aside, among them August Vilmar (1800–68), theological professor at Marburg, and Professor Cosack (1861) of East Prussia. The latter insisted that this hymn is not a relic nor a didactic-dogmatic poem; a teacher is not lecturing in it. It is the song of a soul, filled with the peace of the Gospel, over the rediscovered fundamental truths of the Christian faith.

Originally in 14 stanzas, the translation here given is an altered and updated version of that which appeared in *The Lutheran Hymnal* (1941).

ES IST DAS HEIL is the anonymous, sturdy and beautiful tune that appeared with the Speratus text in *Etlich Christlich lider* (Wittenberg, 1524) as well as in the Erfurt *Enchiridia* (1524) and in Johann Walter's *Geystliche gesangk Buchleyn* (Wittenberg, 1524). In the Erfurt *Enchiridia*, where it is coupled to "Nun freut euch, lieben Christen-gemein" (*LW* 353), a note indicates that the tune was used with the Easter hymn "Frewt euch, yhr frawen und yhr man, das Christ ist auferstanden," thus in pre-Reformation times, a fact attested by a goodly number of 16th-century witnesses (Zahn 4430). The book that appeared in Nürnberg in 1536, namely, *Schöne auserlesene Lieder* by Heinrich Fink (c. 1445–1527), director of the royal orchestra in Krakow, Stuttgart, Augsburg, Salzburg, and Vienna, contains the tune in the original Mixolydian mode. (See essay: The Church Modes, p. 832.)

Paul G. Bunjes prepared the setting for *Lutheran Worship* (1982).

DRAWN TO THE CROSS, WHICH YOU HAVE BLESSED — 356

Genevieve M. Irons wrote this hymn in 1880 with the caption, "Consecration of self to Christ." In 1884 it appeared in her *Corpus Christi*, a Roman Catholic manual for Holy Communion.

DUNSTAN, also called JUST AS I AM, was composed by Joseph Barnby in 1883 and it appeared in *The Home and School Hymnal* (1893) of the Free Church of Scotland. The tune's alternate title is the result of using it with Charlotte Elliott's hymn, "Just As I Am" (*LW* 359).

Herbert Gotsch prepared the setting for inclusion in *Lutheran Worship* (1982).

357 I TRUST, O CHRIST, IN YOU ALONE

I trust, O Christ, in you alone;
No earthly hope avails me.
You will not see me overthrown
When Satan's host assails me.
No human strength, no earthly pow'r
Can see me through the evil hour,
For you alone my strength renew.
I cry to you!
I trust, O Lord, your promise true.

Allein zu dir, Herr Jesu Christ,
Mein Hoffnung steht auf Erden;
Ich weiss, dass du mein Tröster bist,
Kein Trost mag mir sonst werden.
Von Unbeginn ist nichts erkor n,
Auf Erden war kein Mensch gebor'n,
Der mir aus Nöten helfen kann,
Ich ruf dich an,
Zu dem ich mein Vertrauen han.

My sin and guilt are plaguing me;
Oh, grant me true contrition
And by your death upon the tree
Your pardon and remission.
Before the Father's throne above
Recall your matchless deed of love
That he may lift my dreadful load,
O Son of God!
I plead the grace your death bestowed.

Mein' Sünd' sind schwer und übergross
Und reuen mich von Herzen,
Derselben mach mich quitt und los
Durch deinen Tod und Schmerzen,
Und zeig mich deinem Vater an,
Dass du hast gnug für mich gethan,
So werd ich frei der Sündenlast,
Herr, halt mir fest,
Wes du dich mir versprochen hast.

Confirm in us your Gospel, Lord,
Your promise of salvation.
And make us keen to hear your Word
And follow our vocation:
To spend our lives in love for you,
To bear each other's burdens too.
And then, at last, when death shall loom,
O Savior, come
And bear your loved ones safely home.

Gib mir nach dein'r Barmherzigkeit
`Den wahren Christenglauben,
Auf dass ich deine Süssigkeit
Mög inniglich anschauen,
Vor allen Dingen lieben dich
Und meinen Nächsten gleich als mich.
Am letzten End dein Hilf mir send,
Damit behend
Des Teufels List sich von mir wend.

Both Julian and Wackernagel attribute the authorship of this hymn to Johann Schneesing, an attribution accepted by W. G. Polack. However, it was Friedrich Spitta who, in 1903, established Konrad Hubert as the author.

Appearing first in an undated Nürnberg broadsheet, perhaps 1540 or 1541, in the Strassburg hymnals from 1545 on it has the beautiful heading "A prayer-hymn to Christ, our only Savior, for the remission of sins and the increase of faith and true love." While it is a beautiful hymn on repentance, it is truly also a hymn of faith in its expression of love. In Valentin Babst's *Geystliche Lieder* (Leipzig, 1545) Luther connected it to confession with the heading "The common confession in the form of a hymn."

Gilbert E. Doan prepared the English text for inclusion in *Lutheran Book of Worship* (1978).

ALLEIN ZU DIR. On a broadsheet titled *Eyn Schönn Lied von Vnser heiligenn Tauff* (Wittenberg, c. 1541) this fine tune appeared anonymously with this text. In 1545 both appeared in Valentin Babst's *Geystliche Lieder* (Leipzig), the last hymnal publication that Luther supervised.

Jan O. Bender prepared this harmonization for inclusion in *Lutheran Book of Worship* (1978).

SEEK WHERE YOU MAY TO FIND A WAY 358

Seek where you may
To find a way,
Restless, toward your salvation.
My heart is stilled,
On Christ I build,
He is the one foundation.
His Word is sure,
His works endure;
He overthrows
All evil foes;
Through him I more than conquer.

Seek whom you may
To be your stay,
None can redeem his brother.
All helpers failed;
This man prevailed,
The God-man and none other,
Our Servant-King
Of whom we sing.
We're justified
Because he died,
The guilty being guiltless.

Seek him alone,
Do not postpone;
Let him your soul deliver.
All you who thirst,
Go to him first
Whose grace flows like a river.
Seek him indeed
In ev'ry need;
He will impart
To ev'ry heart
The fullness of his treasure.

My heart's delight,
My crown most bright,
O Christ, my joy forever.
Not wealth nor pride
Nor fortune's tide
Our bonds of love shall sever.
You are my Lord;
Your precious Word
Shall guide my way
And help me stay
Forever in your presence.

Such', wer da will,
Ein ander Ziel,
Die Seligkeit zu finden;
Mein Herz allein
Bedacht soll sein,
Auf Christum sich zu gründen.
Sein Wort ist wahr,
Sein Werk ist klar,
Sein heil'ger Mund
Hat Kraft und Grund,
All' Feind' zu überwinden.

Such', wer da will,
Nothelfer viel,
Die uns doch nichts erworben;
Hier ist der Mann,
Der helfen kann,
Bei dem nie was verdorben!
Uns wird das Heil
Durch ihn zuteil,
Uns macht gerecht
Der treue Knecht,
Der für uns ist gestorben.

Ach sucht doch den,
Lasst alles stehn,
Die ihr das Heil begehret!
Er ist der Herr
Und keiner mehr,
Der euch das Heil gewähret.
Sucht ihn all' Stund'
Von Herzensgrund,
Sucht ihn allein,
Denn wohl wird sein
Dem, der ihn herzlich ehret.

Mein's Herzens Kron',
Mein' Freudensonn'
Sollst du, Herr Jesu, bleiben;
Lass mich doch nicht
Von deinem Licht
Durch Eitelkeit vertreiben!
Bleib du mein Preis,
Dein Wort mich speis;
Bleib du mein' Ehr',
Dein Wort mich lehr',
An dich stets fest zu gläuben!

This hymn was written by Georg Weissel in 1623 for his installation as pastor in Königsberg on the Third Sunday in Advent. On the previous Sunday he had dedicated the newly built church for which he had written another hymn beginning "Gross Heil da widerfahret." Both these hymns appeared in Johann Stobäus' *Festlieder durch das gantze Jahr* (part 1, Elbing, 1642). Today "Seek Where You May" is more generally sung as a faith and justification hymn than as one for Advent. With "Lift Up Your Heads, You Mighty Gates" (*LW* 23), it stands as a masterpiece.

The translation is an altered and updated form of that prepared by Arthur Voss for inclusion in *The Lutheran Hymnal* (1941).

SUCH, WER DA WILL is the tune composed by Johann Stobäus, the talented cantor and friend of Weissel, that appeared with the latter's text in the above-mentioned *Festlieder*. Originally it had been composed by him in 1613 to go with the text "Wie's Gott bestellt, mir's wohl gefällt" for the wedding of a friend.

Thomas Gieschen prepared the harmonization for inclusion in *Lutheran Worship* (1982).

359 JUST AS I AM, WITHOUT ONE PLEA

Charlotte Elliott included this hymn in her *The Invalid's Hymn Book* (1836). She added a seventh stanza (here omitted) that same year in her *Hours of Sorrow Cheered and Comforted*. Headed with John 6:37, it has been called "the world's greatest soul-winning hymn" and has been translated into numerous languages.

Several stories are told concerning the origin of the hymn, the most likely of which was told by the author's niece. In 1834 Elliott was staying with her brother Henry V. Elliott, pastor in Brighton, England. One night, while the family members were busy readying things for a bazaar to raise funds for the building of St. Mary's Hall at Brighton for the education of the daughters of the poorer clergy, Charlotte was haunted by a sense of her helplessness. An invalid all her life, she could not help with the bazaar preparations, and she lay awake all night, "tossed about with many a conflict, many a doubt." The next day she wrote the text which, it has been said, has done more for the furtherance of Christianity than any number of bazaars.

WOODWORTH, the most popular setting for this hymn in America, was composed by William Bradbury and included in the *Mendelssohn Collection, or Third Book of Psalmody* (New York, 1849), which Bradbury edited with Thomas Hastings (*LW* 349). The tune was there set to "The God of love will soon indulge" by Elizabeth Scott.

The harmonization is from the *Service Book and Hymnal* (1958).

NOW I HAVE FOUND THE FIRM FOUNDATION 360

Now I have found the firm foundation
Which holds my anchor ever sure,
Laid long before the world's creation
In Christ my Savior's wounds secure,
Foundation which unmoved will stay
When all this world will pass away.

It is that mercy never ending
Which far our human thought transcends
Of him who, loving arms extending,
To wretched sinners condescends;
His heart with pity still will break
Both if we seek him or forsake.

Our ruin God has not intended;
For our salvation he has yearned;
For this his Son to earth descended
And now to heaven has returned.
Thus he is patient evermore
And knocks at our heart's bolted door.

O depth of love, to me revealing
The sea where my sins disappear!
In Christ my wounds find perfect healing,
There is no condemnation here;
For Jesus' blood through earth and skies
Forever "Mercy! Mercy!" cries.

I never will forget this crying;
In faith I trust it all my days,
And when because of sins I'm sighing,
Into my Father's heart I gaze,
For in his heart is surely found
Free mercy without end and bound.

Lord, I will stand on this foundation
As long as I on earth remain;
This will engage my meditation
While I the breath of life retain.
And then, when face to face with you,
I'll sing your mercy great and true.

Ich habe nun den Grund gefunden,
Der meinen Anker ewig hält.
Wo anders als in Jesu Wunden?
Da lag er vor der Zeit der Welt,
Der Grund, der unbeweglich steht,
Wenn Erd' und Himmel untergeht.

Es ist das ewige Erbarmen,
Das alles Denken übersteigt;
Es sind die offnen Liebesarme
Des, der sich zu dem Sünder neigt,
Dem allemal das Herze bricht,
Wir kommen oder kommen nicht.

Wir sollen nicht verloren werden,
Gott will, uns soll geholfen sein;
Deswegen kam der Sohn auf Erden
Und nahm hernach den Himmel ein;
Deswegen klopft er für und für
So stark an unsre Herzenstür.

O Abgrund, welcher alle Sünden
Durch Christi Tod verschlungen hat!
Das heisst die Wunde recht verbinden,
Da findet kein Verdammen statt,
Weil Christi Blut beständig schreit:
Barmherzigkeit! Barmherzigkeit!

Darein will ich mich gläubig senken,
Dem will ich mich getrost vertraun
Und, wenn mich meine Sünden kränken,
Nur bald nach Gottes Herzen schaun;
Da findet sich zu aller Zeit
Unendliche Barmherzigkeit.

Bei diesem Grunde will ich bleiben,
Solange mich die Erde trägt;
Das will ich denken, tun und treiben,
Solange sich ein Glied bewegt.
So sing' ich einstens höchst erfreut:
O Abgrund der Barmherzigkeit!

This hymn, originally in 10 stanzas, was written in 1722 by Johann A. Rothe as a birthday gift for Lord von Schweinitz in Leube near Görlitz, in whose house he was at the time serving as a teacher. In 1725 there appeared the so-called Berthelsdorf hymnal titled *Sammlung geistlicher und lieblicher Lieder*, followed by new printings in 1726 and 1727 with an appendix or supplement. It is in the latter that Rothe's hymn appears. Unquestionably it is the sublime hymn of God's mercy, as witnessed by the numerous occurrences of this word. Stanza 1 was undoubtedly suggested by Hebrews 6:19: "We have this hope as an anchor for the soul, firm and secure." The German expression "O Abgrund" likely has reference to the echo indicated in Psalm 42:7: "Deep calls to deep in the roar of your waterfalls," equivalent of the Latin "Abyssus abyssum invocavit" (Abyss calls to abyss). The spiritual implication appears to be: The abyss of mankind's sins calls to the abyss of God's mercy.

Since this hymn was originally thought to have been the product of Nicolaus L. von Zinzendorf (*LW* 362, 386), founder of the reorganized Moravian Church, or United Brethren, its acceptance into hymnals was a somewhat slow process.

O DASS ICH TAUSEND ZUNGEN HÄTTE. For comments on this tune see hymn 448.

Richard W. Gieseke prepared the harmonization for *Lutheran Worship* (1982).

361 ROCK OF AGES, CLEFT FOR ME

Augustus Toplady, under his *nom de plume* of "Minimus," closed an article in the October 1775 issue of *Gospel Magazine* with four lines:

> Rock of Ages, cleft for me,
> Let me hide myself in thee!
> Foul, I to the fountain fly:
> Wash me, Saviour, or I die.

While he may have completed the hymn at that time, the full four stanzas did not appear in print until the following March. In that issue of *Gospel Magazine* Toplady made "spiritual improvements" on a piece about the national debt, intending to show that the sinner's debt can never be repaid. Based on the assumption that people commit a sin every second of their lives, Toplady's article calculates that an 80-year-old will have accumulated 2,522,880,000 sins. He ended the article with "Rock of ages, cleft for me," there titled "A living and dying prayer for the holiest believer in the world." The title probably had reference to John Wesley's (*LW* 280, 362) teaching that perfect holiness was attainable in earthly life.

Knowing Toplady's furious theological battle with the Wesleys, it is all the more remarkable that the idea for this hymn was drawn from Charles Wesley's *Hymns on the Lord's Supper* (Bristol, 1745). In its 11th edition and its 30th year by the time Toplady published "Rock of Ages," the collection had certainly come under Toplady's scrutiny. Therein he found, in the preface:

> O Rock of Israel, Rock of Salvation, Rock struck and cleft for me, let those two Streams of Blood and Water which once gushed out of thy side, bring down Pardon and Holiness into my soul. And let me thirst after them now, as if I stood upon the Mountain whence sprang this Water; and near the Cleft of that Rock, the Wounds of my Lord, whence gushed this sacred Blood.

And hymn 27 begins, "Rock of Israel, cleft for me." Wesley's imagery, of course, comes from the Bible, as does Toplady's phrase "Rock of ages," found in the marginal note of Isaiah 26:4 in the King James Version. To complete the symmetry, Toplady later published his hymn in *Psalms and Hymns* (1776), side by side with Wesley's "Jesus, Lover of My Soul" (*LW* 508).

Toplady himself approved some changes in the fourth stanza, which originally read:

> *Whilst* I draw this fleeting breath,
> When mine *eye-strings break* in death,
> When I soar *through tracts* unknown,
> See thee on thy judgment throne,
> Rock of Ages, cleft for me,
> Let me hide myself in thee.

Lutheran Worship follows the revised text.

As to the origin of the hymn, which Oliver Wendell Holmes once called "the Protestant Dies Irae," Percy Dearmer notes:

> We have only to add that the story of his making the hymn when he took refuge in the cleft rock of Burrington Combe in the Mendips, was invented about the year 1850—perhaps by some one who thought that one little lie would hardly count among a total of 2,522,880,000 sins.

TOPLADY. Thomas Hastings' tune was first published in *Spiritual Songs for Social Worship* (Utica, 1832), edited by Hastings and Lowell Mason (*LW* 115, et al.). Also called DEVOTION and ROCK OF AGES, it was written in the key of D for this text. While TOPLADY is the standard setting for "Rock of Ages" in this country, the more popular tune in ENGLAND is REDHEAD NO. 76, otherwise known as PETRA and GETHSEMANE (*LW* 110).

JESUS, YOUR BLOOD AND RIGHTEOUSNESS 362

Count Nicolaus L. von Zinzendorf, founder of the reorganized Moravian Church, or the United Brethren, wrote the original of this hymn in 33 stanzas while returning home in 1739 from having visited a Moravian mission on the island of St. Thomas in the West Indies. That same year he published it in appendix 8 to his *Das Gesang-Buch der Gemeine in Herrn-Huth*, a hymnal first published in 1735. Zinzendorf's stanza 1 was undoubtedly based on the first stanza of a hymn generally ascribed to Paul Eber (*LW* 189, 428) but undoubtedly much older than that, beginning "In Christi Wunden schlaf ich ein" (see *TLH* 585), an ardent and childlike prayer for a blessed end. It is not without a bit of poignancy and nostalgia that the present writer quotes the first stanza of

Zinzendorf's text, since it is one of the prayers that his sainted mother taught him when a tiny child to serve as a bedtime prayer:

> Christi Blut und Gerechtigkeit,
> Das ist mein Schmuck und Ehrenkleid,
> Damit will ich vor Gott bestehn,
> Wenn ich zum Himmel werd eingehn.

Stanza 1 of the hymn under discussion, in John Wesley's version, hardly captures the thought and import of the original.

When Zinzendorf's long hymn came to the attention of John Wesley, who had learned about the Moravians en route to Georgia, he put his hand to translating it, a translation in 24 stanzas that he published in *Hymns and Sacred Poems* (1740), of which this hymn in *Lutheran Worship* (1982) is a cento. The altered and updated text was prepared by the Inter-Lutheran Commission on Worship for inclusion in *Lutheran Book of Worship* (1978). A fine, comforting hymn, until recently it has graced the contents of numerous denominational hymnals in various different centos.

ST. CRISPIN is a rather typical Victorian tune composed by George J. Elvey as a setting for Charlotte Elliott's "Just As I Am" (*LW* 359). Its repetitive rhythmic pattern is not a little enervating.

The harmonization is from *The Lutheran Hymnal* (1941), slightly altered.

363 ALL MANKIND FELL IN ADAM'S FALL

This is a slightly altered and updated form of Matthias Loy's free translation in long meter of Lazarus Spengler's hymn "Durch Adams Fall ist ganz verderbt Menschlich Natur und Wesen." Originally in nine stanzas of eight lines, Spengler's hymn first appeared in Walter's *Geystliche gesangk Buchleyn* (Wittenberg, 1524), Johann Walter's choir book.

In the Reformation era this hymn, similar to Paul Speratus' hymn "Salvation unto Us Has Come" (*LW* 355), was held in high regard. As a teaching and confessional hymn of the evangelical faith, the first two lines previously cited are directly quoted in the Formula of Concord, Solid Declaration I, 1, in the discussion of Original Sin. Regarding Spengler's hymn Julian says:

> During the Reformation period it attained a wide popularity as a didactic and confessional hymn. . . . It is one of the most characteristic hymns of the time, conceived in the spirit of deep and earnest piety, eminently scriptural, and setting forth the Reformation teachings in concise and antithetical form, but is, however, too much like a system of theology in rhyme.

Pietism, the Enlightenment, and even the confessional revival of the 19th century, as in the case of the Speratus hymn previously mentioned, found little to commend it. As late as 1853 an Eisenach draft, listing 150 *Kernlieder* (common core hymns), failed to include it. Subsequent hymnals likewise omitted it. Thus its inclusion (in seven stanzas) in the present-day hymnals of the Lutheran territorial churches in Germany (*Evangelisches Kirchengesangbuch*) was greeted as somewhat of a newcomer.

Matthias Loy's free translation appeared in *The Lutheran Hymnal* (1880) of the Ohio Synod and in *The Lutheran Hymnal* (1941).

WENN WIR IN HÖCHSTEN NÖTEN SEIN. For comments on this tune see hymn 428.

The harmonization was prepared by George Leonard, a *nom de plume* of Paul G. Bunjes.

OH, HOW GREAT IS YOUR COMPASSION 364

Oh, how great is your compassion,
Faithful Father, God of grace,
That with all our fallen race
In our depth of degradation
You had mercy so that we
Might be saved eternally!

Your great love for this has striven
That we may, from sin made free,
Live with you eternally.
Your dear Son himself has given
And extends his gracious call,
To his supper calls us all.

Firmly to our soul's salvation
Witnesses your Spirit, Lord,
In your sacraments and Word.
There he sends true consolation,
Giving us the gift of faith
That we fear not hell nor death.

Lord, your mercy will not leave me;
Ever will your truth abide.
Then in you I will confide.
Since your Word cannot deceive me,
My salvation is to me
Safe and sure eternally.

I will praise your great compassion,
Faithful Father, God of grace,
That with all our fallen race
In our depth of degradation
You had mercy so that we
Might be saved eternally.

Ach, wie gross ist deine Gnade,
Du getreues Vaterherz,
Dass dich unsre Not und Schmerz,
Dass dich aller Menschen Schade
Hat erbarmet väterlich,
Uns zu helfen ewiglich!

Du hast uns so hoch geliebet,
Dass der Mensch soll aller Pein
Frei und ewig selig sein,
Dass dein Sohn sich selbst hingibet
Und beruft uns allzumal
Zu dem grossen Abendmahl.

Ja, dein werter Geist bezeuget
Durch die Tauf' und Abendmahl
Unser Heil im Himmelssaal,
Der die Herzen zu dir neiget,
Weil er uns den Glauen schenkt,
Dass uns Höll' und Tod nicht kränkt.

Weil die Wahrheit nicht kann lügen,
Will ich dir vertrauen fest,
Weil du keinen nicht verlässt;
Weil dein Wort nicht kann betrügen,
Bleibt mir meine Seligkeit
Unverrückt in Ewigkeit.

Lob sei dir für deine Gnade,
Du getreues Vaterherz,
Dass dich meine Not und Schmerz,
Dass dich auch mein Seelenschade
Hat erbarmt so väterlich;
Drum lob' ich dich ewiglich.

This hymn by Johannes Olearius first appeared in his *Geistliche Singe-Kunst* (Leipzig, 1671) and was intended for encouragement from the Holy Gospel (Luke 14:16–24: Parable of the Great Banquet) for the Second Sunday after Trinity Sunday (Third Sunday after Pentecost) of the Old Standard Series.

The translation by August Crull is given here in revised and updated form.

ACH WAS SOLL ICH SÜNDER MACHEN is a folk tune of uncertain origin. It appeared in a secular collection of songs entitled *Schäffer-Belustigung, oder zur Lehr und Ergetzlichkeit angestimmter Hirthenlieder* (Altdorf, 1653) where it was set to the song "Sylvius gieng durch die Matten" ("Sylvius went through the meadows"). The tune gets its name from having been borrowed by Johann Flitner, deacon near Greifswald, and included in his *Himmlische Lustgärtlein* (1861) set to his hymn "Ach, was soll ich Sünder machen," a hymn that enjoyed popular use in some parishes in their confessional services.

The setting was prepared by Wilhelm Quampen, a *nom de plume* of Paul G. Bunjes.

365 CHRIST BE MY LEADER

Timothy Dudley-Smith, bishop of Thetford, England, wrote this hymn, based on John 14:6, at the invitation of Canon H. C. Taylor, editor of the Anglican Hymn Book. The hymn, written in July 1961, has several "alliterative references to Christ as victor over darkness, doubt and death."

SLANE is an Irish folk tune from Patrick Weston Joyce's *Old Irish Folk Music and Songs: A Collection of 842 Irish Airs and Songs hitherto Unpublished* (Royal Society of Antiquaries of Ireland, 1909) set to the ancient ballad, "With my love on the road." The tune appeared in the revised *Church Hymnary* (1927) and since that time it has been closely associated with "Be thou my vision." It is one of those attractive and expansive tunes that provides beautiful music for occasional use.

Slane is the name of a hill about 10 miles from Tara in County Meath in Ireland. According to the account in the *Confessions of St. Patrick*, it was there that the saint lit the paschal fire in full view of the king, Loegaire mac Neill, despite the king's order that this fire to celebrate the annual pagan spring festival was to be lit on Tara hill by the king himself. Noticing Patrick's fire, the angry king summoned the saint to appear before him the next day (Easter) and explain his action. Wearing his miter and carrying his crozier, Patrick then led his white-robed companions to Tara, chanting Easter litanies and the breastplate hymn (*LW* 172). Thus was the Gospel brought to the royal seat.

The harmonization was prepared by Wilhelm Quampen, a *nom de plume* of Paul G. Bunjes.

I LAY MY SINS ON JESUS 366

Horatius Bonar first published this children's hymn in his *Songs in the Wilderness* (Kelson, 1843), under the title "The Fulness of Jesus." It is said to have been written about two years before, when the author was assistant in St. John's Church, Leith. Intended as "something which children could sing and appreciate in divine worship," it may have been the first hymn Bonar ever wrote. He himself admitted "that it might be good Gospel, but that it was poor poetry." The circumstance that it became popular does not hide the fact that the poet had to strain himself severely to find rhymes for "Jesus." Moreover, the resultant feminine rhymes are not exactly felicitous.

MUNICH (KÖNIGSBERG) is based on a melody from the third edition of the Meiningen *Gesangbuch* (1693), set to "O Gott, du frommer Gott." Mendelssohn adapted it for "Cast thy burden upon the Lord" in *Elijah*, 1847, and it is his form and harmonization that, as here, have been adopted by hymnal editors. For this text the meter has been altered.

WHEN OVER SIN I SORROW 367

When over sin I sorrow,
Lord Christ, I look to you;
From you I comfort borrow
That your death my death slew.
Dear Lord, your precious blood was spilt
For me, oh, most unworthy,
To take away my guilt.

Oh, what a wondrous off'ring!
See how the Master spares
His servants, and their suff'ring
And grief for them he bears.
God comes down from his throne on high
For me, his guilty creature,
And deigns as man to die.

My manifold transgression,
Forgiven, harms me none
Since Jesus' blood and Passion
For me God's grace has won.
His lifeblood all my debt has paid;
Of hell and all its tor ments
I am no more afraid.

Lord, I will now forever
Your way with honors pave,
For by your cross, O Savior,
God all my sins forgave.
I'll spend my breath in songs of thanks

Wenn meine Sünd' mich kränken,
O mein Herr Jesu Christ,
So lass mich wohl bedenken,
Wie du gestorben bist
Und alle meine Schuldenlast
Am Stamm des heil'gen Kreuzes
Auf dich genommen hast!

O Wunder ohne Massen,
Wenn man's betrachtet recht:
Es hat sich martern lassen
Der Herr für seinen Knecht;
Es hat sich selbst der wahre Gott
Für mich verlornen Menschen
Gegeben in den Tod.

Was kann mir denn nun schaden
Der Sünden grosse Zahl?
Ich bin bei Gott in Gnaden,
Die Schuld ist allzumal
Bezahlt durch Christi teures Blut,
Dass ich nicht mehr darf fürchten
Der Höllen Qual und Glut.

Drum sag' ich dir von Herzen
Jetzt und mein Leben lang
Für deine Pein und Schmerzen,
O Jesu, Lob und Dank,
Für deine Not und Angstgeschrei,

For all your guiltless suff'ring And your self-giving death.	Für dein unschuldig Sterben, Für deine Lieb' und Treu'.

Seldom have two poets worked together so harmoniously as Justis Gesenius and David Denicke (*LW* 385). Involved in the preparation of the Hanoverian hymnbooks, they, following the tenor of the times, felt constrained to modify hymns according to Martin Opitz's (*LW* 85) rules of German verse. Later poets of the Enlightenment unfortunately frequently mutilated some of the priceless hymn texts beyond recognition. While Gesenius and Denicke did not go that far—they enhanced some of the old texts with skill and good taste—it is sometimes difficult to determine which texts are the product of one or the other, since they did not affix their names to a given text.

As for the source of "When over sin I sorrow," hymnologist Johann Kasper Wetzel (fl. 1750), in his *Analecta hymnologica*, attests Justis Gesenius to be the author, a hymn that first appeared in eight stanzas in the Hanover *Gesangbuch* of 1646. Catherine Winkworth prepared a translation of this moving hymn on Christ's vicarious atonement, in five stanzas, for her *Chorale Book for England* (1863), the first stanza of which appears here in altered and updated form. Stanzas 2, 3, and 4 are altered and updated versions of the corresponding stanzas in *The Lutheran Hymnal* (1941).

HERR CHRIST, DER EINIG GOTTS SOHN. For comments on this tune see hymn 72.

The harmonization is by George Leonard, a *nom de plume* of Paul G. Bunjes.

368 MY HOPE IS BUILT ON NOTHING LESS

Edward Mote wrote this hymn in about 1834. His account of its writing appears in *The Gospel Herald* (London), where he writes:

> One morning it came into my mind as I went to labour, to write a hymn on the "Gracious Experience of a Christian." As I went up Holborn I had the chorus . . . In the day I had four verses complete, and wrote them off.

Mote then called on a parishioner whose wife was ill. The husband, accustomed to singing a hymn in his private devotions, was unable to find his hymnbook, so Mote offered the completed four stanzas. The dying woman was so taken with the hymn that Mote, after leaving a copy with her, later finished off two more stanzas and had a thousand copies printed in leaflet form.

This was the first publication of the hymn, which the author sent on anonymously to *Spiritual Magazine*; from there it appeared in an 1836 collection of hymns published by Rees of Crown Street, Soho. That same year Mote himself published it with a few alterations in *Hymns of Praise: A New Selection of Gospel Hymns, combining all the*

Excellencies of our Spiritual Poets, with many Originals (London), a volume that included a hundred of Mote's originals.

In the original, stanza 1 read:

Nor earth, nor hell, my soul can move,
I rest upon unchanging love;
I dare not trust the sweetest frame,
But wholly lean on Jesus' name.

Also omitted here is stanza 5:

I trust his righteous character,
His council, promise, and his power;
His honor and his name's at stake
To save me from the burning lake.

The text given here is that prepared by the Inter-Lutheran Commission on Worship for inclusion in *Lutheran Book of Worship* (1978).

MAGDALEN was composed by Sir John Stainer in 1873 for John Wesley's (*LW* 280, 362) translation of Gerhard Tersteegen's "Gott ist gegenwärtig" (*LW* 206), beginning "Thou hidden love of God, whose height." Stainer called his tune REST. Although Stainer ordinarily insisted that his tunes be used with the texts for which they were written, partly to ensure that the tune name would fit, he made an exception with this one for *Hymns Ancient and Modern* (1875), where it was set to "The saints of God, their conflict past" by W. D. Maclagan.

Under the name MAGDALEN the tune is often used with Kipling's "Recessional." It is also called BEATI.

The setting is from *The Lutheran Hymnal* (1941).

THROUGH JESUS' BLOOD AND MERIT 369

Through Jesus' blood and merit
I am at peace with God;
What, then, can daunt my spirit,
However dark my road?
My courage shall not fail me,
For God is on my side;
Though hell itself assail me,
Its rage I may deride.

There's nothing that can sever
From this great love of God;
No want, no pain whatever,
No famine, peril, flood.
Though thousand foes surround me,

Ich bin bei Gott in Gnaden
Durch Christi Blut und tod.
Was kann mir endlich schaden?
Was acht' ich alle Not?
Ist er auf meiner Seiten,
Gleichwie er wahrlich ist,
Lass immer mich bestreiten
Auch alle Höllenlist.

Was wird mich können scheiden
Von Gottes Lieb' und Treu'?
Verfolgung, Armut, Leiden
Und Trübsal mancherlei?
Lass Schwert und Blösse walten,

For slaughter mark his sheep,
They never shall confound me,
The vict'ry I shall reap.

Oh, neither life's temptation
Nor death's so trying hour
Nor angels of high station
Nor any other pow'r
Nor things that now are present
Nor things that are to come
Nor height, however pleasant,
Nor depth of deepest gloom

Nor any creature ever
Shall from the love of God
This wretched sinner sever;
For in my Savior's blood
This love has its foundation;
God hears my faithful prayer
And long before creation
Owns me his child and heir.

Man mag durch tausend Pein
Mich für ein Schlachtschaf halten,
Der Sieg bleibt dennoch mein.

Dass weder Tod noch Leben
Und keiner Engel Macht,
Wie hoch sie möchte schweben,
Kein Fürstentum, kein' Pracht,
Nichts dessen, was zugegen,
Nichts, was die Zukunft hegt,
Nichts, welches hoch gelegen,
Nichts, was die Tiefe trägt,

Noch sonst was je erschaffen
Von Gottes Liebe mich
Soll scheiden oder raffen;
Denn diese gründet sich
Auf Christi, Tod und Sterben.
Ihn' fleh' ich gläubig an,
Der mich, sein Kind und Erben,
Nicht lassen will noch kann.

This hymn by the gifted Simon Dach, originally in six stanzas, was written on the death of Count Achatius of Dohna, February 6, 1651. Based on Romans 8:31ff., although written on the occasion of death, it is one of those hymns by him that Christians used as a prayer in preparation for death while still in good health and perhaps the prime of life.

The text is an altered form of that which appeared in *The Lutheran Hymnal* (1941), the translation of which was a composite.

LOB GOTT GETROST MIT SINGEN. For comments on this tune see hymn 257.

The harmonization is from *The Lutheran Hymnal* (1941).

370 BLEST THE CHILDREN OF OUR GOD

A number of preachers associated with George Whitefield (1714–70), founder of Calvinistic Methodism, became hymn writers. Among them is Joseph Humphreys, author of this hymn beginning "Blessed are the sons of God" and published in *Sacred Hymns for the Use of Religious Societies* (Bristol, 1743). There it appeared in eight four-line stanzas:

Blessed are the sons of God.
They are bought with Christ's own blood,
They are ransomed from the grave,
Life eternal they shall have.

God did love them in his Son
Long before the world begun;

They are lights upon the earth,
Children of a heavenly birth;
Born of God, they hate all sin,
God's pure seed remains within.

They have fellowship with God,
Through the Mediator's blood;

They the seal of this receive
When on Jesus they believe.

They are justified by grace,
They enjoy a solid peace;
All their sins are washed away,
They shall stand in God's great day.

They produce the fruits of grace
In the works of righteousness.
They are harmless, meek, and mild,
Holy, humble, undefiled.

One with God, with Jesus one,
Glory is in them begun.

Though they suffer much on earth,
Strangers quite to this world's mirth,
Yet they have an inward joy,
Pleasure which can never cloy.

They alone are truly blest,
Heirs of God, joint heirs with Christ;
With them numbered may I be
Here and in eternity!

Richard Conyers, vicar of Helmsley in Yorkshire, was the first to use the final two lines as a refrain, combining the other 30 lines of the hymn into five six-line stanzas in his *A Collection of Psalms and Hymns* (1767). Augustus Toplady (*LW* 361) then reorganized the hymn into six four-line stanzas with the same two-line refrain. This version, which appeared in his *Psalms and Hymns for Public and Private Worship* (1776), is the basis for most modern centos.

VOLLER WUNDER, a tune by Johann Georg Ebeling, first appeared in 1666 in a book confined to Paul Gerhardt's texts and entitled *Pauli Gerhardi Geistliche Andachten, bestehend in 120 violinen und general-bass*, where it was set to Gerhardt's wedding hymn, "Voller Wunder, Voller Kunst, Voller Weisheit, Voller Kraft." Routley is correct in characterizing Ebeling's tunes (see also *LW* 419, 423) as having "an attractive and youthful brightness" (*The Music of Christian Hymnody*). Originally the tune looked like this (Zahn 3371):

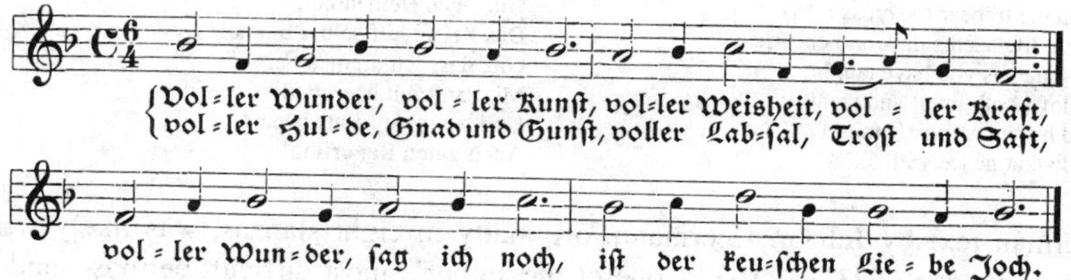

Paul G. Bunjes prepared the harmonization for inclusion in *Lutheran Worship* (1982).

371 O GOD, MY FAITHFUL GOD

O God, my faithful God, True fountain ever flowing, Without whom nothing is, All perfect gifts bestowing: Give me a healthy frame, And may I have within A conscience free from blame, A soul unstained by sin.	O Gott, du frommer Gott, Du Brunnquell guter Gaben, Ohn' den nichts ist, was ist, Von dem wir alles haben: Gesunden Leib gib mir, Und dass in solchem Leib Ein' unverletzte Seel' Und rein Gewissen bleib'.
Give me the strength to do With ready heart and willing Whatever you command, My calling here fulfilling. Help me do what I should With all my might, and bless The outcome for my good, For you must give success.	Gib, dass ich tu' mit Fleiss, Was mir zu tun gebühret Wozu mich dein Befehl In meinem Stande führet! Gib, dass ich's tue bald, Zu der Zeit, da ich soll, Und wenn ich's tu', so gib, Dass es gerate wohl!
Keep me from saying words That later need recalling; Guard me lest idle speech May from my lips be falling; But when within my place I must and ought to speak, Then to my words give grace Lest I offend the weak.	Hilf, dass ich rede stets, Womit ich kann bestehen, Lass kein unnützes Wort Aus meinem Munde gehen; Und wenn in meinem Amt Ich reden soll und muss, So gib den Worten Kraft Und Nachdruck ohn' Verdruss!
When dangers gather round, Oh, keep me calm and fearless; Help me to bear the cross When life seems dark and cheerless; Help me, as you have taught, To love both great and small And by your Spirit's might To live at peace with all.	Find't sich Gefährlichkeit, So lass mich nicht verzagen; Gib einen Heldenmut, Das Kreuz hilf selber tragen! Gib, dass ich meinen Feind Mit Sanftmut überwind' Und, wenn ich Rats bedarf, Auch guten Rat erfind'!

The German text by Johann Heermann, originally in eight stanzas, was likely written sometime between 1623 and 1630—one of the author's most difficult periods—and was published in his *Devoti Musica Cordis* (Breslau, 1630), headed "Daily Prayer." Fischer in *Kirchenlieder-Lexicon* writes:

> It is one of the poet's most widely used and signally blessed hymns and has been not unjustly called his Master Song. If it is somewhat "home-baked," yet it is excellent, nourishing bread. It gives a training in practical Christianity and specially strikes three notes—godly living, patient suffering, and happy dying.

Winkworth's translation first appeared in *Lyra Germanica* (second series, 1858), and again in *Chorale Book for England* (1863). The first four stanzas of her translation appear here in altered and updated form.

WAS FRAG ICH NACH DER WELT. For comments on the tune see hymn 418.

Richard W. Gieseke prepared the harmonization for inclusion in *Lutheran Worship* (1982).

O GOD, FORSAKE ME NOT 372

O God, forsake me not!
Your gracious presence lend me;
Oh, lead your helpless child;
Your Holy Spirit send me
That I my course may run.
Be you my light, my lot,
My staff, my rock, my shield.
O God, forsake me not!

O God, forsake me not!
Take not your Spirit from me;
Do not allow the night
Of sin to overcome me.
Increase my feeble faith,
Which you yourself have wrought.
Be you my strength and pow'r.
O God, forsake me not!

O God, forsake me not!
Lord, hear my supplication!
In ev'ry evil hour
Help me resist temptation;
And when the prince of hell
My conscience seeks to blot,
Be then not far from me.
O God, forsake me not!

O God, forsake me not!
My heart your grace addressing,
O Father, God of love,
Grant me your heav'nly blessing
To do when duty calls
Whatever you allot,
To do what pleases you.
O God, forsake me not!

O God, forsake me not!
Lord, I am yours forever.
The true faith grant to me;
Grant that I leave you never.
Grant me a blessed end
When my good fight is fought;
Help me in life and death.
O God, forsake me not!

Ach Gott, verlass mich nicht,
Gib mir die Gnadenhände!
Ach führe mich, dein Kind,
Dass ich den Lauf vollende
Zu meiner Seligkeit;
Sei du mein Lebenslicht,
Mein Stab, mein Hort, mein Schutz:
Ach Gott, verlass mich nicht!

Ach Gott, verlass mich nicht,
Regiere du mein Wallen,
Ach lass mich nimmermehr
In Sünd' und Schande fallen!
Gib mir den guten Geist,
Gib Glabenszuversicht,
Sei meine Stärk' und Kraft:
Ach Gott, verlass mich nicht!

Ach Gott, verlass mich nicht,
Ich ruf' aus Herzensgrunde.
Ach Höchster, stärke mich
In jeder bösen Stunde;
Wenn mich Versuchung plagt
Und meine Seel' anficht,
So weiche nicht von mir:
Ach Gott, verlass mich nicht!

Ach Gott, verlass mich nicht,
Ach, lass dich doch bewegen,
Ach Vater, kröne doch
Mit reichem Himmelssegen
Die Werke meines Amts,
Die Werke meiner Pflicht,
Zu tun, was dir gefällt:
Ach Gott, verlass mich nicht!

Ach Gott, verlass mich nicht,
Ich bleibe dir ergeben.
Hilf mir, o grosser Gott,
Recht glauben, christlich leben
Und selig scheiden ab,
Zu sehn dein Angesicht!
Hilf mir in Not und Tod:
Ach Gott, verlass mich nicht!

When Johann Martin Schamelius, head pastor and hymnologist in Naumberg, Germany, was preparing the production of the Naumberg *Gesangbuch*, he undoubtedly desired to include a hymn by Salomo Franck of Weimar, who, at the height of his popularity, was secretary of the consistory as well as librarian and court poet. Perhaps he invited Franck to submit a hymn. At any rate, when the hymnal appeared in 1714, Salomo Franck's "Ach Gott, verlass mich nicht" appeared anonymously in the appendix to the second part. It wasn't until 1724, however, when Schamelius produced his commentary to the hymns, that he mentioned Franck as the author. Based on Psalm 38:21 and Psalm 71:9, 18, it is indeed a notable prayer-hymn, utilizing not only the metric pattern (67 67 66 66) of Johann Heermann's "O God, My Faithful God" (*LW* 371), but also some of its thoughts. It was only in the 19th century that Franck's hymn began to be extensively used in hymnals.

The translation is an altered and updated form of that by August Crull which appeared in *The Lutheran Hymnal* (1941).

WAS FRAG ICH NACH DER WELT. For comments on the tune see hymn 418.

The harmonization was prepared by George Leonard, a *nom de plume* of Paul G. Bunjes, for inclusion in *Lutheran Worship* (1982).

373 RENEW ME, O ETERNAL LIGHT

Renew me, O eternal Light, And let my heart and soul be bright, Illumined with the light of grace That issues from your holy face.	Erneure mich, o ew'ges Licht, Und lass von deinem Angesicht Mein Herz und Seel' mit deinem Schein Durchleuchtet und erfüllet sein!
Remove the pow'r of sin from me And cleanse all my impurity That I may have the strength and will Temptations of the flesh to still.	Ertöt in mir die schnöde Lust, Feg aus den alten Sündenwust; Ach rüst mich aus mit Kraft und Mut, Zu streiten wider Fleisch und Blut!
Create in me a new heart, Lord, That gladly I obey your Word. Let what you will be my desire, And with new life my soul inspire.	Schaff in mir, Herr, den neuen Geist, Der dir mit Lust Gehorsam leist't Und nichts sonst, als was du willst, will; Ach Herr, mit ihm mein Herz erfüll!
Grant that I only you may love And seek those things which are above Till I behold you face to face, O Light eternal, through your grace.	Auf dich lass meine Sinnen gehn, Lass sie nach dem, was droben, stehn, Bis ich dich schau', o ew'ges Licht, Von Angesicht zu Angesicht!

This hymn by Johann F. Ruopp, originally in 16 stanzas, first appeared in 1704 in a little hymnal entitled *Jesus Lieder*, secretly published by Ruopp and his friend Johann Friedrich Haug, both ardent supporters of Pietism and promoters of the *collegia pietatis*, private study and devotional assemblies. Appearing here are stanzas 1–3, and 8 of the original, the stanzas that Freylinghausen (*LW* 23, et al.) included in his *Neues Geistreiches Gesangbuch* (1714), a collection of 815 hymns.

The text translation, prepared by the Inter-Lutheran Commission on Worship for inclusion in *Lutheran Book of Worship* (1978), is an altered and updated form of that by August Crull (*LW* 34, et al.) which first appeared in the *Evangelical Lutheran Hymn-Book* (1889).

HERR JESU CHRIST, MEINS. For comments on the tune see hymn 262.

Paul G. Bunjes harmonized the tune for inclusion in *Lutheran Worship* (1982).

SAVIOR, THY DYING LOVE 374

This hymn by Sylvanus D. Phelps first appeared in 1862 in *The Watchman and Reflector*, a Baptist journal of which Phelps was editor. Later it was included in Robert Lowry's *Pure Gold* (1871), a compilation of Gospel songs and hymns. It was Robert Lowry, a Baptist minister, who wrote the tune SOMETHING FOR JESUS originally designated for this hymn. On the occasion of Phelps's 70th birthday Lowry sent the following note:

> It is worth living 70 years even if nothing comes of it but one such hymn as "Saviour, thy dying love." . . . Happy is the man who can produce one song which the world will keep on singing after its author shall have passed way.

WINTERTON was composed by Joseph Barnby in 1892. Its saccharine character marks it as one of his lesser tunes. The close association of text and tune since the *Evangelical Lutheran Hymn-Book* (1912), the first official English hymnal of the Synod, prompted the Commission on Worship to continue the union. Most hymnals use SOMETHING FOR JESUS.

Ralph C. Schultz prepared the harmonization for *Lutheran Worship*.

YOU WILL I LOVE, MY STRENGTH 375

You will I love, my strength, my tower; You will I love, my hope, my joy; You will I love with all my power, With fervor time cannot destroy. You will I love, O light divine, So long as life is mine.	Ich will dich lieben, meine Stärke, Ich will dich lieben, meine Zier, Ich will dich lieben mit dem Werke Und immerwährender Begier; Ich will dich lieben, schönstes Licht Bis mir das Herze bricht.
You will I love, my life, my Savior, You are my best, my truest friend; You will I love and praise forever,	Ich will dich lieben, o mein Leben, Als meinen allerbesten Freund; Ich will dich lieben und erheben,

For never shall your kindness end. Your love for me casts out my fear, You are my Savior dear.	Solange mich dein Glanz bescheint; Ich will dich lieben, Gotteslamm, Als meinen Bräutigam.
I thank you, Jesus, sun from heaven, Whose radiance has brought light to me; I thank you, who has richly given All that could make me glad and free. I thank you that my soul is healed With love that you revealed.	Ich danke dir, du wahre Sonne, Dass mir dein Glanz hat Licht gebracht; Ich danke dir, du Himmelswonne, Dass du mich froh und frei gemacht; Ich danke dir, du güldner Mund, Dass du mich machst gesund.
Oh, keep me watchful, then, and humble, And never suffer me to stray; Uphold me when my feet would stumble, And keep me faithful to your way. Fill all my nature with your light, O Radiance strong and bright!	Erhalte mich auf deinen Stegen Und lass mich nicht mehr irregehn; Lass meinen Fuss auf deinen Wegen Nicht straucheln oder stille stehn; Erleucht mir Leib und Seele ganz, Du starker Himmelsglanz.
You will I love, my crown of gladness; You will I love, my God and Lord, Within the darkest depths of sadness, And not for hope of high reward— For your own sake, O Light divine, So long as life is mine!	Ich will dich lieben, meine Krone, Ich will dich lieben, meinen Gott; Ich will dich lieben ohne Lohne, Auch in der allergrössten Not. Ich will dich lieben, schönstes Licht, Bis mir das Herze bricht.

This hymn by Johann Scheffler, originally in eight stanzas, first appeared in *Heilige Seelen-Lust oder Geistliche Hirten-Lieder* (Breslau, 1657). Scheffler, the mystic, the "Angelus Silesius," at the time of his conversion from Lutheranism to Roman Catholicism, wrote a series of devotional songs of an almost medieval richness. Although many of them are unsuitable for Lutheran worship, this is one of several of his hymns on the subject of the soul's clinging love to the Savior that is unsurpassed. Another included in *Lutheran Worship* (1982) is " 'Come, Follow Me' Said Christ the Lord" (*LW* 379). Utilizing as the *incipit* the thought in Psalm 18:1, "I love you, O Lord, my strength," it is a hymn perfect in style and beauty of rhythm, concise and profound, exhibiting a mysticism that is kept within bounds. The thought of loving God "not for hope of high reward" in stanza 5 is reminiscent of Bernard of Clairvaux's (*LW* 113, 274) insistence that God be loved for his own sake, completely without regard for one's own reward—"Sine intuitu praemii." Incidently, German mysticism was not without its influence on the hymnody of Pietism and in turn on the Wesleys.

The translation is an updated and slightly altered form of that which appeared in *The Lutheran Hymnal* (1941) by Catherine Winkworth from her *Chorale Book for England* (1865).

ICH WILL DICH LIEBEN first appeared with Scheffler's text in Johann König's *Harmonischer Lieder-Schatz* (1738).

Alfred Fremder prepared the harmonization for inclusion in *Lutheran Worship* (1982).

LOVE IN CHRIST IS STRONG AND LIVING 376

Both text by Dorothy Schultz and music by her husband Ralph C. Schultz were written for the marriage of their daughter Debra to Kevin Cook, July 15, 1978. The singing talent of the wedding party, comprised of family members and friends from the Concordia College Choir, suggested a choral piece rather than the customary wedding solo. Hence this was originally written in ABA form as a piece for choir accompanied by strings and oboe.

When this work came to the attention of the Commission on Worship, the commission suggested that Ralph C. Schultz modify the ABA form so that all three stanzas might be sung to the melody of the A section.

DOROTHY is named after the author of the text, namely, Dorothy R. Schultz.

Ralph C. Schultz prepared the harmonization for inclusion in *Lutheran Worship* (1982).

HOPE OF THE WORLD 377

For the 1954 General Assembly of the World Council of Churches in Evanston, Illinois, the Hymn Society of America invited hymn writers to submit new texts to celebrate the event. This hymn by Georgia Harkness was chosen from nearly 500 entries. It was published that same year in the July issue of *The Hymn* and in a Hymn Society collection titled *Eleven Ecumenical Hymns* (1954).

DONNE SECOURS was composed or adapted by Louis Bourgeois for the Genevan Psalter of 1551 (see essay: Metrical Psalms, p. 825). There it was set to Marot's version of Psalm 12, "Donne secours, Seigneur, il en est heure." E. O. Douen included the Dorian mode tune (see essay: The Church Modes, p. 832) in a list of the most beautiful and original melodies in that psalter.

The harmonization is adapted from a setting by Claude Goudimel that appeared in *Worship Supplement* (1969). The use of this tune with this text was not the choice of Georgia Harkness (who preferred ANCIENT OF DAYS [*SBH* 581]), but of the Hymn Society of America.

378 MY FAITH LOOKS TRUSTINGLY

This is perhaps the most famous hymn of Congregationalist minister Ray Palmer, unique in the warmth of its devotion to the person of Christ. Originally in six stanzas, it was written in 1830 shortly after graduating from Yale College, while teaching in a select school for young ladies in New York. A year later, on a street in Boston, he met Lowell Mason, who invited him to contribute to a hymnal that he and Thomas Hastings (*LW* 349) were about to publish. Stepping into a nearby store, Palmer wrote out a copy of this hymn and gave it to Mason. Entitled "Self-consecration," it appeared in *Spiritual Songs for Social Worship* (1832).

The text appears here in updated and altered form.

OLIVET. Impressed with Palmer's text when it was given him in a Boston store, Lowell Mason composed this tune for it, a tune that appeared with Palmer's text in *Spiritual Songs for Social Worship* and that became universally associated with his text. The aforementioned book constituted a collection described by its editors as "devotional songs for use of families and social religious meetings," a collection that they hoped would counteract the "insipid, frivolous, vulgar, and profane melodies" being sung in revival meetings. Although not intended for church use, its use in various prayer meetings and other services, and its resultant popularity, evoked an increased demand for its inclusion in the authorized denominational hymnals. Thus few present-day hymnals omit it.

While Lowell Mason may, by modern standards, be a composer of indifferent merit, when compared to his contemporaries, such tunes as OLIVET and MISSIONARY HYMN (*LW* 320, 322) are seen to be models of austerity and restraint.

The harmonization of OLIVET is from *The Hymnal 1940*.

"COME, FOLLOW ME," SAID CHRIST, THE LORD 379

"Come, follow me," said Christ, the Lord,
"All in my way abiding;
Your selfishness throw overboard,
Obey my call and guiding.
Oh, bear your crosses, and confide
In my example as your guide.

"I am the light; I light the way,
A godly life displaying;
I help you walk as in the day;
I keep your feet from straying.
I am the way, and well I show
How you should journey here below.

"My heart is rich in lowliness;
My soul with love is glowing;
My lips the words of grace express,
Their tones all gently flowing.
My heart, my mind, my strength, my all
To God I yield; on him I call.

"I teach you how to shun and flee
What harms your soul's salvation;
Your heart from ev'ry guile to free,
From sin and its temptation.
I am the refuge of the soul
And lead you to your heav'nly goal."

Then let us follow Christ, our Lord,
And take the cross appointed
And, firmly clinging to his word,
In suff'ring be undaunted.
For those who bear the battle's strain
The crown of heav'nly life obtain.

Mir nach! spricht Christus, unser Held,
Mir nach, ihr Christen alle!
Verleugnet euch, verlasst die Welt,
Folgt meinem Ruf und Schalle,
Nehmt euer Kreuz und Ungemach
Auf euch, folgt meinem Wandel nach!

Ich bin das Licht, ich leucht' euch für
Mit heil'gem Tugendleben.
Wer zu mir kommt und folget mir,
Darf nicht im Finstern schweben.
Ich bin der Weg, ich weise wohl,
Wie man wahrhaftig wandeln soll.

Mein Herz ist voll Demütigkeit,
Voll Liebe meine Seele;
Mein Mund, der fleusst zu jeder Zeit
Von süssem Sanftmutsöle;
Mein Geist, Gemüte, Kraft und Sinn
Ist Gott ergeben, schaut auf ihn.

Ich zeig' euch das, was schädlich ist,
Zu fliehen und zu meiden
Und euer Herz von arger List
Zu rein'gen und zu scheiden.
Ich bin der Seelen Fels und Hort
Und führ' euch zu der Himmelspfort'.

So lasst uns denn dem lieben Herrn
Mit Leib und Seel' nachgehen
Und wohlgemut, getrost und gern
Bei ihm im Leiden stehen!
Denn wer nicht kämpft, trägt auch die Kron'
Des ew'gen Lebens nicht davon.

This hymn by Johann Scheffler, the second of his in *Lutheran Worship* (1982), first appeared in six stanzas in the fifth part of his *Heilige Seelenlust oder Geistliche Hirten-Lieder* (Breslau, 1668), headed "She (The Soul) encourages to follow Christ." The authorship of stanza 4, which first appeared in 1695 in *Geistliche Lieder und Lobgesänge*, is unknown. This hymn, based on Matthew 10:38–39 and 16:24, is considered a masterpiece in biblical didactic poetry. Credit must be given Johann A. Freylinghausen (*LW* 23, et al.) for introducing Scheffler's hymns to the Lutheran Church.

The translation is an altered and updated form of that by Charles W. Schaeffer which first appeared in the *Evangelical Lutheran Hymn-Book* (1912).

MACHS MIT MIR, GOTT (EISENACH, SCHEIN, LEIPZIG) first appeared in Bartholomäus Gesius' *Das ander Theil des anderen newen Operis Geistlicher Deutscher Lieder* (Frankfurt-an-der-Oder, 1605) as the setting for "Ein wahrer Glaub' Gottes Zorn stillt." Johann Schein (*LW* 421) prepared the present form of the tune for his "Machs mit mir, Gott," published in broadsheet in 1628 (Zahn 2383) and later included in the second edition of his *Cantional Oder Gesang-Buch Augsburgischer Confession* (Leipzig, 1645).

Walter Gresens prepared the harmonization for inclusion in *Lutheran Worship* (1982).

380 FORTH IN YOUR NAME, O LORD, I GO

Few are the denominations that fail to include this ardent hymn of dedication to Christian service by Charles Wesley that first appeared in his *Hymns and Sacred Poems* (Bristol, 1749). There it was included in the section "Hymns for Believers" and headed "Before Word." In his *A Collection of Hymns for the use of the People called Methodists* (London, 1780) John Wesley omitted his brother's third stanza, a stanza that admittedly lacks the quality of the others and hence has also been omitted here:

Preserve me from my calling's snare,
And hide my simple heart above,
Above the thorns of choking care,
The gilded baits of worldly love.

Hymnal editors have had some difficulty with the rather awkward-to-sing last line of stanza 2, where Wesley's original read "And prove thine acceptable will." While some have simply omitted the stanza, the text here given has been generally accepted. Pronouns referring to the deity have also been updated.

While here listed under the more general category of Love and Obedience, the text is appropriate for the close of corporate worship, confirmation, ordination and installation services. What an excellent morning prayer before one begins work!

LAKEWOOD was composed by Barry L. Bobb for this text, to be used at the ordination of Ronald Roma in 1980. On this occasion it was used in a four-part choral setting with organ and brass.

Paul G. Bunjes prepared this harmonization for inclusion in *Lutheran Worship* (1982).

381 LET US EVER WALK WITH JESUS

Let us ever walk with Jesus, Follow his example pure, Through a world that would deceive us	Lasset uns mit Jesu ziehen, Seinem Vorbild folgen nach, In der Welt der Welt entfliehen,

And to sin our spirits lure.
Onward in his footsteps treading,
Pilgrims here, our home above,
Full of faith and hope and love,
Let us do our Father's bidding.
Faithful Lord, with me abide;
I shall follow where you guide.

Let us suffer here with Jesus
And with patience bear our cross.
Joy will follow all our sadness;
Where he is, there is no loss.
Though today we sow no laughter,
We shall reap celestial joy,
All discomforts that annoy
Shall give way to mirth hereafter.
Jesus, here I share your woe;
Help me there your joy to know.

Let us gladly die with Jesus.
Since by death he conquered death,
He will free us from destruction,
Give to us immortal breath.
Let us mortify all passion
That would lead us into sin;
Then by grace we all may win
Untold fruits of his creation.
Jesus, unto you I die,
There to live with you on high,

Let us also live with Jesus.
He has risen from the dead
That to life we may awaken.
Jesus, since you are our head,
We are your own living members;
Where you live, there we shall be
In your presence constantly,
Living there with you forever.
Jesus, let me faithful be,
Life eternal grant to me.

Auf der Bahn, die er uns brach,
Immer fort zum Himmel reisen,
Irdisch noch, schon himmlisch sein,
Glauben recht und leben fein,
In der Lieb' den Glauben weisen!
Treuer Jesu, bleib bei mir;
Gehe vor, ich folge dir!

Lasset uns mit Jesu leiden,
Seinem Vorbild werden gleich!
Nach dem Leiden folgen Freuden,
Armut hier macht dorten reich.
Tränensaat, die erntet Lachen,
Hoffnung tröstet mit Geduld.
Es kann leichtlich Gottes Huld
Aus dem Regen Sonne machen.
Jesu, hier leid' ich mit dir,
Dort teil deine Freud' mit mir!

Lasset uns mit Jesu sterben!
Sein Tod uns vom andern Tod
Rettet und vom Seelverderben,
Von der ewiglichen Not.
Lasst uns töten, weil wir leben,
Unser Fleisch, ihm sterben ab,
So wird er uns aus dem Grab
In das Himmelsleben heben.
Jesu, sterb' ich, sterb' ich dir,
Dass ich lebe für und für.

Lasset uns mit Jesu leben!
Weil er auferstanden ist,
Muss das Grab uns wiedergeben.
Jesu, unser Haupt du bist,
Wir sind deines Leibes Glieder;
Wo du lebst, da leben wir.
Ach, erkenn uns für und für,
Trauter Fruend, für deine Brüder!
Jesus, dir ich lebe hier,
Dorten ewig auch bei dir.

Sigismund von Birken wrote this notable hymn, and its first appearance was in his *Geistliche Weihrauchkörner oder Andachtslieder* (Nürnberg, 1652). Although it can serve both as a hymn on our Lord's Passion and as one emphasizing the Christian's love and obedience, its allusion to Romans 6 might also prompt consideration as appropriate for Holy Baptism.

The English text was prepared by the Inter-Lutheran Commission on Worship for inclusion in *Lutheran Book of Worship* (1978).

LASSET UNS MIT JESU ZIEHEN (Zahn 7916) was composed by Georg Gottfried Boltze for the hymn of thanksgiving, "Sollt ich meinen Gott nicht singen" (*LW* 439), by Paul Gerhardt and included in Johann Kühnau's *Vierstimmige alte und neue Choralgesänge* (1790).

The harmonization is from *The Lutheran Hymnal* (1941).

382 "TAKE UP YOUR CROSS," THE SAVIOR SAID

Charles W. Everest wrote this hymn in 1833, when he was but 19 years of age. Originally in six stanzas, it was published by him in that year in his *Visions of Death, and Other Poems*. Its first inclusion in a hymnal appears to have been in *Sabbath School and Social Hymns of the Reformed Protestant Dutch Church of the United States of America* (New York, 1843). Thereafter it appeared in various altered forms in a number of hymnals, including *Hymns Ancient and Modern* (1861). This version was prepared by the Inter-Lutheran Commission on Worship for inclusion in *Lutheran Book of Worship* (1978).

NUN LASST UNS DEN LEIB BEGRABEN appeared in Georg Rhau's *Newe deudsche geistliche Geseng CXIII, mit vier und fünf Stimmen, für die gemeinen Schulen* (Wittenberg, 1544) as the setting for "Nun lasst uns den Leib begraben," a text attributed to Michael Weisse (*LW* 18; see *TLH* 596). As customary at the time, this fine tune was considerably more rhythmic in character compared to the soon thereafter simplified form as also here exhibited.

Jan O. Bender originally prepared this harmonization for inclusion in *Lutheran Book of Worship* (1978).

383, 384 ALL WHO WOULD VALIANT BE

John Bunyan's original poem, "Who would true Valour see," was printed in the second part of *The Pilgrim's Progress* (1684), and was included in Paxton Hood's *Our Hymn Book* (1873). Percy Dearmer reworked the poem for *The English Hymnal* (1906), beginning "He who would valiant be," the editors thinking the original wording inappropriate to a hymn. The text in both *Lutheran Book of Worship* (1978) and *Lutheran Worship* (1982) follows Dearmer's except in number; this has been changed from singular to plural.

Several scholars have noted with puzzlement the similarity between Bunyan's text and the song "Under the greenwood tree" in *As You Like It*, both in meter and in certain phrases; it appears unlikely, however, that Bunyan was familiar with Shakespeare.

MONKS GATE was adapted by Ralph Vaughan Williams from a folk tune he heard at the village of Monk's Gate, near Horsham, West Sussex, England. It was first published in *The English Hymnal* (1906), set to Dearmer's revision of Bunyan's text. While it can perhaps be considered as a fine tune, a striking example in modern hymnody of syncopation and cross rhythm, one cannot but agree with Austin Lovelace that the tune is a misfit to this text, a text that is dactylic (´ ˘ ˘) in nature, whereas the tune appears to be iambic (˘ ´). A better wedding of text and tune, in the estimation of this writer, is below.

The harmonization of MONKS GATE is also that prepared by Ralph Vaughan Williams for inclusion in *The English Hymnal*.

ST. DUNSTAN'S, by C. Winfred Douglas, captures the spirit of meter and text to a much better degree than does MONKS GATE. Douglas explains his composition thus:

> Bunyan's burly song strikes a new and welcome note in our *Hymnal*. The quaint sincerity of the words stirs us out of our easygoing dull Christianity to the thrill of great adventure. The balladlike rhythm requires special musical treatment incompatible with a mechanical regularity of measures. The tune is, therefore, in free rhythm, following the words. It should have a quality of sturdiness which always reminds the writer of St. Paul valiantly battling through manifold disaster in "the care of all the churches." (*The Hymnal 1940 Companion*)

The tune, first published with Douglas' harmonization in the Episcopal *Hymnal* (1918), was composed on December 15, 1917, while returning by train from New York City to his home at St. Dunstan's cottage, on the grounds of the Community of St. Mary, Peekskill, New York. This combination was repeated in *The Hymnal 1940* and in *The Hymnal 1982*. In both hymnals MONKS GATE is designated as the alternate tune.

The harmonization in *Lutheran Worship* (1982) is also by Douglas.

HOW CAN I THANK YOU, LORD 385

How can I thank you, Lord,
For all your loving-kindness,
That you have patiently
Endured my sinful blindness!
When dead in many sins
And trespasses I lay,
I kindled, holy God,
Your anger ev'ry day.

It is your work alone
That I am now converted;
Against the sin in me
You have the pow'r asserted.
Your mercy and your grace,
Which rise afresh each morn,
Have turned my stony heart
Into a heart newborn.

Lord, you have raised me up
To joy and exultation
And clearly shown the way

Was kann ich doch für Dank,
O Herr, dir dafür sagen,
Dass du mich mit Geduld
So lange Zeit getragen,
Da ich in mancher Sünd'
Und Übertretung lag
Und dich, du frommer Gott,
Erzürnte alle Tag'!

Dass ich nun bin bekehrt,
Hast du allein verrichtet;
Du hast des Satans Reich
Und Werk in mir vernichtet.
Herr, deine Güt' und Treu',
Die an die Wolken reicht,
Hat auch mein steinern Herz
Zerbrochen und erweicht.

Du hast mich aufgericht't
Und mir den Weg geweiset,
Den ich nun wandeln soll;

That leads me to salvation.
My sins are washed away;
For this I thank you, Lord,
That in my heart and soul
I have all sin abhorred.

Dafür, Herr, sei gepreiset!
Gott sei gelobt, dass ich
Die alte Sünd' nun hass'
Und willig, ohne Furcht,
Die toten Werke lass'.

Grant that your Spirit's help
To me be always given
Lest I should fall again
And lose the way to heaven.
Grant that he give me strength
Against infirmity;
May he renew my heart
To serve you willingly.

Damit ich aber nicht
Aufs neue wider falle,
So gib mir deinen Geist,
Dieweil ich hier noch walle,
Der meine Schwachheit stärk'
Und in mir mächtig sei
Und mein Gemüte stets
Zu deinem Dienst erneu'.

O Father, God of love,
Accept my supplication;
O Savior, Son of God,
Grant me your full salvation;
O Holy Spirit, be
My ever faithful guide
That I may serve you here
And there with you abide.

O Gott, du grosser Gott,
O Vater, hör mein Flehen!
O Jesu, Gottes Sohn,
Lass deine Kraft mich sehen!
O werter Heil'ger Geist,
Sei bei mir allezeit,
Dass ich dir diene hier
Und dort in Ewigkeit!

Included in the *Kirchengesangbuch für Evangelish Lutherische Gemeinden* (1847), the first official hymnal of the Synod, as well as in its later editions (1848, 1857, 1917), and in the *Evangelical Lutheran Hymn-Book* (1912), the first official English hymnal of the Synod, and in its successor *The Lutheran Hymnal* (1941), this hymn by David Denicke, given its popularity with congregations, was also chosen for inclusion in *Lutheran Worship* (1982). The hymn's first appearance, in eight stanzas, was in the Hanoverian *New Ordentlich Gesangbuch* (1648) entitled "Thanksgiving and Prayer of a Convert." In their simplicity, Denicke's hymns exude a certain warmth and power that flow from a deep spiritual heart.

The translation is an altered and updated form of that by August Crull in *The Lutheran Hymnal* (1941).

O GOTT, DU FROMMER GOTT (MUNICH) first achieved a definitive form when it was set to the text "O Gott, du Frommer Gott" in the 1693 Meiningen hymnal, *Newvermehrtes und zu Übung christlicher Gottseligkeit*. Snatches of it had appeared in several earlier collections (Zahn 5148). Representing one of the many tunes set to the aforementioned text, it is in the isometric form (see essay: Polyrhythmic and Isometric Chorales, p. 822), one of the two different chorale forms beginning to appear in the latter half of the 17th century, the other being the solo-aria style.

The harmonization is an altered form of that which appeared with this text in *The Lutheran Hymnal* (1941).

JESUS, STILL LEAD ON 386

Jesus, still lead on
Till our rest be won;
And although the way be cheerless,
We will follow calm and fearless;
Guide us by your hand
To our fatherland.

If the way be drear,
If the foe be near,
Let no faithless fears o'ertake us,
Let not faith and hope forsake us;
Safely past the foe
To our home we go.

When we seek relief
From a long-felt grief,
When temptations come alluring,
Make us patient and enduring;
Show us that bright shore
Where we weep no more.

Jesus, still lead on
Till our rest be won;
Heav'nly leader, still direct us,
Still support, console, protect us,
Till we safely stand
In our fatherland.

Jesu, geh voran
Auf der Lebensbahn,
Und wir wollen nicht verweilen,
Dir getreulich nachzueilen.
Führ uns an der hand
Bis ins Vaterland!

Soll's uns hart ergehn,
Lass uns feste stehn
Und auch in den schwersten Tagen
Niemals über Lasten klagen;
Denn durch Trübsal hier
Geht der Weg zu dir.

Rühret eigner Schmerz
Irgend unser Herz,
Kümmert uns ein fremdes Leiden,
O so gib Geduld zu beiden;
Richte unsern Sinn
Auf das Ende hin!

Ordne, unsern Gang,
Jesu, lebenslang!
Führst du uns durch rauhe Wege,
Gib uns auch die nöt'ge Pflege.
Tu uns nach dem Lauf
Deine Türe auf!

This is a cento of two hymns written by Count Nicolaus L. von Zinzendorf, namely, "Seelenbräutigam, o du Gottes Lamm" (not to be confused with Adam Drese's "Seelenbräutigam, Jesu, Gottes Lamm"), comprised of 11 stanzas, and the morning hymn "Glanz der Ewigkeit, Gott und Herr der Zeit," comprised of 15 stanzas. As a cento it appeared in the Moravian Christian Gregor's *Gesangbuch zum Gebrauch der Evangelischen Brüdergemeinen* (Barbee, 1778).

The translation by Jane Borthwick, herein updated in slightly revised form, first appeared in the *Free Church Magazine* (1846) and again, somewhat altered, in her *Hymns from the Land of Luther* (first series, 1854). It is a notable hymn on the Christian life, voicing trust in divine mercy and willing obedience to the Lord's leading.

SEELENBRÄUTIGAM was composed by Adam Drese for his own text, "Seelenbräutigam, Jesu, Gotteslamm," given in *Geistreiches Gesangbuch* (Darmstadt, 1698).

Paul G. Bunjes prepared the harmonization for *Lutheran Worship* (1982).

387 PRAISE AND THANKS AND ADORATION

Praise and thanks and adoration,
Son of God, to you we give,
For you chose to serve creation,
Died that Adam's heirs might live.
Dear Lord Jesus, guide my way;
Faithful let me day by day
Follow where your steps are leading,
Find adventure, joys exceeding!

Hold me ever in your keeping,
Comfort me in pain and strife;
Through my laughter and my weeping
Lift me to a nobler life.
Draw my fervent love to you;
Constant faith and hope renew
In your birth, your life and Passion,
In your death and resurrection.

Lov og Tak og evig Äre
Ske dig Guds enbaarne Sön,
Som en Tjener vilde väre,
Kommen ud af Davids Kjön!
Söde Jesu, lär du mig,
At jeg vandrer rettelig,
Og i dine Fodspor träder,
Ja udi din Vei mig gläder.

Lad mig aldrig dig forsage,
Om end Kors og Kummer mig
Skal i denne Verden plage,
Men at jeg dog hjertelig
Elsker dig indtil min Död,
Og forlindrer al min Nöd
Ved din Födsel, Död og Smerte,
Tag dem aldrig fra mit Hjerte!

This hymn by Thomas Kingo first appeared in his *En Ny Kirke-Psalmebog* (Vinterparten, 1689). Based on John 21:19–24, the Gospel for the Third Christmas Day, it was to serve as the closing hymn to that day's corporate worship.

The translation, based on that by Kristen Kvamme which appeared in *The Lutheran Hymnary* (1913), was prepared by the Inter-Lutheran Commission on Worship for inclusion in *Lutheran Book of Worship* (1978).

FREU DICH SEHR. For comments on the tune see hymn 28.

The harmonization was prepared by George Leonard, a *nom de plume* of Paul G. Bunjes.

388 THE MAN IS EVER BLESSED

This is Isaac Watts' metrical paraphrase of Psalm 1 that appeared in his *Psalms of David Imitated in the Language of the New Testament* (London, 1719), a work reflecting his protest against the dullness and crudity and the total lack of New Testament Gospel in the metrical psalmody of his day, the result of Calvin's influence.

ST. MICHAEL. For comments on this tune see hymn 249.

The harmonization is from *The Hymnal 1940*.

MAY WE YOUR PRECEPTS, LORD, FULFILL 389

This hymn by Edward Osler first appeared in *Psalms and Hymns* (1836), of which Osler was co-editor with W. J. Hall. The updated and slightly altered text was prepared by the Inter-Lutheran Commission on Worship for inclusion in *Lutheran Book of Worship* (1978).

Written in the effective 886 886 meter, with the rhyme scheme of AABCCB (as is also Osler's other hymn in *Lutheran Worship*, no. 261), the hymn exhibits a splendid statement of love and obedience, two acts that are today often contrasted, the latter considered in a legalistic spirit. But this antithesis is a false one. True love takes delight in obeying (cf. 1 John 5:3). Those who know and understand such love in the Christian sense are always eager to obey God's commandments.

MERIBAH. Lowell Mason composed this tune in 1839 and named it for the place where Moses struck the rock and water poured out (Ex. 17:5–7).

The harmonization is from *The Lutheran Hymnal* (1941).

FOR JERUSALEM YOU'RE WEEPING 390

This hymn by Anna Hoppe, based on the Gospel reading for the Tenth Sunday after Trinity Sunday in the Old Standard Series (Luke 19:41–48), was written in 1919. Thereafter it was included in *The Hymnal* (Rock Island, 1925) of the Evangelical Lutheran Augustana Synod.

FREU DICH SEHR. For comments on the tune see hymn 28.

The harmonization was prepared by George Leonard, a *nom de plume* of Paul G. Bunjes.

I WALK IN DANGER ALL THE WAY 391

I walk in danger all the way.
The thought shall never leave me
That Satan, who has marked his prey,
Is plotting to deceive me.
This foe with hidden snares
May seize me unawares
If I should fail to watch and pray.
I walk in danger all the way.

Jeg gaar i Fare, hvor jeg gaar,
Min Själ skal altid tänke,
At Satan allevegne staar
I Veien med sin Länke;
Hans skjulte Helved-Brand
Mig let forvilde kand,
Naar jeg ei paa min Skanse staar;
Jeg gaar i Fare, hvor jeg gaar.

I pass through trials all the way,
With sin and ills contending;
In patience I must bear each day
The cross of God's own sending.
When in adversity
I know not where to flee,
When storms of woe my soul dismay,
I pass through trials all the way.

And death pursues me all the way,
Nowhere I rest securely;
He comes by night, he comes by day,
He takes his prey most surely.
A failing breath, and I
In death's strong grasp may lie
To face eternity today
As death pursues me all the way.

I walk with angels all the way,
They shield me and befriend me;
All Satan's pow'r is held at bay
When heav'nly hosts attend me;
They are my sure defense,
All fear and sorrow, hence!
Unharmed by foes, do what they may,
I walk with angels all the way.

I walk with Jesus all the way,
His guidance never fails me;
Within his wounds I find a stay
When Satan's pow'r assails me;
And by his footsteps led,
My path I safely tread.
No evil leads my soul astray;
I walk with Jesus all the way.

My walk is heav'nward all the way;
Await, my soul, the morrow,
When God's good healing shall allay
All suff'ring, sin, and sorrow.
Then, worldly pomp, begone!
To heav'n I now press on.
For all the world I would not stay;
My walk is heav'nward all the way.

Jeg gaar i Trängsel, hvor jeg gaar;
Mod Synden skal jeg stride,
Om Gud med Korsets Ris mig slaar,
Det skal jeg taalig lide,
Tidt ingen Vei jeg ser,
Hvor jeg kan vandre meer,
Naar modgangs Taage om mig staar;
Jeg gaar i Trängsel, hvor jeg gaar.

Jeg gaar til Döden, hvor jeg gaar,
Og veed mig ikke sikker,
Ei nogen Dag og Time, naar
Han har mig alt i Strikker.
Et lidet Aandefang
Kan ende al min Gang,
At jeg i Evigheden staar;
Jeg gaar til Döden, hvor jeg gaar.

Jeg gaar blandt Engle, hvor jeg gaar;
De skal mig vel bevare,
Slet intet Satans Magt formaar
I saadan Himmel-Skare.
Bort Verdens Suk og Sorg!
Jeg gaar i Engle-Borg.
Trods nogen rörer mig et Haar!
Jeg gaar blandt Engle, hvor jeg gaar.

Jeg gaar med Jesum, hvor jeg gaar,
Han har mig ved sin Side,
Han skjuler mig med sine Saar,
Og hjälper mig at stride,
Hvor han sit Fodspor lod,
Der setter jeg min Fod;
Trods al den Deel, mig ilde spaar,
Jeg gaar med Jesum, hvor jeg gaar.

Jeg gaar til Himlen, hvor jeg gaar;
Frimodig da mit Hjerte!
Kun did, hvor du en Ende faar
Paa al din Synd og Smerte!
Bort Verdens Lyst og Pragt,
Til Himlen staar min Agt!
Al Verdens Eie jeg forsmaar,
Jeg gaar till Himlen, hvor jeg gaar.

This hymn by Hans A. Brorson, Lutheran pastor and bishop, appeared in *Nogle Salmer om Troens Frugt* (1734). Scripture passages that might be considered as being the basis for the successive stanzas are: 1 Peter 5:8; John 16:33; Psalm 90:5–6; Psalm 34:7; John 8:12; Hebrews 13:14 and Philippians 3:20.

The translation is a slightly altered form of that by Ditlef G. Ristad that first appeared in *The Lutheran Hymnary* (1913) and thereafter in *The Lutheran Hymnal* (1941).

DER LIEBEN SONNE LICHT UND PRACHT is, with slight changes, the sturdy and moving tune that appeared in Freylinghausen's *Geistreiches Gesangbuch* (fourth edition, 1708) set to a text by Christian Scriver beginning with the same words. The tune itself, however, is considerably older. It is said that Christian Scriver one night heard a frivolous folk text sung to this fine tune. Shocked at such misuse, he sat down and wrote a nine-stanza evening hymn to this tune, five stanzas of which are presently contained in the *Evangelisches Kirchengesangbuch* of the Lutheran territorial churches in Germany.

The setting included in *Lutheran Worship* (1982) was prepared by George Leonard, a *nom de plume* of Paul G. Bunjes.

OH, THAT THE LORD WOULD GUIDE MY WAYS 392

Based on Psalm 119, this hymn, originally in six stanzas, appeared in Isaac Watts's *Psalms of David Imitated* (London, 1719). The text is a slightly altered form of that prepared by the Inter-Lutheran Commission on Worship for inclusion in *Lutheran Book of Worship* (1978).

EVAN. This is an adaptation by Lowell Mason of a tune by William H. Havergal, which was published in 1847 as the setting for Robert Burns' "O thou dread power, who reign'st above." Mason shortened the tune and changed the rhythm, publishing the result as EVA in his *New Carmina Sacra* (1850); later that year he changed the name to EVAN for his *Cantica Laudis*. Havergal was not pleased with Mason's abridgement, calling it "a sad estrangement" and adding that he did not know the reason for the name. In 1872 Mrs. Havergal wrote to Mason, suggesting that a Scottish stream called Evan might have prompted the name; but Mason, who was ill at the time, never responded to her letter and died shortly after receiving it. Mrs. Havergal's hypothesis seems unlikely in view of the fact that Mason published the tune as EVA before ever visiting Scotland.

The setting is from *The Worshipbook* (1972) of the United Presbyterian Church.

JESUS! OH, HOW COULD IT BE TRUE 393

This hymn, originally in seven stanzas, by Joseph Grigg, a minister of the Presbyterian Church, is one of his *Four Hymns on Divine Subjects wherein the Patience and Love of our Divine Saviour is Displayed* (1765). In 1861 Daniel Sedgwick collected Grigg's hymns in *Hymns on Divine Subjects*, in which it was stated that this poem was "composed when the author was ten years of age." It was not without numerous revisions that the hymn was included in various hymnals. The version here given is an altered and updated version of that which appeared in John Rippon's (*LW* 272, 411)

Collection of Hymns from the Best Authors (1787), where it was said to have been altered by a certain Benjamin Francis.

FEDERAL STREET. While conducting a music class in Salem, Massachusetts, Lowell Mason (*LW* 115, et al.) asked if anyone in the group had tried his or her hand at composition. Henry K. Oliver came forth with a tune that he had composed in 1832. Thereafter Mason included it in his *Boston Academy Collection of Church Music* (1836). At the great Peace Jubilee in Boston, 1872, Oliver led some 20,000 people as they sang FEDERAL STREET to his text, "Hail gentle peace." The name of the tune represents the street on which Oliver lived in Salem, Massachusetts.

The harmonization is from *The Lutheran Hymnal* (1941), slightly altered.

SON OF GOD, ETERNAL SAVIOR 394

Somerset Lowry's five-stanza hymn was first published in the February 1894 issue of *Good Will*, thereafter in the *Christian Social Union Hymn Book* (1895). Lowry later granted permission to the editors of *Songs of Praise* (1925) to substitute "birth among us" for "birth incarnate" in the first and last stanzas, and "Hush the storm of strife and passion" in place of "Oh! the past is dark behind us" in the cento's third stanza. Omitted is Lowry's stanza 4:

Dark the path that lies behind us,
Strewn with wrecks and stained with blood;
But before us gleams the vision
Of the coming brotherhood.
See the Christlike host advancing,
High and lowly, great and small,
Linked in bonds of common service
For the common Lord of all.

In addition, slight alterations include the substitution of "Word made flesh" for "Son of Man" in the first and last stanzas, and updating of the language. The text was prepared by the Inter-Lutheran Commission on Worship for inclusion in *Lutheran Book of Worship* (1978).

IN BABILONE. For comments on the tune see hymn 164.

This arrangement is by Julius Röntgen, from *The Hymn Book* (1971) of the Anglican Church of Canada and the United Church of Canada.

O FOUNT OF GOOD, FOR ALL YOUR LOVE 395

The following appeared in 1755 in Philip Doddridge's posthumous *Hymns, Founded on Various Texts in the Holy Scriptures*, entitled "On relieving Christ in the Poor":

Jesus, my Lord, how rich thy grace,
Thy bounties how complete!
How shall I count the matchless sum,
How pay the mighty debt?

High on a throne of radiant light,
Dost thou exalted shine:
What can my poverty bestow,
When all the worlds are thine?

Thy face, with rev'rence and with love
We in thy poor would see;
But thou hast brethren here below,
The partners of thy grave,
And wilt confess their humble names
Before thy Father's face.

In them thou may'st be clothed and fed,
And visited and cheered;
And in their accents of distress
My Savior's voice is heard.

O let us rather beg our bread
Than keep it back from thee.

Edward Osler then revised the hymn for the *Mitre Hymn Book* (1836), where it began, "Fount of all good, to own thy love." Various further alterations by hymnal editors have brought the text to its present form, which is largely an altered and updated version of that in the *Worship Supplement* (1969).

SONG 67. While the appearance of this tune, with a bass line by Orlando Gibbons, in George Wither's *Hymnes and Songs of the Church* (1623), would seem to indicate Gibbons as the composer, this has been disputed since the melody was discovered in Prys' earlier Welsh psalter, *Llyfr y Psalmau* (1621). Some now believe it to be an old psalm tune; Erik Routley notes, "It is an excellent tune, but not on either external or internal evidence ascribable to [Gibbons]" (*The Music of Christian Hymnody*). The name SONG 67 is derived from Wither's book, where it was set to hymn 67:

When one among the Twelve there was,
That did thy Grace abuse;
Thou left'st him, Lord, and in his place,
Did'st just Matthias chuse.

Gibbons' bass line is used in *Lutheran Worship*; the other parts of the harmonization were provided by Paul G. Bunjes.

396 O GOD, WHOSE WILL IS LIFE AND GOOD

Written especially for medical missionaries, this hymn by Hardwicke D. Rawnsley, originally beginning "Father, whose will is life and good," was published in *A Missionary Hymn Book* (London, 1922) of the Society for the Promotion of Christian Knowledge. Rawnsley's fourth stanza is omitted:

For still his love works wondrous charms,
And, as in days of old,
He takes the wounded in his arms
And bears them to the fold.

The text here given is that which appeared in *Lutheran Book of Worship* (1978), except for alterations in stanzas 3 and 4.

The subject of health and healing represents a somewhat new aspect in the history of the Synod's hymnals. Such concerns in the local congregation have been, and continue to be, expressed in the special petitions embodied in the Prayer of the Church. It is worthy of note that Jesus' instruction to his disciples included both preaching and healing. Thus the object of God's redemptive act in Christ is to the human being as a whole. Since health is indivisible, the church has the unique opportunity to relate its theology to the problems of health, thus involving the Christian congregation as a therapeutic community. As for "faith healing" or "divine healing" as practiced by some today, this more often than not distorts biblical truth by offering physical health as the ultimate gift of God rather than as a penultimate one. It is the privilege of the medical profession to convey God's love in a special manner.

LEUPOLD is an adaptation by its composer Leland Sateren of a tune that he composed for a choir selection with a text beginning "Turn not thy face," published by Augsburg Publishing House in 1964. An earlier four-part setting had been published in 1956. The tune's name was chosen by Sateren to honor Ulrich Leupold, a beloved professor, scholar, musician, and friend, a member of the Inter-Lutheran Commission on Worship.

The harmonization is that prepared by Leland Sateren for inclusion in *Lutheran Book of Worship* (1978).

O GOD OF MERCY, GOD OF LIGHT 397

This text by Godfrey Thring appeared as an offertory hymn in his *A Church of England Hymn Book adapted to the daily services of the Church throughout the year* (London, 1880), a book produced as a protest against the various "party hymn-books" being issued and as setting a higher standard. Headed "Which, now, of these three was neighbor unto him that fell among the thieves?" the first line originally read "O God of mercy, God of might." This text, with several alterations, was prepared by the Inter-Lutheran Commission on Worship for inclusion in *Lutheran Book of Worship* (1978). It is one of three hymns in *Lutheran Worship* (1982) with the meter of 888 6, a variation of long meter (88 88) that comes off rather well.

JUST AS I AM by Joseph Barnby, also called BARNBY and DUNSTAN (see *LW* 356), appeared in the *Home and School Hymnal* (London, 1892), composed for Charlotte Elliott's "Just as I Am, Without One Plea" (*LW* 359). The tune exhibits some of the less endearing aspects of Victorianism, of which Barnby is a representative.

The harmonization is an altered form of that prepared by Larry Jon Houff for inclusion in *Lutheran Book of Worship* (1978).

GOD OF GRACE AND GOD OF GLORY 398

Harry Emerson Fosdick wrote this stirring hymn for the opening service of Riverside Church in New York City, October 5, 1930; it was sung again at the church's dedication the following February. The text was published in H. Augustine Smith's *Praise and*

Service (1932). The obligations of "this hour" certainly extend beyond the occasion that inspired it, namely, as an ongoing challenge to Christian discipleship.

While Fosdick's theology was somewhat irregular, this hymn reflects a faith that cannot be faulted. Apropos are the words of Armin Haeussler:

> Soon after the *Hymnal* came off the press, in 1941, our Hymnal Committee was taken to task in print by a critic of another denomination, who held that the theology of Fosdick and Whittier is too liberal. While we may not subscribe to everything written by them, it certainly cannot be denied that men of the Fosdick and Whittier type are animated by the spirit of Christ. We have always welcomed constructive criticism, but when we called at the home of our critic and asked him what he objected to as a good Christian in "God of Grace and God of Glory," he failed to make a reply. We might have asked: Do you refuse to buy a piece of furniture because it may have been manufactured by a Roman Catholic, or a suit of clothes because it may have been made by a Jew? To his probable answer that a hymn is not in the same category, since it may teach false doctrines, let us reply that Catholics and Protestants have often taken hymns from each other and used them, sometimes with no change whatever in the wording, for the very good reason that they could find nothing objectionable in them, in fact, regarded them as very helpful. Our critic himself was very inconsistent, for he put . . . a number of . . . hymns by Unitarian authors into his own compilation. Let us follow the principles of Christian sportsmanship in hymnody as elsewhere and give due credit for every brilliantly executed hymnic touchdown. (*The Story of Our Hymns*)

CWM RHONDDA. For comments on the tune see hymn 220. Fosdick's hymn was originally sung to REGENT SQUARE, a favorite of his. The present combination of text and tune—in the opinion of this writer, the more felicitous—first appeared in *The Methodist Hymnal* (1935), a procedure that necessitated repeating the last line of each stanza.

The harmonization by Paul G. Bunjes differs from that which he prepared for hymn 220.

399 YOUR HAND, O LORD, IN DAYS OF OLD

Written by Edward H. Plumptre in 1864, this hymn was first printed as a leaflet entitled "A Hymn used in the Chapel of King's College Hospital." Plumptre included it in the second edition, 1865, of his *Lazarus and Other Poems*. Thereafter it appeared in the 1868 Appendix to *Hymns Ancient and Modern* (1961) with a reference to Matthew 14:35–36. (On the subject of health and healing see *LW* 396.)

The text here given is a somewhat altered form of that prepared by the Inter-Lutheran Commission on Worship for inclusion in *Lutheran Book of Worship* (1978).

OLD 107th. Louis Bourgeois' tune for Clement Marot's versification of Psalm 107 in the Genevan Psalter (1574) appeared thus:

In the Scottish Psalter of 1564 (see essay: Metrical Psalms, p. 833), where the tune was again set to Psalm 107, the rhythmic form was altered. It is that altered form that is here used in *Lutheran Worship* (1982). Archibald Jacob notes:

> It is a noble tune, with a modal flavour, and a wide, majestic sweep of phrase; the later version is, as can be seen, near enough to the earlier to preserve all its original character.

The harmonization is from *The Worshipbook: Services and Hymns* (1972) of the Presbyterian Church.

O SON OF GOD, IN GALILEE 400

This hymn by Anna Hoppe, originally in six stanzas, beginning "O thou who once in Galilee," appeared in the *American Lutheran Hymnal* (1930). Recognizing its usefulness in its concern for the physically afflicted, it was included in *Worship Supplement* (1969), where it was set to SALEM, a tune by Richard W. Hillert (*LW* 273, et al.). This updated and altered text was prepared by the Inter-Lutheran Commission on Worship for inclusion in *Lutheran Book of Worship* (1978). Interestingly, this text is included in the third edition of *Worship: A Hymnal and Service Book for Roman Catholics*.(1986):

TWENTY-FOURTH. Also known as CHELMSFORD and PRIMROSE, this tune was first published in 1813, both in John Wyeth's *A Repository of Sacred Music, Part II*, and in Robert Patterson's *Church Music*. While Wyeth claims first publication, Patterson's collection was registered seven months earlier and thus can be considered the original source of the tune.

Attribution of the melody is no less confusing. Wyeth gives the name *Chapin* in connection with it, but there were at least seven different Chapins involved in church music at the time; this tune has been accredited to both Lucius Chapin and his brother Amzi. In an article in *Journal of Research in Music Education* (Fall 1960), Charles Hamm attributes the tune to Lucius.

The harmonization of this plaintive tune is somewhat altered from that by Robert Leaf in *Lutheran Book of Worship* (no. 126).

FORGIVE US, LORD, FOR SHALLOW THANKFULNESS 401

This notable hymn with its societal concerns was written by William W. Reid, Sr., at one time director of the department of news service of the Methodist Board of Missions and past executive secretary of the Hymn Society of America. Its first appearance was in *My God Is There, Controlling, and Other Hymns and Poems* (New York, 1965).

SURSUM CORDA was composed by Alfred M. Smith in 1941 for Henry Montagu Butler's text "Lift Up Your Hearts" (*EpH* 482). It was one of the some 5,000 anonymous manuscripts received for consideration by the editors of *The Hymnal 1940* of the Protestant Episcopal Church. Its smooth prevailing stepwise movement (conjunct) suits the prayerful text rather well.

The harmonization is the work of Paul G. Bunjes.

LORD OF GLORY, YOU HAVE BOUGHT US 402

When Eliza S. Alderson submitted this hymn to the editorial committee of *Hymns Ancient and Modern*, she requested that her brother, John B. Dykes, be asked to write a tune for it. Dykes, surprised to learn that his sister had written the hymn, was unsatisfied with her four stanzas. He then added the fifth stanza by repeating the first four lines of stanza 1 and finishing up with four lines of his own composition.

The resulting hymn was first published in the 1868 Appendix to *Hymns Ancient and Modern* (1861), where it was set to Dykes's new tune CHARITAS. The text here given, an altered and updated form of that appearing in *The Lutheran Hymnal* (1941), was prepared by the Inter-Lutheran Commission on Worship for inclusion in *Lutheran Book of Worship* (1978).

HYFRYDOL. For comments on the tune see hymn 286.

The harmonization was prepared by Paul G. Bunjes.

PRAISE AND THANKSGIVING 403

Albert Bayly wrote this hymn in June 1961, and its first appearance was in the *Rodborough Hymnal* (1964), published by the Rodborough Tabernacle Congregational Church. In 1967 it was included in the author's collection of hymns entitled *Again I Say Rejoice* with the following note:

This was written to meet the need for harvest thanksgiving hymns which remind us that we can thank God for his gifts rightly only if we are ready to do his will by sharing those gifts with others, so they can rejoice with us.

BUNESSAN is an attractive and popular tune that originated in the Celtic highlands of Scotland. It was taken down by Alexander Frazer from a wandering highland singer and first published by him in *Songs and Hymns of the Gael* (1888). In the Irish *Church Hymnal* (1917) it was used with Mary Macdonald's "Child in the Manger."

Wilhelm Quampen, a *nom de plume* of Paul G. Bunjes, prepared the harmonization for *Lutheran Worship* (1982).

404 TAKE MY LIFE, O LORD, RENEW

Through all the polemics and unsettlements of 19th century England, poets of the Evangelical School continued to disseminate the teachings that had been best in the piety and philanthropy of the English people, and much of their hymnody has passed into the currency of the church's worship. There come to mind such poets—many of whom are women—as Charlotte Elliott (*LW* 359), Jeanette Threlfall (*LW* 106), James Montgomery (*LW* 50, et al.), Thomas Kelly (*LW* 116, 118), and Horatius Bonar (*LW* 173, et al.).

Included in this group is also Frances R. Havergal, chief among the poets of Christian consecration, author of "Take My Life, O Lord, Renew," a hymn so dear to the church's heart. Translated into many languages and included in most hymnals, it had its origins in a prayer meeting at Areley House, England, February 4, 1874, and is thus described by her in a letter:

> I went for a little visit of five days. There were 10 persons in the house, some unconverted and long prayed for, some converted but not rejoicing Christians. He gave me the prayer, "Lord, give me all in this house!" And he just did. Before I left the house everyone had got a blessing. The last night of my visit . . . I was too happy to sleep, and passed most of the night in praise and renewal of my own consecration, and these little couplets formed themselves and chimed in my heart one after another till they finished with "Ever, only, ALL for thee!" (Dearmer, *Songs of Praise Discussed*)

As indicated in the foregoing, this hymn was originally arranged in a series of couplets—thus 12 stanzas of two lines—each couplet expressing one detail of the all-inclusive first-couplet word, "life": time, hands, feet, voice, lips, wealth, mind, will, heart, and love. The text ends with a reintegration of these details, namely, myself.

The hymn was first published in the appendix of Charles E. Snepp's *Songs of Grace and Glory* (1874), appearing later in Havergal's *Loyal Responses* (1878). The text appears here in altered and updated form.

PATMOS (CONSECRATION). Havergal expressed the wish that her hymn be sung to this tune, composed by her father, William H. Havergal, the pioneer of reform in metrical psalmody. From an unpublished manuscript in 1869 it was published two years later in his *Psalmody*.

The harmonization is by Paul G. Bunjes.

Note: Errors occurring in the second measure in the first printing of *Lutheran Worship* (1982) were corrected in a subsequent printing.

WE GIVE YOU BUT YOUR OWN 405

"The Poor Man's Bishop," William W. How, wrote this hymn in 1858. It was published in *Psalms and Hymns* (1864), edited by How and T. B. Morrell, under the heading of Proverbs 19:17: "He that hath pity upon the poor lendeth unto the Lord."

Concerning this text, hymn writer George Matheson wrote: "[It] sounds the real humanitarian note to the fatherless and widows. Hymnology is feeble and ineffective when it ignores the humanitarian side of religion." Others have favorably compared How's attitude on stewardship to that demonstrated in Wordsworth's "O Lord of heaven" (1863). The latter reads in part:

> Whatever, Lord, we lend to thee
> Repaid a thousandfold will be;
> Then gladly will we lend to thee,
> Who givest all.

This is an altered and updated text of that which appeared in *The Lutheran Hymnal* (1941).

It is refreshing to note that the former rather prevalent custom in some congregations of singing stanza 1 of this hymn (to an "ad nauseam" degree!) in place of the designated offertory texts has fallen into desuetude, and that the newer general offertories in, for instance, Divine Service II, other appropriate hymns, or choir settings of classic offertories are being sung instead.

ENERGY. Originally called ST. ETHELWALD, the tune was composed by William H. Monk for *Hymns Ancient and Modern* (1861), where it was set to Charles Wesley's "Soldiers of Christ, Arise." McCutchan in *Hymn Tune Names* notes, "ENERGY is a much better name for the tune than ST. ETHELWALD, for the saint whose name the tune bears was anything but a fighting man."

The harmonization is by Wilhelm Quampen, a *nom de plume* of Paul G. Bunjes.

406 IN YOU, LORD, I HAVE PUT MY TRUST

In you, Lord, I have put my trust;
Leave me not helpless in the dust,
Let me not be confounded.
Let in your Word
My faith, O Lord,
Be always firmly grounded.

Oh, listen, Lord, most graciously
And hear my cry, my prayer, my plea,
Make haste for my protection;
For woes and fear
Surround me here.
Help me in my affliction.

You are my strength, my shield, my rock,
My fortress that withstands each shock,
My help, my life, my tower,
My battle sword,
Almighty Lord,
What can resist your power?

With you, Lord, I have cast my lot;
O faithful God, forsake me not,
To you my soul commending.
Lord, be my stay
And lead the way
Now and when life is ending.

All honor, praise, and majesty
To Father, Son, and Spirit be,
Our God forever glorious,
In whose rich grace
We run our race
Till we depart victorious.

In dich hab' ich gehoffet, Herr,
Hilf, dass ich nicht zuschanden werd'
Noch ewiglich zu Spotte!
Das bitt' ich dich,
Erhalte mich
In deiner Treu', mein Gotte!

Dein gnädig Ohr neig her zu mir,
Erhör mein' Bitt', tu dich herfür,
Eil bald, mich zu erretten!
In Angst und Weh
Ich lieg' und steh',
Hilf mir in meinen Nöten!

Du bist mein' Stärk', mein Fels, mein Hort,
Mein Schild, mein' Kraft (sagt mir dein wort),
Mein' Hilf', mein Heil, mein Leben,
Mein starker Gott
In aller Not;
Wer mag mir widerstreben?

Herr, meinen Geist befehl' ich dir;
Mein Gott, mein Gott, weich nicht von mir,
Nimm mich in deine Hände!
O wahrer Gott,
Aus aller Not
Hilf mir am letzten Ende!

Glori, Lob, Ehr' und Herrlichkeit
Sei Gott Vater und Sohn bereit,
Dem Heil'gen Geist mit Namen.
Die göttlich' Kraft
Mach' uns sighaft
Durch Jesum Christum! Amen

This hymn, originally in seven stanzas, by Adam Reusner (Reissner), friend and adherent of Protestant mystic Kaspar von Schwenkfeld (c. 1490–1561), first appeared in the second edition of the *Form und Ordnung Geistlicher Gesäng und Psalmen* (Augsburg, 1533) issued by Jacob Dachser, a man with anabaptist leanings. Johannes Zwick included it in his *Neues Gesangbüchle* (1537); Luther followed suit in including it in Valentin Babst's *Geystliche Lieder* (Leipzig, 1539), the last hymnal publication that Luther supervised.

Based on Psalm 31:1–5, it concludes with the last words of the crucified Christ on the cross: "Into your hands I commit my spirit," momentous words that others have repeated on their death beds, namely, Stephen, the first martyr (Acts 7:59), Polycarp of Smyrna (c. 59–c. 156), Bernard of Clairvaux (*LW* 113, 274), John Hus (*LW* 236), and Martin Luther (*LW* 13, et al.). As the latter lay dying in Eisleben, awakened with chest pains at one o'clock in morning, and later when he felt his end to be near, he uttered the words: "In manus tuas commendo spiritum meum; redemisti me, deus veritatis."

Truly this hymn strikes a valiant Christian note. Nelle considers it a counterpart to Luther's "A Mighty Fortress" (*LW* 297, 298), a hymn highly regarded by Pietism.

The translation is an altered and updated form of that by Catherine Winkworth in her *Chorale Book for England* (1863), where she reproduced six stanzas, omitting the final doxology.

IN DICH HAB ICH GEHOFFET. This fine rhythmic chorale tune first appeared in Georg Sunderreiter's *Himmlische Harfen* (Nürnberg, 1581).

Paul G. Bunjes provided the harmonization.

IF GOD HIMSELF BE FOR ME 407

If God himself be for me,
I may a host defy;
For when I pray, before me
My foes, confounded, fly.
If Christ, my head and master,
Befriend me from above,
What foe or what disaster
Can drive me from his love?

I build on this foundation,
That Jesus and his blood
Alone are my salvation,
The true, eternal good.
Without him all that pleases
Will vain and empty prove.
The gifts I have from Jesus
Alone are worth my love.

Christ Jesus is my splendor,
My sun, my light, alone;
Were he not my defender
Before God's awesome throne,
I never should find favor
And mercy in his sight
But be destroyed forever
As darkness by the light.

Though earth, Lord, break asunder,
You are my Savior true;
No fire or sword or thunder
Shall sever me from you;
No danger, thirst, or hunger,
No pain or poverty,
No mighty princes' anger
Shall ever vanquish me.

No angel and no gladness,
No high place, pomp, or show,
No love, no hate, no badness,
No sadness, pain, or woe,

Ist Gott für mich, so trete
Gleich alles wider mich,
So oft ich ruf' und bete,
Weicht alles hinter sich.
Hab' ich das Haupt zum Freunde
Und bin geliebt bei Gott,
Was kann mir tun der Feinde
Und Widersacher Rott'?

Der Grund, da ich mich gründe,
Ist Christus und sein Blut,
Das machet, dass ich finde
Das ew'ge wahre Gut.
An mir und meinem Leben
Ist nichts auf dieser Erd';
Was Christus mir gegeben,
Das ist der Liebe wert.

Mein Jesus ist mein' Ehre,
Mein Glanz und helles Licht.
Wenn der nicht in mir wäre,
So dürft' und könnt' ich nicht
Vor Gottes Augen stehen
Und vor dem strengen Sitz;
Ich müsste stracks vergehen
Wie Wachs in Feuershitz'.

Die Welt, die mag zerbrechen,
Du stehst mir ewiglich,
Kein Brennen, Hauen, Stechen
Soll trennen mich und dich,
Kein Hungern und kein Dürsten,
Kein' Armut, keine Pein,
Kein Zorn der grossen Fürsten
Soll mir ein' Hindrung sein.

Kein Engel, keine Freuden,
Kein Thron, kein' Herrlichkeit,
Kein Lieben und kein Leiden,
Kein' Angst und Herzeleid,

No scheming, no contrivance, No subtle thing or great Shall draw me from your guidance Nor from you separate.	Was man nur kann erdenken, Es sei klein oder gross, Der keines soll mich lenken Aus deinem Arm und Schoss.
For joy my heart is ringing; All sorrow disappears; And full of mirth and singing, It wipes away all tears. The sun that cheers my spirit Is Jesus Christ, my king; The heav'n I shall inherit Makes me rejoice and sing.	Mein Herze geht in Sprüngen Und kann nicht traurig sein, Ist voller Freud' und Singen, Sieht lauter Sonnenschein. Die Sonne, die mir lachet, Ist mein Herr Jesus Christ; Das, was mich singen machet, Ist, was im Himmel ist.

On the Fourth Sunday in Lent (*Laetare*), 1651, Pastor Johannes Berkow of the *Marienkirche* in Berlin was laid to rest, having suddenly died from a stroke on his way from the cemetery back to the church after having buried one of his members. Provost Behr preached the funeral sermon for Berkow, based on Romans 8:31–39. In attendance was Paul Gerhardt. Impressed with Behr's sermon, upon his return home he sat down to write this heroic hymn, a hymn considered to be worthy to be placed next to Luther's "A Mighty Fortress." Its first published appearance was in Johann Crüger's (*LW* 19, et al.) *Praxis pietatis melica* (Frankfurt, 1656).

Apropos are the words of Richard Lauxmann in Koch's *Geschichte des Kirchenlieds*:

> The hymn bears the watchword of the Lutheran Church with [St.] Paul, "If God is for us, who can be against us?" One is reminded of Philip Melanchthon's last words as he, worn out by the numerous conflicts after Luther's death and by the many bitter and heavy experiences, lay dying on April 19, 1560, and as he once more raised himself in bed and cried, "If God is for us, who can be against us?" When someone asked him whether there was anything he desired, he replied, "Nothing except heaven!" and gave up his spirit. In this spirit it [the hymn] has been headed "A Christian Hymn of Consolation and of Joy" and as such it has spoken to the hearts of many troubled people and strengthened them with renewed courage in their fight of faith.

The final stanza of the original 15 (here stanza six) has enjoyed great favor with many Christians.

Stanzas 1–3, and 6 were prepared by the Inter-Lutheran Commission on Worship for inclusion in *Lutheran Book of Worship* (1978), to which stanzas 4 and 5 were added by the Commission on Worship. For the most part, these stanzas were largely based on the original translation by Richard Massie (*LW* 123, et al.) as contributed to William Mercer's (*LW* 492) *The Church Psalter and Hymn Book* (1857).

IST GOTT FÜR MICH. For comments on the tune see hymn 337.

The harmonization is from the *Württembergisches Choralbuch* (1953).

I AM TRUSTING YOU, LORD JESUS 408

This was the favorite hymn of the author, Frances Ridley Havergal, which she wrote in September 1874 and included in her *Loyal Responses* (1878). Slight alterations were necessary to update the personal pronouns.

STEPHANOS. Henry W. Baker composed this tune for John Mason Neale's (*LW* 31, et al.) "Art thou weary, art thou languid," which was included in the 1868 Appendix to the original edition of *Hymns Ancient and Modern* (1861). The tune is named after St. Stephen the Sabaite (725–94), to whom Neale originally attributed the Greek hymn from which he made his translation. Some time later Neale admitted that his hymn actually contained very little of the original Greek.

The setting is by Thomas Gieschen, originally done for *Lutheran Book of Worship* (1978).

FROM GOD CAN NOTHING MOVE ME 409

From God can nothing move me; He will not step aside But always will reprove me And be my constant guide. He stretches out his hand In evening and in morning, Providing his forewarning Wherever I may stand.	Von Gott will ich nicht lassen, Denn er lässt nicht von mir, Führt mich auf rechter Strassen, Da ich sonst irrte sehr, Reichet mir seine Hand. Den Abend wie den Morgen Tut er mich wohl versorgen, Sei, wo ich woll', im Land.
When those whom I regarded As trustworthy and sure Have long from me departed, God's grace shall still endure. He cares for all my needs, From sin and shame corrects me, From Satan's bonds protects me; Not even death succeeds.	Wenn sich der Menschen Hulde Und Wohltat all' verkehrt, So find't sich Gott gar balde, Sein' Macht und Gnad' bewährt, Hilfet aus aller Not, Errett't von Sünd' und Schanden, Von Ketten und von Banden, Und wenn's auch wär' der Tod.
When in my darkest hour, I can on him rely; I have from him the power All evil to defy. For God alone has might, And I shall never fear it; My body, soul, and spirit Belong to him by right.	Auf ihn will ich vertrauen In meiner schweren Zeit; Es kann mich nicht gereuen, Er wendet alles Leid. Ihm sei es heimgestellt; Mein Leib, mein' Seel', mein Leben Sei Gott dem Herrn ergeben, Er mach's, wie's ihm gefällt!
Praise God with hearts and voices, For both are gifts from him; A troubled world rejoices	Lobt ihn mit Herz und Munde, Welch's er uns beides schenkt! Das ist ein' sel'ge Stunde,

Each time we worship him.
The days we spend on earth
Without our God are wasted,
For we shall not have tasted
His joy in endless birth.

Darin man sein gedenkt.
Sonst verdirbt alle Zeit,
Die wir zubring'n auf Erden;
Wir sollen selig werden
Und bleib'n in Ewigkeit.

Yet even though I suffer
The world's unpleasantness,
And though the days grow rougher
And bring me great distress,
That day of bliss divine,
Which knows no end or measure,
And Christ, who is my pleasure,
Forever shall be mine.

Darum, ob ich schon dulde
Hier Widerwärtigkeit,
Wie ich's auch wohl verschulde,
Kommt doch die Ewigkeit,
Die aller Freuden voll;
Dieselb' ohn' alles Ende,
Dieweil ich Christum kenne,
Mir widerfahren soll.

We were by God created
In his own time and place
And by his Son persuaded
To follow truth and grace.
The Spirit guides our ways
And faithfully will lead us
That nothing can impede us.
To God be all our praise!

Das ist des Vaters Wille,
Der uns geschaffen hat.
Sein Sohn hat Guts die Fülle
Erworben uns und Gnad.
Auch Gott der Heilig Geist
Im Glauben uns regieret,
Zum Reich der Himmel führet.
Ihm sei Lob, Ehr und Preis!

While Ludwig Helmbold was lecturing on poetry at the University of Erfurt, he was a frequent house guest of Pancratius Helbich, professor of medicine, whose wife Regina was godmother to Helmbold's eldest daughter. When in 1563 a severe plague broke out in Erfurt, causing thousands of inhabitants to leave the city, Helbich decided to flee with his family. The sad parting occasioned the writing of this comforting hymn by the talented Ludwig Helmbold, dedicated to Regina Helbich. Reflecting Psalm 73:23, this is a splendid hymn of trust, perhaps Helmbold's best hymn. First published as a broadsheet, it soon found its way into various hymnals.

Gerald Thorson prepared the translation for inclusion in *Lutheran Book of Worship* (1978).

VON GOTT WILL ICH NICHT LASSEN is a tune that first appeared in a French collection entitled *Recuel de plusieurs chansons divise en trois parties* (Lyons, 1557) to a text beginning "Une jeune fillette." Popular in Holland, it was a tune used for love songs and beggars songs. In Germany the tune first appeared in 1560 as a hunting song to the text:

Einmal tät ich spazieren
sonderbar allein.
Was tät mich da verführen
ein Weglein, das war klein,
das saubr und lustig war;
darim da tät ich finden
mit meinen schnellen Winden (hunting dogs)
ein Tierlein in dem Gras.

The first, in 1563, to associate this tune to a sacred text (a process called *contrafacta*), it later appeared with Helmbold's text in Joachim Magdeburg's (*LW* 414) *Christliche und tröstliche Tischgesenge mit vier Stimmen* (Erfurt, 1572), where it appeared thus (Zahn 5264b):

Helmbold began the tune on note G.

The harmonization in *Lutheran Worship* (1982) is from the *Württembergisches Choralbuch* (1953).

HAVE NO FEAR, LITTLE FLOCK 410

LITTLE FLOCK. This text, based on Luke 12:32, and tune first appeared in *Five Hymns* (St. Louis, 1973), for which Heinz Werner Zimmermann composed the music and the first stanza, requesting Marjorie Jillson to complete the text.

The harmonization is by William Jensen Reynolds, from the *Baptist Hymnal* (1975).

HOW FIRM A FOUNDATION 411

Ascribed to "K" in John Rippon's *A Selection of Hymns from the Best Authors* (London, 1787), this hymn is sometimes thought to be by Richard Keene, precentor in Rippon's church; but this is not certain, and most hymnals still list it as "Author unknown."

The text, originally in seven stanzas, appeared in Rippon's *Selection* under the heading "Exceeding Great and Precious Promises." This slightly altered and updated text given here was prepared by the Inter-Lutheran Commission on Worship for inclusion in *Lutheran Book of Worship* (1978).

FOUNDATION appeared anonymously with this text in Joseph Funk's *A Compilation of Genuine Church Music* (Winchester, Virginia, 1832), where it was called PROTECTION. In *The Sacred Harp* (Hamilton, Georgia, 1844), it was ascribed to "Z. Chambless" and called BELLEVUE. Various other names have been showered upon this tune which, nonetheless, because of its long association with the above text, is usually known as FOUNDATION.

Charles H. Heaton prepared the harmonization for inclusion in *Lutheran Book of Worship*.

Although written by an English author, this hymn, for almost two centuries, has enjoyed its greatest success in the United States. Strangely, up to now it appears to have lacked its own distinctive tune. In bygone days ADESTE FIDELES (*LW* 41) was a popular vehicle, perhaps the result of its use thus in *Temple Melodies* (1851), edited by Darius E. Jones (1815–81), a business man associated with Lowell Mason (*LW* 115, et al.). Considering it too Christmas-like, the Intersynodical Committee that produced *The Lutheran Hymnal* (1941) decided to use FIRM FOUNDATION (*TLH* 427), a tune composed by Bernhard Schumacher (*LW* 112), one of its committee members. *The Hymn Book* (1971) of the Anglican Church of Canada and the United Church of Canada as well as the *Lutheran Hymnal* (1973) of the Lutheran Church of Australia use ST. DENIO, the tune commonly associated with "Immortal, Invisible, God Only Wise" (*LW* 451). On the other hand, practically all the other hymnals of mainline churches produced in the last decade have opted for FOUNDATION. *The Hymnal 1982* of the Protestant Episcopal Church goes a step farther in offering LYONS as an alternate tune (hymn 637), a tune attributed to Johann Michael Haydn (1737–1806), that was designated for Rippon's text in its previous *The Hymnal 1940*, a tune that serves rather well. Presumably FOUNDATION may now gradually become the established tune for Rippon's "How firm a foundation." Since it is based on the pentatonic scale, the singing of this hymn may be enhanced by singing it in either a two-part (women/men) or four-part (soprano, tenor, alto, bass) canon, beginning after four beats: "How firm* a foundation . . ."

412 THE KING OF LOVE MY SHEPHERD IS

Henry W. Baker's paraphrase of Psalm 23 first appeared in the 1868 Appendix to *Hymns Ancient and Modern* (1861). This is an example of the application of Christian truths to psalmody, particularly stanza 3 and the last line of stanza 4, "Thy cross before to guide me." The words of stanza 3 were the last that his friends heard him whisper on his death bed. Baker's hymn is in part a recast of George Herbert's (1593–1633) paraphrase beginning:

> The God of love my shepherd is
> And he that doth me feed;

While he is mine, and I am his,
What can I want or need?

ST. COLUMBA. Named for the highly revered Irish saint, this tune was included in C. V. Stanford's *Complete Collection of Irish Music as noted by George Petrie* (1902), where it was annotated, "Irish Hymn sung on the dedication of a chapel—County of Londonderry." (The Protestant Cathedral in Londonderry is also called St. Columba.) The Church of Ireland's *Church Hymnal* (1874) had included a simpler version of the tune. Stanford originally gave the triplet in the second phrase as an eighth note and two 16th notes, but later changed it in his harmonization of the tune for the 1904 edition of *Hymns Ancient and Modern*. Unfortunately, few congregations have been taught proper treatment of the triplet, and some of the delightful effect is therefore lost. Singing the notes with precision and sensitivity will bring out the tune's charming lilting quality.

St. Columba is discussed in the biography section as reputed author of hymn 271, "Christ Is the World's Redeemer."

The harmonization is from the *Service Book and Hymnal* (1958), slightly altered.

LORD, YOU I LOVE WITH ALL MY HEART 413

Lord, you I love with all my heart;
Oh, let me not from you depart,
With tender mercy cheer me.
Earth has no joy for which I care,
Heaven itself were void and bare
If I can't have you near me.
And should my guilt my heart subdue,
Let nothing shake my trust in you.
You are the portion I desire;
Your sacrifice my soul inspire.
Lord Jesus Christ,
My God and Lord, my God and Lord,
Forsake me not! I trust your Word.

Lord, all I am or have, you gave;
From stubbor n ego, Lord, you save,
My selfish ways rejecting.
So let me give myself to you,
To all my fellow creatures too,
Your grace, your love reflecting.
Let no false teaching me beguile
Nor Satan's lies my soul defile;
In all my crosses comfort me
That I may bear them patiently.
Lord Jesus Christ,
My God and Lord, my God and Lord,
Let me be yours, my soul restored!

Then let at last your angels come,
To Abram's bosom bear me home

Herzlich lieb hab' ich dich, o Herr,
Ich bitt', woll'st sein von mir nicht fer n
Mit deiner Güt' und Gnaden.
Die ganze Welt nicht freuet mich,
Nach Himmel und Erd' nicht frag' ich,
Wenn ich dich nur kann haben;
Und wenn mir gleich mein Herz zerbricht,
So bist doch du mein' Zuversicht,
Mein Teil und meines Herzens Trost,
Der mich durch sein Blut hat erlöst.
Herr Jesu Christ,
Mein Gott und Herr, mein Gott und Herr,
In Schanden lass mich nimmermehr!

Es ist ja, Herr, dein G'schenk und Gab'
Mein Leib und Seel' und was ich hab'
In diesem armen Leben.
Damit ich's brauch' zum Lobe dein,
Zu Nutz und Dienst des Nächsten mein,
Woll'st mir dein' Gnade geben!
Behüt mich, Herr, vor falscher Lehr',
Des Satans Mord und Lügen wehr,
In allem Kreuz erhalte mich,
Auf dass ich's trag' geduldiglich!
Herr Jesu Christ,
Mein Herr und Gott, mein Herr und Gott,
Tröst mir mein' Seel' in Todesnot!

Ach, Herr, lass dein' lieb' Engelein
Am Letzten End' die Seele mein

That I may die unfearing.
Within my earthen chamber keep
My body safe in peaceful sleep
Until your reappearing.
And then from death awaken me
That my own eyes with joy may see,
O Son of God, your glorious face,
My Savior and my ground of grace!
Lord Jesus Christ,
Oh, hear my prayer; oh, hear my prayer,
Your love surround me ev'rywhere.

In Abrahams Schoss tragen!
Der Leib in sein'm Schlafkämmerlein
Gar sanft, ohn' ein'ge Qual und Pein,
Ruh' bis am Jüngsten Tage.
Alsdann vom Tod erwecke mich,
Dass meine Augen sehen dich
In aller Freud', o Gottes Sohn,
Mein Heiland und mein Gnadenthron!
Herr Jesu Christ,
Erhöre mich, erhöre mich,
Ich will dich preisen ewiglich!

This hymn by Martin Schalling first appeared in *Kurtze und sonderliche Newe Symbola etlicher Fürsten von Gastriz* (Nürnberg, 1571). Written about 1567 "For the Dying," it is the only hymn by Schalling in common usage. According to James Mearns in Julian's *Dictionary*, it "justly ranks among the classic hymns of Germany." Based on Psalm 18 and 73, Koch speaks of it as "a jewel of the Church from the heart of Schalling."

The translation was prepared by Henry Lettermann for *Lutheran Worship.*

HERZLICH LIEB. This tune, by an unknown composer, appeared in Bernhard Schmid's *Zwey Bücher einer neuen Künstlichen Tabulatur auf Orgel und Instrument* (Strassburg, 1577). J. S. Bach (*LW* 89) brings his *Passion According to St. John* to a heartwarming and thrilling conclusion with the chorus singing stanza 3 of this beautiful chorale.

Paul G. Bunjes prepared the harmonization for inclusion in *Lutheran Worship* (1982).

414 WHO TRUSTS IN GOD A STRONG ABODE

Who trusts in God a strong abode
In heav'n and earth possesses;
Who looks in love to Christ above,
No fear that heart oppresses.
In you alone, dear Lord, we own
Sweet hope and consolation,
Our shield from foes, our balm for woes,
Our great and sure salvation.

Though Satan's wrath beset our path
And worldly scorn assail us,
While you are near, we shall not fear;
Your strength will never fail us.
Your rod and staff will keep us safe
And guide our steps forever;
Nor shades of death nor hell beneath,
Our lives from you will sever.

In all the strife of mortal life
Our feet will stand securely;

Wer Gott vertraut, hat wohl gebaut
Im Himmel und auf Erden.
Wer sich verlässt auf Jesum Christ,
Dem muss der Himmel werden.
Darum auf dich all' Hoffnung ich
Ganz fest und steif tu' setzen.
Herr Jesu Christ, mein Trost du bist
In Todesnot und Schmerzen.

Und wenn's gleich wär' dem Teufel sehr
Und aller Welt zuwider,
Dennoch so bist du, Jesu Christ,
Der sie all' schlägt danieder;
Und wenn ich dich nur hab' um mich
Mit deinem Geist und Gnaden,
So kann fürwahr mir ganz und gar
Wed'r Tod noch Teufel schaden.

Dein tröst ich mich ganz sicherlich,
Denn du kannst mir wohl geben,

Temptation's hour will lose its pow'r,
For you will guard us surely.
Our God, renew with heav'nly dew
Our body, soul, and spirit
Until we stand at your right hand
Through Jesus' saving merit.

Was mir ist not, du treuer Gott,
In dies'm und jenem Leben.
Gib wahre Reu', mein Herz erneu',
Errette Leib' und Seele!
Ach höre, Herr, dies mein Begehr,
Lass meine Bitt' nicht fehlen!

The *incipit* of this hymn, "Wer Gott vertraut, hat wohl gebaut," a popular German saying, sometimes inscribed in church windows and even on private homes, constituted the germ for stanza 1 of this notable hymn by the Lutheran pastor Joachim Magdeburg and first published in his *Christliche und tröstliche Tischgesänge, mit vier Stimmen* (Erfurt, 1572). After the initial 10 pages of instructions and admonitions to his two sons, there follow in the book *Hymns for the Seven Days of the Week*, the last which, for Saturday evening, contains this one-stanza hymn. Stanzas 2 and 3 first appeared in Seth Calvisius' *Harmoni Cantionum Ecclesiasticarum* (Leipzig, 1597). Benjamin H. Kennedy (1804–89), brilliant English classical scholar, made a free translation of the entire hymn in his *Hymnologi Christiana* (London, 1863), a translation that served as the basis for the text here given, prepared by the Inter-Lutheran Commission on Worship for inclusion in *Lutheran Book of Worship* (1978).

WAS MEIN GOTT WILL is not the tune that originally appeared with Magdeburg's single-stanza hymn in *Christliche und tröstliche Tischgesänge*; his hymn was set to a melody which he himself may have composed (see Zahn 8027a). WAS MEIN GOTT WILL, attributed to Claudin de Sermisy, was, however, in Magdeburg's book, set to "Was mein Gott will, das g'scheh allzeit" (What my God wills is always best), a hymn text with which the tune had long association in German hymnody. In *Trente et quatre Chansons musicales* (Paris, c. 1529), published by Pierre Attaingnant, the first French music printer, this tune was the setting for the secular song "Il me souffit de tous mes maulx." Moreover, the tune was included in the *Souter Liedekens Thantwerpen* (Antwerp, 1540) as the setting for the Flemish version of Psalm 140.

Bach's frequent use of this tune—in Cantatas 65, 72, 92, 103, 111, 144 as well as in the *St. Matthew Passion*—indicates that it must have been a favorite of his. It appears here, as well as in present hymnals of the Lutheran territorial churches in Germany, in its early rhythmic form (see essay: Polyrhythmic and Isometric Chorales, p. 822).

The harmonization in *Lutheran Worship* (1982) is from the *Choralbuch* (1955).

ALL DEPENDS ON OUR POSSESSING 415

All depends on our possessing
God's free grace and constant blessing,
Though all earthly wealth depart.
They who trust with faith unshaken

Alles ist an Gottes Segen
Und an seiner Gnad' gelegen,
Über alles Geld und Gut.
Wer auf Gott sein' Hoffnung setzet,

By their God are not forsaken
And will keep a dauntless heart.

He who to this day has fed me
And to many joys has led me
Is and ever shall be mine.
He who did so gently school me,
He who daily guides and rules me
Will remain my help divine.

Many spend their lives in fretting
Over trifles and in getting
Things that lack all solid ground.
I shall strive to win a treasure
That will bring me lasting pleasure
And that now is seldom found.

When with sorrow I am stricken,
Hope anew my heart will quicken,
All my longing shall be stilled.
To his loving-kindness tender
Soul and body I surrender,
For on God alone I build.

Well he knows what best to grant me;
All the longing hopes that haunt me,
Joy and sorrow, have their day.
I shall doubt his wisdom never;
As God wills, so be it ever;
I commit to him my way.

If my days on earth he lengthen,
God my weary soul will strengthen;
All my trust in him I place.
Earthly wealth is not abiding,
Like a stream away is gliding;
Safe I anchor in his grace.

Der behält ganz unverletzet
Einen freien Heldenmut.

Der mich hat bisher ernähret
Und mir manches Glück bescheret,
Ist und bleibet ewig mein.
Der mich wunderlich geführet
Und noch leitet und regieret,
Wird forthin mein Helfer sein.

Viel' bemühen sich um Sachen,
Die nur Sorg' und Unruh' machen
Und ganz unbeständig sind.
Ich begehr' nach dem zu ringen,
Was mir kann Vergnügen bringen
Und man jetzt gar selten find't.

Hoffnung kann des Herz erquicken;
Was ich wünsche, wird sich schicken,
So es anders Gott gefällt.
Meine Seele, Leib und Leben
Hab' ich seiner Gnad' ergeben
Und ihm alles heimgestellt.

Er weiss schon nach seinem Willen
Mein Verlangen zu erfüllen,
Es hat alles seine Zeit.
Ich hab' ihm nichts vorzuschreiben;
Wie Gott will, so muss es bleiben,
Wenn Gott will, bin ich bereit.

Soll ich länger allhier leben,
Will ich ihm nicht widerstreben,
Ich verlasse mich auf ihn.
Ist doch nichts, das lang bestehet,
Alles Irdische vergehet
Und fährt wie ein Strom dahin.

An unknown author is responsible for this fine hymn of trust in God, included in the Nürnberg *Andächtiges Haus-Kirch . . . Gesängen* (1676). Dated about 1673, the hymn attempts, in a scriptural way, to present a Gospel-oriented way of life in poetic form. The text might have been enhanced had it included a look to the eventual heavenly glory, rather than simply ending with the passing away of earthly things. Catherine Winkworth included her translation in *Lyra Germanica* (second series, 1858) and again, set to this tune, in the *Chorale Book for England* (1863). This is an altered and updated version of that which appeared in *The Lutheran Hymnal* (1941).

ALLES IST AN GOTTES SEGEN. This tune, based on a melody by Johann Löhner, has appeared in various forms since 1691. In that year Löhner's tune was published in *Der Geistlichen Erquick-Stunden . . . Poetischer Andacht-Klang* (Nürnberg), set to Heinrich Arnold Stockfleth's (1643–1708) "Wunderanfang! herrlichs Ende!" Johann König included a revised version of the tune in his *Harmonischer Lieder-Schatz* (Frankfurt-am-Main, 1738), from which form it has evolved into that given in *Lutheran Worship.*

The harmonization is from *The Lutheran Hymnal* (1941), slightly altered.

THE LORD'S MY SHEPHERD, I'LL NOT WANT

416

Of unknown authorship, this popular paraphrase of Psalm 23 was published in the Scottish Psalter of 1650 (*The Psalms of David in Meeter*), the only psalter officially recognized by the Church of Scotland and the culmination of a century of metrical psalmody. (See essay: Metrical Psalms, p. 825.)

BELMONT (ENTREATY, BERNARD, VIGILS) appears to have been adapted from the first half of an anonymous tune in William Gardiner's *Sacred Melodies* (1812) set to Isaac Watts' "Come hither, all ye weary souls":

In a catalog appended to his *Music and Friends* (1838) Gardiner claims it as his own composition, and well it may be. The present adaptation to common meter was first made in Severn's *Psalm and Hymn Tunes for the Use of St. Mary's Church, Islington.* Thereafter it appeared in *A Church Hymn and Tune Book* (1859), in Routledge's *Church and Home Metrical Psalter and Hymnal*, in *Psalms and Hymns for Divine Worship* (1867), and in the 1868 Appendix to *Hymns Ancient and Modern* (1861).

Although Gardiner did not name the tune, BELMONT may have reference to the Beaumont family, whose stately home Beau-mannor was not far from Gardiner's home in Leicester.

George Leonard, a *nom de plume* of Paul G. Bunjes, prepared the harmonization for *Lutheran Worship* (1982).

417 THE LORD'S MY SHEPHERD, LEADING ME

While the version of Psalm 23 from the Scottish Psalter of 1650 (*LW* 416) undoubtedly continues to remain the most beloved and popular in English-speaking Christendom, the Commission on Worship, seeking somehow to include the tune BROTHER JAMES' AIR in *Lutheran Worship* (1982), welcomed the suggestion by its Hymn Text and Music Committee to include Henry L. Letterman's refreshingly new, six-line version to go with that tune.

BROTHER JAMES' AIR. This beautiful tune was composed by James Leith Macbeth Bain and as here given is an adaptation of a choral arrangement by Gordon Jacob, published in London in 1934. The locution Brother James is the name given James Bain by his friends and acquaintances.

The harmonization is by George Leonard, a *nom de plume* of Paul G. Bunjes.

418 WHAT IS THE WORLD TO ME

What is the world to me
With all its vaunted pleasure
When you, and you alone,
Lord Jesus, are my treasure!
You only, dearest Lord,
My soul's delight shall be;
You are my peace, my rest.
What is the world to me!

The world seeks to be praised
And honored by the mighty
Yet never once reflects
That they are frail and flighty.
But what I truly prize
Above all things is he,
My Jesus, he alone.
What is the world to me!

The world seeks after wealth
And all that mammon offers
Yet never is content
Though gold should fill its coffers.
I have a higher good,
Content with it I'll be:
My Jesus is my wealth.
What is the world to me!

What is the world to me!
My Jesus is my treasure,
My life, my health, my wealth,
My friend, my love, my pleasure,

Was frag' ich nach der Welt
Und allen ihren Schätzen,
Wenn ich mich nur an dir,
Herr Jesu, kann ergötzen!
Dich hab' ich einzig mir
Zur Wollust vorgestellt,
Du, du bist meine Ruh';
Was frag' ich nach der Welt!

Die Welt sucht Ehr' und Ruhm
Bei hocherhabnen Leuten
Und denkt nicht einmal dran,
Wie bald doch diese gleiten;
Das aber, was mein Herz
Vor andern rühmlich hält,
Ist Jesus nur allein;
Was frag' ich nach der Welt!

Die Welt sucht Geld und Gut
Und kann nicht eher rasten,
Sie habe denn zuvor
Den Mammon in dem Kasten;
Ich weiss ein besser Gut,
Wonach mein Herze stellt:
Ist Jesus nur mein Schatz,
Was frag' ich nach der Welt!

Was frag' ich nach der Welt,
Mein Jesus ist mein Leben,
Mein Schatz, mein Eigentum,
Dem ich mich ganz ergeben,

My joy, my crown, my all,
My bliss eternally.
Once more, then, I declare:
What is the world to me!

Mein ganzes Himmelreich,
Und was mir sonst gefällt.
Drum sag' ich noch einmal:
Was frag' ich nach der Welt!

This hymn on the "Renunciation of the World" (1 John 2:15–17) by Georg M. Pfefforkorn first appeared anonymously in eight stanzas, in the *Stettinisches Vollständiges Gesang-Buch* (Alten-Stettin, 1671), but with his name in the Naumburg *Gesang Buch* (1715).

The translation is an updated version of that which appeared in *The Lutheran Hymnal* (1941), namely, an altered version done by August Crull.

WAS FRAG ICH NACH DER WELT is an anonymous tune that first appeared in *Himmels-Lust und Welt-Unlust* compiled by Ahasverus Fritsch (Leipzig, 1679), where it was set to "Die Wollust dieser Welt" by Jacob J. Schütz (Zahn 5206a). The tune's appearance in *Geistreiches Gesang-Buch* (Darmstadt, 1698) exhibits a structure more in conformity with present usage (Zahn 5206b); it is in the somewhat unusual iambic pattern of 67 67 66 66, with its short lines, a meter that had been earlier used by Martin Rinkart in his "Now Thank We All Our God" (*LW* 443). It is suggested that the pulse of the tune not be distorted by the tendency to halt at the ends of the seven-syllable lines.

The harmonization is by Wilhelm Quampen, a *nom de plume* of Paul G. Bunjes.

EVENING AND MORNING 419

Evening and morning,
Sunset and dawning,
Wealth, peace, and gladness,
Comfort in sadness;
These are your works and bring glory to you.
Times without number,
We wake or we slumber,
Your eye observes us,
From danger preserves us,
Shining upon us a love that is true.

Abend und Morgen
Sind seine Sorgen;
Segnen und mehren,
Unglück verwehren
Sind seine Werke und Taten allein.
Wenn wir uns legen,
So ist er Zugegen;
Wenn wir aufstehen,
So lässt er aufgehen
Über uns seiner Barmherzigkeit Schein.

Father, oh, hear me,
Pardon and spare me;
Calm all my terrors,
Blot out my errors
That by your eyes they may no more be scanned.
Order my goings,
Direct all my doings;
As best it may be,
Retain or release me;
All I commit to your fatherly hand.

Gott, meine Krone,
Vergib und schone,
Lass meine Schulden
In Gnad und Hulden
Aus deinen Augen sein abgewandt.
Sonsten regiere
Mich, lenke und führe,
Wie dirs gefället;
Ich habe gestellet
Alles in deine Seliebung und Hand.

Ills that still grieve me
Soon are to leave me;
Though billows tower

And winds gain power,
After the storm the fair sun shows its face.
My joys increasing,
My peace never ceasing,
These I shall treasure
And share in full measure
When in his mansions God grants me a place.

To God in heaven
All praise be given!
Come, let us offer
And gladly proffer
To the Creator the gifts he will prize,
Gladly receiving
Our fruits of believing.
Hymns that adore him
Are precious before him
And to his throne like sweet incense arise.

This beautiful hymn by Paul Gerhardt first appeared in a collection of Gerhardt's hymns published by Johann G. Ebeling entitled *Pauli Gerhardi geistliche Andachten* (Berlin, 1667). Stanzas 1–2 here given are from a translation of stanzas 4 and 8–12 of the original German hymn, a translation prepared by Richard Massie (*LW* 123) and contributed to William Mercer's (*LW* 206) *The Church Psalter and Hymn Book* (1857). Stanzas 3–4, here given in an updated form, are from an English text beginning "The sun ascending, to us is leading" by Herman Brueckner (*LW* 206) in 1918 and included in the *American Lutheran Hymnal* (1930). This is an altered and updated text of that prepared by the Inter-Lutheran Commission on Worship for inclusion in *Lutheran Book of Worship* (1978).

DIE GÜLDNE SONNE was composed by Johann Ebeling for this German hymn and first published in 1667 together with it.

Chorale composers of the 17th century frequently devised melodic progressions to underline, stress, or portray the meaning of specific words, a technique called tone painting, or pictorialism. Notice the effect, even in the English translation, of the descending melodic line in stanza 1 to "Times without number, We wake or we slumber" in contrast to the subsequent descending motif to "Your eye observes us, From danger preserves us."

The harmonization is from the *Württembergisches Choralbuch* (1953).

IF YOU BUT TRUST IN GOD TO GUIDE YOU 420

If you but trust in God to guide you
And place your confidence in him,
You'll find him always there beside you
To give you hope and strength within.
For those who trust God's changeless love
Build on the rock that will not move.

What gain is there in futile weeping,
In helpless anger and distress?
If you are in his care and keeping,
In sorrow will he love you less?
For he who took for you a cross
Will bring you safe through ev'ry loss.

In patient trust await his leisure
In cheerful hope, with heart content
To take whate'er your Father's pleasure
And all-discerning love have sent;
Doubt not your inmost wants are known
To him who chose you for his own.

Sing, pray, and keep his ways unswerving,
Offer your service faithfully,
And trust his word; though undeserving,
You'll find his promise true to be.
God never will forsake in need.
The soul that trusts in him indeed.

Wer nur den lieben Gott lässt walten
Und hoffet auf ihn allezeit,
Den wird er wunderlich erhalten
In allem Kreuz und Traurigkeit.
Wer Gott, dem Allerhöchsten, traut,
Der hat auf keinen Sand gebaut.

Was helfen uns die schweren Sorgen?
Was hilft uns unser Weh und Ach?
Was hilft es, dass wir alle Morgen
Beseufzen unser Ungemach?
Wir machen unser Kreuz und Leid
Nur grösser durch die Traurigkeit.

Man halte nur ein wenig stille
Und sei nur in sich selbst vergnügt
Wie unsers Gottes Gnadenwille,
Wie sein' Allwissenheit es fügt.
Gott, der uns sich had auserwählt,
Der weiss auch gar wohl, was uns fehlt.

Sing, bet und geh auf Gottes Wegen,
Verricht das Deine nur getreu
Und trau des Himmels reichem Segen,
So wird er bei der werden neu;
Denn welcher seine Zuversicht
Auf Gott setzt, den verlässt er nicht.

Georg Neumark in his *Thränendes Haus-Kreuz* (1681) writes of his unexpected appointment as a private tutor at a time when he was vainly seeking employment:

> This good fortune, which came so suddenly and, as it were, from heaven, gladdened my heart so that I, on the first day, to the glory of my God, composed the well-known hymn "Wer nur den lieben Gott lässt walten," for I had ample reason to thank God heartily for this unexpected grace, both then and to the end.

The appointment was in the home of Stephan Henning, a judge in Kiel, which places the hymn's date of origin in the winter of 1641/42. A favorite legend, therefore, which has Neumark composing the hymn after the return of his viola da gamba in 1653, is probably a fabrication.

Catherine Winkworth's translation, based on her earlier version ("Leave God to order all thy ways") in *Lyra Germanica* (first series, 1855), is from the *Chorale Book for England* (1863). This altered and updated text of hers, omitting stanzas 4–6, was prepared by the Inter-Lutheran Commission on Worship for inclusion in *Lutheran Book of Worship* (1978).

WER NUR DEN LIEBEN GOTT LÄSST WALTEN. The tune is also by Georg Neumark, probably written at the same time as the text. The two were published together in Neumark's *Fortgepflanzter musikalisch-poetischer Lustwald* (Jena, 1657). Beloved in Germany, the tune became familiar in England due to its appearance in Mendelssohn's *St. Paul* and in *Hymns Ancient and Modern* (1861), where it is called BREMEN. J. S. Bach based a cantata on this tune.

The setting is from the *Service Book and Hymnal* (1958).

This great hymn of trust is part of the rich development of hymns of personal devotion—the result of the Thirty Years' War (1618–48)—that gave German hymnody a certain crowning glory, exhibited in such poets as Martin Rinkart (*LW* 443), Johann Heermann (*LW* 95, et al.), Paul Gerhardt (*LW* 19, et al.), and Johann Scheffler (*LW* 375, 379). This is before such devotion developed into Pietism, which, in its worst aspects, produced an unhealthy, passionate, amatory address to the earthly figure of the Lord Jesus.

421 IN GOD, MY FAITHFUL GOD

In God, my faithful God,
I trust when dark my road;
Great woes may overtake me,
Yet he will not forsake me.
It is his love that sends them;
At his best time he ends them.

My sins fill me with care,
Yet I will not despair.
I build on Christ, who loves me;
From this rock nothing moves me.
To him I will surrender,
To him, my soul's defender.

If death my portion be,
It brings great gain to me;
It speeds my life's endeavor
To live with Christ forever.
He gives me joy in sorrow,
Come death now or tomorrow.

"So be it," then, I say
With all my heart each day.
Dear Lord, we all adore you,
We sing for joy before you.
Guide us while here we wander
Until we praise you yonder.

Auf meinen lieben Gott
Trau' ich in Angst und Not,
Der kann mich allzeit retten
Aus Trübsal, Angst und Nöten,
Mein Unglück kann er wenden,
Steht all's in seinen Händen.

Ob mich mein' Sünd' anficht,
Will ich verzagen nicht;
Auf Christum will ich bauen
Und ihm allein vertrauen;
Ihm tu' ich mich ergeben
Im Tod und auch im Leben.

Ob mich der Tod nimmt hin,
Ist Sterben mein Gewinn,
Und Christus ist mein Leben.
Dem tu' ich mich ergeben;
Ich sterb' heut oder morgen,
Mein' Seel' wird er versorgen.

Amen, zu aller Stund'
Sprech' ich aus Herzensgrund.
Du wollest uns tun leiten.
Herr Christ, zu allen Zeiten,
Auf dass wir deinen Namen
Ewiglich preisen. Amen.

Ascribed to Sigismund Weingärtner, about whom little is known, this fine hymn, originally in five stanzas, first appeared in *766 Geistliche Psalmen* (Wittenberg, Nürnberg, 1607). Its brief yet courageous and fresh content prompted its inclusion in numerous hymnals. Notice that in the German the first and last stanzas begin with the letter A; the two (originally three) in-between stanzas with O, thus reminiscent of Revelation 1:8 as well as constituting an acrostic, a popular literary device in this period.

The translation by Catherine Winkworth, here considerably altered over that which appeared in *The Lutheran Hymnal* (1941), is from her *Chorale Book for England* (1863).

AUF MEINEN LIEBEN GOTT. Originally composed by the Roman Catholic composer Jacob Regnart for the secular song, "Venus, du und dein Kind seid alle beide blind," the tune first appeared in 1574 in *Kurtzweilige Teutsche Lieder zu Drei Stimmen* (Nürnberg). Bartholomäus Gesius restructured it somewhat and was the first to couple it to a spiritual text. Melchior Vulpius was the first to set it to this text in *Ein schön geistlich Gesangbuch* (Jena, 1609); and Johann Schein, in 1627, gave the tune its present form. Its strong and confident character fit the text rather well.

The setting is by Paul G. Bunjes.

WHAT GOD ORDAINS IS ALWAYS GOOD

422

What God ordains is always good:
His will is just and holy.
As he directs my life for me,
I follow meek and lowly.
My God indeed
In ev'ry need
Knows well how he will shield me;
To him, then, I will yield me.

What God ordains is always good:
He never will deceive me;
He leads me in his own right way,
And never will he leave me.
I take content
What he has sent;
His hand that sends me sadness
Will turn my tears to gladness.

What God ordains is always good:
His loving thought attends me;
No poison can be in the cup
That my physician sends me.
My God is true;
Each morning new
I trust his grace unending,
My life to him commending.

What God ordains is always good:
He is my friend and father;
He suffers naught to do me harm
Though many storms may gather.

Was Gott tut, das ist wohlgetan!
Es bleibt gerecht sein Wille;
Wie er fängt meine Sachen an,
Will ich ihm halten stille.
Er ist mein Gott,
Der in der Not
Mich wohl weiss zu erhalten,
Drum lass' ich ihn nur walten.

Was Gott tut, das ist wohlgetan!
Er wird mich nicht betrügen,
Er führet mich auf rechter Bahn;
So lass' ich mich begnügen
An seiner Huld
Und hab' Geduld,
Er wird mein Unglück wenden,
Es steht in seinen Händen.

Was Gott tut, das ist wohlgetan!
Er wird mich wohl bedenken;
Er, als mein Arzt und Wundermann,
Wird mir nicht Gift einschenken
Für Arzenei;
Gott ist getreu,
Drum will ich auf ihn bauen
Und seiner Güte trauen.

Was Gott tut, das ist wohlgetan!
Er ist mein Licht und Leben,
Der mir nichts Böses gönnen kann;
Ich will mich ihm ergeben

Now I may know Both joy and woe; Someday I shall see clearly That he has loved me dearly.	In Freud' und Leid; Es kommt die Zeit, Da öffentlich erscheinet, Wie treulich er es meinet.
What God ordains is always good: Though I the cup am drinking Which savors now of bitterness, I take it without shrinking. For after grief God gives relief, My heart with comfort filling And all my sorrow stilling.	Was Gott tut, das ist wohlgetan! Muss ich den Kelch gleich schmecken, Der bitter ist nach meinem Wahn, Lass' ich mich doch nicht schrecken, Weil doch zuletzt Ich werd' ergötzt Mit süssem Trost im Herzen, Da weichen alle Schmerzen.
What God ordains is always good: This truth remains unshaken. Though sorrow, need, or death be mine, I shall not be forsaken. I fear no harm, For with his arm He shall embrace and shield me; So to my God I yield me.	Was Gott tut, das ist wohlgetan! Dabei will ich verbleiben; Es mag mich auf die rauhe Bahn Not, Tod und Elend treiben, So wird Gott mich Ganz väterlich In seinen Armen halten, Drum lass' ich ihn nur walten.

This splendid Cross and Comfort hymn was undoubtedly written by Samuel Rodigast, perhaps in 1674, while a member of the philosophy faculty at the University of Jena. Its first appearance was in the appendix to a collection published in 1674 in Hamburg by Johann Jacob Rebenlein entitled *Geistliche Lieder und Psalmen Doktor Martin Luthers und Anderer frommen Christen, jetzt aufs neu wieder eingedicht' und mit herrlichen Liedern vermehrt*. Well-versed that he was in churchly poetry, Rodigast undoubtedly took a page from a hymn ascribed to Pastor Johann Michael Altenburg (1584–1640) in which each stanza began with "Was Gott thut, das ist wohlgethan."

The metric pattern 87 87 877 of the hymn under discussion (incidently, incorrectly listed as 87 87 888 at the hymn itself) that Rodigast chose is as old at least as in Burkard Waldis' (c. 1485–c. 1557) metrical version of Psalm 20. The text here given is from the *The Lutheran Hymnal* (1941), slightly altered.

WAS GOTT TUT was likely composed by Severus Gastorius, first substitute, later cantor in Jena's city school. The eminent organist and composer Johann Pachelbel (1653–1706) used the tune in a cantata and a partita for keyboard that he composed, a tune that became immensely popular and was included in numerous hymnals. The tune was a favorite of Frederick Wilhelm III of Prussia, and at his funeral it was played as mourning music. J. S. Bach (*LW* 89) used the tune in Cantatas 12, 69, 75, 98, 100, and 144 and in one of his wedding cantatas.

Paul G. Bunjes harmonized the tune for inclusion in *Lutheran Worship* (1982).

WHEN I SUFFER PAINS AND LOSSES 423

When I suffer pains and losses, Lord, be near, Let me hear Comfort under crosses. Point me, Father, to the heaven Which your Son For me won When his life was given.	Warum sollt' ich mich denn grämen? Hab' ich doch Christum noch, Wer will mir den nehmen? Wer will mir den Himmel rauben, Den mir schon Gottes Sohn Beigelegt im Glauben?
Under burdens of cross-bearing, Though the weight May be great, Yet I'm not despairing. You designed the cross you gave me; Thus you know All my woe And how best to save me.	Schickt er mir ein Kreuz zu tragen, Dringt herein Angst und Pein, Sollt' ich drum verzagen? Der es schickt, der wird es wenden! Er weiss wohl, Wie er soll All mein Unglück enden.
Christians, let us be undaunted. Ev'ry day Hurl away That which us once haunted. Is it true that death defeats us? No! Rejoice, For Christ's voice Then in peace will greet us.	Unverzagt und ohne Grauen Soll ein Christ, Wo er ist, Stets sich lassen schauen. Wollt' ihn auch der Tod aufreiben, Soll der Mut Dennoch gut Und fein stille bleiben.
What at last does this world leave us But a hand Full of sand Or some loss to grieve us? See what rich and noble graces Our Lord shares With his heirs In the heav'nly places.	Was sind dieses Lebens Güter? Eine Hand Voller Sand, Kummer der Gemüter. Dort, dort sind die edlen Gaben, Da mein Hirt, Christus, wird Mich ohn' Ende laben.
Savior, Shepherd, my Defender, I belong To the throng Blood-bought for that splendor. Having you, I want no other Light of heav'n To be giv'n, My dear God and Brother.	Herr, mein Hirt, Brunn aller Freuden, Du bist mein, Ich bin dein, Niemand kann uns scheiden: Ich bin dein, weil du dein Leben Und dein Blut Mir zugut In den Tod gegeben.

This laudable hymn of comfort by Paul Gerhardt, originally in 12 stanzas, appeared in the 1648 edition of Johann Crüger's (*LW* 19, et al.) *Praxis pietatis melica* headed "A Christian's Hymn of Joy." Next it appeared in *Geistliche Lieder und Psalmen* (Berlin, 1653), edited by Crüger and Christof Runge (1619–81). While the hymn reflects numerous passages in Scripture, both Old and New Testaments, Psalm 73:23–26 seems to constitute the prevailing basis.

The metric pattern of 8336 D, similar to that in "Once again my heart rejoices," is an effective invention of Paul Gerhardt. Polack mentions that the Salzburg Lutherans, some of whom later settled in Georgia, 1734, sang this hymn as they marched through Swabia, having been expelled from their native land by Roman Catholic authorities. It is said that on his deathbed Gerhardt spoke the stanza beginning "Kann uns doch kein Tod nicht töten," as a comfort to himself and his loved ones.

F. Samuel Janzow prepared the translation for inclusion in *Lutheran Worship* (1982).

WARUM SOLLT ICH MICH DENN GRÄMEN. The tune that Johann Crüger set to Gerhardt's text (Zahn 6455a) failed to last. Instead, Johann G. Ebeling's tune WARUM SOLLT ICH MICH gradually became wedded to the text after its appearance in 1666 in the edition of Gerhardt's hymns that Ebeling issued. (Zahn 6456a)

Alfred Fremder and George Leonard, a *nom de plume* of Paul G. Bunjes, prepared the harmonization for inclusion in *Lutheran Worship* (1982).

424 REJOICE, MY HEART, BE GLAD AND SING

Rejoice, my heart, be glad and sing,
A cheerful trust maintain;
For God, the source of ev'rything,
Your portion shall remain.

He is your treasure, he your joy,
Your life and light and Lord,
Your counselor when doubts annoy,
Your shield and great reward.

Why spend the day in blank despair,
In restless thought the night?
On your creator cast your care;
He makes your burdens light.

Did not his love and truth and pow'r
Guard ev'ry childhood day?
And did he not in threat'ning hour
Turn dreaded ills away?

He only will with patience chide,
His rod falls gently down,
And all your sins he casts aside;
In ocean depth they drown.

His wisdom never plans in vain
Nor falters nor mistakes.
All that his counsels may ordain
A happy ending makes.

Wohlauf, mein Herze, sing und spring
Und habe guten Mut!
Dein Gott, der Ursprung aller Ding',
Ist selbst und bleibt dein Gut.

Er ist dein Schatz, dein Erb' und Teil,
Dein Glanz und Freudenlicht,
Dein Schirm und Schild, dein' Hilf' und Heil,
Schafft Rat und lässt dich nicht.

Was kränkst du dich in deinem Sinn
Und grämst dich Tag und Nacht?
Nimm deine Sorg' und wirf sie hin
Auf den, der dich gemacht!

Hat er dich nicht von Jugend auf
Versorget und ernährt?
Wie manchen schweren Unglückslauf
Hat er zurückgekehrt!

Du strafst uns Sünder mit Geduld
Und schlägst nicht allzusehr,
Ja endlich nimmst du unsre Schuld
Und wirfst sie in das Meer.

Er hat noch niemals was versehn
In seinem Regiment;
Nein, was er tut und lässt geschehn,
Das nimmt ein gutes End'.

Upon your lips, then, lay your hand, And trust his guiding love; Then like a rock your peace shall stand Here and in heav'n above.	Ei nun, so lass ihn ferner tun Und red' ihm nichts darein, So wirst du hier in Frieden ruhn Und ewig fröhlich sein.

Appearing first in the now lost 1652 edition of Johann Crüger's *Praxis pietaties melica* and thereafter in *Geistliche Lieder und Psalmen* (Berlin, 1653), edited by Christof Runge and Johann Crüger, this great hymn by Paul Gerhardt, originally in 18 stanzas, beginning "Ich singe dir mit Herz und Mund," has often been extolled as a poetic masterpiece in its language and economy of words; small wonder that it has been popular since its publication.

Stanzas 13, 14, 15, 16, 9, 17, and 18 are here given in an altered and updated translation of that by John Kelly as these appeared in *The Lutheran Hymnal* (1941).

ICH SINGE DIR is the delightful tune first appearing in Balthasar König's *Harmonischer Liederschatz* (Frankfurt, 1738) set to Gerhardt's text beginning with the same words.

The harmonization is from *The Lutheran Hymnal* (1941), slightly altered.

THE WILL OF GOD IS ALWAYS BEST 425

The will of God is always best And shall be done forever; And they who trust in him are blest, He will forsake them never. He helps indeed In time of need, He chastens with forbearing; They who depend On God, their friend, Shall not be left despairing.	Was mein Gott will, das g'scheh' allzeit, Sein Will', der ist der beste; Zu helfen den'n er ist bereit, Die an ihn glauben feste; Er hilft aus Not, Der fromme Gott, Und züchtiget mit Massen. Wer Gott vertraut, Fest auf ihn baut, Den will er nicht verlassen.
God is my comfort and my trust, My hope and life abiding; And to his counsel, wise and just, I yield, in him confiding. The very hairs, His Word declares, Upon my head he numbers. By night and day God is my stay, He never sleeps nor slumbers.	Gott ist mein Trost, mein' Zuversicht, Mein' Hoffnung und mein Leben. Was mein Gott will, dass mir geschicht, Will ich nicht widerstreben. Sein Wort ist wahr, Denn all mein Haar Er selber hat gezählet. Er hüt't und wacht Und hat wohl acht, Auf dass uns gar nichts fehlet.
Lord, this I ask, oh, hear my plea, Deny me not this favor: When Satan sorely troubles me, Then do not let me waver. Oh, guard me well, My fear dispel, Fulfill your faithful saying:	Noch eins, Herr, will ich bitten dich, Du wirst mir's nicht versagen: Wenn mich der böse Geist anficht, Lass mich, Herr, nicht verzagen; Hilf, steur und wehr, Ach Gott, mein Herr, Zu Ehren deinem Namen!

He who believes Indeed receives An answer to his praying.	Wer das begehrt, Dem wird's gewährt. Drauf sprech' ich frölich: Amen.
When life's brief course on earth is run And I this world am leaving, Grant me to say, "Your will be done," Your faithful Word believing. My dearest friend, I now commend My soul into your keeping, From sin and hell, And death as well, By you the vict'ry keeping.	Nun, muss ich Sünd'r von dieser Welt Hinfahr'n in Gottes Willen Zu meinem Gott: wann's ihm gefällt, Will ich ihm halten stille. Mein' arme Seel' Ich Gott befehl' In meiner letzten Stunden. Du frommer Gott, Sünd', Höll' und Tod Hast du mir überwunden.

This hymn first appeared anonymously in 1554 in a broadsheet issued by Friedrich Gutknecht in Nürnberg. A Dresden print of 1557 contains only stanzas 1–2, and 4. The fact that some evangelical hymnals in Europe contain these three plus a fourth doxological stanza, and that others substituted the doxological stanza with what is here the third stanza, seems to indicate that this may originally have been a hymn consisting of stanzas 1–2, and 4. The origin of stanza 3 (listed as stanza 4 in the *Evangelisches Kirchengesangbuch*), as well as the aforementioned doxological stanza, remains a mystery.

As to the authorship of stanzas 1–2, and 4, a Danish psalmbook issued by Hans Thomissön in 1569 is the first to give an author, namely, Margrave Albrecht von Brandenburg. Evidence points to the fact that this is Duke Albrecht of Prussia (1490–1568) who, incidentally, was also Margrave of Brandenburg. Nelle opines that Albrecht von Brandenburg (1522–57), brave in war but dissolute in character, hence known as the "German Alcibiades" (c. 450–404 B. C., Athenian general and politician), could hardly be the author. On the other hand, Albrecht of Prussia, the last grand master of the various ruling Hohenzollerns, a pious, princely reformer of the Prussian Church, is known to have written sacred poetry. Thus Friedrich Spitta (1852–1924), at one time professor of New Testament and practical theology in Strassburg, rediscoverer of the hymns of Albrecht of Prussia, is undoubtedly right when he ascribes this beautiful hymn of trust and comfort to him, a fact, of course, that contradicts both *The Lutheran Hymnal* (1941) and *Lutheran Worship* (1982), although admittedly the former only *ascribes* the hymn to Albrecht von Brandenburg.

As to the circumstances surrounding the writing of "The Will of God Is Always Best," Spitta advances the credible opinion that Albrecht wrote it on the death of his beloved Danish wife Dorothea, who died in 1547. This occasion left him so broken in spirit that he despaired of his life. Fortunately he was able to draw comfort and strength from God's Word and thus submit to God's good and gracious will.

The translation is from *The Lutheran Hymnal* (1941), slightly altered.

WAS MEIN GOTT WILL is the tune by Claudin de Sermisy associated with the secular song "Il me suffit de tous me maulx" that appeared in Paris in 1529 under the title *Trente et quatre chansons musicales*. Its appearance with this text occurred first in

Joachim Magdeburg's *Christliche und tröstliche Tischgesenge* (1572) and thereafter in various German songbooks of Seth Calvisius, 1597, and Michael Praetorius (*LW* 14, et al.). The frequent use of this noble tune by J. S. Bach (*LW* 89) in the *St. Matthew Passion* and in various cantatas exhibits his fondness for it. Notice that here the tune is in the isometric form, whereas at *LW* 414 it is in the originally conceived rhythmic form.

The harmonization of the isometric form is by Paul G. Bunjes.

GOD MOVES IN A MYSTERIOUS WAY 426

William Cowper's poem was first published anonymously in John Newton's (*LW* 217, et al.) *Twenty-six letters on Religious Subjects; to which are added Hymns* (London, 1744), where it was titled "Light Shining Out of the Darkness." The title may have had reference to Cowper's mental instability, but there was confusion as to the hymn's authorship until 1779, when Newton again printed it in the *Olney Hymns*, Book III. Here it was signed "C," meaning Cowper was the author.

The date of publication is given by Newton as July 6, 1774, and it is assumed that the hymn was written about that time. Because Cowper suffered from an attack of suicidal mania in October 1773, one legend would have it that the hymn was written immediately after he was prevented from drowning himself in the Ouse River; but this story is given scant attention by scholars. It is thought probable that the lines were composed either before the attempted suicide, as James Montgomery (*LW* 50, et al.) says, "in the twilight of departing reason"; or after April 1774 when, claims biographer Southey, "in some of his most melancholy moments he used to compose lines descriptive of his own unhappiness."

The hymn as printed in *Lutheran Worship* (1982), made up of stanzas 1, 4, 6, and 3 of the original, was prepared by the Inter-Lutheran Commission on Worship for inclusion in *Lutheran Book of Worship* (1978). Considered by many as the finest hymn on God's providence ever written, it has found its way into numerous hymnals, including the most recent.

DUNDEE. For comments on this tune and its harmonization see hymn 283.

ENTRUST YOUR DAYS AND BURDENS 427

Entrust your days and burdens
To God's most loving hand;
He cares for you while ruling
The sky, the sea, the land.
He that in clouds and tempest

Befiehl du deine Wege,
Und was dein Herze kränkt,
Der allertreusten Pflege
Des, der den Himmel lenkt!
Der Wolken, Luft und Winden,

Finds breakthrough for the sun Will find right pathways for you Till trav'ling days are done.	Gibt Wege, Lauf und Bahn, Der wird auch Wege finden, Da dein Fuss gehen kann.
Rely on God your Savior And find your life secure. Make his work your foundation That your work may endure. No anxious thought, no worry, No self-tormenting care Can win your Father's favor; His heart is moved by prayer.	Dem Herren musst du trauen, Wenn dir's soll wohlergehn; Auf sein Werk muss du schauen, Wenn dein Werk soll bestehn. Mit Sorgen und mit Grämen Und mit selbsteigner Pein Lässt Gott sich gar nichts nehmen, Es muss erbeten sein.
Take heart, have hope, my spirit, And do not be afraid. From any low depression, Where agonies are made, God's grace will lift you upward On arms of saving might Until the sun you hoped for Delights your eager sight.	Hoff, o du arme Seele, Hoff und sei unverzagt! Gott wird dich aus der Höhle, Da dich der Kummer plagt, Mit grossen Gnaden rücken; Erwarte nur die Zeit, So wirst du schon erblicken Die Sonn' der schönsten Freud'.
Leave all to God's direction; His wisdom rules for you In ways to rouse your wonder At all his love can do. When his plans are maturing, Then wonder-working pow'rs Will banish from your spirit What gave you troubled hours.	Ihn, ihn lass tun und walten, Er ist ein weiser Fürst Und wird sich so verhalten, Dass du dich wundern wirst, Wenn er, wie ihm gebühret, Mit wunderbarem Rat Die Sach' hinausgeführet, Die dich bekümmert hat.
How blest you heir of heaven To hear the song resound Of thanks and jubilation When you with life are crowned. In your right hand your maker Will place the victor's palm, And for God's great deliv'rance You'll sing the vict'ry psalm.	Wohl dir, du Kind der Treue! Du hast und trägst davon Mit Ruhm und Dankgeschreie Den Sieg und Ehrenkron'. Gott gibt dir selbst die Palmen In deine rechte Hand, Und du singst Freudenpsalmen Dem, der dein Leid gewandt.
Lord, till we see the ending Of all this life's distress, Faith's hand, love's sinews strengthen, With joy our spirits bless. As yours, we have committed Ourselves into your care On ways made sure to bring us To heav'n to praise you there.	Mach End', o Herr, mach Ende An aller unsrer Not, Stärk unsre Füss' und Hände Und lass bis in den Tod Uns allzeit deiner Pflege Und Treu' empfohlen sein, So gehen unsre Wege Gewiss zum Himmel ein.

This great hymn of comfort and hope, originally in 12 stanzas, was written by Paul Gerhardt perhaps during his pastoral ministry in Mittenwalde, a small town south of Berlin. Its first published appearance was in the eighth edition of Johann Crüger's (*LW* 19, et al.) *Praxis pietatis melica* (Frankfurt-am-Main, 1653). Based on Psalm 37:5, "Befiehl dem Herrn deine wege, und hoffe auf ihn; er wird's wohl machen," in Luther's German translation of the Bible, the text is an acrostic, that is, each stanza begins with the successive word in the psalm passage. This, of course, is not evident in usual English translations of the hymn, much less here in but six stanzas. Actually, this is more than an ordinary acrostic in which the poet exhibits his poetic talents and technique. Here Gerhardt attempts to capture and amplify the piety of the psalmist himself for the Christian's life. And he has done this with singular success! Lauxmann, in Koch's *Geschichte des Kirchenlieds*, calls it the most "comforting of all hymns that have resounded on Paul Gerhardt's golden lyre, sweeter to many souls than honey and the honeycomb." Small wonder that it became such a favorite in German and Scandinavian churches, and that it made its way into English hymnals, largely the result of John Wesley's translation in his *Early Hymns and Sacred Poems* (1739). It was sung at the cornerstone laying of First Lutheran Church in Philadelphia, May 2, 1743; Queen Luise of Prussia, when the kingdom was overrun by Napoleon, wrote in her diary, December 5, 1806, some verses from Goethe's *Wilhelm Meister*. Thereafter, drying her tears, she sang this hymn to the accompaniment of her harpsichord.

A cursory check on some of the latest hymnals reveals that it has been retained in *The Hymnal 1982* of the Protestant Episcopal Church; included in *Rejoice in the Lord* (1985) of the Reformed Church in America; and also in *The Australian Hymn Book* (1977). Produced initially for Anglicans, Congregationalists, Methodists, and Presbyterians, this book, with Catholic Supplement, is also used by Roman Catholics.

F. Samuel Janzow prepared the translation for inclusion in *Lutheran Worship* (1982).

Of the 133 hymns that Gerhardt wrote, 29 can be counted as specifically Cross and Comfort hymns. The remaining can generally be designated as festival hymns. Essentially "Christ" hymns, the latter emphasize his person and his work from beginning to end. Having personally experienced in his heart justification by faith through the work of the Holy Spirit, Gerhardt decorates and crowns the festivals of the church year with the great and objective truths of salvation. Here the Second and Third articles of the Apostles' and Nicene Creeds especially come into play.

In the Cross and Comfort hymns, on the other hand, it is essentially the governance of God the Father that is presented. Although he knows of no other way to the Father than through his Son in the working of the Holy Spirit, here, in these hymns, Gerhardt is a theologian of the First Article, knowing full well, of course, that one does not confess the first without the second and the third. Hence, in 58 of his 133 hymns, Gerhardt makes no specific mention of Christ the Savior, and in a number of others Christ is mentioned perhaps only once. In "Entrust your days and burdens," for instance, no mention is made of Christ. And how sadly this has been misinterpreted!—as though the hymn is not Christian, only religious; as if an orthodox Jew could sing it! In response it must be stated that this hymn is like the Lord's Prayer, which is and remains unquestionably a Christian prayer, although Christ and justification by faith are not specifically mentioned therein. Moreover, certainly the background to "Entrust your days and burdens" is distinctly Christian.

It might prove profitable to mention that this non-mention of Christ is not unique with Gerhardt nor with his contemporaries. About this time, with the beginning of Pietism, there arose a goodly number of hymns, such as "What God Ordains Is Always Good" (*LW* 422), "All Depends on Our Possessing" (*LW* 415), and others that focus on the theology of the First Article. Moreover, it might be well, as Gerhardt did, to consider the Cross and Comfort hymns as "comfort and joy hymns," to borrow an expression from Gerhardt himself. That such hymns also sing of the Savior, it is sufficient to point to "Why Should Cross and Trial Grieve Me" (*TLH* 523) and "If God Himself Be for Me" (*LW* 407), hymns that border on being hymns of praise and thanksgiving.

HERZLICH TUT MICH VERLANGEN. For comments on this tune and its harmonization see hymn 113.

428 WHEN IN THE HOUR OF DEEPEST NEED

When in the hour of deepest need
We know not where to look for aid;
When days and nights of anxious thought
No help or counsel yet have brought,

Our comfort then is this alone:
That we may meet before your throne
And cry to you, O faithful God,
For rescue from our sorry lot.

For you have made a promise true
To pardon those who flee to you,
Through him whose name alone is great,
Our Savior and our advocate.

And so we come, O God, today
And all our woes before you lay;
For sorely tried, cast down, we stand,
Perplexed by fears on ev'ry hand.

Oh, from our sins hide not your face;
Absolve us through your boundless grace!
Be with us in our anguish still!
Free us at last from ev'ry ill!

So we with all our hearts each day
To you our glad thanksgiving pay,
Then walk obedient to your Word,
And now and ever praise you, Lord.

Wenn wir in höchsten Nöten sein
Und wissen nicht, wo aus noch ein,
Und finden weder Hilf' noch Rat,
Ob wir gleich sorgen früh und spät:

So ist dies unser Trost allein,
Dass wir zusammen insgemein
Dich rufen an, o treuer Gott,
Um Rettung aus der Angst und Not.

Die du verheissest gnädiglich
Allen, die darum bitten dich
Im Namen dein's Sohns Jesu Christ,
Der unser Heil und Fürsprech ist.

Drum kommen wir, o Herre Gott,
Und Klagen dir all unsre Not,
Weil wir jetzt stehn verlassen gar
In grosser Trübsal and Gefahr.

Sieh nicht an unsre Sünde gross,
Sprich uns derselb'n aus Gnaden los,
Steh uns in unserm Elend bei,
Mach uns von allen Plagen frei,

Auf dass von Herzen können wir
Nachmals mit Freuden danken dir,
Gehorsam sein nach deinem Wort,
Dich allzeit preisen hier und dort!

One of the great hymns of the Reformation era, Paul Eber's hymn of trust is said to be founded on the Latin hymn by Joachim Camerarius (1500–74), his noted teacher at the *Gymnasium* in Nürnberg, which in turn is based on the prayer of Johoshaphat recorded in 2 Chronicles 20:6–12. The Latin reads:

In tenebris nostrae et densa caligine mentis,
Cum nihil est toto pectore consilii,
Turbati erigimus, Deus, ad Te lumina cordis

Nostra, tuamque fides solius erat opem.
Tu rege consiliis actus, Pater optime, nostros,
Nostrum opus ut laudi serviat omne Tuae.

Although Eber's text appeared in a prayer book entitled *New Betbüchlein* (Dresden, 1566), it must have been written prior to its use in 1547. The outbreak of the Smalcald War shortly after Luther's death in 1546 brought difficult and fearful days for the citizens of Wittenberg and its university, where Eber was professor. When on Ascension Day 1547, after the Battle of Mühlberg, the Wittenbergers, having received word from their captive elector Johann Friedrich to turn their city over to the forces of Emperor Charles V, Johann Bugenhagen, the town pastor, had the church bells rung to call the people to prayer. In the service, in which he preached and led the people, kneeling, in fervent prayer, Eber's hymn "Wenn wir in höchsten nöten sein" was sung. On the repeated advice of the elector, the order to turn over the city was carried out. Fortunately for the people and the university, the emperor treated them with surprising mildness.

Catherine Winkworth's translation, here slightly revised and in updated form, appeared in her *Lyra Germanica* (second series, 1858) and again in her *Chorale Book for England* (1863).

WENN WIR IN HÖCHSTEN NÖTEN SEIN. First published in the French, or Genevan, Psalter, this splendid melody is believed to be by Louis Bourgeois himself. It may have been included in the 1543 edition (*Cinquante pseaumes en francois*), but no copies of this edition are extant. The 1545 edition did include the tune, set to "Leve le coeur, ouvre l'oreille," a metrical form of the Ten Commandments by Clement Marot, the popular court poet and satirist under Francis I.

The tune's association with Eber's text began with *Das Gebet Josaphat* (Wittenberg, 1567). J. S. Bach's last work, blind and sick that he was, was to dicate a chorale prelude on this tune, though with the text, "Before Thy Throne".

The harmonization is from the *Württembergisches Choralbuch* (1953).

I LEAVE ALL THINGS TO GOD'S DIRECTION 429

I leave all things to God's direction,
For he loves me in wealth or woe;
His will is good, and his affection,
His tender love is true, I know.
My strength, my fortress rock is he:
What pleases God, that pleases me.

My God has all things in his keeping,
He is my ever faithful friend;
He gives me laughter after weeping,

Ich halte Gott in allem stille,
Er liebet mich in Freud' und Schmerz.
Wie gut ist Gottes Vaterwille,
Wie freundlich sein getreues Herz!
Er ist mein Hort und meine Zier:
Was Gott gefällt, gefällt auch mir.

Mein Gott weiss alles wohl zu machen,
Er ist der ewig treue Freund,
Er lässt mich nach dem Weinen lachen,

And all his ways in blessing end.
His love endures eternally:
What pleases God, that pleases me.

The will of God shall be my pleasure
While here I live life's interim;
My will is wrong beyond all measure,
It does not will what pleases him.
The Christian's motto then must be:
What pleases God, that pleases me.

God knows what must be done to save me,
His love for me will never cease;
And all my sins my Lord forgave me
With purest gold of loving grace.
His will supreme must ever be:
What pleases God, that pleases me.

My God desires each soul's salvation,
My soul he too desires to save;
Therefore with Christian resignation
All earthly troubles I will brave.
His will be done eternally:
What pleases God, that pleases me.

Was er nur tut, ist wohl gemeint,
Sein Lieben währet für und für.
Was Gott gefällt, gefällt auch mir.

Sein Wille bleibet mein Vergnügen,
Solang ich leb' auf dieser Welt.
Was kann mein eigner Wille tügen,
Der das nicht will, was Gott gefällt?
Ich denk' an meine Christgebühr:
Was Gott gefällt, gefällt auch mir.

Er will und wird mich ewig lieben,
Er weiss, was Seelen nützlich sei,
Er hat mich in die Hand geschrieben
Mit lauterm Golde seiner Treu'.
Weg, eigner Wille, weg mit dir!
Was Gott gefällt, gefällt auch mir.

Gott will, dass mir geholfen werde,
Er will der Seelen Seligkeit;
Drum reiss' ich mich von dieser Erde
Durch wahre Gottgelassenheit.
Sein Will' geschehe dort und hier.
Was Gott gefällt, gefällt auch mir.

This laudable hymn of trust in God by the talented Salomo Franck first appeared in his *Geistliche Poesie* (Weimar, 1685) headed "The soul resigns itself to the divine will." Franck's propensity for brief refrains in his poetry, whether at the beginning, or end, or both, of each stanza, thus to concentrate the thrust of each hymn, is here exhibited in the striking end-refrain, "What pleases God, that pleases me."

The translation is an altered and updated form of that by August Crull in *The Lutheran Hymnal* (1941).

WER NUR DEN LIEBEN GOTT. For comments on this tune see hymn 420.

The harmonization is from *The Lutheran Hymnal* (1941), slightly altered.

OUR FATHER, WHO FROM HEAVEN ABOVE 430

The nine-stanza length of Martin Luther's metrical paraphrase of the Lord's Prayer (*LW* 431) prompted the Commission on Worship to include in *Lutheran Worship* (1982) this three-stanza version by Henry L. Lettermann. In examining it and noting its laudable qualities, one cannot but agree with the old saying, "In der Beschränkung zeigt sich der Meister" ("In exercising restraint, one shows himself/herself to be a master").

While chanting the Lord's Prayer in its commonly accepted scriptural text or singing it in a metrical, or hymn-like form, has traditional warrant (Luther in his German Mass provided the presiding minister with a chant setting for both the Lord's Prayer and the Verba, resulting in a distinctive Lutheran use in all lands), the use of homemade, interpolated, responsive spoken forms of the Lord's Prayer in corporate worship—more didactic than prayer-like—should be discouraged. Apropos is the dictum of Aidan Kavanagh: " . . . the liturgy declaims and proclaims something rather than [that] it analyzes or teaches something." (*Elements of Rite*, p. 57)

VATER UNSER. For comments on the tune see hymn 431.
The setting is the work of Paul G. Bunjes.

OUR FATHER, WHO FROM HEAVEN ABOVE 431

Our Father, who from heav'n above
Has told us here to live in love
And with our fellow Christians share
Our mutual burdens and our prayer,
Teach us no thoughtless word to say
But from our inmost heart to pray.

Your name be hallowed. Help us, Lord,
In purity to keep your Word
That to the glory of your name
We walk before you free from blame.
Let no false teaching us pervert;
All poor deluded souls convert.

Your kingdom come. Guard your domain
And your eternal righteous reign.
The Holy Ghost enrich our day
With gifts attendant on our way.
Break Satan's pow'r, defeat his rage;
Preserve your Church from age to age.

Your gracious will on earth be done
As it is done before your throne,
That patiently we may obey

Vater unser in Himmelreich,
Der du uns alle heissest gleich
Brüder sein und dich rufen an
Und willst das Beten von uns hab'n,
Gib, dass nicht bet' allein der Mund,
Hilf, dass es geh' von Herzensgrund!

Geheiligt werd' der Name dein,
Dein Wort bei uns hilf halten rein,
Dass auch wir leben heiliglich,
Nach deinem Namen würdiglich.
Behüt uns, Herr, vor falscher Lehr',
Das arm' verführte Volk bekehr!

Es komm' dein Reich zu dieser Zeit
Und dort hernach in Ewigkeit;
Der Heil'ge Geist uns wohne bei
Mit seinen Gaben mancherlei;
Des Satans Zorn und gross' Gewalt
Zerbrich, vor ihm dein' Kirch' erhalt!

Dein Will' gescheh, Herr Gott, zugleich
Auf Erden wie im Himmelreich;
Gib uns Geduld in Leidenszeit,

In good or bad times all you say. Curb flesh and blood and ev'ry ill That sets itself against your will.	Gehorsam sein in Lieb' und Leid; Wehr und steur allem Fleisch und Blut, Das wider deinen Willen tut!
Give us this day our daily bread And let us all be clothed and fed. From warfare, rioting, and strife, Disease, and famine save our life That we in honest peace may live, To care and greed no entrance give.	Gib uns heut' unser täglich Brot, Und was man braucht zur Leibesnot; B'hüt uns, Herr, vor Unfried' und Streit, Vor Seuchen und vor teurer Zeit, Dass wir in gutem Frieden stehn, Der Sorg' und Geizes müssig gehn!
Forgive our sins, let grace outpour That they may trouble us no more; We too will gladly those forgive Who harm us by the way they live. Help us in each community To serve with love and unity.	All unsre Schuld vergib uns, Herr, Dass sie uns nicht betrübe mehr, Wie wir auch unsern Schuldigern Ihr' Schuld und Fehl' vergeben gern; Zu dienen mach uns all' bereit In rechter Lieb' und Einigkeit!
Lead not into temptation, Lord, Where our grim foe and all his horde Would vex our souls on ev'ry hand. Help us resist, help us to stand Firm in the faith, armed with your might; Your Spirit gives your children light.	Führ uns, Herr, in Versuchung nicht; Wenn uns der böse Geist anficht Zur linken und zur rechten Hand, Hilf uns tun starken Widerstand, Im Glauben fest und wohlgerüst't Und durch des Heil'gen Geistes Trost.
Deliver us from evil days, From every dark and trying maze; Redeem us from eternal death, Console us when we yield our breath. Give us at last a blessed end; Receive our souls, O faithful friend.	Von allem übel uns erlös, Es sind die Zeit und Tage bös; Erlös uns von dem ew'gen Tod Und tröst uns in der letzten Not; Bescher uns auch ein selig End', Nimm unsre Seel' in deine Händ'!
Amen, that is, it shall be so. Make our faith strong that we may know We need not doubt but shall receive All that we ask, as we believe. On your great promise we lay claim. Our faith says amen in your name.	Amen, das ist, es werde wahr! Stärk unsern Glauben immerdar, Auf dass wir ja nicht zweifeln dran, Was wir hiermit gebeten hab'n Auf dein Wort in dem Namen dein; So sprechen wir das Amen fein.

Having furnished congregations two hymns on the Ten Commandments ("Here Is the Tenfold Sure Command," *LW* 331, and "Man, wouldst thou live all blissfully," Leupold, p. 281); a versification of the Creed ("We All Believe in One True God, Maker," *LW* 213); a hymn on Holy Baptism ("To Jordan Came the Christ, Our Lord," *LW* 223); two hymns on the Lord's Supper ("Jesus Christ, Our Blessed Savior," *TLH* 311, and "O Lord, We Praise You," *LW* 238), there was missing only a versification of the Lord's Prayer to complete the chief parts of the catechism. With the appearance of "Our Father, Who from Heaven Above" in Valentin Schumann's *Geistliche Lieder auf neugebessert und gemehrt* (Leipzig, 1539), Luther supplied this need. It may have been published as a broadsheet previous to this.

Luther is not the first to create a versification of the Lord's Prayer. Others, both in the Middle Ages and the 16th century, had done so. Luther's version, however, takes first place in that each stanza begins with almost a literal rendering of each petition (the doxology excepted), followed by the catechetical meaning of each and concluding with an Amen stanza.

It is not a little interesting to note that this is one of Luther's two hymns (the other is "The angel troop came near," Leupold, p. 307) for which a facsimile of the original draft in Luther's own hand is available (Moser, *Die Melodien der Lutherlieder*, p. 81). The facsimile shows Luther's textual revisions and corrections, also the tune that he originally intended for the text.

The translation is by F. Samuel Janzow.

VATER UNSER. This is the tune that appeared in Schumann's hymnal mentioned above. In some respects it exhibits an affinity to the tune Michael Weisse used for his version of the Lord's Prayer, "Begehren wir mit Innigkeit," that appeared in the 1531 hymnal of the Bohemian Brethren (Leupold, p. 296; Zahn 3792). Its more subdued and devotional character can readily be seen when compared to the tune that Luther originally intended, which looked like this:

W. G. Polack considers "Our Father, Who from Heaven Above" to be Luther's finest hymn, placing it above "A Mighty Fortress" (*LW* 298) and "From depths of Woe" (*LW* 230). It appeared in English as early as 1560 in *Psalmes of David* by R. Cox and in the 1568 edition of John Wedderburn's *Gude and Godlie Ballates*. It was added to the Scottish Psalter (1595).

Richard W. Gieseke prepared the harmonization.

432 ETERNAL SPIRIT OF THE LIVING CHRIST

In the January 1974 issue of *The Hymn*, a publication of the Hymn Society of America, this beautiful hymn on prayer appeared on the cover. Regarding its origin's significance Frank von Christierson, the author, states:

> "Eternal Spirit of the living Christ" is a deeply devotional hymn, the outpouring of my heart to Christ, who is the center and life of my faith. It just came to me one morning, and I wrote as I felt led. I have often felt that Paul's frequent use of the expression "in Christ" is entirely typical of him, and should be typical of every Christian life. Also this hymn expresses my strong feeling that I can't begin to say to God what is really in my heart, but I think he understands (Stulken, *Hymnal Companion*).

ADORO TE DEVOTE. This tune takes its name from the plainsong tune traditionally sung with St. Thomas Aquinas' (c. 1224–75) hymn, "Adoro te devote, latens veritas" ("Humbly I adore you, verity unseen," *LBW* 199). Although sometimes listed as a 13th-century tune, it is undoubtedly of later date. Cyril Pocknee, for instance, claims that it cannot be found prior to the *Paris Processional* (1697), where it was set to a neo-Gallican version of Aquinas' hymn (*French Diocesan Hymns and Their Melodies*, New York, 1954). Moreover, the tune gives a strong flavor of major tonality, suggesting the I-IV-V harmonies that became established in the 17th century.

The harmonization was prepared by Paul G. Bunjes for *Lutheran Worship* (1982).

The fluent rhythm of plainsong in contrast to the recurring pulse of metrical hymnody, together with the employment of the old church modes (see essay: The Church Modes, p. 832), makes the singing of these plainsong tunes by congregations difficult unless thoroughly studied and rehearsed prior to their use in corporate worship. Choirs, on the other hand, given rehearsal time, can readily master these splendid tunes, the oldest in point of time in church hymnals. The singing of such tunes should be light, smooth, and fairly rapid. The rhythm and pace of good reading represent a satisfactory norm. The tune remains subservient to the text. Although plainsong was originally sung in unison and without accompaniment, *Lutheran Worship*, not unlike other hymnals, has added accompaniment to facilitate the singing. Such accompaniment, however, should be subdued, light in texture, or even delicate, and in no way hamper the freedom of the congregation or choir, or detract from the predominance of the melody.

Should congregations or choirs hesitate to attempt the tune ADORO, TE DEVOTE, lest this notable text go unsung, SURSUM CORDA (*LW* 401) will admirably serve as an alternate tune.

COME, MY SOUL, WITH EVERY CARE 433

This fine hymn on prayer, originally in seven stanzas, was written by John Newton, the spirited, energetic, indomitable Calvinistic Anglican curate of Olney, for inclusion in the *Olney Hymns* (1779), Book 1, the hymnal prepared by him and his assistant William Cowper, the poet, for the weeknight evangelical prayer meetings that had met with such great success.

Written in the most common and useful 77 77 trochaic (´ ˘) pattern, there is something attractive about the terseness of short lines and strong downbeats. Moreover, as a means of invocation, trochaic imperatives such as "Come, my soul," "Lord, your rest," "Let your love," "Lead me to," and the like are excellent.

The text here given is in altered and updated form.

VIENNA (RAVENNA, ST. BONIFACE) by Justin Heinrich Knecht first appeared in the *Volständige Sammlung . . . Vierstimmige Choralmelodien für das neue Württembergisches Landgesangbuch* (Stuttgart, 1779), edited by Knecht and J. F. Christmann (Zahn 1238), where it was set to J. A. Schlegel's "Ohne Rast und unverweilt." In the original the second note of phrase three is lowered a half step. Although highly regarded as a musician by his contemporaries, Knecht's music lacked vitality, and today he is remembered only for a few chorale tunes.

The harmonization is an altered form of that contained in *The Hymnal 1940* of the Protestant Episcopal Church.

CHRISTIANS, WHILE ON EARTH ABIDING 434

These two stanzas constitute stanzas 5 and 6 of an English version, beginning "Guardian of pure hearts and hearer," a hymn included in The *Hymnal* (1901) of the Augustana Synod. Stanza 2 of this hymn by Jesper Svedberg is a metrical paraphrase of the Aaronic benediction (Num. 6:24–26), originally beginning "Herre, signe du och raade." Johan Olof Wallin, in 1816, revised stanza 2 and expanded it to six stanzas, beginning "Du som fromma hjartan vaardar."

Source of the present translation, somewhat altered, is unknown.

WERDE MUNTER. For comments on this tune and its harmonization see hymn 263.

435 ALL PEOPLE THAT ON EARTH DO DWELL

This world-famous metrical version of Psalm 100 appeared in 1561, both in the Anglo-Genevan Psalter (*Four Score and Seven Psalmes of David in English Mitre*) and in John Day's *Psalmes of David in English Metre*, known as the English Psalter. The following year, 1862, it was included in the *Whole Booke of Psalmes*, the so-called Old Version, or "Sternhold and Hopkins," set to the present tune (see essay: Metrical Psalms, p. 825).

Some of the early psalters ascribed this text to Thomas Sternhold, while others gave the credit to William Kethe. Because of its appearance in the Anglo-Genevan Psalter, and because a number of Kethe's original works were added to early editions of "Sternhold & Hopkins," Kethe seems most likely as the author. Various other reasons are given for this assumption, including the meter of the text; Sternhold almost invariably used common meter. Moreover, the ascription to Kethe in the British Museum copy of the Anglo-Genevan Psalter is rather strong evidence of his authorship.

Kethe's original wording has been altered in two places by most hymnal editors. In the third line of stanza 1, the original ran, "Him serve with *fear*, his praise forthtell"; it is thought that *mirth* gives a closer approximation of the Hebrew psalmist's word. Likewise "folk" is sometimes changed to "flock" in the third line of stanza 2; the word originally appeared as "folck." Reading this as a misprint, some editors have chosen "flock" as more fitting for the context; but the real meaning of this line in the psalm is "We are his people [folk], the sheep of his pasture." Therefore *Lutheran Worship* retains the original. According to the *Oxford English Dictionary*, the strange expression "For why?" in stanza 4, meaning "because," is a correct translation of Psalm 100:5.

The doxological fifth stanza, based on one in common meter by Tate and Brady in their so-called New Version, was added by John Mason Neale (*LW* 31, et al.).

OLD HUNDREDTH. Louis Bourgeois' tune is the only one preserved intact throughout the history of metrical psalmody. It first appeared in the Genevan Psalter of 1551, where it was set to Theodore de Beze's version of Psalm 134, but it was quickly taken up as the setting for Kethe's Psalm 100 in the Old Version of 1562. This is undoubtedly the most famous of psalm tunes, whether early or late.

The harmonization was prepared by George Leonard, an *nom de plume* of Paul G. Bunjes.

ALL CREATURES OF OUR GOD AND KING 436

From the "Canticle of the Sun" by St. Francis of Assisi, William H. Draper prepared this rather free metrical paraphrase for the children's Whitsuntide Festival at Leeds.

Francis' poem, the first religious poem in the Italian language, has been called by the French composer Gabriel Faure (1845–1924) as "the first greetings of the Italian Renaissance to the Nature she had found again." It was written in the summer of 1225 when Francis was lying ill and unattended in a straw-thatched hut at San Damiano, his discomfort compounded by the scampering of mice that made it impossible for him to sleep; and yet he was still able to compose this tribute of praise to the Creator who made the earth and the creatures his servant so loved.

In contrast to the Italian text, which praises God for his various creations, Draper's paraphrase turns the meaning around and asks all those creations to praise their Lord, a poetic device called apostrophic, that is, addressing inanimate objects, sometimes persons (cf. Ps. 148, for instance). Regarding this hymn, S. Paul Schilling says that "Few hymns are more positive regarding the worth of earthly life." Asked at a later time when his hymn was composed, Draper was unable to recall the exact date; it was sometime during his stay at Adel, Yorkshire, where he was rector from 1899–1919. It first appeared in 1926 in *Hymns of the Spirit*, a little book containing 10 hymns.

LASST UNS ERFREUEN. For comments on this tune and harmonization see hymn 131.

ALLELUIA! LET PRAISES RING 437

Alleluia! Let praises ring!
To God the Father let us bring
Our songs of adoration.
To him through everlasting days
Be worship, honor, pow'r, and praise,
Whose hand sustains creation.
Singing, ringing:
Holy, holy,
God is holy;
Spread the story
Of our God, the Lord of glory.

Alleluia! Let praises ring!
Unto the Lamb of God we sing,
In whom we are elected.
He bought his Church with his own blood,
He cleansed her in that blessed flood,
And as his bride selected.
Holy, holy
Is our union
And communion.

Halleluja! Lob, Preis und Ehr'
Sei unserm Gott je mehr und mehr
Für alle seine Werke;
Von Ewigkeit zu Ewigkeit
Sie in uns allen ihm bereit
Dank, Weisheit, Kraft und Stärke!
Klinget, singet:
Heilig, heilig,
Freilich, freilich,
Heilig ist Gott,
Unser Gott, der Herr Zebaoth!

Halleluja! Preis, Ehr' und Macht
Sei auch dem Gotteslamm gebracht,
In dem wir sind erwählet,
Das uns mit seinem Blut erkauft,
Damit besprenget und getauft
Und sich mit uns vermählet!
Heilig, selig
Ist die Fruendschaft
Und Gemeinschaft,

His befriending Gives us joy and peace unending.	Die wir haben Und darinnen uns erlaben.
Alleluia! Let praises ring! Unto the Holy Ghost we sing For our regeneration. The saving faith in us he wrought And us unto the Bridegroom brought, Made us his chosen nation. Glory! Glory! Joy eternal, Bliss supernal; There is manna And an endless, glad hosanna.	Halleluja! Gott Heil'ger Geist Sei ewiglich von uns gepreist, Durch den wir neugeboren, Der uns mit Glauben ausgeziert, Dem Bräutigam uns zugeführt, Dem Hochzeitstag erkoren! Eia, ei da, Das ist Freude, Da ist Weide, Da ist Manna Und ein ewig Hosianna!
Alleluia! Let praises ring! Unto our triune God we sing; Blest be his name forever! With angel hosts let us adore And sing his praises more and more For all his grace and favor! Singing, ringing: Holy, holy, God is holy; Spread the story Of our God, the Lord of glory!	Halleluja! Lob, Preis und Ehr' Sei unserm Gott je mehr und mehr Und seinem grossen Namen! Stimmt an mit aller Himmelsschar Und singet nun und immerdar Mit Freuden: Amen, Amen! Klinget, singet: Heilig, heilig, Freilich, freilich, Heilig ist Gott, Unser Gott, der Herr Zebaoth!

This anonymous but beautiful hymn demonstrates the strange and interesting evolution of some hymns in arriving at their final form. The roots of this text are in Martin Rinckart's (*LW* 443) *Leibliche, Geistliche, und Himmliche Braut Messe* (Bridal Mass), 1642, in which he created stanzas to the tune WIE SCHÖN LEUCHTET based on Revelation 21 and 22. In 1655 an anonymous poet created a new version of this text, turning it into a burial hymn. Finally, in 1698, this hymn appeared in the *Geistreiches Gesangbuch* (Darmstadt) as a hymn of praise to the Holy Trinity. As such it was included in numerous hymnals and soon became popular. Strangely, it is lacking in the present hymnals of the Lutheran territorial churches in Germany.

Except for the supplanting of the Hebrew Hallelujah with the Latin Alleluia, the text is that of the composite translation contained in *The Lutheran Hymnal* (1941).

WIE SCHÖN LEUCHTET. For comments on this tune see hymn 73.

Richard W. Gieseke prepared the harmonization for inclusion in *Lutheran Worship* (1982).

438 EARTH AND ALL STARS

This hymn was written by Herbert Brokering in 1964 for the 90th anniversary of St. Olaf College, Northfield, Minnesota. Regarding its contents Brokering says:

> I tried to gather into a hymn of praise the many facets of life which merge in the life of community. So there are references to building, nature, learning, family, war, festivity.

EARTH AND ALL STARS was composed by David N. Johnson for Brokering's text. The harmonization was done for *Lutheran Worship* (1982) by Paul G. Bunjes.

Both text and tune of this hymn were included in *Twelve Folksongs and Spirituals* (1968), in *Contemporary Worship I* (1969), and again in *Lutheran Book of Worship* (1978). Originally comprised of six stanzas, the Commission on Worship requested the author—and he obliged—to write a concluding doxological stanza for inclusion in *Lutheran Worship* (1982). The *Psalter Hymnal* (1987) of the Christian Reformed Church has a complete revision by the author generally changing the use of "loud" to "come."

The apostrophic character of this text, exhibiting the poetic device in which the poet addresses inanimate objects, and sometimes persons, is reminiscent of certain psalms (cf. for instance Psalm 148).

I WILL SING MY MAKER'S PRAISES 439

I will sing my Maker's praises
And in him most joyful be,
For in all things I see traces
Of his tender love to me.
Nothing else than love could move him
With such deep and tender care
Evermore to raise and bear
All who try to serve and love him.
All things else have but their hour,
God's great love retains its pow'r.

He so cared for and esteemed me
That the Son he loved so well
He gave for me to redeem me
From the quenchless flames of hell.
O Lord, spring of boundless blessing,
How then could my finite mind
Of your love the limit find
Though my efforts were unceasing?
All things else have but their hour,
God's great love retains its pow'r.

All that for my soul is needful
He with loving care provides,
Nor is he of that unheedful
Which my body needs besides.
When my strength cannot avail me,
When my pow'rs can do no more,
Then will God his strength outpour;
In my need he will not fail me.
All things else have but their hour,
God's great love retains its pow'r.

Sollt' ich meinem Gott nicht singen?
Sollt' ich ihm nicht fröhlich sein?
Denn ich seh' in allen Dingen,
Wie so gut er's mit mir mein'.
Ist doch nichts als lauter Lieben,
Das sein treues Herze regt,
Das ohn' Ende hebt und trägt,
Die in seinem Dienst sich üben.
Alles Ding währt seine Zeit,
Gottes Lieb' in Ewigkeit.

Sein Sohn ist ihm nicht zu teuer,
Nein, er gibt ihn für mich hin,
Dass er mich vom ew'gen Feuer
Durch sein teures Blut gewinn'.
O du unergründ'ter Brunnen,
Wie will doch mein schwacher Geist,
Ob er sich gleich hoch befleisst,
Deine Tief' ergründen können?
Alles Ding währt seine Zeit,
Gottes Lieb' in Ewigkeit.

Meiner Seele Wohlergehen
Hat er ja recht wohl bedacht.
Will dem Leibe Not zustehen,
Nimmt er's gleichfalls wohl in acht.
Wenn mein Können, mein Vermögen
Nichts vermag, nichts helfen kann,
Kommt mein Gott und hebt mir an
Sein Vermögen beizulegen.
Alles Ding währt seine Zeit,
Gottes Lieb' in Ewigkeit.

Since there's neither change nor coldness	Weil denn weder Ziel noch Ende
In God's love that on me smiled,	Sich in Gottes Liebe find't,
I now lift my hands in boldness,	Ei, so heb' ich meine Hände
Coming to you as your child.	Zu dir, Vater, als dein Kind,
Grant me grace, O God, I pray you,	Bitte, woll'st mir Gnade geben,
That I may with all my might,	Dich aus aller meiner Macht
All my lifetime, day and night,	Zu umfangen Tag und Nacht
Love and trust you and obey you	Hier in meinem ganzen Leben,
And then, after this life's end,	Bis ich dich nach dieser Zeit
Ever praise you, God, my friend.	Lob' und lieb' in Ewigkeit.

This hymn, originally in 12 stanzas, first appearing in the still lost third edition of Johann Crüger's *Praxis pietatis melica* (Berlin, 1648), is certainly numbered among Paul Gerhardt's finest hymns. It is a heartfelt hymn of thanks in praise of the everlasting love of God according to the benefits and favors enunciated in the three articles of the Apostles' Creed. Although not evident in this cento, consisting of stanzas 1, 3, 5, and 12 of the original, it is, as someone has said, a catalog of bodily and spiritual benefits and favors of the Lord.

This is an altered and updated version of the composite translation contained in *The Lutheran Hymnal* (1941).

SOLLT ICH MEINEM GOTT is the tune composed by Johann Schop that first appeared in Johann Rist's (*LW* 122, et al.) *Himmlische Lieder* (Lüneberg, 1641) set to Rist's Easter hymn "Lasset uns den Herren preisen, o ihr Christen überall" It is Rists's metric form that Gerhardt took over for his text. Despite the numerous tunes composed for Gerhardt's text, this is the tune that eventually became wedded to his text, a tune that, as a Lutheran chorale, deserves high praise.

Richard W. Gieseke prepared the harmonization included in *Lutheran Worship* (1982).

440 FROM ALL THAT DWELL BELOW THE SKIES

In his *Psalms of David Imitated* (1719), Isaac Watts included three paraphrases in different meters of Psalm 117, his favorite. This hymn is his long meter version, unaltered except for the updated personal pronouns and the added alleluias to fit the tune. The final doxological stanza by William How was appended by the Commission on Worship.

LASST UNS ERFREUEN. See hymn 131 for notes on this chorale tune and its harmonization.

Milgate makes an interesting observation about the ecumenical character of Christian hymnody:

Probably no hymn better shows that God is no respecter of persons when it comes to providing hymns for his people: in the form given here [exclusive of stanza 3] it is a Hebrew hymn translated by an Independent (Congregational) minister, set to a tune from a Catholic hymnal arranged by an agnostic for a Church of England hymn book, and sung by Christians of every denomination.

WE SING THE ALMIGHTY POWER OF GOD 441

This laudable hymn first appeared in Isaac Watts's *Divine and Moral Songs* (1715), where it was entitled "Praise for Creation and Providence." Although noticeably absent in present-day hymnals, it appears in *The Psalter Hymnal* (1987) of the Christian Reformed Church.

ICH SINGE DIR. For comments on the tunes see hymn 151.

The harmonization was prepared for *Lutheran Worship* (1982) by Wilhelm Quampen, a *nom de plume* of Paul G. Bunjes.

IN YOU IS GLADNESS 442

In you is gladness Amid all sadness, Jesus, sunshine of my heart. By you are given The gifts of heaven, You the true Redeemer are. Our souls are waking; Our bonds are breaking. Who trusts you surely Has built securely And stands forever. Alleluia! Our hearts are pining To see your shining, Dying or living To you are cleaving Now and forever. Alleluia!	In dir ist Freude In allem Leide, O du süsser Jesu Christ! Durch dich wir haben Himmlische Gaben, Du der wahre Heiland bist; Hilfest von Schanden, Rettest von Banden. Wer dir vertrauet, Hat wohl gebauet, Wird ewig bleiben. Halleluja. Zu deiner Güte Steht unser G'müte, An dir wir kleben Im Tod und Leben; Nichts kann uns scheiden. Halleluja.
If he is ours, We fear no powers, Not of earth or sin or death. He sees and blesses In worst distresses; He can change them with a breath.	Wenn wir dich haben, Kann uns nicht schaden Teufel, Welt, Sünd oder Tod; Du hasts in Händen, Kannst alles wenden, Wie nur heissen mag die Not.

Wherefore the story
Tell of his glory
With hearts and voices;
All heav'n rejoices
In him forever.
Alleluia!
We shout for gladness,
Win over sadness,
Love him and praise him
And still shall raise him
Glad hymns forever.
Alleluia!

Drum wir dich ehren,
Dein Lob vermehren
Mit hellem Schalle,
Freuen uns alle
Zu dieser Stunde.
Halleluja.
Wir jubilieren
Und triumphieren,
Lieben und loben
Dein Macht dort droben
Mit Herz und Munde.
Halleluja.

This is originally one of the two sacred texts that Johann Lindemann, cantor in Gotha, included in his *Amorum Filii Dei Decades Duae* (Erfurt, 1598), set to tunes from Gastoldi's *Balletti a cinqve voce* (1591). Some of the 20 songs in Lindemann's collection were perhaps little congratulatory songs of thanks addressed to his ruler Johann Kosimir in Gotha. The translation by Catherine Winkworth, here given in slightly altered and updated form, first appeared in her *Lyra Germanica*, (second series, 1858). The use of "since" instead of "if" in the first line of stanza 2 may clarify its meaning.

IN DIR IST FREUDE is the delightful dance tune set to the text "A leita vita, Amor cünuita" in Gastoldi's *Balletti* (1591).

The harmonization by Jan Bender is from *Worship Supplement* (1969).

This hymn is most effectively sung in a brisk, swinging tempo.

443 NOW THANK WE ALL OUR GOD

Now thank we all our God
With hearts and hands and voices,
Who wondrous things has done,
In whom his world rejoices;
Who from our mothers' arms
Has blest us on our way
With countless gifts of love
And still is ours today.

Nun danket alle Gott
Mit Herzen, Mund und Händen,
Der grosse Dinge tut
An uns und allen Enden,
Der uns von Mutterleib
Und Kindesbeinen an
Unzählig viel zugut
Und noch jetzund getan!

Oh, may this bounteous God
Through all our life be near us,
With ever joyful hearts
And blessed peace to cheer us
And keep us in his grace
And guide us when perplexed
And free us from all harm
In this world and the next!

Der ewig reiche Gott
Woll' uns bei unserm Leben
Ein immer fröhlich Herz
Und edlen Frieden geben
Und uns in seiner Gnad'
Erhalten fort und fort
Und uns aus aller Not
Erlösen hier und dort!

All praise and thanks to God
The Father now be given,
The Son, and him who reigns

Lob, Ehr' und Preis sei Gott
Dem Vater und dem Sohne
Und dem, der beiden gleich

With them in highest heaven,	Im höchsten Himmelsthrone,
The one eternal God,	Dem dreieinigen Gott,
Whom earth and heav'n adore;	Als es im Anfang war
For thus it was, is now,	Und ist und bleiben wird
And shall be evermore.	Jetzund und immerdar!

Known as the "German Te Deum," this famous hymn was written by Martin Rinckart during the horrors of the Thirty Years' War (1618–48). The little town of Eilenburg in Saxony, where he was Lutheran pastor, was once sacked by the Austrians and twice by the Swedes. A ravaging plague took the lives of some 8,000 residents. Having lived through such sorrow and misfortune, Rinckart could still thank and praise the Lord.

This famous hymn appeared in Rinckart's *Jesu Hertz-Büchlein* (Leipzig, 1663); it may have been included in the first edition of 1636, but no copy has been found to verify this. The oldest text now available is in Johann Crüger's 1648 edition of *Praxis pietatis melica*. The first two stanzas are evidently based on the apocryphal book of Ecclesiasticus 50:22–26:

> And now bless the God of all things,
> the doer of great deeds everywhere,
> Who has exalted our days from the womb
> and acted towards us in his mercy.
> May he grant us cheerful hearts
> and bring peace in our time,
> in Israel for ages on ages.
> May his mercy be faithfully with us,
> may he redeem us in our time. (Jerusalem Bible)

The third stanza was added as a doxology. Entitled "Tischgebetlein" (Short Table Prayer), it was intended that the hymn be sung as grace at family meals.

The translation by Catherine Winkworth, here slightly altered and updated, appeared in her *Lyra Germanica* (second series, 1858) and again in her *Chorale Book for England* (1863).

NUN DANKET ALLE GOTT. This tune, from Johann Crüger's *Praxis pietatis melica* (1647), is generally accepted to be by Crüger himself. His initials appear in connection with the tune in Christoph Runge's *D. M. Luther's und anderer vornehmen geistreichen und gelehrten Männer geistliche Lieder und Psalmen* (Berlin, 1653), of which Crüger was music editor. Although it is universally associated with Rinckart's text, attempts to attribute the tune to Rinckart have failed for lack of supporting evidence.

This stately hymn has been widely sung in worship at celebrations of praise and thanksgiving as well as on national occasions of thanksgiving.

The setting is from the *Choralbuch* (1955).

444 PRAISE TO THE LORD, THE ALMIGHTY

Praise to the Lord, the Almighty,
the King of creation!
O my soul, praise him, for he is
your health and salvation!
Let all who hear
Now to his temple draw near,
Joining in glad adoration!

Praise to the Lord, who o'er all
things is wondrously reigning
And, as on wings of an eagle,
uplifting, sustaining.
Have you not seen
All that is needful has been
Sent by his gracious ordaining?

Praise to the Lord, who will
prosper your work and defend you;
Surely his goodness and mercy
shall daily attend you.
Ponder anew
What the Almighty can do
As with his love he befriends you.

Praise to the Lord! Oh, let all
that is in me adore him!
All that has life and breath,
come now with praises before him!
Let the amen
Sound from his people again.
Gladly forever adore him!

Lobe den Herren, den mächtigen König
der Ehren!
Meine geliebete Seele, das ist mein
Begehren.
Kommet zuhauf!
Psalter und Harfe, wacht auf!
Lasset die Musikam hören!

Lobe den Herren, der alles so
herrlich regieret,
Der dich auf Adelers Fittichen
sicher geführet,
Der dich erhält,
Wie es dir selber gefällt.
Hast du nicht dieses verspüret?

Lobe den Herren, der deinen Stand
sichtbar gesegnet,
Der aus dem Himmel mit Strömen
der Liebe geregnet!
Denke daran
Was der Allmächtige kann,
Der dir mit Liebe begegnet!

Lobe den Herren, was in mir ist
lobe den Namen!
Alles, was Odem hat, lobe mit
Abrahams Samen!
Er ist dein Licht,
Seele, vergiss es ja nicht!
Lobende, schliesse mit Amen!

This great hymn by Joachim Neander, sometimes called the "Paul Gerhardt of the Calvinists," based essentially on Psalm 103:1–6 and Psalm 150, first appeared in his *A und Ω. Joachimi Neandri Glaub- und Liebes-übung* (Bremen, 1679). As the soul's ardent praise to God, it is one of the most beloved such hymns in German and English-speaking countries alike. Personal in nature throughout, it is a hymn appropriate for birthdays and other festive occasions in the life of the individual Christian as well as for celebrations in the life of the Church.

The translation, based on that published by Catherine Winkworth in her *Chorale Book for England* (1863)—in which she combined the thoughts of the original stanzas 3 and 4 into a single third stanza—is, except for one change, the text prepared by the Inter-Lutheran Commission on Worship for inclusion in *Lutheran Book of Worship* (1978). That change appears in the final line of stanza 3, where *Lutheran Worship* has changed *LBW*'s "If with his love he befriend you" to "As with his love he befriends you."

LOBE DEN HERREN. Neander successfully adapted the tune that first appeared in *Ander Theil des Ernewerten Gesangbuch* (Stralsund, 1665), where it was set to a text by Ahasuerus Fritsch, "Hast du denn, Liebster, dein Angesicht gänzlich verborgen." No composer's name is given; some historians believe it to be by Johann Flittner (1618–78); others are of the opinion that it was based on an earlier secular tune. The tune appeared as follows (Zahn 1912a):

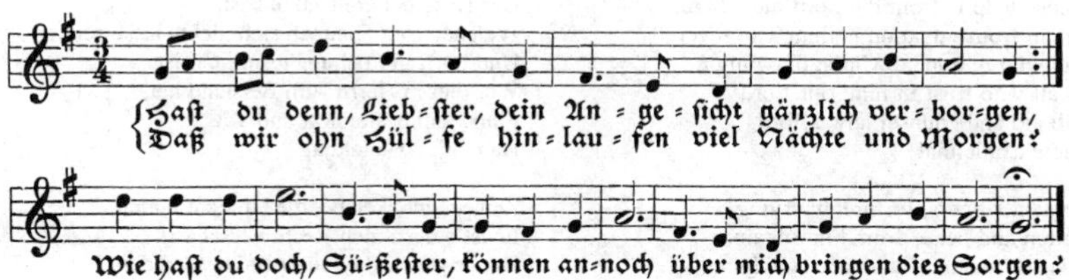

When it appeared with Neander's text in 1679, it was in a considerably different form (Zahn 1912c):

The present form of the tune is basically that found in Winkworth's *Chorale Book for England*, whose music was edited by William S. Bennett and Otto Goldschmidt, except that instead of even notes on "Now to his temple draw near" (st. 1, for example), the rhythm on "temple draw near" is | ♩. ♪ ♩ | 𝅗𝅥. | .

The harmonization is from the *Choralbuch* (1955).

PRAISE THE ALMIGHTY 445

Praise the Almighty, my soul, adore him!
Yes, I will laud him until death;
With songs and anthems I come before him
As long as he allows me breath.
From him my life and all things came;
Bless, O my soul, his holy name.
Alleluia, alleluia!

Lobe den Herren, o meine Seele!
Ich will ihn loben bis in Tod;
Weil ich noch Stunden auf Erden zähle,
Will ich lobsingen meinem Gott.
Der Leib und Seel' gegeben hat,
Werde gepriesen früh und spat.
Hallelujah! Hallelujah!

Trust not in rulers; they are but mortal; Earth-born they are and soon decay. Vain are their counsels at life's last portal, When the dark grave engulfs its prey. Since mortals can no help afford, Place all your trust in Christ, our Lord. Alleluia, alleluia!	Fürsten sind Menschen, vom Weib geboren, Und kehren um zu ihrem Staub; Ihre Anschläge sind auch verloren, Wenn nun das Grab nimmt seinen Raub. Weil denn kein Mensch uns helfen kann, Rufe man Gott um Hilfe an! Halleluja! Halleluja!
Blessed, oh, blessed are they forever Whose help is from the Lord most high, Whom from salvation nothing can sever, And who in hope to Christ draw nigh. To all who trust in him, our Lord Will aid and counsel now afford. Alleluia, alleluia!	Selig, ja selig ist der zu nennen, Des Hilfe der Gott Jakobs ist, Welcher vom Glauben sich nichts lässt trennen Und hofft getrost auf Jesum Christ. Wer diesen Herrn zum Beistand hat, Findet am besten Rat und Tat. Halleluja! Halleluja!
Penitent sinners, for mercy crying, Pardon and peace from him obtain; Ever the wants of the poor supplying, Their faithful God he will remain. He helps his children in distress, The widows and the fatherless. Alleluia, alleluia!	Zeigen sich welche, die Unrecht leiden, Er ist's der ihnen Recht verschafft. Hungrigen will er zu Speis' bescheiden, Was ihnen dient zur Lebenskraft. Die hart Gebundnen macht er frei, Seine Genad' ist mancherlei. Halleluja! Halleluja!
Praise, all you people, the name so holy Of him who does such wondrous things! All that has being, to praise him solely, With happy heart its amen sings. Children of God, with angel host Praise Father, Son, and Holy Ghost! Alleluia, alleluia!	Rühmet, ihr Menschen, den hohen Namen Des, der so grosse Wunder tut! Alles, was Odem hat, rufe Amen! Und bringe Lob mit frohem Mut. Ihr Kinder Gottes, lobt und preist Vater und Sohn und Heil'gen Geist! Halleluja! Halleluja!

This great hymn of praise and trust by Johann D. Herrnschmidt first appeared in Freylinghausen's *Neues geistreiches Gesangbuch* (Halle, 1714). Based largely on Psalm 146, it there appeared in eight stanzas.

The translation by Alfred E. R. Brauer first appeared in the Australian *Lutheran Hymn-Book* (1925). Brauer's stanzas 1–4, a combination of stanzas 5–6, and stanza 8 appeared, slightly altered, in *The Lutheran Hymnal* (1941). Stanzas 1–3, and 8, in altered and updated form, were included in *Lutheran Book of Worship* (1978). *Lutheran Worship* (1982) preserves these but adds Brauer's stanza 5, altered and updated, as stanza 4.

LOBE DEN HERREN, O MEINE SEELE, a sturdy, moving tune, first appeared in the 1665 Appendix to *Neu-vermehrte Christlich Seelenharpf* (Ansbach, 1664), where it was set to the hymn, "Lobet den Herren, aller Herren." This anonymous tune has been inseparably united with Herrnschmidt's text ever since its appearance in the above-mentioned Freylinghausen hymnal. Zahn (4995) lists numerous interesting versions of the tune as they appeared in various hymnals.

The harmonization is by Carl F. Schalk as prepared for and included in *Lutheran Book of Worship* (1978).

JEHOVAH, LET ME NOW ADORE YOU 446

Jehovah, let me now adore you,
For where, Lord, is there such a God as you?
With joyful songs I come before you;
Oh, let your Spirit teach my heart anew
To praise you in his name through whom alone
Our songs can please you through your blessed Son!

O Father, draw me to my Savior
That your dear Son may draw me then to you;
Your Spirit guide my whole behavior
And sanctify my sense and reason too
That, Lord, your peace may not from me depart
But wake sweet melodies within my heart.

While, Lord, my heart, in prayer ascending,
Through your own Holy Spirit reaches you;
Your heart, O Father, kindly bending,
Sends answ'ring love my spirit to renew,
Rejoicing my petition to fulfill
Which I have made according to your will.

And what your Spirit, Lord, has taught me
To seek from you must needs be such a prayer
As you will grant through him who bought me
And raise me up to be your child and heir.
In Jesus' name I boldly seek your face
And take from you, my Father, grace for grace.

Dir, dir Jehova, will ich singen,
Denn wo ist doch ein solcher Gott wie du?
Dir will ich meine Lieder bringen,
Ach gib mir deines Geistes Kraft dazu,
Dass ich es tu' im Namen Jesu Christ,
So wie es dir durch ihn gefällig ist.

Zeuch mich, o Vater, zu dem Sohne,
Damit dein Sohn mich wieder zieh' zu dir;
Dein Geist in meinem Herzen wohne
Une meine Sinne und Verstand regier',
Dass ich den Frieden Gottes schmeck' und fühl
Und dir darob im Herzen sing' und spiel'.

Wenn dies aus meinem Herzen schallet.
Durch deines Heil'gen Geistes Kraft und Trieb,
So bricht dein Vaterherz und wallet
Ganz brünstig gegen mich vor heisser Lieb',
Dass mir's die Bitte nicht versagen kann,
Die ich nach deinem Willen hab' getan.

Was mich dein Geist selbst bitten lehret,
Das ist nach deinem Willen eingericht't
Und wird gewiss von dir erhöret,
Weil es im Namen deines Sohns geschieht,
Durch welchen ich dein Kind und Erbe bin.
Und nehme von dir Gnad' um Gnade hin.

Bartholomäus Crasselius' German hymn, originally in eight stanzas, was first published in *Geistreiches Gesangbuch* (Halle, 1697), and later appeared in Freylinghausen's *Geistreiches Gesangbuch* (1704). Among the prayer-hymns that originated in Pietism, this is undoubtedly one of the finest.

The translation is an altered and updated form of Catherine Winkworth's that appeared in her *Chorale Book for England* (1863).

DIR, DIR, JEHOVAH is an altered form of the tune set to "Wer nur den lieben Gott lässt walten" in the *Musikalisches Handbuch, der geistlichen Melodien* (Hamburg, 1690) by an unknown composer. It has been coupled with this text since its first publication in Freylinghausen's *Geistreiches Gesangbuch* (1704). In England the tune was altered to long meter for "Ride On, Ride On in Majesty" (*LW* 105) and is called WINCHESTER NEW (*TLH* 161). It is also known variously as FRANKFORT or CRASSELIUS.

The harmonization was prepared by George Leonard, a *nom de plume* of Paul G. Bunjes.

447 SONGS OF PRAISE THE ANGELS SANG

It must be remembered that until the Oxford Movement, which began about 1833, was well advanced, the Church of the England was reluctant to admit hymns in corporate worship; metrical psalmody was still the vogue (see essay: Metrical Psalms, p. 825). In some dioceses hymns were episcopally forbidden; there was organized, vocal opposition to anything but psalmody. In others, hymns were introduced without episcopal sanction, usually by the inclusion of hymns in psalm collections. Such was Thomas Cotterill's *A Selection of Psalms and Hymns for public and private use* (Newcastle, 1810). Popularly received and happily used in some dioceses, six more editions quickly followed. When, however, in 1819, the eighth and enlarged edition appeared, a book that Cotterill and James Montgomery had compiled together—it contained 60 of James Montgomery's hymns, including "Songs of praise the angels sang"—a storm of protest ensued over the use of hymns at St. Paul's Sheffield, where Cotterill had been incumbent for two years, as well as throughout the diocese. Suit was brought against Cotterill in the diocesan court at York for using hymns (of human composure) in the worship services. Archbishop Harcourt, sensing that the situation demanded a compromise, offered to approve a new edition if the eighth were withdrawn. That was done, and the following new edition, smaller and less markedly evangelical, prepared under the eye of Archbishop Harcourt and at his expense, was supplied to the Sheffield church, each copy bearing the inscription: "The gift of his grace the Lord Archbishop of York." Suffice it to state that, following the York settlement, new hymn books appeared apace. The Church of England soon reached the stage of substantial recognition of hymnody.

As to the hymn of Montgomery's under discussion, it is to be noted how neatly the expression "songs of praise" occurs no less than 10 times! What might appear disquietingly redundant when read, becomes something like that of a fugal subject when sung (Stanley Osborne). In this splendid hymn, one of numerous hymns of Montgomery's rich legacy to the church, he calls upon the Christian, as Polack says, "to praise God and to follow the example of the angels, who sang in praise of the creation (Job 38:7) and at the birth of Christ (Luke 2:14) and who will sing at the final consummation of all things." Most hymnals have changed the third line of stanza 1, originally reading "When Jehovah's work begun," to "When creation was begun" as given here. Other slight alteration have been made. While included in the general category of Praise and Adoration, the hymn would appear appropriate also for the Sunday(s) after Christmas.

INNOCENTS (DURHAM, ALL SAINTS', AN ANCIENT LITANY). There has not been a little speculation as to the origin of this bright little tune. Some have attributed it to Handel (*LW* 53); others to Samuel Webbe the Younger (1740–1816). In its present form it appeared in *The Parish Choir* (1850), a monthly journal of The Society for Promoting Church Music (1846–51), an organization of Anglican Church musicians connected with the Oxford Movement interested in improving the choir music in corporate worship. Erik Routley (*Companion to Congregational Praise*) credits the tune to William Monk (*LW* 405, 490), editor of *The Parish Choir* (1850) and music editor of *Hymns Ancient and Modern* (1861). The name AN ANCIENT LITANY is the result of the tune's having been set to "Little flowers of martyrdom," a hymn for the festival of The Holy Innocents, December 28. Some music editors appear to consider the tune of French origin.

The harmonization is an altered form of that in *The Lutheran Hymnal* (1941).

OH, THAT I HAD A THOUSAND VOICES 448

Oh, that I had a thousand voices To praise my God with thousand tongues! My heart, which in the Lord rejoices, Would then proclaim in grateful songs To all, wherever I might be, What great things God has done for me.	O dass ich tausend Zungen hätte Und einen tausendfachen Mund, So stimmt' ich damit in die Wette Vom allertiefsten Herzensgrund Ein Loblied nach dem andern an Von dem, was Gott an mir getan!
O all you pow'rs that he implanted, Arise, keep silence now no more; Put forth the strength that God has granted! Your noblest work is to adore. O soul and body, join to raise With heartfelt joy our maker's praise.	Was schweigt ihr denn, ihr meine Kräfte? Auf, auf, braucht allen euren Fleiss Und stehet munter im Geschäfte Zu Gottes, meines Herren, Preis! Mein Leib und Seele, schicke dich Und lobe Gott herzinniglich!
You forest leaves so green and tender That dance for joy in summer air, You meadow grasses, bright and slender, You flow'rs so fragrant and so fair, You live to show God's praise alone. Join me to make his glory known.	Ihr grünnen Blätter in den Wäldern, Bewegt und regt euch doch mit mir! Ihr schwanken Gräschen in den Feldern, Ihr Blumen, lasst doch eure Zier Zu Gottes Ruhm belebet sein Und stimmet lieblich mit mir ein!
All creatures that have breath and motion, That throng the earth, the sea, the sky, Come, share with me my heart's devotion, Help me to sing God's praises high. My utmost pow'rs can never quite Declare the wonders of his might.	Ach alles, alles, was ein Leben Und einen Odem in sich hat, Soll sich mir zum Gehilfen geben, Denn mein Vermögen ist zu matt Die grossen Wunder zu erhöhn, Die allenthalben um mich stehn.
Creator, humbly I implore you To listen to my earthly song Until that day when I adore you, When I have joined the angel throng And learned with choirs of heav'n to sing Eternal anthems to my king.	Ach nimm das arme Lob auf Erden, Mein Gott, in allen Gnaden hin! Im Himmel soll es besser werden, Wenn ich bei deinen Engeln bin. Da sing' ich dir in höhern Chor Viel tausend Halleluja vor.

This cento from Johann Mentzer's original 15-stanza hymn "O dass ich tausend Zungen hätte" first appeared in Johann A. Freylinhausen's (*LW* 182, et al.) *Geistreiches Gesangbuch* (Halle, 1704). One of the most widely popular hymns in the 19th century, it supplanted many of the great hymns of praise stemming from the Reformation. As for the occasion of this great hymn, some have opined that Mentzer wrote it in 1704 after finding a new wife, his wife having died when giving birth to twins, thus leaving him with six small children. Lauxmann (Koch, *Geschichte des Kirchenlieds*) has it that he wrote it after his house was destroyed by fire. In any case, it reflected the fact that the Christian has reason to give thanks and praise to God in all circumstances. Certain expressions in the hymn appear to indicate that he was acquainted with a hymn by Johann Scheffler (*LW* 375, 379) beginning "Hätt ich jetzt hunderttausand Zungen," included in his *Heilige Seelenlust* (Breslau, 1657), a book highly regarded in pietistic circles. When Mentzer addresses and calls upon inanimate objects of nature to praise God—forest leaves, grasses, flowers, etc.—a poetic device called apostrophic (cf. for instance Psalm 148), he seems to have taken a page from a hymn by Johann Franck (*LW* 233, et al.):

> Alle Gräslein auf den Feldern,
> alles, was in Gärten blüht,
> alle Blümlein in den Wäldern,
> alles, was man grünen sieht,
> muss, wenn gleich die Menschen schweigen
> deinen Ruhm und Macht bezeugen.

The translation of this cento, consisting of stanzas 1, 3, 4, 5, and 15, was prepared by the Inter-Lutheran Commission on Worship for inclusion in *Lutheran Book of Worship* (1978). It is based on the composite translation in *The Lutheran Hymnal* (1941), derived from those stanzas of H. H. Mills in his *Horae Germanicae* (1845) and from those of Catherine Winkworth in her *Lyra Germanica* (first series, 1855).

O DASS ICH TAUSEND ZUNGEN HÄTTE. This fine chorale tune, appearing in Johann Balthasar König's *Harmonischer Liederschatz* (Frankfurt, 1738) set to Angelus Silesius' "Ach sagt mir nichts von Gold und Schätzen" (Zahn 2806) is undoubtedly the work of König. When some years later it was set to Mentzer's text by Johann Christoph Kühnau (1735–1822), German composer and conductor, it became inseparably wedded to it.

The harmonization is from the *Württembergisches Choralbuch (1953).*

449 WHEN IN OUR MUSIC GOD IS GLORIFIED

This jubilant hymn, one of very few that speaks about church music and its significance in worship, is the hymn by which F. Pratt Green is perhaps best known in America. Written in 1972 at the request of eminent hymnologist John Wilson, who wanted such a text for music festivals set to Charles Stanford's tune ENGELBERG (see *LBW* 189), it has become widely popular for such occasions. Hence it has been included in many hymn books, set to various tunes, and used as an anthem text by a number of American composers. It appeared on the front cover of *The Hymn* (July 1973) and was included in *New Church Praise* (Edinburgh, 1975). In its orginal form the first line read "When in man's music, God is glorified," juxtaposing "man" and "God" to emphasize the unusualness of the next phrase.

FREDERICKTOWN was written and harmonized by Charles R. Anders for inclusion in *Lutheran Book of Worship* (1978). The tune is named after his birthplace.

In *Rejoice in the Lord* (1985), hymnal of the Reformed Church in America, editor Erik Routley suggests SINE NOMINE (*LW* 191) as an alternate tune for the above text, then with only two alleluias.

THE GOD OF ABRAHAM PRAISE 450

It was Moses Maimonides (1130–1205), renowned Hebrew scholar, who summed up the essential doctrines of Judaism in 15 articles of faith. Two centuries later, Daniel ben Judah, a liturgical poet and writer who lived in Rome in the mid-14th century, arranged these articles in metrical form, which became known as the *Yigdal*, or Doxology. This was, and still is, sung antiphonally by precentor and congregation in Jewish worship, usually at the close of the Sabbath eve service and other festivals. Julian (pp. 1149–50) gives the Hebrew text plus the following literal translation:

> Extolled and praise be the living God, who exists unbounded by time.
> He is one of unparalleled unity, invisible and eternal.
> Without form or figure—incorporeal—holy beyond conception.
> Prior to all created things,—the first, without date or beginning.
> Lo! He is Lord of the world and all creation, which evince his greatness and dominion.
> The flow of his prophetic spirit has he imparted to men selected for his glory.
> No one has appeared in Israel like unto Moses; a prophet, beholding his glorious semblance.
> God has given the true law to his people, by the hands of his trusty prophet.
> This law God will never alter nor change for any other.
> He perceives and is acquainted with our secrets—sees the end of all things at their very beginning.
> He rewards man with kindness according to his work; dispenses punishment to the wicked, according to his misdeeds.
> At the end of days by him appointed, will he send our Messiah, to redeem those who hope for final salvation.
> God, in his great mercy, will recall the dead to life. Praised be his glorious name for evermore.

Hearing the *Yigdal* sung in the Great Synagogue, Duke's Place, London, Thomas Olivers, a Wesleyan preacher from Wales, while staying as a guest at the house of John Bakewell in Westminster, made an English metrical version of it in 12 stanzas, which he published on an undated leaflet (c. 1770) entitled *A Hymn to the God of Abraham. In Three Parts. Adapted to a splendid air, sung by the Priest, Signior Leoni . . . at the Jew's Synagogue in London*. Regarding this metrical version Oliver said to a friend, "Look at this, I have rendered it from the Hebrew, giving it, as far as I could, a Christian character." Later, Charles Wesley included this text in his *A Pocket Hymn Book for the use of Christians of all denominations* (London, 1785). In his *Christian Psalmist*

(1825) James Montgomery (*LW* 50, et al.) says of it, "There is not in our language a lyric of more majestic style, more elevated thought, or more glorious imagery." Earl Selbourne describes it as "An ode of singular power." The text here given represents stanzas 1 through 7 plus 9 and 11 of those edited by the Inter-Lutheran Commission on Worship for inclusion in *Lutheran Book of Worship* (1978).

YIGDAL (LEONI) is an adaptation of the tune to which *Yigdal* was sung when Thomas Olivers first heard it. It was Olivers who stipulated that the tune be called LEONI for Meyer Lyon, or Meier Leon (1751-97), cantor of Duke's Place synagogue, who transcribed the tune for him. It is through this version that both text and tune passed into Christian hymnody. Of sustained quality and grandeur, few present-day hymnals omit it, although invariably in greatly reduced number of stanzas.

The harmonization is from *The Hymnal 1940* of the Protestant Episcopal Church.

451 IMMORTAL, INVISIBLE, GOD ONLY WISE

Walter Chalmers Smith, distinguished minister and scholar in the Free Church of Scotland, included this hymn in his *Hymns of Christ and the Christian Life* (1867), based on 1 Timothy 1:17: "Now to the King eternal immortal, invisible, the only God, be honor and glory for ever and ever." Besides a number of rhythmic irregularities, the hymn as it appeared in this collection included a curious printer's error: the third line of stanza 3 read, "Thy blossom and flourish only are we." W. Garrett Horder (1841–1922), editor of *Congregational Hymns* (1884), persuaded Smith to make some alterations for his collection, to its improvement.

The fourth stanza as it now appears is a cento of the original's final three stanzas, which read:

> Today and tomorrow with thee still are now;
> Nor trouble, nor sorrow, nor care, Lord, hast thou;
> Nor passion doth fever, nor age can decay,
> The same God for ever as on yesterday.
>
> Great Father of glory, Father of light,
> Thine angels adore thee, veiling their sight;
> But of all thy good graces this grace, Lord, impart—
> Take the veil from our faces, the veil from our heart.
>
> All laud we would render; O help us to see,
> 'Tis only the splendor of light hideth thee;
> And now let thy glory to our gaze unroll
> Through Christ in the story, and Christ in the soul.

A few other changes have been made in the process of updating the text for inclusion in *Lutheran* Worship (1982).

ST. DENIO. Known in Wales as JOANNA, this hearty and straightforward tune is based on a Welsh folk melody popular in the late 18th and early 19th century. First associated with "Can Mlynedd i 'Nawr'" ("A Hundred Years from Now") and "Y Gog Lwydlas," a song about the cuckoo, it was apparently adapted for use as a hymn tune by John Roberts, editor of *Caniadau y Cyssegr* (Songs for Worship), 1839. There the tune was called PALESTINA. Prior to Roberts' simplification, the melody, according to the *Journal of the Welsh Folk Song Society* I (1911), ran thus:

Gustav Holst set the melody to "Immortal, invisible" in *The English Hymnal* (1905). It is not known why it was given the name ST. DENIO, the Latin form of "St. Dennis."

The harmonization from *Worship Supplement* (1969) is by Richard W. Hillert.

SING PRAISE TO GOD, THE HIGHEST GOOD 452

Sing praise to God, the highest good,
The author of creation,
The God of love who understood
Our need for his salvation.
With healing balm our souls he fills
And ev'ry faithless murmur stills:
To God all praise and glory!

What God's almighty pow'r has made,
In mercy he is keeping;
By morning glow or evening shade
His eye is never sleeping;
Within the kingdom of his might
All things are just and good and right:
To God all praise and glory!

We sought the Lord in our distress;
O God, in mercy hear us.
Our Savior saw our helplessness
And came with peace to cheer us.

Sei Lob und Ehr' dem höchsten Gut,
Dem Vater alle Güte,
Dem Gott, der alle Wunder tut,
Dem Gott, der mein Gemüte
Mit seinem reichen Trost erfüllt,
Dem Gott, der allen Jammer stillt.
Gebt unserm Gott die Ehre!

Was unser Gott geschaffen hat,
Das will er auch erhalten,
Darüber will er früh und spät
Mit seiner Gnade walten.
In seinem ganzen Königreich
Ist alles recht und alles gleich.
Gebt unserm Gott die Ehre!

Ich rief dem Herrn in meiner Not:
Ach Gott, vernimm mein Schreien!
Da half mein Helfer mir vom Tod
Und liess mir Trost gedeihen.

For this we thank and praise the Lord,
Who is by one and all adored:
To God all praise and glory!

Drum dank', ach Gott, drum dank' ich dir!
Ach danket, danket Gott mit mir!
Gebt unserm Gott die Ehre!

All who confess Christ's holy name,
Give God the praise and glory.
Let all who know his pow'r proclaim
Aloud the wondrous story.
Cast ev'ry idol from its throne,
For God is God, and he alone:
To God all praise and glory!

Ihr, die ihr Christi Namen nennt,
Gebt unserm Gott die Ehre!
Ihr, die ihr Gottes Macht bekennt,
Gebt unserm Gott die Ehre!
Die falschen Götzen macht zu Spott.
Der Herr ist Gott, der Herr ist Gott!
Gebt unserm Gott die Ehre!

This buoyant hymn of praise and thanksgiving, with its beautiful, brief refrain, was written by Johann J. Schütz and first appeared in a tract entitled *Christliches Gedenkbüchlein zur Beförderung eines anfangenden neuen Lebens* that he published in 1673 at Frankfurt-am-Main. Based on Deuteronomy 32:3–4, the original hymn consisted of nine stanzas. Here the cento includes stanzas 1, 3–4, and 8.

Although Schütz tended toward the mystic in Pietism and espoused a separatistic attitude, these are not evident in this lively hymn. The author envisions a congregation about him whom he instructs and encourages to join him in praise to God. Small wonder that this hymn was soon included in many German hymnals.

The translation by Frances E. Cox appeared in the *Lyra Eucharistica* in 1864 and in her own *Hymns from the German* of the same year. Originally beginning with "All praise to God who reigns above," the text was adapted for *Lutheran Book of Worship* (1978) and taken over from there into *Lutheran Worship* (1982).

LOBT GOTT DEN HERREN, IHR. This forceful, swinging, invigorating tune was originally composed by Melchior Vulpius for the hymn beginning with "Lobt Gott den Herren, ihr Heiden all" by Joachim Sartorius (c. 1548–1600). This text, a new-testamentized paraphrase of Psalm 117 for the Epiphany of our Lord, first appeared in Sartorius' book entitled *Der Psalter gesangeweise* (Breslau, 1591). Vulpius' tune was coupled to this text in his *Ein schön geistlich Gesangbuch* (Jena, 1609). This felicitous union is retained in the presently used *Evangelisches Kirchengesangbuch* of the Lutheran territorial churches in Germany. The interesting rhythmic pattern of this tune, namely, ♩♩♩|♩. ♪♩|♩♩♩|𝅗𝅥. , as with other Vulpius tunes and those of his contemporaries, a pattern so characteristic of many social songs of the 16th century, makes such chorales a joy to sing and easy to remember.

The harmonization is from *The Lutheran Hymnal* (1941).

453 MY SOUL, NOW PRAISE YOUR MAKER

My soul, now praise your Maker!
Let all within me bless his name
Who makes you full partaker
Of mercies more than you dare claim.

Nun lob, mein' Seel', den Herren,
Was in mir ist, den Namen sein!
Sein' Wohltat tut er mehren,
Vergiss es night, O Herze mein!

Forget him not whose meekness
Still bears with all your sin,
Who heals your ev'ry weakness,
Renews your life within;
Whose grace and care are endless
And saved you through the past;
Who leaves no suff'rer friendless
But rights the wronged at last.

He offers all his treasure
Of justice, truth, and righteousness,
His love beyond our measure,
His yearning pity o'er distress;
Nor treats us as we merit
But sets his anger by.
The poor and contrite spirit
Finds his compassion nigh;
And high as heav'n above us,
As break from close of day,
So far, since he has loved us,
He puts our sins away.

For as a loving mother
Has pity on her children here,
God in his arms will gather
All those who him like children fear.
He knows how frail our powers,
Who but from dust are made.
We flourish as the flowers,
And even so we fade;
The wind but o'er them passes,
And all their bloom is o'er.
We wither like the grasses;
Our place knows us no more.

His grace remains forever,
And children's children yet shall prove
That God forsakes them never
Who in true fear shall seek his love.
In heav'n is fixed his dwelling,
His rule is over all;
You hosts with might excelling,
With praise before him fall.
Praise him forever reigning,
All here who hear his Word—
Our life and all sustaining.
My soul, oh, praise the Lord!

Hat dir dein' Sünd vergeben
Und heilt dein' Schwachheit gross,
Errett't dein armes Leben,
Nimmt dich in seinen Schoss,
Mit rechtem Trost beschüttet,
Verjüngt dem Adler gleich.
Der Kön'g schafft Recht, behütet
Die leiden in sein'm Reich.

Er hat uns wissen lassen
Sein herrlich Recht und sein Gericht,
Dazu sein' Güt, ohn' Massen,
Es mangelt an Erbarmung nicht.
Sein'n Zorn lässt er wohl fahren,
Straft nicht nach unsrer Schold,
Die Gnad' tut er nicht sparen,
Den Blöden ist er hold.
Sein' Güt' ist hoch erhaben
Ob den'n, die fürchten ihn.
So fern der Ost vom Abend,
Ist unsre Sünd' dahin.

Wie sich ein Mann erbarmet
Über sein' junge Kinderlein,
So tut der Herr uns Armen,
So wir ihn kindlich fürchten rein.
Er kennt das arm' Gemächte
Und weiss, wir sind nur Staub,
Gleichwie das Gras, von Rechte,
Ein' Blum' und fallend Laub.
Der Wind nur drüber wehet,
So ist es nimmer da:
Also der Mensch vergehet,
Sein End', das ist ihm nah.

Die Gottesgnad' alleine
Bleibt stet und fest in Ewigkeit
Bei seiner lieben G'meine,
Die steht in seiner Furcht bereit,
Die seinen Bund behalten.
Er herrscht in Himmelreich.
Ihr starken Engel, waltet
Sein's Lobs und dient zugleich
Dem grossen Herrn zu Ehren
Und treibt sein heil'ges Wort,
Mein Seel' soll auch vermehren
Sein Lob an allem Ort.

This hymn by Johann Gramann (Graumann or Poliander) was written, according to the great Lutheran theologian Martin Chemnitz, one of the authors of the Formula of Concord, at the request of Albrecht the Elder, Duke of Prussia, a follower of Luther's and staunch supporter of the Reformation. Incidently, Chemnitz was for a time the duke's librarian in Königsberg. Albrecht reportedly asked for a hymn based on his favorite psalm, Psalm 103, a beautiful psalm in praise of the God of all grace. The result, in the words of W. G. Polack, "is without question one of our most majestic and fervent hymns of praise, one that should be in the repertory of every Lutheran congregation." The hymn is also important in that it constitutes the first significant German metrical setting of a psalm, a type of versification that had been begun and popularized by Clement Marot (*LW* 399), scholar and favorite poet at the French court of Francis I (see essay: Metrical Psalms, p. 825). To the pious, humble Duke Albrecht, who served his people and carried on his work not without some opposition and vexation, this hymn must have been of matchless encouragement and consolation. Composed in Königsberg as early as 1530, by 1548 someone had already added a fifth stanza, a stanza that still today is included in the *Evangelisches Kirchengesangbuch* of the Lutheran territorial churches in Germany.

First printed about 1540 at Nürnberg as a broadsheet, it was included in Hans Kugelmann's *Concentus novi* (1540) in four stanzas.

The translation, prepared by the Inter-Lutheran Commission on Worship for inclusion in *Lutheran Book of Worship* (1978), is an altered and updated form of that by Catherine Winkworth in her *Chorale Book for England* (1863).

The hymn was used by Gustavus Adolphus April 24, 1632, during the Thirty Year's War as well as at the first restored Protestant worship service in Augsburg. At the conclusion of that war, October 25, 1648, it was sung in thanksgiving by the residents at Osnabrück, Westphalia.

NUN LOB, MEIN SEEL. This tune appeared in Kugelmann's *Concentus novi* (1540) coupled to Gramann's text, from which its name is derived. As in the case of nearly all of Kugelmann's tunes, this is one of three hymn tunes drawn from the 16th-century love song, "Weiss mir ein Blumlein blaue."

The harmonization was prepared by Wilhelm Quampen, a *nom de plume* of Paul G. Bunjes.

454 BEFORE JEHOVAH'S AWESOME THRONE

This hymn, a metrical paraphrase of Psalm 100, first appeared in Isaac Watts's *Psalms of David Imitated* (1719). Originally in six stanzas, the first stanza read:

> Sing to the Lord with joyful Voice;
> Let every Land his Name adore;
> The British Isles shall send the Noise
> Across the Ocean to the Shore.

Only stanza 3 of this hymn as here given in updated form is by Watts. With the exception of the updating of pronouns, a slight change in stanza 4, and the change of "awful" to "awesome," the other stanzas given here represent the revision by John Wesley (*LW* 280, 362) included in the *Collection of Psalms and Hymns* published at Charlestown in 1736.

OLD HUNDREDTH. For comments on the tune see hymn 216.
The harmonization is by Paul G. Bunjes.

REJOICE, O PILGRIM THRONG 455

Edward H. Plumptre wrote this splendid hymn, based on Psalm 20:5 and Philippians 4:4, for the annual choir festival at Peterborough Cathedral in May 1865 and included it in the second edition of his *Lazarus and Other Poems* (1864). Its first appearance in a hymnal was in the 1868 Appendix to *Hymns Ancient and Modern* (1861). Originally in 11 stanzas, beginning "Rejoice, ye pure in heart," it has been widely used as a processional or recessional hymn. The text was prepared by the Inter-Lutheran Commission on Worship for inclusion in *Lutheran Book of Worship* (1978).

MARION was composed by Arthur H. Messiter for this hymn text and named after his mother. First published in the *Hymnal with Music as Used in Trinity Church* (New York, 1893), edited by Messiter while serving at Trinity as organist-choirmaster, it constitutes the only setting for Plumptre's text in the majority of denominational hymnals in the United States, though some hymnals have begun using the sturdy tune VINEYARD HAVEN written by Richard W. Dirksen in 1974.
The harmonization is from the *Service Book and Hymnal* (1958).

GOD BROUGHT ME TO THIS TIME AND PLACE 456

God brought me to this time and place Surrounded by his favor. He guarded all my nights and days, His kindness did not waver. His peace as sentinel he gave My spirit's health and joy to save. To this day he has blessed me.	Bis hieher hat mich Gott gebracht Durch seine grosse Güte; Bis hieher hat er Tag und Nacht Bewahrt Herz und Gemüte; Bis hieher hat er mich geleit't, Bis hieher hat er mich erfreut, Bis hieher mir geholfen.
All honor, thanks, and praise to you, O Father, God of heaven, For mercies ev'ry morning new, Which you have freely given. Inscribe this on my memory: My Lord has done great things for me; To this day he has blessed me.	Hab Lob und Ehre, Preis und Dank Für die bisher'ge Treue, Die du, o Gott, mir lebenslang Bewiesen täglich neue! In mein Gedächtnis schreib' ich an: Der Herr hat grosse Ding' getan An mir und mir geholfen.
Oh, help me ever, God of grace, Through ev'ry time and season, At ev'ry turn, in ev'ry place—	Hilf ferner auch, mein treuer Hort, Hilf mir zu allen Stunden! Hilf mir an all und jedem Ort,

Redemptive love the reason.
Through joy and pain and final breath
By Jesus' life and saving death
Help me as you have helped me.

Hilf mir durch Jesu Wunden;
Hilf mir im Leben, Tod und Not
Durch Christi Schmerzen, Blut und Tod:
Hilf mir, wie du geholfen!

This hymn of praise by Emilie Juliane, countess of Schwarzberg-Rudolstadt, still popular today in the Lutheran territorial churches in Germany, first appeared in her devotional book *Tägliches Morgen-, Mittags- und Abend- Opffer* (Rudolstadt, 1699), to be sung on "Wednesdays after the meal." Clearly in evidence as its basis are such Scripture references as 1 Samuel 7:12: "Then Samuel took a stone and set it up between Mizpah and Shen. He named it Ebenezer, saying, 'Thus far has the Lord helped us' "; Psalm 126:3: "The Lord has done great things for us, and we are filled with joy"; and perhaps Revelation 5:13b: "To him who sits on the throne and to the Lamb be praise and honor and glory and power, for ever and ever."

The translation is by F. Samuel Janzow.

ALLEIN GOTT IN DER HÖH. For comments on this tune see hymn 215.

The harmonization is by Wilhelm Quampen, a *nom de plume* of Paul G. Bunjes.

457 OH, BLESS THE LORD, MY SOUL

This hymn by Isaac Watts, a metrical paraphrase of Psalm 103:1–7, first appeared in his *Psalms of David Imitated* (London, 1719). Written in short meter (66 86)—the other two being common meter (86 86) and long meter (88 88)—it is the least used pattern in the English psalters (see essay: Metrical Psalms, p. 825) because it leaves no room for wordiness or expansion of thought in the first line. The abruptness of its first line, however, usually attracts attention, most often in the form of exhortation, as here: "Oh, bless the Lord, my soul."

This hymn is sometimes confused with a hymn by James Montgomery (*LW* 50, et al.), which also begins with the same opening line.

ST. THOMAS. For comments on this tune and its harmonization see hymn 12.

The harmonization is from *Lutheran Book of Worship* (1978), slightly altered.

458 OH, WORSHIP THE KING

This famous hymn by Robert Grant, originally in six stanzas, is based on William Kethe's paraphrase of Psalm 104 in the Anglo-Genevan Psalter of 1561, beginning with "My soule, praise the Lord, Speake good of his Name." Grant's text first appeared in Edward Bickersteth's *Christian Psalmody* (1833). A few alterations have occurred over the years in the use of this hymn. Stanza 6, line 4 originally read ". . . shall lisp to thy praise." Moreover, the entire text has been updated in *Lutheran Worship*.

For shear literary grace and beauty and grand sweep of structure, this undoubtedly ranks among the finest hymns in the English language. Associated with the early 19th-century Romanticists, Grant cared about the beauty and expressiveness of words, of rhyme and meter. Notice, for example, the visual-verbal images: "Pavilioned in splendor and girded with praise," "Whose robe is the light, whose canopy space," and "His chariots of wrath, the deep thunderclouds form." It is regrettable to note the rather frequent omission of Grant's final stanza of praise and adoration in some recent hymnals.

"Oh, worship the King" is a rather unusual blend of both metrical psalmody (see essay: Metrical Psalms, p. 825) and its free use. The first three stanzas are a careful versification of the opening verses of Psalm 104; the last three are freely developed thoughts—God's care, love, and providence to human beings, the crowning jewels of his creation—based on the remaining verses of the psalm.

HANOVER, named after George III, of the house of Hanover, when he ascended the British throne, is a moving tune also variously known by other names—BROMSWICH, ALIFF STREET, ST. MICHAEL'S, TALLE'S (a misspelling of TALLIS), and PSALM 149. It first appeared anonymously in *A Supplement to the New Version of the Psalms by Dr. Brady and Mr. Tate* (sixth edition, 1708), edited by William Croft. Although now universally credited to Croft, for many years it was attributed to Handel, despite the fact that Handel didn't arrive in England until two years after the tune's first publication. The popularity of the tune was greatly increased by its inclusion in *Hymns Ancient and Modern* (1861).

Croft's tunes are important from the historical standpoint, for they represent the earliest examples of the English psalm tune as distinguished from the Genevan; they require quicker movement in singing, and the glorious rhythmic impulse of HANOVER and its triple meter delightfully mark and exhibit its distinct originality.

The setting is from *The Hymn Book* (1971) of the Anglican Church of Canada and the United Church of Canada, slightly altered.

FORTH IN THE PEACE OF CHRIST 459

This notable recessional hymn by James Quinn first appeared with this tune in *Hymns for Celebration* (London, 1979). Based as it is on 1 Peter 2:9 and Revelation 5:10, it speaks of the life of a Christian as king, priest, and prophet in a sound, biblical and effectively poetic manner.

LLEDROD, or LLANGOLLEN, is an impressive old Welsh tune of uncertain origin that first appeared in *Llyfr Tonau Cynnulleidfaol* (1859), a Welsh hymnal. Its cheerful, vigorous, and unusual and spirited rhythm complements the text rather well. Routley finds it to be a tune that in the third line bursts "the bounds of the meter" (*The Music of Christian Hymnody*).

460 WHEN MORNING GILDS THE SKIES

When morning gilds the skies,
My heart awaking cries:
May Jesus Christ be praised!
When evening shadows fall,
This rings my curfew call:
May Jesus Christ be praised!

When mirth for music longs,
This is my song of songs:
May Jesus Christ be praised!
God's holy house of prayer
Has none that can compare
With "Jesus Christ be praised!"

To him, my highest and best,
I sing when love-possessed:
May Jesus Christ be praised!
Whate'er my hands begin,
This blessing shall break in:
May Jesus Christ be praised!

No lovelier antiphon
In all high heav'n is known
Than "Jesus Christ be praised!"
There to th'eternal Word
Th'eternal psalm is heard:
Oh, Jesus Christ be praised!

Let all of humankind
In this their concord find:
May Jesus Christ be praised!
Let all the earth around
Ring joyous with the sound:
May Jesus Christ be praised!
Sing, sun and stars of space,
Sing, all who see his face,
Sing, "Jesus Christ be praised!"
God's whole creation o'er,
Today and evermore
Shall Jesus Christ be praised!

Beim frühen Morgenlicht
Erwacht mein Herz und spricht,
Gelobt sei Jesus Christus!
So sing ich früh und spät,
Bei Arbeit und Gebet,
Gelobt sei Jesus Christus!

Was tönt der schönste Klang
Der lieblichste Gesang?
Gelobt sei Jesus christus!
In Gottes heiligem Haus
Sprech ich vor allem aus,
Gelobt sei Jesus Christus!

Ihm, meinem höchsten Gut,
Sing ich in Liebesglut,
Gelobt sei Jesus Christus!
Bei jedem Anbeginn
Ruf ich mit Herz und Sinn,
Gelobt sei Jesus Christus!

Im Himmel selbst erschallt,
Mit heiligem Gewalt!
Gelobt sei Jesus Christus!
Des Vaters ewigem Wort,
Ertönet ewig dort:
Gelobt sei Jesus Christus!

Ihr Menschenkinder all
Singt laut im Jubelschall:
Gelobt sei Jesus Christus!
Rings um den Erdenkreis,
Ertöne Gott zum Preis:
Gelobt sei Jesus Christus!
Singt Himmel, Erd' und Meer,
Und aller Engel Heer:
Gelobt sei Jesus Christus!
Es schalle weit und breit,
In Zeit und Ewigkeit:
Gelobt sei Jesus Christus!

Bäumker (IV, No. 45) indicates that this joyful hymn of praise, originally in German, was included in the *Katholisches Gesangbuch für den öffentlich Gottesdienst im Miszthume Würzburg* (1828). The fact that it is identified with several opening lines, namely, "Beim frühen Morgenlicht," "Wach ich fröh Morgens auf," "Wach ich am

Morgen auf," is strong evidence for its possible earlier existence. The translation by Robert Bridges, slightly altered, appeared in *The Yattendon Hymnal* (1899), of which he was editor in collaboration with Harry Ellis Wooldridge. The text reminds one of Psalm 65: 8b: ". . . where morning dawns and evening fades you call forth songs of joy."

The opening line should not limit the use of this hymn to morning occasions. For other situations the hymn may well be given the title "May Jesus Christ Be Praised!"

LAUDES DOMINI. Joseph Barnby originally wrote this tune to Edward Caswall's translation of this German hymn text. Among the seven Barnby tunes in *Lutheran Worship*, this tune, with its verve and vitality, is, in the estimation of this writer, easily the best.

The harmonization is from the *Service Book and Hymnal* (1958).

PRAISE GOD, FROM WHOM ALL BLESSINGS FLOW 461

This doxological text is stanza 5 of *LW* 478.

OLD HUNDREDTH. For comments on this tune see hymn 216.

The harmonization here used is from the *Württembergisches Choralbuch* (1953).

462 THE DAY IS SURELY DRAWING NEAR

The day is surely drawing near
When Jesus, God's anointed,
In all his power shall appear
As judge whom God appointed.
Then fright shall banish idle mirth,
And hungry flames shall ravage earth
As Scripture long has warned us.

The final trumpet then shall sound
And all the earth be shaken,
And all who rest beneath the ground
Shall from their sleep awaken.
But all who live will in that hour,
By God's almighty, boundless pow'r,
Be changed at his commanding.

May Christ our intercessor be
And through his blood and merit
Read from his book that we are free
With all who life inherit.
Then we shall see him face to face,
With all his saints in that blest place
Which he has purchased for us.

O Jesus Christ, do not delay,
But hasten our salvation;
We often tremble on our way
In fear and tribulation.
Oh, hear and grant our fervent plea;
Come, mighty judge, and set us free
From death and ev'ry evil.

Es ist gewisslich an der Zeit,
Dass Gottes Sohn wird kommen
In seiner grossen Herrlichkeit,
Zu richten Bös' und Frommen.
Dann wird das Lachen werden teu'r,
Wenn alles wird vergehn in Feu'r,
Wie Petrus davon schreibet.

Posaunen wird man hören gehn
An aller Welt ihr Ende,
Darauf bald werden auferstehn
All' Toten gar behende;
Die aber noch das Leben han,
Die wird der Herr von Stunden an
Verwandeln und verneuen.

Derhalben mein Fürsprecher sei,
Wenn du nun wirst erscheinen,
Und lies mich aus dem Buch frei,
Darinnen stehn die Deinen,
Auf dass ich samt den Brüdern mein
Mit der geh' in den Himmel ein,
Den du uns hast erworben.

O Jesu Christ, du machst es lang
Mit deinem Jüngsten Tage!
Den Menschen wird auf Erden bang
Von wegen vieler Plage.
Komm doch, komm doch, du Richter gross,
Und mach uns in Genaden los
Von allem Übel! Amen.

The great medieval sequence, "Dies irae, dies illa" ("Day of Wrath, O Day of Mourning," *TLH* 607), generally credited to Thomas de Celano (c. 1200–55), friend and biographer of Francis of Assisi (c. 1182–1226), furnished the basis for this anonymous, freely translated seven-stanza hymn, one of two hymns that appeared together in 1565, beginning with "Es ist gewisslich an der Zeit." Having come to the attention of Bartholomäus Ringwaldt, Lutheran pastor at Langenfeld, Germany, his interest in Christ's second coming, the result of his study of Revelation, prompted him to revise the hymn, a revision that appeared in his *Handbüchlin. Geistliche Lieder und Gebetlein* (Frankfurt-an-der-Oder, 1586) with the heading "A hymn about the Day of Judgment, improved by Bartholomäus Ringwaldt." The hymn became very popular and was frequently sung by congregations and individual Christians amid the horrors of the Thirty Years' War (1618–48). The final stanza in particular became firmly imprinted in the prayerful hearts of many.

The translation was prepared by the Inter-Lutheran Commission on Worship for inclusion in *Lutheran Book of Worship* (1978). It is an altered and updated form of that by Philip A. Peter that appeared in the *Evangelical Lutheran Hymnal* (1880).

ES IST GEWISSLICH (or NUN FREUT EUCH, but not to be confused with the tune at *LW* 150 and 353) is the later Ionian parallel tune set to "Nun freut euch liebe Christen g'mein," which appeared in Joseph Klug's *Geistliche Lieder* (Wittenberg, 1535, perhaps already in the extant 1529 edition). It is considered a recast of the old folk tune, "Wach auf, meins Herzen ein Schöne, zart allerliebste mein." Tradition has it that Luther noted it after hearing it sung by an itinerant artisan.

The harmonization is from the *Württembergisches Choralbuch* (1953).

THE CLOUDS OF JUDGMENT GATHER 463

The clouds of judgment gather,
The time is growing late;
Be sober and be watchful,
Our judge is at the gate:
The judge who comes in mercy,
The judge who comes in might
To put an end to evil
And diadem the right.

Hora novissima, tempora pessima sunt; vigilemus.
ecce minaciter imminet arbiter ille supremus,—
imminet, imminet, ut mala terminet, aequa coronet,
recta remuneret, anxia liberet, aethera donet.

Arise, O true disciples;
Let wrong give way to right,
And penitential shadow
To Jesus' blessed light:
The light that has no evening,
That knows no moon or sun,
The light so new and golden,
The light that is but one.

Curre, vir optime; lubrica reprime, praefer honesta,
fletibus angere, flendo merebere caelica festa
luce replebere iam sine vespere, jam sine luna;
lux nova lux ea, lux erit aurea, lux erit una.

The home of fadeless splendor,
Of blooms that bear no thorn,
Where they shall dwell as children
Who here as exiles mourn;
The peace of all the faithful,
The calm of all the blest,
Inviolate, unfading,
Divinest, sweetest, best.

Patria splendida, terraque florida, libera spinis,
danda fidelibus est ibi civibus, hic peregrinis.
tunc erit omnibus inspicientibus ora Tonantis
summa potentia, plena scientia, pax rata sanctis.

Oh, happy, holy portion,
Relief for all distressed,
True vision of true beauty,
Refreshment for the blest!
Strive now to win that glory,
Toil now to gain that light;
Send hope ahead to grasp it
Till hope be lost in sight.

O sacra potio, sacra refectio, visio pacis,
mentis et unctio, nullaque mentio ventris, edacis!
hac homo mititur, ambulat, utitur, ergo fruetur;
pax rata, pax ea, spe modo, postea re, capietur.

For comments on the text see hymn 309.

The translation of Bernard's hymn here used was prepared by the Inter-Lutheran Commission on Worship for *Lutheran Book of Worship* (1978), based on that by John

Mason Neale which he published in *The Rhythm of Bernard de Morlais, Monk of Cluny, on the Celestial Country* (1858).

DURROW is a traditional Irish tune associated with a County Limerick sea song entitled "Captain Thomson." It is unique in that it is a hexatonic (six-tone) melody—the sixth degree (A♭) of the c minor scale is not used. Moreover, the frequent repetition of certain patterns, the wide range, the skips down from B♭ to g and from f to d, the repeated notes at the end of phrases 2 and 4, give the melody a distinctive quality that will be most readily noticed and enjoyed if, once learned, the congregation is permitted to sing a stanza without accompaniment.

The harmonization was done by William France for *The Hymnbook* (1971) of the United Church and Anglican Church of Canada.

464 A MULTITUDE COMES FROM THE EAST AND THE WEST

A multitude comes from the east and the west
To sit at the feast of salvation
With Abraham, Isaac, and Jacob, the blest,
Obeying the Lord's invitation.
Have mercy upon us, O Jesus!

O God, let us hear when our shepherd shall call
In accents persuasive and tender,
That while there is time we make haste, one and all,
And find him, our mighty defender.
Have mercy upon us, O Jesus!

All trials shall be like a dream that is past;
Forgotten all trouble and mourning.
All questions and doubts have been answered at last,
When rises the light of that morning.
Have mercy upon us, O Jesus!

The heavens shall ring with an anthem more grand
Than ever on earth was recorded;
The blest of the Lord shall receive at his hand
The crown to the victors awarded.
Have mercy upon us, O Jesus!

Der mange skal komme fra Öst og fra Vest,
Og siddes tilbords i Guds Rige
Med Abraham, Isak og Jakob til Gjest
Hos ham, som böd ind os at stige.
Miskunde dig over os, Jesu!

Gud lade os höre med Kjärligheds Brand
Vor Hyrdes hans Lokking saa blide,
At vi maatte skynde os, Kvinde og Mand,
Og sanke os til ham i Tide!
Miskunde dig over os, Jesu!

Da glemmes det Kors, som paa Jorden jeg bar,
Da slukner saa mildelig Sorgen,
Da bliver opklaret, hvad gaadefuldt var,
Da rinder den lyse Dags Morgen.
Miskunde dig over os, Jesu!

Da toner der gjennem den himmelske Hal
En Lovsang, som ikke har Mage.
For Stolen og Lammet de Salige skal
Sin Krone for Kampen modtage.
Miskunde dig over os, Jesu!

This hymn by Magnus B. Landstad, based on the Parable of the Great Banquet (Luke 14:15–24), the Gospel for the Second Sunday after Trinity Sunday in the Old Standard Series, first appeared in his *Udkast til Kirke-Salmebog* (1861). It ranks as one of his best hymns.

The translation, an altered and updated version of that by Peter O. Strömme that appeared in *The Lutheran Hymnary* (1913), was prepared by the Inter-Lutheran Commission on Worship for inclusion in *Lutheran Book of Worship* (1978).

Congregations of the Missouri Synod learned this hymn from its inclusion in *The Lutheran Hymnal* (1941).

DER MANGE SKAL KOMME first appeared anonymously in the *Riddarholmskyrkan handskrivna Koralbok* (1694) and thereafter in *Then Svenska Psalmboken* (Stockholm, 1697), where it was set to "Himmelriket liknas widt tijo jungfruer." A fine tune, it goes well with Landstad's text.

The harmonization is a slightly altered form of that which Paul G. Bunjes prepared for *Lutheran Book of Worship* (1978).

465 OUR FATHER, BY WHOSE NAME

Recognizing the need for a prayer-hymn on the family, F. Bland Tucker wrote this hymn in 1939 for inclusion in *The Hymnal 1940*, the authorized hymnal of the Protestant Episcopal Church, at which time he was a member of the editorial committee. Notice how each stanza addresses a person of the Trinity: Father, Christ, and Spirit.

RHOSYMEDRE (LOVELY). This beautiful Welsh tune is from *Original Sacred Music, Composed and Arranged by the Rev. John Edwards, B. A., Jesus College, Oxford,* published about 1840, the first of two such volumes, where it appeared with an extended alleluia. In *The English Hymnal* (1906) it was called LOVELY; in *Songs of Praise* (1931) RHOSYMEDRE, the name of the Welsh parish in which the composer ministered from 1843 on. Ralph Vaughan Williams (*LW* 59, et al.) wrote a beautiful organ prelude on it as one of *Three Preludes founded on Welsh Hymn Tunes* (1920), the other two being BRYN CALFARIA (*LW* 281) and HYFRYDOL (*LW* 286, 402). The unexpected rhythmic variety in the last two phrases gives RHOSYMEDRE a certain distinctiveness.

The harmonization is from *The Hymnal 1940*.

466 OH, BLESSED HOME WHERE MAN AND WIFE

Oh, blessed home where man and wife Together lead a godly life, By deeds their faith confessing! There many happy days are spent, There Jesus gladly will consent To tarry with his blessing.	I Hus og Hjem, hvor Mand og Viv Bo sammen et gudfrygtigt Liv Med Börn i Tugt og äre, Der leves mangen lyksom Dag, Der vil hos dem med Velbehag Den Herre Kristus väre.
If they have given him their heart, The place of honor set apart For him each night and morrow, Then he the storms of life will calm, Will bring for ev'ry wound a balm, And change to joy their sorrow.	Har du ham givet Själ og Sind, Og er han kjärlig buden ind, Og sat i höiest Säde, Da bliver Levestunden god, Da raader han paa Vaande Bod, Og vender Sorg til Gläde.
And if their home be dark and drear, The cruse be empty, hunger near, All hope within them dying, Let them despair not in distress; See, Christ is there the bread to bless, The fragments multiplying.	Og sidder du i mörke Hus Med tomme Fad og törre Krus, Og dine Smaa paa Skjödet, Og ser med Graad den sidste Rest, Naar Nöd er störst, er Hjälpen näst, Hvor han velsigner Brödet.
O Lord, we come before your face; In ev'ry home bestow your grace On children, father, mother. Relieve their wants, their burdens ease, Let them together dwell in peace And love to one another.	Vor Bön idag til ham vi bär: O Herre Jesu, kom og vär Hos Ägtemand og Kvinde! Hjälp deres Smaa i Verden frem, Sign deres Bord og Hus og Hjem, Og lys din Fred derinde!

Magnus B. Landstad included this beautiful presentation of the Christian home having Christ at its head in his *Udkast til Kirke-Salmebog* (1861). It is based on John 2:1–11, the Gospel for the Second Sunday after the Epiphany in the Old Standard Series of pericopes.

The translation by Ole T. Arneson, written in 1908 and included in *The Lutheran Hymnary* (1913), is given here in slightly altered and updated form.

KOMMT HER ZU MIR. For comments on this tune and its harmonization see hymn 261.

OH, BLEST THE HOUSE 467

Oh, blest the house, whate'er befall,
Where Jesus Christ is all in all!
For if he were not dwelling there,
How dark and poor and void it were!

Oh, blest that house where faith is found
And all in charity abound
To trust their God and serve him still
And do in all his holy will!

Oh, blest that house; it prospers well!
In peace and joy the parents dwell,
And in their children's lives is shown
How richly God can bless his own.

Then here will I and mine today
A solemn cov'nant make and say:
Though all the world forsake his Word,
My house and I will serve the Lord.

Wohl einem Haus, wo Jesus Christ
Allein das all in allem ist!
Ja, wenn er nicht darinnen wär',
Wie elend wär's, wie arm und leer!

Heil, wenn sich Mann und Weib und Kind
In einem Glaubenssin verbind't
Zu dienen ihrem Herr n und Gott
Nach seinem Willen und Gebot!

Wohl solchem Haus! Denn es gedeiht;
Die Eltern werden hoch erfreut,
Und ihren Kindern sieht man's an,
Wie Gott die Seinen segnen kann.

So mach' ich denn zu dieser Stund'
Samt meinem Hause diesen Bund:
Trät' alles Volk von Jesu fern:
Ich und mein Haus stehn bei dem Herrn!

This hymn was written in eight stanzas by Christoph Carl Ludwig von Pfeil. Entitled "Delightful Picture of a House that Serves the Lord. On the Parents of Jesus," it was written for the First Sunday after the Epiphany, 1746, and first published in the *Evangelisches Gesangbuch* (Memmingen, 1782).

Catherine Winkworth shortened the hymn to six stanzas in her *Chorale Book for England* (1863) translation by omitting stanza 6 of the original and combining the thoughts of stanzas 3 and 4 into one.

WO GOTT ZUM HAUS. For comments on this tune and its harmonization see hymn 340.

468 FEED YOUR CHILDREN, GOD MOST HOLY

Feed your children, God most holy,
Comfort sinners poor and lowly;
You our Bread of Life from heaven,
Bless the food you here have given!
As these gifts the body nourish,
May our souls in graces flourish
Till with saints in heav'nly splendor
At your feast our thanks we render.

Speis uns, o Gott, deine Kinder,
Tröste die betrübten Sünder,
Sprich den Segen zu den Gaben,
Die wir jetzund vor uns haben,
Dass sie uns zu diesem Leben
Stärke, Kraft und Nahrung geben,
Bis wir endlich mit den Frommen
Zu der Himmelsmahlzeit kommen!

A popular prayer in the homes of German Christians for asking the blessing before meals, as well as a regularly sung prayer at social gatherings of Christians, this hymn by Johann Heermann first appeared in his *Geistlicher Poetischer Erquickstunden Fernera Fortsetzung* (Nürnberg, 1656) without lines 7–8. These were added by someone when the entire single-stanza hymn appeared in the *Halberstädter Gesangbuch* (1712).

The translation, here in updated form, is that which appeared in *The Lutheran Hymnal* (1941), based on a translation in the *Australian Lutheran Hymn-Book* (1925).

SCHMÜCKE DICH. For comments on this tune see hymn 239.

The setting is from *The Lutheran Hymnal* (1941).

469 HOLY FATHER, IN YOUR MERCY

This hymn was written by Isabella S. Stevenson on the day when her invalid brother sailed for South Africa in 1869. Privately printed, it came into the hands of an officer on *H. M. S. Bacchante*, the ship on which King George and his brother made an around-the-world trip in 1881–82. Used there in public worship, the royal princes sent home a copy to their mother. As a result it was sung by the royal family at home during this trip. The hymn was included in the *Supplement* (1889) to *Hymns Ancient and Modern* (1861) and it won new popularity in World War I.

The text has been somewhat altered in the process of updating the pronouns referring to the deity.

STEPHANOS. For comments on the tune see hymn 408.

The harmonization is from *The Hymnal 1940* of the Protestant Episcopal Church.

LORD JESUS CHRIST, THE CHILDREN'S FRIEND 470

This fine hymn on Christian elementary education by Henry L. Lettermann is the result of his lifelong interest in and devotion to that noble cause.

TALLIS' CANON. For comments on this tune and its harmonization see hymn 484.

SHEPHERD OF TENDER YOUTH 471

This hymn is a free paraphrase by Henry M. Dexter of one of the earliest known Christian hymns, "A Hymn to Christ the Savior," ascribed to Clement of Alexandria and appended to his treatise called Παιδαγωγός ("The Instructor"). The original hymn is actually a series of titles and metaphors addressed to Christ, some taken from Scripture, some Clement's own invention. The original begins Στόμιον πώλων ἀδαῶν ("Bridle of colts untamed").

While working on a sermon in 1846 on the topic "Some prominent characteristics of early Christians," based on the text "Remember the days of old, consider the generations long past" (Deut. 32:7a), Dexter thought interest in the subject might be quickened by turning the ancient poem into a hymn and having it sung by his congregation (Congregational) in the service. His English text, here updated, first appeared in *The Congregationalist*, of which he was editor, on December 21, 1849.

ITALIAN HYMN. For comments on this tune see hymn 169.
The harmonization was prepared by Ralph Schultz.

LET CHILDREN HEAR THE MIGHTY DEEDS 472

This is Issac Watts' version of the first few verses of Psalm 78, a hymn that was included in his *Psalms of David* (1719). Along with Psalms 105, 106, and 136, Psalm 78 is one of the four great national hymns in the Psalter, the purpose of which is to rehearse God's hand in the early history of the nation so that future generations might be warned against a repetition of past failures. Watts' text has here been slightly altered, updated, and expanded with the addition of stanza 4, contributed by Bernard Schumacher for inclusion in *The Lutheran Hymnal* (1941).

NUN DANKET ALL. For comments on this tune and its harmonization see hymn 200.

473 YOU PARENTS, HEAR WHAT JESUS TAUGHT

You parents, hear what Jesus taught
When little ones to him were brought:
Forbid them not, but heed my plea
Permitting them to come to me.

Obey your Lord and let his truth
Be taught your children in their youth
That they in church and school may dwell
And learn their Savior's praise to tell.

For if you love them as you ought,
To Christ your children will be brought.
If thus you place them in his care,
All in your family well shall fare.

Höret, ihr Eltern, Christus spricht:
Den Kindlein sollt ihr wehren nicht,
Dass sie sich meinen Armen nahn,
Denn ich will segnend sie empfahn.

Gehorchet ihm und bringt sie her,
Dass man von Jugend auf sie lehr'
In Kirchen und in Schulen wohl,
Wie man Gott gläubig ehren soll!

Habt ihr sie lieb mit treuem Sinn,
So führet sie zu Jesu hin.
Wer dies nicht tut, ist ihnen feind,
Wie gross auch seine Liebe scheint.

This hymn by Ludwig Helmbold, the most versatile, prolific German poet in behalf of Christian education, first appeared in his *Crepundia Sacra oder christliche Liedlein* (Mühlhausen, 1578). Originally in six stanzas, it is here a cento, consisting of stanzas 1, 4–5 of the author's original, in the rather free translation that William M. Czamanske prepared for inclusion in *The Lutheran Hymnal* (1941).

HERR JESU CHRIST, DICH ZU UNS WEND. For comments on the tune see hymn 201.
The setting is from *The Lutheran Hymnal* (1941).

474 HOW SHALL THE YOUNG SECURE THEIR HEARTS

This is a slightly altered and updated version of the hymn by Isaac Watts that appeared in *The Lutheran Hymnal* (1941). Originally in eight stanzas, it first appeared in Watts' *The Psalms of David Imitated* (London, 1719).

ST. PETER (CHRIST CHURCH). For comments on the tune see hymn 279.
The harmonization is from *The Hymnal 1940* of the Protestant Episcopal Church.

475 GRACIOUS SAVIOR, GENTLE SHEPHERD

This hymn demonstrates the sometimes strange textual evolution of various hymns. The nucleus of this hymn is in some verses by Jane E. Leeson, talented poet of children's hymns, in her *Hymns and Scenes of Childhood* (1842), a book that included "Shepherd in thy bosom folded," "Loving Shepherd of thy sheep," and "Infant sorrow, infant weakness." The text "Gracious Savior, gentle Shepherd," appearing in Jonathan Whittemore's Baptist *Supplement to All Hymn-Books* (London, 1850), was evidently constructed by him from the aforementioned hymns. It appears here in altered and updated form.

SIEH, HIER BIN ICH. This fine chorale tune is from the *Geistreiches Gesangbuch* (Darmstadt, 1698), where it was set to Joachim Neander's (*LW* 198, 206) "Sieh hier bin ich, Ehrenkönig."

Fred L. Precht prepared the harmonization for inclusion in *Lutheran Worship* (1982).

I PRAY YOU, DEAR LORD JESUS 476

I pray you, dear Lord Jesus,
My heart to keep and train
That I your holy temple
From youth to age remain.
Oh, turn my thoughts forever
From worldly wisdom's lore;
If I but learn to know you,
I shall not want for more.

O Jesu, gid du vilde
Mit Hjerte danne saa,
Det baade aarl' og silde
Dit Tempel väre maa!
Du selv min Hjerne vende
Fra Verdens kloge Flok,
Og lär mig dig at kjende,
Saa har jeg Visdom nok!

This represents the final stanza of "Hvor storer dog den Gläde," a hymn by Thomas Kingo to the child Jesus in the temple that first appeared in 1699. An ordinance of the Norwegian Church authorities, dated October 10, 1819, stipulated that this stanza be sung at church dedication services, a custom still observed in some areas.

Norman A. Madson prepared the translation for *The Lutheran Hymnal* (1941), a text that appears here in slightly altered and updated form.

JEG VIL MIG HERREN LOVE is from Hartnack Zinck's *Koral-Melodier* (1801) for the *Evangelisk-Christelige Psalme-Bog*, where it was set to H. Thomissön's text beginning with the same words.

Melvin Rotermund prepared the harmonization for inclusion in *Lutheran Worship* (1982).

477 LORD, HELP US EVER TO RETAIN

Lord, help us ever to retain
The Catechism's doctrine plain
As Luther taught the Word of truth
In simple style to tender youth.

Help us your holy Law to learn,
To mourn our sin and from it turn
In faith to you and to your Son
And Holy Spirit, Three in One.

Hear us, dear Father, when we pray
For needed help from day to day
That as your children we may live,
Whom you baptized and so received.

Lord, when we fall or go astray,
Absolve and lift us up, we pray;
And through the Sacrament increase
Our faith till we depart in peace.

Herr Gott, erhalt uns für und für
Die reine Katechismuslehr',
Der jungen, einfältigen Welt
Durch deinen Luther vorgestellt:

Dass wir lernen die Zehn Gebot',
Beweinen unsre Sünd' und Not
Und doch an dich und deinen Sohn
Glauben, im Geist erleuchtet schon;

Dich, unsern Vater, rufen an,
Der allen helfen will und kann,
Dass wir als Kinder nach der Tauf'
Christlich vollbringen unsern Lauf;

So jemand fällt, nicht liegen bleib',
Sondern zur Beichte komm' und gläub',
Zur Stärkung nehm' das Sakrament.
Amen, Gott geb' ein selig End'!

Ludwig Helmbold's concern for Christian education and the importance he attached to Luther's Small Catechism prompted this children's hymn, a hymn that appeared in his *Dreiszig Geistliche Lieder auf die Fest durch's Jahr* (Mühlhausen, 1585).

The translation is an altered and updated version of that done by Matthias Loy that appeared in the *Lutheran Hymnal* (1880) of the Ohio Synod.

HERR JESU CHRIST, MEINS. For comments on the tune see hymn 262.

The harmonization is from *The Lutheran Hymnal* (1941), slightly altered.

AWAKE, MY SOUL, AND WITH THE SUN 478

As prebendary of Winchester Cathedral and College, with which he was connected for a time, Thomas Ken prepared a *Manual of Prayers for Use of the Scholars of Winchester College* (1674) in which the schoolboys were told, "Be sure to sing the Morning and Evening Hymn in your chamber devoutly, remembering that the psalmist, upon happy experience, assures you that it is a good thing to tell of the loving kindness of the Lord early in the morning and of his truth in the night season." Since, however, the actual hymn texts—for "morning," "evening," and "midnight"—were not published until their inclusion in the appendix to the second edition of A *Manual of Prayers* in 1695, it is likely that these hymns were first sung from printed manuscripts. The first two, namely, "Awake, My Soul, and with the Sun" and "All Praise to Thee, My God, This Night" (*LW* 484) have enjoyed wide usage in English hymnals, and the familiar doxology for both constitutes perhaps the most famous and frequently sung stanza—to the tune of OLD HUNDREDTH (*LW* 216, et al.)—in the corporate worship of all Christendom. Although there are numerous doxological stanzas in existence (invariably the final stanza of a hymn; but see *LW* 173), this is truly *The Doxology*.

The form of "Awake, My Soul, and with the Sun" here given is an updated cento, the original having consisted of 14 stanzas plus the doxology. Similarly "All Praise to Thee My God, This Night" (*LW* 484) is a cento of the first three stanzas and the concluding doxology of what originally was a hymn of 11 stanzas plus the doxology. Both hymns underwent various revisions and alterations by Ken himself; the latter, especially, has been divided, subdivided, and rearranged in various ways over the years.

MORNING HYMN (MAGDELINE or HIPPOLYTUS). Although John Hawkins, Ken's great-nephew and biographer, says that Ken used to "sing his Morning Hymn to his lute, daily before he put on his clothes," it is not exactly known to what tune or tunes. The tune MORNING HYMN, to which it has been almost inseparably wedded, was not in existence until many years later. Composed by Francois H. Barthélémon for Ken's text at the request of Jacob Duche (1737–98), chaplain of the Female Orphan Asylum, Westminster Bridge Road, London, it was entitled "New Jarusalem" [*sic*] and first published in the Supplement to *Hymns and Psalms Used at the Asylum for Female Orphans printed for W. Gawler, Organist to the Asylum* (n.d., c. 1788). Later it was bound with the original collection.

In *Songs of Praise Discussed* Archibald Jacob says of it:

> The tune attained popularity, probably because its undistinguished phrases, being musical commonplaces, were easy to catch and remember; but on the score of quality, it does not deserve it's fame.

With that the present writer can hardly differ. Popularity and long association with Ken's text, however, prompted its inclusion in *Lutheran Worship* (1982). The noted hymnologist Erik Routley (1917–82) evidently agrees with the assessment of Archibald Jacob. *Rejoice in the Lord* (1985), the hymnal of the Reformed Church in America, of which Routley was editor, sets Ken's text to an English traditional melody called HERONGATE, with MELCOMBE (*TLH* 504) suggested as an alternative. Both are creditable tunes that, included in most current hymnals, unfortunately did not find a place in *Lutheran Worship* for lack of space.

479 O HOLY, BLESSED TRINITY

O holy, blessed Trinity, Divine, eternal Unity, O Father, Son, and Holy Ghost, This day your name be uppermost.	O heilige Dreifaltigkeit, O hochgelobte Einigkeit, Gott Vater, Sohn und Heil'ger Geist, Heut' diesen Tag mir Beistand leist'!
My soul and body keep from harm, And over all extend your arm; Let Satan cause me no distress Nor bring me shame and wretchedness.	Mein' Seel', Leib, Ehr' und Gut bewahr', Dass mir kein Böses widerfahr' Und mich der Satan nicht verletz', Noch mich in Schand' und Schaden setz'!
The Father's love shield me this day; The Son's pure wisdom cheer my way; The Holy Spirit's joy and light Drive from my heart the shades of night.	Des Vaters Huld mich heut' anblick', Des Sohnes Weisheit mich erquick', Des Heil'gen Geistes Glanz und Schein Erleucht' mein's finstern herzens Schrein!
My Maker, hold me in your hand; O Christ, forgiven let me stand; Blest Comforter, do not depart, With faith and love enrich my heart.	Mein Schöpfer, steh mir kräftig bei, O mein Erlöser, hilf mir frei, O Tröster wert, weich nicht von mir, Mein Herz mit Lieb' und Glauben zier'!
Lord, bless and keep me as your own; Lord, look in kindness from your throne; Lord, shine unfailing peace on me By grace surrounded; set me free.	Herr, segne und behüte mich, Erleuchte mich, Herr, gnädiglich! Herr, heb auf mich dein Angesicht Und deinen Frieden auf mich richt!

Martin Behm wrote this splendid morning hymn and published its seven stanzas in his *Kriegesmann, das ist gründlicher Unterricht, wie sich ein Christlicher Kriegsmann verhalten solle* (Leipzig, 1593). Later, in *Centuria secunda precationum rhythmicarum* (Wittenberg, 1608), Behm recast the hymn in eight stanzas. The hymn here given consists of stanzas 1–5 of that recast.

The translation is an altered and updated form of that done by Conrad H. L. Schuette, in the *Lutheran Hymnal* (1880) of the Ohio Synod.

STEHT AUF, IHR LIEBEN KINDERLEIN. For comments on this tune and its harmonization see hymn 327.

CHRIST, WHOSE GLORY FILLS THE SKIES 480

This beautiful morning hymn (though not only for mornings), radiating the joy that dispels all gloom, called by James Montgomery (*LW* 50, et al.) "one of Charles Wesley's loveliest progeny," was first published by the Wesley brothers in *Hymns and Sacred Poems* (1740). Charles Wesley explained his use of "sun of righteousness" by citing Malachi 4:2: "For you who revere my name, the sun of righteousness will rise with healing in its wings." George Eliot, pen name for Mary Ann Evans (1819–80), in *Adam Bede*, the tragic love story in which her father serves as the model character, describes (in chapter 38) how Seth Bede, the young Methodist, on leaving his brother one Sunday morning in February, "walked leisurely homeward, mentally repeating one of his favorite hymns." It was this hymn!

John Wesley (*LW* 280, 362) radically changed the opening stanza to read

> O disclose thy lovely face,
> Quicken all my drooping powers!
> Gasps my fainting soul for grace,
> As a thirsty land for showers;
> Haste, my Lord, no longer stay,
> Come, my Jesus, come away.

The text here given represents the original. Set in the popular and useful trochaic 77 77 77, its combination of strong opening words in the lines as well as its use of antithesis (light and dark) add up to form an excellent hymn. Radiating as it does the true joy that dispels all gloom, few present-day hymnals overlook its inclusion.

RATISBON is the tune that appeared in J. G. Werner's *Choralbuch zu den neuen Sächsischen Gesangbüchern vierstimmig für die Orgel* (Leipzig, 1815) set to the words "Jesu, meines Lebens Leben" (*LW* 94). The tune (Zahn 6801) is undoubtedly, however, considerably older than 1815, and it is possibly derived from a tune by Joachim Neander in his *Choralbuch* of 1680. It is one of the chorale tunes with a distinct name, namely, RATISBON, rather than simply being identified by the opening words of the text to which it might have become coupled. Ratisbon is the early name for Regensburg, Germany, a town located at the junction of the rivers Regen and Danube.

The harmonization is from the *Service Book and Hymnal* (1958).

O SPLENDOR OF THE FATHER'S LIGHT 481

Early testimony, namely, a letter of Fulgentius of Ruspe (d. 533), as well as later writers, such as Bede in the eighth century and Hincmar in the ninth, indicate that the original Latin of this hymn is undoubtedly the work of St. Ambrose. More conclusive than such external evidence, however, is the close similarity in thought and expression to sections in his known works. Mearns in Julian describes this as "a beautiful morning hymn to the Holy Trinity but especially to Christ as the light of the world, and a prayer for help and guidance throughout the day." As such it was anciently used for Lauds (sunrise) on Mondays.

This new, fresh, composite translation was prepared by Gracia Grindal for inclusion in *Lutheran Book of Worship* (1978).

SPLENDOR PATERNAE, named so from the *incipit* of the Latin text, is the plainsong tune not only in general use with this hymn but also with other ferial (week day) hymns sung at Lauds.

The setting is from the *Service Book and Hymnal* (1958).

482 FATHER, WE PRAISE YOU

Father, we praise you, now the night is over,
Active and watchful, standing now before you;
Singing we offer prayer and meditation;
Thus we adore you.

Monarch of all things, fit us for your mansions;
Banish our weakness, health and wholeness sending;
Bring us to heaven, where your saints united
Joy without ending.

All-holy Father, Son, and equal Spirit,
Trinity blessed, send us your salvation;
Yours is the glory, gleaming and resounding
Through all creation.

Nocte surgentes vigilemus omnes,
semper in psalmis meditemur, atque
viribus totis Domino canamus dulciter hymnos.

Ut pio regi pariter canentes
cum suis sanctis mereamur aulam
ingredi coeli, simul et beatam ducere vitam.

Praestet hoc nobis Deitas beata
Patris ac Nati pariterque sancti
Spiritus, cujus reboatur omni gloria mundo.

This hymn is generally attributed or ascribed to Gregory the Great, or Gregory I (fl. 590–604), the last of the church fathers and the first of the popes, although some scholars credit it to Alcuin (1735–1804), the leading intellectual at Charlemagne's court. Included in the Roman, York, Sarum, Aberdeen, and other breviaries, it is generally assigned to Matins (after midnight) or Nocturns during the Trinity Season. It clearly began as a hymn for Sunday nocturns (Saturday night), since "Nocte surgentes" means "rising by night."

Written in the sapphic meter, 11 11 11 5, the favorite of Latin hymn writers, in which each of the 11s is subdivided into a combination of five and six syllables, the five being a combination of a dactyl (´ ˘ ˘) and a trochee (´ ˘), and the six being entirely trochaic (´ ˘ ´ ˘ ´ ˘), the stress of the accented beginnings and trochaic endings in such an arrangement reflects rather intense meditative qualities.

The translation, here given in altered and updated form, was that made by Percy Dearmer for inclusion in *The English Hymnal* (1906).

CHRISTE SANCTORUM. For comments on the tune see hymn 175.
The harmonization was prepared by Carl F. Schalk.

WITH THE LORD BEGIN YOUR TASK 483

With the Lord begin your task; Jesus will direct it. For his aid and counsel ask; Jesus will perfect it. Ev'ry morn with Jesus rise, And when day is ended, In his name then close your eyes; Be to him commended.	Fang dein Werk mit Jesu an, Jesus hat's in Händen. Jesum ruf zum Beistand an, Jesus wird's wohl enden. Steh mit Jesu morgens auf, Geh mit Jesu schlafen, Führ mit Jesu deinen Lauf, Lasse Jesum schaffen!
Let each day begin with prayer, Praise, and adoration. On the Lord cast ev'ry care; He is your salvation. Morning, evening, and at night Jesus will be near you, Save you from the tempter's might, With his presence cheer you.	Morgens soll der Anfang sein, Jesum anzubeten, Dass er woll' dein Helfer sein Stets in deinen Nöten. Morgens, abends und bei Nacht Will er stehn zur Seiten, Wenn des Satans List und Macht Dich sucht zu bestreiten.
With your Savior at your side, Foes need not alarm you; In his pro mises confide, And no ill can harm you. All your trust and hope repose In the mighty master, Who in wisdom truly knows How to stem disaster.	Wenn dein Jesus mit dir ist, Lass die Feinde wüten! Er wird dich vor ihrer List Schützen und behüten. Setz nur das Vertrauen dein In sein' Allmachtshände Und glaub' sicher, dass allein Er dein Unglück wende!
If your task be thus begun With the Savior's blessing, Safely then your course will run, Toward the promise pressing. Good will follow ev'rywhere While you here must wander; You at last the joy will share In the mansions yonder.	Wenn denn deine Sach' also, Mit Gott angefangen, Ei, so hat es keine Not, Wirst dein Zweck erlangen: Es wird folgen Glück und Heil Hier in diesem Leben, Endlich wird dir Gott dein Teil Auch im Himmel geben.

This great hymn of trust in the Lord for his help to cope with life's responsibilities appeared anonymously in *Morgen- und Abendsegen*, published in Waldenburg in 1734.

The translation, prepared by the Inter-Lutheran Commission on Worship for inclusion in *Lutheran Book of Worship* (1978), is an altered and updated version of that done by W. Gustave Polack for *The Lutheran Hymnal* (1941).

FANG DEIN WERK appeared in Kornelius H. Dretzel's (*LW* 224) *Des Evangelischen Zions Musicalische Harmonie* (Nürnberg, 1731), coupled to the text "Schwing dich auf zu deinem Gott." Therein, according to Zahn (6352), the tune appeared thus:

Lutheran Worship, taking its cue from the *Lutheran Book of Worship* and other sources, credits Peter Frank (Franck), Lutheran pastor in Germany, as composer of this notable tune. This is due to the appearance of this tune with Peter Frank's text, "Christus, Christus, Christus ist, dem ich mich ergebe," in Johann Belthazar König's *Harmonischer Lieder-Schatz* (1738). Zahn questions drawing such a conclusion. A brief biography of Peter Frank, however, is included in this volume, largely for completeness.

The harmonization was prepared by Donald A. Busarow for inclusion in *Lutheran Book of Worship* (1978).

ALL PRAISE TO THEE, MY GOD, THIS NIGHT 484

This is Thomas Ken's famous Evening Hymn written along with the Morning Hymn discussed at hymn 478. The opening line originally read "Glory to thee, my God, this night," an opening which some hymnals continue to use.

TALLIS' CANON (also known as BERWICK, BRENTWOOD, EVENING HYMN, or SUFFOLK). About 1561, toward the close of Queen Mary's turbulent reign, Matthew Parker, archbishop of Canterbury, completed his first collection of the Psalms entitled *The whole Psalter translated into English Metre, which contayneth an hundred and fifty Psalmes*. Printed, but promptly suppressed, only a few copies were distributed among the archbishop's friends and, as a result, are today still extant. In sort of an appendix to this book Thomas Tallis furnished nine tunes arranged in four parts, one in each of the church modes (see essay: The Church Modes, p. 832), and one set to the hymn "Veni, creator Spiritus." Moreover, he gave an explanation of each mode. Concerning the eighth mode, that used in the tune now long known as TALLIS' CANON, he said it "goeth milde: in modest haste." Written in strict canon form (see *LW* 254) with the tenor leading, the tune was originally twice as long as now, every section being repeated before proceeding to the next. In Parker's Psalter it was set to his metrical paraphrase of Psalm 67. A facsimile of this is given in *The Hymnal 1940 Companion*, p. 122. The present shortened four-phrase form appeared in Ravenscroft's *Whole Booke of Psalmes* (1621). Its first appearance with Thomas Ken's text was presumably in the *Harmonious Companion* (1732) by Smith and Prellieur.

The harmonization is from the *Pilgrim Hymnal* (1931).

NOW REST BENEATH NIGHT'S SHADOW 485

Now rest beneath night's shadow
The woodland, field, and meadow;
The world in slumber lies.
But you, my heart, awaking
And prayer and music making,
Let praise to your creator rise.

The radiant sun has vanished,
Its golden rays are banished
From dark'ning skies of night;
But Christ, the sun of gladness,
Dispelling all our sadness,
Shines down on us in warmest light.

Now all the heav'nly splendor
Breaks forth in starlight tender

Nun ruhen alle Wälder,
Vieh, Menschen, Städt' und Felder,
Es schläft die ganze Welt;
Ihr aber, meine Sinnen,
Auf, auf, ihr sollt beginnen,
Was eurem Schöpfer wohlgefällt!

Wo bist du, Sonne, blieben?
Die nacht hat dich vertrieben,
Die Nacht, des Tages Feind.
Fahr hin! Ein' andre Sonne,
Mein Jesus, meine Wonne,
Gar hell in meinem Herzen scheint.

Der Tag ist nun vergangen,
Die güldnen Sternlein prangen

From myriad worlds unknown; And we, this marvel seeing, Forget our selfish being For joy of beauty not our own.	Am blauen Himmelssaal; So, so werd' ich auch stehen, Wenn mich wird heissen gehen Mein Gott aus diesem Jammertal.
Lord Jesus, since you love me, Now spread your wings above me And shield me from alarm. Though Satan would devour me, Let angel guards sing o'er me: This child of God shall meet no harm.	Breit aus die Flügel beide, O Jesu, meine Freude, Und nimm dein Küchlein ein! Will Satan mich verschlingen, So lass die Englein singen: Dies Kind soll unverletzet sein!
My loved ones, rest securely, For God this night will surely From peril guard your heads. Sweet slumbers may he send you And bid his hosts attend you And through the night watch o'er your beds.	Auch euch, ihr meine Lieben, Soll heute nicht betrüben Kein Unfall noch Gefahr. Gott lass' euch ruhig schlafen, Stell' euch die güldnen Waffen Ums Bett und seiner Helden Schar.

This famous evening hymn by Paul Gerhardt, a pearl in Lutheran hymnody, first appeared in the second edition of Johann Crüger's *Praxis pietatis melica* (Berlin, 1647). From its very beginning it became one of the most loved and well-known hymns of Christian devotion throughout Germany, the result of its childlike spirit, its simplicity of expression, its sublime language, and its deep Christian perception.

During the so-called Enlightenment in 18th-century Germany, the hymn became the object of much criticism and sarcasm. Regarding stanza 1, it was asked: How can the dead woods rest, which never are awake, and how can the world lie in slumber? We know that when one half of the world retires to sleep the other half awakes from it! Again, in 1780 a new hymnal, tainted with the spirit of the Enlightenment, was introduced in Prussia for corporate worship. When four Lutheran congregations in Berlin objected to the use of this hymnal, they received an exemption, January 18, 1781, with the addition of a personal handwritten note from King Frederick the Great stating, "Anyone can believe what he wishes, as long as he is honest. As for the hymnal, everyone is free to sing 'Now all the woods are sleeping,' or any similar foolish and dumb stuff. But the pastors must not forget to be tolerant, for they will not be prosecuted." Even the conservative Claus Harms (1778–1855), archdeacon of St. Nikolai Church at Keel, in a printed brochure about the new hymnal, said he missed a "kernel of thanks" in the hymn. Actually, the entire hymn is expressive of thanks!

Stanza 4 here given (stanza 8 of the original nine-stanza hymn) has long served as a children's bedtime prayer.

The translation, based on that in *The Lutheran Hymnal* (1941), was prepared by the Inter-Lutheran Commission on Worship for inclusion in *Lutheran Book of Worship* (1978). Here it is a composite of hymns 276 and 282 in that book. One change was made in *Lutheran Worship* (1982) in stanza 5: instead of the lines "Though evil would assail me, Your mercy will not fail me; I rest in your protecting arm," as in *The Lutheran Hymnal*, the Commission on Worship opted for the more literal translation of the German as contained in the *Evangelical Lutheran Hymn-Book* (1912), the first official hymnal in the Synod, reading, "Though Satan would devour me Let angel guards sing o'er me: This child of God shall meet no harm."

O WELT, ICH MUSS DICH LASSEN. For comments on the tune see hymn 85. The harmonization was prepared by Paul G. Bunjes.

O GLADSOME LIGHT, O GRACE 486

O gladsome Light, O Grace
Of God the Father's face,
Eternal splendor wearing:
Celestial, holy, blest,
Our Savior and our guest,
Joyful in your appearing.

Day has not faded quite;
We see the sunset light,
Our evening hymn outpouring,
Father, incarnate Son,
Who our redemption won,
Spirit of both adoring.

Glory to you belongs
And praise of holy songs,
O Three in One, Life-giver;
Therefore, our God most high,
We worship, glorify,
And praise your name forever.

Φῶς ἱλαρὸν ἁγίας δόξης,
᾿Αθανάτου Πατρὸς οὐρανίου,
῾Αγίου, μάκαρος,
᾿Ιησοῦ Χριστέ,
᾿Ελθόντες ἐπὶ τὴν ἡλίου δύσιν,
᾿Ιδόντες φῶς ἑσπερινόν,
῾Υμνοῦμεν Πατέρα καὶ Υἱόν
Καὶ ῞Αγιον Πνεῦμα Θεοῦ.
῎Αξιόν σε ἐν πᾶσι καίροις
῾Υμνεῖσθαι φωναῖς ὁσίαις,
Υἱὲ Θεοῦ,
Ζωὴν ὁ διδούς,
Διὸ ὁ κόσμος σε δοξάζει.

This is one of the oldest Christian hymns extant, dated about 200. St. Basil of Caesarea (d. 379) alludes to it as an old anonymous hymn. The only hymn that might be older is "Shepherd of Tender Youth," the paraphrase of a hymn ascribed to St. Clement of Alexandria (*LW* 471). "O Gladsome Light, O Grace" originated in the Greek Church, where it is still sung at the lighting of the lamps for the service of Vespers and is hence known as the "Candlelight hymn." Notice its use in Evening Prayer (*Lutheran Worship*, pp. 251–52) with the translation beginning "Joyous light of glory".

There are numerous English translations of this hymn, including those made by John Keble ("Hail, gladdening light") and by Longfellow in his *The Golden Legend* (1851). The translation here used is a slightly altered version of that by Robert Bridges, poet laureate of England. He had written it for the congregation at Yattendon, England, to which he belonged, and where he lived and worked as superintendent of music.

NUNC DIMITTIS was composed or adapted by Louis Bourgeois for a metrical paraphrase of the Song of Simeon, or Nunc Dimittis, and included in his *Pseaulmes cinquante de David Roy et Prophete*, published at Lyon in 1547. This admirable melody entered various early Lutheran hymnals and appeared in the *Catholische geistliche Nachtigall* (1666). It was sung in England due to its inclusion in the Anglo-Genevan Psalter of 1558; it was brought back into currency by Bridges' use of it for his translation.

The harmonization is by Claude Goudimel, one of the greatest of 16th-century tonemasters.

487 O TRINITY, O BLESSED LIGHT

O Trinity, O blessed Light, O Unity of princely might: The fi'ry sun is going down; Shed light upon us through the Son.	O Lux beata, Trinitas Et principalis unitas, Iam sol recedit igneus, Infunde lumen cordibus.
To you our morning song of praise, To you our evening prayer we raise; We praise your light in ev'ry age, The glory of our pilgrimage.	Te mane laudum carmine, Te deprecamus vespere; Te nostra supplex gloria Per cuncta laudet saecula.
All glory be to God above And to the Son, the prince of love, And to the Spirit, One in Three! We praise you, blessed Trinity.	Deo Patri sit gloria Eiusque soli Filio Sancto simul cum Spiritu Nunc et per omne saeculum.

By the ninth century this hymn was attributed to St. Ambrose of Milan despite the fact that the hymn had no place in the services of the Milan church. This attribution rests on Hincmar of Rheims' treatise *De una et non Trina Deitate* (1857), wherein this hymn is one of the 12 hymns regarded by the Benedictine editors as undoubtedly being the work of Ambrose. It may actually be an anonymous early Latin composition. Its almost universal use was at Vespers (sunset) on Saturday, and sometimes also at Lauds (sunrise) or Vespers on Trinity Sunday.

The English translation was prepared by Gracia Grindal for inclusion in *Lutheran Book of Worship* (1978). It should be noted that the last line of stanza 1 is almost certainly in error as it reads, strangely suggesting by the word "your" that there is a Son of the Trinity. Changing the word "your" to "the" may perhaps be considered a simple way to rectify the problem.

STEHT AUF, IHR LIEBEN KINDERLEIN. For comments on this tune and its harmonization see hymn 327.

SUN OF MY SOUL, O SAVIOR DEAR 488

Some of the classic hymns of the Christian Church were never intended as hymns by their authors but were devotional poems. Such is the case with "Sun of my soul, O Savior Dear," by the Anglo-Catholic John Keble, taken from his *Christian Year*, which he published anonymously in 1827. The popularity of this devotional book in its simple sincerity, despite its many faults (Wordsworth suggested going over the work with Keble to correct the English), led to numerous poems and centos being used as hymns in various books, of which "Sun of My Soul, O Savior Dear" is perhaps the most widely loved. The poem, originally in 14 stanzas and headed with Luke 24:29, describes the benighted traveler pushing on after the sun has set. The cento in *Lutheran Worship* includes stanzas 3, 7–8, 12–14 in altered and updated form.

HURSLEY is adapted from a melody in the *Katholisches Gesangbuch* (Vienna, c. 1774), where it was set to "Grosser Gott, wir loben dich" (see *LW* 171). Having gone through several variations before reaching its present form, with the last line repeated, in David Weyman's *A Sequel to Melodia Sacra* (Dublin, c. 1844), it first accompanied Keble's words in the *Metrical Psalter* (1855) of W. J. Irons and Henry Lahee.

Keble considered the tune a suitable setting for his hymn, and it has remained a standard despite efforts to replace it. Herbert S. Oakeley (1830–1903) composed another tune, called ABENDS, for this text because of his aversion to HURSLEY. He once wrote:

> One of my reasons for disliking it [HURSLEY] is the resemblance it bears to a drinking song, "Se vuol ballare", in Mozart's *Nozze di Figaro*. As Mozart produced that opera in 1768 he is responsible for the opening strain, which suits his Bacchanalian words very well. But to hear "Sun of my soul, thou Saviour dear" sung to a lively tune, unsuitable to sacred words, often has the effect of driving me out of church.

The tune is named for a town near Winchester, England, where Keble was vicar for 30 years. The harmonization in *Lutheran Worship* (1982) is by Wilhelm Quampen, a *nom de plume* of Paul G. Bunjes.

BEFORE THE ENDING OF THE DAY 489

Before the ending of the day,
Creator of the world, we pray!
Your grace and peace to us allow
And be our guard and keeper now.

Te lucis ante terminum,
Rerum creator, poscimus
Ut solita clementia
Sis praesul ad custodiam.

From evil dreams defend our sight,
From all the terrors of the night,
From all deluding thoughts that creep
On heedless minds disarmed by sleep.

Procul recedant somnia
Et noctium phantasmata,
Hostemque nostrum comprime,
Ne polluantur corpora.

O Father, this we ask be done
Through Jesus Christ, your only Son,
Who with the Holy Ghost and you
Shall live and reign all ages through.
Amen

Praesta, Pater omnipotens,
Per Iesum Christum Dominum,
Qui tecum in perpetuum
Regnat cum Sancto Spiritu.

Long used by the Western Church at Compline, or Prayer at the Close of the Day (see *LW* pp. 263–269), this office hymn, of unknown origin, dates from about the seventh century. Although appearing in the earliest Ambrosian manuscripts, it is not attributed to Ambrose (*LW* 13). Due to its popularity, numerous translations of it have been made. This translation, adapted from that by John Mason Neale in his *The Hymnal Noted* (1852), was prepared by the Inter-Lutheran Commission on Worship for inclusion in *Lutheran Book of Worship* (1978). *Lutheran Worship* (1982), however, has retained Neale's opening line instead of using that in *Lutheran Book of Worship*: "To you, before the close of day."

JAM LUCIS is a simple, syllabic plainsong tune (one of the few such syllabic tunes) with a compass of only four notes, in Mode VI (see essay: The Church Modes, p. 832). Its name is derived from its long association with "Jam Lucis orto sidera" ("Now that the daylight fills the sky," *LBW* 268), a traditional office hymn for Prime. In some English hymnals this tune is arranged in four-part Anglican chant, for instance, in *The Church Hymnary* (London, 1927).

The harmonization is that prepared by Carl F. Schalk for inclusion in the *Worship Supplement* (1969).

490 ABIDE WITH ME

This hymn, originally in eight stanzas, was written by Henry F. Lyte either in 1820, at the death of a friend of the author, or in 1847, just prior to Lyte's own death.

According to T. H. Bindley in a letter to the *Spectator* (October 1925), Lyte visited William Augustus LeHunte in 1820, who on his deathbed kept repeating the words "Abide with me." Lyte wrote the hymn shortly thereafter and gave a copy of it to LeHunte's brother, Sir Francis, from whose estate the manuscript passed into Bindley's hands.

On the other hand, Lyte's family and his gardener, Charles Potter, assert that he wrote the hymn in 1847 on the evening of his last sermon and Holy Communion at Lower Brixham, Sunday, September 5, 1847. He walked out to the cliffs behind Berry Head House that evening to contemplate the ocean, and was reminded by the sunset of Luke 24:29: "Abide with us: for it is toward evening, and the day is far spent" (KJV).

He then wrote the hymn, completing the editing in France, where he died in November. A letter from Lyte to a friend named Julia that same year, in which he enclosed the hymn in leaflet form and referred to it as his "latest effusion," seems to corroborate this story, although the letter was dated August 25, 1847, while he was supposed to have written the hymn on September 5 that year.

Lyte's daughter, in her preface to his posthumously published *Remains*, refers to the latter history, but she does not actually say that he wrote the hymn at that time. It is possible that Lyte wrote "Abide with me" in 1820 but polished it somewhat before finally presenting it for publication in 1847. In any case, its first appearance in printed form was in a leaflet published in September 1847; its popularity is attributed to its appearance in the Church of England's first hymnal, *Hymns Ancient and Modern* (1861).

EVENTIDE. William H. Monk composed this tune for "Abide with Me." Conflicting stories surround the composition as well as the text. Monk's wife claims he wrote it at a time of great sorrow, when he was watching a sunset with her. Other sources state that Monk, the music editor for *Hymns Ancient and Modern* (1861), penned the lines in less than ten minutes' time after a meeting of the hymnal's editorial committee.

"Abide with Me" was originally set to a tune written by the author Henry F. Lyte. His tune was as follows:

It is interesting to note that the melodic line always moves in a direction opposite to that taken by Monk in EVENTIDE.

The harmonization is from the *Service Book and Hymnal* (1958).

NOW THE DAY IS OVER 491

Sabine Baring-Gould wrote this hymn, originally in eight stanzas, in 1865 for the children of Horbury Bridge parish, where he was curate at the time. It was first published in *The Church Times*, February 16, 1867, and thereafter in the Appendix (1888) to the original edition of *Hymns Ancient and Modern* (1861).

MERRIAL is not the tune originally written by Sabine Baring-Gould for his text. Rather, EUDOXIA was the title of the tune that he specifically wrote for this text. Based as it was on a German melody that he had heard as a child but never identified, it was the tune that became, and continues to be, current in most hymnals. *The Lutheran Hymnal* (1941) chose to use it. Its predecessor, however, the *Evangelical Lutheran Hymn-Book* (1912), elected to use MERRIAL by Joseph Barnby. Seeing less merit in EUDOXIA than in MERRIAL, the Commission on Worship chose the latter for use in *Lutheran Worship* (1982).

MERRIAL was written by Joseph Barnby in 1868, and he coupled it to Sabine Baring-Gould's text in his *Original Tunes to Popular Hymns* (1869). Robert G. McCutchan's *Hymn Tune Names* has an interesting observation regarding the title MERRIAL. He notes that "Emmelar" was the title for this tune given in Charles Robinson's *Laudes Domini* (1884). The word was meant to represent M. L. R., the initials of Robinson's daughter, later changed to MERRIAL for "Mary L."

The harmonization is from the *Service Book and Hymnal* (1958).

492 GOD, WHO MADE THE EARTH AND HEAVEN

This is *really* a composite hymn! Stanza 1 is that of Reginold Heber's single-stanza evening hymn from his *Hymns, written and adapted to the Weekly Church Service of the Year* (1827). Richard Whately included this single stanza with a second stanza (here st. 3) in his *Sacred Poetry adapted to the Understanding of Children and Youth* (Dublin, 1838). Whately's stanza is a free translation of the antiphon to the Nunc Dimittis at Compline: "Salva nos, Domine, vigilantes; custodi nos dormientes; ut vigilemus in Christo, et requiescamus in pace." (See *LW* p. 268ff. for a translation of this text.) William Mercer added two stanzas of his own (here sts. 2 and 4) in his *Church Psalter and Hymn Book* (1864).

The altered and updated text was prepared by the Inter-Lutheran Commission on Worship for inclusion in *Lutheran Book of Worship* (1978).

AR HYD Y NOS, meaning "on length of night," or "the livelong night," is the traditional Welsh melody commonly known as "All Through the Night," first appearing in Edward Jones' *Musical Relicks of the Welsh Bards* (Dublin, 1784). The ballad was sung by the harpist with his listeners joining in the refrain "Ar hyd y nos" (see the facsimile in *The Hymnal 1940 Companion* [1949]). Tradition has it that Heber was staying in a Welsh house which maintained a harpist. One evening the harpist played this melody in the hall, and Heber, retiring to a corner, wrote the hymn "God who madest earth and heaven" to be sung to it. His sister Mary is said to have arranged and included it in her choir book at Hodnet Church.

The harmonization by Ralph Vaughan Williams is from *The English Hymnal* (1906).

SING TO THE LORD OF HARVEST 493

This hymn by John S. B. Monsell first appeared in the author's *Hymns of Love and Praise for the Church's Year* (second edition, 1866).

WIE LIEBLICH IST DER MAIEN. Johann Steurlein's tune was originally set to the secular song, "Mit Lieb bin ich umfangen," in 1575. It was first linked with a sacred text in Gregor Gunderreitter's *Davids Himlische Harpffen* (Nürnberg, 1581).

Edward Klammer, former manager of the music division of Concordia Publishing House, encountered this tune on a search for a new Thanksgiving anthem. He relates:

> Back in the 1950s I was studying the contents of *Handbuch der deutschen evangelischen Kirchenmusik* [1941] edited by Konrad Ameln, Christhard Mahrenholz, Wilhelm Thomas, and Carl Gerhardt. . . . I came across the melody and four-part setting of "Wie lieblich ist der Maien." The text is by Martin Behm (1557–1622 [*LW* 79, 479]). We (Concordia Publishing House) needed a new anthem, and that "May-melody" struck me as being a good tune for a Thanksgiving anthem. So I proceeded to look for a text which would fit the meter and the spirit of the melody. I sent both to Healey Willan who composed "Sing to the Lord of Harvest" c. 1954, which turned out to be one of our all-time best sellers. (quoted in Stulken, *Hymnal Companion to the Lutheran Book of Worship*)

The harmonization by Jan O. Bender first appeared in the *Worship Supplement* (1969). Interestingly, Edward Klammer and *Worship Supplement* evidently started something, for the hymn and tune now appears in *The Hymn-Book* (1971) of the Anglican Church of Canada and the United Church of Canada; in *Rejoice in the Lord* (1985) of the Reformed Church in America; and in the *Psalter Hymnal* (1987) of the Christian Reformed Church.

WE PRAISE YOU, O GOD 494

Julia Cady Cory writes regarding the origin of this hymn:

> Years before I was married, the organist of the Brick Presbyterian Church of New York City, knowing of my interest in hymnology, came to me and told me that he had a very fine Netherlands melody associated with most militaristic and unchristian words. He lamented the fact, and requested me to

> write more suitable words, which could be used for the Thanksgiving service at the Brick Church. The hymn, as you see it today, was the result (Hostetler).

The song here described as "militaristic and unchristian" was "Wilt heden nu treten voor God den Heere," a Dutch patriotic song that arose in the long and bitter struggle of the Dutch against their Spanish oppressors, lasting through most of the 16th century. The English translation by Theodore Baker (1851–1934), for many years literary editor and translator for G. Schirmer, Inc., New York City, is still included in some English-language hymnals as "We gather together to ask the Lord's blessing" (82 *EpH* 433, *PH* 21). Cory denies the suggestion that her hymn is based on the Dutch: "[the words] are *not* a paraphrase of any words, but were written 'out of my head' to fit the music."

The first congregational use of the hymn was in 1902 at Brick Church and at New York's Church of the Covenant. A few weeks later the author's father, J. Cleveland Cady, asked his daughter to add a fourth stanza for use at the Christmas service at the Church of the Covenant. This stanza, updated as those above, read:

> Your love you did show us, your only Son sending,
> Who came as a babe and whose bed was a stall,
> His blest life he gave us and then died to save us;
> We praise you, O Lord, for your gift to us all.

KREMSER. The tune for which Cory composed her lyrics is an arrangement by Eduard Kremser, director of a male singing society in 19th-century Vienna, of a Netherland folk melody he found in *Nederlandtsche Gedenck-Clanck* (Haarlem, 1626). Kremser included this arrangement, set to a German translation of "Wilt heden nu treten voor God den Heere" (see above), in his *Sechs altniederländische Volkslieder* (Leipzig, 1877). He ended this piece with the words "Mach uns frei!" for a climactic finale still used by glee clubs today.

The harmonization is from the *Service Book and Hymnal* (1958).

495 COME, YOU THANKFUL PEOPLE, COME

Henry Alford first published this hymn in *Psalms and Hymns* (1844). In his hymnal *The Year of Praise* (1867) he extended the hymn to seven eight-line stanzas. It has gone through many alterations, of which the author frequently complained. He particularly disliked the revisions in *Hymns Ancient and Modern* (1868), and therefore announced that the four stanzas in his *Poetical Works* (1865) constituted the authorized text. The present text, with very slight changes to update the second-person pronouns, is from Alford's *Year of Praise*.

The Hymnal 1940 Companion states,

The English Harvest Festival, for which this was written, corresponds to the American Thanksgiving Day, save that it is a movable feast, varying between villages according to the season. It is a true Harvest Thanksgiving, with farmers and gardeners bringing the best specimens of their produce to decorate the church. Alford describes the American corn vividly in the second stanza, but it is more likely that he had some other grain in mind, for the English equivalent of American corn is maize.

ST. GEORGE'S, WINDSOR. Sir George Job Elvey (1816–1893) composed this tune, which is so named to distinguish it from Henry J. Gauntlett's tune ST. GEORGE. Elvey was organist at St. George's Chapel, Windsor, for 47 years. This tune was first published in H. Thorne's *A Selection of Psalm and Hymn-tunes* (London, 1858), where it was the setting for James Montgomery's (*LW* 50, et al.) "Hark, the Sound of Jubilee."

The harmonization is from *The Hymnal 1940* of the Protestant Episcopal Church.

LORD, TO YOU IMMORTAL PRAISE 496

This harvest hymn, an altered and updated cento from Anna L. Barbauld's nine four-line stanzas, first appeared in W. Enfield's *Hymns for Public Worship* (Warrington, 1772), titled "Praise to God in Prosperity and Adversity." In its altered form all references to "Praise in Adversity" have been deleted. Enfield was a friend of the author's family and a mentor to the author herself.

DIX. For comments on the tune see hymn 75.

The harmonization is an altered form of that at hymn 52 in the *Service Book and Hymnal* (1958).

497 GOD BLESS OUR NATIVE LAND

In 1815 the following patriotic song for Saxony by Siegfried A. Mahlmann was published in Wilhelm Fink's *Zeitung für die elegante Welt*:

Gott segne Sachsenland,
Wo fest die Treue stand
In Sturm und Nacht!
Ew'ge Gerechtigkeit,
Hoch über'm Meer der Zeit,
Die jedem Sturm gebeut,
Schütz' uns mit Macht!

Blühe, du Rautenkranz,
In schöner Tage Glanz
Freudig empor!
Heil, Friedrich August, dir!
Heil, guter König, dir!
Dich, Vater, preisen wir
Liebend im Chor!

Was treue Herzen flehn,
Steigt zu des Himmels Höh'n
Aus Nacht zum Licht!
Der unsre Liebe sah,
Der unsre Thränen sah,
Er ist und huldreich nah,
Verlässt uns nicht!

Gott segne Sachsenland,
Wo fest die Treue stand
In Sturm und Nacht!
Ew'ge Gerechtigkeit,
Hoch über'm Meer der Zeit,
Die jedem Sturm gebeut,
Schütz' uns mit Macht!

Charles T. Brooks, while studying at Harvard Divinity School, prepared a rather free translation of two stanzas in about 1832; John S. Dwight, a Boston music critic, then made alterations to Brooks's text, resulting in a version that appeared in Lowell Mason's (*LW* 115) and George Webb's (*LW* 305) *The Psaltery* (1845).

The text here given is a slightly altered form of that contained in *The Psaltery*, a text which was prepared by the Inter-Lutheran Commission on Worship for inclusion in *Lutheran Book of Worship* (1978). (See Julian, p. 1566, for a complete history of English texts.)

NATIONAL ANTHEM (AMERICA, GOD SAVE THE QUEEN). To unravel the skein regarding the origin of this tune is not an easy task. The text to which it was attached was first published anonymously in the *Harmonia Anglicana* (1743), an earlier impression of the *Thesaurus Musicus* (1744), the first stanza which began with "God save our Lord the King." Both text and tune appeared in *The Gentleman's Magazine* (October 1745) in an arrangement by Thomas Arne, English composer and violinist, and again in the second edition of the *Thesaurus Musicus* (1745), wherein the tune appears almost in its present form. Popularity of the tune is attested by its having been frequently adopted to serve as national anthems, for instance, in Germany in 1760 for "Heil dir im Siegerkranz"; in Austria in 1792 for "Heil! Kaiser Joseph, Heil!" (displaced by an anthem with Haydn's tune in 1797; see AUSTRIA, hymn 294); in the United States with Samuel F. Smith's "My Country, 'tis of thee." Neither have various composers overlooked its felicitous use: Handel in his *Occasional Oratorio* (1746); Beethoven in *The Battle of Vittoria, or Wellington's Victory* (1813), and in his setting for George Thomson in *Twelve Songs of Various Nationality* (Edinburgh, 1815), about which he wrote in his diary: "I must show the British what a Godsend they have in their

'God save the King'"; Carl Maria von Weber in his *Overture of Jubilation* (1818); Brahms in his *Song of Triumph* (1872), to mention but a few.

The harmonization is from the *Service Book and Hymnal* (1958), slightly altered.

O GOD OF LOVE, O KING OF PEACE 498

This is one of the many hymns that the fine hymn writer Henry W. Baker contributed to the epoch-making, first edition of *Hymns Ancient and Modern* (1861), a book produced under his chairmanship. As a hymn for times of war it bore the caption: "The Lord shall give his people the blessing of peace." Its lasting quality is attested by its inclusion in almost every recently-published hymnal.

ACK, BLIV HOS OSS, also called PAX, is the tune coupled to the Swedish text beginning with these words that appeared as below in the *Then Svenska Psalm-Boken* (Stockholm, 1697):

Compared to the jerky quality of this tune, the present form of the tune has a refreshing and expansive smoothness.

Carl F. Schalk prepared the harmonization, originally for inclusion in *Lutheran Book of Worship* (1978).

CHRIST, BY HEAVENLY HOSTS ADORED 499

Although generally not included in hymnals published in the last two decades, this hymn's popularity and use for Thanksgiving and/or the Nation, having appeared in the Synod's previous two official English hymnals—*The Evangelical Lutheran Hymn Book* (1912) and *The Lutheran Hymnal* (1941)—prompted the Commission on Worship to include it in the present hymnal.

This altered and updated cento, from an originally eight-stanza hymn by Henry Harbaugh, pastor of the Reformed persuasion, first appeared in his *Poems* (1860), where it was entitled "A National Litany." As such it fervently and beautifully prays for such things that make for a blessed nation.

ST. GEORGE'S WINDSOR. For comments on this tune and its harmonization see hymn 88.

500 BEFORE YOU, LORD, WE BOW

Francis Scott Key, United States district attorney for three terms, author of "The Star-Spangled Banner," probably wrote this hymn for the Fourth of July celebration of 1832.

The text, slightly altered from the original, was prepared by the Inter-Lutheran Commission on Worship for inclusion in *Lutheran Book of Worship* (1978).

DARWALL'S 148TH. For comments on the tune see hymn 179.

The harmonization is from the *Service Book and Hymnal* (1958), slightly altered.

501 GOD OF OUR FATHERS

Written in 1876 for the Fourth of July centennial celebration in Brandon, Vermont, this hymn was submitted anonymously to the compilers of the 1892 Protestant Episcopal *Hymnal*, with the assurance that the author's name would be given if the hymn were accepted. Daniel C. Roberts, then rector of St. Thomas Episcopal Church in Brandon, was duly given credit for the text.

Alterations were made to update the personal pronouns by the Inter-Lutheran Commission on Worship for inclusion in *Lutheran Book of Worship* (1978). The final two lines of stanza 4 originally read:

> Fill all our lives with love and grace divine,
> And glory, laud, and praise be ever thine.

NATIONAL HYMN was composed by George W. Warren for the above text, to be sung at the celebration of the centennial of the United States Constitution in New York in 1887. It was included in Tucker and Rosseau's *Hymnal Revised and Enlarged* (1894), a music edition of the 1892 Episcopal *Hymnal*.

The harmonization is from the *Service Book and Hymnal* (1958).

LORD, WHILE FOR HUMANKIND WE PRAY 502

Written as a national hymn for England, this hymn was first published by its author, John R. Wreford, "with other loyal and patriotic pieces." It was among the 55 hymns Wreford contributed to J. R. Beard's *Collection of Hymns for Public and Private Worship* (1837), and may have been intended to honor Queen Victoria, who ascended to the throne that year.

Wreford's second stanza has been omitted:

> Our fathers' sepulchers are here,
> And here our kindred dwell,
> Our children, too; how should we love
> Another land so well?

The text above is a slightly altered and updated form of that which appeared in *The Lutheran Hymnal* (1941).

ST. FLAVIAN. For comments on the tune see hymn 342.

The harmonization is from the *Service Book and Hymnal* (1958).

503 NOW THE LIGHT HAS GONE AWAY

This song by Frances R. Havergal appeared in *Songs for Little Singers* (1870), a song she wrote while at Leamington, October 17, 1869. In its quiet simplicity and naivete it reminds one of the numerous little so-called spiritual songs that arose in 19th-century Germany, which, as Nelle says, "stand as a forget-me-not under the rose of the German church hymn."

MÜDE BIN ICH gets its name from a German children's evening song, a German spiritual song, to which it was set in Theodore Fliedner's *Liederbuch für Kleinkinder-Schulen* (Kaiserswerth, 1842). Paul G. Bunjes prepared the setting for *Lutheran Worship* (1982).

504 GO TELL IT ON THE MOUNTAIN

This text was taken over by the Commission on Worship from *Lutheran Book of Worship* (1978). Among several versions of this joyous Negro spiritual (for comments on the Negro spiritual see *LW* 505), this version is the work of John W. Work II as included in *American Negro Songs and Spirituals* (New York, 1940), a collection that he edited. An early traditional version reads:

When I was a seeker
I sought both night and day,
I asked the Lord to help me,
And he showed me the way.

He made me a watchman
Upon a city wall,
And if I am a Christian
I am the least of all.

Interestingly, James Baldwin, a young black veteran of World War II, used this first line for an autobiographical novel in 1953 dealing with problems of the African American in contemporary American life. As a result of its wide acceptance, he became one of America's leading novelists and a brilliant interpreter of racial tensions and conflicts.

GO TELL IT is the traditional tune to this Negro spiritual. While it may, as George Pullen Jackson points out in *White and Negro Spirituals*, bear some resemblance to early white spirituals, it nevertheless is a tune possessing its own individuality and spirit, a tune that young people take great delight in singing.

The harmonization was prepared by Hugh Porter for inclusion in the *Pilgrim Hymnal* (1958), of which he was music co-editor with his wife Ethel F. Porter.

WERE YOU THERE 505

This is one of two Negro spirituals of the four in *Lutheran Book of Worship* (1978) that the Commission on Worship chose to include in *Lutheran Worship* (1982). Today widely recognized as one of America's finest contributions to hymnody, there is hardly a major denominational hymnal that fails to include several examples of the Negro spiritual. Rightly does Margaret Just Butcher state:

> The spirituals, though ostensibly naive and simple, are intrinsically profound. Underneath broken words, childlike imagery, and peasant simplicity, lie an epic intensity and a tragic depth of religious emotion for which the only equal seems to be the spiritual experience of the Jews, the only analogue the Psalms. The spirituals stand as one of the great expressions of religious emotion.

Taken in addition to time-honored hymns, Negro spirituals certainly can help provide a balanced diet for Christian worship. Under the direction of J. W. Work II (*LW* 504), it was the "Jubilee Singers" of Fisk University, Nashville, Tennessee, from 1871–78, who brought these powerful religious songs to the attention of the nation and the world.

Although possibly derived from an earlier white spiritual, songs such as "Have you heard how they crucified our Lord?" and "Saw ye my Savior," most authorities credit "Were you there" to the blacks in slavery. With grace, simplicity, and poignancy this spiritual brings to the mind of each worshiper his/her personal involvement in the events of the Lord's crucifixion for the eternal salvation of the lost and dying world.

WERE YOU THERE. Except for one note, the note on "you" in the last phrase, this is a haunting tune in the pentatonic (five tone) scale represented on the successive black keys of the piano beginning on G♭, or by omitting the fourth and seventh notes of any major scale.

The harmonization is by C. Winfred Douglas, as prepared for *The Hymnal 1940* of the Protestant Episcopal Church.

506 THERE STANDS A FOUNTAIN WHERE FOR SIN

This text by William Cowper, probably written in 1771, first appeared in Conyer's *Collection of Psalms and Hymns* (1772). Thereafter it was included in the famous *Olney Hymns* (1779), produced jointly by John Newton (*LW* 217, et al.) and William Cowper, with the heading "Praise for the Fountain Opened." Few hymns have evoked keener controversy, largely the result of the imagery of stanza 1, reflecting Zechariah 13:1; and few hymns have been so altered by hymnbook editors. The illustrious hymnist James Montgomery (*LW* 50, et al.) wrote: "I entirely rewrote the first verse. . . . The words are objectionable as representing a fountain being *filled*, instead of *springing up*. I think my version is unobjectionable." His version began:

From Calvary's cross a fountain flows
Of water and of blood,
More healing than Bethesda's pool
Or famed Siloam's flood.

His revision, however, failed to gain wide acceptance. What some consider as overdrawn imagery and intense emotion has undoubtedly contributed to the omission of this hymn in various contemporary hymnals.

In light of the foregoing the Commission on Worship decided to use stanza 1 as amended by Nathaniel Micklem (1888–1976) except for one change, namely, the use of "stands" instead of "springs." Thus, with the exception of stanza 1, the text is identical to that contained in *The Lutheran Hymnal* (1941).

COWPER. Numerous tunes have been coupled to Cowper's text. Of the two that appeared in *The Lutheran Hymnal* (1941), COWPER was selected more for its popularity than for its quality. It was composed by Lowell Mason specifically for this hymn text, and first published in Thomas Hastings' *Spiritual Songs for Social Worship* (1832).

The harmonization is from *The Lutheran Hymnal* (1941).

507 BEAUTIFUL SAVIOR

Beautiful Savior,
King of creation,
Son of God and Son of Man!
Truly I'd love thee,
Truly I'd serve thee,
Light of my soul, my joy, my crown.

Fair are the meadows,
Fair are the woodlands,
Robed in flow'rs of blooming spring;

Schönster Herr Jesu,
Herrscher aller Herren,
Gottes und Mariä Sohn!
Dich will ich lieben,
Dich will ich ehren,
Meiner Seelen Freud' und Kron'.

Schön sind die Wälder,
Schöner die Felder
In der schönen Frühlingszeit.

Jesus is fairer,
Jesus is purer,
He makes our sorr'wing spirit sing.

Fair is the sunshine,
Fair is the moonlight,
Bright the sparkling stars on high;
Jesus shines brighter,
Jesus shines purer
Than all the angels in the sky.

Beautiful Savior,
Lord of the nations,
Son of God and Son of Man!
Glory and honor,
Praise, adoration
Now and forevermore be thine!

Jesus ist schöner,
Jesus ist reiner,
Der unser traurigs Herz erfreut.

Schön leucht't der Monden,
Schöner die Sonne
Als die Sternlein allzumal.
Jesus leucht't schöner,
Jesus leucht't reiner,
Als all die Engel im Himmelssaal.

Alle die Schönheit
Himmels und der Erde
Ist nur gegen ihn als Schein.
Keiner soll nimmer
Lieber uns werden
Als er, der schönste Jesus mein!

Appearing first about 1662 in a Westphalian manuscript, it was in 1677 that it was anonymously included in a hymnal, namely, in the German Roman Catholic *Münster Gesangbuch.* Called by Nelle "a small Catholic sacramental song," it was set to a tune, so he says, that was borrowed from a Mozart violin sonata," and appeared thus (Zahn 3975):

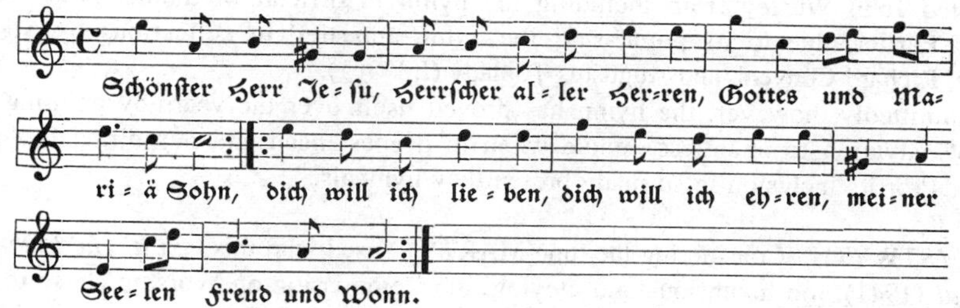

A transcription of this is offered as the first tune to hymn 346 in *The Hymnal 1940* of the Protestant Episcopal Church.

The anonymous translation beginning "Fairest Lord Jesus," which first appeared in Richard Storrs Willis' (*LW* 62) *Church Chorals and Choir Studies* (1850), is the translation generally used in other than Lutheran hymnals. The present translation, identical to that in *The Lutheran Hymnal* (1941) and the *Lutheran Book of Worship* (1978), was prepared by Joseph A. Seiss and included in the *Sunday School Book for the use of Evangelical Lutheran congregations* (Philadelphia, 1873).

SCHÖNSTER HERR JESU (CRUSADER'S HYMN, ST. ELIZABETH) is the tune that appeared with the German text in a book of Sileasian folk songs entitled *Schlesische Volkslieder* (Leipzig, 1842). The title CRUSADER'S HYMN is a vestige of an earlier unfounded assumption.

The harmonization is from the *Service Book and Hymnal* (1958), slightly altered.

508 JESUS, LOVER OF MY SOUL

The general popularity of this hymn prompted the Commission on Worship to include it in *Lutheran Worship* (1982), although not included in *Lutheran Book of Worship* (1978) nor even in the official Methodist hymnal until nine years after the death of its author Charles Wesley. Based on the author's conviction that the Christian must leave the direction of his life to God—the aphorism, "Let go and let God"—the hymn first appeared in *Hymns and Sacred Poems* (1740) in five stanzas as here, with the title "In time of prayer and temptation," later changed to "In temptation." The text was written two years prior to that, shortly after Charles Wesley's "conversion." As a poem it presents difficulties in that there is no logical development in its imagery. Moreover, its amatory and intimate text (a far cry from Samuel Crossman's "My song is love unknown" [*LW* 91]), something that Charles Wesley had caught from Count Zinzendorf's (*LW* 362, 386) Moravians, although not as bad as their often shockingly coarse, whimsical allegories, and perverted spiritualization, these traits evidently prompted John Wesley from including the hymn in official Methodist books until 1797. Earlier, due to its popularity, the hymn appeared in collections by Martin Madan, Richard Conyers, and Augustus Toplady (*LW* 361).

Admittedly, however, the hymn has proved itself over the years by pointing the way of salvation to countless people when in deepest need and despair, a fact that accounts for its inclusion in so many present-day hymnals.

ABERYSTWYTH. Considering the tune MARTYN, used with this text in *The Lutheran Hymnal* (1941), too lugubrious and cloying, the Commission on Worship chose to use ABERYSTWYTH, the tune used with Wesley's text in almost all present-day hymnals in America as well as in other parts of the world. Written by Joseph Parry for the Welsh hymn, "Beth sydd i mi yn y leyd," when he was professor of music at the new University College at Aberystwyth, a seaside resort and foremost university town in Wales, he set the tune to Wesley's text as a conclusion to his cantata *Cerwiden. Ail Llyfr Tonau ac Emynau* (1879) was the first hymnal to include it. Especially effective is the pitch-height accent in the second-to-last phrase. Of the 400 or so song tunes that Parry composed, this is the only one, however, to win lasting recognition. The tune must move, but not too fast.

The harmonization is from the *Hymnal for Colleges and Schools* (New Haven, 1956).

AMAZING GRACE! HOW SWEET THE SOUND 509

This hymn by John Newton, described by himself on his tombstone, "once an Infidel and Libertine, a servant of slavers in Africa," was first published in the *Olney Hymns* (1779) in six, four-line stanzas, with the caption "Faith's review and expectation" and the reference to 1 Chronicles 17:16–17. Printed here are, in order, stanzas 1, 4, 3, and 5. Omitted here (besides st. 6) is stanza 2, the first two lines of which read: " 'Twas grace that taught my heart to fear, And grace my fears relieved." This omission was prompted by the probable misunderstanding of the two different meanings of the word "fear"—the first in accord with Luther's explanations of the Ten Commandments, a "God-fearing" as applied to Christians motivated by the Gospel; the second referring to the trembling fear when confronted with God's Law, a fear removed only by the forgiveness through Christ's atonement.

NEW BRITAIN. This pentatonic (five-tone) tune has appeared with numerous apparently arbitrary names: SYMPHONY, SOLON, HARMONY GROVE, and REDEMPTION. As a folk tune it was undoubtedly sung with various embellishments, especially in the South. Its first-known printed form was in *Virginia Harmony* (1831), compiled by James P. Carrell and David S. Clayton. The present form is a slightly altered version of that which appeared in Edwin O. Excell's (1851–1921) *Make His Praise Glorious* (1900). Paul G. Bunjes prepared the harmonization for *Lutheran Worship* (1982).

This haunting tune and its text of profound religious meaning has become exceedingly popular the last two decades or so. Most recently published hymnals include the hymn. Widely used also today in secular situations, one cannot but wonder with S. Paul Schilling whether its real import is always grasped: "the forgiving love that can find the lost, give sight to the blind, and lead sinners from wretchedness to their true home in God."

BE STILL, MY SOUL 510

Be still, my soul; the Lord is on your side;
Bear patiently the cross of grief or pain;
Leave to your God to order and provide;
In ev'ry change he faithful will remain.
Be still, my soul; your best, your heav'nly Friend
Through thorny ways leads to a joyful end.

Stille, mein Wille! Dein Jesus hilft siegen;
Trage geduldig das Leiden, die Not;
Gott ist's, der alles zum besten will fügen,
Der dir getreu bleibt in Schmerzen und Tod.
Stille, mein Wille! Dein Jesus wird machen
Glücklichen Ausgang bedenklicher Sachen.

Be still, my soul; your God will undertake
To guide the future as he has the past.
Your hope, your confidence let nothing shake;

Stille, mein Wille! Der Herr hat's in Händen;
Hält sich dein Herz nur im Glauben an ihn,
Wird er den Kummer bald wenden und enden;

All now mysterious shall be bright at last. Be still, my soul; the waves and winds still know His voice who ruled them while he dwelt below.	Herrlich wird endlich, was wunderbar schien. Stille, mein Wille! Dein Heiland wird zeigen, Wie vor ihm Meer und Gewitter muss schweigen.
Be still, my soul; though dearest friends depart And all is darkened in the vale of tears; Then you will better know his love, his heart, Who comes to soothe your sorrows and your fears. Be still, my soul; your Jesus can repay From his own fullness all he takes away.	Stille, mein Wille! Wenn Freunde sich trennen, Die du so zärtlich und innig geliebt, Wirst du die Freundschaft des Höchsten erkennen, Der sich zum eigentum treulich dir gibt. Stille, mein Wille! Dein Jesus ersetzet, Was dich beim Sterben der Liebsten verletzet.
Be still, my soul; the hour is hast'ning on When we shall be forever with the Lord, When disappointment, grief, and fear are gone, Sorrow forgot, love's purest joys restored. Be still, my soul; when change and tears are past, All safe and blessed we shall meet at last.	Stille, mein Wille! Es kommen die Stunden, Dass wir beim Herrn sind ohn' Wechsel der Zeit; Dann ist das Scheiden, der Kummer verschwunden, Ewige Freundschaft vergütet das Leid. Stille, mein Wille! Nach zeitlichem Scheiden Sehn wir uns wieder ohn' Schmerzen und Leiden.

This is a cento consisting of stanzas 1–2, 4, and 5 of the original six-stanza poem by Catharina von Schlegel that appeared in the *Neue Sammlung geistlicher Lieder* (Wernigerode, 1752). This was a collection of 818 hymns and songs, more than half of which written by Count Heinrich Er nst von Stolberg-Wernigerode. As a hymn of trust in God in the midst of life's difficulties, it is opined that Catharina von Schlegel evidently had in mind Psalm 46:10: "Be still, and know that I am God."

The translation is an updated version of that by Jane L. Borthwick in her *Hymns from the Land of Luther* (second series, 1855).

Having enjoyed a certain popularity from its appearance under the category of Carols and Spiritual Songs in *The Lutheran Hymnal* (1941)—it was not included in the *Evangelical Lutheran Hymn-Book* (1912), the precursor of *TLH*—prompted the Commission on Worship to include it in *Lutheran Worship* (1982), although in itself the hymn lacks something to be desired. While the metric pattern of four 10s so frequently sounds like poems set to tunes as an afterthought (Charles Wesley wrote poems but not hymns to this meter), six 10s, as here, pushes the matter to precarious limits. The length of the lines and the involved thought process causes the mind to wander before arriving at the ends of stanzas. Moreover, the rhyme scheme of ABAB in the first four lines as here, occurring in such long lines, spreads the rhymes so far apart as to lose their effect. Admittedly, lines five and six, rhyming as they do (CC), redeems the situation a bit in the first four lines. Finally, this writer agrees with Austin Lovelace that this wedding of text and tune "is quite wearisome . . . since the rhythm of the music and the words are at constant odds. One is constantly aware of holding on inordinately long to peculiar syllables (ly, fu-, te-, con-)."

As for the comforting thoughts of the text, however, relative to God's providence, certainly no fault can be found.

FINLANDIA. Search for the tune to which "Stille, mein Wille" may originally have been sung was unsuccessful. Undoubtedly, some of the popularity attached to the English translation of Catharina von Schlegel's text is due to its connection with this adaptation of the choralelike theme in Jean Sibelius' tone poem *Finlandia*, a work composed in honor of his native land when it was chafing under the repressive measures of the Russian empire in 1899. FINLANDIA appeared with the present text in *The Church Hymnary* (revised edition, 1927), authorized by the Church of Scotland and other Presbyterian bodies in England, Australia, New Zealand, and South Africa. Congregations in the Missouri Synod were first introduced to this hymn and tune by its inclusion in T*he Lutheran Hymnal* (1941).

The harmonization is from *The Hymnbook* (1955) of the Presbyterian Church.

IN THE HOUR OF TRIAL 511

This hymn by James Montgomery, dated October 13, 1834, and first distributed in manuscript to his friends, was not published until 1853 when it appeared in the author's *Original Hymns for Public, Private, and Social Devotion* with the caption "Prayers on Pilgrimage." Considerably altered, especially stanzas 3 and 4, by Frances A. Hutton in her *Supplement and Litanies* (n.d.), it was further modified by Godfrey Thring (*LW* 218, et al.) in *The Church of England Hymnbook* (revised edition, 1882). The text here given is identical to that in *The Lutheran Hymnal* (1941).

ST. MARY MAGDALENE. John B. Dykes, the typical Victorian composer, wrote this tune for this trochaic (´ ˘) 65 65D text, and it appeared in Chope's *The Congregational Hymn and Tune Book* (1862). While the trochaic meter is in itself excellent, the constant starting and stopping in such short lines as here is not a little enervating, as is also the monotonous rhythmic pattern of ♩ ♩ ♩ ♩ | 𝅗𝅥 𝅗𝅥.

The harmonization is from *The Hymnal* (1933) of the Presbyterian Church.

LORD, TAKE MY HAND AND LEAD ME 512

Lord, take my hand and lead me
Upon life's way;
Direct, protect, and feed me
From day to day.
Without your grace and favor
I go astray;
So take my hand, O Savior,
And lead the way.

Lord, when the tempest rages,
I need not fear;
For you, the Rock of Ages,
Are always near.
Close by your side abiding,
I fear no foe,

So nimm denn meine Hände
Und führe mich
Bis an mein selig Ende
Und ewiglich.
Ich mag allein nicht gehen,
Nich einen Schritt;
Wo du wirst gehn und stehen,
Da nimm mich mit.

In dein Erbarmen hü`lle
Mein schwaches Herz
Und mach es gänzlich stille
In Freud und Schmerz;
Lass ruhn zu deinen Füssen
Dein armes Kind:

For when your hand is guiding, In peace I go.	Es wird die Augen schliessen Und glauben blind.
Lord, when the shadows lengthen And night has come, I know that you will strengthen My steps toward home, And nothing can impede me, O blessed Friend! So, take my hand and lead me Unto the end.	Wenn ich auch gleich nichts fühle Von deiner Macht, Du führst mich doch zum Ziele, Auch durch die Nacht. So nimm denn meine Hände Und führe mich Bis an mein selig Ende Und ewiglich.

"The most folklike of all spiritual songs—in contrast to the church song (hymn)," so Nelle says, this hymn of infinite trust in divine guidance has long been a favorite as a confirmation hymn in the Lutheran Church. Written by Julie von Hausmann, it first appeared in volume one of *Maiblumen Lieder einer Stillen im Lande, dargereicht von G. Knak* (1862).

The rather free translation was prepared by the Inter-Lutheran Commission on Worship for inclusion in *Lutheran Book of Worship* (1978). Stanza 1 is based on a translation by Herman Brueckner (*LW* 419) and included in the *American Lutheran Hymnal* (1930); stanzas 2 and 3 are based on a translation done by Rudolph A. John in 1912.

SO NIMM DENN MEINE HÄNDE first appeared in volume three of Friedrich Silcher's *Kernlieder für Schule und Haus* (Tübingen, 1842) set to "Wie könnt ich ruhig schlafen."

The harmonization is from the *Service Book and Hymnal* (1958).

513 JESUS, SAVIOR, PILOT ME

Edward Hopper was asked to write an original hymn for an anniversary of the Seamen's Friend Society in New York, May 10, 1880. Not realizing that the above hymn was already familiar to the group, having been published anonymously in the *Sailor's Magazine* and in the *Baptist Praise Book* in 1871, he instead presented this text and thus revealed himself as its author. Pastor of New York's Church of the Sea and Land, Hopper wrote the text in six stanzas for the sailors who attended his services. Included here are stanzas 1, 5–6.

PILOT was written for this text in 1871 by John E. Gould, who picked out the tune on the piano on the eve of his departure for Europe on what, as it turned out, was his last earthly voyage. Its first published appearance was in *The Baptist Praise Book* (1871).

Paul G. Bunjes prepared the harmonization for inclusion in *Lutheran Worship* (1982).

NEARER, MY GOD, TO THEE 514

Sarah Flower Adams submitted this original hymn with 12 others to William Johnson Fox for his *Hymns and Anthems* (1841), compiled for the use of his congregation at Finsbury, England, which, although unaffiliated, was generally considered to be Unitarian. Based on the story of Jacob at Bethel (Gen. 28:10–22), this hymn was at one time a cause of great concern because of its Unitarian origin (although the author was a Baptist all her life) and because the name of Christ did not appear in it. The compilers of the *Baptist Hymn-Book* (1842) asked Arthur T. Russell (*LW* 72, 248) to add a more Christ-centered stanza, and were rewarded with the following:

Christ alone beareth me
Where Thou dost shine;
Joint heir He maketh me
Of the divine:
In Christ my soul shall be
Nearer, my God, to Thee,
Nearer to Thee.

Hervey Doddridge Ganse, an American Presbyterian clergyman, about 1890, retained Stanza 1 and added the remaining three stanzas as they appear in *Lutheran Worship* (1982).

The story of the singing of "Nearer, my God, to thee" by the passengers, of whom 1,635 were lost, of the English ship *Titanic* in 1912 has become legendary. Argument has arisen concerning the use of the tune BETHANY during that experience, as historians claim that BETHANY has never been associated with this text in England; but the substance of the legend remains the same.

BETHANY. Lowell Mason composed this tune for "Nearer, my God, to thee" in 1856, and the hymn's popularity in America is usually credited to the tune. BETHANY was first published in the Andover *Sabbath Hymn and Tune Book* (1859). In 1868 Mason related to a friend the following account:

> When we were compiling the collection known as the *Sabbath Hymn and Tune Book*, they [i.e., Edward A. Park and Austin Phelps] applied to me for a musical setting for the hymn, "Nearer, my God, to thee." The metre was irregular. But one night some time after, lying awake in the dark, eyes wide open, through the stillness of the house the melody came to me, and the next morning I wrote down the notes of BETHANY.

The similarity between BETHANY and the familiar air "Oft in the stilly night" suggests that Mason's tune may have been a subconscious adaptation. An earlier form of this melody, "The Auld House," was found in John Greig's *Scots Minstrelsie*, as sung by Lady Caroline Nairne (1766–1845).

The harmonization is from the *Evangelical Lutheran Hymn-Book* (1912), predecessor to *The Lutheran Hymnal* (1941).

515 I'M BUT A STRANGER HERE

This spiritual song by Thomas R. Taylor was evidently written shortly before his early death of consumption. It was published in his *Memoirs and Select Remains* (1836), to be sung to the tune ROBIN ADAIR.

HEAVEN IS MY HOME (ST. EDMOND, SAINTS' REST) was composed by Arthur S. Sullivan. Sullivan may have been a gifted master of melody when it came to his operas, but his hymn tunes, such as this one, exhibit a real poverty of melodic line. They, so Routley observes, evidence "the disastrous rubbish which a musician of outstanding gifts thought appropriate for church use." (*The Music of Christian Hymnody*)

The harmonization is from *The Lutheran Hymnal* (1941), slightly altered.

516 WHAT A FRIEND WE HAVE IN JESUS

Joseph Scriven penned this spiritual song, about 1855, near Port Hope, Ontario, Canada, to comfort his mother in a time of sorrow. It was never intended that it be printed. A friend who had come one day to visit him in his illness happened to discover it, and Scriven acknowledged that he was the author, stating, "The Lord and I did it between us." First published anonymously in Horace L. Hastings' *Social Hymns, Original and Selected* (1865), in Hastings' *Songs of Pilgrimage* (1886), however, it is attributed to Joseph Scriven. In the meantime Ira D. Sankey found the hymn in a pamphlet of Sunday School hymns published in Richmond, Virginia, and he included it in his *Gospel Hymns and Sacred Songs* (1875), which he compiled with Philip P. Bliss, incorrectly attributing it to Horatius Bonar (*LW* 173, et al.). The mistake was detected and corrected in the 1887 edition of *Gospel Hymns* edited by Sankey, McGranahan, and Stebbens.

CONVERSE, also known as ERIE and WHAT A FRIEND, was composed by Charles C. Converse for Scriven's text, and the combination appeared in *Silver Wings* (Richmond, 1870), a booklet of Sunday School hymns that Converse had compiled.

Aside from the overall glibness and triviality of the tune, it suffers especially from the rhythmic standpoint. The incessant rhythmic pattern, ♩. ♪ ♫♫ | 𝅗𝅥 𝅗𝅥, with all the voice parts moving in that same pattern, leaves one exhausted by the sameness. Stanley Osborne's reharmonization with a strong moving bass line remarkably obviates this sameness (cf. *If Such Holy Song*, p. 548). In the few present-day hymnals that include this hymn text, some, for example, keep CONVERSE (*Rejoice in the Lord* [1985]; *Lead Me, Guide Me* [1987]; *The United Methodist Hymnal* [1989]; *The Hymn Book* [1971]). As for the usage in other hymnals: the *Psalter Hymnal* (1987) has BEACH SPRING (from *The Sacred Harp*, 1844); *The Australian Hymn Book* (1976) offers SICILIAN MARINERS and BLAENWERN. Admittedly the wedding of Scriven text and CONVERSE has become so established that perhaps Osborne's suggestion of a stronger and better reharmonization of this tune is the wiser solution.

The harmonization in *Lutheran Worship* (1982) is from *The Hymn Book* (1971) of the Anglican Church of Canada and the United Church of Canada.

I AM JESUS' LITTLE LAMB 517

I am Jesus' little lamb,
Ever glad at heart I am;
For my Shepherd gently guides me,
Knows my need and well provides me,
Loves me ev'ry day the same,
Even calls me by my name.

Day by day, at home, away,
Jesus is my staff and stay.
When I hunger, Jesus feeds me,
Into pleasant pastures leads me;
When I thirst, he bids me go
Where the quiet waters flow.

Who so happy as I am,
Even now the Shepherd's lamb?
And when my short life is ended,
By his angel host attended,
He shall fold me to his breast,
There within his arms to rest.

Weil ich Jesu Schäflein bin,
Freu' ich mich nur immerhin
Über meinen guten Hirten,
Der mich wohl weiss zu bewirten,
Der mich liebet, der mich kennt
Und bei meinem Namen nennt.

Unter seinem sanften Stab
Geh' ich aus und ein und hab'
Unaussprechlich süsse Weide,
Dass ich keinen Mangel leide;
Und sooft ich durstig bin,
Führt er mich zum Brunnquell hin.

Sollt' ich denn nicht fröhlich sein,
Ich beglücktes Schäfelein?
Denn nach diesen schönen Tagen
Werd' ich endlich hingetragen
In des Hirten Arm und Schoss:
Amen, ja mein Glück ist gross!

This model and popular children's song by schoolteacher Henrietta Luise von Hayn appeared in the Moravian hymnal, *Neues Brüder Gesangbuch* (1778), where it was in the category of Holy Communion.

This is a composite translation of the numerous such that have appeared, the text that was included in *The Lutheran Hymnal* (1941).

WEIL ICH JESU SCHÄFLEIN BIN is the tune that appeared with the above text in the *Brüder-Choral-Buch* (1784).

Paul G. Bunjes prepared the harmonization for inclusion in *Lutheran Worship* (1982).

518 ONWARD, CHRISTIAN SOLDIERS

Sabine Baring-Gould wrote this hymn, originally in six stanzas, late at night on Whitsunday (Pentecost), 1865, for a schoolchildren's procession to take place the following day. Published in *The Church Times* later the same year, it has become one of the most well-known and popular Christian marching songs. The author confessed, 30 years after his hymn's initial publication, "It was written in great haste, and . . . nothing has surprised me more than its popularity."

A story, probably apocryphal, is told concerning distress over the processional cross image in the refrain. As a procession was about to begin in one of his churches, a bishop told his parishioners not to carry the cross; "whereupon," claims Percy Dearmer, "the choir men conspired to end each chorus with the words 'Left behind the door.'"

Baring-Gould's original setting for this hymn was an arrangement from the slow movement of Haydn's Symphony in D, No. 15.

ST. GERTRUDE. Arthur S. Sullivan composed this tune for above text. The first appearance of text and tune joined was in *The Hymnary* (1872), although ST. GERTRUDE was published in the December 1871 issue of *The Musical Times*. Sullivan dedicated the tune to Mrs. Gertrude Clay-Ker-Seymer, in whose home he was a frequent guest.

The harmonization is from the *Service Book and Hymnal* (1958).

519 HOW GREAT THOU ART

This hymn, popularized by the Billy Graham Crusades, has entered various hymnals by a rather circuitous route.

Inspired by the beauty of the Swedish meadows and lakes after a summer thunderstorm in 1885, Carl Boberg wrote the original Swedish text. The first two stanzas are reminiscent of the psalmist's words, "The heavens declare the glory of God; the skies proclaim the work of his hands" (Ps. 19:1). In 1907 Manfred von Glehn, a resident of Estonia, made a German translation beginning with "Wie gross bist du." Five years later Ivan S. Prokhanoff, a clergyman often referred to as the "Martin Luther of Russia," published a Russian version of this German hymn in St. Petersburg and included it in a collection of spiritual songs translated from various languages under the title *Symbols*. In 1922 several of Prokhanoff's hymn booklets were combined into one volume and published in Russian by Prokhanoff's friends of the American Bible Society. The book was entitled *The Songs of a Christian*. In 1927 this volume was reprinted in Russia and there it came to the attention of Stuart K. Hine and his wife, an English missionary couple, who used it in their evangelism efforts in western Ukraine.

After singing it in Russian for many years, Stuart Hine translated the first three stanzas into English. With the outbreak of World War II, the Hines returned to Britain where, in 1948, the fourth stanza was added.

In 1949 Stuart Hine included this hymn in a Russian Gospel magazine that he published. This resulted in numerous requests for reprints of the hymn by missionaries all over the world. One of these reprints was given to George Beverly Shea during the 1954 Billy Graham London crusade, and it was first sung in the Toronto, Canada, crusade of 1955. Its popularity soon prompted its use in American crusades.

O STORE GUD is a Swedish tune of unknown origin, first published in *Sanningsvittet* in 1891, a weekly edited by Carl G. Boberg, where it appeared in triple meter, as arranged by Eric A. Edgren. In 1894 it appeared in the *Svenska Missionsförbundets Sangbok* in duple meter, much as it appears in *Lutheran Worship.* The harmonization is by Stuart Hine.

REJOICE, REJOICE THIS HAPPY MORN HE IS ARISEN! GLORIOUS WORD 520

Rejoice, rejoice this happy morn,
A Savior unto us is born,
The Christ, the Lord of glory!
His lowly birth at Bethlehem
The angels from on high proclaim
And sing redemption's story!
My soul,
Extol
God's great favor;
Bless him ever
For salvation;
Give him praise and adoration!

He is arisen! Glorious word!
Now reconciled is God, my Lord;
The gates of heav'n are open.
My Jesus did triumphant die,
And Satan's arrows broken lie,
Destroyed hell's fiercest weapon.
Oh, hear
What cheer!
Christ victorious,
Rising glorious,
Life is giving.
He was dead but now is living!

Os er idag en Frelser föd,
Guds Salvede i vores Kjöd,
En Herre til Guds Äre.
Nu er han föd i Davids Stad,
Den Sön, som Englene tilbad,
Velsignet evig väre!
Min Själ,
Kjend vel
Denne Naade,
Fri fra Vaade,
Mä dit Öie
Ved Opgangen af det Höie!

Han er opstanden! Store Bud!
Min Gud er en forsonet Gud,
Min Himmel er nu aaben!
Min Jesu seierrige Död
Fordömmelsernes Pile bröd,
Og knuste Mörkets Vaaben.
O Rost,
Min Tröst!
Ved hans Seier,
Som jeg eier,
Helved bäver;
Han var död, men se, han lever!

These two hymns, both by Birgitte K. Boye, appeared in 1778 in *Salmebog, eller en Samling af gamle og ny Salmer, til Guds Aere og Hans Menigheds Opbyggelse* (A hymnal, or a collection of old and new hymns, for the honor of God and the edification of his Church). Both hymns had liturgical significance in the Scandinavian Church, and were designated to be sung before the reading of the sermon text on their respective festivals, Christmas and Easter. They appeared in *The Lutheran Hymnary* (Minneapolis, 1913) in the present translations.

"Rejoice, rejoice this happy morn" was translated by Carl A. Doving. George A. T. Rygh prepared the translation of "He is arisen!" The hymns appear as one number in *Lutheran Worship* in order to save space and because both are set to WIE SCHÖN LEUCHTET. They represent a last-minute inclusion in *Lutheran Worship*, which explains the erroneous classification of Spiritual Songs.

WIE SCHÖN LEUCHTET. For comments on this tune and its harmonization see hymn 73.

The setting is from the *Choralbuch* (1955).

BIOGRAPHICAL INFORMATION ON THE AUTHORS, COMPOSERS, TRANSLATORS, AND ARRANGERS

ADAMS, SARAH FLOWER (1805–1848), born in Harlow, Essex, was the second daughter of Benjamin Flower, the radical editor of *The Cambridge Intelligencer* and later of *The Political Review,* and who was imprisoned for criticizing the politics of the Bishop of Llandaff. Sarah and her sister Eliza were both unusually talented, Sarah as a poet, Eliza as a musician. Eliza often wrote tunes for Sarah's songs. The sisters hosted in their home many distinguished friends, including poet Robert Browning. In 1834 Sarah married civil engineer William Bridges Adams and moved to London. She aspired to be an actress, and her 1837 portrayal of Lady MacBeth in the Richmond Theater was highly acclaimed, but failing health ended her stage career.

She contributed 13 hymns to William Johnson Fox's *Hymns and Anthems* (1841), for which collection Eliza served as music editor. In the same year Sarah published her major literary work, *Vivia Perpetua*, a five-act dramatic poem concerning Christianity vs. heathenism. Her catechism for children with hymns, *The Flock at the Fountain*, went to press in 1845. Her hymns were described by her friend Mrs. Bridell Fox as "the spontaneous expression of some strong impulse of feeling." Adams died in August 1848, and the hymns sung at her funeral were her poems set to her sister's music.

AUTHOR: 514 Nearer, My God, to Thee (st. 1)

ADDISON, JOSEPH (1672–1719), was born May 1, 1672, son of rector Lancelot Addison of Milston, Wiltshire, England, who later became the dean of Lichfield. Educated at Charterhouse, Queen's College, and Magdalen College, Oxford, Joseph Addison studied law and politics and earned the Master of Arts degree in 1693. He joined the Whig party and soon became a prominent figure therein, with the help of his mentor Charles Montague (afterward Lord Halifax).

His political pull gained for him in 1699 a pension, which he lost after the death of William III in 1703. To overcome this difficulty, Addison wrote a highly acclaimed poem on Marlborough's victory at Blenheim, a work that brought him preferment to various successive offices of state.

With the fall of the Godolphin Ministry in 1710, Addison gained time to write the essays that made him famous. When Sir Richard Steele, a boyhood friend of his, brought out his publication *The Tatler,* Addison quickly became a contributor. He initiated the nonpolitical daily *Spectator* when *The Tatler* closed in 1711. The stated purpose of the *Spectator* was to "bring philosophy out of the closets and libraries, schools and colleges; to dwell in the clubs and assemblies, at tea tables and in coffee houses."

Addison's four hymns, undoubtedly inspired by Isaac Watts (*LW* 53, et al.), were all appended to essays in the *Spectator* in the same year, 1712. In 1713 his tragedy *Cato* was produced, and a comedy called *The Drummer* was published soon thereafter. His last literary effort was a party paper issued in 1715 to 1716 called *The Freeholder*; his *Evidences of Christianity* was never completed.

His political career again blossomed with the accession of George I in 1714. He held several government offices and married Charlotte, Countess of Warwick; then, in 1717, he was promoted to assistant secretary of state under his old friend Sunderland.

Alexander Pope criticized Addison's performance in this position, saying that he was unable to issue an order for "endeavoring to word it too finely."

Reportedly Addison's deathbed advice to his wayward nephew, Lord Warwick, was to "See in what peace a Christian can die." His peaceful death occurred June 17, 1719. Samuel Johnson said of him,

> Whoever wishes to attain an English style, familiar but not coarse, and elegant but not ostentatious, must give his days and nights to the volumes of Addison.

AUTHOR: 196 When All Your Mercies, O My God

AHLE, JOHANN RUDOLPH (1625–73), was born December 24, 1625, in Mühlhausen, Thuringia. Educated at the Universities of Göttingen and Erfurt, his gifted musical ability soon prompted his election as cantor at St. Andreas' Church and director of the music school at Erfurt in 1646. Three years later he was given the prestigious position of organist at St. Blasius' Church, Mühlhausen, to succeed Johann Vockerodt. Ahle's son would later succeed his father as organist, and as such became the predecessor of J. S. Bach (*LW* 89). In 1656 Ahle was elected to the town council; in 1661 he was elected mayor, a position he held until his death July 8, 1673, at the age of 48.

Besides being a good poet, Ahle was especially a well-educated and talented organist and composer. Together with Heinrich Albert and others, he was instrumental in originating and introducing into the church what were called sacred arias, a type of song reflective of Italian opera. In the course of his career he wrote over 400 such arias for Sundays, festivals, and other special days in the church year. These became especially popular in Thuringia and Saxony, and they represent Ahle's greatest and lasting influence on the congregational hymn. The publications of Ahle include *Compendium pro tenellis* (Erfurt, 1648), a treatise on singing designed as an aid to building an excellent choir; *Thuringischen neugeflantzten Lustgarten (*Mühlhausen, 1657), *Neue geistliche, auf die hohen Festtage durch's gantze Jahr gerichtete Andachten* (Mühhausen, 1662), *Neue geistliche, auf die Sonntage durch's gantze Jahr gerichtete Andachten* (Mühlhausen, 1664). *Fünfzehn neuer geistlicher Arien* (Mühlhausen, 1660) was followed with the publication of five supplements, the last in 1669.

COMPOSER: 202, 226 LIEBSTER JESU, WIR SIND HIER

ALBRECHT VON PREUSZEN (1490–1568), was born in Ansbach, Franconia. In 1511 he was chosen Grand Master of the German Knightly Order. In a troublesome and futile war over the feudal right of Poland, he sought and found help in an evangelical sermon of Andreas Osiander the Elder (1498–1552) that he heard in Nürnberg sometime in 1522. At once he became sympathetic to Luther's cause. As a result of Luther's support of Albrecht's desire for political and religious changes in Prussia, in September

1523 the first evangelical service was conducted in Königsberg. Having become Albrecht, Duke of Prussia in 1525, he now permitted evangelical churches to be established; he encouraged the production of congregational hymnals and choirbooks. Following a period of extensive and wise planning, he established the University of Königsberg.

Albrecht was undoubtedly one of the most pious rulers that Germany ever had, and he exercised a religious tolerance to groups that sought refuge in his domain—Bohemian Brethren, Reformed from the Netherlands, Schwenkfeldians—that was not a little unique for his time. He died in 1568 at the castle in Tapiau.

AUTHOR: 425 The Will of God Is Always Best

ALDERSON, ELIZA (1818–1889), was a sister of John B. Dykes (*LW* 168, et al.). Born August 16, 1818, at Hull, England, she showed early artistic talent. As a young girl she wrote Sunday school hymns for St. John's Church, Hull, where her grandfather, Thomas Dykes, was pastor. In 1850 she married W. T. Alderson, chaplain to the West Riding Home of Correction, Wakefield. Here she wrote most of her hymns. Only 12 of her many hymns were published, titled *Twelve Hymns* (n.d.). Alderson became an invalid two years before her death on March 18, 1889.

AUTHOR: 402 Lord of Glory, You Have Bought Us

ALEXANDER (HUMPHREYS), CECIL FRANCES (1823–95), was born in 1823 (some older sources give 1818) in Ireland, Redcross Parish, County Wicklow, the daughter of Major John Humphreys. Already as a little girl she began to write poetry, and her love for children is exhibited by her perhaps most famous and important work, *Hymns for Little Children* (1848), for which John Keble (*LW* 488) wrote a preface. This work appeared in over one hundred editions. Regarding the type of hymns suggested by the title, she was of the opinion that "a namby-pamby, childish style is most unpleasing to children," and that "it is surprising how soon they can understand and follow a high order of poetry." Her poems and hymns were designed primarily for the children in her Sunday School classes and were used to illustrate and explain the basic doctrines of Christianity, especially the Apostles' Creed.

In 1850 Cecil Frances Humphreys married William Alexander, then a curate in Londonderry, who in 1867 became bishop of Derry and Raphoe, and in 1896 archbishop of Armagh and primate of all Ireland (and like his wife, a talented poet). His wife's abiding concern for children was evidenced when, upon moving to Londonderry with her husband, she founded the Girls' Friendly Society.

Among her many other books are *Verses from Holy Scripture* (1846), *Narrative Hymns for Village Schools* (1853), *Poems on Subjects in the Old Testament* (Part I, 1854; Part II, 1857), and *Hymns Descriptive and Devotional* (1858). She contributed to a number of hymn collections and in all wrote over 200 hymns and over 200 poems.

She died in Londonderry October 12, 1895. In 1896 her husband, Archbishop Alexander, who survived her by 16 years, published a selection of her best work under the title *Poems by Cecil Frances Alexander*.

AUTHOR: 58 Once in Royal David's City
TRANSLATOR: 172 I Bind unto Myself Today

ALFORD, HENRY (1810–1871), was the compiler of the first comprehensive English commentary on the Greek New Testament (1844–61), the standard critical commentary of the late 19th century. He was born in London October 7, 1810, attended Ilminster Grammar School, and received the Bachelor of Arts degree from Trinity College, Cambridge, in 1832. He later became a fellow of the college. He was ordained a priest and appointed curate of Ampton in 1833; in 1835 vicar of Wymeswold, Leicestershire. Called to Quebec Chapel in London in 1853, he became dean of Canterbury in 1857. His health failed with the workload placed upon him, and he died January 12, 1871, in Canterbury.

Alford was a member of the New Testament Revision Committee and a prolific writer. He created and edited for a time *The Contemporary Review* and authored *Plea for the Queen's English*. His hymnological work spanned translations and selections as well as original hymns and poetry.

AUTHOR: 495 Come, You Thankful People, Come

ALINGTON, CYRIL ARGENTINE (1872–1955), was born October 23, 1872, in Candlesby, Lincolnshire, son of a Church of England minister. Educated at Marlborough and Trinity College, Oxford, he became a fellow of All Souls' College, Oxford, and assistant master at Marlborough and Eton. He was ordained a deacon in 1899, and a priest in 1901. Among his various other positions, he became headmaster of Shrewsbury School in 1908, of Eton in 1916, and chaplain to the King in 1921. He was dean of Durham from 1933 to 1951, when he retired.

A distinguished scholar and writer, Alington authored over 40 works in theology as well as essays, novels, and poems. He died May 16, 1955, at St. Weonards, Herefordshire.

AUTHOR: 129 Good Christian Friends, Rejoice and Sing

ALLEN, OSWALD (1816–78), was born at Kirkby Lonsdale, Westmoreland, England, son of a banker. A diseased spine resulted in his being an invalid all his life. In 1848 his health was such that he was able to accept a position in his father's bank, a move that ultimately led to his succeeding his father as the bank's manager. It was during the severe winter of 1859 to 1860 that he wrote and compiled his *Hymns of the Christian*

Life (London, 1869), a collection of 148 hymns, some previously written, all from his own pen. The rigors of that winter, together with the suffering caused by his malady, combined to give his hymns a soft, tender, comforting cast. He died at his birthplace in 1878.

AUTHOR: 347 Today Your Mercy Calls Us

ALLENDORF, JOHANN LUDWIG KONRAD (1693–1773), was born at Josbach, near Marburg, Germany, February 9, 1693, the son of a Lutheran pastor. After studying under August Hermann Francke (1663–1727) in Halle, he became a tutor in the household of Count Erdmann von Promnitz at Sorau in Niederlausitz. When in 1724 the count's daughter married the prince of Anhalt-Cöthen, Allendorf followed her to Cöthen as the court preacher. There he became the focus of a circle of Pietistic hymn writers. After the death of his first wife, the prince married her younger sister. When she died in 1750, the need for a Lutheran Court preacher ceased, for the prince was of the Reformed confession.

Another of Count Erdmann's daughters had married into the family of the pious Count Christian Ernst von Stolberg. He summoned Allendorf to Wernigerode to assist in two churches there. Later Allendorf became a member of the consistorial council in Wernigerode-Röschenrode and, from 1759 on, pastor of St. Ulrich in Halle. There he served as a faithful, beloved curate of souls until his death June 3, 1773.

Allendorf's hymns appeared principally in *Einige gantz neue auserlesene Lieder* (Halle, c. 1733) and *Einige gantz neue Lieder zum Lobe des Dreyeiningen Gottes und zur gewünschten reichen Erbauung vieler Menschen* (Cöthen, 1736). The latter, known as the *Cöthnische Lieder*, contained 132 hymns by Allendorf in its fourth edition.

AUTHOR: 78 Jesus Has Come and Brings Pleasure

ALLWARDT, ERICH BAUM (1905–), has been in retirement in St. Louis since 1973, after 25 years in the pastoral ministry and 17 years as manuscript editor at Concordia Publishing House, St. Louis. Born May 13, 1905, in Sandusky, Ohio, he attended parochial school in Woodville, Ohio, and the Woodville Normal and Academy of the Evangelical Lutheran Joint Synod of Ohio and Other States. Here he earned his high school diploma, a certificate of music in piano and harmony, and a year of college credits. In 1926 he earned his Bachelor of Arts degree from Capital University, Bexley, Ohio. After a year of factory work he studied one year at Capital Seminary and two years at Concordia Seminary, St. Louis, graduating in 1930. His year of internship was served at St. John's Lutheran Church, Collinwood, in Cleveland, where his future wife, Olga Grapatin, was a member. Married in 1932, the couple has six children.

From 1931 to 1944 Allwardt was first resident pastor of Trinity Church, Willoughby, Ohio, then became pastor of Immanuel Church, Decatur, Indiana (1944–50), and of St. John's, Evanston, and Grace, Bristow, Indiana (1950–56). In

1951 he organized Emmanuel Church, Tell City, Indiana, a daughter of the Evanston congregation. From 1948–56 he was editor of the *Central District News,* Part II of the *Lutheran Witness.*

Allwardt retired from the publishing house at the end of 1973 but continued there with part-time work. In 1980 he was asked to become chief manuscript editor for *Lutheran Worship* (1982). Since then he has written historical articles for *Concordia Historical Institute Quarterly* and has transliterated and translated German correspondence for the Institute's archives.

TRANSLATOR: 66 Every Year the Christ Child

AMBROSE, ST. (c. 340–97) was born at Trier, Germany, the son of a prefect of the Roman province of Gaul. After the death of his father in 353, the mother and children moved to Rome. Here Ambrose studied law and soon distinguished himself in the court of the pretorian prefect of Italy. In 374 he was appointed consul of the Liguria and Aemilia districts in northern Italy, which demanded his moving to Milan. In the conflict between those holding the catholic faith and those of the Arian heresy, he displayed such courage and wisdom that upon the death of the bishop of Milan in 374 he was elected bishop by acclamation of the people and, though only a catechumen, he was forthwith baptized and a week later, December 7, 374, consecrated bishop. In this office Ambrose exhibited both gentleness and firmness. He courageously and successfully defied the Roman rulers in their repeated attempts to dominate the church. He was also largely responsible for winning over St. Augustine, a Manichaean heretic, to the Christian faith.

Scholar, statesman, theologian that he was, he is especially known and remembered for his significant contribution to the Christian Church in the area of hymnody and music. In fact, the real history of hymns in the West begins with him. It was in the basilica in Milan, beset with Arian opponents, that Christians heard the first strains of catholic hymnody in which, with simplicity and beauty, dignity, directness, and evangelical fervor, Ambrose set forth the doctrines of the orthodox faith. Cast in eight four-line stanzas—the familiar classical iambic dimeter that later became known as the Ambrosian metre—these hymns, congregational in character, became popular in the truest sense and soon found their way into the Milanese and other liturgies. Eventually they found a permanent place in the Roman office.

How deeply the appeal of their music could touch the soul is attested by St. Augustine:

> What tears I shed over the hymns and canticles when the sweet sound of the music of your church thrilled my soul! As the music flowed into my ears and your truth trickled into my heart, the tide of devotion swelled high within me, and the tears ran down, and there was gladness in those tears (*Confessions*, ix. 6).

The immense popularity of these hymns encouraged imitation, and a host of hymns in the same form came to be known as Ambrosian hymns, creating uncertainty as to which of these are actually by Ambrose. Of the more than 90 such hymns, investigation has established that 14 are undoubtedly by Ambrose. Credit is also given Ambrose for introducing to the West the practice of antiphonal singing. Worn out by labors and anxieties for the cause of Christ, Ambrose of Milan died April 4, 397.

AUTHOR: 13 Savior of the Nations, Come
481 O Splendor of the Father's Light
487 O Trinity, O Blessed Light

ANNA SOPHIA of Hesse-Darmstadt (1638–83), daughter of the staunch Lutheran Landgrave Georg II of Hesse-Darmstadt, was born in Marburg, December 17, 1638. She became so thoroughly grounded in the Holy Scriptures and the church fathers that, it is stated, she could put many theologians to shame. At the age of 18 she was elected prioress of a Lutheran convent in Quedlinburg. Here she lived a quiet, secluded life in Christ, suffering frequent asthma attacks and struggling with herself to remain in Christ. Her innermost thoughts are expressed in a series of scholarly, devotional poems and hymns that dwell on the friendship of the soul with Christ and are included in a devotional book entitled *Der treue Seelen-Freund Christus Jesus*, published in 1658.

AUTHOR: 339 Speak, O Lord, Your Servant Listens

ANDERS, CHARLES R. (1929–), was born in Frederick, Maryland, July 29, 1929. He holds a Bachelor of Arts degree (1950) from Wittenberg University, Springfield, Ohio; a Bachelor of Music degree (1951) from St. Olaf College, Northfield, Minnesota; Bachelor of Divinity (1954) from Hamma School of Theology, Springfield, Ohio; and a Master of Music in musicology from Indiana University (1962).

Ordained in 1954, Anders became assistant pastor of Lutheran Church of the Redeemer, Atlanta. Three years later he began service at Advent Lutheran in Greenwood, Indiana, remaining there until 1962, when he was called as assistant director of the Commission on Worship of the Lutheran Church in America. He served from 1967–75 as a member of the Hymn Music Committee of the Inter-Lutheran Commission on Worship preparing the *Lutheran Book of Worship* (1978). From 1973–75 he was music editor at Augsburg Publishing House, Minneapolis.

Returning to the parish ministry, he was pastor of All Saints Lutheran Church, Tamarac, Florida, from 1975–82. He is currently serving as senior pastor of Diamond Lake Lutheran Church, Minneapolis.

Anders has contributed articles to church music publications as well as composing hymn tunes and choral compositions.

COMPOSER: 449 FREDERICKTOWN

ANTHES, JOHANN A. (1789–1842) [*TLH* and *LBW* list the name as Friedrich K. Anthes, b. 1812], was born October 9, 1789, at Kronberg, Germany, son of teacher and cantor Gottfried A. Anthes. Instructed in music by his father, in 1810 he became teacher and cantor-adjunct in Weilburg, and in 1817 teacher of music in a teacher-training college at Idstein, where he died May 19, 1843.

Considered to be a first-rate musician, he was commissioned to produce a *Choralbuch* to the then-recently issued Nassau hymnal of 1842, a task which he accepted, but which sudden death in 1843 terminated. When the book appeared in 1847, it contained a number of tunes acknowledged as composed by him.

COMPOSER: 345, 347 ANTHES

ARENDS, WILHELM ERASMUS (1677–1721), was born February 6, 1677, the son of a Lutheran pastor, at Langestein, near Halberstadt. In 1707 Wilhelm became pastor at Crottorf, near Halberstadt, and in 1718 pastor of St. Peter and St. Paul Church in Halberstadt. Here he served until his death May 16, 1721.

As a student of August Hermann Francke in Halle, he belongs to the Pietistic school of poets.

AUTHOR: 303 Rise To Arms! With Prayer Employ You

ARNESON, OLE T. (1853–1917), was born near Highlandville, Iowa, May 4, 1852. He attended the Winona Public School, Winona, Minnesota, and from 1876–79 he served as principal of the public school at Spring Grove, Minnesota. From mailing clerk to shipping clerk he finally became manager of the book department of Skandinaven in Chicago. His interest in hymnody led him to translate many hymns from the Norwegian language. He died June 3, 1917.

TRANSLATOR: 466 Oh, Blessed Home Where Man and Wife

BACH, JOHANN SEBASTIAN (1685–1750), was born at Eisenach in eastern Germany on March 21, 1685, in the shadow of the Wartburg Castle, where Luther translated the New Testament. At the age of six he began attending the Latin school in Eisenach, where he also sang in the church choir. Upon the death of his father four years later he was sent off to live with his brother Johann Christoph, organist in Ohrdruf and former student of Johann Pachelbel (1653–1706), from whom he received a sound musical education. At the age of 15 he left his brother's home to become a scholarship singer at St. Michael's Church in Lüneberg. While there he studied organ and composition with the German composer and organist Georg Böhm (1661–1733) and often walked 30 miles to hear the famed organist Adam Reinken (1623–1722). In 1703 at the age of 18 he was appointed organist at St. Boniface in Arnstadt, where he remained until 1707. It was while here that he made a four-month visit to Lübeck to study with the eminent Dietrich Buxtehude (1637–1707). After one year as organist at St. Blasius Church in Mühlhausen, which he left because of some conflict with Pietists, he became court organist at Weimar and later concert master of the Duke's chamber orchestra, his first major position. From 1717–23 he served as court musician to Prince Leopold of Anhalt-Cöthen. Despite the lively young duke who was his pupil, Bach disliked the Calvinistic opposition to the use of music in the church. Thus during his stay here his composing was largely restricted to chamber and keyboard works. Bach's last position was that of cantor at St. Thomas' School in Leipzig, a position that composers and organists Georg Philipp Telemann (1681–1767) and Johann Graupner (1683–1760) had turned down. Here his task was to train the choirboys, provide music for special occasions, conduct the music every Sunday at St. Thomas, St. Nicholas, and two lesser churches, and teach Latin.

In the course of his lifetime Bach produced a prodigious amount of vocal, choral, instrumental and keyboard music—two great Passions, the Mass in B minor, about 300 cantatas for the church year, 26 preludes and fugues, 143 chorale preludes for organ, six concerti grossi (Brandenburg), four orchestral suites, concertos for various instruments, partitas, suites, and sonatas for clavier and chamber combinations, 48 preludes and fugues for clavier, motets, and other works. Considering music the handmaid of theology, he pursued this goal with an insatiable thirst for perfection and a formidable knowledge of the Bible. He wrote as though God himself were scrutinizing every note and phrase, beginning most manuscripts with the abbreviation *JJ,* Latin for "Jesus, help," and ending them with *SDG,* Latin for "To God alone be glory."

Bach was twice married, the first time to his distant cousin Maria Barbara Bach, and after her death to Anna Magdalena Wülken, the young daughter of a court trumpeter. He fathered twenty children. With the life expectancy of those times, less than half of them grew into adulthood. A number of his sons became distinguished musicians.

Blinded by a minor stroke, Bach spent the last year of his life dictating music to two young students. Blind and sick, his last such effort was to dictate an expanded version of the organ chorale based on Paul Eber's (1511–69) hymn "Wenn wir in höchsten Nöten sein" (*LW* 428). Bach, however, provided this organ chorale with the text "Vor deinen Thron trit ich hiermit":

Before Thy throne I come and pray:
Cast not Thy sinful child away!
Do not Thy gracious help remove
From me who needs forgiving love!

A blessed end do Thou, Lord give;
And then, that I with Thee may live,
Awaken me by Thy great power.
Amen. Oh, help me in this hour!

(Gurlitt, *Johann Sebastian Bach*, p. 133.)

He died in Leipzig July 28, 1750. At his funeral the boys of St. Thomas sang, and the bells of the four churches peeled to the passing of him who would later be considered one of the "three Bs" in the musical world—Bach, Beethoven, Brahms—as well as being called the Fifth Evangelist.

COMPOSER: 89 POTSDAM

BACKER, BRUCE R. (1929–), was born December 12, 1929, at New Ulm, Minnesota, and educated at St. Paul's Evangelical School and at Martin Luther Academy, then an integral part of Dr. Martin Luther College, a teacher training institution of the Wisconsin Evangelical Lutheran Synod, both in the same city. In 1947 he entered the college, receiving the Teacher's Diploma from the then-three year college in 1950. Transferring to Northwestern College, Watertown, Wisconsin, he graduated in 1952 with a Bachelor of Arts degree in preparation for the holy ministry. Thereafter he entered the Wisconsin Lutheran Seminary, Thiensville, in 1953, and Northwestern University, Evanston, Illinois, in the summer of that year, graduating cum laude from the seminary in June 1956, and with honors from Northwestern University in August of that year.

Assigned as assistant instructor to the faculty of Dr. Martin Luther College in 1956, first at its remote site in Fond du Lac, Wisconsin, and then in New Ulm, Minnesota, two years later he was given a full professorship, thus succeeding his father Emil D. Backer, who had served there from 1924–57. He teaches pipe organ, Lutheran liturgy, hymnody, and choral conducting, and chairs the organ department. In addition he has devoted himself to revising the teaching of music theory, developing a curriculum for organ instruction, introducing a course in music listening and in Lutheran worship, for which he published a text in 1988.

In 1959 he began studies with Johannes Riedel toward the Doctor of Philosophy degree in musicology at the University of Minnesota. Having completed the course work and qualifying examinations in 1967, he, however, discontinued the program in 1970. He has been a student, both intensively and intermittently, of the renowned organist and teacher Heinrich Fleischer for these many years.

Since 1981 Backer has served the Wisconsin Evangelical Lutheran Synod as a member of its Commission on Worship and more recently as a member of its Joint Hymnal Committee until 1988. In connection with this service he has composed numerous hymn tunes.

Married to Virginia Spaude, he is the father of five children.

COMPOSER: 144 TRIUMPH

BAHNMEIER, JONATHAN FRIEDRICH (1774–1841), was born July 12, 1774, the son of J. C. Bahnmeier, the town preacher at Oberstenfeld, Württemberg. Following his theological studies at Tübingen, he became assistant to his father. After serving in two other minor positions, in 1815 he was appointed professor of education and homiletics at Tübingen. Four years later, because of his innocent close relationship to a German students' association formed for political purposes, he was deprived of his professorship and appointed dean and town preacher at Kirchheim-unter-Teck. There he labored tirelessly and effectively for 21 years, not only as a caring pastor and distinguished preacher but also in behalf of Christian education, missions, and Bible distribution. His poetic gifts and his having published two collections of hymns and miscellaneous songs for various occasions prompted his membership on the committee that compiled the *Württemberg Gesangbuch* (1842). While visiting a school at Brucker he suffered a stroke that resulted in his death a few days later at Owen, August 18, 1841.

AUTHOR: 321 Spread the Reign of God the Lord

BAIN, JAMES L. MACBETH (c. 1840–1925), was born in Scotland. A mystical writer, poet, and spiritual healer, he passed from orthodox faith to agnosticism, to a revelation of all-pervading Divine Love. Introduced to the Christo Theosophic Society, he finally felt restored to his lost faith in all its simplicity. In his "rapture of faith restored" he wrote poems and tunes, including apparently BROTHER JAMES' AIR. The brotherhood of healers formed by Bain for treating both physical and spiritual illness often sang to patients as part of the healing process. Bain published *The Brotherhood of Healers. Being a Message to All Practical Mystics . . . and an Introduction to the Study of the Essential Principles of Spiritual, Psychic and Mental Healing* (1906). The last years of his life were spent caring for people in the slums of Liverpool and at a children's home. He died September 19, 1925.

COMPOSER: 417 BROTHER JAMES' AIR

BAJUS, JOHN (1901–71), was born April 5, 1901, at Raritan, New Jersey. He graduated from the then-Concordia Institute (now Concordia College), Bronxville, New York, in 1921 and from Concordia Seminary, St. Louis, in 1925. As a pastor he for a time served the Granite City-West Frankfurt-Staunton, Illinois, parish, followed by a number of years at Zion Lutheran Church, Chicago. A charter member of the Slovak Luther League when it was organized in 1927, he was its president from 1928–30, its field secretary from 1928–30, and again from 1933–35. He was the first editor of its *Courier* from 1929–46. Beginning in 1949 he served a number of years as first vice-president and statistician of the Slovak Evangelical Lutheran Church. He was a member of the Intersynodical Committee on Hymnology and Liturgics for the Synodical Conference of North America, the committee that produced *The Lutheran Hymnal* (1941). As such he achieved recognition as a translator of Slovak hymns and poems. He died at Norridge, Illinois, August 14, 1971.

TRANSLATOR: 146 Lo, Judah's Lion Wins the Strife

BAKER, HENRY WILLIAMS (1821–77), was born May 27, 1821, in London, the eldest son of Vice-Admiral Sir Henry Lorraine Baker. Educated at Trinity College, Cambridge, he was ordained in 1844 and became vicar of Monkland, near Leominster, on the English-Welsh border, in 1851. Eight years later he succeeded to the baronetcy, which benefice he held until his death, February 12, 1877. His last touching words were those of stanza 3 of his exquisite rendering of Palm 23, "The King of love my shepherd is" (*LW* 412):

Perverse and foolish oft I strayed,
But yet in love he sought me
And on his shoulder gently laid
And home rejoicing brought me.

Baker, credited with having written 33 hymns, is remembered as the chief promoter of *Hymns Ancient and Modern* (1861), a project in which from the first, and for twenty years, he was engaged as chairman of the committee and acknowledged as the leader responsible for the preparation and development of that epoch-making book. As editor he exercised his right of freely altering contributions, so freely that one contributor who took exception to his changes said sarcastically that H. A. and M. should be taken to mean "Hymns Asked for and Mutilated." In defense of Baker it must be stated that many of his alterations have been generally approved. He desired to restore to the devotional life of the church the treasures of early Latin hymnody and thus was instrumental in securing the many fine translations of J. M. Neale (*LW* 31, et al.). The immense popularity of the book—sales of well over 60 million—is ample proof of Baker's taste and ability, a tribute to his judgment of assessing the needs of the Anglican Church. He himself contributed both translations and original hymns, some of which are among the most cherished devotional treasures of the Church. Celibacy of the clergy was part of his high church belief, and he died unmarried. He published *Family Prayers for the use of those who have to work hard* and a *Daily Text Book* for the same group.

AUTHOR:	412	The King of Love My Shepherd Is
	498	O God of Love, O King of Peace
TRANSLATOR:	36	Of the Father's Love Begotten
	188	Sweet Flowerets of the Martyr Band
COMPOSER:	408, 469	STEPHANOS

BARBAULD, ANNA LAETITIA AIKIN (1743–1825), learned to read at two years of age, and studied under Philip Doddridge (*LW* 29, et al.). Her father John Aikin, a dissenting minister at Kibworth, England, tutored at the dissenting academy there.

She was married in 1774 to her father's student Rochemont Barbauld, a dissenting minister of French Protestant descent. Pastor of a congregation at Palgrave in Suffolk, he opened a school there at which his wife taught. Pastor Barbauld suffered from mental illness and, after he reportedly attacked her, Mrs. Barbauld had him committed to a sanatorium. He escaped in 1808 and drowned himself.

Anna Barbauld, at the insistence of her brother, John Aikin, devoted her talents to writing. Her first volume of *Poems* was published in 1773, and in the same year she brought out *Miscellaneous Pieces in Prose* in collaboration with John who, when she showed reluctance to publish her poems, took them to the printer himself. Deeply concerned with children's welfare, she adopted her brother's son Charles and wrote *Early Lessons* (1781) for him. She died at the age of 81, on March 9, 1825.

AUTHOR: 496 Lord, to You Immortal Praise

BARING-GOULD, SABINE (1834–1924), was the eldest son of the squire of an estate called Lew-Trenchard, at Exeter, England. After spending much of his early life in France and Germany, he received his Bachelor of Arts and Master of Arts degrees from Clare College, Cambridge, and later became an honorary fellow of the college.

Assistant master of the choir school of St. Barnabas' Church in Pimlico, 1857, and at Hurstpierpoint College, Sussex, until 1864, when he was ordained deacon. Attaining priesthood in 1865, he was appointed to the curacy of Horbury parish, near Wakefield, serving also the mission at Horbury Bridge until 1867, when he was preferred to the incumbency of Dalton, Yorkshire. In 1871 he became rector of East Mercer, Essex, but remained only one year, retiring in 1872, for the remainder of his life, to Lew-Trenchard, which he inherited from an uncle.

In the same year he published three of his principal works, including the first volume of his most ambitious literary venture, *Lives of the Saints* (15 volumes). He exercised his prerogative as lord of the manor by appointing himself as the rector, when the position became vacant through the death of an uncle. The net annual income from the position meant very little to a man of his financial means, for it was only 117 pounds; however, it gave him the opportunity of preaching and of supervising more effectively the spiritual life of almost 300 persons.

In 1868 he married Grace Taylor, a girl who had worked as a millhand. This happy marriage produced 15 children.

Baring-Gould was probably the most prolific of all English authors—the literary catalogue of the British Museum lists more titles by him than by any other British writer of his time—though he will be remembered most as the author of the hymn, "Onward, Christian soldiers." He died at Lew-Trenchard at the age of ninety on Jan. 2, 1924.

AUTHOR: 491 Now the Day Is Over
518 Onward, Christian Soldiers

BARNBY, JOSEPH (1838–96), was born in York, England, August 12, 1838, the son of a church organist. He was a chorister at Yorkminster at the age of seven, an organist and choirmaster at 12, and a student at the Royal Academy of Music at 16. Following his studies at the Royal Academy he served as organist at St. Michael's, Queenhithe; St. James the Less, Westminster; St. Andrew's, Welles Street, where his choir reached a degree of perfection second to none in London. From 1871–86 he was at St. Anne's, Soho, where he established annual Lenten performances of Bach's *St. John Passion.* Moreover, in 1871 he conducted the *St. Matthew Passion* with full orchestra in Westminster Abbey, the first performance of that work in an English church.

From 1875–92 he served as precentor and director of music instruction at Eaton College. From 1861–76 he was music advisor to Novello, Ewer, and Company, music publishers, who in 1867 established for him what became known as Barnby's Choir. Later he conducted the Royal Choral Society. In 1892 he became principal of the Guild Hall School of Music and was knighted. He died suddenly on January 28, 1896, shortly after conducting a rehearsal of G.F. Händel's (*LW* 53) *Judas Maccabaeus.*

Barnby produced a prodigious amount of music: the oratorio *Rebecca*, anthems, services, chants, vocal solos, part songs, and 246 hymn tunes, many of which were popular at the turn of the century but today are considered to exemplify the less endearing aspects of Victorianism. He was music editor of five hymnals, the most notable of which was *The Hymnary* (1872), for the high church party of Benjamin Webb, vicar of St. Andrew's Church, where Barnby served as organist and choirmaster. He helped edit the *Cathedral Psalter* (1873).

COMPOSER: 253 O PERFECT LOVE
318 GALILEAN
356 DUNSTAN
374 WINTERTON
397 JUST AS I AM
460 LAUDES DOMINI
491 MERRIAL

BARNES, EDWARD SHIPPEN (1887–1958), was born in Seabright, New Jersey, September 14, 1887. He earned his Bachelor Arts degree at Yale University, where he studied music under Horatio Parker, Harry Benjamin Jepson, and David Stanley Smith. Further music study was pursued under Vincent d'Indy and Abel Decaux at the Schola Cantorum in Paris, where he also studied privately with Louis Vierne. He served as organist and choirmaster at the Church of the Incarnation and Rutgers Presbyterian Church in New York City, at St. Stephen's Church in Philadelphia, and at the First Presbyterian Church in Santa Monica, California. In 1954 he retired to Idyllwild, California, where he died February 14, 1958.

In addition to his *Method of Organ Playing*, the cantatas: *The Comforter* and *Remember Now thy Creator,* and *Bach for Beginners,* Barnes wrote a number of organ and choral works as well as anthems and services for the Episcopal Church. He also contributed to the *Handbook to the Hymnal of the Presbyterian Church* (1935).

ARRANGER: 55 GLORIA

BARTHÉLÉMON, FRANCOIS HIPPOLITE (1741–1808), was born in Bordeaux, France, July 27, 1741, to a French government officer and a wealthy Irish lady. Educated at the best schools, he joined the army as an officer in the Irish Brigade, where he exhibited noteworthy skill in fencing and in the tangentially related art of music.

Encouraged by his colonel to pursue a career that would afford more opportunities than did the armed forces, Barthélémon found himself accompanying the Earl of Kelly, an amateur composer and admirer, to England. There Bartel, as his friends called him, distinguished himself not only as a composer and violinist, but as a conductor at the King's Theatre, at Marleybone and Vauxhall Gardens. In 1776 Barthélémon and his wife, singer Mary Young, presented concerts in Germany, Italy, and France. Among other distinguished appearances, they were invited to perform for a select party at the Versailles palace and, as a result, urged to remain at the French court. In 1777 the two returned to England. On his second visit to London, Franz Joseph Haydn (*LW* 294) became their close friend. Haydn gave lessons to their only daughter, Cecilia, and on one occasion accompanied singer Mary Barthélémon at a benefit concert. Back in London Mrs. Barthélémon became a patroness of the chapel of the Asylum for Female Orphans. She arranged to introduce her husband to the Swedenborgian chaplain, Jacob Duché, and the two became close friends. When Duché began compiling a collection of psalms and hymns for use at the asylum, he naturally called on Barthélémon to assist; and in the course of this collaboration, Barthélémon's single immortal tune, now known as MORNING HYMN, was set to Thomas Ken's "Awake, my soul, and with the sun," a union that has enjoyed worldwide use.

A stroke in his later years robbed Barthélémon of much of his ability, and he died in London July 20, 1808. In addition to his several compositions for the theater, he composed quartets for strings, violin duets and concertos, keyboard lessons and preludes, plus some glees and catches.

COMPOSER: 478 MORNING HYMN

BAYLY, ALBERT FREDERICK (1901–84), was born September 6, 1901, at Bexhill-on-Sea, Sussex, England, and educated at St. Mary Magdalene School, St. Leonard's, and Hastings Grammar School. Bayly trained as a shipwright at the Royal Dockyard School, Portsmouth, but later decided to study at Mansfield College, Oxford (1925–28), and become a minister of the Congregational church. Upon graduation in 1928 he became assistant minister of Whitley Bay Congregational Church, taking charge also of Fairway Hall, Monseaton, Northumberland, a new branch established by the Whitley Bay congregation. Thereafter he served a number of congregations: Morpeh Congregational Church (1938–46); Hollingreave Church in Burnley (1946–50); Swanland Congregational Church in East Yorkshire (1950–56); Eccleston Congregational Church, St. Helens, Lancashire (1956–62); and Thaxted Congregational Church,

Essex (1962–72). He retired to Chelmsford, Essex, in 1968). He died July 26, 1984, returning home after attending at Chichester the annual conference of the Hymn Society of Great Britain.

Bayly wrote his first hymn, "Rejoice, O people, in the mounting years," in 1945 for the Triple Jubilee of the London Missionary Society. Encouraged by its success, he continued to write hymns that he eventually published in four collections: *Rejoice, O People* (1951), *Again I Say Rejoice* (1967), *Rejoice Always* (1971), and *Rejoice in God* (1978). It is to his credit that few hymnals published since 1950 lack one or more hymns from his pen. In 1968 Westminster Choir College, Princeton, New Jersey, made him an honorary fellow, and on May 31, 1978, he was honored at a special service in Westminster Abbey. Being one of the first of the new wave of hymn writers to emerge after the second World War, Cyril Taylor described Bayly as "the last of the old and the first of the new."

AUTHOR: 403 Praise and Thanksgiving

BECK, THEODORE(1929–), was born April 17, 1929, in River Forest, Illinois. He attended the American Conservatory of Music, Chicago, where he studied piano with Kurt Waniek, and Concordia College, River Forest, graduating with the Bachelor of Arts degree in 1950. Two years later he earned the Master of Music degree from Northwestern University, Evanston, Illinois, meanwhile teaching organ at Concordia (1950-53). Since 1953 he has been teaching music theory and organ at Concordia Teachers College, Seward, Nebraska. Beck achieved the Doctor of Philosophy degree from Northwestern in 1961.

He served as a member of the music committee for the *Worship Supplement* (1969) to *The Lutheran Hymnal* (1941). For several years he has been a member of the Music Editorial Advisory Committee of Concordia Publishing House. His choral and organ music has been published by Concordia, Augsburg, Chantry Press, and The Choristers Guild. Married to Carol Schall in 1950, he is the father of three children.

ARRANGER: 26 CONSOLATION
57 TEMPUS ADEST FLORIDUM
133 HERZLICH TUT MICH ERFREUEN
183 ROK NOVÝ
281 BRYN CALFARIA

BEDE, The Venerable (673–735), was born near the monasteries of Wearmouth and Jarrow. Orphaned as a child, at the age of seven his relatives gave him to Abbot Benedict (Biscop) and afterwards to Ceolfrid, to be educated. In his nineteenth year he was admitted to the diaconate; in his 30th, to the priesthood, both by the hands of Bishop John of Beverley and at the bidding of Abbot Ceolfrid. Bede, the scholar, grammarian, philosopher, poet, biographer, historian, and divine, spent the greater part of his life at Jarrow, hardly leaving the monastery. There he died May 26, 735.

Bede was above all a student of history and theology, and a teacher whose aim it was to teach his pupils the knowledge necessary both to salvation and to the understanding of Christian theology and history. To this end he wrote a series of textbooks and treatises that were used in western Europe's schools for many centuries. The work that contributed most to his fame is the *Ecclesiastical History of the English People*, a well-arranged and straightforward account of the establishment and growth of the Christian Church in England. In this work he mentions that he is the author of a *Liber hymnorum diverso metro sive rhythmo,* a book containing both metrical and rhythmical hymns. Unfortunately this book has not survived, but Blume and Dreves in their *Analecta hymnica*, vol. 50, include no less than 16 hymns considered to be genuine Bede hymns.

AUTHOR: 149 A Hymn of Glory Let Us Sing

BEHM, MARTIN (1557–1622), was born September 16, 1557, in Lauben, Silesia, the son of the town overseer. During a severe famine in 1574 a close relative, Dr. Paul Fabricius, an imperial physician and professor at Vienna, took the young Behm to that city to shield him from hunger and death. There Behm served as a tutor for two years. In 1576 he went to Strassburg, drawn there by Johann Sturm, renowned humanist and pedagogue, rector of the newly founded Lutheran university. Here, to pursue his university studies, Behm worked as a graduate assistant and received financial help from Johann Sturm. Upon the death of his father in May 1580, Behm left Strassburg to return home. At Easter, 1581, he was appointed assistant in the town school and the following September 20 he was ordained deacon of Holy Trinity Church, the main Lutheran church in Lauben. In November of 1582 he married Ursula, daughter of cloister administrator Casper Römer. The union was blessed with 11 children. One son, as deacon, later became a colleague of his father.

When, in July 1584, the senior pastor, Sigismund Schwabe, was advanced to Breslau, the town council kept the position nominally vacant for two years. Thereafter, June 1586, Behm was appointed chief pastor. In this position he served tirelessly and faithfully for 36 years, seeing his Christian people through a fierce earthquake in 1590, a devastating pestilence in 1613, and the horrors of war in 1619.

Behm also became a renowned preacher, and his church was frequently filled with people from abroad. Steeped in the Lord's Passion and its salvific significance for sinful mankind, the 150 passion sermons that he preached in 1614 entitled *Spectaculum passionis Jesu Christi* became popular favorites. Moreover, he took special delight in the Psalter and in the course of 18 years he preached 463 sermons on it.

In his sermons on the Gospels Behm cultivated the habit of turning the leading thoughts into rhymed prayers that he then recited to the congregation. As a result he enriched the Church with some 500 hymns, most of which were published in three volumes: *Centuria precationum rhythmicarum* (Wittenberg, 1606); *Centuria secunda precationum rhythmicarum* (Wittenberg, 1608); and *III. Centuria precationum rhythmicarum* (Wittenberg, 1615).

After preaching on the Tenth Sunday after Trinity Sunday in 1621 he was suddenly stricken with an illness that confined him to his bed for 24 weeks until his death February 5, 1622.

AUTHOR: 79 O Jesus, King of Glory
479 O Holy Blessed Trinity

BELSHEIM, OLE GULBRAND (1861–1925), was born at Vang Valdres, Norway, August 26, 1861. Having come to America as a boy of five, he attended Luther College, Decorah, Iowa; Northfield Seminary, and Augsburg Seminary, Minneapolis. He held Lutheran pastorates successively at Milwaukee, Wisconsin; Albert Lea, Minnesota; Grand Meadow, Minnesota; and Mandan, North Dakota. It was as a member of the committee for *The Lutheran Hymnary* (1913) that he translated this hymn. He also translated Laache's *Catechism* into English in 1894, and for two years he served as editor of the *Christian Youth.* He died February 12, 1925.

TRANSLATOR: 333 God's Word Is Our Great Heritage

BENDER, JAN O. (1909–), was born in Haarlem, The Netherlands. At his father's death the family moved to Lübeck, Germany, when Jan was 13 years of age. His music studies included work with Karl Straube (1873–1950), at one time organist and cantor at the *Thomaskirche* in Leipzig, and with Hugo Distler (1908–40), the renowned composer and organist in Lübeck and Amsterdam. For 26 years Bender was organist and choirmaster for several churches in Germany, including seven years (1953–60) at St. Michael's, Lüneberg, where J.S. Bach was once a choir boy.

Coming to the United States in 1960, Bender taught music at Concordia College, Seward, Nebraska, for five years, moving to Springfield, Ohio, in 1965 for an associate, and then full, professorship at Wittenberg University. In 1976 he returned to Germany, traveling again to the United States three years later to teach at Valparaiso University, Valparaiso, Indiana, and later Gustavus Adolphus College, St. Peter, Minnesota. Since 1982 he and his wife Charlotte have been living in Hanerau, Holstein, West Germany.

Bender was awarded the Doctor of Letters degree by Concordia Seward in 1975; in the same year he received the Canticum Novum award from Wittenberg University, and became a fellow in the Hymn Society of America. His music publications number over 1,100 pieces in his opus numbers 1–90; he prepared a number of hymn settings for *Lutheran Book of Worship* (1978) and *Worship Supplement* (1969). His settings in *Lutheran Worship* (1982) were done for either of the foregoing hymnals.

COMPOSER: 319 WITTENBERG NEW

ARRANGER:	72	HERR CHRIST, DER EINIG, GOTTES SOHN
	126	SONNE DER GERECHTIGKEIT
	357	ALLEIN ZU DIR
	382	NUN LASST UNS DEN LEIB BEGRABEN
	442	IN DIR IST FREUDE
	493	WIE LIEBLICH IST DER MAIEN

BERNARD OF CLAIRVAUX (1091–1153), was born at his father's castle in the Fontaines region of what is now France. His father, a knight named Tesselin, died in the First Crusade. After being educated at Chatillon, he decided to join the Cistercians at the monastery in Citeaux, in 1113, taking with him an uncle and two brothers, whom he had won over. Two years later he founded the more famous Cistercian community at Clairvaux (Beautiful Valley), of which he was the first abbot, where he remained until his death.

Bernard's persuasiveness and influence, with the backing of Henry I of England and Emperor Lothar of Germany, enabled Innocent II to make good his claim to the papacy over against the rival claim of Anacletus II. In the appointments to high church offices Bernard's influence was also clearly in evidence.

The year 1140 saw Bernard prosecuting, at the Council of Sens, logician Peter Abelard (1079–1142), who championed dialectic and rationalism in the Church's doctrine, an act which led to Abelard's excommunication. Bernard's impassioned eloquence in behalf of the Second Crusade caused masses to answer the call, a crusade that ended in disaster, with Germany's King Conrad III and King Louis VII of France returning defeated and disgraced with but a miserable remnant who had escaped death. Bernard issued a heartfelt apology for his part in recruiting people, which apology is among his works still extant. Weary of dissension and reproach, he died in 1153.

The hymns commonly attributed to St. Bernard cannot be proven, although some experts feel their style is unmistakably his. Author Richard C. Trench (1807–86) speaks of Bernard of Clairvaux as "the stayer of popular commotions, the queller of heresies, the umpire between princes and kings, the counsellor of popes, the founder . . . of an important religious order, the author of a crusade." Martin Luther (*LW* 13, et al.) called him "the greatest monk that ever lived."

AUTHOR (attr.):	113	O Sacred Head, Now Wounded
	274	O Jesus, King Most Wonderful

BERNARD OF CLUNY (twelfth century). Little is known about his life except that he entered the monastery at Cluny during the abbacy of Peter the Venerable (1122–56) and that he wrote one of the greatest medieval hymns known.

The famous monastery of Cluny, near Macon in Burgundy, France, was founded by William the Pious, Duke of Aquitaine, in 910. In the 11th and 12th centuries it exercised great influence in the life of the church. Its leading figures came from noble families who enjoyed the confidence of sovereigns and popes alike. In the middle of the 12th century, when the influence of the order—according to the strict Benedictine rule—reached its height, the number of Cluniac houses reached 314, scattered in France, Italy, Germany, England, Scotland, and Poland.

It was at Cluny that Bernard wrote the poem upon which his fame rests, namely, *De Contemptu Mundi* (On the contemptibleness of the world), which he dedicated to Peter the Venerable, and which has become the source of a number of famous hymns, of which the two listed below are among the best known.

AUTHOR: 309 Jerusalem the Golden
463 The Clouds of Judgment Gather

BIANCO DA SIENA (c. 1350–1434), whose birthdate is unknown, was probably born at Anciolina in the Val d'Arno, Italy. He spent his early years as an apprentice in the wool trade in Siena. In 1367 he entered the newly instituted order of Jesuates, a group of unordained followers of the rule of St. Augustine, founded that year by John Columbinus of Siena (suppressed by Pope Clement IX in 1668). Bianco appears to have lived in Venice in his late years and there he died. His hymns (*Laudi Spirituali*) were published in 1851; some have been translated into English by Dr. Littledale.

AUTHOR: 162 Come Down, O Love Divine

BIRKEN (BETULIUS), SIGISMUND von (1626–81), was born May 5, 1626, at Wildenstein, near Eger in Bohemia, where his father was an evangelical pastor. In 1629 his father, together with other pastors, had to flee Bohemia because of their faith, and the family established residence in Nürnberg. Following his schooling at the *Egidien Gymnasium* in Nürnberg, Sigismund entered the University of Jena in 1643 to study law and theology. Lack of funds prompted his return to Nürnberg in 1645. Shortly thereafter, in recognition of his poetical ability, he was admitted as a member of the Pegnitz Shepherd and Flower Order. Before the close of 1645 he was appointed tutor to the princes of Brunswick-Lüneburg at the Wolfenbüttel court. While here he was crowned poet. A year later, tired of court life, he traveled for two years, during which time he not only met the famous poet Johann Rist (*LW* 122, 244, 248), but was also admitted by Philipp von Zesen to membership in the German Rose Society, a prestigious group of poets. Upon his return to Nürnberg, November 20, 1648, just at the time that the Peace of Westphalia was concluded, he was again employed as a private tutor. In 1654, in recognition of his poetic gifts, Emperor Ferdinand III raised him to the rank of nobility, and in 1658 he was accepted as a member of the Fruitbearing Society. Four years later, on the death of Georg Philipp Harsdörffer, he became chief shepherd of the Pegnitz order, to which he imparted a distinctly religious cast. He died June 12, 1681, the result of a stroke.

Although Sigismund von Birken wrote approximately 48 hymns, their baroque, bucolic character and imagery generally limited their acceptance in hymnals to the two here listed.

AUTHOR: 109 Jesus, I Will Ponder Now
381 Let Us Ever Walk with Jesus

BLACKER, MAXWELL J. (1822–88), was born May 22, 1822. Educated at Merton College, Oxford, where he also earned the Master of Arts degree, he was ordained in 1848 and held several curacies, including that of St. Barnabas, Pimlico. He died June 11, 1888.

The *Hymner* of the Plainsong and Medieval Society contained numerous of his translations from the Latin.

TRANSLATOR: 323 Only-Begotten, Word of God Eternal

BOBB, BARRY L. (1951–), is presently director of music publications at Concordia Publishing House, St. Louis, Missouri. Born August 18, 1951, in Seymour, Indiana, he received his early education at the local parochial school and public high school and earned the Bachelor of Science degree from Concordia College, River Forest, Illinois, in 1973. He also holds the Master of Church Music degree from his alma mater. He has studied organ with the late Herbert Gotsch (*LW* 85, 356) and Thomas Gieschen (*LW* 358, 408) and composition with Richard Hillert (*LW* 71, et al.). Prior to assuming his present position, he served Christ Community Lutheran School in St. Louis and Salem Lutheran School in Affton as teacher. Barry Bobb has also served Christ Lutheran Church, Orland Park, Illinois; Salem Lutheran, Affton, Missouri; and Mt. Calvary Lutheran, Brentwood, Missouri, as minister of music. Married to Donna Lynn Ferrebee, he is the father of two boys.

As a composer he has had several choral works published and was a contributor to *The Concordia Hymn Prelude Series*, a 42-volume work for organ completed in 1986. He is the coauthor of *Proclaim: A Guide for Planning Liturgy and Music* (1985) for the parish pastor and church musician.

COMPOSER: 380 LAKEWOOD
ARRANGER: 165 KOMM, O KOMM, DU GEIST DES LEBENS

BOBERG, CARL GUSTAF (1859–1940), was born August 16, 1859, at Mönsteras, on the southeast coast of Sweden, the son of a shipyard carpenter. At the age of 19, having worked several years as a sailor, he experienced a conversion and felt the urge to begin preaching. Following two years' attendance at the Bible School in Kristinehamm, he became a lay preacher in his hometown. His talents, both as a speaker and writer, caused his becoming editor, from 1890–1916, of the weekly *Sanningsvittnet* and his election to the Swedish Parliament, wherein he served from 1912–31. He died at Kalmer on January 7, 1940.

AUTHOR: 519 How Great Thou Art

BOGATZKY, KARL HEINRICH VON (1690–1774), was born September 7, 1690, in Jankowe, near Mielitsch in Lower Silesia, the son of an army officer of a noble Hungarian family. With the frequent absences of his father, his mother and grandmother were largely responsible for his Christian upbringing. At the age of 14 he served as a page at the ducal court of Weissenfels. With the father's desire that he become a soldier, young Karl was stationed for a time in Breslau. His aversion to that life, coupled with a lengthy illness, prompted his move to the University of Jena to study jurisprudence. Influenced by Pietism, in 1715 he entered the University of Halle to study theology, a move that caused a complete break with his father. Poor health prohibited his entering the active ministry, so he devoted his time to religious writing and speaking at private gatherings. Following the death of his wife of eight years, in 1740 he moved to the court of the pious Duke Christian Ernst, where he wrote a few of his works. Upon the death of the duke in 1745, he moved to the orphanage in Halle, where his friend G. A. Francke gave him a free room. Here he taught Latin students, conducted regular devotions, and continued his writing. He died June 15, 1774.

Among his writings are *Das güldne Schatzkästlein der Kinder Gottes* (Breslau, 1718), a work that the English divine John Berridge (1716–93) recast in English and titled *The Golden Treasury,* which became a favorite book of devotion in Great Britain. His *Betrachtungen und Gebete über das ganze neue Testament* appeared in seven volumes (Halle, 1756–61).

As a poet, although his output was considerable—411 hymns in all—he was not exceptionally gifted, and the quality of his work is uneven. He assisted in the production of the influential collection of *Coethen Hymns* (1736), and among his better hymns it must be admitted that he speaks with a sincerity and warmth of faith far superior to the often sweet sentimentality of other contributors to that collection.

AUTHOR: 315 Awake, Thou Spirit of the Watchmen

BOLTZE, GEORG GOTTFRIED. Little information is available about him except that he was cantor and school teacher at an orphanage in Potsdam about 1750. He was still living in 1789.

COMPOSER: 381 LASSET UNS MIT JESU ZIEHEN

BONAR, HORATIUS (1808–1889). Generally regarded as the most eminent of the hymn writers of Scotland, Bonar was also a preacher of great fame and power. The son of a tax collector, he was born in Edinburgh, December 19, 1808, and received his education under Thomas Chalmers at the High School and University of Edinburgh. Although he had actually begun pastoral work sometime before his ordination, as minister-assistant at Leith, in 1837 he was ordained and settled at Kelso, on the river Tweed, near the English border, succeeding his father-in-law Robert Lundie.

Bonar found in Thomas Chalmers, his teacher, distinguished as social reformer, mathematician, theological professor, ecclesiastical statesman, and especially as a preacher, the primary stimulus for his intellectual and spiritual life. A descendant of a family which had been represented in the Church of Scotland for over two centuries, Bonar's one striking move was in joining Chalmers and others in forming the Free Church of Scotland at the time of the Disruption in 1843. Just then there was a good deal of unrest throughout the church, caused by the action of "patrons" who held as their property the right of naming the parish minister, and too often put in their nominee against the vehement protest of the congregation. This led to the Great Disruption of 1843, and Bonar with many of his friends was among the 451 ministers who withdrew from the Establishment and formed "the Free Church of Scotland." Bonar and his parish were exceptional in being able to retain their property, and he continued at Kelso as the devoted pastor of the church, now "Free," until 1866.

Those quiet years at Kelso no doubt made him what he was intellectually and spiritually. For many years he was one of the editors of *The Border Watch*, the official Free Church paper. The University of Aberdeen honored him with a Doctor of Divinity degree in 1853. A trip to Egypt and Palestine from 1855–56 aroused his great interest in the Jews and in prophecy. The second coming of Christ was much on Bonar's mind all of his life, and he became an ardent "premillenarian," believing that our Lord was to return in person, soon, suddenly, and with power, to destroy antichrist and restore Israel, and to inaugurate an earthly kingdom of a thousand years. The Advent hope became an absorbing passion. In its light he lived and worked, and to spread it he wrote tracts and books, and for 25 years edited *The Quarterly Journal of Prophecy*.

This sense of detachment from the present world, this homesickness for heaven, this hopeful but pensive expectation of the Second Coming, are behind his hymns and make them what they are. Few men knew the Bible as thoroughly as he. Although a Calvinist, his faith showed more latitude in everyday life than his creedal subscription. His first hymns were written for children, of whom he was very fond. Thrown off rather casually, usually on railroad trains, with no attempt to polish them, Bonar's hymns showed imperfections, such as awkward rhymes and faulty rhythm; however, as someone has said:

> They have gone round the world, have been sung in churches of all communions, have been learned by little children, and hung as lights over the thickly closing waters of death.

Because of the earlier influence of Thomas Chalmers on his life, Bonar found special pleasure therefore in becoming, in 1866, first pastor of the Chalmers Memorial Church, Grange, Edinburgh. In 1883 he became moderator of the General Assembly of the Free Church of Scotland.

Some of Bonar's hymns are truly classical. No less than 100 are to be found in the various hymnals of the English-speaking countries today. His works include *Songs for the Wilderness* (1843); *The Bible Hymn Book* (1845); *Hymns, Original and Selected* (1846); *Hymns of Faith and Hope* (1857), second series 1861; *The Song of the New Creation* (1872); *Hymns of the Nativity* (1879), and other books. However, of his 10 tracts or volumes of hymns (1843-1881) seven were published before his church authorized hymn singing, and his hymns were sung in almost every communion but his own. He died at Edinburgh, July 31, 1889.

AUTHOR: 173 Glory Be to God the Father
243 Here, O My Lord, I See You Face to Face
348 I Heard the Voice of Jesus Say
366 I Lay My Sins on Jesus

BORTHWICK, JANE (1813–97), was born in Edinburgh, Scotland, April 9, 1813, the elder daughter of James Borthwick, manager of the North British Insurance Office. Having traveled widely on the Continent and, encouraged by her father to use her linguistic gifts in translating, she and her sister Sarah Findlater translated and published 122 German hymns, in four series—1854, 1855, 1858, and 1862—under the title, *Hymns from the Land of Luther,* to which she contributed 69 translations and her sister 53. Jane also wrote some original hymns, many of which were published in *Thoughts for Thoughtful Hours* (1857). A member of the Free Church of Scotland, she took an active interest in various missionary endeavors both at home and abroad. She died September 7, 1897. Julian says of her:

> These translations, which represent relatively a larger portion of hymns for the Christian Life and a smaller for the Christian Year than one finds in Miss Winkworth, have obtained a success as translations and an acceptance in hymnals only second to Miss Winkworth's. . . . Hardly a hymnal has appeared in England or in America without containing some of these translations.

TRANSLATOR: 386 Jesus, Still Lead On
510 Be Still, My Soul

BÖSCHENSTAIN, JOHANN (1472-1539?), was born at Essling, Württemberg. As an ordained priest and an outstanding student of the renowned humanist Johann Reuchlin (1455–1522), he became an instructor of Hebrew at Ingolstadt in 1505. Here Andreas Osiander (the Elder, 1498–1552), the priest who later introduced the Reformation in

Nürnberg, attended his lectures on the Psalms. From Ingolstadt Böschenstain went to Augsburg where, in 1518, Elector Frederick the Wise called him as professor of Hebrew and Greek to Wittenberg University, where Philipp Melanchthon (*LW* 189) was a student of his. Within the next three years he went to Nürnberg, Heidelberg, and Antwerp. A brief stay in Zurich afforded Ulrich Zwingli (1484–1531) occasion to study Hebrew under him. In 1523 Böschenstain settled in Augsburg where he became a royal licensed teacher of Hebrew. The date and place of his death is uncertain. Some authorities give Augsburg, 1539; others, Nördlingen, 1540.

Among his works are a Hebrew grammar (1514), *The Seven Penitential Psalms* (Latin, 1520; German, 1536), the *Prayer of Solomon* (1523) and four hymns.

AUTHOR: 108 From Calvary's Cross I Heard Christ Say

BOUMAN, HERBERT J. A. (1908–81), son of a Lutheran pastor, was born July 21, 1908, in Freeman, South Dakota. After completing studies at Concordia College, St. Paul, Minnesota, he entered Concordia Seminary, St. Louis, where he received the Bachelor of Divinity degree in 1955 and a Master of Sacred Theology degree in 1960. That same year Concordia Theological Seminary, Springfield, Illinois, honored him with the Doctor of Divinity degree. As a Lutheran pastor he served Our Savior Lutheran Church, Canton, Ohio; St. John, Geneva, Ohio; St. John, Decatur, Indiana; and Immanual, Sheboygan, Wisconsin. As a theological professor he taught at Concordia College, Fort Wayne, Indiana; Concordia Seminary, St. Louis, Missouri; Luther Seminary, St. Paul, Minnesota; and the Lutheran Seminary, Porto Alegre, Brazil.

Bouman's talents led to other opportunities of service. He chaired the Board of Appeals of The Lutheran Church—Missouri Synod (1947–62); he served as secretary of the Synodical Conference (1956–62); he was a member of the Synod's Commission on Doctrinal Unity (1953–62); the Commission on Theology and Church Relations (1962–69); and the Division of Theological Studies of the Lutheran Council in the U.S.A. (1961–66).

In addition to articles in various professional and theological journals, sermons, and devotional literature, he did a number of translations: four volumes of *Luther's Works*, American Edition; Edmund Schlink's *Theology of the Lutheran Confessions* and his *The Doctrine of Baptism*; Hans-Werner Gensichen's *We Condemn: How Luther and 16th-Century Lutheranism Condemned False Doctrine*; Walter V. Loevenich's *Luther's Theology of the Cross*; and C. F. W. Walther's *Law and Gospel*. At the time of his heart attack and ensuing death on November 28, 1981, he had just translated the first chapter of Günther Stiller's *Johann Sebastian Bach and Liturgical Life in Leipzig*, a translation that was continued for a while by Daniel F. Poellot, completed by Hilton C. Oswald, and published by Concordia Publishing House in 1984.

TRANSLATOR: 54, part 2, The glorious angels came today

BOUMAN, PAUL B. (1918–), was born in Hamburg, Minnesota. He earned a Bachelor of Science in Education at Concordia Teacher's College, River Forest, Illinois, and a Master of Music degree from Northwestern University, Evanston, Illinois. Additional musical study was pursued at the Westphalian Church Music School in Hereford, Germany. He was teacher and director of music at Ebenezer Lutheran Church, Milwaukee, Wisconsin (1939–45); St. Paul Lutheran, Melrose Park, Illinois (1945–53); Grace Lutheran Church, River Forest, Illinois (1950–83);

Bouman's children's choir has won numerous awards, and he has presented rehearsal demonstrations to various chapters of the American Guild of Organists and other conferences. He is the composer of a number of choral works and is represented by organ selections in the *Parish Organist* (1953-66) and *The Concordia Hymn Prelude Series* (1986).

He is the recipient of the Spiritus Christi Medal from his alma mater; the Te Deum Award from Zion Lutheran Church, Dallas, Texas; and the Doctor of Humane Letters degree from Christ Seminary-Seminex, St. Louis, Missouri.

Married to Victoria Bartling of Milwaukee, this union was blessed with five children.

Presently retired and living in Oak Park, Illinois, with his wife, he continues to write and conduct church music and children's choir workshops.

ARRANGER: 83 O GROSSER GOTT
246 DU LEBENSBROT, HERR JESU CHRIST

BOURGEOIS, LOUIS (c. 1510–c. 1561). From his birth in Paris, little is known of him before 1541 when he went to Geneva with John Calvin (1509–64). There he became cantor at the churches of St. Pierre and St. Jervais and in 1545 master of the choristers in succession to Guillaume Franc. His fame rests largely on the fact that, beginning in 1542, he was entrusted with the important task of writing, selecting, and arranging the music for the various editions of the Genevan (French)Psalter, a task that continued for 15 years. The most notable collection appeared in 1547 with the title *Pseaulmes cinquante de David Roy et Prophete,* published at Lyon, a book that reflected Bourgeois' work on the psalms to that date. It is not certain whether the tunes were composed by him or merely arranged by him in four-part harmony. In appreciation for his services and in recognition of his high character and gratuitous teaching of the children, the Genevan authorities admitted him to the rights of citizenship. His last psalter, containing 83 psalms, was printed at Geneva in 1551. It occasioned his imprisonment for altering certain well-known tunes without authorization. Within 24 hours, however, Calvin secured his release (the alterations were later officially approved). Salary problems, coupled with the refusal of Genevan congregations to allow part-singing, and Calvin's opposition to printing harmonized tunes, led Bourgeois, in 1552, to leave Geneva for Paris, where, after 1561, nothing is known of him.

Bourgeois, a sensitive and consummate musician, preserved and shaped some of the finest hymn tunes still in use. Apropos are the words of poet laureate Robert Bridges (1844–1930; *LW* 486):

> Historians who wish to give a true philosophical account of Calvin's influence at Geneva ought probably to refer a great part of it to the enthusiasm attendant on the singing of Bourgeois's melodies.

COMPOSER/ARRANGER:	216, 245, 435, 454, 461	OLD HUNDREDTH
	363, 428	WENN WIR IN HÖCHSTEN NÖTEN SEIN
	486	NUNC DIMITTIS

BOURNE, GEORGE HUGH (1840–1925), was born November 8, 1840, at St. Paul's Cray, Kent, the son of an Anglican clergyman. Educated at Eaton and Christ Church College, Oxford, culminating in a Doctor of Civil Law degree in 1871, he was ordained deacon in 1863, becoming curate of Sandford-on-Thames. The following year he was ordained priest. In 1866 he became headmaster of St. Andrew's School, Chardstock Devon; in 1886 he became warden of St. Edmond's College, Salisbury. Bourne served as sub-dean at Salisbury Cathedral from 1887 until 1901, when he became treasurer and an honorary canon in the cathedral chapter (prebendary). In 1874 he published privately *Seven Post-Communion Hymns* for use in the chapel of St. Edmund's. He died at St. Edmond's December 1, 1925.

AUTHOR:	281	Lord, Enthroned in Heavenly Splendor

BOWRING, JOHN (1792–1872), was born of Puritan parents in Exeter, October 17, 1792; educated at the grammar school of Moreton, Hampstead; and then employed by his father in his trade, which was the manufacture of coarse woolens for China and the Spanish peninsula. Bowring became one of the world's outstanding linguists, claiming to read 200 and speak 100 languages. In French only did he have an instructor. Spanish, Italian, Portuguese, German and Dutch were learned by his own efforts, before he reached the age of 16.

Subsequent to this mercantile life, young Bowring essayed the political, and soon became the associate of Jeremy Bentham, and also a contributor to the radical *Westminster Review*. Still keeping up his study of languages, he first acted as Bentham's literary executor and the editor of his collected works, and then published translations from various Continental sources. In 1825 he succeeded Bentham as the editor of the *Westminster Review*. From this period dates the diplomatic and literary career of this gifted and learned man. In 1828 he received the Doctor of Letters degree from the University of Groningen.

In 1835 he was elected to Parliament as a Radical from Kilmarnock advocating free trade; in 1841 he was returned there from Bolton on a similar issue.

His labors for foreign nations were only recognized after a time. In 1849 he became British consul at Canton, afterward superintendent of trade and minister plenipotentiary to China, 1853, and finally governor, commander-in-chief, and vice-admiral of Hong Kong and its dependencies.

Queen Victoria knighted him in 1854, and from this date the decorations and orders bestowed upon him were many. Siam, the Philippine Islands, and Italy experienced some of his best endeavors for their advancement. His mind was always vigilant, and, in spite of weakness induced by the attempted arsenical poisoning of himself and family in China, he toiled on incessantly until a week or so before his death. He was accustomed to reply to every remonstrance: "I must do my work while life remains to me; I may not long be here." In all benevolent and Christian enterprises he was indefatigable. He was a strenuous advocate of prison reform, but deep beneath all else ran the undertone of Christian praise. At 80 years of age he was frequently known to begin the day with some new song of adoration and thanksgiving.

Theoretically, Sir John Bowring was a Unitarian. Practically, he was a devoted and evangelical believer. Bowring's varied writings, including hymns, are contained in 36 volumes. The writing of hymns was somehow worked into his many activities as a recreation, and he published two collections of them, *Matins and Vespers* (1823) and *Hymns* (1825), which, of all his writings, have proved to be the most enduring. Unitarian hymnbooks in England and America first printed his hymns, but other denominations soon brought a number into common use.

He died November 23, 1872. His tombstone bears the appropriate words of his own hymn: "In the cross of Christ I glory."

AUTHOR: 101 In the Cross of Christ I Glory

BOYE, BIRGITTE KATERINE (1742–1824), was born March 7, 1742, in Gentofte, Denmark, to Jens Johansen of the royal service. In her youth she was promised to Herman Hertz, a king's gamekeeper, whom she married in 1763 upon his appointment as forester in Vordingborg. Though she had four children, she nevertheless found time to devote herself to the study of foreign languages. She became proficient enough in French, English, and German to read original poetry in these languages and to prepare translations of hymns.

In 1773 the Society for the Advancement of the Liberal Arts requested all interested persons to submit sacred poetry, to be considered for inclusion in a successor to Thomas Kingo's (*LW* 100, et al.) hymnal. Birgitte contributed 20 hymns, of which 18 were eventually included in the hymnal. Produced in 1778 by Bishop Ludvig Harbol and Prince Fredrik's secretary Ove Guldberg, this became known as "Guldberg's hymnal," although its full title was *Salmebog, eller en Samling af gamle og ny Salmer, til Guds Aere og Hans Menigheds Opbyggelse* (A hymnal, or a collection of old and new hymns, for the honor of God and the edification of his church).

While the hymnal was being compiled, the office of forester was abolished. The hardships thus brought upon the Hertz family caused Birgitte to appeal to Guldberg, who mentioned the family's plight to Prince Fredrik. The prince then arranged for the two sons to be educated at his own expense and later, when Hertz died, he himself supported the widow and her children. Birgitte was remarried in 1778 to Hans Boye, a custom house worker from Copenhagen. When Guldberg prepared an unauthorized hymnal of his own, he asked Boye to contribute to it; 124 of her original hymns eventually appeared in this volume, as well as 24 translations.

Boye died October 17, 1824, after surviving her second husband. Besides Guldberg's hymnals, her verses appeared in her own *Davids Psalmer i en fri Oversaettelse* in three volumes (1781–85). This collection contained settings of the first 89 psalms. Many of her dramatic works were performed at special royal events, and she wrote nationalistic poetry as well.

AUTHOR: 520 Rejoice, Rejoice This Happy Morn
He Is Arisen! Glorious Word!

BRADBURY, WILLIAM BATCHELDER (1816–68), was born at York, Maine, October 6, 1816. In 1830 he went to Boston where, as a complete novice, he began his studies in harmony, organ, and voice at the Boston Academy of Music. There Lowell Mason (*LW* 115), one of his teachers, took great interest in him, giving him various teaching assignments. Bradbury served as organist in churches in Boston and Brooklyn before becoming organist and choir director of First Baptist Church in New York City in 1841. Free singing classes and large-scale youth music festivals that he instituted and directed influenced the introduction of music into the public schools of New York. With Lowell Mason and Thomas Hastings (*LW* 361) he participated in numerous music festivals, conventions, and institutes. The years 1847–49 saw him in Europe, studying under some of the great teachers of the day. In 1854, with his brother and a German piano maker, he established the Bradbury Piano Company in New York City, a company that merged with the Knabe firm in 1917. He died in Montclair, New Jersey, January 7, 1868.

Bradbury's enormous output (59 publications between 1841–67) perhaps accounts for the fact that his music was frequently criticized and belittled as being "sugared American psalmody" and meager in quality. But his tunes, many written for religious social gatherings and not for corporate worship, appealed to people and supported evangelists with the earliest examples of the gospel song.

COMPOSER: 359 WOODWORTH

BRAUER, ALFRED ERNEST RICHARD (1866–1949), was born August 1, 1866, near Fernwood (formerly Blumberg), South Australia. While attending Prince Alfred College (Wesleyan) as a law student, he decided to alter course and study theology. He received

preparatory theological instruction from Pastor Strempel of Hahndorf (later St. Michael's, Ambleside). Having enrolled at Concordia Theological Seminary, Springfield,
Illinois, in the fall of 1887, he graduated in 1890 and accepted a call to the Dimboola parish in the Australian state of Victoria. Here he established and served a number of congregations until 1896, when he was called to the Lutheran school in Handorf where Pastor Strempel, now his father-in-law, was pastor of St. Michael's. Upon Strempel's election to the presidency of the Australian Lutheran Synod, Brauer was appointed his secretary and called to St. Michael's as associate pastor. With the death of Pastor Strempel, Brauer became head pastor, a position he held until, in 1921, he accepted the call to St. John's, Melbourne. Here he served until his resignation in 1942. He died at Melbourne, October 18, 1949.

Brauer was for many years editor of the *Australian Lutheran*, founded in 1913, and chairman of the committee that produced the *Australian Lutheran Hymn-Book* (1925), to which he also contributed a number of translations. His chief literary work, however, to which he devoted many years of effort, is *Under the Southern Cross*, a history of the Evangelical Lutheran Church of Australia. Postwar difficulties prevented its publication until 1956.

TRANSLATOR: 445 Praise the Almighty

BRIDGES, MATTHEW (1800–1894), was born at Maldon, Essex, on July 14, 1800. Educated in the Church of England, in 1828 he published *The Roman Empire Under Constantine the Great,* a polemic against the Roman Catholic Church. In 1848, under the influence of the Oxford Movement and John Henry Newman, he joined the Roman Church. He moved to Quebec, Canada, but returned to England a short time before his death, which occurred at his home at the Convent of the Assumption, Sidmouth, Devon, October 6, 1894. Many of his hymns were first brought into use in America by Henry Ward Beecher's *Plymouth Collection* (1855).

AUTHOR: 278 Crown Him with Many Crowns

BRIDGES, ROBERT SEYMOUR (1844–1930), was born October 23, 1844, at Walmer, Kent, England. As a son of a wealthy and distinguished family, he was educated at Eaton and Corpus Christi College, Oxford. After traveling abroad for a time, he studied medicine at St. Bartholomew's Hospital, London, where, after completing the requirements, he became a casualty physician. He also practiced privately and served as a physician at London's Great Northern Hospital. Already in 1873 his *Shorter Poems* showed that he had unusual gifts of another kind, and in 1882, partly also due to ill health, he retired from medical practice and settled in Yattendon, Berkshire. In 1884 he married Mary Monica Waterhouse, daughter of an architect, and together they lived in Yattendon while he devoted himself to literature and music. It was here that he, in collaboration with Harry Ellis Wooldridge, edited the *Yattendon Hymnal* (1899). Containing 100 hymns in four parts, for which he selected and matched texts and tunes, no less than 44 of the hymns were either written, adapted, or translated by him. James Moffatt (1870–1944), noted Scottish scholar, described the collection as "easily the most distinguished of individual contributions to modern hymnody."

In 1907 Bridges moved to Boar's Hill, in Oxford, where he lived with his family until his death April 21, 1930.

Bridges was truly a scholar of great learning and a skilled and cultivated musician. Small wonder that he was appointed poet laureate in 1913 and, on the publication of his *Testament of Beauty* in 1929, given the Order of Merit. Recognizing his singular talents, the University of Michigan invited him and his wife as guests for three months and awarded him an honorary doctorate. Similar honors were accorded him by Oxford, St. Andrews, and Harvard Universities.

TRANSLATOR: 460 When Morning Gilds the Skies
486 O Gladsome Light, O Grace

BRIGGS, GEORGE WALLACE (1875–1959), was born in Kirkby, Northamptonshire, England, December 14, 1875. As a student at Emmanuel College, Cambridge, from which he also graduated, he gained high honors in the classical studies. Ordained by the Church of England, he briefly served a parish in Wakefield, Yorkshire. From 1902–09 he was chaplain in the Royal Navy. Thereafter he was vicar of St. Andrew's, Norwich, 1909–18; rector of Loughborough, 1918–27; canon of Leicester Cathedral, 1927–34; and canon of Worcester Cathedral from 1934 until his retirement in 1956. He died December 30, 1959, at Hindhead, Surrey.

Briggs was widely involved in educational work, especially in the publication of books of prayers and hymns for schools. Included among such works are *Prayers and Hymns for Use in Schools* (1927); *The Little Bible* (1931); *The Daily Service* (1936), a book that exerted a marked influence on the worship services in English schools; *Songs of Faith* (1945); and *Hymns of the Faith* (1957), a compilation for use in Worcester Cathedral. He also wrote a few tunes for his own hymns.

Briggs was closely associated with Percy Dearmer in the production of *Songs of Praise* (1925) and was cofounder of the Hymn Society of Great Britain and Ireland, of which he was chairman of the executive committee for many years. In 1915 he came to the United States, where he lectured at Berkeley, California, and New Haven, Connecticut, and made a presentation at the Hymn Society of America meeting in New York City.

AUTHOR: 343 God Has Spoken by His Prophets

BROKERING, HERBERT FREDERICK, (1926–) was born at Beatrice, Nebraska, on May 21, 1926. The son of a Lutheran pastor, he studied at Wartburg College and

Wartburg Seminary, Waverly, Iowa, and at Lutheran Theological Seminary, Columbus, Ohio. He holds a Master of Arts degree in child psychology from the University of Iowa, and has pursued further studies in religious education at the University of Pittsburgh. In Germany, at the Universities of Kiel and Erlangen, he also followed a theological course of study.

Parishes in Cedarhurst, New York, in Pittsburgh, and in San Antonio, Texas, have all claimed Brokering as their pastor during his 10 years in the parish ministry. From 1960–70 he worked at the national offices of the American Lutheran Church, in the department of parish education. Presently Brokering acts as a freelance resource person and consultant on creative worship and pan-denominational ministry. For 16 years he has taught creative worship at seminaries, mostly at Luther Northwestern in St. Paul, Minnesota.

In recent years Brokering has led seven pilgrimages into Eastern Block churches, primarily into the former German Democratic Republic. He has also collaborated with Roland Bainton in Renaissance-Reformation festivals throughout the United States and Japan.

Married and the father of four children, Brokering writes every day. He has authored more than 30 books, including *Lord, Be With* (1969), *Surprise Me, Jesus* (1973), *Wholly Holy* (1980), and, with Bainton, *Pilgrimage to Luther's Germany* (1980). He has published more than 40 anthems; concerning his song texts, he writes,

> All my songs are written off living situations, events, persons, physical times. I focus on something that fills my senses, and the spirit is on the move, bringing order out of chaos.

AUTHOR: 438 Earth and All Stars

BROOKS, CHARLES TIMOTHY (1813–83), was born June 20, 1813, at Salem, Massachusetts, and educated at Harvard Divinity School, graduating in 1835. It was as a student at the latter that he translated "God bless our native land" from the German. Ordained by the Unitarian Church, he served parishes in Maine and Vermont until 1837, when he became pastor in Newport, Rhode Island, where he served for 34 years, resigning in 1871 because of poor eyesight. He died June 14, 1883. Among other things, Brooks furnished texts for Lowell Mason's (*LW* 115, et al.) singing books.

TRANSLATOR: 497 God Bless Our Native Land (st. 1)

BROOKS, PHILLIPS (1835–93), was born in Boston on December 13, 1835. He was educated in the usual fashion at Boston Latin School and Harvard, graduating in 1855. After trying unsuccessfully to teach at the Latin School, he entered the Virginia (Episcopal) Theological Seminary at Alexandria and was ordained in 1859.

After serving 10 years in Philadelphia, first at the Church of the Advent and later at Holy Trinity, in 1869 Brooks accepted the repeated call to Trinity Church in Boston. There he embarked on an extremely successful ministry, his moving and thoughtful sermons as well as his warm personality drawing many new members. In 1871 land was purchased for the erection of a new church building in Copley Square, but before its completion the Boston fire of 1872 destroyed the old structure on Summer Street. Despite the Unitarianism which threatened to engulf all of New England, Brooks continued to preach the Gospel to Trinity congregation from an auditorium, his fame spreading until he became the best-known American pastor of his time. Even the intellectual community found reason to approve of Brooks; Oliver Wendell Holmes and others visited Trinity often.

Devoted to children, Brooks wrote several hymns intended for them, including "O Little Town of Bethlehem." His familiarity with hymnody can be traced to his childhood, when Phillips and his brothers would recite a newly memorized hymn before the assembled family each week. It is said that Phillips Brooks knew over 200 hymns by memory by the time he entered college.

Brooks was also fond of traveling. He visited the Holy Land in 1865, made trips to Japan and India, and frequently traveled to England, where he preached widely, establishing a friendship with Arthur Stanley, Dean of Westminster Abbey, and preaching by special request to Queen Victoria. Back home in Boston, he declined offers of professorships and various other preferments until he was named Bishop of Massachusetts in 1891. Death occurred less than two years later, on January 23, 1893.

Several volumes of Brooks' sermons have been published and have enjoyed outstanding sales. Says hymnologist Louis F. Benson:

> The word that seems best to describe him is 'great.' He was great in his physical proportions, great in the endowments of genius, great in the power to work, extraordinarily great in his personal influence over men, greatest of all in the moral elevation of his character and his ever-deepening spirit of consecration to Christ's service (*Studies of Familiar Hymns,* first series).

AUTHOR: 59, 60 O Little Town of Bethlehem

BRORSON, HANS ADOLPH (1694–1764), was born June 20, 1694, in Randrup, Denmark, son of a Lutheran pastor. After graduating from the Ribe Latin School, he entered the University of Copenhagen, where he took up theology, philology, history, and philosophy. When illness forced him to leave the university in 1717, he became the family tutor in the home of his uncle District Superintendent Klausen of Logum Kloster. Improved in health, he passed his final theological examination in October 1721. Ordained in 1722, he accepted a call to Randrup, his native city. There he served until 1729, when he was called to Tonder, a Danish-German parish, where he worked closely with Johann Herman Schräder, pastor, pietist, and hymn writer. Since the hymns were sung in German, whether the services were in German or Danish, Brorson assumed the task of providing the congregation with some Danish hymns. Following his first publication, *Jule-Psalmer*, he prepared other small collections for the church year, all of which were gathered into a single volume entitled *Troens rare Klenodie* (1739), which enjoyed six editions during his lifetime. Appointed district superintendent in 1739 and bishop of Ribe in 1741, he served with distinction and was accorded much love and respect. Despite ill health, he continued to write hymns, which his son published in 1765 in a collection entitled *Svane-Sang*, a year after his father's death on June 3, 1764.

Brorson is one of Denmark's greatest hymn writers, contributing hymns and translations numbering in the hundreds. Not to be overlooked is the significant work, a revision of Thomas Kingo's (*LW* 100, et al.) hymnal, *Den my Salemebog* (The New Hymn Book), which Erik Pontoppidan published in 1740, a work that Brorson had projected and to which he had contributed extensively.

AUTHOR: 192 Behold a Host Arrayed in White

BROWNE, SIMON (c. 1680–1732), was born in Shepton-Mallet, Somersetshire, England. After studying for the Independent ministry at the academy at Bridgewater, he began to preach at the age of 20. He became pastor of an Independent charge in Portsmouth, and then, in 1716, of the Independent Chapel in Old Jewry, London. Isaac Watts (*LW* 53, et al.) was his near neighbor, being at that time pastor in Berry Street.

In 1723 Browne was afflicted with a hypochondriacal malady which took the form of a delusion that he could not *think*. In that year he had lost his wife and son and was greatly distressed. But the compelling cause was thought to be an attack made on him by a highway robber whom he accidently killed in the struggle. This had a most serious effect on his mind. Frequently after this he was tormented with a desire to destroy himself, and he always maintained that his mental powers were gone. Yet, though he would not patiently suffer any contradiction of this idea, he wrote a defense of Christianity, a work on the Trinity, a dictionary, and continued Matthew Henry's *Commentary* by his exposition of the First Epistle of St. Paul to the Corinthians. He left 266 hymns as his legacy to Christian praise.

In his hymn writing Browne was a great admirer and imitator of Watts. Sometimes he conveys lines bodily from Watts, confessing, "I have borrowed my stamina from others." His publications number over 20. Of these works, he is known to hymnology through his *Hymns and Spiritual Songs, in Three Books, designed as a Supplement to Dr. Watts*, (1720, 1741, 1760). It contains 166 hymns, seven doxologies, and a preface of some historical interest.

AUTHOR: 161 Come, Gracious Spirit, Heavenly Dove

BROWNLIE, JOHN (1859–1925), was born August 6, 1859 (though some give as early as August 3, 1857), in Glasgow, Scotland, where he was educated at the university and at the Free Church College. Serving first as assistant minister to the Free Church, Portpatrick, Wigtownshire, he later became senior minister. His great interest in education resulted in his becoming chairman of the governors of Stanraer High School. He is especially remembered, however, for his contributions to hymnody, both original and in translation, the latter as a result of his special study of Latin and Greek hymnology. His publications include *Hymns of our Pilgrimage* (1889); *Hymns of the Pilgrim Life* (1890); *Pilgrim Songs* (1892); *Hymns of the Early Church* (1896); *Hymns from East and West* (1898); and *Hymns of the Greek Church* (fourth series). Moreover, he prepared the *Hymns and Hymn Writers of the Church Hymnary*, a companion to *The Church Hymnary* (1898), the hymnal of the Presbyterian Church of the United Kingdom.

AUTHOR: 26 The King Shall Come

BRUECKNER, HERMANN H. M. (1866–1942), was born March 11, 1866, in Grundy County, Iowa, the son of a Lutheran pastor. Ordained in 1888, he served congregations in Illinois, Michigan, Kentucky, and Wisconsin before moving to Iowa City, where he served a parish for 15 years, during which period he also earned the Master of Arts degree at the University of Iowa (1917). The next nine years were spent working part-time at the university and pursuing graduate studies. In 1926 he was called to Hebron College (an American Lutheran institution, now closed), Hebron, Nebraska, where he taught French, German, English, and Christian doctrine. Wartburg Seminary, Dubuque, Iowa, awarded him the honorary Doctor of Divinity degree in 1938. His marriage to Leonore Schneider in 1899 was blessed with five children. After her death in 1920, he was married to Dorothy Staehling of Waverly, Iowa, in 1922. He retired professor emeritus from Hebron College in 1941 and died January 25, 1942.

TRANSLATOR: 206 God Himself Is Present
419 Evening and Morning

BRUN, JOHAN NORDAHL (1745–1816), was born March 21, 1745, in Bynesset, Norway, the son of a merchant. At the behest and under the guidance of his mother, he had read through the Holy Scriptures twice by the time he was 11 years of age. His half-brother, a candidate of theology in Copenhagen, induced him to study theology and tutored him in that pursuit. After studying at the local Latin school and thereafter at the university in Trondhjem, Brun became the family tutor to Councillor Meinche (Mennche) and accompanied his son to Sor, Denmark. There, after three months' preparation, he took the theological examinations and came out with the lowest grade possible. He returned to Norway and, after spending three years in Trondhjem as an instructor, preacher, and poet, he went back to Copenhagen in 1767. Another three months of arduous study led to his passing the theological examinations. His return to Trondhjem saw him tutoring and writing poetry. In 1771 he was appointed private secretary to Bishop Johannes Ernst Gunnerus (1718–73) and accompanied him to Copenhagen on official business, a relationship, however, that lasted only a brief period. Now in Copenhagen, he entered the contest for the best Danish tragedy and won with his *Zarine*. Another play on the subject of Norwegian history, plus his output of nationalistic songs, made him a popular leader of Norwegian students in Copenhagen. Ordained in 1772, he became assistant pastor at Bynesset; two years later he was appointed senior pastor of Koskirken in Bergen. In 1804 he was consecrated bishop of the Bergen diocese. He died July 26, 1816.

As an active and energetic bishop, a powerful and orthodox preacher, Brun constituted a formidable force in combating the inroads of Rationalism in the Lutheran Church.

AUTHOR: 222 How Blest Are They Who Hear God's Word

BUCHANAN, ANNABEL MORRIS (1889–1983), was born in Groesebeck, Texas. After graduating from the Landon Conservatory of Music in Dallas in 1907, she attended the Guilmant Organ School in New York City and studied privately with Emil Liebling, William C. Carl, John Powel, and others. Before her marriage in 1912 to John Preston Buchanan, a lawyer and writer, she taught piano, organ, theory, and composition in colleges in Oklahoma, Texas, and Virginia. Her work in the field of American folk music was distinguished and extensive. She was president of the Virginia Federation of Music Clubs from 1927–30, and cofounder and director of the White Top Music Festival and Conference from 1931–41. She held various offices in the National Federation of Music Clubs and the National League of American Pen Women, and was a member of the American Guild of Organists.

Besides collecting valuable folk music materials and writing a number of original compositions, her publications include *Adventures in Virginia Folk Ways*, *American Folk Music*, *Book of American Composers*, and *American Folk Music Booklet*.

A broken hip necessitated her leaving her apartment in New York City in 1976 and moving to Parkview Convalescent Center in Paducah, Kentucky, where she died in 1983. Her extensive and valuable collection of books, manuscripts, and recordings were donated to the University of North Carolina, Chapel Hill, in 1978.

ARRANGER: 307 LAND OF REST

BUNJES, PAUL G. (1914–), was born in Frankenmuth, Michigan, September 27, 1914. He attended Concordia College, River Forest, Illinois, from 1933–36, and graduated with a Bachelor of Arts degree from Valparaiso University, Valparaiso, Indiana, in 1941. Three years later he received the Master of Music degree from the University of Michigan, Ann Arbor.

Bunjes attended several universities for course work and enrichment, including a half year in Europe, particularly Germany. During the latter he did research in polyphonic music of the Reformation era, specifically George Rhau's *Postremum Vespertini Officii Opus*, published in 1970 by Bärenreiter as *Musikdrucke Rhau V*. For 16 years he was an elementary teacher and administrator at St. Lorenz, Frankenmuth, Michigan, and Zion in Wausaw, Wisconsin. He has been on the faculty of Concordia River Forest since 1951, and chaired the music department from 1961–77.

In 1966 Bunjes achieved the Doctor of Philosophy degree from Eastman School of Music, University of Rochester, New York. Other honors include a Doctor of Letters degree from Concordia College, Seward, Nebraska, in 1982; the title Distinguished Professor of Music at Concordia River Forest in 1984; and, also in 1984, his induction into Chicago's Senior Citizens' Hall of Fame. For more than 30 years, with only slight interruptions, he served on the Commission on Worship of the Lutheran Church—Missouri Synod, culminating in his music editorship of *Lutheran Worship* (1982). In addition he served on the Inter-Lutheran Commission on Worship for a number of years.

Bunjes' music compositions are legion, including numerous works for organ, chorus, and orchestra. He has contributed articles to *Lutheran Education* and *Church Music*, serving also on the editorial staff of the latter journal; he authored *The Service Propers Noted*, *The Formulary Tones Annotated*, *The Praetorius Organ*, and *Postremum Vespertini*, all published between 1960 and 1970. He is a designer of organs as well, having designed over 110 pipe organs for churches and for college and university chapels since 1948.

Represented by numerous harmonizations in *Lutheran Worship*, Bunjes' work appears under his own name as well as the *noms de plume* Wilhelm Quampen and George Leonard. Regarding his use of pen names, Bunjes notes:

> Inasmuch as I was registered under my given name and two pseudonyms at the copyright office of the Library of Congress, a transfer of the copyrights to Concordia Publishing House suggested the retention of the composer appellations "as is." Most of the elements of the two pseudonyms are the Christian names of my baptismal sponsors. The use of pseudonyms is reminiscent of the Reformation time when, for example, the name "Melanchthon" replaced "Schwarzerd," "Jonas" replaced "Koch," and "Praetorius" replaced "Schultheiss."

ARRANGER:	13	NUN KOMM, DER HEIDEN HEILAND
	15	PICARDY
	16	MARIA IST GEBOREN
	21	TRÖSTET, TRÖSTET, SPRICHT DER HERR
	25	AUS MEINES HERZENS GRUNDE
	30	GOTTES SOHN IST KOMMEN
	31	VENI EMMANUEL
	32, 259	O HEILAND, REISS DIE HIMMEL AUF
	33	NUN KOMM, DER HEIDEN HEILAND
	36	DIVINUM MYSTERIUM
	37	VOM HIMMEL HOCH

38 VOM HIMMEL HOCH
63 DIES EST LAETITIAE
66 ALLE JAHRE WIEDER
77 LOBT GOTT, IHR CHRISTEN
78 JESUS IST KOMMEN, GRUND EWIGER FREUDE
79, 102 VALET WILL ICH DIR GEBEN
82 FREUT EUCH, IHR LIEBEN
84 O DURCHBRECHER
87 DEO GRACIAS
95, 100 DER AM KREUZ
103 HERR JESU CHRIST, WAHR MENSCH UND GOTT
104 VEXILLA REGIS
106 ELLACOMBE
107 GOTTLOB, ES GEHT NUNMEHR ZU ENDE
108 DA JESUS AN DES KREUZES
119 HERZLIEBSTER JESU
122 O TRAURIGKEIT
124 CHRIST IST ERSTANDEN
140 VRUECHTEN
145 ES IST GENUG
153, 232 ACH GOTT UND HERR
154 KOMM, HEILIGER GEIST, HERRE
158 VENI CREATOR SPIRITUS
163 DEN SIGNEDE DAG
170 GOTT DER VATER WOHN UNS BEI
176, 244 ACH GOTT VOM HIMMELREICHE
177 WACHET AUF
184 NUN LASST UNS GOTT DEM HERREN
185 MIT FRIED UND FREUD
194 KING'S LYNN
198 UNSER HERRSCHER
200 NUN DANKET ALL
209 KYRIE, GOTT VATER
213 WIR GLAUBEN ALL
214 JESAIA, DEM PROPHETEN
220 CWM RHONDDA
230 AUS TIEFER NOT I
233 HERR, ICH HABE MISSGEHANDELT
234 VATER UNSER
236 JESUS CHRISTUS, UNSER HEILAND
237 JESUS CHRISTUS, UNSER HEILAND
239 SCHMÜCKE DICH
241 PICARDY
242 ICH STERBE TÄGLICH

245 OLD HUNDREDTH
252 RESIGNATION
261 KOMMT HER ZU MIR
262, 373 HERR JESU CHRIST, MEINS
270 JESU, MEINE FREUDE
274 HIDING PLACE
277 EINS IST NOT
279 ST. PETER
282 ANGEL'S STORY
288 ES WOLLE GOTT UNS GNÄDIG SEIN
291 KIRKEN DEN ER ET GAMMELT HUS
292 THE SAINTS' DELIGHT
298 EIN FESTE BURG
300, 466 KOMMT HER ZU MIR
301 ISTE CONFESSOR
309 EWING
323 ISTE CONFESSOR
329 ERHALT UNS, HERR
331 IN GOTTES NAMEN FAHREN WIR
339 WERDE MUNTER
340, 467 WO GOTT ZUM HAUS
341 O HERRE GOTT
352 DIE HELLE SONN LEUCHT
355 ES IST DAS HEIL
369 LOB GOTT GETROST MIT SINGEN
370 VOLLER WUNDER
380 LAKEWOOD
386 SEELENBRÄUTIGAM
395 SONG 67
398 CWM RHONDDA
401 SURSUM CORDA
402 HYFRYDOL
404 PATMOS
406 IN DICH HAB ICH GEHOFFET
413 HERZLICH LIEB
421 AUF MEINEN LIEBEN GOTT
422 WAS GOTT TUT
425 WAS MEIN GOTT WILL
430 VATER UNSER
432 ADORO TE DEVOTE
438 EARTH AND ALL STARS
454 OLD HUNDREDTH
464 DER MANGE SKAL KOMME
472 NUN DANKET ALL

	485	O WELT, ICH MUSS DICH LASSEN
	503	MÜDE BIN ICH
	509	NEW BRITAIN
	513	PILOT
	517	WEIL ICH JESU SCHÄFLEIN BIN

As George Leonard (*nom de plume*):

ARRANGER:	35	GELOBET SEIST DU
	48	QUEM PASTORES
	50	REGENT SQUARE
	58	IRBY
	70	WHILE SHEPHERDS WATCHED
	116	O MEIN JESU, ICH MUSS STERBEN
	136	HEUT TRIUMPHIERET GOTTES SOHN
	147	ERSCHIENEN IST DER HERRLICH TAG
	157, 189	KOMM, GOTT SCHÖPFER
	173	WORCESTER
	218	REGENT SQUARE
	235	ST. LUKE
	248	AUS TIEFER NOT II
	250	HERR JESU CHRIST, DICH ZU UNS WEND
	267	CHRISTUS, DER IST MEIN LEBEN
	306	JERUSALEM, DU HOCHGEBAUTE STADT
	310	ERSCHIENEN IST DER HERRLICH TAG
	315	DIR, DIR, JEHOVAH
	321	GOTT SEI DANK
	344	ACH BLEIB BEI UNS
	345	ANTHES
	363	WENN WIR IN HÖCHSTEN NÖTEN SEIN
	367	HERR CHRIST, DER EINIG GOTTS SOHN
	372	WAS FRAG ICH NACH DER WELT
	387, 390	FREU DICH SEHR
	391	DER LIEBEN SONNE LICHT UND PRACHT
	416	BELMONT
	417	BROTHER JAMES' AIR
	423	WARUM SOLLT ICH MICH DEN GRÄMEN
	435	OLD HUNDREDTH
	446	DIR, DIR, JEHOVAH

As Wilhelm Quampen (*nom de plume*):

ARRANGER:	19	WIE SOLL ICH DICH EMPFANGEN
	20	WO SOLL ICH FLIEHEN HIN
	39	FRÖHLICH SOLL MEIN HERZE SPRINGEN
	40	FREUET EUCH, IHR CHRISTEN SPRINGEN
	45	CHRISTE REDEMPTOR
	46	GARTAN
	52	PUER NOBIS
	113, 427	HERZLICH TUT MICH VERLANGEN
	150	NUN FREUT EUCH
	181, 456	ALLEIN GOTT IN DER HÖH
	182	GOTT SEI DANK
	197	ERHALT UNS, HERR
	202	LIEBSTER JESU, WIR SIND HIER
	207	GOTT SEI DANK
	212	WIR GLAUBEN ALL AN EINEN GOTT
	226	LIEBSTER JESU, WIR SIND HIER
	249	ST. MICHAEL
	266	JESUS, MEINE ZUVERSICHT
	269	MEINEN JESUM LASS ICH NICHT
	302	STRAF MICH NICHT
	327, 479, 487	STEHT AUF, IHR LIEBEN KINDERLEIN
	336	ES IST GEWISSLICH
	354, 453	NUN LOB, MEIN SEEL
	364	ACH, WAS SOLL ICH SÜNDER MACHEN
	365	SLANE
	403	BUNESSAN
	405	ENERGY
	418	WAS FRAG ICH NACH DER WELT
	441	ICH SINGE DIR
	459	LLEDROD
	488	HURSLEY

BUSAROW, DONALD A. (1934–), was born April 10, 1934, in Racine, Wisconsin. Following his graduation from Concordia Teachers College, River Forest, Illinois, he continued music study at the Cleveland Institute of Music, earning a Master of Music degree, and at Michigan State University, from which he earned the Doctor of Philosophy degree. The study of music composition was pursued with Marcel Dick, Jere Hutcheson, and Jan Bender (*LW* 319, et al.).

Busarow presently serves as professor of music at Wittenberg University in Springfield, Ohio, where he teaches theory, composition, organ, and courses in church music. He is the university organist and director of chapel music. In 1982 he was appointed director of the Wittenberg University Choir; he serves also as director of music at St. Matthew Lutheran Church in Dayton, Ohio.

His compositions are listed in the catalogs of Concordia Publishing House, Augsburg-Fortress Publishing House, Morning Star Music Publishers, Chantry Music Press, and GIA of Chicago. In 1980 he was awarded first prize in the International Horn Society composition for his composition, "Death, Be Not Proud," a work for soprano, horn, and piano. The sacred opera *Esther*, was commissioned by Wittenberg University and premiered in 1980. Of special interest are over thirty publications of hymn settings for choir, congregation, instruments, and organ. Numerous settings of liturgical works for choir have been commissioned by publishers. Four volumes of chorale preludes for two instruments and organ have been published along with his set of accompaniments for thirty canonic hymns, over 40 organ pieces, and a collection of wedding solos. Several of his hymn harmonizations appear in the *Lutheran Book of Worship* (1978) as well as here in *Lutheran Worship* (1982).

In recent years Busarow has been highly active as workshop clinician, both organ and choral, and his hymn festivals and recitals have gained wide popularity throughout the country.

ARRANGER:	22	JEFFERSON
	142	ORIENTIS PARTIBUS
	483	FANG DEIN WERK

BUNYAN, JOHN (1628–1688), was born November 30, 1628, at Elstow, near Bedfordshire, England. His father, a tinker, had a fixed residence and was able to send John to a village school to learn reading and writing. Born in a time of severe Puritanism, Bunyan often had dreams of fiends trying to drag him away, and similar terrors. At about age seventeen, when his father died, he joined the Parliamentary Army, from which he was released in 1647. During his military career one of his friends was killed while marching on a siege in Bunyan's place; from that time on he considered himself saved by an act of Providence.

Although Bunyan described himself as the "chief of sinners," it is apparent from various biographies that his worst crimes in his youth were on the order of bell-ringing and dancing, which were forbidden by his church. He married, a couple of years after his release from the army, a woman who brought to the union only her piety and two religious books. These had a shattering effect on Bunyan who, by means of a lively imagination and a neglected education, was particularly susceptible to fear of judgment. Stricken with a nervous disorder as a result of his extreme guilt and remorse, he joined in 1653 a Nonconformist (Baptist) congregation in Bedford under the leadership of John Gifford. Bunyan and his family moved to Bedford in 1655; a short time later his wife died, leaving him in charge of four children. He became a deacon of the church and, two years later, after the death of Gifford, began to preach.

A highly effective speaker, Bunyan gained in popularity among Baptists (dubbed "Bishop of Bedford" by some), but drew criticism and opposition from other quarters.

With the Restoration in 1660 he was jailed for, in the words of the warrant, having "in contempt of his Majestie's good laws preached or teached at a Conventicle meeting or assembly . . . in other manner than according to the Liturgie or Practice of the Church of England." He had married again shortly before his arrest; his wife pleaded for his release, but, despite his family's plight, Bunyan refused to give up preaching. One critic agreed with him that his gift ought not to be concealed, but claimed Bunyan's real gift lay in repairing kettles. So Bunyan was sentenced to 12 years in the Bedford county jail; there he made laces to support his children, preached to fellow prisoners, and began writing. In all he wrote nine books during this imprisonment, of which his autobiographical *Grace Abounding to the Chief of Sinners* (1666) was the most prominent. Toward the end of his incarceration he was allowed to come and go more or less at will. His complete freedom was attained in 1672 with the passage of the Declaration of Indulgence.

Bunyan immediately began preaching again and, when the Declaration was repealed in 1675, found himself again in danger, for he was again imprisoned, this time for six months, during which stay he began his famous allegory, *The Pilgrim's Progress*. This book, published in 1678, soon gained widespread popularity among the Puritanical commoners of the time. Bunyan himself saw his manuscript as an unimportant diversion, to occupy only his spare moments, not as a major work of lasting value. He published the second part of *Pilgrim's Progress* in 1684; in the meantime he had produced *The Life and Death of Mr. Badman* (1680) and *The Holy War* (1682).

Bunyan died of pneumonia on August 31, 1688, after riding in the rain in an attempt to reconcile a father and son.

Almost continually engaged in controversy with other church leaders, Baptists as well as other sects, Bunyan approved of singing in church at a time when it was considered antiscriptural. His *Solomon's Temple Spiritualized*, published in 1688, speaks of congregational singing as a divine institution. Among his other works were *A Few Sighs from Hell* (1658); *The Doctrine of Law and Grace Unfolded* (1659); and A *Book for Boys and Girls: or, Country Rhimes for Children* (1686), a series of verses with morals (or as they are called "Comparisons") appended, two of which had music provided. In a shortened form and with the title *Divine Emblems: or Temporal Things Spiritualized* it continued to be published until the beginning of the 19th century.

AUTHOR: 383, 384 All Who Would Valiant Be

CAMPBELL, ROBERT (1814–68), was born December 19, 1814, in Troehraig, Ayrshire. Pursuing a profound interest in theology, he attended the University of Glasgow. His change of heart to study law and become a lawyer, however, prompted him to seek that degree at the University of Edinburgh. Originally a Presbyterian, at an early age he joined the Episcopal Church of Scotland and became a devout churchman, deeply concerned with the education of poor children.

In 1848 he began translating a series of Latin hymns that he submitted to John Mason Neale (*LW* 31) and others for criticism. Two years later a selection of these, with some original hymns and a few by others, appeared in his *Hymns and Anthems for Use in the Holy Services of the Church within the United Diocese of St. Andrews, Dunkeld, and Dunblane*. This became known as *St. Andrews Hymnal*, a book used in the diocese for a number of years. In 1852 Campbell entered the Roman Catholic Church and continued his service to the young and the poor. He died in Edinburgh December 29, 1868.

TRANSLATOR: 126 At the Lamb's High Feast
156 Creator Spirit, Heavenly Dove

CARWITHEN, ROBERT, (1933–) organist, composer, conductor, carillonneur, is a graduate of Philadelphia's Curtis Institute of Music and Princeton's Westminster Choir College. For 26 years he was the organist and choirmaster of First Presbyterian Church in Germantown, Philadelphia, Pennsylvania, and founder of The Oratorio Choir there.

He has been a recording artist and carillonneur for the Schulmerich Carillons, Sellersville, Pennsylvania, and has arranged over 1,000 hymns and secular songs for the carillon.

Carwithen has distinguished himself in the field of choral and instrumental music. He has arranged many anthems for chorus and for chorus and instruments, has been involved in both choral and instrumental clinics across the United States, and has made several recordings.

Carwithen has been a student, in organ, with Marie Madeleine Duruflé, André Isoir, Zavier Darasse in France.

Presently he is organist and director of music at the First Presbyterian Church in Philadelphia and professor of organ at Westminster Choir College, Princeton, New Jersey.

ARRANGER: 169 ITALIAN HYMN

CASWALL, EDWARD (1814–78), was born July 15, 1814, at his father's vicarage in Yately, Hampshire, England. Educated at Marlborough and Brasenose College, Oxford, where he earned the Bachelor of Arts degree in 1836 and the Master of Arts in 1838. Writing lively satirical sketches during his student days caused him to be considered a humorist. Ordained deacon at Wells in 1838, and priest at Bath in 1839 in the Church of England, he served brief curacies until, in 1840, he was appointed perpetual curate at Stratford-sub-Castle, near Salisbury. Attracted to the Oxford, or Tractarian, Movement in its interest in Roman Catholic doctrine, sacraments, worship, and life, he resigned his position, went to Rome with his wife, where, in 1847, they were received into the Roman Catholic Church. Subsequent to his wife's death of cholera in 1849, Caswall entered the Oratory of St. Philip Neri at Edgbaston, Birmingham, to work with John Henry Newman (1801–90), one of the founders of the Oxford Movement, first as novice, then as subdeacon and deacon until 1852, when he was reordained as a priest.

There he devoted himself to ministering to the sick and the poor and to translating early Latin hymns from the Roman breviaries as well as writing some original hymns. These were published in his *Lyra Catholica* (1849); *The Mask of Mary, and Other Poems* (1858); *A May Pagent and Other Poems* (1865); and a collection of these, many in revised form, in *Hymns and Poems* (1873). Standing next to the masterful translations of Greek and Latin hymns by John Mason Neale (*LW* 31, et al.) are the fine translations of Edward Caswall. He died January 2, 1878, and was buried five days later at Redwall, near Bromsgrove.

TRANSLATOR:	18	Hark! A Thrilling Voice Is Sounding
	98	Glory Be to Jesus
	156	Creator Spirit, Heavenly Dove
	274	O Jesus, King Most Wonderful

CAWOOD, JOHN (1775–1852), was born at Matlock, Derbyshire, England, March 18, 1775. He was the son of a farmer and had little education as a child. At 18 he was engaged for menial service by Mr. Cursham of Sutton-in-Ashfield, Nottinghamshire. After three years' study under the direction of the Rev. Edward Spencer of Winkfield, Wiltshire, in a classical course, he entered St. Edmund Hall, Oxford, in 1797, where he received the Bachelor of Arts degree in 1801 and was ordained in the same year. Thereafter he became successively curate of Ribsford and Dowles, and incumbent of St. Ann's Chapel of Ease, Bewdley, Worcestershire. The latter was a perpetual curacy to which he was appointed in 1814. He died November 7, 1852.

His hymns, 17 in all, were never published by himself. Of these, nine were included in Cotterill's *Selection of Psalms and Hymns* (eighth edition, 1819). Most of these have passed into other collections.

AUTHOR:	342	Almighty God, Your Word Is Cast

CHANDLER, JOHN (1806–76), was born at Witley in Surrey, June 16, 1806. After earning his Bachelor and Master of Arts degrees at Corpus Christi College, Oxford, he was ordained deacon by the Church of England in 1831 and priest in 1832. In 1837 he succeeded his father as vicar of Whitley; later he was appointed rural dean. He died at Putney July 1, 1876.

Chandler's prose works include the *Life of William Wykeham* (1842), *Horae Sacrae: Prayers and Meditations from the writings of the divines of the Anglican Church* (1854), plus numerous sermons and tracts. His most lasting work, however, was his translation of Latin hymns, inspired largely by his interest in accompanying the ancient prayers of the Church with hymns from the same period. The appearance of some translations from the *Paris Breviary* (1736) along with their Latin originals, published by Isaac Williams in the *British Magazine,* caught his attention. Securing a copy of the *Breviary* together with a copy of George Cassander's *Hymni Sacri* of 1556, he went to work. In 1837 he published his first volume of translations entitled *The Hymns of the Primitive Church, now first Collected, Translated and Arranged.* It contained 100 hymns, for the most part ancient, with a few additions from the *Paris Breviary*. Unaware that some of the hymns he had translated were not so ancient, in 1841 he republished this volume under the more appropriate title of *The Hymns of the Church, mostly primitive, Collected, Translated, and Arranged for Public Use.*

TRANSLATOR: 12 The Advent of Our God
14 On Jordan's Bank the Baptist's Cry
151 O Christ, Our Hope
290 Christ Is Our Cornerstone

CHAPIN, LUCIUS (1760–1842), was born in Springfield, Massachusetts, a descendant of Deacon Samuel Chapin, who emigrated from England to America in 1636. As a leader in the congregation, his father often led the singing. At the age of 15 Lucius enlisted as a fifer in the Continental Army in Boston. He served at Ticonderoga and spent the historic winter of 1777–78 with Washington at Valley Forge. Thereafter he fought in the battle of Monmouth. Following his discharge from the armed forces he offered his services as a singing master and conducted classes in various states on the eastern seaboard. As a solid, dedicated Presbyterian, Lucius considered himself a missionary for the cause of both religion and church music. Married to Susan Rousseau of Staten Island, in 1794 he settled in Vernon, Kentucky, where he worked for the next 40 years developing and promoting singing schools. His brother Amzi joined him for a time, and thereafter returned to New England. It is likely that the compiler of *Kentucky Harmony* (1816), Ananias Davisson, may have received his music training from one or both of the Chapin brothers. In 1835 Lucius retired and moved to Hamilton County, Ohio, where he died December 24, 1842.

COMPOSER: 400 TWENTY-FOURTH

CHATFIELD, ALLEN WILLIAM (1808–96), was born October 2, 1808, at Chatteris, Cambridgeshire, England, the son of the then-vicar of Chatteris. Educated at Charter House and Trinity College, Cambridge, he graduated in 1831 with high classical honors. Ordained in 1832, he became vicar of Stotfold, Bedfordshire, and, in 1848, vicar of Much Marcle, Herefordshire.

Besides his published sermons and his rendering into Greek, in various meters, of the Litany (classic Western form), the Te Deum, and other liturgical pieces from the *Book of Common Prayer*, he is especially remembered for his *Songs and Hymns of the Earliest Greek Christian Poets, Bishops, and others, translated into English verse* (1876). He died at Much Marcle January 10, 1896.

TRANSLATOR: 231 Lord Jesus, Think on Me

CHRISTIERSON, FRANK VON (1900–), was born on Christmas Day, 1900, in Lovisa, near Helsinki, Finland, in a house previously owned by Jean Sibelius. At the age of five he moved with his family to the United States, graduating from Stanford University with a Bachelor of Arts degree in psychology. For three years he served as youth work director at First Presbyterian Church, San Luis Obispo, California. Graduating from San Francisco Theological Seminary in 1929, he was ordained by the presbytery of Santa Barbara, receiving the Master of Arts degree the following year from the same institution.

Christierson served as pastor of Calvary Presbyterian in Berkeley for 14 years, going on to become founding pastor of Trinity, North Hollywood, where he remained for 16 years. He then became founding pastor of Celtic Cross, Citrus Heights, California, staying there five years until his retirement in 1965.

Since that time, Christierson served five interim pastorates in northern California and Nevada, then, in 1971, serving as part-time assistant pastor at First Presbyterian Church, Roseville, California, where he ministered to the sick and elderly. He became a fellow of the Hymn Society in America in 1983, and received the Distinguished Alumnus Award from San Francisco Theological Seminary in 1984.

He is the author of more than 140 hymns, 18 published by the Hymn Society of America, while several have found their way into such major denominational hymnals as the Methodist *Book of Hymns* (1964), *The Hymnal* (1974) of the United Church of Christ, the Presbyterian *Worshipbook* (1972), and the *Book of Worship for United States Forces* (1974).

Married to Frances May Lockhart in 1925, he has a son, a daughter, and a granddaughter.

AUTHOR: 432 Eternal Spirit of the Living Christ

CLARKE, JEREMIAH (c. 1669–1707), started out as a chorister in the Chapel Royal, John Blow director. From 1692–95 he was organist at Winchester College. In 1695 he was appointed organist of St. Paul's Cathedral and in 1703, master of the choristers. He and William Croft, both students of John Blow, were sworn in as gentlemen-extraordinary of the Chapel Royal in 1700; in 1704 they were appointed joint organists.

A gifted, sensitive musician, given to periods of despondency, Clarke took his own life with a pistol, presumably over a hopeless passion for a beautiful lady in a station far above him.

Clarke composed songs, anthems, hymn tunes, cantatas, instrumental and keyboard music, as well as music for the theater. The *Beggars Opera* by John Pepusch (1667–1752) includes one of his songs. The popular "Trumpet Voluntary," for many years attributed to Henry Purcell, is now said to be Clarke's "Prince of Denmark's March." The "Trumpet Tune in D" is said to be his. In the *Yattendon Hymnal* (1899) Robert Bridges (*LW* 460, 486) included nine of Clarke's tunes with these comments:

> He [Clarke] seems to have been the inventor of the modern English hymn tune. His tunes are beautiful and have the plaintive grace characteristic of his music and melancholy temperament. They are first in merit of their kind, as they were first in time; . . . their neglect is to be regretted.

Both Bridges and Ralph Vaughan Williams (*LW* 59, et al.) did much to remedy this neglect. The latter included six of Clarke's tunes in *The English Hymnal* (1906).

COMPOSER: 235 ST. LUKE

CLAUSNITZER, TOBIAS (1619–1684), was born at Thurm, near Annaberg, Saxony. After studying at several universities, including theology at Leipzig, he received the Master of Arts degree in 1643. The following year he became chaplain to the Swedish regiment stationed in Leipzig during the Thirty Years' War. As such he preached the sermon at St. Thomas' Church to celebrate the accession of Christina to the Swedish throne. He also had the honor of preaching the sermon of thanksgiving at the field service ordered by General Wrangel, at Weiden, in the Upper Palatinate, January 1, 1849, at the conclusion of the Peace of Westphalia. Shortly thereafter he became the first pastor at Weiden and subsequently a member of the consistory and inspector of the district. He died May 7, 1684, at Weiden.

AUTHOR: 202 Dearest Jesus, at Your Word
212 We All Believe in One True God, Father

CLEMENT OF ALEXANDRIA (c. 170–c. 220), whose full name was Titus Flavius Clement, is considered one of the most eminent fathers of the early Eastern Church. A diligent student of Greek literature and philosophy, he was a stoic and an eclectic. It was while a student of Pantaenus, head of the famous Catechetical School at Alexandria, that Clement embraced Christianity. When the former retired from missionary work in Arabia and India, Clement became the school's head, c. 190, a position he retained until 203, when he was forced to leave Alexandria and retire in Palestine because of the violent persecution in the reign of Septimius Severus.

Clement's chief works are *Exhortation to the Heathen (Protrepticius)*, *The Tutor (Paedagoogos)*, and the *Miscellanies (Stromateis)*, all written to demonstrate Christianity to be the true philosophy, centered in Christ, the Logos.

AUTHOR (attr.): 471 Shepherd of Tender Youth

COFFIN, CHARLES (1676–1749), was born at Buzancy in the Ardennes in northern France and educated at Deplessis College of the University of Paris. In 1701 he became a member of the faculty at the College of Doirmans-Beauvais in the University of Paris, and its principal in 1712, succeeding the historian Charles Rollin. From 1718–23 he was rector of the University of Paris. Thereafter he returned to his former position at Doirmans-Beauvais.

As early as 1727, when he published a number of Latin hymns, he became noted as a writer of such hymns. In 1736 he published a volume of 100 hymns entitled *Hymni Sacri Auctor Carolo Coffin,* some of which appeared in the *Paris Breviary* in the same year. In fact, Coffin played an important role in the production of this *Breviary*, a work ordered by the Archbishop of Paris that included a number of hymns by French poets aimed at supplying "modern" hymns for worship in the observance of the canonical, or prayer, hours. Coffin died June 20, 1749.

Coffin's hymns, characterized as "direct and fitted with the spirit of grace," are remarkable also for their pure latinity and scripturalness. In 1775 Lenglet of Paris published a complete edition of his poems in two volumes.

AUTHOR: 12 The Advent of Our God
14 On Jordan's Bank the Baptist's Cry

COLUMBA (c. 521–97), one of the most renowned of the early saints of Scotland, was born at Garton, County Donegal, the son of a notable Irish family. Educated in the monastic schools of Moville and Clonard, he was also pupil of the aged bard Gemman, whose influence may be sensed in the Latin hymns and Celtic poems ascribed to Columba. Ordained to the priesthood about 551, Columba founded a number of churches in Ireland before leaving on a missionary trip to Scotland with 12 companions, all blood relatives. The group landed at Iona, a small island to the west of Scotland, which became the home of the small community as well as the starting point for a most successful missionary endeavor on the mainland, especially among the Picts. When not engaged in missionary or diplomatic expeditions, Columba's headquarters continued to be at Iona, where he had frequent visitors. By preaching and pious example he and his followers converted the whole of northern Scotland and established numerous monasteries. The day prior to his death saw him copying the Psalter. Arriving at the words "They that love the Lord shall lack no good thing," he paused and said, "Here I must stop; let Baithin do the rest." Baithin was the cousin whom he had chosen as his successor. Columba died June 8, 597.

Columba's influence, however, continued until it came to dominate the churches of Scotland, Ireland, and Northumbria. For 75 years or more Celtic Christians in those lands upheld certain Columban traditions of order and ritual in opposition to Rome itself, and Columba's rules for the monasteries held sway until supplanted by the milder ordinances of St. Benedict of Nursia (c. 480–c. 543).

AUTHOR (attr.): 271 Christ Is the World's Redeemer

CONKEY, ITHAMAR (sometimes J. or John Conkey; 1815–67). Of Scotch ancestry, he was born in Shutesbury, Massachusetts, May 5, 1815; he died at Elizabeth, New Jersey, April 30, 1867. A versatile musician, after serving as organist at the Central Baptist Church in Norwich, Connecticut (1849–50), he went to New York City, where he had a distinguished career as a church soloist and was considered an authority on oratorio singing. He served successively as bass soloist at Calvary Episcopal Church, New York; member of the choir, Grace Church, New York; and from 1861 on, as bass soloist and conductor of the quartet-choir of the Madison Avenue Baptist Church, New York.

COMPOSER: 101 RATHBUN

CONVERSE, CHARLES CROZAT (1832–1918), was born October 7, 1832, in Warren, Massachusetts, a descendant of one of the early settlers in Woburn, Massachusetts. After a thorough education in English and the classics in the United States, he studied philosophy and law in Germany, as well as music, under some eminent musicians at the Leipzig Conservatory. There he also became a friend of Franz Liszt (1811–86) and Louis Spohr (1784–1859). On returning to the States in 1859 he studied for the legal profession at Albany University, where he graduated in 1861. From 1875 until his retirement to Highwood, New Jersey, he practiced law in Erie, Pennsylvania. He died in Highwood, October 18, 1918.

Converse was a man of numerous talents. Besides enjoying a successful law career, he was a partner in the Burdett Organ Company; he was a composer, editor, philologist, and writer. Of the songs, hymn tunes, chamber music, oratorios, and symphonic works that he composed, only the tune CONVERSE, or ERIE, appears to have survived. And this is perhaps attributable to the popular text to which it has been almost inseparably joined, at least in American hymnals. The tune itself, with its incessant recurring rhythmic pattern, is not of great merit. The composer's serious study of music in Leipzig appears in stark contrast to the caliber of this tune. Someone has said that it has "most of the merits without the disadvantages of the gospel song."

COMPOSER: 516 CONVERSE

COOK, JOSEPH SIMPSON (1859–1933), was born in Durham County, England, December 4, 1859. After graduating from Weslyan College of McGill University in Montreal, Canada, he became a minister in the Methodist Church, and later in the United Church of Canada. He died May 27, 1933, in Toronto.

AUTHOR: 57 Gentle Mary Laid Her Child

CORY, JULIA BULKELY CADY (1882–1963), was born November 19, 1882, the daughter of J. Cleveland Cady, a noted architect in New York City and an active member of the Brick Presbyterian Church there. Julia Cory, educated at Brearley School and Reynold's School in New York City, also became a member of the Brick Presbyterian Church. Later, when she lived in Englewood, New Jersey, she was a member of the First Presbyterian Church of that city. Married to Robert Haskell Cory in 1911, she became the mother of three sons. She died May 1, 1963.

AUTHOR: 494 We Praise You, O God

COSIN, JOHN (1594–1672), was born November 30, 1594, at Norwich, England. Educated at Caius College, Cambridge, he took holy orders and was appointed chaplain to the bishop of Durham. He subsequently became prebendary of Durham and archdeacon of East Riding of Yorkshire. In 1634 he became master of Peterhouse, Cambridge, and vice-chancellor of the university in 1640. His famous *Collection of Private Devotions in the Practice of the Ancient Church called the Hours of Prayer* (1627), virulently attacked by the Puritans, caused him to be deprived of his benefices. He then fled to France, where he was chaplain to the exiled members of the royal family. With the restoration of Charles II in 1660 he returned to England and became dean and later bishop of Durham. During his episcopate he spent large sums on the cathedral, the library, and in various works of charity. He helped in the final revision of *The Book of Common Prayer* (1662), in which his translation of the "Veni, Creator Spiritus" was included. He died January 15, 1672, at Westminster.

TRANSLATOR: 157, 158 Come, Holy Ghost, Our Souls Inspire

COWPER, WILLIAM (1731–1800), was born November 15, 1731, in the rectory of Great Berkhamsted, England. His father John Cowper was rector of the parish as well as a chaplain to George II. His mother, Ann Donne, a descendent of the poet John Donne (1573–1631), died when he was but six years of age. Following his education at Westminster, where he studied law, he was apprenticed to an attorney at age eighteen and admitted to the bar in 1754; but he never actually practiced law. From 1759–63 he was commissioner of bankrupts. His first mental breakdown and attempted suicide was caused by his being nominated to a clerkship in the House of Lords and his anxiety over the preliminary examination before the House. This resulted in spending 18 months in the asylum at St. Alban's, during which detention he was "converted" in the evangelical manner; that is, he realized a personal contact with Christ and sin forgiven. Following his release he went to live at Huntingdon, where he met and became a fast friend to the Reverend Morely and Mrs. Unwin, who took him in as a boarder. This happy relationship was interrupted by the accidental death of Mr. Unwin. Meeting the Reverend John Newton of Olney, when he called to offer his sympathy, ushered in a new life for Cowper. Newton prevailed upon him and Mrs. Unwin to move to Olney, where he and Newton conducted village prayer meetings, visited the poor and sick, distributed the alms supplied by a wealthy friend of Newton's, and wrote the historic *Olney Hymns* (1779), containing 67 of his texts.

Unfortunately, the depression returned and led him to another attempted suicide. The malady gradually waned by the time his cousin, Lady Hesketh, brought him to Weston in 1786. In 1794 he was granted an annual pension of £300, and the following year he moved with Mrs. Unwin, by then a helpless invalid, to East Dereham. Her death again brought on despair and resulted in writing his last poem, *The Castaway*. Cowper's greatest and best known work was *The Task*, written during one of the brighter periods of his life. From this previously mentioned despair Cowper never fully recovered. He died April 25, 1800.

AUTHOR: 426 God Moves in a Mysterious Way
506 There Stands a Fountain Where for Sin

COX, FRANCES ELIZABETH (1812–97), English poet and author, was born at Oxford, May 10, 1812, and died at Headington on September 23, 1897. Her *Sacred Hymns from the German*, published in 1841, was succeeded in 1864 by a revised and enlarged collection entitled *Hymns from the German*. She shares with Catherine Winkworth the honor of being the best translators of German hymns into English.

TRANSLATOR: 139 Jesus Lives! The Victory's Won
277 One Thing's Needful
452 Sing Praise to God, the Highest Good

CRASSELIUS, BARTHOLOMÄUS (1667–1724), was born February 21, 1667, at Wensdorf near Glaucha, Saxony. While a pupil of August Herman Francke at the University of Halle, he became a thoroughly convinced Pietist. Small wonder that as a Lutheran pastor, first at Nidda, in Wetteravia, Hesse, and thereafter from 1708 on in Düsseldorf, his bold and determined advocacy of Pietism resulted in his becoming entangled in numerous controversies. He died November 10, 1724, in Düsseldorf.

AUTHOR: 446 Jehovah, Let Me Now Adore You

CROFT, WILLIAM (1678–1727), was born in Nether Ettington, near Stratford-on-Avon, England, and baptized there December 30, 1678. At the Chapel Royal, he became a chorister, pupil and protege of John Blow. In 1700 he became organist at St. Anne's Church, Soho, and gentleman extraordinary of the Chapel Royal, sharing that post with Jeremiah Clarke. In May 1704 they jointly succeeded Francis Pigott (c. 1665-1704) as organist of the chapel and, when Clarke died in 1707, Croft became sole organist. After John Blow's death in 1708, Croft became not only composer and master of children of the Chapel Royal, but also organist of Westminster Abbey. In 1712 he relinquished his post at St. Anne's. The following year he received the Doctor of Music degree from Oxford University. The work submitted for the degree consisted of two odes for solo voices, chorus, and orchestra entitled *With Noise of Canon* and *Laurus cruentas,* celebrating the Treaty of Utrecht (1713–14), ending the War of Spanish Succession. He died August 14, 1727, at Bath and was buried close to Henry Purcell in Westminster Abbey. His epitaph concludes: "Having resided among mortals for 50 years, behaving with utmost candour . . . he departed to the heavenly choir . . . that being near, he might add to the concert of angels his own hallelujah."

Although in earlier life Croft composed for the theater and also wrote sonatas, songs, and odes, he is especially remembered for his sacred music—hymn tunes, anthems, services—and it is in this area that he made for himself one of the greatest names in English music history. The burial service he composed, hardly surpassed for solemn grandeur, is a noble classic of moving simplicity, into which, without apparent incongruity, he overtly incorporated Henry Purcell's beautiful anthem "Thou knowest, Lord, the secrets of our hearts." Also deserving of mention is his ground-breaking *Musica sacra* (1724), a two volume collection of his anthems, engraved in the form of a score rather than in the hitherto customary separate parts.

COMPOSER:	180	ST. ANNE
	458	HANOVER

CRONENWETT, EMANUEL (1841–1931), was born February 22, 1841, near Ann Arbor, Michigan, the son of George Cronenwett, a pastor in that area. Educated for the Lutheran ministry at Capitol University, Columbus, Ohio, he was ordained and served at Carrollton, Ohio, where he ministered also to seven congregations in four countries. Next he served congregations at Waynesburg, Wooster, and Delaware, Ohio, and during the last 54 years of his long ministry he was pastor at Butler, Pennsylvania. Grove City (Pennsylvania) College honored him with the Doctor of Divinity degree. As a hymnist he was both an author and translator. He died at Butler, Pennsylvania, March 9, 1931.

TRANSLATOR:	189	Lord, God, to You We All Give Praise
AUTHOR:	340	We Have a Sure Prophetic Word

CROSSMAN, SAMUEL (c. 1624–83), was born in Bradfield Monachorum in Suffolk, England. He received the Bachelor of Divinity degree in 1660 from Pembroke College, Cambridge, and was appointed vicar of All Saints', Sudbury, where, in addition to his Anglican congregation, he also served a Puritan church. Because of this, he was ejected under the Act of Uniformity of 1662, but later returned to the Church of England and was episcopally ordained in 1665.

He served for two years as one of the king's chaplains, and in 1667 was appointed vicar of St. Nicholas Church and prebendary of Bristol Cathedral, of which he became dean shortly before his death on February 4, 1683.

Crossman's writings include a small pamphlet, *The Young Man's Meditation, or some few Sacred Poems upon Select Subjects and Scriptures* (1664), reprinted in 1863 by D. Sedgwick, and two sermons for the "Days of public Humiliation for the execrable Murder of King Charles I" (1681). Crossman is one of the first English authors before Issac Watts to write hymns of human composition over against strict metrical psalmody. (See essay: Metrical Psalms, p. 825.)

AUTHOR: 91 My Song Is Love Unknown

CRUCIGER, ELIZABETH (c. 1500–35), was born of a noble Polish family with the surname Meseritz. Religious persecution prompted the family to move to Wittenberg, where Elizabeth met Caspar Cruciger (Kreutziger), a student at the University of Wittenberg, whom she married in 1524.

As a result of his piety and discretion, Luther loved Cruciger as his own son; he considered him one of his most promising students. Upon completion of his studies in 1525, at the age of 21, Cruciger became rector of the newly, evangelical-founded St. John's School and also preacher at St. Stephen's Church in Magdeburg. Three years later he was called to the philosophical faculty at Wittenberg University. At the wish of Luther, however, he transferred to the theological faculty, where he expounded both the Old and New Testaments and, in 1533, at the behest of Elector Johann Friedrich, was promoted to Doctor of Theology.

Elizabeth was a pious, devoted wife and mother, a friend of Katherine Luther; Luther's hymns were loved and used for edification in the Cruciger household. After but 11 years of marriage, Elizabeth died in May of 1535. Although she undoubtedly wrote other hymns, she is remembered only for one.

AUTHOR: 72 The Only Son from Heaven

CRÜGER, JOHANN (1598–1662), the son of an innkeeper, was born April 9, 1598, in Gross-Breesen, Brandenburg. He studied at schools in Guben, Sorau, Breslau, the Jesuit school in Olmütz, and finally at the Poets' School in Regensburg. There he pursued the study of music under Paul Homberger, a former pupil of the great organist and composer at St. Mark's in Venice, Giovanni Gabrielli (c. 1533–1612). In 1620 he enrolled at the University of Wittenberg, engaged not only in theological but also in music studies. In 1622 he was appointed cantor of St. Nicholas Church in Berlin and teacher in the *Gymnasium* of the Gray Cloister, the two positions in which he remained until his death on February 23, 1662.

In 1657 the famous poet Paul Gerhardt (1607–76) became a deacon at St. Nicholas, and the friendship that developed between the two lasted until Crüger's death. Next to Luther, Crüger is perhaps the most important musician and composer of hymn tunes of the Lutheran Church. He created and stylized no less than 122 chorale tunes (21 to Gerhardt's texts, at least 18 of which are still popular today). He published five monumental collections of hymns, beginning with the *Neues vollkömmliches Gesangbuch Augsburgischer Confession* (Berlin, 1640), a work that contained 161 hymns in four parts. There followed *Geistliche Kirchenmelodien* (Berlin, 1649), containing the same number (109 of which with instrumental accompaniment); *Geistliche Lieder und Psalmen* (Berlin, 1653), a collection of 92 tunes without texts; and the *Psalmodia sacra* (Berlin, 1658), containing 150 psalms by Ambrosius Lobwasser (1515–85) and 184 tunes with instrumental accompaniment. His chief contribution to hymnody, however, was his *Praxis pietatis melica* (Berlin, 1644), which went through 45 editions, thus constituting the most significant collection of 17th-century hymnody. Its final edition, appearing nearly a hundred years later, contained over 1,300 hymns.

Crüger's dual role of cantor and teacher is also reflected in his publications—his hymn collections and treatises intended for school use. In one of the latter, his *Synopsis Musica*, he discusses the church modes in the then "new" terms, dividing them into the *naturaliores* (Ionian, Lydian, and Mixolydian) and *molliores* (Dorian, Phrygian, and Aeolian), in other words, the major and minor keys. He emphasizes the importance of the triad and the teaching of counterpoint from the harmonic-chordal rather than from the contrapuntal standpoint (Riedel).

The influx of Huguenots into Berlin under the blessing of Elector Frederick William swelled the ranks of Calvinism. Thus Crüger's activities touched both Lutherans and Calvinists. The previously mentioned *Psalmodia sacra* (1658) was produced by Crüger at the behest of the elector for the benefit of the members of the Reformed faith. Crüger's own work was in turn influenced by this assignment. The structure of some chorale tunes, as well as their metric, rhythmic, and harmonic patterns, reflect the style of the French psalters (Riedel).

Crüger exhibited a felicitous method of merging the objective chorales of the Luther tradition with the more subjective hymns of Pietism. His hymnals were useful for both church and home. Moreover, he was the first to use the then-new "figured bass."

COMPOSER:	19	WIE SOLL ICH DICH EMPFANGEN
	39	FRÖHLICH SOLL MEIN HERZE SPRINGEN
	119	HERZLIEBSTER JESU
	128	AUF, AUF, MEIN HERZ
	139, 266	JESUS, MEINE ZUVERSICHT
	174, 443	NUN DANKET ALLE GOTT
	184	NUN LASST UNS GOTT DEM HERREN
	200, 204, 472	NUN DANKET ALL
	233	HERR, ICH HABE MISSGEHANDELT
	239, 468	SCHMÜCKE DICH
	270	JESU, MEINE FREUDE

CRULL, AUGUST (1845–1923), was born January 27, 1845, in Rostock, Germany, the son of a lawyer. Shortly after he entered the *Gymnasium* in Rostock, his father died, and his mother married Albert Friedrich Hoppe, who later became editor of the St. Louis edition of *Luther's Works* (1880–97). Having come to the United States with his family, Crull attended Concordia College at St. Louis and Fort Wayne, graduating in 1862. Thereafter he attended Concordia Seminary, St. Louis, receiving his diploma three years later. After serving as assistant pastor of Trinity Lutheran Church, Milwaukee; director of the Lutheran High School, Milwaukee; and pastor of the Lutheran Church in Grand Rapids, Michigan, in 1873 he became professor of German at Concordia College, Fort Wayne. There he remained until his retirement in 1915, when he returned to Milwaukee, where he died April 17, 1923.

Crull's translations are included in many American Lutheran hymnals.

TRANSLATOR:	34	Come, O Precious Ransom
	109	Jesus, I Will Ponder Now
	145	I Am Content! My Jesus Ever Lives
	153	Draw Us to You
	174	The Lord, My God, Be Praised
	287	Abide with Us, Our Savior
	352	God Loved the World So that He Gave
	364	Oh, How Great Is Your Compassion
	372	O God, Forsake Me Not
	373	Renew Me, O Eternal Light
	385	How Can I Thank You, Lord
	418	What Is the World to Me
	429	I Leave All Things to God's Direction

CUMMINGS, WILLIAM HAYMAN (1831–1915), was born August 22, 1831, in Sidbury, Devonshire, England. As a boy he sang in the choirs of St. Paul's Cathedral and the Temple Church, London. In 1847 he was appointed organist at Waltham Abbey and in that year he sang in the premiere performance of Mendelssohn's *Elijah*, conducted by the composer. Cummings' adaptation of a theme from Mendelssohn's *Festgesang* (1840) to "Hark! the herald angels sing" dates from this time. Acclaimed as a tenor soloist, Cummings frequently sang the principal tenor parts in Bach's Passions and other works; he sang for the Birmingham Festival in 1864, even filling engagements in the United States. From 1879–96 he was professor of singing at the Royal Academy of Music, and for a time he conducted the Sacred Harmonic Society and was precentor at St. Anne's, Soho. In 1896 he was selected to succeed Joseph Barnby (*LW* 253, et al.) as principal of the Guildhall School of Music, where he modernized the curriculum. Here he remained until his retirement in 1910. In 1900 Trinity College, Dublin, awarded him an honorary Doctor of Music degree.

Cummings' works include an anthem, a morning service, and a cantata, *The Fairy Ring*. He contributed to Groves *Dictionary of Music and Musicians*. Since modern research has supplanted his biography of Henry Purcell (*LW* 186), Cummings is today especially remembered for the magnificent music library, some 4,500 pieces, that he collected. Unfortunately this collection was dispersed by auction, a cruel fate against which he himself had warned while living.

ARRANGER: 49 MENDELSSOHN

CUTLER, HENRY STEPHEN (1824–1902), was born October 13, 1824, in Boston. Following his early schooling and training there, he went to Frankfurt-am-Main, Germany, where he studied music, the while traveling in England, visiting cathedral services and becoming exposed to the liturgical practices and ideals of the Oxford Movement. Returning to Boston, he served for a time as organist and choirmaster of Grace Church (no longer in existence) before going to the Church of the Advent. Here his choir of men and boys became distinguished not only for its fine singing but also for its becoming one of the first vested (in surplices) choirs in the United States.

In 1858 he went to Trinity Church in New York City. Here he dismissed the two women in the existing choir, he organized and trained the men and boys. His choir chanted psalms, sang other parts of the liturgical service, and became vested in surplices. Embarking on a month-long concert tour with three members of Trinity Choir, his return was greeted with the termination of his position, June 30, 1865, on grounds of "absence without leave." Thereafter he served churches in Brooklyn, Providence, Philadelphia, and Troy before his retirement in 1885 and his return to Boston, where he died December 5, 1902.

Cutler's works include anthems, service and organ music, *The Trinity Psalter* (1864) and *Trinity Anthems* (1865). In 1864 Columbia University honored him with a Doctor of Music degree.

COMPOSER: 304 ALL SAINTS NEW

CZAMANSKE, WILLIAM MARTIN (1873–1964), was born August 26, 1873, at Granville, Wisconsin. Following his graduation from Concordia College, Milwaukee, in 1894, he entered Concordia Seminary, St. Louis, graduating in 1898. Ordained that same year, he served Lutheran churches in Madelia, Minnesota, 1898–1902; West Henrietta, New York, 1902–04; Rochester, New York, 1904–10; and Sheboygan, Wisconsin, 1910–51, when he retired and where he died in 1964.

Besides contributing poems to the *Lutheran Witness*, *Sunday School Times*, *Etude*, *Expositor*, *Northwestern Lutheran*, and other church publications, he served as a member of a subcommittee of the Committee on Hymnology and Liturgics for the Synodical Conference of North America, the committee that produced *The Lutheran Hymnal* (1941).

AUTHOR: 325 For Many Years, O God of Grace

DACH, SIMON (1605–59), was born July 29, 1605, at Memel, 72 miles northeast of Königsberg, Prussia. When his study of theology and philosophy at the cathedral school in Königsberg was terminated because of the pestilence, he spent three years at the University of Wittenberg. In 1623 he went to Magdeburg to become more exposed to the liberal arts. The Thirty Years' War, together with a plague that broke out, prompted him to flee to Königsberg, there to pursue his studies in philosophy and theology. While there he became a close friend of Abraham Calov (1612-86), teacher and theologian, staunch defender of orthodoxy. In ill health and meager circumstances, Dach met and became a friend of Robert Roberthin, through whose help he was now able to spend less time teaching and more time writing poetry. In 1633 Dach became assistant rector at Königsberg cathedral school. Through the influence of Roberthin, in 1639 Dach was appointed professor of poetry at Königsberg. His position, which involved the interpretation of Latin poets, was approached with great joy. In the furtherance of his work he read Thomas á Kempis (*LW* 275), and such Lutheran systematicians and devotional authors as Johann Arndt (1555-1621), Johann Gerhardt (1582–1637), Nikolas Hunnius (1585–1643), Johann Meyfart (*LW* 306), and Philipp Nicolai (*LW* 73, 177). In 1641 he married Regina, daughter of the court attorney Christoph Pohl, who bore him seven children. The death of his dear friend and benefactor Robertin in 1648 prompted Dach to turn from secular to religious poetry, and so he now began his hymn writing, producing about 150 in all. The Thirty Years' War and its attendant vicissitudes created in him a yearning for the heavenly mansions, a feeling expressed in many of his hymns.

Dach was undoubtedly the most gifted of a group of prominent Prussian theologians, scientists, and poets known as the Königsberg circle, or school. He died April 15, 1659.

AUTHOR: 268 Oh, How Blest Are You
369 Through Jesus' Blood and Merit

DACHSTEIN, WOLFGANG (c. 1487–1553), was born in Offenburg, Southeast of Strassburg, and in 1503 he enrolled at Erfurt at the time Luther was studying there. Some time later he entered the Dominican Order at Strassburg and in 1521 he was chosen to be organist at St. Thomas' Church. Espousing the Reformation cause in the summer of 1523, he left the Dominican Order and gained his Strassburg civil rights. Married in 1524, in 1541 he became organist at the cathedral in Strassburg and in 1542 teacher of music at the recently established *Gymnasium Argentinense*. Seven years later, in order to remain cathedral organist, he returned to the Roman Church. He died March 7, 1553, in Strassburg.

In addition to coediting the *Teutsch Kirchenamt* with his friend Matthäus Greiter (c. 1495–1550), German composer and cantor, Dachstein is also credited with several tunes in the Genevan Psalter. (See essay: Metrical Psalms, p. 825.)

COMPOSER: 111 AN WASSERFLÜSSEN BABYLON

DAMAN (DAMON), WILLIAM (GUILIEMO) (c. 1540–c. 1591), was organist of the Chapel Royal under Queen Elizabeth. The work for which he is best known, prepared for the use of his friend John Bull, citizen and goldsmith of London, was published by John Day with the title *The Psalmes of David in English meter, with notes of four parts set unto them by Guilielmo Daman* (1579). With only a few exceptions, the tunes used in this book are those that had appeared in previous books—the Anglo-Genevan Psalter of 1556, the English of 1562, and the Scottish of 1564. The Daman volume consists of four books, one for each voice part, and the harmony is simple note-against-note. Daman evidently considered the simple harmony not worthy of his ability and reputation, for he withdrew the book and destroyed the remaining copies with the result that it is now very rare. He then undertook the task of revising the harmonies, and in 1591 a second and more elaborate edition was published entitled *The former (second) Booke of the Musicke of M. William Daman, late one of her majesties Musitions: contayning all the tunes of Davids psalms as they are ordinarily soung in the Church, most excellently by him composed into four parts*. This work is in eight books, the first four of which have the melody in the tenor, the second four in the soprano.

COMPOSER: 99, 231 SOUTHWELL

DARWALL, JOHN (1731–89), was baptized January 13, 1731 in the rectory of Houghton, Staffordshire, England. Following his graduation with a Bachelor of Arts degree from Brasenose College, Oxford, in 1756, he was ordained and appointed curate in 1761 at St. Matthew's Church, Walsall, Staffordshire. Becoming vicar there in 1769, he remained in that position until his death December 18, 1789.

As an enthusiastic amateur musician he composed some sonatas for the piano and tunes in two parts, treble and bass, for each of the 150 psalms in the New Version of the Psalms (1696), popularly known as the "Tate and Brady," only one of which remained in use. (See essay: Metrical Psalms, p. 825.)

COMPOSER: 179, 217, 290, 500 DARWALL'S 148TH

DAY (DAYE, or DAIE), JOHN (1522–1584), one of the earliest and most successful music printers, was born at Dunwich, Suffolk, England. After learning his trade in London, he began printing in 1546, moving his shop to Aldersgate three years later. He printed the first edition of what is known as Queen Elizabeth's Prayer Book; the first edition of Foxe's *The Book of Martyrs;* the first church music book in English, *Certaine Notes set forth in foure and three parts to be song*; Archbishop Parker's translation of the *Psalmes* (1560), the first by one person of the whole Psalter in English metre; the first edition of *The Whole Booke of Psalms* (1562), known as the Old Version or Sternhold and Hopkin's Psalter, plus 36 separate editions of this psalter, the result of a monopoly granted him by the crown in 1559 (whether or not he played any part in the choice of the psalm tunes is difficult to determine); and *The Whole*

Psalmes, in four partes, which may be sung to all musical instruments, probably the earliest psalter in which the proper tunes were harmonized and to which the eminent English composer Thomas Tallis (*LW* 254, et al.) contributed.

Day must have employed journeymen of great skill, for his music books show a clean, crisp impression with spacious layout and good registration. An astute businessman, he acquired various printing monopolies on which he built a virtual printing empire. Moreover, a zealous supporter of religious reform, he suffered imprisonment for his loyalty to it; for a time he was forced to live abroad. Following his death at Walden, Essex, July 23, 1584, his son Richard carried on the business.

PRINTER: 342 ST. FLAVIAN

DEARMER, PERCY (1867–1936), was born in London, February 27, 1867, and educated at Westminster School and Christ Church, Oxford, earning the Bachelor of Arts degree in 1890 and the Master of Arts degree in 1896. Ordained deacon in 1891 at Rochester Cathedral and priest the next year, he filled curacies until he was made vicar of St. Mary's, Primrose Hill, London, where he served from 1901–15 with Martin Shaw as his organist. Here he was able to put into effect his ideas concerning liturgy and church music. Having organized, with Scott Holland, the Christian Social Union, he served as its secretary for 21 years. He was also chairman of the League of Arts. In 1915 he enlisted as chaplain with the Serbian nursing service to British Forces, for which he was awarded the Serbian Red Cross decoration. Returning to England in 1916, he became a lecturer for the YMCA, visiting India, Burma, and North America. In 1919 he was appointed professor of ecclesiastical art at King's College, London, holding that position until his death May 29, 1936, in Westminster. Oxford University honored him with the Doctor of Divinity degree, and in 1931 he became canon of Westminster.

A man of boundless energy and wide interests, he produced, among other things, the *Parson's Handbook* (1899); *Everyman's History of the English Church* (1899); *Everyman's History of the Prayer Book (1912),* and the *Story of the Prayer Book* (1934). With Ralph Vaughan Williams he produced the epochal *The English Hymnal* (1906). With Williams and Shaw he produced *Songs of Praise* (1925); *The Oxford Book of Carols* (1928); and *Songs of Praise Enlarged* (1931), for which he compiled the handbook *Songs of Praise Discussed* (1933). Because of his hymnals English congregations were introduced to many American hymns.

TRANSLATOR:	175	Father Most Holy
	482	Father, We Praise You
AUTHOR:	383, 384	All Who Would Valiant Be

DECIUS, NIKOLAUS (c. 1485–c. 1546), probably born at Hof in upper Franconia, Bavaria, in 1501 he matriculated at the University at Leipzig, where he earned the Bachelor of Arts degree. Entering the service of the Church, in 1519 he became provost of the Benedictine Monastery at Steterburg, near Brunswick. While here he wrote a commentary on Matthew's Gospel; he also began to lean toward the cause of the Reformation. The year 1522 saw him briefly as a teacher in Hanover, a period in which he probably wrote three hymns in Low German (*Plattdeutsch*), with melodies based on corresponding Gregorian chants. In 1523 he went to study at the University of Wittenberg and, recommended by Luther, he became pastor of St. Nicholas Church, Stettin. He is mentioned as a deacon at Liebstadt in 1530, moving to Mühlhausen in 1534. In 1540 he became deputy cantor to Hans Kugelmann (c. 1495–1542), composer and kapellmeister, and assistant court preacher to Duke Albrecht of Prussia in Königsberg, where he remained until 1543 when, perhaps as chaplain, he joined a campaign against the Turks. Returning to Mühlhausen thereafter, nothing more is known about him after 1546.

AUTHOR:	208	Lamb of God, Pure and Sinless
	215	All Glory Be to God on High
COMPOSER:	208	O LAMM GOTTES, UNSCHULDIG
	215, 456	ALLEIN GOTT IN DER HÖH

DENICKE, DAVID (1603-80), was born in Zittau, Saxony, January 1, 1603, the son of a city magistrate. After studying law at the universities of Wittenberg and Jena he became a tutor in law for a time in Königsberg before traveling through Holland, England, and France. In 1629 he became tutor to the sons of Duke Georg of Brunswick-Lüneberg. In 1639 he was appointed head of the religious establishment in Bursfeld and in 1642 he became a member of the consistory in Hanover, where he died April 1, 1680. Denicke was coeditor with his friend J. Gesenius (*LW* 367) of various Hanoverian hymn books published between the years 1646–49.

AUTHOR:	385	How Can I Thank You, Lord.

DEXTER, HENRY MARTYN (1821–90), was born August 13, 1821, at Plympton, Massachusetts. Following his graduation from Yale College in 1840, he attended the Andover Theological Seminary, from which he graduated in 1844. He then served as pastor of congregations in Manchester, New Hampshire, and in Boston, Massachusetts. In 1867 he discontinued his pastoral work to become editor of the *Congregationalist* and *Recorder*. Dexter was not only a rather prolific writer, he was also considered an authority on the history of Congregationalism. He died November 13, 1890.

TRANSLATOR:	471	Shepherd of Tender Youth

DIX, WILLIAM CHATTERTON (1837-98), was born in Bristol, June 14, 1837, the son of William John Dix, surgeon who wrote the *Life of Chatterton*, the Bristol poet, after whom his son was named. Educated at Bristol Grammar School, William became manager of a marine insurance company in Glasgow as well as being a scholarly layman. On retirement he lived in Clifton with a married daughter. He died September 9, 1898, and was buried in the parish church at Cheddar, Somerset.

Dix's hymns were published in *Hymns of Love and Joy* (1861), *Altar Songs, Verses on the Holy Eucharist* (1867), *A Vision of All Saints* (871), and *Seekers of a City* (1878). Several of his hymns are translations from the Greek.

AUTHOR: 61 What Child Is This
75 As with Gladness Men of Old
345 Come unto Me, Ye Weary

DOAN, GILBERT EVERETT, JR. (1930–), served as chairman of the Committee on Hymn Texts of the Inter-Lutheran Commission on Worship and also as secretary of that commission from 1972 until its dissolution in 1978. Born at Philadelphia, Pennsylvania, on September 14, 1930, Doan prepared at Deerfield Academy, received the Bachelor of Arts degree in geology from Harvard College (1952), the Bachelor of Divinity degree from Lutheran Seminary at Philadelphia (1955), and the Master of Arts degree in American civilization from the University of Pennsylvania (1962). Wagner College awarded him the Doctor of Divinity in 1984.

Doan served as campus pastor at Philadelphia (1955–61) and as northeast regional director of the National Lutheran Campus Ministry (1961–84). In 1984 he accepted the call to the pastorate of the Lutheran Church of the Holy Communion, Philadelphia. He has published a book on the preaching of Fredrick W. Robertson as well as essays and a number of reviews on homiletical and liturgical subjects.

TRANSLATOR: 45 O Savior of Our Fallen Race
92 O Lord, Throughout These Forty Days
215 All Glory Be to God on High
314 O Christ, Our Light, O Radiance True, stanzas 1, 3–5
357 I Trust, O Christ, in You Alone

DOANE, GEORGE WASHINGTON (1799–1859), was born, on May 27, 1799, the year Washington died. Shortly after his birth, the family moved from Trenton, New Jersey, to New York City and then, when the boy was 10, to Geneva, New York, where he attended prep school. He graduated with high honors from Union College, Schenectady, in 1818.

Headed at first for a career in law, he studied briefly in the law office of Richard Harison in New York, but then abandoned the practice for the ministry. Thus in 1819 Doane became a candidate for the priesthood in New York, supporting his mother and sisters by teaching in the meantime. He was ordained deacon April 19, 1821, and became assistant pastor of Trinity Church, New York. His ordination to the priesthood took place August 6, 1823.

In 1824 Doane accepted a professorship at the newly established Washington College (now Trinity College) in Hartford, Connecticut; in 1828 he became assistant pastor of Trinity Church, Boston, accepting the rectorship there on the death of his predecessor; in 1832 he was elected bishop of New Jersey.

Doane's first book appeared in 1824, entitled *Songs By the Way, Chiefly Devotional, with Translations and Imitations*, which included his best known hymns. A man of much learning and forceful character, he was one of the great American prelates of his time. He was also sympathetic with the Tractarian Movement and edited an American edition of John Keble's *Christian Year* (1834). He died April 27, 1859, after a brief illness.

AUTHOR: 283 You Are the Way; to You Alone

DODDRIDGE, PHILIP (1702–51), was born June 26, 1702, the youngest of 20 children, and one of two to survive infancy. His mother was the daughter of a Bohemian Lutheran pastor who had escaped to England to avoid persecution. After the death of his parents in 1715 he came under the care of Pastor Samuel Clark at St. Albans. At the suggestion of his uncle, who was steward for the Duke of Bedford, the Duchess offered to support Doddridge at Cambridge so that he might take holy orders in the Church of England, but he declined the offer and instead entered Jenning's Dissenting Academy at Kibworth. In 1723 Doddridge was chosen pastor at Kibworth. Six years later he was appointed minister of the Castle Hill Meeting in Northampton, a parish comprised of poor, hardworking people, where he remained for 22 years. In 1729 he opened a Dissenting academy in Market Harborough on the advice of Isaac Watts (*LW* 53 et al.) The wide range of subjects—daily reading in Hebrew and Greek, algebra, trigonometry, Watts' logic, outline of philosophy and copious theology—were taught mostly by Doddridge himself. In 1736 the University of Aberdeen honored him with the Doctor of Divinity degree.

Doddridge won the friendship of Isaac Watts (*LW* 53, et al.); he was sympathetic to the work of Charles Wesley (*LW* 15, et al.), his brother John (*LW* 280, 362), and George Whitefield, and was greatly admired as a person and as a divine. He was cofounder of the hospital in Northampton; the Doddridge Memorial Chapel was built there in his honor. He died October 26, 1751, in Lisbon where he had gone in the hope of finding relief from the consumption which he suffered.

Doddridge wrote a goodly number of theological works, of which *The Rise and Progress of Religion in the Soul* became a classic of devotion for the Independents. His hymns, some 400 in all, were published after his death, by his friend Job Orton in *Hymns, Founded on Various Texts in the Holy Scriptures* (1755). These hymns, like those of Watts, were largely used as extensions and reinforcement of the sermon topic of the day.

AUTHOR: 29 Hark the Glad Sound
228 Our Children Jesus Calls
395 O Fount of Good, for All Your Love

DOUGLAS, CHARLES WINFRED (1867–1944), was born in Oswego, New York, on February 15, 1867. At the age of 16 he became organist at the local Presbyterian church. He attended Syracuse University and graduated with the Bachelor of Music degree in 1891. He stayed on at Syracuse as vocal instructor for a year, going in 1892 to New York City where he played organ and directed the choirs of the Church of Zion and St. Timothy. Returning to Syracuse to study theology, Douglas was ordained deacon in 1893, and became for a short time curate of the Church of the Redeemer in New York City, including duties as music director; he also taught at St. John's School there.

Because of health considerations, in 1894 Douglas moved to Denver, Colorado, as minor canon of the Cathedral of St. John in the Wilderness. Soon lung trouble forced him to spend more time outdoors, and he went to Evergreen, Colorado. Married in 1896, Douglas and his physician wife, Mary Josepha Williams, provided the land for a mission congregation in Evergreen, founded August 6, 1899, as the Church of the Transfiguration.

After a trip to England in 1901, Douglas suffered a setback in his health and retired to the desert with the Native Americans of the Southwest. Given the name "Tall Pine Tree" by the Hopis, he became a recognized authority on Native American arts and culture, later collaborating with President Theodore Roosevelt on improving methods of education for Native Americans.

From 1903–06 Douglas again traveled in England, France, and Germany, studying church music especially with the Benedictines of Solesmes. This solid foundation in Gregorian chant led Douglas to prepare many adaptations of plainsong masses, and to his election to the presidency of the American Plainsong Society. From 1906 on he was director of music for the Community of St. Mary at Peekskill, New York, where he was able to apply his knowledge of plainsong to English adaptation. At his own expense and using a type font he developed for plainsong notation, Douglas published many outstanding works on the subject, including the *Monastic Diurnal* (1932), the music edition of which was nearly complete at his death.

Douglas was named canon residentiary at St. Paul's Cathedral, Fond du Lac, Wisconsin, in 1907, and honorary canon in 1911. The Summer School of Church Music at Cambridge and Wellesley, Massachusetts (1915–24), brought Douglas as a lecturer to the attention of a much larger audience than he had previously enjoyed. Awarded the Doctor of Music degree in 1917 by Nashotah Seminary, Wisconsin, he founded the Evergreen Conference in 1923 and served as its vice-president for the remainder of his life, assisting also in the planning for its School of Church Music. In 1934 he "retired" to become chaplain of the western Community of St. Mary in Kenosha, Wisconsin, and was named honorary canon of St. John's Cathedral in Denver.

Hale Lecturer at Seabury-Western Seminary in 1935, Douglas delivered a series of lectures on church music so successfully that they were published in 1937 as *Church*

Music in History and Practice, later revised in 1962 by Leonard Ellinwood and still used as a text for students of church music.

Both priest and musician, Douglas was able to combine the two professions to approach the ideal of church musicianship. A member of the Joint Commission on Worship of the Episcopal Church, he served as music editor of the *Hymnal* of 1916 and *The Hymnal 1940*. At first he chaired the committee producing *The Hymnal 1940 Companion* but, due to the pressure of editing the hymnal, he resigned this post. However, he was still instrumental in compiling the *Companion*, and indeed was consulting with his successor in Santa Rosa, California, when he died of a heart attack January 18, 1944.

Douglas left behind a long list of publications, including the following: *The Choral Service*, with Wallace Goodrich (1927); *The American Psalter* (1929); and the *Plainsong Psalter* (1932). He was music editor of *The American Missal* (1931) and author of *The Midnight Mass and other poems* (1933); he composed a *Magnificat* for eight-part chorus unaccompanied (1940); *The Chorales from the Organ Works of Brahms* (1939–44), and various original organ preludes. He also edited a *Mission Hymnal* (1913); *Selected Hymns and Carols*, Northwestern University, third edition 1936, together with a *Brief Commentary*, Northwestern University, the same year. Other publications include *Ordinary and Canon of the Mass* (1913); *The Canticles at Evensong* (1915); *The Order of Matins* (1916); *The Psalms of David* (1917); the *St. Dunstan's Psalter* and *The Ceremonial Noted* (1923); *The St Dunstan Kyrial* (1933); and *A Missionary Service Book* (1937). Some of his carols and choral works were published posthumously.

COMPOSER:	384	ST. DUNSTAN'S
ARRANGER:	384	ST. DUNSTAN'S
	505	WERE YOU THERE
TRANSLATOR:	54	He Whom Shepherds Once Came Praising
	76	O Chief of Cities, Bethlehem
	315	Awake, Thou Spirit of the Watchmen

DÖVING, CARL (1867–1937), was born at Norddalen, Norway, March 21, 1867. He served as a teacher in the Schreuder Mission before he emigrated to America in 1890. Here he attended Luther College, Decorah, Iowa, and thereafter Luther Seminary, St. Paul, Minnesota. He served parishes at Red Wing and Montevideo, Minnesota, and Brooklyn, New York. His last position was that of city missionary in Chicago.

Döving was a linguist of note. As a missionary in Chicago, he conversed with infirmary patients in German, Icelandic, Norwegian, Swedish, Danish, and Greek. His linguistic and literary gifts were put to good use as a member of the Hymnary Committee of the Norwegian Lutheran Church. He translated many German and Scandinavian hymns into English, 32 of which are contained in *The Lutheran Hymnary* (1913). He died October 2, 1937.

TRANSLATOR: 234 To You, Omniscient Lord of All
291 Built on the Rock
520 Rejoice, Rejoice This Happy Morn

DRAPER, WILLIAM HENRY (1855–1933), was born December 19, 1855, at Kenilworth, Warwickshire, England. Educated at Cheltenham College and Keble College, Oxford, where he received the Bachelor of Arts degree in 1877 and the Master of Arts three years later, he was ordained in 1880 and served as assistant curate at St. Mary's, Shrewsbury (1880–83); vicar at Alfreton (1883–89); vicar of the Abbey Church, Shrewsbury (1889–99); rector of Adel, Leeds (1899–1919); Master of the Temple, London (1919–30); and vicar of Axbridge (1930–33). His deep interest in hymns prompted him to translate over sixty from Latin and Greek. He published *The Victoria Book of Hymns* (1897); *Hymns for Holy Week*, translations from hymns from the Greek Church (1899); *A Memorial Service*, containing four hymns (1898); and *The Way of the Cross* (n.d.). He edited *Seven Spiritual Songs* by Thomas Campion (1919) and *Hymns for Tunes by Orlando Gibbons* (1925). He died August 9, 1933, at Clifton, Bristol, England.

TRANSLATOR: 436 All Creatures of Our God and King

DRESE, ADAM (1620–1701), was born December 15, 1620, in Weimar, Germany. His first post was that of musician at the court of Duke Wilhelm IV at Saxe-Weimar. To further his education the duke sent him to Warsaw to study under the renowned Italian conductor (kapellmeister) Marco Sacchi. On his return to Weimar the duke made him his court conductor. Upon the duke's death in 1662, Drese accompanied the duke's youngest son, Bernard, to Jena, where, in 1672, Drese became mayor of Jena. Following the death of Bernard in 1678, Drese became conductor at the court of Prince Günther in Arnstadt.

It was while in Arnstadt that Drese was deeply moved and drawn to God by the writings of Philip Jakob Spener (1635–1735), father of Pietism, as well as Luther's commentary on Romans, and he soon opened his home to the private devotional meetings of the Pietists. Here his hymns were sung before they appeared in print. To further the cause of a living, vital Christianity—the *desideratum* of Pietism—he also produced a devotional tract to which Spener wrote the foreword.

Drese was both a poet and musician. His so-called *Jesus-gesänge* appeared in the *Geistreiches Gesangbuch* (Halle, 1695-97) and in a second edition (Darmstadt, 1698). Other tunes of his remain in the *Musikalisches Lustwäldern* (1652–57) of court poet Georg Neumark (*LW* 420), whom Drese met in Weimar. His involvement with the Pietists caused him to burn all the operas he had written, though a collection of his instrumental music survives.

Drese died in Arnstadt, February 15, 1701.

COMPOSER: 386 SEELENBRÄUTIGAM

DRETZEL, KORNELIUS HEINRICH (1697–1775), was born in 1697 at Nürnberg, the son of an organist. At the age of 14 he was already organist of the Frauenkirche there. He then went to St. Ägydien in 1719. Dretzel's work, clearly evidencing the influence of J. S. Bach's (*LW* 89) style, may indicate that he perhaps studied under Bach at Weimar prior to 1717. From St. Ägydien he went to St. Laurenz in 1743, and from there to the most important post of all, to St. Sebald, where he succeeded W. H. Pachelbel (1686–1764), the eldest of son of Johann Pachelbel. He died May 7, 1775, in Nürnberg, where he spent his entire life.

Distinguished as a contrapuntist and composer of fugues, his *Des evangelischen Zion's musicalische Harmonie, oder Evangelisches Choralbuch* (Nürnberg, 1731), containing 900 melodies with basso continuo, the most complete collection up to that time, is of great hymnological importance.

COMPOSER: 224, 351 O DASS ICH TAUSEND ZUNGEN HÄTTE

DRYDEN, JOHN (1631–1700), was born of Puritan stock August 9, 1631, at Aldwinkle, Northamptonshire. Educated at Trinity College, Cambridge, the first verses to bring him fame were his *Heroic Stanzas on the Death of Oliver Cromwell* (1658). Two years later, however, he became a Royalist, celebrating the Restoration with two works, *Astrea Redux* and *A Panegyric on the Coronation* (1670), and was subsequently made poet laureate, a post he held until the accession of William in 1688. Three years earlier, on the accession of James II, he had become a Roman Catholic, writing *The Hind and the Panther* as an apologia. Refusing to take the oath to Protestant William and Mary at the Revolution, he sacrificed his position and pension. He died May 18, 1700, and was buried at Westminster Abbey beside Geoffry Chaucer (c. 1340–1400).

His works include plays, poems, odes, satires, and a translation of Juvenal, Virgil, Bocaccio, and other poets. In addition to his translation of "Veni, creator spiritus," he is believed to have been translator of a number of other Latin hymns which appeared (after his death) in *The Primer of Office of the B. V. Mary, in English* (1706).

TRANSLATOR: 167 Creator Spirit, by Whose Aid

DUDLEY-SMITH, TIMOTHY (1926–), was born December 26, 1926, in Manchester, Derbyshire, England, the son of a schoolmaster. After attending Holm Leigh School in Buxton and Tonbridge School, he went to Pembroke College at Cambridge, from which he earned the Bachelor of Arts degree in 1947 and the Master of Arts in 1951. Ordained deacon in 1950 and priest in 1951 in the diocese of Rochester, he was curate of St. Paul's Cumberland Heath, Kent, 1950–53; head of the Cambridge University Mission, Bermondsey, 1953–55; and honorary chaplain to the bishop of Rochester, 1953–60. From 1953 on he was commissioned as a public preacher in the diocese of Rochester, and from 1953–62 in the diocese of Southwark. In 1955 he became editorial secretary of the Evangelical Alliance and founder-editor of its magazine *Crusade* (1955). From 1959–65 he was assistant secretary, and from 1965–73 senior secretary, of the Church Pastoral Aid Society. In July 1973 he was appointed archdeacon of Norwich; and in 1981 he was consecrated Bishop of Thetford, a suffragan to the Bishop of Norwich.

An author of over 80 hymns, these have been included in such hymnals as *100 Hymns for Today* (1969); *Psalm Praise* (1973); *Hymns II* (1976); and *Westminster Praise* (1976). His texts with commentary are included in two collections: *Lift Every Heart* (1984) and *Songs of Deliverance* (1988).

AUTHOR: 365 Christ Be My Leader

DUFFIELD, GEORGE (1818–88), was born September 12, 1818, in Carlyle, Pennsylvania, the son of a Presbyterian clergyman. After graduating from Yale University in 1837, he proceeded to Union Theological Seminary, New York City, graduating in 1840. Ordained an elder, he served parishes successively in Brooklyn, New York; Bloomfield, New Jersey; Philadelphia; Adrian, Michigan; Galesburg, Illinois; Saginaw, Ann Arbor, and Lansing, Michigan. Knox College, Galesburg, Illinois, honored him with an honorary doctorate.

A man of independent means, he was devoted to building up small congregations and doing mission work. His declining years were spent with his son Samuel W. Duffield, a minister and noted hymnologist, the author of *English Hymns, their Authors and History* (1886) and *Latin Hymn Writers and their Hymns* (1889). He died in Bloomfield, New Jersey, July 6, 1888.

AUTHOR: 305 Stand Up, Stand Up for Jesus

DWIGHT, JOHN S. (1813–1893), was born May 13, 1813, in Boston. Following his studies at Harvard and Harvard Divinity School, he was ordained in 1836 and became pastor of the Unitarian Congregation at Northampton, Massachusetts, where he served only one year. Shyness to express his religious feelings prompted him to resign his position. This finally led to his avoidance of attending public worship altogether. In 1852 he founded *Dwight's Journal of Music* to improve musical standards, a journal which he owned and edited for 30 years. He was also one of the founders of the Harvard Musical Association. He died September 5, 1893.

TRANSLATOR: 497 God Bless Our Native Land (st. 2)

DWIGHT, TIMOTHY (1752–1817), was born May 14, 1752, at Northampton, Massachusetts. The grandson of Jonathan Edwards, he entered Yale at age 13, graduating in 1769. He was successively a grammar-school teacher, tutor, chaplain in the

Revolutionary Army (where he won the admiration of George Washington), Congregational pastor, and president of Yale, a position in which he inaugurated a new and brilliant era for the college. His frank chapel addresses and sermons on "Theology Explained and Defended" won a new respect among the students for the truth and relevance of the Christian faith, and not only at Yale, but also at Dartmouth, Amherst, and Williams. In addition to his duties as president he taught classes in ethics, metaphysics, logic, theology, literature, and oratory.

As one of New England's most illustrious sons, Dwight was also the foremost hymnologist of his time. At the request of the General Association of Connecticut he revised Watts' (*LW* 53, et al.) *The Psalms of David Imitated* (1719), so as to accommodate them to the American scene, adding 33 of his own hymns and paraphrases, a book used extensively in both Congregational and Presbyterian churches in Connecticut. He died January 11, 1817, in Philadelphia.

AUTHOR: 296 I Love Your Kingdom, Lord

DYKES, JOHN BACCHUS (1823–76), was born March 10, 1823, at Hull, England, the son of a banker and the grandson of a well-known evangelical clergyman. At the age of 10 he was already assistant organist at his grandfather's church. In 1847 he received the Bachelor of Arts degree from St. Catherine's, Cambridge, where he helped found the University Musical Society. Ordained that same year, he served briefly at Malton, Yorkshire, becoming minor canon and a short time later precentor at Durham Cathedral in 1849. In 1861 the University of Durham honored him with the honorary Doctor of Music degree; the next year he became vicar of St. Oswald's, Durham. During his ministry here, his pastoral concerns and winning personality won him many friends. His then-high-church tendencies conflicted with the low-church ideas of the bishop, who hence denied him parish assistance. Ongoing strife with the bishop, coupled with the heavy workload, brought on Dyke's death in his 53d year, January 22, 1876, at Ticehurst, Sussex.

Dyke's success, so Routley says,

> was bound up with, and parallel to, the success of *Hymns Ancient and Modern* itself. He has seven tunes in the 1861 edition, 24 in the 1868, 56 in the 1875 edition (*The Music of Christian Hymnody*).

In all he wrote some 300 hymn tunes. He may not have been the ablest of Victorian hymn tune composers, but he was easily the most successful in the popular imagination with his congregational and choral sense. Benson says that, together with Monk Elvey, Gauntlett, and others, Dykes

> crystallized the musical tendencies of the time into a definite form of Anglican hymn tune, with restrained worship and yet appealing to the taste of the people (*The English Hymn*).

COMPOSER: 168 NICAEA
276 BEATITUDO
511 ST. MARY MAGDALENE

EBELING, JOHANN GEORG (1637–76; some sources give 1620–76), a notable musician of the 17th century despite the brevity of his life, was born July 8, 1637, in Lüneberg, Germany. Like Johann Crüger (*LW* 19, et al.) he was one of the "singers of Paul Gerhardt." In 1662 he succeeded Johann Crüger as cantor of St. Nicholas Church in Berlin and as faculty member and director of music at the Greyfriars *Gymnasium*, Berlin. It was as an associate of Paul Gerhardt (*LW* 19), who at this time was deacon at St. Nicholas, that Ebeling published, first in a series of 10 parts with 12 hymns in each, then in a complete edition, *Pauli Gerhardi geistliche Andachten, bestehend in 120 Liedern . . . also dutzendweise mit neuen sechsstimmigen Melodeyen gezieret* (Berlin, 1666–67). Of the 120 tunes, all but seven are considered to have been composed by Ebeling. The harmonizations, without exception, are all his. A second collection of hymns, *Evangelischer Lustgarten Herrn Pauli Gerhardts*, was published in 1669. In 1668 he became professor of music, Greek, and poetry, as well as cantor, at the Caroline *Gymnasium* in Stettin, Pomerania, where he served until his death in 1676.

With the publication in 1657 of *Archaeologiae Orphicae sive Antiquitates Musicae* (Stettin), Ebeling became recognized as a learned music scholar, a development that started him off on a brief but eventful career. But he was also a gifted tune maker. The lively folk rhythms that he sometimes employs, and thus preserves, often give his tunes the character of spiritual arias. Paul Gerhardt was fortunate to have had two professional musicians as colleagues, namely, Johann Crüger and Johann Ebeling, who competed to adorn his noble hymn texts with music of equal quality.

COMPOSER: 370 VOLLER WUNDER
419 DIE GÜLDNE SONNE
423 WARUM SOLLT ICH MICH DENN GRÄMEN

EBER, PAUL (1511–69), was born November 8, 1511, at Kitzingen, Bavaria, son of a master tailor. In 1523 he was sent to the *Gymnasium* at Ansbach but was forced by an illness to return home. He was physically deformed for life as the result of being thrown from a horse. In 1532 Eber entered Wittenberg University where, among others, he enjoyed Luther (*LW* 13, et al.) and Melanchthon (*LW* 189) as teachers. In 1536 he became lecturer in the philosophical school and eight years later professor of Latin grammar. Three years prior to the latter appointment, he married Helena Küffnerin, who bore his 14 children, of which but two sons and daughters outlived him.

In 1557 Eber was appointed professor of Hebrew at Wittenberg University and preacher of the Castle Church in Wittenberg; in 1558, following the death of Johann Bugenhagen (1485–1558), he succeeded him as town pastor of Wittenberg and general superintendent of electoral Saxony. In 1559 he received the Doctor of Theology degree.

When Melachthon died, Eber preached the funeral sermon based on 1 Thessalonians 4:13-18. In the ensuing theological struggles, especially regarding the Sacrament of the Lord's Supper, in which the follower's of Melanchthon were accused of Crypto-Calvinism, Eber had to endure numerous suspicions and attacks. Following the death of his wife in July 1569, lingering sorrow and ill-health finally resulted in Eber's death on December 10, 1569.

Next to Luther, Paul Eber is undoubtedly the most important and exceptionally-gifted poet of the Wittenberg circle. His hymns, some of them written for his own children, are distinguished by their tender, childlike spirit and simplicity. Of the 17 or so hymns credited to him, not a single one made its way into the early hymnals provided by Luther and his colleagues.

TRANSLATOR: 189 Lord God, to You We All Give Praise
AUTHOR: 428 When in the Hour of Deepest Need

ECCARD, JOHANN (1553–1611), was born at Mühlhausen in Thuringia. As a pupil in the Latin School in Mühlhausen he probably received his first music training from the young cantor Joachim von Burck. His membership in the Kapelle of the Weimar court and thereafter in the Bavarian Hofkapelle in Munich led him to study with the celebrated Orlando di Lasso. His return to Mühlhausen in the winter of 1573-74 gave him occasion to form an association with poet Ludwig Helmbold (*LW* 409, et al.), who had been there as deacon since 1571. In 1557 and 1558 he served as musician in the household of Jacob Fugger in Augsburg; in 1579 he entered the service of Margrave Georg Friedrich of Brandenburg at Königsberg until 1608, when Joachim Friedrich gave him sole charge of the music at his principal residence in Berlin. There he remained until his death in 1611.

Eccard's work centers largely on the development of the Lutheran chorale during the second half of the 16th century: transferring the melody from the tenor to the highest part, simply harmonized; and freely treating the chorale in an elaborate polyphonic style. Together with Leonard Lechner (c. 1533–1606), Hassler (*LW* 133, 427), and Praetorius (*LW* 14, et al.) in particular, he was one of the principal Protestant composers of the chorale motet. Capable of realizing the full implications of the text in word-note relationships and varied textures, he was able to reflect the intrinsic warmth of, for instance, Helmbold's verse.

COMPOSER: 103 HERR JESU CHRIST, WAHR MENSCH UND GOTT

EDWARDS, JOHN DAVID (1805–85), was born at Penderlwyngach, Gwnnw's, Cardiganshire, December 19, 1805 (though some give 1806). He graduated from Jesus College, Oxford, in 1830; was ordained deacon in 1832 and priest in 1833. Appointed vicar of Rhosymedre, Ruabon, in 1843, he ministered there in North Wales until 1885. He died at the Llanddoget rectory, Denbighshire, November 24, 1885.

His *Original Sacred Music*, the first book of hymn tunes for Anglican congregations in Wales, appeared in two volumes, the first in 1836, the second in 1843. Although he composed a considerable amount of music, he is especially remembered only for the tune listed below.

COMPOSER: 465 RHOSYMEDRE

ELLERTON, JOHN (1826–93), was born in Clerkenwell, London, on December 16, 1826. Educated at King William's College, Isle of Man, and Trinity College, Cambridge, he became associated with Frederick D. Maurice and the Oxford Movement, which helped to temper his Evangelical fervor with respect for high church forms. He is said to have had "the subjective piety of the Evangelical, the objective adoration of the High, the intellectual freedom of the Broad," hence no affiliation with any single one of the Anglican Church's three parties.

He received the Bachelor of Arts degree in 1849 and was ordained in 1850. From his first curacy in Eastbourne, Sussex, he went in 1852 to Brighton, where he wrote his first hymns for the children of the parish, and stayed until 1860, when he became chaplain to Lord Crewe and vicar of Crewe Green, Cheshire. During his ministry there he became interested in social welfare, as the population was mostly made up of steel workers at the London and Northwestern Railway Company, as well as farmers and laborers on Lord Crewe's estate. Ellerton was instrumental in reorganizing the Mechanics' Institute of the Railway Company, he himself teaching English and Bible history. He also supplemented his meager income by conducting services in a hall in town each Sunday. Most of his hymns were written while incumbent at Crewe Green.

In 1872 he became rector successively of Hinstock, Shropshire; St. Mary's, Barnes, in Surrey (1876–86); and White Roding in Essex. Before this last appointment he fell ill and spent a year in Switzerland and Italy, never totally regaining his health. He was named canon of St. Alban's in Hertfordshire in 1892, but was never installed due to his paralysis. Visiting Torquay, Devonshire, in 1893, he died there on June 15, 1893.

Ellerton, a friend of the poet Wordsworth, refused to copyright any of his hymns, contending that if they were "counted worthy to contribute to Christ's praise in the congregation, one ought to feel very thankful and humble" (Haeussler). Organizer of one of the first choral societies in the Midlands, he was dedicated to hymnody, and repeated many of his favorite hymns on his deathbed. He wrote 86 original hymns and translated many others. He was consulted in an editorial capacity on every major hymnal produced during the last three decades of his life. He served as coeditor for *Church Hymns* (1871) with William W. How (*LW* 182, et al.), and edited *Children's Hymns and School Prayers* (1874) and the *London Missionary Hymn Book* (1885). He also aided the compilers of both the 1875 and 1889 editions of *Hymns Ancient and Modern*. In addition he compiled *Hymns for Schools and Bible Classes* in 1859, and published his own hymns in *Hymns, Original and Translated* (1888). In 1881 his *Notes and Illustrations of Church Hymns* appeared in a folio edition.

AUTHOR:	221	Savior, Again to Your Dear Name
	251	O Father, All Creating
TRANSLATOR:	43	From East to West
	135	Welcome, Happy Morning

ELLIOTT, CHARLOTTE (1789–1871), was born March 18, 1789, at Clapham, Surrey, England, the granddaughter of Henry Venn, one of the members of the famous Clapham sect which gathered around William Wilberforce. Her father, Henry Venn Elliott, was an Evangelical clergyman who moved from Clapham to Brighton, a stronghold of "vital religion" in Victorian times. Already at an early age she not only began to write humorous poems, but she exhibited a keen interest in music and painting. At the age of 32, stricken with a severe illness, she was left an invalid for the rest of her life. In 1822, after meeting César Malan (1787–1864), the Swiss evangelist (author of the popular German spiritual song, "Harre, meine Seele"), who paid a visit to her father, she devoted most of her time and energies to religious and humanitarian pursuits. She wrote 150-some hymns, of which "Just as I am, without one plea" (*LW* 359), written while residing at her brother's house in Brighton, is the most well known. Her hymns exhibit the tenderness born of much suffering and resignation. They appeared in her *Invalid's Hymn Book* (several editions, 1834–54), an earlier work compiled by Miss Kiernan of Dublin but which Charlotte Elliott reedited and republished, adding 32 of her own hymns. Among other works containing hymns were *Hours of Sorrow Cheered and Comforted* (1836), *Hymns for a Week* (1839), and *Thoughts in Verse on Sacred Subjects* (1869). She died September 22, 1871, in Brighton.

AUTHOR:	359	Just as I Am, Without One Plea

ELVEY, GEORGE JOB (1816–93) was born in Canterbury, England, on March 27 or 29, 1816. He studied under his elder brother Stephen and Highmore Skeats at Canterbury Cathedral, and then later at the Royal Academy of Music, becoming an accomplished organist by age 17. At age 19 he succeeded Skeats, whose daughter he later married, as organist and master of the boys at St. George's Chapel, Windsor, selected by King William IV over such other competitors as Samuel S. Wesley (*LW* 251, et al.). Elvey received the Bachelor of Music degree from Oxford in 1838 and the doctorate in 1840, by special dispensation of the chancellor. His position at St. George's Chapel gave him special direction over music for many royal events, and he was knighted in 1871 after composing a Festival March for the marriage of Princess Louise. Elvey died December 9, 1893, and was buried outside the west front of St. George's Chapel.

COMPOSER:	88, 495, 499	ST. GEORGE'S, WINDSOR
	278	DIADEMATA
	362	ST. CRISPIN

ENGEL, JAMES E. (1925–1989), was born March 21, 1925, in Milwaukee, Wisconsin. After attending Bethlehem Lutheran School and Milwaukee Lutheran High School, he earned the Bachelor of Science degree from Concordia College, River Forest, Illinois, in 1946, and some years later the Master of Music degree from Northwestern University, Evanston, Illinois, with further music education at the University of Wisconsin, Madison. He taught grade school at Bethlehem Lutheran in Milwaukee, at St. John's Lutheran, Racine, Wisconsin, at Concordia College, Milwaukee, and at Fox Valley Lutheran High School in Appleton, Wisconsin. At the time of his death, April 17, 1989, the victim of lung cancer, he was professor of organ and music theory at Dr. Martin Luther College, New Ulm, Minnesota, a position he held since 1975. Married to Norma Engel, he was the father of four children.

As a composer he contributed 22 organ compositions to the *Concordia Hymn Prelude Series*; he wrote and edited a significant number of choir and organ compositions published by Augsburg, Fortress, Chantry Press, Concordia, Morning Star, and Northwestern Publishing House. For Dr. Martin Luther College he prepared a *Manual for the Beginning Church Organist* and two sets of chorale preludes for the beginning student. His *An Introduction to Organ Registration* was published by Concordia in 1986.

ARRANGER: 144 TRIUMPH

ESTE (EST, EASTE, EAST), THOMAS (c. 1540–c. 1608), was the most important English music printer and publisher of his time. In 1591 he printed a new and enlarged edition of Daman's *Psalms*. In 1592 for an edition of the entire psalter, he collected (perhaps commissioned) harmonizations by ten leading composers of the time, including Allison, Blanks, Cavendish, Cobbold, Douland, Farmer, Farnaby, Hooper, Johnson, and Kirbye. It was entitled *The whole book of Psalmes, with their wonted tunes in four parts*, a book distinguished for the quality of its music and credited with being the first in which specific names were given to the tunes.

PRINTER: 196 WINCHESTER OLD

EVEREST, CHARLES WILLIAM (1814–77), was born May 27, 1814, at East Windsor, Connecticut. After graduating from Trinity College, Hartford, in 1838, he was ordained in 1842 and served as rector of the Episcopal church in Hampden, Connecticut, for 31 years. During this time he also managed an important school, and for a few years acted as agent of the Society for the Increase of the Ministry. He died January 11, 1877, at Waterbury, Connecticut.

AUTHOR: 382 "Take Up Your Cross," the Savior Said

EWING, ALEXANDER C. (1830–95), was born in the parish of Old Machar, Aberdeen, January 3, 1830, the son of Alexander Ewing, lecturer on surgery at Marischal College in Aberdeen. Here young Alexander studied law for a time, but when he found that he had no real bent for a legal career, he went to Heidelberg to study music in Germany. Although he never became a professional musician, he was an excellent pianist; he played the violin, cello, and cornet, and was a gifted linguist. He took a major part in the activities of the Haydn Society of Aberdeen and sang in the Aberdeen Harmonic Choir, both of which were directed by the distinguished William Carnie. It was after a rehearsal of the latter that Alexander Ewing went up to Carnie to say that he had written a hymn tune, which he would like to have the choir try, and he offered to pass out the voice parts. Such was the debut of EWING, the tune that has enjoyed such a long and popular career, both in England and America.

During the Crimean War (1853–56) Ewing joined the commissariat department of the army, was stationed at Constantinople, attained the rank of lieutenant colonel, and later served in south Australia and China. In 1867, a year after his return to the British Isles, he married Juliana Horatia Gatty, author of many well-known books for children.

Ewing died in Taunton, July 11, 1895. The one tune by which he is now known was not only sung at his funeral, but on the following Sunday it was sung in most of the churches in Taunton.

COMPOSER: 309 EWING

FABRICIUS, JACOB (1593–1654), born in Köslin, Pomerania, he studied in Frankfurt-an-der-Oder and thereafter taught school for a time. Next he became the Lutheran pastor in Köslin, then court-preacher in Stettin (today Szczecin in northwest Poland on the Oder River). In 1630–32, during the Thirty Years' War (1618–48), he accompanied Gustavus Adolphus as his court and field preacher. From 1634 on he was general superintendent of Pomerania as well as, from 1642 on, pastor at St. Mary's Church in Stettin. He died in 1654.

AUTHOR: 300 Do Not Despair, O Little Flock

FARLANDER, ARTHUR W. (1898–1952), was born in Germany, April 21, 1898, and in 1919 he came to the United States, where he attended the James Millikin University, Decatur, Illinois; University of Chicago Divinity School; the Evangelical Theological Seminary, Chicago; and the Church Divinity School of the Pacific. Ordained deacon in 1926 and priest the following year, he was rector of All Saints' Church, San Francisco (1927–30); dean of St. James Cathedral, Fresno, California (1930–36); and rector of the Church of the Incarnation, Santa Rosa, California, from 1936 until his death January 23, 1952. He was a member of the committee for *The Hymnal 1940* and *The Hymnal 1940 Companion*.

TRANSLATOR: 315 Awake, Thou Spirit of the Watchmen

FARRELL, MELVIN, (1930–) born at St. Paul, Minnesota, in 1941 his family moved to Seattle, Washington. After attending minor seminary at St. Edward's, Kenmore, Washington, he went to the Theological College, Washington, D.C., for major seminary studies. Having earned his Master of Arts degree in Philosophy in 1953, his Master of Arts degree in Literature in 1956 at the University of Washington, and his Licentiate in Sacred Theology in 1957 at the Catholic University, Washington, he was ordained to the priesthood in 1957. He taught at St. Edward's Seminary, Seattle, for 10 years, becoming principal of the high school department in 1962. Six years later he returned to the Catholic University to pursue a doctorate in theology, which he obtained in 1970. After serving one year as president of St. Thomas Seminary College, Seattle, two years as rector of St. Patrick's Seminary, Menlo Park, and two years as director of formation for the Sulpician Province, in 1975 he became president-rector of the St. Thomas Seminary, Seattle. Two years later he was appointed research secretary for a special task force commissioned by the archbishop of Seattle to study the feasibility of a newly designed theology program of priestly formation. Active in religious education at the University of Seattle, he has conducted workshops and retreats for the continuing education of priests.

Among his published works are *First Steps to the Priesthood* (1960), *Getting to Know Christ* (1963), *Theology for Parents and Teachers* (1973), *Teaching the Good News Today* (1974), *The Christian Message at a Glance* (1975), and *A Catechism for Parents and Teachers* (1977). His activity as a hymn writer, begun in 1953, has resulted in the inclusion of his work in several hymnals, some most recently in *Today's Missal* (Catholic Truth Society, Portland, Oregon).

TRANSLATOR: 17 O Lord of Light, Who Made the Stars

FAWCETT, JOHN (1740–1817), was born near Bradford, Yorkshire, England, January 6, 1740. At the age of 16 he heard evangelist George Whitefield speak. The sermon, whose text he never forgot, impressed him so much that he became associated with the Methodists for a time, attending the Church of England with them. In 1758 he joined the Baptist church at Bradford, and in 1763, after being ordained by the Baptist Church, he took charge of a small congregation of illiterate farmers and shepherds in the nearby tiny village of Wainsgate. There being no parsonage, he and his wife Mary stayed with first one and then another of the parishioners. Paid only 20 pounds annually, Fawcett, however, devoted himself to his people, and the congregation witnessed phenomenal growth. A vacancy at Carter's Lane Baptist Church in London in 1772 offered Fawcett the opportunity for advancement and a higher salary to support his family, and he accepted. When, however, he and Mary were saying their farewells at Wainsgate, they were so overcome by the emotion in the parting that they decided to stay.

Fawcett's ministry in Wainsgate lasted 54 years. In 1777 he also took charge of a new chapel in Hebden Bridge. During the course of his ministry at these two places he opened a school to train Baptist preachers, built a new meeting house, founded the Northern Education Society (now Rawdon College), and wrote a number of prose works. His 166 hymns, collected and published in 1782 as *Hymns Adapted to the Circumstances of Public Worship and Private Devotion*, were written to be sung at the conclusion of his sermons. In the hymnal's preface he declares:

> I blush to think of these plain verses falling into the hands of persons of an elevated genius, and refined taste. To such, I know, they will appear flat, dull and unentertaining. . . . If it may be conducive, under divine blessing to warm the heart or assist the devotion of any humble Christian in the closet, the family, or the house of God, I shall therein sincerely rejoice, whatever censure I may incur from the polite world (Reynold's, *Companion to Baptist Hymnal*).

Besides his collection of *Hymns*, Fawcett authored *The Christian's Humble Plea for his God and Savior* (1772), which gained wide recognition; *Advice to Youth on the Advantages of Early Piety* (1778); and a commentary on Holy Scripture, *The Devotional Family Bible,* published in 1811, the year in which Brown University, Providence, Rhode Island, awarded him the honorary Doctor of Divinity degree.

A stroke suffered in February of 1816 paralyzed Fawcett and brought his pastoral work to an end. He died July 25, 1817.

AUTHOR: 218 Lord, Dismiss Us with Your Blessing
295 Blest Be the Tie That Binds
332 How Precious Is the Book Divine

FILITZ, FRIEDRICH (1804–76), was born March 16, 1804, in Arnstadt, Germany. After earning his Doctor of Philosophy degree, he lived in Berlin from 1843–47, where he worked with Ludwig Christian Erk, music director and seminar instructor, and with whom he published the *Vierstimmige Choralsätze der vornehmsten Meister des 16. und 17. jahrhunderts* (Essen, 1845). This constituted another effort, among others, toward liturgical reform and churchly renewal after the disastrous effects of Pietism and Rationalism. After moving to Berlin, in 1847 he prepared and published a four-part chorale book, consisting of 223 tunes, for the *Allgemeines Evangelisches Gesang-und Gebetbuch zum Kirchen- und Hausgebrauch,* a hymnal that his friend Baron Christian von Bunsen had published in 1846. In 1848 Filitz moved to Munich, where he died December 8, 1876.

COMPOSER: 98 WEM IN LEIDENSTAGEN

FORTUNATUS, VENANTIUS HONORIUS CLEMENTIANUS (520–609), was born at Ceneda, near Treviso, Italy, and educated in the classics at Ravenna and Milan. During his school years he was afflicted with eye trouble, which was miraculously cured, so the story goes, by the application of oil from the altar of St. Martin of Tours. Either in gratitude for the cure or to escape an apparently imminent barbarian invasion, Fortunatus left about the year 565 to travel in Gaul, eventually paying his respects at St. Martin's shrine at Tours.

Having made the acquaintance of the Frankish king Sigbert, Fortunatus accompanied him on extensive travels in the capacity of scribe, friend, and poet, repaying hospitality at various courts with flattering verse in honor of his hosts. His true feelings may not have been reflected in these odes, as he later wrote:

> I had for auditors, barbarians incapable of knowing the difference between a raucous voice and a sweet one, and of distinguishing the song of a swan from the cry of an owl. . . . I sang my verses while my auditors kept time by clapping their hands and committing a thousand follies fit to revolt even the god Bacchus (Bailey, *The Gospel in Hymns*).

Eventually Fortunatus settled at Poitiers, where he enjoyed the friendship of Queen Rhadegunde. Born to royalty in Thuringia, Rhadegunde had been captured by the Franks in 529 when they conquered her homeland and murdered her family. She was forced to marry their king, Clothair I, but as soon as possible she left him for a convent she had founded outside Poitiers. Chiefly because of her influence and that of her adopted daughter Agnes, the abbess, Fortunatus joined the priesthood.

Made bishop of Poitiers in 599, Fortunatus spent the last years of his life in that capacity. He died wealthy and famous in the year 609.

Inspired by the mysticism of the age, Fortunatus wrote several poems about the cross of Christ. He also authored a number of lives of saints, including St. Martin of Tours. Of his religious poetry, F. J. Raby in *Christian-Latin Poetry* states, "He was moved to express himself in the terms of that erotic mysticism which became more common at a later date." He has been called "the last of the classical poets and the first of the troubadours."

AUTHOR: 103, 104 The Royal Banners Forward Go
117 Sing, My Tongue
125 Hail Thee, Festival Day (Easter)
135 Welcome, Happy Morning
148 Hail Thee, Festival Day (Ascension)
159 Hail Thee, Festival Day (Pentecost)

FOSDICK, HARRY EMERSON (1878–1969), was born May 24, 1878, in Buffalo, New York, where he received his elementary schooling. After graduating from Colgate University in 1900 with a Bachelor of Arts degree, he was ordained and served as pastor of First Baptist Church, Montclair, New Jersey, from 1904–15. In 1904 he earned the Bachelor of Divinity degree from Union Theological Seminary; in 1908 the Master of Arts degree from Columbia University. That year he became a lecturer on Baptist principles and polity at Union Theological Seminary; in 1911 instructor in homiletics. From 1915–46 he was professor of practical theology. Meantime, he became associate minister at First Presbyterian Church in 1919. When in 1926 he was asked to subscribe to the Westminster Confession, refusing to give up his liberal views, he resigned his position. That year he became pastor at Park Avenue Baptist Church, later Riverside Church, where he remained, preaching to large congregations until his retirement in 1946. He died in New York, October 5, 1969.

Through his radio broadcasts and books Fosdick influenced thousands of people. The latter include *The Meaning of Prayer* (1919), *The Modern Use of the Bible* (1924), *A Guide to Understanding the Bible* (1938), *On Being a Real Person* (1938), his autobiography *The Living of These Days* (1956), and *A Book of Public Prayers* (1960).

AUTHOR: 398 God of Grace and God of Glory

FOSTER, FREDERICK WILLIAM (1760–1835), was born in Bradford, England, August 1, 1760, and educated at the educational center of the Moravian Brotherhood, Fullneck, Yorkshire, and at the Moravian College in Saxony at Barbee, near Magdeburg. In 1781 he became assistant master at Fullneck and somewhat later, minister and provincial superintendent. As both a translator of German hymns and author of original English hymns, he edited the *Moravian Hymnbook* (1801), its supplement (1808), and its revised edition (1826). He died at Ockbrook, near Derby, April 12, 1835.

TRANSLATOR: 206 God Himself Is Present

FRANCE, WILLIAM E. (1912–), was born April 21, 1912, near New Liskeard, Ontario, the son of a Baptist minister. Receiving his early music instruction from his mother, at the age of 17 he became organist at the Avondale United Church, Tillsonburg. His study of piano, organ, and composition continued under various teachers, including Healey Willan, until in 1941 he graduated from the University of Toronto with a Bachelor of Music degree. In the succeeding years he has served a number of churches as organist and choirmaster. He was a member of the subcommittee on hymn tunes in the production of *The Hymn Book* (1971) of the Anglican Church of Canada and the United Church of Canada. His published works for organ and piano, together with his songs, part songs, and anthems, number over 70.

ARRANGER: 463 DURROW

FRANCIS OF ASSISI (c. 1182–1226), known to his contemporaries as the "troubadour of God," was born in Assisi, Italy, son of a prosperous cloth merchant. A self-indulgent youth, he spent his time in gaiety and frivolous living until a serious illness in 1202 changed his life and awakened within him the desire to turn his back on wealth and devote his life to prayer, poverty, and to the care of the outcast and the poor. Organizing a group of men outside the city of Assisi, sworn to poverty, he sent them out two-by-two to preach and relieve distress, thus founding the order of the Franciscans, sanctioned by the Pope in 1210. Numerous miraculous tales have arisen concerning Francis, including that of the sacred stigmata, the wounds of the Savior in his own hands, feet and side. He loved birds, beasts, flowers, and all nature. He and his followers lived among the poor, even helping them with some of their daily tasks. Their life was one of self-sacrifice and love to do battle against the gross wickedness of the day. A lover of music, Francis adopted Italian secular song to suit his purposes, creating the historic, folklike *laudi spirituali,* which endured in history to the 17th century. He died October 4, 1226, at Assisi, Italy.

AUTHOR: 436 All Creatures of Our God and King

FRANCIS, BENJAMIN (1734–99), was born in Wales. Baptized at the age of 15, he began to preach at 19. After studying at Bristol Baptist College, he moved to Horsley in Gloucestershire to serve a parish, where he remained until his death in 1799, despite frequent efforts on the part of various London churches to secure him as a pastor. A writer especially of Welsh hymns, he published a collection in 1774 entitled *Alleluia*, to which he contributed 103 hymns. In the second volume, 1776, he contributed an additional 91 hymns.

AUTHOR: 393 Jesus! Oh, How Could It Be True

FRANCK, JOHANN (1618–77), was born June 1, 1618, the son of Johann Franck, attorney and town-councillor at Guben, Brandenburg, Germany. Following the death of his father when young Johann was but two years of age, an uncle and town judge, Adam Tielke, adopted him and saw to his early education. In 1637 he enrolled at the University of Königsberg to study law. There it was Simon Dach (*LW* 268, 369), professor of poetry and later rector of the university, who recognized and cultivated the poetic gifts of Franck. At the urgent request of his mother, Franck returned to Guben in 1640, primarily to be near her during the trying days of the Thirty Years' War (1618–48). There he soon began to practice law and, having won the confidence of the people, in 1648 he was elected town-councillor, in 1661 mayor, and finally, as town-deputy to the Diet of Lower Lusatia. Despite his many responsibilities, he did not neglect his poetic gifts; he continued friendly relations and communication with Simon Dach, his beloved teacher and friend; with August Buchner, professor of poetry at Wittenberg University; and with especially two musicians—Johann Crüger (*LW* 19, et al.), his friend and countryman, and Christoph Peter, cantor at the main church in Guben. He died in that city June 18, 1677.

Franck was one of the most significant poets of his day, second only to Paul Gerhardt (*LW* 19, et al.). His hymns are notable for their warmth and sincerity, simplicity of style, and biblical expression. He marks the transition from the objective to the more individual, subjective and mystical type of hymn. His emphasis on the union of the faithful soul with Christ makes him a precursor of the so-called Jesus hymn.

Franck wrote approximately 110 hymns, many of which appeared in various editions of Crüger's *Praxis pietatis melica,* all of which were included in his *Geistliche Sion*, published in Guben in two sections, the first (1672) containing his hymns, the second (1674) his secular works.

AUTHOR: 233 Lord, to You I Make Confession
239 Soul, Adorn Yourself with Gladness
270 Jesus, Priceless Treasure

FRANCK, MELCHIOR (c. 1573–1639), was born in Zittau, on the borders of Saxony and Silesia. A student of Hans Leo von Hassler (*LW* 113, 427), in 1603 he became Kapellmeister to the Duke of Koburg, a position that he held until his death June 1, 1639.

With Hassler and Michael Praetorius, Franck ranks as a master in his day. A prolific composer of both sacred and secular works, especially many fine lieder and chorale motets, he contributed greatly to improving the instrumental accompaniment of songs, something to which little attention had previously been given. His works appeared in various collections, the best-known of which is perhaps *Geistlichen Musikalischen Lustgartens* (1616).

COMPOSER: 306 JERUSALEM, DU HOCHGEBAUTE STADT

FRANCK, SALOMO (1659–1725), was born March 6, 1659, at Weimar, the son of a government secretary. After studying at the University of Jena, he held several governmental appointments before becoming librarian at the Weimar court of the pious Duke Wilhelm Ernst, as well as curator of the duke's medal and coin collection and his court poet. A sincere, devout Christian, Franck had his share of family afflictions and misfortunes, a fact often exhibited in his hymns, numbering a total of approximately 330. They are characterized and distinguished for their neatly flowing language, excellent verse structure, learned from Johann Rist (*LW* 122, et al.), and their adaptation to popular understanding and congregational singing. Franck also wrote a goodly number of cantata texts, comprised of recitatives, arias, and chorales, some of which J. S. Bach (*LW* 89) used for his cantatas. As a member of the Fruitbearing Society, Franck also put his hand to writing secular poems. He died July 11, 1725, and at his funeral service the sermon was based on a text that he himself had chosen, namely, "Do not rejoice that the spirits submit to you, but rejoice that your names are written in heaven." (Luke 10:20)

Franck's published works include *Geistliche Poesie* (Weimar, 1685), *Geist-und Weltliche Poesien* (Jena, 1711), and *Evangelisches Andachts-Opfer* (Weimar, 1715).

AUTHOR: 372 O God, Forsake Me Not
429 I Leave All Things to God's Direction

FRANK (FRANCK), PETER (1616–75), was born September 27, 1616, in Schleusingen, Germany. After completing his studies at the *Gymnasium* in his hometown, he began the study of theology at the University of Jena in 1636. Four years later saw him at the university in Altdorf. After serving two years as a private tutor, he was appointed pastor in Thüngen. Subsequent churches that he served were at Rossfeld, Rodach, Gleussen, and Herreth. Skilled in Latin, he not only wrote German but also Latin poetry. A number of his hymns found their way into local hymnals. One hymn that became rather widely accepted was "Christus, Christus, Christus ist, dem ich mich ergebe," written for the burial of a pastor. He died June 22, 1675.

COMPOSER (attr.): 483 FANG DEIN WERK

FRANZÉN, FRANS M. (1772–1847), was born February 9, 1772, at Uleåborg, Finland, of Swedish parentage. After earning a Master's degree at the Äbo Academy, he entered the University of Upssala to pursue the Doctor of Philosophy degree. In 1794 he became academic librarian at Åbo, four years later professor in the history of literature. When, in the Napoleonic wars, Sweden lost Finland to Russia, Franzén, like many other Swedes living in Finland, returned to Sweden, becoming pastor of the Kumla parish in 1812. It was now that his talent at hymn writing began to blossom, and he became associated with Archbishop Johan Olof Wallin (*LW* 199, 434) in the preparation of *Svenska Psalm-Boken* of 1819, described by Ryden as a masterpiece from the golden age of Swedish hymnody, a work to which he contributed 29 hymns. When in 1825 Franzén became pastor of St. Clara Church, Stockholm, he was soon elected secretary of the Swedish Academy, membership in which he had held since 1808. Appointed bishop of the diocese of Härnosänd, he worked tirelessly as a pastor and forceful preacher until his death August 14, 1847.

AUTHOR: 27 Prepare the Royal Highway

FRANZMANN, MARTIN HANS (1907–76), was born at Lake City, Minnesota, on January 29, 1907. He studied at Northwestern College, Watertown, Wisconsin, earning the Bachelor of Arts degree in 1928 and continuing his studies at Wisconsin Lutheran

Seminary, Thiensville, Wisconsin. In 1936 he accepted a professorship at his alma mater, remaining at Northwestern for 10 years.

He joined the faculty of Concordia Seminary, St. Louis, in 1946; nine years later he was appointed chairman of the exegetical theology department. For more than 20 years Franzmann continued postgraduate studies at the University of Chicago. He received the honorary Doctor of Divinity degree from Concordia Seminary, Springfield, Illinois, in 1958.

He continued also to serve the Missouri Synod in a number of ways: as a member of the Synodical Advisory Committee on English Bible Versions (1950–1956); as chairman of the Synodical Conference (1952–56); as vice-chairman of the Committee on Doctrinal Unity (1950–62); as representative of the Missouri Synod to the Lutheran World Federation in 1962; and as a member of the Commission on Theology and Church Relations (1962–69). A Daniel L. Shorey Traveling Fellowship took him to Greece for a time; he later traveled to England, where he was ordained October 4, 1969, and became a theology tutor at Westfield House in Cambridge, an institution of the Evangelical Lutheran Church of England for the training of its pastors. He died at Cambridge March 28, 1976. Erik Routley in his *Companion to Westminster Praise* calls him "the most penetrating and trenchant American hymn writer of his generation." The words of William Schmelder, one of Franzmann's students, serve a fitting tribute:

> For us who knew him as a teacher, he was one who opened for us the fullness and the depths of the Biblical texts; who taught us as his students to emulate Moses when reading the Word of God; whose posture as an interpreter was: take off your shoes, you are standing on holy ground. He was a man of culture, whose eloquence is noted in the hymns which appear in the *Worship Supplement.* If anyone had a way with words Martin Franzmann did, but always in the service of the Word.
>
> But I suppose most of all, we shall remember him as a Christian gentleman, one whose teaching and preaching, whose life, whose being, whose poetry, whose elegance and eloquence had been given shape because of the death and resurrection of Jesus Christ (Memorial Service, April 2, 1976).

Franzmann's writings include *Follow Me: Discipleship According to Saint Matthew* (1961; reprinted in Concordia Heritage series, 1982); *Ha! Ha! Among the Trumpets* (1966); *Concordia Commentary: Romans* (1968); *Pray for Joy* (1970); *Alive with the Spirit* (1973); and *The Revelation to John* (1976). He was editor of the *Concordia Bible with Notes: The New Testament* (1971) and coeditor with Walter Roehrs of the *Concordia Self-Study Commentary* (1971). His hymn text, "In Adam we have all been one," appears in *More Hymns for Today* (1980), the second supplement to *Hymns Ancient and Modern* (revised, 1950).

TRANSLATOR: 134 With High Delight Let Us Unite
AUTHOR: 259 Preach You the Word

292 In Adam We Have All Been One
319 O God, O Lord of Heaven and Earth
328 Thy Strong Word
346 O Kingly Love, That Faithfully

FRANZMANN, WERNER H. (1905–), was born August 11, 1905, in Lake City, Minnesota, the older brother of Martin Franzmann (*LW* 259, et al.). Following his graduation from Northwestern College, Watertown, Wisconsin, in 1925, and from the Wisconsin Lutheran Seminary, Thiensville, in 1929, he became an assistant instructor at the above-mentioned college for one year (1929–30) and thereafter Lutheran pastor at Coloma, Michigan (1930–42). From there he went to Michigan Lutheran Seminary, Saginaw, to serve as professor of religion, English, and Latin. His literary and scholarly talents led to his becoming editor-in-chief at Northwestern Publishing House (1968–72), Milwaukee, Wisconsin, publishing arm of the Wisconsin Evangelical Lutheran Synod, of which he had been a member from his youth. The urge to serve as parish pastor one more time before retiring led him to accept the call of a parish in Ann Arbor, Michigan, where he served from 1968–72, when he returned to Westfield, Wisconsin.

Commissioned by the Board for Parish Education of the Wisconsin Evangelical Lutheran Synod, he wrote the *Bible History Commentary*, the Old Testament volume of which appeared in 1981, the two New Testament volumes in February 1989. Though aimed especially at Christian day schools and Sunday school teachers, the work has enjoyed widespread use among pastors and professors as well.

As to Franzmann's hymn writing, though he had translated a number of German hymns in earlier days, he did not write a hymn until he was 52 years of age, while editor of *The Northwestern Lutheran*. Desirous of including a hymn in the festival issues, he decided to put his hand to this task. To his surprise, they were appreciated. As a result he has written 17 hymns.

AUTHOR: 144 Triumphant from the Grave

FREMDER, ALFRED (1920–), composer, conductor, and pianist, was associate professor of practical theology, coordinator of music and cultural activities, and chaplain at Concordia Seminary, St. Louis from 1979–91. Prior to his tenure at St. Louis he was professor of composition and piano and composer in residence at Texas Wesleyan College in Fort Worth. He has also taught at Arizona State University, North Texas State University, and at Bethany Lutheran College in Mankato, Minnesota, where he was department chairman and conductor of the Bethany Choir.

Born March 14, 1920, in Sioux City, Iowa, he received his pre-seminary training at Concordia College, Milwaukee, from 1934–40. At Concordia Seminary he received the Bachelor of Arts degree in 1942 and his Theological Diploma in January of 1945. In the field of music Fremder holds the Master of Arts degree in composition from the

University of Minnesota, where he studied with composers Earl George and Paul Fetler. He received his Doctor of Philosophy degree in composition and theory from North Texas State University, where he studied with composers William P. Latham and Martin Mailman. From 1960–68 he served as president of the Society of Arizona Composers. His piano study was principally with Liborius Semmann of Milwaukee and pianist Artur Schnabel.

Fremder was a member of the Commission on Worship of the Lutheran Church—Missouri Synod from 1978–86. He served as chairman of the Hymn Text and Music Committee from 1978–82 and as chairman of the Commission on Worship from 1980–82, the years *Lutheran Worship* was prepared for publication.

Fremder has written for various media. His major works include *The Passion according to St. Mark* for chorus, orchestra, and narrator, which had its first performance at Trinity Cathedral, Phoenix, in 1964; a mass for chorus and orchestra entitled *Tetelestai*, commissioned and performed for the 1976 bicentennial celebration of the United States (the *Credo* from *Tetelestai*, performed October 1, 1989, by the St. Louis Symphony Orchestra and Chorus, Leonard Slatkin, conductor) and *Concerto for Piano and Orchestra*, performed in 1974 by Norwegian pianist Eva Knardahl with the Oslo Philharmonic Orchestra, Sverre Bruland, conductor, and broadcast over Norwegian National Radio on July 4th of that year.

In a 1976 bicentennial national competition for which over 100 entries were submitted, Fremder's *Concerto for Piano and Orchestra* won first prize and his *Landi Variations* for two pianos was given honorable mention.

At the invitation of the Korean Lutheran Church Fremder served as exchange professor at Luther Seminary near Seoul from March through June 1987. He became professor emeritus of Concordia Seminary on July 1, 1991.

ARRANGER: 375 ICH WILL DICH LIEBEN
423 WARUM SOLLT ICH MICH DENN GRÄMEN

FREY, STEPHANIE KRISTIN (1952–), was born October 8, 1952, in Waterloo, Iowa. The family having moved to Madison, Wisconsin, she graduated from the James Madison Memorial High School there. After earning the Bachelor of Arts degree in English, cum laude, from Luther College, Decorah, Iowa, in 1974, she joined the staff at Augsburg Publishing House, Minneapolis, as an editorial assistant. She continued working there part-time while enrolled in the Master of Divinity program at Luther Seminary, St. Paul, Minnesota (M. Div. 1982). From 1982–86 she served christ the King Lutheran Church, Mankato, Minnesota. She presently serves as pastor of First Lutheran Church, St. James, Minnesota.

AUTHOR: 211 My Soul Now Magnifies the Lord

FREYLINGHAUSEN, JOHANN ANASTASIUS (1670–1739), son of the mayor of Gandersheim, in the province of Brunswick, Germany, was born December 2, 1670. In 1689 he enrolled at the University of Jena to pursue the study of theology. There he made the acquaintance of an "awakened" student by the name of J. Homeyer, who encouraged Freylinghausen to read the works of Martin Luther, Johann Arndt (1612–1694), and Philip Spener (1635–1705), the man who first gave direction to the Pietistic movement. As a result, so Freylinghausen stated, "he saw the light and perceived many pleasant stirrings of the heart."

Having heard about the fervent sermons of August Herman Francke (1663–1727) in Erfurt, Freylinghausen moved to that city, where he enjoyed the association of Francke and attended the lectures of both Francke and J. J. Breithaupt, the two prominent Pietist leaders of the time. In 1692 when these two were called to the University of Halle as professors of theology, he followed them there. In Halle he became a colleague to Francke, first in the church at Glaucha, a suburb of Halle, where for 20 years, from 1695–1715, he served without salary, next as an assistant to Francke at St. Ulrich's in Halle. In 1715 he married Francke's only daughter, Anastasia, whose baptismal sponsor he was. As assistant to his father-in-law, the organizing genius of Pietism, Freylinghausen helped direct the *Paedagogium* and the *Waisenhaus* (orphanage) in Halle. Upon Francke's death in 1727, Freylinghausen succeeded him in that office, taking also full charge of St. Ulrich and the other institutions that Francke had established. Freylinghausen died February 12, 1739, the result of his fourth and final stroke.

Though an effective and persuasive preacher, Freylinghausen's fame rests primarily on his contribution to the field of hymnody. Among the works of the poets of the Halle, or Pietist, circle, his hymns rank as the finest. In 1704 he published his *Geistreiches Gesangbuch*. Originally containing 683 hymns and 174 tunes, before long this collection grew to more than 750 hymns and 250 tunes. In 1714, he published the *Neues geistreiches Gesangbuch*, a collection of 815 hymns. The 1704 hymnal went through 19 editions; the 1714, through four. Today the more commonly known editions are those of 1741 and 1771, in which the former two are combined into one.

Although the numerous editions appeared in connection with and under the auspices of the Francke orphanage, the appellation "Halle hymns" also includes the hymns originating in the circles of Halle University, the seat of Pietism. The Freylinghausen collections exemplify Pietism at its best. The hymns pulsate with new life and vigor. Subjective in character, they are concerned about the spiritual well-being of the common man. Old hymns, even some of the early Latin hymns, hymns and tunes by contemporaries, the authorship of many uncertain, are included. The tunes—appealing, sweet, bright, often dazzling in character—stand in sharp contrast to the traditional church hymnody. As a skilled musician, Freylinghausen not only composed a number of the tunes (approximately 22), he also reworked and embellished the tunes of others.

The use of these hymns, under his direction, in the Wednesday and Saturday afternoon orphanage song-and-prayer periods readily contributed to their becoming current in other pious circles. They were not only for use in corporate worship, but also to be sung at home, at Christian entertainments, and while traveling.

In the history of the chorale, among other things, two important influences of Freylinghausen are to be noted: (1) the chorales are intended as unison song accompanied by a keyboard instrument; (2) the harmonies are given in figured bass. Thus the Freylinghausen methods presage the keyboard improvisation and melodic ornamentation of the great Johann Sebastian Bach (Riedel, *The Lutheran Chorale*).

COMPOSER (?): 23 MACHT HOCH DIE TÜR
182, 207, 321 GOTT SEI DANK
315, 446 DIR, DIR JEHOVAH

FREYSTEIN, JOHANN BURKARD (1671–1718), was born April 18, 1867, at Weissenfels, the son of A. S. Freystein, vice-chancellor of Duke August of Saxony and inspector of the *Gymnasium* at Weissenfels. Educated at the University of Leipzig, where he studied law, mathematics, philosophy, and architecture, he resided in Berlin and Halle before going to Dresden as an assistant to a lawyer. After earning the Doctor of Laws degree at Jena University in 1695, he began his own legal practice in Dresden. In 1703 he became counselor at Gotha, but returned to Dresden in 1709 as a member of the court council and counselor of justice. In 1713 he was also appointed a member of the Board of Works.

Influenced by Philip J. Spener's sermons, he, as a pious lawyer, wrote a number of hymns that enjoyed wide use. He died of dropsy at Dresden, April 1, 1718.

AUTHOR: 302 Rise, My Soul, to Watch and Pray

FRIESE, HEINRICH. Little information is available about this man other than that he was organist perhaps at the *Jacobuskirche* in Hamburg and that he collected and published the *Choral-Gesang-Buch*, containing 140 tunes with bass line but without figures. No place or date of publication is given except the handwritten 1703 in an extant copy. This volume saw two editions.

COMPOSER: 120 O WELT, SIEH HIER

FRITSCH, AHASVERUS (1629–1701), was born December 16, 1629, at Mücheln near Merseburg, the son of the town's mayor. His early youth was spent during the Thirty Years' War (1618–48), a period that caused him and his family untold suffering and woe. Despite the death of his father, his mother sent him to the *Gymnasium* at Halle. In 1650 he went to Jena University, where he studied under the learned jurist J. Georg Adam Struve. Financial difficulties interrupted his studies, but he finally finished the requirements in 1654. In 1657 he became tutor of the young count Albert Anton von Schwarzburg-Rudolstadt, and in 1661 the University of Jena honored him with a Doctor of Law degree. Later he became chancellor of this university and president of the Rudolstadt consistory. He died of a stroke on August 24, 1701.

Fritsch was a conscientious, upright and skilled statesman who wrote a host of significant things on social and political matters; he was a pious and humble Christian whom Philip J. Spener (1635–1705) lauded. He edited two hymn collections.

COMPOSER: 187, 371, 372, 418 WAS FRAG ICH NACH DER WELT

FUNCKE, FRIEDRICH (1642–99), was born at Nossen in the Harz, Germany, and educated at Freiberg and Dresden. He first served as cantor at Perleberg; then, beginning in 1664, as cantor at Lüneberg. It was to this city that August Herman Francke (1663–1727), one of the leaders of Pietism, came in 1687 to study privately with Lutheran superintendent Kaspar Herman Sandhagen (1639–1697), after he had been recognized as a lecturer by Leipzig University. Here Franke experienced that inner conversion, about which he later could say that Lübeck was the place of his natural birth; Lüneberg the place of his spiritual birth. Neither did Sandhagen nor Funcke totally escape the influence of Pietism. Occupied as the former was with the Book of Revelation, toward the end of his life he was accused of having chiliastic tendencies. Fortunately Funcke did not suffer that fate. While in Lüneberg he collaborated with Sandhagen and, with the cooperation of the publisher Johann Stern, produced the *Lüneberg Gesangbuch* in 1686, to which Funcke contributed a goodly number of tunes as well as some texts.

In 1694 Funcke became pastor at Römstadt, where he died October 20, 1699.

AUTHOR: 153 Draw Us to You

GANSE, HERVEY DODDRIDGE (1822–91), was born February 27, 1822, near Fishkill, New York, moving to New York City in 1825. Following his graduation from Columbia College in 1839, he studied theology at New Brunswick, New Jersey, becoming ordained in 1843. From 1843–56 he was pastor of a Dutch Reformed congregation in Freehold, New Jersey; from 1856–76 pastor of the Northwest Reformed Dutch Church, New York City. In January 1876 he became pastor of the First Presbyterian Church, St. Louis, where he served until his death in 1891.

Ganse wrote no less than six hymns that found their way into either *Hymns of the Church* (1869) or *Hymns and Songs of Praise* (1874), hymnals of the Dutch Reformed Church.

AUTHOR: 514 Nearer, My God, to Thee (sts. 2, 3, 4)

GARDINER, WILLIAM (1770–1853), was born March 15, 1770, in Leicester, England, the son of a stocking manufacturer, a business in which he himself became successful.

As a hobby, music increasingly took up his time. Already in his youth, under the *nom de plume* of W. G. Leicester, he published a collection of his own songs and duets. His frequent business travels to the Continent afforded him occasion to meet Mozart (1756–91), Haydn (*LW* 294), and Beethoven (1770–1827). In the hope of replacing both the Old and New Versions of the Psalms (see essay: Metrical Psalms, p. 825), his six-volume *Sacred Melodies* (1812–38) was an attempt to match the finest texts to the best tunes, mostly adopted from great composers. These volumes enjoyed considerable popularity and became a source for hymnal compilers. They influenced Lowell Mason (*LW* 115, et al.) in his *Boston Handel and Haydn Society's Collection*, where he not only used Gardiner's tunes but also his method of adapting older material for hymn tunes. Gardiner was the first to introduce Beethoven's music to England. He published his reminiscences, *Music and Friends* (1838), and also wrote a book on acoustics entitled *The Music of Nature*. He died February 16, 1853, in Leicester.

COMPOSER: 416 BELMONT

GASTOLDI, GIOVANNI GIACOMO (c. 1556–c. 1622), was born at Carvaggo, Italy. In 1572 he was a young subdeacon at Santa Barbara, the ducal chapel of the Gonzaga family in Mantua; a short time later he became deacon and a singer in the cappella. Undoubtedly a student of Giaches de Wert, he became *maestro di cappella* while Wert was ill. In 1592 he succeeded Wert and remained in charge of the music at Santa Barbara until the end of 1608, when he apparently moved to Milan in a secular capacity. His later life is obscure.

Although Gastoldi composed in a variety of genres, he is largely remembered for his famous ballettos, pieces "to sing, play, and dance," many of which with a fa-la-la refrain. His *Balletti a cinqve voce* (1591) went through numerous editions in Italy and beyond, and their influence can be noticed in the works of Claudio Monteverdi (1567–1643), in the *Lustgarten* of Hans Leo Hassler (*LW* 113, 427), and in the ballets of Thomas Morley in England. Gastoldi's rhythmic phrases are regular; his harmony is diatonic with frequent cadential progressions, and practically completely divorced from the modal system. He died about 1622.

COMPOSER: 442 IN DIR IST FREUDE

GASTORIUS (BAUCHSPIES), SEVERUS (1646–82), was born at Öttern, near Weimar. After attending the Latin School at Weimar, where his father taught, he attended the University of Jena. In 1670 he became substitute-cantor for Andreas Zöll, whose daughter he married in 1671; in 1677, on Zöll's death, he became cantor, a position he held until his own early death on May 8, 1682.

Gastorius is primarily remembered for his tune WAS GOTT TUT, modeled on a tune by Werner Fabricius that appeared in E. C. Homburg's (*LW* 94) *Geistliche Lieder* (Jena,

1659). He also published five funeral motets which exhibit the influence of W. C. Briegel (1626–1712) and Johann M. Bach (1648–94).

COMPOSER: 422 WAS GOTT TUT

GATES, MARY CORNELIA (1842–1905) was born February 14, 1842, at Rochester, New York, the daughter of William S. Bishop. After receiving a good education, she became a faculty member of Leroy Female Seminary. In 1873 she married Merrill Gates, a prominent educator, who, in 1882, became president of Rutger's College, and nine years later president of Amherst. Mary Gates was long an active member of the Women's Board for Foreign Missions of the Reformed Church in America (Dutch Reformed); both she and her husband served their denomination in other capacities. She contributed to *The Independent*, *The Atlantic Monthly*, *The Christian Intelligencer*, and *The Youth's Companion*. Her *Hymns of Nature and Songs of the Spirit* was published in 1908. She died December 17, 1905.

AUTHOR: 316 Send Now, O Lord, to Every Place

GAUNTLETT, HENRY JOHN (1805–76), was born July 9, 1805, in Wellington, Shropshire, England, the son of a curate. At the age of nine he became organist of his father's church at Olney, Buckinghamshire. On the insistence of his father he became a lawyer, a profession he followed until 1844, when he gave it up to devote himself to music. He was organist in turn at St. Olave's, Southwark; Christ Church, Newgate Street; Union Chapel, Islington; and St. Bartholomew the Less, Smithfield. He died at Kensington, February 21, 1876.

Gauntlett is the senior and the most prolific of the Victorian musicians. It is said that he wrote thousands of tunes, many when not at his best. He was in great demand for editing the music of various hymnals. Much of his work is contained in *The Congregational Psalmist* (first edition, 1858; last edition, 1886), compiled for Union Chapel, Islington, which contains numerous strong, bright tunes and simple congregational anthems on a broad scale. The work was commendable in its congregational aspect, despite some often trite, key-tied, dull, unimaginative tunes. His contribution to the reform of church music and the promotion of hymnody, however, was undeniably great, and it is undoubtedly IRBY, the compelling tune of "Once in royal David's city," that makes Gauntlett immortal.

But he is also known for other music achievements. He extended the pedal of the English pipe organ; in 1851 he took out a patent for applying electric or magnetic action to the organ. Felix Mendelssohn (*LW* 49), who chose him as organist for the first performance of *Elijah* at Birmingham, 1846, wrote of him:

> His literary attainments, his knowledge of the history of music, his acquaintance with acoustical laws, his marvelous memory, his philosophical

> turn of mind, as well as his practice experience, rendered him one of the most remarkable professors of the age.

The Archbishop of Canterbury conferred on him the Doctor of Music degree, the first granted by this prelate in 200 years.

COMPOSER: 58 IRBY

GELLERT, CHRISTIAN FÜRCHTEGOTT (1715–1769), was born July 4, 1715, in Hainichen, Saxony, the son of a Lutheran pastor and poet. He attended the Fürstenschule at Meissen beginning in 1729, and afterward the University of Leipzig. Here he studied theology and assisted his father for a time, but "congenital timidity" and a poor memory (preaching from a manuscript was forbidden) convinced him to give up on the pastoral ministry after four years of study.

Gellert became private tutor in the family of Herr von Luttichau in 1739, returning to Leipzig two years later to oversee a nephew enrolled there as well as resuming his own course of studies. He attained the Master of Arts degree in 1744 and the following year accepted a post on the philosophical faculty.

Appointed extraordinary professor of philosophy in 1751, Gellert began lecturing on poetry and rhetoric, later on ethics. He became a very popular lecturer, filling his classrooms to capacity and counting Goethe and Lessing among his students—surprisingly, for his religious views would not have been readily accepted in that age of Rationalism had Gellert not been an extraordinarily genuine and charismatic speaker.

Gellert's literary ventures included the organizing of the "Leipziger Dichterbund," a group of poets that published the *Bremische Beiträge*, and the contributing of several comedies and a novel to this publication (1745–46). In addition he began a series of *Tales and Fables*, published in book form in 1746 and 1748, that won him acclaim as a German classicist and went through many reprints and translations.He is best known for his hymns, of which 54 appeared in his *Geistliche Oden und Lieder* (Leipzig, 1757). His biographer writes:

> Never did he attempt a spiritual poem without carefully preparing himself, and striving with all his soul to experience previously the truth of his utterances. He then chose his most ecstatic moments for composition, and as soon as his ardor cooled he laid aside his pen until the golden moments came again.

His popularity among Roman Catholics, due in part to his hymn writing, caused several to try and persuade Gellert to join that church, but he remained a devout Lutheran until his death December 13, 1769.

AUTHOR: 139 Jesus Lives! The Victory's Won

GEORGE, GRAHAM (1912–) was born in Norwich, England, April 11, 1912, and emigrated to Canada in 1928. He was a student of Alfred Whitehead in his undergraduate years, receiving the Bachelor of Music degree in 1936 from the University of Toronto, and the Doctor of Music three years later.

George continued his music education at Yale University, in the Netherlands, and in Paris, pursuing philosophy studies as well. He spent a year directing music at West Hill High School in Montreal, but his music career was interrupted by overseas service in the Canadian Army from 1941–45. Afterward he taught for a short while in the Montreal public schools, going in 1946 to Queen's University, Kingston, Ontario. There he served as professor of music (and resident musician in the early years) from 1946–77. In addition to his academic duties he prepared and conducted annual performances of operas, symphonic and choral works from 1946–72, retiring from the university in 1977 as professor emeritus.

As organist, George has served at various parishes in and around Montreal and Kingston. His is a fellow and an associate of the Canadian College of Organists, and an associate of the Royal College of Organists, over which he presided from 1972–74.

Founder of the St. Francis Madrigal Singers of Sherbrooke, Quebec, George has been in demand as a conductor with the Queen's Symphony and the Kingston Symphony Orchestra as well as the Kingston Choral Society. His compositions include orchestral works, choral music, vocal solos, chamber, music, keyboard works, and works for stage, radio, and film scores. He has received numerous awards and commissions. His *Tonality and Musical Structure* was published in 1970 and reprinted in paperback in 1976. He is married and the father of four sons.

COMPOSER: 105 THE KING'S MAJESTY
299 GRACE CHURCH, GANANOQUE

GERHARDT, PAUL (1607–76), was born March 12, 1607, in Gräfenhainichen, a small village between Halle and Wittenberg. His father, Christian Gerhardt, mayor of the village, died before Paul reached maturity. His mother was a Lutheran pastor's daughter and a pastor's granddaughter from Eilenburg, the home of Martin Rinckart (*LW* 443).

As a result of the Thirty Years' War (1618–48), Paul experienced considerable suffering during his youth. From 1622–27 he attended the court school at Grimma, an institution in which a solid Lutheranism held sway. On January 2, 1628, he began the study of theology at the University of Wittenberg, where he remained until 1643, when he moved to Berlin. Here he became family tutor in the home of Andreas Berthold, an attorney. In this capacity he established noteworthy relationships with M. Schirmer, Johann Crüger (*LW* 19, et al.) and frequently helped his pastor friends by filling their pulpits. During this period of candidacy for the holy ministry his poetic gifts blossomed to the fullest. From 1647–66 no less than 28 hymns appeared.

In 1651 Gerhardt was called to Mittenwalde, a small town south of Berlin, as provost. Before assuming this position he was ordained in Berlin, subscribing to the Formula of Concord. Mittenwalde suffered heavily during the war, both from fire and plague, affording Gerhardt frequent opportunity to comfort people through his poetry. It was here that his hymns began to attract attention, and they soon were adopted into the hymnbooks of Brandenburg and Saxony. In his fourth year at Mittenwalde he married Anna Maria Berthold, the daughter of Andreas Berthold.

Dire financial straits, coupled with unpleasantness because of the jealousy of a colleague, prompted Gerhardt to accept the call to be the third assistant pastor (deacon) of St. Nicholas Church in Berlin. There he soon acquired great influence as a favorite, popular preacher and a personality honored and beloved. He continued also to write hymns as an associate of Johann Crüger.

This was a period of bitter conflict between Lutherans and Calvinists. When conferences between the two parties, arranged by the Calvinist elector Friedrich Wilhelm the Great, failed, the elector issued an edict forbidding clergy to attack each other's doctrine and confession. Later he demanded that all Lutheran clergy sign a document compelling them to follow the order of the edict. When, on February 9, 1666, Gerhardt, convinced that such an act would constitute a compromising of his faith, refused to sign, he was deposed from office and even prohibited from conducting any function of his office in private. This was unquestionably the most difficult period in his life. Just prior to this he had lost four of his five children and his beloved wife was seriously ill.

Petitions from citizens prompted the elector to reinstate him on the condition that he preach in accordance with the aforementioned edict. But Gerhardt refused. Charitable members of the congregation now constituted his sole support. In 1668 his wife Anna Maria died. Now only a young son remained. In 1669 Gerhardt was appointed archdeacon of Lübben, where he spent the closing years of his life in much unhappiness, the result of family affliction and the unkindness of rude and unsympathetic people. He died June 7, 1676. The inscription on his portrait in the Lutheran church at Lübben reads: "Theologus in cribo Satanae versatus" (A divine sifted in Satan's sieve).

Gerhardt's hymns, about 133 in all, can well be considered among the greatest works of art in the German language, and he is indeed the foremost hymnwriter of the Lutheran Church. The hymns of no German writers have found their way into the English language more than those of Gerhardt. They mark the transition from the objective to the more subjective in hymn writing and are the pure and spontaneous utterance of a fervent faith in Christ Jesus.

AUTHOR:	19	O Lord, How Shall I Meet You
	39	Once Again My Heart Rejoices
	48	Come, Your Hearts and Voices Raising
	111	A Lamb Alone Bears Willingly
	113	O Sacred Head, Now Wounded
	120, 121	Upon the Cross Extended
	128	Awake, My Heart, with Gladness
	184	Now Let Us Come Before Him
	280	Jesus, Your Boundless Love So True
	407	If God Himself Be for Me

419 Evening and Morning
423 When I Suffer Pains and Losses
424 Rejoice, My Heart, Be Glad
427 Entrust Your Days and Burdens
439 I Will Sing My Maker's Praises
485 Now Rest Beneath Night's Shadow

GERIKE, HENRY VICTOR (1948–) was born August 17, 1948, in Parkers Prairie, Minnesota, the oldest of six children of Rev. Victor and Lila Gerike.

A graduate of both Concordia Academy (1966) and Concordia College, St. Paul, Minnesota (1970) with a Bachelor of Arts degree, he received the Master of Church Music degree from Concordia College, River Forest, Illinois, in August 1983. From Concordia Seminary, St. Louis, Missouri, he received the Master of Divinity degree in 1991.

Organ instructors have included Paul Manz (*LW* 195) and Herbert Gotsch (*LW* 85, 356); composition has been studied with Richard Hillert (*LW* 18, et al.).

Service to the Church has included 15 years as teacher and music director in several parishes and schools: Concord Lutheran School, Pagedale, Missouri (1970–75); Unity Lutheran Church, Bel Nor, Missouri (1970–75); St. Paul's Lutheran Church and School, Aurora,, Illinois (1975–79); Grace English Lutheran Church and School, Chicago, Illinois (1979–85). From 1973–75 Gerike served as director of the St. Louis Lutheran Children's Choir. He was the cofounder and chairman of The Lutheran Parish Musicians Guild of St. Louis, and later of the Guild of Northern Illinois. Additional service includes serving on the program and worship committees of conferences of the Missouri, Northern Illinois, and English Districts of The Lutheran Church—Missouri Synod. Presently, he serves as director of the Concordia Seminary Chorus, St. Louis, Missouri.

Recognition was granted him in the 1977 *Who's Who in Religion*. A number of his organ compositions are included in the *Concordia Hymn Prelude Series*. His choral compositions have been published by Mark Foster Music Company, Concordia Publishing House, and G.I.A. Publications. His hymn tune ASCENDED TRIUMPH, written for use with Jaroslav Vajda's text, "Up through Endless Ranks of Angels" (*LW* 152), has been included in both *Lutheran Book of Worship* (1978) and *Lutheran Worship* (1982).

COMPOSER: 152 ASCENDED TRIUMPH

GERMANUS (c. 634–c. 734), was born in Constantinople of a patrician family. Ordained to the priesthood in 668, he became one of the clergy at the "Great Church," St. Sophia, and later leader of the clergy there. He gained great influence from his reputation for piety and learning. He promoted the Quinisext, or Trullan, Council of 692, after which he was appointed to the metropolitan see of Cyzicus. In 715 he was appointed patriarch of Constantinople; during his tenure he was a staunch opponent of the iconoclasts. Consequently he was forced to resign in 730 because he refused to yield to the iconoclastic Emperor Leo III, the Isaurian. Germanus is supposed to have died at the age of 95.

AUTHOR: 51 A Great and Mighty Wonder

GESENIUS, JUSTUS (1601–73), was born July 6, 1601, at Essbeck, Hanover, where his father was pastor. Studying theology both at Helmstedt and Jena, he was awarded the Master of Arts degree in 1628. The following year he became pastor of St. Magnus' Church in Brunswick; in 1636 court chaplain and preacher at Hildesheim Cathedral; in 1642 councillor and general superintendent of Hanover.

As coeditors of the Hanoverian hymnbook (1646–60), Gesenius and David Denicke (*LW* 385) recast, mostly for the better, many of the tried and true Lutheran hymns according to the poetical canons of Martin Opitz (*LW* 85). Gesenius was an accomplished and influential theologian, a renowned preacher, who distinguished himself on behalf of the catechetical instruction of the laity.

AUTHOR: 367 When over Sin I Sorrow

GESIUS (GESE, GÖSE, GÖSS), BARTHOLOMÄUS (c. 1555–1613), was born in Müncheberg, Germany. With some interruptions he studied at the University of Franfurt-an-der-Oder; he may also have studied at the University of Wittenberg. In 1582 he was for a short time cantor at Müncheberg, after which he probably returned to Frankfurt. Next he was domestic tutor to Freiherr Hans Georg von Schönaich of Carolath in Muskau and Sprottau (Upper Lusatia), a prominent poet, some of whose works Gesius set to music. While here he was offered the post of cantor at the *Marienkirche* in Frankfurt. Having assumed this position in 1593, he remained there until his death of the plague in 1613.

Gesius perhaps acquired his musical training either from Christoph Zacharias, organist at the Marienkirche, or from the Cantor Gregor Lang. Representing Lutheran theology, his output for church and school is comprised largely of settings of pre-Reformation Latin songs and Protestant hymns in the cantus firmus technique, as illustrated in his *Psalmodia Choralis*, containing 631 hymn tunes. This work, as well as his *Geistliche deutsche Lieder* (1601), probably influenced Michael Praetorius (*LW* 14, et al.), who from 1585–90 studied in Frankfurt and who in his last three years had been organist at the Marienkirche.

Both in his *St. John Passion* (1588) and *St. Matthew Passion* (1613), Gesius played an important part in the history of that musical form—a mixed type between the German dramatic Passion and the motet Passion. His settings of the Magnificat (1607) contributed to popular German Christmas traditions from the late Middle Ages to J. S. Bach (*LW* 89).

COMPOSER: 379 MACHS MIT MIR, GOTT
ARRANGER: 421 AUF MEINEN LIEBEN GOTT

GIARDINI, FELICE de (1716–96), was born April 12, 1716, in Turin, Italy. His early musical training was given him as a chorister in the Milan Cathedral. Returning to Turin, he studied violin with the famed Giovanni B. Somis, who had been a pupil of Corelli and Vivaldi. After an extended concert tour in Italy, Germany, and France, he settled in London, England, in 1752. Here he soon took a leading role as a violinist, harpsichordist, teacher, leader of Italian opera, and composer of sorts. The Countess of Huntingdon commissioned four hymn tunes from him for Martin Madan's *Lock Hospital Collection* (1769). He led the orchestra for the Three Choirs Festival from 1770–76. In 1784 he accompanied the British ambassador to the Sardinian court at Naples. Five years later he returned to England, only to discover that he had lost his place in public appreciation. Russia, to which he next betook himself in the hope of better fortune, proved as cold as London, and in Moscow he sank under poverty, disappointment, and distress. There he died June 8, 1760.

Capricious in character, having few friends but numerous enemies, Giardini was still a great artist, a musician who takes his rightful place in English music history.

COMPOSER: 169, 317, 471 ITALIAN HYMN

GIBBONS, ORLANDO (1583–1625), was born in Oxford, England, and baptized on Christmas Day, 1583. Member of a family of musicians, at age 13 he joined the choir of King's College, Cambridge, where his brother Edward was master of the choristers. In 1604 he accepted the position of organist at the Chapel Royal in London, becoming a Bachelor of Music in 1606 from Cambridge. Oxford University granted him the Doctor of Music degree in 1622, in which year he was also awarded an honorary doctorate by his alma mater.

One of the greatest "old style" polyphonic writers, Gibbons had a talent for composing many different types of works, including secular vocal and instrumental ensembles, madrigals, anthems, and keyboard pieces. Of the latter, some of his best work was written for the virginal, a 16th-century type of harpsichord, on which, as a performer, he was unrivaled. In 1619 Gibbons was appointed the King's musician for the virginals.

Gibbons became organist at Westminster Abbey in 1623, where he was in charge of the music for the funeral of James I in 1625. Later that year he traveled to Canterbury under orders from Charles I, to provide music for the arrival from France of Charles' bride-to-be, Henrietta Maria; but in Canterbury Gibbons suffered a stroke and died before the ceremony, on Pentecost Day, June 5, 1625. He was buried in Canterbury Cathedral.

In addition to his various individual works, Gibbons published a collection of *Madrigals and Motets* (1612) and wrote the melodies with figured bass for George Wither's (c. 1588–1667) *Hymnes and Songs of the Church* (1623).

COMPOSER: 166, 256 SONG 13
211 SONG 34
395 SONG 67

GIESCHEN, GERHARD (1899–1987), was born June 28, 1899, in Helenville, Wisconsin. Educated at Northwestern College, Watertown, Wisconsin, and Lutheran Theological Seminary, Thiensville, Wisconsin, he was ordained in 1922 by the then-Evangelical Lutheran Joint Synod of Wisconsin and Other States and served pastorates at Rib Falls and Marshfield, Wisconsin. In the latter he served as assistant pastor and principal of the congregation's day school. When, in the depression of the early 30s the congregation could not afford to maintain its school, Pastor Gieschen found himself without a call. It was then that St. John's Church, Leigh, Nebraska, a member of the then-United Lutheran Church in America, with the approval of the president of the Nebraska Synod, extended to him a call, which he accepted. Here he served from 1933–40. His next parish was at Wayne, Nebraska (1940–42); then Our Redeemer, Omaha (1942–47); and thereafter St. Peter, Forest Park, Illinois (1947–50). In the summer of 1950 Gieschen was called to be an assistant professor at Central Lutheran Theological Seminary, Fremont, Nebraska. One and a half years later he was appointed full professor of systematic theology, serving in a number of capacities, including faculty secretary, choir director, and as acting president (1964–67) when E. B. Keisler retired in 1964. Midland College, Fremont, Nebraska, honored him with the Doctor of Divinity degree in 1952.

Following the merger in 1962 which resulted in the formation of the Lutheran Church in America, four seminaries of predecessor church bodies were brought together to create the Lutheran School of Theology at Chicago (LSTC). At that time Gieschen retired and was included as professor emeritus of systematic theology at LSTC. The last years of his life were spent in Sun City, Arizona, where he died June 22, 1987, survived by his wife Lucille, his sons Donald, Roger, David, and Gary, and daughter Eunice Lipps.

TRANSLATOR: 85 Arise and Shine in Splendor

GIESCHEN, THOMAS E. (1931–), was born in Wauwatosa, Wisconsin, July 11, 1931. He was educated at Wisconsin Conservatory of Music and Wisconsin State Teachers College, Milwaukee, going on to study organ with Paul Bunjes (*LW* 131, et al.) and to receive a Bachelor of Science in education at Concordia College, River Forest, Illinois.

Gieschen continued his training with Robert Noehren at the University of Michigan and with Barrett Spach at Northwestern University, Evanston, Illinois, attaining the Master of Music degree in 1958 and the Doctor of Music 10 years later. Married to Roselyn Newman in 1952, he served for three years as teacher and director of music at Gethsemane Lutheran Church, Detroit. In 1955 he went on to Emmaus Lutheran Church in Milwaukee, where he held the same position.

Now professor of music and chairman of the music department at his alma mater, Concordia College, where he has taught since 1957, Gieschen has also been active at the organ. Our Redeemer Lutheran Church in Chicago employed his services as organist/choirmaster from 1957–71, and he was associate organist at the Evangelical Lutheran Church of St. Luke, Chicago, from 1976–78. Organ consultant and recitalist, he was a contributing editor of *Church Music*. His published works also include original compositions and arrangements, and he has edited choral and organ music.

ARRANGER:	358	SUCH, WER DA WILL
	408	STEPHANOS

GIESEKE, RICHARD W. (1952–), was born May 15, 1952, in Elgin, Illinois, where he attended public school until his matriculation at Concordia Teachers College (now Concordia University), River Forest, Illinois. There he studied composition with Richard Hillert (*LW* 18, et al.) and Carl F. Schalk (*LW* 17, et al.), earning the Bachelor of Arts degree in 1974 and the Master of Church Music in 1978. He has also studied at Westminster Choir College, Princeton, NJ, and at Concordia Seminary, St. Louis.

Gieseke was teacher and music director at St. Peter's Lutheran Church, Evansville, Illinois, 1974 to 1975, going on to St. Louis as teacher and director of music at Word of Life Lutheran School, where he served until 1989. During his years at Word of Life he has also held positions as minister of music at various churches in the St. Louis area. In 1989 he joined the Editorial Services department of Concordia Publishing House, St. Louis with responsibilities in music, curriculum, and worship products.

The catalog of his works comprises choral pieces with various instrumental ensembles, hymns, solo vocal works, organ compositions, and concertatos, many of which have been published by Concordia Publishing House, G.I.A. Publications, Chicago, and Morning Star Music Publishers. He has also edited and arranged various works of major composers. He provided numerous harmonizations for inclusion in *Lutheran Worship* and in *Songs of God's Love* as well as organ settings for the *Concordia Hymn Prelude Series*—all published by Concordia.

He is also a member of the Hymn Society of America.

Married to Susan Diane Rosemann, he is the father of two daughters.

ARRANGER:	27	BEREDEN VÖG FÜR HERRAN
	28	FREU DICH SEHR
	120	O WELT, SIEH HIER
	121	O WELT, ICH MUSS DICH LASSEN
	123	CHRIST LAG IN TODESBANDEN
	151	ICH SINGE DIR
	166	SONG 13
	174	NUN DANKET ALLE GOTT
	186	WESTMINSTER ABBEY
	263, 434	WERDE MUNTER

303 WACHET AUF
317 ITALIAN HYMN
326 O GROSSER GOTT
343 REX GLORIAE
360 O DASS ICH TAUSEND ZUNGEN HÖTTE
371 WAS FRAG ICH NACH DER WELT
431 VATER UNSER
437 WIE SCHÖN LEUCHTET
439 SOLLT ICH MEINEM GOTT

GILMAN, SAMUEL (1791–1858), was born February 16, 1791, at Gloucester, Massachusetts. After receiving his early education at the academy in Atkinson, New Hampshire, he attended Harvard, graduating in 1811. Several years were then spent as clerk at a bank in Salem before returning to Harvard in 1817 to serve as a tutor. In 1819 he was called to serve as pastor of the Unitarian church at Charleston, South Carolina, a position he held until his death February 9, 1858, while on a visit at Kingston, Massachusetts.

TRANSLATOR: 227 This Child We Now Present to You

GLÄSER, CARL GOTTHILF (1784–1829), was born May 4, 1784, in Wessenfels, Germany. After receiving his early music instruction from his father, he attended St. Thomas' School in Leipzig, where he studied music under John Adam Hiller and August Eberhard Muller, who taught him the pianoforte, and under Campagnoli, who taught him the violin. In 1801 he began to study law at the Leipzig University, but being more interested in music than in briefs, he gave up jurisprudence and settled in Barmen, where he taught piano, violin, and voice, directed choruses, and opened a music shop. In addition he composed motets, school songs, and instrumental music until his death April 16, 1829.

COMPOSER: 350 AZMON

GOTSCH, HERBERT (1926–84). Following his graduation from the then-Concordia College (now Concordia University), River Forest, Illinois, in 1948, he served as a Lutheran teacher, organist, and choir director at congregations in Pasadena, California; Detroit and Saginaw, Michigan, until he joined Concordia's faculty in 1958. After studying for a time at Chicago Musical College, he proceeded to Northwestern University, Evanston, Illinois, from which he received the Master of Music degree in 1949 and the Doctor of Music degree in 1965. An outstanding teacher and accomplished organist, respected as such by his students, he played dedication recitals on church organs throughout the Midwest. His annual recital at Concordia was a prominent part of the school's musical tradition. Besides his teaching and recital work, he authored numerous articles for church music publications which exhibited his scholarship and encyclopedic knowledge. At the time of his death, March 8, 1984, caused by brain cancer, he was editing a 42-volume series of choral preludes for organ, of which 29 volumes had been completed and published by Concordia Publishing House with the title *The Concordia Hymn Prelude Series*. Richard Hillert (*LW* 71, et al.), a colleague, edited the remaining volumes 30–42.

ARRANGER: 85 O WELT, ICH MUSS DICH LASSEN
356 DUNSTAN

GOUDIMEL, CLAUDE (c. 1520–72), was born in Besancon in the south of France. In 1549 his first book of chansons was published in Paris where, two years later, he became an editor and later joint-publisher with Nicolas du Chemin, under whose label many of Goudimel's works appeared.

Born a Roman Catholic, Goudimel eventually converted to the Reformed Church, probably around 1558. In that year he completed his masses, the last work he composed for the Roman Catholic Church.

Goudimel's settings of the Genevan Psalter represent his most memorable work. The first complete psalter in an entirely homophonic setting appeared in 1564 as *Les CL Pseaumes de David, nouvellement mis en musique a quatre parties par Claude Goudimel*. A second edition appeared the following year with four parts in simple counterpoint, brilliantly done, followed in 1565–6 by an edition in motet form for three to eight voices. Ambrosius Lobwasser used Goudimel's settings for his *Der Psalter . . . in Deutsche Reyme verstendiglich und deutlich Gebracht* (1573). The discovery of Goudimel's music in the 1551 *Pseaumes in Forme de Motets* stirred up the question of the tunes' composition; some feel that Goudimel merely harmonized familiar melodies. His psalm settings were used by both the Reformed and Roman Catholic Churches until their use was forbidden by the latter.

For a time Goudimel lived with the Huguenot colony at Metz but, fearing persecution, the colony began to disperse between 1565 and 1568. Goudimel returned to his native Besancon, later going to Lyons, where he became a victim of the St. Bartholomew's Day massacre and died August 27 or 28, 1572.

In addition to his psalm harmonizations, Goudimel composed chansons, motets, and five masses. Nearly all the psalm books published throughout the following two centuries included music by Goudimel.

ARRANGER: 377 DONNE SECOURS
486 NUNC DIMITTIS

GOULD, JOHN EDGAR (1822–75), was born at Bangor, Maine. His interest in music and composing saw him, at the age of 30, in an established music store on Broadway in

New York City and having published four books of songs, two of them in collaboration with Edward L. White. After his marriage Gould moved to Philadelphia where he became a partner in a successful retail piano and music business with William G. Fischer, composer of the tune for "I love to tell the story."

Gould died suddenly in Algiers, Africa, March 4, 1875, while on a European and North African tour.

COMPOSER: 513 PILOT

GRAMANN (GRAUMANN, POLIANDER), JOHANN (1487–1541), was born July 5, 1487, in Neustadt, in the Bavarian Palatinate. After earning the Master of Arts degree in 1516 and the Bachelor of Divinity degree in 1520 at Leipzig University, he was appointed rector of St. Thomas' School in Leipzig, where J.S. Bach (*LW* 89) would later become kapellmeister. In 1519, impressed with Luther's (*LW* 13, et al.) emphasis on Scripture and the dictates of conscience in the disputation among Eck, Luther, and Karlstadt, Gramann decided to leave Leipzig and go to Wittenberg to join Luther and Melanchthon in the cause of the Reformation. In 1523 he was appointed preacher at Würzburg; two years later, at the outbreak of the Peasants' War, he was appointed preacher to the nunnery of St. Clara in Nürnberg. On Luther's recommendation, Margrave Albrecht of Brandenburg called on Gramann to help introduce the cause of the Reformation in Prussia. In 1525 Gramann became pastor of the Altstadt church in Königsberg. Here he worked faithfully to establish a sound foundation for the Lutheran faith. In opposing the Anabaptists and the Schwenkfeldians—the radical elements of the Reformation—he incurred the displeasure of the count. In a disputation with the Anabaptists and Schwenckfeldians Gramann won the day. He also played an active role in the church visitation of 1531 as well as in the establishing of Lutheran schools in the province. Gramann died at Königsberg, April 29, 1541, the result of a massive stroke.

Of the 17-some hymns in the small hymnal that Paul Speratus (*LW* 355) compiled for the early Lutherans in Königsberg, it is only conjecture which are from the hand of Gramann, except for the hymn given below, perhaps the earliest Lutheran hymn of praise.

AUTHOR: 453 My Soul, Now Praise Your Maker

GRANT, ROBERT (1779–1838), was born in Bengal, India, the son of Charles Grant, sometime member of Parliament for Iverness, director of East India Company, and an Indian philanthropist. Following his graduation from Magdalen College, Oxford, of which be became a fellow, he was called to the bar in 1807, and became king's sergeant in the court of the Duchy of Lancaster. As a member of Parliament he represented in succession Elgin Burghs, Inverness Burghs, Norwich, and Finsbury. Having been made privy councillor in 1831, two years later he became Judge Advocate General and then the civil governor of Bombay in 1834, at which time he was also knighted. He died at Dalpoorie, July 9, 1838.

Grant's hymns contributed to *The Christian Observer* and to H. V. Elliott's *Psalms and Hymns* (Brighton, 1835). His brother Lord Glenelg collected and published 12 of his hymns in *Sacred Poems* (London, 1839). Julian says Grant's hymns "are marked by . . . graceful versification and deep and tender feelings."

AUTHOR: 93 Savior, when in Dust to You
458 Oh, Worship the King

GREEN, FREDERICK PRATT, (1903–), was born September 2, 1903, in the village of Roby, now part of Liverpool, England. Moving with his family to Wallasey just before World War I, he first attended the grammar school there; in 1917 he transferred to Rydal, the Methodist school at Colwyn Bay. After spending four years in his father's leather manufacturing business, in 1924 he entered the Wesleyan Methodist ministry, having trained at Didsbury College, Manchester. During his active pastoral ministry of 42 years, he served various churches, chiefly in Yorkshire and London. For five years he was superintendent of the Dome Mission in Brighton, at a time when the evening congregation was perhaps the largest in Britain. He was chairman of the York and Hull District from 1957–64, and he served at Sutton until his retirement to Norwich in 1969.

Although Green did not begin to write poetry until beyond 40 years of age, he is a poet of distinction whose poems have appeared in, for instance, *The New Yorker*, *The Listener*, and the *Oxford Book of Twentieth-Century Verse*. He has published three collections of poems: *This Unlikely Earth* (1952), *The Skating Parson* (1963), and *The Old Couple* (1976).

He was over 60 years of age when the committee responsible for preparing *Hymns and Songs* (1969), a supplement to the Methodist Hymn Book, invited him to serve on their committee and to write hymns for specific tunes as well as help to fill certain gaps in subject matter.

Few hymnals since 1969 have overlooked Green's outstanding contribution to hymnody. He has been a major contributor to *Cantate Domino* (1975), the international hymnal of the World Council of Churches. He wrote the hymn authorized to be sung in churches of all denominations in celebration of the Silver Jubilee of Queen Elizabeth II in 1977. That same year he was appointed to edit the hymnbook *Partners in Praise* (Abingdon, 1979), and in 1982 he was made a fellow of The Hymn Society of America as well as being awarded an honorary doctorate by Emory University, Atlanta, Georgia, in the Humanities for his contribution to hymnody. That same year Hope Publishing House brought out *The Hymns and Ballads of Fred Pratt Green*. Of interest are his words:

> Coming to hymn-writing after experience as a poet, I have learned to distinguish between these two activities. One writes poetry to please oneself; one writes hymns as a servant of Christ and of his Church. Only one thing matters: that the hymn shall be right for use in worship.

AUTHOR: 449 When in Our Music God Is Glorified

GREGORY I (c. 540–604), known as Gregory the Great but who viewed himself as the "servant of the Church's servants," was born into a wealthy patrician family. He received an excellent education in law, thus preparing him for public service. In 573 he became prefect of Rome, but when his father died in 575 leaving him a fortune, he devoted his wealth to the founding of six monasteries on family lands in Sicily, and he himself became a Benedictine monk. While on a mission to Britain in 590, he was recalled back to Rome to become pope, much against his will. He sent Augustine, who later became the first archbishop of Canterbury, to Britain to evangelize that land. He was also a great liturgical reformer, revising and shaping the Mass as well as simplifying and codifying plainsong, later named for him Gregorian chant, one of four "local dialects" of Western church music, the other three being Milanese, Gallican, and Mozarabic. Through his influence and that of his missionaries, this music was spread far and wide, and it became the standard music throughout the entire Western churches.

AUTHOR (attr.): 482 Father, We Praise You

GRESENS, WALTER FREDERICK (1937–) was born September 9, 1937, in Chicago, Illinois. He attended Concordia College, River Forest, Illinois, and was graduated in June 1959; he has done graduate work at the University of Wisconsin and Andrews University in Berrien Springs, Michigan. His first call was to Emmaus Lutheran Church, Milwaukee, Wisconsin, where he served as teacher and music director to June 1969. He then served in the same capacity at Trinity Lutheran Church, St. Joseph, Michigan. In 1978 he accepted a call to St. John Lutheran Church, Rochester, Michigan, where he presently serves as minister of music. He has served as chairman of the Worship Committee of the Michigan District and has conducted workshops for organists in that district. His choral compositions have been published by Augsburg-Fortress and Concordia Publishing House.

ARRANGER: 111 A Lamb Alone Bears Willingly
379 "Come, Follow Me," said Christ, the Lord

GRIEG, EDVARD HAGERUP (1843–1907), was born in Bergen, Norway, June 15, 1843, son of the British consul at Bergen. At the age of 15, on the advice of Ole Bull (1810–80), great Norwegian violinist and composer, Edvard was sent to the Leipzig Conservatory, where he studied under such notables as Moscheles, Hauptmann, and Reinecke. In 1863 he went to Copenhagen, the cultural center of Norwegian as well as Danish life, where he met Hans Christian Anderson, whose poems he set to music in his *Melodies of the Heart*. Introduced to Norwegian folk music by Ole Bull in 1864, he devoted his talents toward Norwegian national music and gave a successful concert of such music in 1866, which catapulted him to fame and his career. Appointed conductor of the Harmonic Society, he was blessed with students, and the following year he established the Norwegian Academy of Music. Franz Liszt praised his Piano Concerto in A Minor; acquaintance with Lindeman's (*LW* 96, 291) *Fjeldmelodier* served as the basis for 25 piano pieces. The founding in 1871 of the Christiania Musical Society for the promotion of orchestral music was due in part to his help; 1876 saw the first performance of his incidental music for Henrik Ibsen's *Peer Gynt*. His appointment as conductor of the Bergen Harmonic Society, a position he held from 1880–82, constituted his last such public service. From then on his time was spent composing new and revising former works, and embarking on extended concert tours that took him to Denmark, Holland, Germany, France, England, Poland, and Czechoslovakia. He died suddenly September 4, 1907, while boarding a steamer that was to take him to London for some concert engagements.

Grieg created a new national art. He did for Norway what Chopin had done for Poland, Liszt for Hungary, and Dvorak for Bohemia.

ARRANGER: 192 DEN STORE HVIDE FLOK

GRIGG, JOSEPH (c. 1722–68), the son of poor parents, first earned his living as a mechanic until he was 25 years old, when he entered religious work. In 1743 he became an assistant minister to Pastor Thomas Bures of the Presbyterian Church, Silver Streak, London. Upon the death of Bures in 1747, Grigg married a woman of some wealth and resided at St. Albans, where he devoted himself to literary work. He died at Walthamslow, Essex, October 29, 1768.

The author of 40-some hymns, he is today remembered especially for "Behold a stranger at the door" (*TLH* 650) and the one listed below.

AUTHOR: 393 Jesus! Oh, How Could It Be True

GRINDAL, GRACIA (1943–), was born May 4, 1943, at Powers Lake, North Dakota. In 1955 the family moved from North Dakota to Salem, Oregon, where Gracia attended high school; she went on to major in English and history at Augsburg College, Minneapolis, graduating in 1965.

Grindal spent a year in Oslo, Norway, before returning to the United States to study at the University of Arkansas, Fayetteville. She received the Master of Fine Arts degree in 1969, spending the summer as an editorial assistant at Augsburg Publishing House, Minneapolis. In 1968 she joined the English faculty at Luther College, Decorah, Iowa, where she taught for 16 years. Since 1984 Grindal has been affiliated with Luther-Northwestern Theological Seminary, St. Paul, Minnesota, from which she earned a Master of Arts degree in 1983. Here she is presently associate professor of pastoral theology and ministry.

Her publications include *Pulpit Rock* (1976), *Sketches Against the Dark* (1981), and *Singing the Story* (1982, 1983); in addition she has contributed articles and poems to such periodicals as the *Christian Century, The Cresset, College English*, and *Dialog*. She was a member of the Hymn Text Committee of the Inter-Lutheran Commission on Worship from 1973–78 and holds membership in the Hymn Society of America. She is currently working on an opera libretto and a movie script.

TRANSLATOR: 67 Lo, How a Rose Is Growing
192 Behold a Host Arrayed in White
481 O Splendor of the Father's Light
487 O Trinity, O Blessed Light

GRÜBER, FRANZ XAVIER (1787–1863), was born at Unterweizberg near Hochburg, Austria, November 25, 1787, the third son of a poor weaver. Having studied violin in his youth and organ with Georg Hartdobler, organist at Burghausen, at the age of 18 he was sufficiently proficient to accompany choral services from a figured bass. He taught at the secondary school in Arnsdorf from 1807–29, serving also as organist at St. Nikolaus in Orberndorf from 1816–29. Thereafter he taught at Berndorf until 1833, when he became director of music at Hallein, near Salzburg. He died June 7, 1863.

All his children studied music, and his eldest son, Felix, a teacher in the principal school in Hallein, was also a composer. His grandson Franz became kapellmeister at Salzburg cathedral.

Although Franz Gruber wrote over 90 compositions, he is today remembered only for the tune to "Silent Night."

COMPOSER: 68 STILLE NACHT

GRUNDTVIG, NIKOLAI FREDERICK SEVERIN (1783–1872), was born September 8, 1783, the son of a Lutheran pastor at Udby, Denmark. At the age of nine he was sent to Pastor L. Feld of Thyregod, a country parish in Jyland, to be educated. Having passed the *examen artium* after six years, he entered the University of Copenhagen, where he came under the influence of Rationalism, graduating in 1803 "without spirit and without faith." He spent the next three years tutoring for a wealthy family. Later in one of Copenhagen's schools, he taught history, which gradually led to his becoming convinced of the truth of Christianity. His father's illness resulted in his being invited to assist him. Grundtvig's trial sermon for ordination, however, in which he attacked the spirit of Rationalism among the Danish clergy, delayed his ordination for a year. Ordained in 1811, he became assistant to his father. In 1821 King Frederick VI appointed him pastor at Presto, and the following year he became assistant pastor of Our Savior's Church, Kristianhavn. As a result of a libel suit for charging Professor H. N. Clausen with false doctrine, Grundtvig was forced to resign his office in 1826. During the next three years he made several trips to England to study Old Anglo-Saxon manuscripts, and for 10 years he was without a parish. In 1839 he was fully reinstated and appointed pastor in Vartov. Soon gaining recognition as an eloquent and forceful preacher, he drew large numbers of people to attend his services. His interest in raising the educational standards led him to establish folk schools in Rödding and other cities. These proved so popular, they were copied in Sweden, Norway, and Finland, earning for him the title "the father of the public school in Scandinavia." His greatness in church and state is attested by the fact that when Denmark became a monarchy in 1848, Grundtvig served as a member of the constitutional assembly. Moreover, when his golden jubilee as a pastor was celebrated, representatives came from all departments of Denmark's church and state as well as from other Scandinavian countries, at which time he was also given the title of bishop. He died September 2, 1872, having delivered his final sermon on the day before his death.

Grundtvig is undoubtedly the most important Scandinavian hymn writer of the 19th century, ranking with Brorson (*LW* 192, 391) and Kingo (*LW* 100, et al.). He published *Kraedlinger* (1815), *Songs for the Danish Church* (1837), and *Festsalmer* (1850). After his death his hymns and poems were published in five volumes entitled *Hymns and Spiritual Songs*. His hymns, of which "Built on the rock" is perhaps the most popular, are characterized by a strong emphasis on the Word of God and the Holy Spirit and an uncompromising forthrightness in doctrine.

AUTHOR: 291 Built on the Rock
333 God's Word Is Our Great Heritage

GRYPHIUS (GREIFF), ANDREAS (1616–1664), was born October 2, 1616, at Gross-Glogau in Silesia, the son of a Lutheran archdeacon. Educated in Fraustadt (1631–34) and thereafter at the *Gymnasium* in Danzig (1634–36), he became a tutor in the house of Baron Georg von Schönborn for a time. It was through the baron's influence that he was crowned with a laurel wreath as one of the imperial poets. When the Counter-Reformation forced him to flee to Holland, he entered Leyden University in 1639. Here he was given opportunity to lecture on dramatic poetry and permitted the publication of his various epigrams and sonnets. News of the death of a beloved brother and sister brought on a period of ill health, a time in which he wrote some of his finest, soul-stirring hymns. After regaining his health he traveled through France, Italy, Holland, and Germany, broadening his knowledge of language as well as enjoying the plaudits as a poet and the reputation of being the creator of German tragedy. Finally settling in Fraustadt in 1647, he married the daughter of a respected merchant in 1649. After the Peace of Westphalia in 1648, Silesia breathed with new life, and in 1650 Gryphius was appointed trustee of the principality of Glogau, an office that he faithfully and zealously discharged until his death of a paralytic stroke July 16, 1664.

A man of sterling character and genuineness, as a poet Gryphius certainly ranks with Martin Opitz (*LW* 85) and Johann Heermann (*LW* 95, et al.) among the best of the Silesian circle.

AUTHOR: 337 Preserve Your Word, O Savior

GURNEY (BLOMFIELD), DOROTHY FRANCES (1858–1932), was born in London, October 4, 1858, the daughter of the Reverend Frederick George Blomfield and granddaughter of Bishop Blomfield of Chester and London. In 1897 she married Gerald Gurney, the eldest son of Archer Gurney, rector and hymn writer of some merit. At first an actor by profession, Gerald Gurney was later ordained by the Church of England. In 1919, however, Dorothy and her husband were received into the Roman Church at Farnborough Abbey. The author of three volumes of verse, she is perhaps best known today for the hymn listed below. She died June 15, 1932.

AUTHOR: 253 O Perfect Love

HAMILTON, JAMES (1819–96), was born April 18, 1819, at Glendollar, Scotland, and educated at Corpus Christi College, Cambridge. Ordained in 1845, he became rector of St. Barnabas', Bristol, in 1866, and vicar of Doulting, Somerset, in 1867.

AUTHOR: 181 Across the Sky the Shades of Night

HAMMERSCHMIDT, ANDREAS (c. 1611–75), was born at Brüx in Bohemia, about 1611, the son of a saddler. Bohemia's return to Roman Catholicism during the Thirty Years' War (1618–48) prompted the family to move to Freiberg, Saxony. From July 1633–34 he was organist in the service of Count Rudolf von Bünau at the castle at Wiesenstein, Saxony, where Stephen Otto was cantor. In 1634 he became organist of St. Peter's Lutheran Church in Freiberg, succeeding Christoph Schreiber, and in 1639 organist of St. John's Church in Zittau, again as successor to Schreiber, a position of considerable importance that he held until his death October 29, 1675.

St. John's contained three organs opposite each other, thus providing ideal possibilities for the concerted style of music-making. His position required that he compose and perform vocal music to organ accompaniment. He directed the soloists from the school choir and the instrumental ensemble of the town musicians. The liturgical choral music was left to the cantor. Besides enjoying a large number of music pupils, Andreas was often called upon as an organ expert. All these activities enabled him to live a rather affluent life. He was undoubtedly one of the most distinguished composers of church music in the 17th century, and his contribution to choir and congregational music is most noteworthy. Representative of his work are the various parts of his *Musicalische Andachten* (1639ff.), *Fest-, Buss- und Danklieder* (1658), and *Kirchen- und Tafel-Musik* (1662). A friend of Christian Keimann (*LW* 40), rector of and teacher at the Zittau *Gymnasium*, Hammerschmidt provided musical settings to many of Keimann's hymns.

COMPOSER: 40 FREUET EUCH, IHR CHRISTEN

HANDEL, GEORG FRIEDRICH (1685–1759), was born at Halle February 23, 1685, the son of a barber-surgeon to Duke Augustus of Saxony, who preferred that Georg become a lawyer. The Duke of Saxe-Weissenfels, however, impressed with hearing him play the chapel organ, arranged that he study with Fredrich W. Zachau, organist at the *Liebfrauenkirche,* Halle. After three years of concentrated music studies, Handel spent a year in Berlin, and thereafter, in 1697, he became organist at the cathedral church in Halle. From 1702–03 he studied law at the University of Halle, but left there to go to Hamburg, where he played violin in the opera orchestra and began his career as a composer of opera. His first opera *Almira* was produced in 1705. The next four years saw him in Italy, where he met Arcangelo Corelli (1653–1713), composer and violinist, and the two Scarlatti brothers—Alessandro (1660–1725) and Francesco (1666–1741)—both eminent composers. It was in Italy that Handel experienced numerous triumphs. In 1710 he became music director to the Elector of Hanover. A trip to England in 1710 so fascinated him that in 1713 he returned to it and made it his home, becoming naturalized as a British subject in 1726. When the Elector of Hanover became George I of Great Britain and Ireland, any hard feelings he might have had over Handel's previously leaving him were evidently dispelled, for he doubled Handel's salary. For 30 years Handel concentrated almost wholly on composing operas—the vogue at that time—46 in all. During one interval he was music director to the Duke of Chandos at Cannons, nine miles from London. There he composed the Chandos Te Deums and anthems for the Duke's private chapel. It was only when opera waned and financial woes beset him that Handel turned to writing oratorios, 32 in all, which, in exhibiting his genius for drama and grandeur, set the pattern for such compositions for a century or more. After the *Messiah,* composed in 24 days, was so enthusiastically received when presented for the first time in Dublin in 1741, Handel lived a life of popular favor. In 1737 he suffered a paralytic stroke, and by 1753 he was completely blind. Despite this he continued to play the harpsichord and organ and direct his oratorios. He died April 14, 1759, in London and was buried in Westminster Abbey.

Handel's productiveness seemed to know no limits. In addition to his operas and oratorios, he composed instrumental, organ, and harpsichord music, choral and solo vocal music, and even three hymn tunes set to Charles Wesley's texts (see John Wilson, "Handel and the hymn tune," *The Hymn* [October 1985]: 18–23). The most complete edition of his works, numbering 93 volumes, is that edited by Friedrich Chrysander for the Händel Gesellschaft, namely, *G. F. Händels Werke* (Leipzig und Bergedorf bei Hamburg, 1858–1902).

COMPOSER: 53 ANTIOCH

HANSEN, FRED C. M. (1888–1965), was born June 25, 1888, in Velje, Denmark. Two years later he came to United States with his parents. After graduating from Dana

College in 1910 and Trinity Seminary in 1914, both located in Blair, Nebraska, he served a number of congregations: in Davenport and Audubun, Iowa; Milwaukee; Council Bluffs; and Chicago. As a leading pastor in the United Evangelical Lutheran Church—one of two American Lutheran church bodies of Danish origin—he was president of the Iowa district from 1939–43 and of the Illinois district from 1944–48. In 1958 he retired to Blair, Nebraska, where he died April 4, 1965.

While pastor in Audubon, Iowa, he and Pastor P. E. Jensen helped establish the Lutheran Bible Camp at Lake Okoboji, Iowa, a place still popular today for conferences and retreats. Besides editing several monthly church papers, he served on the various hymnal committees of his church, the last as the member of a commission that produced the *Service Book and Hymnal* (1958), in all instances contributing original hymns as well as translations.

TRANSLATOR: 291 Built on the Rock

HARBAUGH, HENRY (1817–67), was born October 24, 1817, of Swiss parents, in Franklin County, Pennsylvania. Educated at Marshall College, Mercersberg, and ordained by the Reformed Church in 1843, he served successively as pastor at Lewisberg, Lancaster, and Lebanon, Pennsylvania. In 1864 he became professor of theology at the Mercersberg Seminary, serving as editor of the *Guardian*, *The Mercersberg Review*, and the *Reformed Church Messenger*. As a leader of the liturgical movement within the Reformed Church, he published *Hymns and Chants for Sunday Schools* (Lebanon, 1861). He died December 27, 1867.

AUTHOR: 499 Christ, by Heavenly Hosts Adored

HARDING, JAMES PROCKTOR (1850–1911), was born May 19, 1850, at Clerkenwell, London. While working many years in the English civil service, as an amateur musician he also served for 35 years as organist and choirmaster at St. Andrew's Church, Thornhill Square, Islington, in London. Through the Gifford Hall Mission in Islington he and his brother spent much time and money in behalf of the physical and spiritual well-being of the poor. He composed anthems, services, and part songs, many of which were for the children's festivals at the mission.

COMPOSER: 86 MORNING STAR

HARKNESS, GEORGIA ELMA (1891–1974), was born April 21, 1891, at Harkness, New York. After receiving the Bachelor of Arts degree from Cornell University in 1912, she continued studies at Boston University, earning the Master of Arts and Master of Religious Education degrees in 1920 and the Doctor of Philosophy degree in 1923. Following her ordination by the Methodist Church in 1926, she pursued further studies at Harvard, Yale, and Union Theological Seminary. From 1922–27 she was professor of philosophy at Elmira College in New York; thereafter for two years at Mount Holyoke College. From 1939–50 she was professor of applied theology at Garrett School of Theology, Evanston, Illinois, as such the first woman in the country to hold a full professorship at a theological seminary. She next was professor of applied theology at Pacific School of Religion, Berkeley, California, from 1950–61, during this time spending a year teaching at Union Theological Seminary, Manila, and also some time teaching at the International Christian University, Mitaka, Japan.

Harkness was chosen church-woman of the year in 1958 and was honored with the Doctor of Letters degree from Elmira College in 1962. As a writer, teacher, and lecturer, active on various committees and in conferences, she exercised considerable influence in the Methodist Church. Her writings include 37 books, among them *Prayer and the Common Life* (1947); *The Modern Rival of Christian Faith* (1952); *Christian Ethics* (1957); *The Providence of God* (1960); *The Ministry of Reconciliation* (1971); and *Women in Church and Society* (1972).

She died August 30, 1974, at Claremont, California.

AUTHOR: 377 Hope of the World

HARWOOD, BASIL (1859–1949), born April 11, 1859, in Woodhouse, Olveston, Gloucestershire, England, was educated at Charterhouse, Trinity College, Oxford, earning the Bachelor of Music degree in 1880; Bachelor of Arts degree in 1881; Master of Arts degree in 1884; and Doctor of Music degree in 1896. Before accepting the post of organist at St. Barnabas, Pimlico, in 1883, he spent a period of study under Carl Reinecke and Salomon Jadassohn at the Leipzig conservatory. Thereafter he became organist at Ely Cathedral (1887-92) and Christ Church Cathedral, Oxford (1892–1909). While here he was also *Choragus* (leader of a chorus) of the university, precentor of Keble College, and first conductor of the Oxford Orchestral Association and of the Oxford Bach Choir. He was also music editor of the *Oxford Hymn Book* (1908).

After retiring to Woodhouse in 1909, he busied himself by composing a considerable amount of church music—anthems, church services, organ pieces, and two sonatas. His hymn tunes—actually more like anthems for choir than tunes for congregations—of which he composed some 90, appeared in some English hymnals, but today appear to enjoy little currency (see *LBW* 77).

Harwood died at Kensington, London, April 3, 1949.

ARRANGER: 74 DEUS TOURUM MILITUM

HASSLER, HANS LEO (1562–1612), was born in Nürnberg, Germany, and baptized August 17, 1562 (some sources indicate 1564 as his birth year). He studied music first with his father, Isaak Hassler, a gem worker and well-known musician, and later (1584) in Venice with Andrea Gabrieli (c. 1520–1586). Here Hassler became friends with

Gabrieli's nephew, composer Giovanni Gabrieli (c. 1557–1612), and picked up knowledge of the polychoral style so popular among Venetian composers.

In 1585, after a year and a half in Venice, Hassler was employed by Octavian Fugger, prince and art patron of Augsburg, as organist. He was appointed musical director in 1600, the year Octavian died, but the following year he chose to become organist at the *Frauenkirche* (later, chief music director) in his native Nürnberg. Married in 1604, he went to Ulm; from there he went on to serve Emperor Rudolph at Prague.

Hassler's final position was that of organist to Christian II, Elector of Saxony, at Dresden, where he moved in 1608. He was plagued with tuberculosis in his latter years, and died while accompanying the elector to the imperial election at Frankfurt, June 8, 1612.

Using the compositional methods he learned in Italy, Hassler helped found the German school of choral music. His works include some organ pieces as well as numerous secular and sacred choral works. The best-known of his secular works, *Lustgarten neuer Deutscher Gesäng* (1601), wherein the tune HERZLICH TUT MICH VERLANGEN was first published, contained compositions for instrumental ensemble as well as vocal music. Himself a Lutheran, Hassler wrote much of his sacred music for the Roman Church, including a volume of masses (1599) and two collections of motets, *Cantiones sacrae* (1591) and *Sacri concentus* (1601). For the Lutheran Church, his *Psalmen und christliche Gesänge* (1607) included 52 motet-form settings of chorale melodies; other, simpler, chorale tunes were collected in *Kirchengesänge*, *Psalmen und geistliche Lieder* (1608).

COMPOSER: 113, 427 HERZLICH TUT MICH VERLANGEN

HASTINGS, THOMAS (1784–1872), was born at Washington, Connecticut, October 15, 1784. His father, a physician and farmer, moved the family to the frontier at Clinton, New York, when Thomas was 12 years old. A nearsighted albino, Hastings taught himself music while attending a country school in Clinton, and at 18 was directing the village choir. In 1823 he went to Utica where, in addition to directing the Oneida County choir, he edited and published a weekly religious journal, *The Western Recorder*.

Hastings was dedicated to the upgrading of American music, particularly hymns. Believing the European style of composition and notation superior, he set about reforming church music on the basis of "scientific" principles. In 1832 a group of churches in New York City asked him to come to help improve their psalmody; there he remained, doing much to establish the city's prominence in music publishing, until his death on May 15, 1872.

Composer of about 1,000 hymn tunes, Hastings also wrote texts to fit some of his tunes. He collaborated with Lowell Mason (*LW* 53, et al.) in the production of *Spiritual Songs for Social Worship* (1832). In addition he compiled some 50 other collections from the *Utica Collection* (later combined with Solomon Warriner's *Springfield Collection* and retitled *Musica Sacra*, 1816) to *Church Melodies* (1858). With Lowell

Mason (*LW* 115, et al.) and William Bradbury (*LW* 359) he is considered one of the more influential of 19th-century American church musicians. Despite the seriousness with which he pursued his ideals, his tunes lack the character and his harmonizations exhibit less skill than those of Lowell Mason.

AUTHOR: 349 Delay Not, Delay Not, O Sinner, Draw Near
COMPOSER: 361 TOPLADY

HATTON, JOHN (c. 1710–1793), sometimes known as John of Warrington, was born at Warrington, England. He lived for a time in St. Helen's, in the township of Windle, Lancashire, on a street he gave to the single tune by which his name is known. His funeral took place in the Presbyterian Chapel, St. Helen's, December 13, 1793.

COMPOSER: 264, 312 DUKE STREET

HAUSMANN, JULIE von (1825 or 26–1901), was born into a family of German background in the city of Riga, Latvia, a Baltic province. Shortly after her birth the family moved to Mitau, where her father taught in the *Gymnasium*. Julie was one of seven sisters. Ill health prompted her to give up the idea of a career, and, after the death of her mother in 1859, she devoted herself to the care of her blind father, who had been town councillor. In 1861, the family moved back to Riga, where her father died. After his death Julie often went to Germany, and from 1866–70 she lived in Biarritz, in southern France, with an older sister who there was organist in the English church. After 1870 both sisters resided with two other sisters in St. Petersburg, Russia, where the oldest sister Elizabeth was head of the girls' school of St. Anne's Church, to which was connected a pension house. There the four sisters lived and worked happily together for a number of years. During that time Julie was not only busily engaged in writing poetry, but also in performing works of charity. After the death of her youngest sister in 1896, and her oldest sister in 1898, Julie and another sister moved to a seaside resort at Wössö, Estonia, where Julie died August 15, 1901.

The single work that Julie herself published was a devotional book entitled *Hausbrot*. It was while caring for her father at Riga, that, through her friend Olga von Karp, some of Julie's poetry came to the attention of Gustav Knak, a mission-minded and poetically gifted Lutheran pastor in Berlin. Pleased with what he saw, he requested that he see the entire collection of her work. Julie consented to their publication, provided that it be published without her name for the benefit of a hospital and orphanage in Hong Kong. The collection was thus published with the title *Maiblumen, Lieder einer Stillen im Lande, dargereicht von G. Knak*. The first volume, published in 1862, included "So nimm denn meine Hände." Three more volumes followed, the last published by Knak's son.

AUTHOR: 512 Lord, Take My Hand and Lead Me

HAVERGAL, FRANCES RIDLEY (1836–79), was born December 14, 1836 at Astley, Worcestershire, England. Her father, William Henry Havergal, vicar of Astley, nicknamed her "Little Quicksilver" because of her precocious intelligence. When she was seven years old she wrote verses which were published in the religious periodical *Good Words*. Born into a Calvinist household, she worried in her early years about being one of the "elect," but at age 14 she went through the requisite conversion. Never very healthy, Havergal was privately tutored in England and in Düsseldorf, Germany. She learned to speak French and German as well as Latin, Greek, and Hebrew, and was extremely talented in music, and had committed the entire New Testament, Psalms, Isaiah and the minor prophets to memory. A devoted evangelist, she felt her mission was to "sing for Jesus" and to draw others closer to him.

Her bright, vivacious personality attracted many admirers. It has been suggested that it was her character rather than the intrinsic value of her poetry which caused her work to be so widely accepted. Many of her hymns were originally published in leaflets which she periodically collected into volumes, such as *Ministry of Song* (1869), *Under the Surface* (1874), and *Loyal Responses* (1878).

Havergal was very active with missionary and aid societies. She taught Sunday school, gave Bible readings in the servants' hall, and corresponded with many people. In 1878 she traveled with her sister to South Wales, where she came down with a cold that developed into pneumonia. She died June 3, 1879, and was buried next to her father in the Astley churchyard.

Following her death her sister collected her works into one volume, and they appeared in *Poetical Works* (1884).

AUTHOR:	282	O Savior, Precious Savior
	404	Take My Life, O Lord, Renew
	408	I Am Trusting You, Lord Jesus
	503	Now the Light Has Gone Away

HAVERGAL, WILLIAM HENRY (1793–1870), was born January 18, 1793, at High Wycombe, Buckinghamshire. Educated at St. Edmund's Hall, Oxford, where he received the Bachelor of Arts degree in 1815 and the Master's in 1819, he was ordained a deacon in 1816 and priest the following year. After holding two curacies in Gloucestershire, he was given the rectory of Astley, Worcestershire, in 1829. As a result of a serious carriage accident he was forced to resign his calling soon afterwards, affording him opportunity to pursue his music studies. He reissued Ravenscroft's *Whole Booke of Psalms* (1844) and compiled his best known work, *Old Church Psalmody* (1847), works that contributed to purify metrical psalmody. In 1842 he was able to assume the rectorship of St. Nicholas, Worcester, and in 1845 he received an honorary canonry in the cathedral there. Impaired health caused him in 1860 to accept the quiet living of Shareshill near Wolverhampton; in 1867 he resigned to retire at Leamington, where he died April 19, 1870. In striving to improve the church's music in his day, he composed a goodly number of hymn tunes, arranged some ancient tunes, published *A History of the Old Hundredth Psalm Tune, with Specimens* (1854); A *Hundred Psalm and Hymn Tunes* (1859), of his own compositions; and *Fireside Music*, a collection of songs, rounds, and carols.

COMPOSER: 392 EVAN
404 PATMOS

HAWEIS, THOMAS (1734–1820), was born at Redruth, Cornwall, England, January 1, 1734. Of aristocratic ancestry, he easily joined the ranks of hymnwriters associated with Selina Shirley, Countess of Huntingdon.

Educated at Truro Grammar School, Haweis was bound as an apprentice to a surgeon and pharmacist, but at about age 14 he came under the influence of Samuel Walker, curate of St. Mary's Church in Truro. Walker recognized his talent for speaking and nurtured Haweis' spiritual nature to the point that Haweis turned from medicine to ministry.

He enrolled in Christ Church College and then Magdalen College, Oxford, but received no degree. He was ordained in 1757 and appointed curate of St. Mary Magdalen's Church, Oxford, and chaplain to the Earl of Peterborough; but in spite of his success and popularity, his Methodist leanings caused his removal from the curacy after a few years.

Haweis then became an assistant to Martin Madan at Locke Hospital in London. From 1764 to his death in 1820 he was rector of All Saints, Aldwinkle, Northamptonshire. In 1768 he also became chaplain to the Countess of Huntingdon's chapel at Bath and manager of the college she founded in Wales.

Although he received no degree at Oxford, he graduated with the Bachelor of Laws degree from Cambridge in 1772, when he became a fellow of Christ's College; a university in Scotland added the Doctor of Medicine degree to his titles.

In 1792 Haweis published *Carmina Christo—or Hymns to the Saviour. Designed for the use and comfort of those who worship the Lamb that was slain,* containing 141 original hymns to which he added 115 more in 1808. *Carmina Christo* was a companion volume to Lady Huntingdon's *Select Collection of Hymns*, which she published with her cousin, Walter Shirley, for use in her private chapel. As a friend of John Newton, he edited Newton's autobiography. Haweis also wrote a church history, a translation of the New Testament and a biblical commentary.

In 1795 Haweis contributed to the founding of the London Missionary Society. Later, when advancing age brought failing health, he retired to Bath, where he died February 11, 1820.

COMPOSER (attr.): 29 CHESTERFIELD

HAYDN, FRANZ JOSEF (1732–1809), was born March 31, 1732, at Rohrau, near the Hungarian border in Eastern Austria, the son of a wheelright. He received his early music training from his uncle and in the Roman Catholic choir school of St. Stephen's,

Vienna. He taught himself counterpoint and received a few lessons in composition from Nicola Porpora (1686–1768), an Italian composer. After two years of service at the chapel of Count von Morzin, a Bohemian nobleman, in 1861 he entered the service of Prince Paul Anton Esterhazy, head of a wealthy and powerful Hungarian noble family. Enjoying this position most of his life, he had the financial security and musical resources to compose and perform his vast output of timeless music: for court orchestra, theatres, chamber groups, and the like. He made two visits to England, where he received a Doctor of Music degree from Oxford, and spent two seasons (1791–92; 1794–95) conducting concerts and composing new works. His enormous output includes 104 symphonies, 83 string quartets, 52 piano sonatas, 18 operas, four oratorios, 14 masses, in addition to other chamber music, songs, arias, cantatas, and liturgical pieces. His Christian piety prompted him to conclude his music manuscripts with *Laus Deo* or *Soli Deo Gloria*. Since he wrote no hymn tunes as such, those that exist are adapted from larger works.

COMPOSER: 294 AUSTRIA

HAYN, HENRIETTA LUISE von (1724–82), was born at Idstein, Nassau, May 22, 1724, the daughter of a ducal chief ranger. Deeply pious as a young child, after her confirmation, however, this piety waned in her being caught up in worldly matters. A chance exposure to Count Nicolaus von Zinzendorf's (*LW* 362, 386) Berlin lectures, as well as word about the activities of the United Brethren, brought her back to her Christian faith. Thus at the age of 20 she was received into the Moravian community at Herrnhag, where she became teacher of the girls' school. Later she transferred to the community at Grosshennersdorf, and thereafter, in 1751, to Herrnhut. From 1766 until her death she cared for the invalid sisters of the community.

A gifted poet, her verses reflect her deep love for Christ. Of her 40-some hymns or portions thereof, 28 appeared in the *Brüder Gesangbuch* (1778). She died August 27, 1782.

AUTHOR: 517 I Am Jesus' Little Lamb

HEATON, CHARLES HUDDLESTON (1928–), was born in Centralia, Illinois, and received a Bachelor of Music degree in 1950 from DePaul University, Greencastle, Indiana. After earning the Master of Sacred Music degree at Union Theological Seminary, New York City, in 1952, he served in the United States Army for two years. Having earned the Doctor of Sacred Music degree from Union in 1957, he became minister of music at Second Presbyterian Church, St. Louis, until 1972, during which time he directed music at Temple Israel and lectured at Eden Theological Seminary. Since 1972 he has been organist and choir director at East Liberty Presbyterian Church, Pittsburgh, Pennsylvania.

Heaton edited the *Hymnbook for Christian Worship* (1970); he published *How to Build a Church Choir* (1958) and *A Guide to Worship Services of Sacred Music* (1962). He has been active both as a fellow of the American Guild of Organists and as a member of the Hymn Society of America. Married to Jane Pugh of Centralia, Illinois, he is the father of three children.

ARRANGER: 411 How Firm a Foundation

HEBER, REGINALD (1783–1826), the son of an Anglican clergyman, was born at Malpas, Cheshire, on April 21, 1783. He entered Brasenose College, Oxford, at the age of 17, immediately excelling academically. In his first year he won the chancellor's prize for the best Latin poem with "Carmen Seculare." His poem "Palestine" took the Newdigate prize and established him as a first-rank poet; upon reading it, Sir Walter Scott made only one suggestion, that the temple tools be mentioned. Heber then added the lines:

> No hammer fell, no pond'rous axes rung;
> Like some tall palm, the mystic fabric sprung.
> Majestic silence!

"Palestine" is the only prize verse to have earned a permanent place in English literature.

Ordained in 1807, Heber accepted from his elder half-brother Richard the living of Hodnet, where his father had been rector until his death two years earlier. Richard had amassed a library of some 147,000 books, which enhanced his brother's education to a great extent. Reginald Heber declined Hodnet's existing vicarage, instead building for himself a large estate, where his position was that of both pastor and squire. He stayed in Hodnet 16 years, writing most of his hymns during that time.

Feeling that the lack of hymns in the Church of England was hurting its ministry, Heber cast about for a suitable supplement to Sternhold and Hopkins (see essay: Metrical Psalms, p. 825). After considering Cowper's *Olney Hymns*, he finally decided to compile a hymnal himself, leaning upon his friends Walter Scott, Southey, and Henry Milman (*LW* 105) to contribute. Heber envisioned hymns for all the festivals of the church year, with the following criteria: (1) the hymn must be part of the liturgy of the Church and must therefore adapt itself to the church calendar; (2) the hymn should come after the Nicene Creed and complement the message of the sermon; (3) it should be a literary masterpiece.

Of the literary giants invited to prepare hymns, only Milman came through. Heber's manuscript collection eventually contained 98 hymns, 12 by Milman, 29 by other writers, and 57 by Heber. He sought authorization for its publication from the bishop of London, but was denied it; the volume was published after Heber's death as *Hymns written and adapted to the Weekly Church Service of the Year* (1827), a work that not only popularized the use of hymns in the Anglican communion but also gave a new literary quality to its hymnody.

Bampton lecturer in 1815 and preacher at Lincoln's Inn in 1822, Heber seemed destined for honors in his church. His concern for the pastoral ministry extended into missionary work when, at the age of 40, he was called to become bishop of Calcutta. One of his dearest friends was in charge of choosing a successor to the late Bishop Middleton. He wrote, asking Heber's recommendation and hinting that Heber himself would be enthusiastically welcomed, were it not for great opportunities for Heber at home in England. After twice refusing the call, Heber accepted the third time, feeling it came from God.

Deeply troubled by the Hindu religion, Heber labored for three years in the established Church of India and among the unconverted. His was the honor of ordaining the first native Indian pastor. On a visit to Trichinopoly, where he confirmed 42 new members, Heber died of a stroke on April 3, 1826.

Some of his hymns were published between 1811 and 1816 in a series in the *Christian Observer*. The rest appeared in the aforementioned posthumous *Hymns*, edited by his widow.

AUTHOR:	86	Brightest and Best of the Stars of the Morning
	168	Holy, Holy, Holy
	304	The Son of God Goes Forth to War
	322	From Greenland's Icy Mountains
	492	God, Who Made the Earth and Heaven

HEERMANN, JOHANN (1585–1647), was born at Raudten near Wohlau, in Silesia, October 11, 1585, the fifth and only surviving child of a poor furrier. Afflicted with a severe childhood illness, his mother vowed that, if spared by the Lord, she would have him educated for the holy ministry. Heermann attended schools at Raudten, Wohlau, Fraustadt, and the St. Elizabeth *Gymnasium* at Breslau, as well as the *Gymnasium* at Brieg. While at Fraustadt he tutored the sons of Pastor Valerius Herberger, a task that afforded him opportunity for rich spiritual development in the Herberger household. At Brieg he became tutor to Baron Wenzel von Rothkirch's two young sons, whom, in 1609 he accompanied to the University of Strassburg. An eye infection, however, forced Heermann to return to Raudten the following year. On the recommendation of Baron Wenzel, in 1611 he was appointed deacon of Köben, a small town not far from Raudten, and within a year he was promoted to the pastorate. A throat infection finally ended his preaching in 1634. Four years later he retired to Lissa in Posen, where he died February 17, 1647.

Heermann suffered intensely during the Thirty Years' War (1618–48). Silesia, belonging to Roman Catholic Austria, was frequently subjected to extensive fighting and pillage. More than once Heermann lost all his personal effects; on several occasions he narrowly escaped death. In 1631 Silesia was struck by a severe pestilence in which some 500 people died in Köben alone. Despite his personal afflictions and tribulations and the terrible calamities of the Thirty Years' War, he served as a faithful and caring pastor, he continued to write hymns of trust and confidence in the Lord, about 400 in all, hymns that caused him to be acknowledged as the finest German hymn-writer between Luther and Gerhardt. As early as 1608 Rudolph II (1552–1612), emperor of the Holy Roman Empire, crowned him poet laureate in recognition of his singular talents. Heermann can well be considered as marking the transition from the objective hymns of the Reformation to the more subjective hymns of the period that followed.

AUTHOR:	95	Grant, Lord Jesus, that My Healing
	119	O Dearest Jesus, What Law Have You Broken
	314	O Christ, Our Light, O Radiance True
	371	O God, My Faithful God
	468	Feed Your Children, God Most Holy

HELD, HEINRICH (1620–59), was born July 21, 1620, the son of Valentin Held, Guhrau, Silesia. As a child his parents moved to Fraustadt, then a part of Poland, to escape persecution by Roman Catholics. It was during his attendance at the *Gymnasium* in Thorn that his poetic talents began to blossom. Pursuing the study of jurisprudence at Königsberg and Rostock, and after traveling to Holland, England, and France, he settled down in Fraustadt as a practicing lawyer. It was here that he received the poet laureate award. The vicissitudes of the Thirty Years' War prompted him to move to Altdamm, a suburb of Stettin, where, in 1657, he became city clerk and shortly thereafter treasurer and councillor. With the siege of Altdamm in 1659 Held became ill and was taken to Stettin. There he died on August 16, 1659.

Held ranks among the best of Silesian hymn writers. His only extant poetical work is his *Deutscher Gedichte Vortrab* (Frankfort-an-der-Oder, 1643).

AUTHOR:	33	Let the Earth Now Praise the Lord
	165	Come, Oh, Come, O Quickening Spirit

HELMBOLD, LUDWIG (1532–98), was born January 13, 1532, at Mühlhausen, Thuringia, the son of a woolen manufacturer. Educated at the universities of Leipzig and Erfurt, receiving the Bachelor of Arts degree in 1550, he thereafter served as headmaster of St. Mary's School in Mühlhausen. Returning to Erfurt for further study, he completed the Master of Arts degree in 1554 and remained there as lecturer until his appointment in 1561 as associate rector of the St. Augustin *Gymnasium* in Erfurt. The plague that broke out in 1563 took the lives of some 4,000 inhabitants of Erfurt, causing the university to be closed. When in 1565 it reopened, Helmbold was appointed dean of the philosophical faculty; the following year he was crowned poet laureate by Emperor Maximilian II. Here Helmbold remained until 1570, when, in his concern for upholding the Lutheran faith, he suffered hatred and personal criticism from various quarters which resulted in his resignation. Though now 39 years of age, he began the study of theology to prepare himself for the Lutheran ministry. In 1571 he became deacon and later pastor of St. Mary's Church in Mühlhausen, his hometown. In this quiet and peaceful situation he authored numerous Latin and German poems and hymns. In 1586, having been elected superintendent of Mühlhausen, he assumed the pastorate at St. Blasius' Church, faithfully serving there until his death April 8, 1598.

Helmbold's poetic works number some 400, appearing in such publications as *Geistliche Lieder* (Mühlhausen, 1575); *Crepundia Sacra oder Christliche Liedlein* (Mühlhausen, 1578), a small hymnal for schools; and *Neue Christliche Lieder* (Erfurt, 1595). His concern for Christian education led him to write a metrical version of the entire Augsburg Confession.

AUTHOR: 409 From God Can Nothing Move Me
473 You Parents, Hear What Jesus Taught
477 Lord, Help Us Ever to Retain

HEMY, HENRI FREDERICK (1818–88), was born November 12, 1818, at Newcastle-on-Tyne, the son of German parents. He served for many years as organist of St. Andrew's Roman Catholic Church in Newcastle and was also professor of music at Tynemouth as well as teacher of singing and piano at St. Cuthbert's College, Ushaw, Durham. His *Crown of Jesus Music* (1862), in four parts, containing Latin hymns, chants, masses, and service music—little of which was original with him—was widely used in Roman Catholic churches. His *Royal Modern Tutor for the Piano Forte* (1858) became popular with piano teachers and went through numerous editions. He died June 10, 1888, at Hartlepool.

TRANSLATOR: 55 Angels We Have Heard on High

HERMAN (HEERMANN), NIKOLAUS (c. 1480–1561), is known both as a poet and composer. Undoubtedly these talents reflect his environment, namely, Joachimsthal in Bohemia, just over the mountains from the border of Saxony. In the Reformation period this little mountain city not only thrived as a result of its mining industry, but it was also noteworthy for its adoption of the evangelical cause and its fostering of the arts, notably the rich hymnody of the Bohemian Brethren. Whether Herman was actually a native of this place is uncertain. About 1518 he became a teacher in the Latin school there; some time later he assumed the positions of cantor and organist in the local Lutheran church. In the latter capacity he established a close and helpful relationship with his pastor, Johann Mathesius, who as a student at Wittenberg University was frequently the table companion of Martin Luther. When Mathesius preached a noteworthy sermon, Herman often straightway embodied its leading thoughts in a hymn. The hymns of Herman, however, were not primarily written for corporate worship, but were intended for boys and girls in school, to nurture their faith, to give them an anchor in the storms of life, and to instill in them the "mind of Christ" (1 Cor. 2:16).

Plagued with a severe case of gout, Herman retired early, and it is in the last 14 years of his life that most of his hymns were written. Essentially they appeared in two collections: *Die Sontags Evangelia über das ganze Jahr, in Gesänge verfasset für die Kinder und christliche Hausväter* (1560) and *Die Historien von der Sintflut* (1562). These two collections contained 176 hymns. Included in the first was the previously composed (1554) Christmas hymn, "Let all together praise our God" (*LW* 44), and the great Easter hymn, based upon the Medieval antiphon, "That Easter day with joy was bright" (*LW* 147). What some consider the finest of his hymns, "When my last hour is close at hand" (*TLH* 594:1–4), appeared in the second collection. Herman's poetry is of the popular, childlike, picturesque type.

Herman was a musician of no meager talents. As a cantor he took pains to reintroduce plainsong; as an organist he was perceived as a master by the assembled congregation. He was of the strong opinion that as a church musician he was essentially a servant of the Word. His compositions leaned heavily upon earlier models of first rank, and his chorales reflect the character of the Wittenberg and Strassburg styles. They thus take their place among the best of the Reformation period.

Herman died in Joachimsthal on May 3, 1561.

AUTHOR:	44	Let All Together Praise Our God
	235	As Surely as I Live, God Said
COMPOSER:	44, 77	LOBT GOTT, IHR CHRISTEN
	147, 310	ERSCHIENEN IST DER HERRLICH TAG
	327, 479, 487	STEHT AUF, IHR LIEBEN KINDERLEIN

HERNAMAN, CLAUDIA FRANCES, *née* Iboston (1839–98), was born at Addlestone, Surrey, England, October 19, 1838. Married to J. W. D. Hernaman, Anglican clergyman and inspector of schools for the king, her interest in the religious education of children led her to prepare about 150 original hymns and translations of various Latin and German hymns especially adapted to children. These she published in her *Child's Book of Praise* (1873), *Christmas Carols for Children* (1884, 1885), and *The Crown of Life* (1886). She died October 10, 1898, in Brussels, Belgium.

AUTHOR:	16	Hosanna Now Through Advent
	92	O Lord, Throughout These Forty Days

HERRNSCHMIDT, JOHANN DANIEL (1675–1723), was born April 11, 1675, at Bopfingen, Württemberg, Germany, the son of a deacon who later became the town clergyman in that community. In the autumn of 1700, having earned his master's degree at the University of Altdorf, Herrnschmidt went to Halle where, under the influence of August Herman Francke (1663–1727) and other leaders of Pietism, he became one of the "awakened" university students. Two years later he was called away from Halle to serve as assistant to his father. In 1712 Prince Georg August called him to be superintendent, court preacher, and member of the consistory at Idstein. In that same year he earned the Doctor of Theology degree at Halle. After four years of faithful and prudent service, he was appointed professor of theology at Halle University, and the following year, 1716, subdirector of the Pädagogium and Orphanage where Francke was director. He died at Halle, February 5, 1723.

Herrnschmidt belongs to the more significant of the Halle circle of poets. His hymns, while not always examples of the best poetry, are steeped in Scripture and exceptional in godly sincerity. Of the 17 hymns that he wrote, disseminated and popularized by their inclusion in Freylinghausen's two hymnbooks (1704 and 1714), the one here listed is certainly a pearl.

AUTHOR: 445 Praise the Almighty

HERZBERGER, FREDERICK WILLIAM (1859–1930), was born October 23, 1859, in Baltimore, Maryland, the son of a Lutheran pastor. Following his graduation in 1882 from Concordia Seminary, St. Louis, he first served as a missionary in Arkansas, where he was instrumental in founding six congregations. After further service in Carson, Kansas, Chicago, and Hammond, Indiana, he became the first city missionary of the Missouri Synod in the city of St. Louis. His concern for and organizational ability resulted in the founding of the Society for Homeless Children, the Lutheran Altenheim, and the Lutheran Convalescent Home of St. Louis. Notable are also his endeavors in behalf of the Associated Lutheran Charities, the Wheatridge Sanitarium, and the Bethesda Home at Watertown, Wisconsin. He died at St. Louis on August 26, 1930.

Author of *The Family Altar*, Herzberger was also an able poet.

TRANSLATOR: 263 Send, O Lord, Your Holy Spirit

HEY, JOHANN WILHELM (1789–1854), was born March 27, 1789, at Leina, a village between Gotha and Reinhardsbrunn, Germany, where his father was a Lutheran pastor. After completing his studies at the *Gymnasium* in Gotha, where he became thoroughly grounded in the classics—English, Dutch, Spanish, Italian languages were eventually not foreign to him—he studied theology at the universities of Jena and Göttingen. In 1818 he became a Lutheran pastor at Töttelstadt; in 1827 court preacher at Gotha. His sound Gospel sermons in a time when Rationalism was holding sway created a situation that led to his leaving Gotha after five years to become superintendent of Ichtershausen, a position that gave him oversight over all Lutheran churches and ministers in that ecclesiastical district. In this capacity he served as a true and sincere servant of Christ without denying the truth of the gospel. He died May 19, 1854. Reflecting his exemplary ministry, Deacon Tümpel from Gotha preached the funeral sermon based on

Hebrews 13:7: "Remember your leaders, who spoke the word of God to you. Consider the outcome of their way of life and imitate their faith."

Hey was a talented poet, whose efforts were largely devoted to the children's world. He is especially remembered for his two collections of poems for children entitled *Fabeln für Kinder* (1833, 1837), to which was added a "Serious Appendix"containing religious and moral songs.

AUTHOR: 66 Every Year the Christ Child

HEYDER, FRIEDRICH CHRISTIAN (1677–1754). Little is known of him other than that he was born in Merseburg, Germany, in 1677. In 1699 he became a deacon, and from 1706–41 he served as a pastor in Zorbig, near Halle, where he died in 1754.

AUTHOR: 242 I Come, O Savior, to Your Table

HILLERT, RICHARD WALTER (1923–), was professor of music from 1959–90 at Concordia College (now Concordia University), River Forest, Illinois. At his retirement he was given the title Distinguished Professor Emeritus. Born March 14, 1923, in Granton, Wisconsin, he was educated in local parochial and public schools and received the Bachelor of Science in Education degree from Concordia River Forest in 1951. He also holds Master of Music (1955) and Doctor of Music (1968) degrees from Northwestern University, Evanston, Illinois. He studied composition with Matthew Nathaniel Lundquist, Anthony Donato, and with the Italian composer, Goffredo Petrassi at the Berkshire School of Music, Tanglewood, Massachusetts. He was teacher and director of music at Bethlehem Lutheran Church, St. Louis, from 1951–53, and at Trinity Lutheran Church, Wausau, Wisconsin, from 1953–59. Married to Gloria Bonnin, he is the father of three children.

The catalog of his compositions comprises works in many forms, including songs, piano pieces, large organ works, chamber, orchestral, cantatas, concertatos, and choral pieces both unaccompanied and with various instrumental ensembles. Notable among his contributions is the liturgical music for congregation which appeared first in the *Worship Supplement* (1969) to *The Lutheran Hymnal* (1941), with settings of the Eucharist, Matins, and Vespers. Later work as a member of the Liturgical Music Committee of the Inter-Lutheran Commission on Worship from its beginning in 1967 led to the writing of numerous pieces of liturgical music: psalm tones, canticles, hymn harmonizations and new hymn tunes, and settings of the Venite, Te Deum, and "Create in me" as well as Setting One for the Holy Communion in *Lutheran Book of Worship* (1978), which became Divine Service II, First Setting, in *Lutheran Worship* (1982). He served as music editor for *Worship Supplement* and *Lutheran Book of Worship*. More recently he has served as music editor of volumes 30–42 of the *Concordia Hymn Prelude Series*. Among his publications of liturgical music for congregational, choral, and instrumental performance, perhaps the best known is the "Festival Canticle: Worthy is

Christ." His hymnic and liturgical works also appear in *Worship III* and in *The Hymnal 1982* of the Episcopal Church, *The United Methodist Hymnal* (1989), and *The Presbyterian Hymnal* (1990). Included in his legacy to the church are his many compositions as well as his numerous students who are active in composing music for the church.

He was assistant editor of *Church Music* (1966–80), a magazine for which he wrote numerous articles related to church music. Other major articles have appeared in *Response, Keywords in Church Music, Journal of Sacred Music, Lutheran Education, Handbook of Church Music*, and in *The Musical Heritage of the Church.* Memberships include Pi Kappa Lambda, the national music honor society, and the Hymn Society of America. His Sonata for Piano (1961) received first prize from the Chicago Chapter of the International Society of Contemporary Music. An article, "Composers in the Church: Richard Hillert," appears in *Church Music* 72,1. His biography is included in the 1985 edition of *International Who's Who in Music*. A *Catalog of the Works of Richard Hillert* was published in River Forest in 1983.

COMPOSER:	71	SHEPHERDING
	273	GRANTON
	324	RIVER FOREST
	346	KINGLY LOVE
ARRANGER:	18	FREUEN WIR UNS ALL IN EIN
	43	CHRISTUM WIR SOLLEN LOBEN SCHON
	47	IN DULCI JUBILO
	54	QUEM PASTORES
	69	NARODIL SE KRISTUS PÁN
	129	GELOBT SEI GOTT
	130	O FILII ET FILIAE
	199	VI LOVA DIG, O STORE GUD
	223	CHRIST UNSER HERR
	451	ST. DENIO

HINE, STUART WESLEY KEENE (1899–), was born July 25, 1899, in London, England, where he attended Coopers Company School. Having passed his entrance examination for Oxford University, he failed, however, to matriculate. After serving in World War I, he and his wife became engaged in missionary activities in East Poland, Czechoslovakia, and the Crimea. In pursuing this work they produced gospel literature in various languages. Their last years together were spent in Somerset, England, where his wife passed away in 1985. Stuart now resides in Essex.

TRANSLATOR/AUTHOR/ARRANGER: 519 How Great Thou Art

HOFF, ERIK CHRISTIAN (1832–94), was born January 21, 1832, in Bergen, Norway. Educated to be a school teacher, he studied music while teaching in Bergen. Having accepted a teaching position in Oslo in 1862, in 1864 he became organist there in the *Garnisonskirke*. Six years later he abandoned teaching to devote all his time to music. His interest in the chorale brought him to join the proponents of the rhythmic chorale (see essay: Polyrhythmic and Isometric Chorale, p. 822) over against the isometric form. Enamored and intrigued with Hoff's organ playing, King Oscar suggested that he publish a chorale book. This he set about doing at the very time that Ludwig Lindemann (*LW* 96, 291) was editing the chorale book of the newly-authorized *Kirkesalmebog* of Magnus Landstad (*LW* 234, et al.). Hoff's plan was to include tunes for all the hymnals in use in Norway at the time, even some used by the daughter church in America, the Norwegian Evangelical Lutheran Synod. Unfortunately, in his bid to the Norwegian chorale book committee to give equal recognition to his and Lindemann's book—thus to afford congregations a wider choice, especially the rhythmic chorale forms that Lindemann had rejected—Hoff lost out. He did, however, manage to have his book published privately under the title *Melodibog til samtlige authoriserede Salmeboger* (1878), a book of 265 tunes that drew upon both Swedish and Danish traditions, containing also a number of new tunes and 61 by Hoff. One of the most enduring of his tunes is the one listed below. He also composed organ pieces, male chorus numbers, and children's songs. He died December 8, 1894.

COMPOSER: 205 GUDS MENIGHED, SYNG

HOLDEN, OLIVER (1765–1844), was born September 18, 1765, in Shirley, Massachusetts. Moving with his family to Charlestown when he was 21, he found work as a carpenter, rebuilding the city burned by the British after the Battle of Bunker Hill. His building operations and real estate transactions proved highly successful and profitable. Moreover, his great interest in music found expression in leading and directing singing schools and choirs, writing music, compiling tune books, and selling music as a sideline in the general store he owned and operated. His generosity found expression in donating land for the site of a Baptist church as well as his constructing, practically unaided, a Puritan church where he preached from 1818 to 1833. During this time he was also a member of the Massachusetts House of Representatives.

Included in his publications, which he edited alone or with others, are: *The American Harmony* (Boston, 1792); *Union Harmony* (Boston, 1793); *The Modern Collection of Sacred Music; Sacred Dirges; Hymns and Anthems, Commemorative of the Death of George Washington*; and *Plain Psalmody* (all in 1800); and *The Charleston Collection of Sacred Songs* (Boston, 1803). *The Massachusetts Compiler* (Boston, 1795), a collection of tunes which he helped edit with Hans Gram and Samuel Holyoke, has been called "the most progressive work on psalmody which appeared in America before 1800." In fact, after the death of singing master and composer William Billings (1746–1800), Holden was the most popular American composer of psalm and hymn tunes. He wrote hymn texts as well as tunes, of which CORONATION is undoubtedly the most celebrated. He died at Charlestown, September 4, 1844.

COMPOSER: 272 CORONATION

HOLST, GUSTAV(US) THEODORE (1874–1934), was born September 21, 1874, at Cheltenham, of English blood on his mother's side, of Swedish on his father's side. Originally intent on a career as a pianist, poor health caused him to alter his coarse, and at the age of 17 he became organist at Wyck Rissington, Gloucestershire. At 19 he entered the Royal College of Music where he stayed for five years, studying composition with Charles Stanford (1852–1924) and forming a lifelong friendship with Ralph Vaughan Williams (*LW* 59, et al.). Holst also studied the trombone, and for a number of years he played it in theatre orchestras, in the Scottish Orchestra, and later in the orchestra of the Carl Rosa Opera Company. This experience prompted Archibald T. Davison of Harvard University to count Holst, in 1957, among "the first orchestrators of this age." In 1903 he became a music master in London and Reading, and in 1918 a teacher in composition at the Royal College of Music. During World War I, when his health prevented his enlisting, he went to the Middle East for the Y.M.C.A. to organize and direct musical activities for the members of the armed forces. He visited America in 1923; was Cramb Lecturer at the University of Glasgow in 1925; and lecturer in composition at Harvard in 1932. That same year he conducted the Boston Symphony in three concerts featuring his own compositions. He died at Ealing, Middlesex, on May 25, 1934. Percy Choles (1877–1958), English writer on music and encyclopedist, says that Holst had the power "of communicating a love for the finest music to any body of men, women, or children with whom he might happen to meet."

His works include *The Planets*, a suite for full orchestra; *The Hymn of Jesus* (two choruses and semi-chorus), his only large sacred work; *Ode to Death*, to Walt Whitman's text; an Ave Maria for ladies chorus; and five operas. His love for folk music is reflected in the number of arrangements he made of folk tunes, and in its influence in his own music.

ARRANGER: 135 PRINCE RUPERT

HOMBURG, ERNST CHRISTOPH (1605–81), was born at Mihla near Eisenach. As a practicing attorney in Naumburg, he began to write secular poems, including love and drinking songs. In 1648 he became a member of the Fruitbearing Society; a short time later a member of the Elbe Swan Order founded by Johann Rist (*LW* 122, et al.). Considered by his contemporaries as a poet of first rank, it was not until troubles arising from his own illness and that of his wife, plus other afflictions, that he turned to hymn writing. He wrote nearly 150 hymns primarily for his own private use to strengthen his life of faith and trust in the Lord. His hymns appeared in *E. C.*

Homburg's Geistliche Lieder, Erster Theil and Ander Theil (1659). He died June 2, 1681, in Naumberg.

AUTHOR: 94 Christ, the Life of All the Living

HOPKINS, EDWARD JOHN (1818–1901), was born into a musical family on June 30, 1818, in Westminster, London, England. His father was a clarinet player; an uncle was bandmaster of the Scots Guards; and one of his cousins was an organ builder. As a result, Edward picked up a good music education at an early age; when he was eight, he began singing at the Chapel Royal, at St. James', and at St. Paul's Cathedral. Most Sundays he was shuttled back and forth between the latter two churches, spending his whole day at services.

After four years as organist of Mitcham Church, Surrey, and short terms of such duty at St. Peter's, Islington, and St. Luke's, Berwick Street, Soho, Hopkins went to Temple Church in 1843, where he remained for 55 years, until his retirement. He became active in the Royal Society of Musicians and the Philharmonic Society, and helped organize the Royal College of Organists.

Hopkins also established himself as a composer and editor. His first book of tunes was *The Temple Choral Service-Book* (1867), including original tunes and arrangements. He served as senior editor of *The Organist and Choirmaster*, and as music editor of several hymnals, including those of the Congregational Church, the Presbyterian Churches of England and Canada, and the Free Church of Scotland. He collaborated with E. F. Rimbault on the production of a textbook, *The Organ: Its History and Construction* (1855), and contributed articles to *Grove's Dictionary of Music and Musicians*.

Composer of anthems, hymn tunes, and chants, Hopkins is best remembered for his simpler hymn tunes, although he seemed to prefer unusual meters. His chants, on the other hand, collected in the *Cathedral Psalter* (1855), contributed not a little to the baneful "Anglican thump," the result of his pointing of the psalm texts.

The Archbishop of Canterbury awarded Hopkins the honorary Doctor of Music degree in 1822, followed in 1826 by a similar honor from Trinity College, Toronto. He retired at the age of 80 and died three years later, February 4, 1901.

COMPOSER: 221 ELLERS

HOPPE, ANNA BERNARDINE DOROTHY (1889–1941), was born May 7, 1889, in Milwaukee. Beginning with patriotic verses as a child, at the age of 25 she began writing spiritual poetry in earnest, most of which was done commuting to church or to work and in spare time. Her livelihood was derived from work in business offices as a stenographer. Having received only an elementary education, she was largely a self-taught poet. Interest in her hymns came as a result of their appearance in several religious periodicals, notably the *Northwestern Lutheran*, a publication of the Evangelical Lutheran Synod of Wisconsin, Minnesota, Michigan, and Other States

(Wisconsin Evangelical Lutheran Synod) of which she was a member. As a Lutheran, American hymn-writer, her hymns enjoyed ready acceptance in various hymnals of the early 20th century—23 in *The Hymnal* (1925) of the then-Augustana Synod, eight in the *American Lutheran Hymnal* (1930), and two in *The Lutheran Hymnal* (1941). Through the influence of Dr. Adolph Hult of Augustana Seminary, Rock Island, Illinois, her *Songs for the Church Year* appeared in 1928. She was also adept at translating German hymns. She died August 2, 1941, in the city of her birth.

AUTHOR: 390 For Jerusalem You're Weeping
400 O Son of God, in Galilee

HOPPER, EDWARD (1818–88), was born February 17, 1818, in New York City; he studied at New York University and Union Theological Seminary, graduating in 1842. Ordained by the Presbyterian Church, he served congregations in Greenville, New York; Sag Harbor, Long Island; and the Church of the Sea and Land (Seamen's mission), in New York City's harbor area, where he had contact with many sailors. Lafayette College awarded him the honorary Doctor of Divinity degree in 1871. He died suddenly of a heart attack April 23, 1888.

His hymns were published anonymously. The one below appeared in *The Sailor's Magazine*, March 3, 1871, and in *The Baptist Praise Book* of the same year.

AUTHOR: 513 Jesus, Savior, Pilot Me

HORN, EDWARD TRAILL III (1909–), was born July 4, 1909, in Philadelphia, the grandson of E. T. Horn, one of the architects of the Common Service of 1888. Educated in the public schools of New York City and Ithaca, New York, he attended Cornell University, where he earned the Bachelor of Arts degree. Graduate study in the field of economics and sociology was pursued from 1930–31 and again from 1944–48 at Cornell and at the University of Pennsylvania. In the meantime he attended the Lutheran Theological Seminary at Philadelphia, leading to his ordination in 1934, the year in which he also married Sophia W. Oldach of Hilton, New York. Later, after she died, he married Carol Hancock Mills in 1983. Following his ordination he served as pastor of The Lutheran Church of Ithaca, as well as Lutheran university chaplain at Cornell University for nine years; as assistant professor of preaching and church administration at the Lutheran Theological Seminary, Philadelphia for three years; and from 1945 until his retirement in 1977 as pastor of Trinity Lutheran Church, Germantown, Pennsylvania.

Notable have been his contributions in the field of worship: member of the Common Service Book Committee, United Lutheran Church, 1937–57; member of the commission that produced the *Service Book and Hymnal* (1958); member of the Commission on Worship, Lutheran Church in America; member of the Inter-Lutheran Commission on Worship that produced the *Lutheran Book of Worship* (1978). A popular and frequent lecturer and preacher, he also produced such publications as *Altar and Pew* (1951); *The Christian Year* (1956); and *The Church at Worship* (1957).

TRANSLATOR: 165 Come, Oh, Come, O Quickening Spirit

HORN, (ROH, Bohemian; CORNU, Latin), JOHANN (c. 1490–1547), was born in Domaschitz, Bohemia. In 1518 he was ordained and appointed preacher to the community of the Bohemian Brethren (*Unitas Fratrum*) at Jungbunzlau. Appointed third senior, or elder, to Bishop Skoda in 1529, three years later, at the Synod of Brandeis, he was appointed bishop. A staunch supporter of Luther, in 1522 he and Michael Weisse (*LW* 18) journeyed to Wittenberg to discuss doctrinal concerns of the Brethren with Martin Luther (*LW* 13, et al.). Horn's collections of Czech hymns, *Pisnechval bozskych*, published in Prague in 1541, contained 481 hymns and 300 tunes, a notable book for its contents. He also prepared a revised edition of Michael Weisse's *New Gesangbuchlen* of 1531 and prepared *Ein Gesangbuch der Brüder inn Behemen und Merherrn* (Nürnberg, 1544).

Having served a congregation at Jungbunzlau for many years, he died there on February 11, 1547.

AUTHOR: 30 Once He Came in Blessing
COMPOSER: 141 GAUDEAMUS PARITER

HOUFF, LARRY JON (1944–), was born July 1, 1944, in Lorain, Ohio. While pursuing his 1966 Bachelor of Music degree at Wittenberg University, Springfield, Ohio, he studied organ with Frederick Jackish (*LW* 338) and Elmer Blackmer, and composition with Jan Bender (*LW* 319, et al.). In 1971 he received a Master of Divinity degree from Waterloo Lutheran Seminary, Waterloo, Ontario. Ordained in 1972, he became assistant pastor and director of music at First Lutheran Church, Springfield, Ohio. Prior to taking that post he held positions as part-time lecturer in church music at Waterloo Lutheran University, Waterloo Lutheran Seminary, Wittenberg University, and as organist at parishes in Waterloo, Kitchener, and St. Jacob's, Ontario, and in Springfield, Ohio. In the production of *Lutheran Book of Worship* (1978) he was a member of the Inter-Lutheran Commission on Worship. Married to Gundula Glüer, he is the father of two children.

ARRANGER: 397 JUST AS I AM

HOW, WILLIAM WALSHAM (1823–97), was born near Shrewsbury, England, on December 13, 1823. He took his Bachelor of Arts degree from Wadham College, Oxford, in 1845, and the Master of Arts degree in 1847, after which he studied theology at Durham. Ordained deacon in 1846, he became curate of St. George's, Kidderminster; he attained priesthood in 1847 and the following year was appointed curate of Holy Cross, Shrewsbury. In 1851 he became rector of Whittington, a farming village on the Welsh border. In 1853 he was appointed rural dean of Oswestry; in 1860, honorary canon of St. Asaph's cathedral, becoming in 1869 proctor of the diocese. He traveled to Rome in 1865 as chaplain of the English Church. All of How's 56 hymns were written at Whittington, between 1858–71; many were written for children, whom he held especially dear.

"The children's bishop" was only one of How's nicknames. After his consecration by Queen Victoria in 1879 as Bishop of Bedford (which diocese covered the slums of East London), he devoted himself so completely to his work among the poverty-stricken residents that he became known as "the poor man's bishop." Others called him "the omnibus bishop," because he, unlike most bishops, lived among his people and rode in buses rather than carriages.

Totally lacking in personal ambition, How refused the bishopric of Manchester and later that of Durham, both prestigious and lucrative positions, without even mentioning the offers to his wife. In 1889 he became the first bishop of Wakefield in West Yorkshire, working with the factory and mill workers of the West Riding. He falls within that group of clergymen known as "Broad Anglicans." In 1887 he preached a sermon on "The Bible and Science" in which he reconciled biblical Creation with the theory of evolution. His arguments were so convincing that scientist Thomas Huxley (1825–95), a devoted Darwinian, made room in his theories for Christianity; and thus How aided in keeping many evolutionists in the Anglican fold.

A close friend of John Ellerton (*LW* 43, et al.), How served as coeditor with him and music editor Arthur Sullivan (*LW* 515, 518) for *Church Hymns* (1871), which hymnal, published by the Society for the Promotion of Christian Knowledge, was at that time the closest rival of *Hymns Ancient and Modern* (1861). Earlier, in 1854, How had collaborated with Congregationalist Thomas Morrell to produce *Psalms and Hymns*; that same year he published *Daily Family Prayers for Churchmen.*

On vacation in western Ireland, How died August 10, 1897, and was buried in the Whittington churchyard.

AUTHOR:	182	Jesus Name of Wondrous Love
	191	For All the Saints
	335	O Word of God Incarnate
	405	We Give You But Your Own
	440	From All That Dwell Below the Skies (st. 3)

HOWARD, SAMUEL (1710–82), born in London in 1710, was a chorister at the Chapel Royal under William Croft (*LW* 180, 458). Later he became a pupil of Handel's (*LW* 53) rival, Johann C. Pepusch (1667-1752), German composer and theorist, and held organist positions at St. Bride, Fleet Street (1736–82) and St. Clement Dane, The Strand (1769–82) He received the Doctor of Music degree from Cambridge in 1769. Writing for the theatre as well as for the church, he composed music that became popular at the time, and assisted William Boyce in compiling *Cathedral Music* (1760–73). He died July 13, 1782, in London.

COMPOSER: 316 ISLEWORTH

HUBERT, KONRAD (1507–77), was born in 1507 in Bergzabern, Pfalz, and spent his early school years in Heidelberg. While attending the University of Basel he was won over to the cause of the Reformation. The year 1531 saw him in Strassburg as a deacon and private secretary to Martin Bucer (1491–1551), the man who introduced the Reformation in that city. Engaged not only in editing Bucer's large hymn collection of 1541, as well as the Strassburg editions of 1560 and 1572, he also prepared a book of Latin songs for children and wrote hymns on his own. Following a middle course between Lutheran and Reformed theology, in 1563 he was relieved of his position as assistant at St. Thomas Church in Strassburg. From then on until his death April 13, 1577, he continued to work on Bucer's various writings with the help of Johan Sturm (1507–89) and the English archbishop, Edmund Grindell (1518–83).

AUTHOR: 357 I Trust, O Christ, in You Alone

HUGHES, JOHN (1873–1932) was born November 22, 1873 at Dowlais, Glamorgan (Wales). The following year his family moved to Llantwit Fardre, Pontypridd. In 1885 he began to earn a living as a door boy at Glyn Colliery, a local mine. A lifelong member of the Salem Baptist Church, Pontypridd, he eventually succeeded his father as deacon and precentor, while serving in an official capacity with the Great Western Railway. He died May 14, 1932, at Llantwit Fardre.

Hughes wrote several hymn tunes as well as two anthems and a number of Sunday school marches, but he is best remembered for his composition CWM RHONDDA.

COMPOSER: 220, 398 CWM RHONDDA

HUS, JOHN (c. 1369–1415), the great Bohemian church reformer, was born in Hussinecz, Bohemia. Educated at the University of Prague, he became lecturer there, and later rector of that institution. As a priest at Bethlehem Chapel, Prague, founded for the preaching of God's Word in the language of the people, he fearlessly attacked corruption at all levels in the church; his defense and championing of John Wycliffe's (1320–84) reform ideas made him suspect of heresy. In 1409 he was forbidden to preach; in 1412 he was excommunicated. He then went into hiding and turned to writing. Cited to appear before the Council of Constance, 1414, and promised safe-conduct, he was captured and thrown into prison. Asserting that the Church is the communion of all who are predestined to salvation, and that Christ and not the pope is the head of the universal Church, the Council tried and condemned him as a heretic, July 6, 1415, and had him burned at the stake. His ashes were cast into the Rhine.

Hus' inability to accept the authority of the church where it went against his conscience and his understanding of Holy Scripture foreshadowed the advent of modern man and the 16th century Reformation. His works include *De Ecclesia*, *De Causa Boemica,* plus letters and sermons.

AUTHOR: 236, 237 Jesus Christ, Our Blessed Savior

IRELAND, JOHN (1879–1962), was born at Bowden, Cheshire, August 13, 1879, the son of Alexander and Anne Elizabeth Ireland, well-known authors who numbered among their friends Thomas Carlyle, Leigh Hunt, and Ralph Waldo Emerson. A somewhat painful and unhappy childhood, followed by the death of both parents, contributed to the lonely, introspective side of Ireland's personality. Educated at Leed's Grammar School, the Royal College of Music (where he studied with Sir Charles Stanford), and Durham University, he became one of the most distinguished of the English composers of his generation. His career also included serving St. Luke's, Chelsea, as organist for 22 years, and teaching composition at the Royal College of Music for 16 years, where his pupils included Benjamin Britten and Alan Bush. Although preeminent as a writer of songs and piano music, he also composed in the larger forms—orchestral works such as a piano concerto; *The Forgotten Rite*, an orchestral poem; *A London Overture*; and the film score for *The Overlanders*. Although his 90-some songs are of unequal quality, the best of them are among the finest of this century.

In 1932 Durham University honored him with a doctorate. He died at Rock Mill, Washington, Sussex, June 12, 1962.

COMPOSER: 91 LOVE UNKNOWN

IRONS, GENEVIEVE MARY (1855–?), was the daughter of William J. Irons, a clergyman and hymnologist of the Church of England, prebendary of St. Paul's Cathedral. Although she contributed a number of pieces to various publications, including a manual for Holy Communion entitled *Corpus Christi* (1884), she is chiefly remembered for her reverent hymn of consecration.

AUTHOR: 356 Drawn to the Cross, Which You Have Blessed

ISAAC, HEINRICH (c. 1460–c. 1517) may have been a Netherlander, but more probably was born in Germany. He went to Italy, where he became organist at the Church of San Giovanni, Florence. He was also organist of the Medici Chapel (1477–93), and music director to the sons of Lorenzo the Magnificent, one of whom was later to become Pope Leo X. Following the death of his patron Lorenzo, he appears to have remained in Italy for some years, enjoying his fame. He left for Vienna in 1496, and from 1497–1515 he was music director to Emperor Maximilian I at Innsbruck. He retired with an annual pension of 150 florens, returned to Italy, but failed to secure a renewal of favor, despite a recommendation to Duke Ercole of Ferrara. The last trace that history gives of him is at San Lorenzo Maggiore in Rome, "old, and sick, and without means." He died in Florence.

Isaak was a prolific composer, writing in all forms current in his day—sacred and secular songs, masses, motets, and instrumental works. His *Choralis Constantinus*, which contained music settings of the propers for the entire church year, is, in the words of Gustav Reese, "the most imposing musical creation of the entire pre-Reformation period in Germany." Not to be overlooked is the fact that Isaak, together with Ludwig Senfl (c. 1492–1555), his pupil and successor at the court of Maximilian I, and Hans Leo Hassler (*LW* 113, 427), is considered one of the great composers of German secular songs. The occasional placing of the melody in the soprano marks him as an innovator.

COMPOSER: 85, 121, 485 O WELT, ICH MUSS DICH LASSEN (INNSBRUCK)

JACKISCH, FREDERICK F. (1922–), was born in Chicago and received a Bachelor of Science degree from Concordia College, River Forest, Illinois, and his Master of Music degree from Northwestern University, Evanston, Illinois.

Jackisch received a Lutheran World Federation grant in 1964 for the study of church music in Germany, which led to his giving organ recitals in Stuttgart, Herford, and Berlin. He earned the Doctor of Philosophy degree from Ohio State University in 1966, and accepted the position of exchange professor of organ at the Berliner Kirchenmusikschule for the fall of 1968.

As a director of music Jackisch has served Lutheran parishes in New Orleans and Fort Wayne, Indiana. He is currently director of graduate study, professor of church music, and organist at Wittenberg University, Springfield, Ohio, as well as director of the Chapel Choir. From 1966–78 he served as chairman of the Hymn Music Committee of the Inter-Lutheran Commission on Worship; in addition, he has been a recitalist for several chapters of the American Guild of Organists.

COMPOSER/ARRANGER: 338 WALHOF

JACOBS, HENRY EYSTER (1844–1932), was born November 10, 1844, at Gettysburg, Pennsylvania, the son of Michael Jacobs (1808–71), pastor and professor of mathematics and natural science at Pennsylvania. Educated at Pennsylvania College and Gettysburg Lutheran Seminary, he taught for two years at the above-mentioned college and served as home missionary in Pittsburgh for a year prior to his call in 1868 to serve as pastor at Philipsburg, Pennsylvania, and principal of Thiel Hall. From 1870–83 he was Latin professor at Pennsylvania College, after which he succeeded Charles Porterfield Krauth (1823–83) as professor of systematic theology at the Evangelical

Lutheran Seminary, Philadelphia. In 1895 he became dean of that institution. As a member of the conservative General Council, Jacobs was one of the founders of the United Lutheran Church in America, which in 1918 merged the General Council with the General Synod and the United Synod of the South. Both scholar and author, he, with G. F. Spieker, translated Leonard Hutter's *Compendium of Lutheran Theology* and with C. A. Hay, H. F. Schmid's *Doctrinal Theology of the Lutheran Church.* He also translated *The Book of Concord, with Historical Appendixes*, two volumes (1882–83). Other works include *The History of the Evangelical Lutheran Church in the United States; Elements of Religion; Martin Luther, the Hero of the Reformation*; and *A Summary of Christian Faith*. He was editor of the *Lutheran Church Review* (1882–96); *Works of Martin Luther* (six volumes, 1915); and the *Lutheran Commentary* (12 volumes, 1900). He died July 7, 1932.

AUTHOR:	250	Lord Jesus Christ, We Humbly Pray

JANZOW, F. SAMUEL, (1913–) was born in Calgary, Alberta, on July 17, 1913. He attended Concordia College, St. Paul, Minnesota (1930–32), and Concordia Seminary, St. Louis (1932–36). Ordained in 1936, for 11 years he served as pastor of Luther-Tyndale and Holy Trinity churches in London, England.

In 1948 he received the Master of Arts degree in English from the University of Minnesota, Minneapolis. He became pastor of Trinity Lutheran Church, Trimont, Minnesota, serving there until 1954, when he accepted a professorship in English and theology at Concordia Teachers College, River Forest, where he taught until retirement. There he served also as editor of *Motif: A Literary Journal* (1961–1978). In 1968 he earned the Doctor of Philosophy degree from the University of Chicago. Married to Lydia Marie Pieper, he has a son and a daughter.

Articles by Janzow have appeared in various periodicals, including *The Campus Pastor, Lutheran Education, Concordia Journal*, and *Costerus*. He wrote the psalm versifications and paraphrases for *Psalms for the Church Year* (Augsburg, 1975) and the hymn translations for the six-volume *Hymns of Martin Luther* (Concordia, 1978–80, 1982). His *Getting Into Luther's Large Catechism*, a guide for popular study, appeared in 1978; his *Sing Glorias for All His Saints*, a collection of hymns for the saints' days in the church year, appeared in 1983, both published by Concordia.

Appointed to the newly organized Commission on Worship of The Lutheran Church—Missouri Synod in 1978, he served with distinction as both author and translator, not only as a member of the commission itself, but as a member if its Hymn Texts and Music Committee. He and his wife live, presently retired, in Michigan City, Indiana.

AUTHOR:	71	From Shepherding of Stars
	252	Lord, when You Came as Welcome Guest
	310	Look Toward the Mountains
TRANSLATOR:	13	Savior of the Nations, Come

21	"Comfort, Comfort," Says the Voice
23, 24	Lift Up Your Heads, You Mighty Gates
25	O People, Rise and Labor
35	We Praise, O Christ, Your Holy Name
44	Let All Together Praise Our God
47	Now Sing We, Now Rejoice
52	From Heaven Came the Angels Bright
95	Grant, Lord Jesus, that My Healing
122	O Darkest Woe
124	Christ Is Arisen
176	The Bridegroom Soon Will Call Us
184	Now Let Us Come Before Him
185	In Peace and Joy I Now Depart
213	We All Believe in One True God, Maker
214	Isaiah, Mighty Seer, in Spirit Soared
230	From Depths of Woe I Cry to You
236, 237	Jesus Christ, Our Blessed Savior
265	In the Very Midst of Life
269	Jesus, Shepherd, in Your Arms
288	May God Embrace Us with His Grace
321	Spread the Reign of God the Lord
331	Here Is the Tenfold Sure Command
336	Grant, Holy Ghost, that We Behold
344	Lord Jesus Christ, Will You Not Stay
423	When I Suffer Pains and Losses
427	Entrust Your Days and Burdens
431	Our Father, Who from Heaven Above
456	God Brought Me to This Time and Place

JILLSON, MARJORIE ANN, (1931–), was born October 29, 1931, in Detroit, Michigan. In 1953 she completed a Bachelor of Arts degree in religion at the College of Wooster, Ohio. For five years she worked for the federal government at Gallaudet College, Washington, before returning to Detroit, where she was employed as a dental secretary for eight years.

Three Simple Melodies (1971)) includes texts by Jillson set to music by Heinz Werner Zimmermann (*LW* 410), with whom she collaborated also on *Five Hymns* (1971). For the latter work Zimmermann prepared the music settings and the first stanzas, requesting Jillson to complete the texts.

Jillson, who has struggled with thyroid illness for the greater part of her life until now, adds that "the present holds greater promise for better health. All of this influenced how and why I wrote, especially, perhaps, noticeable in 'Have No Fear, Little Flock.'"

She presently resides in St. Clair Shores, Michigan.

AUTHOR: 410 Have No Fear, Little Flock (sts. 2, 3, 4)

JOHN OF DAMASCUS (c. 675 or 696–c. 749 or 754), one of the great early theologians and poets, perhaps the greatest of the Greek Church, was born in Damascus toward the close of the seventh century. Here he and his adopted brother, Cosmas the Melodist, were educated by a captive Italian monk. After succeeding his father as *logothete*, (chief representative of the Christians to the Mohammedan caliph), he and his brother, about 716, gave away their possessions and retired to the monastery of St. Sabas, between the Dead Sea and Jerusalem. There he was ordained a priest by the Church of Jerusalem, spending his life writing theological works in defense of orthodox faith—used extensively by the 13th-century Latin scholastics—and hymns. In the latter field he was chief exponent of the then-newly developed canon, writing a number of these for the Greek festivals of the church, along with other hymns. The best known of his canons is the Easter, or Golden Canon (*LW* 133). Similar to the efforts of Gregory I (*LW* 482) toward liturgical reform in the West, John of Damascus is credited with inventing the eight *echoi*, or modes (see essay: The Church Modes, p. 832), and producing the *Ocotechos*, a book of chants in the eight modes for a cycle of eight Sundays.

AUTHOR: 133 The Day of Resurrection
141 Come, You Faithful, Raise the Strain

JOHN, MARQUESS OF BUTE (1847–1900), otherwise known as John Patrick Crichton-Stuart, was born September 12, 1847, at Mount Stuart in County Bute, Scotland, and educated at Christ Church, Oxford. Renouncing Presbyterianism, he joined the Roman Catholic Church in 1868. Rector of St. Andrews (1892–98), provost of Rothesay (1896–99), and for a time president of University College, Cardiff, Wales, in 1892 he became lord lieutenant of the County of Bute. Glasgow University (1879), Edinburgh University (1882), and St. Andrews (1893) honored him with the Doctor of Laws degree. His interest and knowledge in matters of worship and liturgy resulted in the translation of numerous works from the early church, including his four-volume translation of *The Roman Breviary* (1879). He died October 9, 1900, at Dumfries House, and his heart was buried at the Mount of Olives.

TRANSLATOR: 76 O Chief of Cities, Bethlehem (st. 5)

JOHNSON, DAVID N. (1922–1987), a native of San Antonio, Texas, was born June 28, 1922. His Bachelor of Music degree was earned at Trinity University, San Antonio; his Master of Music and Doctor of Philosophy degrees at Syracuse University. With the American Guild of Organists he holds an associate degree. He served as chairman of the music department of St. Olaf College, Northfield, Minnesota, as university organist at

Syracuse University, as organist and choir director of Trinity Episcopal Cathedral, Phoenix, and as professor of Music at Arizona State University. He died August 2, 1987.

His publications, consisting largely of organ and choral works, number well over 300 and have been published by Augsburg Fortress and Concordia Publishing House as well as other publishers.

COMPOSER: 438 EARTH AND ALL STARS

JOSEPH, THE HYMNOGRAPHER (c. 800 or 810–883 or 886), was born at Syracuse, Sicily, where he received his early education at the Sicilian school of poets. He left Sicily for the monastic life at Thessalonica. After being ordained a presbyter, he went to Constantinople and sided with the "orthodox" party in the struggle with the iconoclastic emperor, Leo the Armenian. While on his way to Rome to solicit the support of the pope, he was captured by pirates and taken to Crete. When finally released, he returned to Constantinople, where in 850, he founded a monastery connected to the Church of St. John Chrysostom (c. 345–407), patriarch of Constantinople. Because of his strenuous defense of icons, he was banished to Chersonae by the emperor Theophilus (reign 829–42). Upon the death of that emperor, Joseph was recalled by Empress Theodora and made keeper of the sacred vessels in the Great Church of Constantinople. Credited with having written 1,000 canons, he is the most prolific of the Greek hymn writers, after whom Greek hymnody declined.

AUTHOR (attr.): 190 Stars of the Morning, So Gloriously Bright

JULIANE, EMILIE (1637–1706), countess of Schwarzburg-Rudolstadt, was born August 16, 1637, at Heidecksburg, the castle of her father's uncle, Count Ludwig Günther of Schwarzburg-Rudolstadt, where her father (Count Albert Friedrich) and his family had to seek refuge during the Thirty Years' War (1618–48). After the death of her father and mother, 1641 and 1642 respectively, Emilie Juliane was adopted by her aunt, who was also her godmother and who had become the wife of Count Ludwig Günther. Educated at Rudolstadt with her cousins, in 1665 she married her cousin Albert Anton. This marriage of 42 years was blessed with two children, the second of which died in infancy. A pious woman, daily nurtured by God's Word, and having received a sound background in poetry and hymnody as a child, she became the most productive of German women hymn writers. Some 600 hymns are attributed to her, hymns reflecting her deep love for the Savior. She published several collections during her lifetime, including *Kühlwasser in grosser Hitze des Kreuzes* (Rudolstadt, 1685), *Tägliches Morgan-, Mittags-, und Abend-Opffer* (Rudolstadt, 1685), and after her death, December 3, 1706, several collections were published by various interested individuals.

AUTHOR: 456 God Brought Me to This Time and Place

JULIAN, JOHN (1839–1913), was born January 27, 1839, at Topcliffe, Yorkshire, eldest son of Thomas Julian of St. Agnes, Cornwall. Privately educated, he was ordained deacon by the Church of England in 1866, and priest the following year. In 1876 he became vicar of Wincobank; from 1905 on he was vicar of Topcliffe, while canon of York from 1901 on. Recognizing his talents, Durham University honored him with the Master of Arts degree in 1887; Archbishop Benson of Canterbury awarded him the Doctor of Divinity degree in 1894; and Howard University, Washington, D.C., honored him with the Doctor of Laws degree in 1894. He is remembered especially for his monumental *A Dictionary of Hymnology* (1891), also for presiding over its revision in 1907. In the preparation of this work he estimated that he examined 400,000 hymns, and even today his work remains the source-book on the subject. He himself wrote a few hymns, which he modestly omitted to mention in his dictionary. In addition he published *Concerning Hymns* (1874) and *Outgrowth of some Literary, Scientific and other Hobbies* (1899). He died January 22, 1913, at Topcliffe.

AUTHOR: 83 O God of God, O Light of Light

KEBLE, JOHN (1792–1866) was born April 25, 1792, at Fairford, Gloucestershire, England, where his father was vicar of Coln St. Aldwyn's. Beginning his career as a brilliant student at Oxford, he was ordained a priest by the Church of England, thereafter serving a number of relatively obscure parishes all his life. His writings, however, contributed toward a spiritual awakening in the church of his time. His *Christian Year: Thoughts in Verse for the Sundays and Holydays throughout the Year* (1827), for instance, went through 96 editions in his lifetime and became a devotional companion to the *Book of Common Prayer*. Keble became professor of poetry at Oxford (1831–41), which required little of him beyond one lecture per term. Other works of Keble include *A Life of Bishop Wilson* (1863) and *Academical and Occasional Sermons* (1847).

In 1833 Keble delivered the famous assize sermon at Oxford on "National Apostasy," which John Henry Newman (1801–90) considered the beginning of the Oxford Movement, aimed, as Keble expressed in one of the four "Tracts for the Times" that he wrote, to direct people to "deep submission to authority, implicit reverence for catholic tradition, firm belief in the divine prerogative of the priesthood, real nature of the sacraments, and the danger of speculation." The fact that Newman and some other 50 clergymen left the Church of England and joined the Roman Catholic Church was one of great sorrow to Keble.

In 1836 he returned to Hursley and remained there until failing health prompted him to move to Bournemouth in 1863, where he died March 29, 1866. To perpetuate his memory, Keble College was founded at Oxford in 1869, the same year that 12 volumes of his sermons were published as well as *Letters of Spiritual Counsel* and *Miscellaneous Poems* .

In the popular sense of the word "hymn," Keble can scarcely be called a hymn writer. He did not intend or wish that his poems be used in public worship. It was others who included them, mostly as centos, in popular hymn collections.

AUTHOR: 488 Sun of My Soul, O Savior Dear

KEIMANN, CHRISTIAN (1607–62), was born February 27, 1607, at Pankratz, Bohemia, where his father was a Lutheran pastor. After attending the *Gymnasium* in Zittau, he entered the University of Wittenberg in 1627, from which he graduated with a Master of Arts degree in 1634. In the meantime, the ravages of the Thirty Years' War (1618–48) forced his father, mother, five brothers and a sister to flee Bohemia and live in exile in Zittau.

Shortly after completing his studies at the University of Wittenberg, Keimann was appointed assistant master of the *Gymnasium* in Zittau by the town council; in 1638 he became its rector. The ensuing years were not a little difficult in coping with the continuing disruption of the Thirty Years' War. But they were also very fruitful and rewarding for this patient, caring, loving, gifted teacher and rector. Besides producing a number of instructive books in arithmetic, logic, rhetoric, Latin, and Greek, he sought to instill in his students a familiarity with God's Word through his poetry. Thus he produced a few plays based on Holy Scripture and 13 hymns, most of which came into popular church use. His hymns, in their fresh, joyful spirit and notable form, rank among the best of the 17th century. Andreas Hammerschmidt, organist at the *Johanneskirche* in Zittau, preserved many by composing settings for them. Keimann died of a stroke January 13, 1662.

AUTHOR: 40 Oh, Rejoice, All Christians, Loudly

KELLY, JOHN (1831–90), Presbyterian minister and hymn translator, was born at Newcastle-on-Tyne on October 5, 1833.. Educated at the University of Glasgow, he next studied theology at Bonn from 1852–54, at New College in Edinburgh from 1856–57, and at the Theological College of the English Presbyterian Church (1860), London, by which church he was ordained. Refusal by the medical advisor of the Foreign Mission Committee for service in the India Mission of his church prompted him to accept pioneer mission work at Tiverton. There he established a congregation which he served from 1864–68. He next served at Hebburn-on-Tyne for eight years and thereafter at Streatham from 1876–80. In 1881 he left the active ministry to serve as tract editor for the Religious Tract Society (founded 1799).

In 1867 Kelly published his translations in *Paul Gerhardt's Spiritual Songs*, and in 1885 the Religious Tract Society published his *Hymns from the Present Century from the German*. Afflicted with cancer, Kelly was advised to move to Braemer, in Scotland, for health's sake. There he died on July 19, 1890.

TRANSLATOR: 120, 121 Upon the Cross Extended
128 Awake, My Heart, with Gladness
424 Rejoice, My Heart, Be Glad

KELLY, THOMAS (1769–1855), was born in Kellyville, County Queens, Ireland, July 13, 1769. The son of a judge, he was educated at Trinity College, Dublin, intending to follow his father to the bar. However, his study of Hebrew led him into an interest in theology, and he decided to give up the worldly in favor of the spiritual. After a period of enthusiasm bordering on fanaticism, during which time he endangered his life by his asceticism, Kelly encountered the doctrine of justification by faith alone and found himself freed of the sin that had weighed him down.

Ordained by the Church of Ireland(Anglican) in 1792, Kelly embarked on a career of fervent evangelical preaching and quickly fell into disfavor with the established church's hierarchy. In the company of evangelist Rowland Hill he was inhibited by the archbishop from preaching in any Dublin churches. Undaunted, Kelly continued to speak in various unconsecrated buildings and eventually established several chapels of his own, having married a woman of substantial means and sympathy. A separate sect, now extinct, gathered around Kelly's magnetic preaching.

He was active in many good causes, and was particularly esteemed by the poor because of his service to them during the Irish Famine (1845–49). A man of great learning (an excellent Bible scholar and well-versed in classical and oriental languages), he wrote 767 hymns during his 60 years of ministry.

Kelly was afflicted with a stroke that caused his death on May 14, 1855, at the age of 85. He compiled *A Collection of Psalms and Hymns extracted from Various Authors* (Dublin, 1802) and his original hymns were published in *Hymns on Various Passages of Scripture*. This volume went through seven editions, from 1804–53, each successive edition containing additional hymns.

AUTHOR: 116 Stricken, Smitten, and Afflicted
118 We Sing the Praise of Him Who Died

KEMPIS, THOMAS À (1379-1471), was the son of a peasant whose family name was Hammerken. Educated in the poor scholar's house attached to the Brethren of Common Life at Deventer, Holland, he became known as Thomas from Kempen (Thomas à Kempis). The Brethren of Common Life, founded in 1375 by Gerold Groote, whose biography was written by Thomas, was a lay fellowship dedicated to Christian service as exemplified in the life of Christ. The aims of this organization were spelled out in *The Imitation of Christ*, a renowned work of which Thomas was undoubtedly the editor or compiler. First printed in 1471—one of the earliest printed books—it is said to have been translated into more languages than any other book except the Bible.

Received into this Brotherhood in 1398, a year later Thomas entered a monastery at Mount St. Agnes, near Zwolle. In 1413 he was ordained priest; in 1425 sub-prior. Here he remained until his death in 1471, writing a chronicle of his monastery, several biographies, tracts, and hymns.

AUTHOR (attr.): 275 Oh, Love, How Deep

KEN, THOMAS (1637–1711), was born at Berkhampstead, Hartfordshire, England, in July of 1637. Orphaned at a young age, he went to live with his stepsister and her husband, Izaak Walton, author of *The Compleat Angler* (1653), the classic on fishing.

In 1656 Ken matriculated at what is now Magdalen College, Oxford. The following year he became a fellow of New College, Oxford, where mistreatment of Anglican worship was severe. Cromwell's death in 1658 ushered in a return to pre-Puritan ways, and Ken, now devoted to the high church party, received the Bachelor of Arts degree in 1661 and the Master of Arts degree three years later. Ordained in 1662, he was appointed rector of Little Eaton, Essex. Three years later he became domestic chaplain to Bishop Morley, a friend of Izaac Walton. Indebted to the Waltons for their hospitality when he was under indictment as a loyalist, the bishop arranged that Ken become a fellow at Winchester College in 1666, and rector of Brighton, Isle of Wight, in 1667. Two years later Ken returned to Winchester as prebendary of the cathedral, chaplain to the college and to Bishop Morley. It was during this period that he prepared *A Manual of Prayers for the Use of the Scholars of Winchester College* in which he suggested the use of three hymns for "Morning," "Evening," and "Midnight." He later wrote such hymns (LW 478, 484) and published them separately in 1692, including them in the appendix to the second edition of *A Manual of Prayers* (1695).

Ken became a Doctor of Divinity in 1679 and was appointed chaplain to Princess Mary (later queen), wife of William of Orange, at The Hague. His outspoken criticism, however, of a case of immorality at the court led to his dismissal from that post. He returned to Winchester and, at Morley's death in 1684, was appointed chaplain to Charles II. On June 29, 1685, Ken was consecrated bishop of Bath and Wells; eight days later he was called to minister to the king, who lay dying of a stroke.

The accession of James II brought turbulent times. As bishop, Ken ministered to prisoners and sufferers. Refusing to sign James II's *Declaration of Indulgence*, securing toleration for dissenters and papists, Ken was one of the seven bishops imprisoned in the Tower of London but acquitted at their trial. Refusing to take the oath of allegiance to William of Orange in 1691, he was deprived of his see. He then retired to the home of his friend Lord Weymouth, at Longleat, Wiltshire. In 1703 Queen Anne offered to restore Ken to the position vacated by the death of his previous successor, Richard Kidder, but Ken refused and was given an annual pension. He died March 19, 1711, and, according to his request, was buried at Frome Church, "under the east window of the chancel, just at sunrising." His immortal "Awake, my soul, and with the sun" (*LW* 478) was sung at dawn on that occasion.

Besides the previously mentioned *Manual of Prayers*, he wrote *The Practice of Divine Love*. His poetical works, in four volumes, were published in 1721 and republished by Pickering in 1868 with the title *Bishop Ken's Christian Year or Hymns and Poems for the Holy Days and Festivals of the Church.*

AUTHOR: 461 Praise God, from Whom All Blessings Flow
478 Awake, My Soul, and with the Sun
484 All Praise to Thee, My God, This Night

KENNEDY, BENJAMIN HALL (1804–99), was born November 6, 1804, at Summer Hill, near Birmingham, England. Educated at King Edward's School, Shrewsbury School, and graduating with honors from St. John's College, Cambridge, in 1827, he was successively a fellow of St. John's (1828–36), headmaster of Shrewsbury School (1836–66), Regius Professor of Greek at Cambridge University, and canon of Ely. Ordained in 1829, he also served for a time as prebendary of Lichfield Cathedral and rector of West Felton, Salop. In 1880 he had the unique honor of being elected an honorary fellow of St. John's College for the second time, after 58 years.

A man of brilliant scholarship and vast and accurate learning, he published numerous works of classical learning: *The Psalter, or Psalms of David in English Verse* (1860); *Hymnologia Christiana* (1863), containing nearly 200 translations from German, recasts of other hymns, psalm paraphrases, and original hymns. He died April 6, 1899.

TRANSLATOR: 414 Who Trusts in God a Strong Abode

KETHE, WILLIAM (?–c. 1593 or 94), was probably a native of Scotland, but neither the date nor the place of his birth is known. Living in exile in Frankfort and Geneva during the reign of Roman Catholic Queen Mary from 1553–58, he was afterwards employed as an envoy from Geneva to the other English-speaking congregations on the Continent. When the exiles left Geneva in 1559, he may have been one of the few left behind to "finish the Bible and the psalms both in metre and prose." In 1563 he was chaplain to the forces under the Earl of Warwick at Newhaven (Havre) and again in 1569 in the North. From 1561–93 he was rector of Childe Okeford in Dorset and died probably around 1593.

As a facile rhymer he wrote some popular religious ballads as well as metrical versions of the Psalms, 25 of which were included in the Anglo-Genevan Psalter of 1561, all of which were adopted in the Scottish Psalter of 1564–65. (See essay: Metrical Psalms, p. 825.)

AUTHOR: 435 All People That on Earth Do Dwell

KEY, FRANCIS SCOTT (1779–1843), was born August 9, 1779, at Pipe's Creek, Maryland, and received his education at St. John's College, Annapolis, graduating in

1796. After studying law for many years he served as district attorney for the District of Columbia. Active in the Episcopal Church, he served as vestryman and lay reader of St. John's Church, Georgetown, D.C., and vestryman of Christ Church, Georgetown, when that parish was organized. At one time he seriously considered taking holy orders. He helped organize the Domestic and Foreign Missionary Society in 1820 and was a delegate to the General Convention from 1814–26. He died January 11, 1843, in Baltimore. His hymns and poems were published in Miller and Osbourn's *Lyra Sacra* (1832) and in his collected poems published in 1857.

AUTHOR: 500 Before You, Lord, We Bow

KINGO, THOMAS HANSEN (1634–1703), was born December 15, 1634, at Slangerup, Denmark. His grandfather, a tapestry weaver, had emigrated from Scotland near the end of the 17th century. Young Thomas attended the Latin school in his hometown for 10 years before transferring to a school in Hillerod, near Frederiksborg, where his talent for poetry soon showed itself. The school's principal, Albert Bartholin, recognizing this unusual talent, took Kingo into his home. Kingo chose to study Danish literature, a fine background for one who was to become one of Denmark's greatest hymn writers.

After studying for the ministry at the University of Copenhagen, Kingo graduated in 1658 and tutored privately until his ordination in 1661. His first pastorate was a small country parish near Vedby. In 1668 he returned to lead the flock in his hometown of Slangerup.

Though his secular poetry began to attract attention about this time, his real fame came in 1673 with the publication of the first part of his *Aandeligt Sjunge Chor*, or "Spiritual Songs." The dedication of this volume to King Christian V stated that the Danish people need not depend wholly on hymns of foreign origin for their worship. Kingo justified the practice of setting his lyrics to popular tunes, writing, "If a pleasing melody set to a song of Sodom delights your ear, how much more, if you are a true child of God, should not that same melody delight your soul when sung to a song of Zion!"

Kingo's poetic gift thus came to the attention of the Danish king, who made the author a member of the nobility in June of 1679. After the appearance of the second part of his "Spiritual Songs" in 1681, Kingo received an honorary doctorate in theology the following year; and on March 27, 1683, he was appointed by the king to prepare a hymnbook for the Church of Denmark to replace the one which had been in use for over a century. This appointment included very specific instructions: some of Kingo's original hymns could be included, but tampering with old favorites should be kept to a minimum, and the works of Martin Luther (*LW* 13, et al.) were to be left alone.

In response to the king's directive, Kingo produced in 1689 the *Vinterparten*, or Advent to Easter section, of a proposed hymnal, containing 267 hymns of which Kingo had authored 136. A royal brief dated January 25, 1690, commanded that the hymnal be used throughout Denmark, but this was rescinded by a second brief on February 22. Kingo's book, which he had published at his own expense, was rejected, and Søren Jonassen, dean of Roskilde, was commissioned to compile another hymnbook.

Jonassen's effort, containing none of Kingo's hymns, was also disapproved, whereupon the king appointed a commission to produce the authorized hymnal. Kingo, again in the court's favor, worked closely with the commission; 85 of his hymns were chosen for inclusion in the final product, which carried his name on the title page and was popularly known as "Kingo's Hymnal."

Kingo died October 14, 1703. His remains were buried in a small village churchyard near Odense. Of his work Bishop Skaar has said:

> Among his finest hymns in 'Spiritual Songs' must be mentioned the morning and evening hymns with their accompanying prayers and the table and Communion hymns. His hymns based on the Gospel and Epistle lessons, especially, express in striking phrases the thoughts that stir the hearts of Lutheran believers as they behold the life of the Savior upon earth.

AUTHOR: 100 On My Heart Imprint Your Image
225 All Who Believe and Are Baptized
245 O Jesus, Blessed Lord, My Praise
387 Praise and Thanks and Adoration
476 I Pray You, Dear Lord Jesus

KINNER, SAMUEL (1603–68), was born in Breslau, Germany (now in Poland). After practicing medicine here for a time, he entered the service of Duke of Liegnitz-Brieg as counselor and court physician, serving in this capacity until his death August 10, 1668, at Brieg.

AUTHOR: 246 Lord Jesus Christ, You Have Prepared

KIRBYE (KIRBY), GEORGE (c. 1560–1634), was born most likely in Suffolk, England. He was the house musician to Sir Robert Jermyn at Rushbrooke Hall near Bury St. Edmunds, and perhaps church warden at St. Mary's. Essentially an English madrigalist, an impeccable craftsman of unfailing taste, he was one of the most important contributors to Este's psalter entitled *The Whole Booke of Psalmes* (1592), supplying most of the harmonizations therein. In 1597 he himself published what he called the "first fruites of my poore knowledge in Musicke," a set of 24 madrigals for four, five, and six voices. The volume was dedicated to the daughters of Sir Robert Jermyn of Rushbrooke where Kirby lived as music master. A man of substance, he died October 1634 at Bury, St. Edmunds.

COMPOSER (attr.): 196 WINCHESTER OLD

KIRKPATRICK, WILLIAM J. (1838–1921), was born February 27, 1838, in Duncannon, Pennsylvania. Trained as carpenter, he studied music with his father, and played the violin, cello, flute, and organ. After serving in the Civil War (1861–65) as a fife major, he became a furniture dealer in Philadelphia, a vocation in which he was engaged for some 16 years. At the age of 21 he edited and compiled *Devotional Melodies* (1859), his first venture in that field, an activity that eventually resulted in the compilation of some-100 books, published largely by John J. Hood Company, Philadelphia, books to which he contributed numerous gospel song tunes. A lifelong Methodist, he was first a member of Wharton Street Methodist Episcopal Church and later director of music for 11 years at Grace Methodist Episcopal Church, both in Philadelphia. There he died September 29, 1921.

COMPOSER: 64 CRADLE SONG

KITCHIN, GEORGE WILLIAM (1827–1912), was born December 7, 1827, at the Naughton rectory, Suffolk, England, the son of a rector. Educated at Ipswich Grammar School, at King's College School, and Christ Church, Oxford, he graduated with the Bachelor of Arts degree in 1850. Ordained by the Church of England, 1852, he became headmaster of a preparatory school in Twyford, Hampshire, returning to Christ Church, Oxford, as censor and tutor in 1863. He became dean of Winchester (1883–94) and dean of Durham (1894–1912), and from 1909 on he served as chancellor of the University of Durham. He published books on historical, biographical, and archeological subjects, the most important being his three-volume *History of France*. He died October 13, 1912, at Durham.

AUTHOR: 311 Lift High the Cross

KITSON, CHARLES HERBERT (1874–1944), was born November 18, 1874, the son of James Kitson, and educated at Ripon School and Selwyn College, Cambridge, where he was an organ scholar. He served as organist at St. John the Baptist, Leicester, 1901–13; at Christ Church Cathedral, Dublin, 1913–20; as professor of music at University College, Dublin, 1915–20; and the Royal Irish Academy of Music, 1918–20. Thereafter he held several posts as an examiner for degrees in music in the universities of Oxford, Wales, and London, and as a professor at the Royal College of Music. His publications include: *The Art of Counterpoint; Applied Strict Counterpoint; Studies in Fugue; The Evolution of Harmony; Rudiments of Music; Invertible Counterpoint; Elementary Contrapuntal Harmony*; *Irish Hymnal* (1919, coeditor).

ARRANGER: 271 MOVILLE

KLUG, JOSEPH (c. 1490–1552). Little is known about Klug's early life except that he was the son of Peter Klug, who for a time worked for the large Anton Koberger printing establishment in Nürnberg.

By the summer of 1523, Klug was operating the print shop in Wittenberg recently established by the painter Lukas Cranach (1472–1533) and goldsmith Christian Döring (d. 1533). Soon Klug was printing items under his own name. Among other innovations, he pioneered the use of metal type in the printing of a Hebrew grammar. The publication for which he is most remembered is the *Geistliche Lieder* (Wittenberg, 1529), authorized by Luther himself (*LW* 13, et al.) and for which he also wrote a foreword. Although not extant, its contents can be reconstructed through its reprints by Rauscher (Erfurt, 1531) and Gutknecht (Nürnberg, 1531), and through the altered new editions of 1533, 1535, 1543. For a number of years the content and organization of the Klug hymnal served as a model for others that followed.

Klug also published a number of Luther's shorter works, Bugenhagen's *Brunswick Church Order* (1528), some works of Philipp Melanchthon (*LW* 189), Justus Jonas, Casper Cruciger, and others. Following his death in June 1552, Klug's son Thomas took over his printing business. This venture, however, ended with his death May 27, 1563.

Joseph Klug was only one person among others who published works in behalf of the Reformation. Numbered among such are Georg Rhau (*LW* 382), Michael Lotter (b. 1499), and Hans Lufft (1495–1584).

PRINTER:	124	CHRIST IST ERSTANDEN (1533)
	156, 157, 189	KOMM GOTT SCHÖPFER (1533)
	197, 329, 334	ERHALT UNS, HERR (1543)
	236	JESUS CHRISTUR, UNSER HEILAND (1533)
	336, 462	ES IST GEWISSLICH (1529)
	340, 467	WO GOTT ZUM HAUS (1533)

KNAPP, WILLIAM (1698–1768). Precise information in regard to this composer has been difficult to obtain, owing to the fact that the records of the parish in which he was born were destroyed by fire in 1762. Of German descent, born at Wareham, Dorset, in 1698, he was a glover by trade, though he became a musician of no mean ability. He is reported to have been an organist as well as a composer, and the author of two books, *A Set of New Psalm Tunes and Anthems in Four Parts* (1738), and *The New Church Melody* (1754).

He was parish clerk at St. James' Church, Poole (1729–68), and was described as a "country psalm-singer." Among the former duties of a parish clerk was that of singing the responses in church services and making the announcement before the hymn: "Let us all sing to the glory of God." His tenure of this office, while a George Savage was the sexton, gave occasion to the following lines in *The London Magazine*, 1742, contributed by a fellow townsman of Poole, named H. Price:

From pounce and paper, ink and pen,
Save me, O Lord, I pray;
From Pope and Swift and such-like men,
And Cibber's annual lay;
From doctors' bills and lawyers' fees,
From ague, gout and trap;
And what is ten times worse than these,
George Savage and Will Knapp.

In addition to *A Sett of New Psalm-tunes and Anthems in four parts* (London, 1738), Knapp also prepared *The New Church Melody* (1753).

He died at Poole in 1768 and was buried on September 26 "somewhere near the old town wall."

COMPOSER: 161 WAREHAM

KNECHT, JUSTIN HEINRICH (1752–1817), was born September 30, 1752, at Biberach, Germany. After gaining a classical education at the college of the convent in Esslingen, where he also learned to play a number of orchestral instruments and was given opportunity to study organ with a teacher who introduced him to the works of Bach (*LW* 89), Telemann (1681–1767), and Handel (*LW* 53), he served for a time as professor of literature in Biberach. In 1792 he gave that up to become organist and musical director of the town. A pioneer in the use of program notes, which he introduced in 1790 for his orchestral concerts, in 1807 he was appointed director of the court and theatre orchestra in Stuttgart. Two years later he resigned this position, the result of criticism and the realization that he failed to have the proper qualifications. The remainder of his life was spent in Biberach.

A brilliant organist, Knecht enjoyed a considerable reputation as a composer, teacher, and theorist. With J. F. Christmann he coedited *Vollständige Sammlung... Choralmelodien* (1799), which included 97 melodies of his own. The list of compositions takes up four columns in Eitner's *Quellen-Lexikon*—works for the stage, incidental music for plays, vocal compositions, and church music for organ and choirs—most, except for a few chorale tunes, are little known.

COMPOSER: 433 VIENNA

KNUDSEN, PEDER (1819–63), son of a parish singer in Voga, Norway, was a talented musician who became proficient on various instruments, especially the violin. Johann Behrens, prominent musician in Christiania (now Oslo), became interested in him and secured his services as choral director in Holinestraud. Knudsen became civic music director at Kragerö in 1854, and as such was in charge of the music in all its schools. Here he also organized the Midsummer Eve music festivals. In 1859 he became organist and choirmaster in Olesund, and it was there that he composed the tune for Marie Wexelsen's "Jeg er saa glad hver julekveld." He died in 1863, shortly before Christmas.

COMPOSER: 56 JEG ER SAA GLAD

KOCHER, CONRAD (1786–1872), was born December 16, 1786, at Ditzingen, Württemberg, Germany. In St. Petersburg as a tutor at the age of 17, where he heard the music of Haydn (*LW* 294) and Mozart (1756–91), he decided on music as a career. A friendship with Muzio Clementi (1752–1832), English composer, keyboard player and teacher of Italian birth, confirmed him in this intention, and he went to Rome in 1819. A study of Palestrina's (c. 1525–94) works led him to strive for a general reform of church music in Germany. Returning there, he founded a School of Sacred Song in Stuttgart, an institution that stimulated and popularized four-part singing throughout Württemberg and its environs. Becoming organist in *Stiftskirche* in Stuttgart (1827–65), he devoted himself to devising various hymnals, to which he contributed some new tunes. His works include two operas; an oratorio; *Die Tonkunst in der Kirche* (1823), a treatise on church music; and he compiled a large collection of chorales in *Zions Harfe* (1855). The University of Tübingen honored him with the Doctor of Philosophy degree in 1852. He died March 12, 1872, in Stuttgart.

COMPOSER: 75, 496 DIX

KÖNIG, JOHANN BALTHASAR (1691–1758), was baptized at Waltershausen, near Gotha, January 28, 1691. At the age of 12 he went to Frankfurt-am-Main as a chorister. During the years 1711–21 he trained under Georg Philipp Telemann (1681–1767). Eventually he succeeded Telemann as director of the municipal music and was in charge of music at *Barfüsserkirche* and St. Katharine's, Frankfurt and taught singing at the *Gymnasium.*

König's *Harmonischer Liederschatz* (1738), was the largest and most influential collection of tunes published in the 18th century. Of the 1,784 tunes in the main section of the book, 361 were new.

He died March 31 and was buried at Frankfurt April 2, 1758.

COMPOSER: 80, 228 FRANCONIA
95 DER AM KREUZ
415 ALLES IST AN GOTTES SEGEN (adapt.)

KOREN, ULRIK VILHELM (1826–1910), was born December 22, 1826, in Bergen, Norway. After attending the Bergen cathedral school he entered the University of Christiania (now Oslo) in 1844. Following his graduation he taught for a time until, in 1853, he received a call to serve as pastor of a small group of Norwegians in Little Iowa (later Washington Prairie, Iowa), near Decorah. He was ordained, and then with his wife Else *née* Hysing, he crossed the ocean to assume his pastoral work in December of that year. As such he was the first Norwegian pastor to settle west of the Mississippi. While caring for his flock, he also served as secretary, then as vice-president of the Norwegian Synod from 1855–74. In that year he became president of the Iowa District, a position he held until 1894, when he became president of the Norwegian Lutheran Synod of America, a position he held until his death December 19, 1910, all the while still serving his congregation in Iowa. A man of many interests, he helped to establish the Grieg Singing Society, the first mail route out of Decorah, and the Norwegian Mutual Insurance Company.

Interested in church music and hymnody, it was through his influence and efforts that the *Rythmisk Koralbog* was published with 27 original hymns and 21 translations of Koren's.

AUTHOR: 205 Oh, Sing Jubilee to the Lord

KRETZMANN, PAUL EDWARD (1883–1965), was born August 24, 1883, in Farmers Retreat, Indiana. After graduating from Concordia College, Fort Wayne, in 1902, he attended Concordia Seminary in St. Louis for two years, thereafter moving west for health reasons. He taught in Lutheran schools in Colorado and Kansas, and was ordained to the office of the public ministry in 1906. He became, first, pastor of St. Peter's Church, Shady Bend, Kansas, and later of Emmaus Church in Denver.

Kretzmann taught science and mathematics at Concordia College, St. Paul, Minnesota, for seven years, moving back to St. Louis in 1919 to become editor and production manager at Concordia Publishing House. In 1923 he joined the faculty at Concordia Seminary in St. Louis, where he taught courses in New Testament interpretation and religious education until his resignation in 1946. He went on to serve as pastor of St. John's Church, Forest Park, Illinois.

Leaving the Lutheran Church—Missouri Synod in 1948 because of a doctrinal dispute, Kretzmann later joined the group that formed the Orthodox Lutheran Church, presiding over its Minneapolis seminary for a time. He died July 13, 1965, at Minneapolis, survived by his wife, Louise, and five children.

Best known of Kretzmann's works is his four-volume *Popular Commentary of the Bible* (1921–24); other published works include *Christian Art* (1921), *Teaching of Religion* (1934), and *What Lutheran Sunday School Teachers Should Know* (1928). He served as coeditor of the *Concordia Cyclopedia* (1927).

TRANSLATOR: 187 When All the World Was Cursed

KRIEGER, ADAM (1634–66), was born January 7, 1634, at Driesen in the Neumark, Prussia. A student of Samuel Scheidt (1587–1654) in Halle and also Heinrich Schütz (1585–1672) in Dresden, in 1655 he became organist at St. Nicholas' in Leipzig. Two years later he was appointed court organist in Dresden. He died June 30, 1666, at the age of 32.

A poet as well as a talented composer, he is remembered especially for his *Neue Arien* (Dresden, 1669), songs for two, three, and five voices on his own texts with instrumental ritornelli between each stanza.

COMPOSER: 277 EINS IST NOT

KRIEGER, W. HARRY (1914–74), was born in Marion, Illinois, May 2, 1914. He received his undergraduate training at St. Paul's College, Concordia, Missouri, going on to attend Concordia Seminary, St. Louis, from which he graduated in 1939. In 1941 he became pastor of Messiah Lutheran Church in Columbia, South Carolina; during World War II he became an army chaplain, serving with the 38th Infantry Division in the Pacific and the Army of Occupation in northern Japan. Krieger was decorated with the Bronze Star Medal and the Purple Heart, among other awards.

Trinity Church in Traverse City, Michigan, called Krieger as its pastor in 1948; he remained there 13 years before becoming, in 1961, the full-time president of the Michigan District of The Lutheran Church—Missouri Synod. After four years of presidency, he accepted the call to Trinity Lutheran in Jackson, Michigan, serving as its pastor until his death January 13, 1974.

Krieger held a number of positions in the The Lutheran Church—Missouri Synod, including membership on the Board of Missions in North, South, and Central America; the Commission on Literature; chairman of the Board of Control, Concordia College, Ann Arbor, Michigan; fourth vice-president of the Synod (1965–69); and fifth vice-president (1972–74). He married the former Edith Krueger and fathered four children.

AUTHOR: 326 Our Fathers' God in Years Long Gone

LANDSTAD, MAGNUS BROSTRUP (1802–80), was born in Maasö, Finmarken, Norway, October 7, 1802, where his father was pastor in this extreme northern point of Norway. Educated by his father, he entered the University of Christiania (Oslo) in 1822, completing his theological studies in 1827. It was during his student days that he became interested in hymn writing through the accidental auction purchase of *Freuden-Spiegel des Ewigen Lebens* by Philipp Nicolai (*LW* 73, 177) and Bishop A. Arrebo's *Hexaemeron* (The Glorious and Mighty Works of the Creation Day). First appointed resident vicar of the Lutheran Church at Gausdal, in 1834 he became pastor at Kviteseid. While here he composed three hymns for the Reformation festival. At this time he also began to collect folk songs. Five years later he succeeded his father at Seljord. In 1841 he published his *Hjertesuk* (Heartthrobs, or Prayers).

In 1848 the Norwegian ecclesiastical authorities requested Landstad to prepare a hymnal for the Church of Norway, a request he declined because of the heavy workload at Seljord. Called to Fredrikshald in 1849, he was given an assistant that he might accept and work on the hymnal project, which he did. In 1859 he was called to Sandeherred, where he continued to serve until his retirement in 1876.

In 1861 the first edition of the *Udkast til Kirke-Salmebog* appeared. Criticism about the omission of certain hymns and that the language was too "radical" (the use of Norwegian rather than the conventional Danish), prevented wide acceptance. Landstad, however, continued to revise his old work, and finally on October 16, 1869, Landstad's *Hymnary* was authorized for use at corporate worship in the Church of Norway. Within the year it had made its way into 642 of the 923 parishes. His own parish at Sandeharred, however, dominated by a group of pietists, refused to accept the new hymnal. The hymnal was notable not only for his original hymn texts and translations of Latin and German hymns, but also its use of many Norwegian poets, thus making it a national hymnal.

Landstad died October 9, 1880, in Christiania, having written about 175 hymns. His hymnal was not replaced until the 20th century when it was reedited and greatly enlarged as Landstad's *Reviderte Salmebog*.

AUTHOR: 234 To You, Omniscient Lord of All
464 A Multitude Comes
466 Oh, Blessed Home Where Man and Wife

LAWES, HENRY (1595–1662), was born at Dinton, Wiltshire, England, in December 1595, and baptized January 1, 1596. A pupil of Giovanni Coperario (John Cooper, who was music master of the children of James I), Lawes was appointed an epistoler (reader of the epistle at the Communion service) of the Chapel Royal, January 1, 1626, and a gentleman of the Chapel in November of the same year. He became music master to the family of the Earl of Bridgewater, and was commissioned by the earl to write and direct a masque in honor of the festivities when he became lord president of Wales. Lawes asked John Milton to prepare the text, and on Michaelmas night, September 29, 1634, *Comus* was given its first performance at Ludlow Castle. Milton was from then on his friend, and addressed a sonnet to him beginning:

> Harry, whose tuneful and well-measured song,
> First taught our English music how to span
> Words with just note and accent...

Lawes excelled as a songwriter, and published several volumes of *Ayres and Dialogues for one, two, and three voices*. His best writing is found in his stage productions and in his 300 or more songs. He was highly esteemed by his contemporaries, especially by poets, because of his careful attention to text-setting, and he developed a style known as *aria parlante*, a style of melody midway between aria and recitative. Included in his church music are about 20 anthems. His hymn tunes were contributed to Sandys' *Psalms*, and to *Choice Psalms put into Musick for three Voices* (1648), published with his brother, William (1602–45), for use of the Chapel Royal and the Royal Court of Charles I. During the Protectorate, Lawes lost all his court appointments, but regained them in 1660 with the Restoration, when he wrote an anthem for the coronation of Charles II. He died October 21, 1662, in London and is buried in the cloisters of Westminster Abbey.

Ralph Vaughan Williams brought Lawes' tunes into circulation in England and America when he included five of them in *The English Hymnal* (1906).

COMPOSER (attr.): 243 FARLEY CASTLE

LEAF, ROBERT, (1936–) was born February 20, 1936. After earning a Bachelor of Music Education degree from MacPhail College of Music, Minneapolis, he studied composition with Paul Fetler. Having published nearly 100 choir selections as well as having taught public school music, he lives in Minneapolis, where he continues to compose.

ARRANGER: 400 TWENTY-FOURTH

LEESON, JANE ELIZABETH (1809–81). Little is known about her. Born in London, she is the only hymn writer in general currency from the Catholic Apostolic Church, to whose hymnal she contributed nine hymns and translations. Remembered especially for two children's hymns, "Loving Shepherd of the sheep" (*EH* 602) and "Savior, teach me day by day" (*EpH* 428), both considered real classics of children's hymnody, many of her hymns were the outcome of prophetic utterance, a supposed revival of the ancient "gift of prophecy" mentioned in 1 Corinthians 14. These hymns have not survived. Later in life she joined the Roman Catholic Church, at which time she wrote several books for children, largely of a devotional character, including *Infant Hymnings, Songs of Christian Chivalry* (1848), and *The Child's Book of Ballads* (1849).

She died November 18, 1881, at Leamington in Warwickshire.

AUTHOR: 475 Gracious Savior, Gentle Shepherd
TRANSLATOR: 137 Christ the Lord Is Risen Today; Alleluia

LETTERMANN, HENRY L. (1932–), was born February 28, 1932, at Pittsburgh, Pennsylvania. Following his elementary education at First Evangelical Lutheran School, Sharpsburg, Pennsylvania, he attended Concordia High School, and thereafter the then-Concordia Teacher's College (now Concordia University), River Forest, Illinois, where he received the Bachelor of Science degree in 1954. After teaching at the Junior High School of Trinity Lutheran Church, Fort Lauderdale, Florida (1954–56), and at the Lutheran High School Central, St. Louis, Missouri (1956–59), he became instructor of English at Concordia College, River Forest, in 1959. Here, while furthering his education—Master of Arts degree from the University of Chicago (1959);

Doctor of Philosophy degree from Loyola University, Chicago (1974)—he rose through the ranks to become full professor.

Besides his classroom responsibilities, his interest in education of the young, coupled with his poetic talents, resulted in his contributing numerous texts of children's songs that appeared in the Concordia Music Education series published by Concordia Publishing House as well as numerous carols published in *Lutheran Education*, the organ of the Lutheran Education Association, of which he is a member. Pastors have frequently called on him to write hymns for anniversary observances. As a member and secretary of the Hymn Text and Music Committee of the Synod's Commission on Worship that prepared *Lutheran Worship* (1982), he contributed both original texts and translations from the German. Later, from 1984–87, he served as a member of the commission itself.

Unfortunately, a serious illness in July 1985 caused Lettermann to resign his professorship and seek early retirement. He and his wife Betty, the parents of a grown son and daughter, presently live in Dunedin, Florida.

AUTHOR:	63	Who Are These That Earnest Knock
	320	On Galilee's High Mountain
	324	As Moses, Lost in Sinai's Wilderness
	417	The Lord's My Shepherd, Leading Me
	430	Our Father, Who from Heaven Above
	470	Lord Jesus Christ, the Children's Friend
TRANSLATOR:	108	From Calvary's Cross I Heard Christ Say
	111	A Lamb Alone Bears Willingly
	197	Lord, Open Now My Heart to Hear
	246	Lord Jesus Christ, You Have Prepared
	413	Lord, You I Love with All My Heart

LEMKE, AUGUST (1820–1913). Little is known about this man who came to America from Germany and, in 1847, became Christian day school teacher, organist, and choir director for Trinity Lutheran Church, Milwaukee, Wisconsin. It was while serving in this capacity that he wrote the tune for Georg Weissel's text, "Macht hoch die Tür, die Tor' macht weit ("Lift up your heads, You mighty gates"), that would later be called MILWAUKEE. In 1851 Lemke resigned his position and took up a secular occupation. Nothing further is known of him, except that he died November 1, 1913.

COMPOSER:	24	MILWAUKEE

LINDEMAN, LUDVIG MATTIAS (1812–87), was born November 28, 1812, in Trondhjem, Norway. He first studied piano, organ, and theory with his father Ole Andreas Lindemann, organist for 57 years at the Church of Our Lady and editor of the first Norwegian choral book, *Koralbog* (1835). Already at the age of 12 Ludvig frequently substituted for his father at the organ. After completing his liberal arts studies, he entered the seminary in Christiania (Oslo) in 1833. While there he often substituted for his brother as organist at Our Savior's Church, as well as playing 'cello in the Christiania theater orchestra. Having decided to choose music as his vocation rather than theology, in 1839 he succeeded his brother as organist of Our Savior's, a position that he held for the rest of his life. As the outstanding organ virtuoso of his day in Norway, in 1871 he was invited to play several recitals for the dedication of the new organ in the Royal Albert Hall, London. Although he gave up theology for music, he continued his association with the seminary in Christiania as professor of singing and church music. In 1848 he was married to Aminda Magnhilde Brynie, and in 1883 with his son Peter, he founded what is today the Oslo Conservatory, the first music conservatory in Norway.

Beginning in 1848 Lindeman traveled throughout Norway collecting folk tunes. By 1880 the collection of tunes numbered over 2,500, many of which were preserved in a series of volumes, *Aeldre og nyere norske fjeldmelodier* (1853–67)—a source for later composers such as Edvard Grieg (*LW* 192).

When Landstad's (*LW* 234, et al.) *Hymnary* was authorized for use in 1869, Lindeman assumed the task of editing a chorale book to accompany it. In 1872 he completed the task, having introduced the use of quarters, dotted quarters, and eighth notes (instead of the accustomed half-note style of notation) in order to restore life and rhythm to singing. Despite strong reaction to his changes, his *Koralbog, indelholdende de i Landstads Salmebog forekommende Melodier* was authorized for used in 1877. It quickly won acceptance, due in part to the use of some of his own tunes as alternates for established ones. His interest in liturgy was evident when he published *Norsk Messebog* (1870), which gave the foundations of chanting liturgical texts, based in part on Luther's (*LW* 13, et al.) instructions in the *Deutsche Messe* (1526). A gifted composer of melodies, Lindeman is known for various publications: *Melodier til W. A. Wexels Christilige Psalmer* (1840), *Martin Luthers aandelige Sange, samt 25 Salmer fra det 16. og 17. Aarhundred, ordenede af M. B. Landstad* (1859), *Melodier til Hauges Salmebog* (1875) and *Hoimesseliturgi* (1877). He died May 23, 1887.

COMPOSER:	96	NAAR MIT IE
	291	KIRKEN DEN ER ET GAMMELT HUS

LINDEMANN, JOHANN (1549–1631), was born in 1549 in Thuringia, Germany, son of Cyriacus Lindemann, a noted educator trained at Wittenberg. After studying at the *Gymnasium* in Gotha, he attended the University of Jena from 1568–70, when he was awarded the Master of Arts degree. Thereafter he became cantor in Gotha (1580), a position he held until he retired in 1631. He died November 6, 1631.

Lindemann was a relative of Martin Luther (*LW* 13, et al.)—Luther's mother was born Margarete Lindemann; her brother was Johann Lindemann's grandfather. In addition to his work in music, Lindemann was noted as one of the signers of Formula of Concord (1577).

AUTHOR: 442 In You Is Gladness

LITTLEDALE, RICHARD FREDERICK (1833–90), was born September 14, 1833, in Dublin, Ireland, the son of a merchant. Educated at Trinity College, Dublin, where he earned a Doctor of Laws degree, and at Oxford, where he earned a Doctor of Civil Law degree, he was ordained a deacon in 1856 and a priest in 1857, serving St. Matthew's, Thorpe Hamlet, Norfolk, and thereafter St. Mary the Virgin, Crown Street, Soho. When ill health forced him to give up this work, he devoted his time to literary work, publishing almost 50 books, chiefly on theological, historical, liturgical, and hymnological subjects. A devoted high churchman and friend of John Mason Neale, he wielded considerable influence by his *Plain Reasons Against Joining the Church of Rome* in 1880. A versatile linguist, he not only wrote original hymns but translated texts from Danish, Swedish, Greek, Latin, Syriac, German, and Italian. Many of these appeared in *The Peoples Hymnal*, which he edited in 1867 with James Edward Vaux. With him he also prepared the *Priest's Prayerbook* (1864) and *The Altar Manual* (1863-77). He also compiled *Carols for Christmas and Other Seasons* (1863). He died January 11, 1890, in London.

TRANSLATOR: 162 Come Down, O Love Divine

LÖHNER, JOHANN (1645–1705), a contemporary Johann Pachelbel (1653–1706), was born December 21, 1645, in Nürnberg, Germany. With the death of his parents at age 15, he was adopted by his brother-in-law G. C. Wecker, under whose tutelage he became a musician. After traveling to Vienna, Salzburg (where he played for the archbishop), and Leipzig (to hear Sebastian Knüpfer), he returned to his hometown of Nürnberg, where he sang as a tenor in various churches and served as organist at the *Frauenkirche*. In 1682 he became organist of the *Spitalkirche* and in 1694 of the *Lorenzkirche*, where he remained until his death April 2, 1705.

Löhner's works include a number of hymn tunes and numerous songs for one voice and simple continuo that he wrote as devotional music for the home. His most significant work is perhaps the *Auserlesene Kirch- und Tafel-Music*, containing 12 works for solo voice, two violins, and continuo. His last published work is a collection of 21 canons and two four-part motets.

COMPOSER: 415 ALLES IST AN GOTTES SEGEN

LONGFELLOW, HENRY WADSWORTH (1807–82) was born February 27, 1807, at Portland, Maine, into a family which traced its ancestry to Plymouth Pilgrims. His early education took place in Portland, When he was 15, he enrolled in Bowdoin College, Brunswick, Maine, graduating in 1825 with his classmate and friend, Nathaniel Hawthorne. While still in school, he published poetry in several national magazines, which led him to choose writing over law for his vocation. Because of his ability in translation, he was offered a professorship at Bowdoin on the condition he study in Europe. Returning from Europe, he taught at Bowdoin from 1829–35, when he accepted a professorship at Harward. Again, he went to study in Europe, accompanied by his wife, Mary Storer Potter, whom he had married in 1831. His wife died in 1835 at Rotterdam. He returned to Harvard, where he taught for 18 years. In 1843 Longfellow married Frances Elizabeth Appleton, who died from an accident in 1861. Throughout his career he continued his work of translation, which also encouraged his work in poetry. Among his works are included: *Poems of Slavery* (1842); *Poets and Poetry of Europe* (1845); *Evangeline* (1847); *The Song of Hiawatha* (1855); *The Courtship of Miles Standish* (1858); *Tales of a Wayside Inn* (1863); *Christus: A Mystery* (1872), a trilogy on the beginnings of Christianity. Though never a hymnist, as was his brother Samuel (*LW* 166), nevertheless a number of his poems have been adapted for purpose. He died March 24, 1882, at Cambridge, Massachusetts.

TRANSLATOR: 268 Oh, How Blest Are You
COLLECTOR: 486 O Gladsome Light, O Grace

LONGFELLOW, SAMUEL (1819–92), brother of the famous Henry Wadsworth Longfellow, was born June 18, 1819, in Portland, Maine, and earned the Bachelor of Arts degree from Harvard in 1839. Equally distinguished as a Unitarian minister and as a hymn writer, he was pastor of the Unitarian Church, Fall River, Massachusetts (1848–51); of the Second Unitarian Church, Brooklyn, New York (1853–60); and from 1860–83 of the Unitarian Church in Germantown, Pennsylvania. While pastor in Brooklyn, he instituted a series of vesper services that became widely popular in other communions and that led to the publication of *Vespers* (1859).

Among his other works are *A Book of Hymns and Tunes* (1860); *A Book Of Hymns For Public and Private Devotion* (1846), which he coedited with Samuel Johnson; and *Hymns of the Spirit* (1864). Following his retirement in 1884, he prepared his brother's biography, which was published in 1886. Like his friend S. Johnson, Longfellow shifted from Unitarianism to a free thinking Universalism, in which Christianity had no special place.

He died October 3, 1892, in Portland, Maine.

AUTHOR: 166 Holy Spirit, Light Divine

LÖWENSTERN, MATTHÄUS APELLES von (1594–1648), was born April 20, 1594, at Neustadt, Silesia, the son of a saddler. In 1625 he was appointed treasurer and director of the choir at Bernstadt by Duke Heinrich Wenzel of Münsterberg; in 1626 he was appointed director of the Princes School at Bernstadt; in 1631 he was made counsel, secretary and director of finances. Later he became counsel for emperors Ferdinand II and Ferdinand III; the latter made him a noble. His last position was as councillor of state at

Oels to Duke Carl Friedrich of Münsterberg, a brother of the aforementioned nobles. He died April 11, 1648 at Breslau.

Löwenstern's 30 hymns—set to his own tunes—were written in imitation of some of the older verse forms, such as the sapphic and alcaic, and, as he said, for the furtherance of the praise of God and the edification of his church. Though he never published these hymns himself, some friends collected and published them in 1644 under the title *Spring Blossom, from 30 Flowers that grew in a quiet little Graden, but which were plucked somewhat too early.*

AUTHOR: 301 Lord of Our Life

LOWRY, SOMERSET THOMAS CORRY (1855–1932), was born in Dublin, March 21, 1855, the son of a lawyer. Educated at Repton School and Trinity Hall, Cambridge, from which he graduated with a Bachelor of Arts degree in 1877 and Master of Arts degree in 1880, he was ordained deacon in 1879 and priest the following year. Thereafter he served in several parishes before going to St. Augustine's in Bournemouth as vicar in 1900. He became rector of Wonsten in 1911 and vicar at St. Bartholomew, Southsea, in 1914. In 1919 he retired in Bournemouth. He died at Torquay January 29, 1932.

A scholar and author, Lowry's published works include *The Work of the Holy Spirit* (1894), *Convalescence* (1897), *Lessons from the Passion* (1899), and *The Days of our Pilgrimage* (1900). His 60-some hymns were published from time to time in various periodicals, nearly all of which were included in his *Hymns and Spiritual Songs* (1910).

AUTHOR: 394 Son of God, Eternal Savior

LOY, MATTHIAS (1828–1915), was born in Cumberland County, Pennsylvania, March 17, 1828, the fourth of seven children. His mother, a Lutheran, gave the children their Christian elementary education. When only 14 years of age, Loy was apprenticed to Baab and Hummel, printers in Harrisburg, a position he held for six years, at the same time attending school. Charles W. Schaeffer (*LW* 379), Lutheran pastor in Harrisburg, urged him to pursue the holy ministry as his vocation. This prompted Loy to study Latin and Greek with the principal of the Harrisburg Academy, where he later became a regular student. Next he left for Circleville, Ohio, to print a German semimonthly paper for the United Brethren Publishing House. On the suggestion, however, of the Lutheran pastor in Circleville, he decided to enter the seminary of the Evangelical Lutheran Synod of Ohio at Columbus. During his seminary days he was an avid reader of *Der Lutheraner*, edited by C. F. W. Walther (*LW* 138). Upon his graduation in 1849 Loy was called to a congregation in Delaware, Ohio. In 1860 he was elected president of the Joint Synod of Ohio and four years later he was appointed editor of the *Lutheran Standard*. Then, having served 16 years in the parish ministry, he accepted the call to be professor of theology at Capital University, Columbus, Ohio, March 1865. Three years later he resigned as president of the Ohio Synod. William F. Lehmann, professor at the Columbus seminary who had been vice-president, succeeded him. It was at this time that Loy declined the call to become English professor of theology at Concordia Seminary, St. Louis. Two years later, upon the death of Lehman, Loy returned to Ohio as president of Capital University and, again, as president of the Ohio Synod. He retired in 1902 and died January 26, 1915.

In addition to editing the *Lutheran Standard* Loy started the *Columbus Theological Magazine* in 1881. He fostered the formation of the Synodical Conference, organized in 1872, and he wrote four books: *The Doctrine of Justification* (1868), *Sermons on the Gospel* (1888), *Christian Church* (1896), and *The Story of My Life* (1905). In addition to the 20 hymns that he wrote, he prepared many translations of German hymns.

AUTHOR:	329	The Law of God Is Good and Wise
	330	The Gospel Shows the Father's Grace
TRANSLATOR:	235	As Surely As I Live, God Said
	249	Your Table I Approach
	257	Let Me Be Yours Forever
	363	All Mankind Fell in Adam's Fall
	477	Lord, Help Us Ever to Retain

LUISE, HENRIETTA (1627–1667), Electress of Brandenburg, daughter of Fridrich Heinrich, Prince of Nassau-Orange and Stadtholder of the United Netherlands, was born at 'S Granvenhage (The Hague), Nov. 27, 1627. She received a careful Christian training in literature and also domestic economy. On Dec. 7, 1646, she married Elector Fridrich Wilhelm of Brandenburg, who was then residing at Cleve. In the autumn of 1649 she set out with her husband and child, Wilhelm Heinrich, on the way to Berlin, but in the inclement weather the child became ill and died at Wesel, Oct. 24, 1649. It was not till April 10, 1650, that she went to Berlin. On the birth of her second son, Carl Emil (d. 1674), at Oranienburg, near Berlin, on Feb. 16, 1655, she founded an orphanage there as a thank-offering (now the Oranienburg Orphanage at Berlin). On July 11, 1657, her third son, who became King Friedrich I of Prussia, was born at Königsberg. After the birth of her youngest son, Ludwig, at Cleve, in 1666, she never entirely recovered. In the spring of 1667 she was conveyed to Berlin, where she died there June 18, 1667.

Henretta Luise was a woman of noble character; a devoted wife who accompanied her husband in many of his expeditions, and was his right-hand counsellor in matters of state; and a true mother of her people, introducing the culture of the potato, founding model farms, establishing elementary schools, and in many ways interesting herself in restoring their welfare after the ravages of the Thirty Years' War. She was, like the Elector, a member of the Reformed Church, but earnestly desired to promote peace between the Lutheran and Reformed communions, and exerted herself especially on behalf of Paul Gerhardt. Another of her efforts in this direction was by means of the *Union Hymn Book*, which Christoph Runge edited at her direction and published in 1653. In this book, four hymns appeared with her name.

AUTHOR (attr.) 266 Jesus Christ, My Sure Defense

LUNDEEN, JOEL WALDEMAR (1918–), was born May 24, 1918, in Yuchow, Honan, China, the son of missionary parents. After one year at Augsburg College, Minneapolis, he transferred to Augustana College, Rock Island, Illinois, where he completed the Bachelor of Arts degree in 1940. Having earned the Master of Divinity degree at Augustana Theological Seminary, Rock Island, he was ordained in 1945, and first served for two years at Peace Lutheran Church, Arlington, Virginia. In 1945 he and Doris M. Nordling, a nurse, were united in marriage and are the parents of four sons. After combining the parish ministry with teaching for a number of years in New Jersey and Kansas, he served as library director and church archivist at Augustana Seminary from 1958–67; then as library director at the Lutheran School of Theology, Chicago, (1968–75), where he also taught hymnology and worship. From 1967–83 he was associate archivist for the Lutheran Church in America.

He is past president of the Augustana Historical Society and the Lutheran Historical Conference. From 1957–62 he served as secretary of the Commission on Worship of the Augustana Church; for 10 years he was member of the Sub-Committee on Hymn Texts of the Inter-Lutheran Commission on Worship that prepared *Lutheran Book of Worship* (1978); in 1965 he became a member of the Hymn Society of America. His talent in music, enhanced by receiving an organ scholarship at Augustana College, found expression in frequently serving as organist in various churches in Minneapolis, Quad-Cities, and Chicago. In 1985 Bethany College, Lindsborg, Kansas, honored him with the Doctor of Humanities degree.

Included in his publications are sermons, Bible studies and devotional materials; articles on church music and Augustana church history; the *Archival Responsibilities of the Seminary and Church College Librarians* (1962–64); and *Preserving Yesterday for Tomorrow: A Guide for the Archives of the LCA* (1977); and the comprehensive index to the 54 volume American Edition of *Luther's Works* published by Fortress Press in 1986.

Retired since 1983, he and his wife live in Grand Forks, North Dakota.

TRANSLATOR: 199 We Worship You, O God of Might
208 Lamb of God, Pure and Sinless

LUTHER, MARTIN (1483–1546), was born November 10, 1483, in Eisleben, the son of miner Hans Luther and Margarete, *née* Ziegler. His education, not without considerable hardship, was mainly gained at Magdeburg, Eisenach, and the University of Erfurt, where he earned the Master of Arts degree in 1505. Following a short time at the Erfurt Law School, he entered the Black Cloister of the Augustinians in Erfurt and was ordained a priest in 1507. He then was sent as lecturer to the recently founded University of Wittenberg, where he continued his studies as he lectured on moral philosophy. In 1509 he was recalled to Erfurt to assist his old Augustinian teacher

Johannes Nathin in instructing novitiates. Being sent to Rome in 1510 on affairs of his order, he was shocked by the worldliness of some of the Italian clergy. Not long after his return to Wittenberg in 1512 he became Doctor of Theology and professor of Scripture. Conflict with the church began with Dominican Friar Tetzel's selling of indulgences in Wittenberg and Luther's response in the posting of his 95 theses on the door of the Castle Church there October 31, 1517. Summoned to Rome to answer for his theses, Luther's university and the Elector of Saxony refused to let him go. His treatise, *The Babylonian Captivity of the Church* (1520), prompted Pope Leo to issue a papal bull against him, which Luther publicly burned at Wittenberg. Emperor Charles V summoned him to appear before the Diet of Worms (1521), where Luther refused to retract his doctrines, and thus was placed under the imperial ban. On the return trip to Wittenberg, the elector, fearing for his safety, had his friends "capture" him and take him to the Wartburg Castle where, among other writings, he began his translation of the Bible (completed in 1534). In 1522, to calm various iconoclastic disorders, he returned to Wittenberg and its university. Three years later he married Katharina von Bora, a former nun.

Luther's work in hymnody grew largely out of his concern for liturgical reform. As early as 1523 in his *Formula Missae* he bemoans the lack of vernacular songs that people might sing during the Mass, and he encourages German poets to compose evangelical hymns for this purpose. Soon poets rose to supply the need, following Luther's example; there began that great stream of hymnody that lasted for two centuries.

Printing with movable metal type, invented by Johann Gutenberg about 1449, made it possible quickly to print and disseminate the hymns of the early Reformation. The hymn tunes and texts of the late medieval and Lutheran traditions appear largely in books printed between 1524 and 1545. The few 1523 publications were in broadsheet form. Beginning with 1524 the majority of hymnbooks appear with text and tune, thus designed for unison singing; others appear with text lined out for more voices, thus designed for choir use. Among the chief one-voice hymnals is the *Etlich Christlich lider Lobgesang* (Wittenberg, 1524), commonly known as the *Achtliederbuch* from its contents—four hymns by Luther, three by Paul Speratus (*LW* 355), and one by an unnamed author. This book enjoys the distinction of being, what might be called, the first Lutheran hymnal. Next came the two known as the Erfurt *Enchiridia*, also in 1524—the first entitled *Enchiridion oder eyn Handbuchlein*, the second, *Eyn Enchiridion oder Handbuchlein*. These first three small hymnbooks were designed that congregations might begin learning the hymns by following the choir's singing of them. Then there are Joseph Klug's (LW 124, et al.) two significant editions of *Geistliche Lieder*, (Wittenberg,1529), of which no copy is extant, and the 1533 edition. Not to be overlooked are Michael Weisse's (*LW* 18) *Ein New Gesengbuchlen* (1531), a collection for the Bohemian Brethren, and Valentin Schumann's (*LW* 37, 38) *Geistliche Lieder auffs newgebessert und gemehrt* (Leipzig, 1539). Valentin Babst's *Geystliche Lieder* (Leipzig, 1545) is considered to be the finest and most representative hymnal of this period. It contained 89 hymns plus an additional 40 in the appendix and is the last hymnal publication that Luther had opportunity to supervise.

Of the multi-voiced hymnals for choir, two especially deserve mention. The first is Johann Walter's *Geystliche gesangk Buchleyn* (Wittenberg, 1524), Luther's first official hymnbook publication, which was actually a collection of polyphonic motets with the *cantus firmus*, or melody, in the tenor. Of the 38 hymns in this collection, 28 are by Luther, approximately two-thirds of his total output. The popularity of this book evoked four more editions—1525, 1537, 1544, and 1551, each an improvement over its predecessor. The second hymnal, Georg Rhau's (*LW* 382) *Newe deudsche geistliche Gesenge* (Wittenberg, 1544), constitutes an anthology of choral settings by favorite composers of the Renaissance and Reformation eras. It is estimated that from 1524 to Luther's death in 1546 no less than 100 hymnals were published in Germany.

Great impetus was given congregational singing with Luther's issuance of his vernacular service, the *Deutsche Messe*, in 1526 with its simple metrical paraphrases, or hymn versions, of the ordinary of the Mass. In the course of time the Kyrie became "Kyrie, God Father in heaven above," the Gloria "All glory be to God on high" or "All glory be to God alone," the Credo "We all believe in one true God," the Sanctus "Isaiah, mighty seer, in spirit soared," and the Agnus Dei "O Christ, the Lamb of God." (Cf. Divine Service III, *Lutheran Worship*, pp. 197–198.)

Luther's hymns, so far as their source is concerned, can conveniently be grouped into five categories. The Psalter furnished immediate inspiration for the first group. The most celebrated and well-known in this class is "A mighty fortress is our God" (*LW* 297–98), suggested by Psalm 46. Then there are the less bold paraphrases such as "From depths of woe" (*LW* 230), based on Psalm 130. Second, there are paraphrases of other portions of Scripture such as "Isaiah, mighty seer, in spirit soared" (*LW* 214), based on Isaiah 6:1-4, "In peace and joy I now depart" (*LW* 185), and "Our Father, who from heaven above"(*LW* 431). Third, there are the transcriptive translations of Latin office hymns and antiphons, approximately 12 in number. There are, for example, the "Come, Holy Ghost, God and Lord" (*LW* 154), based on "Veni, sancte Spiritus;"and "From east to west" (*LW* 43), derived from "A solis ortus cardine." The next group includes the pre-Reformation *Leisen*, songs which Luther recast and revised, examples of which are "To God the Holy Spirit let us pray" *LW* 155) and "Triune God, oh, be our stay" (*LW* 170). Finally, there are the original hymns such as "Flung to the heedless winds" (*TLH* 259), commemorating the burning at the stake in Brussels in 1523 of the two Augustinian monks Heinrich Vose and Johann Esch, the first martyrs of the Reformation. Included in this category is also "Dear Christians, one and all, rejoice" (*LW* 353), a clear and forceful expression of the whole plan of God's salvation for sinful mankind.

Luther's speech is that of the people—idiomatic, penetrating, often coarse and rugged. But it is the speech of a tremendously earnest mand concerned with a momentous religious cause. The simple, homemade, domestic form of these chorales went straight to the heart of the common man. They speak the great truths of salvation not in dry doctrinal tones or individualistic reflection but in the form of testimony and confession.

As for the tunes of Luther's hymns, musicologists today are inclined to ascribe his authorship to most, if not all, of the new tunes that appeared with his hymns, particularly in the Wittenberg hymnals, and they credit him with having arranged some of the older tunes. Luther was an accomplished amateur musician who had a fine voice as a boy, and who became an expert player on the flute and the lute. His music education was such that he knew and followed medieval concepts of both the theory and ethical implications of music. He not only preserved and extended the music traditions of his day, he was also an innovator, especially in his use of the church modes, the tonal system of his day. In this respect it is his use of the later and newer modes, especially the Ionian, that show him to have been in step with the advanced thinking of his day. Moreover, as Riedel says, these modes brought new, brighter, less austere sounds within the walls of the churches. (See essay: The Church Modes, p. 832.)

Luther's frequent discourses on music show that his musical philosophy was carefully thought out, logical, sincere, and applicable to situations of life and churchly activity. Familiar are his statements of esteem for music:

> Next to the Word of God music deserves the highest praise.
>
> I am strongly persuaded that after theology there is no art that can be placed on a level with music; for besides theology, music is the only art capable of affording peace and joy of the heart, like that induced by the study of the science of divinity.

For Luther, the spoken, proclaimed, and preached Word of God is of first importance. This is the "living voice of the Gospel"—God speaking to mankind. Faith comes from what is heard. Music is first and foremost an event that is heard. It resembles the Word as the miracle of God that we hear, for, as he insisted, "the notes instill life into the texts." In the preface to a collection of part-songs he wrote:

> Indeed, upon mankind, not upon any other creatures, has been bestowed not only a voice, but also the gift of speech, in order that mankind might know that it is to praise God with words and music.

In praising the great Renaissance composer Josquin des Prez (c. 1440–c. 1521)) "as a master of notes," Luther states that "God has his Gospel preached also through the medium of music." Commenting on the last words of David (2 Sam. 23:1) he says: "Music and notes, which are wonderful gifts and creations of God, do help gain a better understanding of the text, especially when sung by a congregation and when sung earnestly." Thus in all his hymns and liturgical compositions Luther used music, not to entertain or embellish, but to proclaim the Word of God.

Luther was frequently beset with illness and in his closing years he often wished for death. Nevertheless, pressing duties and numerous requests kept him busy. In February of 1546 he was asked to negotiate peace between the princes of Mansfeld. Thus, in the cold of winter he set out for Eisleben with his sons and Justus Jonas, provost of the Castle Church and professor of canon law at the University of Wittenberg. A swollen stream with ice floes delayed the group in Halle for three days before permitting a dangerous crossing. Difficult negotiations finally led to a compromise agreeable to both princes. The following day Luther rested comfortably; he was in good spirits, he conversed freely about death, resurrection, and eternal life. That evening he retired early. Shortly after midnight he awakened with severe pains. He remarked to Justus Jonas: "I'll be happy to remain here in Eisleben, where I was born and baptized." As a cold sweat engulfed him, he earnestly repeated the text of John 3:16. With the words, "Father, into your hands I commend my spirit," he passed away shortly before 3 a. m. on February 18, 1546. His funeral procession traveled from Eisleben over Halle to Wittenberg, where he was buried in the Castle Church.

AUTHOR:	13	Savior of the Nations, Come
	35	We Praise, O Christ, Your Holy Name
	37	From Heaven Above to Earth I Come
	38	Welcome to Earth, O Noble Guest
	52	From Heaven Came the Angels Bright
	123	Christ Jesus Lay in Death's Strong Bands
	154	Come, Holy Ghost, God and Lord
	155	To God the Holy Spirit Let Us Pray
	170	Triune God, Oh, Be Our Stay
	185	In Peace and Joy I Now Depart
	210	All Glory Be to God Alone
	213	We All Believe in One True God, Maker
	214	Isaiah, Mighty Seer, in Spirit Soared
	219	Grant Peace, We Pray, in Mercy, Lord
	223	To Jordan Came the Christ, Our Lord
	230	From Depths of Woe I Cry to You
	238	O Lord, We Praise You
	265	In the Very Midst of Life
	288	May God Embrace Us with His Grace
	297, 298	A Mighty Fortress Is Our God
	331	Here Is the Tenfold Sure Command
	334	Lord, Keep Us Steadfast in Your Word
	353	Dear Christians, One and All
	431	Our Father, Who from Heaven Above
COMPOSER:	185	MIT FRIED UND FREUD
	214	JESAIA, DEM PROPHETEN
	230	AUS TIEFER NOT I
	234, 280, 430, 431	VATER UNSER
	297, 298	EIN FESTE BURG

LYON, MEYER (c. 1751–97), also known by his liturgical name, Michael Leoni, was born perhaps in London. He became a popular tenor at Covent Garden and Drury Lane, as well as cantor at various London synagogues, including the Great Synagogue, Aldgate,

London. Singing in Handel's (*LW* 53) *Messiah*, however, made him unpopular with fellow-Jews in London, a fact which may have prompted him to proceed to Dublin in 1778. There, in his attempt to popularize his opera, he went bankrupt. Returning to London, he failed to find the favor he previously enjoyed. In 1787 he went to Jamaica and became *chazzan* of the Ashkenazic (English and German) Synagogue in Kingston. There he spent the remainder of his life. Though he wrote several pieces for the theater and for use in the Jewish ritual, he is especially remembered for the ancient Hebrew tune (YIGDAL) which he arranged and gave to a friend in the Church of England.

ARRANGER: 450 YIGDAL

LYTE, HENRY FRANCIS (1793–1847), was born near Kelso, Roxburghshire, Scotland, June 1, 1793. Orphaned at an early age, he was educated as a charity student at an Irish boys' school, the Portora, the Royal School of Enniskillen, and finally at Trinity College, Dublin. Here he augmented his limited funds by three times winning the prize for English poetry. He graduated in 1814, intending to go into medicine, but instead was ordained in 1815 and received a curacy near Wexford, Ireland.

Moving to Marazion in 1817, Lyte was called in 1818 to the nearby home of a friend and fellow clergyman who was dying and felt unprepared. He and Lyte turned to the writings of St. Paul, where they both found the comfort, peace, and hope they sought. The friend died in peace; Lyte relates: "I was greatly affected by the whole matter, and brought to look at life and its issue with a different eye than before; and I began to study my Bible and preach in another manner than I had previously done." He took charge of the family of his departed friend from that point.

By his own account "jostled from one curacy to another," Lyte was transferred to Lymington, Hampshire, in 1819, and to Lower Brixham, Devonshire, in 1823. By this time he had married the daughter heiress to the estate of the Reverend W. Maxwell of Bath.

Lower Brixham, famous as the 1688 landing place of William of Orange in his effort to drive out Catholic James II, was a rough, uncouth fishing village. Lyte spent 24 years there in devoted service, organizing a Sunday school, training teachers, and writing hymns. When William IV visited the place shortly after his accession, Lyte and his surpliced choir met the king with song which so pleased his majesty that he presented the curate with Berry Head House, which at one time had served as a hospital for the troops quartered in that area. Eager to share the Psalms with his parishioners, Lyte wrote most of his 81 hymns in this new home.

Asthmatic and tending to be tubercular, Lyte's health failed in 1844, forcing him to spend subsequent winters in Nice on the French Riviera, although summers he returned to Brixham. His long absences allowed dissensions in the parish; some members left to join the Plymouth Brethren; and his choir dispersed. Insisting it was better to "wear out than to rust out," he struggled to keep both his flock and his health on the right path, but upon his return to Nice in 1847, he died on November 20.

Lyte's *Tales on the Lord's Prayer in Verse*, which he wrote while at Lymington (1819–23), was first printed in 1826. He also published *Poems, Chiefly Religious* (1833) and *Spirit of the Psalms* (1834). Additional poems were published posthumously.

AUTHOR: 490 Abide with Me

MACGREGOR, DUNCAN (1854–1923), was born September 18, 1854, at Fort Augustus, Inverness-shire, England, the son of a schoolmaster who was a noted Gaelic scholar. Following his education at the parish school, Dunnichen, Forfarshire, and the University of Aberdeen, he served as a missionary at Drumoak and Kincardine o'Neil, Aberdeenshire, in the North Isles, and Orkney. In 1881 he was ordained at Inverallochy, an Aberdeenshire fishing village, where he spent the rest of his life. He died October 8, 1923.

As a liturgiologist Macgregor was the leading authority on worship in the early Scottish Church. Among his published works are *The Scald, or, The Northern Ballad-Monger*; *The Gospel of the Scots,* a lecture delivered in St. Paul's Cathedral; *St. Columba*; and *The Celtic Inheritance of the Church of Scotland.*

TRANSLATOR: 271 Christ Is the World's Redeemer

MADSON, NORMAN A. (1886–1962), son of Andrew J. Madson and Mar, *nee* Hoverson, was born November 16, 1886, at Manitowoc, Wisconsin. He was educated at Wittenberg Academy, Wittenberg, Wisconsin; Luther College, Decorah, Iowa; the University of Chicago; and Luther Seminary, Hamline, Minnesota. Ordained November 14, 1915, he served as traveling missionary of the Norwegian Synod on the Iron Range in Northern Minnesota (1915–16); instructor at Luther College (1916–18); U.S. Army chaplain (1918–19); pastor at Bode, Iowa (1919–25), and at Princeton, Minnesota (1925–1946); professor and first dean of Bethany Lutheran Theological Seminary, Mankato, Minnesota (1946-60).

Married August 31, 1918, to Elsie Haakonson, the couple was blessed with three daughters.

Madson served in the following church offices: secretary, Bethany Lutheran College Association (1927–29); president of the Norwegian Synod in 1935 (resigned because of ill health) and again from 1942–46; editor of the *Lutheran Sentinel* (1927–29); member of the Norwegian Synod's Union Committee (1938–57), of the Intersynodical Committee on Hymnology and Liturgics (1929–1942), and of the Missionary Board of the Evangelical Lutheran Synodical Conference of North America (1946–1950).

He is the author of *Ved Betlehemskrybben* (1935), a collection of Christmas festival sermons in the Norwegian language; *Evening Bells at Bethany* (1948), a collection of chapel addresses at Bethany College; *Evening Bells at Bethany II* (1952);

Preaching to Preachers (1952); and many conference and convention essays and a host of articles for the *Evangelisk Luthersk Tidende* and the *Lutheran Sentinel*. In 1951 he was awarded the honorary Doctor of Divinity degree from Concordia Theological Seminary, Springfield, Illinois. After his retirement in 1960 he continued to live in Mankato, Minnesota, until his death December 10, 1962.

TRANSLATOR: 56 I Am So Glad when Christmas Comes
476 I Pray You, Dear Lord Jesus

MAGDEBURG, JOACHIM (c. 1525–c. 1583), was born at Gardelegen in the Altmark, Germany. After spending two years at Wittenberg University, in 1546 he became rector at the school in Schöningen, Brunswick, and in 1547 pastor in Dannenberg in Lüneberg. Two years later, finding it too difficult to exist on his meager salary, he moved to Salzwedel in the Altmark. There he allied himself with Illyricus Flacius (Matthias Flach, 1520–75) in an attack on the Roman Church. Refusing to adopt the Roman ceremonies prescribed in the Augsburg Interim of 1548, he was banished from the electorate of Brandenburg in 1552. It was through his friend Johann Aepinus, that he received the appointment of deacon at St. Peter's in Hamburg. After losing that post because of a disagreement with the successor of Aepinus, he went to the city of Magdeburg. There, in collaboration with Flacius, Magdeburg published the multi-volume church history up to the year 1300 called *The Magdeburg Centuries*. After a brief pastorate in Ossmanstedt in Thuringia, where he was dispossessed as a follower of Flacius, he was appointed military chaplain at Raab in Hungary, ministering to German-speaking troops. Forced to leave because of a Confession of Faith that he and 18 other evangelical clergy submitted to the Austrian Diet, in 1571 he went to Erfurt. It was while here that he published his *Christliche und tröstliche Tischgesänge, mit vier Stimmen* (1572). In 1581 he became pastor at Efferding, Austria, a position that lasted but two years, again the result of his support of Flacius. From then on nothing is known of him.

AUTHOR: 414 Who Trusts in God a Strong Abode

MAHLMANN, SIEGFRIED AUGUST (1771–1826), was born in Leipzig, Germany, May 13, 1771. After studying law at the University of Leipzig, he traveled throughout Europe, returning to Leipzig, where he purchased a bookstore in 1802. From 1805 to 1816 he edited the *Zeitung für die elegante Welt*; from 1810–18 he wrote for the *Leipziger Zeitung*. Besides writing serious poems, he also wrote a number of songs that became popular with German children. He died December 16, 1826, at Leipzig.

AUTHOR: 497 God Bless Our Native Land (German text)

MAJOR, JOHANN (1564–1654), was born at Reinstädt, near Orlamünde, Germany. Becoming deacon at Weimar, then, in 1605, pastor and superintendent at Jena, he finally became professor of theology at the University of Jena. In this position he coedited *Das Weimarische Bibelwerk*, which had first been published in Nürnberg in 1640, contributing also the commentary on Acts and the first three chapters of John.

AUTHOR: 232 Alas, My God, My Sins Are Great

MANT, RICHARD (1776–1848), was born February 12, 1776, at Southampton, the son of the rector of All Saints'. Educated at Winchester and Trinity College, Oxford, he became a fellow of Oriel in 1801. Ordained in 1802, after various curacies he became vicar of Coggeshall, Essex, in 1810; Bampton Lecturer in 1811; domestic chaplain to the archbishop of Canterbury in 1813; rector of St. Botolph's, Bishopsgate, London, in 1816; and in addition, of East Horsley in 1818. He was consecrated bishop of Killaloe, Ireland, in 1820, and in 1823 moved to the see of Down and Connor, to which, in 1833, that of Dromore was added.

A voluminous writer in the field of hymnody as well as in Scripture and church history, his hymns were collected in *The Book of Psalms in an English Metrical Version* (1824); *The Holy Days of the Church* (1828, 1831); and *Ancient Hymns from the Roman Breviary . . . to which are added Original Hymns* (1837).

He died November 2, 1848, in Ballymoney, County Antrim, Ireland.

AUTHOR: 195 For All Your Saints, O Lord

MANZ, PAUL O. (1919–), cantor of the Evangelical Lutheran Church of Saint Luke, and professor of church music at Christ Seminary-Seminex at the Lutheran School of Theology in Chicago, Illinois, was born May 10, 1919, in Cleveland, Ohio. He studied with Albert Riemenschneider, Edwin Arthur Kraft, Edwin Eigenschenck and Arthur B. Jennings, and received a Master of Music degree from Northwestern University, Evanston, Illinois. He was awarded a Fulbright grant to study organ, improvisation and composition at the Royal Flemish Conservatory of Music in Antwerp, Belgium, where he worked with Flor Peeters and earned the first prize with highest distinction. An extension of his grant permitted him to continue his studies in Frankfurt, Germany, with Helmut Walcha. Before coming to Chicago, he held posts in Fond du Lac, Wisconsin; Emmanuel Lutheran Church, St. Paul, Minnesota; the University of Minnesota, Minneapolis, Minnesota; Macalester College, St. Paul, Minnesota; and Concordia College, St. Paul, Minnesota. He was chairman of the Music Department of Concordia College, St. Paul for 20 years and cantor of Mount Olive Lutheran Church in Minneapolis for 37 years.

His position as cantor extends his ministry beyond the bounds of his local parish and seminary and enables him to serve the whole church as composer, recitalist, teacher, lecturer, and leader in worship. He has concertized extensively in the United

States, Canada, and Europe, including a three-month tour with the Roger Wagner Chorale in 1964 as guest organist and accompanist, and has become especially well-known for his exciting and inspiring hymn festivals. He has appeared with several major symphony orchestras as guest artist and has appeared as lecturer and recitalist at regional and national conventions of the American Guild of Organists; he has participated in many organ seminars and clinics and served as organist for the Third Assembly of the Lutheran World Federation. In 1968 he was invited to be the American recitalist at festivities honoring Flor Peeter's retirement from active teaching, and in 1973 he was conference chairman of the International Youth Music Festival in Berlin. He received a Doctor of Letters degree from Concordia College, Seward, Nebraska; a Doctor of Music degree from Carthage College, Kenosha, Wisconsin; a Doctor of Humane Letters degree from Christ Seminary-Seminex of Chicago, Illinois; a St. Caecelia Medal from Boys' Town, Omaha, Nebraska; and the Cantare Con Spirito Sonare medal from Gustavus Adolphus College, St. Peter, Minnesota.

In 1983 he was asked to return to Belgium to celebrate the 60th anniversary of Flor Peeters as organist at the Cathedral of St. Rombaut. At this occasion he was one of the four speakers invited to speak to the assembly.

In addition to his series of chorale improvisations for organ, his compositions include a number of choral works and some compositions for choir and congregation with organ and instruments. He has nine recordings of organ, improvisations, literature, and instruments. He is a past dean of the Twin Cities Chapter of the American Guild of Organists, and past president of the Lutheran Society for Worship, Music and the Arts. Married in 1943 to Ruth Mueller, he and his wife are parents of three children of their own, and four by adoption after the death of their parents, the Rev. and Mrs. Herbert J. Mueller.

ARRANGER: 195 FESTAL SONG

MARCH, DANIEL (1816–1909), was born at Milbury, Massachusetts, July 21, 1816. Following his graduation from Yale in 1840, he was ordained by the Presbyterian Church in 1845, but later joined the Congregational Church, serving several of its parishes including Woburn, Massachusetts, where he died March 2, 1909. *He authored Night Scenes in the Bible; Walks and Homes of Jesus; and Home Life in the Bible.*

AUTHOR: 318 Hark, the Voice of Jesus Calling

MAROT, CLÉMENT (c. 1496–1544), was born at Cahors, France, about 1496, thus becoming a contemporary of Martin Luther (*LW* 13, et al.). After working as a clerk in the law courts of Paris, he became secretary to Marguerite d' Angoulème, sister of Francis I and later Queen of Navarre. It may have been from her that he learned and endorsed Lutheran or Huguenot (Calvinist French Protestants) views. When in 1526 and again in 1527 he was imprisoned for his Lutheran views, he petitioned King Francis I, who interceded on his behalf and appointed him *valet de chambre*. The 1534 Protestant poster campaign implicated Marot and, fearing arrest, he fled to Marguerite's court at Navarre, returning to Paris in 1536. It was perhaps at her instigation that the highly educated and talented poet Marot began to translate some psalms in metrical form in contrast to simple paraphrasing. His first translations, set to old French tunes and popular secular songs and circulated in manuscript form, created a sensation and attained extraordinary favor at the dissolute court. They became the fashion of the hour, each of the royal family and the courtiers selecting a favorite. This fashion, however, was short-lived, for the theological doctors of the Sarbonne, heresy hunters who were suspicious that there was some connection between Marot's psalms and the detestable Protestant doctrines, caused Marot in 1543 to flee for safety to John Calvin's (1509–64) religious commonwealth at Geneva. Calvin, a year earlier, had already adopted 35 of Marot's psalms for congregational use. Marot then translated 20 more in metrical form, which were characteristicly dedicated to the ladies of France. In 1543 Marot's *Fifty Psalms* were published at Geneva, a collection that formed the basis for later Calvinist psalters.

Marot's psalms, like his chansons, are constructed in strophes with alternating masculine and feminine rhyme, with an infinite variety in structure, meter, and versification. After Marot's death, Calvin requested Théodore de Bèze (1519–1605) to translate and versify the remaining hundred. Bèze was a man who had become a convert to the Reformed doctrines and had been appointed professor of Greek in the new University of Lausanne. His versifications hardly measured up to the subtle, graceful style and rhythmic verve of Marot's work. He finished the work in several installments, and the completed Genevan Psalter appeared in 1562. Subsequent psalters that emanated from Geneva under Calvin's leadership have had a wide and enduring significance, and the music of Louis Bourgeois (*LW* 216, et al.) and others has been the source of some of the most magnificent tunes in the Church's musical heritage. (See also essay: Metrical Psalms, p. 825.)

COMPOSER (attr.) : 399 Your Hand, O Lord, in Days of Old

MARRIOTT, JOHN (1780–1825), was born at Cottesbach, near Lutterworth, Leicestershire. Educated at Rugby and Christ Church, Oxford, he was ordained in 1804 and became private tutor to George Henry, Lord Scott, son of the fourth Duke of Buccleuth, at Dalkeith Palace, Scotland. When the young duke died at the age of 10, Marriott became domestic chaplain to the father. In 1808 the duke appointed him the rector of Church Lawford, Warwickshire, a post he held for the rest of his life. Continuous residence there, however, became impossible because of his wife's poor health. Thus he went to live in Devon, where he served curacies at St. James' and St. Lawrence's in Exeter and at nearby Broadclyst.

Marriott himself published none of his hymns during his lifetime; those that did appear were printed without his permission. He wrote two volumes of sermons, one published posthumously. A close friend of Sir Walter Scott, the latter dedicated to him the second canto of *Marmion* and included some of Marriott's ballads in his *Ministrelsy of the Scottish Border* (1802–05).

Marriott died at St. Giles in the Fields, London, March 31, 1825.

AUTHOR: 317 God, Whose Almighty Word

MASON, ARTHUR JAMES (1851–1928), was born May 4, 1851, in England and educated at Trinity College, Cambridge, earning the Bachelor of Arts degree in 1872 and the Doctor of Divinity degree in 1890. In 1873 he became a fellow and the following year a tutor at Trinity College. Ordained in 1874, he served as canon missionary at Truro, then as vicar of All Hallows, Barking, London, in 1884. In 1895 he became canon of Canterbury Cathedral and also professor of divinity at Cambridge and fellow of Jesus College. He was master of Pembroke College from 1903–12 and vice-chancellor of the University of Cambridge from 1908–10.

Mason's works include a translation and four original hymns in the 1889 Supplement to *Hymns Ancient and Modern* (1861). He prepared for publication A. S. Walpole's *Early Latin Hymns*, on which he and Walpole had worked for over 20 years. He wrote *The Persecution of Diocletian* (1875); *Historic Martyrs of the Primitive Church* (1903); and *The Church of England and Episcopacy* (1914).

He died April 24, 1928, in Canterbury.

TRANSLATOR: 245 O Jesus, Blessed Lord, My Praise

MASON, LOWELL (1792–1872), was born January 8, 1792, at Medfield, Massachusetts. As a child he learned to play any instrument placed before him; by age 16 he was giving voice lessons and leading his church choir.

In 1812 he moved to Savannah, Georgia, where he studied music composition and harmony with the well-schooled F. L. Abel while working first in a dry goods store and then in a bank. Organist and choir director of the Independent Presbyterian Church, he compiled with Abel's assistance a collection of church music which he tried to market in Philadelphia during a leave of absence from the bank. Finding no one in Philadelphia to publish his book, he tried Boston, with no success there either until he ran into a man named George K. Jackson, a member of the Boston Handel and Haydn Society. Jackson became very enthusiastic about Mason's work, and convinced the Society to back the project. The volume, an immediate success, was published in 1821 as the first edition of the *Boston Handel and Haydn Society Collection of Church Music*; it went through 22 editions as an influential publication in the history of American hymnody.

This publication marked a turning point in Mason's life. After taking care of business in Savannah, he took up residence in Boston in 1827. He became the president and conductor of the Handel and Haydn Society (1827–32), and was director of music at Second Presbyterian (1831–44) and at Central Church (1844–51) before he settled at the Bowdoin Street Church, where the Rev. Lyman Beecher, father of Harriet Beecher

Stowe, was pastor. The choir under Mason's direction gained professional admiration, adding to Mason's increasingly high reputation.

Firmly established in Boston, Mason began lecturing and teaching vocal music. He published several volumes of hymns, including *The Juvenile Psalmist, or The Child's Introduction to Sacred Music* (1829), the first book of its kind for Sunday schools. When he resigned in 1832 from the Boston Handel and Haydn Society, he joined George Webb (*LW* 305) in founding the Boston Academy of Music. In the same year he collaborated with Thomas Hastings (*LW* 361) in the production of *Spiritual Songs for Social Worship*.

Mason was dedicated to music education for children, and he worked to establish training schools for teachers. In 1837 he traveled to Europe, where he studied the highly acclaimed teaching methods of Johann Pestalozzi (1746–1827). The year 1838 saw Boston public schools incorporating the teaching of vocal music into the curriculum, largely due to Mason's influence.

Mason returned to Europe in 1851 for a two-year lecture tour. In Germany he met Johann Nägeli, publisher of the works of Beethoven and Clementi. Nägeli made available numerous publications as yet unknown in America, which music later inspired some of Mason's 1,000 hymn tunes. Most of the names Mason gave his tunes were biblical names from the Old Testament.

Compiler of at least 80 manuals and music collections, Mason amassed a small fortune on the basis of their sales. His tune-book *Carmina Sacra* (1841) sold an estimated half million copies. In 1855 New York University granted him the honorary Doctor of Music, the second degree of its type ever awarded by an American university. In 1853 he moved to Orange, New Jersey, where he started a church and Sunday school while continuing his composing and writing. It was there that he died on August 11, 1872, leaving his entire library to Yale University.

COMPOSER:	115	HAMBURG
	227	UXBRIDGE
	295	BOYLSTON
	320, 322	MISSIONARY HYMN
	378	OLIVET
	389	MERIBAH
	506	COWPER
	514	BETHANY
ARRANGER:	53	ANTIOCH

MASSIE, RICHARD (1800–87), was born June 18, 1800, at Chester, England, the son of R. Massie, rector of St. Bride's. In 1834 he married Mary Ann Hughes of Blache Hall, Chester, a union that ended with her death seven years later.

A man of wealth and leisure, with two inherited estates—Pulford Hall, Coddington, Cheshire, and another near Wrexham, Denbighshire—he devoted himself to literature and gardening while living at the former.

In addition to publishing *Martin Luther's Spiritual Songs* (1854), a book containing Luther's hymns in English dress, he published *Lyra Domestica* (two series, 1860 and 1864) containing translations respectively of the first and second series of the *Psalter und Harfe* (two parts, 1833 and 1843) of Carl J. P. Spitta (1801–59). He also contributed versions of numerous German hymns to William Mercer's *Church Psalter and Hymn Book* (1854) as well as to other hymnals. He died March 11, 1887, at Pulford Hall, Coddington.

TRANSLATOR: 123 Christ Jesus Lay in Death's Strong Bands
156 Creator Spirit, Heavenly Dove
170 Triune God, Oh, Be Our Stay
353 Dear Christians, One and All
407 If God Himself Be for Me
419 Evening and Morning

MAUDE, MARY FAWLER (1819–1913), was born in London, England, in 1819, the daughter of George Henry Hooper, of Stanmore, Middlesex. During her teen years she wrote *Scripture Manners and Customs, Scripture Topography*, and *Scripture Natural History*, a series of widely used textbooks published by the Society for the Promotion of Christian Knowledge and based on the descriptions of travelers in the Middle East. In 1841 she married Joseph Maude, who took over the vicarage of Chirk Ruabon, North Wales, and became an honorary canon of St. Asaph's Cathedral.

Maude devoted her life to the work of visiting, caring for the sick, and supporting her husband's ministry. She taught classes for the Welsh miners of her husband's parish, and the hymns she wrote, of which only the hymn below remains in common usage, were intended as classroom aids. In 1848 she published *Twelve Letters on Confirmation*, including the aforementioned hymn, and the remainder of her published hymns appear in her *Memorials of Past Years* (1852).

In 1887 her husband died and Maude moved to Overton, where she taught a class for young men. She lived to be 93 years old, and continued in her work until her death July 30, 1913.

AUTHOR: 256 Yours Forever, God of Love

McCOMB, WILLIAM (1793–1873), was born in Coleraine County, Londonderry, Ireland, in 1793. As a layman, who for many years was a bookseller in Belfast, he published *The Dirge of O'Neill* (1816), and *The School of the Sabbath* (1822). These, together with smaller pieces, were collected and published in 1864 and entitled *The Poetical Works of William McComb*. He died in 1873.

AUTHOR: 285 Chief of Sinners, Though I Be

McFARLAND, JOHN T. (1851–1913), was born January 2, 1851, at Mount Vernon, Indiana. Educated at Iowa Wesleyan University and Simpson College, he graduated from the Boston University School of Theology and then served parishes in Iowa, Illinois, Rhode Island, New York, and Kansas. He served as Secretary of the Sunday School Union, and in 1904 became the editor of Sunday school literature for the Methodist Episcopal Church, for which he introduced the idea of graded Sunday school lessons. He died at Maplewood, New Jersey, December 22, 1913.

AUTHOR (attr.): 64 Away in a Manger (st. 3)

MEDLEY, SAMUEL (1738–99), was born June 23, 1738, at Cheshunt, Hertfordshire, England, the son of a schoolmaster who was a friend of Isaac Newton. Apprenticed to an oil dealer in London, but dissatisfied with such a business, he entered the Royal Navy. Severely injured in a battle with the French fleet off Port Lagus, 1759, he had to retire from active service and was taken to the home of his grandfather. The latter's prayers plus a sermon of Isaac Watts (*LW* 53, et al.) read to him led to his conversion, and he joined Eagle Street Baptist Church, London. After successfully conducting a school for a time and beginning to preach, in 1767 he was called to be pastor of the Baptist congregation at Watford. Five years later he became pastor at Byron Street Church, Liverpool, which he served for 27 years until his death July 17, 1799, the result of his impaired health from the early war injury.

Medley wrote a considerable number of hymns, appearing first in magazines or leaflets. These he gradually collected into *Hymns* (Bradford, 1785); *Hymns on Select Portions of Scripture* (Bristol, 1785), a second edition of the previous volume, enlarged in 1787; and *Hymns. The Public Worship and Private Devotion of True Christians Assisted in some Thoughts in Verse* (London, 1800). *A Memoir*, written by his daughter Sarah in 1833, contained 44 additional sacramental hymns. Although a goodly number of his hymns were popular among the Baptists, particularly those of a Calvinistic cast, only the single hymn listed below is contained in the *Baptist Hymnal* (1975).

AUTHOR: 264 I Know that My Redeemer Lives

MEINHOLD, JOHANN WILHELM (1797–1851), was born at Netzelkow, on the island of Usedom, February 27, 1797, the son of a Lutheran pastor. After four years at the University of Greifswald, Germany, in 1820 he became rector of the Usedom's town school. Several years later he was appointed to the pastorate of Coserow and in 1828 to that of Crummin in Usedom. Four years after receiving the Doctor of Divinity degree from Erlangen in 1840, he became pastor at Rehwinkel, near Stargard. A staunch conservative, theological controversies of the time, plus his own leaning to Roman Catholicism, prompted him to resign his office in 1850 and to retire to Charlottenburg, suburb of Berlin. There he died November 30, 1851.

Meinhold's hymns and poems appeared in his *Gedichte* (Leipzig, 1823) as well as in occasional publications, though he is perhaps best known for his historical romance *Maria Schweidler, die Bernstein hexe* (1843).

AUTHOR: 269 Jesus, Shepherd, in Your Arms

MELANCHTHON, PHILIPP (1497–1560), was born February 16, 1497, at Bretten, near Karlsruhe, Germany, the son of Georg Schwartzerd, armorer for Emperor Maximilian. While young Philipp was attending Latin School at Pforzheim from 1507–09, his teacher, Johann Reuchlin, changed Philipps's last name to Melanchthon (Greek for "black earth," which is the meaning of Schwartzerd in German) as a compliment to his promising student. From 1509–11 Melanchthon attended Heidelberg University, where he received his Bachelor of Arts degree. The next two years saw him at Tübingen University, where he earned the Master of Arts degree January 25, 1514. Four more years were spent there doing research, writing, and teaching.

In 1518 Melanchthon accepted the call to teach Greek language and literature at Wittenberg University, a position offered him on the recommendation of Reuchlin. Meeting Luther and becoming involved with the Reformation changed the course of his life. In September 1519, after presenting his notable baccalaureate theses, he received the Bachelor of the Bible degree, actually his last degree, for he did not earn the Doctor of Theology degree, nor was he ever ordained.

Melanchthon came to Wittenberg as a biblical humanist and educator. Within a short time he gained the respect of both faculty and students. His lectures at times were attended by as many as 800 hearers. His relationship to Luther, although occasionally strained, constituted perhaps one of the most famous friendships in history. The two worked side by side, strengthening and supporting each other. Melanchthon's major work in systematic theology, the *Loci communes theologici*, his part in framing the *Augsburg Confession* (1530) and its *Apology* (1531), and his influence with respect to the *Formula of Concord* (1577) have proved to be monumental contributions to the cause of Lutheranism. His involvement in the visitation of the churches of electoral Saxony (1525–27) and the subsequent Articles of Visitation (1528) established a sound educational system in that territory. In fact, Melanchthon enjoys the distinction of being the great educator of the Reformation movement. Moreover, he made vital contributions through his participation in imperial diets, colloquies, and other meetings where theological and practical problems of the church were discussed. Unfortunately, while Luther matured with increasing age and reached ever greater clarity in his theological assertions, Melanchthon underwent changes and made concessions that, in the mind of some, left uncertainty regarding his enduring greatness as a Lutheran theologian and churchman.

Melanchthon's role in the music history of the Lutheran Church is greater than that in the development of hymnody. The curriculum that he prepared for the elementary schools in Saxony assigned an hour daily to the study of music. Since he was a humanist and classicist, the few hymns he wrote were in Latin and thus of little influence.

Melanchthon died a lonely man on April 19, 1560, and was laid to rest in the Castle Church of Wittenberg, opposite Luther's pulpit-side grave.

AUTHOR: 189 Lord God, to You We All Give Praise

MENDELSSOHN-BARTHOLDY, JAKOB LUDWIG FELIX (1809–47), was born February 3, 1809, at Hamburg, Germany, the son of a wealthy banker. The name Bartholdy was added to the family name by the composer's father when he abandoned Jewry for the Lutheran faith. Thus Felix was baptized in a Lutheran church. His grandfather was the famous Jewish philosopher Moses Mendelssohn, and his mother a very refined and cultured woman.

As a boy Felix exhibited remarkable musical gifts. He appeared as a concert pianist in 1818, and in 1819 his setting of Psalm 19 was publicly performed. By 16 he had composed a number of symphonies and the *Octet for Strings*, Op. 20; at 17 the overture to *A Midsummer Nights Dream*, Op. 21, was produced. It was from a manuscript copy that Mendelssohn became acquainted with J. S. Bach's (*LW* 89) *St. Matthew Passion*, a large-scale work considered almost impossible to perform. A plan for its revival matured, however, and in 1829, 100 years after its original performance, Mendelssohn conducted this magnificent work at the *Singakadamie* in Berlin, an occasion that ushered in the modern cultivation of Bach's music. That same year he made his first of 11 visits to England, visits in which he met various important musicians, became known in its social life, and was afforded opportunity to conduct various concerts featuring his own compositions as well as the works of others. In 1833 he became city director of music in Düsseldorf, where he cultivated Handel's oratorios. Within two years five of them were presented in his own arrangements. A short time later he was given the coveted position of conductor of the Leipzig Gewandhaus orchestra, an organization that he built into the first of the great modern symphony orchestras. In this endeavor he acted not only as conductor, but also as soloist, especially as pianist and organist. From 1842–43 he assisted in organizing the Leipzig Conservatory, where he then became teacher of piano and composition with Robert Schumann (1810–56), the quintessential Romantic composer, as his assistant. Mendelssohn resigned the Gewandhaus position in 1846 and died in Leipzig November 4, 1847, the result of frequent strokes. His death threw Europe into mourning; in Leipzig it was as though a king had died.

Mendelssohn was truly one of the most naturally gifted musicians of the 19th century, and he left a prodigious array of music for piano and organ, concertos for piano and violin, overtures and incidental music, chamber works, songs, oratorios and sacred works for choir, 13 early string symphonies, and five symphonies of his mature years. Especially remembered are his *Songs Without Words*, his oratorios *Elijah* and *St. Paul*, his incidental music to *A Midsummer Nights Dream*, Op. 21 and 61, and his *Reformation Symphony*, Op. 107, composed for the Berlin celebrations planned in remembrance of the Reformation and in commemoration of the Augsburg Confession, celebrations that failed to take place. He was a man of most charming disposition, making all who came in contact with him his ardent friends and admirers. Towards his fellow artists he was free from envy, always encouraging those in whom he discovered talent.

COMPOSER: 49 MENDELSSOHN

MENTZER, JOHANN (1658–1734), was born July 27, 1658, at Jahmen near Rothenburg in Silesia. Following his study of theology at the University of Wittenberg, he was, from 1691 on, briefly pastor in Merzdorf, later in Hauswalde. In 1698 he became pastor in Chemnitz, near Bernstadt, Saxony, in the neighborhood of Herrnhut, where Zinzendorf (*LW* 362, 386) gave refuge to the persecuted Moravians, and whose friend he became. Here he remained until his death February 24, 1734. A gifted poet, Mentzer sometimes, however, carried the emotional element to extreme, particularly in his Passion and repentance hymns. His output numbers some 32 hymns.

AUTHOR: 293 Lord Jesus Christ, the Church's Head
448 Oh, that I Had a Thousand Voices

MERCER, WILLIAM (1811–73), was born at Barnard Castle, Durham, England, and educated at Trinity College, Cambridge, from which he received the Bachelor of Arts degree in 1835. In 1840 he was appointed to the parish of St. George's, Sheffield, where he remained until his death at Leavy Greave, Sheffield, August 21, 1873.

Mercer is known chiefly for the work which he edited with John Goss (1800–80), English organist, composer, and teacher, entitled *The Church Psalter and Hymn Book* (1854), enlarged in 1856, and followed by an Appendix in 1872. This volume was for many years the most used and influential hymnal in England. St. Paul's Cathedral, for instance, continued to use it 10 years after the appearance in 1861 of *Hymns Ancient and Modern*. It is a book to which Mercer contributed several translations and paraphrases from Latin and German.

TRANSLATOR: 206 God Himself Is Present
AUTHOR: 492 God, Who Made the Earth and Heaven (sts. 2, 4)

MESSITER, ARTHUR H. (1834–1916), was born April 1, 1834, in Frome Selwood, Somersetshire, England. Educated in England, where he studied piano and voice privately and became a piano teacher, he came to the United States in 1863. Here he sang for a time as a volunteer in the choir of Trinity Church, New York, then served successively as organist of four churches in Philadelphia. In 1866 he accepted the appointment of organist and choirmaster of Trinity Church, where he succeeded Henry S. Cutler (*LW* 304) and remained until his retirement in 1897. There his music program, in the best English cathedral tradition, gained wide recognition, and his choir work "went far toward counteracting the pernicious influence of 'quartet choirs'" (*The Hymnal 1940 Companion*). Recognizing Messiter's pursuit of excellence, St. Stephen's College, Annandale, New York, honored him with a Doctor of Music degree.

As for other accomplishments, the music edition of the *Episcopal Hymnal* of 1893 was his work; he edited a *Psalter* (1889); *The Choir Office-Book* (1891), composed several anthems; and wrote *A History of the choir and music of Trinity Church, New York* (1906).

He died July 2, 1916, in New York City.

COMPOSER: 455 MARION

MEYER, ANNA MAGDALENA (1867–1941), was born November 14, 1867, in Alt-Rüdnitz, Neumark, Germany, the daughter of George and Ottilie Plehn. A teacher of the Lutheran school at Alt-Rüdnitz, her father resigned in 1869 and emigrated to St. Louis with his wife and four children. Upon completion of theological study at the Practical Seminary, which later became Concordia Seminary, Springfield, Illinois, he was admitted to the holy ministry in 1871. After serving for several years at Lake Ridge and Tecumseh, Michigan, he served at Chippewa Falls, Wisconsin, for 22 years. It was here that Anna Meyer attended Christian day school and the local high school, thereafter teaching school for a number of years. In July 1893 she was united in marriage to Christian Meyer, Lutheran pastor in Howard, South Dakota. After serving congregations in Nebraska, Illinois, and Wisconsin, he died in 1939.

Anna Meyer wrote a number of original hymns as well as translations from the German, items that were occasionally published in church periodicals. She died August 18, 1941, at Milwaukee, Wisconsin.

TRANSLATOR: 138 He's Risen, He's Risen

MEYER, FRANZ HEINRICH CHRISTOPH (1705–67), was born February 8, 1705, in Hanover, Germany, the son of Franz David Meyer, organist at the Castle Church. This was a position that Franz David's father had held, an office that Franz Heinrich held, and that his two sons eventually held. Commissioned to provide new hymns for the enlarged edition of the Hanover *Kirchengesangbuch* (1740) resulted in the creation and inclusion of the tune below.

COMPOSER: 255 MEIN SCHÖPFER, STEH MIR BEI

MEYFART, JOHANN MATHESIUS (1590–1642), was born November 9, 1590, in his grandfather's house in Jena while his mother was there on a visit. His father was pastor in Walswinkel near Gotha, Germany. Meyfart attended the universities of Jena and Wittenberg. From the former he received his master's degree in 1611 and his doctorate in theology in 1624. In 1616 he became professor at the *Gymnasium* in Koburg and in

1623 its director. His zeal for strengthening the Christian life led him to write a number of devotional works: *Tuba Poenitentiae Prophetica* (1625); *Tuba Novissima* (1626); *Höllisches Sodoma* (1629); *Himmlisches Jerusalem* (1630); and *Das Jüngste Gericht* (1632). In these impressive and relatively forward-looking works Meyfart exhibited himself to be, as he was frequently portrayed, "a German Dante, full of learning and fantasy, an individual that one would seldom encounter anywhere." (Koch)

The publishing of *De Disciplina Ecclesiastica* in 1633, a dissertation on church discipline, evoked such a negative reaction among his colleagues, they complained to the governing body. In consequence Meyfart accepted the position offered him by the pious Duke Ernst of Gotha to be professor of theology at the University of Erfurt, an institution that, as a result of the victory of Gustavus Adolphus, was to be restructured along Lutheran lines. In 1635 Meyfart became its rector. The following year, after becoming also pastor of the Augustinian church at Erfurt, he wrote a memorandum proposing how to steer the course of the practices of the clergy, worship, and church discipline. This created more divisions and unrest. The embittered Meyfart died at Erfurt, January 26, 1642.

AUTHOR: 306 Jerusalem, O City Fair and High

MICHEELSEN, HANS FRIEDRICH (1902–73), was born June 9, 1902 in Hennstedt (Dittmarschen), Germany. His early musical training in playing the piano, organ, trumpet, and violin was given him by his father, Hinrich, the teacher-cantor and organist in Hennstedt. Though he began his studies in 1919 at the Uetersen *Gymnasium* with the hope of becoming a musician, he bowed to his father's wish that he become a teacher. Thus he graduated in 1921 as a teacher, but because of lack of teaching positions, he became a private tutor. This afforded him time to be organist at the Paulskirche, Brunbüttelkoog, and to study organ with Max Brode. Music theory and counterpoint were studied with Paul Kickstadt, who encouraged Micheelsen to apply at the Berlin *Musik-Hochschule*. Accepted in 1933, he studied with Paul Hindemith with whom he shared a desire to create useful music for non-professional musicians. In 1935 he was appointed cantor and organist at the St. Matthäuskirche, Berilin-Tiergarten. During this time he composed several large-scale choral works. He heard his *Weihnachts historie* performed at the 1937 Berlin Festival of German Church Music along with music of Hugo Distler and Ernst Pepping, his contemporaries. In 1938 he was called to Hamburg to direct the newly-founded *Landeskirchlichen Kirchenmusikschule* and to be its teacher of composition. He was drafted into the German army in 1941 and forced to serve in the infantry at the Russian front. Returning to Hamburg in 1945, he set about rebuilding the church music school and its curriculum. Micheelsen retired 23 years later to devote himself to composition and his hobby of gardening. He returned to village of his birth, Hennstedt, in 1972, serving as organist in the same church his father had served. On November 23, 1973, he died of cancer.

Micheelsen's works include a *Deutsche Messe* (German Mass); chorale cantatas and liturgical motets; two Passions (*St. John*, 1968; *St. Matthew*, 1946); oratorios; organ works based on chorales and seven *Orgelkonzerte* (organ concert pieces). Not unlike Heinrich Schütz, for whom he had great admiration, Micheelsen's choral music greatly emphasized the text. He wrote several hymn tunes, three of which were included in the *Evangelishes Kirchingesangbuch* (1950).

COMPOSER: 21 TRÖSTET, TRÖSTET, SPRICHT DER HERR

MILLER, EDWARD (1735–1807), was born October 30, 1735, at Norwich, England. Though he at first followed his father in the paving trade, he ran away from home to study music. A music pupil of Charles Burney at King's Lynn, he for a time played flute in Handel's (*LW* 53) orchestra. Described as a "warm-hearted, simple-hearted, right-hearted man," for over 50 years he was organist of Doncaster Parish Church (1756–1807). Dissatisfaction with the existing state of church music prompted him to publish an edition of *The Psalms of David* (1790) with tunes; *Thoughts on the Present Performance of Psalmody* (1791); *The Psalms of Watts and Wesley...for the use of Methodists* (1801); *Psalms of David set to New Music* (1801); and *Sacred Music . . . an Appendix to Dr. Watts' Psalms and Hymns* (1802). With the assistance of his son, the Reverend W. E. Mueller, he produced *David's Harp* (1805), the most important Methodist tune-book issued between 1789 and 1876. In addition to hymn tunes, he wrote a number of smaller works, including six sonatas for harpsichord. In 1786 he received the Doctor of Music degree from Cambridge. He died September 12, 1807 at Doncaster.

COMPOSER (adapt.): 114 ROCKINGHAM OLD

MILLER, JOHN (JOHANNES MÜLLER) (1756–90), was born in Germany at Groshennersdorf near Herrnhut, Saxony, the son of Lutheran parents. Educated at the Moravian grammar school, Niesky, and the Moravian Theological College at Barbee, near Magdeburg, in 1781 he came to Fullneck, the educational center of the Moravians in England, as assistant preacher and chaplain. Seven years later he married and became minister of the neighboring congregation in Pudsey. He died of tuberculosis in 1790, at the age of 34. With Frederick Foster (*LW* 206) Miller revised older translations and prepared new ones for the 1789 edition of *The Moravian Hymn Book.*

TRANSLATOR: 206 God Himself Is Present

MILMAN, HENRY HART (1791–1868), was born in London February, 10, 1791, the son of Sir Francis Milman, physician to King George III. Educated at Greenwich, Eton, and Brasenose College, Oxford, where he had an illustrious literary career winning several prizes, after earning his Bachelor of Arts degree in 1814 and his Master's in 1816, he was ordained deacon and shortly thereafter, in 1817, priest, becoming vicar of

St. Mary's, Reading, that same year. From 1821–31 he was professor of poetry at Oxford; in 1827 he became Bampton lecturer; in 1835 he received a canonry of Westminster, with the rectorship of St. Margaret's. Here he remained until 1849, when he became dean of St. Paul's Cathedral, where he initiated the great services under the dome.

Successful as a playwright, his work as an historian was certainly the most important, beginning with his *History of the Jews* (1829); his edition of Edward Gibbon's *The History of the Decline and Fall of the Roman Empire* (1839); his *History of Christianity to the Abolition of Paganism in the Roman Empire*; followed by his *History of Latin Christianity* (1854). His *Poetical Works* were collected in three volumes, and his 13 hymns appeared in Reginald Heber's *Hymns Written and Adapted to the Weekly Church Service of the Year* (1827) and in his own publication *Selection of Psalms and Hymns* (1837). His last book, *The Annals of St. Paul's Cathedral*, was published after his death September 24, 1868, which occurred at Sunninghill, Berkshire.

AUTHOR: 105 Ride On, Ride On in Majesty

MOHR, JOSEPH (1792–1848), was born December 11 or 22, 1792, in Salzburg, the son of Joseph Mohr, a mercenary soldier, and Anna *née* Schoiberin, a Salzburg seamstress. As a youth he was a chorister at the Salzburg Cathedral, where the Mozarts had served some years previous; later he attended Salzburg University. Ordained a priest by the Roman Catholic Church in 1815, he became an assistant priest at St. Nikolaus Church in Oberndorf. It was during his brief service there, from 1817–19, that he wrote "Stille Nacht." After serving a number of parishes in the Salzburg diocese, he became priest at Hintersee (1828–37) and at Wagrein (1837–48). He died December 4, 1848.

AUTHOR: 68 Silent Night, Holy Night

MOLANUS, GERHARD WALTHER (Wolter) (1633–1722), was born at Hameln, Germany, November 1, 1633. After attending the University of Helmstädt, where he studied with George Calixtus (1586–1656), whose theology is said to have been syncretistic, he became professor of mathematics at the University of Rinteln in 1650, and later in 1665 professor of theology. In 1674 he became head of the Hanover Consistory and finally in 1677 general superintendent of the entire electorate of Braunschweig-Lüneburg. He died September 15, 1722, in Hanover.

It was under his direction that the large Hanover *Gesangbuch* appeared in 1698, to which he contributed the preface.

AUTHOR: 249 Your Table I Approach

MÖLLER, JOHANN JOACHIM (1660–1733), was born in Sommerfeld, Germany, and died in 1733 as archdeacon at Krossen, near the Bober and Oder rivers.

AUTHOR (attr.): 145 I Am Content! My Jesus Ever Lives

MONK, WILLIAM HENRY (1823–89), was born March 16, 1823, at Brompton, London, England. He studied music under Thomas Adams and G. A. Griesbach, and took his first position in 1841 as organist at Eaton Chapel, Pimlico. From there he went to St. George's, Albemarle Street (1843–45) and Portman Chapel, Marylebone (1845–47). In 1847 he took over as choirmaster at King's College, London, becoming organist in 1849 and professor of vocal music upon the resignation of John Hullah in 1874. Two years later he was appointed a professor in the National Training School for Music and in Bedford College. For 37 years he served as organist at St. Matthias, Stoke Newington, where he held daily choral services with a volunteer choir.

Devoted to hymn singing, Monk edited the music for the first two editions of *Hymns Ancient and Modern* (1861 and 1868). He collaborated with others in the 1875 and 1880 editions; the 1889 edition had just been sent to press when he died, March 1, 1889. Because *Hymns Ancient and Modern* was the Church of England's first departure from the Psalms and psalm tunes, Thomas Hardy noted as a lad the mutilation of the old psalm tunes and later recorded his disapproval:

> Stripped of some of your old vesture
> By Monk or another. Now you wore no frill,
> And at first you startled me. But I know you still,
> Though I missed the minim's waver
> And the dotted quaver.

Besides *Hymns Ancient and Modern*, Monk edited music for *The Scottish Hymnal* (1872 ed.); Wordsworth's (*LW* 88, 203) *Hymns for the Holy Year* (1862), and *The Book of Common Prayer, with Plain Song and Appropriate Music*. He also took over editorship of the periodical *Parish Choir* in 1840, remaining in that capacity until 1851. In 1882 Durham University honored him with the Doctor of Music degree.

COMPOSER: 405 ENERGY
490 EVENTIDE

MONSELL, JOHN SAMUEL BEWLEY (1811–1875), son of the archdeacon of Londonderry, was born March 2, 1811, at St. Columb's, Derry, Ireland. He was educated at Trinity College, Dublin, attaining the Bachelor of Arts degree in 1832. Two years later he was ordained deacon, and priest in 1835; he first served as chaplain to church historian Richard Mant (1776–1848; *LW* 195), bishop of Down, Connor, and Dromore. He went on to become chancellor of the diocese of Connor, later serving as rector of Ramoan. In 1853 he moved to England as vicar of Egham in Surrey, becoming rector of

St. Nicholas, Guildford, in 1870. Monsell's death occurred at Guildford, Surrey, April 9, 1875, when, inspecting some repairs being made on his church, he was struck by a piece of falling masonry.

Author of at least 300 hymns, which he said should be "fervent and joyous," Monsell wrote that "We are too distant and reserved in our praises." John Julian in his *Dictionary of Hymnology* agrees that Monsell's hymns "are as a rule bright, joyous, and musical," adding that "they lack massiveness, concentration of thought, and strong emotion. A few only are of enduring excellence." His poems were published in 11 volumes, including *Hymns and Miscellaneous Poems* (1837); *Parish Musings and Devotional Poems* (1850); *Spiritual Songs for the Sundays and Holidays throughout the Year* (1857); *Hymns of Love and Praise for the Church's Year* (1863); *Litany Hymns* (1869); *The Parish Hymnal* (1873), and *Nursery Carols* (1873). His most popular work was *Our New Vicar* (1867).

AUTHOR:	260	Lord of the Living Harvest
	299	Fight the Good Fight
	493	Sing to the Lord of Harvest

MONTGOMERY, JAMES (1771–1854), son of Moravian preacher John Montgomery, was born November 4, 1771, at Irvine, Ayrshire, Scotland. He received his early education at a settlement of United Brethren in Bracehill, near Ballymena, Ireland, where his parents moved when he was four years old. Later, when his parents sailed as missionaries for the West Indies, he was trained for the ministry at a boy's boarding school run by the Brethren of Fulneck, Yorkshire. There he fell behind in his studies due to his poetry writing during class, and he eventually dropped out and went to work in a bakeshop. In 1787 he ran away and supported himself by selling a poem for a guinea, which sustained him until he was employed in a chandler's shop in Mirfield, near Wakefield. Bored by the work there, he left for London to write; but, as he was unable to find a publisher, he again turned to clerking, this time at Wath.

In 1792 he moved to Sheffield and went to work for Joseph Gales, printer of the *Sheffield Register*, whose political opinions forced him to leave England in 1794. Montgomery took over the paper and changed its name to the *Sheffield Iris*. A determined republican in that era of the French Revolution, he was jailed for publishing an original poem celebrating the fall of the Bastille. Upon his release he printed an article disagreeing with the way a local riot had been handled, and again he was imprisoned. These two terms of confinement gave him time to write much of the poetry for which he is known. He became well-known in Sheffield, outspoken in his support for foreign missions and the Bible Society, and fearless in his denunciation of evils such as the slave trade, child-chimney-sweeps, and state lotteries. He also advocated the teaching of writing in Sunday schools.

Montgomery, although raised in the Moravian church, spent some time "free thinking"; he worshiped with Anglicans, Independents, Baptists and Methodists, and cooperated with the outlawed Roman Catholics, Unitarians, and Quakers, but returned finally to the Moravians.

In 1825 he gave up ownership of the paper and became a founder of and regular contributor to the *Eclectic Review*. He lectured on poetry at Sheffield and at the Royal Institution, London; these lectures were published in 1833. In the same year the British government awarded him a literary pension of £200 a year. He purchased an estate called the Mount on the western side of Sheffield; there he lived until his death on April 30, 1854

Montgomery is best known for his 400-some hymns, which were mostly written early in his life. Many of the hymns appeared in Thomas Cotterill's *Selection of Psalms and Hymns for Public and Private Use, adapted to the Festivals of the Church of England*...(8th edition, 1819) and in his own books: *Songs of Zion* (1822), *The Christian Psalmist* (1825), and *Original Hymns for Public, Private, and Social Devotion* (1852). He also turned his hand to longer poems of a more sociological nature, such as *The West Indies* (1810), a poem in honor of Britain's abolition of slave trade. Other major works include *Prison Amusements* (1796), *The Ocean* (1805), and *The World Before the Flood* (1812).

AUTHOR:
50 Angels from the Realms of Glory
82 Hail to the Lord's Anointed
96 Come to Calvary's Holy Mountain
110 Go to Dark Gethsemane
207 To Your Temple, Lord, I Come
262 We Bid You Welcome in the Name
447 Songs of Praise the Angels Sang
511 In the Hour of Trial

MORISON, JOHN (1749 or 50–98), was born in Cairnie, Aberdeenshire, Scotland. After graduating from King's College, Aberdeen, he held several teaching positions in Caithness before going to Edinburgh for further study, especially Greek. It was probably while teaching in Thurso school that he met John Logan who, on his arrival in Edinburgh, introduced him to Dr. MacFarlane, a member of the Committee of Assembly engaged in preparing a revised edition of the Scottish *Translations and Paraphrases*. Encouraged to submit some versions, Morison offered 24, seven of which were accepted in more or less altered form. Appointed to the parish of Canisbay in 1779, he was ordained nine months later and served in this, his only charge. In 1781 he was appointed a member of the *Committee for Revision of the Translations and Paraphrases*, to which he had earlier contributed. In 1792 the University Edinburgh honored him with the Doctor of Divinity degree. He died June 12, 1798, at Canisbay.

AUTHOR:
77 The People That in Darkness Sat

MOTE, EDWARD (1797–1874), was born January 21, 1797, in London. Having gone astray in his youth, the preaching of John Hyatt converted him, and two years later he joined the Baptist Church. Until he entered the Baptist ministry at the age of 55, he had pursued the trade of cabinetmaker. From 1852 until his death November 13, 1874, he was pastor of the Baptist Church at Horsham, Essex.

In 1836 Mote published *Hymns of Praise. A New Selection of Gospel Hymns, combining all the excellencies of our spiritual poets, and many originals. For the use of all spiritual worshippers,* containing about 100 hymns written by him. Benson in his *The English Hymn* regarded this hymnal as "an anthology of Calvinistic praise."

AUTHOR: 368 My Hope Is Built on Nothing Less

MOULTRIE, GERARD (1829–85), was born September 16, 1829, at Rugby, Warnickshire, England. Educated at Rugby School and Exeter College, Oxford, where he earned the Master of Arts degree in 1856, he was ordained by the Anglican Church and became assistant master and chaplain of Shrewsbury School. After holding various chaplaincies, in 1869 he became vicar of Southleigh, and four years later warden of St. James' College, Southleigh, where he died April 25, 1885.

Both a hymn writer and translator of Greek, Latin, and German hymns, his works include *Hymns and Lyrics for the Seasons and Saints' Days of the Church* (1867), *The Espousals of St. Dorothea and Other Verses* (1870), and *Cantica Sanctorum, or Hymns for the Black Letter Saints' Days in the English and Scottish Calendars* (1880).

TRANSLATOR: 241 Let All Mortal Flesh Keep Silence

NEALE, JOHN MASON (1818–66), was born January 24, 1818, in Bloomsbury, London, England. His father, a clergyman and fellow of St. John's College, Cambridge, died when John was five years old, and the boy was therefore brought up solely by his mother. He attended Sherborne Grammar School and then was tutored privately until 1836, when he accepted a scholarship to Trinity College, Cambridge.

A brilliant student, Neale gained numerous honors and distinctions; he was elected fellow and tutor of Downing College and, as a graduate, won the Seatonian Prize for sacred poetry 11 times. Although both his parents had been "pronounced evangelicals," while at Cambridge he was drawn into the high-church Oxford movement and became one of the founders of the Ecclesiological, or Cambridge-Camden, Society. His degree, attained in 1840, was not adorned with honors because of the ruling, rescinded the following year, that honors in Classics could be given only to those who qualified in mathematics, and Neale was no mathematician.

After graduation, Neale was ordained and, in 1842, he married the daughter of an evangelical clergyman. He spent three months as chaplain to Downing College, hoping for a curacy at St. Nicholas, Guildford, but the bishop, perhaps holding Neale in disfavor because of his high church associations, refused to approve the appointment.

Instead, he was assigned in 1843 to the small parish of Crawley in Sussex. He remained there only six weeks and was never installed. Due to ill health he was forced to spend the next three winters in Madeira where, fortunately, the great resources of a large library at Funchal were available to him and he was able to amass a fortune in material for his subsequent writings.

Upon his return in 1846, Neale was offered the provostship of St. Ninian's, Perth, which he declined because of the climate and the effect it might have on his health. Instead, he was appointed warden of Sackville College, a home for the indigent elderly men in East Grinstead. Because of high church practices, Neale was suspended from performing the functions of his office by his superior, the Bishop of Chichester, in 1847, which inhibition lasted until 1863. Thus he was forced to accept a position from which, because the appointment came from Earl De la Warr, he could not be removed even by the bishop. So Neale, the most learned hymnologist and liturgiologist of his time, labored in obscurity, spending his spare time on the writings and translations that added so much to the study of hymnology.

Neale had published three volumes of original poetry: *Hymns for Children* (1842), of which he claimed, "Long ago I determined that if no one else did anything to free our poor children from the yoke of Watts, I would try"; *Hymns for the Young* (1844), intended for older children; *Hymns for the Sick* (1843); and a third series of *Hymns for Children* (1846) before his arrival in East Grinstead. Shortly thereafter he began work on the five-volume *History of the Holy Eastern Church* (1847–73). His chief fame, however, is due to his translations from the Greek and Latin, of which he produced more than 200. His translations of Latin hymns were contained in *Mediaeval Hymns and Sequences* (1851); *The Hymnal Noted* (1852 and 1854), in which 94 of the 105 hymns were prepared by Neale; and *Hymns, Chiefly Mediaeval, on the Joys and Glories of Paradise* (1865), in which he laid out the translation side-by-side with the original. These translations, which followed the meter and rhyme scheme of their Latin counterparts almost without fail, brought down on him the wrath of the Roman Catholic Church, which claimed he had falsified the texts by deliberately omitting any trace of Roman doctrine—this of a man whose own Anglican Church had once suspected him of Roman sympathies! In his translations from the Greek that appeared in his *Hymns of the Eastern Church* (1862), Neale broke new ground.

Neale would accept no copyright for his sacred verse, claiming that "a hymn, whether original or translated, ought, the moment it is published, to become the common property of Christendom, the author retaining no private right in it whatever." Although he was never honored by his own church or country, for his pioneering in hymnody he was granted an honorary Master of Arts degree in 1853 and the honorary Doctor of Sacred Theology degree in 1861 by Trinity College, Hartford, Connecticut.

He was actively involved in establishing the Sisterhood of St. Margaret and, from this, several auxiliary institutions: an orphanage, a school for girls, and a home for fallen women. His last public act was to lay the foundation of a new convent for the Sisterhood on St. Margaret's Day, July 20, 1865. His health gave way the following spring, and five months later he died, August 6, 1866, age 48, at East Grinstead.

TRANSLATOR:	31	Oh, Come, Oh, Come, Emmanuel
	36	Of the Father's Love Begotten
	51	A Great and Mighty Wonder
	74	From God the Father, Virgin-Born
	81	When Christ's Appearing Was Made Known
	87	Oh, Wondrous Type! Oh, Vision Fair
	102	All Glory, Laud, and Honor
	103, 104	The Royal Banners Forward Go
	117	Sing, My Tongue
	130	O Sons and Daughters of the King
	133	The Day of Resurrection
	141	Come, You Faithful, Raise the Strain
	147	That Easter Day with Joy Was Bright
	190	Stars of the Morning, So Gloriously Bright
	240	Draw Near and Take the Body of the Lord
	309	Jerusalem the Golden
	489	Before the Ending of the Day

NEANDER, JOACHIM (1650–80), was born at Bremen, Germany, the child of a master in the *Paedagogium* in that city. Descended from a long line of distinguished clergymen, after completing studies at the *Paedagodium*, he attended the *Gymnasium* in Bremen, where his student life was riotous and profligate. The concern and earnestness of Pastor Theodore Under-Eyck of St. Martin's in Bremen caused Neander to change his ways. After tutoring five young sons of wealthy merchants at Frankfurt-am-Main, he accompanied them to the University of Heidelberg. Here he became acquainted with two confirmed Pietists, Jakob Spener and Johann J. Schuetz (*LW* 452). In the spring of 1674 Neander was appointed rector of the Latin School at Düsseldorf, an institution under the supervision of a contentious Reformed pastor. Difficulties between the two men led to Neander's dismissal. His promise to abide by the rules of the church and school led to his reinstatement. Five years later he became lay assistant of Pastor Under-Eyck at St. Martin's. The following year, May 31, 1680, he died of consumption (tuberculosis).

Neander was a great lover of nature. In fact, the valley of the Düssel near Mettmann, where Neander used to take long hikes, was later named Neanderthal for him. Moreover, it was in this valley, in 1856, that the skeleton of the so-called Neanderthal man was discovered.

Neander is regarded as the foremost hymn writer of the German Reformed Church. He wrote approximately 60 hymns, many included in his collection, *Alpha and Omega* (1680).

AUTHOR:	444	Praise to the Lord, the Almighty
COMPOSER:	198	UNSER HERRSCHER (NEANDER)
	206	WUNDERBARER KÖNIG

NELSON, HORATIO BOLTON (1823–1913), was born August 7, 1823, at Brickworth House, Witshire, the son of Thomas Bolton of Birnham, Norfolk, England. (On succeeding to the title of second Earl, Thomas Bolton assumed the name of his renowned and celebrated uncle, Admiral Viscount Nelson.) Horatio attended Trinity College, Cambridge, receiving his Master of Arts degree in 1844. Succeeding to the title in 1835, it was in 1845 that he took his seat, the year that he married Mary Jane Diana, the daughter of the second Earl of Normanton. He became the "father" of the Nelson House in 1909.

Included in his publications is *A Form of Family Prayer with special Offices for the Seasons* (1852) and *A Calendar of Lessons for Every Day in the Year* (1858). With John Keble (*LW* 488) he edited the *Salisbury Hymn-Book* (1857), which in its second form appeared in 1868 as the *Sarum Hymnal*. The source of "By all your saints in warfare," originally beginning with "From all thy saints in warfare," is from his *Hymns for Saints' Days, and other Hymns, By a Layman* (1864).

He died at Trafalgar House, the victim of dropsy, and was buried March 1, 1913.

AUTHOR:	193, 194	By All Your Saints in Warfare

NEUMARK, GEORG (1621–81), was born March 16, 1621, in Langensalza, Thuringia, Germany, the son of a clothier. Educated at the *Gymnasia* of Schleusingen and Gotha, in 1641 he was on his way to the University of Königsberg when he was attacked by a band of thieves who robbed him of all his possessions. Numerous fruitless quests of employment, while suffering extreme poverty, finally resulted in his becoming a tutor in the home of Judge Stephen Henning. It was at this point that he wrote the hymn below. At last he saved sufficient money to attend the University of Königsberg, where he studied law and poetry, the latter under the famous Simon Dach (*LW* 268, 369). After leaving the university he earned only a meager living in Warsaw, Thorn, Danzig, and Hamburg. Finally, in 1652, he returned to Thuringia as a court poet, librarian, and registrar to Duke Wilhelm II of Saxe, Weimar, and later custodian of the ducal archives. In 1656 Neumark became secretary of the prestigious Fruitbearing Society. He was not only a poet but also a musician. He died July 18, 1681, after becoming blind in his final year.

AUTHOR:	420	If You But Trust in God to Guide You
COMPOSER:	420, 429	WER NUR DEN LIEBEN GOTT

NEUMEISTER, ERDMANN (1671–1756), was born at Üchteritz, near Weissenfels, May 12, 1671. He received his elementary schooling in Pforta and studied at the University of Leipzig, receiving his Master of Arts degree in 1695. Thereafter he spent two years lecturing at the university before becoming assistant pastor of a Lutheran congregation at Bad Bibra. The following year he became full pastor and assistant superintendent of the Eckartsberg district. After serving as tutor to the daughter of Duke Johann George, as well as assistant court preacher at Weissenfels, he went to Sorau as senior court preacher, member of the consistory, and superintendent. Here he met the composer Georg Philipp Teleman (1681–1767). From 1715 until his death on August 18, 1756, he was pastor of St. James' Church, Hamburg.

A staunch defender of Lutheran orthodoxy over against Pietism, Neumeister became known as an earnest and eloquent preacher.

He also ranks high as a hymn writer of the 18th century, not only for quantity (some 650) but also their quality. In 1718 he published his *Evangelische Nachklang*, containing hymns for the Sundays and festivals of the entire church year. A year prior to his death a complete collection of his spiritual poems, about 715 in all, was published with the title *Herrn Erdmann Neumeisters Psalmen und Lobgesänge* (Hamburg, 1755).

Neumeister is also noted as a writer of church cantata texts and as having thus contributed to the development of this form, especially to the cantatas of J. S. Bach, his contemporary, for whom he wrote some of their texts.

AUTHOR: 229 Jesus Sinners Will Receive
354 I Know My Faith Is Founded

NEWBOLT, MICHAEL ROBERT (1874–1956), was born in Dymock, Gloucestershire. After earning the Bachelor of Arts (1895) and Master of Arts (1912) degrees at St. John's College, Oxford, he was ordained deacon in 1899 and priest in 1900. He served as assistant curate of Wantage (1899–1905); as vicar of St. Mary's, Iffley, (1905–10); as principal of the Missionary College at Dorchester (1910–16); as perpetual curate of St. Michael and All Angels in Brighton (1916–27); and as canon of Chester Cathedral (1927–46). In that year he was licensed to preach in the diocese of Oxford, and he moved to Bierton, Aylesbury, Buckinghamshire, where he died February 7, 1956. His books include *The Manifold Wisdom of God*; *Healing*; and *The Bible and the Ministry.*

REVISER: 311 Lift High the Cross

NEWTON, JOHN (1725–1807), prodigal son of a sailing merchant, was born July 24, 1725, in London. His mother, a devout Dissenter, intended for him to be trained for the ministry, but she died when he was seven years old. John received only two years of education, learning by heart the Westminster Catechism with all its Scripture texts and all of Isaac Watts' (*LW* 53, et al.) hymns for children. However, the severe discipline at school and at home caused him to lose interest in scholarship, and on his 11th birthday he joined his father for five voyages in the Mediterranean.

At age 17 he fell in love with Mary Catlett, the 14-year-old girl his mother had planned for him to marry, and lost a contract because of spending too much time with her; and, walking along the dock dressed in a seaman's outfit to gain her admiration, he was pressed into the navy aboard the man-o'-war "Harwich."

Newton's father was unable to get him released, but he arranged for John a midshipman's berth and officer training. During his military service Newton tried several times to adhere to his mother's religious principles, praying, reading Scripture, and even fasting, but some skeptical literature finally convinced him to discard them. After a time Newton deserted from the navy, and was caught, whipped, and demoted to a common sailor. Because of his superior attitude as a midshipman, he was disliked by the other sailors and therefore treated badly. The memory of his girlfriend was, by his own account, the only thing keeping him from suicide; until finally, when a mischievous midshipman cut down his hammock and dropped him to the deck, he asked to be transferred to a Guinea trading vessel. The navy, glad to be rid of him, agreed.

Once in Africa, Newton left the ship and went to work for a slaver off Sierra Leone, where he imagined he could do as he pleased; but he found himself treated as badly as the slaves, owning nothing but the clothes on his back and given nothing to eat but what the slaves would share with him. He wrote of his misery to his father, and finally was transferred to another trader elsewhere on the island. His life here was tolerable, and when at length a ship arrived, dispatched by his father to rescue him, he was indifferent. The ship's captain tricked him into returning to England by telling him lies about a supposed inheritance.

Lodged in the ship's cabin with nothing to do, Newton read Thomas à Kempis' (*LW* 275) *Imitation of Christ* and began to reflect on his forgotten religious training. The ship became waterlogged in a storm, and, manning the pumps for hours on end, Newton prayed "like the cry of the ravens, which yet the Lord does not disdain to hear." (Duffield, *English Hymns*) Newton dates his spiritual birth from that experience on March 10, 1748.

Upon arrival in England Newton went to work for the ship's captain who had lured him back. He married Mary Catlett on February 1, 1750, and became the captain of a slave ship. At this time the moral ramifications of slaving still went unquestioned, and Newton found no difficulty in reconciling his new faith with his occupation. After six years in slave trade he met another ship's captain, through whom Newton met many religious people in London. He became a tide surveyor at Liverpool while studying Greek and Latin and awaiting a call to the ministry. He heard Whitefield preach and considered the Dissenting church, but finally decided on the Established.

On December 16, 1758, he was appointed to a curacy, but the Archbishop of York refused to ordain him, "because he was much too earnest about religion to be readily entrusted with a commission to teach it, except as a matter of favour to a great man" (Sir George Otto Trevelyan, *The American Revolution*). Lord Dartmouth, a friend and helper of Lady Huntingdon, brought pressure upon the church in Newton's behalf, and he was ordained deacon on April 29, 1764, and priest in the following year. He went to Lord Dartmouth's village of Olney, where he carried on an evangelical ministry, begging from Lord Dartmouth the use of a large mansion for Thursday Bible studies, and teaching his growing congregation to sing hymns as well as the standard Sternhold and Hopkins Psalms. His neighbor William Cowper (*LW* 426, 506) became a dear friend, and Newton enlisted Cowper's help in writing hymns. *Olney Hymns* was published in 1779, containing 280 hymns by Newton and 68 by Cowper. This hymnal, although it had no tunes, filled a need felt by the common people for a textbook of the evangelical faith which could be read, sung, and memorized. It was a landmark in the development of the hymn in the Church of England.

In 1780 Newton moved to St. Mary Woolnoth parish, London. Though he never retired, he would, in his old age, be accompanied at the pulpit by a servant who helped him read his texts. He died December 21, 1807, and was buried beneath his church of St. Mary Woolnoth, where his tombstone was inscribed with his own words:

"John Newton
Clerk
Once an Infidel and Libertine
A Servant of Slaves in Africa
was
by the Rich Mercy of our Lord and Saviour
Jesus Christ
Preserved, Restored, Pardoned,
and Appointed to Preach the Faith
he had long labored to destroy."

Newton's remains, along with the tombstone, were moved in 1893 to the cemetery at Olney, because of excavations at the London site.

Besides *Olney Hymns*, Newton published "An Authentic Narrative" on his life. Written in collaboration with Richard Cicero, this possibly exaggerated autobiography was intended to show that even the worst of sinners (as Newton thought of himself) was a candidate for salvation.

AUTHOR:	217	On What Has Now Been Sown
	279	How Sweet the Name of Jesus Sounds
	294	Glorious Things of You Are Spoken
	433	Come, My Soul, with Every Care
	509	Amazing Grace! How Sweet the Sound

NICHOLSON, SYDNEY HUGO (1875–1947), was born February 9, 1875, in London, England, the son of Sir Charles Nicholson, who, in 1833, had emigrated to Sydney, Australia, where he became a wealthy businessman, founder and first chancellor of the University of Sydney, and who, later in life, returned to England where he married.

Young Sydney, named for Sydney, Australia, was educated at Rugby School and New College, Oxford, from which he received the Master of Arts and Doctor of Music degrees. At the Royal College of Music he studied under Walter Parratt and Charles V. Stanford. While a student there, he served as organist at Barnet Parish Church from 1897. In 1903 he became organist of Lower Chapel, Eton College, and in 1904 of Carlisle Cathedral. Having moved to Manchester Cathedral in 1908, he became chief music advisor to *Hymns Ancient and Modern* (1861), editing the music of the 1916 Supplement. In 1919 he succeeded Sir Frederick Bridge as organist of Westminster Abbey. Retiring from the abbey position in 1928, he devoted himself to the founding of the St. Nicholas College of Church Music, first located at Chiselhurst, near London, and then serving as its director until his death May 30, 1947. In 1945 this school became the Royal School of Church Music and was transferred to Canterbury. In 1954 it was moved to Addington Palace at Croyden, Surrey.

Nicholson played a large and important part in the history of *Hymns Ancient and Modern*, not only as music editor under W. H. Frere in 1913, but also as a proprietor and, from 1938–47, as chairman. He was awarded the Archbishop of Canterbury's Doctor of Music degree in 1928.

As for his publications, with G. L. H. Gardiner he published *A Manual of English Church Music* (1923). He himself wrote *Quires and Places where they Sing* (1933); and *Peter: the Adventures of a Chorister* (1944); as well as numerous essays on church music. He composed some hymn tunes, a service in D♭, some anthems, songs, and two light operas.

COMPOSER: 311 CRUCIFER

NICOLAI, PHILIPP (1556–1608), son of a Lutheran pastor, was born August 10, 1556, at Mengeringhausen in Waldeck. The name Nicolai is the result of his father's dropping the family name Rafflenböl in favor of his father's Christian name Nicolaus. Included in Philipp's early education was the significant time spent in Mühlhausen, where he was exposed to the poetic and music influences of Ludwig Helmbold (*LW* 409, et al.) and Joachim von Burgk, respectively. Helmbold went to great pains to introduce his pupils to classical Latin poetry and he encouraged them to imitate such fine examples of the art. Nicolai's theological education, made possible by the kindness of the Count of Waldeck, was begun with a year at the University of Erfurt in 1575 and continued at the University of Wittenberg, where he graduated in 1579. Fifteen years later he received a Doctor of Divinity degree from that institution. Following his graduation he spent four years assisting his father at Mengeringhausen; thereafter, in 1583, he was called to serve a congregation in Herdecke in the Ruhr. Because of strong Roman Catholic influence and sentiment there, he resigned his position three years later. After serving one year in Niederwildungen, he became head pastor of Altwildungen and also court preacher to Countess Margareta of Waldeck and tutor to her son, Wilhelm Ernst. It was here that he became involved in the Sacramentarian controversy, firmly upholding the Lutheran position. Next he became pastor at Unna, Westphalia, where he again was drawn into controversy, this time with the Calvinists. Several months after he assumed office in Unna, the city fell victim to a ravaging plague that, in the course of seven months, took the lives of no less than 1,400 people. In these days of sorrow and mourning, Nicolai was moved to write and publish his *Frewden-Spiegel dess Ewigen Lebens* (1599). Included in this work were three hymns, two being "Wachet auf" and "Wie schön leuchtet der Morgenstern," what respectively were to become known as the king and queen of chorales. While at Unna, the invasion of the Spanish caused Nicolai to flee in December of 1598, but he was able to return the following April.

In 1606, at age 44, Nicolai married the widow of his fellow clergyman, Peter Dornberger, who brought with her a son and a daughter. In August of 1601 he was installed as head pastor of St. Katherine's in Hamburg, where for the last seven years of his life he enjoyed a large sphere of activity. The people of Hamburg were happy to have such a pillar of the Lutheran Church as their pastor, a man who also here withstood the onslaught of Calvinists and papists. He died of fever on October 26, 1608.

Nicolai was both a gifted poet and composer. He was a preacher of great power, an influential churchman, and, his controversial writings notwithstanding, a kind, peace-seeking, and lovable person.

AUTHOR:	73	O Morning Star, How Fair and Bright
	177	Wake, Awake, for Night Is Flying
COMPOSER:	73, 160, 325, 437, 520	WIE SCHÖN LEUCHTET
	177, 303	WACHET AUF

NOEL, CAROLINE MARIA (1817–77), was born April 17, 1817, at Teston, Kent, the daughter of Gerard Thomas Noel, an Anglican priest and hymn writer. At age 17 she wrote her first hymn, and during the next three years a dozen or so more. After that she wrote nothing until, about 20 years later, as an invalid she recommenced writing for the distinct purpose of comforting others. Her first publication appeared in 1861 entitled *The Name of Jesus and Other Verses, for the Sick and Lonely*. This was enlarged in succeeding editions with the title *The Name of Jesus and Other Poems*, the last edition, containing 78 pieces, published in 1878, after her death.

She died December 7, 1877, at St. Marleybone, London, and was buried near the Abbey Church of Romsey, near the side of her father, where he had previously been vicar.

AUTHOR: 178 At the Name of Jesus

OAKELEY, FREDRICK (1802–80), was born September 5, 1802, at Shrewsbury, England, the son of Charles Oakeley, one time Governor of Madras. In 1624 he received the Bachelor of Arts degree from Christ Church College, Oxford, and two years later he was ordained by the Church of England. Elected to a chaplain-fellowship at Balliol College in 1827, that same year, after hearing a sermon by Charles Loyd on the Anglican Prayer Book, he decided to join the Oxford Movement. He was prebend of Lichfield Cathedral in 1832, preacher at Whitehall in 1837, and minister of Margaret Chapel (later All Saints'), Margaret Street, London, in 1839, where Richard Redhead (*LW* 110, 285) was organist and choirmaster. Their mutual liturgical efforts prompted the chapel sometimes to be called the Tractarian Cathedral. By 1845 Oakely's theological views were such that, given the Anglican Church's proceedings against him, he resigned all his appointments, joined John Henry Newmann (1801–90), who helped found the Oxford Movement at Littlemore, and was received into the Roman communion. Following his reordination he worked for many years among the poor in Westminster, where, in 1852, he became a canon in the pro-Cathedral. His last years were spent as a parish priest in Islington, London. There he died January 29, 1880.

His writings include *Whitehall Chapel Sermons* (1837), *The Church of the Bible* (1857), *Historical Notes on the Tractarian Movement* (1865), and four volumes of verse.

TRANSLATOR: 41 Oh, Come, All Ye Faithful

OLEARIUS, JOHANN GOTTFRIED (1635–1711), was born September 25, 1635, at Halle, Germany, the son of Gottfried Olearius, Lutheran pastor of St. Ulrich's Church. Following his schooling at the *Gymnasium* in Halle, in 1653 he entered Leipzig University, where, after pursuing brief studies also at Tübingen, Marburg, and Jena, he received the Master of Arts degree in 1656. Two years later he was ordained and became assistant to his father at St. Mary's Church in Halle. In 1662 he became deacon and as such, in 1685, inspector of the second section of the Saale District. Three years later he was appointed chief pastor, superintendent and consistorial councillor at Arnstadt as well as professor of theology in the local *Gymnasium.* Arnstadt received him with much joy and love. Shortly after celebrating his 50th anniversary in the office of the holy ministry in 1708, he lost his eyesight. From then on until his death on May 21, 1711, he had people read devotional literature to him.

It was in his earlier years, as far back as his student days, that Johann G. Olearius wrote most of his hymns. They appeared largely in his *Primitiae poeticae oder Erstlinge an deutschen Liedern und Madrigalien* (Halle, 1664) and in the expanded second edition entitled *Geistliche Singe-Lust* (Arnstadt, 1697). His later years were spent writing devotional literature.

AUTHOR: 34 Come, O Precious Ransom
187 When All the World Was Cursed

OLEARIUS, JOHANNES (1611–84), was born September 17, 1611, at Halle, the son of Johann Olearius (Latin for Oelschlaeger), who was the first of a long family line of famous and gifted German Lutheran theologians. Johannes' mother was the daughter of Pastor Nicander at St. Ulrich in Halle. Barely 11 years old, he lost both parents within a single year, and it was only through the kindness of Andreas Sartorius, a lawyer in Halle, that young Johannes was taken into his home and afforded the opportunity to attend the *Gymnasium* in Halle. In 1629 he enrolled at the University of Wittenberg, from which he received the Master of Arts degree in 1632 and Doctor of Theology in 1643. As early as 1632 he began to lecture, and in 1635 he became assistant to the philosophical faculty at Wittenberg University. From 1637–43 he served as superintendent at Querfurt, during which time he married Catherine Elisabethe Merk, who bore him five sons, all of whom eventually earned the doctorate or licentiate in theology. In 1643 Duke August of Sachsen-Weissenfels appointed him to be his court preacher and father confessor at Halle. In 1657 he became a member of the consistory, the churches' governing body, and in 1664 general superintendent. When, in 1680, a change in administration occurred, Duke Johann Adolf appointed Olearius to similar positions in Weissenfels, where he remained until his death on April 14, 1684.

Among the works that Johannes Olearius produced are his commentary on the entire Bible (Leipzig, 1681), numerous devotional books, and a translation of the *Imitatio Christi* by Thomas à Kempis (c. 1379–1471); (*LW* 275). His *Geistliche Singe-Kunst* (Leipzig, 1671) constituted the most comprehensive collection of hymns up to that time—1,218 hymns in seven volumes, of which 296 bore his initials. As one of the most significant and prolific poets of his time, Olearius' hymns reflect the orthodoxy of the days of Luther and Selnecker. After him one sense new sounds, namely, those of Pietism.

AUTHOR:	28	Comfort, Comfort, These My People
	174	The Lord, My God, Be Praised
	197	Lord, Open Now My Heart to Hear
	364	Oh, How Great Is Your Compassion

OLIVER, HENRY KEMBLE (1800–85), was born November 24, 1800, at Beverly, Massachusetts. From childhood on, music had a strong hold on him; it remained a lifelong and primary interest, in spite of not making it his profession.

After attending Boston Latin School and Phillips Academy, Andover, he spent two years at Harvard and graduated from Dartmouth in 1818, which in 1883 awarded him an honorary Doctor of Music degree. For 24 years he taught school in Salem, beginning in 1818. As organist, he served St. Peter's Church, Salem, for two years before serving North Church, Salem, for 24 years. About 1849, he began his tenure of 12 years at Lawrence's Unitarian Church. He founded the Salem Oratio Society, the Salem Glee Club, and the Mozart Association, of which he was also president, organist, and director.

A leader in civic affairs, he was mayor of both Lawrence (1859–61) and Salem (1877–80), state treasurer from 1861–65, organizer and developer of the Massachusetts Bureau of Statistics and Labor (1867–73), a pioneer institution of its kind. In addition, he served as adjutant general of Massachusetts from 1844–48, and superintendent of the Atlantic Cotton Mills of Lawrence from 1848–58. He died in Salem, August 12, 1885.

With Tuckerman and Bancroft he published the *National Lyre* (1848); his collection *Hymn and Psalm Tunes* first appeared in 1860; *The Original Hymn Tunes* in 1875.

COMPOSER:	393	FEDERAL STREET

OLIVERS, THOMAS (1725–99), was born at Tregynon, Montgomeryshire, Wales. Following the death of his parents when but four years old, he was passed from one relative to another, receiving little formal education. While apprenticed to a shoemaker, his life became so dissolute that by the age of 18 he was forced to leave his hometown. After short stays in Shrewsbury and Wrexham, he traveled to Bristol, where he heard George Whitefield preach from the text "Is not this a brand plucked out of the fire?" (Zech. 3:2), a sermon that changed the course of his life. He settled in Bradford-on-Avon as a shoemaker, returned to Tregynon to pay his debts and became a member of the Methodist Society. John Wesley (LW 280, 362) recognizing his potential, enlisted Olivers as one of his itinerant preachers in 1753. For the next 22 years he traveled through England, Scotland, and Ireland. Uneducated as he was, in 1775 Wesley appointed him supervisor of the *Arminian Magazine*, only to remove him in 1789 because "the errata were insufferable and pieces were inserted in the magazine without his knowledge." He spent the rest of his life in retirement in London, where he suddenly died in March 1799.

Olivers belongs to that small group of authors associated with only one hymn, though he wrote two others and is the arranger of the tune HEMSLEY (*LBW* 27).

AUTHOR: 450 The God of Abraham Praise

OLSEN, NORMAN PETER (1932–), the son of Norwegian immigrants, was born February 15, 1932, at Union City, New Jersey. After completing a Bachelor of Arts degree at Concordia College, Moorhead, Minnesota, in 1954, he received a Bachelor of Theology degree from Luther Theological Seminary, St. Paul, Minnesota, in 1959. During his theological studies he served a two-year internship at First Lutheran Church, Decorah, Iowa.

Olsen has served various pastorates in Minnesota since his ordination, including Cyrus and Kensington (1959–63); Benson (1963–65); Glencoe (1965–73); and Grace Lutheran, Luverne (1973–81). Since 1981 he has served at Bethlehem Lutheran Church in Mankato. He is married and the father of four adult children.

Olsen's hymn writing is of recent origin. In 1975, at the suggestion of his senior choir director, Dolly Talbert, he wrote a Lenten hymn, "Follow Me," which was set to music by Mrs. Talbert. Other hymns followed: "Break Gently, O Dawn" and "The First Day" for Easter; "Unto God My Rock" for the congregation's centennial celebration; and "When Seed Falls on Good Soil," another hymn for Lent. Mrs. Talbert prepared tunes for each of these hymns, and in 1976 they were included in a private publication for Grace Church, entitled *Sing*. Since then he has written other hymns. Olsen notes,

> Our venture into hymn writing has taken on an added dimension, beyond our own personal enjoyment: we hope to encourage others and revive the Church's gift of hymnody, so that along with the grand old hymns of the Christian community, the 20th-century Church may also sing of *her* faith, *her* mission, and *her* times.

AUTHOR: 338 When Seed Falls on Good Soil

OLSSON, OLOF (1841–1900), was born March 31, 1841, in Karlskoga, Värmland, Sweden. Prior to ordination, he studied music with the organist Västergötland and continued his regular studies at Fjellstedt's Mission Institute, Uppsala; the Mission Institute of Leipzig, Germany; and Uppsala University. Ordained in 1863, he served as pastor in the diocese of Karlstad, Sweden, until 1869, when he came to America to serve as pastor in Lindsborg, Kansas, during which time he was also a member of the Kansas Legislature from 1871–72. He was professor at Augustana College and Seminary, Rock Island, Illinois, from 1876–88, and was its president from 1891 until his death May 12, 1900. While at this institution he organized the Handel Oratorio Society. He served as author or editor of a number of publications for the Augustana Synod, as well a leader in producing its first English-language hymnal in 1901.

TRANSLATOR: 107 The Death of Jesus Christ, Our Lord

ONDERDONK, HENRY USTIC (1789–1858), was born March 16, 1789, in New York and studied medicine at Columbia College and at the University of Edinburgh, from which he received his Doctor of Medicine degree in 1810. For a while he was associated with Dr. Valentine Mott in behalf of the *New York Medical Journal*, but in 1815 he abandoned medicine for the ministry. He took holy orders in the same year and was for a while rector of St. Anne's Church, Brooklyn, New York, a rectorship that came after two years of missionary work. On October 27, 1827, Onderdonk was consecrated at Philadelphia and acted as assistant bishop of Philadelphia to Bishop White until 1836, when he succeeded White as chief bishop of the diocese. Suspended from office by the House of Bishops on the ground of intemperance, he was restored in 1856. He served American hymnody as an author and compiler and was a member of the committee which compiled the *American Prayer Book Collection* of 1826. He died at Philadelphia, December 6, 1858.

ADAPTOR/TRANSLATOR: 228 Our Children Jesus Calls

OPITZ, MARTIN (1597–1639), was born December 23, 1597, at Bunzlau, Silesia. After one year at the University of Frankfort-an-der-Oder, in 1619 he went to Heidelberg, where he studied literature and philosophy. After a brief period as professor of philosophy at the *Gymnasium* in Weissenburg, he led a rather wandering life in the service of various territorial noblemen. As a reward for the requiem poem on the death of Charles Joseph of Austria in 1625, he was crowned laureate by Emperor Ferdinand II, who later also ennobled him. In 1629 he was elected to the Fruitbearing Society, the most important of literary societies aiming to reform the German language. On a diplomatic mission to Paris on behalf of Burgrave Carl Hannibal von Dohna, for whom he was private secretary, he met Hugo Grotius, Dutch poet, jurist, and classical scholar. From 1635 until his death, August 20, 1639, he lived in Danzig (Gdansk) where Wladyslaw IV of Poland made him his secretary and historiographer.

As head of the Silesian circle of poets, Opitz was regarded as the greatest German poet, the "father of German poetry," at least in respect to its form. His influential *Buch von der Deutschen Poeterey* (Brieg, 1624) established rules for the purity of language, style, verse, and rhyme. It insisted on word stress rather than syllable counting. His poems follow his own rigorous rules and are mostly didactic and descriptive. His work served as a foundation for greater poets of his generation. Among other things, he versified the Epistle readings for the Sundays and festivals of the church year (editions of 1624, 1628, 1639) according to the meters in the French Psalter, in which "Arise and shine in splendor" appeared; he versified some psalms in the meters of Clement Marot (*LW* 399) and Theodore de Béze (1519–1605), John Calvin's versifiers (see essay: Metrical Psalms, p. 825). His complete works were issued in three volumes at Frankfurt and Leipzig in 1724.

AUTHOR: 85 Arise and Shine in Splendor

OSLER, EDWARD (1798–1863), was born January 30, 1798, at Falmouth, England. Brought up as a Dissenter, he was educated for the medical profession. Having served at the Swansea Infirmary and House of Industry from 1819–25, and thereafter as surgeon in the navy, he then settled in London about 1836. Severing his Dissenter connections, he became associated with William John Hall in publishing *Psalms and Hymns adapted to the Service of the Church of England* (1836) that, by its cover, became known as the *Mitre Hymnal*. Osler contributed 15 psalm versions and 50 hymns, some of both adapted from earlier authors. Later, Lord Selborne's *Book of Praise from the best English Hymn Writers* (1862) and Orby Shipley's *Lyra Euchristica* (1864) included some of his other hymns. From 1841 until his death in Truro, March 7, 1863, he was on the staff of the Society for Promoting Christian Knowledge and editor of the *Royal Cornwall Gazette*.

AUTHOR: 261 Lord of the Church, We Humbly Pray
389 May We Your Precepts, Lord, Fulfill
395 O Fount of Good, for All Your Love

OWEN, WILLIAM ('of Prysgol') (1813-93), was born December 12, 1813, in Bangor, Carnarvonshire, Wales, where from the age of 10 he worked, like his father, in the famed Penryhn slate quarries of Bethesda. At 18 he composed his first tune for a then-popular hymn text. Criticized for his daring, he was told to write new tunes to new texts. BRYN CALFARIA is such a new tune, coupled to the Welsh hymn "Gwaed y groes sy'n cody fynny."

In 1852/54 Owen published *Y Perl Cerddorol* (The Pearl of Music), which contained a number of compositions, mostly hymn tunes. Popularity of the work soon prompted further editions of 1886 and 1892. He conducted several choirs and was precentor at Caeathraw Chapel. Owen died at Caernarvon, July 20, 1893.

COMPOSER: 281 BRYN CALFARIA

PALESTRINA, GIOVANNI PIERLUIGI SANTE da (c. 1525–94), was born in the town of Palestrina, 23 miles east of Rome, to a wealthy citizen. His early musical training occurred at Santa Maria Maggiore, Rome, where as a choir boy, he came under the influence of the great Dutch master Orlando de Lassus (1532–94). In 1544 he was appointed organist at the cathedral of Palestrina and was married in 1544. When his bishop became Pope Julian III in 1551, Palestrina was brought with him to be the choir master of the Julian Chapel in the Vatican. In 1555 the pope made him a member of the Pontifical Choir, Sistine Chapel. In the fluid conditions of the Counter Reformation, other appointments followed: choirmaster at St. John Lateran (1557); St. Mary Major (1560); director of music at the Roman Seminary (1565), where two of his sons were students. In 1571 he returned to the Julian Chapel as choirmaster, remaining there until his death February 2, 1594. After the death of his first wife, he decided to enter the priesthood. He changed his mind, however, and married the widow of a prosperous furrier and leather merchant. A proposal to reappoint him to the Pontifical Choir in the early 80s was defeated because of his second marriage. He now devoted himself to composition.

Most of his music was sacred in character. Each of the two complete editions of his works that have been published contains over 30 volumes of masses, motets, and other liturgical music, plus some sacred and secular madrigals. His style was officially held by the Council of Trent (1545–63) to be the ideal at which all other composers should aim.

COMPOSER: 143 VICTORY

PALMER, RAY (1808–1887), the son of a judge, was born November 12, 1808, in Little Compton, Rhode Island. Educated at home, Ray, at the age of 13,was forced by harsh financial circumstances to start work clerking in a dry-goods store in Boston. During his two-year employment there, he underwent deep religious experiences and joined the Congregational Church. Encouraged by his pastor, Palmer resolved to enter the ministry. After three years at Phillips Academy, Andover, he attended Yale and graduated in 1830.

After further study in New York and New Haven, he was ordained in 1835. His first pastorate was at Bath, Maine, where he remained for 15 years. He stayed approximately the same length of time with a congregation in Albany, New York before becoming secretary of the Congregational Union of New York, a position he held from 1865–78. Failing health forced his retirement to Newark, New Jersey; connected with the

Belleville Congregational Church, he became its pastor in charge of visitation. Palmer died March 29, 1887, reciting hymns even on his deathbed. A devout man, with cheerful, bouyant spirit, he was loved by all who knew him.

The best of Palmer's 38 hymns, by his own admission, were written in his youth. His writings include several volumes of religious verse and devotional essays, among which are *Spiritual Improvement* (1839); *Hymns and Sacred Pieces, with Miscellaneous Poems* (1865); *Hymns of My Holy Hours and Other Pieces* (1868); and his complete *Poetical Works* (1876).

AUTHOR: 378 My Faith Looks Trustingly

PARRY, JOSEPH (1841–1903), was born May 21, 1841, at Cyfarthfa Merthyr Tydfil, Wales, into a family of such poor circumstances that before the age of 10 he had to discontinue school to work in the iron industry. In 1854 his family emigrated to Danville, Pennsylvania, where he received his first music lessons in classes conducted by fellow Welsh workmen, who then subscribed to send him to a music college at Geneseo, New York, in 1861. Returning to Wales in 1862, he took an organist's post and competed in several Eisteddfodau (Welsh festivals of the singing arts) winning prizes in 1863–64, 1866. Friends in America and Wales raised funds to enable him to continue his musical studies at the Royal Academy of Music (1868–71). From 1871–73 he conducted a music school in Danville, Pennsylvania; then he was appointed professor of music at the newly founded University College, Aberystwyth (1873–79). He ran private music schools in Aberystwyth (1879–81) and in Swansea (1881–88) before he was appointed lecturer and then professor at University College of South Wales, Cardiff.

Parry wrote oratorios, cantatas, anthems, some instrumental music, as well as 400 hymn tunes. For a number of years, he wrote one hymn tune every Sunday. He died February 17, 1903, at Penarth, Glamorgan.

COMPOSER: 93, 508 ABERYSTWYTH

PATRICK (c. 372, 386, or 389–c. 461 or 466), the patron saint of Ireland, was born near what is now Dumbarton in North Britain. His father Calpurnius, a deacon and member of the town council, was undoubtedly of noble Roman descent, hence the name Patricius (patrician). At the age of 16 Patrick, with others, was carried off to Ireland and sold as a slave. During this captivity he learned the Irish language and became an ardent Christian. On his escape and return to Britain after six years, he was ordained deacon and priest in Gaul. About 425 he returned to Ireland as a missionary, devoting his life to the conversion of its people to the Christian faith. In 432 he was consecrated Ireland's second bishop, and by the time of his death in 461 at Saulpatrick, Ireland had a strong and active church.

St. Patrick's two important writings are his *Confession* and *The Letter to Carolicius.*

AUTHOR (attr.): 172 I Bind unto Myself Today

PERRONET, EDWARD (1726–92), was born at Sundridge, Kent, into a family of French Huguenots (Calvinist French Protestants) who had come to England to escape persecution after the revocation in 1685 of the Edict of Nantes (1598). Wesley (*LW* 280, 362) and his brother Charles (*LW* 15, et al.) for nearly 40 years, even to the point of being call "the archbishop of Methodism." His son Edward, however, originally intent on taking holy orders, by 1749 had committed himself (with his brother Charles) to work with the Wesleys as an itinerant preacher. In that year, accompanying John Wesley in Bolton, Lancashire, a mob attacked the house where they were staying and beat them mercilessly. In 1775 John took issue with the Wesleys on their insistence that their preachers not administer the sacraments, but rather that they encourage their followers to receive the sacraments in their respective parishes of the Church of England. Contrariwise, Perronet asserted that, as a divinely-called minister, he had the right to administer the sacraments. In 1757 he published *The Mitre; a Sacred Poem,* a scathing satire in which he attacked the abuses in the Church of England. This roused John Wesley's anger, and he demanded that the book be suppressed. Relationship with the Wesleys was subsequently broken off.

Perronet then joined the Countess of Huntingdon's Connexion as minister in a chapel in Watling Street, Canterbury. His constant attacks on the Church of England, however, also displeased the Countess. Thus, Perronet, a zealous, fiery, and energetic preacher, ended his days as pastor of a small Independent, or Congregational, chapel in Canterbury, where he died on January 2, 1792. Despite his violent temper, he is said to have possessed a warm, devotional spirit as well as poetic talent.

Perronet's hymns were published anonymously in three small volumes; *Select Passages of the Old and New Testament, versified* (1756); *A Small Collection of Hymns, Canterbury* (1782); and *Occasional Verses, Moral and Sacred* (1785). All his hymns, except the one below, undeservedly have fallen by the wayside.

AUTHOR: 272 All Hail the Power of Jesus' Name

PETER, PHILIP ADAM (1832–1919), was born at Homburg-von-der-Hohe, Hesse-Nassau, Germany, January 2, 1832. Educated at the Corydon Academy of Indiana and trained for the Lutheran ministry by E. S. Henkel in Corydon, he was ordained pastor by the Joint Synod of Ohio and Other States in 1858. He served St. Paul's, Olean, Indiana, from 1869–74; thereafter he served three Indiana parishes simultaneously: St. Matthew's, Ithaca; Trinity in Franklin Township; and Immanuel near Philipsburg until ill health hindered his work. Retiring in 1908, he died February 9, 1919.

In addition to his parish responsibilities, Peter served for nine years as secretary of the Southern District, and as secretary of the Western District for another eight. His publications include a *History of the Reformation of the Sixteenth Century* (1889); *St. Paul, The Great Apostle to the Gentiles* (1901); and translations of a number of hymns.

TRANSLATOR: 462 The Day Is Surely Drawing Near

PETERSEN, VICTOR OLOF (1864–1929), was born September 24, 1864, in Skede, Smaland, Sweden. He came to America in 1867 and studied at Augustana College and Academy, Rock Island, Illinois, graduating in 1889. After a short time of teaching physics and chemistry at Augustana College, his brief study of chemistry at Harvard resulted in his being given a full professorship. Becoming secretary of the Rock Island Tropical Plantation Co. in 1906, from 1907–13 he managed the Chalchijapa Plantation in southern Mexico. Engaged thereafter in the real estate and insurance business in Rock Island, in 1920 he was called to be professor of chemistry at Huron College, Huron, South Dakota, where he remained until his death in 1929.

As a lover of hymnody, he translated a number of hymns from Swedish sources.

TRANSLATOR: 20 O Bride of Christ, Rejoice

PFEFFERKORN, GEORG MICHAEL (1645–1732), was born March 16, 1645, at Iffta, a small village near Eisenach, where his father was a Lutheran pastor. After studying at the universities of Jena and Leipzig he served for a time as private tutor in Altenburg and thereafter became a member of the teaching staff at the local *Gymnasium*. His piety and talents prompted Duke Ernst the Pious of Gotha to appoint him as private tutor of his three sons. In 1676 Duke Friedrich I appointed him pastor of Friemar, near Gotha, and in 1682 a member of the consistory and superintendent at Gräfen-Tonna, also near Gotha. Here the Lord blessed his work and granted him a long life—he was 86 when he died March 3, 1732.

His poetic works appeared during his early teaching years: *Poetisch-philosophischen Fest und Wochenlust* (Altenburg, 1667), for which he was crowned poet, and *Anweisung zur Verskunst* (1669).

AUTHOR: 418 What Is the World to Me

PFEIL, CHRISTOPH CARL LUDWIG VON (1712–84), was born January 12, 1712, at Grünstadt near Worms, where his father was then in the service of Count Leiningen. After completing his studies at the universities of Halle and Tübingen, he was appointed in 1732 Württemberg secretary of the legation at Regensburg, a position he later resigned because of political differences, retiring to his estate in Deufstettin near Crailsheim. Made a baron by Emperor Joseph II, in 1765 he received the cross of the

Red Eagle Order from Frederick the Great. An intermittant fever confined him to his bed from August 1783 to his death February 14, 1784, at Deufstetten.

Pfeil was a man of deep and genuine piety. His hymn writing began after a spiritual experience on the 10th Sunday after Trinity Sunday, 1730, and it continued to be his favorite activity, thus making him one of the most productive of German hymn writers. His published hymns number about 950, included in such publications as *Lieder von der offenbarten Herrlichkeit und Zukunft des Herrn* (Esslingen, 1741) and *Evangelische Glaubens-Herzensgesänge* (Dinkelsbühl, 1783).

AUTHOR: 467 Oh, Blest the House

PHELPS, SYLVANUS DRYDEN (1816–95), was born in Suffield, Connecticut, May 15, 1816, and was educated at the Connecticut Literary Institute and Brown University, where he graduated in 1844. Two years later, after study at Yale Theological Seminary, he became pastor of First Baptist Church, New Haven, where he labored for 28 years, also publishing numerous prose works and volumes of poetry. His *Holy Land, with Glimpses of Europe and Egypt, A Year's Tour* (1862) was widely read and passed through nine editions in 25 years. He died November 23, 1895.

Phelps is today chiefly remembered as the father of William Lyon Phelps, renowned author and for many years professor of English literature at Yale University, and as the author of the following hymn.

AUTHOR: 374 Savior, Thy Dying Love

PLUMPTRE, EDWARD HAYES (1821–91), was born August 6, 1821, at Bloomsbury, London. Educated at King's College, London, and University College, Oxford, he graduated in 1844 and became a fellow at Brasenose College, Oxford. Taking holy orders in the Church of England in 1846, he soon became prominent as a preacher and theologian. After holding such important positions as chaplain of King's College, London (1847–68); dean of Queen's College, Oxford; prebendary of St. Paul's Cathedral; professor of pastoral theology (1853–63) and professor of New Testament exegesis at King's College (1864–81); and rector of Pluckley, Kent, he was appointed dean of Wells Cathedral in 1881, a position which he held the last 10 years of his life. During his career he was several times select preacher at Oxford; Grinfield lecturer on the Septuagint, Oxford; and examiner in theological schools there. He was a member of the Old Testament Company of Revisors of the Authorized Version of the Bible. He published numerous notable works on the classics, history, divinity, biblical criticism, and biography; several volumes of verse; translations of Sophocles, Aeschylus, and Dante; and in 1888 a fine biography of Bishop Ken (*LW* 461, et al.).

Plumptre's hymns were often written for special occasions in his parish churches and elsewhere; some appeared in his own books of verse, for instance, *Lazarus, and Other Poems* (1864); others were contributed to various hymnals. Julian says of him:

> As a writer of sacred poetry he ranks very high. His hymns are elegant in style, fervent in spirit, and broad in treatment. . . . The rhythm of his verse has a special attraction to musicians, its poetry for the cultured, and its stately simplicity for the devout and earnest minded.

He died in the deanery at Wells, Sommerset, February 1, 1891.

AUTHOR: 399 Your Hand, O Lord, in Days of Old
455 Rejoice, O Pilgrim Throng

POLACK, WILLIAM GUSTAVE (1890–1950), was born December 7, 1890, in Wausau, Wisconsin. He studied at Concordia College, Fort Wayne, Indiana, and Concordia Seminary, St. Louis, graduating from the latter in 1914. Ordained in 1914 by the Rev. C. A. Frank, founder and first editor of the *Lutheran Witness*, Polack assumed duties as assistant pastor under Frank at Trinity Lutheran Church, Evansville, Indiana. The same year he married Iona Mary Gick; the union was blessed with six children. In 1921 Polack succeeded Frank as pastor of Trinity.

Polack remained in Evansville four more years; in 1925 he accepted the call as professor of theology at Concordia Seminary, St. Louis, where he chiefly taught liturgics and church history. At the same time he joined the staff of the *Lutheran Witness*, for which he was associate editor for 25 years. He also donated much of his time to Concordia Historical Institute, and edited the *Concordia Historical Quarterly* from 1927–49. He was an associate of *The Cresset*, a review of art and literature of the Walther League; and from 1928–39 he was editor of the *Concordia Junior Messenger*. He served for some time as member and chairperson of the Board for Young People's Literature of The Lutheran Church—Missouri Synod, and as secretary (1927–37) and president (1945–49) of the Concordia Historical Institute and editor of its quarterly (1927–49).

He became chairman of the Committee on Hymnology and Liturgics of the The Lutheran Church—Missouri Synod in 1929, and the following year organized the Intersynodical Committee on Hymnology and Liturgics for the Synodical Conference of North America—which group prepared *The Lutheran Hymnal* (1941), to which he contributed three original hymns and nine translations. Instrumental in the publication of this hymnal and service book, Polack authored the *Handbook to The Lutheran Hymnal* (1942) as well. That same year Valparaiso University, Valparaiso, Indiana, honored him with the Doctor of Divinity degree.

Polack died of a brain tumor on June 5, 1950. He was buried at Clear Lake Lutheran Chapel, Clear Lake, Indiana, a congregation he had helped establish in 1938 near his resort home there.

Equally facile in German and English, Polack translated hymns and poetry as well as producing several prose works, including *The Building of a Great Church* (1926); *Into All the World: The Story of Lutheran Foreign Missions* (1930); *The Story of Luther*

(1931); *The Story of C. F. W. Walther* (1935); *Fathers and Founders* (1938); and *Beside Still Water*, published after his death in 1950.

TRANSLATOR: 66 Every Year the Christ Child (sts. 2–3)
209 Kyrie, God Father
210 All Glory Be to God Alone
341 O God, Our Lord, Your Holy Word
483 With the Lord Begin Your Task

POLLOCK, THOMAS BENSON (1836–96), was born May 28, 1836, at Strathalan, Isle of Man. A graduate of Trinity College, Dublin (B.A. 1859; M.A. 1863), where he won the vice-chancellor's prize for English verse, in 1861 he was ordained and became a curate of St. Luke's, Leek, Staffordshire, and of St. Thomas', Stamford Hill, London. In 1865 he joined his brother J. S. Pollock at St. Alban's Mission, Borderly, Birmingham, where they worked together for 30 years. Poor as was the area, a large congregation was gathered, and a church was built that was the finest in the city. To better serve the people, the brothers engaged three assistant clergy, six lay readers, and four sisters; and St. Albans became the high church stronghold of Birmingham. After 30 years as curate, Thomas succeeded his brother as vicar, but his health, broken by the strenuous demands of the parish, led to his death 10 months later.

Pollock was a successful writer of hymns in the form of metrical litanies, many of which were published in his *Metrical Litanies for Special Services and General Use* (Oxford, 1870). He was a member of the committee that compiled *Hymns Ancient and Modern* (1861), the most popular and widely sold of all English hymnals. He died December 15, 1896.

AUTHOR: 112 Jesus, in Your Dying Woes

POPE, ALEXANDER (1688–1744), was born May 22, 1688, in London, the son of a wholesale linen merchant who was Roman Catholic. As a result of a severe illness, Pope developed a physical deformity at the age of 10, a deformity from which he later recovered, but not without the effect of a certain distorted view of life. Though he attended Winchester briefly, he was largely self taught, becoming one of the most eminent writers and satirists of his generation. His *Rape of the Lock* (1712), a brilliant mock-heroic poem, won him a wide reputation. His independence was earned with his translation of the *Illiad* (1715–20) and *Odyssey* (1725–26). He died May 30, 1744, and was buried in the parish church at Twickenham.

AUTHOR: 313 Rise, Crowned with Light

PORTER, HUGH (1897–1960), was born September 18, 1897, in Heron Lake, Minnesota, the son of a Methodist minister, and grew up in towns in Colorado, Illinois, and Indiana. At the age of 14 his music training and ability were such that he already held a regular organ position. Having earned a Bachelor of Music degree from the American Conservatory of Music in Chicago (1920), he went on to earn a Bachelor of Arts degree at Northwestern University in Chicago in 1924. That year he went to New York, having been granted a fellowship by the Julliard Musical Foundation, at which time he privately studied piano with Howard Wells (1918–20), organ with Wilhelm Middelshulte (1918–20), Lynnwood Farnam (1924–27), and T. Tertius Noble (1924–27). From 1920–52 he, among other activities, taught at the American Conservatory (1920–23); at New York University (1925–28); he served as organist of the New First Congregational Church of Chicago (1920–23); of Calvary Episcopal Church and Church of the Heavenly Rest in New York City (1924–30); of Second Presbyterian Church, New York (1931–35); and of the Sunday worship at Union Theological Seminary (1947–60). As a fellow of the American Guild of Organists (1932), he was a well-known recitalist throughout the United States.

Torn between music and the pastoral ministry, in 1927 he entered Union Theological Seminary as a ministerial student. When, in 1928, the seminary's School of Sacred Music was founded, he was one of the first to enroll. Here he received the Master of Sacred Music degree in 1930; the Doctor of Music degree in 1944. He was a member of the faculty from 1931 until his sudden death in 1960. During his 15 years as director of the School of Sacred Music he did much to broaden its program and enhance its reputation. With his wife Ethel F. Porter, he served as music editor of the *Pilgrim Hymnal* (1958). She thereafter coauthored the *Guide to the Pilgrim Hymnal* (1966) with Albert C. Ronander, minister of the United Church of Christ and executive secretary of the committee that compiled the *Pilgrim Hymnal.*

ARRANGER: 504 Go Tell It on the Mountain

POTT, FRANCIS (1832–1909), was born December 29, 1832, at Southwark, London, and educated at Brasenose College, Oxford, where he received the Bachelor of Arts degree and the Master's in 1857. Ordained in 1856, he became curate of Bishopsworth, Somerset; of Ardingley and Ticehurst, Sussex. He was rector of Norhill, Bedfordshire, from 1866–91, when he retired because of increasing deafness and went to live at Speldhurst, Kent, near Tunbridge Wells, where he died October 26, 1909.

Pott was a member of the original committee that produced *Hymns Ancient and Modern* in 1861. That year he also published *Hymns Fitted to the Order of Common Prayer*. His interest in the reform of chanting led him to publish *The Free Rhythm Psalter* (1898), a book that turned out to be too elaborate for general use.

TRANSLATOR: 143 The Strife Is O'er, the Battle Done

PRAETORIUS, MICHAEL (c. 1571–1621), was born at Kreuzburg-an-der Werra, Thuringia, Germany, on February 15, about 1571, the son of Michael Schultheiss (of which Praetorius is the latinization), a Lutheran pastor and teacher. In the controversy that broke out after the Augsburg Interim (1548), Praetorius' father was numbered among the strict Lutherans. As a result, he lost his position and had to move a number of times. One such move took the family to Torgau, where in the *Lateinschule* young Michael was taught music by Michael Voigt, the successor to Johann Walter (*LW* 265). In 1582 Praetorius matriculated at the University of Frankfort-an-der-Oder, where his brother Andreas was professor of theology. In 1587 he became organist at the *Marienkirche* in Frankfort; in 1595 organist and 1604 kapellmeister to Duke Heinrich Julius of Brunswick, who had his residence in Wolfenbüttel. While here he married Anna Lakemacher, who bore him two sons. Following the duke's death, his successor permitted Praetorius to be away frequently for considerable periods of time. This brought him to Kassel, to Dresden, where he met Heinrich Schütz (1585–1672) and became acquainted with the latest Italian music, to Magdeburg, to Halle, and other places.

As the son and grandson of Lutheran theologians he remained a firm, committed Christian all his life. According to the sermon preached at his funeral, he sometimes regretted that he had not studied for the holy ministry. One cannot but be impressed with his enormous creative power and, considering his relatively short life, his astonishing output—three major works: *Musae Sioniae*, nine volumes published between 1605 and 1610, containing chorale arrangements of more than 1,200 compositions, from simple to polychoral settings; *Hymnodia Sionia* (1611), in which canonic technique plays so prominent a role; and the three-volume theoretical, historical treatise, *Syntagma Musicum* (1615–19), the second volume of which contains detailed information about the instruments of his day, particularly a thorough treatment of the organ. Aside from its documentary value, the *Syntagma Musicum* reflects the great diffuseness of instrumentation in the early Baroque, the prominent place given the organ, the variety of tone color in the performance of polyphonic music, and the *alternatim praxis*, all of which reached a high point in Germany in the lifetime of Praetorius.

He died February 15, 1621, at Wofenbüttel, near Brunswick.

COMPOSER: 14, 52, 81 PUER NOBIS
244 ACH GOTT VOM HIMMELREICHE

F. B. P. (16th,century) The conjecture that these initials stand for Francis Baker, Pater (Priest or Presbyter), a Roman Catholic priest imprisoned at the Tower of London and sentenced to death about 1593, is totally unfounded. Julian rejects this and various other attempts to identify this author.

AUTHOR: 307 Jerusalem, My Happy Home

PRECHT, FRED L. (1916–), was born June 22, 1916, at St. Clair Minnesota. After attending Concordia Academy and Concordia College (1936), St. Paul, Minnesota, he entered Concordia Seminary, St. Louis, Missouri. At his graduation in June 1940 he was assigned to serve as assistant professor at Concordia Theological Seminary, Springfield, Illinois, teaching various courses as well as directing the Concordia Seminary Choir. Here he served until the spring of 1943, when he accepted the call to serve as pastor of St. John's Lutheran Church, Alma City, Minnesota. A year later he received the call to return to Concordia Seminary as professor of worship and music and conductor of the seminary choir.

He earned the Bachelor of Music (1951) and Master of Music (1953) degrees from Northwestern University, Evanston, Illinois, and pursued graduate studies at Concordia Seminary, St. Louis, earning the Master of Sacred Theology degree (1961), the Doctor of Theology degree (1965).

In addition to teaching various courses in the field of corporate worship at the Springfield seminary, he also served for many years as dean of the chapel. The seminary choir which he conducted, besides its annual concert tours in the United States, made three European concert tours (1954, 1958, 1966).

He was a member of the Synod's Commission on worship (1965–76); the editorial board of *Church Music*; and the Inter-Lutheran Commission on Worship (1968–75), serving on its Liturgical Texts Committee and later on its Liturgical Music Committee. He served as executive director of The Lutheran Church—Missouri Synod Foundation (1968–71), and then headed the department of seminary relations at Concordia Theological Seminary Springfield, Il., until his move to St. Louis in July 1976.

In 1979 he was installed as executive secretary of the Synod's Commission on Worship which was entrusted with the task of revising the *Lutheran Book of Worship* (1978). This resulted in the appearance of *Lutheran Worship* (1982). He also edited the companion volumes to the new hymnal that were produced by the commission: *Lutheran Worship: Altar Book* (1982); *Lutheran Worship: Agenda* (1984); and *Lutheran Worship: Little Agenda* (1985). He was also associate editor of *Lutheran Worship Notes*, a newsletter for congregations.

A member of the Hymn Society of America, the North American Academy of Liturgy, and the Societas Liturgica, he has been elected to the Pi Kappa Lambda, the national music honor society of Northwestern University. The Aeterna Moliri (Building for Eternity) medal was awarded him, May 28, 1983, by Concordia College, St. Paul, Minnesota, for "churchmanship . . . characterized by moral and intellectual courage . . . and contributions to the church . . . of lasting worth."

Since his official retirement, July 1, 1987, concluding 44 years of service to the Synod as such, he has devoted his time to preparing the manuscript for this *Companion to Lutheran Worship* and with his wife Louise lives in Fairview Heights, Illinois.

ARRANGER: 284 O DURCHBRECHER
475 SIEH, HIER BIN ICH

PRICHARD, ROWLAND HUW (HUGH) (1811–87), born January 14, 1811, at Y Graienyn, near Bala, Merionethshire, was named after his grandfather, the bard Rowland Huw. He spent most of his life in Bala as a well-known precentor. In 1880 he moved to to Holywell to be a loom-tender's assistant at the Welsh Flannel Manufacturing Company's mills. When he was 33 years old, his *Cyfaill y Cantorion* (The Singer's Friend) was published, comprised mainly of his own compositions. Many of his hymn tunes were also published in various Welsh periodicals. He died at Holywell, Flintshire, January 25, 1887.

COMPOSER: 286, 402 HYFRYDOL

PRUDENTIUS, AURELIUS CLEMENS (348–c. 413), was born in northern Spain, probably at the town of Saragossa. He attended the imperial schools, where he studied the Latin poets Virgil and Horace as well as law and rhetoric. He went on to become a lawyer and later a judge; when Theodosius came to power, he called Prudentius to Rome for a court office.

Prudentius was impressed with the imperial city, especially the evidence of Christianity found there. However, at the age of 57, feeling the vanity and worldliness of his official life, he decided to retire and begin a life of seclusion and self-denial. His major activity became writing, which he undertook solely for the praise and glory of God. He championed political causes for the same reasons: his two-volume poem "Against Symmachus" was a blow in the battle against pagan imagery in the Senate chamber, and he was also instrumental in putting an end, in 404, to gladiatorial exhibitions.

The two major works of Prudentius are the *Peristephanon*, a collection of 14 poems honoring the martyrs of Spain, Rome, and Africa; and the *Cathemerinon*, a series of 12 very long hymns, ranging in length from 80 to 220 lines, for the various hours of the day. These were among the most widely read devotional books in the Middle Ages; centos from them were used extensively in early breviaries and hymns. The three hymns by Prudentius contained in *Lutheran Worship* (1982) are all drawn from the latter.

Historians and hymnologists have always accorded Prudentius the highest praise, and Luther once expressed the desire that his poetry be studied in German schools.

AUTHOR:
36 Of the Father's Love Begotten
76 O Chief of Cities, Bethlehem
188 Sweet Flowerets of the Martyr Band

PURCELL, HENRY (1658 or 59–95), was born at Westminster, London, the son of a Gentleman of the Chapel Royal and successor to Henry Lawes (*LW* 243). The boy's musical education was given him by his father and then by an uncle. From 1669–73 he was a chorister at the Chapel Royal, studying under Matthew Locke, Henry Cooke, and Pelham Humphrey. In 1673 he was apprenticed to organ builder and keeper of the royal instruments John Hingston. In 1674 he also studied with John Blow, Humphrey's successor at the Chapel Royal. In 1677 he succeeded Matthew Locke as "composer to the king's violin," and was organist in Westminster Abbey (1679–95) succeeding John Blow, and organist at the Chapel Royal 1682–95). He succeeded Hingston in 1683 as keeper of the royal instruments, and was responsible for the music at the coronation of James II in 1685, and of William and Mary in 1689. On his death, November 21, 1695, he was accorded full ceremonial burial in the Abbey.

Purcell's official duties prompted him to write a goodly amount of music, including three services, three Latin anthems, 15 full anthems and 50 verse anthems, and some organ music. His anthem "Thou knowest, Lord" was written for the funeral of Queen Mary II, and of its first performance Thomas Tudway (c. 1650–1726), English composer and musicologist, wrote:

> I appeal to all that were present, as well as such as understood music, as those that did not, whether they ever heard anything so rapturously fine and solemn and so heavenly in operation, which drew tears from them all; and yet a plain, natural composition; which shows the pow'r of music, when 'tis rightly fitted and adapted to devotional purposes.

COMPOSER: 186 WESTMINSTER ABBEY

PUSEY, PHILIP (1799–1855), was born June 25, 1799, at Pusey, England, the son of the first Viscount Folestone, who assumed the name of Pusey instead of Bouverie. His elder brother was the famous Edward Bouverie Pusey, renowned leader of the Oxford Movement. Educated at Eton and Christ Church, Oxford, Philip, however, left without taking his degree, settling on his estate and devoting himself to agriculture and public service and becoming one of the founders of the Royal Agricultural Society. He was a Conservative of the House of Commons, successively for Rye, Sussex, Chippenham, Wiltshire, Casshel, and Birkshire. He was a connoisseur of art, a collector of prints and etchings, a copious contributor to the reviews, and one of the founders of the London Library. Interested in hymnology and a keen hymnologist, in opposition to his famous brother, he wanted to supplant the Sternhold and Hopkins version of the Psalms (see essay: Metrical Psalms, p. 825) with Milman's (*LW* 105) hymns. He died at Oxford July 9, 1855.

TRANSLATOR: 301 Lord of Our Life

PYE, HENRY JOHN (1825–1903), was born in 1825 at Cliffton Hall, Staffordshire, England. Receiving the Bachelor of Arts degree from Trinity College, Cambridge, in 1848, and the Master of Arts four years later, he took holy orders and became rector of Cliffton-Campville, Staffordshire. While here he prepared and published *Hymns* (1851), a collection for use of his congregation. In 1868, however, he and his wife, the sole daughter of Bishop S. Wilborforce (1759–1833), English philanthropist and politician, founder of the Anti-Slavery Society, joined the Roman Catholic Church. He died January 3, 1903.

AUTHOR: 186 In His Temple Now Behold Him

QUINN, JAMES (1919–), born April 21, 1919, in Glasgow, was educated at St. Aloysius' College and Glasgow University, where he received the Master of Arts degree in 1939. Entering the Society of Jesus that same year, he was ordained to the priesthood in 1950. He served as translator and consultant to the International Commission on English in the Liturgy (ICEL) and as secretary of the Secretariat for Christian Unity of the Bishops' Conference of Scotland. After teaching at Heythrop College, Preston Catholic College, and Wimbledon College, he was appointed spiritual director to Beda College, Rome, in 1966.

His publications include *New Hymns for All Seasons* (London, 1969) and *Eucharistic Hymns* (Dublin, 1982). He has attempted to create texts which are "richly scriptural, doctrinally sound, and liturgically correct." His texts have been characterized by a sensitivity to language resulting in works that contain "resonances that gradually disclose their depth of content through constant use" (Milgate, *Songs of the People of God*).

AUTHOR: 459 Forth in the Peace of Christ

QUITMEYER, ELIZABETH (1911–), was born June 20, 1911, in Detroit, Michigan, where her father, Henry A. Quitmeyer, was a teacher at the Lutheran School for the Deaf. Elizabeth was one of 10 children, all of whom were taught the German language in their home, where vocal and instrumental music also held an important place.

At the age of 25 Quitmeyer suddenly became very ill; over 15 years she struggled with her health, enduring five years in the hospital. She writes,

> When too weak to hold even a small book, or to retain what I had just read, I did remember what I had memorized: verses from Scripture, catechism and hymns came to mind often. It was then that I tried to write verse for family and friends' birthdays, and later for the hospital paper.

Stronger, but still limited in strength, she was employed for 22 years in a business office. She continued writing verse and translating German texts. In 1963 her translation, "Lord, In Thy Name I Rest Me," from Bonifacius Stoelzlen (1603–67), appeared in *This Day* under the heading "Songs Before Unknown," a section devoted to contemporary hymn writers.

In 1974 failing health made an early retirement necessary. Quitmeyer writes,

> Emphysema, a common aftermath of the surgery and treatments, now keeps me housebound in cold and windy weather and on hot summer days, especially when very humid. Though needing oxygen most of the time, writing hymns or translating is still a joy. . . . Every day is a gift, and I try to remember day by day that 'What God ordains is always good; his mercy fails me never.'

She continues to live in Detroit, Michigan.

TRANSLATOR: 223 To Jordan Came the Christ, Our Lord

RAMBACH, JOHANN JACOB (1693–1735), was born February 24, 1693, in Halle, Germany. After attending the *Gymnasium* in Glaucha, he came home for a while to help his father, a carpenter, support the family. In 1712 he entered the University of Halle, the seat of Pietism, to study theology, during which he assisted J. H. Michaelis in preparing an edition of the Hebrew Bible. From 1720–23 he was a private tutor in Jena, after which he became a professor of theology at Halle University; and in 1727 he became the successor of August Herman Francke as overseer of an orphanage, as well as preacher at the *Schulkirche*. Four years later, at the invitation of the Duke of Hesse, he became the principal theological professor and superintendent at Giessen. Here his preaching and teaching were not well received. On April 19, 1735, at the age of 42, he died of a violent fever.

As a theologian, preacher, devotional writer, and issuer of hymnals, Rambach was highly regarded. As a poet of church hymns—he wrote over 180—he has been characterized as a forerunner of Christian F. Gellert (*LW* 139). Unfortunately, Rambach did not escape the influence of Rationalism, in Germany, the Enlightenment (*Aufklärung*), for one notices nuances of this in some of his hymns as well as an emphasis on the humanity of Christ at the expense of his divinity.

His works include *Geistliche Poesien* (Halle, 1720, 1735, 1753), containing cantatas, devotional madrigals, sonnets, and hymns; *Poetische Festgedanken* (Jena, 1723); *Geistreiches Haus-Gesangbuch* (Frankfort and Leipzig, 1735); the posthumously-published *Gesammelte Geistliche Lieder* (1740), and the *Anthologie Christlicher Gesänge*, his greatest work in six volumes.

AUTHOR: 224 Baptized into Your Name Most Holy
255 My Maker, Now Be Nigh

RAWNSLEY, HARDWICKE DRUMMOND (1851–1920), was born September 28, 1851, at Shiplake, Henley-on-Thames, England, the son of an Anglican clergyman. After receiving the Bachelor of Arts degree in 1875 and the Master of Arts in 1883, both at Balliol College, Oxford, he was ordained in 1875 and served as curate of St. Barnabas, Bristol (1875–78); vicar at Low Wray, Lancashire (1878–83); vicar at Crosthwaite (1883–97); and honorary canon of Carlisle (1893).

His love of nature impelled him to organize the National Trust for Places of Historic interest and Natural Beauty. His works include some hymns and some books of poetry, and 12 books on the English Lake District. He died May 28, 1920, at Gresmere.

AUTHOR: 396 O God, Whose Will Is Life and Good

READ, DANIEL (1757–1836), was born November 16, 1757, in Rehobeth, near Attleboro, Massachusetts. After serving as a soldier during the Revolutionary War, he went to New Haven, where he began his business career as a maker of ivory combs, and where he formed a partnership with Amos Doolittle, an engraver, to publish and sell books. Interested in public affairs, he was also a stockbroker for a bank and director of the library of New Haven, Connecticut, where he died December 4, 1836.

Included in his works are *The American Singing Book, An Introduction to Psalmody* (1790); *The Columbian Harmonist* (1793); and *The New Haven Collection of Sacred Music* (1817). He founded of the *American Musical Magazine* (1786), the first publication of its kind in America.

COMPOSER (attr.): 118 WINDHAM

REDHEAD, RICHARD (1820–1901), was born March 1, 1820, at Harrow-on-the-Hill, Middlesex, and became a chorister at Magdalen College, Oxford. From 1839–64 he was organist and choirmaster at Margaret Chapel (later All Saints', Margaret Street), London, sometimes called the Tractarian Cathedral, where he and rector Frederick Oakely (*LW* 41) devoted much attention to music, choir, and the liturgy. Both were deeply involved in the Oxford Movement; together they edited *Laudes Diurnae* (1843), the first Gregorian psalter for use in the Anglican Church. This, and Redhead's *Ancient Hymn Melodies and Other Church Tunes* (1853), his most famous publication, greatly contributed to the revival of church music. Included among his many other works are *Church Music* (chants and responses); *Hymns for Holy Seasons; The Celebrant's Office Book*; *The Parish Tune Book*; and *The Book of Common Prayer with Ritual Song*.

For 30 years, from 1864–94, he was organist and choir director at the Church of St. Mary Magdalene, Paddington, where his skill with boys' voices and sensitive service playing brought him renown. He died April 27, 1901 at Hellingley, Hailsham, Sussex.

COMPOSER: 110, 285 GETHSEMANE

REDNER, LEWIS HENRY (1831–1908), was born December 14, 1831, at Philadelphia, Pennsylvania, where he attended public school and eventually became a wealthy real estate broker. Active in church, Sunday school, and music, he served as organist in four Philadelphia churches. He was at Holy Trinity (1861–64) when Phillips Brooks (*LW* 59, 60) was rector there, thus providing the tune and harmonization for "O little town of

Bethlehem." After resigning from Holy Trinity Church, he devoted the next 19 years to serving Holy Trinity's mission chapel as organist, superintendent of the Sunday school, and precentor. He remained a member of Holy Trinity for the rest of life, serving as a member of the vestry for 37 years and establishing an endowment fund that still supports its work in the city. He died August 20, 1908, in Atlantic City, where he had gone to recuperate from an illness.

COMPOSER: 60 ST. LOUIS

REED, ANDREW (1787–1862), was born at St. Clement Danes, London, November 27, 1787, the son of a watch maker, who was also a Congregationalist lay preacher. After graduating from Hackney College in 1811, he entered the Congregational ministry as pastor of New Road Chapel, St. George's-in-the East, London, where he had been brought up and was a member. Growth of the congregation necessitated a larger edifice in 1831, and the church was renamed Wycliffe Chapel. Here he remained until his retirement in 1861. A brilliant organizer, ardent humanitarian as well as an effective preacher, he was largely instrumental in founding six benevolent institutions in London devoted primarily to helping needy children.

In 1817 Reed published a *Supplement* to Watts' hymns, a work that was enlarged and published as *The Hymn Book* in 1825. This included 21 of his own hymns and 20 of his wife's that appeared anonymously and were not credited until publication of the *Wycliffe Chapel Supplement* in 1872. In 1842 he published *Hymn Book prepared from Dr. Watt's Psalms and Hymns and Other Authors, with some Originals.*

Yale University honored him with the Doctor of Divinity degree when, in 1834, he and J. Matheson were sent to visit Congregational churches in the United States. He died February 25, 1862, at Hackney, London.

AUTHOR: 166 Holy Spirit, Light Divine

REES, TIMOTHY (1874–1939), was born August 15, 1874, at Llanon, Dyfed, Wales. After attending Ardwyn School, Aberystwyth, and St. David's College, Lampeter, from which he received the Bachelor of Arts degree in 1896, he studied for the priesthood at St. Michael's College, Aberdare. Ordained in 1897, he became curate at Mountain Ash, Glamorganshire. From there he returned to St. Michael's College as lecturer and chaplain, serving thus from 1901–06, when he became a member of the Anglican Community of the Resurrection, Mirfield, Yorkshire. During World War I he saw service as a chaplain and was awarded the Military Cross. After the war he returned to Mirfield and was principal of the College of the Resurrection (1922–28), and examining chaplain to the Bishop of Bangor (1925–28). He went on numerous foreign missions for his church prior to being consecrated bishop of Llandoff in 1931. Here he remained until his death April 29, 1939.

AUTHOR: 164 Holy Spirit, Ever Dwelling

REGNART, JACOB (c. 1540–99), was perhaps born at Douai, France, where he probably received his first musical education as a chorister in the Prague *Hofkapelle* of Archduke Maximilian. After Maximilian's election as emperor and two years' study in Italy, he was appointed music teacher to the chapel choristers. Following Maximilian's death and the disbanding of his household, Emperor Rudolph II made Regnart a member of his Hofkapelle, which soon moved to Prague. Shortly advanced to vice-kapellmeister, he continued to publish a great deal of music, both sacred and secular.

In 1582, persuaded by Archduke Ferdinand to become his vice-kapellmeister, he moved to Innsbruck; three years later he was advanced to kapellmeister. Under his leadership the Innsbruck Court was reorganized and the musical standard raised by importing new Netherlands singers together with Italian solo singers and instrumentalists. Committed to Catholic reform, he produced his motet collection *Mariale* (1588) and another collection of motets in collaboration with three of his brothers. By now Regnart had become a man of wealth, and it was only Ferdinand's death that prevented his elevation to the nobility for his outstanding services. That honor, however, was realized by the action of Archduke Matthias in 1596. After Ferdinand's death and the subsequent disbanding of the Hofkapelle, Regnart moved to Prague, where he again entered imperial service as vice-kapellmeister under Monte. Here he died October 16, 1599.

Regnart's music—sacred and secular vocal, instrumental—continued to be highly regarded after his death and appeared in a number of anthologies. His greatest success as a composer came as a result of his *Schöner kurzweiliger Teutscher Lieder* for three voices that originally appeared in three volumes (1576, 1577, 1579). In the style of Italian villanellas, they not only became immensely popular but also very important for the development of the Lied.

COMPOSER: 421 AUF MEINEN LIEBEN GOTT

REID, SR., WILLIAM WATKINS (1890–1983), was born in Ballinasloe, Ireland, October 15, 1890. When he was 10 years old he came to the United States with his family. In 1904 he moved from the Bronx, New York, to Whitestone, Long Island, where he resided until 1979 when he moved to Wesley Village, Jenkins Township, Pennsylvania. Educated at New York University, earning a Bachelor of Science degree in 1915, a Master of Arts degree in 1917, he became a reporter for several New York city newspapers. In 1919 he began a lifetime career of service to Methodist missions in the areas of journalism and public relations. Following his retirement in 1961 as director of the department of news service of the Methodist Board of Missions, New York City, he became executive secretary of the Hymn Society of America. He was a member and trustee of the Epworth United Methodist Church, Whitestone, New York, and served on numerous committees in the New York United Methodist Conference. Listed for several years in *Who's Who in America*, he also served as president of the National Religious Publicity Council and the Hymn Society of America, to whose work he gave himself extensively, serving as editor of *The Hymn* (1966–76), writing the Society's history (1962; 1972), and even being one of the founding members in the 1920s.

A talented hymn writer, he wrote more than 70 hymns (some under the pseudonym Benjamin Caufield), 65 of which were published by the Hymn Society of America in *My God Is There, Controlling, and Other Hymns and Poems* (New York, 1965). He died February 18, 1983.

AUTHOR: 401 Forgive Us, Lord, for Shallow Thankfulness

REINAGLE, ALEXANDER ROBERT (1799–1877), was born August 21, 1799, in Brighton, England. After studying music with his father at Oxford, he later became a teacher there and well-known figure in musical circles. Organist at the church of St. Peter's-in-the-East, Oxford (1822–53), he composed a number of sacred pieces and psalm tunes, and at least one piano sonata. He also wrote and compiled a number of teaching manuals for violin and cello. In 1846 he married Caroline Orger, a pianist and teacher, who also wrote some technical works for the piano. He died April 6, 1877, at Kidlington, near Oxford.

COMPOSER: 279, 474 ST. PETER

REUSNER (REISZNER), ADAM (1496–c. 1575), was born at Mündelsheim (Mindelheim), in Swabian Bavaria. His studies at Wittenberg University were made possible by the generosity of Captain Georg von Frundsberg, very likely the result of his being a companion of Frundsberg's second son, Melchior. At Wittenberg he studied Greek and Hebrew under Johann Reuchlin. Sometime later he became private secretary to Frundsberg. In this capacity he accompanied Frundsberg and his troops on the campaign into Italy in 1527, helping Charles V fight Pope Clement VII. In honor of Georg von Frundsberg, Reusner wrote his pithy "Captain's Psalm," a hymn text based on various verses of Psalm 31, a work that was included in an Augsburg hymnal in 1533 and later taken up by Luther in the Babst *Gesangbuch* (1545).

Reusner next accompanied Frundsberg to Ferrare, Italy, where the intellectual elite lived. Here he became acquainted with the genial humanist Jakob Ziegler, whom he accompanied to Strassburg. There he met Kaspar von Schwenkfeldt (c. 1489–1561), one of the so-called radical reformers, whose friend and adherent he became. After residing a while in Frankfurt-am-Main, he returned to Mündelsheim, where he died, close to the age of 80.

Reusner wrote hymns as early as 1530. A manuscript in Wolfenbüttel entitled *Tägliches Gesangbuch . . . durch A. Reusner*, a collection of old and new hymns, some representative of Schwenkfeldtianism, contains no less than 40 of his own hymns.

AUTHOR: 406 In You, Lord, I Have Put My Trust

REUTER, FRIEDRICH (FRITZ) OTTO (1863–1924), was born October 11, 1863, in Johannsbach, in the Erzgebirge of Saxony, Germany. After his confirmation he studied at the Teachers' Seminary in Waldenburg, graduating in 1884. His first employment was as assistant teacher at Oberlungwitz, near Chemnitz. Three years later he accepted the position of teacher, organist, and choir director in Klingenthal. From there he served one year at Rheinsdorf, near Zwickau. In 1893 he went to Lichtenstein-Kallenberg, where he was cantor until 1904. When for conscience' sake he felt he could no longer serve in the state church of Germany, he joined the Lutheran Free Church of Saxony. After teaching for a year at a private boys' school in Berlin, in 1905 he accepted the call to the Christian day school of the Lutheran congregation in Winnipeg, Canada. Two years later he went to Bethlehem Lutheran Church in Chicago. The following year, in 1908, he accepted the call extended him by the Evangelical Lutheran Synod of Wisconsin and Other States (Wisconsin Synod) to serve as professor of music at Dr. Martin Luther College, New Ulm, Minnesota.

Reuter was a musician of no meager talents, and his influence as a teacher on the music in the Lutheran church was considerable, due in part to some of the well-known musicians with whom he studied: Reichert in Waldenburg; Schneider and Schreck in Leipzig; Reinberger in Munich; and Thiel of the *Akademisches Institut für Kirchenmusik* in Berlin. He died June 9, 1924.

COMPOSER: 293, 333 REUTER

REYNOLDS, WILLIAM JENSEN (1920–), was born April 2, 1920, in Atlantic, Iowa, the nephew of the Baptist musician Isham E. Reynolds. In September the family moved to Oklahoma where William's father, George Washington Reynolds, was a church music director and evangelistic singer; the younger Reynolds attended Oklahoma Baptist University and Southwest Missouri State College, (B.A. 1942). Choosing to study music, he entered Southwestern Baptist Theological Seminary, Fort Worth, attaining the Master of Sacred Music degree in 1945, as well as the Master of Music from North Texas State College in 1946. During this time he worked as a part-time church music director.

From 1946–47 Reynolds served as minister of music at First Baptist Church in Ardmore, Oklahoma, going on to spend eight years at First Baptist in Oklahoma City. In 1955 he was hired by the church music department of the Baptist Sunday School Board in Nashville, becoming music editor the following year, director of editorial services in 1962, and department head in 1971.

Since 1980 Reynolds has served on the faculty of the School of Church Music of Southwestern Baptist Theological Seminary. He was a member of both hymnal committees that produced the *Baptist Hymnal* 1956 and 1975, serving as general editor of the 1975 book. He also authored the companions to both hymnals: *Hymns of Our Faith* (1964) and *Companion to the Baptist Hymnal* (1976).

A former president of the Hymn Society of America, Reynolds has published numerous materials, including choral music as well as hymnological studies. His *A Survey of Christian Hymnody* appeared in 1963; *Christ and the Carols* in 1967; and *Congregational Singing* in 1975. In 1968 he prepared a reprint of the 1859 edition of *The Sacred Harp.*

Reynolds has served as music director for meetings of the Southern Baptist Convention, the Baptist World Alliance, and the Baptist Youth World Conference.

ARRANGER: 410 LITTLE FLOCK

RHABANUS MAURUS (c. 776–856), was born at Mainz, Germany, educated at Fulda, and then ordained deacon in 801. After studying at Tours, France, with Alcuin (735–804), the greatest scholar of his time, he returned to Fulda and became head of the monastery there, making it one of the leading schools in Germany. Ordained priest in 814, he served as abbot of Fulda from 822–42. Political turmoil caused him to give up this position and retire to prayer and literary work until 847, when he was called to be archbishop of Mainz. He died February 4, 856, and was buried at the monastery of St. Alban, Mainz.

One of the principal theologians of the Carolingian era, he was a prodigious writer, producing a study of grammar, a collection of homilies for the church year, two penitentials, a pedagogical dictionary, extensive commentaries on the Bible, and some Latin poetry, perhaps including the hymns below.

AUTHOR (attr.): 156 Creator Spirit, Heavenly Dove
157, 158 Come, Holy Ghost, Our Souls Inspire
167 Creator, Spirit, by Whose Aid

RHAU, GEORG (1488–1548), was born at Eisfeld-an-der-Werra. After receiving his Bachelor of Arts degree in philosophy at the University of Wittenberg in 1514, he became cantor at the St. Thomas School in Leipzig, a position that J. S. Bach (*LW* 89) assumed some years later. In 1521 he was a school teacher in Eisleben, where he taught music; in 1524 he established a publishing business in Wittenberg with the basic intent that he furnish the early Lutheran congregations a broad and comprehensive repertory for their musical needs. As a friend of Luther (*LW* 13, et al.), he espoused Luther's concept of educating the youth through music. His activities as a composer are somewhat uncertain, except that, while cantor in Leipzig, he wrote a 12-part Mass to introduce the famous debate between Luther and Eck. Among the numerous works that he published—for Vespers, for the Mass, and for the various liturgical and nonliturgical purposes—his *Newe deudsche geistliche Gesenge . . . für die gemeinen Schulen* (*LW* 382), published in 1544, an anthology of the works of 19 different composers, exhibits not only the variety of early Protestant styles, but constitutes the most important such

Lutheran collection prior to the *Musae Sioniae* (1605–12) of Michael Praetorius (*LW* 176, et al.). Dedicated to the mayor and council of his hometown of Eisfeld, Rhau, as indicated in the title, compiled the collection for the training of youth in the citizen-supported Latin schools of the larger cities, thus supplying selections to be learned and sung by them in corporate worship. At least six of the composers represented in this collection were definitely or probably Roman Catholics, a fact that indicates a certain over-arching character of music at that time, regardless of nationality and confession.

PUBLISHER: *Newe deudsche geistliche Gesenge* (Wittenberg, 1544)
382 NUN LASST UNS DEN LEIB BEGRABEN

RILEY, JOHN ATHELSTAN LAURIE (1858–1945), was born August 10, 1858, at Paddington, London, and educated at Eton College and Pembroke College, Oxford. A man of means, after leaving the university he traveled extensively—to the Near East, to Persia, Turkey, Kurdistan, and Europe—gathering information for articles on the churches of the Eastern Mediterranean included in his book *Athos, or the Mountain of the Monks* (1887). His work as chairman of the Anglican and Eastern Church Association earned him the Order of St. Sava and his appointment as commander of the Order of King George I of Greece. Active in behalf of public education and a staunch supporter of the high church opinion in the Church of England, he was for many years vice-president of the Alcuin Club. Joining a group in 1901 interested in producing a more high church "supplement" to *Hymns Ancient and Modern* (1861), he helped in what became *The English Hymnal* (1906), to which he contributed three original hymns plus seven translations from the Latin and one from the Greek. Besides his book *Concerning Hymn Tunes and Sequences* (1915), his illustrated lectures counteracted criticism and helped publicize *The English Hymnal.*

His purchase in 1932 of a mansion on Jersey, one of the Channel islands, provided him comfort in his retirement years until his death on November 17, 1945.

AUTHOR: 308 Ye Watchers and Ye Holy Ones

RINCKART, MARTIN (1586–1649), was born in Eilenburg, Saxony, April 23, 1586, the son of a cooper. After attending the local Latin school, in 1601 he became foundation scholar and chorister at St. Thomas' School in Leipzig. Next he enrolled as a theological student at the University of Leipzig, graduating in 1616. After holding various appointments for a number of years—master of the *Gymnasium* at Eisleben; cantor at the St. Nicholas Church; deacon at St. Anne's Church in the Neustadt of Eisleben (1610); pastor at Erdeboren—in 1617 he became archdeacon at Eilenburg, his birthplace, where he spent the rest of his life.

During those years, the Thirty Years' War (1618–48) raged on, and Eilenburg, a walled city, became a haven for vast multitudes of people fleeing the horrors of war.

Thousands died from famine and plague, including his wife. For some time Rinckart was the only pastor in the city, sometimes reading the burial service for as many as 70 persons in a day. Yet in the midst of these calamities he maintained his courage and trust in the Lord. He died December 8, 1649, having received little gratitude for his services.

Rinckart was not only a devout, caring pastor and a talented poet, he was also a gifted musician and effective dramatist.

AUTHOR: 443 Now Thank We All Our God

RINGWALDT (RINGWALT, RINGWALD), BARTHOLOMÄUS (1532–99), was born November 28, 1532, Frankfurt-an-der-Oder. Ordained in 1557, he was pastor of two Lutheran parishes before he settled in 1566 as pastor of Langenfeld near Sonnenburg, Brandenburg. This was the time of the Crypto-Calvinistic Controversy, a period after the death of Philipp Melanchthon (1560; *LW* 189) when Lutheranism was split into two camps: one group comprised of the followers of Melanchthon who tried to suppress Luther's views on the Lord's Supper and replace them with Calvin's while still confessing loyalty to Lutheranism; the other group comprised of followers of Luther's views, namely, belief in the real presence of Christ's body in the sacrament. Taking his stand with the latter group, Ringwaldt, together with others such as Nikolaus Selnecker (*LW* 257, 344) and Ludwig Helmbold (*LW* 409, et al.), was concerned with upholding the biblical doctrine. Thus he boldly testified to the truth, not only to his congregation but also in the hope of winning outsiders to Christ, in whose behalf he issued *Newe Zeittung* (Amberg, 1582) as well as an expanded version of the same entitled *Christliche Warnung des Treuen Eckarts* (Frankfurt-an-der-Oder, 1558), both of which appeared in numerous editions and exerted considerable influence.

Ringwaldt was one of the most prolific hymn writers of the 16th century, credited with having written approximately 150 hymns. Considered an excellent poet by his contemporaries, his language is lofty, penetrating, and impressive. Granted, in his concern to lead and nourish his flock with the solid Word of God and to bring the world to true repentance, the lyrical aspect is generally suppressed by the didactic. Evident in some of his hymns are the conflagrations, floods, calamities, and heartaches that he suffered.

His hymn publications include *Trostlieder, in Sterbensläufften zu gebrauchen* (1577); *Evangelia, auf alle Sonntag und Fest* (1581); and *Handbüchlin. Geistliche Lieder und Gebetlin* (1582).

AUTHOR: 336 Grant, Holy Ghost, that We Behold
462 The Day Is Surely Drawing Near

RIST, JOHANN (1607–67), was born March 8, 1607, at Ottensen, near Hamburg, Germany, the son of a Lutheran pastor. At 20 he graduated from the *Gymnasium Illustri* at Bremen, after which he entered the University of Rinteln, where, under the influence of Josua Stegmann (*LW* 287), he began to take an interest in hymnology. As a tutor to the sons of a Hamburg merchant he next accompanied them to the University of Rostock, where he studied Hebrew, mathematics, and medicine. In the spring of 1635 Rist married and, having received the appointment as pastor at Wedel, near Hamburg, on the Elbe River, he settled there. Although he had several opportunities to go to larger parishes, he devoted most of his life to the people and the church in Wedel, serving as both the pastor and the physician of the parish. Crowned poet laureate in 1644 by Emperor Ferdinand III, a year later he was raised to the rank of nobility by the same ruler. In the same year he was also admitted to membership in the Fruitbearing Society, previously organized by Martin Opitz (*LW* 85).

Rist was a voluminous and many-sided writer. His hymns, numbering approximately 680, were never sung in his home church during his lifetime but were widely used throughout the rest of Germany in both Protestant and Roman Catholic communions. His hymns for Advent and for Holy Communion, in their scriptural, objective, and edifying nature, are considered the best. In addition to his hymns, Rist was the author of historical writings and plays depicting the sufferings brought about by the Thirty Years' War, during which he lost his scientific and musical instruments.

He died August 31, 1667, in Wedel, the result of a severe fever.

AUTHOR: 122 O Darkest Woe
244 O Living Bread from Heaven
248 Lord Jesus Christ, Life-Giving Bread

RISTAD, DITLEF GEORGSON (1863–1938), was born November 22, 1863, at Overhallen, Norway. Having attended the Kläbu Normal School, he became a teacher at the Namsos Middle School in Norway. In 1887 he came to America and attended Luther Seminary and the University of Chicago. After serving several Lutheran parishes in Wisconsin, from 1901–19 he served successively as president of Albion Academy, of Park Region Luther College, and of the Lutheran Ladies' Seminary, Red Wing, Minnesota.

His work in the area of hymnody consisted of his editing the *Lutheran Sunday-school Hymnal*, serving on the committee for the *Lutheran Hymnary* and the *Lutheran Hymnary Junior*, and publishing a volume of poems in the Norwegian language. He died September 20, 1938.

TRANSLATOR: 391 I Walk in Danger All the Way

ROBERTS, DANIEL CRANE (1841–1907), was born November 5, 1841, in Bridgehampton, Long Island, New York. Having graduated from Kenyon College, Gambier, Ohio, in 1857, he served with the 84th Ohio Volunteers during the Civil War. In 1865 he was ordained deacon by the Protestant Episcopal Church and priest in 1866.

After serving various parishes in Vermont and Massachusetts, in 1878 he was appointed vicar of St. Paul's Church, Concord, New Hampshire, where he served for 23 years. For many years president of the New Hampshire State Historical Society, in 1885 Norwich University honored him with the Doctor of Divinity degree. He died October 31, 1907, at Concord.

AUTHOR: 501 God of Our Fathers

ROBERTS, JOHN (1822–77), was born December 22, 1822, at Tanrhiwfelen, Penllwyn, near Aberystwyth. After pursuing a variety of occupations, in 1856 he began to preach, and in 1859 he was ordained by the Calvinistic Methodist Church. After serving at Merthyr and Aberdare, he went to Capel Goch, Llanberis, where he founded the Snowdon Temperance Union. In 1859 he founded the great institution in Wales known as *Gymanfa ganu*, or singing festival, the purpose of which was to encourage love for the hymn and hymn tune. That same year he published *Llyfr Tonau Cynulleidfaol* (Book of Congregational Tunes), the epoch-making and recognized tune book of the Calvinistic Methodists. He served as editor (1861–73) of *Y Cerddor Cymreig*, a monthly music magazine; of *Telyn y Plant* (1859–61), a publication for children; and *Cerddor y Solffa* (1869–74). G. Parry Williams says of him:

> As a musician he was unique; incomparable as a musical critic and instructor and an arranger of congregational hymn tunes; and as a conductor of sacred music festivals he was in a special sense God's gift to Wales.

He died May 6, 1877, at Vron, near Carnarvon.

ARRANGER: 137 LLANFAIR

ROBINSON, JOSEPH ARMITAGE (1858–1933), was born January 9, 1858, at Keynsham, near Bath, England. Educated at Christ's College, Cambridge, he received his Bachelor of Arts degree in 1881, Master of Arts degree in 1884, Bachelor of Divinity degree in 1891, and Doctor of Divinity degree in 1896. Ordained a deacon in 1881 and a priest in 1882, he served as domestic chaplain to the bishop of Durham; from 1884–90 as dean of Christ's College; from 1888–92 as assistant curate at Great St. Mary's in Cambridge; and from 1893–99 as Norrisian Professor of Divinity. Beginning in 1899 he was rector of St. Margaret's, Westminster, for one year, and canon of Westminster for three years. He was dean of Westminster from 1902–11, when he became dean of Wells. Here he served until his death at Upton Noble, Somerset, May 7, 1933.

Among his publications are the *Cambridge Texts and Studies*, begun in 1891, which he originated and of which he was first editor, and the commentary on *Ephesians* (1903).

AUTHOR: 89 How Good, Lord, to Be Here

RODE, WALDEMAR (1903–1960), was born August 6, 1903, in Hamburg, Germany, the son of a merchant whose forebears included a number of theologians. Following his studies at the universities of Freiburg, Marburg, and Göttingen, he served first as a preacher at St. Michael's in Hamburg. From 1929 to his retirement he served as Lutheran pastor in Hamburg-Uhlenhorst.

AUTHOR: 21 "Comfort, Comfort," Says the Voice

RODIGAST, SAMUEL (1649–1708), the son of a Lutheran pastor, was born October 19, 1649, in Gröben, near Jena. Educated in Weimar and thereafter at the University of Jena, where in 1671 he earned the Master of Arts degree and in 1676 he became an adjunct of Jena's philosophical faculty. From 1680 on he served as conrector and later as rector at the *Gymnasium* of the Gray Cloister in Berlin. There he remained, despite offers from the University of Jena, until his death March 29, 1708.

AUTHOR: 422 What God Ordains Is Always Good

RÖNTGEN, JULIUS (1855–1932), was born May 9, 1855, in Leipzig, Germany, where he studied music with Friedrich Lachner, E. F. Richter, Louis Plaidy, and Carl Reinecke. In 1877 he went to Amsterdam, where he became piano teacher at the music school, which later became a conservatory. From 1912–24 he was director of the Amsterdam Conservatory. Prior to that, from 1884–86, he was conductor of the choral society Excelsior; from 1886–98 he was conductor of the Amsterdam Toonskunstkoor. As a pianist he gave many recitals. In 1924 he retired to devote his efforts entirely to composition. He died at Utrecht September 13, 1932.

A prolific composer of the late Romantic school, his works include 12 symphonies, chamber music, three piano concertos, three operas, and film scores. Acquainted with Johannes Brahms and Edvard Grieg (*LW* 192), he published a biography of the latter in 1930, the same year in which he was awarded an honorary doctorate by the University of Edinburgh.

ARRANGER: 394 IN BABILONE

ROSSETTI, CHRISTINA GEORGINA (1830–94), was born at St. Pancras, London, December 5, 1830, the daughter of Gabriele Rossetti, an Italian refugee who became professor of Italian at the new University of London. Educated at home in a circle of literary people and artists, she began to write poetry in her early girlhood, some of her earliest work being published in 1850 in *The Germ*, the magazine of the pre-

Raphaelites, of which her brother W. M. Rossetti was one of the founders. For a short time she helped her mother with a small day school in North London. Strikingly beautiful as well as gifted and talented, she often sat as a model for such artists as Holman Hunt, Milais, Maddox Brown, and her brother Dante Gabriel. She twice rejected proposals of marriage, one because her suitor became a Roman Catholic. She lived a quiet, secluded life, writing and tending her mother, who lived until 1886, and befriending the poor children connected with the church near Regent's Park, where she worshiped. After a long illness, she died at Torrington Square, St. Giles, London, December 29, 1894.

Her poetry appeared in *Goblin Market and Other Poems* (1862), *The Prince's Progress* (1866), *Sing-song for Children* (1872), *A Pagent and other Poems* (1881), and *Verses* (1893); her *New Poems* appeared posthumously in 1896. Her devotional books, mainly in prose, include *Time Flies, a Reading Diary* (1885), *Seek and Find* (1879), *Called to be Saints* (1881), and *The Face of the Deep* (1892), a commentary on the Apocalypse.

AUTHOR: 46 Love Came Down at Christmas

ROTERMUND, MELVIN E. (1927–). Teacher and parish music director in Lutheran parishes since 1950, Rotermund has served St. John Lutheran Church, Decatur, Illinois; Zion Lutheran Church, Chicago; and presently serves St. Andrew Lutheran Church, Park Ridge, Illinois. He was born in Alma, Missouri, where his father was a Lutheran school teacher. Elementary school training was in Christ Lutheran School in St. Louis and in Altamont, Illinois, where he was confirmed and also attended high school. He attended Concordia Teachers College, River Forest, Illinois, attaining the Bachelor of Science degree in 1950 and the Master of Arts in 1959.

Rotermund has served on numerous Northern Illinois District committees for conferences, on the building committee of Luther High School South in Chicago, on a high school and district accreditation committees, and local and district worship projects. More than a dozen of his anthem arrangements for choirs as well as a volume of handbell hymn arrangements have been published. Several of his hymn preludes are included in the *Concordia Hymn Prelude Series*. He was one of three arrangers for the *Songs of God's Love* (1984) children's hymnal.

In 1951 Rotermund was married to Marilyn Deffner. He is the father of two daughters.

ARRANGER: 476 JEG VIL MIG HERREN LOVE

ROTHE, JOHANN ANDREAS (1688–1758), was born May 12, 1688, at Lissa, Silesia, the son of a Lutheran pastor. Having studied theology at and graduated from the University of Leipzig, he delayed, for reasons of conscience, to enter the parish ministry. Instead, he chose to become tutor in the house of Hans Christoph von

Schweinitz near Leuba, at the same time occasionally preaching in the vicinity of Görlitz. Hearing him preach, Nicolaus von Zinzendorf (*LW* 362, 386) offered him the pastorate at Berthelsdorf, where the Moravian settlement at Herrnhut was situated, and he was installed in 1772. For 15 years Rothe enjoyed a very fruitful ministry. His insistence on sound, biblical doctrine, coupled with his efforts to make Lutherans out of these Moravians, displeased Zinzendorf. As a result, Rothe accepted a call to Hermsdorf, near Görlitz, where he assumed the pastoral office in 1737. Two years later he became assistant pastor at Thommendorf, near Bunzlau, becoming head pastor in 1742. Here he remained until his death July 6, 1758.

A highly gifted and esteemed man, a learned and pious theologian, Rothe is credited with having written about 40 hymns. Though many of them may not be considered great poetry, they evidence a tenderness of feeling and a joyful acknowledgement of God's grace in Christ.

AUTHOR: 360 Now I Have Found the Firm Foundation

RUOPP, JOHANN FRIEDRICH (1672–1708), was born the end of February 1672 at Strassburg, Alsace-Lorraine, the son of a shoemaker. From 1689–92 he was a student of theology and poetry at the universities of Strassburg and Jena, where he became enamored with Pietism. After serving as a vicar in Lampertheim, in 1692 he became pastor at Goxweiler, near Strassburg. In 1699 he became assistant to his stepbrother in the village of Breuschwickersheim, where he was held in high regard as a scholar. It was while at Goxweiler that he prepared and had published a collection of hymns titled *Jesuslieder*. After three years of attempting, together with his colleagues, to spread a "living Christianity"—the desideratum of Pietism—he was removed from office and forced to leave Alsace-Lorraine. Finding refuge in Halle, the hotbed of Pietism, he became food inspector at the orphanage and adjunct to the theological faculty. He died May 26, 1708.

From Ruopp's collection, Freylinghausen (*LW* 23, et al.) included seven hymns in his *Neues geistreiches Gesangbuch* (1714).

AUTHOR: 373 Renew Me, O Eternal Light

RUPPRECHT, OLIVER C. (1903–), attended Concordia Seminary, St. Louis, and was ordained in 1927. He served as pastor of Redeemer Lutheran Church, Evansville, Indiana, until 1937, when he joined the faculty of Concordia College at Milwaukee (now Concordia University Wisconsin, Mequon). He has been associated with the college throughout the remainder of his professional career, until his retirement in 1979.

Specializing in church hymnody and religious art, Rupprecht lectured extensively on various phases of theology, church music, art history, and Christian education, and served as guest lecturer in summer courses at Concordia College (now Concordia University), River Forest, Illinois, and at Concordia Teachers College, Seward,

Nebraska. For more than 15 years he traveled extensively with multimedia presentations under the general title "Twentieth-Century Living and Great Religious (Musical and Pictorial) Art."

A member of the Hymn Society of America, Rupprecht served in a consultative capacity in the production of *Lutheran Worship* (1982). For 12 years he was a member of the Catechism Committee of the Lutheran Church—Missouri Synod, and for five years he served on the Committee on Religion in Public Schools. In 1978 he was awarded the honorary Doctor of Letters degree by Concordia Seminary, St. Louis.

As well as numerous hymn texts and translations, Rupprecht has written articles appearing in various periodicals and is coauthor of *The Musical Heritage of the Church*, Vol. 3, and of *Spiritual Growth and Professional Competence* (1954). A member of the Riemenschneider Bach Institute, he has prepared analyses and evaluations of a number of Bach cantatas as well as a full-length, published commentary on the *Mass in B Minor*. He was commissioned by the music department of Valparaiso University to translate the critical biography of J. S. Bach by Wilibald Gurlitt, one of Europe's leading experts on Bach. The work was published in 1956 as *J. S. Bach: The Master and His Work*.

TRANSLATOR: 78 Jesus Has Come and Brings Pleasure
136 Today in Triumph Christ Arose

RUSSELL, ARTHUR TOZER (1806–74), was born March 20, 1806, at Northampton, the son of Thomas Clout, a Congregational pastor who changed his surname to Russel. Educated at Merchant Taylors' school, London; Manchester College, York; and St. John's College, Cambridge, he was ordained in 1829 and became curate of Great Grandsen, Hunts. Thereafter he served as vicar of Caxton from 1830–32; of Whaddon from 1852–66; of St. Thomas, Toxteth Park, Liverpool, where he served only a year; of Wrockwardine Wood, Shropshire, where he stayed until 1874. For a few months prior to his death on November 18, 1874, he was rector of Southwick near Brighton.

Russel began his ecclesiastical career as an extreme high churchman. The study of St. Augustine, however, made him a moderate Calvinist. As such he became an effective critic of both the high and the broad church. A prolific writer of both theological and biographical subjects, his best prose work is perhaps the *Memorials of the Life and Works of Bishop Andrewes* (1859). He was an author of approximately 140 original hymns, a translator of numerous German hymns, and a composer of a number of hymn tunes. His published works in this field include *Hymn Tunes, Original and Selected, from Ravenscroft and Other Musicians* (c. 1840); *Hymns For Public Worship* (1848); and *Psalms and Hymns, partly Original, partly Selected, for the Use of the Church of England* (1851), a collection containing numerous German hymns, the entire volume arranged along the lines of the old Lutheran hymnbooks.

TRANSLATOR: 72 The Only Son from Heaven
248 Lord Jesus Christ, Life-Giving Bread

RYDEN, ERNEST EDWIN (1886–1981), was born September 12, 1886, in Kansas City, Missouri. After graduating from Augustana College, Rock Island, Illinois in 1910, he studied for the holy ministry at Augustana Seminary, becoming ordained in 1914. That year he married Agnes E. Johnson, also a graduate of Augustana College. He first served Grace Lutheran Church, Jamestown, New York, the first English-speaking congregation of the Augustana Synod east of Chicago. In 1915, Grace Lutheran of the Augustana Synod merged with Holy Trinity Church of the same city, when he became their pastor. This newly merged congregation now began to use the *Church Book* (1868) of the General Council, which contained an English liturgy based on the better liturgies of the 16th century, a liturgy that anticipated the Common Service of 1888. From 1920–34 Ryden served as pastor of Gloria Dei Lutheran Church, St. Paul, Minnesota. While here he presented weekly programs on hymns of the church over the St. Paul radio station KSTP. He was head of the English Association of Churches of the Augustana Synod; and president of the Board of Christian Service, an organization which established three orphanages in Minnesota and Bethesda Hospital in the city of St. Paul.

Next saw Ryden in Rock Island, Illinois, where he served as editor of *The Lutheran Companion* from 1934–61, when publication was discontinued. For five years during that time he also was editor of the *Lutheran Outlook* of the American Lutheran Church. From 1934–42 he was president of the American Lutheran Conference; for 20 years he was a member of the Board of Directors of Augustana College, which college honored him with the Doctor of Divinity degree in 1930. In 1935 he was delegate to the Lutheran World Convention in Paris; in 1948 a representative at the World Council of Churches Assembly in Copenhagen. That year Sweden also honored him with the Royal Order of the North Star.

In 1964 Ryden became pastor and later pastor emeritus, of Emmanuel Lutheran Church, North Grosvenor Dale, Connecticut. He died January 1, 1981, in Providence, Rhode Island.

Besides being author and translator of 40 hymns, he was coeditor of *The Hymnal* (1925) of the Augustana Synod; secretary of the Joint Commission for the *Service Book and Hymnal* (1958) from 1945–58; author of *The Story of Our Hymns* (1935) and *The Story of Christian Hymnody* (1958); and the article "Lutheran Hymnbooks since the Reformation," in the *Lutheran Encyclopedia* (1964). Editors of other denominational hymnals have recognized his talents and included his hymns and translations: *The Hymnal of the Evangelical Covenant Church* (1950), *The Methodist Hymnal* (1946), and *Worship: A Hymnal and Service Book for Roman Catholics* (1986).

AUTHOR: 327 How Blessed Is This Place, O Lord

RYGH, GEORGE ALFRED TAYLOR (1860–1943), was born March 21, 1860, in Chicago, Illinois. After graduating from Luther College, Decorah, Iowa, in 1881, he studied at Luther Seminary, St. Paul, Minnesota, and thereafter at Capital University, Columbus, Ohio. From 1884–89 he was pastor of a Lutheran congregation in Portland, Maine. The following years he alternated regularly between the ministry and teaching professions, among others, serving as pastor in Chicago (1899–1910), teacher at St. Olaf College (1910–13), Northfield, Minnesota, and finally as pastor in Minneapolis (1920–30). Northfield, Minnesota, became the place of his retirement. From 1909–14 Rygh served as editor of the *United Lutheran*; in 1925 he became editor of the *Lutheran Herald*. He served as a member of the Hymnary Committee of the Norwegian Lutheran Church, for which he translated a number of hymns that were included in the *Lutheran Hymnary* (1913). In 1917 Newberry College, Newberry, South Carolina, honored him with the Doctor of Letters degree. He died July 16, 1943.

TRANSLATOR: 225 All Who Believe and Are Baptized
339 Speak, O Lord, Your Servant Listens
520 Rejoice, Rejoice, This Happy Morn
He Is Arisen! Glorious Word!

SATEREN, LELAND BERNHARD (1913–), was born October 13, 1913, in Everett, Washington. He attended Augsburg College, Minneapolis, graduating in 1935 with a Bachelor of Arts degree. For three years he was music director of the public schools of Moose Lake, Minnesota, traveling in 1937 to Europe to research choral literature. Going on to postgraduate studies at the University of Minnesota, he meanwhile served as music director at the university radio station, KUOM, attaining the Master of Arts degree in 1943.

Sateren spent three years as educational director in the Civilian Public Service before returning to Augsburg College in 1946. Since 1950 he has been professor of music and, until 1973, chairman of the music department there. Of Norwegian extraction, he directed the Augsburg Choir, with which he toured Scandinavia and Central Europe in 1965 and again in 1975; in the 1975–76 academic year he was choral director and teacher of music composition and conducting at the Conservatory of Music in Bergen, Norway. He also conducted summer choral workshops in Scandinavia during the 1970s and 80s.

A sabbatical in 1961 allowed Sateren to pursue a study of 34 college and university choirs in the northeastern United States; in 1966 he was able to complete a study of fourteen European choirs. A member of various professional organizations including the American Choral Directors Association (ACDA) and the Hymn Society of America, Sateren is the only person to have worked with both the committees producing the *Service Book and Hymnal* (1958) and *Lutheran Book of Worship* (1978).

As a composer, Sateren has written over 300 choral works and published works on choirs and choral music, as well as having contributed articles to professional magazines. Honors include a Doctor of Humane Letters from Gettysburg College, (Gettysburg, Pennsylvania), and a Doctor of Music from Lakeland College, (Sheboygan, Wisconsin), both in 1965; the St. Olaf Medal conferred by King Olav of Norway in 1971; and the first F. Melius Christiansen Memorial Award of the Minnesota chapter of the ACDA, 1974. By proclamation of Governor Albert H. Quie, February 3,

1979, was celebrated as "Leland B. Sateran Day" throughout the State of Minnesota, where Sateran and his wife reside.

ARRANGER: 247 THE ASH GROVE
COMPOSER: 396 LEUPOLD

SAVONAROLA, GIROLAMO (1452–98), one of the forerunners of the Reformation, born in Ferrara, Italy, was intended for the medical profession. The vast cultural ferment ushered in by the Italian Renaissance, however, combined with an unhappy love affair, impelled him to become a Dominican friar, a preacher of repentance in Florence, fearlessly attacking the ungodliness and licentiousness of the times as well as the worldly conquests of Pope Alexander VI, a member of the notorious Borgia family. Convinced that the Renaissance was developing into a glorified form of paganism that was creeping into the church, he preached in fierce and uncompromising terms, and his sermons soon gained him many supporters. To the poor whose rights he championed, he became another St. Francis. The death of Lorenzo the Magnificent in 1492 with its resultant political upheaval made Savonarola virtually the ruler of Florence. Like Calvin in Geneva, he sought to build up a theocracy. Indecent books and pictures were burned; lewd carnival songs banned. His *Laudi Spirituali* (Spiritual Songs), set to the same tunes and meter as those banned, were written to replace them. Failing to bribe Savonarola into silence with the red hat of a Cardinal, the pope excommunicated him. With the support of the secular courts he was arrested, cruelly tortured, and on May 23, 1498, hung and his body burned.

A collection of Savonarola's hymnic poems was published in Florence in 1862 entitled *Poesie di Fra Girolamo Savonarola tratte dall' Autographo*, some of which had been included in the *Laudi Spirituali* compiled by Fra Serafino Razzi and published in Venice in 1563.

AUTHOR: 90 Jesus, Refuge of the Weary

SCHAEFER, WILLIAM JOHN (1891–1976), was born January 30, 1891, at Manitowoc, Wisconsin. After completing two years at Northwestern College, Watertown, Wisconsin, he entered Concordia Theological Seminary, Springfield, Illinois (now at Fort Wayne, Indiana), graduating in 1913. He served congregations at Garrison, Nebraska; Colome, South Dakota; and Milwaukee, Wisconsin. In 1935 he was appointed associate editor of the *Northwestern Lutheran*, the official periodical of the Joint Synod of Wisconsin and Other States, of which he later became managing editor. He was a member of the Intersynodical Committee on Hymnology and Liturgics which prepared *The Lutheran Hymnal* (1941). He died in 1976 at Milwaukee, Wisconsin.

TRANSLATOR: 293 Lord Jesus Christ, the Church's Head
337 Preserve Your Word, O Savior

SCHAEFFER, CHARLES WILLIAM (1813–96), was born May 5, 1813, in Hagerstown, Maryland, but after his father, a Lutheran pastor, died, the family moved to Carlisle, Pennsylvania. In 1829, after his mother married the Reverend Benjamin Keller, the family moved to Germantown, Pennsylvania, where Charles attended Germantown Academy. He graduated from the University of Pennsylvania (1832) and the Theological Seminary at Gettysburg, Pennsylvania. After successively serving congregations in Barren Hill (1835–40), Harrisburg (1940–49), and Germantown (1849–74), Pennsylvania, in 1864 he became professor at the Lutheran Theological Seminary in Philadelphia, where he served until his retirement in 1894. For many years he served as president of the Lutheran Ministerium of Pennsylvania. He was also for a time president of the General Synod and General Council; he served as trustee of the University of Pennsylvania from 1859 until his death March 15, 1896, in Philadelphia.

TRANSLATOR: 379 "Come, Follow Me" Said Christ, the Lord

SCHALK, CARL FLENTGE (1929–), was born September 26, 1929, in Des Plaines, Illinois. He received his undergraduate education at Concordia College (now Concordia University), River Forest, Illinois, earning the Bachelor of Science degree in education in 1952. In 1958 he received the Master of Music degree from the Eastman School of Music, Rochester, New York, and in 1965, the Master of Arts and Religion from Concordia Seminary, St. Louis.

From 1952–58 Schalk served as teacher and director of music at Zion Lutheran Church, Wausau, Wisconsin. He was director of music for the International Lutheran Hour from 1958–65. Since 1965 he has taught church music on both the undergraduate and graduate levels at Concordia River Forest.

A lecturer and clinician at numerous church music workshops and pastoral conferences, Schalk also serves as a member of the Music Editorial Advisory Committee of Concordia Publishing House. He was editor of *Church Music* magazine (1966–80), and served as a member of the Inter-Lutheran Commission on Worship Hymn Music Committee which prepared the *Lutheran Book of Worship* (1978). He presently serves as a member of the Research Committee for the Hymn Society of America, and is a member of the board of the National Association of Pastoral Musicians. His choral compositions and hymn settings for congregational use are widely used throughout the country.

Schalk edited the two-volume set, *Key Words in Church Music* and *Handbook of Church Music* (1978); authored *The Roots of Hymnody in The Lutheran Church—Missouri Synod* (1965); *Music in Lutheran Worship* (1983); *The Pastor and the Church Musician* (1984), and *Luther on Music: Paradigms of Praise* (1988). He edited an annotated volume of *Source Documents in American Lutheran Hymnody* (1978) and has prepared a *Catalog of Hymnals and Choralebooks in the Klinck Memorial Library* (1975). He serves as editor of the Church Music Pamphlet Series published by Concordia Publishing House. Numerous articles by Schalk have appeared in various religious periodicals such as the *Christian Century*, *Concordia Theological Monthly*,

Pastoral Music, *Lutheran Education*, and *Currents in Theology and Mission*. Concordia College, Seward, Nebraska, honored him with the Doctor of Laws degree; Concordia College, St. Paul, Minnesota, with the Doctor of Humanities degree.

He and his wife, Nöel Donata *née* Roeder, are the parents of three children.

COMPOSER:	117	FORTUNATUS NEW
ARRANGER:	17	CONDITOR ALME SIDERUM
	117	FORTUNATUS NEW
	134	MIT FREUDEN ZART
	164	IN BABILONE
	172	ST. PATRICK'S BREASTPLATE
	175	CHRISTE SANCTORUM
	211	SONG 34
	215	ALLEIN GOTT IN DER HÖH
	219	VERLEIH UNS FRIEDEN
	238	GOTT SEI GELOBET UND GEBENEDEIET
	243	FARLEY CASTLE
	275	DEO GRACIAS
	353	NUN FREUT EUCH
	445	LOBE DEN HERREN, O MEINE SEELE
	482	CHRISTE SANCTORUM
	489	JAM LUCIS
	498	ACH, BLIV HOS OSS

SCHALLING, MARTIN (1532–1608), was born April 21, 1532, at Strassburg. As a student at the University of Wittenberg, he became a favorite pupil of Philipp Melanchthon (*LW* 189) and a good friend of Nicolaus Selnecker (*LW* 257, 344). After earning his Master of Arts degree he remained in Wittenberg for a time as lecturer until, in 1544, he became a deacon at Regensburg. In the theological controversies that followed the death of Martin Luther (*LW* 13, et al.), Schalling often found himself at odds with various factions. His preaching against the tenets of Matthias Flacius (1520–75) caused him to lose his position in Regensburg in 1558. As a deacon at Amberg, Bavaria, he was expelled with other Lutheran pastors when Elector Friedrich III decided to adopt Calvinistic theology in worship. Fortunately the elector's son, Duke Ludwig, continuing as a Lutheran, permitted Schalling to minister to the Lutherans at Vilseck, near Amberg. When Ludwig became regent of Oberpfalz, he recalled Schalling to Amberg in 1576 as court preacher and superintendent. Upon the death of Ludwig's father in 1576, Ludwig, now as elector of Pfalz, appointed Schalling as general superintendent of the Oberpfalz as well as court preacher at Heidelberg. Pressed to sign the Formula of Concord of 1577, Schalling refused, considering it too harsh with the followers of Melanchthon. This resulted in his banishment from the court at Heidelberg and his being confined to his house at Amberg from 1580–83, when he was finally deprived of his offices. After staying at Altdorf for some time, in 1585 he was appointed pastor of St. Mary's Church in Nürnberg, where he remained until blindness caused him to retire. He died December 19, 1608, at Nürnberg.

AUTHOR: 413 Lord, You I Love with All My Heart

SCHARLEMANN, DOROTHY HOYER (1912–), was born December 6, 1912, in the parsonage of Emmaus Lutheran Church in Denver, Colorado. She studied at St. John's College, Winfield, Kansas, and Harris Teachers College, St. Louis, earning a Bachelor of Science degree in education from the University of Illinois, Champaign/Urbana. She credits her father and husband, both Lutheran clergymen, as well as her mother with "less formal, but more vital, education" in church history, hymn singing, and scriptural meaning. She writes,

> Exposure to the sometimes vapid hymnology of general Protestant churches during an 11 year stint as chaplain's wife with the United States Air Force strengthened [my] appreciation of the Lutheran heritage, which was reinforced by the experiences of the next 30 years as professor's wife at Concordia Seminary, St. Louis, where student chapel and choruses, as well as the St.Louis Bach Society, greatly enlarged [my] musical and hymnological horizons.

Since her husband Martin's death in 1982, she has retired to Santa Barbara, California, well cared for by three sons in that state and a daughter in New York City.

AUTHOR: 254 May God the Father of Our Lord

SCHEFFLER, JOHANN (1624–77), was born of Lutheran parents in Breslau, Silesia, presently since World War II a part of Poland. After studying medicine at the universities of Breslau, Strassburg, Leyden, and Padua, he became private physician to Duke Silvius Nimrod of Württenberg-Öls. Here he associated with mystic Jakob Böhme's adherents, whose writings had interested him as a boy. Bequeathed a large library, he became acquainted with the writings of other mystics. Considered a heretic by the Lutheran clergymen, and discovering his thought and attitude compatible with Roman Catholic theology, he joined the Roman Church in 1653, later adopting the name Angelus Silesius, derived from the Spanish mystic Joan ab Angelis and from his native Silesia. In 1654 he became court physician to Emperor Ferdinand III, a profession he soon gave up when he took orders and joined the monastery of St. Matthias in Breslau.

A highly gifted poet, Scheffler's hymns, written largely before his conversion, were mostly contained in his *Heilige Seelenlust oder Geistliche Hirten-Lieder* (Breslau, 1657). Zinzendorf (*LW* 362, 386) included many of them in his *Christ-Catholisches Singe und Bet-Büchlein* (1727).

AUTHOR: 375 You Will I Love, My Strength
379 "Come, Follow Me," Said Christ, the Lord

SCHEIDT, CHRISTIAN LUDWIG (1709–61), was born in Waldenburg, Germany. From 1724–30 he attended the Universities of Altdorf and Strassburg; thereafter he studied theology at Halle and philosophy at Göttingen. It is said that he studied at Halle to understand the things of God, namely, spiritual matters; that he attended Göttingen to understand the thoughts and works of men. Shortly after his graduation from Göttingen he was made a Doctor of Laws and appointed a member of its faculty. Later he taught at the University of Copenhagen. He died in 1761 at Hanover, where he at the time was councillor and librarian.

AUTHOR: 351 By Grace I'm Saved

SCHEIN, JOHANN HERMAN (1586-1630), was born at Grünhain, near Annaberg, Saxony, January 20, 1586. Not long thereafter, at the death of his father, a Lutheran pastor, his family moved to Dresden where, at the age of 13, Schein was accepted as a soprano into the Hofkapelle of the Elector of Saxony. Here he became thoroughly acquainted with both sacred and secular choral music in Latin, German, and Italian. In 1603 he was admitted to *Schulpforta,* the famous electoral school near Naumburg that specialized in music and the humanities. At the University of Leipzig, in 1607 he began the study of law and liberal arts for four years. After serving as a private tutor to the Wolffersdorff family for two years, in 1615 he became kapellmeister at the Court of Duke Johann Ernst of Sachse-Weimar. His tenure there was happy but short, for in 1616, after an audition, he returned to Leipzig to succeed the famous Seth Calvisius (1556–1615) as cantor at St. Thomas' Church and School, where he remained the rest of his life.

Schein was first married to Sidonia Hosel, a native of Grünheim, who bore him five children, of which only the elder son survived into adulthood. Seven months after Sidonia's death he married Elizabeth von der Perre, daughter of a painter who had worked on the decoration of the organ in the St. Nicholas' Church. At least four of the five children of this union died in infancy. In addition to his familial sorrows Schein suffered from poor health—tuberculosis, gout, scurvy, and kidney stones. Two visits to the springs at Carlsbad were of no help, and he died in Leipzig on November 19, 1630.

Schein wrote a prodigious amount of music, largely vocal; songs both sacred and secular; German and Latin motets; occasional pieces for weddings and funerals; and an instrumental collection that marked a high point in the history of the variation suite. His last and perhaps best-known sacred collection was the *Cantional Oder Gesang-Buch Augsburgischer Confession*, published in Leipzig in 1627. The tradition of arranging Lutheran hymns in four-part harmony with the melody in the soprano had begun with Lucas Osiander already in 1586 and had flourished in the meantime. This *Cantional* was the largest to date; it included most of the hymns in use at Leipzig, arranged according to the liturgical year. In compiling this work Schein served as editor, arranger, author, and composer.

Wolfgang C. Printz (1641–1717), German music theorist, historian, and novelist, singled out Schütz, Schein, and Scheidt as the three best composers of their time. As close friends, Schütz visited Schein on his deathbed and at his request composed a motet on the text "Das ist je gewisslich wahr."

ARRANGER: 421 AUF MEINEN LEIBEN GOTT

SCHIRMER, MICHAEL (1606–73), was born July 18, 1606, in Leipzig, the son of an inspector of wine casks. After attending the St. Thomas' School in Leipzig, where Johann Schein (*LW* 421) was at the time director of music, he entered the University of Leipzig in 1619, where he earned both the Bachelor of Arts and Master's degrees. First serving as director of the *Gymnasium* in Freiburg, he shortly thereafter assumed a pastorate in Stiegnitz. In 1636 he went to Berlin as assistant director of the Greyfriars *Gymnasium*, serving in this capacity until, in 1651, he was made associate rector.

The horrors of the Thirty Years' War (1618–48), the pestilence and poverty, together with other trials and disappointments—he lost his only daughter in death at the age of nine; his wife and 25-year-old son within the span of less than a year—these brought on a severe depression. Yet he labored faithfully as administrator, teacher, scholar, and staunch Lutheran. His singular poetic gifts and talents—whether in Greek, Latin, or German languages—resulted in his being crowned poet laureate. Having resigned his position in 1668, he remained in Berlin until his death May 4, 1673.

His works include scriptural plays (*Der verfolgte David*), *Biblische Lieder und Lehrsprüche* (Berlin, 1650), *Biblische Trostsprüche, in Deutsche Reime Übersetzt* (Berlin, 1652), and *Trost und Lehrsprüche . . . in Teutsche Reime Verfasst* (Berlin, 1650). His hymns, about five in number, exhibit unmistakably the influence of Johann Heermann (*LW* 95, et al.), and he can well be considered the precursor of Paul Gerhardt (*LW* 19, et al.) in the transition from the objective hymns of the Reformation to the later more subjective type.

AUTHOR: 160 O Holy Spirit, Enter In

SCHLEGEL, CATHARINA AMALIA DOROTHEA VON (1697–?), is mentioned by Koch as being a canoness or head of a Lutheran nunnery in Cöthen, Germany. Her correspondence with Count Heinrich Ernst von Stolberg-Wernigerode during the years 1750–52 seems to indicate that she was in some capacity attached to the ducal court in Cöthen. Nothing else is known about her life.

AUTHOR: 510 Be Still, My Soul

SCHMOLCK, BENJAMIN (1672–1737), was born December 21, 1672, at Brauchitschdorf in the principality of Liegnitz, Silesia, where his father served as one of the pastors of a Lutheran church for 46 years. While attending the *Gymnasium* in Lauban, one of the prominent educational centers in Silesia, he was taught by Pastor George Wende, a remarkable educator. At the age of 16 his father permitted him to preach a sermon in his church. Impressed with this young man's ability, Nicolaus Heinrich von Haugwitz, a prominent layperson of the parish, promised him a sizable stipend that allowed him to enroll at the University of Leipzig, where orthodoxy had triumphed over Pietism, and the beginnings of the Enlightenment were in evidence.Here he came under the influence of Johannes Olearius (*LW* 28, et al.) whose teaching was of a "living Christianity," but not pietistic. During his final years at the university Schmolck readily supported himself as a poet and in 1697 was even crowned poet laureate.

When in 1697 his aged father needed help in his parish, Schmolck traded his shining career for service in the little village of Brauchitschdorf. In 1701 he was ordained in Liegnitz; in 1702 he married Anna Rosina Rehwald, daughter of a merchant in Lauban. Later that year he became pastor of *Friedenskirche* in Schweidnitz, an exceptionally difficult parish, the result of the counter-Reformation and the terms of the Peace of Westphalia. According to the latter, only three pastors were permitted to serve the church at Schweidnitz, which included no less than 36 villages. Here Schmolck served the rest of his life, his final years beset with a stroke and partial paralysis. He died February 12, 1737.

Schmolck wrote no less than 1,180 hymns, most of which appeared in his popular books of devotion: *Flammen der Himmlisch-Gesinnten Seele* (1704); *Die Lustige Sabbat in der Stille zu Zion* (1714); *Kirchen-Gefährte* (1732); and *Klage und Reigen* (1734). Most of his hymns were done too hurriedly and hence lacked the quality and content expected of a first-class poet, as he himself admitted, "When you shake the tree too often, unripened fruit falls to the ground." The chief worship service of his day on Sunday afforded pastors like Schmolk opportunity to introduce their own hymns to the congregation. People came to church without a hymnbook; they sang the designated hymn of the day by heart. After the sermon the pastor could readily acquaint the congregation with a hymn of his own making, a hymn that might frequently gather the thoughts expressed in the sermon. Schmolck's poetry exhibits the influence of Daniel Caspar von Lohenstein, and as such he is often classified as belonging to the second Silesian school of poets. He stands completely in the orthodox tradition with its emphasis on sin and grace. His use of Scripture, his poetic skill, his simple structure, his stress on the personal relationship with God, and his coupling of hymns to well-known and simple tunes (110 times to WER NUN DEN LIEBEN GOTT [*LW* 420, 429]); 80 times to MEINEN JESUM LASS ICH NICHT [*LW* 34, 269]) caused his hymns to be loved by congregations.

AUTHOR: 198 Open Now Thy Gates of Beauty
226 Dearest Jesus, We Are Here

SCHOP, JOHANN (c. 1595–c. 1667), probably born in Hamburg, he became a member of the court orchestra in Wolfenbüttel in 1615. Thereafter he went to the Danish court in Copenhagen (1618), where he became renowned as a performer and teacher. The historian Johann Mattheson (1681–1764) spoke of him as an artist without equal in his time and as one of the finest of the first half of the 17th century. Schop was also an excellent performer on the organ, lute, and the German zink (a 15th/16th century reed instrument in the form of a straight or slightly bent tube of wood or ivory, with six finger holes and a cup-shaped mouthpiece). After 1621 Schop held various positions in Hamburg: as town violinist and organist, later *Ratsmusikdirektor* (borough musician) and organist at St. James' Church. He died in Hamburg.

As a close friend and fellow townsman of Johann Rist (LW 122, et.al.), he provided musical settings for Rist's *Himmlische Lieder* (1641–1643). Manfred Bukofzer speaks of these two of the North German school whose "sacred and secular miniature songs in very popular style" contributed greatly to the literature of that period, the second great flowering in the history of the German song (Bukofzer, *Music in the Baroque Era*). Schop also composed considerable occasional music, suites, sacred concertos, and instrumental music.

COMPOSER: 263 WERDE MUNTER

SCHRÖDER, JOHANN HEINRICH (1667–99), was born October 4, 1667, at Hallerspringe, near Hanover. While a student at University of Leipzig he came under the influence of August H. Francke (1663–1727), whose lectures he attended. In 1696 he became pastor in Möseburg, near Neuhaldenstein. Shortly thereafter he married Tranquilla Sophia Wolf, a staunch Pietist, who less than a year later died in childbirth. Two years later, June 30, 1699, Johann was called home.

He contributed four hymn texts to *Geistreiches Gesang Buch* of Halle (1697), of Darmstadt (1698), and of Freylinghausen (1704). His hymns are considered by Julian to be "good examples of the early hymns of the Pietists."

AUTHOR: 277 One Thing's Needful

SCHRÖTER, LEONHART (1532–1601), was born at Torgau, Germany, and received his early music training from Johann Walter (*LW* 265). Additional schooling was had in Annaberg and the ducal school in Meissen. From 1561–76 he was town cantor in Saalfeld (Thuringia), except for two years when he lost his position because of his sympathy for the Philippists (supporters of Melanchthon's [*LW* 189] doctrines), who were not considered true Lutherans. During those two years he was librarian at the Wolfenbüttel court. While at Saalfeld he became associated with Ludwig Helmbold (*LW* 409, et al.) in Mühlhausen, an important Lutheran poet of his day. From 1576–95 Schröter was cantor at the Alstadt *Lateinschule* in Magdeburg, a highly regarded position previously occupied by Martin Agricola (1486–1556) and Gallus Dressler

(1533–c. 1580). Here he achieved prominence as a composer of settings for both Latin and German texts.

Except for his Latin texts, such as in his *Hymni Sacri* (1587), which he set strictly in the Reformation polyphonic style, his homophonic writing exhibits a closer alliance between music and text, resulting in a more personal expression as practiced by the Flemish Orlando di Lasso (c. 1532–94) at the Bavarian court. His publications include *Geistliche Lieder* (1562); *Cantiones Suavissimae* (1576–80); and his exceptional and well-known *Four-and eight-voice Christmas songs* (1586–87). His few psalm settings contributed to the early Protestant motet. He died in 1601.

COMPOSER: 82 FREUT EUCH, IHR LIEBEN

SCHUETTE, CONRAD HERMANN LOUIS (1843–1926), was born June 17, 1843, at Vorrel, Hanover. Having come to America in 1854, he studied theology at Capital University, Columbus, Ohio, and was ordained in 1865. That same year he married Victoria M. Wirth of Columbus. After serving St. Mark's Lutheran Church, Delaware, Ohio, where Matthias Loy (LW 235, et al.) had served earlier, in 1872 he became professor of mathematics and natural philosophy; in 1880 professor of theology; and in 1890 president of Capital University. From 1881–94 he was pastor of Christ Church, Pleasant Ridge (now Bexley), Ohio. In 1894 he was elected president of The Joint Synod of Ohio and Other States, a position he held until 1924.

Capital University honored him with the Doctor of Divinity degree in 1898. He was one of the founders of The National Lutheran Council, serving as its president from 1923–25. A frequent contributor to church periodicals of the Ohio synod, he published *The Church Members' Manual*; *Church, State, and School*; *Before the Altar*; and *Exercises Unto Godliness*. To the Ohio Synod *Hymnal* of 1880 he contributed five original hymns and several translations from the German. He died August 11, 1926, at Columbus, Ohio.

TRANSLATOR: 479 O Holy, Blessed Trinity

SCHULTZ, DOROTHY RUTH *née* NICKEL (1934–) Born June 9, 1934, in Bessemer, Michigan, became interested in writing, especially poetry and verse, in elementary school. This interest was pursued during her years at Luther Institute, Chicago, where she served as assistant editor of the school newspaper, and at college, where she was a news and feature writer.

Her education includes three years at Concordia College, River Forest, Illinois; a Bachelor of Arts degree from Concordia College, Bronxville, New York; and a Master of Science in Education degree from the College of New Rochelle, New York. Married to Ralph C. Schultz (*LW* 146, et al.) in 1954, she began teaching at St. Mark's Lutheran School in Cleveland, Ohio. The couple moved to Bronxville, New York, in 1961, when

Ralph was called to teach music and chair the Department of Music at Concordia College there.

In the 1960s Dorothy Schultz was commissioned by the editors of the Concordia Music Education series to prepare original lyrics for the music materials in the series. She later collaborated with her husband for the published works "Sing for Joy," used as the theme for the Concordia College Choir of Bronxville for almost a decade, and "Love in Christ," written on the occasion of their daughter Deborah's marriage in 1978.

AUTHOR: 376 Love in Christ Is Strong and Living

SCHULTZ, RALPH C. (1932–), was born in Dolton, Illinois, June 23, 1932. His music study began at an early age, stimulating an ongoing interest in musical composition. He earned a Bachelor of Music degree from the Cosmopolitan School of Music in Chicago in 1954, at the same time earning the Bachelor of Science in Education at Concordia College, River Forest, Illinois.

Upon graduation Schultz married Dorothy Ruth Nickel, and the couple began teaching careers in Cleveland, Ohio, Ralph serving also as organist and choir director at Trinity Lutheran Church there. In the summer of 1955 he began to study composition with Ross Lee Finney and organ with Robert Noehren at the University of Michigan. Influenced by Noehren, Trinity Church in 1957 installed the first major tracker action organ in America. Built by Rudolf von Beckerath, the instrument gained an international reputation and became the model for what has become a revival of interest in the tracker organ in America.

Transferring to the Cleveland Institute of Music, Schultz received the Master of Music degree in theory and composition in 1960, meanwhile conducting the Cleveland Lutheran Chorus and Orchestra. The following year he accepted the call to teach music and chair the Department of Music at Concordia College, Bronxville, New York. He began doctoral studies in music education at Teachers College of Columbia University, but his interest in church music led him to transfer to Union Theological Seminary, where he earned the Sacred Music Doctorate in 1967. He returned to Union as lecturer in conducting from 1968–71.

Schultz assumed the presidency of Concordia College, Bronxville in 1976. He has also served as a member of the synodical Commission on Worship that produced *Worship Supplement* (1969), that helped produce the *Lutheran Book of Worship* (1978), and that produced *Lutheran Worship* (1982). Recently he served The Lutheran Church—Missouri Synod as a member of the President's Commission on Higher Education.

Throughout his career as a composer, Schultz has been closely identified with music for the church, but he has also written sonatas for piano, pieces for strings, and a suite for orchestra entitled *The Intelligent Man*. In addition to numerous organ pieces, Schultz has composed extensively for choirs, both children and adult. Major compositions for choir include the *Lutheran Chorale Mass*, with orchestra; *To Him be the Glory*, with orchestra; *Praise God with Hearts and voices*, with orchestra; *O Sing*

Unto the Lord with a New Song, with instruments; and *Sing for Joy*, with instruments. He and his wife (*LW* 376) collaborated on many children's pieces for the Concordia Music Education series. Their collaboration has thus far produced special music for the weddings of three of their six children.

COMPOSER: 146 BRONXVILLE
376 DOROTHY
ARRANGER: 187 WAS FRAG ICH NACH DER WELT
325 WIE SCHÖN LEUCHTET
374 WINTERTON
471 ITALIAN HYMN

SCHUMACHER, Bernard (1886–1978), was born November 7, 1886, at Watertown Wisconsin, where he also attended Northwestern College. His education continued at Concordia Teachers College, Addison, Illinois; Johns Hopkins University and Peabody Institute, Baltimore, Maryland. After serving as teacher in Lutheran Christian day schools for a number of years, he became superintendent of the South Wisconsin District of the then-Lutheran Synod of Missouri, Ohio, and Other States. He was secretary of the Intersynodical Committee on Hymnology and the Liturgics that prepared *The Lutheran Hymnal* (1941), and chairman of its Subcommittee on Tunes. He retired at Wauwatosa, Wisconsin, where he died on February 26, 1978.

Included among his works are *Eventide* (1917) and *King Victorious* (1924), two sacred cantatas; *Select Songs: Songs for School and Home* (1922) and *Music Reader for Lutheran Schools* (1933), both of which he coauthored; *Book of Accompaniments to Songs in the Music Reader for Lutheran Schools* (1933); and *Lutheran Organist* (1927), which he coauthored; plus various compositions for organ and choir.

COMPOSER: 112 SEPTEM VERBA
AUTHOR: 472 Let Children Hear the Mighty Deeds (st. 4)

SCHÜTZ, JOHANN JAKOB (1640–90), was born September 7, 1640, at Frankfurt-am-Main, Germany. After completing his studies at Tübingen University, he became a licensed attorney, practicing both civil and canon law in Frankfurt. His zeal for church law prompted Phillip J. Spener (1635–1705), the father of Pietism, to admit that he learned much from him. One of the early and most trusted followers of Spener, Schütz suggested what later became the *Collegia Pietatis*, namely, private devotional gatherings in homes. A learned and pious man, the influence of Spener, his overly pietistic wife, and the peculiarities of chiliasm finally caused him to sever relationship with the Lutheran Church and to join the Separatist Moravians. He died at Frankfurt on May 22, 1690.

Five hymns in the *Christliches Gedenckbüchlein* (1675) are usually ascribed to him.

AUTHOR: 452 Sing Praise to God, the Highest Good

SCRIVEN, JOSEPH MEDLICOTT (1819–86), was born in Seapatrick, County Down, Ireland, September 10, 1819. Educated at Trinity College, Dublin, and Addiscombe Military College, Surrey, at the age of 25 he went to Canada, after his fiancee was drowned on the eve of their wedding day. Here he taught school for a while at Woodstock and Brantford, Ontario, before moving to Bewdley, near Rice Lake, where again a second engagement was terminated by the death of his fiancee shortly before the wedding day.

As a member of the Plymouth Brethren he was determined to live according to the precepts of Christ's Sermon on the Mount and in close communion with him. Without an actual home of his own, he moved from place to place into the homes of others; he spent much of his time in Christian service, doing menial tasks for the handicapped, the sick, and the poor. Depression, poverty, and illness were his lot. During one night of his illness in October 1886, he left the house and was found dead the next morning, October 10, in the nearby waters of Rice Lake.

AUTHOR: 516 What a Friend We Have in Jesus

SEARS, EDMOND HAMILTON (1810–76), was born April 6, 1810, in Sandisfield, Massachusetts. Following his graduation from Union College, Schenectady, New York, he attended Harvard Divinity School, from which he graduated in 1837. Thereafter he served a number of small Unitarian churches near Boston, namely, Wayland (1838) and Lancaster (1840). Ill health compelled him to return to Wayland, where he devoted himself to writing. He died January 16, 1876, at Weston, Massachusetts.

Despite his affiliation with these churches, Sears claimed to be orthodox in his beliefs, although it is said that he had been considerably influenced by Emmanuel Swedenborg (1688–1772), a prolific theosophical writer and the father of the Swedenborgians. He published several books during his lifetime, including *Regeneration* (1854), *Foregleams of Immortality* (1858), and *The Heart of Christ* (1872). Elizabeth Barret Browning (1806–61), famous poet of Victorian England, was a great admirer of his.

AUTHOR: 62 It Came upon the Midnight Clear

SEDULIUS, COELIUS (c. 450), was perhaps born in Rome. The little that is known about his life is gathered from two letters by him written to a certain Macedonius, in which he records his early interest in literature and that he was a late convert to Christianity. He appears to have become a priest, dedicated to attract the heathen to Christ through his writings, among other works: *Carmen Paschale*, a poem based on the Gospels, dedicated to Macedonius; *Opus Pachale*, the Gospel story in prose; and *Paean alphabeticus de Christo*, an acrostic hymn of 23 four-line stanzas in iambic dimeter, from which the following "A solis ortus cardine" and "Hostis Herodes impie" are derived.

AUTHOR: 43 From East to West
81 When Christ's Appearing Was Made Known

SEISS, JOSEPH AUGUSTUS (1823–1904), originally Seuss, was born March 18, 1823, at the German Moravian settlement of Graceham, Maryland, the son of a miner. Confirmed a member of the Moravian Church, he eventually enrolled at Gettysburg College in 1839 and was licensed by the Evangelical Lutheran Synod of Virginia in 1842, after privately being tutored in theology. After serving various parishes in Virginia and Maryland, he became pastor of St. John's Lutheran Church in Philadelphia (1858–74), where he remained until he, with some of his parishioners, established the Church of the Holy Communion in western Philadelphia (1874–1904), where he died June 20, 1904.

Seiss served as president of both the Pennsylvania Ministerium and the General Council. He was author or editor of some 80 works, including *The Last Times* (1856); *The Evangelical Psalmist* [1859]; *Ecclesia Lutherana* (1868); *Lecturers on the Gospels* (1868-72); *Lecturers on the Epistles* (1885); as well as works on the Lutheran liturgy and hymn collections.

TRANSLATOR: 507 Beautiful Savior

SELNECKER, NIKOLAUS (1532–92), was born December 5, 1532, at Hersbruck, near Nürnberg. At the age of 12 he was already organist of the *Burgkapelle* there. As a student at Wittenberg University, from which he earned the Master of Arts degree in 1554, he was a favorite pupil of Philipp Melanchthon (*LW* 189). Serving first as a private teacher in Wittenberg, in 1557 he was appointed second court preacher and tutor to the court at Dresden and becoming ordained in 1558. His defense of confessional Lutheranism over against the Crypto-Calvinists at the court caused him to leave, and in 1565 he became professor of theology at the University of Jena. Theological disputes again caused his departure to become professor of theology at Leipzig University and pastor of St. Thomas' Church. Here, as both a theologian and musician, among other things, he was the leading figure in developing the great motet choir in St. Thomas', later made famous by J. S. Bach (*LW* 89). In 1570 he was given leave of absence to go to Wolfenbüttel as court preacher, but was recalled to Leipzig in 1574. He became involved in bitter doctrinal disputes regarding the Lord's Supper, and, together with Martin Chemnitz (1522–86) and Jakob Andreä (1528–90), he prepared the Formula of Concord, which was published in 1577. The accession of Christian I as elector in 1588, a ruler who favored Calvinism, again deprived Selnecker of his offices in Leipzig, and he became superintendent at Hildesheim. On the death of Christian I, he was recalled to Leipzig, where he died May 24, 1592.

His theological works, which champanioned orthodox Lutheran doctrine, number no less than 175, with 94 in Latin and 81 in German. No less prolific was he as a hymn writer, his output numbering about 150, many of them based on the Psalms, from which he had drawn such comfort in his days of theological dispute. Of his numerous hymn publications, of which he frequently wrote both words and music, the chief collection is the *Christliche Psalmen, Lieder und Kirchengesenge* (Leipzig, 1857).

AUTHOR: 257 Let Me Be Yours Forever (st. 1)
344 Lord Jesus Christ, Will You Not Stay

SELTZ, MARTIN LOUIS (1909–67), was born December 20, 1909, near Gibbon, Minnesota, the son of Lutheran pastor Carl Seltz and Doris (*née* Sauer). He attended Concordia College, St. Paul, Minnesota, graduating in 1928 and continuing his studies at Concordia Seminary, St. Louis, until graduation in 1934. From 1929–31, he was an instructor at Concordia College, St. Paul.

For three summers, 1932–34, Seltz was musical director at Lutherland Camp in Pennsylvania. Following ordination he served as pastor of Trinity Lutheran Church, Hill City, Minnesota, moving to St. Paul Church in Waseca six years later. Married to the former Helen Spittler in 1945, they moved the following year to Boone, Iowa, where he served Trinity congregation for 14 years.

While at Trinity, Seltz became active with the Iowa District West, serving on its board of directors and as its secretary of education and superintendent of schools. The family, now including four children, moved in 1961 to Elmhurst, Illinois, to work with Immanuel Church; the following year Seltz was appointed to the Commission on Worship, Liturgics, and Hymnology. At that time the commission was beginning work on *Worship Supplement* (1969). Seltz, acquainted from childhood with the German language, began translating hymn texts to be included in that volume, some of which would be included in *Lutheran Book of Worship* (1978). His widow writes, "Translating German texts was a special joy to Martin. If he had lived, I'm sure his retirement would have been happily spent in further translations!" As a member of the Missouri Synod's Commission on Worship he also served on the Inter-Lutheran Commission on Worship, which produced the *Lutheran Book of Worship.*

Seltz accepted the pastorate of Concordia in South St. Paul, Minnesota, in 1965, two years before his death on October 5, 1967.

TRANSLATOR: 32 O Savior, Rend the Heavens Wide
54 He Whom Shepherds Once Came Praising

SERMISY, CLAUDIN de (c. 1490–1562), most probably was born in France. Word of him first appears in 1508 when he was appointed *clerc musicien*, a post that implied ordination to the priesthood and choir membership at Sainte-Chapelle du Palais in Paris. In that same year Louis XII called him to be *chanteur* in the Chapel de musique du Roy, the French equivalent of gentleman of the royal chapel. In 1515 he was one of the musicians present at the funeral of Louis XII. In the aforementioned capacity Sermisy was present at three historic occasions: in 1515 he accompanied Francois I to a meeting with Pope Leo X in Boulogne, where the French chapel singers competed with the papal choir; in 1520 he was present when Francois I met with Henry VIII at the Field of Cloth of Gold; and again in 1532 when the two met at Boulogne. That same year Sermisy was appointed *sous-maître* of the chapel, a position that gave him responsibility for feeding, maintaining, and training the boy singers. In 1553 he was made canon of Sainte-Chapelle, an office that entitled him to a residence plus large salary and obligated him to officiate at certain ceremonies. He died in Paris, October 13, 1562.

As a composer Sermisy exhibits a wide range of talent—masses, motets, and some 200 chansons—and his works were evidently popular, judging from their many reprints.

COMPOSER (attr.): 425 WAS MEIN GOTT WILL

SIBELIUS, JEAN (1865–1957), was born into a Swedish-speaking family December 8, 1865, at Tavestehus, Finland, the son of a medical doctor. In 1885 he entered the University of Helsingfors (Helsinki) to study law but gave it up the following year to develop his natural aptitude for music at the Helsingfors Conservatory, where he became a pupil of Martin Wegelius in composition. After traveling and studying in Berlin and Vienna, he taught composition at the Helsingfors Conservatory and at the Philharmonic Orchestra School. When he was 32 the Finnish Government gave him an annual grant for life so that he might be free to compose. Thus he came to be identified as the national composer of Finland and known chiefly for his dramatic works, suites, songs, symphonies, (seven) symphonic poems in which he exhibits an exceptional sense of form and mastery of the orchestra. His development from one work to the next was less predictable than that of almost any other 19th or early 20th century symphonist. His early years as a violinist acquainted him with the full range of expressive devices, resulting in imaginative and resourceful writing. His symphonic poem *Finlandia* was composed in 1899 for a great patriotic demonstration in favor of the freedom of the press when the Finns were struggling against Russian domination. His visit to the United States to conduct some of his works at the Norfolk Festival resulted in Yale University honoring him with the Doctor of Music degree.

He died at Järvenpää in 1957 at the age of 91.

COMPOSER: 510 FINLANDIA

SILCHER, FRIEDRICH (1789–1860), was born June 27, 1789, in Schnaith, Württemberg, the son of a school teacher and organist. After being taught music by his father, he spent three years with the learned musician N. F. Auberlen, organist at Fellbach (near Stuttgart), who taught him to be a teacher equipped with a thorough knowledge of music. In 1806 he became a teacher's assistant in Schorndorf and thereafter a private tutor in Ludwigsburg. In 1811 he settled in Stuttgart as a piano teacher, giving private lessons and continuing his study of piano and composition with Conradin Kreutzer. His association with Carl Maria von Weber (1786–1826), composer, conductor, pianist and critic, influenced him toward Romanticism. In 1817 he accepted a position at the University of Tübingen, which he held for 43 years. There he first established the orchestral society, using it to present Haydn oratorios in the *aula* of the university. Considering himself, however, deficient in the orchestral field, and convinced that choral song constituted his forte, he established and organized the university's choral society (*Liedertafel*) in 1829. In 1852 the university conferred an honorary doctorate on him. On his retirement in 1860 he was awarded the Knight's Cross of the Order of Peace. He died in Tübingen August 26, 1860.

Silcher is remembered primarily for his work in behalf of folk songs and their use as a genre both for performance and for popular music education. Because choral societies were formed and the cause of school music was thus fostered, he collected and arranged folk songs from Germany and other countries and composed some 250 songs modelled along the lines of Mozart, Weber, and Mendelssohn (*LW* 49), but folklike in style. As these became widely disseminated, they often began to be considered as original folk songs rather than composed. On the centenary of his death a critical edition of his works—*Sammlung deutscher Volkslieder*, 12 volumes—was published and a Silcher archive opened in Schnaith in 1956. Other works include a *Württemberg Choralbuch, Geschichte der evangelischen Kirchengesänge* (1844), and *Kernlieder für Schule und Haus* (Tübingen, 1842).

COMPOSER: 66 ALLE JAHRE WIEDER
512 SO NIMM DENN MEINE HÄNDE

SLOAN, JOHN MORRISON (1835–?), was born May 19, 1835, at Stairaird, Ayrshire. After earning his Master of Arts degree at the University of Glasgow, Edinburgh, he served successively as collegiate minister of the Free Church, Dalkeith, 1864; minister of the South Freechurch, Aberdeen, 1868; collegiate minister of Anderston Free Church, Glasgow, 1878; and minister of Grange Free Church, Edinburgh, 1890. In the course of his ministry he contributed a number of original hymns as well as translations from the German to Anglican hymnals of the late 19th century.

TRANSLATOR: 303 Rise! To Arms! With Prayer Employ You

SMART, HENRY THOMAS (1813–79), was born October 26, 1813, in London, the son of a well-known violinist, orchestra director, music publisher, and piano manufacturer. Already as a youngster he exhibited a remarkable aptitude for music, but he found practice too irksome. Frequent visits in leisure hours to the organ firm of Robson and Flight resulted in becoming knowledgeable in organ construction, which served him later when he designed and supervised the building of many notable organs. After refusing a commission in the Indian army, he worked in a law firm, but four years later gave this up to devote his life to music. Although he had some formal music instruction from his father and from William H. Kearns, a prominent violinist in England, he was largely self-taught. He became one of England's most eminent organists of the 19th century, distinguished not only in performance, but also in improvisation, service playing and composition. Besides being organist in a number of prominent Anglican churches in London, he composed choral works sung at many English festivals, service music, hymn tunes, organ pieces, cantatas, an opera, and several hundred part songs, many of them for women's voices. A strong advocate of congregational singing, he favored unison singing over against part singing. He served as music critic to the *Atlas*, a weekly journal; and as music editor of *The Chorale Book* (1858) and the *Presbyterian Hymnal* (1875); he contributed tunes to *Hymns Ancient and Modern* (1861) and to the English Presbyterian *Psalms and Hymns for Divine Worship* (1867).

After he became completely blind at age 52, his daughter took down all his compositions. He died in London July 6, 1879.

COMPOSER: 50, 218 REGENT SQUARE
343 REX GLORIAE

SMITH, ALFRED MORTON (1879-1971), was born in Jenkintown, Pennsylvania, May 20, 1879. After graduating from the University of Pennsylvania in 1901, he entered the Philadelphia Divinity School, graduating with a Bachelor of Arts degree in 1905 and earning a Bachelor of Sacred Theology degree in 1911. Ordained deacon in 1905 and priest in 1906, he served briefly at St. Peter's Church, Philadelphia, and then went to California as assistant at St. Luke's, Long Beach. From 1906 to 1916 he served at St. Matthias' Church, Los Angeles, and for two years in the City Mission, when he entered the army as a chaplain, serving in France and entering Germany along with the Army of Occupation. In 1919 he returned to Philadelphia and was appointed to the staff of the Episcopal City Mission. During this ministry of 35 years he acted also as chaplain at the Eastern State Penitentiary, at Sleighton Farm School, at Valley Forge Military Academy, and at city hospitals. For eight years he served as assistant at St. Clement's and for three years as associate priest at St. Elizabeth's Church. Retiring to Jenkintown in 1954, he later moved to Druim Moir, the Houston Foundation's home for retired clergy at Chestnut Hill, and finally to Brigantine, where he died February 26, 1971.

It was not until his adult years that Smith finally began to study harmony and the cello. His music ability developed to the point where he was composing and playing in a community orchestra. Besides composing a few hymn tunes and carols, of which SURSUM CORDA is undoubtedly the best tune, he composed two masses, the *Missa de Sancto Matthia* (1936) and the *Missa de Sancto Clement* (1948).

COMPOSER: 401 SURSUM CORDA

SMITH, WALTER CHALMERS (1824–1908), was born December 5, 1824, in Aberdeen, Scotland. Educated at the University of Aberdeen, where he earned the Master of Arts degree, he studied theology at New College, Edinburgh, and was ordained and installed in 1850 as pastor of the Free Church of Scotland congregation at Chadwell Street, Islington, London. He later served as minister of Orwell Free Church, Milnathort, Kincross-shire; of Free Tron Church, Glasgow; and of the Free High Church, Edinburgh. He served as the moderator of the Assembly of the Free Church of Scotland in its Jubilee Year in 1892, retiring the following year. He died at Kinbuck, Perthshire, September 19, 1908.

A man of catholic and scholarly interests, Smith's published works include *The Bishop's Walk* (1860); *North Country Folk* (1883); *A Heretic, and Other Poems* (1891); and *Poetical Works* (1902). To him poetry was "the retreat of his nature from the burden of his labors," a means of expressing what could not be done so in the pulpit.

AUTHOR: 451 Immortal, Invisible, God Only Wise

SMITHERS, NATHANIEL B.(1818–96), was born in Dover, Delaware, October 8, 1818, the elder of two surviving sons of a Methodist notary. His mother died when he was about five; six years later the father and sons moved to Maryland. Having shown early aptitude in scholastics, "repeating passages from Virgil when most children are prattling nursery rhymes," Nathaniel was sent to West Nottingham Academy. He graduated early, at the age of 15, and entered the newly founded Lafayette College in Easton, Pennsylvania. His knowledge of Latin progressed so dramatically that his teacher claimed he could be taught no more.

Graduating in 1836, Smithers first spent a year teaching at Snow Hill, Maryland, before turning to the study of law at Carlisle, Pennsylvania. He was admitted to the Pennsylvania bar in 1840, and to the Delaware bar the following year.

After several years of building up his practice, Smithers married his first cousin, Mary Elizabeth Smithers, in March of 1853. Four children were born to the couple, two of them dying in infancy. Mrs. Smithers died of consumption in 1867, leaving her husband to care for the children as well as his burgeoning law practice. Eventually this hectic pace settled down enough to permit him some time for literary pursuits, and in 1879 he published the first volume of his translations of Latin hymns. His skill at translation was so facile that, when Bret Harte's poem "Plain Language from Truthful James" appeared in print, Smithers produced a Latin version that had scholars believing Harte's to be the translation rather than the original. Smithers enjoyed his joke for a while before admitting authorship of the Latin copy.

Granted the honorary Doctor of Laws degree both by his alma mater, Lafayette College, and by Dickinson College, Smithers was elected to various political positions throughout his career, from clerk in the Delaware State Assembly in 1845 to U.S.

congressional representative in 1863. He was a staunch abolitionist and prohibitionist, casting his votes according to his conscience. Following the War Between the States, he served on the Special Committee on Reconstruction of the Union. He retired in 1895 from his second appointment as Secretary of State. Death from Bright's disease occurred on January 16, 1896.

TRANSLATOR: 76 O Chief of Cities, Bethlehem (sts. 1, 2, 4)

SOHREN (SOHR, SOHRER), PETER (c. 1630–c. 1692), was born in Germany, perhaps the son of Daniel Sohren, pastor in Lenzen, near Elbing. Cantor and organist at the *Dreikönigskirche,* Elbing, and for a time cantor and schoolmaster at nearby Dirschau, he was an assiduous composer and compiler of Protestant hymn tunes. In 1668, five years after Johann Crüger's (*LW* 19, et al.) famous *Praxis pietatis melica*, Sohren published an enlarged edition of it, contributing numerous tunes with figured bass and using the same title. The title page noted that he was the "Best old school and mathematics teacher of the Christian congregation of Heilige Leichnam in the Royal City of Elbling in Prussia." Offended at the lack of recognition given him, he later produced a second collection entitled *Musicalischer Vorschmack der Jauchtzenden Seelen* (Hamburg, 1683), a volume containing 1,117 texts and 430 melodies. Though Sohren's tunes are often more rhythmically varied and colorful in contrast to the more staid examples of the congregational hymn, few of them were regularly used in the 18th century.

COMPOSER: 246 DU LEBENSBROT, HERR JESU CHRIST

SPEE, FRIEDRICH VON (1591–1635), was born in Kaiserswörth, Germany, a small city near Düsseldorf, of which his father was magistrate. In 1610, at the age of 19, he joined the Society of Jesus. Following his priestly ordination he served as teacher of grammar and philosophy at a Jesuit college in Cologne. In 1627, at the order of his superiors, he served as a priest in Würzberg and Bamberg. There his life was embittered with the sad duty of ministering to and accompanying innocent people—no less than 158 in Würzberg alone during the years 1627–28—who were sentenced to be burned at the stake as the result of the prevalent witchcraft trials. His speaking-out and writing against such trials finally brought them to an end. In 1631 he was sent to Rinteln, in Lower Saxony, where he was in charge of a Roman Catholic mission. The year 1635 saw him in Trier, a city held by the French army but soon besieged both by the armed forces of Spain and the imperial troops. When in May of that year these forces stormed into the city, Spee risked his life to help the wounded and to care for the sick and dying, both physically and spiritually. Exhausted by such rigors, he was stricken with a fever; he died August 7, 1635, in the presence of his saddened Jesuit brothers.

The hymns of Spee are characterized by deep feeling, glowing inspiration, pleasing sound, and refined form. Shortly before his death he brought together most of his handwritten hymns, or poems, under the title *Trutz-Nachtigal oder geistlichs-Poetisch Lust Waldlein.* These were published by one of his former students 14 years after Spee's death and eventually went through a number of editions.

AUTHOR: 32 O Savior, Rend the Heavens Wide

SPEGEL, HAQUIN (1645–1714), was bishop of Skara and later bishop of Linköping prior to being elevated to the archbishopric of Uppsala, Sweden, in 1711. As a hymnist he collaborated with others in the hymnal prepared by Jesper Svedberg.

AUTHOR: 107 The Death of Jesus Christ, Our Lord

SPENGLER, LAZARUS (1479–1534), was born March 13, 1479, at Nürnberg, the ninth of the 21 children of the clerk at the Imperial Court of Justice. After spending two years at the University of Leipzig, the death of his father in 1496 prompted his return to Nürnberg, where he was given a position in the town clerk's office. In 1507 he became town clerk; in 1516 town councillor.

An avid and ardent supporter of the Reformation, he became one of its leaders in the Nürnberg area. As such he was named with Luther (*LW* 13, et al.) and other friends in Pope Leo X's Bull of Excommunication, June 15, 1520. Ignoring the Bull, Spengler was one of the representatives at Luther's appearance at the Diet of Worms in April 1521. After consultation with Luther and Melanchthon (*LW* 189), it was through Spengler's efforts that the Benedictine religious establishment at St. Aegidien was turned into an Evangelical *Gymnasium,* opened as such by Melchanthon in May 1526. It was Spengler who brought about the visitation of the church in the Nürnberg area in 1528, an action that resulted in the publication of a church order (*Kirchenordnung*) in 1532. Moreover, he upheld strict Lutheranism in the negotiations at the Diet of Augsburg in 1530.

Spengler died at Nürnberg, September 7, 1534.

AUTHOR: 363 All Mankind Fell in Adam's Fall

SPERATUS (Latin: HOFFER), PAUL (1484–1551), was born December 13, 1484, in Röthlen near Ellwangen in Württemberg. After spending quite some time at Paris and at various Italian universities studying the humanities, in 1518 he became a preacher at Dinkelsbühl, Bavaria, where he avidly read some of Luther's (*LW* 13, et al.) early works. In the following two years he served as preacher at Würzburg and Salsburg, but in each place he was forced to leave for openly expressing his evangelical views. Shaking the dust from his feet, so he wrote, he married Anna—thus becoming one of the first priests to break the vow of celibacy—and set out for Vienna, where he lived as a private individual and earned his Doctor of Theology degree. A sermon based on

Romans 12:1–5 that he preached on the First Sunday after the Epiphany, January 12, 1522, in which he defended and praised marriage and courageously and joyfully expounded the doctrine of justification by faith—at the very time when Luther's books were being burned in Vienna!—caused the theological faculty of the University of Vienna to brand him as a heretic. Forced to leave Vienna, he spent a brief period in Ofen, where the Reformation had taken root, and from there, invited by the abbot of the Dominican cloister in Iglau, Moravia, he became preacher at the cloister church. King Ludwig, however, summoned him to Olmütz, where in 1523 he was imprisoned on bread and water for 12 weeks, even threatened with death by fire. Finally freed through the good offices of Duke Albrecht of Prussia (*LW* 425) and Queen Maria of Hungary, he went to Wittenberg toward the close of 1523. Here, among other things, he helped Luther prepare the so-called *Achtliederbuch* and translated Luther's *Formula Missae* (1523) into German. On the recommendation of Luther, Speratus became court preacher for Duke Albrecht at Königsberg, East Prussia, in May 1525. In this capacity he drew up the *Kirchenordnung* (containing the liturgy and rules of church governance) for Prussia and he visited the congregations in the province to see that its stipulations were carried out.

In 1530 he assumed the bishop's office in Pomerania with a residence at Marienwerder. In this poverty-stricken area he served with tireless devotion and energy, steadfast in adhering to the evangelical truth until his death August 12, 1551.

AUTHOR: 355 Salvation unto Us Has Come

STAINER, JOHN (1840–1901), was born June 6, 1840, at Southwark, London. A chorister at St. Paul's Cathedral (1848–56), he studied the organ with George Cooper, received the Bachelor of Music degree at Oxford in 1859, and became organist at St. Michael's College Tenbury (1857–59), at Magdalen college, Oxford (1860–72), and at the University College (1861–72). Taking his Bachelor of Arts degree from St. Edmund Hall in 1864 and the Master's in 1866, he was already a Doctor of Music in 1865. In 1872 he went to St. Paul's Cathedral, succeeding John Goss, a position he held until 1888. At the same time he was conductor of the Royal Choral Society (1873–88), professor of organ and later principal of the National Training (now Royal) College of Music (1875–82). In 1888 he was knighted and in the following year elected Heather Professor of Music at Oxford. Durham University had already honored him with the Doctor of Music degree in 1888; Oxford University with the Doctor of Classical Letters in 1895. He retired from the Heather position in 1899, and was made Master of the Musicians Company the following year. He died March 31, 1901, in Verona, while on a trip to Italy.

Stainer wrote over 150 hymn tunes, many anthems, and two cantatas, including the celebrated *Crucifixion* (1887). His text book on organ playing remained a classic for over 50 years. He was closely connected with *Hymns Ancient and Modern*, being appointed to its tunes committee in 1870, and was consultant for other hymnals. He edited the *Church Chant Book* (1891), the *Church Hymnary* (1888), *A Choir Book for the Office of Holy Communion* (1871), and was joint editor of *The Cathedral Prayer*

Book with Music (1891), and (with J. H. Bramley) of *Christmas Carols New and Old* (1871), some harmonies of which even today are still considered standard. In 1879 he published *The Music of the Bible* and did musical research, especially on 15th century music. He did much to improve the standard of repertory and performance in Anglican church music. In the preface to his collected *Hymn Tunes* (1901) he almost apologizes for his hymn tunes, which, in the estimation of Erik Routley, are sometimes beautiful, sometimes "abysmal," sometimes "genially popular" (*The Music of Christian Hymnody*).

COMPOSER: 368 MAGDALEN

STEELE, ANNE (1716–78), was the daughter of William Steele, a timber merchant who was lay preacher of the Baptist Church in Broughton, England. Already as a child she exhibited her poetic gift by writing little poems with which she often entertained her father's visitors. A hip injury she suffered as a child, from which she never fully recovered, plus the great sorrow when her fiancée drowned on the day she was to have been married, weakened her constitution but deepened the note of resignation in her piety. She loved her village home, where she spent her life in works of benevolence until her death in November 1778.

In 1770 she published her *Poems on Subjects chiefly Devotional* in two volumes, under the name of Theodosia. Following her death an additional volume was published containing a preface by Caleb Evans of Bristol Baptist College. These three volumes contain 144 hymns. Julian says of her hymns: "Although few of them can be placed in the first rank of lyrical compositions, they are almost uniformly simple in language, natural and pleasing in imagery, and full of genuine Christian feeling." Routley considers her "the mother not only of English women hymn writers, but also of all those who turn their own sorrow to the profit of the singing congregations" (*Hymns and Human Life*).

AUTHOR: 350 The Savior Calls; Let Every Ear

STEGMANN, JOSUA (1588–1632), was born September 14, 1588, at Sülzfeld, near Meiningen, Germany, the son of a Lutheran pastor. After earning the Master of Arts degree at the University of Leipzig, he became an adjunct of its philosophical faculty. In 1617 he was appointed superintendent of the Schaumburg district, pastor at Stadthagen, and also professor of the *Gymnasium* there. That same year he received the Doctor of Divinity degree from the University of Wittenberg. When, in 1621, the *Gymnasium* at Stadthagen was changed into a university and transferred to Rinteln, Stegmann became professor of theology there. The Thirty Years' War (1618–48) forced him to leave Rinteln in 1623. Returning to Rinteln two years later, he was appointed overseer of the Lutheran clergy of Hesse-Schaumburg. The Edict of Restitution issued by the emperor in 1629 caused him untold woe. Harassed by both Benedictine monks, who now claimed to be rightful professors of the university, and by soldiers, who demanded a refund of his salary— these contributed to his early death August 3, 1632.

AUTHOR: 287 Abide with Us, Our Savior

STEURLEIN (STEUERLEIN), JOHANN (1546–1613), was born July 5, 1546, the son of Caspar Steurlein, the first Lutheran pastor in Smalcald (Schmalkalden), Germany. After completing his study of law in 1569, he was appointed town clerk of Wasungen, between Smalcald and Meiningen, where he encouraged young Melchior Vulpius (*LW* 109, et al.) in his work. In 1589 he became secretary in the chancery at Meiningen, then notary public; and finally mayor of Meiningen (1604), where he died May 5, 1613.

A gifted poet (cf. *TLH* 125), Emperor Rudolph II crowned him as such in recognition of his having rhymed both the Old and New Testaments in German. He was also an excellent musician, as such publishing a number of tunes and harmonizations in *Geistliche Lieder* (1575) and *Sieben und Zwantzigk neue geistliche Gesenge* (1588).

COMPOSER: 493 WIE LIEBLICH IST DER MAIEN

STEVENSON, ISABELLA STEPHANA (1843–90), was born at Cheltanham, Gloucestershire, the daughter of an army officer. Here she spent her entire life. For many years an invalid, her one and only hymn was written under the stress of personal anxiety. She was a devoted member of the Church of England.

AUTHOR: 469 Holy Father, in Your Mercy

STOBÄUS, JOHANN (1580–1646), was born July 6, 1580, in Graudenz, West Prussia, the son of a musician. Having received his early music training from Johann Eccard (*LW* 103), the kapellmeister in Königsberg, Kneiphof, he also attended the university there beginning in 1600, sang bass in the chapel choir, and in 1602 became cantor of the church and the cathedral school. In 1626 he succeeded his teacher Johann Eccard as kapellmeister, where he served until his death September 11, 1646.

Stobäus published *Cantiones Sacrae* (1624) and *Geistliche Lieder auf gewöhnliche Preuss, Kirchenmelodeie*n(1634). With Eccard and Heinrich Albert, Stobäus was considered one of the best north German composers.

COMPOSER: 358 SUCH, WER DA WILL

STOLSHAGEN (STOLSHAGINS), KASPAR (1550–94). Little is known about him other than that he was born in Bernau, near Berlin. In 1574 he became Lutheran pastor in

Stendal, and in 1589 preacher at Iglau, in Moravia, where he died in 1594. He was known also for his poetry and hymns.

AUTHOR: 136 Today in Triumph Christ Arose

STONE, SAMUEL JOHN (1839–1900), was born April 25, 1839, in Whitmore, Staffordshire, England. Educated at the Charterhouse School, he went to Pembroke College, Oxford, where he earned the Bachelor of Arts degree in 1862 and the Master's in 1872. Ordained in the Church of England, he served as curate of Windsor from 1862–70, and of St. Paul's Haggerston from 1870–74, succeeding his father as vicar of Haggerston in 1874. In 1890 he became the rector of All-Hallows-by-the-Wall, London, where he remained until his death November 19, 1900. During his tenure at Windsor, he sided with the conservatives in the cause of biblical orthodoxy which was being challenged by liberals led by John Colenso, the Bishop of Natal. This episode provided Stone the opportunity of writing the hymn below, for which he is best known.

Included in his works are *Lyra Fidelium* (1866); *The Knight of Intercession and Other Poems* (1872); *Sonnets of the Christian Year* (1875), originally published in *The Leisure Hour*; *Order of the Consecutive Church Service for Children, with Original Hymns* (1883); a collection of his original pieces and translations as *Hymns* (1886); and *Iona* (1898). His *Collected Poems and Hymns* was edited posthumously by F. G. Ellerton with a memoir. Stone served on the committee that prepared the 1909 edition of *Hymns Ancient and Modern*.

AUTHOR: 289 The Church's One Foundation

STRODACH, PAUL Z. (1876–1947), was born March 27, 1876, in Norristown, Pennsylvania. Educated at Muhlenberg College, Allentown, Pennsylvania, where he received the Bachelor of Arts degree in 1896 and the Master's in 1899, he entered the Lutheran Theological Seminary, Mt. Airy, Philadelphia, from which he graduated in 1899. Between 1899, the year he was ordained, and 1912 he served congregations in Trenton, New Jersey; Easton and Washington, Pennsylvania; and Canton, Ohio. From 1912–21 he served Grace, Roxborough, Philadelphia, and then was pastor of Holy Trinity, Norristown, Pennsylvania (1921–26); literary editor of Lutheran Publication House, Philadelphia (1926–46); member of the Church Book Committee of the General Council (1913–18), which produced the *Common Service Book* (1917), the official service book of the United Lutheran Church in America; and member of the Joint Commission that prepared the *Service Book and Hymnal* (1958), from its organization in 1945 until his death May 30, 1947, in Easton.

As a liturgical scholar and author, Strodach published *The Church Year* (1924); *The Collect for the Day* (1939); *The Road He Trod* (1932); *Lift Up Your Hearts* (1934); and a number of devotional books including *Oremus: Collects, Devotions, Litanies from*

Ancient and Modern Sources (1925), as well as sermons and a collection of Christmas carols. He was known also for his magnificent illuminations in the medieval style.

AUTHOR: 131 Now All the Vault of Heaven Resounds

STRÖMME, PEER OLSEN (1856–1921), was born September 15, 1856, at Winchester, Wisconsin. After earning the Bachelor of Arts degree at Luther College, Decorah, Iowa, in 1876, and graduating from Concordia Seminary, St. Louis, in 1879, Strömme held pastorates at Mayville, North Dakota; Ada, Minnesota; and Nelson, Wisconsin. He also served as superintendent of schools of Norman County, Minnesota; as teacher at St. Olaf College, Northfield, Minnesota; and principal of Mt. Horeb Academy, Mt. Horeb, Wisconsin. Strömme not only edited various Norwegian newspapers, periodicals, and the *Minnesota Times*, but authored several books, wrote many poems, and translated numerous hymns. He died September 15, 1921.

TRANSLATOR: 100 On My Heart Imprint Your Image
464 A Multitude Comes

SULLIVAN, ARTHUR SEYMOUR (1842–1900), was born May 13, 1842, at Lambeth, London, the son of an Irish musician who became master of the band at the Royal Military College, Sandhurst, and later professor of brass band at Kneller Hall, the Royal Military School of Music. By the time Arthur was eight he could play most band wind instruments. From 1854–57 he was a chorister in the Chapel Royal, under the guidance of Thomas Helmore. He studied at the Royal Academy of Music in London (1856–58) and at the Leipzig Conservatory (1858–61). Before he taught at the National Training School for Music (forerunner of the Royal College of Music), 1876–81, he served as organist of St. Michael's, Chester Square, London (1861–67), and of St. Peter's, Cranley Gardens, South Kensington (1867–72). During 1866, he and George Grove went to Leipzig to discover and study Schubert's manuscripts. In 1867 the success of his first operetta *Cox and Box* turned his attention to the theatre, where he achieved lasting fame as the partner of W. S. Gilbert. His works includes songs, serious operas, operettas, orchestral and choral music, and oratorios. His 56 hymn tunes were written between 1867 and 1874. He was music editor of *Church Hymns* (1874), knighted in 1883, and made a Chevalier of the Legion of Honor. He died in London, on May 13, 1842.

COMPOSER: 515 HEAVEN IS MY HOME
518 ST. GERTRUDE

SVEDBERG, JESPER (1653–1735), the first important hymn writer of Sweden, was born August 28, 1653, near Falun, Sweden, the son of a miner. Educated at Uppsala and

Lund universities and ordained in 1683, he became chaplain of the royal cavalry regiment in Stockholm. Impressed by his work, King Karl XI elevated him to court preacher. In 1609 he became dean and pastor at Vingaker; two years later professor and dean of the cathedral in Uppsala. Commissioned by the king in 1691 to prepare a new hymnbook, Svedberg submitted the book two years later to the archbishop and theological faculty for examination. With but minor revisions the contents was approved and printed in 1694. Within a short time it was condemned by Bishop Carl Carlson as containing "innumerable heresies of a theological, anthropological, Christological, soteriological, and eschatological nature." Revised by a commission appointed by the king, the book was printed in 1695, omitting 75 hymns, mostly those of Svedberg and Haquin Spegel (*LW* 107), and including six new ones. This hymnal remained in use until 1819, when Wallin's *Svenska Psalm-Boken* was issued. Humiliated and disappointed over the rejection of his hymnal, this revision still bore Svedberg's stamp, and the *Psalmbok* of 1937 still included 33 of his hymn texts. In 1703 he was consecrated bishop of Skara, an office he held until his death July 26, 1735. His son was the famous mystic and philosopher, Emmanuel Swedenborg.

AUTHOR: 434 Christians, While on Earth Abiding (st. 1)

SYNESIUS OF CYRENE (c. 365/75–c. 414) was born at Cyrene, near modern Benghazi, of a wealthy and illustrious family. After studying at Alexandria under the Neoplatonist philosopher Hypatia, he devoted himself to philosophy and the life of a country gentleman. When his country was invaded by Libyan nomads, he raised a volunteer army for the defense of Cyrene. In 397 he went to Constantinople to persuade Emperor Arcadius to take steps to meet the danger of the Gothic invasion, but, as Edward Gibbon states, "The court of Arcadius indulged the zeal, applauded the eloquence, and neglected the advice of Synesius" (*Decline and Fall of the Roman Empire*, 1952). On his return he married a Christian and was converted in 401. Though he was consecrated bishop of Ptolemals in 410 in response to the will of the people—an honor that he accepted with much hesitation—there was little of the ecclesiastic in his makeup. He was no ascetic, he adhered to the married state, he loved sport and the open-air life.

It is questioned to what extent he remained a Neoplatonist and how thoroughly he accepted Christian orthodoxy. His 10 odes, written in various classical meters, are, however, of singular beauty, and interesting as expressing Christian devotion seen through the eyes of a Platonist philosopher.

AUTHOR: 231 Lord Jesus, Think on Me

TALLIS, THOMAS (c. 1505–85), has been called "the father of English cathedral music," his life spanning the entire period in English music from Robert Fayrfax (1464–1521) to Orlando Gibbons (*LW* 166, et al.). Born probably in Leicestershire, little is known of his early life until 1532 when he is noted as a "player of organs" at

Dorer Priory. He conducted the choir at St. Mary-at-Hill, London (1537), which moved shortly thereafter to Waltham Abbey, Essex, until the dissolution of monasteries in 1540. Becoming a lay clerk at Canterbury Cathedral and by 1543 a Gentleman of the Chapel Royal at Greenwich, he remained in royal service until his death at Greenwich, Kent, on November 23, 1585. In 1557 Queen Mary granted him a 21-year lease on the manor of Minster, Isle of Thanet, and in 1575 Queen Elizabeth granted Tallis and his pupil William Byrd (c. 1540–1623) a 21-year monopoly on music printing and music paper—though this operation was never financially successful.

About 1560 Archbishop Matthew Parker prepared *The whole Psalter translated into English Metre, which contayneth an hundreth and fifty Psalmes*, the first versification of the entire book of Psalms to be done by one person and probably the first psalter printed by John Day. For this psalter Thomas Tallis provided nine tunes, with the nature of the first eight modes (see essay: The Church Modes, p. 832) described in the *Psalter* as follows:

The first is meeke: devout to see,
The second is sad: in maiestyy,
The third doth rage: and roughly brayth,
The fourth doth fawne: and flattry playth,
The fyfth deligth: and laugheth the more,
The sixth bewayleth: it weepeth full sore,
The seventh tredeth stout: in froward race,
The eighth goeth milde: in modest pace.

His chief glory was in writing choral church music, often of 10 on a grand scale, as demonstrated by his motet *Spem in alium* for eight five-part choirs.

COMPOSER: 254, 470, 484 TALLIS' CANON
348 THIRD MODE MELODY

TATE, NAHUM (1652–1715), was the son of the Rev. Faithful Teate of Dublin. Educated at Trinity College, Dublin, in 1672 he settled in London and became engaged in writing. He published *Poems on Several Occasions* (1677), and as a poet and dramatist wrote with Dryden the second part of *Absalom and Achitophel* (1681). For the theatre he produced largely mangled versions of other men's plays, including some of Shakespeare's. His chief original poem was *Panacea, or a Poem on Tea* (1700). He also published *Characters of Virtue and Vice* (1691). In 1692 he became poet laureate; in 1702 historigrapher-royal. His chief claim to fame is his collaboration with Nicholas Brady in the production of the New Version of the Psalms (1696), popularly called "Tate and Brady" (see essay: Metrical Psalms, p. 825), a book in which it is impossible to distinguish the work of one from the other. In comparison with the ruggedness of the Old Version, the "Tate and Brady" produces an effect of tameness, of spiritless in the extreme. Yet it was used for more than 200 years in the Church of England. In his *Essay on Psalmody* (1710), Tate defended the New Version against all attacks.

Of an intemperate and improvident disposition, Tate died August 12, 1715, within the precincts of Mint, Southwark, where he had sought refuge from his creditors.

AUTHOR: 70 While Shepherds Watched

TAYLOR, R. E. (?–1938). Little is known about him other than, being of Congregational persuasion, he was a hospital missionary in Melbourne, Australia, and an admirer of Martin Luther (*LW* 13, et al.) and his teachings.

TRANSLATOR: 255 My Maker, Now Be Nigh

TAYLOR, THOMAS RAWSON (1807–35), was born May 9, 1807, at Ossett, near Wakefield, England, the son of an English Congregational minister. Apprenticed to a merchant at the age of 15, after a brief time he worked in a print shop, the proprietor of which was a man of great piety, who greatly affected the young man's religious convictions. At the age of 18, Taylor, with the proprietor's consent, left the print shop to study for the Congregational ministry at the Airedale Independent College. Upon the completion of his studies he became pastor of Howard Street Chapel in Sheffield. After serving less than a year, ill health caused him to resign. Having regained his health somewhat, he became classical tutor at the Airedale Independent College, a work he continued until his death of consumption March 7, 1835.

AUTHOR: 515 I'm But a Stranger Here

TERSTEEGEN, GERHARD (1697–1769), was born November 25, 1697, at Mörs (Meurs) in Rhenish, Prussia, the son of a pious merchant of the Reformed faith. As a young student at the *Gymnasium* in Mörs, he became well versed in the ancient languages, including Hebrew. He was to become a pastor of the Reformed Church, but his father's death in 1703 created financial difficulties. Thus in 1713 he served an apprenticeship to his brother-in-law, a merchant in Mühlheim, and after four years he started a business for himself, which in 1719 he gave up for a more quiet trade, namely the weaving of silk ribbons.

After some years of spiritual depression, during which he ceased attending Reformed services because of the irreligious life of some of the church members, Tersteegen began in 1725 to speak at the prayer meetings of Wilhelm Hoffmann. He gave up his career as a silk weaver and began to teach among Quietists. About 1727 a house at Otterbeck, between Mühlheim and Elberfeld, was acquired as a retreat where "awakened souls" could retire under his spiritual direction.

Amidst these various activities Tersteegen found time to translate works of medieval and later mystics and Quietists, to write devotional books and hymns, and to keep up a wide correspondence. He died at Mühlheim, April 3, 1769, the result of a severe case of dropsy.

His works include *Weg der Wahrheit* (1750), a collection of tracts; *Geistliche Brosamen von des Herrn Tischgefallen* (1769–73), 33 addresses delivered between 1753–56; and *Geistliches Blumengärtlein* (Frankfurt und Leipzig, 1729), which, enlarged in successive editions, contained 111 hymns, properly so called. Despite the fact that Tersteegen remained outside the institutionalized church, the hymns in this collection are broad in scope (the Church and sacraments excepted); they live and move in the church year; their poetry repeatedly and directly leads into God's house. Mystic that he was, Tersteegen's speech is straightforward and clear. He ranks with Joachim Neander (*LW* 198) and Friedrich Adolph Lampe as one of the three most important hymn writers of the Reformed Church in Germany.

AUTHOR: 206 God Himself Is Present

TESCHNER, MELCHIOR (1584-1635), was born April 29, 1584, at Fraustadt, Silesia (now Wschowa, Poland). He studied theology, philosophy, and music at Frankfurt-an--der-Oder (1602–05), where Bartholomäus Gesius (*LW* 379, 421) was one of his teachers. In 1605 he became cantor at Schmiegel, and then, after further study at the universities of Helmstedt and Wittenberg, cantor of the Lutheran *Zum Kripplein Christi* Church at Fraustadt (1609–14). Here he worked with Valerius Herberger (1562–1627), who wrote the hymn "Valet will ich dir geben" ("Farewell I Gladly Bid Thee," *TLH* 407) after surviving a plague. For this text Teschner composed two five-part settings which were published in Leipzig in 1615. From 1614 until his death on December 1, 1635, Teschner was pastor of the church at Oberpritschen, near Fraustadt. He is otherwise known as the composer of two wedding songs published respectively at Liegnitz in 1614 and Leipzig in 1619.

COMPOSER: 79, 102 VALET WILL ICH DIR GEBEN

THEODULF OF ORLÉANS (c. 750/60–821). Born in northern Spain of Gothic lineage, Theodulf received a thorough education including not only Christian history and works, but also "heathen" poets like Virgil and Ovid.

Having established a reputation for literary genius, Theodulf was called to the court of Charlemagne at Aachen about 781, who made Theodulf Abbot of Fleury and Bishop of Orléans. He established schools in connection with the monasteries and churches of Orléans and tuition-free schools in poorer towns and villages, run by priests. He also set about reforming the churches of his diocese, imposing strict discipline on the clergy. Because of this, Charlemagne sent him in 798 to tour Gaul as one of the *missi dominici*, inspectors and observers of church life. Theodulf described his experiences with bribery and corruption in a lengthy poem.

Charlemagne died in 814 and was succeeded by Louis the Pious, who imprisoned Theodulf for alleged complicity in a plot to overthrow the throne. Incarcerated in the monastery of St. Aubin at Angers, Theodulf continued to write verse to fill the time. In one poem he charges the muse to visit Theodulf's friend, the bishop of Autun, and to say,

> I am the muse of Theodulf, come from the dungeon of his prison-house, where he is consumed with love for thee. There he lies, an exile, helpless and poor, sad, troubled, and in want, despised and cast down. . . . He reads nothing, he cannot teach, he cannot fulfil his duty of praise to the Lord, the father of all, the king of heaven and earth.

Raby relates: "For Theodulf, his muse was his companion and his consolation. Poetry and art were for him necessities of life."

Theodulf died in 821, probably of poison. Historians differ on the circumstances: some say he was freed shortly before his death, returning to his see; others claim he died in prison.

AUTHOR: 102 All Glory, Laud, and Honor

THILO, VALENTIN (1607–62), was born April 19, 1607, at Königsberg. In 1624 he began the study of theology and rhetoric with Samuel Fuchs at the University of Königsberg. When, in 1632, Fuchs retired, he recommended that Valentin Thilo succeed him as professor of rhetoric. Considering himself too young for that position, at the request of Thilo the position was held open for two years while he continued his studies at the University of Leyden. Returning to Königsberg in 1634 with a Master of Arts degree, he was installed as professor of rhetoric at this outstanding educational institution, later made famous by Immanuel Kant (1724–1804).

In 1643 Thilo married Catharine, widow of Jacob Sahm, judge of Königsberg, who bore him a son Albert and a daughter Maria. While still in their youth, both were stricken with disease and died, a bitter sorrow for their parents.

In his 28 years of teaching, Thilo was elected dean of the philosophical faculty five times; he served twice as the rector of the university. He wrote two books on rhetoric and was held in honor and respect by his grateful students. With his friends Heinrich Albert (1604–51), composer and hymnist, and Simon Dach (*LW* 268, 369), and others, Thilo was a member of the Prussian poetic circle. His hymns appeared mostly in the *Preussische Fest-Lieder* (Elbing, 1642, 1644) and in *Neu Preussischer vollstaendiges Gesangbuch* (Königsberg, 1650). Focusing largely on the festivals of the church year, they were quickly taken over into numerous German hymnals.

Plagued with gout the last years, Thilo died July 27, 1662.

AUTHOR: 25 O People, Rise and Labor

THOMISSÖN, HANS (1532–73), was born in Hygom, Denmark, in 1532, the son of a pastor. Educated at the University of Copenhagen, in 1553 he went to Wittenberg as a tutor for three young noblemen. While there he earned a Master of Arts degree at the University of Wittenberg in 1555. Appointed as rector of the school in Ribe, Denmark, it was his task to rehearse and conduct the student choir that sang at the cathedral. Four years later he was appointed to the faculty at the University of Copenhagen as well as pastor of *Vor Frue Kirke* (Church of Our Lady), Copenhagen. In 1569 Thomissön published *Den danske Psalmebog*, an enlarged and somewhat altered version of Claus Mortensön's *En ny Handbog* (A New Handbook), published in Rostock by L. Dietz in 1529 (*LW* 199). Commanded by the king to be used in all churches, *Den danske Psalmebog* became the standard hymnal in use in Denmark and Norway for the next 130 years. Thomissön died December 22, 1573, in Copenhagen, and was buried at Vor Frue Kirke.

PUBLISHER: 222 OM HIMMERIGES RIGE

THORSON, GERALD (1921–), was born June 8, 1921, in Menomonie, Wisconsin. He holds a Bachelor of Arts degree from Augsburg College (1943), where his studies included English, German, and Greek; a Master of Arts from the University of Minnesota (1948); and a Doctor of Philosophy degree in English and comparative literature from Columbia University (1957). In addition he has pursued studies in linguistics and Scandinavian culture at the University of Wisconsin, French at Grenoble University, and Norwegian literature and history at Oslo University.

Thorson served the United States military from 1943–46, first in the Infantry and then with the Office of the United States Military Government for Bavaria. In 1946 he joined the faculty of Augsburg College, becoming chairman of the English department in 1952 and of the humanities division in 1958. In 1964 Thorson moved to St. Olaf College, Northfield, Minnesota, as chairman of the English department, adding to his duties the chair of the language and literature division in 1973. He has also served as lecturer in English at Wagner College, New York (1951–52); visiting professor of American literature at the University of Iceland (1961–62); and guest professor of American literature at Konstanz University, Germany (1970–71).

He was Minnesota state chairman of the National Council of Teachers of English Achievement Awards Program from 1958–60. The Lutheran Society for Worship, Music, and the Arts enjoyed his services as chairman of the Commission on Literature and Drama (1958–61) and as chairman of its board of publications (1962–65). He has held memberships on the International Board of Moderators of Lambda Iota Tau, a literary honor society (1959–61); the Hymn Text Committee of the Inter-Lutheran Commission on Worship that produced *Lutheran Book of Worship* (1968-77); and the editorial advisory board of the *Journal* of the Society for the Study of Multi-Ethnic Literatures in the United States (1977–84).

Author of articles, poems, reviews, editorials, and essays, for 10 years Thorson was associate editor of *Response* magazine (1960–70). Honors and awards include

George Sverdrup and Torger Thompson fellowships, a Fulbright lectureship, Norwegian Information Service Travel Grant, a Faculty Growth Award from the American Lutheran Church, the Distinguished Alumnus Citation from Augsburg College, and a St. Olaf College Humanities Grant. He retired in 1986, after 40 years of teaching.

TRANSLATOR: 163 O Day Full of Grace
409 From God Can Nothing Move Me

THRELFALL, JEANETTE (1821–80), the daughter of a wine merchant and a gentlewoman whose parents had opposed the marriage, was born March 24, 1821, in Blackburn, Lancashire, England. Orphaned at a young age, she lived with an aunt and uncle in Blackburn and later with their daughter's family in Westminster. Two accidents left her an invalid, but her poetry displays only a spirit of cheerfulness and courage. She died November 30, 1880, at her cousin's home in Westminster.

Of Threlfall's 35 poems, some were published anonymously in periodicals, others were collected in 1856 in a volume titled *Woodsorrel, or, Leaves from a Retired Home*. In 1875, 15 of these verses, together with 55 others, were selected for inclusion in a second collection, *Sunshine and Shadow*.

AUTHOR: 106 Hosanna, Loud Hosanna

THRING, GODFREY (1823–1903), was born March 25, 1823, son of the rector of Alford, Somerset, England. Educated at Shrewsbury and Balliol College, Oxford, he was ordained deacon in 1846, and priest the following year. After serving as curate at Strathfield-Turgis, then at Strathfieldsaye, he succeeded his father at Alford-with-Hornblotton in 1858. Appointed rural dean at Wells Cathedral in 1867, he served there 25 years, becoming prebend of East Harptree in 1876.

In 1893 Thring retired, and 10 years later he died, September 13, 1903, at Guildford. It is said of *A Church of England Hymn Book* (1880), of which he was editor, that it "set a higher literary standard than any other hymn book of its time." He also published *Hymns and Sacred lyrics* in 1874.

AUTHOR: 218 Lord, Dismiss Us with Your Blessing (st. 3)
278 Crown Him with Many Crowns
397 O God of Mercy, God of Light

TISSERAND, JEAN (d. 1494), was a preaching friar of the Minorite order who became rather well-known in Paris. Besides writing several Latin hymns, he founded an order for penitent women and wrote an office and a history in commemoration of members of his order that were martyred in Morocco in 1220.

AUTHOR (attr.): 130 O Sons and Daughters of the King

TOPLADY, AUGUSTUS MONTAGUE (1740–78), was born at Farnham, Surrey, England, on November 4, 1740. His father, Major Richard Toplady, was killed at Carthagena a few months after his son's birth, leaving Augustus to be reared by his mother, who tended to spoil young Augustus, a precocious and somewhat neurotic child. At age 12 he began to preach to anyone who would listen; at age 15 he began to write hymns, which he collected and published as a 19-year-old.

Educated at Westminster School, Toplady helped his mother claim an estate in Ireland, where they moved in time for him to enroll in Trinity College, Dublin. In August of 1756 Toplady attended a revival meeting in a barn, where he heard Wesleyan evangelist James Morris preach. Of the experience he later wrote,

> Strange that I, who had so long sat under the means of grace in England, should be brought near to God in an obscure part of Ireland, amidst a handful of God's people, met together in a barn, and under the ministry of one who could hardly spell his name.

Toplady underwent a spiritual awakening as a result of that meeting, and he decided to enter the ministry. At first he clung to the Armenian theology of the Methodists, and the doctrine of free grace for all. However, upon studying the Thirty-Nine Articles, he found them Calvinistic; much study and reflection caused him to drop the idea of free grace in favor of election theology. He was ordained by the Church of England on June 6, 1762, signing his name to the articles five times to show his ardent agreement.

In this time of hot theological debates, Toplady was bound to disagree with John Wesley and the Methodist point of view. The two men carried on a conflict in pamphlets, letters, and tracts. Toplady recklessly called Wesley "the most rancorous hater of the gospel-system that ever appeared in this island"; Wesley countered by remarking, "I do not fight with chimney-sweepers. . . . I should only foul my fingers." Toplady continued a vituperative "smear campaign" against Wesley until his death; in his final illness he declared that, were he on his deathbed, he "would not strike out a single line" he had written with regard to Wesley.

Toplady, plagued by tuberculosis, never tired of working and ministering. From his first curacy in Blagdon, Somerset, in 1762, he traveled in 1764 to Farley Hungerford. Later he became vicar of three tiny villages in Devonshire, including Broadhembury, where he compiled his *Collection of Psalms and Hymns* of 1776, made up of 419 hymns from various sources. Those of other writers were altered as needed to suit Toplady's purposes; he also included some original hymns. The fact that Toplady chose to use hymns in his services shows that his early Methodism still had some effect on him. During this time Toplady was also editor of the *Gospel Magazine*, in which he produced the idea that our sins are like the national debt (March, 1776).

The chilly, damp climate of Devonshire had an ill effect on Toplady's delicate health, and he tried to find a position in London. Failing that, he nevertheless moved to

London and preached whenever opportunity arose, until some friends were able to get for him the Huguenot chapel in Orange Street, Leicester-fields. Preaching there on Sunday and Wednesday evenings, Toplady led his flock until he became too hoarse to do more than announce his text. Told by his physician that his condition was improving, Toplady disagreed: "No, no; I shall die, for no mortal could endure such manifestations of God's glory as I have, and live." The next day, August 11, 1778, Toplady died while singing one of his own hymns.

Besides his *Psalms and Hymns for Public and Private Worship* (1776), Toplady published *Poems on Sacred Subjects* (1759), *Hymns and Sacred Poems on a variety of Divine Subjects* (1860), and a *Historic Proof of the Doctrinal Calvinism of the Church of England* (1774). The latter followed a pamphlet printed in 1769, *The Church of England vindicated from the charge of Armenianism.*

At his own request, Toplady was buried beneath the gallery of Tottenham Court Chapel, which was frequently a gathering place for the Wesleyans.

AUTHOR: 361 Rock of Ages, Cleft for Me

TRANOVSKÝ, JIRI (JURAJ) (1591–1637), was born April 19, 1591, in a village near Tesin in Silesia, of Polish descent. After studying at Kolberg (1605–07), he proceeded to Wittenberg University, where he was already writing poetry in Czech and Latin. Going to Bohemia in 1612, which at the time was united with Silesia and which afforded Lutherans the freedom to worship, he accepted a teaching position at the *Gymnasium* near St. Michael (*Sv. Mikulás*) Church in Prague. He held two other teaching positions and was married to Anna Polani prior to 1616, when he was ordained and began serving a Lutheran congregation in Medziriecie. With the accession of Ferdinand II of Bohemia, toleration of Lutherans came to an end. Tranovský and his congregation suffered the horrors of the Thirty Years' War (1618–48), with famine and pestilence taking the lives of thousands of people, including three of his children. He himself was imprisoned for a time in 1624. Exiled in 1625, he returned to his native Silesia, where he became court preacher to the castle in Bielsko. The occupation of upper Silesia forced him to leave again, and he became court preacher to Orava Castle in 1628. Waning health prompted him to gather, arrange, and complete his Latin hymns, resulting in the publication of his *Odarum Sacrarum* (1629), which contained 150 Latin texts for congregational singing together with several tunes of his making. In 1631 he became senior pastor at *Sväty Mikulás*. Here he produced his two greatest works, The *Phiala Ordoramentorum* and the *Pisne duchovni stare i move . . . cili Cithara Sanctorum* (1636), popularly known by Slovak Lutherans as the "Tranoscius." He died May 29, 1637.

AUTHOR: 132 Make Songs of Joy

TUCKER, FRANCIS BLAND (1895–1984), a collateral descendant of George Washington, was the youngest of 13 children born to a "family of clergymen"; his father, Beverly D. Tucker, was bishop of Southern Virginia, two brothers became bishops of the Episcopal Church, and several nephews went on to become clergymen. Born January 6, 1895, in Norfolk, Virginia, Francis was educated at Lynchburg High School and the University of Virginia (B.A. 1914), going on to Virginia Theological Seminary. Ordained a deacon in 1918, he was with the American Expeditionary Forces in France in World War I, returning to complete his third year at the seminary and attaining the Master of Divinity degree in 1920.

He served rectorships at St. Andrew's Church in Lawrenceville, Virginia (1920–25) and St. John's in Georgetown, Washington, D.C. (1925–45) before arriving in Savannah, Georgia. Here he served 22 years as rector of Christ Church. In 1944 he was granted a doctorate of divinity by Virginia Theological Seminary, and in 1945 was elected bishop of the Diocese of Western North Carolina, but he declined the post, saying that his ministry in Savannah was not yet completed.

Tucker was the only person to have served on both the committee for *The Hymnal 1940* and that for its successor, *The Hymnal 1982*, as well as being a contributor to both. He was very active as well in civic affairs, including a study of the federal food surplus/food stamp programs in 1961, the board of the Family Service Agency (now the Department of Family and Children Services), and civil rights activities in the 1960s. He belonged to a number of patriotic organizations such as the Society of Colonial Wars and the Sons of Confederate Veterans.

Tucker died January 1, 1984, five days before his 89th birthday. His wife, Mary Laird Tucker, preceded him in death by 11 years. An obituary in the *Savannah Morning News*, January 4, 1984, states:

> He was a leader in so many ways—in Savannah, in the Diocese of Georgia, in the national church; but mainly, he was a leader in reconciling sinners with God. If only that could be said of every one of God's people, Peace would reign on Earth.

AUTHOR: 465 Our Father, by Whose Name

VAJDA, JAROSLAV JOHN (1919–), the son of a Lutheran pastor, was born April 28, 1919, in Lorain, Ohio, but grew up in Emporia, Virginia; Milwaukee, Wisconsin; and East Chicago, Indiana. Following his graduation in 1938 from Concordia Junior College, Fort Wayne, Indiana, he entered Concordia Seminary, St. Louis, Missouri, in 1939, after working in the Indiana Harbor Steel mills to earn tuition money. He vicared at Sts. Peter and Paul Lutheran Church in Central City, Pennsylvania (1942–43), and graduated from the seminary with the Bachelor of Arts and Master of Divinity degrees in 1944. His first call was to Holy Trinity Lutheran Church, Cranesville, Pennsylvania (a bilingual, Slovak and English parish), where he ministered from 1945–49. From 1949–53 he served Our Blessed Savior Lutheran Church in Alexandria, Indiana. In 1953 he moved to Tarentum, Pennsylvania, where he supervised a relocation and building of a church in Brackenridge, Pennsylvania, concluding his ministry at St. John's Lutheran

Church (also bilingual) in 1963. From 1959–63, he was also editor of *The Lutheran Beacon* of the Synod of Evangelical Lutheran Churches. In 1963 he went to St. Louis, Missouri, where he became editor of *This Day* magazine, a monthly family religious publication. From 1971, when *This Day* ceased publication, to 1986 he was book editor and developer for Concordia Publishing House. Married to Louise Mastaglio of Milwaukee, Wisconsin, in 1945, he is the father of three children.

Vajda, whose original and translated hymns and poems have appeared in print in the United States and abroad, began writing poetry at the age of 18, and three years later made his translation of the 32-sonnet sequence "A Song of Blood" of Slovakia's greatest poet Hviezdoslav. His Bachelor of Divinity thesis, "A History of the *Cithara Sanctorum* by Juraj Tranovsky," was written in 1944. His interest in poetry, hymnody, and music provided background for his work on the Commission on Worship of The Lutheran Church—Missouri Synod (1960–78) and on the Inter-Lutheran Commission on Worship (1967–78), working particularly with hymn texts. Among his translations are *Bloody Sonnets* (1950); *Slovak Christmas* (1960); *Janko Kral* (1972); *An Anthology of Slovak Literature* (1977), as well as a number of hymns and translations in the *Worship Supplement* (1969) to *The Lutheran Hymnal* (1941), and in the *Lutheran Book of Worship* (1978). *Now the Joyful Celebration*, a collection of original hymns, carols, songs, and translations, was published in 1987; its sequel appeared in 1991. "Now the Silence" (*LBW* 205) has appeared in six major American and Canadian hymnals and has been translated into Welsh and Slovak. In 1991 he published *Something to Sing About*, a study of hymns and worship.

In 1987 Concordia College, Seward, Nebraska, honored him with a Doctor of Letters degree; in 1988 he was named a fellow of the Hymn Society of America; and in May 1990, Concordia College, St. Paul, Minnesota, also honored him with a Doctor of Letters degree.

AUTHOR:	152	Up Through Endless Ranks of Angels
	273	Amid the World's Bleak Wilderness
TRANSLATOR:	132	Make Songs of Joy
	183	Greet Now the Swiftly Changing Year
	420	If You But Trust in God to Guide You (contributor)

VAUGHAN WILLIAMS, RALPH (1872–1958), probably the most significant English composer of the 20th century, was born October 12, 1872, at Down Ampney, Gloucestershire, where his father was vicar. He was educated at Charter House, the Royal College of music, and Trinity College, Cambridge (1892–95). Returning to Royal College of Music, London, he studied with Charles Stanford (1852–1924), Charles Hubert Parry (1848–1918), and Charles Wood (1866-1926) and became a close friend of Gustav Holst (*LW* 135). He was organist of St. Barnabas, South Lambeth (1895–98), extension lecturer for Oxford University, and professor of composition at the Royal College of Music from 1920. At the outbreak of World War I in 1914 he joined the Royal Army as a private, later receiving a commission in the artillery.

His works include nine symphonies, rhapsodies, fantasias, suites, concertos, string quartets, songs, stage music, opera and film. His choral-orchestral works of large dimension, for example, *The Magnificat* (1932), and the *Dona Nobis Pacem* (1936), have enjoyed considerable popularity and are perhaps numbered among his most notable achievements. Not to be overlooked, however, is his interest in collecting and editing for publication English folk songs and carols, many of which he adapted as hymn tunes. These, as well as his interest in Old English music from the Tudor period to Henry Purcell (1658–1695), greatly influenced his own compositions. His gift of melodic invention coupled with a noble style mark his works, as a whole, with laudable originality and striking beauty.

In 1919 Oxford University awarded him the honorary degree of Doctor of Music; in 1951 the University of Bristol did likewise. He was music editor of *The English Hymnal* (1906), a noteworthy collection of the best hymns in the English language up to that time, and, with Martin Shaw (1875–1958), editor of *Songs of Praise* (1926) and *The Oxford Book of Carols* (1928).

He died at St. Marylebone, London, August 26, 1958.

COMPOSER:	59	FOREST GREEN
	125, 148, 159	SALVE FESTA DIES
	162	DOWN AMPNEY
	178	KING'S WESTON
	191	SINE NOMINE
	193, 194	KING'S LYNN
	383	MONKS GATE
ARRANGER:	64	CRADLE SONG
	65	SUSSEX CAROL
	76	TRUTH FROM ABOVE
	131, 149, 308, 436, 440	LASST UNS ERFREUEN
	492	AR HYD Y NOS

VETTER, DANIEL (d. c. 1721), was born in Breslau, Germany, and studied under organist and composer Werner Fabricius, whom he succeeded in 1679 as organist at St. Nicholas Church in Leipzig. In his biography of J. S. Bach, Philip Spitta, describing the state of music in Leipzig just before Bach went there as cantor, sheds a little light on Vetter by stating:

> There was no remarkable musician there at that time; the only one, besides Kuhnau, who had done anything important in his own branch of art, was Daniel Vetter . . . as organist to the church of St. Nicholas.

Vetter is remembered for his organ and klavier hymn accompaniment in Italian tablature notation, *Musicalische Kirchen- und Haus-Ergötzlichkeit, bestehend in den gewöhnlichen geistlichen Liedern, so durch's gantze Jahre beim öffentlichen*

Gottesdienst gesungen werden, Erster Theil (Leipzig, 1695); Zweiter Theil (Leipzig, 1713).

COMPOSER: 188 DAS WALT GOTT VATER

VETTER (STREJC), GEORG (1536–99), was born at Zabreh, Moravia. Educated at the Universities of Königsberg and Tübingen, he was ordained a priest by the United Brethren in 1567, thereafter serving a congregation at Weisswasser in Moravia. In 1575 he became pastor of a congregation at Weisskirchen, where, due to his excessive authoritarianism, he remained only five years. In 1590 he moved to Gross-Seelowitz, where he served until his death January 25, 1599.

In addition to the six hymns of his included in his *Kirchengeseng darinnen die Heubtartickel des Christlichen Glaubens gefasset* (1566), Vetter prepared in 1587 a Czech version of the Calvinist psalms with Claude Goudimel's (*LW* 377, 486) settings. Vetter played a significant role in producing the Kralice Bible translation, a work of great import comparable to Luther's (*LW* 13, et al.) German Bible.

AUTHOR: 134 With High Delight Let Us Unite

VOSS, ARTHUR PAUL (1899–1955), was born May 19, 1899, at Bay City, Michigan. In 1905 he was brought to Milwaukee with his parents, his father having accepted the call to Grace Lutheran Church as teacher. Educated at Concordia College, Milwaukee, he thereafter entered the Lutheran Theological Seminary at Wauwatosa, Wisconsin, an institution of the Joint Synod of Wisconsin and Other States. His first and only pastorate was at St. James Lutheran Church, Milwaukee, a newly organized congregation, in which he served for 33 years.

In 1954 he accepted the call to be professor at the Theological Seminary in Thiensville, where he taught church history, symbolics, and homiletics. Additional service to the synod included: chairman of the Board of Trustees; president of the Southeast Wisconsin District; member of the Intersynodical Committee on Hymnology and Liturgics that prepared *The Lutheran Hymnal* (1941); and representative on the Intersynodical Relations Committee of the Synodical Conference. He was also for many years an associate editor of *The Northwestern Lutheran.*

Voss died October 19, 1955, of a heart attack while attending a meeting of the General Synodical Committee.

TRANSLATOR: 358 Seek Where You May to Find a Way

VULPIUS, MELCHIOR (c. 1560/70–1615), was born at Wasungen, near Meiningen, Thuringia, about 1560. He taught Latin at the school in Schleusingen, where he became cantor and known as a composer. From 1596 until his death on August 7, 1615, he was cantor at Weimar. One of his first publications was the *Kirchengeseng und geistliche Lieder Dr. M. Luthers* (Leipzig, 1604), of which the second enlarged edition bore the title *Ein schön geistlich Gesangbuch* (Jena, 1609). Even more distinguished than some of the original chorale tunes contained in the latter work were the contrapuntal settings that were published in his *Cantiones Sacrae* (1602 and 1604). In 1610 he published a German translation, with additions, of Heinrich Faber's *Musicae Compendium*. Several years later he composed a setting of the Passion according to St. Matthew. Following his death, other hymns of his were published in the *Kantional* (Gotha, 1646), a type of hymnbook containing four-part homophonic settings of both traditional and new chorale tunes, in which the melody was placed in the soprano, in contrast to the procedure in the previous century when the melody of the chorale motets resided in the tenor.

Vulpius is one of the most inventive and significant composers of the 16th century, especially because of his nearly 200 motets and about 400 hymns.

COMPOSER:	109	JESUS KREUZ, LEIDEN UND PEIN
	129	GELOBT SEI GOTT
	267, 287	CHRISTUS DER IST MEIN LEBEN
	352	DIE HELLE SONN LEUCHT
	452	LOBT GOTT DEN HERREN, IHR

WADE, JOHN FRANCIS (c. 1710/11–86), was an English Roman Catholic layman who devoted most of his life copying and selling manuscripts of plainsong and other early music plus teaching Latin and church song. These activities were carried on at Douai, in Northern France, a place of refuge for those loyal to the Roman Catholic faith who fled England after the abdication of James II. Here was also located an English college. He died August 16, 1786, at Douai. A volume of his collected manuscripts (1751) is preserved at Stonyhurst College, near Blackburn, Lancashire.

AUTHOR:	41	Oh, Come, All Ye Faithful
COMPOSER:	41	ADESTE FIDELES

WALDER, JOHANN JAKOB (1750–1817), was born January 11, 1750, at Wetzikon in the canton of Zurich, where his pastor taught him to love music and where he later studied composition. By the age of 25 his melodies began to appear in various collections. In 1785 he turned to politics, and in succeeding years he served in various government positions. He died March 18, 1817.

COMPOSER:	332	WALDER

WALKER, WILLIAM (1809–75), was born May 6, 1809, near Cross Keys, South Carolina, the son of Welsh immigrants. At the age of 18 his family moved to Cedar Spring near Spartanburg. After a period of rudimentary schooling, he became a member of a Welsh-Baptist church and began to teach in singing schools. Known as "Singin Billy" Walker—to distinguish him from two other men in Spartanburg with the same name—he pursued this career the rest of his life in the Carolinas, Georgia, Tennessee, while also collecting and organizing folk songs, many of Welsh, Scotch, Irish, and English origins. Associated with his brother-in-law Benjamin Franklin White (they were married to the Golightly sisters Amy and Thurza), evidence indicates that the two prepared a collection of hymns, in four-shape notation with symbols for mi, fa, sol, la, entitled *Southern Harmony*, but only Walker's name appeared on the title page when it came out in 1835, after which time he always signed his name "William Walker, A. S. H." (Author of *Southern Harmony*). The resultant rift between the two prompted White to move to Harris County, Georgia, where, in 1844, he published *The Sacred Harp*, which contained some of the same material as *Southern Harmony*. Both became immensely popular in the rural South, for they contained hymns that had been perpetuated for generations. In 1845 Walker published the *Southern and Western Pocket Harmonist*, also in four-shape notation. *The Christian Harmony* appeared in 1867 and *Fruits and Flowers* in 1873, both in seven-shape notation with a distinctive pattern for each note of the scale. It is said that *Southern Harmony* and *The Christian Harmony* are still used in western Kentucky.

William Walker died in Spartanburg September 24, 1875.

COMPOSER/ARRANGER: 22 JEFFERSON

WALLIN, JOHAN OLOF (1779–1836), was born at Stora Tuna, Dalarna province, Sweden, October 15, 1779, the son of a sergeant major in the Dalarna regiment. Despite poverty and poor health, he studied at the University of Uppsala, where he earned the Doctor of Philosophy degree at the age of 24. Ordained in 1806, he served a number of parishes, becoming a gifted and effective preacher, a college lecturer in 1807, a bishop in 1824, and archbishop of Sweden in 1837. He died June 30, 1839, in Uppsala.

Wallin is Sweden's greatest sacred poet, holding the place in Swedish hymnody similar to that held by Isaac Watts in English hymnody. In 1809 he became a member of the committee appointed by the Swedish parliament to prepare a new hymnal to replace the one in use since 1695. Prepared in haste over a period of approximately three years, the book met with severe criticism. Asked to revise the book, Wallin labored to see the book appear in 1819 with the title *Den Svenska Psalmboken*, a book officially authorized by King Karl XIV. Of a total of 500 hymns, 128 were originals by Wallin, 23 his translations, and no less than 178 were revisions by him. His famous Christmas hymn, "All hail to you, O blessed morn" (*LBW* 73), is sung at dawn on Christmas Day in almost every church in Sweden. This *Psalmboken* was a hymnal that remained in use for over a 100 years, with only an appendix added in 1920. When, in 1937, the

Psalmbok finally supplanted it, over a third of its 600 hymns were originals, translations, or revisions by Wallin.

AUTHOR: 199 We Worship You, O God of Might
434 Christians, While on Earth Abiding (st. 1)

WALTER (WALTHER), JOHANN (1496–1570), was born at Kahla in Thuringia. A choirboy during or after his school days in Kahla and Rochlitz, while at Leipzig University, between 1521–25, he was a bass in the *Hofkapelle* of Friedrich the Wise, Elector of Saxony. In 1526 he became cantor of a school in Torgau, where his task was to instruct the boys in music and organize the singing in the parish church. After the Smalcald War (1547) and the subsequent transfer of the electoral title, Walter's allegiance to the Elector Moritz of Saxony took him from Torgau to Dresden to direct the *Hofkapelle* from 1548 until he was pensioned in 1554. Shortly thereafter, he returned to Torgau, where he died March 25, 1570.

Walter's importance for music history rests on a number of activities. In 1524 his *Geystliches gesangk Buchleyn* was published, the first Lutheran collection of choral music, with a preface written by Martin Luther. The book's success is attested by its numerous editions and continuations. His work paved the way for succeeding generations. Moreover, in 1525 (with his colleague Conrad Rupsch) Walter spent three weeks in Luther's home advising and assisting him in adapting the old music and preparing the music for the *Deutsche Messe* (German Mass) to be published and distributed. In addition Walter assisted the cause of the Reformation in organizing church music for several towns in Saxony, a work that had its effects far beyond its borders. Walter's hymns, most of which appeared in *Das Christlich Kinderlied D. Martini Lutheri* (Wittenberg, 1566), contributed little to congregational song, for they were perhaps sung mainly in daily school prayers.

Walter remained a strict supporter of the Lutheran cause, a fact reflected in his letters from Dresden and in some of his late works from Torgau.

AUTHOR: 176 The Bridegroom Soon Will Call Us
COMPOSER: 265 MITTEN WIR IM LEBEN SIND

WALTER, WILLIAM HENRY (1825–1923), was born in Newark, New Jersey, and already as a boy was organist at a Presbyterian church and Grace Episcopal Church of the same city. After studying with Edward Hodges—English organist renowned for his playing technique and organ mechanical skills, an artist who lived for a time in the New York area—Walter became organist successively at St. John's Chapel, St. Paul's Chapel, and Trinity Chapel in New York City, remaining in the last position until 1869. In 1865, a year after honoring him with a Doctor of Music degree, Columbia University appointed him their organist.

As a composer of anthems, hymn tunes, and service music, his published works include *Chorals and Hymns* (1857), a *Manual of Church Music* (1860), and *The Common Prayer with Ritual Song* (1868).

He died in 1893 in New York City.

COMPOSER: 195 FESTAL SONG

WALTHER, CARL FERDINAND WILHELM (1811–87), was born October 25, 1811, in Langenschursdorf, Saxony. Of a long line of Lutheran pastors, Walther received his early schooling in his home village and in Hohenstein. After graduating from the *Gymnasium* at Schneeberg in 1829, he began the study of theology at the University of Leipzig. Following his graduation in 1833, he served for a time as a private tutor. In 1837 he was ordained and installed as pastor of the Lutheran congregation at Bräunsdorf, Saxony. Perplexed by the opposition of the church authorities and the rationalistic stance of the church in Saxony, he left his charge after one year to emigrate to America with 750 confessional Lutherans of the area, under the leadership of Pastor Martin Stephan, arriving in St. Louis in February 1839. His first charges in Perry County, Missouri, were at Dresden and Johannesberg. In the spiritual and economic turmoil of those early years he emerged as a sound theological and spiritual leader. In 1841 he succeeded his deceased brother as pastor of Trinity Lutheran Church, in the Soulard district of St. Louis. Here he developed a strong pastoral and preaching ministry.

Walther was instrumental in establishing a publishing concern (later to become Concordia Publishing House); he founded *Der Lutheraner* and edited *Lehre und Wehre*, two publications that gave a strong, confessional impetus to American Lutheranism. He helped organize and became the first president of the Evangelical Lutheran Synod of Missouri, Ohio, and Other States in 1847, serving in that capacity from 1847–50 and again from 1864–78. When the log cabin college in Perry County was moved to St. Louis as Concordia Seminary, he became its permanent professor of theology, serving also as its president until his death in 1887. The free conferences with other Lutherans that Walther proposed in the hope of uniting all biblical and confessional-minded Lutherans resulted in the establishment of the Evangelical Lutheran Synodical Conference in 1872, with Walther as its first president for two years.

An accomplished pianist and organist, Walther wrote a number of songs and hymns. Moreover, in his concern for orthodox hymnody credit must be given him for the publication in 1847 of the first hymnal for the Saxon immigrants, the *Kirchengesangbuch für Evangelisch-Lutherische Gemeinden ungeänderter Augsburgischer Confession*, containing 437 hymns. The recapture of the rhythmic form of the chorale also owes much to his interest and influence. He died May 7, 1887.

AUTHOR: 138 He's Risen, He's Risen
COMPOSER: 138 WALTHER

WALWORTH, CLARENCE AUGUSTUS (1820–1900), was born in Plattsburg, New York, May 30, 1820. After graduating from Union College, Albany, he was admitted to the bar in 1841. Originally a Presbyterian, he studied briefly at the General Theological Seminary, New York, with the intent of ordination by the Protestant Episcopal Church but his interest in the Oxford Movement led him to join the Roman Catholic Redemptorist Order. After a period of study in Belgium and at Witten, Holland, he was ordained to the priesthood taking the name Clarence Alphonsus. Returning to the United States to do mission work, he became one of the founders of the Order of Paulists, of which he was a member until going to St. Peter's Church, Troy, New York, to serve as priest. His last 34 years were spent as rector of St. Mary's, Albany, the last 10 years of which he was stricken with blindness. He died September 19, 1900.

He published *The Gentle Sceptic* (1863); *The Oxford Movement in America* (1895); and *Andiatorocte of the Eve of Lady Day and Other Poems* (1888), as well as being vocal against the evils of the expanding industrial complex and the music of political power.

TRANSLATOR: 171 Holy God, We Praise Your Name

WARREN, GEORGE WILLIAM (1828–1902), was born August 17, 1828, in Albany, New York. Educated at Racine College in Wisconsin, and a self-taught musician, he served 12 years as organist at St. Peter's Church, Albany; two years at St. Paul's, Albany; and 10 years at Holy Trinity Church, Brooklyn. From 1870–1900 he was organist at St. Thomas' Church, New York City. In addition to composing a number of hymn tunes that were included in his *Hymns and Tunes as Sung at St. Thomas' Church* (1888), he also composed a number of services and anthems. He alma mater honored him with a Doctor of Music degree. He died March 17, 1902, in New York.

COMPOSER: 501 NATIONAL HYMN

WATTS, ISSAC (1674-1748), was born July 17, 1674, at Southampton, the son of a Nonconformist deacon, a clothier by trade, who was twice imprisoned for his beliefs. Young Issac learned Greek, Latin, and Hebrew under John Pinhorn, rector of All Saints' and master of the Free-School at Southampton. Instead of accepting the offer to enter one of the universities with a view to ordination by the Church of England, in 1690 he entered an Independent, or Nonconformist, academy at Stoke Newington, the high educational standards of which left a permanent mark on his mind. The "academies," which paralleled the English universities, arose because the Church of England refused Nonconformists admission to the established universities. In 1694, after completing his academy studies, he returned home. There he spent the next two years writing the bulk of his *Hymns and Spiritual Songs* (1707–09) in response to a challenge by his father to improve the standard of praise, hitherto restricted to metrical psalmody, much of poor quality, about which Watts had complained. For the next six years he was tutor in the family of an eminent Puritan, Sir John Hartopp. In 1699 he was chosen assistant minister of the distinguished Independent congregation in Mark Lane, London, and in 1702 he was ordained and became its pastor. Under his leadership the congregation grew to the point that Samuel Price was appointed his assistant and later his copastor. Intensive study and work caused Watts' health to fail and from 1712 until his death, 36 years later, he lived a quiet life of a semi-invalid as the guest of Sir Thomas Abney, alderman and one-time Lord Mayor of London, devoting his efforts to the production of theological and philosophical works as well as hymns. His *Improvement Of The Mind* was praised by Samuel Johnson (1709-84), an outstanding figure of English life and letters; his *Logic* served as a standard university textbook for a 100 years. In 1728 the University of Edinburgh honored him with a Doctor of Divinity degree. He died November 25, 1748, at the Abney home in Stoke Newington and was buried in Bunhill Fields, the Puritan cemetery. In 1779 a monument was erected to him in Westminster Abbey.

The influence of Calvinism caused English congregational song to be limited to metrical psalmody, namely, versified psalms that remain close to the biblical text (see essay: Metrical Psalms, p. 825). It was against the dullness and crudity of expression and the total lack of New Testament Gospel in such metrical psalmody that Watts protested. Thus he is generally regarded as the father of English hymnody. His hymns, about 600 in number, were mostly published in his *Horae Lyricae* (1705), *Hymns and Spiritual Songs* (1707), *The Psalms of David Imitated in the Language of the New Testament and apply'd to the Christian State and Worship* (1719), and *Divine Songs attempted in Easy Language, for the Use of Children* (1715), a pioneer hymnal for children. Although not the first English hymn-writer, credit must be given Watts for bringing about the change from psalmody to hymnody in the English Church. Moreover, his hymns contributed greatly to make hymn singing a powerful devotional force, especially in Nonconformist circles, where hitherto the use of music in worship, except for metrical psalmody, had been regarded with suspicion.

AUTHOR:
53 Joy to the World
97 Alas! and Did My Savior Bleed
99 Not All the Blood of Beasts
114, 115 When I Survey the Wondrous Cross
180 Our God, Our Help in Ages Past
200 This Is the Day the Lord Has Made
204 Come, Let Us Join Our Cheerful Songs
312 Jesus Shall Reign
388 The Man Is Ever Blessed
392 Oh, that the Lord Would Guide My Ways
440 From All That Dwell Below the Skies
441 We Sing the Almighty Power of God
454 Before Jehovah's Awesome Throne
457 Oh, Bless the Lord, My Soul
472 Let Children Hear the Mighty Deeds
474 How Shall the Young Secure Their Hearts

WEBB, BENJAMIN (1819–85), was born November 28, 1819, in London. Educated at St. Paul's School, he thereafter attended Trinity College, Cambridge, (Bachelor of Arts degree in 1842; Master's in 1845). Ordained by the Church of England in 1843, he was assistant curate of Keneston, Gloucestershire (1843–44); of Christ Church, St. Pancras (1847–49); and of Bransted, Kent (1849–51). He served as perpetual curate of Sheen, Staffordshire, from 1851–62, and vicar of St. Andrew's, Wells Street, London, from 1862 until his death, November 27, 1885, at St. Marylebone, London.

Webb, with his friend John Mason Neale (*LW* 31, et al.), was one of the founders of the Cambridge Ecclesiological Society; he edited the *Ecclesiologist* (1842–68) as well as being general editor of the Society's publications. He wrote and edited numerous books on theological and ecclesiological subjects, notably *Continental Ecclesiology* (1847); he collaborated with Neale in *An Essay on Symbolism* and *A Translation of Durandus*, scholastic philosopher and theologian (c. 1270–1322). He was one of the original editors of Neale's *The Hymnal Noted* (1852), translating some hymns for it; he was coeditor with Canon W. Cooke of *The Hymnary* (1872), to which he contributed some original hymns.

TRANSLATOR: 275 Oh, Love, How Deep

WEBB, GEORGE JAMES (1803–87), was born June 24, 1803, at Rushmore Lodge, near Salisbury, England, the son of a prosperous farmer. After serving for a time as organist of a church in Falmouth, in 1830 he emigrated to Boston, Massachusetts, where he became, and remained for 40 years, organist of Old South Church. With Lowell Mason (*LW* 115, et al.) he was a founder of the Boston Academy of Music in 1833, where both taught, Webb being in charge of secular music studies. He became famous as a choral conductor and orchestral teacher, and was president of the Boston Handel and Haydn Society from 1840–43. He published a number of song books, both secular and sacred, including: *The Odeon* (1807) with Mason; *The Massachusetts Collection of Psalmody* (1840); *The American Glee Book* (1841); *The Psaltery* (1845); and, with Mason, *The New Odeon*, *The National Psalmist* (1848). He served as editor of *The Music Library* (1835–36) and of *The Musical Cabinet* (1837–40).

Already in 1835 he became a Swedenborgian, joining the Church of New Jerusalem. As such he edited that church's liturgical service book (1836) as well as its revisions of 1854 and 1876; he wrote a book on *Vocal Technics* and collaborated in another on *Voice Culture*.

In 1870 he followed Mason to New York City and took up residence in Orange, New Jersey. From 1876–85, when living in New York, he resumed his teaching. Retiring to Orange, New Jersey, in 1885, he died there October 7, 1887.

COMPOSER: 305 WEBB

WEBBE, SAMUEL, JR. (1768–1843), was born in London on October 15, 1768. He studied music with his father and later with composer Muzio Clementi. Organist at Paradise Street Unitarian Church in Liverpool in 1798, he later returned to London to teach music, and when his father died in 1816, he succeeded him as organist for the Spanish Embassy Chapel. Finally, moving back to Liverpool, he served there in the Roman Catholic churches of St. Nicholas (1818) and St. Patrick (1819). In 1808 he published a *Collection of Psalm Tunes* for four voices; his other publications include *Convito Armonica*, selections from several composers, and several books of vocal music exercises. He collaborated with his father on the *Collection of Motetts and Antiphons* in 1792. Samuel Webbe, Jr., died in Hammersmith, Middlesex, on November 25, 1843.

COMPILER/REVISER: 29 CHESTERFIELD

WEGELIN, JOSUA (1604–40), was born January 11, 1604, in Augsburg. After attending the University of Tübingen, where he received the Master of Arts degree in 1626, he was for a time pastor at Budweiler before being appointed fourth deacon of the Franciscan church at Augsburg. The Edict of Restitution, enacted by Emperor Ferdinand III, forced him and other Lutheran pastors to leave Augsburg. This edict was instigated by the Benedictine monks, who, after settling in Rinteln in 1630, claimed to be the rightful professors and demanded that the old church lands be restored to them, especially the property previously belonging to the nunnery at Rinteln, property which had been designated for the support of the Lutheran professors. In 1632 Wegelin was recalled to be archdeacon of the Franciscan church in Augsburg, when Gustavus Adolphus (1594–1632), Swedish king, took over the city in the Thirty Years' War (1618–48). The following year he was appointed preacher at the Hospital Church of the Holy Spirit. In 1635 the war forced him again to flee, and he found refuge in Pressburg, Hungary, where he held office as pastor. He died there September 14, 1640.

AUTHOR: 150 On Christ's Ascension I Now Build

WEINGÄRTNER, SIGISMUND (17th century) is generally identified as a preacher in or near Heilbronn on the Neckar River. Others suggest he may have lived in or near the cloister of Heilbronn in Franconia. Two hymns are credited to him in the *Geistliche Psalmen*, a hymnal containing 766 psalms (actually psalm paraphrases), published in Nürnberg and Wittenberg in 1607, one of which was "Auf meinen lieben Gott."

AUTHOR (attr.): 421 In God, My Faithful God

WEISSE, MICHAEL (c. 1480–1534), was born in Neisse, Silesia. He entered Kracow University in 1504, became a priest, and thereafter a monk in Breslau. Moved by

Luther's writings, in 1518 he left the monastery with two other monks and joined the Bohemian Brethren (*Unitas Fratrum*), becoming the preacher of the German Brethren at Landskron, Bohemia and Fulness, Moravia. On two occasions, in 1522 and 1525, he, along with Johann Horn (*LW* 30, 141), was sent to visit Luther to explain to him the theology of the Bohemian Brethren. The Brethren commissioned Weisse to provide a hymnal for the German Bohemian Brethren, which in 1531 appeared, entitled *Ein Neugesängbuchleyn*. It contained 16 Czech and four Latin hymns in translation, plus 137 hymns from his own hand. The influence of this work on Lutheran hymnody is evidenced by the fact that no less than three-quarters of its hymns appeared in various Lutheran hymn books in the 16th and 17th centuries.

For a time the Brethren leaned toward the Zwinglian doctrine of the Lord's Supper. This is evidenced also in some of the hymns in the aforementioned hymnal. Later the Brethren leaned toward Luther's theology of this sacrament. Weisse thus undertook to rework and bring out a hymnal reflecting Luther's doctrine. But he died while engaged in this task, and it was left to Horn and his colaborers to finish the hymnal. It appeared in 1544 and contained 32 new hymns.

Among the German poets of the Bohemian Brethren Weisse stands as the most excellent leader. Luther, with whom Weisse was personally acquainted, called him "a first-rate poet." He died March 19, 1534, at Landskron.

COMPOSER/COMPILER:	18	FREUEN WIR UNS ALL IN EIN
	30	GOTTES SOHN IST KOMMEN (sometimes attr.)

WEISSEL, GEORG (1590–1635), was born at Domnau near Königsberg, Prussia, the son of Johann Weissel, judge and mayor of the town. After attending the University of Königsberg (1608–11), a school that was spared the devastation of the Thirty Years' War (1618–48), he studied for brief periods at Wittenberg, Leipzig, Jena, Strassburg, Basel, and Marburg. Appointed rector of the school at Friedland near Domnau in 1614, he resigned after only three years that he might resume his studies in theology at the University of Königsberg. In 1623 he became pastor of the newly built Alt-grossgart Church in Königsberg, a position he held until his death August 1, 1635.

Weissel was a gifted poet, writing about 23 hymns, and his work inspired others, among them Simon Dach (*LW* 268, 369).

AUTHOR:	23, 24	Lift Up Your Heads, You Mighty Gates
	358	Seek Where You May to Find a Way

WESLEY, CHARLES (1707–88), the 18th and last child of Samuel and Susannah Wesley, was born at Epworth, Lincolnshire, December 18, 1707. In 1716 Charles went to Westminster School, where his home and board were provided by his elder brother Samuel, an assistant teacher at the school. Five years later Charles was elected to a Westminster studentship at Christ Church College, Oxford, where he earned his

Bachelor and Master of Arts degrees, as well as becoming a fellow. With George Whitefield and, a little later, his elder brother John (*LW* 280, 362), he formed the Holy Club and established its discipline of methodical work and worship that led to the nickname "Methodists." After earning his Master's degree in 1729, he became a college tutor. In 1735, shortly after receiving deacon's and priest's orders on successive Sundays, he, in the company of missionaries Benjamin Ingham and his brother John, set off for the new colony of Georgia, U.S.A., where he was to serve as secretary to General Oglethorpe. On board the ship were 26 German Moravians, who, with their bishop, planned to colonize in the New World. Their staunch faith in the face of treacherous weather, and their singing of hymns in their daily services made a lasting impression on the Wesleys. After a brief stay in Georgia, Charles returned to England in 1736; not long thereafter he came under the influence of Zinzendorf (*LW* 362, 386) and other Moravians, especially the later Bishop Peter Böhler (1712–75), with the result that on Whitsunday, May 21, 1738, he experienced an evangelical conversion. In that same year he became curate at St. Mary's, Islington. Opposition of the lay parish officers, however, incited the vicar of St. Mary's to prohibit Wesley's preaching. Thus, like his brother John, he became a freelance evangelist and itinerant preacher, in which his wife, the former Sarah Gwynne, accompanied him. Charles had his concerns about the relation of Methodism to the Church of England; thus when his brother John, because of opposition by the established Church, ordained ministers, Charles strongly disapproved of this sectarian action. In 1756 Charles settled in Bristol and in 1771 he moved to London, in both instances devoting himself to the care of the various Methodist societies as well as ministering to the prisoners in Newgate. He died in London March 29, 1788, still a priest of the Established Church, and was buried in Marylebone churchyard.

Charles Wesley, the "Sweet Bard of Methodism," is unsurpassed both in the quantity and overall quality of his hymns. Whereas Watts produced the large total of approximately 600 hymns, Charles Wesley left no less than 6,500. Charles' unusual fluency—he could enhance any occasion and drive home a lesson by quickly writing a hymn—resulted in a vast deal of worthless verse, once the immediate purpose had been served. John Wesley, who revised and winnowed his brother's work, once said "some bad, some mean, some most excellently good." Hymns like "Hark! the herald angels sing" (*LW* 49), "Christ the Lord is risen today" (*LW* 142), "Oh, for a thousand tongues to sing" (*LW* 276), and "Lo, he comes with clouds descending" (*LW* 15), judged by any standards, must be ranked with the finest. Moreover, Charles Wesley ushered in two new kinds of hymns: (1) the hymn of Christian experience—every mood and emotion of the soul; admittedly, very autobiographical; and (2) the evangelistic hymn—simple, direct, and tender hymns, entreating sinners to return to God, yet devoid of the triviality and vulgarity of so many later revival hymns.

AUTHOR:	15	Lo, He Comes with Clouds Descending
	22	Come, O Long-Expected Jesus
	49	Hark! The Herald Angels Sing
	127	Jesus Christ Is Risen Today

142 Christ the Lord Is Risen Today
179 Rejoice, the Lord Is King
276 Oh, for a Thousand Tongues to Sing
286 Love Divine, All Love Excelling
380 Forth in Your Name, O Lord, I Go
480 Christ, Whose Glory Fills the Skies
508 Jesus, Lover of My Soul

WESLEY, JOHN BENJAMIN (1703–91), elder brother of Charles (*LW* 15, et al.) and the son of Samuel Wesley, was born June 17, 1703, at Epworth, Lincolnshire. Educated at Charterhouse and Christ Church, Oxford, he took holy orders in 1725 and a short time later became a fellow of Lincoln College in 1726. Returning to Lincolnshire a year later to serve as a curate to his father, in 1729 he was summoned back to Lincoln College, Oxford, to help with tutoring. There he found the small group of "Methodists" that had already been formed by his brother, and became their leader.

In 1735 he joined his brother Charles and the governor, General Oglethorpe, to Savannah, Georgia, as missionary for the Society for the Propagation of the Gospel. During the voyage he came into contact with a group of German Moravians, whose piety and singing of hymns so impressed him, he began to translate some of their hymns—from Zinzendorf's (*LW* 362, 386) *Herrnhaut Gesangbuch* (1735) and Freylinghausen's (*LW* 23, et al.) two Pietist collections, *Geistreiches Gesangbuch* (1704) and *Neues geistreiches Gesangbuch* (1714)—into English. In 1737 he published a selection of these at Charlestown in a *Collection of Psalms and Hymns*. Returning to England in 1738, it was in May of that year, at a meeting in Aldersgate Street, London, where someone was reading Luther's preface to the Epistle to the Romans, that he felt his heart "strangely warmed" and experienced the great spiritual change that made him a fervent evangelist, in the course of which he traveled 225,000 miles and preached over 40,000 sermons. Finding pulpits in the Established Church closed to him, he preached, following the practice of George Whitefield, in the open air. The first Methodist chapel was built at the Horse Fair, Bristol, in 1739.

Scarcely less astonishing was his literary activity. He translated large portions of the classics, wrote grammars, dictionaries, and histories, edited the works of John Bunyan (1628–88), Richard Baxter (1615–91), and others, and brought out a "Christian Library" of 50 volumes for use by his itinerant preachers, who were known as "Mr. Wesley's preachers."

John Wesley was also a genius at organizing. By gradually forming his converts into permanent congregations, he ushered in a new era in the religious, social, educational history of the working class. He and his brother, however, deeply regretted the circumstances that forced them unwillingly to form a new denomination. Their initial aim was to revive the Church of England, and they regarded their evangelical services as extra-liturgical services of that Church, though, of course, the bishops took a different view. It is significant to note that John and Charles published only one hymn collection apiece for the use of Methodists; their other volumes were intended for Christians of all denominations.

As for John's influence in the area of hymnody, it is largely as a translator of German hymns from the *Herrnhaut Gesangbuch* that he has made a lasting contribution. He had a way of toning down the oftentimes overly subjective hymns of Halle and Herrnhut in favor of the more objective doctrines of the Church.

TRANSLATOR: 280 Jesus, Your Boundless Love So True
362 Jesus, Your Blood and Righteousness

WESLEY, SAMUEL SEBASTIAN (1810–76), was born August 14, 1810, in London, the son of Samuel Wesley and the grandson of Charles Wesley (*LW* 15, et al.), the great hymn writer. His father named him in honor of his hero, Johann Sebastian Bach. At the age of 10 he became a chorister at the Chapel Royal. At the age of 16 he was given his first organist position; he served several churches prior to becoming organist at Hereford Cathedral in 1832. He was organist at Exeter Cathedral (1835–42), and it was while serving here that he earned his Doctor of Music degree at Oxford in 1839. Thereafter he served Leeds Parish Church (1842–49), Winchester Cathedral (1849–65), and Gloucester Cathedral (1865–76). While at Gloucester he completed his *European Psalmist* (1872), one of the most notable collections of tunes in the 19th century. Of the 733 tunes contained therein, 130 were of his own composition. Offered the choice between knighthood and a civil list pension, he chose the latter in 1873, something he enjoyed only three years before his death April 19, 1876, at Gloucester.

Samuel Wesley was, like his father, one of England's leading organists of the 19th century. He strove to improve the standard of church music and the standing of church musicians, the appalling conditions of which he exposed in *A Few Words on Cathedral Music and the Musical System of the Church, with a Plan of Reform* (1849). He was also one of the first organists to insist on a full pedal board in his instrument. His compositions include services, anthems, chants, and hymn tunes.

COMPOSER: 251, 260, 289 AURELIA

WESTENDORF, OMAR (1916–), was born February 24, 1916, in Cincinnati, Ohio. At the age of 20 he began his career as church organist and choirmaster at St. Bonaventure Church, Cincinnati, a position he held for over 40 years. He earned the Bachelor of Music degree in 1950 and the Master of Music degree several years later from the College-Conservatory of Music of the University of Cincinnati. Organizer and director of the freelance Bonaventure Choir, a group frequently appearing in concerts and heard on numerous recordings, he was also music instructor in several Cincinnati schools and director of the Bishop's Choir at the Cathedral in Covington, Kentucky. Having founded the World Library of Sacred Music in 1950 and the World Library Publications in 1957, he served as its chairman and president until his resignation in 1976, when he established a consultation agency on liturgical music.

Westendorf has written over 35 hymns. His "Gift of Finest Wheat," beginning "You satisfy the hungry heart," was the official hymn of the 41st Eucharistic Congress in Philadelphia, 1976, having won first prize for that honor in an international contest. It now appears in the third edition of *Worship* (1986), a Hymnal and Service Book for Roman Catholics; in the *Psalter Hymnal* (1987) of the Christian Reformed Church; in *The United Methodist Hymnal* (1989); and in *Lead Me, Guide Me* (1987), the African American Catholic Hymnal. He has compiled four successive hymnals, culminating in the *People's Mass Book* (1964), the first vernacular hymn and service book for Roman Catholics, resulting from the worship decisions of Vatican Council II (1962–65). He was consultant for the production of *The Book of Worship for the United States Forces* (1974). His *Music Lessons for the Man in the Pew* is intended as an aid to sight reading choral music.

Westendorf is married and the father of three children.

AUTHOR: 247 Sent Forth by God's Blessing

WEXELSEN, MARIE (1832–1911), was born September 20, 1832, at Ostre Toten, Norway. At the age of 20 she began writing poetry and her hymns became well-known throughout Norway. She lived in Trondhjem for many years and died there in 1911.

AUTHOR: 56 I Am So Glad when Christmas Comes

WHATELY, RICHARD (1787–1863), was born February 1, 1787, at St. Marylebone, London. A delicate child, he received his early education at a private school near Bristol. After attending Oriel College, Oxford, where he had a brilliant career while earning his degrees, culminating in the Doctor of Divinity degree, and being elected a fellow in 1811, he was ordained a priest. He remained in Oxford as tutor until 1823, when he accepted the living at Halesworth, Suffolk. Having returned to Oxford in 1825 as principal of St. Alban's Hall, in 1829 he became professor of political economy at Oxford; in 1831 he was appointed archbishop of Dublin. He was a member of the Royal Irish Academy, and in 1833 took a seat in the House of Lords.

Included in his writings are *Elements of Logic* (1826), which went through numerous editions; *Historic Doubts Relative to Napoleon Bonaparte*, a clever answer to David Hume's (1711–76) contention that no amount of evidence can prove a miracle; *Essays on Some of the Peculiarities of the Christian Religion* (1825); and *On Some of the Difficulties of the Writings of St. Paul* (1828). Lacking an ear for music as well as a sense of the artistic or natural beauty, it is, however, said that "his acute intellect enlightened every subject that he touched, and his powers of exposition and illustration have hardly ever been surpassed." He died October 8, 1863, in Dublin.

AUTHOR: 492 God Who Made the Earth and Heaven (st. 3)

WEYSE, CHRISTOPH ERNST FRIEDRICH (1774–1842), was born March 5, 1774, in Altona, Denmark, the son of an herb peddler and captain in the militia, and of a mother who was a pianist. Following his early piano studies, he soon became regarded as a prodigy. After studying in Copenhagen with J. A. P. Schulz (1747–1800), then-music director of the Royal Theatre and Opera, he for a time was a concert pianist. Disliking that life, he served as organist at the Reformed church in Copenhagen from 1794–1805, during which time he composed a number of symphonies and piano pieces, while also teaching voice. In 1805 the University of Copenhagen appointed him organist of Vor *Frue Kirke*, a position he held until his death October 8, 1842.

From 1819 on he was court composer, producing mostly sacred cantatas; he was titular professor at the University of Copenhagen in 1816, and was honored with an honorary doctorate in 1842.

One genre above all for which he is remembered is his songs—the wholly unsophisticated type plus the more expressive romance; the two later merged into a single personal idiom, some used to the texts of Bernhardt S. Ingemann (1789–1862; *TLH* 481), the famous Danish author and poet. These songs, collected and published in two volumes after Weyse's death, are said to have formed a musical counterpart to the "golden age" of early Romantic poetry in Denmark.

COMPOSER: 163 DEN SIGNEDE DAG

WHINFIELD, WALTER GRENVILLE (1865–1902), was born November 6, 1865, at South Elkington, Lincolnshire. Educated at Magdalen College, Oxford, he received his Bachelor of Arts degree in 1889, and Bachelor of Music degree in 1890. He was ordained deacon in 1890, and priest in 1891. Curate of West Hackney in 1890, he transferred to Eastbourne in 1891; then relocated to Bromsgrove, Worcester, in 1898. He was the founder and first vicar of the new parish of Dodford, near Bromsgrove. In 1902 he published a collection of hymn tunes. He died April 26, 1919, at Dodford.

COMPOSER: 173 WORCESTER

WHITTEMORE, JONATHAN (1802–60), was born April 6, 1802, in England. As a Baptist minister he published the *Supplement to all Hymn Books* (London, 1850). He died October 31, 1860.

AUTHOR/EDITOR: 475 Gracious Savior, Gentle Shepherd

WILDE, JANE FRANCESCA, *née* ELGEE,(1826–96), was born at Wexford on the southeast coast of Ireland, the daughter of an archdeacon. Having married Dr. William Wilde, a Dublin oculist, she became the mother of Oscar Wilde (1854–1900), Irish poet, witt, and dramatist. Caught up in the Irish nationalist movement, despite her Protestant and conservative background, she contributed to *The Nation* under her *nom de plume*, "Speranza;" she published several books on old Irish customs and legends including *The American Irish*. She died February 3, 1896, at Chelsea.

TRANSLATOR: 90 Jesus, Refuge of the Weary

WILLIAMS, AARON (1731–76), seems to have spent most of his time in and around London as a music engraver, teacher of music and psalmody, and compiler and publisher of psalm tune collections. At one time he was also clerk of the London Wall Scots Church.

Included among his collections are *The Royal Harmony* (1776); *Harmonia Coelestis (or the harmony of heaven imitated, a collection of scarce and much esteemed anthems)*, sixth edition, 1775; *Psalmody in Miniature, in three books, containing the tenor and bass of all the tunes generally used in churches, chapels, or discenting congregations* (1778). *The Universal Psalmodist* (1763) saw numerous editions, including an American edition by Daniel Bailey at Newburyport, Massachusetts, entitled *The American Harmony* (1769).

COMPOSER: 12, 296, 457 ST. THOMAS

WILLIAMS, ROBERT (c. 1781–1821), was born at Mynydd Ithel, Llanfechell, on the island of Anglesey in North Wales, where he spent his entire life. Blind from birth, he earned a living as a skilled basketmaker. It is said that he had such a keen ear he could accurately jot down a tune after a single hearing. He was evidently also a popular singer. The tune below appeared in his manuscript book, and it is not known whether he actually composed the tune—he was a gifted musician—or whether it was something he jotted down after hearing it.

COMPOSER (attr.): 137 LLANFAIR

WILLIAMS, PETER (1722–96), was born January 7, 1722, at Llansadurnin, Carmarthenshire, Wales. Educated at the Carmarthen Grammar School, he was influenced by the preaching of George Whitefield (1714–70) and studied for the ministry. Ordained in 1744, he first served the curacy of Eglwys Cummin, where he also taught school; but the Church of England, suspicious of his evangelistic tendencies, moved him from parish to parish until in 1746 he joined the Calvinistic Methodists.

Williams became an itinerant preacher with this group, which later charged him with heresy and disowned him. He continued to preach at the chapel he had built on his own land in Water Street, Carmarthen, until his death on August 8, 1796, at a farm called Gelli Ladnais in the parish of Llandyfeilog, Carmarthenshire.

Williams' contribution to Welsh literature includes the first Welsh Bible commentary, published at his own expense (1767–70); a concordance published in 1773; and, with David Jones in 1790, John Canne's Bible with marginal notes. He printed a Welsh hymnal in 1759 in addition to his *Hymns on Various Subjects* (1771).

TRANSLATOR: 220 Guide Me Ever, Great Redeemer

WILLIAMS, THOMAS JOHN (1869–1944), was born at Ynysmendwy, Pontardawe, Glamorgan. He studied at Cardiff with David Evans. Although insurance was his main occupation, he served as organist and choirmaster at Zion Church in Llanelly from 1903–13, and thereafter as organist at Calfaria, Llanelli (1913–31). He wrote a goodly number of hymn tunes and some anthems. He died in Llanelli, Carmarthenshire, April 24, 1944.

COMPOSER: 328 EBENEZER

WILLIAMS, WILLIAM (1717–91), was born at Cefn-y-Coed, Llanfairarybryn, Carmarhtenshire, Wales, on February 11, 1717. His father, a prosperous farmer, saw to it that the boy received a good education; he attended Llwynllwyd Academy (later, the Presbyterian College) in Carmarthen, intending to study medicine. However, at the age of 20 Williams heard evangelist Howell Harris (one of George Whitefield's preachers) speak to a group of people after a church service in Talgarth, and he was moved to enter the ministry.

Ordained a deacon by the Church of England in 1740, Williams nevertheless found that his sympathies lay with the revival movement. Rather than pursue the priesthood, he became a Calvinistic Methodist and took all Wales as his parish, logging an average of 3,000 miles a year for the next 45 years as a traveling preacher. His intimate knowledge of the Welsh countryside thus gained became the basis for much of the imagery in his hymns.

Wales, a country of singers and storytellers, was badly in need of hymns in the native tongue to help animate the revival process. Soon after the formation of the Calvinistic Methodists, Harris held a hymn writing contest among the preachers of his acquaintance; Williams won, and soon became recognized as the poet laureate of the Welsh revival. Often described as "the Watts of Wales," he wrote in all over 800 hymns in Welsh and more than 100 in English.

Williams died January 11, 1791, at Pantycelyn, the parish of his birthplace. In addition to his numerous hymns, he left two long poems, *Theomemphus* and *Golwg ar Deyrnas Crist* (A View of the Kingdom of Christ), as well as several prose works. His collections include *Alleluia* (1744); *Hosanna i Fab Dafydd* (1754); *Hosanna to the Son of David* (1759); *Y Môr o Wydr* (1762); and *Gloria in Excelsis* (1772).

AUTHOR: 220 Guide Me Ever, Great Redeemer

WILLIS, RICHARD STORRS (1819–1900), was born February 10, 1819, in Boston, the son of Nathaniel Willis, founder of *The Youth's Companion.* In the autobiographical sketch that he wrote for the publishers Bigelow and Brown in 1887, now preserved in the Library of Congress, he tells of his student activities at Yale University: president of the Beethoven Society; arrangements and original compositions done for the student orchestra; Bachelor of Arts degree earned in 1841. Following his graduation, he describes six years of study in Germany under Warlensee, Hauptmann, and Mendelssohn (*LW* 49, 366). Returning to New York in 1848, he decided to go into journalism, thereafter serving as music critic for the *New York Tribune*, the *Albion*, and *The Musical Times*. From 1852–64 he edited *The Musical Times, The Musical World*, and *Once a Month*.

Numbered among his publications are *Church Chorals and Choir Studies* (1850); *Our Church Music* (1856), *A Practical Handbook for Pastors and Musicians; Waif of Song* (1876); and *Pen and Lute* (1883). He also issued several collections of songs and choir music that he titled *Miscellaneous Lyrics*.

After 1861 he moved to Detroit, where he died May 7, 1900.

COMPOSER: 62 CAROL

WILSON, HUGH (c. 1764–1824), was born at Fenwick, near Kilmarnock, Scotland, the son of a cobbler. Apprenticed to his father, he studied mathematics and music in his spare time, and became sufficiently qualified to teach for extra income. His two hobbies were making sun dials and writing hymn tunes. He sometimes led the psalmody in the Secession Church. About 1800 he moved to Pollockshaws, where he held responsible positions in the cotton mills. Next he moved to Duntocher, where he worked in the mills as a draughtsman and calculator. Here he also managed the Secession Church and became cofounder of the first Sunday school. He died August 14, 1824, and was buried at Old Kilpatrick. Though he wrote and adapted many psalm tunes, only two survive, because shortly before his death he directed that all his music manuscripts should be destroyed.

COMPOSER: 97 MARTYRDOM

WINKWORTH, CATHERINE (1827/29-1878), was born at Ely Place, Holborn, London on September 13, 1827 or 1829. She spent most of her youth near Manchester, moving with her family in 1862 to Clifton, near Bristol.

Winkworth was a pioneer in women's issues, especially higher education for women; she spent much of her energy promoting Clifton High School for Girls and the Clifton Association for the Higher Education of Women. She served also as governor of Red Maid's School, Bristol, and a member of the Cheltenham Ladies' College.

Winkworth's translations of German hymns, however, continue to bring her recognition, which are generally regarded as faithful to the original language while possessing literary merit on their own. Her works were prolific, and many are still in use (usually in somewhat altered form) in modern hymnals. To Winkworth belongs some of the credit for a revitalized interest in German hymnody, because of the volume and availability of her translations. Her *Lyra Germanica* appeared in two series, 1855 and 1858, followed by the *Chorale Book for England* (1863), particularly noteworthy because the chorale tunes were included with the original and translated texts. To complete her library of works from the German, in 1869 she published *Christian Singers of Germany*, a handbook of sorts containing biographies of the hymn writers.

Winkworth died suddenly of heart disease during a vacation in Monnetier, France, July 1, 1878.

TRANSLATOR:	28	Comfort, Comfort These My People
	30	Once He Came in Blessing
	33	Let the Earth Now Praise the Lord
	39	Once Again My Heart Rejoices
	40	Oh, Rejoice, All Christians, Loudly
	42	Let Us All with Gladsome Voice
	79	O Jesus, King of Glory
	94	Christ, the Life of All the Living
	119	O Dearest Jesus, What Law Have You Broken
	122	O Darkest Woe
	160	O Holy Spirit, Enter In
	177	Wake, Awake, for Night Is Flying
	198	Open Now Thy Gates of Beauty
	201	Lord Jesus Christ, Be Present Now
	202	Dearest Jesus, at Your Word
	212	We All Believe in One True God, Father
	224	Baptized into Your Name Most Holy
	226	Dearest Jesus, We Are Here
	232	Alas, My God, My Sins Are Great
	233	Lord, to You I Make Confession
	244	O Living Bread from Heaven
	266	Jesus Christ, My Sure Defense
	270	Jesus, Priceless Treasure
	302	Rise, My Soul, to Watch and Pray
	306	Jerusalem, O City Fair and High
	314	O Christ, Our Light, O Radiance True
	321	Spread the Reign of God the Lord

334 Lord, Keep Us Steadfast in Your Word
367 When over Sin I Sorrow
371 O God, My Faithful God
406 In You, Lord, I Have Put My Trust
415 All Depends on Our Possessing
420 If You But Trust in God to Guide You
421 In God, My Faithful God
428 When in the Hour of Deepest Need
442 In You Is Gladness
443 Now Thank We All Our God
444 Praise to the Lord, the Almighty
446 Jehovah, Let Me Now Adore You
453 My Soul, Now Praise Your Maker
467 Oh, Blest the House

WOODD, BASIL (1760–1831), was born August 5, 1760, at Richmond, Surrey, England. Educated at Trinity College, Oxford, in 1783 he was ordained by the Church of England and was chosen lecturer of St. Peter's Cornhill the following year. In 1785, having become morning preacher at Bentinck Chapel, Marylebone, he purchased the lease of this proprietary chapel and, in addition, he became rector of Drayton Beauchamp, Buckinghamshire, in 1808. He held these two positions until his death in 1831.

Woodd is especially remembered for having brought more closely together in the Church of England the Evangelicals, who cared most for hymn singing, and the moderate Prayer Book group, who wished to retain metrical psalmody (see essay: Metrical Psalms, p. 825), but supplemented with hymns on holy days and occasions. Woodd's interesting book, *The Psalms of David, and other portions of the Sacred Scriptures, arranged according to the order of the Church of England, for every Sunday in the Year; also for Saints' Days, Holy Communion, and other services*, published in London in 1794, actually turned out to be a companion to the *Book of Common Prayer*. The metrical psalm was designated to serve as the Introit; then followed one or more hymns adapted to the Epistle or Gospel; then hymns for Communion, Baptism, and other church offices and occasions. Thus this became an important book that stamped hymnody with the mark of the Anglican Church rather than of a religious party.

AUTHOR: 84 Hail, O Source of Every Blessing

WOODFORD, JAMES RUSSELL(1820–85), was born April 30, 1820, at Henley-on-Thames and educated at Merchant Taylors' School, London, and Pembroke College, Cambridge. Ordained in 1843, he was for a time second master in Bishop's College, Bristol, and curate of St. John the Baptist in the same city. In 1845 he became incumbent of St. Savior's Church, Coalpit Heath, and of St. Mark's, Easton, Bristol;

rector of Kempsford, Gloucestershire (1855); vicar of Leeds (1868–73); honorary chaplain to the Queen; several times select preacher at Oxford; and in 1873 consecrated bishop of Ely in Westminster Abbey. He died October 24, 1885.

His published works include sermons and *Hymns arranged for the Sundays and Holy Days of the Church of England* (1852, 1855). He was joint editor of *The Parish Hymn Book* (1863, 1875). His original hymns and translations from the Latin appeared in these books.

AUTHOR: 80 Within the Father's House

WOODWARD, GEORGE RATCLIFFE (1848–1934), was born December 27, 1848, at Birkenhead, England. After earning his Bachelor of Arts degree in 1872 and Master of Arts in 1875 at Caius College, Cambridge, he took holy orders in the Church of England and was successively curate at St. Barnabas', Pimlico, London (1874–82); vicar of Little Walsingham, Norfolk (1882–88); rector of Chelmondiston, Suffolk (1888–94); curate again at St. Barnabas' (1894–99); licentiate preacher diocese of London (1899–1903); and curate of St. Mark's at Marleybone Road, London (1903–06).

Scholar, musician, editor, and accomplished linguist, he translated numerous hymns from Greek, Latin, and German; he composed and arranged numerous hymn tunes; in collaboration with Charles Wood, teacher of harmony and counterpoint at the Royal College of Music, he compiled three series of *The Cowley Carol Book* (1901, 1902, 1919) as well as two editions of the *Songs of Syon* (1904, 1910), a unique contribution to English hymnody and an invaluable source book. Much of the music which *The English Hymnal* (1906) introduced in England was the result of Woodward's research. In 1910 he produced an edition of the *Piae Cantiones* (1582) for the Plainsong and Early Church Music Society. With Charles Wood he prepared *An Italian Carol Book* (1920) and the *Cambridge Carol Book* (1924). For the Society for Promoting Christian Knowledge he published translations of *Hymns of the Greek Church* (1922). In 1924 he was honored with the Lambeth Doctor of Music degree.

He retired to Highgate, St. Pancras, London, where he died March 3, 1934.

AUTHOR: 140 This Joyful Eastertide
ARRANGER: 14, 81 PUER NOBIS

WORDSWORTH, CHRISTOPHER (1807–85), was born October 30, 1807, at Lambeth, London, son of the master of Trinity College, Cambridge, and nephew of the renowned English poet, William Wordsworth. Educated at Winchester School and Trinity College, Cambridge, where he was acknowledged as a scholar and athlete, he was ordained by the Church of England and served as headmaster of Harrow (1836–50), vicar of Stanford-in-the-Vale, Berkshire (1850–69), canon of Westminster (1844), and in 1869 was consecrated Bishop of Lincoln, a position he held until shortly before his death on March 20, 1885, at Harewood, Yorkshire.

A recognized Greek scholar and prolific writer on many learned subjects, he wrote a commentary on the entire Bible and a work on church history. His numerous and spontaneous hymns were largely composed during his travels and written on scraps of paper. In his *Holy Year: or Hymns for Sundays, Holidays, and Other Occasions throughout the Year* (1862), containing 117 original hymns and 82 others, he sought to provide hymns for every season of the Christian year. His conviction that every doctrinal subject arising in worship should be treated lyrically resulted, however, in not a little didactic and doctrinaire verse.

AUTHOR: 88 Songs of Thankfulness and Praise
203 O Day of Rest and Gladness

WORK II, JOHN W. (c. 1871–1925), was born August 6, about 1871, in Nashville, Tennessee. While a student at Fisk University, Nashville, where he majored in history and Latin, he also studied voice and sang in the Mozart Society and developed an interest in Negro spirituals. Following his graduation in 1895 he spent a year in public school teaching, a year at Harvard University, and a year as library assistant at Fisk University. Having earned his Master's degree at Fisk in 1898, he was appointed instructor of Latin and Greek there. His interest in preserving, studying, and performing Negro spirituals prompted him, with the help of his brother Fredrick Jerome Work (1879–1942), to collect, harmonize, and publish several collections of slave songs and spirituals, the earliest of which was *New Jubilee of Songs as Sung by the Fisk Jubilee Singers* (1901). As a descendant of an ex-slave, his *Folk Song of the American Negro* (1907) is one of the earliest treatises on Black folk music. His lectures throughout the country, as well as his articles in leading periodicals, contributed greatly to the general appreciation of this genre. In addition, he trained and performed as tenor soloist with the Jubilee Singers and organized the Fisk Jubilee Quartet, which later recorded for the Victor Company. A change in administration at Fisk, coupled with negative feelings about Black folk music, caused his resignation in 1923. He then served for two years as president of Roger Williams University in Nashville until his death September 7, 1925.

AUTHOR: 504 Go Tell It on the Mountain (stanzas)

WORTMAN, DENIS (1835–1922), was born April 30, 1835, in Hopewell, New York. After earning his Bachelor of Arts degree at Amherst in 1857, in 1860 he attended the theological seminary of the Reformed Church in New Brunswick, New Jersey. Thereafter he served Reformed churches in Brooklyn, Philadelphia, Schenectady, Fort Plain, and Saugeries, New York. His prominence in that denomination is attested by his being appointed secretary of ministerial relief, a position he held for 17 years, and his election to the presidency of the General Synod of the Reformed Church in America. Union College, Schenectady, conferred the Doctor of Divinity and Doctor of Humane

Letters degree upon him. He was the author of *Reliques of Christ* (1888) and *The Divine Processional* (1903).

He died August 28, 1922, at East Orange, New Jersey.

AUTHOR: 258 God of the Prophets, Bless the Prophets' Sons

WREFORD, JOHN REYNELL (1800–81), was born December 12, 1800, at Barnstaple, Devon, England. Educated at Manchester College, York, for the Unitarian ministry, he became colleague-minister of the New Meeting, Birmingham, in 1826, but was compelled to resign after five years because of voice failure. He then opened his school at Edgbaston, Birmingham. The later years of his life were spent in retirement at Bristol.

Among his writings are *A Sketch of the History of Presbyterian Nonconformity in Birmingham* (The Unitarian Variety) and several volumes of devotional verse. In 1837 he contributed 55 hymns to a book that met with no success even among Unitarians, namely, J. R. Bard's *Collection of Hymns for Public and Private Use*, a novel effort to reconstruct Unitarian hymnody from materials exclusively Unitarian. Thus it rejected all trinitarian and evangelical hymns, thereby sacrificing some of the great hymns of the church. He died July 2, 1881, at St. Maryleborne, London.

AUTHOR: 502 Lord, While for Humankind We Pray

YOUNG, JOHN FREEMAN (1820–85), was born October 30, 1820, at Pittson, Kennebec County, Maine. Having attended Wesleyan University, Middletown, Connecticut, and Virginia Theological Seminary in Alexandria, he was ordained a deacon by the Protestant Episcopal Church in 1845 and priest in 1846. After serving dioceses in Texas, Mississippi, Louisiana, and New York, in 1867 he was elected and consecrated bishop of the diocese of Florida, a position he held until his death of pneumonia November 15, 1885. An energetic and mission-minded prelate, he not only promoted education by establishing and reopening schools in the south, but he also distinguished himself as a notable hymnologist and liturgiologist. Among other things, he published *Hymns and Music for the Young* (1860–61) and edited *Great Hymns of the Church*, published posthumously in 1887 by John Henry Hopkins, Jr.

TRANSLATOR: 68 Silent Night, Holy Night

ZIMMERMANN, HEINZ WERNER (1930–), was born in Freiburg, Germany, on August 11, 1930. At age 16 he studied composition with Julius Weismann, continuing his music studies with Wolfgang Fortner at the Heidelberg School of Sacred Music, from 1950–54, and with Thrasyboulos Georgiades at Heidelberg University. The State Music Academy at Freiburg granted him a state diploma in composition and music theory.

Zimmermann taught theory and composition at the Heidelberg School of Sacred Music from 1954–63, going on to serve as director of the Berlin School of Sacred Music in West Berlin. During this time he made two lecture tours of the United States and taught one term at Wittenberg University, Springfield, Ohio, on a Fulbright grant. He also lectured at New College, Oxford University, for a summer term.

Recipient of a number of composition prizes and commissions, Zimmermann was awarded the Doctor of Music degree by Wittenberg University in 1967. He has published numerous works, especially choral music with instrumental accompaniments. His *Missa Profana* for mixed choir and soloists with Dixieland jazz band and orchestral accompaniment premiered in Minneapolis in 1981. The following year the International Bach Academy, Stuttgart, awarded him the Johann Sebastian Bach-Preis in composition for his *St. Thomas Cantata*.

The first cantata of Zimmermann's current project, a cantata series on "The Bible of Spirituals," was performed by the West Berlin Philharmonischer Chor in 1986. The series is based on texts of American spirituals; this premiere cantata is titled *The Hebrew Chillen's Hallelu*.

COMPOSER: 410 LITTLE FLOCK

ZINCK, HARTNACK (1746–1833), was born July 2, 1746, in Husum, Denmark. First serving as cantor in Hamburg, in 1787 he became singing-master at the Royal Theatre in Copenhagen. From 1789–1801 he was also organist at Our Savior's Church in Christianshavn, and in the latter year he published the *Koral-Melodier* for the *Evangelisk-Christelege Psalme-Bog*. He died February 15, 1833.

COMPOSER (attr.): 476 JEG VIL MIG HERREN LOVE

ZINZENDORF, NICOLAUS LUDWIG von (1700–60), was born May 26, 1700, Dresden, the son of a wealthy nobleman whose family had Pietistic sympathies. Part of his early education was given by Phillipp Spener, the head of the Pietists and his godfather, at the Adelspädagogium at Halle (1710–16). He graduated from Wittenberg University in 1719 to become court Poet to the Saxon court.

Zinzendorf first became interested in the Moravian Brethren when he met one of the members of this persecuted sect, a carpenter who hoped to relocate his community in Saxony. Zinzendorf offered his newly purchased estate of Berthelsdorf to house the Moravians, or *Unitas Fratrum* (United Brethren), and in 1722 the settlement was established. Nestled beneath the mountain called "Hutberg" or "Shelter Mountain," the new home of the Moravians was renamed Herrnhut, meaning "Shelter of the Lord." In 10 years the colony grew to number 600, having become a haven for persecuted Christians from Moravia and Bohemia, with Zinzendorf as its superintendent. Criticized for his association with the Moravians who were in disfavor with the predominantly Lutheran country, in 1734 he was examined for soundness of doctrine at Tübingen and, found to be sound, he was granted a license to preach; thus in 1737 he was consecrated a Moravian bishop. Banished from Saxony in the same year on the charge of false doctrine, he established other missions in Germany, Holland, Great Britain, and America. When in 1748 his banishment was repealed, he returned to Herrnhut, where he spent the rest of his life; he died May 9, 1760, a poor man, his entire fortune having been spent on religious work.

Dedicated to spreading the Gospel, their evangelical fervor made the United Brethren one of the dominant religious forces of the 17th century. The "hours of song" that Zinzendorf introduced in Herrnhut and other localities, probably fashioned after the Halle practices under Francke, suggest that such song sessions were to him the focal points of spiritual and congregational life. Zinzendorf wrote hymns from the time he was 12 years old until his death, and some 2,000 hymns are attributed to him, some of them good, most too subjective and emotional for congregational use, others, dwelling so deeply and descriptively on the wounds and sufferings of Christ as to be almost irreverent. This accounts for the very small number of his hymns in use today. Granted, the hymnbooks he edited for the Moravian Brethren proved to be effective tools for their missionaries and inspired the Wesley's to use and compose hymns for their congregations.

AUTHOR: 362 Jesus, Your Blood and Righteousness
386 Jesus, Still Lead On

ESSAYS

The Matter of Alterations

In the discussion of hymn texts in this volume, some hymns are noted as being "updated." This term indicates that the Elizabethan-Jacobaean English, the language of the King James Version of the Bible with its *thee*, *thou*, *thy*, *thine*, and *ye* (and their concomitant old verb forms) has been made contemporary with the use of *you* and *your*. This is in line with the decision of the Commission on Worship, to whom the task of producing a new hymnal was entrusted, to use the New International Version of the Bible, the translators of which

> judged that to use these archaisms (along with the old verb forms . . .) would violate accuracy in translation. Neither Hebrew, Aramaic nor Greek uses special pronouns for the persons of the Godhead. A present-day translation is not enhanced by forms that in the time of the King James Version were used in everyday speech, whether referring to God or man. (Preface, The Holy Bible, *New International Version*)

Despite the fact that the German language has polite forms of pronouns (*Sie*, *Ihrer*, *Ihnen*, *Sie*), neither Luther in his German Bible translation nor the German hymn writers used such forms to address the persons of the Godhead. Please note, however, that not all hymns in the old English idiom have been updated in *Lutheran Worship* (1982), for some, considered to be classic, and others, requiring too extensive a recast because of rhyme problems, have been permitted to stand.

Other hymns are noted as being "altered," meaning that uncopyrighted original texts have been changed. This applies also to copyrighted texts whose authors have given permission for such changes. Altering hymn texts has been a way of life on the part of hymnal editors, as the reaction of Charles Wesley to the numerous alterations in his "Hark! The Herald Angels Sing" (*LW* 49) demonstrates:

> Now they are perfectly welcome to do so, provided they print them just as they are. But I desire they would not attempt to mend them; for they really are not able. Therefore I must beg of them one of these two favours: either to let them stand just as they are, to take them for better or worse; or to add the true reading in the margin, or at the bottom of the page, that we may no longer be accountable either for the nonsense or for the doggerel of other men.

Yet in this matter Charles himself took the liberty of altering the hymns of George Herbert and Issac Watts as he pleased. John Wesley, while in Georgia as a young man, was cited by a grand jury at Savannah in 1737 for making alterations in the metrical psalms and introducing unauthorized psalms and hymns. Augustus Toplady and Martin Madan freely changed Charles Wesley; Reginald Heber made free with Jeremy Taylor; and John Keble was a notorious offender.

Many great hymns would not be included in a given hymnal were alterations impossible, and the reasons for doing so are many and varied. One major form of alteration is the omission of stanzas too numerous for singing hymns in their entirety.

Time restrictions because of multiple services prevent the singing of numerous stanzas. Less stanzas permit the inclusion of more hymns in a hymnal. "Jerusalem, the golden" (*LW* 309) and "The Clouds of Judgment Gather" (*LW* 463), for instance, are from a 12th-century poem of almost 3,000 lines by Bernard of Cluny entitled *De Contemptu Mundi* (On the Contempt of the World). Paul Gerhardt's "Entrust your days and burdens" (*LW* 427), originally in 12 stanzas, has been reduced to six stanzas. In omitting stanzas, care must be exercised that the thought patterns not be disturbed.

Doctrinal concerns frequently necessitate amending words, phrases, or lines. Stanza 3 of Issac Watts' "Lord, We Confess Our Numerous Faults" (*TLH* 382) originally contained the Calvinistic line "But we are saved by sovereign grace." Changing it to "But we are saved by God's free grace" made it agree with the Lutheran, scriptural doctrine. Reflecting both the Armenian doctrine of free will and the Wesleyan doctrine of perfectionism (freedom from sin is possible in this life), Charles Wesley's "Love Divine, All Love Excelling" (*LW* 286) has undergone considerable change. "Let us find the second rest" in stanza 2 was soon changed to "promised rest" in many hymnals, though the United Methodist *Book of Hymns* (1969) did reinstate "second." "Take away the power of sinning" (st. 2) became "love of sinning" or "bent to sinning" in many 18th-century hymnals. (See *LW* 62 in this volume for another example of alteration because of theology.)

Occasionally entire stanzas are deleted from a hymn for doctrinal reasons. The confusion over the two words "fear" and "fears" in John Newton's "Amazing Grace" (*LW* 509, st. 2) prompted the Commission on Worship to drop the entire stanza, which reads:

> Twas grace that taught my heart to fear,
> And grace my fears relieved;
> How precious did that grace appear
> The hour I first believed.

It does not help to insist that "fear" is reverence, as understood by Martin Luther in his explanations of the Commandments, and that "fears" is being afraid. It is God's Law and not his grace that makes the heart to fear in the sense of making afraid or becoming conscience-smitten. Hymnal editors are not exempt from exercising care in properly distinguishing Law and Gospel. (See *LW* 329 and 330.)

Some hymns are altered because certain words have taken on meanings that today offend aesthetic sensibilities. Usage in the 18th-century could permit Issac Watts to call himself a worm in "Alas, and Did My Savior Bleed" (*LW* 97), for this simply implied that he was of little importance, or significance. Today's use of that word, applied to a person, makes that person the object of contempt and loathing. Thus, *Lutheran Worship* followed the lead of *The Baptist Hymnal* (1975) in changing "for such a worm as I" to "for sinners such as I." Similarly, *Lutheran Worship* adopted the change of "awefull" to "awesome" in "Before Jehovah's Awesome Throne" (*LW* 454) as it appeared in *Lutheran Book of Worship* (1978). The Presbyterian *Worshipbook* (1972) changed the opening words to "Before the Lord Jehovah's Throne."

Expressions that might evoke a chuckle or negate a certain liturgical propriety are subjected to alterations. Stanza four, for instance, of John Fawcett's "Blest Be the Tie that Binds" (*LW* 295), originally read:

When we asunder part,
It gives us inward pain;
But we shall still be joined in heart,
And hope to meet again.

The Lutheran Hymnal (1941) has it thus:

When here our pathways part,
We suffer bitter pain;
Yet one in Christ and one in heart,
We hope to meet again.

The Church Hymnary (rev. ed., 1927), reads:

When for awhile we part,
This thought will soothe our pain,
That we shall still be joined in heart
And one day meet again.

The Hymnal 1940 is more to the point:

When we at death must part,
Not like the world's, our pain;
But one in Christ, and in one in heart
We part to meet again.

Lutheran Worship (1982) omitted this stanza for lack of space.

The Lutheran Hymnal (1941) paid tribute to C. F. W. Walther, the first president of The Lutheran Church—Missouri Synod, for his leadership and concerns in behalf of good hymnody, by including his text and tune, "He's risen, He's risen" (*TLH* 198). In the English translation of Anna M. Meyer, the last two lines of the first stanza read:

Break forth, hosts of heaven, in jubilant song,
And earth, sea, and mountain, the paean prolong.

The merits of this Easter hymn prompted the Commission on Worship to include it in *Lutheran Worship*, updated and revised, by changing "paean prolong" to "praises prolong."

When *Lutheran Book of Worship* (1978) and *Lutheran Worship* (1982) were produced, feelings were not as strong as today about the traditional use of masculine nouns and pronouns referring to God, and the use of *man*, *men*, and *mankind* to designate both men and women. Assertions of male dominance in some quarters have today led to the issuance of inclusive language revisions of lectionary readings, historical canticles, and hymn texts, to a degree at least on an experimental basis. With respect to retaining masculine pronouns for the deity, it should be remembered that "Father" is a *name* of God, not a metaphorical image, a name God gives himself. *He* names human fathers and families, not vice-versa. Thus the Commission on Worship did not hesitate to continue using masculine pronouns for God, for they are in the inspired biblical text. Criticizing the *Lectionary for the Christian People* (1988) by Gordon Lathrop and Gail Ramshaw, Richard John Neuhaus in the *Forum Letter* of February 1989 states:

The consistent elimination of 'He' in reference to God is a basic, if not implicitly heretical, deviation from the Christological and Trinitarian decisions of the ecumenical councils solemnly affirmed by the Augsburg Confession.

The Commission on Worship moved toward a language that affirms both men and women. Thus, for example, it accepted "Good Christian Friends (not "men"), Rejoice and Sing" (*LW* 129); the changes in "Hark! The Herald Angels Sing" (*LW* 49, st. 3)—"Born that we (not "man") no more may die, / Born to raise each child (not "the sons") of earth"; in "Our God, Our Help in Ages Past" (*LW* 180, st. 5) "Soon bears us all away" instead of "Bears all its sons away"; in "Joy to the World" (*LW* 53, st. 2)"Let all (not "men") their songs employ," changes made by the Inter-Lutheran Commission on Worship for inclusion in *Lutheran Book of Worship* (1978).

Thus, not a few of the best-loved hymns in Christendom are the result of considerable alteration, besides "Hark! the Herald Angels Sing" (*LW* 49), and the Advent hymn "Lo, He Comes With Clouds Descending" (*LW* 15). The important thing about alterations is that they be instinctively well done, with a sure eye on the context, and that they preserve the artistic qualities and intent of the originals. Actually, the reprehensible aspect of altering is failing to note that the text, or tune, for that matter, has been altered.

Concerning Amens

The use of amen to conclude a hymn is rare in the history of hymnody. Certain liturgical pieces in plainsong (Gregorian chant), such as the Gloria Patri, Gloria in Excelsis, and the Nicene Creed, plus some office hymns, depending on the content, append an amen. An amen imbedded within the final stanza of a hymn occurs occasionally, especially in German Lutheran hymns. But amens appended to such hymns is a rarity.

A cursory examination of some hymnals produced in the early part of the 20th century reveals a rather arbitrary appending of the amen, evidently reflecting the whims of the editors and compilers. The *Common Service Book of the Lutheran Church* (1917), prepared by the United Lutheran Church in America, appends an amen to every hymn. *The Service Book and Hymnal* (1958), prepared by a committee representing eight separate Lutheran bodies that later merged into the American Lutheran Church and into the Lutheran Church in America (now merged into the Evangelical Lutheran Church in America), appends the amen on a selective basis, usually to hymns of prayer and praise. The hymnal of the Baptists and Disciples, namely, *Christian Worship, A Hymnal*, and *The Lutheran Hymnal*, both of which appeared in 1941, conclude every hymn with an amen. The fact has generally been forgotten that, from the very beginning, this procedure evoked rather strong negative reactions in The Lutheran Church—Missouri Synod as well as in the Synodical Conference, with the result that many pastors decried and limited such usage. The *Evangelical Lutheran Hymn-Book* (1912), the first official English hymnal of the Synod, used no amens.

Among recent hymnals that omit amens are *The Lutheran Hymnal* (1973), produced by the Lutheran Church of Australia; the *Australian Hymn Book* (1976), an ecumenical hymnal prepared by a committee representing Anglicans, Congregationalists, Methodists and Presbyterians; and *The Hymnal 1982* of the Episcopal Church. Those hymnals that foster a judicious use of the amen include *The Hymnal of the United Church of Christ* (1974), the *Baptist Hymnal* (1977), and the *Broadman Hymnal* (1977), generally only appending amens to hymns of prayer and/or praise, to doxologies, and to certain "liturgical" hymns and chants.

In the light of the foregoing examples, the Commission on Worship decided to use no amens except with certain liturgical hymns and early Latin hymns, the latter coupled to plainsong tunes (see *LW* 17, 45, 65, 104, 158, 208, 213, 219, 432, 481, 489). Should an amen be desired to conclude a given hymn of prayer or praise (certainly not in the case of primarily reflective or didactic hymns), this should be left to the discretion of the pastor and/or the organist, who is capable of playing a plagal cadence, the chord structure of which is IV-I for such amen.

Polyrhythmic and Isometric Chorales

The chorale as developed in the Protestant Reformation and in the following centuries constitutes a significant and lasting contribution to the church in the cause of the Gospel. Rightly has Ulrich Leupold said, "The sudden bursting forth of the Lutheran chorale is one of the most thrilling chapters in the history of the Reformation." Moreover, in their acceptance, assimilation, and development of all phases of pre-reformation music, the reformers not only transformed these traditions in the service of the Reformation but also assured the timeliness of such music in any age.

Originally referring to the Latin (Gregorian) plainsong of the Western Church with the locution "choral," the term "chorale" became the designation for the vernacular, unison congregational hymn of the evangelical church. In the chorale there is a certain economy of musical materials: simple tunes; a tendency to replace the church modes with a new tonality (see essay: The Church Modes, p. 840); strophic musical and textual forms; a close relationship of tune and text—a tune written for a given text is identified by the opening words of that text; straightforward language and essentially syllabic melodic style; a wider vocal compass with jumps and leaps when compared to the step-wise progression of plainsong; and the emphasis on word rhythm with its variety of note values that defy a set meter and produce the effect of a rhythmic "drive." It is the latter characteristics that essentially exhibit the polyrhythmic nature of the early Lutheran chorales with their ruggedness and vigor, their pleasantly unsymmetrical pattern, a rhythm, as Routley says, "so marked and so urgent as to make harmony, or even aminimum accompaniment, virtually unnecessary for a successful performance."

The polyrhythmic chorale tune was often derived from the tenor line of mixed-voice, polyphonic motets of the 16th century. Few of these melodies use bar lines, for there is a mixture of duple and triple meters within each piece. A musical slowing down, or rhythmic "brake," is often applied as approach to, or in preparation of, the candence of a phrase and/or of the end of the composition. This brake is the *hemiola* (Greek: *hemiolios*, the whole and the half), a rhythmic device with notes based on a relationship of 3:2 or 2:3—substituting, for instance, three half notes for two dotted-half notes. An especially good example of the use of hemiola is "Lo, How a Rose Is Growing" (*LW* 67).

Many chorales employ the barform from the tradition of the *Meistersänger*. A poetic as well as a musical structure, the barform consisted of three parts: a *Stollen* (two poetical sections or musical phrases); a repeat of the *Stollen*; and the *Abgesang* (usually three contrasting sections, sometimes including a quotation from part of the *Stollen),* with one of the following as a resulting pattern:

A (ab)	A (ab)
A (ab)	A (ab)
B (cde[fg])	B (cd[ef] b)

Use of the barform facilitated the easy learning of the tunes and texts. Many of the chorales of the Reformation reflect this barform structure, for example, "All Glory Be to God on High" (*LW* 215), "The Day Is Surely Drawing Near" (*LW* 462),"From Depths of

Woe I Cry to You" (*LW* 230), "Lo, How a Rose Is Growing" (*LW* 67), and "A Mighty Fortress Is Our God" (*LW* 298).

Illustrated below in the polyrhythmic version of "A Mighty Frotress Is Our God" are the barform and the triple inserts in the grid of duple rhythm.

The free, pliable, irregular rhythmic flow, so characteristic of the early German choral and Genevan psalter tunes, stands in stark contrast to the rigid isometric restructuring exhibited in the chorale harmonizations of J. S. Bach (*LW* 89) and in the tunes of Pietism (see Freylinghausen [*LW* 23, et al]). The isometric versions of the chorales removed the rhythmic subtleties and replaced them with basically equal note values and straight 3/4 or 4/4 time. The result is a taming of the melody and a smoothing or flattening of the syncopations and melodic jumps, which may be seen by comparing the *isometric* form of "A Mighty Fortress Is Our God" (*LW* 297) with the original, *polyrhythmic* form of the same tune (*LW* 298).

The above comments in no way diminish the superlative artistry of J. S. Bach. Though his chorale harmonizations constitute the heart of his entire liturgical output—most prominently displayed in his passions and cantatas—Bach actually composed no chorale tunes. While the preface to Georg Schmelli's (1676–1762) unsuccessful *Musicalishes Gesangbuch* (Leipzig, 1763) implies that of the 954 hymns contained therein the 69 with figured bass were either composed or improved by Bach, research shows that only three tunes can perhaps be attributed to him: "Vegiss mein nicht," "Dir, dir, Jehovah," and "Komm, süsser Tod"—all three of which are arias and not chorales. Bach arranged and harmonized the chorale tunes in the contrapuntal style of his day for choir and not congregational purposes. In so doing he altered the character of what was originally a unison tune for congregation—a type of tune dependent on melodic line and rhythm for its impact—making it depend more on harmonic elaboration for beauty and effectiveness.

That *Lutheran Worship* contains a large number of chorales in their original polyrhythmic form is due in no small measure to Carl Ferdinand Wilhelm Walther (*LW* 138), "a theologian, churchman, and a musician of a century ago, who prepared a German hymnal . . . and who prevailed upon H. F. Hölter, who prepared its Choralbuch, to publish its chorales in their original rhythmic form," (Buszin). Through the pages of *Der Lutheraner*, of which he was editor, Walther promoted not only a concern for a confessionally orthodox hymnody, but also for the use of the chorales in their original rhythmic form in order to invigorate hymn singing in The Lutheran Church—Missouri Synod.

Metrical Psalms

In the complex Reformation movement of the 16th century there were two contrasting, but at times partially interblending, forms of Protestantism, the one begun in Saxony by Martin Luther (1483–1546), the other begun in Switzerland by Ulrich Zwingli (1484–1531). The occasions that precipitated reform were not quite the same in both, nor did the two act in concert. Both aimed at the reform of certain abuses in the church and both initially expected to remain in that historic church. Matters, however, took a different turn. Serving as army chaplain in the war between opposing Swiss cantons, Zwingli met an early death. Leadership then moved from Zurich, where he had served as priest, to Geneva, where John Calvin (1509–64) assumed the leadership role. Although these two types of Protestantism began about the same time, the Lutheran matured some 20 years before the Calvinistic. In the course of time, Lutheranism spread widely in Germany and into the Scandinavian countries; Calvinism ranged in Switzerland, France, the Low Countries, and the British Isles, penetrating also certain areas in Germany. It gave rise to the French Huguenots, the Dutch Reformed, the Scotch Presbyterian, and the English Puritans.

Luther's love for and appreciation of music and its worship function developed out of the basic tenets that practical music was first of all a gift of God used in praise of God; secondly, an aid in the exercise of devotion and piety for the faithful Christian; and finally, an educational tool for the spreading of the Gospel (Blume). His insistence on participation on the part of the congregation led him to play a prominent role as creator, arranger, and promoter of the congregational hymn. (For additional thoughts on Luther and music see his biography, p. 684.)

Of the three reformers discussed here—Luther, Zwingli, Calvin—Zwingli was perhaps the most musically gifted; but, because of his exclusion of all musical elements in worship, he stood in stark contrast to Luther's views on music and worship. Zwingli's position is due in part to his understanding of prayer: "In your devotion you should be alone. Devotion is falsified by the participation of man" (final address to the First Zurich Disputation, January 21, 1523). To him corporate worship was the collective devotion of individuals, not the body of Christ, the Church, at a given place. Singing distracted the individual's meditation. This attitude of music and worship thus brought about the demolition of organs in the Zurich cathedral as well as in various churches in German-speaking Switzerland.

John Calvin (1509–64), of northern France, first educated for the priesthood and then for the profession of law, very early became known as a learned theologian. At the age of 27 he published his *Institutes of the Christian Religion*, a work that was to be regarded as the monumental systematization of Reformed theology. In 1536 he settled in Geneva, Switzerland, where he established a theocratic form of government and developed the presbyterian system of ecclesiastical government.

Calvin shared with Luther the idea that music had a duty to fulfill as a spiritual power, but he was far from being sympathetic to Luther's unsophisticated pleasure in the power of music. Lest music be misused in the service of vanity and sensuality, Calvin omitted chanting at the altar, polyphony, and the use of instruments. Unison, unaccompanied congregational singing in the vernacular thus constituted the only form of service music. To him a return to primitive usage, with its utmost simplicity and reverence, was the desideratum. Except for a few paraphrases from other portions of Scripture, the ancient Hebrew psalms, received from God and in turn offered to God, satisfied that requirement. For popular, congregational use, however, these psalms needed to be metricized and coupled to suitable and attractive tunes. This idea was not original with him, for he had become acquainted with the versification of psalms by Clément Marot (1495–1544; *LW* 399), scholar and favorite poet at the French court of Francis I, works set to folk song or chanson tunes. These had created a sensation, the singing of which became the fashion of the hour not only at the French court but far beyond. Moreover, during Calvin's three-year exile in Strassburg, where he served as pastor of a small French congregation, he had been exposed to the happy and vigorous singing of some Lutheran congregations. The publication of Marot's rhymed psalms in 1542, renderings of Scripture in the vernacular, led authorities to indict this versifier for heresy, causing him to flee for his life to Geneva. This first collection included metrical versions of 30 selected psalms. At the urging of Calvin he completed 19 more plus versions of the Decalog and Nunc Dimittis. After a year or so in Geneva, he left for Savoy. In August 1544 he suddenly died at Turin, possibly, as some suspected, the result of poisoning.

Five years later Théodore de Bèza (1519–1605) arrived in Geneva, joining the ranks of the Reform. Recognizing his ability, Calvin prevailed upon him to complete what Marot had begun. Although his poetic talents were not on a par with those of Marot, credit must be given him for the fidelity and zeal of his labors to complete the project. He became Calvin's colleague in theology, first rector of the college in Geneva, and, after Calvin's death, the foremost leader of the developing Reformed Church.

The completed Genevan (French) Psalter, *Pseaumes de David mis en rime francaise par Clément Marot & Théodore de Bèza*, was published in Paris in 1562. It contained 125 tunes for the 150 psalms and several canticles. While the origin of the texts is known, not so the origin of the tunes, especially of the various editions that preceded this 1562 publication. A goodly number were written by Louis Bourgeois (*LW* 216, et al.), a musician of rare capacity and distinction, whom Calvin brought from Paris with the instruction to prepare music that "should be simple, to carry the weight and majesty suitable to the subject, and to be fit to be sung in church." He wrote some marvelous tunes, as well as organizing the music education of the students and children. Though he was the first to make polyphonic arrangements of the Genevan psalm tunes, the most important of such settings were made by Claude Goudimel (*LW* 377, 486), one of the most prominent French composers of his time. His adherence to the Huguenot cause cost him his life in the infamous Massacre of St. Bartholomew, when from August 28–31, 1572, the Huguenot population of Lyon was decimated. Some of the tunes in this Genevan Psalter were adaptations of popular airs, others can be traced to Strassburg and Lutheran influence. Their creation undoubtedly followed the general 16th-century procedure of arranging, modifying, and oftentimes transforming existing tunes. Melodically, these tunes, depending on their varied historical sources, are in the church modes (see essay: The Church Modes, p. 832), with a frequent tendency toward the popular major and minor patterns.

It is in their musical and verbal rhythm that one discovers the most characteristic element in these Genevan tunes. In part isometric, but also in part rhythmic, or polyrhythmic, the latter is especially noticeable in the variety of ways in which the virtually limited use of whole and half notes succeed one another. No Genevan tune can, for instance, be divided into four-square, four-beat units. Within the 125 tunes in this Psalter, there are 110 different poetic meters, each requiring a specific tune form.

The numerous editions, translations, and publications stemming from the Genevan Psalter attest to its popularity and significance in the long history of metrical psalmody.

As for hymnody in the Reformation in England, Lutheranism, with its distinctive doctrines and popular hymnody, gained no appreciable foothold. About 1539, a book that appeared to have been influenced by Luther was published by Miles Coverdale (c. 1488–c. 1568), the great translator of the Bible, entitled *Goostly psalmes and spiritualle songes*. Suppressed in 1539, but restored in 1546, it may not have exerted much impact in the development of English psalmody. Of interest is its examples of early English versification, for it contained versified, or metrical, forms of a number of psalms, of the Magnificat, Nunc Dimittis, Lord's Prayer, Creed, Ten Commandments, as well as translations and versifications of some Latin and early German hymns of Luther and his colleagues.

About 1548 Thomas Sternhold (1500–49), groom of King Henry VIII's (d. 1547) robes, to counteract the profane and obscene songs of his fellow courtiers, published a collection of 19 metrical psalms that he had done, dedicating them to young King Edward VI, Henry's successor. A second edition of 37 psalms appeared in 1549. All were in the old ballad, or common, meter (8686, doubled or tripled) except for two. With the death of Sternhold several months later, John Hopkins (d. 1570), a clergyman and schoolmaster in Suffolk, assumed the task and contributed 60 versions.

Roman Catholic Queen Mary's accession to the throne in 1553 prompted many leaders of the Reformation to flee to Geneva to escape persecution. There England's developing metrical psalmody came under the influence of French translations and tunes. In 1556 a collection of 51 metrical psalms appeared that constituted the second section of a rival version of the Prayer Book used by the exiles in Geneva. It was entitled *The form of prayers and ministration of the Sacraments, Etc. used in the Englishe Congregation at Geneva; and approved by the famous and godly learned man, John Calvin.* In addition to 44 psalm versions by Sternhold and Hopkins, this book included a metrical form of the Ten Commandments plus seven psalms by William Whittingham, Hebrew scholar and brother-in-law of Calvin; it became known as the Anglo-Genevan Psalter. Three more editions were to appear in quick succession (1558, 1560, 1561) before the appearance in 1562 (the same year as the Genevan Psalter) of the monumental English collection of metrical psalms published in London by John Day (*LW* 342, 502) with the long, descriptive title *The Whole Book of Psalmes, collected into English metre by T. Sternhold, John Jopkins, and others: conferred with the Ebrue with apt notes to sing withal. Faithfully perused and allowed according to th' ordre appointed in the Quene's Maiesties' Iniunctions. Very mete to be used of all sorts of people privately for their solace & comfort; laying apart all ungodly songes and ballades which tende only to the nourishing of vyce, and corrupting of youth.* Of the 156 metrical psalm versions contained in this book (Psalms 23, 50, 51, 100, 125, and

136 were repeated) 44 were by Sternhold, 63 by John Hopkins, 28 by John Norton, 14 by William Whittingham, and seven by William Kethe (*LW* 435). As to the meters used, 134 were in common, or ballad, meter, a fact that, according to Waldo Seldon Pratt, laid a "paralyzing hand on English hymnodic verse for at least three centuries"; five in short meter; and three in long meter, with the remainder in peculiar meters of Genevan origin. It is interesting to note that, whereas the French Psalter contained 125 tunes for the 150 psalms, the John Day collection contained only 50, supplied by a number of skilled musicians. The tunes were such as did not rely on harmony and thus could readily be learned and sung in unison. This complete Psalter became known as the Old Version or, more popularly as "Sternhold and Hopkins," thus distinguished from the New Version of Tate and Brady (see below). A number of tunes from it still in use reflect this in their titles: OLD HUNDREDTH (*LW* 216, et al.; originally to Psalm 134 in the Genevan Psalter (1562), but in the Old Version to Psalm 100) and OLD 124TH (*LW* 240, et al., abbr.). (For the sources of WINCHESTER OLD and ROCKINGHAM OLD see *LW* 196 and 114). The popularity of this Psalter is attested by the fact that by the mid-19th century it had been reprinted 300 times.

In 1563 John Day, who himself had been in exile in Geneva, published a four-part harmonized version of his earlier book, with the tune in the tenor. Other influential collections were the two Daman psalters (1579, 1591), Este's (1592), and Ravenscroft's (1621). The second of Daman's is important in that it placed the tune in the soprano line (occasionally in the alto) instead of in the tenor. Daman composed his own settings, whereas the psalters of Day, Este (see biography), and Ravenscroft draw on the work of numerous composers. Such harmonized psalters were largely used in situations other than in corporate worship.

When the exiles returned to Scotland after the death of "Bloody Mary," their practice of psalm-singing went with them. John Wedderburn prepared Scotland's first psalter entitled *Gude and godlie Ballatis*, probably published about 1546. Wedderburn, a Scottish priest suspected of heresy, had fled Dundee to Wittenberg, where, studying under Luther and Melanchthon, he became an ardent supporter of the Reformation. Containing not only metrical versions of 22 psalms but also some daring and amusing satires, spiritual meditations, and a few translations of several of Luther's and other Reformation hymns, it became so popular that, for a time, it appeared as though the Lutheran model of hymnody might become the vehicle of praise in the new church. John Knox, however, the founder of Scotch presbyterianism, insisted on a different route. Having served two years as pastor of an English-speaking congregation of refugees in Geneva, in 1559, when he returned to Scotland, he brought with him the Anglo-Genevan Psalter. After making considerable revisions in imitation of the French Psalter, this psalter was issued as part of *The Book of Common Order* in 1564, and it remained the authorized Scottish Psalter until 1650, when the General Assembly approved and authorized a new version of this psalter, unfortunately without providing tunes. As a result, the music in the churches was perhaps largely confined to a limited number of common tunes (tunes previously not attached to any particular psalm) known by heart to the precentors and worshipers. The 1595 edition of *The Book of Common Order* had two interesting features, namely, a brief prayer appended to each psalm, reflecting it's basic thought, plus a set of metrical versions of the Gloria Patri in a variety of meters, thus affording such an ascription of praise to conclude each psalm.

Various psalters accompanied the immigrants in early American history. The Huguenots brought the Genevan collection to Florida; the Dutch settlers in New Amsterdam brought a translation of the French Psalter by Peter Dathleen, using the tunes of Louis Bourgeois. To the Separatist Puritans, nothing was more sacred in corporate worship than the singing of God's own Word in the form of metrical psalms. It was the Ainsworth Psalter, entitled *Book of Psalmes: Englished both in Prose and Metre*, that came with them on the Mayflower and that set the pattern in the 17th century. The first book of any kind printed in New England was the *Bay Psalm Book*, printed by Stephen Daye in Cambridge, Massachusetts, in 1640. Prepared by a number of clergy, the goal was to make a most literal and exact version of the original Hebrew over against the more free versions exhibited in some of the European editions. The following lines from Psalm 23 demonstrate the awkwardness of this attempt:

> The Lord to mee a shepherd is,
> want therefore shall not I
> Hee in the folds of tender-grasse,
> doth cause mee down to lie:
> To waters calme mee gentle leads
> Restore my soule doth hee:
> hee doth in paths of righteousness:
> for his names sake leads mee.

No tunes were included in the early editions of the *Bay Psalm Book*, only references to tunes in other well-known English psalters.

Among the many attempts to produce an acceptable metrical version of the psalms, no version became authorized in England until, in 1696, two Irishmen, Nahum Tate (*LW* 70), poet laureate, and Nicholas Brady, royal chaplain, produced *A New Version of the Psalms of David, fitted to the tunes used in Churches*, a book that became known as the New Version, or, more popularly, the "Tate and Brady." In the pursuit of literary and poetical excellence (in that day's style), the English Reformation principle of adhering closely to the Hebrew gave way to rhetorical paraphrase, approximating the procedure of hymn writing.

Here are a few lines of Psalm 42 from the Old Version in contrast to the New Version:

> Like as the heart doth pant and bray, the well-springs to obtain;
> So doth my soul desire alway with thee, Lord, to remain.
> My soul doth thirst, and would draw near the living God of might;
> Oh, when shall I come and appear in presence of his sight? (vv. 1-2)
>
> For I did march in good array with joyful company;
> Unto the temple was our way to praise the Lord most high;
> My soul, why art thou sad always and frets thus in my breast?
> Trust still in God, for him to praise I hold thee ever best. (vv. 4b-5)

While the New Version was accepted in many parish churches and in fashionable centers like London, it never enjoyed the widespread and enthusiastic use of the Old

Version. Tate himself relates that at family prayers in the home of a friend one of the maids explained her non-participation and silence by saying, "If you must know the plain truth, sir, as long as you sung [*sic*] Jesus Christ's psalms, I sung along with ye; but now that you sing psalms of your own invention, ye may sing by yourselves." Again, when a certain bishop was once asked what a drysalter was, he replied, "Oh, Tate and Brady, of course" By the beginning of the 18th century metrical psalmody had about run its course. The dull practice of "lining out" each line by the parish clerk, singing the words and music for the congregation to repeat; the stifling effect of neglecting other forms of church music; the monotonous overuse of the common meter, so characteristic of English psalter collections—these gradually created a feeling of apathy and ushered in a desire for something new and better. That desire saw it's beginnings fulfilled in the efforts of Issac Watts (*LW* 53, et al.). Although Watts was not the first to react to the intolerable conditions—John Patrick, preacher to the Charterhouse, London, for instance, attempted to Christianize the psalms with the publishing of his *A Century of Select Psalms and Portions of the Psalms of David, especially all those of Praise* in 1679 (actually paraphrases rather that translations)—Watts wrote and acted with a determined aggressiveness that meant to conquer. In the preface to one of his hymns he describes the deplorable situation:

> To see the dull indifference, the negligent and thoughtless air that sits upon the faces of the whole assembly while the psalm is on their lips, might tempt even a charitable observer to suspect the fervour of inward religion; and it is much to be feared that the minds of most of the worshippers are absent and unconcerned.

As a result of his example and influence, freer paraphrases of psalmody and other portions of Holy Scripture, hymns of "humane composure," as one writer put it, or hymns simply suggested by Scripture began their course, paving the way for the development, growth, and output of English hymnody that continues to the present day.

This centuries-long period of the psalters, however, should not be lightly dismissed, for it has contributed some splendid, much loved texts and tunes that continue to grace the contents of today's numerous denominational hymnals. Texts from the Old Version include "All people that on earth do dwell" (*LW* 435); from the Scottish Psalter of 1650 there is "The Lord's my shepherd, I'll not want" (*LW* 416). As for tunes, mention has been made above of two from the Old Version. In addition there are SOUTHWELL (*LW* 99, 231) and ST. FLAVIAN (*LW* 342, 502). Included from the French Psalters are OLD HUNDREDTH (*LW* 216, et al.; see above), OLD 107TH (*LW* 399), FREU DICH SEHR (*LW* 28, 387, 390), WENN WIR IN HÖCHSTEN NÖTEN SEIN (*LW* 363, 428), MIT FREUDEN ZART (*LW* 134), and DONNE SECOURS (*LW* 377). Tunes from the New Version are ST. ANNE (*LW* 180) and HANOVER (*LW* 458). The Scottish Psalter of 1615 has contributed DUNDEE (*LW* 283, 426); the edition of 1635, CAITHNESS (*LW* 92).

Watts's influence should perhaps not be overly exaggerated. He was not always inspired; he wrote too much always to be at his best; he invented no new meters. Moreover, there existed some good metrical psalm versions that had accumulated for over a century and a half, of which William Kethe's world famous version of Psalm 100 is a good example (see *LW* 435). Some excellent hymns had been pioneered by Cosin (*LW* 157, 158), Crossman (*LW* 91), Ken (*LW* 461, 478, 484), Tate (*LW* 70), and others. One is minded to agree with the eminent Presbyterian hymnologist Louis Benson that Watts "could have compiled an English hymn-book out of existing materials, whose excellence would not be questioned today" (*The English Hymn*). His indomitable spirit, his spiritual, intellectual, poetic resources, his example of putting the joyous Gospel into verse, plus the peoples' weariness with the current psalm versions—these combined to accord Watts such a prominent place in the history of English hymnody.

The Church Modes

The present system of transposing scales, each major or minor scale having the same succession of whole steps and half steps as each of its fellows, dates back no farther than the 17th century. Prior to that a system was developed, called church or ecclesiastical modes, that dominated European music for 1,100 years.

The modal system originally consisted of four "authentic" and four "plagal" modes. The compass of each of the authentic modes lies between the keynote, called the "final," and the octave above, and, in their untransposed state, includes the notes and the successive intervals, or steps, represented by the white keys on the pianoforte. The first authentic mode begins on D, the second on E, and so on. Each authentic mode has a corresponding plagal, consisting of the last four notes of the authentic mode transposed an octave below, and followed by the first five notes of the authentic, the final being the same in the two related modes.

The ranges of these eight modes, known by their Greek names, may be represented as follows:

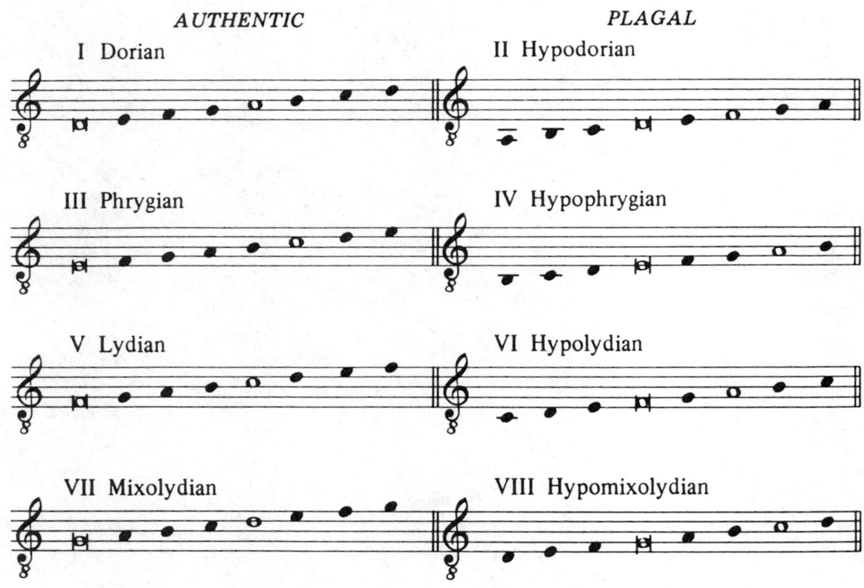

Although theorists in the Medieval and Renaissance periods insisted that these modes be strictly followed, in practice, however, the B was often changed to B♭ in modes I or II, and V and VI. Such changes gradually led to the creation of today's major and minor scales. In 1547, just one year after Martin Luther's (*LW* 13, et al.) death, the

Swiss monk and music theorist Henricus Glareanus recognized these modifications and considered them as four additional modes, namely:

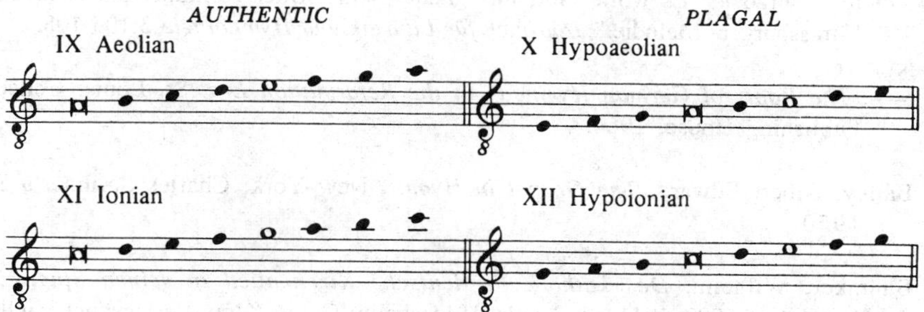

It is Glareanus who is also credited with having given the modes their Greek names rather than heretofore being identified by their numbers. The different succession of whole steps and half steps in each of these church modes has a marked effect on the sound to one's ear. To many people modal music and modal harmonizations sound sadlike, perhaps even morbid. A more apt characterization might be one of reverence and sturdiness. Such, for instance, is the impression one receives by the music of the Russian composers of the 19th century, much of which is strongly modal in character. But there is also a brighter aspect to this system. The Ionian mode, for instance, is the modern major scale. Tempo and rhythm can also contribute to this aspect.

This modal system continued to be used by some composers for another 400 years, and even today continues to appear in the work of some composers. This is due, in part, to the tonal variety and beautiful effects this system affords in contradistinction to the customary, more limited major and minor scales.

The popular terms church modes, or ecclesiastical modes, can lead to the misconception that they are the property of the church. These locutions are largely the result of associating the modes with such ecclesiastical figures as St. Ambrose (*LW* 13, et al.) and Gregory the Great (*LW* 482) and the connection the modes had and continue to have to plainsong, or Gregorian chant. Moreover, the history of music is inextricably bound up with the history of the church during the first 16 centuries or more. While the church helped to classify and codify the modal system in its use of it, minstrels, troubadors, folk music, and instrumental music all used the system, for no other system was known at the time.

Select Bibliography

Ameln, Conrad. " 'Es wolle Gott uns gnädig sein': Über Herkunft und Gestalt der 'Strassburger' Melodie." *Jahrbuch für Liturgik und Hymnologie* 3:105-108.

——. *The Roots of German Hymnody of the Reformation Era.* St. Louis: Concordia Publishing House, 1964.

Bailey, Albert Edward. *The Gospel in Hymns.* New York: Charles Scribner's Sons, 1950.

Bäumker, Wilhelm. *Das katholische deutsche Kirchenlied in seinen Singweisen.* Reprint of 1883–1911 ed. 2 vols. Hildesheim: Georg Olms Verlagsbuchhandlung, 1962.

Bennett, William Sterndale, and Otto Goldschmidt, eds. *The Chorale Book for England: The Hymns from the Lyra Germanica and Other Sources. Translated by Catherine Winkworth.* London: Longman, Green, Longman, Roberts, and Green, 1865.

Benson, Louis F. *Studies of Familiar Hymns*, First Series. Reprint of 1917 ed. Philadelphia: Westminster Press, 1926.

——. *Studies of Familiar Hymns*, Second Series. Philadelphia: Westminster Press, 1923.

——. *The Hymnody of the Christian Church.* New York: George H. Doran Co., 1927.

Benton, Elizabeth G. "Hymn Notes." *Journal of Church Music* 7, 7 (July–August 1965): 15.

Bernard, J. H., and R. Atkinson. *The Irish Liber Hymnorum.* 2 vols. London: Harrison and Sons, 1898.

Bishop, Selma L. *Isaac Watts, Hymns and Spiritual Songs 1707–1748.* London: Faith Press, 1962.

Blume, Friedrich, et al. *Protestant Church Music: A History.* New York: W. W. Norton, 1974. (A translation of Blume, *Geschichte der Evangelischen Kirchenmusik*, 1964, together with articles and revisions by Ludwig Finscher, Georg Feder, Adam Adrio, Walter Blankenburg, Torben Schousboe, Robert Stevenson, and Watkins Shaw.)

Bodine, William Budd. *Some Hymns and Hymn Writers.* Philadelphia: The John C. Winston Co., 1907.

Bonner, Clint. *A Hymn Is Born.* Chicago: Wilcox and Follett Company, 1952.

Bradley, Ian. *The Penguin Book of Hymns*. New York: Viking Penguin Inc., 1989.

Brady, N., and N. Tate. *New Version of the Psalms of David*. London: G. E. Eyre and W. Spottiswoode, n.d.

Brawley, Benjamin. *History of the English Hymn*. New York: The Abingdon Press, 1932.

Büchner, Arno, and Siegfried Fornaccon, revisers. *Die Lieder unserer Kirche* by Johannes Kulp. Sonderband, *Handbuch zum Evangelischen Kirchengesangbuch*. Göttingen: Vandenhoeck & Ruprecht, 1958.

Bucke, Emory Stevens; Gealy, Fred D.; Lovelace, Austin C.; and Young, Carlton R. *Companion to the Hymnal: A Handbook to the 1964 Methodist Hymnal*. Nashville: Abingdon Press, 1970.

Bukofzer, Manfred F. *Music in the Baroque Era*. New York: W. W. Norton and Co., 1947.

Butcher, Margaret Just. *The Negro in American Culture*. New York: A. Knopf, Inc., 1956.

Buszin, Walter E. "The Rhythmic Chorale in America." *The Hymn* 13, 3 (July 1962): 71–84.

Companion to the Hymnal of the Service Book and Hymnal. Minneapolis: The Commission on Liturgy and Hymnal, 1976.

Dearmer, Percy, and Archibald Jacob. *Songs of Praise Discussed*. London: Oxford University Press, 1933.

Dickinson, Edward. *Music in the History of the Western Church*. New York: Charles Scribner's Sons, 1927.

Doane, William Croswell. *The Life and Writings of George Washington Doane, with a Memoir by his son, William Croswell Doane*. Vol. 1. New York: D. Appleton and Company, 1860.

Douglas, Charles Winfred. *Church Music in History and Practice*. rev. ed. New York: Charles Scribner's Sons, 1962.

Dreves, G. M., and C. Blume, eds. *Analecta hymnica medii aevi*. 55 vols. Leipzig: Fues Verlag and O. R. Reisland, 1886–1922.

Dudley-Smith, Timothy. *Lift Every Heart: Collected Hymns, 1961–1983, and Some Early Poems*. Carol Stream, Il: Hope Publishing Co., 1984.

Duffield, Samuel Willoughby. *English Hymns: Their Authors and History*. New York: Funk & Wagnalls, 1886.

Ellinwood, Leonard, ed. *The Hymnal 1940 Companion*. 2d ed., rev. New York: The Church Pension Fund, 1951.

Evangelical Lutheran Hymn-Book. Authorized by the Evangelical Lutheran Synod of Missouri, Ohio, and Other States. St. Louis: Concordia Publishing House, 1912.

Evangelisches Kirchengesangbuch. Stammausgabe. Kassel: Bärenreiter Verlag, 1955.

Evangelisches-Lutherisches Gesangbuch für Kirche, Schule und Haus. Verlag der Evang.-Lutherischen Synode von Wisconsin u.a. Staaten. Milwaukee: Northwestern Publishing House, n.d.

Fallersleben, Hoffman von. *Geschichte des Deutschen Kirchenliedes*. Hanover: Carl Rumpler, 1861.

Fischer, A. F. W. *Kirchenlieder-Lexicon*. Gotha: Friedrich Andreas Perthes, 1878.

Frost, Maurice, ed. *Historical Companion to Hymns Ancient and Modern*. London: Wm. Clowes and Sons, Ltd., 1962.

Gurlitt, Wilibald. *Johann Sebastian Bach: The Master and His Work*. Trans. Oliver C. Rupprecht. St. Louis: Concordia Publishing House, 1957

Haeussler, Armin. *The Story of Our Hymns, The Handbook to the Hymnal of the Evangelical and Reformed Church*. St. Louis: Eden Publishing House, 1952.

Hostetler, Lester. *Handbook to the Mennonite Hymnary*. Newton, Kansas: Board of Publications of the General Conference of the Mennonite Church of North America, 1949.

Hughes, Charles W. *American Hymns Old and New: Notes on the Hymns and Biographies of the Authors and Composers*. New York: Columbia University Press, 1980.

Hummel, Horace D. *The Word Becoming Flesh*. St. Louis: Concordia Publishing House, 1979.

Hymns and Ballads of Fred Pratt Green, The. Carol Stream, Illinois: Hope Publishing Company, 1982.

Jones, Francis Arthur. *Famous Hymns and their Authors*. Detroit: Singing Tree Press, 1970.

Julian, John, ed. *A Dictionary of Hymnology*. Reprint of 1907 ed. 2 vols. New York: Dover Publications, 1957.

Kavanagh, Aidan. *Elements of Rite: A Handbook of Liturgical Style*. New York: Pueblo Publishing Co., 1982.

Koch, Eduard Emil. *Geschichte des Kirchenlieds und Kirchengesangs der christlichen, insbesondere der deutschen evangelischen Kirche*. 8 vols. Stuttgart: Chr. Belser'chen Verlagshandlung, 1866–71.

Leaver, Robin. *The Theological Character of Music in Worship*. St. Louis: Concordia Publishing House, 1989.

Liber Usualis, The. Edited by the Benedictines of Solesmes. Tournai (Belgium): Desclée and Co., 1934.

Liemohn, Edwin. *The Chorale Through 400 Years of Musical Development as a Congregational Hymn*. Philadelphia: Muhlenberg Press, 1953.

Leupold, Ulrich, ed. *Liturgy and Hymns*. Vol. 53, *Luther's Works, American Edition*. Philadelphia: Fortress Press, 1965.

Lovelace, Austin C. *The Anatomy of Hymnody*. New York and Nashville: Abingdon Press, 1965.

Lucke, Wilhelm, ed. Vol. 35, *D. Martin Luthers Werke*. Kritische Gesammtausgabe. Weimar: Hermann Böhlaus Nachfolger, 1923.

Lutheran Book of Worship. Prepared by the churches participating in the Inter-Lutheran Commission on Worship. Minneapolis: Augsburg Publishing House; Philadelphia: Board of Publication, Lutheran Church in America, 1978.

Lutheran Hymnal, The. Authorized by the Synods Constituting the Evangelical Lutheran Synodical Conference of North America. St. Louis: Concordia Publishing House, 1941.

Marks, Harvey B. *The Rise and Growth of English Hymnody*. New York: Fleming H. Revell Company, 1938.

McCutchan, Robert Guy. *Hymn Tune Names*. New York: Abingdon Press, 1957.

Milgate, Wesley. *Songs of the People of God*. London: Collins Liturgical Publications, 1982.

Moffatt, James, and Miller Patrick, eds. *The Handbook to the Church Hymnary*. London: Oxford University Press, 1935.

Moser, Hans Joachim. *Die Melodien der Lutherlieder*. Leipzig: Gustav Schlüssman, 1935.

Music, David W. "Hans Leo Hassler." *Journal of Church Music,* 25,1 (January 1983): 9–10.

Nelle, Wilhelm. *Geschichte des deutschen evangelischen Kirchenliedes*. 4th ed. Hildesheim: Georg Olms Verlagsbuchhandlung, 1962.

Osborne, Stanley L. *If Such Holy Song, The Story of the Hymns in The Hymn Book 1971*. Whitby, Ontario: The Institute of Church Music, 1976.

Patrick, Millar. *The Story of the Church's Song*. Revised for American use by James Rawlings Sydnor. Richmond, Virginia: John Knox Press, 1976.

——. *Four Centuries of Scottish Psalmody*. London: Oxford University Press, 1939.

Parry, K. L., and Erik Routley. *Companion to Congregational Praise*. London: The Independent Press, 1953.

Pilgrim Hymnal. Boston: The Pilgrim Press, 1931.

Pocknee, Cyril E. *The French Diocesan Hymns and Their Melodies*. New York: Morehouse-Gorham, 1954.

Polack, W. G. *The Handbook to the Lutheran Hymnal*. St. Louis: Concordia Publishing House, 1942.

Putnam, Alfred P. *Singers and Songs of the Liberal Faith*. Boston: Roberts, 1875.

Raby, F. J. E. *A History of Christian-Latin Poetry*. 2d ed. Oxford: The Clarendon Press, 1953.

Reed, Luther D. *The Lutheran Liturgy*. Rev. ed. Philadelphia: Fortress Press, 1960.

Reese, Gustave. *Music in the Renaissance*. New York: W. W. Norton and Company, Inc., 1954.

Reeves, Jeremiah Bascom. *The Hymn as Literature*. New York: The Century Co., 1924.

Rest, Friedrich. *The Cross in Hymns*. Valley Forge, Pennsylvania: The Judson Press, 1969.

Reynolds, William Jensen. *Companion to Baptist Hymnal*. Nashville: Broadman Press, 1976.

——. *Hymns of Our Faith: A Handbook for the Baptist Hymnal*. Nashville: Broadman Press, 1964.

Riedel, Johannes. *The Lutheran Chorale: Its Basic Traditions*. Minneapolis: Augsburg Publishing House, 1967.

Ronander, Albert C., and Ethel Porter. *Guide to the Pilgrim Hymnal*. Philadelphia: United Church Press, 1966.

Routley, Erik. *Hymns and Human Life*. New York: Philosophical Library, 1952.

——. *Hymns and the Faith*. London: John Murray, 1955.

——. *The Music of Christian Hymnody*. London: Independent Press Limited, 1957.

Ryden, E. E. *The Story of Christian Hymnody*. Rock Island, Illinois: Augustana Press, 1959.

Sadie, Stanley, ed. *The New Grove Dictionary of Music and Musicians*. 20 vols. London: Macmillan Publishers Limited, 1980.

Sampson, George. *The Century of Divine Songs*. London: H. Milford, [1943].

Schalk, Carl. *Key Words in Church Music*. St. Louis: Concordia Publishing House, 1978.

——. *Luther on Music*. St. Louis: Concordia Publishing House, 1988.

——. *The Roots of Hymnody in The Lutheran Church—Missouri Synod*. St. Louis: Concordia Publishing House, 1965.

Schilling, S. Paul. *The Faith We Sing*. Philadelphia: The Westminster Press, 1983.

Scholes, Percy A. *The Oxford Companion to Music*. 9th ed. London: Oxford University Press, 1955.

Service Book and Hymnal of The Lutheran Church in America. Music Edition. Authorized by the churches cooperating in the Commission on the Liturgy and the Commission on the Hymnal. Minneapolis: Augsburg Publishing House; Rock Island: Augustana Book Concern; Blair, Nebraska: Lutheran Publishing House; Hancock, Michigan: Finnish Lutheran Book Concern; Philadelphia: United Lutheran Publication House; Columbus, Ohio: Wartburg Press, 1958.

Stevenson, Robert M. *Patterns of Protestant Church Music*. Durham, North Carolina: Duke University Press, 1953.

Stulken, Marilyn Kay. *Hymnal Companion to the Lutheran Book of Worship.* Philadelphia: Fortress Press, 1981.

Trench, Richard C. *Sacred Latin Poetry.* London: Macmillan and Co., 1864.

Vajda, Jaroslav. *Now the Joyful Celebration: Hymns, Carols, and Songs.* St. Louis: Morning Star, 1987.

—. *So Much to Sing About: Hymns, Carols, and Songs.* St. Louis: Morning Star, 1991.

Wackernagel, Philipp. *Das deutsche Kirchenlied von der ältestan Zeit bis zu Anfang des XVIII Jahrhunderts.* 5 vols. Reprint of 1841 ed. Hildesheim: Georg Olms Verlagsbuchhandlung, 1964.

Warren, Michael C. "Isaac Watts." *Journal of Church Music* 23, 9 (November 1981):7–10.

Watson, Richard and Kenneth Trickett. *Companion to Hymns and Psalms.* Petersborough, England: Methodist Publishing House, 1988.

Webster, Donald. *Our Hymn Tunes: Their Choice and Performance.* Edinburgh: The Saint Andrew Press, 1983.

Williams, Thomas J. "Orientis Partibus." *The Hymn* 6, 4 (October 1955): 126–127.

Wilson, John. "Handel and the Hymn Tune." *The Hymn* 36, 4 (October 1985): 218–223.

Winkworth, Catherine, trans. *Lyra Germanica, Second Series: The Christian Life.* 7th ed. London: Longmans, Green, Reader, and Dyer, 1869.

—, trans. *Songs for the Household. Lyra Germanica, First Series, retitled.* New York: R. Worthington, 1882.

Winterfeld, Carl von. *Über Herstellung des Gemeine- und Chor-gesanges in der evangelischen Kirche.* Geschichtliches und Vorschläge. Leipzig: Breitkopf und Härtel, 1848.

Wither, George. *Hymns and Songs of the Church.* London: Reeves & Turner, 1895.

Worship Supplement. Authorized by the Commission on Worship of The Lutheran Church—Missouri Synod and Synod of Evangelical Lutheran Churches. St. Louis: Concordia Publishing House, 1969.

Zahn, Johannes. *Die Melodien der deutschen evangelischen Kirchenlieder aus den Quellen geschöpft und mitgeteilt.* 6 vols. Reprint of 1889 ed. Hildesheim: Georg Olms Verlagsbuchhandlung, 1963.

Abbreviations and Terms Used in *Lutheran Worship* and *Lutheran Worship Hymnal Companion*

abbr.	abbreviated
adapt.	adapted
alt.	altered
arr.	arranged
attr.	attributed to
b.	born
c.	*circa*, about
©	copyright
cent.	century
cento	a hymn comprised of separate stanzas of a longer original
cf.	*confer*, compare
coll.	collected
CM	common meter (4 lines: 86 86)
composite	a combined translation from the works of various authors
CP	*Congregational Praise* (1931)
d.	died
D	double (occurs after a meter pattern)
EH	*The English Hymnal* (1906)
EKG	*Evangelisches Kirchengesangbuch*, Stammausgabe (1955)
EpH	*The Hymnal 1940*
82EpH	*The Hymnal 1982*
et al.	and others
fl.	*floruit*, flourished
harm.	harmonized by
i.e.	*id est*, that is
LBW	*Lutheran Book of Worship* (1978)
LM	long meter (4 lines: 88 88)
LW	*Lutheran Worship* (1982)
n.d.	no date
para.	paraphrased by
PH	*Pilgrim Hymnal* (ninth printing, 1963)
PM	peculiar (varied) meter
SBH	*Service Book and Hymnal* (1958)
SM	short meter (4 lines: 66 86)
st.	stanza
sts.	stanzas
TLH	*The Lutheran Hymnal* (1941)
tr.	translated by
vs.	*versus*, against
WS	*Worship Supplement* (1969)

Scripture References in Hymns and Spiritual Songs

Hymns and Spiritual Songs with Scripture References

12 Zech. 9:9; Eph. 4:22; Phil. 2:7
13 John 1:14
14 Num. 6:25; Is. 40:3, 7; Matt. 3:1-6
15 John 19:37; Rev. 1:7
16 Matt. 21:9; Mark 13:26-27; Eph. 3:16-17
17 Ps. 30:10-12; 86:3-6; Acts 4:24-30;Col. 1:14-17
18 John 1:35-36; Rom. 13:11-12; Rev. 4:11; 11:15, 19
19 Matt. 21:1-9
20 Matt. 21:5; Luke 19:37-38; 1 John 4:13-16
21 Is. 40:1-8
22 Is. 9:6; Luke 1:67-75; 2:29-32
23 Ps. 24:7-9
24 Ps. 24:7-9
25 Luke 3:4-5
26 Matt. 25:31; Rev. 22:20
27 Ps. 24:7-9; Is. 40:3-4; Matt. 21:8-9
28 Is. 40:1-8
29 Is. 40:3; 61:1-2; Luke 4:17-19
30 Luke 4:17-19
31 Ex. 19:9-13; Ps. 80:14-19; Is. 7:14; 11:1; 59:20
32 Is. 64:1
33 Ps. 98:3-4; Luke 24:27; Acts 3:24-26; 13:32-33; 1 Peter 1:10-11
34 Ps. 49:7-8; Matt. 20:28; 21:5; 1 Tim. 2:6; Rev. 5:9
35 John 1:14
36 1 Tim. 3:16; Rev. 1:8; 4:11
37 Luke 2:1-20
38 Luke 2:1-20
39 Luke 2:8-14
40 Matt. 1:10-11; Luke 2:10-14; 2 Cor. 8:9
41 Luke 2:15
42 Ps. 118:15; Is. 52:9; Rom. 5:10-11; 2 Cor. 8:9; 1 Peter 1:8
43 Ps. 95:1-6; Luke 1:26-31; 2:7-11; Phil. 2:5-7
44 Luke 2:1-14; John 10:9
45 John 1:1-5
46 1 John 4:9-21
47 Luke 2:1-14
48 Ps. 107:10-22; Luke 2:15
49 Is. 9:6; 61:1-3; Mal. 4:2; Luke 2:14
50 Matt. 2:1-3; Luke 2:7-14; 1 Tim. 3:16
51 Luke 2:8-14; 1 Tim. 3:16
52 Luke 2:10-11
53 Ps. 98; Is. 55:13; Luke 2:10
54 Matt. 2:1-11; Luke 2:7-20
55 Matt. 2:11; Luke 2:7-20
56 Matt. 2:1-11; Luke 2:7-20
57 Luke 2:7-11
58 Luke 2:4-7; Rev. 7:9-12
59 Micah 5:2
60 Micah 5:2
61 Matt. 2:1-11; Luke 2:1-20
62 Gen. 11:9; Is. 9:4-5; Luke 2:13-14
63 Luke 2:4-16
64 Luke 2:7
65 Luke 2:10-14, 20
66 Luke 2:4-7
67 Is. 11:1-2
68 Luke 2:7-15
69 Rom. 5:11; 8:32-33; 1 John 4:9, 14
70 Luke 2:8-14
71 Luke 2:9-12
72 John 6:38-39; 1 John 4:9; Rev. 22:16
73 Rev. 22:16
74 John 1:14; 1 John 4:14
75 Is. 60:19; Matt. 2:1-11; Rev. 21:23

76 Matt. 2:1-2, 10-11
77 Is. 9:2; Matt. 4:16
78 Is. 12; Luke 2:68-79; 1 John 1:1-2
79 Matt. 2:1-12
80 Luke 2:41-52
81 Matt. 2:1-12; Luke 3:21-22; John 2:1-11
82 2 Sam. 7:12; Ps. 72
83 Ps. 24:7; 43:3; Luke 2:14; Rev. 5:12; 19:4-6
84 Is. 60:3-6; Matt. 2:11
85 Is. 60:1-6
86 Matt. 2:1-11
87 Matt. 17:1-8; Luke 9:28-36
88 Is. 61:1-3; Matt. 2:1-2; 3:13-17; 4:1-11; 1 Peter 1:20
89 Matt. 17:1-8; Mark 9:2-6; Luke 9:28-36
90 Mark 15:29-30
91 Is. 53; Matt. 11:5; 21:8-9; 27:21-22
92 Matt. 4:1-11; Mark 1:12-13; Luke 4:1-13
93 Deut. 21:8; Ps. 86:3; Matt. 4:1-11; 27:50, 60; Luke 18:13
94 Matt. 26:64-67; 27:33-46
95 Is. 53:4-5; 1 Peter 2:24
96 Is. 25:6-8; Zech. 13:1; Matt. 11:28; 27:33-35
97 Luke 23:44-46; Rom. 12:1; 1 Peter 2:24
98 Gen. 4:10; 1 Peter 1:19
99 Heb. 10:4
100 Gen. 1:27; Matt. 27:37; Luke 23:38; Rom. 8:29
101 Gal. 6:14
102 Ps. 24:7-9; 118:26; Matt. 21:6-9, 15, 16
103 Ps. 96:10
104 Ps. 96:10
105 Ezek. 1:26; Zech. 9:9; Matt. 21:1-9
106 Matt. 21:15
107 Matt. 26:26-29
108 Heb. 5:7
109 Luke 18:31-34
110 Lam. 3:19; Matt. 26:36-39; Luke 24:1-8
111 Is. 53:4-7; John 1:29
112 Matt. 27:46; Luke 23:34, 43, 46; John 19:26-28, 30
113 Ps. 22:6-8; Is. 50:6; Matt. 27:29; John 19:2
114 Gal. 6:14; Phil. 3:8
115 Gal. 6:14; Phil. 3:8
116 Is. 53:3-5
117 Ps. 98:1-2; Is. 52:9-10; Luke 1:68-69; Gal. 6:14; Rev. 12:7-10
118 Gal. 6:14; Phil. 3:8; 1 John 4:8; Rev. 5:12
119 Luke 23:20-24; John 10:11
120 Is. 53; Heb. 9:28; 1 Peter 2:21-25
121 Is. 53; Heb. 9:28; 1 Peter 2:21-25
122 Matt. 27:57-60; Acts 3:15; 1 John 4:9-10
123 Is. 25:8; Acts 2:24; 1 Cor. 5:7b; 15:55; 2 Tim. 1:10
124 1 Cor. 15:17-20
125 Acts 1:9; 2:31-33; Gal. 1:1
126 Ex. 12:22; 14:22; Matt. 26:26-28; Rev. 5:11-13
127 Matt. 28:6; 1 Cor. 15:20; Rev. 1:18
128 Col. 2:15
129 Ps. 118:24; Matt. 2:10; Luke 2:20
130 Matt. 28:1; John 20:24; 26-29
131 Rev. 5:13; 7:11-12
132 Is. 53:4-5; 1 Cor. 15:55-57
133 Ex. 12:22, 26-27; Ps. 118:15; Matt. 28:9
134 Is. 52:9-10
135 Gen. 3:1-15; Acts 5:30-31; 10:40; 1 Peter 3:18-19
136 Ps. 18:46-49; Eph. 1:19-21; 1 Peter 1:3-5
137 Mark 16:6; John 1:29; Rom. 6:9
138 1 Cor. 15:55
139 Rom. 8:11
140 1 Cor. 15:20
141 Ex. 15:1-21; Ps. 106:1-12; Matt. 27:66; Luke 18:33

142 Matt. 27:45; 28:6; Acts 2:29-32; 1 Cor. 15:55-57
143 Ps. 98:1-2; Matt. 27:63; 1 Cor. 15:55-57
144 Acts 2:23-36; 1 Cor. 15:20-26, 55-57
145 John 11:25
146 Rev. 5:5
147 Matt. 28:1-7; Luke 24:36
148 Acts 1:9; 2:31-33; Gal. 1:1
149 Ps. 47:5-9; John 14:9-11; Acts 1:9-11; Col. 3:1
150 John 14:3; Col. 3:1-4
151 Col. 1:20; Heb. 1:2; 1 Peter 2:24
152 Acts 1:9-11
153 Song of Songs 1:4; John 6:44-45; 12:32
154 Luke 11:13; John 16:13; Acts 2:4
155 John 16:13
156 Is. 11:2; John 16:13-15
157 Is. 11:2; John 14:26
158 Is. 11:2; John 14:26
159 Acts 1:9; 2:31-33; Gal. 1:1
160 Is. 11:2; Ezek. 36:27; 1 Cor. 3:16; Rev. 2:10
161 John 16:13-14
162 Ezek. 36:26-28; John 14:16
163 Acts 2:1-4
164 1 Cor. 2:14-16; Eph. 3:7-9
165 Rom. 8:15
166 Luke 4:17-19; John 16:13; 1 Thess. 5:23; 2 Tim. 1:7
167 Gen. 1:2; Is. 11:2; Rom. 8:9; 1 Cor. 3:16
168 Ex. 33:20; Is. 6:2-3; Rev. 4:8-11
169 Ps. 45:3; Is. 61:10; Dan. 7:13-14; John 1:14; 1 Tim. 6:14-16; Rev. 4:8
170 Ps. 7:1; 16:1; 18:18; 31:1-3
171 Is. 6:2-3; Luke 2:14; Rev. 7:9-14
172 Matt. 28:19; Rom. 6:4; 2 Cor. 13:14; 1 Peter 1:2
173 Jude 25; Rev. 1:5-6; 5:12; 7:10-12, 14; 19:1
174 Deut. 32:3; Ps. 5:11-12; 92:1-4
175 2 Cor. 13:14
176 Matt. 25:6
177 Is. 52:1; 62:5-12; Matt. 25:1-13; Rev. 21:21-22
178 Gen. 1:1-3; John 1:1-4; Phil. 2:5-11
179 1 Cor. 15:25; Phil. 2:9-11; Heb. 1:3; 1 Peter 3:22; Rev. 19:6
180 Ps. 61:3; Ps. 90
181 Ps. 121
182 Matt. 1:21; Luke 1:31; Acts 4:12; Phil. 2:9-11
183 Ps. 65:11; 107:8
184 Ps. 18:2-3; 91:1
185 Luke 2:29-32
186 Luke 2:22
187 Luke 1:41, 44; John 1:15-17, 29
188 Matt. 2:13-16; Rev. 14:4
189 Matt. 18:10; Heb. 1:14
190 Job 38:7; Heb. 1:14; Rev. 5:13
191 Heb. 12:1; Rev. 2:10; 14:13; 21:21
192 Rev. 7:13-17
193 Matt. 2:16-18; 9:9; Luke 3:2b-6; 9:11; John 1:40-51; 12:20-22; 15:5; 20:26-28; 21:15-17; Acts 1:12-14; 21-26; 7:59-60; 9:1-6; 12:1-2; Heb. 13:7; Rev. 1:9-10; 7:9-17
194 Matt. 2:16-18; 9:9; Luke 3:2b-6; 9:11; John 1:40-51; 12:20-22; 15:5; 20:26-28; 21:15-17; Acts 1:12-14; 21-26; 7:59-60; 9:1-6; 12:1-2; Heb. 13:7; Rev. 1:9-10; 7:9-17
195 Phil. 1:21; Rev. 7:13-17
196 Ps. 16:5-6, 11-12; 33:1, 5; 68:19
197 Ps. 119:140; 143:8
198 Ps. 100:4; 118:19-26; Is. 26:2-4; 2 Cor. 6:16
199 2 Sam. 7:22-24; Is. 6:2-3; Rev. 7:9-14
200 Ps. 118:24
201 Ps. 43:3-4; 95:2; Is. 6:3
202 Luke 11:28; John 6:63-68; 8:31b-32

203 Ps. 118:24; Is. 6:3; Matt. 28:1; Acts 2:1-4
204 Ps. 95:1-2; Rev. 5:12
205 Ps. 100
206 Is. 62:2-3; Hab. 2:20; John 8:12
207 Ps. 27:4-6; 65:4; Heb. 9:14
208 Ps. 31:16; 33:22; 85:7; Is. 53:6-7; Luke 17:13; John 1:29; 35-36; 1 Cor. 5:7; 1 Peter 1:18-19
209 Ps. 28:2; Is. 46:16-17; Titus 3:4-7
210 Luke 2:14; 19:37-40; Rev. 5:9-14
211 Luke 1:46-55
212 John 11:25-27; Rom. 8:26-27; Heb. 1:1-8
213 Is. 43:1-7; John 1:1-4, 14; Rom. 8:14; 2 Cor. 4:13
214 Is. 6:1-4
215 Luke 2:14; John 1:29; 14:16; 1 John 5:4-9
216 Mark 4:26-29; Luke 8:8
217 Matt. 13:3, 19, 23; Mark 4:26-29; 1 Cor. 3:6
218 Num. 6:24-26
219 2 Thess. 3:16
220 Ex. 13:21; Josh. 3:14; John 6:33
221 Ps. 85:8; 110:2; John 20:19
222 Ps. 1:1-3; 119:1-8; Is. 61:3; Luke 11:28
223 Matt. 28:19; Mark 1:9-11; Luke 3:21-22
224 Matt. 28:19
225 Mark 16:16; Rom. 6:3-5; Col. 2:12-13
226 Mark 10:13-16
227 Luke 18:15-17
228 Mark 10:14-16
229 Luke 15:2-4
230 Ps. 130; Rom. 5:20-21
231 Ps. 51:6-12; 119:133
232 Ps. 38:4
233 Ps. 32:5; 51:3-11; 139:7-10
234 Ezra 9:15; Ps. 51:3; Dan. 9:18-19; Matt. 15:22; Luke 18:13
235 Ezek. 33:11; Matt. 16:19; John 20:21-23
236 John 6:50-57; 1 Cor. 11:23-29; 1 Thess. 1:10; Heb. 10:12
237 John 6:50-57; 1 Cor. 11:23-29; 1 Thess. 1:10; Heb. 10:12
238 1 Chron. 29:20; Ps. 118:1; Rom 5:9
239 John 6:35; Rev. 19:8
240 Ps. 34:8; 1 Cor. 10:16
241 Is. 6:2; Matt. 26:28
242 1 Cor. 11:28
243 Matt. 26:26-28; John 6:35; 1 John 1:7
244 Matt. 26:26-29; John 6:35
245 2 Cor. 9:15
246 1 Cor. 11:23-26
247 Joshua 1:16; 1 Kings 8:66; Luke 8:39; 24:47-53; 1 Cor. 10:16
248 John 6:33-35, 48
249 Mark 14:22-25
250 1 Cor. 10:16-17
251 Ps. 127:1; Matt. 19:4-6
252 John 2:1-11
253 Ruth 1:17; Matt. 19:6; Eph. 5:24-33
254 1 Peter 5:10
255 Ps. 25:4-5; 119:8; 143:10
256 Mal. 3:17
257 Ps. 55:18; Mark 4:18-20; Rom. 6:16
258 2 Kings 2:9; John 20:21-23
259 Luke 8:4-15
260 Luke 10:2
261 Is. 6:7
262 1 Cor. 4:1-2
263 Is. 11:2; Jer. 23:4; John 20:21-23; Acts 11:24; 1 Tim. 1:6
264 Job 19:25-27; John 14:2; Heb. 7:25
265 Gen. 7:21-24; 1 Sam. 20:3; 2 Cor. 1:8-10
266 Job 19:25-27; 1 Cor. 15:35ff
267 Phil. 1:21
268 Phil. 1:21; Rev. 4:10-11; 14:13; 21:4
269 2 Sam. 12:18; Matt. 18:2-3
270 Matt. 13:44-46; 1 Peter 1:18-19

271 Acts 2:21-36; Phil. 2:5-11
272 Heb. 2:9; Rev. 5:9-16; 19:16
273 Ps. 80:8-19; Is. 5:1-7; John 15:1-5
274 Ps. 22:28; 45:1-3; 146:10; Luke 19:38; Phil. 2:10-11; 1 Peter 2:7
275 Eph. 3:17-21; Heb. 2:9-10, 14-18
276 Ps. 96:1-3; Acts 4:12; 1 John 1:7; Rev. 5:11-13
277 Luke 10:42
278 Matt. 28:6; Heb. 2:9; Rev. 5:11-14; 19:12
279 Ps. 18:1; Song of Songs 1:3
280 Ps. 23:4; John 14:15; Gal. 2:20; Eph. 3:16-21
281 1 Cor. 5:7b; Rev. 1;5-6; 5:11-14; 7:9-17
282 Phil. 2:9; 1 Peter 1:8
283 John 14:6
284 Rev. 4:11; 5:9-14
285 Rom. 5:8-11
286 Ps. 85:7-8; 106:4; Rev. 7:15
287 Luke 24:29
288 Ps. 67
289 Eph. 2:20; 4:4-6; 1 Peter 1:18-19
290 1 Kings 9:3; Ps. 95:1-6; 118:22-23;1 Peter 2:4-9
291 Is. 57:15; Acts 17:24; 1 Cor. 3:11-16; Eph. 2:19-22
292 Gen. 3:8; John 10:14; Rom. 5:14
293 Eph. 1:22-23; Col. 2:10
294 Ex. 13:21-22; Ps. 48:1-14; Ps. 87; 132:13-18; Is. 33:20-21
295 Ps. 133; Rom. 12:4-5; Eph. 4:3-6
296 Ps. 26:8; 27:4; Ps. 137; Is. 49:16; Eph. 5:2
297 Ps. 46:1
298 Ps. 46:1
299 1 Cor. 9:24; 1 Tim. 6:12; 1 Peter 5:7
300 Luke 12:32
301 Ps. 79:9
302 Matt. 25:5, 13; 26:41; 1 Thess. 5:5-9
303 Eph. 6:10-18
304 Acts 12:1-5; 1 Tim. 6:12; Rev. 19:11-14
305 Luke 9:23-26; 12:8; 1 Cor. 15:25; Eph. 6:11-17; Rev. 2:10b
306 Matt. 17:1-9; Rev. 7:9-12; 21:2-3
307 Ps. 42:2; 137:1-6; Rev. 21:10-12
308 Ps. 148; Dan. 4:13; Rev. 7:9-12
309 Rev. 21:18-23
310 Ex. 19:16; Is. 2:2-3; Heb. 12:18-24
311 Ps. 60:4; John 3:14; 12:32; Heb. 13:12-15
312 Ps. 72; Matt. 11:28
313 Is. 60
314 Is. 60:1-3; Luke 1:70, 79; John 8:12
315 Is. 52:8; 62:6-7; 2 Thess. 3:1
316 Luke 10:1-2; Rom. 8:37
317 Gen. 1:1-3; John 1:14
318 Is. 6:8; Matt. 20:1-16; Luke 10:2; John 4:35
319 Is. 52:7; John 1:1-7
320 Matt. 28:16-20
321 Ps. 96:1-5; Matt. 22:9-10; Luke 10:2; 24:47-48; Rom. 8:32; 10:15
322 Ps. 96:3; Luke 24:47; Acts 16:9; 26:18
323 1 Kings 8:27-30; Ps. 20:1-5
324 Ps. 22:3-5; 107:4-8; Heb. 11
325 Ps. 26:8; 27:4-5; 84:1; 122:1
326 Ps. 44:1-8; 90:1-2; 107:21-22; 116:17-19; Jer. 33:11
327 Gen. 28:16-18; Ps. 43:4-5; 141:2
328 Gen. 1:3; 2 Cor. 4:6
329 Ps. 19:7-8; 119:129-132
330 John 3:16; 1 John 4:9-10
331 Ex. 20:1-17
332 Ps. 119:105
333 Ps. 16:6; 119:111
334 Ps. 119:10; John 8:31
335 2 Sam. 22:29-33; Ps. 119:105; John 1:14; Rev. 1:20
336 Ps. 19:7; Is. 53:4-5; Rom. 5:1-5; 1 Peter 2:21-25
337 1 Peter 1:5-7; Jude 20-21

338 Matt. 13:8, 23; Mark 4:28; Luke 8:8, 15
339 1 Sam. 3:10
340 2 Peter 1:19
341 1 Peter 1:23-25; Rev. 14:6-7
342 Matt. 13:3-9; 18-23; Mark 4:3-9, 13-20
343 Heb. 1:1-2
344 Luke 24:29
345 Matt. 11:28; John 6:37
346 Job 38:7; Is. 7:14; Matt. 22:1-14
347 Is. 1:18; Luke 15:20-24; John 7:37-38; Rev. 3:8; 22:17
348 Matt. 11:28; John 4:14; 6:35; 8:12
349 Zeph. 1:14; Acts 24:25; Heb. 3:7-14
350 Matt. 11:28
351 Eph. 2:8-9
352 John 3:16
353 Rom. 3:28
354 John 17:8; 2 Tim. 1:12
355 Rom. 3:5; 5:1-2; Gal. 3:16-21
356 John 12:32; 1 Cor. 2:2
357 Rom. 3:25; 1 Peter 2:24
358 John 6:68-69; Acts 4:12
359 John 1:29; 6:37; Rev. 3:17
360 1 Cor. 3:11
361 John 19:34; 1 Cor. 10:4
362 Is. 61:10; Heb. 12:24; 1 John 1:7; Rev. 7:13-14; 19:7-8
363 Rom. 3:12; 5:12-21
364 2 Cor. 9:15; Titus 3:4-7
365 John 8:12
366 John 1:29; Rev. 7:14
367 Heb. 10:14
368 Matt. 24:31; Luke 6:48; Rom. 3:25-26; 1 Tim. 1:1; 1 John 1:7
369 Rom. 8:35-39
370 Ex. 15:13-18; Ps. 107:1-3; Matt. 5:14; Eph. 1:3-8
371 1 Kings 3:5; James 1:17
372 Ps. 38:21-22
373 2 Cor. 3:18; Col. 3:1-10
374 Acts 9:6; Phil. 3:7-8
375 John 14:23
376 Eph. 5:2; Col. 3:13-14; 1 John 4:16
377 Ps. 146:5-10; 1 Cor. 15:57
378 John 1:29; Eph. 3:12; Heb. 12:2; Rev. 21:4
379 Matt. 16:24; 1 Peter 2:21-25
380 Ps. 16:8; Matt. 11:30; John 6:27; 1 Cor. 15:58; Col. 3:17
381 Matt. 16:24; John 11:16; 1 Peter 2:21; 1 John 2:6
382 Matt. 16:24
383 Heb. 11:13-16, 33-40
384 Heb. 11:13-16, 33-40
385 Ps. 50:14; 100:4-5; 107:22; Col. 1:12-14
386 Ex. 15:13; Ps. 25:4-5; 31:3; Luke 5:11; Heb. 4:9
387 Ps. 92:1-2; 106:1; Matt. 16:24; 20:26-28; John 21:19-24; 1 Peter 2:21
388 Ps. 1
389 Matt. 6:10
390 Luke 19:41
391 1 Peter 5:8
392 Ps. 119:5, 33, 133, 176
393 Mark 8:38
394 Heb. 7:25; 1 Peter 1:20-23
395 Ps. 116:12; Matt. 25:40
396 Ps. 146:8; Matt. 10:7-8
397 Deut. 10:12; Micah 6:8; Matt. 25:40; Luke 10:36-37
398 Ps. 80:14-19; 85:7-8
399 Mark 1:32-34
400 Mark 7:32-37
401 1 Kings 8:36a; Ps. 85:5; 106:44-47
402 Acts 20:28, 35
403 Ps. 105:1-2; 107:31-38; Eph. 5:19-20
404 Rom. 12:1-2; Eph. 6:24
405 Ex. 23:19; James 1:27; 1 John 3:17-18
406 Ps. 31:1-5
407 Rom. 8:31-39
408 2 Sam. 22:3; Is. 12:2; Jer. 17:7; Acts 2:38

409 Josh. 24:16; Ps. 73:23
410 Luke 12:32
411 Is. 40:11; 41:10; 43:1-7
412 Ps. 23
413 Ps. 18; 27:9
414 Ps. 73:25-26
415 Prov. 10:22; Eccl. 11:7-10; Matt. 6:19-34; Rom. 8:31-32; Col. 3:1-4
416 Ps. 23
417 Ps. 23
418 1 John 2:15-17
419 Ps. 33:3-6; 104:24
420 Ps. 55:22; Heb. 13:5
421 Ps. 7:1; 25:1-8; 2 Thess. 3:3; Heb. 2:17-18
422 Deut. 32:4; Rom. 8:28; Eph. 2:20-22
423 Ps. 73:23; Heb. 11:13-16; 1 Peter 1:6-9
424 Ps. 27:1-4; 56:8; 73:25-26
425 Matt. 6:10
426 Deut. 33:26; John 13:7; Rom. 11:33; Eph. 1:9
427 Ps. 37:5; 125:1
428 2 Chron. 20:12; Dan. 9:17-19
429 Job 1:21; Rom. 8:28
430 Matt. 6:9-13
431 Matt. 6:9-13
432 Rom. 8:26-27
433 1 Kings 3:5; Ps. 34:15-17; 145:18-19; John 14:13-14
434 Ps. 34:17; Dan. 9:17-19; Matt. 6:9-13; Luke 21:36
435 Ps. 100
436 Ps. 65:8-13; 98:1, 4-9; 145:1; Ps. 148
437 Rev. 19:1
438 Ex. 15:1-2; Ps. 96:1; 149:1-3; Is. 42:10-12
439 Ps. 146; 149:2-4; Eph. 5:19-20
440 Ps. 117
441 Ps. 149
442 John 16:22; Rom. 8:38; 2 Cor. 6:10a; 1 Peter 1:6-9
443 Ps. 68:19; 100:4; 107:21-22; Eccl. 50:22-24
444 1 Chron. 16:23-36; Ezra 3:11; Neh. 9:6; Ps. 91:4; 103:1-11; Is. 40:21
445 Ps. 146
446 John 8:44-46; 16:23; Rom. 8:14-16; Gal. 4:6
447 Neh. 9:5-6; Job 38:7; Ps. 148:1-2
448 1 Chron. 16:31-36; Ps. 126:3
449 1 Chron. 16:4-36; Ps. 150; Mark 14:26
450 Ex. 3:6, 14; Dan. 7:13
451 Ps. 104:1-5, 31-35; Dan. 7:13; 1 Tim. 1:17; 6:15-16
452 Deut. 32:3; Ps. 96:1-8; 121:4
453 Ps. 103; Is. 40:6-8
454 Ps. 100
455 Ps. 20:5; 118:15-26
456 1 Sam. 7:12
457 Ps. 103:1-7
458 Ps. 104
459 1 Peter 2:9; Rev. 5:10
460 Matt. 21:9; Luke 19:37-38; Phil. 2:9-11
461 Ps. 150:1
462 Matt. 25:31-34; Luke 21:25-36
463 Luke 21:36; 1 Cor. 16:13; 1 Peter 5:8; Rev. 21:24
464 Matt. 8:11-12
465 Joshua 24:15; Luke 10:38-39; 19:5-9; John 4:53; Acts 16:32-34; 1 Cor. 13:14
466 Ps. 128
467 Josh. 24:15b; Luke 2:41-52; 10:38-42
468 Ps. 145:15-17
469 Gen. 31:49; 1 Sam. 20:42
470 Ps. 34:11; 78:1-8; 128:3-6
471 Is. 40:11
472 Ps. 78
473 Mark 10:14
474 Ps. 119:9
475 Mark 10:13-16
476 1 John 3:23

477 Ex. 20:1-17; Ps. 119:9-12
478 Ps. 59:16-17; 92:1-4; 108:1-2; 1 Cor. 10:31
479 Gen. 28:18-22; Ps. 5:3; 59:16-17
480 Mal. 4:2; Luke 1:78; 2 Peter 1:19
481 John 1:14; 8:12; 2 Cor. 4:6
482 Ps. 92:1-2
483 Col. 3:17
484 Ps. 57:1; 91:4
485 Ps. 3:5; 4:8; 36:7; 42:8; 139:11
486 John 1:9; 2 Cor. 4:6
487 Ps. 16:9; 113:3; Mal. 1:11
488 Luke 24:29
489 Ps. 91:1-12; Ps. 121
490 Luke 24:29; Rom. 8:19-21; 1 Cor. 15:55
491 Prov. 3:24
492 Gen. 1:1-4; Ps. 121
493 Ps. 65:9-13; 67:5-6; Is. 9:6; John 17:23
494 Ps. 26:12; 95:1-6; 107:31-32; 149:1-2
495 Is. 9:3; Matt. 13:24-30, 37-40
496 Ps. 65:9-13; 68:19; 107:31-38; Hab. 3:17-18
497 Rom. 13:1-7
498 Ps. 25:7; 46:9; 122:6-8; 147:14-15
499 Ps. 33:12; Jer. 29:7; 1 Tim. 2:1-3
500 Ps. 145:1
501 Ps. 44:1-8; Is. 40:26; Rev. 22:5
502 Rom. 13:1-7
503 Ps. 3:5; 4:8
504 Luke 2:7-20
505 Matt. 28:6; Luke 23:33, 53
506 Zech. 13:1
507 Ps. 45:2
508 Ps. 57:1; Is. 32:2, 6-7
509 Rom. 3:22b-24; Eph. 2:4-8
510 Ps. 42:4-11; 46:10
511 Matt. 26:36-38; Luke 22:31-32, 61; John 19:17
512 Gen. 5:24; Ps. 5:8; 27:11; 121:4-7; Is. 43:2
513 Matt. 8:26
514 Gen. 28:10-19
515 Heb. 4:9; 11:13-16
516 Matt. 7:7-8; 21:22; John 15:14-16
517 Is. 40:11; John 21:15
518 Matt. 16:18; Eph. 4:4-6
519 Ps. 92:5
520 Luke 2:10-14 (Christmas)
520 Rom. 4:25; 1 Cor. 15:57 (Easter)

General Index

All references are to *LW* hymn numbers.

Names of tunes are in full capitals. Titles of books and their common designations are in italics.

Original First Lines of Translated Hymns and Spiritual Songs

First Lines of Hymns and Spiritual Songs

---

* *Indented lines indicate first lines by which some hymns may also be known.*